W9-BMG-360

THE IVP BIBLE BACKGROUND COMMENTARY

NEW TESTAMENT

Craig S. Keener

An imprint of InterVarsity Press
Downers Grove, Illinois

InterVarsity Press
P.O. Box 1400, Downers Grove, IL 60515-1426
World Wide Web: www.ivpress.com
E-mail: email@ivpress.com

InterVarsity Press®, is the book-publishing division of InterVarsity Christian Fellowship®, a student movement active on campus at hundreds of universities, colleges and schools of nursing in the United States of America, and a member movement of the International Fellowship of Evangelical Students. For information about local and regional activities, write Public Relations Dept., InterVarsity Christian Fellowship, 6400 Schroeder Rd., P.O. Box 7895, Madison, WI 53707-7895, or visit the IVCF website at <www.intervarsity.org>.

All Scripture quotations, unless otherwise indicated, are the author's own translation.

Cover photograph: Sarah Stone/Tony Stone Images

ISBN-10: 0-8308-1405-1
ISBN-13: 978-0-8308-1405-3

Printed in the United States of America ∞

Library of Congress Cataloging-in-Publication Data

Keener, Craig S.
The IVP Bible background commentary: New Testament/Craig S. Keener.
p. cm.
Includes bibliographical references.
ISBN 0-8308-1405-1
1. Bible. N.T.—Commentaries. I. InterVarsity Press. II. Title.
BS2341.2.K445 1993
225.7—dc20 93-40939
CIP

P 41 40 39 38 37 36 35 34 33 32 31 30 29 28 27 26
Y 21 20 19 18 17 16 15 14 13 12 11 10 09 08 07

This book is dedicated to our brothers and sisters
on the frontline of evangelism in Africa, Asia, Latin America,
the inner cities of North America and the many other places
where followers of Jesus are paying a high price
to proclaim his gospel in truth. Many of them have not had
the time or opportunity to pursue the original cultural context
of the New Testament, but I pray with all my heart
that this book will be useful to them in their service
to our Lord Jesus Christ.

Acknowledgments

When I began studying the Bible, I just wanted to learn the Bible itself in its original languages so I could spend my life living and preaching it; but the more I read it, the more I realized my need for background. Once I realized, over a quarter century ago, that background helped me understand the Bible better, I desperately began looking for a book that would provide it for each passage. Unable to find such a book, I began scouring many books, and then working through countless volumes of ancient sources. After a decade of nearly full-time research, I resolved to provide such a book, if no one else offered the service first, to save ordinary readers most of the years of study it had taken me. At the time of this foreword, it has received almost unanimous praise and sold well over a quarter million copies.

I wrote the *Background Commentary* to serve readers like the young preacher I was when I began my study: many pastors and other readers who lack access to such tools for reasons of time, training or economics. I did not write this book (in contrast to many others) for scholars (who have access to many primary sources) or those pastors who have access to a wide range of commentaries that provide background in more detail. Many of my fellow biblical scholars have, however, expressed regret that this work does not provide scholarly documentation they could follow up. This lack is unfortunate, but given the book's size already and its primary audience, the editorial decision was made not to bog it down with documentation. Scholars will know where to find some of the information, but I am also writing other commentaries (so far two on Matthew, and one each on John, 1 and 2 Corinthians, and Revelation) that provide much of the documentation as well as detail for what is only summarized here. In the end, then, scholars will also get most of the documentation they want.

I am deeply indebted to the professors with whom I studied over the years. I am also deeply indebted to the students I served through campus ministry or teaching, and to the congregations I served, for the opportunity to test out the ideas in this commentary. They are the ones who helped me sift through which elements of background were genuinely important to communicating the message of the biblical text and which were only peripheral.

I should especially acknowledge my editors: Rodney Clapp; Ruth Goring; and Dan Reid. About two years after I decided that InterVarsity Press would be an ideal publisher for a commentary like this if I ever got the time to write it, Rodney asked if I would be interested in writing a book for InterVarsity Press. A few months later, I prayed for the Lord to provide a particular amount of money so I could pay rent and buy groceries while I worked on writing that year, having no idea where the money would come from. Less than twenty-four hours later, Rodney called and surprised me by offering me an unexpected advance. He could not have guessed that the offer came to the exact dollar amount that I had prayed for the night before. I witnessed the Lord's providence while undertaking this work, and pray that it will serve the needs of his church.

Contents

List of Abbreviations

AB	Anchor Bible
GNC	Good News Commentary
GNS	Good News Studies
HNTC	Harper's New Testament Commentaries
ICC	International Critical Commentary
KJV	King James Version
LEC	Library of Early Christianity
NASB	New American Standard Bible
NCB	New Century Bible
NIBC	New International Bible Commentary
NICNT	New International Commentary on the New Testament
NIGTC	New International Greek Testament Commentary
NIV	New International Version
NRSV	New Revised Standard Version
SBLBMI	Society of Biblical Literature: The Bible and Its Modern Interpreters
SBLDS	Society of Biblical Literature Dissertation Series
SBLMS	Society of Biblical Literature Monograph Series
SBLSBS	Society of Biblical Literature Sources for Biblical Study
SNTSMS	Society of New Testament Studies Monograph Series
TDGR	Translated Documents of Greece and Rome
TEV	Today's English Version
TNTC	Tyndale New Testament Commentary
WBC	Word Biblical Commentary
*	Indicates names and terms found in the glossary

How to Use This Commentary

Cultural and historical background can clarify virtually every text in the New Testament, yet much of this material has been inaccessible to nontechnical readers. Although many helpful commentaries exist, no single commentary has focused solely on the background material. Yet it is precisely this element—the background that indicates how the New Testament's writers and first readers would have understood its message—that the nontechnical reader needs as a resource for Bible study (most other elements, such as context, can be deduced from the text itself).

Some surveys of the cultural background of the New Testament exist, but none of these is arranged in a manner that allows the reader to answer all the pertinent questions on a given passage. This deficiency convinced me twelve years ago to undertake this project, which is now long overdue. This book is written in the hope that all Christians will now be able to read the New Testament much closer to the way its first readers would have read it.

A CULTURAL COMMENTARY

Cultural context makes a difference in how we read the New Testament. For instance, since there were plenty of exorcists in the ancient world, ancient readers would not have been surprised that Jesus cast out demons, but since most exorcists employed magic spells or pain compliance techniques to seek to expel demons, Jesus' driving them out "by his word" was impressive. Viewing the conflict concerning head coverings in 1 Corinthians 11 in the broader context of tensions over head coverings between well-to-do and less well-to-do women in first-century Corinth clarifies Paul's teaching in that passage. Understanding ancient views on slavery demonstrates that Paul's teaching, far from supporting that institution, undermines it. Recognizing what Jewish people meant by "resurrection" answers the objections of many skeptics today concerning the character of Jesus' resurrection. And so forth.

The sole purpose of this commentary (unlike most commentaries) is to make available the most relevant cultural, social and historical background for reading the New Testament the way its first readers would have read it. Although some notes about context or theology have been necessary, such notes have been kept to a minimum to leave most of the work of interpretation with the reader.

Knowing the ancient culture is critical to understanding the Bible. Our need to recognize the setting of the biblical writers does not deny that biblical passages are valid for all *time;* the point is that they are not valid for all *circumstances.* Different texts in the Bible address different situations. For instance, some texts address how to be saved, some address Christ's call to missions, some address his concern for the poor, and so on. Before we apply those passages, we need to understand what circumstances they originally addressed.

This is not to play down the importance of other factors in interpreting the Bible. The most important issue, next to the Spirit's application to our hearts and lives, is always literary context:

reading each book of the Bible the way it was put together under the inspiration of the Holy Spirit. This commentary itself is meant only as a tool to provide readers ready access to New Testament background—it is not meant to be the whole story. In my own preaching and teaching, I am more concerned with literary context than with culture. But readers can ascertain the context on their own by studying the Bible itself. For ministers and other Bible readers, application of the Bible is also crucial, but specific applications will differ from culture to culture and from person to person, and these, again, are readily available to readers of the Bible without outside helps.

For the majority of the users of this commentary, who have not studied Greek and Hebrew, a good, readable translation is crucial for understanding the Bible. (For instance, both the NASB, which is more word for word, and the NIV, which is more readable, are very helpful. One might read regularly from the NIV and study more detailed passages from or compare with the NASB.) In contrast to the half-dozen mainly medieval manuscripts on which the King James Version was based, we now have over five thousand New Testament manuscripts, including some from extremely close to the time the New Testament books were written (by the standards used for ancient texts). These manuscripts make the New Testament by far the best-documented work of the ancient world and also explain why more accurate translations are available today than in times past. But the biggest reason for using an up-to-date translation is that it is written in the current English we speak and thus is easier to understand. Understanding the Bible so one can obey its teaching is, after all, the main purpose for reading it.

Other methods of getting into the text itself, like outlining and taking notes, are also useful to many readers. For a more complete guide on how to study the Bible, the reader should consult the helpful book by Gordon Fee and Douglas Stuart, *How to Read the Bible for All Its Worth* (Grand Rapids, Mich.: Zondervan, 1981).

But the one factor in applying the Bible that is not available to most Bible readers is the cultural background. This commentary is meant to fill that need and should be used in conjunction with other important elements of Bible study: an accurate and readable translation, context, prayer and personal application.

Again, this commentary will not be helpful for those who neglect context, a rule of interpretation more basic than culture. It is best to read through each book of the Bible as a whole, rather than skipping from one part of the Bible to another, so one can get the whole message of a particular biblical book. These books were written one at a time to different groups of readers, who read them one book at a time and applied them to their specific situations. One must keep this point in mind when reading, teaching or preaching from the Bible. (Many alleged contradictions in the Bible arise from ignoring context and the way books were written in the ancient world. Ancient writers, like modern preachers, often applied and updated the language, while being faithful to the meaning, by arranging their materials; so the context is usually inspired guidance on how to apply a teaching in the Bible.) It is always important to check the context of a passage in the biblical book in which it occurs before using this commentary.

But once one has examined a passage in context, this commentary will be an invaluable tool. One may use it while reading through the Bible for daily devotions; one may use it for Bible studies or for sermon preparation. The one book orthodox Christians accept as God's Word is the most important book for us to study, and it is hoped that this commentary will aid all believers in their study of God's Word.

Although the format of this book has been tested in the classroom, in Bible studies, from the pulpit and in personal devotions, it may fail to answer some social-cultural questions related to passages of the New Testament. Despite efforts to answer the right questions, it is impossible to anticipate every question; for this reason, some helpful books on ancient culture are listed in the brief bibliography at the end of this introduction.

The reader may also find background relevant to a particular passage under other passages where I had felt it was most important to include it. Because the New Testament itself is composed of books aimed at different audiences (Mark was meant to be read quickly, whereas Matthew was meant to be studied and memorized), my treatment of some books is more detailed than that of others. As the book most foreign to modern readers, Revelation receives the most detailed treatment.

HOW TO USE THIS BOOK

This commentary may be used either for reference or in conjunction with one's regular Bible reading. In reading the Bible devotionally or in preparing sermons or Bible studies, one has two of the most crucial tools for interpretation in the Bible itself: the text and its context. The third most crucial tool, which was already known and assumed by the ancient readers but is unavailable to most modern readers, is the background of the text. This commentary is written to supply that need to the fullest extent possible in a one-volume work.

The most important ancient background for the New Testament's ideas is the Old Testament, especially in its Greek translation. This commentary includes Old Testament background, but because that background is available to all readers of the Bible, the emphasis of the commentary is on other Jewish and Greco-Roman culture of the first century. Early Christian writers naturally also drew on other early Christian traditions, many of which are available to us in the New Testament; but because that material is directly available to the reader, it has been omitted for the most part here. Similarly omitted are notes on background that are transcultural, because readers in all cultures assume this information.

Those who use this commentary in conjunction with personal Bible study should read the biblical passage first and examine its context. Then they may most profitably examine the notes in this commentary; the notes on related passages may also be helpful. Having established what the text was saying to the ancient readers, one has a real feel for the issues being addressed and is ready to move to the stage of personal application.

The situation behind Paul's letter to the Romans provides one example of how one could apply what one learns in this commentary. In that letter, Paul argues that Jews and Gentiles are saved on the same terms and urges reconciliation between them within the body of Christ. In the United States, where many churches are still segregated along lines of race and white Christians have often not taken the time to hear the hurts that black Christians and other minority peoples have faced here, Paul's message of ethnic reconciliation is painfully relevant. Once we grasp the point of the text in its original historical setting, we are in a position to apply that text to both our personal lives and our culture today.

Because the Bible's original message, once understood, speaks to human issues today in a variety of situations and cultures, the way we apply it will vary from person to person and culture to culture. (For instance, if Paul urges the Corinthians to deal seriously with sin, the principle is clear; but different people will have to deal with different sins.) For that reason, most application is left to the reader's common sense and sensitivity to the Holy Spirit.

This point usually applies even where I strongly felt that guidance should be given concerning application. For instance, in my treatment of Matthew 24:15-22 I emphasize those details that were fulfilled in A.D. 66-70. Some people think that certain prophecies in that passage will be fulfilled again; but because that is a theological rather than a cultural-historical issue, I leave that matter to the reader's discretion. In the same way, I am convinced that the background provided for passages on women's ministry should lead modern readers to recognize that Paul does indeed accept the teaching ministry of women. But due to the nature of this work, someone who does not share that conviction can nevertheless profitably use the commentary on those passages without feeling constrained to accept my view. I dare to hope that all sincere believers, grappling with the same context and the same background, are likely to come to similar conclusions in the end.

Most readers will be familiar with words like *priest* and *Palestine*, but terms whose cultural significance may be unfamiliar to the reader are found in the glossary at the end of this book and are marked at least once in a given context with an asterisk. Some recurrent theological terms (like *Spirit, apocalyptic, Diaspora, Pharisee* and *kingdom)* had specific meanings in the ancient world that cannot be mentioned in each text; the regular reader of this commentary should thus become familiar with these terms in the glossary.

HOW NOT TO USE THIS BOOK

Not all background in this commentary is equally helpful for understanding the Bible. Some background is almost self-evident, especially where ancient culture and modern readers' culture overlap. Likewise, not all sources are of equal merit for our purposes. Some sources, particularly rabbinic sources, are later than the New Testament; some of the information from these sources is more helpful whereas other material is less helpful, and I weighed these factors as carefully as possible in writing this commentary. Usually only Old Testament and Apocrypha citations and occasionally citations from the Jewish Pseudepigrapha are explicitly given in this commentary; citing all the rabbinic, Greek and Roman sources would weigh it down too heavily for the general reader.

Some background is included because it appears in standard scholarly commentaries, and readers must judge for themselves how relevant it is for their interpretation. This is a *background* commentary; it does not dictate how readers must understand or apply the text, and readers who disagree with some interpretations I suggest will nevertheless find the commentary useful.

More importantly, the general reader should be aware that parallels between an idea in the New Testament and an idea in the ancient world need not mean that one copied the other—both may have drawn on a familiar saying or concept in the culture. Thus I cite the parallels simply to illustrate how many people in that culture would have heard what the New Testament was saying. For instance, Paul's use of the kinds of arguments used by rhetoricians (professional public speakers) indicates that he was relating to his culture, not that he wrote without the inspiration of the

Holy Spirit. Further, people and sources from wholly unrelated cultures (e.g., Stoics and the Old Testament) may share some concepts simply because those concepts make sense in those cultures (or even most cultures), even if they do not make sense in ours; our own culture often unconsciously limits our understanding of Paul and his contemporaries. Because ancient peoples did not think as we do does not mean that they were wrong; we can still learn much from their insights in areas like rhetoric and human relationships.

Similarly, when I comment that Paul used the language of Stoic philosophers, I do not mean that Paul had adopted Stoicism; public philosophical discourse had been commonly affected by Stoic ideas and terminology. In other cases, the adoption of philosophical language is intentional; outsiders sometimes viewed Christianity as a philosophical school, and Christians were able to use this outside perception as a means to communicate the gospel. Like other writers, Paul could appeal to his culture in the popular language of his day but give that language a new twist.

When I cite a later Jewish tradition that amplifies the Old Testament, I do not mean to imply that the tradition is necessarily true. These citations are to help us feel how the first readers and hearers of the New Testament felt about the Old Testament characters; sometimes New Testament writers also allude to these extrabiblical traditions (Jude 14-15). (One need not assume that New Testament writers always simply recycled earlier Jewish imagery to relate to their culture, however; often a variety of Jewish views existed, and the New Testament writers picked a particular one. Although the New Testament writers had to accommodate the language of their day to communicate their point, neither they nor we need see all that language as inaccurate. Some modern readers assume glibly that ancient worldviews are wrong, but phenomena sometimes attributed to "primitive" worldviews, such as possession by harmful spirits, can now be corroborated by crosscultural evidence; they need not be explained away by modern Western rationalism.)

Finally, we should always be cautious in application; it is important that we apply biblical texts only to genuinely analogous situations. For instance, it is not accurate to read Jesus' attacks on the religious leaders of his day as attacks against all Jewish people, as some anti-Semites have. Jesus and his disciples were themselves Jewish, and such an abuse of the text makes no more sense than using the book of Exodus against Egyptians today (later Old Testament prophets did not, e.g., Is 19:23-25). Jesus' challenges against the piety of religious authorities in his day have nothing to do with their ethnicity; these challenges are meant to confront us as religious people today and warn us not to act as those religious leaders did. The issue was a religious one, not an ethnic one. In other words, we must apply the *principles* of the text in the light of the real issues the biblical authors were addressing and not ignore the passages' historical context.

A POPULAR, NOT A SCHOLARLY, COMMENTARY

Scholars may be disappointed that the text of this work is not documented or nuanced the way a scholarly work would be, but should keep in mind that this book is not written primarily for scholars, who already have access to much of this information elsewhere. But pastors and other Bible readers who have fewer resources and less time available need a concise and handy reference work in one volume at their disposal.

Scholars like to document and investigate all angles of a question, nuancing their language carefully and guarding against attacks by those holding other interpretations of the same texts. This is not possible in a work of this length. Scholars also like to include all available data, which the same limitation also prohibits here. To be useful for most pastors' preaching and most other Christians' Bible study, this work's language needs to be plain and concise.

I have generally ignored scholarly questions that do not deal directly with the issue central to this book, the ancient context of the New Testament. It is important for the purpose of this book to ask what the text as it stands means; it is not important to ask about the sources behind the text and their editing, and I have dealt with those issues only where absolutely necessary. When I have addressed those issues, however, I have done so from orthodox Christian assumptions about Scripture, assumptions which I could amply defend were that my purpose in this book.

The purpose of this book is likewise limited not only to cultural-historical context in general, but also to that which actually sheds light on the New Testament. For instance, to claim that some emphasis of early Christianity is distinctive to Christianity is not to claim that other groups did not have their own distinctive characteristics; but this is a commentary on the New Testament, not a commentary on those other groups.

I have, however, tried to be as fair as possible to the major different views of the background of the New Testament. My own research divides fairly evenly between the Jewish and Greco-Roman contexts of the New Testament, with an emphasis on ancient Judaism as part of the larger Mediterranean culture. I have often labored over a variety of interpretations of the evidence before selecting which interpretation or interpretations I felt were most accurate or most relevant to the text. Not every scholar will agree on every point, but I have endeavored to make the book as accurate and helpful as possible. I hope that this book will both stimulate other students to pursue more detailed scholarship and provide easy access to the world of the New Testament for those whose call in life does not permit them the opportunity to pursue it in more detail.

My comments are based on more than a decade of work especially on the primary literature of the ancient world but also on recent scholarly research in ancient Judaism and Greco-Roman antiquity, as well as on other commentaries. Were I to cite all the sources to which I am indebted, this commentary would run to an unmanageable length, but I acknowledge here that they are many. (One source I have meticulously avoided, due to current scholarly criticism, is Strack-Billerbeck's commentary on the New Testament from rabbinic sources. Most of my beginning work in ancient Judaism was in rabbinic sources, and I trust that the reader will have lost nothing from this omission. Besides being out of date, Strack-Billerbeck suffers from a lack of discrimination between early and late sources, those most and least likely to be representative of early Judaism as a whole, and worst of all, from an unfair portrayal of the spirit of the sources. I have tried to avoid these mistakes insofar as possible in my own work.)

To keep the commentary to manageable length, I have made painful decisions about what material to omit. I have not adduced the many parallels available to turns of phrases or mentioned remote parallels that would not illumine a passage for the minister or general reader. I have often chosen to delete material of uncertain value, even if it is used by many other scholars. (For instance, given the uncertainty of the date of the document called the Similitudes of Enoch, I have not used it as background for Jesus' title "Son of Man," although many scholars do.) I have also tried to avoid duplicating the information available in other commonly used reference works. Because word studies are elsewhere available, I have generally omitted discussions of Greek words except where the meaning of the text depends on the broader cultural context of these words.

Readers may detect some points where my own theology has influenced my reading of a text in a manner that disagrees with their own. I genuinely try to derive my theology and applications only from my study of the biblical text, but if the reverse has occasionally happened, I ask the reader's pardon. This book is meant to be useful, not controversial, and if readers disagree on some points, I hope they will find most of the rest of the commentary helpful nonetheless.

OTHER SOURCES FOR THE CULTURAL CONTEXT OF THE NEW TESTAMENT

The following sources are useful to readers of the New Testament.

General. See especially John E. Stambaugh and David L. Balch, *The New Testament in Its Social Environment*, LEC 2 (Philadelphia: Westminster, 1986); David E. Aune, *The New Testament in Its Literary Environment*, LEC 8 (Philadelphia: Westminster, 1987); Everett Ferguson, *Backgrounds of Early Christianity* (Grand Rapids, Mich.:

Eerdmans, 1987). A helpful anthology of texts is C. K. Barrett, *The New Testament Background: Selected Documents,* rev. ed. (San Francisco: Harper & Row, 1989); a helpful one-volume source of data is *The New Bible Dictionary,* ed. J. D. Douglas, 2nd ed. (Wheaton, Ill.: Tyndale House/Leicester, U.K.: Inter-Varsity Press, 1982); see more fully *The International Standard Bible Encyclopedia,* 4 vols., rev. ed., ed. Geoffrey W. Bromiley (Grand Rapids, Mich.: Eerdmans, 1979-88).

How to Understand the Bible in Its Context. See especially Gordon D. Fee and Douglas Stuart, *How to Read the Bible for All Its Worth: A Guide to Understanding the Bible* (Grand Rapids, Mich.: Zondervan, 1981); compare A. Berkeley Mickelsen and Alvera Mickelsen, *Understanding Scripture* (Peabody, Mass.: Hendrickson, 1992).

Students wishing for a more advanced discussion of modern hermeneutical (interpretive) issues should consult Grant R. Osborne, *The Hermeneutical Spiral: A Comprehensive Introduction to Biblical Interpretation* (Downers Grove, Ill.: InterVarsity Press, 1991).

Judaism: General. E. P. Sanders, *Judaism: Practice and Belief, 63 BCE—66 CE* (Philadelphia: Trinity, 1992).

Judaism: Rabbinic Judaism. The most complete summaries of the views of the ancient rabbis are George Foot Moore, *Judaism in the First Centuries of the Christian Era,* 2 vols. (1927; reprint, New York: Schocken, 1971); and Ephraim E. Urbach, *The Sages: Their Concepts and Beliefs,* 2 vols., 2nd ed. (Jerusalem: Magnes, Hebrew University, 1979). Unfortunately, neither work gives special attention to the development in rabbinic thought; New Testament students must depend on the earliest and most widely attested (preferably in other kinds of sources) traditions. But it does not hurt readers to start with a basic summary of the developed traditions, if one is sensitive to the dates of rabbis cited and the dates of the documents in which the attributions occur, and to the breadth of attestation provided. (The arguments of Jacob Neusner and others in this regard are now generally accepted, although details and levels of skepticism concerning the sources vary.)

Judaism: Surveys of the Documents. One useful work is Samuel Sandmel, *Judaism and Christian Beginnings* (New York: Oxford University Press, 1978); cf. Martin McNamara, *Palestinian Judaism and the New Testament,* GNS 4 (Wilmington, Del.: Michael Glazier, 1983). For a summary of rabbinic literature, see Hermann L. Strack, *Introduction to the Talmud and Midrash* (1931; reprint, New York: Atheneum, 1978). Some more recent and progressive approaches may be sampled in volumes like *Early Judaism and Its Modern Interpreters,* ed. Robert A. Kraft and George W. E. Nickelsburg, SBLBMI 2 (Atlanta: Scholars Press, 1986). Most issues are treated in detail in more specialized works; for instance, see E. P. Sanders, *Paul and Palestinian Judaism* (Philadelphia: Fortress, 1977), for Jewish views on salvation; on the roles of women see Leonard Swidler, *Women in Judaism: The Status of Women in Formative Judaism* (Metuchen, N.J.: Scarecrow, 1976); Judith Romney Wegner, *Chattel or Person? The Status of Women in the Mishnah* (New York: Oxford University Press, 1988).

Judaism: Primary Sources. One should especially read the Old Testament and the Apocrypha (in the latter, especially Wisdom of Solomon and Ecclesiasticus or Sirach); then translations of the Dead Sea Scrolls; and the documents of most relevant date in *The Old Testament Pseudepigrapha,* ed. James H. Charlesworth, 2 vols. (Garden City, N.Y.: Doubleday, 1983-1985), especially 1 Enoch, Jubilees, the Sibylline Oracles (not all from the same period), the Letter of Aristeas and others like 4 Ezra and 2 Baruch. Josephus is invaluable, though due to the sheer volume of his works, one may wish to focus on *Against Apion,* the *Life* and then the *War (The Works of Josephus,* trans. W. Whiston [Peabody, Mass.: Hendrickson, 1987]). Readers may wish to peruse Philo to acquaint themselves with a major Jewish philosopher in the Diaspora; the works of Philo are now available in a one-volume edition (trans. C. D. Yonge; Peabody, Mass.: Hendrickson, 1993). Those who wish to examine rabbinic literature firsthand might start with *Abot* in the Mishnah; many early traditions are also preserved in the Tosefta, Abot de Rabbi Nathan and the tannaitic commentaries on parts of the Pentateuch (Mekilta on Exodus, Sifra on Leviticus, Sifre on Numbers, and Sifre on Deuteronomy). Archaeological data are regularly published in journals but also appear in books such as Eric M. Meyers and James F. Strange, *Archaeology, the Rabbis, and Early Christianity* (Nashville: Abingdon, 1981); collections of inscriptions and papyri are also helpful.

Greco-Roman World: General. See Stambaugh and Balch, *Social Environment;* M. Cary and T. J. Haarhoff, *Life and Thought in the Greek and Roman World,* 4th ed. (London: Methuen, 1946); cf. also Abraham J. Malherbe, *Moral Exhortation: A Greco-Roman Sourcebook,* LEC 4 (Philadelphia: Westminster, 1986); Wayne A. Meeks, *The Moral World of the First Christians,* LEC 6 (Philadelphia: Westminster, 1986).

Greco-Roman World: Secondary Sources. On the way texts were written and understood in the Greco-Roman world, see Aune, *Literary Environment;* cf. also Stanley K. Stowers, *Letter Writing in Greco-Roman Antiquity,* LEC 5 (Philadelphia: Westminster, 1986). On moralists and moral issues, see Malherbe, *Moral Exhortation;* and Meeks, *Moral World.* On Greek religion, see Walter Burkert, *Greek Religion* (Cambridge: Harvard University Press, 1985).

On history, Tacitus, Suetonius and Josephus are quite readable and may be pursued before the secondary sources; many Greek and Roman sources are available in paperback (e.g., through Penguin Books), although those wishing to do more advanced work should locate the Loeb Classical Library editions. Helpful secondary sources include F. F. Bruce, *New Testament History* (Garden City, N.Y.: Doubleday, 1972); and Bo Reicke, *The New Testament Era: The World of the Bible from 500 B.C. to A.D. 100* (Philadelphia: Fortress, 1974). Specialized works, such as those on women in antiquity (e.g., Mary R. Lefkowitz and Maureen B. Fant, *Women's Life in Greece and Rome* [Baltimore: Johns Hopkins University Press, 1982], one collection of texts), are indispensable for more detailed study.

Greco-Roman World: Primary Sources. A broad sampling of documents is available in *The Roman Empire: Augustus to Hadrian,* ed. Robert K. Sherk, TDGR 6 (New York: Cambridge University Press, 1988). For first-century history, one should read Tacitus and Suetonius. For first- and second-century moral thought, one should at least sample Epictetus, Seneca, Plutarch and perhaps a satirist like Juvenal; see also Abraham J. Malherbe, *The Cynic Epistles: A Study Edition,* SBLSBS 12 (Missoula, Mont.: Scholars Press, 1977).

Introductions to New Testament Scholarship. See, for example, Luke T. Johnson, *The Writings of the New Testament: An Interpretation* (Philadelphia: Fortress, 1986); D. A. Carson, Douglas J. Moo and Leon Morris, *An Introduction to the New Testament* (Grand Rapids, Mich.: Zondervan, 1992); Donald Guthrie, *New Testament Introduction* (Downers Grove, Ill.: InterVarsity Press, 1970); George Eldon Ladd, *A Theology of the New Testament* (Grand Rapids, Mich.: Eerdmans, 1974). On the historical reliability of the New Testament, see, e.g., F. F. Bruce, *The New Testament Documents: Are They Reliable?* 5th ed. (Grand Rapids: Eerdmans, 1980).

The Need for a Cultural-Historical Commentary

Many readers will recognize the value of a cultural commentary. But others may, even after reading "How to Use This Commentary," still remain unclear. The following essay elaborates the importance of cultural background in biblical interpretation for those who have not been exposed to this issue previously. Because those already trained in biblical studies will agree with the need for cultural context, this essay is directed solely toward nontechnical readers.

HOW THE BIBLE ITSELF INVITES US TO INTERPRET IT

Readers of the Bible have long realized the value of cultural and historical background for understanding the Bible. The biblical writers themselves assume its importance. For instance, when Mark writes about an issue debated by Jesus and his opponents, he explains the custom involved in it to his Gentile readers, who would not have otherwise known the custom (Mk 7:3-4). Similarly, when Jesus' opponents take an apparent concession in the Law at face value, Jesus says that the *intent* of the Law is what is crucial, and to grasp it one must understand the situation and the state of its original audience (Mk 10:4-5).

Biblical writers can often simply assume the importance of the readers' knowing the situation. (It was understood in the ancient world that the better one knew the situation with which a speech dealt, the better one could understand the speech: see the first-century A.D. Roman rhetorician *Quintilian 10.1.22; one should also keep rereading the speech to catch all the subtle nuances and foreshadowings in it; see Quintilian 10.1.20-21.) For instance, when Paul writes a letter to the Corinthians, he can assume that the Corinthians know what situations he is addressing. Reading 1 Corinthians may be like listening to one side of a telephone conversation, and we can fortunately reconstruct most of the conversation by reading 1 Corinthians. But part of the meaning of the conversation is determined by the situation itself, not just by the words in front of us. What Paul *assumes* his readers will grasp in his writing is as much a part of his meaning as what he *says*. If we cannot relate to the situation he and his readers are assuming, we will have more difficulty understanding his point. A few examples will illustrate this point.

Paul addresses the issue of celibacy in 1 Corinthians 7. There he definitely sounds as if he favors celibacy, and even though he allows marriage as a valid lifestyle, some commentators think he suggests that it is a second-class lifestyle for those who do not have the gift of being able to "control themselves." He certainly makes some valid points about the benefits of singleness, but is he really against marriage in general? First Corinthians 7:1 tells us plainly that Paul is responding to a letter from some of the Christians in Corinth. Because some of these Christians followed a certain view in their culture that opposed marriage, one could just as easily read the chapter as follows: Paul is saying, "You have a good point, and I agree with you that singleness is a good gift from God. But you are taking matters too far if you impose it on married people or on people who should get married."

A clearer example would be how we read Paul's warnings about meat offered to idols. It would be all too easy for readers today to say, "Well, there aren't any idols to sacrifice meat to today, so let's just skip this chapter of 1 Corinthians." But this sidesteps the transcultural issue *behind* the cultural issue. Once we see how concrete the issue was in Corinth—that well-to-do Christians who did not eat this food could offend friends and business associates, and all to keep the less-educated Christians from being hurt in their faith—we can compare it with similar issues today. Some Christians today want a prestigious lifestyle because it attracts other yuppies to a religion that demands little in the way of sacrifice—even if such a religion alienates the homeless and hungry in developing nations and in our North American cities. Considering how to balance the interests of different factions in a church is relevant in many congregations today.

Understanding that the Bible does address issues and motives like those we face today is important. Far from making the Bible less relevant, understanding the situation helps us make it more relevant (sometimes even uncomfortably relevant). It forces us to see that the people with whom Paul dealt were not simply morally unstable troublemakers; they were real people with real agendas like ourselves.

RELEVANCE TO ALL CULTURES

Most of the book God gave us was not directly dictated in the first person (i.e., the Bible does not read as if God were saying: "I'm God, and I am speaking directly to everybody in all times"). Some Bible readers have always wanted the Bible to read that way and like to pretend that this is the proper way to interpret it. But God chose to inspire the Bible in a different form: he inspired his prophets and witnesses to address real situations in their own day as an example for generations that would follow (1 Cor 10:11). If Paul was inspired to write a letter to the Corinthians, whether people today like it or not, that letter is a letter to the *Corinthians,* just as it claims to be.

God gave us eternal principles, but he gave them to us in specific concrete forms, addressing real situations. He gave us those principles in the form of illustrations, to show us how those principles work out in real-life situations, because he wanted to make sure that we would apply them to our own real-life situations. Thus, for example, Deuteronomy 22:8 ("build a parapet around your roof, lest you incur bloodguilt if someone falls off") still teaches us concern for our neighbor's safety, even though most of us no longer have flat roofs on which we entertain our neighbors. The moral today might be, "Make your colleague fasten her seatbelt when she rides with you to work." The example might be different today, but the point is the same; yet until we understand the original example, we cannot recognize the real point we must reapply in our own culture.

We may not like the fact that God gave us his Word in concrete form, because in our culture we are used to thinking abstractly. But in many cultures people think concretely and can read a story or a conversation and learn much more about God than we can learn from reading a series of abstractions. Those cultures are more attuned to the Bible that God chose to give the world than we are. Much of the Bible is historical narrative (i.e., true stories), and much of it is letter or prophecy directed to specific situations. Thus its format is more like a conversation than an abstract philosophical treatise. Even abstract principles like those in Proverbs are expressed in specific cultural forms; for instance, some Egyptian wisdom sayings use almost the same wording as their Hebrew counterparts, because that was how people in that part of the ancient Near East expressed their wisdom at that time.

If God had not chosen to give us the Bible in concrete, cultural forms, what forms would he have used? Is there a neutral language, a universal one not bound by any culture? (Some North Americans seem to think that English is neutral; but had the Normans not ruled English territory for some time, *we* would not speak English now ourselves.) As one scholar put it, if God had just spoken to us in a cosmic wind, how many of us would have understood him? Or as one cartoon put it, if God had revealed the details of quantum physics and the theory of relativity to Moses, instead of "In the beginning God created," would Moses or the Hebrew language have been able to communicate that data to his contemporaries? God is too practical and too concerned about us understanding him to try to communicate with us like that. He worked through all the different cultures—from early in the Old Testament to totally different cultural situations in the New Testament—to communicate his Word.

BEYOND OUR OWN CULTURAL STARTING POINTS

Indeed, God is so involved in the multicultural matrix of history that he did not disdain to step into it himself. The ultimate enculturation of his Word occurred when the Word became flesh, as the prologue of John (1:1-18) declares. Jesus did not come as a cultureless, amorphous, genderless human. He came as a first-century Jewish man, with unique chromosomes and physical features, just as each of the rest of us is unique. His cultural specificity does not mean that he was not *for* all of us; it means instead that he could better identify with all of us as a *particular* person—by being like we are—than by being a general, faceless person who compromised any real humanity for an indistinctive "neutrality." Many Gnostics, who reinterpreted Christianity in later centuries, tried to deny that Jesus really came "in the flesh," but the apostle John is clear that this point is the dividing line between genuine and phony Christians: genuine Christians believe that our Lord Jesus came in the flesh, as a particular historical person (1 Jn 4:1-6). Those who insist on understanding Jesus—or the other people in the Bible—apart from that historical particularity are treading on the outer fringes of Christian faith.

One of the main emphases in the book of Acts is that the gospel is for all peoples and all cultures. The first Christians were surprised to learn that the gospel was for Gentiles as well as Jews, but throughout the book of Acts the Spirit of God was revealing this multicultural mission to the church. That was God's program from the beginning: missions from Jerusalem to the ends of the earth. Those like Stephen and Paul, who already knew more than one culture, were the most ready to participate in God's plan. People who assume that God reveals himself only in one culture (their own) are a couple of millennia behind on their Bible reading! In Acts we find God purposely revealing himself to people of all cultures in terms they understood; thus Paul preaches one way in a synagogue in Acts 13, another way to rural farmers in chapter 14 and still another way to Greek philosophers in chapter 17. The same Paul related to specific issues of ancient culture in his letters, and we cannot ignore those issues if we wish to know what Paul's point was.

When Paul fought for Gentiles to have the right to come to Christ as Gentiles, he was fighting cultural bigots who (in that case) said that one had to be Jewish to be a first-rate Christian. They read the Bible in the light of their own culture and tradition and thought that everybody else should read it the same way they did. They had quite a lot of good company, unfortunately, because their problem was not their Jewishness—Paul was just as Jewish as they were. The problem was that they read the Bible in light of their own cultural assumptions, which is the same problem we all have unless we train ourselves to see beyond those assumptions. Our own backgrounds and the information we start with affect the categories and associations we bring to a text—consciously or unconsciously. By contrast, getting more of the ancient readers' backgrounds helps us to read texts more as they would have read them.

Missionaries today face problems similar to Paul's. (For instance, compare the graphic examples in Don Richardson, *Peace Child* [Ventura, Calif.: Regal Books, 1974], and case studies in more technical works from various perspectives, like Marvin K. Mayers, *Christianity Confronts Culture: A Strategy for Cross-Cultural Evangelism* [Grand Rapids, Mich.: Zondervan, 1974]; Charles H. Kraft, *Christianity in Culture: A Study in Dynamic Biblical Theologizing in Cross-Cultural Perspective* [Maryknoll, N.Y.: Orbis, 1979]; Louis J. Luzbetak, *The Church and Cultures: An Applied Anthropology for the Religious Worker* [Techny, Ill.: Divine Word, 1970; Pasadena, Calif.: William Carey, 1976].) If we read the gospel in the light of our own culture, we are in danger of mixing our culture in with the Bible and then imposing our new concoction on someone else as a condition of being right with God. For instance, missionaries were the first people to introduce divorce into some African societies, thinking that they were creating a remedy for polygamy. They refused to accept these African converts as full Christians until they got rid of their extra wives. In so doing, they not only introduced a new sin and social upheaval into these societies, but they imposed a condition on these new believers that the Bible itself does not demand. Polygamous marriages do not appear in a healthy light in the Bible, and I am not suggesting that polygamy is good. But neither should we simply break up polygamous marriages already in existence, without thought for the husbands, wives, children and others involved. Nowhere does the Bible advocate breaking up such marriages already in existence.

Most missionaries today recognize that Christians in different cultures can learn from one another. Different parts of the Bible appeal to different groups. One part of the Bible unclear to us may be clear to some Shona Christians in Zimbabwe. Or a reading that one group thinks is clear may be a misinterpretation of the text. Hindus who read Jesus' teaching about being "born again" as a reference to reincarnation have missed Jesus' meaning because they have read it from the standpoint of Hindu assumptions. But if we start merely from our own culture's assumptions, we stand as much chance of misreading the Bible as reincarnationist Hindus do. (Hopefully none of us would err so far as the man who suspected that when the Bible called Herod a "fox," it meant that his subjects thought him attractive.)

Some devoutly evangelical Christians in certain Asian and African cultures still venerate their ancestors, and North American Christians generally consider such veneration as pagan. But we North Americans often explain away texts like "You can't serve both God and mammon," and "covetousness is idolatry," so we can live the way we want. Christians in other cultures generally consider our culture's materialism as pagan too. Our cultural blinders let us see other people's sins more easily than our own, and only reading the Scriptures the way the writers were inspired to intend them—rather than the way the Scriptures fit what we already believe—will challenge our own cultural misconceptions.

What common ground can we, as Christian interpreters from a variety of cultures, have? If we want an objective way to interpret the Bible, and if we believe that the writers were inspired to address specific issues of their day, then we need to try to find out what issues they were addressing. To some extent we can figure that out from the texts themselves. We do not have to know what women's head coverings looked like in Corinth to figure out from 1 Corinthians 11 that the question of whether women should wear head coverings was an issue there. Further, some texts can give us background for other texts; for instance, 2 Kings tells us what was going on when Isaiah was prophesying to the people of Israel, and so helps us understand the book of Isaiah.

But such background is not always enough. This is true not only of so-called problem passages but also of passages that we assume we interpret correctly. For instance, when we read that the good seed bears fruit a hundred times over (Mt 13:23), only if we know the average size of an ancient Palestinian harvest do we understand how abundant such a harvest would be. The charge against Jesus posted above the cross, "The King of the Jews," makes a lot more sense if we recognize that the Romans were very nervous about so-called prophets in Judea whom some people thought were messianic kings, because some of these "prophets" had already stirred up a great deal of trouble for Rome.

Further, culture affects even which books strike us as easier to understand; different parts of the Bible appeal to different cultures. Any reader of Leviticus and 1 Timothy could tell that the forms of writing used in these documents are quite different. Leviticus's hygiene codes have parallels in Hittite and other ancient Near Eastern texts; Leviticus was addressing issues of its day. But the subject matter of Leviticus would not have even interested most Greco-Roman readers by the time 1 Timothy was written, whereas all of 1 Timothy's themes and literary forms have parallels in Greco-Roman literature. To modern Western readers, most of the New Testament is much more inviting than Leviticus; but in many cultures, laws concerning what is clean and unclean are important, and Christians in these cultures have taken more interest in some parts of the Bible that we tend to ignore. Of course, we have theological reasons for saying that we do not need to obey Leviticus literally today; but if all Scripture is inspired and profitable for teaching (2 Tim 3:16), it must have some purpose. The question is just, What is that purpose? What point was God communicating to his people? Cultural background helps us figure out what the purpose was.

OBJECTIONS TO USING CULTURAL BACKGROUND

Although everyone knows that the Bible was written in a different time and culture, and most people take that fact into account when they read particular passages, not everyone is consistent in using cultural background. Of course, not all passages in the Bible require much background; our culture still has some features in common with the culture of the Bible. But if we do not know anything about the original culture, we may sometimes assume that we do not need any background for a passage when in fact it would dramatically affect the way we read the text. Even though most people recognize the need to pay attention to cultural background, some people become nervous at the suggestion that they need it.

Some Christians occasionally object that using cultural and historical background is dangerous. "After all," they complain, "you can use culture to twist the Bible around to mean anything." People who raise this objection could cite one of the arguments raised by some apologists for a gay church with whom I have talked. Some gay theological writers claim that Paul argues against homosexual behavior only because at that time it was normally associated with idolatry; thus they suggest that Paul would not oppose homosexual behavior today. With no disrespect intended for these writers, the problem in this case is that the cultural background these writers give is wrong: homosexual behavior was widespread among the Greeks and was practiced by some Romans, and it was by no means specifically linked with idolatry. Although this example is a good argument against *making up* cultural background, it is no reason not to use genuine cultural background.

One might keep in mind that people have been twisting the Bible quite ably for a long time without using any cultural background; it is doubtful that a little historical study would make matters any worse. *Ignoring* the original culture and so reading it in light of our own is a far graver threat to most of us. (For example, the "Aryan Christians" under the Nazis "demythologized" biblical history to make it non-Jewish and hence more palatable to Nazi tastes. This is an extreme example of ignoring original historical context and reinterpreting the Bible to fit one's own culture. It differs from most reinterpretations today only in that the Nazis did it intentionally.)

A more common objection, which I raised myself a decade and a half ago, is that assuming the importance of cultural background might take the Bible out of the hands of nonscholars. At that time I rejected the use of cultural information so thoroughly that I insisted that women should wear head coverings in church, and I even tried to get up enough nerve to engage in some of Paul's "holy kissing." Fortunately, I deferred the kissing idea till I could resolve the issue (I say "fortunately" because someone would have probably hit me). I finally did resolve it, and the more I have studied the world of the Bible, the more I have come to realize that God was being relevant in communicating his Word the way he did. He gave us concrete examples of how his ways address real human situations, not just abstract principles that we could memorize without pondering how to apply them to our lives. If we wish to follow God's example of being relevant, we need to understand what these teachings meant in their original culture before we try applying them to our own.

Cultural background does not take the Bible out of people's hands; it is when we *ignore* cultural context that we take the Bible out of people's hands. To hand people the symbols in Revelation with no explanation of how such symbols were commonly used in the ancient world is like handing the Gospel of Luke in Greek to somebody who cannot read Greek and saying, "Since this is the Word of God, you must understand and explain it." Only a trained scholar or a complete fool would have any idea what to do with it (and the fool's idea would be wrong).

TRANSLATING BOTH LANGUAGE AND CULTURE

Some scholars before the time of Luther decided that the church hierarchy of their day was wrong to keep the Bible in Latin. Most people could not understand the Bible unless scholars translated it for them into their own language. Some of these scholars were martyred for their conviction that the Bible must be available in common people's language; Luther, who translated the Bible into the German of his day, barely escaped this same fate. The best way scholars could help people was not by saying, "Translations are not available for the common people; therefore we take the Bible out of their hands if we say they actually needed such translations all along." The better approach was for such scholars to say, "Translations are not available for the people; therefore we will put the Bible into their hands by doing some hard work and making translations."

Translating can be difficult, as anybody who has studied a foreign language can testify. Some words do not translate directly in a single term; sometimes a word or phrase can have several different meanings, and the translator has to decide which meaning is best for a particular context. There is also more than one way to express an idea in English once one decides what it means. Those of us who have read the whole New Testament in Greek can testify that the same problems obtain there as in any other text we might try to translate. A random check of any passage in two or three Bible translations will verify the difficulty: no two translations will match exactly (otherwise, of course, they wouldn't be separate translations).

When Bible translators go into other cultures they face difficult questions regarding the meanings of words and phrases. For instance, some translators had to explain "Behold, the Lamb of God!" (Jn 1:29) for a culture that had no sheep and thus no words for lambs. The culture did, however, have pigs, and used them for sacrifices. But if they translated it "Behold, the Pig of God!" (which does not ring nicely to our American ears, and certainly would have offended ancient Jewish sensibilties even more), what would happen when they had to translate passages in the Old Testament where pigs were unclean but sheep were not? Perhaps they could best solve the issue by putting a footnote in the text and by translating with some combination of words that communicated the concept as best as possible in their language, like "hairy pig." Old Testament translators have had to resort to similar methods when rendering the Hebrew words for different kinds of locusts into English (Joel 1:4; 2:25). English does not have enough different words for locusts to match all the Hebrew terms, perhaps because the many varieties of locusts were more of an issue for the Israelites than they are for most of us.

But there is a bigger problem than just the words in the text in front of us. What happens when Paul makes an allusion to a whole concept that was important in his day? How do we translate that? Or do we just mention the issue in a footnote? The allusion that Paul makes is part of his meaning, yet sometimes even those who are otherwise competent to translate the text cannot catch the allusions Paul makes.

Some Christian readers during and before the Reformation period tried to figure out the situations that biblical texts were addressing. It was good that many scholars recognized the need to read the New Testament in the context of its own world, rather than viewing it as if it had been written in German or English directly to readers in the Renaissance or some other period. They were not, however, the majority. Most readers still read too much of their own culture into the text, just as we do when we fail to look at it in the light of the original culture. Medieval and Renaissance intellectuals did the same thing; most of us have seen paintings of biblical scenes with Europeans in European dress filling all the roles of the biblical dramas. They were painted as if most of the biblical characters were Europeans, even though we know that few biblical characters were Europeans, and none was northern European.

Fortunately, some knowledge about the ancient world was still available in the Reformation period. Many scholars from medieval days up through the nineteenth century were so competent in the Greek classics that they could catch all sorts of allusions to Greek customs in the New Testament. The problem is that many Greek customs had changed from the time those classics had been written to the time of the New Testament.

Another danger in assuming that all the background to the New Testament was classical Greek may be illustrated from the first few centuries that the New Testament was in circulation. The Gnostics often read the New Testament more in the light of Plato than in the light of the Judaism from which it emerged, and this was the source of many of their doctrines which other Christians rejected as heretical. Plato did have some influence on the world of the New Testament, but he was hardly the most important influence.

Some writers, like John Lightfoot in the 1600s, challenged the predominant classical grid through which the New Testament was being read and offered Jewish texts as New Testament background. Lightfoot bent over backward to cover himself against the attacks of anti-Semites, explaining at some length that he indeed thought these Jewish texts were unspiritual, but that the work was necessary if one were to understand the New Testament.

Today, when anti-Semitism is less popular than in Lightfoot's day, it is more obvious to us that the Greek texts Lightfoot's contemporaries were using were much more pagan than the texts for which he found it necessary to apologize to his readers. Today it is generally recognized that Judaism forms the *primary* context of the New Testament. Its basic, broad context is Greco-Roman society, but Jewish people had lived in and adapted to Greco-Roman culture, paving the way for the first Christians' witness in the context of pagan culture. Further, the first Christians were

Jewish, and outsiders perceived Christianity as a form of Judaism. Moreover, the earliest Christians themselves saw their faith in Jesus as the true fulfillment of the Old Testament hope and hence saw themselves as faithful to Judaism. (Indeed, the New Testament writers affirm that only Christians were faithful to biblical Judaism; although some other Jewish groups also claimed to be the faithful remnant of Israel, these groups do not seem to have survived into subsequent centuries.) Both the specific Jewish and the broader Greco-Roman contexts of the New Testament are crucial for its interpretation, just as a good translation is.

THE WORK THAT REMAINS

Christians, especially those most committed to crosscultural missions, have always recognized the importance of reading the Bible in the light of its original cultural context. But while translations are available to most Christians, the cultural "footnotes" are not. Many helpful commentaries do exist, but no single commentary provides easy access to all the requisite background in one or two volumes. The more volumes in a work, the less accessible it becomes to most readers. Only a small percentage of people who read the Bible today have full sets of commentaries, fewer of them would have access to adequate cultural information in each of those commentaries, and fewer still can regularly take time to sort through them.

Many earlier biblical scholars gave their lives to translate the Bible and so to begin to make it intelligible to whoever wanted to read it; but the work has never been completed. Many Bible readers still have very limited access to the background. Although many tasks demand the attention of Christian biblical scholars, this is surely one of the most important.

The need to understand the cultural context of the Bible should be as clear today as the need for translation was in the Reformation period. In our industrial, Western society, we are moving farther and farther from any vestige of biblical roots; our culture is becoming more and more alienated from the cultures in which the Bible was written and our young people are finding God's Book more and more foreign. It does no good to lament that most people will not visit our churches and learn our Christian language. God has called us to be missionaries in our world, so we must make the Word of God intelligible to our culture. We must not simply read it; we must understand it and explain it. We must explain what the writers meant when they wrote it to cultures long since changed or vanished, and how its message applies to us today.

Most of the church in North America today seems asleep to its mission, largely because we have not allowed the Word of God to speak to us in all its radical power. We have allowed it to be a foreign book, and allowed the people it addresses to be a people far removed from our own lives. The tragedy is that the stakes have never been as high as they are in our generation: the world boasts a population five times as high as it did one and a half centuries ago, when the church was stirring to its missions call in another great move of the Spirit. Now, with millions of international students, visitors and immigrants often moving into regions with a high concentration of Christians, the opportunities are greater than ever before, as is the need. Not only can we send out many of our number as laborers for the harvest; all the rest of us must labor for the harvest here. We cannot afford to sleep.

God is making more than one important demand to his church, but one crucial demand is that we understand his Word. In a culture full of Bibles and teachings, those who value the Bible's authority still need to know and understand it better. Pastors, usually overworked, rarely have the time to investigate all the necessary resources to acquire background for each text on which they preach. Yet the need to understand God's message and to awaken the whole church to his call so we can fulfill the commission our Lord has given us is urgent.

Among the resources God provides for that task are specialists gifted in the body of Christ as teachers who can provide various valid insights to help us understand and apply God's Word. Just as missionaries must learn a language and a culture to communicate God's message to another culture, we need servants of God on the other end, learning the language and culture in which God's Book was written. Such teachers labored in the past to provide translations and labor today to provide other tools to make the treasures of the Bible more widely accessible to all its readers.

That certain segments of the secular academic community privately or publicly deride those who devote scholarship to God's glory or want their conclusions to be of practical value in the world makes it difficult for some scholars, who must answer to such critics, to write for the church. That some Christians have connected research with impiety does not help, either. But a long list of Christian scholars throughout history demonstrates that research can make the biblical message more available—scholars from Justin, Jerome and Augustine, to the monks who led the medieval universities on which modern universities are based, and later Luther, Calvin, Wesley and others. Charles Finney and Jonathan Edwards, leading figures in America's Great Awakenings, were academicians as well as devout servants of God. Likewise, many scholars today have pursued scholarship because this was God's call for them. Many of the tools they developed have aided the preparation of this commentary.

But the biggest task does not fall to scholars alone. All believers are called to hear God's voice in the Scriptures, to start with what is already clear and to go from there. One need not be a scholar to read passages of the Bible in context or to read the cultural footnotes to the Bible that a commentary like this one is meant to provide. May God give us all grace to do our part, to obey Christ our Lord and to reveal him to the needy people of our generation.

GOSPELS

Introduction

Genre. *Genre* means the kind of writing a work is, whether poetry, prophecy, bomb threat, letter, etc. Today it is easy to identify the genre of the Gospels, because four of them are grouped together at the beginning of the *New Testament. But when each Gospel was written, people would have read it as belonging to some genre or genres they already knew. Genre is important because our expectation of the kind of writing something is will influence how we read it (e.g., we take poetry less literally than prose).

The Genre of the Gospels. In earlier times, when scholars had concentrated on classical Greek literature, they thought that the Gospels looked like common people's literature instead of "high" literature. But subsequent studies have shown that literature ranged widely between folk and high literature, and folk literature often imitated high literature. This means of deciding Gospel genre has lost popularity.

In recent times most scholars have come to classify the Gospels as ancient biography. Ancient biographies did not necessarily emphasize the same features that modern biographies do, but they were still a form of historical writing. Some biographers, like *Plutarch and *Livy, certainly spiced up their narratives; others, like *Tacitus (in the *Agricola)* and *Suetonius, kept very close to their sources. Jewish writers could model their biographies after *Old Testament biographical *narratives, which everyone in their day took to be reliable.

Jewish biography exhibits a variety of forms. *Josephus spiced up his autobiography in good Greek style but still expected his readers to take him seriously, and the substance of his account is generally reliable. Some Palestinian Jewish historiography took the form of haggadic *midrash, a sort of narrative commentary expanding on biblical stories (e.g., the book of *Jubilees and *Qumran's *Genesis Apocryphon* expand on Genesis). These works did not directly influence the Gospels; Luke wrote like a good Greco-Roman historian, and none of the Gospels fits the haggadic midrash pattern. But even works such as Jubilees, with its haggadic expansions (often to explain details), deletions (often to whitewash heroes) and so forth, follow the basic outline of their sources at most points; the early Jewish Pseudo-Philo's *Biblical Antiquities* does so even more.

Ancient Historiography. Like many historians, journalists and others today, ancient historians had particular themes they wanted to emphasize. History was full of meaning and was to be written in a way that brought out its meaning. Most historians also sought to recount their narratives in a lively and entertaining way. At the same time, however, historians by definition sought to follow the sense of their sources, to be as accurate as possible. Even those who took the most freedom followed the basic substance of history; and, where they had inadequate sources, they aimed for verisimilitude.

Are the Gospels Accurate? On the continuum between more and less careful writers, the writers of the Gospels are among the most careful. When we see how Matthew and Luke used Mark as a source, it is clear that they followed their sources carefully. Writing for ancient readers, they naturally followed the literary conventions of their day. But the first Gospels were written when eyewitnesses were still in positions of authority in the church and oral tradition could be checked, and this supports their reliability; biographies of roughly contemporary characters were normally far more accurate than those concerning heroes of the distant past. See further comment on Luke 1:1-4.

Sayings. Students carefully learned sayings of their teachers, often taking notes to help them memorize. The sayings were sometimes passed on with the stories in which they occurred, and at other times they were passed on as isolated proverbs (sayings of the wise); later students in *rhetorical schools could also transplant sayings to other appropriate stories about the same teacher. Sayings were often collected, especially by *disciples of a famous teacher. Sayings of one teacher were also sometimes modified or transferred to another teacher after much time had elapsed, but the Gospels were written when Jesus' teachings were still in the memories of the writers' sources, and hence it is unlikely that such changes occurred in the Gospels.

Jesus' words sometimes differ slightly from Gospel to Gospel. We expect such differences, because paraphrasing sayings in one's own words was a standard school exercise and a common writing technique in ancient times. (Those who conclude that different Gospel writers contradict each other because they quote Jesus differently are thus not paying attention to how works were written in antiquity.) At the same time, a particular style and rhythm and sometimes *Aramaic expressions come through Jesus' sayings, indicating that the Gospel writers did not always paraphrase him, even in translation from Aramaic to Greek.

Jesus used many of the Palestinian Jewish teaching techniques of his day, such as *parables and *hyperbole (*rhetorical exaggeration), to make his points graphically. To grasp them the way his first hearers grasped them, his sayings must be read in this light and then understood in the context of the whole of his teachings. For example, readers must adequately recognize both loyalty to parents (Mk 7:9-13) and the greater demands of the *kingdom (Mk 10:29-30). Parables must also be read the way Jesus' Jewish hearers would have understood them. They were illustrations meant to convey truth, but some of the details of most parables are included simply to make the story work, so we should be careful not to read too much into such details.

Literary Techniques. Greek literary conventions permeated most Jewish literature written in the Greek language, and were applied both to historical books (which the Gospels claim to be) and novels alike. Writers of topical biography had complete freedom to rearrange their sources, so it should not surprise us that Matthew and Mark have many events in Jesus' ministry in different order. Although Jesus, like other Jewish teachers, surely repeated the same sayings on separate occasions, some of his sayings probably occur in different places in the Gospels simply because the writers were exercising the freedom ancient biographers had to rearrange their material. This freedom enabled the Gospel writers, like preachers today, to preach Jesus as well as report about him, while still recounting his words and deeds accurately. Ancient Christians already knew, of course, that the Gospels were not in chronological order, as the early Christian teacher Papias plainly remarked about Mark.

How to Read the Gospels. Ancient biographies were meant to be read the whole way through rather than jumping from a passage in one book to a passage in another. Each of the four Gospels was written separately to different readers and was meant to be read on its own terms before the reader moved to a different Gospel. We should therefore work through each Gospel, following the flow of that Gospel's thought.

Ancient biographies often had morals to their stories and set forth the characters as positive or negative examples. Old Testament stories about men and women of God taught morals about faith and how to serve God. The reader is therefore meant to ask at the end of each Gospel story, What is the moral of this story? How does this story help me relate to Jesus better?

Sayings were often passed down as proverbs, which are general principles or graphic ways of making a point; other times they appear in the context of stories where they are applied in a specific way.

Applying the Gospels Today. When we read *narratives, or stories, in the Bible, we should look for the moral or morals of the story that the author wished to emphasize for his audience. We should try to put ourselves in the place of ancient readers and hear the words of Jesus as if we were hearing them for the first time from his own mouth. We should allow Jesus' graphic language to strike us the way it would have struck the first hearers. The Gospels recorded Jesus' sayings to apply them to other generations besides Jesus' own (the writers wrote them down for their own generation, after Jesus had ascended to heaven), expecting the readers to apply them to their own situations. But before we can understand how Jesus' teachings apply to our situations today, we must understand what he actually said in first-century Palestine and what he meant.

The Gospels in This Commentary. Matthew, Mark and Luke overlap significantly (see *Synoptic Gospels in the glossary), and in order to avoid repetition I have sometimes included more background under one of the Gospels than another one. Because readers will learn the most by working their way through one Gospel at a time, however, I have provided sufficient background for interpretation for each of the three Gospels. Mark was meant to be read quickly, like a tract, whereas Matthew was meant to be studied more as a training manual; my comments on Matthew are thus often more detailed, although Matthew and Luke receive less attention where they use Mark. When Matthew and Luke overlap, the commentary is generally more detailed on Matthew. I have treated John independently, because the Fourth Gospel overlaps with the others considerably less than they overlap with one another.

Bibliography. See especially David E. Aune, *The New Testament in Its Literary Environment,* LEC 8 (Philadelphia: Westminster, 1987); Joel B. Green, Scot McKnight and I. Howard Marshall, eds., *Dictionary of Jesus and the Gospels,* (Downers Grove, Ill.: InterVarsity Press, 1992); Robert H. Stein, *The Method and Message of Jesus' Teachings* (Philadelphia: Westminster, 1978).

MATTHEW

Introduction

Authorship. In contrast to, say, Paul's letters, attributions of authorship in the Gospels are generally based on church tradition rather than evidence in the biblical text itself. Although this tradition is usually trustworthy, in the case of Matthew it may be less reliable (since the same tradition also claims that the original Gospel of Matthew was written in Hebrew, which is not true of our First Gospel). The authorship of the First Gospel is thus debated, but we will speak of "Matthew" for convenience's sake and lack of a better designation.

Date. The date of Matthew is debated. Some conservative scholars, like Robert Gundry, date Matthew before A.D. 70 and attribute its authorship to Matthew; other equally conservative scholars date Matthew around 80 and are less certain about authorship. Because Matthew addresses the emerging power of the *Pharisaic *rabbis considerably more than Mark (but still recognizes the power of the *Sadducees and the priesthood), and these rabbis began to achieve some political power in Syria-Palestine mainly after 70, it is reasonable to surmise that Matthew was written in the seventies, although this date is not certain.

Where Matthew Was Written. The most likely locale is in the area of Syria-Palestine, because that is where the rabbis exercised their greatest influence in the seventies and eighties of the first century. But again certainty is not possible.

Setting, Purpose. Matthew addresses the needs of his Jewish-Christian readers, who are apparently in conflict with a Pharisaic religious establishment (cf. 3:7 with Lk 3:7; Mt 5:20; 23:2-39). Members of the early rabbinic movement, mainly successors of the earlier Pharisees, never achieved the power they claimed, but they began to consolidate as much juridical and theological influence as possible, especially in Syria-Palestine, in the years following A.D. 70.

Matthew presents the traumatic destruction of the temple, which had probably occurred recently (see the previous discussion on date), as judgment on the previous Jewish establishment (though it was mainly Sadducean) in chapters 23—24. He wants to encourage his community to evangelize *Gentiles as well as their own people (cf. 1:5; 2:1-12; 3:9; 8:5-13; 15:21-28; 24:14; 28:19). Matthew's collection of Jesus' teachings (especially chaps. 5—7, 10, 13, 18, 23—25) is to be used to make other *disciples for Jesus, just as other Jewish disciples passed on their rabbis' teachings to their own disciples (28:19).

Genre and Sources. Most scholars think that when Matthew wrote his Gospel, Mark was already in circulation. (Not all scholars accept this position, but it is widely viewed as the consensus.) In line with the standard literary practice of the day, Matthew followed one main source, which he regarded as highly reliable—Mark—and then wove in material from other dependable sources around it. Due to space limitations in this commentary, much of the material found in both Matthew and Mark receives more detailed treatment only under Mark.

Biographies were written differently in Matthew's day than they are today. Biographers could write either in chronological order (e.g., Luke follows the order of his sources as carefully as possible) or, more frequently, in topical order. Matthew arranges the sayings of Jesus according to topic, not chronology: the ethics of the *kingdom in chapters 5—7, the mission of the kingdom in chapter 10, the presence of the kingdom in chapter 13, church discipline and forgiveness in chapter 18 and the future of the kingdom in chapters 23—25. Some commentators have argued that Matthew grouped Jesus' sayings into five sections to parallel the five books of Moses (other works were divided into five to correspond with the books of Moses, e.g., Psalms, Proverbs, the *rabbinic tractate Pirke Abot, 2 Maccabees and perhaps *1 Enoch).

Matthew's Message. This Gospel or one of its sources may have been used as a training manual for new Christians (Mt 28:19); rabbis taught oral traditions, but Jewish Christians needed a body of Jesus' teachings in writing for Gentile converts. Matthew repeatedly emphasizes that Jesus fulfills the Jewish Scriptures, and argues from those Scriptures the way a trained scribe would. He portrays Jesus as the epitome of Israel's hopes for his Jewish audience, but also emphasizes missions to the Gentiles: outreach to the Gentiles is rooted both in the *Old Testament and in Jesus' teaching. Matthew is quick to counterattack the religious leaders of his day who have attacked the followers of Jesus; but he also warns of the growing dangers of apostate religious leadership within the Christian community.

Commentaries. W. D. Davies and Dale Allison, *A Critical and Exegetical Commentary on the Gospel according to Saint Matthew,* ICC, 3 vols. (Edinburgh: T. & T. Clark, 1988-), provides some Jewish background. John Meier, *Matthew,* New Testament Message: A Biblical-Theological Commentary (Wilmington, Del.: Michael Glazier, 1981), is good on literary issues, although he would not agree with my emphasis on the specifically Jewish context of Matthew. Those most familiar with Matthew's milieu, however, will recognize that my commentary is less dependent on other commentaries and more indebted to primary sources and to older scholars such as Joachim Jeremias, T. W. Manson, Gustaf Dalman and, more cautiously, Josef Blinzler and J. D. M. Derrett; and to more recent scholars such as E. P. Sanders, Geza Vermes and Martin Goodman. One helpful specialized study is Marshall D. Johnson, *The Purpose of the Biblical Genealogies,* SNTSMS 8, 2nd ed. (Cambridge: Cambridge University Press, 1988), whose treatment includes Matthew 1:2-16; see also C. S. Keener, *. . . And Marries Another: Divorce and Remarriage in the Teaching of the New Testament* (Peabody, Mass.: Hendrickson, 1992), which addresses Matthew 5:17-48 and 19:1-12; and Carl H. Kraeling, *John the Baptist* (New York: Charles Scribner's Sons, 1951), on John the Baptist.

1:1-17
The Background of Jesus

Ancient biographies typically began by rehearsing the noble lineage of their subject. Here Jesus is connected with the history of his people from the beginning (see also comment on Lk 3:23-38).

1:1. The *Messiah was to be a "son [descendant] of David"; "son of Abraham" was applied to Jewish people in general, so Matthew begins by reminding us that Jesus is Jewish. Genealogies could provide unity to a survey of history between major figures (as with Adam, Noah and Abraham in Gen 5, 11). Greek readers often called the book of Genesis "the book of generations," and the title is also used for genealogies and other accounts contained in it (Gen 2:4; 5:1 *LXX). In Genesis genealogies are named for the first person cited, but Matthew's genealogy is named for the person in whom it climaxes, Jesus Christ.

1:2-16. As in *Old Testament genealogies, but in contrast to Luke and Greco-Roman genealogies, Matthew records the names beginning with the oldest and moving to the most recent.

Genealogies reminded Jewish people of God's sovereignty in arranging marriages and providing offspring. Sometimes they explained why a person behaved a particular way (e.g., Moses' descent from lawbreakers like Reuben, Simeon and [directly] Levi helps explain some of his own weaknesses in Exodus 6:12-30). Most important, they were essential to document a person's proper lineage as a pure Israelite (in contrast to some other Galileans, who could be descended from converted *Gentiles), a member of the priesthood, or royalty. Genealogies could also be used as unifying links between major figures in history; Genesis links Adam, Noah and Abraham in this way (Gen 5, 11). Matthew connects Jesus with the Old Testament *narratives about the patriarchs, the Davidic kingly line and the exile.

At least partial genealogical records of important (especially priestly) families were kept in the temple. After the temple was destroyed in 70, anyone could have claimed to be of Davidic descent, but the claim for Jesus was made before 70, when it still could have been checked (Rom 1:3). Even after 70, the evidence for his Davidic descent was still sufficient to provoke trouble for some of Jesus' relatives with the Roman government.

Women did not need to be recorded in ancient genealogies, but Matthew includes four women (1:3, 5-6), three of them Gentiles (Gen 38:6; Josh 2:1; Ruth 1:4) and the other also a Gentile or at least the wife of a Gentile (2 Sam 11:3)—even though he omits the matriarchs prominent in Jewish tradition, Sarah, Rebekah, Leah and Rachel. Thus he hints from the Old Testament that God has always planned missions to all peoples (Mt 28:19).

Scholars have suggested that some ancient genealogies incorporated symbolic material based on the interpretation of biblical texts. Jewish interpreters of Scripture sometimes would modify a letter or sound in a biblical text to reapply it figuratively. Thus the Greek text of Matthew 1:10 reads "Amos" (the prophet) rather than "Amon" (the wicked king—2 Kings 21), and Matthew 1:8 reads "Asaph" (the psalmist) rather than "Asa" (a good king turned bad—2 Chron 16); most translations have obscured this point.

1:17. Matthew omits some names, as was customary in genealogies (in this case perhaps following the Greek translation of the Old Testament); creating patterns like three sets of fourteen made lists easier to remember. Some commentators have argued that

Matthew uses fourteen generations because the numerical value of David's name in Hebrew letters is 14. (Unlike letters in the English alphabet, Greek and Hebrew letters were also used as numerals; the Jewish practice of counting the numerical values of words and deriving meaning from them came to be called *gematria.)* Dividing history into eras was common; a later Jewish text, *2 Baruch, divided history into fourteen epochs.

1:18-25 The Birth of Jesus

Ancient biographers sometimes praised the miraculous births of their subjects (especially prominent in the Old Testament), but there are no close parallels to the virgin birth. Greeks told stories of gods impregnating women, but the text indicates that Mary's conception was not sexual; nor does the Old Testament (or Jewish tradition) ascribe sexual characteristics to God. Many miraculous birth stories in the ancient world (including Jewish accounts, e.g., *1 Enoch 106) are heavily embroidered with mythical imagery (e.g., babies filling houses with light), in contrast with the straightforward narrative style of this passage (cf. similarly Ex 2:1-10).

1:18. Betrothal *(erusin)* then was more binding than most engagements are today and was normally accompanied by the groom's payment of at least part of the bride price. Betrothal, which commonly lasted a year, meant that bride and groom were officially pledged to each other but had not yet consummated the marriage; advances toward anyone else were thus regarded as adulterous (Deut 22:23-27). Two witnesses, mutual consent (normally) and the groom's declaration were necessary to establish Jewish betrothals (in Roman betrothals, consent alone sufficed). Although rings were used in the Roman world, it is not clear whether Palestinian Jews used them in this early period.

Mary would have probably been between the ages of twelve and fourteen (sixteen at the oldest), Joseph perhaps between eighteen and twenty; their parents likely arranged their marriage, with Mary and Joseph's consent. Premarital privacy between betrothed persons was permitted in Judea but apparently frowned upon in Galilee, so Mary and Joseph may well not have had any time alone together at this point.

1:19. The penalty for adultery under Old Testament law was death by stoning, and this penalty applied to infidelity during betrothal as well (Deut 22:23-24). In New Testament times, Joseph would have merely been required to divorce Mary and expose her to shame; the death penalty was rarely if ever executed for this offense. (Betrothals were so binding that if a woman's fiancé died, she was considered a widow; betrothals could otherwise be terminated only by divorce.) But a woman with a child, divorced for such infidelity, would be hard pressed ever to find another husband, leaving her without means of support if her parents died.

But because divorces could be effected by a simple document with two witnesses, Joseph could have divorced her without making her shame more widely known. (It was necessary to involve a judge only if the wife were the one requesting that the husband divorce her.) Much later *rabbinic tradition charges that Mary slept with another man, but Joseph's marrying her (v. 24) demonstrates that he did not believe this was the case.

1:20. In the Old Testament, angels often brought messages in dreams; in Greek literature, deceased people (as well as pagan deities) often brought messages, but this occurs nowhere in the Bible. The Old Testament does mention expert dream interpreters, like Daniel (Dan 1:17; 2:19-45) and Jacob's son Joseph (Gen 37:5-11; 40—41). Most stories from here in Matthew 1 to the end of Matthew 2 involve supernatural guidance (dreams or the star).

1:21. The name Jesus (*Aramaic *Yēshūa'*, Greek *Iēsous)* means "God is salvation" in Hebrew. Parents often intended the names they gave children to have some meaning, but if God gave the name, it had special signficance. The Old Testament taught that God's people would be saved in the time of the *Messiah (Jer 23:5-6), and Jewish readers in the first century would have understood this salvation to mean more than just personal forgiveness. They prayed for the day when God would deliver his people from the consequences of their sins—from subjugation beneath their enemies; many believed that this deliverance would occur when their people as a whole reformed and turned wholeheartedly to God. Jesus came to deliver his people from personal sin and thus to deliver them from its judgment as well.

1:22-23. Matthew cites Isaiah 7:14 and indicates a broad familiarity with Isaiah's context. In that context, Assyria would lay waste Israel and Aram before "a son" was grown (Is 7:14-17); "a son" thus seems to refer to Isaiah's own son (8:3-4). But all the names of Isaiah's children were meant as signs pointing beyond themselves (8:18), and to whom would "Immanuel," or "God with us" (7:14), more aptly point than to the son of David rightly called "Mighty God" (9:6; cf. 10:21; 11:1)?

1:24-25. Joseph acts like Old Testament men and women of God who obeyed God's call even when it went against all human common sense. Marriage consisted of covenant (at the betrothal; the marital contract also involved a monetary transaction between families), a ceremony and consummation, which ratified the marriage, normally on the first night of the seven-day wedding. Joseph here officially marries Mary but abstains from consummating the marriage until after Jesus is born. Jewish teachers thought that men had to marry young because they could not resist temptation (many even blamed a woman's uncovered hair for inducing lust). Joseph, who lives with Mary but exercises self-control, thus provides a strong role model for sexual purity.

2:1-12
The Pagan Seekers

Matthew informs his readers that even at Jesus' birth, the religious teachers who knew the most (2:5) failed to act on the truth, while pagans whom one would never expect to come to the Jewish *Messiah did just that.

2:1. Herod the Great died in 4 B.C.; Jesus was thus born before 4 B.C., rather than in A.D. 1; our calendars are off by several years. "Magi" (not "wise men"—KJV) were pagan astrologers whose divinatory skills were widely respected in the Greco-Roman world; astrology had become popular through the "science" of the East, and everyone agreed that the best astrologers lived in the East. The Old Testament explicitly forbade such prognostication from signs (Deut 18:11; cf. Is 2:6; 47:11-15), prescribing true *prophecy instead (Deut 18:15).

2:2. Astronomers have offered various proposals for the appearance of this star in the first decade B.C. The ancients thought comets and falling stars predicted the fall of rulers; some emperors even banished from Rome astrologers who issued such predictions. By this period many Jewish people accepted the idea that the stars could accurately predict the future. Even though these Magi were pagans, God had chosen to reveal himself to them.

2:3. Many rulers feared astrological signs of their demise; the Emperor Nero later reportedly slaughtered many nobles in the hope that their deaths (rather than his own) would fulfill the prediction of a comet. Jerusalem was an important trade center; the Magi must have come with quite an entourage for the whole city to notice them. Then again, many people resented Herod's rule and rumors could have circulated quickly. King Herod, who was aware of broad currents of thought in the Roman Empire and sponsored pagan temples among Gentile cities in his realm, might have been especially apt to consider the Magi's mission significant.

2:4. The chief priests belonged mainly to the wealthy aristocracy of *Sadducees; "*scribes" in the narrow sense in which the term is used here applies to experts in the Jewish *law, most of whom were also teachers of the law. Herod exercised a great deal of influence over the prominent leaders of the people, having forcibly removed most of his political opponents.

2:5-6. Micah 5:2 predicted Bethlehem as the *Messiah's birthplace, because the Messiah was to be a descendant of David, and Bethlehem had been David's hometown. It was a small town less than a ten-mile walk from Herod's capital, Jerusalem. The Magi had come to Jerusalem because that was where they expected to find any Judean king—perhaps one of Herod's sons. What is remarkable is that the *scribes would know where the Messiah would be born yet not act on that knowledge either positively (Mt 2:11) or negatively (2:16). Because successors of these Jerusalem leaders later sought Jesus' execution (26:3-4, 57), Matthew may be suggesting that the line between taking Jesus for granted and crucifying him is very thin.

2:7-8. Herod's deceit may resemble that of an earlier tyrant, the Pharaoh (possibly Seti I) who instructed the midwives to kill Hebrew boys at birth (Ex 1:16). The midwives could have killed the babies, making them appear as stillbirths, without the mothers' realizing it because of the birthing posture used.

2:9-10. The text might imply only that the star *appeared* to move due to the Magi's own movement. Even had the object been close enough to earth to calculate its relation to Bethlehem, Bethlehem was so close to Jerusalem that any distance would have been negligible unless the object was only a mile high. But the description of God's leading of the Magi by a moving, supernatural sign may recall how God had led his own people by the fire and cloud in the wilderness (Ex 13:21-22).

2:11. Their posture of worship was appropriate toward gods or toward kings in the East (but unlike most Mediterranean peoples, the Magi, though pagan, may not have been polytheists; they may have been Zoroastrian, but scholars debate the exact nature of Zoroastrianism in this period). Incense and myrrh were treasures characteristic of the East that the Mediterranean world typically imported from there (cf. 1 Kings 10:10; Ps 72:10-11, 15).

2:12. Most kings reacted with hostility to potential usurpers and to astrological predictions of their demise. That the Magi had to be warned by a dream not to return to Herod thus suggests their naiveté, an innocence Jews rarely expected of *Gentiles. Most peoples in the ancient world paid attention to special dreams (1:20); some even had rules on how to interpret them; and the Greeks thought that Magi were specially adept at dream interpretation.

The main road they would need to take northward from Bethlehem went directly through Jerusalem, then eastward through Syria. Given the probably large size of their entourage, the Magi could not approach Jerusalem without being noticed, as Herod knew very well. Indeed, no major route could take them homeward without passing through Jerusalem. They probably ventured far south to Hebron, then followed the rugged road to Gaza on the coast, where another road could lead them northward. This route would then have carried them through Nazareth, then Capernaum and on to Damascus.

2:13-15
Egypt and a New Exodus

2:13-14. A very large Jewish community lived in Egypt in this period. Perhaps one-third of Alexandria, located in northern Egypt, was Jewish; with a population estimated at about one million, it was one of the empire's largest cities. Alexandria included a well-to-do Jewish element, schooled in Greek thought; most inhabitants of Egypt, however, were agrarian peasants, some of the poorest in the empire. Other Jewish communities had existed farther south, especially in Elephantine, for centuries. Literature from Palestinian Jews indicates that many of them questioned the devoutness of their Egyptian Jewish kinfolk, although Egyptian Jews considered themselves faithful to God.

The Nile made travel easy within Egypt, but the coastal road to Egypt from Palestine was not the finest, and Egypt would be even harder to reach from Bethlehem without traveling northward to Jerusalem (one would have to take the poorer route southward to Hebron; see comment on 2:12). Egypt had served as a place of refuge in the past (1 Kings 11:40; Jer 26:21). By leaving "at night," Joseph's family made their route of departure impossible to trace; the language might also evoke Jewish readers' memory of Exodus 12:31.

2:15. Matthew builds almost every paragraph from the genealogy to the Sermon on the Mount around at least one text in the Old Testament, explaining some event of Jesus' life from Scripture. In context Hosea 11:1 refers plainly to the Israelites leaving Egypt in the exodus; Matthew applies this text to Jesus because Jesus epitomizes and fulfills Israel's history (Mt 1:1).

Matthew may have borrowed this Israel/Messiah interpretive analogy from Isaiah; Isaiah 42—53 narrows down the mission of Israel as a whole to the one who can ultimately fulfill that mission and suffer on behalf of the whole people—the one whom Christians would later understand to be Jesus.

Herod died in 4 B.C.

2:16-18
Herod's Slaughter: A New Captivity

2:16. Because the only natural route by which the Magi could have returned was through Jerusalem (2:12), Herod knew that the Magi had purposely avoided returning to him. He was known for acts like the massacre described here. A young but popular competitor, a high priest, had a "drowning accident" in a pool that was only a few feet deep. Enraged at his favorite wife, Herod had her strangled; he was deceived into having two innocent sons executed; and on his own deathbed Herod had another son executed (admittedly a guilty one). Although probably fictitious, a purported comment of the emperor is appropriate: Better to be one of Herod's pigs than his son. *Josephus reports that Herod ordered nobles executed at his death to ensure mourning when he died; they were instead released at his death, producing celebration.

One of his fortresses, the Herodium, was within sight of Bethlehem, and he may have dispatched guards from there. Jewish people saw infanticide (killing babies) as a hideous, pagan act; normally applied by the Romans to deformed babies, it had also been used to control oppressed populations (Ex 1:16; 1 Macc 1:60-61; 2 Macc 8:4). Like Moses, Jesus escaped the fate of other male babies (Ex 1:22—2:10), and some Jews were expecting the coming of a prophet "like Moses" (Deut 18:15, 18).

2:17-18. Jeremiah 31:15 refers to the figurative weeping of Rachel, who was buried in Bethlehem (Gen 35:19). Jeremiah said she mourned for her descendants carried off into captivity during the Babylonian exile. Like righteous Jeremiah, Jesus was carried off to Egypt, but Rachel had cause to mourn anew at Herod's murder of her people.

2:19-23
The Nazarene

2:19. On dreams, see comment on 1:20.

2:20-21. Matthew's first readers would have undoubtedly caught the comparison Matthew implies between Jesus and Moses here (cf. Ex 4:19).

2:22. Archelaus, one of Herod's surviving sons, exhibited his father's worst flaws and was also a bad ruler. That his mother was a *Samaritan surely also failed to commend him to his Jewish subjects. His rule was unstable, and the Romans ultimately deposed him and banished him to Gaul (France).

2:23. Archaeological evidence in the region of Nazareth indicates that many people had moved there from Judea, from the area near Bethlehem. Joseph may have had friends or relatives in Nazareth (cf. Lk 2:4). Nazareth was on a major road from the coast to Syria and only a few miles from the culturally diverse city of Sepphoris, which was being rebuilt at this time. Though small, Nazareth would not have been isolated from broader cultural currents of antiquity.

No single text provides Matthew's citation here. But ancient authors sometimes blended texts together, and both Jews and Greeks used plays on words to make points in argumentation, so this text could be a play on the Hebrew word *nētser,* "branch," a title for the *Messiah (Jer 23:5; Zech 3:8; 6:12; cf. Is 11:1). (The only problem with this suggestion is that it assumes Matthew's original readers already knew Hebrew; but perhaps the more skilled among them did.) Or it could be a play on "Nazarene": by changing some letters slightly, it could refer to the Nazirites, a class of people dedicated to God (cf. Num 6:1-21).

3:1-12
Jesus' Forerunner

See Mark 1:2-8 for more detailed comments. Isaiah 40:3, cited in Matthew 3:3, refers to a herald of the new exodus, when God would save his people again from the oppression they suffered.

3:1. "In those days" was a common Old Testament expression, especially in (but not limited to) prophecies concerning the future. Many people in Jesus' day expected a great leader to bring deliverance to God's people from the wilderness, in a new exodus. In times of severe national apostasy in the Old Testament, some prophets (like Elijah) found it necessary to live outside society's boundaries.

3:2. The Jewish people recognized that God ruled the universe in one sense now, but prayed daily for the time when his *kingdom, or rule, would be established over all peoples of the earth. (See further comment on Mk 1:14-15.)

3:3. Isaiah 40:3 is in the context of Isaiah's prophecy of a new exodus, when God would again deliver his people and lead them back to Jerusalem from all the nations among which they were scattered. Highways required adjustment of terrain to make them straight and level, and ancient kings, especially the kings of the East, expected the roads to be well prepared before they would travel on them. Perhaps in the interest of technical accuracy, Matthew deletes Mark's citation of Malachi here (but cf. Mt 11:10).

3:4. John's diet is that of the very poor; although domestic beekeepers were common, John eats only wild honey. (Honey was normally procured by smoking the bees out and then breaking open the honeycomb; honey was the only sweetener for food and was considered the sweetest of tastes.) But *Essenes and other pious Israelites (2 Macc 5:27) ate such diets to avoid unclean food.

John dressed like Elijah (2 Kings 1:8) and other people who lived outside society (some, like *Cynics and *Josephus's Essene tutor Bannus, were more *ascetic); the allusion to Elijah here suggests that the end is near (Mal 4:5-6).

3:5-6. Pagans wanting to convert to Judaism would *repent and be *baptized, but John here treats Jewish people on the same terms as pagans (see further comment on Mk 1:4-5.)

3:7. Ancients thought that some kinds of vipers ate their way out of their mothers (see, e.g., Herodotus, *Plutarch). It was bad enough to be called a viper, but to be called a viper's child was even worse—killing one's mother or father was the most hideous crime conceivable in antiquity.

3:8. *Repentance meant turning from sin. The *Pharisees themselves are known to have questioned professions of repentance if the supposedly repentant person continued sinning. The Old Testament prophets had sometimes described the obedience one owed God, or God's future blessing of his people, in terms of fruit (a natural image in an agricultural society; cf. Is 5:2; 27:6; Hos 10:1, 12-13; 14:7-8; Prov 11:30-31).

3:9. Jewish people commonly believed that they were saved as a people by virtue of their descent from Abraham. The idea of God raising up people from stones would have sounded to John the Baptist's Jewish hearers more like pagan mythology (the Greeks had such a story) than reality, but these words emphasized that God did not need Israel to fulfill his purpose (as in Amos 9:7; cf. Gen 1:24; 2:9). Some scholars have also suggested a wordplay on "children" and "stones" in *Aramaic.

3:10. Jewish literature sometimes used trees (like many other things) to symbolize Israel; at times the Old Testament used trees in parables of judgment against the nations (Is 10:33-34; Ezek 31:2-18; Amos 2:9) or Israel (Is 10:18-19; Jer 11:16; Ezek 15:6). The wood of a thick tree (like a cedar from Lebanon) would have been used for building, but much of the wood from Palestine's many slender fruit trees (e.g., olive or fig trees) would be useful only for small items or, often as here, for fuel.

3:11. Slaves of high-status individuals often had higher status than free persons. A slave (unlike a *disciple, who also served a master) carried the master's sandals; John here claims that he is not worthy even to be Christ's slave.

The prophets had predicted the outpouring of God's *Spirit on the righteous at the time when God established his *kingdom for Israel (Is 44:3; Ezek 39:29; Joel 2:28). They also decreed fire upon the wicked (Is 26:11; 65:15; 66:24; Jer 4:4; 15:14; etc.). In Matthew 3:11, the wicked are baptized, or immersed, in fire (3:10, 12), the righteous in the *Holy Spirit.

3:12. Because the same Greek word can mean both "spirit" and "wind," the picture of wind and fire carries over from 3:11. Winnowing was familiar to all Palestinian Jews, especially to the farmers: they would throw harvested wheat into the air, and the wind would separate the heavier grain from the lighter chaff. The chaff was useless for consumption and was normally burned. Some other writers also described the day of judgment as a harvest (4 Ezra 4:30-32; cf. Jer 51:33; Joel 3:12-14) or the wicked as chaff (Is 17:13; Jer 13:24; 15:7; etc.). That the fire is "unquenchable" points beyond the momentary burning of chaff to something far more horrible (Is 66:24), in spite of the fact that Jewish tradition itself was far from unanimous concerning the duration of hell (see "Gehenna" in glossary).

3:13-17
Jesus' Accreditation by God

See Mark 1:9-11 for further details.

3:13-14. John anticipates Jesus' immediate baptism in the *Spirit (see comment on 3:11).

3:15. Jesus' response seems to stress his identification with Israel in obedience to God's *law (cf. 5:17).

3:16. Many believed that the *Spirit was no longer available in their time; others believed that the Spirit simply did not work as forcefully as in the days of the prophets, until the time of the end. That the Spirit comes on Jesus indicates the inauguration of the messianic era and marks Jesus out as the Spirit-bearer and hence Messiah (3:11).

3:17. Many believed that voices from heaven were the closest anyone came to *prophecy in their time; Jesus has both kinds of witness: the heavenly voice and John's prophecy. Matthew intends his more erudite readers to see allusions not only to a royal *Messiah in Psalm 2:7, but also to the suffering servant of Isaiah 42:1-4 (see comment on Mt 12:18-21).

4:1-11
Jesus Overcomes Israel's Tests

The three texts from Deuteronomy (6:13, 16; 8:3) cited here (4:4, 7, 10) were commands God gave to Israel when he tested Israel for forty years in the wilderness. Unlike Israel of old, Jesus as Israel's representative (1:1; 2:15) passes the tests. Some scholars have compared the battle of wits between Jesus and the devil to the way *rabbinic debates were conducted. Jewish stories also praised those who endured and passed the severest moral tests.

4:1. One of the most common recitations of God's acts in the Old Testament was that he "led" his people in the wilderness (see especially Is 63:14), where they were tested. Although the Old Testament only rarely mentions the devil, his activity as tempter (cf. Job 1—2) had come into focus much more by Jesus' day. The surprising feature here for most Jewish readers would not have been that the devil was providing temptation, but that he was doing it in person.

4:2. Moses also fasted forty day and nights; Jesus may appear here as a new Moses, the new lawgiver (see Mt 5:1-2). Israel also was in the wilderness forty years (see the introduction to this section).

4:3. The ancients attributed this sort of feat to magicians, who claimed to be able to transform themselves into animals and to transform other substances, like stones into bread. Many Jewish people were also hoping for a new exodus led by a new Moses—complete with new manna, or bread from heaven. The devil wants to conform Jesus to contemporary expectations.

4:4. The devil challenges or seeks to define Jesus' sonship (4:3), against God's Word (3:17). But Jesus would have known the context of Deuteronomy 8:3, which he cites: he can depend on God's provision of manna in the wilderness because God is Jesus' Father as God was Israel's (Deut 8:5).

Other Jewish circles (as evident, e.g., in the *Dead Sea Scrolls and later *rabbinic texts) also used the phrase "It has been written" to introduce Scripture.

4:5-6. "The holy city" was a standard title for Jerusalem. The devil takes Jesus to a part of the temple that overlooked a deep valley; a fall from there would have meant certain death. Later *rabbis acknowledged that the devil and demons could handle Scripture expertly. Here the devil cites Psalm 91:11-12 out of context; 91:10 makes clear that God's angelic protection (cf. Mk 1:13) is for events that *befall* his servants, not an excuse to seek out such dangers. The devil phrases his temptation in standard Jewish wisdom language (Wisdom of Solomon 2:18).

4:7. Jesus cites Deuteronomy 6:16, which refers to how the Israelites had tested God at Massah by refusing to accept that God was among them until he wrought a sign for them (Ex 17:7).

4:8-9. This realm did not technically belong to the devil (see Dan 4:32), who owned human hearts only as a usurper. The best the devil could do would be to make Jesus the political, military sort of *Messiah most Jewish people who expected a Messiah were anticipating.

4:10-11. Deuteronomy 6:13, which Jesus cites, prohibits idolatry (see Deut 6:14), a commandment anyone who worshiped the devil would obviously violate.

4:12-17 Foreshadowing the Preaching to Gentiles

4:12-13. Nazareth was a small agricultural village and suburb of the old Galilean capital, Sepphoris; Capernaum was a larger fishing town on the northwest edge of the Sea of Galilee. The trade routes brought *Gentiles through those parts. Capernaum lay in the borders of Naphtali but not Zebulon; Matthew mentions the latter because they occur together in Isaiah 9:1, which he cites in 4:15.

4:14-16. Citing here Isaiah 9:1-2, Matthew undoubtedly knows the context: the light to which it refers is that of the *Messiah (Is 9:6-7). (Matthew again is anticipating the evangelization of non-Jews by foreshadowing it in his narrative.) Many non-Jews in Galilee had been forcibly converted to Judaism in the second century B.C.; they had previously been aligned with Judea's Phoenician enemies (1 Macc 5:15). Subsequently, however, many Judeans settled in Galilee, and its inhabitants were primarily ethnically as well as religiously Jewish. More to the point, Galilee was surrounded on all sides (except its southern, Samaritan border) by *Hellenistic city territories. Capernaum (like Sepphoris and Nazareth farther south) was situated along one of the major trade routes of Palestine, later called "the way of the sea." This was a caravan route from Damascus to Caesarea Maritima, which was on the Mediterranean coast.

4:17. Jesus' message, like John the Baptist's (3:2), is summarized as *repentance to be ready for the *kingdom.

First-century Jewish hearers would have heard in this proclamation a warning of the imminent day of judgment.

4:18-22
Examples of Repentance

Ancient writers often illustrated their teachings (here, 4:17) with *narrative examples. See comment on Mark 1:14-20 for further details.

4:18. Most people in Jewish Palestine depended on salted fish, wheat and barley for sustenance; fish products like fish gravies were thus also common. The fish of the Sea of Galilee included large carp; the fish would be dried, salted or pickled to preserve them. Fishermen were central to the Galilean economy and made a good living by the standards of their culture, far better than the large numbers of peasants who worked the land through much of the Roman Empire. It is thought that the casting net had a narrow end pulled by the boat and a wide end sunk by leads (contrast the larger dragnet of 13:47); nets were probably made of rope or cords woven from flax, papyrus or hemp.

4:19-20. *Disciples normally chose to become students of a particular *rabbi, rather than a teacher calling his own disciples.

4:21-22. Fishermen had more income than average people in Galilee, so James and John left behind a good job. More than that, however, they suddenly left behind their father and the family business; such abandonment could easily bring them dishonor in the community. (Both Jews and Greeks, however, had similar stories and would recognize this sudden departure as a sure sign of radical discipleship.)

4:23-25
Examples of Kingdom Authority

Ancient literature commonly includes not only longer *narrative segments but also summary statements like this passage (also 9:35; 19:1-2; etc.).

4:23. Visiting teachers, especially popular ones, were normally invited to speak in *synagogues, which in this period were led by priests or laymen who were prominent members of their communities.

4:24. Because many Jewish people lived in Syria, Matthew presumably intends Syrian Jews here (Matthew would have eagerly mentioned *Gentiles had they come). The presence of multitudes seeking relief at hot springs (like Hammath-Tiberias) in Galilee testifies to the vast numbers who sought healing in the first century; teachers reputed as healers (usually Gentile magicians) also drew great crowds.

Although some contemporary medical writers (such as the second-century A.D. Greek physician Aretaeus, but unlike the fifth-century B.C. Greek Hippocrates) thought epilepsy was due to demonic activity, Matthew here distinguishes the two.

4:25. The Decapolis, the "Ten Cities," was a *Gentile area that included a large Jewish population.

5:1-12
The Beatitudes, or Blessings

Matthew 5—7 is the first block of teaching material in Matthew, dealing with the ethics of the *kingdom. In 4:17 Jesus summarizes his message: "*Repent, for the kingdom is at hand"; Matthew 5—7 shows in greater detail the repentant lifestyle that characterizes the people of the kingdom. This block is introduced by a common *Old Testament literary form called beatitudes: "Happy are those who . . . , for they shall . . ." (e.g., Ps 1:1). Here the blessings are the promises of the kingdom for those who live the repentant life. Jesus' hearers would have understood them especially as promises for the future time of God's reign; we must read them in the light of the present aspect of the kingdom as well (see "kingdom" in the glossary). The future kingdom was sometimes defined by images from the creation narratives or from Israel's exodus from Egypt, which the Jewish people regarded as their original redemption.

5:1-2. Although one would stand to read Scripture publicly, Jewish teachers would sit to expound it, often with *disciples sitting at their feet. Many scholars have compared the "mountain" (cf. Lk 6:17) here to Mount Sinai, where God through Moses first taught his ethics by the *law (Ex 19—20; cf. Is 2:2-3).

5:3. Ancient writers and speakers would sometimes bracket a section of material by beginning and ending with the same phrase. These blessings thus deal with the gift of the kingdom (5:3, 10).

Many Jewish people believed that the kingdom would be ushered in only by a great war and force of arms; Jesus promises it for the "poor in spirit," the "humble" or "meek" (5:5), the peacemakers (5:9). Poverty and piety were often associated in Judaism; the term *poor* could encompass either physical poverty (Lk 6:20), or the faithful dependence on God that it often produced ("in spirit," as here).

5:4. Mourning was usually associated with either *repentance or bereavement; the conjunction with "comfort" means that the second aspect is in view here. It could mean grief over Israel's sins, but in this context probably refers to the pain of the oppressed. "Comfort" was one of the blessings promised for the future time when God would restore his mourning people (Is 40:1; 49:13; 51:3, 12; 52:9; 54:11; 57:18; 61:2; 66:13).

5:5. Here Jesus cites Scripture (Ps 37:9, 11). Not those who try to bring in the kingdom politically or militarily but those who humbly wait on God will "inherit the earth." The Hebrew of the psalm could mean "inherit the land" in a narrower sense (Ps 25:13), but in Jesus' day Jewish people expected God's people to reign over all the earth, as some other *Old Testament passages suggest.

5:6. Jewish people understood that God would also satisfy his people's needs in the future kingdom (Is 25:6; 41:17-18; 55:2), as he had supplied for them in the exodus when he first redeemed them (Deut 6:11; 8:7-10). But the greatest object of longing should be God (Ps 42:1; 63:1) and instruction in his righteousness (Ps 119:40, 47, 70, 92, 97, 103; Jer 15:16).

5:7. Some later *rabbis uttered similar statements (cf. also Prov 11:17). Like the peacemakers (v. 9), the merciful are not those who seek to bring in the kingdom by force. The mercy Jewish people generally hoped to receive was expected in the day of judgment (cf. Mic 7:18-19).

5:8. The "pure in heart" (Ps 73:1) were those in Israel whose hearts were "clean," or undefiled, those who recognized that God alone was their help and reward (Ps 73:2-28). The righteous would see God on the day of judgment (e.g., Is 30:20), as in the first exodus (Ex 24:10-11).

5:9. Both the Jewish people and the righteous were called "sons of God" in Jewish tradition; the ultimate declaration of that fact would be made in the sight of the nations on the day of judgment. Those *Pharisaic *rabbis who prevailed in Palestinian Judaism after the war of A.D. 66-70 were the ones who emphasized the way of peace rather than the way of revolt espoused by others. But most other Jewish leaders, including all groups in Jerusalem except the Christians and some of the Pharisees, had joined in the spirit of revolt and were killed or came to be viewed as illegitimate leaders after the revolt's failure.

5:10-12. Many of the Old Testament prophets suffered in bringing God's word to Israel (e.g., Jer 26:11); Jewish tradition amplified the number of prophetic martyrs further and made it a major emphasis. The burden of proof was always on the prophet who spoke what people wanted to hear (Jer 28:8-9; cf. 6:14; 8:10-11; 23:17).

Most Jewish people did not believe that prophets still existed in the Old Testament sense, so Jesus' comparing his followers to the prophets indicated that they would have an extraordinary mission. To suffer for God was meritorious (Ps 44:22; 69:7), and Judaism highly honored martyrs for God's *law; yet no other *rabbi called *disciples to die for his own teachings or name.

5:13-16
Real Discipleship

A *disciple of the *kingdom who does not live like a disciple of the kingdom (5:3-12) is worth about as much as tasteless salt or invisible light.

5:13. Various scholars have emphasized different uses of salt in antiquity, such as a preservative or an agent regularly added to manure; but the use of salt here is as a flavoring agent: "if salt has become tasteless" (the Greek word can also mean "become foolish," so it may include a play on words).

Although the salt recovered from impure salt substances taken from the Dead Sea could dissolve, leaving only the impurities behind, the point here is closer to that expressed by a *rabbi at the end of the first century. When asked how one could make saltless salt salty again, he replied that one should salt it with the afterbirth of a mule. Being sterile, mules have no afterbirth, and he was saying that those who ask a stupid question receive a stupid answer. Real salt does not lose its saltiness; but if it did, what would you do to restore its salty flavor—salt it? Unsalty salt was worthless.

5:14. Jewish tradition considered Israel (Is 42:6; 49:6) and Jerusalem (as well as God and the *law) the light of the world. The "city" here may thus be Jerusalem; or it may be any elevated city at night, whose torch lights would make it visible to the surrounding countryside.

5:15-16. The small wicker oil lamps of this period gave little light in the average home, which had few windows; they would be most effective by being set on a lampstand. Something large placed over them would presumably extinguish the light altogether.

5:17-20
The Law Enforced

Jesus' ethical demands (5:3-16) are no weaker than those of the law given by Moses; cf. 5:21-26.

5:17. Jewish teachers said that one "abolished" the law by disobeying it (cf. Deut 27:26), because one thereby rejected its authority. Such highhanded rebellion against the law—as opposed to particular sins—warranted social and spiritual expulsion from the Jewish community. The charge of openly persuading others that the law was no longer in force would be even worse. Jesus opposed not the law but an illegitimate interpretation of it that stressed regulations more than character.

5:18. Jesus refers here to the *yod,* the smallest letter in the Hebrew alphabet. Later *rabbis told the story that when God changed Sarai's name to Sarah, the *yod* that was removed complained to God for generations till he reinserted it, this time in Joshua's name. Jewish teachers used illustrations like this to make the point that the law was sacred and one could not regard any part as too small to be worth keeping.

5:19. Later *rabbis decided that the greatest commandment was honoring one's father and mother, and the least, respecting a mother bird; they reasoned that both merited the same reward, *eternal life (based on "life" in Ex 20:12; Deut 22:7). A modern reader might ask, What happens to the person who breaks one and keeps another? But such a question misses the point of this *hyperbolic language which other Jewish teachers also typically used to say, "God will hold accountable anyone who disregards even the smallest commandment."

5:20. The *Pharisees were the most respected religious people of the day, and the *scribes the supreme experts in the law (especially, no doubt, the Pharisaic scribes). Verses 21-48 show what Jesus' demand for a "higher" righteousness involves. The Pharisees also stressed the right intention of the heart *(kavanah);* Jesus' criticizes not their doctrine but their hearts as religious people. Religious communities led by Pharisaic teachers may have also been opponents of Jewish Christians in Syria-Palestine in Matthew's day, giving Matthew additional incentive to record these words.

5:21-26
Anger as Murder

Six times in verses 21-43 Jesus cites Scripture and then, like a good *rabbi, explains it (5:21, 27, 31, 33, 38, 43). The sort of wording he uses ("You have heard, . . . but I say") was used by other Jewish teachers to establish the fuller meaning of a text, although Jesus speaks with greater authority than Jewish teachers normally claimed.

5:21-22. "Raca" is *Aramaic for "empty-headed one"; the insult is about the same as the one that follows it, "Fool!" The punishments are also roughly equal: the (day of God's) judgment, the heavenly *Sanhedrin or supreme court, and hell. (Jewish literature described God's heavenly tribunal as a supreme court, or sanhedrin, parallel to the earthly one.) "The hell of fire" is literally "the *Gehenna of fire," which refers to the standard Jewish concept of Gehinnom, the opposite of paradise; in Gehinnom the wicked would be burned up (according to some Jewish teachers) or eternally tortured (according to other Jewish teachers). Not only the outward act of murder but also the inward choice of anger that generates such acts violates the spirit of God's law against murder.

5:23-24. Judaism stressed reconciliation between individuals; God would not accept an outward offering if one had oppressed or mistreated one's neighbor and did not make it right. In the *Old Testament God accepted only sacrifices offered with a pure heart toward him and one's neighbor (Gen 4:4-7; Prov 15:8; Is 1:10-15; Jer 6:20; Amos 5:21-24).

5:25-26. Again Jesus returns to the image of the heavenly court. Here he may use the custom of debt imprisonment as another image in the *parable; this was a non-Jewish custom, but Jewish hearers would have known about it among the *Gentiles. No mercy would be shown: the amount of money to be repaid extended to the last (literally) *quadrans,* almost the least valuable Roman coin, the equivalent of only a few minutes' wages. (Details like the "officer" make the parable work as a story but do not symbolize anything in particular. Ancient storytellers did not invest meaning in every detail of their parables; see "parable" in the glossary.)

5:27-30
Lust as Adultery

5:27-28. Other Jewish teachers also looked down on lust; some even went as far as Jesus in regarding it as adultery. The issue is thus not the doctrine of Jesus' hearers but their heart. The Greek word here is the same as in the opening line of the tenth commandment in the *Septuagint (the Greek version of the Old Testament): "You shall not desire your neighbor's wife" (Ex 20:17). The tenth commandment, against coveting, forces Jesus' hearers to internalize Moses' other commandments.

5:29-30. Corporal punishment (cutting off appendages, e.g., Ex 21:24-25) is easier to bear than capital punishment, the decree of eternal death pronounced by the heavenly court. Some Jewish thinkers believed that one would be *resurrected in exactly the form in which one had died (e.g., with limbs missing, as in the case of many martyrs) before being made whole, and Jesus employs this image.

5:31-32
Remarriage as Adultery

Under Jewish law, "adultery" referred only to the wife's misbehavior, not the husband's. Matthew does not agree with this view (5:28); but because his readers must obey the law of their communities, he deals only with the issue of the wife.

Some *Pharisaic *rabbis allowed divorce for almost anything (just as Roman law did); others allowed it only if the wife were unfaithful (see comment on 19:1-10; both Jewish and Roman law *required* divorce for adultery). Yet the stricter rabbis did not view more lenient divorces as invalid. Jesus thus goes beyond the stricter position: not only does he allow divorce only if one's wife is unfaithful, but he regards divorce for any other reason as invalid, thus making remarriage in those cases adulterous. This seems, however, to be *hyperbole (as in 5:29-30), a graphic way of forbidding divorce except when the other partner has already irreparably broken the marriage covenant.

If Jesus' interpretation of the law was stricter than what the law said at face value, no one would have thought that he was therefore contradicting the law; "building a fence" around the law was a standard Jewish practice that involved making certain that the law's intent was not broken.

5:33-37
Integrity, Not Oaths

People swore by all sorts of things other than God to testify that their word was true. They reasoned that if they broke their oath based on any of these lesser things, at least they were not bringing God's name into disrepute. It eventually became necessary for *rabbis to decide which oaths were completely binding. Jesus says that everything by which one could swear is ultimately God's, and demands that people simply be as good as their word. Jesus argues the point in part from Scripture; Isaiah 66:1 declared that heaven is God's throne and earth is his footstool.

Most people in Jewish Palestine had black or dark hair, unless they were older, in which case their hair was turning white; verse 36 would have been heard as referring to God's control over aging. Jesus' rule here is stricter than the letter of the law but in accord with its spirit (Deut 23:21-23; Eccles 5:5). It is possible that the *Essenes also avoided oath-taking after their initial oath to join their sect.

5:38-42
Nonresistance

The language is partly *hyperbole—*disciples did not engage in behavior that would immediately lead to homelessness (cf. 2 Cor 11:20). But hyperbole was meant to provoke hearers to consider the radical nature of what they were being told: Jesus is quite literally calling them to value relationships supremely and regard possessions as nothing. (The point is absolute unselfishness, motivated by love; cf. 5:43-44.)

5:38. The "eye for an eye" and "tooth for a tooth" are part of the widespread ancient Near Eastern law of retaliation. In Israel and other cultures, this principle was enforced by a court and refers to legalized vengeance; personal vengeance was never accepted in the *law of Moses, except as a concession for a relative's murder (Num 35:18-21). The *Old Testament did not permit personal vengeance; David, a great warrior, recognized this principle (1 Sam 25:33; 26:10-11).

5:39. The blow on the right cheek was the most grievous insult possible in the ancient world (apart from inflicting serious physical harm), and in many cultures was listed alongside the "eye for an eye" laws; both Jewish and Roman law permitted prosecution for this offense. A prophet might endure such ill treatment (1 Kings 22:24; Is 50:6).

5:40. The poorest people of the Empire (e.g., most peasants in Egypt) had only an inner and outer garment, and the theft of a cloak would lead to legal recourse. Although conditions in first-century Palestine were not quite that bad, this verse could indicate divestiture of all one's possessions, even (*hyperbolically) one's clothes, to avoid a legal dispute affecting only oneself. Jesus gives this advice in spite of the fact that, under Jewish law, a legal case to regain one's cloak would have been foolproof: a creditor could not take a poor person's outer cloak, which might serve as one's only blanket at night as well as a coat (Ex 22:26-27).

5:41. Roman soldiers had the legal right to impress the labor, work animal or substance of local residents (cf. Mk 15:21). Although impressment may not have happened often in Galilee, it happened elsewhere, and the fact that it could happen would be enough to raise the eyebrows of Jesus' hearers at this example of nonresistance and even loving service to the oppressor.

The Jewish hierarchy favored the status quo with Rome; some revolutionaries wanted to revolt. Most Palestinian Jews in this period wanted freedom but were not revolutionaries. But by A.D. 66 Jewish Palestine was caught up in a war, and by 70 the wisdom of Jesus' course was evident: Rome won the war, and the Jewish people, led to defeat by the revolutionaries, were crushed.

5:42. Beggars were widespread. The Bible stressed giving to those in need (Deut 15:11; Ps 112:5, 9; Prov 21:13). God would take care of the needs of those who helped the poor (Deut 15:10; Prov 19:17; 22:9; 28:8). Biblical laws against usury and especially about lending to the poor before the year of release (Deut 15:9; every seventh year debts were to be forgiven; cf. Lev 25) support Jesus' principle here, but Jesus goes even farther in emphasizing unselfish giving (especially Lk 6:35).

5:43-48
Beyond Nonresistance

5:43-44. The *Old Testament did not explicitly teach hatred for one's enemies (Ex 23:4-5; Prov 25:21-22), although hating God's enemies was a pious way to feel (Ps 139:19-22); some

Jewish groups, like the *Essenes, emphasized hatred toward those outside the covenant. Greek ethics sometimes stressed learning from one's enemies' criticism but also could stress making sure to hurt one's enemies more than one was hurt by them (so Isocrates, a fourth-century B.C. Athenian orator and rhetorician).

Prayer for one's persecutors (except that God would strike them dead!) had not generally characterized even the most pious in the Old Testament (cf. 2 Chron 24:22; Jer 11:20; 15:15; 17:18; 18:23; 20:12; often in Psalms, e.g., 137:7-9). Greek philosophers generally answered their critics harshly and arrogantly.

5:45. Jewish teachers emphasized this universal aspect of God's mercy (they also stressed that the prayers of the righteous could bring rain in times of drought; Jesus' statement does not deny that idea). Some Jewish texts said that by being like God, one would be his children (i.e., imitators; e.g., Ecclus 4:10).

5:46-47. Some Jewish teachers emphasized kindness to pagans (*Gentiles) to draw them to the truth, but most people greeted and (apart from charity) looked after only those they knew. *Tax gatherers were considered among the most apostate Jews; Gentiles were considered (usually rightly) immoral, idolatrous, often anti-Jewish pagans. Jews agreed that one should not be like the pagans (so also the Old Testament: Lev 18:3; Deut 18:9; Jer 10:2).

5:48. This verse summarizes 5:21-47. The *Aramaic word for "perfect" can mean "complete" or "whole," including the nuance of "merciful" (Lk 6:36); in this context, it means fulfilling the requirements of Matthew 5:21-47. The Bible already commanded being holy as God is holy (Lev 11:44-45; 19:2; 20:26), and Judaism (as well as some Greek philosophers) sometimes argued ethics on the basis of imitating God's character.

6:1-4
Secret Charity

6:1. This verse is the thesis statement that introduces the three examples of private piety in 6:2-16. Judaism stressed that one should not perform deeds for the sake of reward but nonetheless promised reward, as Jesus does here; this reward is rendered at the day of judgment, as in Judaism. Prayer, fasting and gifts to the poor were basic components of Jewish piety (Tobit 12:8), and many *rabbis listed qualities (e.g., virtues on which the world was founded) in sets of three.

6:2-4. Greeks and Romans did not support personal charity; wealthy contributions to public projects or to poorer *clients were meant to secure the giver's popularity. In contrast, charity was central to Jewish piety; some writers even said that it saved a person, although later Jewish laws technically did not permit one to give over 20 percent above his tithes.

Some commentators have taken the trumpet sounding literally, but it is *hyperbolic (people did not blow trumpets when giving alms) and may reflect a play on words (charity boxes were often shaped like trumpets). Not letting one's left hand know about the right hand's gift is clearly hyperbole. The language of "having" a reward "in full" is the language of repayment in ancient business receipts.

6:5-15
Secret Prayer

The parallel structure of the larger section (6:1-18) and of this passage on prayer is augmented by the presence of a sample prayer (6:9-13; thus how one should not pray, 6:5, 7-8; and how one should pray, 6:6, 9). Judaism was much more serious about regular prayer than were Greek and Roman religions.

6:5-6. The problem is not public prayer but motives directed toward other people rather than toward God. It was probably common for pious people to recite their prayers individually in the *synagogue; it is not clear that everyone prayed simultaneously in all synagogues as early as Jesus' time. The "chamber" could have been a storeroom; most people did not have private rooms in their houses, and only that room would have a door on it. Standing was a common posture for prayer.

6:7. Jewish scholars were debating the use of fixed prayers in this period; they generally held them to be acceptable if one's intent was genuine. Greek prayers piled up as many titles of the deity addressed as possible, hoping to secure his or her attention. Pagan prayers typically reminded the deity of favors done or sacrifices offered, attempting to get a response from the god on contractual grounds.

6:8. Judaism recognized that God knew everything; the issue here is thus not Jesus' hearers' doctrine but their hearts. Jewish people saw God differently than Greeks saw their gods (even though even monotheistic faith was not always what it should have been). In Judaism, God was a Father who delighted in meeting the needs of his people; Judaism also recognized that God knew all a person's thoughts. Jesus predicates effective prayer on a relationship of intimacy, not a business partnership model, which was closer to the one followed by ancient paganism.

6:9-10. Jewish people commonly addressed God as "Our heavenly Father" when they prayed, although such intimate titles as "Abba" (Papa) were rare (see comment on Mk 14:36). One standard Jewish prayer of the day (the Kaddish) proclaimed, "Exalted and hallowed be his . . . name . . . and may his kingdom come speedily and soon."

Jewish prayers recognized that God's name would be "hallowed," or "sanctified," "shown holy," in the time of the end, when his *kingdom would come, as the Bible also said (Is 5:16; 29:23; Ezek 36:23; 38:23; 39:7, 27; cf. Zech 14:9). In the present God's people could hallow his name by living rightly; if they lived wrongly, they would "profane" his name, or bring it into disrepute among the nations (cf. also Ex 20:7; Jer 34:16; 44:25-26; Ezek 13:19; 20:14; Amos 2:7).

It was understood that after his *kingdom came God's will would be done on earth as in heaven.

6:11. This verse alludes to God's provision of "daily bread" (manna) for his people in the wilderness after he first redeemed them. Prayers for God to supply one's basic needs—of which bread and water are the ultimate examples—were common in the ancient world (cf. Prov 30:8).

6:12. Jewish teaching regarded sins as "debts" before God; the same *Aramaic word could be used for both. Biblical law required the periodic forgiveness of monetary debtors (in the seventh and fiftieth years), so the illustration of forgiving debts would have been a graphic one (especially since Jewish lawyers had found a way to circumvent the release of debts so that creditors would continue to lend).

6:13. Parallels with ancient Jewish prayers, and possibly the *Aramaic wording behind this verse, suggest that the first line means: "Let us not sin when we are tested"—rather than "Let us not be tested" (cf. 4:1; 26:41 in context; cf. Ps 141:3-4). Some scholars have suggested an allusion to the final time of suffering here, which was expected to precede the coming *kingdom. Because Jewish prayers were commonly used in liturgical contexts that ended with a statement of praise, later texts' addition of the benediction ("Thine is the kingdom . . .") to the original text of Matthew is not surprising.

6:14-15. The principle of forgiveness that Jesus states here seems to be that only people of grace know how to accept grace. See comment on 18:21-35.

6:16-18 Secret Fasting

During at least the dry seasons, many of the most pious people fasted (without water, though this was unhealthy) two particular days a week. This fasting was considered meritorious, although *ascetic fasting (e.g., fasting only to "beat down the flesh") was forbidden. Jewish fasting required abstinence not only from food but also from other pleasures, which would include the usual practice of anointing one's head with oil to prevent dry skin; avoiding all these practices made fasting obvious. (Greeks oiled their bodies before exercise and then used a metal utensil called a strigil to scrape off the sweaty dirt accumulated on the oil. But Jews did not practice this custom, and it is not in view here in Mt 6.) God had never settled for outward fasting only (Is 58:3-12; Jer 36:9).

6:19-24 Don't Seek Possessions

One should not value possessions enough to seek them (6:19-24)—or enough to worry about them—because God will provide one's basic needs (6:25-34).

6:19. Ancient teachers like *Hillel, a famous Jewish teacher, generally acknowledged the corruptibility of earthly treasure. Because thieves could dig through walls and steal a strongbox in one's home, well-to-do people usually tried one of several other methods to safeguard their wealth: investing money with moneychangers, depositing it in a temple for safekeeping (even most robbers balked at "robbing gods") or burying it in the ground or in caves, where, however, moth (for expensive apparel) or rust (for coins) could destroy its value in time.

6:20-21. Jewish texts spoke of "laying up treasure" with God (e.g., Tobit 4:7-10). Sometimes this meant that the generous person could trust that God would help him in time of need; sometimes it referred (as here) to treasure in the world to come.

6:22-23. Jesus speaks literally of a "single" eye versus a "bad" or "evil" one. This saying may involve several plays on words. A "single" eye normally meant a generous one but also sets the reader up for 6:24. A "bad" eye in that culture could mean either a diseased one or a stingy one. Many people believed that light was emitted from the eye, enabling one to see, rather than that light was admitted through the eye. Although here Jesus compares the eye to a lamp, he speaks of "diseased" eyes which fail to *admit* light. Such eyes become a symbol for the worthlessness of a stingy person.

6:24. Two masters rarely shared slaves, but when they did it always led to divided interests. "Mammon" is an *Aramaic word for possessions or money, and Jesus seems to be personifying it as an idol, using another ancient figure of speech (personification).

6:25-34 Don't Worry About Possessions

6:25. Most people in antiquity had little beyond basic necessities—food, clothing and shelter. Because their acquisition of these necessities often depended—especially in rural areas—on seasonal rains or (in Egypt) the flooding of the Nile, they had plenty of cause for stress even about food and clothing.

6:26-27. Some ancient philosophers taught about or drew morals from nature as well as from philosophy. Many Jewish teachers said that God's concern in the laws of the Bible was only for humans (although it was clear that God watched over all creation; cf. Ps 104:27). But Jesus' argument was a standard Jewish "how much more" *(qal vahomer)* argument: If God cares for the birds (and *rabbis agreed that he sustained all creation), how much more does he care for humans?

6:28-30. Some commentators have suggested that the flowers here may be anemones, which were purple, the color that many ancient readers would have envisioned for Solomon's royal robes (6:29). Yet such flowers were fuel for the oven. The perishing of grass and flowers as they dried up in each year's summer heat was a natural image for human mortality (cf. Ps 103:15-16; Is 40:6-8).

6:31-33. The pagan world did indeed seek after such necessities, but Jesus reminds his hearers that they could trust their Father (v. 32; see comment on 6:7-8) and should seek the *kingdom (v. 33).

6:34. Other Jewish teachers after Jesus gave the same advice; whether Jesus used a common saying or his teaching in this case became a common saying is hard to determine.

7:1-5
Reciprocal Judgment

7:1-2. The idea of a measuring scale (the image is from the ancient marketplace) was used elsewhere for the day of judgment or divine retribution; "As a man measures it will be measured back to him" occurs a number of times in later Jewish sources and may have been a maxim. For the principle, see 5:7, 6:14-15 and Proverbs 19:17. Compare also the Old Testament principles that false witnesses were to receive the penalty they sought for the accused (Deut 19:18-21) and that God opposed unjust judges (Ex 23:6-8; Deut 16:18-20).

7:2-5. Although ancient eye surgery often involved lancing the eye, here Jesus clearly uses *hyperbole. The imagery is vivid, shocking, ludicrous and probably humorous to Jesus' hearers, but it communicates the point. The prophets had appealed to graphic images, often employing plays on words to communicate their message (e.g., the Hebrew of Mic 1; Jer 1:11-12). The *Old Testament (e.g., Prov 15:32) and subsequent Jewish tradition stressed that people should always be humble enough to accept correction.

7:6-12
Imitating God's Gifts

7:6. Pigs and dogs were considered unclean animals (Prov 26:11; 2 Pet 2:22), which had no appreciation for valuable things (Prov 11:22). Pigs typically ate the vilest foods, and dogs were scavengers, consuming even human blood. Stray dogs were known to growl at those who tossed them food as well as those who ignored them. The image would thus be forceful and beyond dispute for ancient hearers.

The question is what the verse means in the context. Perhaps it means not correcting (cf. Mt 7:1-5) those who would not listen (cf. Prov 23:9). Perhaps it means giving only to those who want what one offers, as God does (Mt 7:7-11); in this case the text returns to the idea of giving and of reciprocity in verse 12.

7:7-8. The boldness with which this

text promises answers to prayer is quite rare in ancient literature.

7:9-11. Jesus adapts a standard Jewish argument here called *qal vahomer:* arguing from the lesser to the greater (if the lesser is true, how much more the greater). Fish and bread were basic staples, integral to the diet of most of Jesus' hearers; they do not stand for the fineries of the wealthy.

7:12. That one should not do to others what one would not wish done to oneself was a common teaching; it occurred in the Jewish book of Tobit, in the teaching of the early Jewish teacher *Hillel and in Greek sources as well.

7:13-27
The Two Ways

7:13-14. Jesus' hearers would have been familiar with the image of "two ways"—one leading to life and the other to death; it was common in Judaism. Jesus' emphasis that few are on the right way occurs in 4 Ezra but is not as common as the general image of the two ways. Most Jewish people believed that Israel as a whole would be saved and that the few who were lost would be exceptions to the general rule.

7:15. Although most educated Jewish people did not believe that prophets had continued in the *Old Testament sense, they believed that false prophets (cf., e.g., Jer 2:8; 5:30) continued; *Josephus mentioned many of them in the first century. The contrast between vicious wolves and harmless lambs or sheep was proverbial.

7:16. Like wheat and barley, grapes and figs were among the most valuable and widely consumed fruits of the earth; thorns and thistles were worthless and troublesome to harvesters, as the Old Testament often mentions. For a figurative use of "fruits" in the Old Testament, see Isaiah 5:6 and comment on Matthew 3:8.

7:17-20. The repetition of "know them by their fruits" (7:17, 20) brackets this illustration; such bracketing was commonly used as a literary device (called *inclusio)* to mark off a paragraph. Prophets were known to be false if they led people away from the true God (Deut 13) or their words did not come to pass (Deut 18:21-22). The *rabbis allowed that prophets might temporarily suspend a teaching of the law the way rabbis themselves would, but if they denied the law itself or advocated idolatry, they were false prophets. Jesus teaches that if they do not live right, they are false (Mt 7:21-23). Cf. Luke 6:43-45.

7:21-23. The miracles Jesus mentions are not necessarily false; it is possible to prophesy by the *Spirit's inspiration and yet be disobedient to God and unsaved (1 Sam 19:20-24). The admonition to depart is from a psalm about the vindication of the righteous (Ps 6:8; cf. 119:115; 139:19).

7:24-27. The *rabbis debated whether hearing or doing the law was more important; most concluded that hearing it was more important, because one could not do it without hearing it. But they did insist that both were necessary.

Again the image is of the day of judgment. The idea of ultimately being judged for hearing but not obeying was familiar (Ezek 33:32-33). But no Jewish teacher apart from Jesus claimed so much authority for his own words; such authority was reserved for the law itself. Some of Jesus' more biblically literate hearers may have thought of Proverbs 24:3 ("by wisdom a house is built") and the contrast between wisdom (which builds a house in 9:1) and folly in Proverbs 9:1-18.

7:28-29
Response of the Masses

The teachers of the law never claimed

as much authority as Jesus had (7:24-27); they derived their authority especially from building on previous tradition.

8:1-4
Touching the Unclean: Leprosy

Matthew groups together nine stories containing ten specific miracles (some commentators have suggested that Matthew wants his readers to remember Moses' ten miracles) in chapters 8—9: three miracles in 8:1-17, then teaching on true discipleship (8:18-22); three more miracles (8:23—9:8), then teaching on true discipleship (9:9-17); and finally three more miracle stories, one of which includes two miracles (9:18-33).

Ancient writers used examples to illustrate points: Jesus' authority over sickness, demons and nature summons people to recognize his authority over their lives. In ancient thought, miracles could call attention to or attest teachers or their views (in contrast to modern rationalistic attempts to deny them).

8:1. The authorities viewed mobile teachers with followings of large crowds as threats to social stability; the Romans were always concerned about uprisings in Jewish Palestine. Readers familiar with this situation in pre-70 Jewish Palestine might recognize here a hint of impending conflict.

8:2. Leprosy was an unattractive skin disease for which the Bible had prescribed quarantine from the rest of society (Lev 13:45-46). Lepers were thus outcasts from society, and most healthy people preferred to ignore them. "Lord" in personal address could also mean "Sir" and need not connote a recognition of Jesus' deity.

8:3. Touching a leper was forbidden, and most people would have been revolted by the thought of it. Indeed, the law enjoined the leper's isolation from society (Lev 13:45-46). See further comment on Mark 1:40-45. The miracle itself would have been viewed as the work of a mighty prophet, however (cf. 2 Kings 5:14).

8:4. Jesus here follows the injunctions detailed in the *Old Testament law of leprosy (Lev 14:1-32). The instructions not to tell anyone else resemble the clandestine activity of some Old Testament prophets; on the messianic secret see further the discussion of Mark's message in the introduction to Mark.

8:5-13
A Non-Jew's Faith

By including this story from his source, Matthew encourages his Jewish Christian readers in the *Gentile mission. Even a single exception should be enough to challenge racist stereotypes.

8:5. The nearest legion of Roman troops was stationed in Syria; many troops were also stationed at Caesarea on the Mediterranean coast and in the fortress Antonia in Jerusalem; Capernaum, as a customs post, would naturally have warranted at least some soldiers. Centurions commanded a "century," but in practice this consisted of sixty to eighty troops, not one hundred. They were the backbone of the Roman army, in charge of discipline.

8:6. On "Lord" see comment on 8:2. During their twenty or so years of service in the Roman army, soldiers were not permitted to marry. Many had illegal local concubines, an arrangement that the army overlooked and the concubines found profitable; but centurions, who might be moved around more frequently, would be less likely to have such informal families than most soldiers. By ancient definitions, however, a household could include servants, and household servants and masters sometimes grew very close—especially if they made up the entire family unit. Centurions were paid much better than lower-ranking troops; servants were too expensive for common soldiers.

8:7. Jesus' response may be read as a question, a challenge, rather than a statement: "Shall I come and heal him?" (cf. 15:26). If one reads it as a statement, it declares Jesus' willingness to cross an important cultural boundary. It seems that pious Jewish people did not normally enter *Gentile homes; see comment on Acts 10:27-29.

8:8. The centurion, who knows that Jewish people rarely entered Gentile homes, concedes Jesus' special mission to Israel (cf. 15:27). At the same time he expresses great faith, for among all the stories (both true and spurious) of healing miracles in antiquity, long-distance healings were rare and considered especially extraordinary.

8:9. The centurion's response demonstrates that he (backed by Rome's authority) understands the principle of authority that Jesus exercises. Roman soldiers were very disciplined and (except in times of mutiny) followed orders carefully; they provided the ultimate model of discipline and obedience in the Roman Empire.

8:10. *Gentiles were generally pagans, with no faith in Israel's God.

8:11. This verse reflects the standard Jewish image of the future banquet in God's *kingdom. Although the Bible declared that it was for all peoples (Is 25:6; cf. 56:3-8), Jewish literature by this period emphasized that it was prepared for Israel, who would be exalted over its enemies. People were seated at banquets according to rank. They "sat" at regular meals but "reclined" (as here) at feasts; table fellowship signified intimacy, so fellowship with the great patriarchs, Abraham, Isaac and Jacob, was thought to represent a future hope for the Jewish people, not for Gentiles, with whom Jewish people did not eat.

8:12. The "rightful" heirs are cast out; other Jewish texts used outer darkness to describe hell, often where mighty evil spirits were imprisoned; the gnashing of teeth may allude to Psalm 112:10.

8:13. Some Jewish stories circulated about miracle workers, but reports of long-distance healings were rare and regarded as extraordinary. This healing would thus have been viewed as especially miraculous.

8:14-17
Messiah the Healer

8:14. Archaeologists have found what is thought to be this home in a site close to the *synagogue. Adult children were expected to care for their aged parents. (For more details see comment on Mk 1:29-34.)

8:15. Some religious men refrained from touching women in general to avoid any possibility of becoming unclean, unless they had means by which they could ascertain their status (based on Lev 15:19). That Peter's mother-in-law was able to "serve" them at table, a common womanly role in antiquity (cf. Lk 10:40), indicates the extent to which she was genuinely healed.

8:16. Exorcists often used magical incantations and sought to manipulate higher spirits into helping them drive out lower ones; in contrast, Jesus simply drives out spirits "with a word."

8:17. In context Isaiah 53:4 emphasizes particularly healing from the ravages of sin (53:5-6; cf. Hos 14:4, etc.), as some other Christian writers noted (1 Pet 2:24-25). But given Isaiah's emphasis on physical restoration in the messianic era (35:5-6) and the connection between physical and spiritual healing in Jewish tradition (cf. also Is 33:24), it makes good sense that Matthew also finds the nuance of physical healing here: Jesus inaugurates the messianic era, making some of its benefits available even in advance of the cross.

8:18-22
Jesus' Demands

8:18. *Disciples generally acted as servants to their *rabbis, following practical orders relevant to the work of the teacher and his school as well as learning his teachings.

8:19-20. Disciples usually sought out their own teachers. Some radical Greek philosophers who eschewed possessions sought to repulse prospective disciples with enormous demands, for the purpose of testing them and acquiring the most worthy. Comparisons with animals constituted a reasonably common teaching technique (e.g., the now famous animal fables attributed to Aesop). Like fishermen and *tax gatherers, carpenters had a much better income than agrarian peasants; Jesus' call, not involuntary poverty, summoned him and his followers to a sacrificial lifestyle.

8:21-22. One of an eldest son's most basic responsibilities (in both Greek and Jewish cultures) was his father's burial. The initial burial took place shortly after a person's decease, however, and family members would not be outside talking with *rabbis during the reclusive mourning period immediately following the death. It has recently been shown that what is in view here instead is the secondary burial: a year after the first burial, after the flesh had rotted off the bones, the son would return to rebury the bones in a special box in a slot in the tomb's wall. The son in this narrative could thus be asking for as much as a year's delay.

Nevertheless, Jesus' demand that the son place him above the greatest responsibility a son had toward his father would have sounded like heresy: in Jewish tradition, honoring father and mother was one of the greatest commandments, and to follow Jesus at the expense of not burying one's father would have been viewed as dishonoring one's father (cf. Tobit 4:3-4).

8:23-27
Lord of Nature

Greek stories about those who could subdue nature were normally about gods or about demigods who had acted in the distant past. Jewish tradition reported some earlier teachers who could pray for rain or its cessation like Elijah. But absolute authority over waves and sea in Jewish tradition belonged to God alone. It is not difficult to understand why the *disciples did not know what to make of Jesus!

8:28-34
Lord over Evil Spirits

Proposals vary on why Matthew has two, and Mark but one, demoniac here (see comment on Mk 5:1-20); one suggestion is that Matthew includes an extra one here because he left one out by omitting the story recorded in Mark 1:21-28. The doubling of characters here would not have violated standard Jewish writing conventions of that time.

8:28. Tombs were ceremonially unclean and were thought to be popular haunts for evil spirits (a belief the spirits were apparently happy to accommodate). Both Gadara (here) and Gerasa (Mk 5:1) were predominantly *Gentile cities in the region of the Decapolis, but Gadara was much closer to the Sea of Galilee (Gerasa, a prominent and magnificent city, was over thirty miles southeast). Roughly six miles to the southeast, Gadara probably controlled the land where this *narrative occurs. Violent behavior is still frequently associated with spirit possession in cultures that recognize the phenomenon.

8:29. "Before the time" means before the day of judgment. Apparently even the demons did not expect the *Messiah to come in two stages, a first and second coming.

8:30. Jewish people lived in this region, but it was predominantly non-Jewish; hence the pigs.

8:31. Ancient stories about demons suggest that they liked to negotiate the least difficult terms if they were going to have to leave one whom they possessed. Hearing that demons would want to inhabit unclean pigs, Jewish listeners would respond, "But of course!"

8:32. In Jewish tradition, demons could die or be bound; because Matthew says nothing to the contrary, his readers would probably assume that these demons have been destroyed or imprisoned.

8:33-34. The *Old Testament *narratives of Elijah and Elisha allowed Jewish people to place some miracle workers in the category of "prophet," but Greeks usually categorized miracle workers as magicians or sorcerers. Because magicians and sorcerers were usually malevolent and Jesus' coming had already cost these *Gentiles from the Decapolis economically (he sank a lot of pork), they were naturally terrified of him.

9:1-8
Authority to Forgive and to Heal

It was common to abridge accounts, as Matthew often does; reciting Mark's story about the paralytic (see comment on Mk 2:1-12), he omits the letting down through the roof.

9:1-2. Many "beds" were mats; thus the paralytics' friends may have carried him on the bed on which he lay all the time. "His own town" here is Capernaum (4:13).

9:3. Judaism believed that only God could forgive sins, but most Jews allowed that some of God's representatives could speak on God's behalf. The *Old Testament penalty for blaspheming God's name—reproaching rather than honoring it—was death (Lev 24:10-23). According to later *rabbinic law, blasphemy technically involved pronouncing the divine name or perhaps inviting people to follow other gods. According to the more common, less technical usage, it applied to any grievous insult to God's honor (cf. Num 15:30). But these legal scholars were mistaken in interpreting Jesus' words as blasphemy, by any definition.

9:4. Judaism recognized that God sometimes revealed to prophets what others were thinking or planning.

9:5-7. Jewish teachers knew that only God could ultimately forgive (on the Day of Atonement in response to sacrifice); but they also recognized that healing ultimately came from God as well. *Josephus shows us that many false prophets in Jesus' day claimed to work miracles but actually failed to work them; some of Jesus' critics may have placed him in this category. His act in front of these witnesses, however, should have challenged them to rethink their case.

9:8. When ancient writers reported accounts of miracles, they generally concluded the account with the amazed response of the crowds who witnessed it.

9:9-13
A Physician for Sinners

9:9. Levi may have been a tax farmer

working for Herod; situated at an office in Capernaum, he was more likely a customs agent, charging import duties on wares brought through this town on important nearby trade routes. Even more than the fishermen, he had a secure and prosperous job, which he surrendered to follow Jesus' call.

9:10. Most people regarded a man of wealth inviting a religious teacher over for dinner as honorable behavior. *Tax gatherers, however, were regarded as collaborators with the Romans and were despised by religious people. Some commentators have argued that "sinners" may refer to all who did not eat food in ritual purity, but the term probably refers to anyone who lived sinfully rather than religiously, as if they did not care what the religious community thought of them.

9:11. Table fellowship indicated intimate relations among those who shared it. The *Pharisees were particularly scrupulous about their special rules on eating and did not like to eat with less scrupulous people, especially people like *tax gatherers and sinners. Here they assume that Jesus, being a wise teacher, ought to share their religious convictions, which they believed were scriptural (Ps 1:1).

9:12. Jesus' reply plays on a common image of the day (comparing physicians and teachers) to make his point. Quick, witty repartee was characteristic of popular teachers in both Jewish and Greek traditions.

9:13. Other *rabbis often said, "Go and learn" or "Come and see" to direct hearers to scriptural proofs for their position. Hosea 6:6 does not reject sacrifice or ritual, but elevates right relationship with God and right treatment of the poor, the oppressed and the outcasts above sacrifice and ritual (cf. similarly 1 Sam 15:22; Ps 40:6; 50:7-15; 51:16; 69:30-31; Prov 21:3).

9:14-17
Appropriate Fasting

9:14. The *law required fasting only on the Day of Atonement, but many other fasts had been added by religious Jews, especially by groups like the *Pharisees. Many of the Pharisees may have fasted two days a week without water, especially during the dry season. Fasting was an important practice to join with prayer or penitence, so it would have been unusual for *disciples (prospective rabbis) to have avoided it altogether. A teacher was regarded as responsible for the behavior of his disciples.

9:15. Wedding feasts required seven days of festivity; one was not permitted to fast or engage in other acts of mourning or difficult labor during a wedding feast. Jesus makes an analogy about the similar inappropriateness of fasting in his own time.

9:16. Again, the issue is the inappropriateness of fasting in the present circumstance. Older clothes would have already shrunk somewhat from washing.

9:17. Wine could be kept in either jars or wineskins. Old wineskins had already been stretched to capacity by fermenting wine within them; if they were then filled with unfermented wine, it would likewise expand, and the old wineskins, already stretched to the limit, would burst.

9:18-26
Touching the Unclean: Blood and Death

Raising the dead was an extraordinary miracle, attributed to Elijah (1 Kings 17:21-22) and Elisha (2 Kings 4:33-35) in the Old Testament. See comment on Mark 5:21-43 for further details.

9:18-19. "Rulers of the *synagogue" were the chief officials in synagogues and were prominent members of their communities. If the setting is still Capernaum (9:1), it is significant that Jesus' following could include both this man and more questionable elements of the community (9:9).

One would fall at the feet of someone of much greater status (like a king) or prostrate oneself before God; thus for this prominent man to humble himself in this way before Jesus was to recognize Jesus' power in a serious way.

9:20-21. This woman's sickness was reckoned as if she had a menstrual period all month long; it made her continually unclean under the *law (Lev 15:19-33)—a social and religious problem in addition to the physical one. If she touched anyone or anyone's clothes, she rendered that person ceremonially unclean for the rest of the day (cf. Lev 15:26-27). Because she rendered unclean anyone she touched, she should not have even been in this heavy crowd. Many teachers avoided touching women altogether, lest they become accidentally contaminated. Thus she could not touch or be touched, she had probably never married or was now divorced, and she was marginal to Jewish society.

In an act of scandalous faith, she touches Jesus' garment's "fringe"—no doubt one of the tassels *(zizith)* worn by Jewish men, in obedience to Numbers 15:38-41 and Deuteronomy 22:12, on the four corners of their outer garment, and later on the prayer shawl *(tallith).* The tassels were made of blue and white cords woven together.

9:22. Many ancient people believed that only teachers closest to God had supernatural knowledge. Jesus uses his supernatural knowledge to identify with the woman who had touched him—even though in the eyes of the public this would mean that he had contracted ritual uncleanness.

9:23-24. Flute players were there to lead the crowd in mourning. Several professional women mourners were required even at the funeral of the poorest person; the funeral of a member of a prominent family like this one would have many mourners. The cathartic release of mourning included shrieking and beating of breasts. Because bodies decomposed rapidly in Palestine, mourners were to be assembled, if possible, immediately upon someone's death; in this case they had gathered before word even reached Jairus that his daughter had died.

9:25-26. The most defiling kind of ritual uncleanness one could contract in Jewish law came from touching a corpse (Num 19:11-22).

9:27-34
Healing Blind Eyes

9:27-31. "Son of David" was the title of the *Messiah, but in most expectations the Messiah was a political or military figure rather than a healer. But these blind men understand a connection between healing and Jesus' identity that was not part of Jewish tradition. God ruled over blindness and sight (Ex 4:11; Prov 20:12) and could answer prophets' prayers to remove and restore human sight (2 Kings 6:18-20).

9:32-34. Elijah and Elisha had done extraordinary healing miracles; David is the only recorded Old Testament figure God used in exorcism (1 Sam 16:23). Matthew 9:33 thus indicates that the crowds were greatly impressed with his miracles.

9:35-38
More Laborers Needed

The works of Jesus in 8:1—9:35 must become those of his *disciples in chapter 10.

9:35-36. Without Moses (Num 27:17) or a king (1 Kings 22:17; 2 Chron

18:16) Israel had been said to be "without a shepherd," or ruler. When Israel was without other faithful shepherds (religious leaders), God himself would become its shepherd (Ezek 34:11-16); the shepherd's ministry included feeding (34:2-3), healing (34:4) and bringing back the lost sheep (34:4-6). Matthew 9:36 thus also implies that those charged with shepherding Israel, its leaders, were failing.

9:37-38. "Harvest" could be used as an image for the end time (cf. comment on 3:12), but the idea here is more like God's witnesses in Isaiah. A late first-century *rabbi said something similar to 9:37; it is uncertain whether it was already a standard Jewish saying, or this rabbi was influenced by a saying that goes back to Jesus, or the parallel is a coincidence.

10:1-4 Sending the Twelve

Israel had twelve tribes, and groups that chose twelve leaders (as in the *Dead Sea Scrolls) did so because they believed that their own group was the true, obedient remnant of Israel.

The lists in Luke and Acts replace Mark and Matthew's "Thaddeus" with "Judas son of James" (cf. also Jn 14:22). Ancient documents show that it was common for people to go by more than one name, so the different lists of *apostles probably do refer to the same people. Nicknames were common, appearing even on tomb inscriptions. "Cananaean" is *Aramaic for "*zealot" (Lk 6:15); thus some translations simply read "Simon the Zealot" here. In Jesus' day, this word could just mean "zealous one," but it may mean that he had been involved in revolutionary activity before becoming Jesus' follower, as it would probably mean when the Gospels were written.

"Apostles" means "sent ones," or commissioned representatives. The analogous Hebrew term was used for business agents, although the general concept is broader than that; a "sent one" acted on the full authority of the sender to the extent that he accurately represented the sender's mission. Commissioning narratives appear in the *Old Testament, as when Moses commissions Joshua to carry on Moses' work and take the Promised Land (Deut 31:23). *Rabbis allowed their senior students to teach while they were still students, to prepare them for their own work as rabbis.

10:5-16 The Mission

10:5. "Way of the *Gentiles" probably means a road leading only to one of the pagan, Greek cities in Palestine; Jewish people normally avoided roads that led into such cities anyway. Galilee was surrounded by Gentile regions except in the south, where it shared borders with Samaria. (On *Samaritans, see comment on Jn 4:1-4.)

10:6. A common Jewish belief was that ten tribes of Israel had been lost and would be found in the time of the end. Here, however, Jesus uses "lost sheep of Israel" in the more common Old Testament sense: they have gone astray from the Lord (Is 53:6; Jer 50:6; cf. Ezek 34:5). The idea that a message was first to Israel did not preclude it later coming to others (Amos 3:2 and context; cf. the oracles against the nations by Isaiah, Jeremiah and others).

10:7-8. That the *apostles' mission is the same as Jesus' is appropriate for "sent ones" (see comment on 10:1-4): they acted within the limits of their authorization. "As I [God] [gave the *law] for free, so you should" was a later Jewish saying applied to teachers of the law; whether it was a proverb Jesus was citing this early we cannot be sure.

10:9-10. They are to travel light, like some other groups: (1) peasants, who often had only one cloak; (2) some traveling philosophers, called *Cynics (probably represented as nearby as Tyre and the Decapolis, *Gentile cities surrounding Galilee); (3) some prophets, like Elijah and John the Baptist. They are to be totally committed to their mission, not tied down with worldly concerns. The "bag" could have been used for begging (so the Cynics used it), though cf. 10:11; on "money belts," see comment on Luke 6:38. It is said that *Essenes received such hospitality from fellow Essenes in various cities that they did not need to take provisions when they traveled.

10:11-13. Showing hospitality by taking in travelers was one of the most important virtues in Mediterranean antiquity, especially in Judaism; Jesus could have drawn on Old Testament precedent for traveling ministers depending on such hospitality (2 Kings 4:8-11); cf. comment on Matthew 10:41. (Indeed, Israelite tradition had required even most wicked kings to respect prophets and to spare them despite their criticisms, which other ancient kings would not have endured.)

To whom and under what circumstances greetings should or should not be given were important issues of social protocol, especially because the common Jewish greeting, "Peace," was really a blessing or wish-prayer meant to communicate peace. Jesus cuts through such issues of protocol with new directives.

10:14-15. Pious Jewish people returning to holy ground would not want even the dust of pagan territory clinging to their sandals; Jesus' representatives here treat unresponsive regions as unholy or pagan. Sodom is set forth as the epitome of sinfulness both in the prophets and in subsequent Jewish tradition; the point here is probably that they rejected God's messengers, albeit lesser ones than Jesus (Gen 19).

10:16. Jewish people sometimes viewed themselves (Israel) as sheep among wolves (the *Gentiles). The contrast between vicious wolves and harmless lambs or sheep was proverbial.

10:17-23
Promise of Persecution

10:17. Local courts, or councils deciding cases, were run by local elders or priests before A.D. 70; in later times *rabbis came to staff them, with a minimum of three judges per court. *Synagogues were the local places of public assembly, and thus provided the natural location for hearings and public discipline. Sometimes discipline was administered in the form of flogging; under second-century rules, Jewish flogging consisted of thirteen harsh strokes on the breast and twenty-six on the back. These words would have struck Jewish Christians as particularly painful, because they signified rejection of their preaching among their own people.

10:18. In Jewish thinking, a Jew betraying any Jew to *Gentile persecutors was a horrendous act. "Governors" are Roman overseers in the provinces; the three levels were propraetors, proconsuls and procurators. "Kings" may refer only to Rome's vassal princes but probably includes Parthian and other rulers from the East, indicating virtually universal persecution.

10:19-20. Jewish people thought of the *Holy Spirit especially as the Spirit of *prophecy who had anointed the prophets to speak God's message.

10:21-22. See Micah 7:5-7 (more explicit in Mt 10:35-36); this family divisiveness also became part of other Jewish images of the end time (e.g., *1 Enoch 100:2). In a culture where family loyalty was essential and honor of parents paramount, these words would have sounded unbelievably harsh.

10:23. A Jewish tradition that may have been in circulation in Jesus' day warns that in the time of final tribulation, Jewish people persecuted for their faith would have to flee from one city to another. The *disciples may have understood his words in these terms. Jesus' point seems to be that they will always have someplace to which they can escape, and some will survive to the end no matter how severe the persecution is (24:22).

10:24-33
Comfort in Persecution

Like most early Christians and zealous Christians in many parts of the world today, Matthew's readers faced persecution and often other dangers as part of their daily lives. Jesus' words would comfort them.

10:24-25. *Disciples were to serve their teachers, in hopes of ultimately becoming master teachers themselves. A slave could attain status if owned by a prominent master, and under rare circumstances (e.g., if owned by a *freedperson), he could attain equal status after—but never before—becoming free and attaining wealth too. Verse 25 contains a play on words: by reading "Beelzebul" as if it meant "master" (*Aramaic *be'el)* of the house (Hebrew *zebul),* Jesus spoke of the "master of the house."

10:26-27. Everything would come to light on the day of judgment, as was widely agreed; there was therefore no point in concealing anything now. The flat rooftops provided the best place for shouting messages out over the crowded streets.

10:28. Fearing (respecting, only in a much stronger way than we use the term *respect)* God was central to Jewish wisdom tradition and is repeatedly stressed in Jewish literature; some Jewish writers made affirmations about martyrdom similar to this passage (*4 Maccabees 13:14-15). Body and soul were instantly destroyed in some Jewish traditions about hell; in others, they were perpetually destroyed and tormented. Contrary to the assertions of many modern scholars, most Jewish people agreed with the Greeks that soul and body were separated by death.

10:29-31. Sparrows were one of the cheapest items sold for poor people's food in the marketplace, the cheapest of all birds. Two were here purchased for an *assarion,* a small copper coin of little value (less than an hour's work); Luke 12:6 seems to indicate that they were even cheaper if purchased in larger quantities. This is a standard Jewish "how much more" argument: If God cares for something as cheap as sparrows, how much more does he care for people!

10:32-33. In Jewish descriptions of the day of judgment, the testimony of righteous persons for or against others bore much weight with God. *Rabbis spoke of God's angels or his attributes of mercy or judgment pleading a case before him. Here Jesus' advocacy before the Father weighs more heavily than anything else in this world.

10:34-39
The Cost of Discipleship

10:34. It was generally believed that there would be great sufferings before the end, and that the *Messiah would lead his people in a triumphant war, followed by a time of peace. Jesus assures his listeners that the promised era of peace is yet some time off and goes on to explain the nature of the current sufferings and conflict.

10:35-36. The context of Micah 7:6, cited here, describes the awful evils in the land and the untrustworthiness of even the closest relatives and friends that would continue until the Lord would come to vindicate those who hoped in him. Given the belief held by many Jewish people that a time of sufferings would precede the end, the *disciples would probably have understood this saying as suggesting that they were already experiencing the sufferings of that time.

10:37. Jesus here expounds on the text just cited (Mic 7:6) to make a point virtually inconceivable to most of his hearers. Loving family members, especially parents, was one of the highest duties in Judaism; the only one who could rightfully demand greater love was God himself (Deut 6:4-5; cf. Deut 13:6-11; 2 Macc 7:22-23).

10:38. A condemned criminal would carry on his back the horizontal beam of the cross out to the site of his execution, generally amid an antagonistic, jeering mob. This verse means a shameful, painful road to a dreadful execution.

10:39. Most Jewish people contrasted the life of this world with the life of the world to come.

10:40-42
Receiving Christ's Messengers

This passage returns to the theme of hospitality toward the messengers of the gospel (10:11-14). The principle here is like that of the appointed messenger or agent in Judaism, who represented his sender to the full extent of his commission. God, his glory and law, and Israel were also connected in this way in Jewish tradition. This principle had always been true of the prophets (e.g., 1 Sam 8:7; cf. Num 14:2, 11; 16:11): one who embraced them embraced their message and thus God's will. Those who provided for them were likewise rewarded (1 Kings 17:9-24; 2 Kings 4:8-37). A cup of water was the only gift the poorest person might have, but it would symbolize enough. Cold water was highly preferred for drinking (see comment on Rev 3:15-16).

11:1-19
More Than a Prophet: The Forerunner

Matthew 11:1 is an epilogue to 9:37—10:42; in 11:2-19, John, like Jesus and the Twelve, becomes a model for Christian discipleship.

11:1. Emissaries would often be sent to prepare people for the coming of a king or other important figure before his arrival. "Cities" is meant in a broad rather than a technical Greek sense: there is no indication that Jesus approached major cities like Sepphoris or Tiberias. Even most of the larger agricultural towns had fewer than three thousand inhabitants, and the Galilean countryside was full of villages.

11:2-3. John's attitude here contrasts strikingly with 3:14. Some commentators have suggested that John is concerned about reports that Jesus has been touching the unclean (8:3; 9:20, 25); to this report Jesus replies with the results of those touches (11:5). More likely, John, like most of his contemporaries, is tempted to think of a *kingdom bringer (3:11) or royal *Messiah rather than a miracle worker, so Jesus vindicates his healing mission with a text about the blessings of the messianic era (11:5). John's *disciples had probably traveled on the main road northward from Herod's fortress Machaerus, where John was imprisoned, through Perea beside the Jordan, to cross into Galilee, where Jesus was teaching.

11:4-6. Jesus cites signs from Isaiah

35:5-6 that refer to the arrival of the messianic era; cf. Isaiah 26:19; 61:1.

11:7. Reeds were fragile (Is 42:3; *3 Maccabees 2:22), so a "reed shaken by the wind" was notoriously weak (1 Kings 14:15) and undependable (2 Kings 18:21; Ezek 29:6).

11:8. Prophets were rarely well-to-do, and in times of national wickedness they were forced to operate outside societal boundaries. (In David's time, Nathan and Gad could be court prophets; but by Ahab's time the court prophets were corrupt, and Elijah and others had to hide out in the wilderness or, in better days, at least remain outside the king's palace.) Royal luxury is not a standard of holiness in the *kingdom.

11:9-10. Many Jews in the first century believed that full-fledged prophets had died out long ago, but they would have been open to the restoration of prophets in the end time. By fulfilling Malachi 3:1, John is more than just any herald of God; he is the direct announcer of the Lord, fulfilling the prophecy of Elijah's return (Mal 4:5-6).

11:11. This statement elevates Jesus' *disciples rather than demeans John (cf. 11:9-10). One may compare the early *rabbinic saying that Johanan ben Zakkai, one of the most respected scholars of the first century, was the "least" of *Hillel's eighty disciples; this saying was not meant to diminish Johanan's status but to increase that of his contemporaries. Calling John the "greatest" was a typically Jewish form of praise, which could be applied to more than one person at a time; rabbis, for instance, could in the same breath speak of both Joseph and Moses as the greatest figures of Israel's history (in the *Old Testament cf., e.g., 2 Kings 18:5; 23:25). Those "born of women" was a familiar Old Testament and Jewish expression for humans (e.g., Job 14:1).

11:12. Revolutionaries, such as those later known as *Zealots, wanted to bring in the *kingdom by military force. Jesus uses their zeal (cf. Prov 11:16) in a figurative way for the single-minded commitment necessary to enter the kingdom; he describes his followers as *spiritual* zealots (cf. Mt 10:34).

11:13. Jewish people sometimes summarized the Bible as "the Law and the Prophets"; many of them believed that after the biblical prophets the prophetic voice was muted until the messianic time. John thus introduces the messianic era.

11:14-15. Malachi 4:5 had promised the return of Elijah, who had reportedly never died (2 Kings 2:11); Elijah's return thus became part of Jewish expectation for the future.

11:16-17. "To what may we compare . . . ?" was a familiar idiom preceding a *rabbinic *parable or argument from analogy.

Spoiled children who pretend to have weddings and funerals (one later game was called "bury the grasshopper") stand for Jesus' and John's dissatisfied opponents; dissatisfied with other children who will not play either game, they are sad no matter what. The term for "mourn" here is "beat the breast," a standard mourning custom in Jewish Palestine. Custom mandated that bystanders join in any bridal or funeral processions.

11:18-19. John the Baptist fit the role of an apparently *ascetic prophet, like Elijah; Jesus follows a model more like David, but both are proper in their place. The charge that John "has a demon" suggests either that he is a false prophet possessed by an evil spirit, or that he is a sorcerer who manipulates a spirit guide; either charge would warrant the death penalty under Old Testament law (Deut 13:1-11; 18:9-20). "Glutton and drunkard" was also a capital charge (Deut 21:20); hence this is a serious accusation.

Some commentators have suggested that 11:19 identifies Jesus with the Jewish image of personified, divine wisdom (cf. 11:25-27); he might, however, simply be claiming that one can recognize that his behavior (11:2) is truly wise by examining it.

11:20-24
Judgment on Cities

Judgment oracles against nations were standard in the *Old Testament prophets (Isaiah, Jeremiah, Ezekiel); they also appear in the Jewish *Sibylline Oracles before and during the *New Testament period. The principle that those who had more light were judged more strictly appears in the Old Testament (cf. Amos 3:2; Jon 4:11).

11:20-21. Jewish people thought of Tyre and Sidon as purely pagan cities (cf. 1 Kings 16:31), but some of their inhabitants who were exposed to the truth had been known to repent (1 Kings 17:9-24). "Sackcloth and ashes" was dressing characteristic of mourning, including the mourning of *repentance. Chorazin was a short walk, less than two miles, from Capernaum.

11:22. According to some Jewish stories about the time of the end ("the day of judgment," as it was often called), the righteous among the pagan nations would testify against the rest of their people, making clear that no one had any excuse for rejecting the truth about God.

11:23. Judgment was often described in the terms Jesus uses here (Is 5:14; *Jubilees 24:31), especially against a ruler who exalted himself as a deity (Is 14:14-15, of the Babylonian king's death).

11:24. See comment on 11:22.

11:25-27
God's Revelation

In Jewish wisdom tradition, it was not those who were wise in their own eyes and leaned to their own understanding who were genuinely wise (Job 12:24-25; Prov 3:5-7; 12:15; 16:2; 21:2; 26:12), but the simple who began with the fear of God (Job 28:28; Ps 111:10; Prov 1:7; 9:10). Matthew 11:27 may attribute the power of predestination (assigned only to God in Jewish sources) to Jesus; as the revealer of God, he assumes a position often assumed by divine Wisdom in Jewish tradition. For the image of infants, cf. 10:42 and 18:1-10; God had always favored the lowly (e.g., 1 Sam 2:3-9).

11:28-30
The True Sabbath

11:28. God offered rest to the weary (Is 40:28-31; cf. the invitation of divine Wisdom in Ecclus 24:19); this was not the promise an ordinary teacher would make.

11:29-30. When a man carried a yoke he would carry it on his shoulders (cf., e.g., Jer 27:2); Judaism applied this image of subjection to obedience. Jewish people spoke of carrying the yoke of God's law and the yoke of his *kingdom, which one accepted by acknowledging that God was one and by keeping his commandments. Matthew intends Jesus' words about rest as a contrast with *Pharisaic sabbath rules in the following passage (12:1-14): the promise of "rest for your souls" comes from Jeremiah 6:16, where God promises to stay his wrath if the people turn to him instead of to the words of the false religious leaders (6:13-14, 20).

Greek literature praised meekness in the sense of gentleness and leniency but not in the sense of self-abasement; aristocrats disdained humility as a virtue, except for the lowly. Jesus, however, identifies with those of low social status, a value more prominent in Jewish piety.

12:1-8
Food on the Sabbath

Other details are noted in Mark 2:23-27, although details in Matthew, written mainly for Jewish Christians, would have sounded less like a sabbath violation to Jewish ears than Mark's wording would. Matthew's structure follows the standard form for many ancient reports of arguments: he summarizes the situation (12:1-2), presents arguments by example (12:3-4), analogy (12:5), comparison (12:6), citation (12:7) and ultimate basis (12:8).

12:1. Jewish law based on Deuteronomy 23:25 (cf. Ruth 2:2-3) provided for the poor to eat food as they passed through a field. The issue here is thus not that the disciples took someone's grain but that they picked it on the sabbath; later *rabbinic law specifically designated this as one of thirty-nine kinds of work forbidden on the sabbath.

12:2. The modern picture of *Pharisees as legalists unfairly trivializes the Pharisees' piety (probably intentionally, so modern legalists will not have to address Jesus' real bases for criticism). Not only the Pharisees but other Jewish people throughout the ancient world honored the sabbath and celebrated it with joy. The Bible itself had forbidden infractions of the sabbath under pain of death, so the Pharisees were naturally disturbed when it appeared that Jesus dishonored the day.

12:3-4. Although highhanded rejection of the sabbath was regarded as rebellion against God, different Jewish groups made arguments for differing interpretations of sabbath laws and were not in a position to legally enforce their views against others. Jesus' arguments here would not have satisfied the Pharisees, but they might have satisified elders or priests serving as judges on local courts.

12:5-6. As we know from later sources, most *rabbis would have questioned an argument based merely on example such as the one in 12:3-4 and Mark 2:25-26; it is significant that Matthew, writing for Jewish readers, has an argument from the *law itself.

The law of Moses commanded work for priests on the sabbath (Num 28:10). This is a Jewish "how much more" argument: if acceptable for the guardians of the temple, how much more for one greater than the temple? The temple had become the central symbol of the Jewish faith, and the suggestion that a human being could be greater than the temple would have struck most ancient Jewish ears as presumptuous and preposterous. Jewish teachers could, however, accept and argue from the principle that some things took precedence over sabbath observance (temple ritual, saving a life, defensive warfare, etc.).

12:7-8. Jesus goes on the offensive here with a still higher principle of the *Old Testament; cf. 9:13.

12:9-14
Healing on the Sabbath

Other details are noted in the comment on Mark 3:1-6. Whereas Mark's argument would not have been as persuasive to *Pharisees, being an argument from analogy from greater to lesser (3:4), Matthew includes a more helpful argument from lesser to greater (12:12).

12:9-10. As one may gather here, informal dialogues could occur in smaller *synagogue gatherings in this period that are quite different from the stricter ritual observed in most churches and synagogues today. The predominant school of *Pharisees in this period, the Shammaites, did not allow praying for the sick on the sabbath; the minority school, however, the Hillelites (who later became predominant), allowed it.

12:11. The *Essenes would have forbidden even rescuing an animal on the sabbath, but many Pharisees and most other Jewish interpreters would have agreed with Jesus. Pits were sometimes dug to capture predators such as wolves, but livestock could fall into them as well. Counterquestions (as here, answering 12:10) were common in the debates of Jewish teachers.

12:12. Jesus here uses a standard Jewish argument, "how much more" *(qal vahomer):* If one is concerned for a sheep, how much more for a person? This, too, was an argument his opponents had to understand, and by analogy it showed the inconsistency of their interpretation of biblical sabbath laws.

12:13-14. *Pharisees, who had little political power in this period, could do no better than plot. Jewish courts could not enforce the death penalty in this period, although the law of Moses allowed it for sabbath violation (Ex 31:14; 35:2). The Pharisees had no power to destroy him, and their own rules did not permit them to seek his execution if he had defeated them in a scriptural argument, but this need not stop them from trying. Even had Matthew's Jewish readers been Pharisees (which is unlikely), they would be forced to see Jesus' opponents as unjust and obstinate here.

12:15-21
The Spirit-Anointed Servant

12:15-16. Withdrawing from this *synagogue with new followers was not actually destroying the synagogue; first-century Palestinian Judaism was very diverse, and not everyone in a synagogue need hold the same views.

12:17-18. The servant passage in Isaiah 42:1-4 in context refers inescapably to Israel, not to the *Messiah, despite a later Jewish tradition applying it to the Messiah (44:1, 21; 49:3). But because God's servant Israel failed in its mission (42:18-19), God chose one within Israel to restore the rest of the people (49:5-7), who would take the remainder of the punishment due Israel (cf. 40:2) in its place (52:13—53:12). Thus Matthew declares that the Messiah takes up the servant mission of Isaiah 42:1-4, and he is marked by the presence of the *Spirit. Matthew translates Isaiah to conform to the language of Matthew 3:17 ("my beloved . . . in whom I am well pleased"), which was otherwise closer to Genesis 22:2.

12:19-21. This passage stresses Jesus' meekness, in contrast to the warlike *Messiah many people hoped for; this was the reason for the messianic secret (on which see the introduction to Mark in this commentary). It was customary to quote only part of a passage, because the more biblically informed hearers would know the context; Matthew wants all of his readers to catch the note on which he concludes: salvation for non-Jews.

12:22-37
Blaspheming the Spirit

See further comment on Mark 3:20-30.

12:22-23. The *Messiah of Jewish expectation, a descendant of David, was not a miracle worker, but since God was with Jesus in such extraordinary ways, it is not difficult to see how messianic hopes would be attached to him. David was also the only exorcist reported in the *Old Testament (1 Sam 16:23).

12:24. Pagan exorcists sought to remove demons by magical incantations. In the second century *rabbis still accused Jesus and Jewish Christians of using sorcery to achieve the miracles that everyone acknowledged they were performing. Sorcery merited the death penalty under Old Testament law (Ex 22:18).

The title Beelzebul, "Lord of the House," probably alludes to "Beelzebub" ("lord of flies," a possible corruption of Baal-zebul), the local deity of Ekron (2 Kings 1:2-3). The title was appropriately applied in early Judaism to *Satan (*Testament of Solomon).

12:25-26. Jesus does not deny the existence of other exorcists here. But a demon's retreat that meanwhile drew attention to another of Satan's servants would only be a strategic retreat; such possible activity of magical exorcists contrasts with the wholesale exorcizing of the masses that Jesus undertakes, which clearly signifies a defeat of Satan (12:29). Quick, witty repartee was characteristic of popular teachers in both Jewish and Greek traditions.

12:27. "Your sons" means "members of your own group" (just as, e.g., "sons of the prophets" in the *Old Testament meant "prophets"). Because some of the Pharisees' associates also cast out demons (by methods that would look more magical than Jesus'), they should consider their charge carefully. On being the judges of others, see comment on 12:41-42.

12:28. It was generally believed that the *Spirit had been quenched or muted in some way after the Old Testament prophets had died, but that this withdrawal of the Spirit would be reversed in the time of the *kingdom, when the *Messiah came. In the context of 12:18, Matthew wishes his readers to hear this text as Jesus' claim to be the Messiah (12:23).

12:29. Many early Jewish sources report that *Satan or demons were "bound," or imprisoned, after God subdued them; magical texts often speak of "binding" demons by magical procedures. Here, however, the *parable about tying up a protective householder means that Jesus had defeated Satan and could therefore plunder his possessions—free the demon-possessed.

12:30. Ancient Jewish teachers stated their points as starkly as possible; this statement and the one in Mark 9:40 both mean "A person is either on one side or the other." Other contrast sayings similar to this one circulated in antiquity.

12:31-32. Jewish teachers commonly taught that one's sufferings in this life could make up for sins; but certain grave sins would be carried over into the world to come. (Some teachers declared similarly that King Manasseh's *repentance allowed him to be forgiven in this world but not in the world to come.) "Highhanded" sins—deliberate rebellion against God—could not be atoned for under *Old Testament law. Blasphemy was punishable by death (Lev 24:10-23).

Jesus thus regards blasphemy against the *Spirit—permanently rejecting his identity (Mt 12:18) as attested by the Spirit's works (12:28)—as the worst of sins. (On the meaning of blasphemy in general, see comment on 9:3-8.)

12:33. For a figurative use of "fruits" in the Old Testament, see comment on 3:8; the fruits here are their words (12:34-37).

12:34-35. Their words (12:36-37) against him revealed their heart; on "offspring of vipers," see comment on 3:7 (cf. also Is 57:3-4; 59:5-8). Other Jewish teachers also often stressed the importance of a right heart (though believing something and being something are not always the same thing, as the lives of many who claim to be Christians today testify). People were characterized by their actions as fools, wise,

sinners, etc., in Jewish wisdom tradition.
12:36-37. Many proverbs emphasize the importance of sound speech and that silence is better than unhealthy speech (e.g., Prov 10:11; 15:4; 17:27-28). But if Judaism associated any words with morality and eternal destiny more than others, they were the basic confession of God's oneness in the Shema' ("Hear, O Israel, the Lord thy God the Lord is one," Deut 6:4; cf. Mk 12:29); of all the unsound speech that could have revealed their hearts, Jesus' opponents revealed their hearts especially by rejecting testimony that was just as critical as the Shema' (12:32).

12:38-45
A Demonized Generation

Here Jesus returns the charge: they, not he, are servants of *Satan.
12:38-41. Jewish discussions of the end times featured converts among the poor who would testify against those who said they were too poor to follow God; converts among the rich, converts among the *Gentiles and so on. Here Jesus appeals to pagans who converted. Some Jewish teachers disliked Jonah for his initial disobedience to God "on behalf of Israel"—they said that he feared that Nineveh's *repentance would leave unrepentant Israel condemned. In the *Old Testament, Nineveh, responsible for permanently destroying the northern kingdom of Israel, epitomized wickedness (e.g., Nahum 2:8; 3:1, 7); but the repentance of Nineveh in Jonah 3:10 also taught that God could spare pagans who turned to him (Jon 1:15-16; 4:10-11) as well as judge his disobedient servants (1:14-15). (Some *rabbis thought that Jonah resented Gentile repentance because it showed up Israel's lack of it.)

"Three days and nights" (Jon 2:1) need not imply complete days; parts of a twenty-four-hour day counted as representing the whole day. In early Jewish law, only after three days was the witness to a person's death accepted.
12:42. Some traditions identified the "Queen of the South," the queen of Sheba (1 Kings 10:1), with the queen of Ethiopia (cf. Acts 8:27).
12:43-45. Jesus' point: Although he is casting out demons, this wicked generation is inviting all the more back in. The desert was a natural haunt of demons in much of Jewish tradition, and "sevenfold" was a traditional way to express severe punishment (Gen 4:15, 24; Lev 26:18), so the hearers would have readily caught Jesus' point.

12:46-50
Jesus' Real Family

See comment on Mark 3:31-34. Fidelity to and respect for one's family were so heavily emphasized that such words must have struck their hearers quite forcefully. Many Jewish interpreters regarded the command to honor father and mother as the most important in the *law.

Family relationships in the ancient world were often defined by hierarchy even more than by kinship ties, so that wives and especially children (and, in wealthy homes, slaves) were expected to obey the father of the household. Jesus can thus define his "mother, brothers and sisters" as those who obey his Father. To disavow literal family members was so repulsive that even using the image would have been culturally offensive. Further, spiritual or figurative kinship language in Judaism (especially "brothers") was viewed ethnically (fellow Israelites).

13:1-9
The Sower, the Seed and the Soils

*Rabbis commonly taught in *parables,

sermon illustrations to communicate their main point or points. This Palestinian Jewish teaching form appears in the *New Testament only in the teaching of Jesus, and thus cannot be attributed to composition by the later *church outside Jewish Palestine.

Most of the Roman Empire's inhabitants were rural peasant farmers or herders. The literate elite often ignored this large population, but Jesus' illustrations show that he ministered frequently among this class. Although Galilee was heavily populated with villages and boasted two major cities (Sepphoris and Tiberias), most of its inhabitants were rural, agrarian peasants.

13:1-2. Jesus gets in the boat for the purpose of relieving the overcrowding, but this would also make him easier to hear; a speaker to a crowd on shore would produce an ideal acoustic situation.

13:3-4. Seed was often (though not always) sown before the ground was plowed; it thus commonly befell any of the fates reported here. A farmer could either cast the seed by hand, as probably here, or let it trickle from holes in a sack carried by an animal. The "path" or "road" is one of the many footpaths through the field.

13:5-6. Much of the land in Palestine has only a thin layer of soil over rock; if the sower had not plowed first, he would not be aware that he wasted seed on this soil until after the fact.

13:7. These thistles were probably unseen, too; instead of having been pulled out, they may have just been cut or burned, leaving roots from which thistles could grow with the seed to choke it out.

13:8. Thirtyfold, sixtyfold and a hundredfold are tremendously good harvests from Galilean soil. The Jordan Valley normally yielded between ten- and a hundredfold, so a hundredfold need not be a miraculous harvest (Gen 26:12; cf. Amos 9:13). But for much of Palestine, the average yield was tenfold (meaning that 10 seeds were harvested for every seed sown), and all the figures Jesus reports here are very good yields.

13:9. *Disciples learned especially by carefully listening to their teachers.

13:10-23
The Sower Explained: Understanding the Word

That some members of the community of *disciples would not persevere fits *Old Testament models; in the Old Testament, some persons, like Saul, turned away from obedience to God, whereas others, like David, persevered through many trials.

13:10. Disciples asked their teacher questions till they understood what he meant.

13:11-13. *Parables were meant to explain a *rabbi's point by illustrating it; however, if the point were not stated, the parable would amount to no more than a story. Rabbis had some more secretive teachings that they thought only their closest disciples could handle, and they reserved these for private instruction. The meaning of Jesus' parables, then, would be understood only by those who chose to become insiders.

13:14-15. The people in Jesus' day were like the people in Isaiah's day who heard the word but could not really hear and repent (Is 6:9-10).

13:16-17. Some Jewish texts describe how the righteous in the *Old Testament longed to see the era of messianic redemption and a fuller revelation of God. Making a statement about someone (here, Jesus) by blessing someone else (here, those who saw him in contrast to the blind of 13:15) was an accepted *rhetorical technique of the day.

13:18-23. Outsiders chose what they would do with the word when it came to them. *Rabbis sometimes said that one would be consumed with either the *law or with the cares of this world (v. 22).

13:24-30
The Story of Wheat and Tares

Wealthy landowners controlled most of the rural land throughout the Roman Empire; their estates were worked either by free peasants or by slaves, whose options in life were roughly the same (except that slaves could also be beaten or sold). Many of Jesus' hearers (13:34) may have been rural farmers on larger estates, who would have readily identified with the difficulty of the situation he described.

13:24. "The kingdom is like a man who . . ." does not mean that the *kingdom is compared only to the man. *Rabbinic *parables often began with, "To what may such and such be compared?" or, "Such and such is like . . ." In these parables the phrase meant that the subject was being explained by the whole analogy that followed, not just by the next word.

13:25-27. The most basic staple of the Palestinian diet (and the ancient diet in general) was bread; thus wheat was critical. But a poisonous weed, a kind of ryegrass known as darnel (usually translated "tares") looked like wheat in the early stages and could only be distinguished from it when the ear appeared.

13:28-29. The fields were normally weeded in the spring, but if the weeds were discovered too late—as here—one would risk uprooting the wheat with them; the master does not want to risk his wheat. Once they were fully grown, however, harvesters could cut the wheat just below the head, leaving the shorter tares to be cut separately.

13:30. Although first-century Palestine was undoubtedly more forested than it became in subsequent times, much of the earlier forest had been cut down, and fuel could not be wasted; once dried, the darnel at least proved useful for something—fuel for burning.

13:31-33
The Stories of Mustard Seed and Leaven

The point of both *parables is that the mighty *kingdom everyone expected could issue from apparently obscure beginnings—like Jesus and the *disciples.

13:31-32. Scholars still dispute what plant is meant by the "mustard seed." Nevertheless, by no conjecture is it the smallest of all seeds that Jesus' listeners could have known (the orchid seed is smaller); the point is that it was recognized as very small and yet yielded a large shrub. Around the Sea of Galilee, it can reach a height of ten feet and has sometimes reached fifteen feet. Its usual height, however, is about four feet; because it would grow anew each year, birds could not nest in it when they built nests in early spring. The *hyperbole Jesus applies to the best image of growth from tiny to large he had available does not change the point, however; the *kingdom might begin in obscurity, but it would culminate in glory.

Even if birds could not nest in the mustard plant, they could perch in it (Matthew's term here was sometimes used that way); Matthew's language here alludes to Daniel 4:12, the splendor of another ruler's kingdom. Sources suggest that Palestinian custom relegated mustard seeds to fields rather than gardens; one may thus contrast Matthew 13:31 with Luke 13:19, each adjusting the image for their respective readerships.

13.33. Roman cities had bakeries, but the image here is that of a rural Galilean woman. Leaven, or yeast, would be mixed through the meal. Three pecks of flour, roughly a bushel, was all that a woman could knead, and the resulting bread would feed about a hundred people.

13:34-35
Secret Teachings

See comment on 13:10-13. Matthew cites Psalm 78:2, where the psalmist describes his knowledge in traditional terms of Hebrew wisdom, then goes on to give its content in the rest of the psalm: the history of God's faithful, saving acts and of his people's rebellion.

13:36-43
The Final Separation of Wheat and Tares

Various groups, like the *Essenes, withdrew from the rest of Judaism to pursue a higher level of purity. But, as all Jewish groups agreed, God alone knew the hearts of all people. Only at the end, at the day of judgment, would the righteous and the wicked be effectively separated. The harvest is used elsewhere (e.g., 4 Ezra 4:30-32; *2 Baruch 70:2; cf. Is 32:13-15; Jer 31:27-28; Hos 2:21-23; 6:11) as a symbol for the end, and Jewish texts sometimes compare hell with a furnace (*1 Enoch 54:6; some manuscripts in 98:3; 4 Ezra 7:36). Other Jewish texts also spoke of the righteous shining with glory in the future kingdom.

13:44-46
The Kingdom's Value

13:44. Treasures were often buried for safekeeping. The most likely circumstance envisioned here is that of a peasant who, while working the field of a wealthy landowner, found the treasure but covered it again lest the landowner claim it for himself. The peasant then invested all his own resources into that field to procure the treasure. Stories of finding lost treasures naturally circulated among the poor; Jesus uses the story line to stir his hearers to seek for a treasure far greater than any on earth.

13:45-46. Divers sought pearls in the Red Sea, Persian Gulf and Indian Ocean, and some pearls could be worth the equivalent of millions of dollars. Jesus' hearers were probably familiar with the basic story line; there seems to have been a folktale that ran similarly, although it did not make the same point about the *kingdom.

13:47-50
The Final Separation of Good and Bad Fish

For further discussion see 4:19; on separation, 13:36-43; for the furnace, see comment on 13:40. Different kinds of nets were used for fishing; dragnets (the kind used here) were much larger than the fishing nets employed in 4:18. It is thought that floats and sinkers were attached to keep one part of the wide end of the net at the surface while the other part dragged below.

13:51-52
Scribes for the Kingdom

The law and wisdom were often compared with treasure (and sometimes with a pearl); *scribes, who were specially conversant with the law, naturally had the "old" treasure, and the message of the *kingdom gave them something new. The image is that of a householder paying out old and new coins kept in a strongbox hidden in his home. Some scholars have suggested that Matthew's Gospel addresses especially Christian scribes whose vocation is to disciple the *Gentiles to the greatest teacher, Jesus (28:19).

13:53-58 Dishonor at Home

See comment on Mark 6:1-6 for more details. The tradition of prophets being rejected by their own town was old (Jer 1:1; 11:21-23), but the theme of prophets being persecuted had developed even further in subsequent Jewish lore.

When Jesus was growing up in Nazareth, the demand for carpenters there was great (to rebuild nearby Sepphoris, which had been burned and its surviving inhabitants enslaved); thus it is not surprising that this was Joseph's occupation. Carpenters engaged in woodwork, such as wooden plows, chairs and the woodwork on roofs. They also engaged in masonry where buildings were made of stone. Nazareth itself was a small village in this period, with perhaps 1,600-2,000 inhabitants; Jesus would thus have been known to most of his townspeople.

14:1-12 Herod Executes John

See Mark 6:14-29 for considerably more detail. This passage refers not to Herod the Great, who died within several years of Jesus' birth, but to Herod Antipas, Herod the Great's son by a *Samaritan mother, and full brother of Archelaus (2:22). He had ruled in Galilee and Perea (the latter was a narrow strip of land on the east of the Jordan) since about 4 B.C., and continued in power till A.D. 39.

14:1. Matthew uses Herod Antipas's actual title, "tetrarch," rather than the sarcastic or loose one Mark gives him ("king"). "Tetrarch" originally meant ruler of one-quarter of some territory, but Romans applied it to rulers of any portion; Herod the Great's kingdom had been divided in 4 B.C. among Archelaus (later supplanted by Roman procurators), Antipas and Philip.

14:2-4. The first-century historian *Josephus also reports Herod Antipas's affair with his sister-in-law Herodias. The tetrarch and his paramour divorced their spouses to marry one another, and Herod thereby offended his former father-in-law, the Nabatean king, ultimately leading to a war in which Herod's honor suffered greatly. John thus surely expected that Herod would resent his preaching, but he preached anyway; Herod could well have taken John's moral preaching as a political criticism.

14:5-6. Jewish people did not normally celebrate birthdays in this period (Josephus declares celebrating birthdays forbidden). But though most Jews considered birthday celebrations a *Gentile custom, the aristocracy evinced considerable Greek influence. At Herod's fortress Machaerus, men and women dined in separate halls, so Herodias would not have directly witnessed Herod's behavior toward her daughter Salome.

14:7. Herod's oath is a drunken one; as a vassal of Rome, he had no authority to compromise any of his territory.

14:8-9. It was an affront to one's honor to break an oath in front of guests, even if (as in this case) Jewish teachers would have absolved the oath.

14:10-11. Jewish law required a trial before execution; here Herod, given power by the Romans, ignores this law. Beheading was the fastest and least painful method of execution and was carried out with a sword. But it was a Greek and Roman custom, contrary to Jewish custom.

14:12. One's son would normally be in charge of the burial; either John had no adult sons (which is probable) or his *disciples were the only ones ready to fulfill this role. Although the whole ancient world (except for some eccentric philosophers) considered lack of proper burial the worst possible fate, Jewish law forbade public mourning for those executed according to Jewish law, and Herod may have resented whoever showed up to claim the body.

14:13-21
Feeding the Five Thousand

See comment on Mark 6:32-44 for more details. The most significant ancient reports of feeding miracles are the reports of Israel's eating manna in the wilderness of Sinai and miracles performed at the hands of prophets (e.g., Elisha in 2 Kings 4:42-44).

14:13-15. Bread and fish were basic staples of the Palestinian diet; meat was more expensive and rarely eaten except at feasts. Teachers were not normally responsible for feeding their *disciples from their own means.

14:16. Ancient students often paid their teachers (though other teachers were self-supporting); it was honorable to invite teachers to dinner and to show them the utmost hospitality. But here Jesus, the teacher, assumes the role of host or provider. (Although *disciples often viewed teachers as father figures, teachers rarely had the resources to provide for disciples out of their own means.) The ancient emphasis on hospitality included providing food as well as shelter for guests.

14:17-18. Compare especially 2 Kings 4:42-43 for the incredulity of prophet-disciples when Elisha tells them to distribute the food to the people.

14:19. It was customary for the head of the household to "bless," or give thanks for, food before a meal.

14:20. One source reports that traveling Jews carried baskets with them; thus the twelve baskets may be the *disciples' own.

14:21. A crowd of five thousand men plus women and children was larger than most of the villages that covered the Galilean countryside.

14:22-33
Walking on the Water

See also Mark 6:45-52. Moses, Joshua, Elijah and Elisha had all done water miracles, parting the sea or the river Jordan; but the only one the *Old Testament said "trod" upon the waters was God himself.

14:22. Because a teacher controlled the duration of the learning situation, it would be understood that Jesus could send the crowds home.

14:23. The pious normally set aside two specific hours a day for prayer; Jesus here spends the whole remainder of the day in prayer (though how long this time was is uncertain, given Matthew's ambiguous use of "evening" here—vv. 15, 23). Mountains were places of prayer for Moses and Elijah; here, away from the crowdedness of Galilean town life, Jesus could find solitude.

14:24. Harsh storms often arise suddenly on the Sea of Galilee.

14:25. The fourth, or final, shift of the night watch was between 3 and 6 a.m.; the watches started at 6 p.m. Jewish people often divided the night into three watches, but the Romans had four.

14:26. Belief in ghosts or disembodied spirits was common on a popular level in antiquity, even though the idea of ghosts contradicted popular Jewish teachings about the *resurrection from the dead.

14:27. Jesus' answer is literally "I am"; although this can easily mean "It is I," it may also allude back to God's self-revelation in Exodus 3:14 and Isaiah 43:10, 13: "I AM."

14:28-32. Despite Peter's failure to follow through, by beginning to walk on water he had done something that not even the greatest prophets of the *Old Testament had done. Walking on water might remind readers of Israel passing through the Red Sea or the Jordan but was a greater miracle. (In one story told by the *rabbis—we cannot determine whether it is as early as Jesus' time—the first Israelite to cross the Red Sea began to sink in the waves but was rescued by Moses' rod, which divided the sea.) For Jesus' rescue, cf. Psalm 18:16 and 144:7.

14:33. The term *worship* was applied to homage offered to pagan kings as well as that offered to deities. Although it could indicate prostration as a sign of respect (e.g., 1 Sam 24:8; 25:23), it is an unusual term to express Jewish *disciples' amazement at a human teacher, even in miracle stories. Ancient miracle stories (including many in the Gospels) often concluded with the observers' awe and praise.

14:34-36 Healings at Gennesaret

The "fringe" of Jesus' garment no doubt refers to the tassels he wore as an observant Jew; see comment on 9:20; cf. 23:5. Ancient literature commonly includes not only longer *narrative segments but also summary statements like this passage (cf. 4:23-25). Gennesaret was a plain on the northwest shore of the Sea of Galilee.

15:1-20 Human Tradition Versus God's Word

See Mark 7:1-23 for more detail.

15:1-2. Contemporary Jewish sources always characterize the *Pharisees as observing the traditions of the elders; in this way they felt they could depend upon a repository of the wisdom of the pious who preceded them. Washing hands before meals was one of the most prominent of those traditions but had no direct basis in Scripture.

15:3. Jesus responds to the Pharisees' question with a counterquestion, as *rabbis often did.

15:4-6. Judaism universally demanded honor of father and mother and included financial support of aged parents as part of this honor. Some, like *Josephus and many *rabbis, regarded this demand as the most important commandment in the Law. The *Pharisees therefore could not have disagreed with Jesus' example; they did not recommend that people fail to support their parents, but their allowance of special vows dedicating things only to "sacred" use created this loophole for those who could have wished to use it (cf. Prov 28:24). Some legal loopholes (such as the *prozbul,* an early rule circumventing the law's cancellation of debts in the seventh year) were intended to uphold the spirit of the law; this one unwittingly undercut even that.

15:7-9. In his day Isaiah attacked those who valued tradition rather than God's message through the Law and the Prophets; the same message was still applicable for Jesus' day.

15:10-11. In a later story Johanan ben Zakkai, a Jewish teacher from the generation after Jesus, admitted privately to his *disciples that outward impurity did not really defile; one should simply keep God's commandments about purity. But this sort of teaching, even if it had been widespread, was not emphasized publicly, lest people fail to keep the ceremonial laws (as happened among some well-to-do Jews in Egypt).

15:12. Although the *Pharisees (from whose teachers most of the later *rabbis seem to have come) had virtually no political power, they were respected and highly influential among the people. Offending them thus did not appear to be prudent.

15:13-14. The images of uprooting (Jer 42:10; 45:4; cf. 1:10; 11:16-19; 12:2; 24:6; 31:28), blindness (15:14; cf., e.g., Deut 29:4; Is 6:10; 42:19) and leaders guiding others astray with falsehood (Is 3:12-15; 9:16) are standard *Old Testament judgment language; the *Dead Sea Scrolls similarly describe the *Qumran community as a shoot planted by God. The image here is that of a farmer preparing his field and ridding it of unwanted weeds (cf. 13:30). The point of Jesus' response to his *disciples is: Do not worry about the *Pharisees' power, because their day of judgment is coming (Mt 3:10).

15:15-20. Such views were rare, and even more rarely divulged publicly; see comment on 15:10-11. Liberal Alexandrian Jews who no longer believed in literal observance of the food laws (Lev 11; Deut 14) were particularly despised by their more conservative colleagues. But everyone would at least have had to agree with Jesus that the heart matters most (see Is 29:13, cited in Mt 15:8-9; cf. also Is 59:13).

15:21-28
Mercy on the Canaanites

15:21. Tyre and Sidon were traditionally pagan territory; Sidon had been the home of Jezebel (1 Kings 16:31). But in the same generation a woman from that region had miraculously received food and healing for her child from the prophet Elijah and so became a full believer in Israel's God (1 Kings 17:8-24). In Jesus' period, one had to pass through territory belonging to Syrophoenicia, as here, to get from Galilee to Caesarea Philippi. Many Jewish people still lived here, however.

15:22. Canaanites, many of whose survivors had been driven northward into Phoenicia during the Israelite conquest, were the most morally despised of Israel's enemies in the *Old Testament; Matthew's characterizing this woman with this term would set Jewish readers on edge if they still had any racist tendencies. But by acknowledging Jesus as "Son of David"—*Messiah—she also acknowledges the right of the kingdom of David (who had also embraced many non-Jews as allies) over the land. How could a Jewish person remain prejudiced against a Canaanite woman such as this one?

15:23-24. Jesus' statement in verse 24 does not preclude a later mission to *Gentiles. The servant of Isaiah 53:6-8 suffers on behalf of the lost sheep of Israel (cf. 40:11; 56:11), but the servant's mission was ultimately to reconcile all nations to God (42:6; 49:6-7).

15:25-28. Certain people in the Old Testament, most notably the Sidonian woman to whom Elijah came (1 Kings 17:18-19) and the Shunammite woman with Elisha (2 Kings 4:28), laid their need before a prophet and would not take no for an answer; God answered their prayers with a yes. (Some Jewish teachers closer to Jesus' time were reported to exercise the same kind of holy chutzpah in praying for rain, etc.) Even those who were most intimate with God approached him with only the greatest respect when praying an insistent prayer (Gen 18:22-32); but they also refused to be deterred.

15:29-31
Lame, Crippled, Blind and Mute Healed

Here Jesus cures many traditional categories of serious ailments. Even in a culture where people did not deny the existence of miracles, these cures were extraordinary. Matthew's summary of such miracles may recall prophecies of

Isaiah (35:5-6; cf. 29:18-19, 23).

15:32-39
The Second Feeding

Jesus' first feeding miracle (see comment on Mt 14:13-21) was not an exception; he was able to repeat it at any time. Magadan (v. 39) was Mary Magdalene's hometown; it has been identified with Tarichea, where many fishermen seem to have worked.

16:1-4
No Sign but Jonah's

16:1. The *Pharisees and *Sadducees differed on most matters. The Pharisees had great popular support, whereas the Sadducees held political power. Together they could make a dangerous team. Probably writing after 70, Matthew often links the various leaders together, though in his day the Pharisees were gaining sole ascendancy in Palestinian religious politics. On such testing, cf. 4:3.

16:2-3. They ask for a sign from heaven in verse 1 (cf. 2 Kings 20:8-9; Is 38:7; 2 Chron 32:24); astrologers used signs in the heavens to predict the fall of emperors, and *rabbis also tried to interpret such signs. Jewish writers like *Josephus believed there were portents in the heavens when disasters were about to occur (cf. also Mt 24:29-30). Some prophets, like Elijah, actually had produced signs from heaven—he called down fire from heaven (1 Kings 18:38)—but most prophetic signs were not so spectacular (Judg 6:17; Is 7:11-14; 8:18; 19:20; 20:3; 37:30; 38:7; 66:19; Ezek 4:3; 12:11; 24:24, 27). Perhaps Jesus' opponents desire a sign to validate that he is a prophet—some rabbis believed that prophets could temporarily even set aside some commandments of the *law, provided they were attested by signs—or perhaps they merely want him to make a prediction. ("Heaven" was a Jewish title for God, so they could simply mean a sign "from God.")

16:4. Like their ancestors who did not heed God's acts already done among them, this generation is evil (Deut 32:5, 20 in context). Signs had already been given them (Mt 16:3), even clearer than God's usual signs from the heavens (16:2), but the final attestation would be the *resurrection (12:40).

16:5-12
Evil Yeast

16:5-6. Jewish tradition sometimes used yeast to symbolize evil. Some Jewish teachers made such comparisons (e.g., describing false teaching as poisoned water); the *disciples should thus have recognized that their *rabbi could speak figuratively. On the *Pharisees and *Sadducees, see comment on 16:1 and glossary.

16:7-11. Like Israel in the wilderness, Jesus' contemporaries quickly forgot God's past provision, and he often called them to remember (e.g., Deut 8).

16:12. The *Sadducees denied the *resurrection (Mt 22:23) and the *Pharisees held to human traditions (15:2-3); throughout Matthew, both oppose Jesus.

16:13-20
The Christ and the Rock

16:13. Caesarea Philippi (a city distinct from the usual *New Testament Caesarea, which was on the coast) was pagan territory, near a grotto devoted to the worship of the Greek deity Pan; Herod had also dedicated a temple for the worship of Caesar there. Thus it was hardly the most expected site for a divine revelation. The city was some twenty-five miles from the Lake of Galilee and about seventeen hundred feet higher, hence the need to stop along the way (15:21); it lay near the source of the Jordan, at the Old Testament Dan, the northern boundary of ancient Israel.

16:14. All these answers about who Jesus is fall into the "prophets" category; though most Jewish teachers held that prophets had ceased, popular expectation of end-time prophets remained strong. Elijah was expected to return (Mal 4:5), and many of Jesus' miracles resembled Elijah's. His judgment oracles (Mt 11:20-24) or downplaying the temple (cf. 12:6; 24:1-2) may have evoked the comparison with Jeremiah.

16:15-16. Peter has the right title, though the wrong concept of what *Messiah means (16:22). David's royal line was adopted by God (2 Sam 7:14), so it was natural for the ultimate successor to his throne to be called God's Son (Ps 2:7; 89:27), as a few Jewish interpreters in this period noticed (e.g., in the *Florilegium* from *Qumran Cave 4, an *Essene commentary on 2 Sam 7).

16:17. "Blessed are you" is a standard form of blessing (cf. comment on Mt 5:1-12). "Barjonah" is *Aramaic for "son of Jonah." "Flesh and blood" was a typical Jewish phrase for "human being(s)." Although all Jews emphasized learning by studying the Scriptures, some also recognized divine illumination (e.g., in the *Dead Sea Scrolls) or revelation (*apocalyptic literature; some *rabbinic mysticism).

16:18. In *Aramaic, "Peter" and "rock" are the same word; in Greek (here), they are cognate terms that were used interchangeably by this period. For the idea of a person as the foundation on which something is built, cf. Isaiah 51:1-2; Ephesians 2:20. (This promise is made to Peter because Peter was the one who confessed Jesus—v. 16; the point is that Peter is the rock in his role as confessor, and others build on the foundation by their proclamation of the same confession.)

The *Old Testament often spoke of those who "built" God's people (e.g., Ruth 4:11; Jer 1:10) and prayed for God to build Israel up (Ps 51:18; 69:35; 147:2; Jer 24:6; 31:4, 28). The "gates of Hades" in the Old Testament (Job 38:17; Ps 9:13) and subsequent Jewish tradition referred to the realm and power of death; death itself would not silence the *church. Against those who presuppose that Jesus could not have planned the church, though he chose twelve disciples as the nucleus of a remnant for Israel (compare the symbolic use of twelve in the *Dead Sea Scrolls), the language of a "church" was already being used for a remnant community among his contemporaries (Dead Sea Scrolls; see "church" in glossary for further information).

16:19. The keeper of the keys was one of the most important roles a household servant could hold (cf. Mk 13:32-34); a high official held the keys in a royal kingdom (Is 22:20-22) and in God's house, the temple. Keys here refer to the authority to admit into the *kingdom (Mt 23:13), based on the knowledge of the truth about Jesus (16:16). The *Qumran community also had officials deciding whether to admit members; the decision was made based on the prospective member's acceptance of the community's rule of life.

Many Jews felt that the Jewish high court acted on the authority of God's tribunal in heaven, in a sense ratifying its decrees. "Binding" and "loosing" (also 18:18) were terms regularly used for *rabbis' legislative authority in interpreting Scripture ("prohibiting" and "permitting"), and thus could apply to judicial situations as well.

16:20. For comment on the messianic secret, see the introduction to Mark's Gospel.

16:21-28
Redefining Messiahship

Peter had divulged Jesus' secret identity (16:16) yet retained a faulty concept of what that identity entailed.

16:21. Even most of the *Old Testament prophets sought to avoid martyrdom insofar as possible and complained about their sufferings (1 Kings 19:3-4; Jer 20:7-18). Although martyrdom was associated with the prophets, it was not their *goal;* but it seems to be Jesus' goal here (cf. especially 20:28).

16:22. Jewish tradition in this period emphasized a triumphant *Messiah; apparently only a century after Jesus' teaching did Jewish teachers begin to accept the tradition of a suffering Messiah in addition to a triumphant one. One of the first rules of ancient discipleship (with noticeably rare exceptions) was: Never criticize the teacher, especially publicly. Here Peter breaks that rule, even on standard cultural grounds.

16:23. The term *stumbling block,* referring to something over which people tripped, had come to be used figuratively for things that led people to sin or stumble in their faith. Jesus identifies Peter with *Satan because he speaks the same temptation: the *kingdom without the cross (4:9-10). *Rabbis sometimes punned on the names of *disciples; here the "rock" (16:18) becomes a "stumbling stone."

16:24. For 16:24-28, see comment on Mark 8:34—9:1. Carrying the horizontal crossbeam en route to crucifixion (where the upright stake already stood awaiting the condemned person) meant enduring mockery and scorn on a path leading to death as a condemned criminal. Crucifixion was the worst form of criminal death, the supreme Roman penalty, inflicted only on the lower classes and slaves; even talk of it could evoke horror.

16:25-26. One's life is worth more than any treasures, which would be worthless if one were not alive to enjoy them (cf. Ps 49:7-8; Ex 30:12).

16:27-28. Jesus alludes to Daniel 7:13-14 and thus applies *Old Testament language for God as judge to himself (Ps 62:12; Prov 24:12; Jer 17:10; 32:19; Ezek 18:30). The reference to angels is probably from Zechariah 14:5, though it also fits the context of the image in Daniel 7:13-14. "Taste death" was idiomatic for "die." Verse 28 is a transition to the proleptic revelation of the *kingdom to follow in 17:1-8 ("proleptic" means that this revelation anticipates the kingdom).

17:1-13
The Glory Shines Again

This passage includes so many allusions to God revealing his glory to Moses on Mount Sinai that most ancient Jewish readers would certainly have caught them. For more details on the passage, see comments on Mark 9:2-10.

17:1. The six days alludes to Exodus 24:16, when God began to speak to Moses from his cloud on the mountain.

17:2. Some Jewish texts described glorious angels or the resurrected righteous in terms like those describing Jesus here, but the strongest allusion to a human appearance being transformed by glory is in Exodus 34:29, where Moses' face radiated glory because of God's revelation of himself to Moses.

17:3. Jewish people expected the return of both Elijah and Moses at the end of the age. Both of them (Ex 24:15-16; 1 Kings 19:8) heard from God at Mount Sinai (also called Horeb).

17:4. Israel had dwelt in tabernacles in the wilderness while the presence and glory of God was among them.

17:5. The cloud of glory overshadowed the mountain in Exodus 24:15 and the tabernacle in 40:34 (the same Greek word is used in the *LXX of Ex 40:35 that Matthew uses here).

To the biblical allusions in Matthew 3:17, the voice in this passage adds Deuteronomy 18:15: When the prophet like Moses comes, "give heed to him."

17:6-8. The *disciples' fear was characteristic of people in the *Old Testament and later Jewish tradition when they experienced revelations of God.

17:9-13. Jewish people believed that Elijah would return before the time of the end to make matters right (Mal 4:5-6); the *resurrection of all the righteous dead was to follow his coming, at the end.

17:14-23
Inadequate Faith for Exorcism

17:14-21. See comments on Mark 9:14-29 for more detail. Like Moses, Jesus must deal with the failure of those he left in charge once he comes down from the mountain (Ex 24:14; 32:1-8, 21-25, 35). "Removing mountains" was a Jewish figure of speech for that which was incomparably difficult (mountains were thought to be the most stable of all things; cf. Ps 46:2; Is 54:10); mustard seeds were used to define a proverbially small quantity. Jesus is thus telling the *disciples that nothing God asks them to do will be impossible if they trust him. (Cf. Zech 4:7.)

17:22-23. Jesus predicts what would have been obvious to the disciples had they known that he planned to drive the moneychangers from the temple courts: he would die (cf. Mt 18:31; 19:22; 26:22). Because the disciples understand his *resurrection to mean the general resurrection at the end of the age (17:9-10), they miss his point.

17:24-27
The Children Are Exempt

17:24. Free adult Jewish men all over the ancient world showed their solidarity with the temple and the Holy Land by paying a half-shekel tax (Ex 30:13-16); in *New Testament times this was two drachmas (as here), or two days' wages. After 70, in Matthew's time, the Romans confiscated this tax for the upkeep of a pagan temple, and some Jews may have refused to pay it on principle; but in Jesus' day, any Jew loyal to Judaism would have paid it. The local collectors of the tax may have wondered about Jesus' position on the matter if he had already betrayed some opposition to the temple (as later in 21:12-14; 23:38—24:15); collectors did not force those living off charity (as they would assume Jesus to be—Lk 8:3) or beggars to pay. Or they may have simply been wondering if he would pay it in this locality or elsewhere, because the *disciples were moving about.

17:25-26. Like a good prophet, Jesus responds to Peter before Peter even brings up the matter (1 Sam 9:20; 1 Kings 14:6; 2 Kings 5:26; 6:32).

The answer to Jesus' question was obvious; the royal family did not tax itself. Jesus' point is thus that the Son of God should not be taxed for the upkeep of his Father's house. (The principle of an exemption was known in Judaism: the temple's attendants, the priests, applied it to themselves, to the chagrin of some of their *Pharisaic contemporaries—*Mishnah *Sheqalim* 1:3-4.) For Matthew's readers this saying would mean: It is not because Jesus is not in solidarity with Judaism (for he is), but rather because he is the *hope* of Judaism, that he need not pay.

17:27. On the basis of solidarity with the rest of the Jewish community, however, Jesus pays the tax. If some of

Matthew's Jewish Christian readers were looking for an excuse to avoid paying the tax in their own day, this text would encourage them to pay it instead.

A stater was worth four drachmas (4 denarii); hence it covered the tax for both Jesus and Peter. Jewish teachers had several stories describing how God rewarded faithful Jews who bought fish and found gems in them; if these stories are as early as the first century (their date is not certain), Peter might be surprised that something similar had actually happened to him. Some fish in the Lake of Galilee had mouths large enough to hold staters; one such fish was what is now called the *Chromis simonis* (named after Simon Peter).

18:1-6
Offending the Children

See comment on Mark 9:33-37 for more information.

18:1. Some Jewish texts speak of different rewards and ranks in the *kingdom. Rank and status were issues that members of ancient society confronted daily.

18:2-4. The most powerless members of ancient society were little children; in most of ancient society, age increased one's social status and authority. In Jewish culture, children were loved, not despised; but the point is that they had no status apart from that love, and no power or privileges apart from what they received as total dependents on their parents. "Converted" may allude to the Jewish idea of turning, returning or *repenting.

18:5. On "in my name" see 10:40.

18:6. "Stumble" was often used metaphorically to refer to sinning or falling away from the true faith. Millstones were used to grind meal. They were extremely heavy, and the term here refers to the heavier kind of millstone turned by a donkey, rather than the lighter kind a woman would use. Jewish people regarded this punishment as the awful sort that pagans might carry out; this makes the image all the more dreadful (cf. *1 Enoch 48:9). Cf. comment on Matthew 26:24.

18:7-14
Offenders of the Powerless

This passage extends the metaphor to all the weak in the *church, certainly including children. Church leaders and members must seek not only to avoid causing stumbling but also to bring back anyone who has stumbled.

18:7-9. Judaism also balanced God's sovereign plan with human choice and responsibility. To the extent that one's poor eyes could cause one to trip, they could be viewed as a sort of stumbling block; on stumbling blocks, see comment on 18:6; on the removal of limbs, cf. comment on 5:29-30 or Mark 9:42-47.

18:10. Jewish readers would generally recognize here the concept of the guardian angel; it was typically believed that every Jewish person had one. Further, angels received their orders from God's throne; but unlike lower angels and mortals, only the highest angels regularly saw God's glory. Those who mistreated these "little ones" would hence be reported directly to God by the greatest angels, and the report would stand them in bad stead in the day of judgment.

18:12-14. One hundred was an average-sized flock in Palestine. Greek and Jewish literature affords other examples of pasturers who had to leave the flock or herd to look for a lost animal (cf. 1 Sam 9:3); a shepherd could leave his own flock with the other shepherds with whom he worked, who would be watching over their own flocks. Religious leaders who failed to care for the broken and powerless are rejected by God (Ezek 34:2-10), and God himself would then seek after the sheep (34:11-16). God's people were commonly described as sheep in the *Old Testament (cf. comment on Jn 10:1-18).

18:15-20 Disciplining Offenders

We should keep in mind that the whole context of this passage on *church discipline is mercy and forgiveness; forgiveness qualifies (but does not annul) the force of this passage on disciplining unrepentant offenders in the Christian community. The contextual emphasis is the hope of bringing back the erring, not confirming them irreparably in their guilt.

18:15. This procedure was standard Jewish custom; the *Dead Sea Scrolls, the *rabbis and others demand that one begin with private reproof. Publicly shaming someone unnecessarily was considered sinful, and Jewish teachers stressed the importance of receiving reproof.

18:16. Deuteronomy 19:15 (cf. 17:6-7) was the standard text Jewish authorities cited for requiring two witnesses. (The *rabbis took this principle so far that one eyewitness was not sufficient even if the eyewitness caught the murderer with the bloody knife in hand.) Strict judicial procedures are being followed at this point because a judicial action is about to take place; Jesus here agrees with the Jewish practice of private rebuke, witnesses and finally, if repentance is not forthcoming, the judicial assembly (18:17).

18:17. A *church by definition would function as an ancient *synagogue would, and ancient synagogues were not only assembly halls for prayer and study but community centers where discipline would be inflicted on an erring member of the community. This discipline could take a variety of forms, including public beating, but the most severe were several levels of dismissal from the community. After the most severe level of discipline the offending member would be treated as a pagan instead of as a Jew. Pagans and *tax gatherers alike—tax gatherers were seen as agents of a pagan government—were excluded from the religious life of the Jewish community. Giving a person a final warning before a court would take action (e.g., Deut 25:8) was an act of mercy.

18:18. Many Jews felt that the Jewish high court acted on the authority of God's tribunal in heaven, in a sense ratifying its decrees (the verb tenses here also indicate that the heavenly court has decided first). Those who judged cases on the basis of God's *law accurately represented his will.

"Binding" and "loosing," terms normally used for tying up or imprisoning versus freeing or releasing, provide a natural metaphor for condemning or acquitting in a court. As terms regularly used for *rabbis' legislative authority in interpreting Scripture, they could naturally apply to judicial situations as well.

18:19-20. The "two or three" must refer to the "two or three witnesses" of 18:16. These verses may refer to the prayer of execration given at a Jewish excommunication; or they could represent prayers for the *repentance and consequent forgiveness of the excommunicated person (see 1 Jn 5:16). In either case, it is of interest to note that the witnesses in the *Old Testament were to be the first to execute the judgment of the court (Deut 17:7); here they are the first to pray.

Ten Jewish males was the minimum quorum to constitute a *synagogue assembly, but it was frequently said that

God's presence was with even two or three who met together to study his law. Jesus' presence is thus presented here as identical with God's (cf. also Mt 1:23; 28:20). (One of the most common names for God among the later *rabbis was "the Place," i.e., the Omnipresent One.)

18:21-35
Forgiving the Forgivers

18:21-22. Seventy times seven (some interpreters read seventy-seven) does not really mean exactly 490 here; it is a typically graphic Jewish way of saying "Never hold grudges." Because true *repentance should involve turning from sin, some later *rabbis limited opportunities for forgiveness for a given sin to three times; Peter might have thought his offer of seven times was generous.

18:23. On "the *kingdom may be compared" see comment on 13:24. The story here is about a *Gentile king, perhaps one of the Greek rulers of Egypt before the Romans conquered it. "Servants" here could mean his upper-level slaves—who were better off than nearly all the free people of Egypt, most of whom were peasants. In this case, however, "servants" probably refers to free provincial satraps, who functioned as the ruler's tax farmers in various regions; they too were vassals of the king. The ruler would allow them to collect taxes for him at a profit, but he demanded efficiency; this was the time of year when he was going to settle their accounts with him.

18:24. Many peasant agricultural workers struggled to pay taxes, but this difficulty did not mitigate the tax collectors' responsibility to submit the requisite amount to the king. Some of the *disciples and perhaps Jesus himself could have smiled as the master storyteller told how far the king had let one of his servants get in debt: ten thousand talents probably represented more than the entire annual income of the king, and perhaps more than all the actual coinage in circulation in Egypt at the time! In one period, the silver talent represented six thousand drachmas, or six thousand days' wages for an average Palestinian worker; ten thousand talents would thus be roughly sixty million days' wages (in another period, 100 million). Although taxes were exorbitant in those days, especially for rural peasants, *Josephus reports the annual tribute from Galilee and Perea under wealthy Herod to be only two hundred talents; it was thus inconceivable that one official could get so far in debt.

Ancient Judaism often viewed sins as debts before God (see comment on 6:12).

18:25. Ptolemaic rulers (kings who ruled Egypt in the Greek period) never accepted excuses. Enslaving family members for the man's debt was a *Gentile practice that the Jewish people in this period found abhorrent. The math does not work here; the price of an average slave was between five hundred and two thousand days' wages, hence the king cannot recoup even one-thousandth of his losses on this sale. But a king with better math skills would not have let the man get so far in debt to begin with!

18:26. "I will repay" was a standard promise in ancient business documents. But in the light of 18:24, this promise is patently impossible.

18:27. Given the ruthlessness of ancient Near Eastern kings and the greatness of the debt, that this ruler would forgive his servant is almost as impossible in the real world as the size of the debt. Sometimes rulers had to forgive Egyptian peasants' past tax debts when failed crops rendered them simply unable to pay, but the sums involved were comparatively small.

18:28. One hundred denarii represented one hundred days of a common worker's wages, which would be a small sum for his fellow tax farmer, after he had finished his accounting with the king (18:23). It was also a ridiculously minuscule sum compared to what the first servant had owed the king. But apparently the forgiven slave, instead of internalizing the principle of grace, had decided to become ruthlessly efficient in his exacting of debts henceforth. Such extreme actions as choking are reported of angry creditors elsewhere in antiquity as well.

18:29-30. Someone in prison could not pay back what he owed (v. 34), unless friends came to his aid with the requisite funds.

18:31-33. The king is naturally angry; the forgiven servant has put another of his servants out of active commission, hence costing the king more lost revenues. The king had gained more advantage by convincing his people of his benevolence than he would have gained profit from the sale of the first servant; but once it was rumored that this first servant, his agent, was acting mercilessly, it reflected badly upon his own benevolence.

18:34. Jewish law did not permit torture, but Jewish people knew that *Gentile kings (as well as Herod) practiced it. Because this servant had fallen from political favor, he would have no allies who would dare come to his aid; and even if he had, given the sum he owed, his situation would have remained hopeless. He would never be released.

18:35. The great contrasts of the *parable are humorous and effective in relaxing the ancient listener's guard, but the horrifying details of debt slavery, torture and so forth bring home the point forcefully. This story would have grabbed the ancient hearer.

19:1-12
Grounds for Divorce

This passage follows the sequence of a *rabbinic debate.

19:1-3. The *Pharisees themselves debated the grounds for divorce implied in Deuteronomy 24:1-4: the school of *Shammai, predominant in Jesus' day, argued that the passage allowed divorce only if one's spouse was unfaithful; the school of *Hillel, which eventually won out, said that a man could divorce his wife if she burned the toast (a later *rabbi of this school added, "Or if you find someone more attractive"!). The success of a protagonist's wisdom under "testing" with difficult questions was an ancient theme (cf. 1 Kings 10:1).

19:4-6. It was standard interpretive practice to counter one proof text by appealing to another. Like the sectarians who wrote the *Dead Sea Scrolls, Jesus appeals to God's original purpose in creation in Genesis 2:24.

19:7. Here Jesus refers to Deuteronomy 24:1, the basic text Jewish interpreters used to discuss grounds for divorce.

19:8. Jewish teachers of the *law recognized a legal category called "concession": something that was permitted only because it was better to regulate sin than to relinquish control over it altogether. Given God's purpose in creation (Gen 2:24), divorce naturally fell into such a category (cf. Mal 2:14-16).

19:9. The school of *Shammai (see comment on 19:1-3) did not permit divorce except for the wife's unfaithfulness (whether successful or attempted), but they did not consider remarriage afterward adulterous. Jesus is more consistent: if one divorces one's spouse without valid grounds (unfaithfulness or analogous sins; cf. 1 Cor 7:10-13), the marriage is not truly dissolved and subsequent marriage is adulterous. This statement (that all subsequent unions are invalid unless the first marriage was dissolved by infidelity) may be *hyperbolic rather than literal, but hyperbole is stated the way it is to make its point forcefully, not to be ignored. Divorce must never be taken lightly.

Because men could divorce women unilaterally but women could demand a divorce only under certain very narrow conditions (and then needed the court's help), Jesus' opposition to this sort of divorce is also a defense of married women.

19:10. Jewish men took the right to divorce for granted. To marry without an escape clause in case it did not work—parents arranged the marriages and partners did not always turn out as expected—made the prospect of marriage itself frightening.

19:11-12. *Rabbis recognized different categories of eunuchs—those born without sexual organs (i.e., made eunuchs by God) and those made eunuchs by people, such as served in Eastern courts. But nothing was as offensive to Jewish sensitivities as making someone a eunuch, a practice that would exclude him from the people of God (Deut 23:1). Perhaps playing on Isaiah 56:4-5, Jesus uses this graphic language to describe a call to singleness for the *kingdom, although singleness, too, was generally outside the mainstream of Jewish social life (see comment on 1 Cor 7).

19:13-15
Blessing the Kingdom's Children

See comment on Mark 10:13-16 for more details; Matthew's form of the story is abbreviated, but abbreviating such accounts was a common practice in ancient writing.

Children were socially powerless and dependent. Some people in the *Old Testament would lay hands on others to bestow a blessing in prayer. Insensitive *disciples trying to keep from the master those seeking his help might remind Jewish hearers of Gehazi, a disciple of Elisha who eventually lost his position (2 Kings 4:27; 5:27).

19:16-22
The Price Was Too High

See Mark 10:17-22.

19:16. Greek traditions also reported aristocratic young men who wanted to study under a famous teacher but were too spoiled to carry out what the teacher demanded.

19:17. Jewish tradition emphasized the goodness of God (e.g., *Philo: "God alone is good") and even used "the Good" as a title for him (as well as for the law); by emphasizing God's unique goodness, Jesus hopes to confront the man with his own need. "Enter into life": "life" was sometimes used as an abbreviation for "*eternal life"—the life of the world to come.

19:18-19. These commandments include the humanward (vs. Godward) ones among the Ten Commandments (except the humanly untestable prohibition of coveting) and the summary of humanward commandments: Love your neighbor as yourself (Lev 19:18; cf. Mt 22:39).

19:20. With the possible exception of the less specific "Love your neighbor as yourself," most Jewish people could claim to have kept the specific commandments just mentioned. "Young man" places him between twenty-four and forty years of age.

19:21. Only a few radical Greek

teachers demanded such things of would-be *disciples. Jesus' demands are more radical than Jewish charity laws permitted (lest the benefactor reduce himself to poverty); later regulations limited charity to twenty percent (which was nonetheless considerable on top of tithes and taxes). This was a severe test, not only of whether the disciple would value the teacher above earthly possessions, but even of his claim to love his neighbor as himself.

19:22. The young man responds as most aristocrats would have responded and did respond when confronted with such demands. The *kingdom is not meant to be an extra blessing tagged onto a comfortable life; it must be all-consuming, or it is no longer the kingdom. For that reason, it appeals more readily to those with less to lose.

19:23-29
A Cost-Benefit Analysis of the Kingdom

See Mark 10:23-31.

19:23-26. Here Jesus clearly uses *hyperbole. His words reflect an ancient figure of speech for the impossible: a very large animal passing through a needle's eye. (A needle's eye in Jesus' day meant what it means today; the idea that it was simply a name for a small gate in Jerusalem is based on a gate from the medieval period and sheds no light on Jesus' teaching in the first century.)

Mainstream Judaism never denied the rich a place in the *kingdom of God; many of its benefactors and leaders were rich. Jesus allows that the rich may, by God's mercy, enter in, but only by giving their wealth to the poor.

19:27-29. "Regeneration" was a term used for the future renewal of the world in Greek circles and naturally applied to Jewish expectations of a new world order (such expectations appear in Is 65:17; 66:22; and in the *Dead Sea Scrolls). That the twelve tribes would be restored was one of the standard Jewish beliefs about the end times. Judges were those who ruled Israel in the *Old Testament before the institution of Israelite kingship.

19:30—20:16
The Last and the First

The agricultural setting of this *parable agrees with what is known from other ancient Palestinian Jewish sources. Other *rabbis also told parables like this one, although Jesus' point is different from the one preserved in similar rabbinic parables; both, however, typically portray God as a king or landowner.

19:30. Ancient literature often employed a framing device called *inclusio* to bracket off sections of material on a particular topic; 19:30 and 20:16 bracket off this parable, which follows naturally on the message of sacrificing in this age in 19:23-29. Most Jewish people believed that the day of judgment would set all things right; the *Gentiles would be cast down and Israel exalted.

20:1. On "the kingdom is like" see comment on 13:24. Wealthy landowners often hired temporary workers, especially during harvest season, when workers were needed for short periods of time. Work began around sunrise, about 6 a.m., before the day became hot.

20:2. Some day laborers were also tenant farmers, with small plots of their own land; others were sons of those owning small pieces of land and had not inherited any of their fathers' land; still others had lost their land and traveled from place to place seeking employment. A denarius was an average day's wage.

20:3. Shortly before 9 a.m. (the time

of day was necessarily reckoned from sunrise) the landowner found day laborers waiting to be hired in the marketplace. If it was harvest season and these men had any land of their own, they might have spent the morning gathering in their own ripe harvest.

20:4. These workers would expect less than a full day's wage.

20:5. The "sixth hour" is the period just before noon, and the "ninth hour" shortly before 3 p.m. The laborers would finish by 6 p.m., so those newly hired would expect to receive considerably less than a full day's wages.

20:6-7. These laborers are hired for only a single hour of work; but the harvest must be gathered in quickly, before the day ends, and the work is not yet done. These verses express the typical urgency surrounding the harvest in ancient times. Not only day laborers looking for work but also idlers were known to congregate at the marketplace.

20:8. Jewish law mandated that laborers be paid the same day, because the wages were often little more than sufficient for a day's needs (Deut 24:14-15).

20:9-15. The wealthy throughout the Mediterranean world often bestowed significant gifts on the poor that were widely praised as beneficent, increasing the public status of the donors. Because status defined roles in ancient society, those who complained about receiving a day's wage for a day's work would be viewed as rude and ungrateful.

An "evil eye" (literally; cf. KJV) meant a "stingy eye" in common idiom (cf. Prov 28:22); suggesting that the laborers were stingy because he was a generous benefactor was a humiliating dismissal. Jewish people all affirmed that God, who alone rightfully owned all things, was beneficent whatever he gave; they acknowledged that only his attribute of mercy would enable even Israel to survive the day of judgment.

Jewish teachers employed a similar folk story about the day of judgment, but they used it to make the opposite point. Israel, who had worked hard, would receive high wages; the *Gentiles, who had labored little, would receive little. In this context, however, Jesus' point challenges those who have wealth and status in this world, Jewish or Gentile, and promises that in the world to come God will redress those who have been oppressed in this world.

20:17-19
Jesus as the Last

In this context of those with low status being exalted, Jesus gives the extreme example: voluntarily submitting to ridicule and execution as a common criminal at the hands of the Romans, to be vindicated by God in the *resurrection.

20:20-28
The Greatest Is the Servant

See comments on Mark 10:35-45.

20:20-21. The indirect intercession of a motherly woman was often more effective than a man's direct petition for himself, in both Jewish and Roman circles (see also 2 Sam 14:2-20; 1 Kings 1:15-21; cf. 2 Sam 20:16-22). In this case, however, it does not work.

20:22-24. The "cup" represents Jesus' death (Mt 26:27-28, 39); Jesus may borrow the image from the "cup of wrath" in the *Old Testament prophets (see comment on Mk 10:38 for references).

20:25. *Gentile ways are as negative an example as possible (5:47; 6:7; 18:17). Israelite kings had been bound by stricter moral conventions than neighboring pagan rulers (cf. Jezebel's more ready abuse of power than

Ahab's). Jewish tradition recognized that most pagan rulers of postbiblical times were tyrants as well.

20:26-27. Inverting the role of master and slave was radical anywhere in antiquity; even the few masters who believed that slaves were theoretically equals did not go as far as Jesus goes here. Jewish *disciples served their *rabbis; in the *Qumran community, those of lesser rank obeyed those of greater rank.

20:28. Here Jesus probably alludes to the suffering servant of Isaiah 53, who offered his life on behalf of the many. It is also a standard Jewish "how much more" *(qal vahomer)* argument: if their master served, how much more ought they to do so.

20:29-34
Taking Time for the Blind

20:29-30. Although the road from Jericho to Jerusalem was notorious for robbers, it was widely used, and larger companies (such as Jesus') would face no threat. Jericho was one of the wealthiest cities of Judea and beggars there would not starve, but their vocation as beggars and dependents still marked them as poor and at the bottom of the socioeconomic scale—"nobodies" who were dependent on the pity of passersby. "Son of David" indicates that they acknowledge Jesus as *Messiah. "Have mercy on us" could be a common cry for alms, though here they seek more.

20:31. Those believing that their trek to Jerusalem was leading to the establishment of the *kingdom could well feel that Jesus had more important things to do than to be stopped by these beggars, whether they just want alms or are seeking something more.

20:32-34. The beggars want more than alms, and Jesus again demonstrates the difference between his *kingdom and the kind most people were expecting.

21:1-11
The Meek King

See Mark 11:1-10 for some other details.

21:1-3. This borrowing of a donkey may be seen in terms of royal emissaries temporarily impressing (demanding the service of) an animal; Jesus as Lord has the right to whatever his followers claim to own. On the historical level, the donkey's owner probably saw it as helpful hospitality to visitors to the feast or perhaps as the honor of helping on his way a famous *rabbi. Some commentators have also suggested that the owner was away and those who kept the house, hearing that "the master" had need of the donkey, thought they were sending it to its real owner; but they surely would have known the other servants in their household, and they recognized that the disciples were not part of the household. Cf. perhaps Genesis 49:10-11.

21:4-7. Colts that had not yet been ridden sometimes accompanied their mothers. Following a common Jewish practice of reading the Hebrew text for all one can get from it, Matthew reads Zechariah 9:9 as referring to two animals instead of referring to the same animal in two ways. The text is messianic, as ancient interpreters generally acknowledged, but applying this part to himself redefines Jesus' messiahship: officials used donkeys for civil, not military, processions (e.g., 1 Kings 1:33). Thus this text is not a "triumphal entry" in the sense of Roman triumphal processions; it is Jerusalem's reception of a meek and peaceful king.

21:8. Festal pilgrims were often welcomed in this way, though the acclamation of 21:9 suggests that in Jesus' case the welcome was on a larger and more significant scale. Cf. Psalm 118:27 (NIV).

21:9. Except for the acclamation "Son of David!" which indicates a recognition of Jesus' ancestry and a hope that he is the *Messiah, their cry is taken from Psalm 118:25-26 ("Hosanna!" means "O save!"). The Hallel, composed of Psalms 113—118, was sung regularly during Passover season and would be fresh on everyone's mind; later generations applied these psalms to the future redemption for which they hoped. Jesus cites Psalm 118 messianically in Matthew 21:42.

21:10-11. Jesus was better known in Galilee than in Judea; ancient sources often note regional divisions between the two.

21:12-17
Challenging the Temple Aristocracy

Like Jeremiah's smashing the pot in the temple centuries before (Jer 19), Jesus' demonstration there was a prophetic act inviting *repentance and warning of the temple's imminent destruction (see comment on Mt 24:1-2).

21:12. *Old Testament *law required visitors to the feast to purchase their sacrifices in Jerusalem, hence sellers of doves and other sacrificial animals were necessary. Because visitors would come with foreign currencies—even most Galilean towns had their own coinage—moneychangers had also become necessary. Although ancient moneychangers normally managed to turn an honest profit, those in the temple reportedly made very little. The issue is not the commerce per se, and possibly not even whether it involves economic exploitation under the guise of religion, so much as *where* the commerce is occurring. Scholars have proposed several theories on the basis of later evidence, including that the sale of animals had been introduced into the Court of the Gentiles very recently; but this theory is uncertain.

21:13. The Old Testament temple did not officially restrict the access of women or non-Jews, but by extending Jewish purity laws the architects of Herod's temple had excluded Jewish women from the Court of Israel, placing them on a lower level, and non-Jews outside even the Court of Women. Non-Jews could enter the Jewish part of the temple only on pain of death, yet the noisy crowds around the merchants' tables no doubt consumed a significant part of the large space in the Court of the Gentiles at the crowded festivals. Jesus here cites Isaiah 56:7, which goes on to speak of the temple being for the *Gentiles as well, a subtlety some of Matthew's more skillful readers might have caught. He also cites Jeremiah 7:11 ("den of robbers"), which addressed religious leaders of Jeremiah's day who thought their vested interests in the temple would protect them from God's wrath and the temple's destruction. It did not.

21:14. Even hereditary priests who were blind or lame were not permitted in the sanctuary (Lev 21:18); this rule was extended in time to exclude all the blind and lame (cf. 2 Sam 5:8; see also the *Dead Sea Scrolls). Second-century *rabbis permitted but did not require blind and lame men to attend the feasts like other men. Although those who controlled the temple would not have opposed their presence in the outer court (see, e.g., Acts 3:2), Jesus' emphasis on ministry to them here makes a countercultural statement.

The powerful *Sadducean priests who ran the temple were generally not looking for a *Messiah; but had they expected him, they would have expected him either to challenge their power militarily or to seek an alliance with them. From the aristocratic standpoint, seeking followers among the weak was a foolish way to try to establish a kingdom.

21:15-17. *Messianic claims threatened the stability of the temple hierarchy as much as overturning the tables would (cf. 27:11).

Because the high priests spoke Greek as their first language, Jesus quotes to them from the Greek translation of Psalm 8:2, which reads "praise," rather than the Hebrew, which has "strength" (slightly less appropriate). Jesus may argue *qal vahomer* ("how much more"): if God can bring strength or praise from the mouths of infants, how much more can he confound the powerful by the mouths of these children?

21:18-22
The Power of Faith

21:18. Jerusalem was full of visitors during Passover season—perhaps as many as 500,000—and many of the visitors consequently had to lodge in the countryside. "Morning" may mean as early as 6 a.m.

21:19-20. By this time of year fig trees near the Mount of Olives would have leaves, but only green fruit with an unpleasant taste appeared this early; edible figs appeared around early June. Often the green fruit would fall off, leaving only leaves.

The sequence of events here differs from Mark (cf. Mk 11:12-14, 20-26); ancient biography was not required to be chronological, and Matthew's changes in Mark's sequence would have been considered negligible. For further details, compare comment on the Markan passage.

21:21-22. From where Jesus and his *disciples are standing, the Mount of Olives and (from its slopes) perhaps the Dead Sea would be visible; thus Jesus' illustration would have been vivid to his disciples. "Removing mountains" was a figure of speech for doing what was virtually impossible; here Jesus promises that nothing would be impossible for them. This promise is reminiscent of the miraculous activity that characterized the ministry of some *Old Testament prophets, like Elijah and Elisha.

21:23-32
The Right Authority

The conflicts with the authorities in the next several chapters reflect standard methods of debate in antiquity: questions and answers, witty responses, and attempts to trap opponents in their own words. See comment on Mark 11:27-33 for more details.

21:23-27. Jesus replies to the authorities' question with a counterquestion, which was common in Jewish debate. He argues that his authority and John's derive from the same source—"heaven" (one Jewish way of saying, "from God"). This response follows the Jewish legal principle that a commissioned messenger acts on the full authority of the one who sent him. The rest of the interaction follows the standard debate procedure of the period.

The chief priests were politicians—less popular than the politically powerless *Pharisees—who had to balance the interests of both their people and the Roman authorities. Thus they had to keep popular opinion in mind when making decisions that might incur the displeasure of the people (21:26).

21:28-30. That a father should have asked his son to go work in the vineyard was natural. That the son should have refused to go would have offended Jewish moral sensibilities: this was an openly disobedient son, and disobedience was a punishable offense.

But failing to go after promising to go was worse than not having promised; this son violated his word to his own father. The son who refused to go but *repented clearly acted preferably (cf. Ezek 18:21-24).

21:31-32. The pious regarded *tax gatherers and prostitutes as outside practicing Judaism. Jesus could not have chosen a much more offensive comparison. The rhetorical question or invitation to reconsider at the end of the *parable was a long-standing technique for challenging hearers (e.g., Is 5:4; cf. 2 Sam 12:1-7). "Way of righteousness" means a righteous lifestyle (Prov 8:20; 12:28; 16:31), which was both John's practice and his message.

21:33-46 The Evil Tenants and the Benevolent Landowner

Much of the rural Roman Empire was controlled by wealthy landowners, whose income from the land allowed them lives of complete leisure. Their estates were generally worked by tenant farmers, who were usually free peasants (as in Egypt), but sometimes by slaves (as in most of Italy). Although landowners gained great honor among the poor if they were benevolent and treated their workers like urban *patrons treated lower-class *clients, such landowners normally had little incentive to do so. They generally lived far away, often in cities, and had little personal contact with their workers. But the landowner in this *parable is so benevolent that aristocrats would have considered him naive.

Jesus addresses those who fancy themselves rulers of Israel (21:23), reminding them that they are merely custodians appointed by God (like the shepherds of Jer 23 and Ezek 34) over his vineyard.

21:33. Jesus' description follows the normal way to prepare a vineyard, but he clearly alludes to Isaiah 5:1-2, where Israel is the vineyard.

21:34. Payments were rendered at harvest time, either by percentage (usually at least 25 percent) or a predetermined amount.

21:35-37. Landowners always had power, socially and legally, to enforce their will on the tenants; a few reportedly even had squads of hired assassins to deal with troublesome tenants. Here the tenants act as if *they* are the ones with power, and they exploit it mercilessly (as opposed to the ideal of a *benevolent* landowner). This attitude fits the Jewish tradition that Israel martyred many of the prophets God sent.

21:38-39. The tenants presume too much about the inheritance. Although they could have seized it under certain legal conditions, the owner could also stipulate—and after their misdeeds certainly would—that someone else inherit the vineyard; or representatives of the emperor could have seized it. The story paints the tenants as incomparably wicked and stupid; yet the tenants are a transparent metaphor for the religious leaders who serve themselves rather than God—as Jesus' hearers know (21:45).

21:40-41. The ancient hearers would wonder why the landowner had not intervened earlier to throw out the tenants. Asking questions was a standard *rabbinic way of involving hearers in the story or teaching; getting hearers of *parables to pronounce judgment on themselves was familiar from the biblical prophets (2 Sam 12:5-7; 14:8-17; 1 Kings 20:40-42).

21:42. This text is from Psalm 118:22-23, part of the Hallel, like 118:25-26 cited in Matthew 21:9. The building referred to is the temple (see Ps 118:18-21, 25-27); as the cornerstone of a new temple, Jesus poses a threat to the builders of the old one (the Jewish aristocracy). (Interpreters disagree as to whether the "cornerstone" refers to the stone located in the corner of the foundation or to the capstone of an arch, but this point is not crucial to the interpretation of the passage.)

21:43. Israel was a "holy nation" (Ex 19:5-6), but the threat of transferring their status to others had been made before (Ex 32:10; Num 14:12). God rejected the builders' rejection (Mt 21:42), and he could replace them (cf. 3:10). "Producing" fruit (cf. 3:8) meant turning over the fruit to the landowner (God), in contrast to the tenants in the *parable (21:33-42).

21:44. "Falling on" the cornerstone reflects Isaiah 8:14-15 (cf. Is 28:16); the stone falling on the offender alludes to Daniel 2:34, 44, where God's *kingdom, portrayed as a rock, crushes its earthly challengers. Jesus here uses a standard Jewish practice of expounding one text (Mt 21:42) by citing others sharing the same key word or concept, in this case, the divine stone. A later *rabbi warned, "If a pot falls on a rock, woe to the pot; if a rock falls on the pot, woe to the pot—either way, woe to the pot!"

21:45-46. The priestly leaders were shrewd politicians who would be careful not to act *publicly* against the people's wishes; the *Pharisees were popular with the people but not popular enough to directly challenge Jesus' own popularity here. The priestly aristocracy and the Pharisees acted in concert only when necessary to preserve their people against dangerous revolutionary sentiments; challenging a common adversary like a *messianic claimant would fit this category.

22:1-14
Honor the King's Son—or Die

22:1-2. On "the kingdom is like" see comment on 13:24. In *parables *rabbis often compared God to a king, whose son represented Israel; the setting was also often a wedding feast for the son. Wedding feasts were frequently large gatherings; a very wealthy person could invite an entire city to one. Coming to a wedding feast required some commitment of valuable time on the part of guests (Jewish hearers would assume a feast lasting seven days, and a king would expect his guests to remain throughout the feast); this commitment would be difficult for peasants working the land. But the honor of being invited by a king—and the terror of displeasing him—would have motivated intelligent invitees to attend. The invited guests may have been aristocratic landowners anyway (22:5), who had the leisure for such activities.

22:3. Following the custom, a preliminary invitation had already been sent (hence "those who had been invited"); the potential guests thus had no excuse.

22:4. The king reiterates the honor of the invitation.

22:5. Ignoring the king would be scandalously rude, would probably suggest treasonous feelings and would certainly invite a king's wrath; this *parable's original hearers would thus feel incensed at these subjects' unbelievable stupidity.

22:6. This behavior would obviously have been illegal even had the servants not belonged to the king; but servants of a king had higher status than most free persons, and as a king's messengers they represented his person. Ancient peoples universally despised the mistreatment of heralds, or emissaries. In addition, the mistreatment of royal representatives was outright treason, constituting a declaration of revolt. Yet this was the treatment God's servant-messengers, the prophets, were known to have received.

22:7. Kings did not always live in the same place as most of their subjects; the burning of the city probably alludes specifically to the destruction of Jerusalem, which was burned in A.D. 70 (see 24:15). Burning a city was the final step in its complete destruction.

22:8-10. Preparations for the wedding of a king's son would be massive, and it would dishonor the son not to have guests present. Thus, as a last resort, the king invites commoners.

22:11-13. Even commoners knew better than to attend a royal feast without appropriate (at least clean) attire; this would be a sign of insolent disrespect to the host (who at this point in the story is in no mood for further disrespect!). Thus even some of those who showed up for the feast (presumably representing Jesus' purported followers, like Judas) dishonored him.

Scholars have suggested a parallel with a later Jewish story in which a king invited guests to a feast without advance notice of the date. In this story, only the diligent subjects were dressed and ready at the door when the date came; the others had to wait outside in shame.

22:14. The last part of the story illustrates the point that many are invited ("called") to a feast, but few are in the end among the chosen.

22:15-22
Caesar and God

Here Jesus' opponents seek to force him to choose between revolution—which would allow them to charge him before the Romans—and accommodation with the Romans—which they suppose he opposes (because he opposed their own leadership in the temple). The success of a protagonist's wisdom under "testing" with difficult questions was an ancient theme (cf. 1 Kings 10:1); Jesus' superior wisdom is demonstrated in 22:15-46.

22:15-16. *Pharisees tended to be nationalistic, whereas Herodians were clients of Herod, the Roman vassal; they worked together only in extraordinary situations. Pharisees would be concerned about Jewish legal requirements to have witnesses for a charge but would be ready to investigate charges concerning Jesus' disloyalty to the *law. That they would test his teaching here is not surprising. The Herodians, who hoped for a restoration of Herodian rule in Judea (which Pilate currently governed), were naturally disturbed by *messianic figures who might cause Rome to tighten its direct control over the land.

22:17. The Pharisees pit the obligations of peace with Rome against the nationalistic, messianic fervor that they assume Jesus has generated; a disastrous tax revolt two decades earlier had shown where such fervor could lead. If he publicly takes the view characterized by those later called *Zealots (no king but God), the Herodians can have him arrested; if he rejects that view (which he does), he may compromise his following.

22:18-22. Jewish Palestine circulated its own copper coins, omitting the image of the deified emperor, which was offensive to Jewish tastes (though after A.D. 6 they were nonetheless *Roman* coins). But foreign coins, which bore the emperor's image and mention of his divine status, were in common circulation in Palestine, where neither gold nor silver coins were permitted to be struck. The silver denarius, probably minted in Lyon, was required to pay taxes in Palestine as elsewhere in the empire, and Jewish people had to use it whether they liked it or not.

Revolutionaries in A.D. 6 had violently protested the use of such coins and incurred terrible Roman retaliation. If Jesus' questioners here are concerned about paying Roman taxes, they obviously ought not to be carrying this coin. Repartee that put one's interrogators in a bad light was characteristic of popular teachers in both Jewish and Greek traditions, and Jesus proves himself among the most effective of ancient teachers.

22:23-33
The God of the Living

22:23. In ancient Judaism the *Sadducees were especially notorious for not believing in *resurrection; *rabbis who considered themselves successors of the *Pharisees often classified Sadducees as heretics for this view (although the Sadducees, who vanished in the years after A.D. 70, were no longer around to respond).

22:24. The Sadducees' question concerns the law of levirate marriage, a custom practiced in many cultures both in antiquity and today (see Deut 25:5). It provides economic and social protection to widows in certain kinds of family-oriented societies where women cannot earn wages. Students of Jewish *law were still expounding this *Old Testament principle in Jesus' day and afterward, though *rabbinic rules differed from the Old Testament in some respects (e.g., the brother married the widow and the children she bore him were now his own).

22:25-27. The Sadducees borrow the story line from the Jewish book of Tobit, where righteous Sarah's first seven husbands died, slain by the jealous demon Asmodeus. Some second-century *rabbis proposed that a two- or three-time widow should not marry again, lest she bring harm on her next husband too (cf. Gen 38:11). Teachers commonly proposed hypothetical situations when defining Jewish law.

22:28. *Rabbinic literature is full of examples of the mocking question posed by pagans, apostates or those they considered heretics, like the *Sadducees.

22:29-33. It was widely agreed that angels did not procreate (it was unnecessary since in most traditions they did not die), nor did they usually eat or drink. "Marry" probably refers to the groom, whereas "be given in marriage" refers to the bride betrothed by her father.

Arguing against their *Sadducean opponents, the *Pharisees commonly tried to prove the *resurrection from the law of Moses (one *rabbi even suggested that the resurrection was taught in every passage in the law; cf. also 4 Maccabees 7:18-19; 16:25; 18:19). Jesus here does the same. He argues that God would not claim to be the God of those who no longer exist; indeed, his faithfulness to his covenant demands that if he is their God after death, death is not the final word for them. One of the most common Jewish prayers of the period recites God's faithfulness to Abraham, Isaac and Jacob as a living reality for their own time.

Jewish teachers sometimes contested their opponents' points by appealing to Scripture with phrases like, "Go and read." The accusation implied in "Have you never read" was even harsher (22:31; cf. 12:3; 19:4; 21:16, 42).

22:34-40
The Greatest Commandments

Following Jewish interpretive technique, Jesus links the two commandments (Deut 6:5; Lev 19:18) by a common key word: "Love." Jewish ethics repeatedly stressed love of God and of others.

22:34-38. This commandment was so important to Judaism that it was regularly recited. In the Greek language, adjectives like "great" had come to be used sometimes for superlatives like "greatest." Deuteronomy 6:5 demanded loving God with all one's "heart, soul and might"; "might" here becomes "mind" (which was implicit in the Hebrew understanding of "heart"), but the image is still "with one's whole person." (*New Testament writers apparently revocalized the Hebrew term for "might" as "mind," a Hebrew term which sounded similar; such revocalization was a common Jewish interpretive practice.)
22:39. Jewish tradition sometimes joined the second commandment with the first.
22:40. Some other teachers also used these commandments as summaries of the law, which is how they also appear in their contexts in the *Old Testament.

22:41-46
David's Lord

By definition, the Christ, or anointed one, was the royal descendant of David (Is 9:7; 11:1; Ps 2; 89; 132). But this view of messiahship lent itself to a revolutionary view of the *kingdom (see comment on 11:10) and was inadequate. The one who would reign in God's kingdom was David's "Lord," not merely his descendant; he would thus be greater than the resurrected David.

When Jewish teachers challenged their hearers to resolve apparent discrepancies in Scripture, they assumed that both texts were true (in this case, Jesus knows that he is both David's son and David's Lord) and were simply asking how to harmonize them. Jesus' opponents apparently have no answer to his question, perhaps because Jewish interpreters did not apply Psalm 110:1 to the *Messiah.

When contemporary literature reports hearers being overawed by a wise speaker's (usually the protagonist's) wisdom, the readers are meant to respect the speaker's wisdom too (e.g., 1 Esdras 4:41-42).

23:1-12
Serve More Humbly Than Pharisees

The other Gospels also record Jesus' disputes with *scribes and *Pharisees (Mk 12:38-40; Lk 11:39-52), but Matthew may emphasize these disputes more than do Mark and Luke because scribes and Pharisees constituted the chief Jewish opposition his readers faced in Syria-Palestine (see the introduction to Matthew). Scribes and Pharisees were originally distinct though overlapping groups (Lk 11:39-52), but those who threatened Matthew's readers were the joint successors of both these groups. Matthew also intends this warning to apply against these opponents' counterparts in the *church (Mt 24:45-51).
23:1-2. Some scholars have pointed to a prominent seat in many *synagogues as a "seat of Moses" (cf. 23:6), but Jesus presumably means this expression figuratively. The *Pharisaic *scribes who articulated the law believed their traditions were rooted in Moses' own teaching and fancied themselves Moses' successors for their own generation.
23:3. Pharisaic teachers normally taught that knowing Scripture took precedence over obeying it, because knowing it was the prerequisite for obeying it; but they themselves would have agreed that one must obey it and not just learn it.
23:4-5. "Phylacteries" are *tefillin,* small boxes affixed by a leather strap to one's head and left hand during morning and evening prayers; Scrip-

ture passages were inserted in these boxes (the practice is based on Deut 6:8). These passages were then recited as part of the prayers; rules concerning this later became stricter under the *rabbis. For the tassels, see Matthew 9:20 and 14:36.

23:6. Seating was critical at banquets; those seated in lower-status places frequently complained, as ancient literature amply attests. The most prominent seats in the *synagogue probably varied in this period before synagogue architecture was standardized; one first-century synagogue seems to suggest a lack of seating rank. But honored seats would have normally been in the most visible place, probably nearest the bema, the platform for the reading of the Law; perhaps distinguished guests were given chairs in synagogues while most hearers remained on mats on the floor. Seating was according to rank in the *Qumran assemblies, the *Sanhedrin and *rabbinic schools.

23:7-8. Greetings ("Peace be with you") were so important socially that specific rules developed how to greet whom when; greetings were an essential courtesy in Greek and Jewish cultures. Not to hail a person superior in understanding the *law was a grievous insult. Marketplaces were the most crowded places in town. "*Rabbi" means "my master" and came to be commonly applied to teachers as a title of respect (something like "Reverend" or "Father" today); they were especially "masters" of their pupils. They were venerated in a variety of ways.

23:9-11. Rabbis were also affectionately and respectfully called "Abba," or "Papa"; they addressed their *disciples as their children, and the rabbis' authority and honor placed them on a higher level than the disciples. Jesus says that only God is to receive such superior respect; all other Christians are peers.

23:12. The principle stated here occurs in Proverbs 25:6-7 with reference to seating at banquets, and elsewhere the principle refers to the future time when God equalizes everyone (Is 2:11-12; 5:15; cf. Ezek 17:24; 21:26.

23:13-28
Woes to the Hypocrites

Like beatitudes (see Mt 5:3-12), woes were an *Old Testament form of prayer. The prophets commonly employed them, and they are akin to "alases" or, perhaps here, curses ("Cursed be . . ." in contrast to the blessing formula, "Blessed be . . ."; cf. Deut 27—28).

*Pharisees were not all of one kind, and the later *rabbis, who generally considered themselves spiritual heirs of the Pharisees, report criticisms of several sorts of Pharisees whose hearts were not right (e.g., "the bruised Pharisee," who kept bumping into things because his eyes were closed to avoid seeing a woman). These reports emphasize that motives are critical; the best motive is fear of the Lord, or (in the more refined version) love of God. *Rabbinic literature regularly condemns hypocrisy and demands proper motives. Jesus' opponents would have agreed with most of his ethics, and perhaps protested that they were not really violating them.

Hypocrites originally meant playactors but by this time the term was also used pejoratively for two-faced people, whose behavior either differed from their belief or varied when they were with different people.

23:13. The image of power to shut someone out is the image of the doorkeeper with the keys to the house; see comment on 16:19.

23:14. This verse is not in all Greek

manuscripts of Matthew; for background on its content, see comment on Mark 12:40.

23:15. *Pharisees did not have missionaries as such, but Jewish people outside Palestine were always eager to make converts among the *Gentiles, and the wing of Pharisaism most influenced by *Hillel was said to be especially open to converting non-Jews to Judaism. Judaism continued to be a missionary religion for centuries, until it was finally stifled by the legislation of Roman Christendom, with which it was in competition (although the Romans had always resented Jewish *proselytism, including in pre-Christian times).

"Child of hell" means someone destined to go there. The problem here is not making converts (28:19) but teaching them wrongly.

23:16-22. Jews were no longer allowed to pronounce the sacred name of God in this period. By swearing lesser oaths, some people hoped to avoid the consequences of swearing by God's name if they could not keep their vow or if their oath turned out to be mistaken. As people swore or vowed by things related to God instead of by God himself, more and more things became substitutes for the divine name and thus became roundabout ways of seeming to swear by God while hoping to buffer the consequences. See comment on 5:33-37.

23:23. The principle that virtues like justice, mercy and faith are most important is familiar from Scripture (Deut 10:12-13; Mic 6:8), and the *rabbis themselves sometimes summarized the *law in terms of general principles like love. Most *Pharisees and other Jewish interpreters like *Philo agreed that there were heavier and lighter parts of the law. They would have responded to Jesus that they attended to minutiae only because even the smallest detail of the law was important to the pious; they taught that one should devote as much attention to the little details as to the principles. But Jesus was not against the law (see Mt 5:19); his point is that they should have learned justice, mercy and covenant faithfulness first (9:13; 12:7).

Tithes were especially used to support the priests and Levites. "Dill" and Luke's "rue" (Lk 11:42) are similar words in *Aramaic, possibly reflecting an original Aramaic source here. The law did not explicitly require tithing these dried green plants. Different groups of *Pharisees debated among themselves whether to tithe cummin.

23:24. The *hyperbole here is humorous and would certainly catch ancient hearers' attention. Wanting to avoid the impurity caused by a dead insect in their drink, Pharisees would strain out an insect as small as a fly (and anything larger than a lentil) before it could die in order to preserve the fluid (cf. Lev 11:32, 34). Pharisees considered gnats, which were smaller than lentils, exempt from this impurity, but the scrupulous Pharisee of Jesus' hyperbole would not have taken any chances. Yet Jesus charges hyperbolically that they would leave a camel (the largest land animal in Palestine and ritually unclean) in the cup and gulp it down. Their attention to the law's details was fine, but they had missed the main point (Mt 23:23).

23:25-26. Ritual purity was important to the Pharisees, so they washed their vessels as well as themselves in ritual baths. The school of *Shammai—the Pharisaic majority in this period—said that the outside of a cup could be clean even if the inside were not; the minority view of *Hillel's followers was that the inside of the cup must be cleansed first. Jesus sides with the school of Hillel on this point, but does this so that he can make a figurative statement about the inside of the heart.

23:27-28. Nothing spread ritual impurity as severely as a corpse (it made anyone who touched it unclean for a week—Num 19:11); *Pharisees believed that one contracted impurity if even one's shadow touched a corpse or grave. Inconspicuous tombs (or limestone ossuaries) would be whitewashed each spring before Passover to warn passersby to avoid them and so avoid impurity; the Pharisees either lacked this telltale warning (Lk 11:44) or pretended that it was a mark of distinction rather than evidence of impurity. "Whitewash" probably alludes to Ezekiel 13:10-12 and 22:28; it may have covered over a wall's weakness but would not stop its collapse.

23:29-39
Killing the Prophets

This is the final woe (23:29).

23:29-30. Ancient Judaism emphasized more often than the *Old Testament had that Israel had martyred its prophets (e.g., Jer 26:20-23; cf. 2 Chron 36:15-16). The Jewish community in this period built tombs as monuments for the prophets and righteous (including some who were not martyred, like David or Huldah).

23:31. Jesus' point here is, "Like father, like son"; corporate sin and guilt continued among the descendants of the wicked unless they repented (Ex 20:5; Deut 23:2-6; 1 Sam 15:2-3; Is 1:4; etc.).

23:32. This is an ironic challenge, typical of the prophets (Is 6:9; Jer 44:25; Amos 4:4-5): Go ahead and sin if you must, but God will judge you for it (Eccles 11:9)!

23:33. Being called vipers, or a kind of venomous snake, was bad enough (Ps 58:4; 140:3; cf. Gen 3). But the offspring of a viper was reputed to eat its way out of its pregnant mother's belly, so calling someone the offspring of vipers could imply that one was guilty of the universally horrifying crime of matricide. In other words, this was worse than just calling someone a viper!

23:34. Prophets were sent by God according to the Old Testament, or by Wisdom (cf. Lk 11:49) in some Jewish traditions; here they are sent by Jesus.

Jewish people commonly believed that fully anointed prophets had ceased at the end of the Old Testament period and would be restored only in the end time. Here Jesus mentions several clerical categories: prophets, wise men (wisdom teachers who circulated proverbs, etc.) and *scribes to explain Scriptures (cf. 13:52). Crucifixion was the severest Roman punishment, reserved for the lowest classes of non-Romans; any Jew who delivered another Jew over to such a punishment was naturally despised by his people. *Synagogue scourgings were a form of discipline inflicted on errant members of the Jewish community (see comment on 10:17); on "city to city" see 10:23.

23:35. Bloodguilt was a serious matter, affecting the whole community and not just the individuals directly responsible (Deut 21:1-9). God himself would avenge it (Deut 32:43; Ps 79:10).

The Hebrew Bible is arranged in a different sequence than our modern English versions of the *Old Testament; in it Zechariah is the last martyr (2 Chron 24:20-22), and Abel is the first, as in our Bibles (Gen 4:8). Jewish tradition expanded the accounts of both martyrdoms, declaring that after Zechariah's death a fountain of blood appeared in the temple that not even the slaughter of thousands of priests could appease (cf. also Gen 4:10

for the outcry of blood).

The Zechariah murdered in the temple was son of Jehoiada the priest (2 Chron 24:22), not Zechariah son of Berechiah (Zech 1:1), who lived much later in Israel's history. But Matthew uses the Jewish interpretive technique of combining key words to coalesce two Zechariahs, referring to one and alluding to the other, as he did with Amon/Amos and Asa/Asaph in his genealogy in chapter 1. (The suggestion of some scholars that "Zechariah" also alludes to a prophet martyred in A.D. 67 is unlikely.)

23:36. "This generation" occurs also in Matthew 11:16; 13:39, 45; and 16:4; see comment on 24:34. This is the generation that would see the destruction of the temple. For the image of generations of guilt climaxing in the guiltiest generation on whom the whole judgment is poured out, see Jeremiah 16:10-13.

23:37. Jewish tradition claimed that Jewish people were under God's wings, and when a Jewish person converted a *Gentile, he or she brought that Gentile "under the wings of God's presence." The *Old Testament also portrays God as an eagle hovering over its offspring (Deut 32:11; cf. Ex 19:4), protecting Israel under his wings (Ps 17:8; 36:7; 57:1; 61:4; 63:7; 91:4) and terrifying Israel's foes in the same way (Jer 49:22). This is one Old Testament image of God's love for his people; here Jesus fills this divine role.

Prophets sometimes addressed Jerusalem directly (Jer 13:27), and repetition of a name in direct address is common in Jewish texts. On "killing the prophets" see comment on 23:29-30.

23:38. The "house" could mean Israel (Jer 12:7), but in this context almost certainly means the temple (e.g., Judith 9:13), which would also be left "desolate" (Mt 24:15) in A.D. 70. In the *Old Testament, the temple was called God's house; perhaps it is called "*your* house" here to declare that God's presence has exited it, as in Ezekiel 10—11.

23:39. On the significance of this citation, see 21:9. The Old Testament prophets and subsequent Jewish tradition suggested that the redemption would not come until after Israel's widespread *repentance (cf. Is 30:19).

24:1-3
Introduction to the Judgment Discourse

Chapter 23 began Jesus' warning of God's judgment against certain elements of the religious establishment; this chapter extends that judgment to the temple itself. After it was destroyed in A.D. 70, many of the Jewish people saw God's hand of judgment in the destruction.

24:1. The Jerusalem temple was one of the most splendid structures of all antiquity and seemed strong and invincible (cf., e.g., Letter of Aristeas 100-101). It was the central symbol of Judaism and was renowned for its beauty. See further comment on Mark 13:1.

24:2. Some Greek philosophers were unimpressed with magnificent structures, but Jesus' response goes far beyond this attitude—he speaks of judgment. Some other Jewish groups (including the *Qumran sect) also expected the temple to be judged; but most Jews, regardless of their other differences, found in the temple a symbol of their Jewish unity and would have been appalled to think that God would allow it to be destroyed (as in Jer 7:4-15). Some stones were left on others (e.g., part of one wall still stands), but this fact does not weaken the force of the *hyperbole: the temple was almost entirely demolished in A.D. 70.

24:3. *Old Testament prophets often grouped events together by their topic rather than their chronology, and in this discourse Jesus does the same. He addresses what are grammatically two separate questions: the time of the temple's destruction and the time of the end.

24:4-14 Coming Events

Preliminary signs indicating the nearness of the end appear in many Jewish *apocalyptic writings (e.g., *2 Baruch 70:7), but much material characteristic of such texts (the final war, Rome's destruction, etc.) is missing here. Most of the preliminary signs that other apocalyptic thinkers expected for the end are explicitly *not* indicators of the end here (Mt 24:6-8).

24:4-5. Many false *messianic figures arose in the first century (and subsequently); they often attracted large and devoted followings. Although *Josephus, writing for Gentile readers, describes them as "false prophets" rather than as messiahs, their political aspirations are usually apparent in his descriptions.

24:6-8. These troubles were associated with the sufferings many Jews thought would immediately precede the end (e.g., 4 Ezra 9:3; 13:31-32; 2 Baruch 27:7; 70:3; Sibylline Oracles 2:22-24; 3:660-61). Some compared these troubles to "birth pangs," or the "birth pangs of the *Messiah" or of the messianic era (e.g., in the *Qumran *Hymns;* cf. Is 13:8; Hos 13:13). For Jesus, they are only the "*beginning* of birth pangs" and characterize life as normal in this age. He describes some of them in *Old Testament language (2 Chron 15:6; Is 19:2; Jer 51:46).

24:9-14. Universal persecution, apostasy and worldwide missions revival mark the final era. These events began to characterize Christianity in the first century, although not yet on a worldwide scale.

Under pressure, many converts to Judaism reverted to paganism, and Jewish texts warn of many Jewish people turning from God in the end time as they had just before the rise of the Maccabees in the second century B.C. Apostasy and especially handing over friends to persecutors were considered horrible crimes.

Thus Jewish readers would have readily understood Jesus' warning about persecution and apostasy here; his teaching concerning the spread of the good news of the *kingdom among all nations, however, runs counter to prevailing Jewish teaching. Although *apocalyptic writers expected persecution by the nations, they did not anticipate a widespread conversion of *Gentiles before the end.

24:15-22 The Events of 66-70

One prerequisite for Christ's return was the series of events fulfilled in A.D. 66-70, events accurately predicted by Jesus.

24:15. The "abomination that brings about desolation" in Daniel 9:27 occurs after the cutting off of the *Messiah (a passage subjected to various interpretations); Daniel 11:31 sounds as if it should have occurred in the second century B.C., and 12:11 at the time of the end, so some interpreters have felt that the *prophecy was accomplished in stages. Some interpreters believe that parts of Daniel's prophecy remain to be fulfilled; others believe that all of it was fulfilled in the first century.

The first-century Jewish historian *Josephus felt that Daniel was fulfilled when *Zealots slaughtered the priests in the temple in A.D. 66, committing a sacrilege for which God brought about the desolation of the temple (human bloodshed in the temple desecrated it;

cf. comment on Mt 23:35). This sacrilege would have been the signal for Christians to flee Jerusalem (24:16); early Christian historians tell us that Christian prophets warned the Jewish Christians to flee Jerusalem at this time.

The temple was left "desolate" in 70, when the Romans destroyed it with fire and then erected their own standards on the site. As Jewish people knew (it is lamented in the *Dead Sea Scrolls), these standards bore the insignia of the Roman emperor, who was worshiped as divine in the Eastern Mediterranean; they would thus have sealed the site's desecration. Jerusalem's citizens had felt that even bringing these standards into Jerusalem temporarily (as Pilate had done roughly three and one-half years before Jesus uttered this warning) defiled the holy city. On several occasions the Jerusalemites had shown that they preferred death to their temple's defilement.

24:16. The mountains were the easiest place in Judea to hide; armies had often used them for waging guerrilla warfare (cf., e.g., 1 Sam 23:26; 1 Macc 2:28). Early Christian tradition indicates that the Jerusalem Christians fled to Pella at the base of mountains to the north; although the Judean hill country lay all about Jerusalem, the route northward to Pella would be through the Jordan Valley. Both the mountains and the route to Pella could have provided places of refuge, but the flight to Pella shows that the mountain saying in 24:16 was not made up after the event.

24:17. The roof, which was flat, was used for prayer, drying vegetables and other functions. The staircase from this roof was on the outside of the house; one could thus descend without entering the house.

24:18. Workers would wear an outer cloak to the fields when they began the day about 6 a.m.; as the day grew warmer, they left their cloaks on the edge of the field.

24:19. Being pregnant or nursing a child made travel much more difficult. Famine would also make pregnancy and nursing much more problematic. Indeed, *Josephus reports that the siege of Jerusalem became so difficult that some women ate their children (as in Lev 26:29; Deut 28:57; 2 Kings 6:29).

24:20. Winter restricted conditions for travel, immobilizing even most armies. In the winter, the otherwise dry creek beds (wadis) were flooded with water and became difficult to cross. Some fugitives from Jerusalem did try to escape the Roman siege in winter and, delayed by these flooded creek beds, were slaughtered.

Jewish law prohibited riding horses, mules and other means of transportation on the sabbath; even one's walking distance was regulated. Transportation and passage would thus be difficult to obtain on the sabbath, especially if residents of Jerusalem wished to flee secretly without being challenged by the patriotic *Zealots. The sabbath could be violated to save life, but those who did not recognize the situation's urgency would not cooperate. (If Jerusalem were besieged in the sabbatical year—Lev 25:1-7—its inhabitants would quickly run out of food; but we may safely assume that the sabbath day, rather than year, is intended here.)

24:21. Here Jesus borrows the language of Daniel 12:1, referring to the final era of tribulation necessary before the dead would be raised (12:11-13). "Never before or again" was sometimes *hyperbolic (cf. Josh 10:14 with Ex 8:13; Num 14:20; 2 Kings 6:18), although *Josephus concurs that the sufferings of 66-70 exceeded any before them in human history.

24:22. Jesus presumably means the 1,260 days of Daniel; the time would be shortened to ensure survivors.

24:23-28
Beware of False Messiahs

24:23-24. Some Jewish false prophets in first-century Palestine drew large followings by claiming that they could perform miracles, such as parting the Jordan or making the walls of Jerusalem fall down; they failed to make good on such promises. In addition, many magicians claimed to work miraculous cures, and some Jewish false prophets probably made similar claims.

24:25. Advance warning was always helpful for affirming faith (Is 48:5).

24:26. Would-be *messiahs most often came in the wilderness, trying to imitate Moses, who had long ago led his people through the wilderness. (Jewish people expected a deliverer like Moses, as in Deut 18:15.) After A.D. 70 and especially after the crushing defeat in A.D. 135, many Palestinian Jews grew more skeptical of messianic claimants (Sadducees already had been).

24:27. False *messiahs could not duplicate this sign. This is the coming of the Lord described by passages like Zechariah 14:3-8, with Jesus filling the role most Jewish readers expected God to fill.

24:28. Jesus' return will not be a secret event; it will be the place of the last battle, leaving his enemies as food for vultures (Ezek 32:4-6; 39:17-20). Being eaten instead of buried was considered a horrible fate (Deut 28:26; 1 Sam 17:44; Ps 79:2).

24:29-31
Final Signs

24:29. This reference to astronomical events is *Old Testament language for the time of God's judgment at the final battle (e.g., Is 13:10; 24:23; 34:4; Ezek 32:7-8; Joel 3:14; Zech 14:6). Similar cosmic language was sometimes applied to judgments or other divine acts in history as well (e.g., Ps 18:6-19; Jer 4:20-28; *Sibylline Oracles). Darkness was apparently a frightful judgment in antiquity (Ex 9:21-23). Both Jew and *Gentile regarded signs in the heavens as portentous, and some signs in the heavens (on a much smaller scale) were reported to have accompanied the fall of Jerusalem.

24:30. This heavenly appearance of the sign of the Son of Man is the ultimate sign of Jesus' coming (24:3). The text combines Zechariah 12:10, where in the end God brings his people to repent of the pain they have caused him, and Daniel 7:13-14, where a representative of suffering Israel would receive the *kingdom from God and reign forever. (Cf. also Rev 1:7.) In the *Dead Sea Scrolls, "clouds" refers to the hosts of angels at God's coming; in the *Old Testament, this image could refer to the cloud of God's glory or to literal clouds.

24:31. Trumpets were used to announce the accession of kings and other great events. In the *Old Testament they were especially used to gather God's people (most frequently for war); the prophets often used the trumpet as a symbol warning of impending battle and devastation (e.g., Jer 4:5, 19, 21; Zeph 1:16). The trumpet had already been used for the gathering of God's people in the end time (Is 27:13), a gathering associated with Israel's salvation (Is 11:12; 43:5; 49:5; 56:8; and commonly in Jewish tradition) and God's final war (Zech 9:14-16). A regularly recited Jewish prayer from this period mentions this future gathering of Israel at the sound of the trumpet; various other ancient Jewish texts agree. It was thus a natural image for the gathering of believers (cf. 1 Cor 15:52; 1 Thess 4:16).

"From one end of heaven to the other" may communicate in a popular image of the day: heaven was a dome over the earth, so this phrase is similar to our equally figurative "from one end of the earth to the other"—i.e., everywhere (cf. Mk 13:27).

24:32-35 Certainty of the Coming

24:32-33. This is the first of seven future-kingdom *parables, paralleling the seven parables on the presence of the *kingdom in chapter 13.

Unlike most Palestinian trees, fig trees lose their leaves in winter; they would have been in leaf by this time of year, however, predicting the fruit that should appear on them in the summer. Jesus had earlier used this tree as a *parable for the temple's destruction (see Mk 11:12-25). But the meaning is ultimately decided by the context: when the signs he had listed (including the temple's destruction) were fulfilled, his coming would be imminent.

24:34. The temple was destroyed roughly forty years after Jesus spoke these words (which refer to the temple's demise rather than to the Second Coming—see comment on 24:3). The *Dead Sea Scrolls anticipated a final, forty-year generation of tribulation before the end; Jesus leaves the period between the final earthly sign (the temple's demise) and his return indeterminate.

24:35. Even Jewish prophets would not speak thus of their own words (Zech 1:5-6); such a claim was made only for God's words, spoken through Moses and the prophets (cf. Jer 31:35-37). Those who claimed that their words were unchangeable believed that they spoke infallibly for God (cf. Zech 1:5-6; comment on Rev 22:18-19; rabbis spoke thus concerning the authority of the *Old Testament).

24:36-44 Uncertainty of the Time of His Coming

24:36. See perhaps Zechariah 14:7. Although God had made the crucial things known to his people, he always kept some mysteries secret (Deut 29:29; cf. 4 Ezra 4:52).

Jewish teachers struggled with a tension between two positions: (1) one could predict when the *Messiah would come, in a time ordained only by God; and (2) one could not predict his coming, but he would come whenever Israel repented and wholly followed God.

24:37-39. Jewish tradition emphasized the evils of Noah's generation in much fuller detail than the Bible had.

24:40-41. In the context of 24:37-39, "taken" presumably means "taken to judgment" (cf. Jer 6:11 NASB, NRSV). Grinding at the mill was a task assigned to women. Wives of *Pharisees were allowed to work together with unreligious women (provided they did not involve themselves in any infringements of Pharisaic purity rules); thus the scenario of women of different convictions working together is not unusual.

24:42-44. Thieves could "break in" by digging through the clay wall of the average Palestinian Jewish home. (A more well-to-do householder with stronger walls would often have servants to watch the doors for him.) A thief who broke in at night, unlike one who broke in during the day, could be killed with impunity because he was regarded as potentially dangerous (Ex 22:2-3).

24:45-51 Watchful Servants

Often a well-to-do householder had a slave who was a "manager," or "steward," managing his estate. Such a high-level slave could be in charge of giving rations to the other servants and could abuse his authority only if the master were not present. (Absentee landowners and householders were common, especially if they owned other estates at a great distance. In some stories of the period, absentee kings, landowners or husbands posed temptations to those remaining behind.)

Some laws viewed slaves as persons, while other laws viewed them as property (for economic matters). Although masters were allowed to beat slaves, it was in their economic interests not to do so often or severely. A slave who abused the other slaves was mistreating his master's "property"; often these other servants were also objects of the master's personal concern. Drunkenness was despised, especially if slaves drank wine and banqueted at the master's expense without his knowledge.

25:1-13 Watchful Bridesmaids

Being a bridesmaid was a great honor; to be insultingly unprepared and shut out of the feast was the stuff of which young women's nightmares were made. Professed believers must endure in faith to the end (24:13).

25:1. On "the kingdom is like" see comment on 13:24. Weddings were held toward evening and torches were used as part of the celebration, which focused on a procession leading the bride to the groom's house. It is unlikely that "lamps" refers to the small Herodian oil lamps, which could be carried in the hand; all the evidence points instead to torches, which were also used in Greek and Roman wedding ceremonies. These torches may have been sticks wrapped with oil-soaked rags. In many traditional Palestinian villages in more recent times, the wedding feast occurs at night after a day of dancing; the bridesmaids leave the bride, with whom they have been staying, and go out to meet the bridegroom with torches. They then escort him back to his bride, whom they all in turn escort to the groom's home.

25:2-7. Torches like these could not burn indefinitely; some evidence suggests that they may have burned for only fifteen minutes before the burnt rags would have to be removed and new oil-soaked rags would need to be wrapped on the sticks of which they were made. Because not all the details of ancient Palestinian weddings are known, it is not clear whether the *parable envisions the lamps as burning while the bridesmaids slept (to avoid the delay of having to rekindle them) or as being lit only after the first announcement of the bridegroom's coming (as many scholars think). Either way, if the bridegroom delayed longer than they anticipated, their lamps would not last unless they had an extra reserve of oil. Bridegrooms were often late, and their comings were repeatedly announced until they arrived.

25:8. The bridesmaids needed sufficient oil to keep the torches lit during the procession to the groom's home and the dancing.

25:9-10. Trying to share the oil would have left too little for any of the torches and ruined the wedding ceremony. It would have been difficult to find dealers at this time of night, however (although some catering shops could have been open if they were near a large city); the foolish bridesmaids were definitely going to be late. The young women were supposed to meet the bridegroom, who would then fetch his bride from her home and lead the whole procession back to his father's house for the feast. The bolt used to shut doors (25:10) was noisy and cumbersome; perhaps it represents an effort to be repeated only if necessary, making new visitors unwelcome (cf. Lk 11:7).

25:11-13. The foolish bridesmaids missed the entire procession back to the groom's house, along with the festive singing and dancing. They also missed the critical element of the Jewish wedding, in which the bride was brought into the groom's home under the wedding canopy. Having insulted the dignity of the host, they were not admitted to the feast, which lasted for seven days following the ceremony.

25:14-30 Making Use of the Interim Time

Wealthy landowners usually delegated the control and multiplication of their wealth to trained accountants, who could be free persons or, as here, servants. In view of the impending day of reckoning, believers must make the wisest use of all that the Lord has entrusted to them, to make it count for him; they must never take their stewardships for granted (24:45-51).

25:14. Well-to-do masters often went on long journeys. Given the uncertainties of transportation in those days, the time of return for even a well-planned trip would be uncertain.

25:15-17. Although the exact value of a talent varied from period to period and place to place, we may estimate the values of these investments at roughly fifty thousand, twenty thousand and ten thousand denarii. Since one denarius was a day's wage, this would be a "small sum" (25:21, 23) only to a very rich master, who would probably entrust his wealth only to his most dependable and prudent servants.

Those with sufficient capital could invest it at a profit; for instance, they could lend it to moneychangers who would use it to turn a profit and give them a substantial share. Lending money at interest was also profitable, given the exorbitant interest rates of the period (although Jewish people were not supposed to charge interest to fellow Jews); one *patron is reported to have lent to an entire city at roughly 50 percent interest! Because most people did not have capital available for investment, those who did could reap large profits.

25:18. One of the safest—and least profitable—ways of protecting one's money was to bury it in the ground; such buried reserves are still occasionally found where someone never returned to retrieve his or her deposits. (In Lk 19, a servant does worse: tying up money in a head cloth instead of burying it was considered gross negligence, because it did not even keep the deposit safe.)

25:19-23. Doubling one's investment was normal, and the servants should have been able to accomplish this. The principle that integrity in smaller matters qualified one to prove one's integrity in larger matters was often invoked in antiquity. Jesus may well have used the *Aramaic term for "joy" that also means "festival" (cf. 25:10); the master threw a feast at his return and honored his helpful servants.

25:24-25. The third slave should have known better; he simply did not care what happened to his master's property (see comment on 25:15-17). The smallest possible investment, providing interest on a savings deposit, could not have endangered the deposit; it would have been as safe as burying the money. The phrase "You have what is yours" was used in Jewish transactions to say, "I am not responsible for this any further."

25:26-27. Although usury, charging

interest on a loan or a deposit, was technically against Jewish law (Ex 22:25; Lev 25:36-37; Deut 23:19-20; Neh 5:7; Ps 15:5; Prov 28:8; Ezek 18:8, 13, 17; 22:12), *Gentiles were not bound to refrain from it; further, Jewish people could charge Gentiles, and many wealthy Jewish aristocrats followed Greek custom more than official Jewish teaching anyway. Just as other *rabbis could tell *parables about kings long after kings had ceased in Jewish Palestine, Jesus could expect his hearers to grasp the full imagery of this parable.

25:28-30. Darkness is elsewhere used as an image for hell (8:12).

25:31-46
Judging Sheep and Goats

25:31. The Son of Man was going to come to reign for God (Dan 7:13-14; cf. the *Similitudes of Enoch, of uncertain date), and some Jewish *apocalypses (perhaps following Greek images of the realm of the dead) described human judges before the final day of judgment. But the description of absolute authority afforded Jesus here fits most precisely the standard Jewish picture of God judging the nations in the day of judgment. For the angels see comment on 16:27.

25:32. God judging the nations (e.g., Is 2:4; Mic 4:3) was a standard part of Jewish expectation for the future. God would distinguish among the sheep (Ezek 34:17). Although sheep and goats grazed together, it is said that Palestinian shepherds normally separated sheep and goats at night because goats need to be warm at night while sheep prefer open air. Sheep were more valuable than goats, and characteristics like this may have may have influenced how these terms would be heard figuratively; for instance, in a pagan dream handbook sheep were associated with good while goats were associated with trouble.

25:33. The right is the preferred side in ancient texts; in the few scenes of judgment where it occurs, the right side is for the righteous and the left for the wicked (e.g., the Testament of Abraham recension A).

25:34. "Inherit the *kingdom" is a familiar phrase; in Jewish tradition, the kingdom was prepared for Israel, who had been predestined by God. The king in Jewish *parables is virtually always God; here it refers to Jesus.

25:35-36. Except for visiting the imprisoned, the deeds Jesus lists are standard righteous deeds in Jewish ethics. Providing for the poor, giving hospitality to the stranger and visiting the sick were basic to Jewish piety.

25:37-39. An unclear statement followed by a counterquestion was a standard method of moving an argument forward (see, e.g., Mal 1:6-7).

25:40. In some Jewish *apocalyptic texts, the nations would be judged for how they treated Israel. In the Bible, God also judged people for how they treated the poor. But given the use of "brothers" or "sisters" (12:50; 28:10; the Greek term can include both genders) and perhaps "least" (5:19; 11:11; cf. 18:4; 20:26; 23:11) elsewhere in Matthew, this passage probably refers to receiving messengers of Christ. Such missionaries needed shelter, food and help in imprisonment and other complications caused by persecution; see comment on 10:11-14. Receiving them was like receiving Christ (on the Jewish principle of agency, see comment on 10:40-42). The judgment of all nations thus had to be preceded by the proclamation of the *kingdom among them (24:14).

25:41-45. Some Jewish traditions (like the *Qumran *War Scroll*) report that Belial (*Satan) was created for the pit; destruction was not God's original purpose for people (4 Ezra 8:59-60). In many Jewish traditions, the demons were fallen angels (cf. comment on 2 Pet 2:4). Jewish tradition was divided on the duration of hell; this passage's description of it as "eternal" was certainly not merely a concession to a universal image in Judaism.

25:46. *Eternal life was promised to the righteous after their *resurrection at the end of the age (Dan 12:2). Some Jewish teachers believed that hell was temporary and that at the end some people would be burned up and others released; other Jewish teachers spoke as if hell were eternal. Jesus here sides with the latter group.

26:1-16
The Givers and the Takers

See comments on Mark 14:1-11 for further details.

26:1-2. Jesus' prediction of crucifixion may not sound harsh to us, due to our familiarity with the story, but it could have only jarred Jesus' *disciples. Inhabitants of the Roman Empire, especially in places like Jewish Palestine, saw crucifixion as the cruelest, most painful and most degrading form of common criminal execution.

26:3-5. A private meeting to plot the execution of a person not yet convicted certainly violated Jewish law. Their fear of a riot at the festival (v. 5), however, was entirely reasonable: under the crowded conditions of the festivals, riots were more likely than at any other time, and hundreds of people had been trampled in tumults at previous festivals. The Roman governor came from Caesarea at the feasts to forestall any trouble, and Roman security was increased during this season. The priestly aristocracy were, above all, guardians of the status quo, and they would have to deal with *messianic pretenders in the most politically expedient way; they dare not arrest Jesus publicly (26:55). On Caiaphas, see comment on John 11:47-48.

26:6. Bethany was one of those villages near Jerusalem where Passover pilgrims could spend the night with hosts. On Simon the "leper" see comment on Mark 14:3.

26:7-9. It was customary to anoint the heads of important guests, but this woman's anointing of Jesus is extraordinary. This perfume (undoubtedly imported from the East) was expensive, worth a year of a common laborer's wages, and had probably been kept in her family as an heirloom. Its fragrance was preserved by its sealing in alabaster (the favored container for perfume). Once the flask was broken, its contents could be used with their full freshness only once.

26:10-11. Jesus' reply probably contains an allusion to Deuteronomy 15:11, which urges generosity to the poor, who will always be in the land. He does not play down giving to the poor but plays up what follows: devotion to Jesus himself must precede and inform all other important and godly agendas.

26:12-13. In Jewish tradition, kings (including, by definition, the *Messiah, or "anointed one"), priests and others had to be anointed for service. But Jesus here stresses a different kind of anointing undoubtedly unintended by the woman: anointing a body for burial (see Mk 16:1).

26:14-16. Chief priests would be easily located, but they would not have been accessible to Judas had his mission been less in line with their plans. The average price of slaves varied from place to place and period to period, but Matthew's biblically informed readers would recognize thirty pieces of silver as the average Old Testament compensation for the death of a slave (Ex 21:32); Judas sells his master cheaply.

26:17-30 Betrayal and Death in the Passover

See comments on Mark 14:12-26 for further details.

26:17. By this period "the Feast of Unleavened Bread," which immediately followed Passover in the Bible, had been extended in popular parlance to include the Passover itself. Representatives from each family would "prepare the Passover" (i.e., have the priests slaughter a lamb for them in the temple), then return with it for the later meal. Others would prepare the other dishes.

26:18-19. Because the Passover had to be eaten within Jerusalem's walls, most homes included guests during the night of the feast.

26:20. The Passover was to be eaten at night. In April, at the time of the Passover, sundown in Jerusalem came by 6 p.m., so their meal could have started then. Table fellowship was intimate at the feast; one or two families normally shared the meal (a minimum of ten persons was required); here Jesus and his closest *disciples make up the family unit. The usual posture at meals was sitting, but reclining on couches (originally a Greek practice) was customary for feasts.

26:21-23. Bitter herbs were dipped into a mixture of nuts, fruit and vinegar to lessen their bitterness. That someone who was betraying a person would "dip in the bowl" with that person would have horrified ancient readers, who saw hospitality and the sharing of table fellowship as an intimate bond.

26:24-25. Those lamenting in Greek tragedies and in the Bible often mourned the day of their birth (Job 3; Jer 20:14-18). Such laments were rhetorical expressions of deep grief, but Jesus here uses the same language as a statement of fact. Other Jewish teachers also observed that it would have been better for a person never to have been born than to have denied the eternal God; it seems to have been a common statement of Jewish wisdom (*rabbis; 4 Ezra 7:69; *1 Enoch 38:2; 2 Enoch 41:2).

26:26. It was customary for the head of the household to give thanks for the bread and wine before any meal, but special blessings were said over bread and wine at the Passover meal. We should not understand "This is my body" literally, just as Jesus' contemporaries did not take literally the standard Jewish interpretation spoken over the Passover bread: "This is the bread of affliction our ancestors ate when they came from Egypt." (Taken literally, that bread would have been centuries old, and it had already been eaten anyway.) The lifting up and explanation of the unleavened bread took place after the first cup.

26:27. Four cups of red wine came to be used in the annual Passover celebrations, and if these were in use by the first century (as is likely), this cup may be the third or fourth. The leader of the group would take the goblet in both hands, then hold it in his right, a handbreadth above the table.

26:28. In the Old Testament, covenants were ratified by the blood of sacrifice; God had also redeemed his people from Egypt by the blood of the Passover lamb. "On behalf of the many" probably alludes to Isaiah 53 (see comment on Mt 20:28). Passover ritual interpreted the cup but did not interpret it as blood, because Jewish law and custom were revolted by the idea of drinking any creature's blood—especially human blood.

26:29. Vows of abstinence were common in Palestinian Judaism: "I will not eat any such and such until this happens," or "I vow that I will not use this until that happens." Jesus vows not to drink wine again until the *kingdom comes, and he apparently abstains from the fourth cup. Jewish tradition commonly portrayed the time of the kingdom as a banquet (based on texts like Is 25:6), when the Bible had promised an unending supply of wine (cf. Amos 9:13-14).

26:30. After the meal, it was customary to sing psalms antiphonally from the Hallel, which consisted of Psalms 113—118. The walk to the Mount of Olives took at least fifteen minutes.

26:31-46
The Other Betrayers

See comment on Mark 14:27-42.

26:31-32. On "stumbling" ("fall away"—NASB) see comment on 18:6. Zechariah 13:7 (the shepherd quotation) is not clearly *messianic (Zech 13:1-9 refers to striking false prophets in judgment, following Deut 13:1-11; cf. Zech 10:2; 11:3, 15-17), but the principle of sheep scattering from a smitten shepherd certainly applies equally well to the divine shepherd (Mt 25:32; cf. 18:12-14).

26:33-35. Ancient sources typically regarded the rooster as a reliable reporter of the advent of dawn, and night guards, shepherds and others who were awake at night were also familiar with other crowings, which, depending on the time of year, varied between 11:30 p.m. and 3:30 a.m. The point is that the denial was imminent.

26:36. They may have arrived at Gethsemane by 10 or 11 p.m. (which was well into the night in that culture). Gethsemane seems to have included an olive grove and probably an olive press (hence its name, which means "oil press"); it was on the western slope or base of the Mount of Olives, facing Jerusalem. Because Passover night had to be spent within the larger boundaries of Jerusalem, which did not include Bethany, they would not return to Bethany that night (21:17).

26:37-38. Jesus' description of his grief draws on *Old Testament language (Ps 42:5-6, 11; 43:5; Jon 4:9; cf. Ps 142:3-6; 143:3-4); compare Matthew 27:46.

26:39. The cup (20:22; cf. 27:48) may allude to the Old Testament image of a cup of judgment given to the nations; see comment on Mark 10:39. Jewish readers would regard applauding God's will even to one's own hurt as virtuous (e.g., 1 Macc 3:59-60; *rabbis; *Dead Sea Scrolls).

26:40. The *disciples were to "stand watch" like the porters, slaves in charge of the door, in the *parable in Mark 13:34-36. It was customary to stay awake late on the Passover night and to speak of God's redemption. They should have been able to stay awake to keep watch; they had probably stayed up late on most other Passovers of their lives. According to a Jewish teaching (which may, however, be later than this period), if anyone in the Passover group fell asleep (not merely dozed), the group was thereby dissolved.

26:41-46. "Temptation" here is "testing"; given the common Jewish religious uses of the word, Jesus is saying: "lest you fall prey to the testing you are about to face." The contrast between "spirit" and "body" simply means that one may mean well on impulse (26:33; cf. the use of "spirit" in many cases in Proverbs), but the body is susceptible to exhaustion. Romans appreciated loyalty to one's sense of duty; Judaism stressed faithfulness to God's law even to the point of dying for it. Thus all ancient readers would have recognized heroism in Jesus' intense faithfulness to his calling.

26:47-56
Completion of the Betrayal

See further comment on Mark 14:43-52.

26:47. Because they are sent by prominent men of Jerusalem, the band that comes to arrest Jesus is probably the temple guard. They come prepared for armed resistance from one they suppose is a *messianic revolutionary.

26:48-50. A kiss was a sign of special affection among family members and close friends, or of a *disciple's honor and affection for his teacher. Judas's kiss is thus a special act of hypocrisy (cf. Prov 27:6). Given ancient values concerning hospitality, friendship and covenant loyalty, any of Matthew's readers encountering this story for the first time would have been horrified by the narration of the betrayal. Judas appears as the most contemptible of traitors; Jesus appears as one unjustly betrayed.

26:51. Although this servant is probably not a Levite and thus unable to minister in the temple anyway, it is worthy of note that those who were missing appendages such as ears were barred from serving in the sanctuary.

26:52. These are not the words of a violent revolutionary (26:47). End-time schemes often included a great battle between the people of light and the people of darkness, and Jesus certainly expected violence (24:1-2); but his own followers were to stay clear of it. Matthew's readers might hear this possibly familiar saying (cf. the *Sentences* of the Syriac Menander 15-19) ironically: the temple authorities' wish to keep peace for the Romans (Mt 26:1-5) invited the sword of judgment at the hands of the Romans in A.D. 66-70.

26:53-54. Legions normally had six thousand soldiers, so Jesus is saying that he could summon around seventy-two thousand angels (a legion per disciple). A human force of this size could have easily crushed the whole temple guard and the Roman garrison in the fortress Antonia; such an angelic force could have easily defeated any human army raised against them. God's heavenly armies occasionally appear in the Old Testament, and they were invincible (e.g., 2 Kings 6:17; cf. 2 Kings 19:35).

26:55-56. Subversives (like the later assassins who slew Jewish aristocrats under cover of the crowds in the temple) did their acts secretly or in a way that would enable them to avoid capture; the Romans and their local agents were always concerned about such groups. Jesus' supposed subversion had been public and unconcealed.

26:57-68
Jesus' Trial

See comments on Mark 14:53-65.

26:57. The full *Sanhedrin normally met in their special meeting hall in the temple, the Chamber of Hewn Stone. In this case, many members of the Sanhedrin hold a secret night meeting without advance notice in the high priest's home, though they are investigating what they will claim is a capital offense. At least according to later *Pharisaic legal ideals, such a meeting was illegal on all these counts: capital trials had to meet during the day, and only after a day had intervened might the court render a verdict. Pharisaic laws forbade executions at feasts except for the most heinous crimes. But the priestly aristocracy would pay little attention to Pharisaic scruples, and they had to hurry before Jesus' popularity with the crowds forced his release or made him more of a hero.

26:58. Trespassing on the high priest's private property required much courage from a Galilean fisherman. The guards are presumably members of the temple guard, probably waiting to see the results of the trial inside. Regardless of whether they had all been assigned guard duty that night, they would have stayed up later than usual because it was Passover.

26:59-60. The virtuous Jewish tradition of diligent cross-examination of witnesses brings the false testimony into question. But once these witnesses had contradicted one another, they should have been declared false and the case against Jesus regarded as fabricated; under Jewish law, in a capital case, false witnesses were supposed to be put to death (see Deut 19:16-21; also the *Dead Sea Scrolls). Even though Rome had not given the *Sanhedrin jurisdiction to execute false witnesses, the Sanhedrin should have at least disciplined them; that the case just goes on demonstrates severe bias among the council members gathered there.

26:61. Many Jewish people expected that God would establish a new, purified temple when he put down the Romans. Outsiders had naturally misinterpreted Jesus' teaching about a new temple and warning about the old temple's destruction as the threat of a mad, *messianic revolutionary. But they still fail the cross-examination.

26:62. In the *Old Testament, a judge would normally stand to render the verdict. At least according to later *rabbinic law, the high priest could not legally force Jesus to convict himself out of his own mouth, but the priestly aristocracy would pay little attention to *Pharisaic regulations even if this rule were already widely held. The official finally asks whether Jesus thinks of himself as a *messiah—hence, to a high priest's mind, as a revolutionary.

26:63. The high priest tries to compel Jesus to speak by appealing to the divine name; thus the phrase "adjure" (KJV, NASB, RSV), "charge under oath" (NIV; cf. NRSV, TEV; cf. also 1 Sam 14:24; 1 Kings 22:16). False oaths in God's name were forbidden in the Old Testament as "taking his name in vain."

26:64. Jesus' statement here is a claim to be not only a mortal messiah but the cosmic ruler of Daniel 7:13-14, the embodiment of Israel's call, the one who would come in glory and reign forever; the phrase "from now on" is especially offensive, because he thereby claims this role in the present, which would imply that he is their judge rather than they being his judges. "Power" was one Jewish title for God.

26:65. One would tear one's clothes as a sign of mourning or *repentance; more to the point here, one who heard the sacred name blasphemed was required to do this. But the high priest must be desperate for a conviction; unless Jesus mentions the sacred Hebrew name of God, or summons them to idolatry (e.g., by calling himself God, which he does not do at this point) or in some other way insults God's dignity, he is not technically guilty of blasphemy. Jesus' association of himself with God could be considered offensive, but the high priest would first have to prove it untrue.

26:66. The high priest was not permitted to judge a case alone; he had to solicit the council's vote. (If later *rabbinic sources give any indication concerning how the *Sanhedrin may have functioned, the clerk may have called for each member's vote by name.) Although they cannot have believed that Jesus had committed blasphemy according to its technical legal definition (see comment on 9:3), they have an important reason to deal with him quickly: he clearly poses a threat to the temple establishment, and as a *messianic claimant he threatens their power and the nation's stability (cf. Jer 26:9, 11).

26:67-68. Unlike public flogging, the behavior represented here—spitting on, striking and taunting a prisoner—was, of course, against Jewish law.

26:69-75
Peter's Final Betrayal

See comment on Mark 14:66-72.

26:69-72. As a servant in an aristocratic household near the temple, this woman had no doubt been at the temple and could have gotten a good look at Jesus' *disciples in the temple courts. "I do not know what you say" is the standard form for denial in Jewish legal texts; calling a known person "the man" was sometimes used contemptuously.

26:73. Galilean accents differed from Judean accents; Galileans were careless with their vowels and failed to clearly differentiate the various guttural consonants. The high priest's servants and temple guard would have lived in Jerusalem and viewed themselves as Judeans. Some scholars have suggested that Judeans associated Galileans with revolutionaries, but the evidence for this suggestion is at best ambiguous; given the ancient mistrust between urban and rural dwellers, however, it is not unlikely that many Jerusalemites looked down on Galileans. But the point here is simply that the hearer assumes—rightly—that *disciples of a Galilean teacher were themselves Galileans.

26:74. The "curses" Peter utters are not vulgar words; rather, he swears by various things that he does not know Jesus (cf. 5:33-37), invoking curses on himself if he is lying. No one considered the uttering of such curses good religious behavior.

26:75. For most people in the ancient Mediterranean, rooster's crowing marked daybreak. Those who were awake much earlier may have recognized an earlier Palestinian rooster crowing between 12:30 and 2:30 a.m.

27:1-10
The Other Betrayer's Remorse

Peter's remorse (26:75) contrasts with that of Judas, who killed himself instead of *repenting (27:5).

27:1-2. The Jewish authorities have to bring Jesus to Pilate, because they were not authorized by the Romans to execute the death penalty themselves. Pilate would be available as early as sunrise; like other Roman officials, he would finish his regular public day before noon.

27:3-4. Some Jewish teachers held that even the recantation of a false witness for the prosecution could not reverse the verdict; the officials here seem less concerned with legal theory than with political expediency, however.

Those who dealt in bribes were accursed under the law (Deut 27:25), and a false witness was liable to the punishment appropriate for the alleged crime of the accused (Deut 19:18-19). Having innocent blood on one's hands meant that one was guilty of murder; in the *Old Testament, this guilt could be expiated only by the blood of the murderer or, if the murderer was unknown, through a sacrifice (Gen 4:10; 9:6; Num 35:33; Deut 21:1-9). God could, however, grant mercy to the *repentant (Gen 4:15; 2 Sam 12:13-14).

27:5. Judas's suicide is an act of despair (cf. Saul—1 Sam 31:4; the traitor Ahithophel—2 Sam 17:23). Greco-Roman tradition considered suicide a nobler way to die than letting others kill one. To some Jewish people it was likewise noble if it was performed to avoid falling into the hands of torturers or to avoid being defiled (e.g., in *Josephus and in *4 Maccabees, possibly under Greek influence). But Judaism, especially strict Palestinian Judaism, normally regarded it as evil. (Ancient readers would thus view Judas's act in a more negative light than they would view that of the jailer in Acts 16:27.)

According to ancient thought, if Judas had hanged himself in the sanctuary he would have defiled it (though he may have just "gone away" to locate a more convenient place). Flinging the money in the temple alludes to Zechariah 11:13 (see comment on Mt 27:9).

27:6. Ancient writers often used irony, and Matthew is no exception: the chief priests are more concerned about the legal technicality of blood money for the treasury than that they issued the money for a judicial murder or that Judas is about to kill himself (cf. 23:23-24). Although the *Old Testament did not explicitly prohibit the use of such money, they are careful to use it for something doubly unclean (burying strangers). Some commentators have suggested that the mention of the treasury could reflect a Hebrew pun on the word translated "potter" (27:7; by a slight change of Hebrew spelling one could read "potter" as "treasury"), but this suggestion is not certain.

27:7-8. Burying people who had no one else to bury them was an act of piety (cf. Tobit). Many Jews from around the world visited Jerusalem or moved there in their old age, and if they died without sufficient funds others would need to pay for their burial; the "strangers" might also include unclean *Gentiles. (There is also a Jewish tradition of burying condemned criminals in such a field.) Thus the high priests no doubt saw their behavior as pious!

27:9-10. Jewish scholars could cite some texts while simultaneously alluding to others. Matthew here quotes Zechariah 11:12-13, but by attributing it to Jeremiah he also alludes to a similar text that he wishes his more skillful readers to catch (Jer 32:6-10; cf. 19:1-4, 10-11). (The quotation is almost verbatim, and it is unlikely that Matthew would have known the text so well yet attributed it accidentally to the wrong author, unless he is using a list of standard *messianic proof texts instead of citing directly from Zechariah, or he is purposely "blending" texts, as I suggest here.) Zechariah 11:12-13 refers to the low valuation God's people had placed on him; they valued him at the price of a slave (Ex 21:32).

27:11-26
The Messiah or the Revolutionary

27:11-13. The charge presented to Pilate is clearly that Jesus claims to be a king, i.e., that he is a revolutionary acting for the overthrow of Rome.

27:14. Jewish martyr stories also report rulers' amazement at martyrs' refusal to compromise. Although most of these stories are fictitious, they reflect not only the genuine astonishment of *Gentiles unfamiliar with Jewish commitment to the details of their law but also the ancient ideal of bravery in standing against tyrants.

27:15-18. Customs like this release of a prisoner varied locally. Roman law recognized two kinds of amnesty: acquittal before the trial and pardon of the condemned; this is the latter. Pilate was not required by law to cooperate, but he had severely irritated the priestly aristocracy and Jerusalemites at the beginning of his tenure and may have wished to avoid further problems. (If the trial is as late as October of A.D. 31, Pilate's main political supporter in

Rome had just been executed, and he was on shaky ground politically; but the events of Mt 27 probably occurred before then.)

27:19. The "judgment seat" seems to have been outside the palace. By this period Roman governors were allowed to take their wives with them to the provinces. Further, although Roman matrons were ideally quiet, many stories praised aristocratic Roman women who privately influenced their husbands to some noble course of action. Dreams were respected in all Mediterranean cultures as sometimes being revelatory (see comment on 1:20; 2:12).

27:20-23. These events occur early in the morning (see 27:1-2), and much of the crowd may not be those whom Jesus had been teaching after arriving from Bethany each day. But ancient literature also reports how quickly the masses often changed allegiances (e.g., in *Tacitus; 1 Sam 11:12). The chief priests were well respected and more visible than Jesus, especially to foreign Jews visiting Jerusalem for the feast and unfamiliar with local politics. Barabbas would also appeal to those drawn to more militant responses to Roman oppression than Jesus provided.

27:24. Washing hands was a typically Jewish (but also sometimes *Gentile) way of declaring one's innocence (Deut 21:6; *Letter of Aristeas 306), but Pilate's words and action absolve his guilt no more than the exactly parallel words of the chief priests in Matthew 27:4, or those of others who acceded to subordinates' unjust demands for the cause of political expediency (e.g., Jer 38:5).

27:25. Once the responsibility for a murder or crime was attached to one person, another was free (cf. Gen 27:13; 2 Sam 3:28-29). Matthew probably relates this cry of the crowd to the *Pharisaic opponents of his community and to the judgment of A.D. 66-70 that crushed the next generation; but he would hardly have approved of the anti-Semitic use to which this verse was subsequently put (cf. 5:39, 43-44).

27:26. Crucifixion was prefaced by scourging, either on the way to the cross or before the victim began the trip to the cross. Tied to a post, the condemned person would be beaten with the *flagellum:* a leather whip with metal knotted into its thongs. This whipping bloodied the victim's back, leaving strips of flesh hanging from the wounds. By weakening the victim's constitution, it would mercifully shorten the time it would take the condemned person to die on the cross.

27:27-44
Executing the King of the Jews

Crucifixion was the most shameful and painful form of execution known in antiquity. Stripped naked—especially shameful for Palestinian Jews—the condemned would be hanged in the sight of the crowds, regarded as a criminal, unable to restrain the excretion of wastes in public and subjected to excruciating torture. Sometimes the victim would be tied to the cross with ropes; in other cases, as with Jesus, he would be nailed to the cross. His hands would not be free to swat away insects attracted to his bloodied back or other wounds. The victim's own weight would pull his body into a position that eventually prohibited breathing. A footstand on the cross allowed him some support, but sooner or later his strength would give out, and (usually after several days) he would die from suffocation.

27:27. The Praetorium in this period was Herod the Great's old palace, where the Roman prefect stayed when he visited Jerusalem. A cohort of six hundred men was normally stationed in Jerusalem (at the fortress Antonia on the Temple Mount), reinforced by troops who accompanied Pilate to the feast in case they were necessary for riot control.

27:28. Nakedness was especially embarrassing to a Jewish person in antiquity. Red robes would be those most readily available, because soldiers wore them; this garment could resemble the purple robe of the pre-Roman Greek rulers of the East. Roman soldiers often played games to pass time: they carved on the stone pavement of the fortress Antonia, where they were garrisoned on the Temple Mount, and knucklebones used as dice have also been recovered there.

27:29. The soldiers' kneeling before Jesus parodies royal homage in the Greek East. The reed is meant to parody a scepter; military floggings often used bamboo canes, so one may have been on hand among the soldiers. "King of the Jews" is an ironic taunt but may also reflect some typical Roman anti-Judaism. "Hail!" was the standard salute to the Roman emperor.

27:30. Spitting on a person was one of the most grievous insults short of violence; Jewish people considered the spittle of non-Jews particularly unclean. The soldiers' spitting on Jesus might parody the kiss of homage expected by rulers of the Greek East.

27:31. Those being crucified by the Romans were stripped naked; Jewish law on stoning stripped a man of all but a loincloth.

27:32. Cyrene, a large city in what is now Libya in North Africa, had a large Jewish community that no doubt included local converts; "Simon" is a Jewish name. Like multitudes of foreign Jews, he had come to Jerusalem for the feast. Roman soldiers could impress any person into service to carry things for them. The condemned person himself normally had to carry the horizontal beam (Latin *patibulum)* of the cross out to the site where the upright stake (Latin *palus)* awaited; but Jesus' back had been too severely scourged for him to do this (see comment on 27:26).

27:33-34. The women of Jerusalem had prepared a painkilling potion of drugged wine for condemned men to drink; Jesus refuses it (cf. 26:29). The myrrh-mixed wine of Mark 15:23, a delicacy and external pain reliever, becomes wine mixed with gall in Matthew; compare Ps 69:21 and the similarity between the *Aramaic word for "myrrh" and the Hebrew word for "gall."

27:35-36. Roman law permitted the execution squad any minor possessions the executed person carried (cf. also Ps 22:18). The custom of casting lots, common in both the *Old Testament and Greek culture, was a common ancient way to make decisions of this nature.

27:37. The condemned person sometimes carried the charge (Latin *titulus)* to the site of execution.

27:38. The word for "robbers" here is the standard term in *Josephus for revolutionaries; presumably they had been colleagues of Barabbas.

27:39. The Gospel writers purposely describe the ridicule in the language of the righteous sufferer of Psalm 22:7.

27:40. Those who pass by repeat *Satan's taunt of Matthew 4:3, 7, still emphasizing their expectation of a political *messiah.

27:41-42. Compare 4:3, 6.

27:43-44. The language of the religious authorities exactly parallels Psalm 22:8; the righteous sufferer himself quotes this psalm in Matthew 27:46 (Ps 22:1).

27:45-56
The King's Death

27:45. The "sixth hour" begins by noon, the "ninth hour" by 3 p.m.; crucifixions rarely ended so quickly. The latter time, when Jesus dies, was close to the time of the evening offering in the temple. Darkness was one of the plagues in Egypt and occurs in the prophets as a judgment for the end time; both Jews and pagans considered eclipses and other darkenings of the sky bad omens.

27:46. Here Jesus quotes Psalm 22:1, which may have been part of the Scripture recitation at this time of day. His opponents do not pause to consider that the psalm ends with the sufferer's vindication and triumph (Ps 22:25-31). Whereas Mark's quotation is in *Aramaic, Matthew's is mainly in Hebrew.

27:47. Because Elijah was thought never to have died, some *rabbis felt that he was sent on errands like the angels, often to deliver pious rabbis from trouble.

27:48. This offer of a wine-soaked sponge may have been an act of mercy, because the wine could act as a painkiller. Perhaps the man thinks Jesus is delirious from pain. But sour wine was usually a remedy for thirst, and it may have been an attempt to revive him to perpetuate his suffering.

27:49. See comment on 27:47.

27:50. "Giving up one's spirit" is used elsewhere to refer to death.

27:51-53. Stories were told of catastrophes occurring at the deaths of pious *rabbis, especially those whose intercession had been vital to the world; on rare occasions, Greek writers also applied such stories to the deaths of prominent philosophers. These events would have communicated Jesus' importance quite well to ancient observers and readers.

27:51. The veil (or curtain—NIV) is probably the one between the holy of holies—inhabited only by God—and the sanctuary where the priests ministered (Ex 26:33). Matthew may intend this tearing of the veil to recall the rending of clothes at the hearing of blasphemy (Mt 26:65). Although the point of the veil's rending may be that by the cross God provides access for all people into his presence, it is more likely that it indicates instead the departure of God from the temple (as in Ezek 10—11). *Apocalypses sometimes mentioned a major earthquake shortly before the coming of the *kingdom.

27:52-53. Although these raisings of the dead saints, like those in the Old Testament, do not mean that they will not die again, they prefigure Judaism's anticipated final *resurrection, when the dead will be raised never to die again. Archaeological evidence indicates that in popular (not official) Judaism, the tombs of saints were venerated.

27:54. Here a pagan—one of the executioners—is the first person after Jesus' death to recognize, to some extent, his identity, although he may mean "*Son of God" quite differently than Jewish people and Christians (including Matthew) would have (cf. Dan 3:25, 29): a semidivine hero, son of a deity, rather than *Messiah.

27:55-56. Family and friends would usually be present at an execution; only the male *disciples would have been in danger as suspected allies of a revolutionary. Women often (though much less than men) performed the office of *patron, or benefactor, supporting religious or other groups. But in ancient Jewish Palestine, for these women to accompany Jesus' disciples could have been scandalous.

27:57-61
Jesus' Burial

27:57-58. Arimathea was only about

twenty miles from Jerusalem. Joseph is said to have been wealthy; he must have been prominent to have secured an audience with Pilate after his official public hours. When buried, crucifixion victims were normally thrown into common graves; they did not receive an honorable burial in their family tomb. Exceptions were often made when relatives asked for the body, but in the case of treason (as claiming to be the Jewish king would be) an exception would not be made unless the deceased had a prominent advocate. Jesus had a posthumous ally in this man of influence, who was not ashamed to go on record as his follower.

"Evening" need not mean sundown and therefore that the sabbath had begun, but there is no reason to think that the sabbath had not begun. In this hot climate under Jewish law the preliminary disposal of the body (including its washing, also practiced by other peoples) took precedence over celebration of the sabbath, even if the rest of the treatment of the body had to wait. Burying the dead was an important duty of the pious in Judaism. Public mourning was important for all the dead but was illegal for anyone who had been executed.

27:59-60. Being wrapped in a fine linen shroud would mark an honorable burial. To bury someone in one's own family tomb was a special act of reverence and affection (cf. 1 Kings 13:30-31; Is 53:12). (Cemeteries and burial plots in this period nearly always belonged to families.) In the first century, the body would normally be left to rot in the tomb's antechamber for the first year; at the end of the year, the bones would be gathered into a box, which would slide into a slot on the wall. This practice probably related to the standard Jewish hope in the *resurrection of the body at the end of the age. The stone rolled in front of the tomb was a carved, disk-shaped stone probably about three feet in diameter, rolled into place in a groove and moved back from the entrance only with great effort.

27:61. Women generally took part in preparing bodies for burial in the ancient world. The oldest tradition for the site of Jesus' grave (the Roman Catholic location of the Holy Sepulcher) is a clearly first-century tomb located inside the walls of Jerusalem since the forties of the first century, even though the *New Testament and Jewish law required that the crucifixion happen outside the city walls. But King Agrippa I expanded the city walls in the forties; at the time of Jesus' crucifixion, that area was still outside the walls. Thus the tradition of the approximate site of Jesus' burial and *resurrection goes back to within ten years of the event. (The traditional Protestant site contains tombs from a much later period and has no evidence to commend it.)

27:62-66. Making Sure He Stayed Buried

The priestly aristocracy, ever politically astute, takes no chances, and despite the sabbath and festival they obtain an audience with Pilate to secure the tomb. It is unclear whether Pilate here provides them with Roman guards or tells them where the tomb is and permits them to post some of their temple guard; the guards' fear of Pilate's reprisals (28:14) indicates that they are probably Roman guards whom Pilate has put at the chief priests' (28:11) disposal. The seal on the stone would make any tampering obvious. That the Jerusalem authorities would have acted thus on the sabbath indicates their special interest in the case as well as the selectiveness of their piety.

28:1-10 The First Witnesses of the Risen Jesus

That women are chosen as the first witnesses is highly significant; the surrounding culture considered their witness worthless. It fits Jesus' countercultural and counterstatus ministry and certainly runs counter to what outsiders would have valued or anything the later *church would have chosen to invent.

28:1. Sabbath ended at sundown on Saturday evening; the women are on their way to the tomb by 6 a.m., as soon as there is enough light for them to see. Jewish mourners as well as pagans were often known to visit tombs within the three days after the burial, to ensure that their relative was dead; given the nature of crucifixion, however, such a precaution would be unnecessary here, and the concerns may be only sentimental.

28:2-4. Angels, especially visibly fiery ones (ancient Judaism typically believed angels were made of fire), generally terrified people (e.g., Judg 6:22-23; 13:19-20; cf. 4 Ezra 10:25-27; *3 Enoch 22:4-9).

28:5-8. Jerusalem was the religious center of Judaism; many Judeans still looked on Galilee as a place of former non-Jews (4:15). Yet Galilee was where some of Jesus' revelations to his *disciples would take place; all four Gospels report that Jesus was better received there.

28:9-10. The witness of women was considered unreliable in that culture, yet Jesus goes against the culture by revealing himself to the women and telling them to bear his message to the other *disciples. This detail is definitely not one that ancient Christians would have invented, because it did not appeal to their culture.

28:11-15 The Final Subversion

Guards faced serious consequences for falling asleep on the job (indeed, Roman guards could be executed), including jobs guarding the corpses of crucifixion victims (see the first-century Roman writer Petronius *Satyricon* 112). But the priestly aristocracy had enough influence to protect their own interests. Like Judas (26:15), the guards act partly on mercenary motives. They should have seen enough to know better than to go along with the religious authorities' plan, but the bribe and the potential penalty they face for allowing Jesus' body to disappear ensures their cooperation. (The officials' promise to protect the guards from Pilate may involve more bribery; Pilate was known to be susceptible to this form of persuasion.) Matthew would be unlikely to report a charge against the *resurrection that had not actually been made (28:15), and his report indicates that the Jerusalem authorities had sought to explain the empty tomb—but had never tried to deny it.

28:16-20 Jesus' Final Orders

28:16. God had often revealed himself on mountains in biblical tradition, especially in the narratives about Moses.

28:17. Some who see Jesus' appearance are doubtful, perhaps because it does not fit current expectations of the end time: all the dead were to be raised together, not the *Messiah first.

28:18. Here Jesus alludes to Daniel 7:13-14.

28:19-20. "Making *disciples" was the sort of thing *rabbis would do, but Jesus' followers are to make disciples for Jesus, not for themselves. Disciples are made here in a twofold way: (1) By *baptizing them. Because baptism was an act of conversion (used for *Gentiles converting to Judaism), it means initiating people to the faith. (2) By teaching them Jesus' commandments recorded in Matthew. Rabbis made disciples by teaching them. Many Jews outside Palestine sought converts among the "nations" (which can also be translated as "Gentiles" or "pagans"). But only a few converts ever studied under rabbis, so the idea of making Gentiles full disciples—followers of Jesus who would learn from and serve him—goes beyond this Jewish tradition. Isaiah predicted that Israel would be a witness to (or against) the nations in the end time (e.g., 42:6; 43:10; 44:8).

Jewish literature only called God omnipresent; Jesus' claim that he would always be with them, coupled with his being named alongside the Father in *baptism (Jewish people did not baptize in the names of people), constitutes a proclamation of his deity.

Mark

Introduction

Authorship. Early church tradition attributes this Gospel to John Mark (Acts 15:37; Col 4:10; 1 Pet 5:13), who was said to have derived his information from Peter. Further, the titles of the Gospels, which attribute them to particular authors, circulated throughout the Roman world from an early period; though the titles are not inspired, their wide circulation indicates that the tradition is early. Because there is no evidence against this attribution, Mark is the most likely candidate for the author.

Date, Setting and Purpose. The most common suggestion is that Mark wrote his Gospel to Roman Christians during the time of the great persecution in Rome, about A.D. 64 (for more discussion see 1 Peter).

Place of Writing. Various proposals for Mark's provenance have been offered: Galilee, Alexandria and, most often, Rome. Mark's audience probably lived outside Palestine and most of them were non-Jewish; Rome is the most likely of these proposals (favored by some early Christian traditions), though it is not certain.

Genre. See the introduction to the Gospels in this commentary.

Why Mark Wrote. Those who heard Mark read in the churches already knew many of the stories about Jesus, whom they worshiped as Lord. Mark connects these stories into a sort of biography of Jesus, following some of the plot movements familiar from Greek tragedy, except with a happy ending, like traditional Jewish stories that emphasized the faithfulness of God. Ancient biographies often made particular moral points through the example of their heroes, and Mark is no exception: he wants his fellow Christians to understand that Christ's call involves both power and suffering in their conflict with *Satan's forces.

Thus Mark wrote to a community that needed to be reminded that God heard prayers and would work through their witness and faith; they also needed to be reminded that this might cost them their lives in persecution. Finally, they could be reminded through the failure of the *disciples in Mark that if they had not yet achieved the radical lifestyle their Lord's words demanded, he would still work with them patiently to help them get to that level of commitment. The most likely situation in the early church proposed for Mark's writing here is the suffering of Roman Christians under Nero starting in A.D. 64.

Mark's Message. Some themes are especially prominent in Mark. One such theme is the so-called messianic secret: Jesus conceals his messianic identity, insofar as possible, from the public. This secrecy may be due to several factors. First, the Christ, or *Messiah, was the Davidic king and officially took this title only at his enthronement. Thus in Mark Jesus is finally "coronated" on the cross. Second—and this is probably more important—Jesus' mission was completely different from any of the political views about messiahs circulating at the time; "messiahship" was thus an inadequate category for him until he could define it by the character of his mission. His mission could be understood only retrospectively, in the light of his death and *resurrection (9:9). One might further compare Jesus' attempts to secure privacy when possible with some prominent *Old Testament prophets. Such prophets often worked clandestinely, not seeking their own glory but only to accomplish their mission (e.g., 1 Kings 11:29; 13:8-9; 21:18; 2 Kings 9:1-10); more of their time may have been spent in the humble lifestyle circles of their own disciples whom they were training (1 Sam 19:20; 2 Kings 4:38; 6:1-3).

A related theme in Mark is the failure of the disciples. Ancient writings would often play down the sensibility of secondary characters to make them foils for the main hero; characters' blindness also was used to heighten tragic elements. In Mark, the disciples are obtuse with regard to Jesus' and their own mission, both the charismatic part (miracle working—4:40; 9:18-19, 28-29) and, more significantly, the suffering part. The *narrative example of their denseness contrasts so forcefully with Jesus' repeated calls to total commitment that they almost serve the literary function of comic relief in the narrative. This theme is so pervasive that the gospel apparently ends on this note (16:7-8).

Commentaries. The most useful to the readers of this commentary will be William L. Lane, *The Gospel According to Mark,* NICNT (Grand Rapids: Eerdmans, 1974); the commentaries by D. E. Nineham, *Saint Mark,* Pelican New Testament Commentaries (Philadelphia: Westminster/London: SCM, 1977), and especially Hugh Anderson, *The Gospel of Mark,* NCB (1976; reprint, Grand Rapids: Eerdmans, 1981), also contain useful cultural information.

1:1-15
Introduction of the One Who Brings the Spirit

Ancient writers often mentioned the main themes of their works in their introductions. The opening of the Gospel of Mark introduces Mark's presentation of Jesus as the proclaimer and bringer of God's *kingdom. In this passage Jesus, endowed with the *Spirit, enters into conflict with *Satan and defeats him; in the rest of the Gospel Jesus drives out demons and heals the sick, is opposed by Satan's religious and political agents, and ultimately overcomes Satan's opposition by the *resurrection. This passage promises that Jesus endows his followers with this same Spirit for the same conflict they must face in proclaiming God's kingdom.

1:1. The Greek term translated "*gospel" refers to the good news a herald would bring, and the Greek translation of Isaiah used the related verb to refer to the good news that God was restoring his people and bringing the *kingdom of God. (Because Jewish readers often named books for their first word or words, some scholars suggest that "the good news of Jesus Christ" is the title of Mark's Gospel; but these words are also simply a natural way to start off a book like this one.)

1:2-3. Jewish teachers often combined several texts or parts of texts, especially if they had a key word or words in common (here, "prepare the way"). Because they were so learned in the Scriptures, they did not have to say which texts they were quoting and often assumed the context without quoting it. Thus Mark cites both Isaiah (40:3) and Malachi (3:1) here, although he mentions only Isaiah. Isaiah refers to preparing the way for God, who is coming to restore his people; Malachi refers to God coming in judgment to set matters straight among his people. Mark applies these texts about God to Jesus.

1:4-5. Like many other ancient peoples, Jewish people practiced ceremonial washings. Their only once-for-all ceremonial washing, however, was the immersion that non-Jews had to go through when they converted to Judaism. Non-Jews who were converting to Judaism would immerse themselves in water, probably under the supervision of a religious expert. John's *baptizing activity fits this model.

Jewish people also practiced "*repentance" when they did something wrong, asking God's forgiveness and determining to change. (The *Old Testament prophets often used this Hebrew idea of "turning" from sin; it involves more than just a "change of mind," which is the literal sense of the Greek term used here.) But the ultimate example of repenting, or turning from a wrong way of living to a right way of living, was when a non-Jew decided to obey the teachings of Israel's God.

To tell Jewish people that they had to be baptized or repent the same way non-Jews did would have been offensive, because it challenged the prevalent Jewish belief about salvation. Most Jewish people thought that if they were born into a Jewish family and did not reject God's law, they would be saved; John told them instead that they had to come to God the same way that non-Jews did. The point of John's baptism is that everyone has to come to God on the same terms.

The Jordan River was the most natural place for John to have the people immerse themselves, but this location may have also evoked Israel's history of salvation (Josh 3—4). John's coming in the "wilderness" could evoke Israel's history, too, especially because Isaiah 40:3 predicted the herald of a new exodus there, and many Jewish people expected the *Messiah to come as a new Moses there.

1:6. Some other poor people in John's day dressed the way he did and ate locusts and honey (the *Dead Sea Scrolls even give directions concerning the eating of locusts). But what is most important here is that the Old Testament emphasizes that Elijah dressed this way and, like John, did not depend on society for his sustenance (cf. 1 Kings 17:4, 9). Elijah was expected to return before the end (Mal 3:1; 4:5-6).

Many Jewish people believed that there had been no true prophets since Malachi and that prophets would not be restored till near the time of the end. But Mark wants us to understand that John is definitely a prophet.

1:7. *Disciples often served their teachers in the same ways that slaves would serve their masters, except for the most menial chores like taking off their masters' sandals. John feels unworthy even to be the *Messiah's slave.

1:8. Some passages in the Old Testament speak of the *Spirit being poured out like water. These passages refer especially to the time of God's *kingdom, when he would cleanse his people and endow them with power to speak for him (Is 44:3; Ezek 36:25-27; Joel 2:28-29). Jewish tradition in Jesus' day still stressed that the Spirit would cleanse and provide prophetic anointing in the end time.

1:9-10. The tearing of the heavens may also indicate that the *kingdom is near (Is 64:1; 65:17). Although ancient writers used the dove symbolically in many diverse ways, it may here allude back to God's promise of a new world (Gen 8:10-12).

1:11. Jewish teachers who believed that God no longer spoke through prophets believed that he now spoke to them by means of a voice from heaven *(bat kol),* although this was not considered as important as *prophecy. Here Mark shows that both a voice from heaven *and* John's prophecy testify to Jesus.

In Jewish stories the voice from heaven occasionally quoted Scripture, and most scholars think that the voice here refers to two or three Scriptures: Psalm 2:7, about the royal *Messiah, the *Son of God; Isaiah 42:1, about the suffering servant; and Genesis 22:2, about Abraham sacrificing his beloved son. The wording of Mark's text is closest to Psalm 2:7 and Genesis 22:2.

1:12-13. It was commonly believed that demons were especially attracted to places like bathhouses, graveyards and deserts. Readers would thus sense the suspense as Jesus battled with *Satan on Satan's own turf. Safety among beasts signified God's protection (Ezek 34:25; Dan 6:22).

1:14-15. The summary of Jesus' message may also be the summary of Mark's *Gospel, or good news (1:1): people should turn their lives over to God (on *repentance, see comment on 1:4-5) if they believe the good news that God is getting ready to fulfill all his promises to his people.

The Jewish people recognized that God ruled the universe in one sense now, but they prayed daily for the day when his *kingdom, or rule, would be established over all peoples of the earth. Then, they believed, everyone would submit to God. Because the Gospels affirm that Jesus must come twice, they recognize that the kingdom comes in two stages: God's future rule is established in the lives of those who obey him in the present, and over all the world when Jesus returns. John, however, was not yet in a position to make this distinction.

1:16-20 Downward Mobility and Jesus' Call

Ancient writers often liked to illustrate their teachings with examples, and Mark is no exception. After telling how Jesus summoned people to turn their lives over to God, he reports a particular example illustrating how some followers of Jesus did so.

A few people in Jewish Palestine were rich; most were relatively poor. Some, like fishermen, tended to fall between the rich and the poor (distinctions were less clearly drawn in Galilee than in much of the empire). James and John were clearly not poor—they had "hired servants" (v. 20), as only well-off people did (although the term could mean rented slaves, it most likely means free hired workers). Peter and Andrew were probably in business with James and John (Lk 5:7-10); we know of other fishing partnerships at that time. This text indicates that none of these *disciples left their business behind because it was going badly; they left behind well-paying jobs.

Many Jewish teachers in Jesus' day felt that the greatest commandment was to honor one's parents. To abruptly leave behind one's family and the family business was a great sacrifice that went against everything the culture taught.

*Disciples usually sought out their own teachers. Because discipleship often involved temporarily laying aside one's livelihood and being apart from one's wife and children, the decision to choose a teacher would have normally been made only after much deliberation, especially when the teacher traveled from place to place instead of staying in one town to teach.

1:21-28 Authority over Demons

The account of the fishermen demonstrates the claims Jesus' authority makes on his followers' lives, but the verses that follow it demonstrate his authority over evil spirits (cf. 1:12-13). The only recorded exorcist in the *Old Testament was David (1 Sam 16:23). Although wandering demons appear frequently in Jewish literature, the only demons that appear in the Gospels (except *Satan—Mk 1:13) are in people they possess (or, as a second choice, in pigs—5:12). The place that Jesus encounters his first demon may shock Mark's readers: it is in a religious institution.

1:21. Most *synagogues were community centers and places of prayer and study. When visiting teachers were present, synagogue leaders would invite them to lecture, especially on the sabbath. Archaeologists have found the site of Capernaum's synagogue, which was built from basalt blocks. Although later synagogues were more ornate, most people in this first-century Galilean synagogue probably sat on mats on the floor.

1:22. Synagogue services were conducted by priests or by what we would call "lay leaders," but those most skilled in the Scriptures undoubtedly contributed their share when the Old Testament was to be expounded. Many local teachers were village *scribes who also wrote down and interpreted legal documents for their village; some of them taught children the Bible. Most teachers would try to expound the *law (normally from their Scripture reading) by explaining the proper way to translate and apply it or by appealing to their traditions. Jesus' teaching went quite a bit further than this kind of exposition.

1:23-24. Demons (also sometimes called "unclean spirits," e.g., *Jubilees

10:1) were often associated with magic, and magicians tried to subdue other spiritual forces by invoking their names. If the demon here is trying to subdue Jesus in this way ("I know who you are" was used to subdue spiritual powers in magical texts), as some scholars have suggested, this ploy does not work. Ancients often recognized that demons had access to supernatural knowledge; it is not surprising that these demons perceive Jesus' true identity, which the people there still do not recognize. "Holy One" was normally a title of God, but "Holy One of God" here probably means something like "God's right-hand agent"; in Jewish literature, demons recognized their inability to harm those who walked close to God.

1:25-27. Demons were rebuked and subdued with orders like "Be silent" (*Testament of Solomon); rebukes in the *New Testament and other ancient literature never involved a *formal* statement like "I rebuke you." Exiting demons usually caused a commotion to make clear that they were leaving, regardless of the person who was casting them out.

Although exorcists—people who tried to chase demons out of other people—also occasionally used phrases like "Come out of so-and-so!" they used the phrases as parts of elaborate magical incantations. They had two main methods of expelling demons: (1) revolting or scaring the demon out (e.g., by putting a smelly root up the possessed person's nose in the hope that the demon would not be able to stand it); (2) invoking the name of a higher spirit to get rid of the lower one. The people are thus amazed that Jesus can be effective by simply ordering the demons to leave. Jewish tradition praised teachers who could draw special insights from the law and sometimes attributed miracle-working powers to popular teachers; but Jesus seems to earn a category by himself ("new teaching").

1:28. Galilee's villages were close together, and close connections among them would allow word to spread rapidly.

1:29-34
The Healer's Popularity

1:29-31. A newly married couple normally lived with the husband's family until they made enough money to move out on their own. Many parents died while their children were young adults, so it is possible that Simon and Andrew took over their parents' home. Simon's father-in-law had probably passed away, and Simon and his wife had taken her widowed mother into their home. Caring for one's extended family was more common then than it is today.

1:32-34. The sabbath ended Saturday at sundown. Mark mentions that it was "after sunset" to let us know that the sabbath is over, because it would have violated the sabbath for anyone to have carried someone on the sabbath. The whole town gathers "at the door" because most homes around Capernaum had only one room, and even a larger home could not have accommodated many people. The doorway may have opened to the street or to a courtyard shared with other homes, as often in Galilean towns. Teachers reputed to work miracles rapidly drew large crowds.

1:35-39
Prayer Alone

1:35-37. This crowdedness also leads to another problem: it would be nearly impossible to find a place to be alone in such ancient towns, with their narrow streets and sometimes ten or twenty people living in the common one-room houses; most town blocks consisted of four homes all facing a common courtyard. Galilee was also heavily populated, and villages were commonly close together. But one could find a place alone in the hills outside one's village if one arose early enough. People got up for work as soon as the sun rose, so Jesus has to get up well before dawn to go out and find a solitary place for prayer.

1:38-39. The word used for the other "towns" suggests large agricultural towns still governed according to regular village structures; these were apparently places that had not yet heard of Jesus. He probably could have drawn the largest crowds in the *synagogues on market days and sabbaths, and in late afternoons or early evenings when laborers had finished their day's work.

1:40-45
Cleansing a Leper

Leprosy was an unattractive skin disease for which the Bible had prescribed quarantine from the rest of society (Lev 13:45-46), although the Bible did not go as far as many Jewish teachers who blamed the disease on the leper's sin (often the sin of slander). Lepers were thus outcasts from the rest of society, the kind of people most healthy people preferred to ignore. Touching a leper was forbidden, and most people would have been revolted by the thought of it.

The leper approaches Jesus with humility, which was the proper *Old Testament way to approach God for prayer, although the fact that he even approaches Jesus also indicates a measure of holy boldness. Acknowledging that God had the right to refuse the prayer and that one depended on his mercy was not in any way a lack of faith (Gen 18:27, 30-32; 2 Sam 10:12; Dan 3:18).

The law had prescribed particular sacrifices if someone's leprosy were cured (Lev 14:1-32). By complying with these regulations, Jesus does nothing to violate the law or to offend the priests. (Later Jewish laws also insisted that the leper be checked by a local priest before going to the temple, but it is not clear whether these prescriptions were in effect in Jesus' day.)

Teachers thought to perform miracles usually had large followings, because many people were sick; the number of people suffering from various afflictions is attested by how many people flocked to hot springs in Galilee that were thought to relieve ailments. Jesus, who performs miracles without the common pagan use of magical incantations, acquires such a large following that for a period of time he cannot accommodate them inside a town (v. 45).

2:1-12
Healed and Forgiven

Just as Jesus violates his culture's religious sensibilities by touching a leper (1:41) and claims more authority than a normal *rabbi would dare accept (cf. 1:17, 27), and just as Mark's *narrative challenges cultural religion by beginning with a demoniac in a house of study and prayer (1:21-28), Jesus' role in this passage challenges the theological categories of his culture's religious establishment.

2:1-2. The capacity of the average Capernaum home may have allowed only about fifty persons standing close together (the longest span in excavated homes is eighteen feet). We thus should not think of literally the whole town inside or just outside the door.

2:3-4. Many "beds" were mats; thus the paralytics' friends may have carried him on the bed on which he lay all the time. The roof was approached by an outside staircase, so they could reach it unimpeded. The roof of single-story homes was sturdy enough for walking but was normally made of branches and rushes laid over the roof's beams and covered with dried mud; thus one could dig through it.

2:5-7. Sins were to be atoned for by offerings in the temple. Judaism taught that only God could forgive sins, but most Jews allowed that some of God's representatives could speak on God's behalf. The passive form, "are forgiven," could be interpreted in this way (Jewish teachers often used the passive form to describe God's activity); but Jesus was not a priest, no one had offered sacrifice, and the *scribes had heard no basis for the pronouncement of forgiveness, not even clear indication of *repentance.

The *Old Testament penalty for blaspheming God's name—reproaching rather than honoring it—was death (Lev 24:10-23). According to subsequent Jewish teaching, blasphemy involved pronouncing the divine name or inviting people to follow other gods. Strictly speaking, therefore, these legal scholars would have been mistaken in interpreting Jesus' words as blasphemy, even by their own rules. But the term was used much more broadly in popular parlance in this period, and they may apply it in the general sense of dishonoring the divine name.

2:8. Because supernatural knowledge was especially attributed to prophets (e.g., 2 Kings 6:12), Jesus' hearers would probably view him here as a prophet; "speaking in one's heart" may be idiomatic (Deut 15:9; 18:21; 30:14). Most Jewish teachers believed that "prophets" in the Old Testament sense had ceased, but most of the people were happy to entertain new prophetic figures, many of whom they saw as harbingers of the end.

2:9-12. Some Jewish teachers accepted miracles as verification that a teacher was truly God's representative; others did not regard miracles as sufficient proof if they disagreed with the teacher's interpretation of Scripture.

Jewish teachers knew that only God could ultimately forgive (on the Day of Atonement in response to sacrifice); but they also recognized that healing ultimately came from God. Both were from God but could be announced through God's agents acting according to his will. *Josephus shows us that many false prophets in Jesus' day claimed to work miracles but actually failed to work them; some of Jesus' critics may have placed him in this category. His act in front of these witnesses, however, should have challenged them to rethink their case.

2:13-17
A Tax Gatherer Follows

As in 2:1-12, Jesus' behavior here runs counter to standards of piety among his Jewish contemporaries.

2:13. Most prominent local teachers taught regular groups of *disciples and also performed other local services in their town. Translocal teachers who had large followings, however, could threaten the establishment as potential revolutionaries.

2:14. Levi may have been a general *tax farmer working for Herod Antipas; situated at an office in Capernaum, however, he was more likely a customs agent, charging import duties on wares brought through this town on important nearby trade routes. Even more than the fishermen, he has a secure and prosperous job, which he abandons to follow Jesus' call.

Some taxes went directly to the Roman government, but tolls and customs taxes (usually levied at 2-3 percent, but multiplied for traders who passed through many territories) supported the cities where they were taken. Even if Levi is a locally valuable customs agent, however, this *narrative shows that he is still regarded as unwholesome; the municipal aristocracy supported Roman interests against those of the Jewish poor.

2:15. *Tax gatherers were regarded as collaborators with the Romans and despised by religious people. Some commentators have argued that "sinners" may refer specifically to those who did not eat food in ritual purity, but the term probably refers to anyone who lived sinfully rather than religiously, as if they did not care what the religious community thought of them.

2:16. Table fellowship indicated intimate relations among those who shared it. The *Pharisees were particularly scrupulous about their special rules on eating and did not like to eat with less scrupulous people, especially people like tax gatherers and sinners. Here they assume that Jesus, being a wise teacher, ought to share their religious convictions.

2:17. Jesus' reply plays on a common image of the day (comparing physicians and teachers) to make his point.

2:18-22
The Right Time to Fast

Again (see 2:13-17) Jesus does not appear religious enough for the traditionalists; but he has a new kind of religious lifestyle in mind.

2:18. The Law required fasting only on the Day of Atonement, but many other fasts had been added by religious Jews, especially by groups like the *Pharisees (many of whom may have fasted without water twice a week, especially in the dry season). Fasting was an important practice to join with prayer or penitence, so it would have been unusual for *disciples (prospective *rabbis) to have avoided it altogether. A teacher was regarded as responsible for the behavior of his disciples.

2:19-20. Wedding feasts required seven days of festivity; one was not permitted to fast or engage in other acts of mourning or difficult labor during a wedding feast. Here Jesus makes an analogy about the similar inappropriateness of fasting in his own time.

2:21-22. Again the issue is the inappropriateness of fasting in the present circumstance. Jesus uses two ordinary facts to make his point. Older clothes had already shrunk somewhat from washing. Wine could be kept in either jars or wineskins; the latter would stretch. Old wineskins had already been stretched to capacity by fermenting wine within them; if they were then filled with unfermented wine, it would also expand, and the old wineskins, already stretched to the limit, would break.

2:23-27
The Right Use of the Sabbath

Jesus' conflicts with the religious establishment in the preceding passages come to a head over details of sabbath observance (2:23—3:6). Their religious priorities differ; whereas the religious establishment may think that Jesus questions the Bible's authority, he demands instead a different way to understand it and so apply it.

2:23-24. Because not many *Pharisees lived in Galilee and they would normally not be in a grainfield on the sabbath—unless they were following Jesus around—it is possible that local religious teachers are responding to reports about what Jesus' *disciples had done, and that Mark applies the more specific term *Pharisees* to them. (Like other ancient writers, Mark was free to update older wording and to omit details irrelevant to the point of his *narrative.) It is also possible that Pharisees had been investigating or traveling with Jesus.

Pharisees would not have been more than a sabbath day's journey from a village where they were staying; thus the disciples, who encounter Pharisees, are surely within walking distance of food in a village, if it had been properly prepared the preceding day. Teachers were held responsible for the behavior of their *disciples, and many *rabbis considered it proper to defend the honor of their disciples.

2:25. Whether or not his opponents agree with Jesus' argument, he has cited biblical precedent for hunger overriding a standard biblical rule; therefore they could not punish him in a local priestly court. Because Jesus is defending his disciples, he mentions "those who were with" David; although it is not clear that anyone was with David (1 Sam 21:1), David claimed that there were others (21:2). Either Jesus accepts David's claim as true, or his point from the standpoint of legal precedent is that the priest accepted David's word and let hunger take precedence over ritual law.

2:26. Abiathar was not yet high priest when David was given the bread, but Mark employs the term in the standard manner of his day: "high priest" was applied to any member of the high priestly family with administrative power, which would have included Abiathar when David came to Ahimelech, Abiathar's father.

2:27. Although Jesus claims the right to interpret sabbath rules as the authoritative *Son of Man (Dan 7:13-14), his opponents no doubt understand him to mean that because the sabbath was made for people (other Jewish teachers also mentioned this point), human beings had authority to do what they needed on the sabbath. ("Son of man" was a standard *Aramaic term for "human being," and his hearers probably assumed he meant this rather than that he claimed to be the Son of Man of Daniel 7:13-14.)

3:1-6
Healing or Killing on the Sabbath

3:1. The muscles and nerves of a "dried" or "withered" hand were inactive; thus the hand, smaller than usual, did not function (1 Kings 13:4; cf. Testament of Simeon 2:12). No cure was known for this paralysis.

3:2. In the teachings of Jewish legal scholars, minor cures were not permitted on the sabbath, although saving a life was a different matter. (Even the strictest observers of the sabbath allowed compromising the sabbath to save life or to fight in a defensive war.) The rule against cures applied to physicians, however, not to healings wrought by God, and *Pharisees disputed among themselves whether prayer for the sick was permitted on the sabbath. Jesus' opponents are therefore going considerably beyond standard Jewish rules to try to convict him.

3:3-5. Jesus might mean that "killing" is permitted on the sabbath, as it was during the Maccabean warfare (second century B.C.); more likely he draws a legal analogy from the principle that one could violate the sabbath to save life but not to kill except in self-defense; by extension, one could do good but not harm. (A possible allusion to 2 Kings 5:7 is less likely.)

3:6. Unintentional violations of the sabbath or issues of disagreement about what constituted work (matters that were debatable in Jewish courts) were normally treated lightly; capital punishment (Ex 31:14; 35:2) was thought appropriate only for those who willfully rejected the sabbath. Jesus' opponents go far beyond their own traditional teachings here. On the Herodians see comment on 12:13.

3:7-12 Increasing Popularity

3:7-8. Idumea was south of Galilee; east of the Jordan River was Perea, and Tyre and Sidon were to the northwest. Like Galilee, Idumea and Perea were religiously Jewish territories once dominated by *Gentiles; Tyre and Sidon were Gentile cities, although it seems most likely here that Jewish residents of those cities are intended (see 7:27).

3:9-12. Finally Jesus has to find another way to deal with the growing crowds (3:9). Any prophet supposed to perform signs drew large crowds in Jewish Palestine, and Jesus seems to have drawn larger crowds than most others. Other "signs prophets" sometimes tried miracles like making the walls of Jerusalem fall down or the Jordan part (they failed), but no prophets since Elijah and Elisha had been reported as doing as many healing miracles as Jesus.

3:13-19 Commissioning Twelve Representatives

3:13. Mountains were often places for communion with God (e.g., the experiences of Moses and Elijah).

3:14-15. Israel consisted of twelve tribes, and if groups chose twelve leaders (as apparently those who wrote the *Dead Sea Scrolls did), they did so because they believed that their own group was the true, obedient remnant of Israel. "*Apostles" means commissioned representatives, the point here being that Jesus' authority to proclaim the *kingdom and expel demons continues through his followers.

3:16-19. Luke (and probably "Q," a source he shares with Matthew) lists "Judas son of James" rather than Matthew's and Mark's "Thaddeus." Ancient business documents show that people were commonly known by several different names, so the different lists of apostles probably do refer to the same people. (The differences in the lists do show that the lists were not copied from one another or standardized, and thus that the tradition of Jesus choosing twelve is older than the particular lists themselves.) Nicknames were common, appearing even on tomb inscriptions.

"Cananaean" is *Aramaic for "*zealot" (Luke 6:15); thus some translations simply read "Simon the Zealot" here. In this period, this term could just mean "zealous one," but it may mean that he had been involved in revolutionary activity (some revolutionaries soon after this time came to be known as "Zealots"). "Boanerges" is a Greek rendering of the Aramaic for "sons of thunder" (*rgs* for Aramaic *r'm*). "Iscariot" may mean "man from Kerioth," but this is unclear; other proposals (e.g., a Greek transliteration of an Aramaic corruption of the Latin *sicarius*, "assassin"; see comment on Acts 21:38) are equally uncertain.

3:20-30 Jesus Raids Satan's House

3:20-22. Exorcists often invoked a higher spirit to get rid of a lower one, so Jesus' opponents accuse him of gaining his power for exorcism from sorcery—relying on *Satan himself. Insanity (3:21) was often associated with demon possession (3:22). Because false teachers were sometimes thought to be inspired by demons and the official penalty for misleading God's people this way was death (Deut 13:5; 18:20), Jesus' family had reason to want to reach him before the legal experts did. (The legal experts could not enforce the death penalty, because Palestine was under Roman domination; but the public charge alone would humiliate the family.) Teachers offended by reports of the events of 2:1—3:6 are now taking the offensive.

3:23-27. Although magical texts sometimes "bind" demons by incantations, Jesus has defeated the strong man simply by his moral victory in the wilderness (1:13) and by commanding demons to leave (1:25-26; cf. Is 49:24-25).

3:28-30. "Blaspheming the *Spirit" here means opposing Jesus' *messiahship so firmly that one resorts to accusations of sorcery to get around the Spirit's signs confirming his identity. Different teachers debated whether some sins were eternally unforgivable; Jesus probably means that their hearts were becoming so hard they would never think to repent.

3:31-34
Jesus' Real Family

Thinking of one's coreligionists as brothers and sisters was common; respecting older persons as mothers or fathers was also widespread. But allowing ties in the religious community to take precedence over family ties was unheard-of in Judaism, except when a pagan converted to Judaism and regarded his new family as more important than his old one. (Like other Jewish teachers, Jesus commonly employs *hyperbole, or *rhetorical exaggeration. He is not rejecting his earthly family altogether but stating his priorities, because they want to declare him mentally incompetent to rescue him from the dangers he is sure to face from religious authorities if he continues on his present path; see 3:21.)

4:1-20
The Parable of the Sower and Four Soils

4:1-2. The acoustic setting from the boat would have been ideal for Jesus' voice to carry to the crowds. Some places in Palestine, such as a cove near Capernaum, have natural acoustics that would allow as many as seven thousand people to hear a person speaking in the center of the cove.

*Rabbis commonly taught in *parables; although the subjects of many parables centered on royal courts, teachers explaining points to common folk probably often used more down-to-earth parables like the harvest stories Jesus uses here.

4:3-7. When seed was sown before the ground was plowed up (as it often was), it commonly befell one of the fates reported here. The "road" is probably the footpath through the field.

4:8. Thirtyfold, sixtyfold and a hundredfold are tremendously good harvests from Galilean soil. The fertile Jordan Valley normally yielded between ten- and a hundredfold, so a hundredfold need not be a miraculous harvest, as some have thought; but for much of Palestine, the average yield was tenfold (meaning that ten seeds were harvested for every seed sown), and all the figures Jesus reports here are very good yields. The yield is worth the sown seed that was wasted (cf. Eccles 11:1-6).

4:9. "Ears to hear" reflects the motif in the *Old Testament prophets that many had ears but were deaf to God's voice (e.g., Is 6:10; 43:8; 44:18; Ezek 12:2).

4:10-11. Jewish teachers normally used *parables to illustrate and explain points, not to conceal them. But if one tells stories without stating the point they were meant to illustrate, as Jesus does here, only those who listen most astutely (4:9) and start with insiders' knowledge could possibly figure out one's point. The members of the *Qumran community believed that God gave secrets to the prophets that they encoded in the Bible, and that God revealed the interpretation of those biblical texts to their own teacher, who shared it only with them. Greek teachers like Plato and sometimes Jewish teachers would leave certain points obscure to keep them from outsiders; only those who were serious enough to persevere would understand.

4:12. The point in the context of Isaiah 6:9-10, which Jesus quotes here, is that God's people had hardened their hearts so that they could not hear him; God thus chose to harden them further (what some have called "penal blindness") by sending them his message anyway.

4:13-14. This most basic message is the foundation for the rest: Jesus' message must be embraced with endurance and without distraction from the world to produce its intended effect.

4:15. Judaism recognized *Satan as the ultimate accuser and tempter; by mentioning him, Jesus immediately notifies his *disciples of the seriousness of forgetting his word. Other *rabbis also taught that forgetting a teaching of Scripture was a serious offense, but they would have resented a teacher who claimed unique authority for his own message.

4:16-17. Judaism valued its heroes of the past who had refused to compromise God's word, even in the face of death. Jesus' description of apostasy when persecuted for the message of the *kingdom thus would evoke the disciples' discomfort and self-examination.

4:18-20. The fruitful "seeds" presumably spread the word and multiply disciples (as well-trained disciples of rabbis were supposed to do when they became teachers in their own right; part of the goal was to increase obedience to the law).

4:21-25
Accountability for the Word

Had another *rabbi uttered the words of 4:22 in this context (contrast Mt 5:15), it would mean bringing forth treasures (special insights) concealed in Scripture. Thus Jesus claims to reveal God's message; he calls his *disciples to understand and build on his teaching.

4:21-23. Jesus is a master of the graphic illustrations in which Jewish teachers sought to excel: invisible light is pointless, and God wants the light of his word to be received. The lamps were small clay lamps that had to be set on a stand to shed much light in a room; a bushel basket placed over the lamp would no doubt extinguish it.

4:24-25. The conventional wisdom was that each person is accountable for what he or she does with what he or she had originally been given; Jesus applies this principle to his own teaching. Thus if the crowds did not obey what light they had received, they would never receive more. The language of "measuring" is the language of weighing food and other commodities at the market; Jewish texts sometimes use it for God's measuring out just judgments in the final day.

4:26-32
A Microcosm of the Future Kingdom

It was commonly realized that God would someday establish his *kingdom, or rule, unchallenged over all the earth.

Jesus and his small band of close followers may have seemed too obscure to contain the future glory of the kingdom, but the seed of the word would continue to spread from them until the final coming of the kingdom. Jesus' teaching challenges prevailing views of how the kingdom would come.

4:26-29. Every farmer would have agreed that God's providence, not the farmer's power, made the grain grow. (Thus pagan and Jewish farmers alike sought divine help for their crops; pagan farmers relied heavily on sacrifices.)

4:30-32. Scholars still dispute what plant is meant by the "mustard seed." Nevertheless, by no conjecture is it the smallest of all seeds that Jesus' listeners could have known (the orchid seed is smaller). The point is that it was proverbially small and yet yielded a large shrub. Around the Sea of Galilee, it can reach a height of ten feet and has sometimes reached fifteen feet, although its usual height is about four feet. Because it would grow anew each year, birds could not nest in it when they built nests in early spring; but small birds could light on it, all that is necessary to fulfill the language here (an allusion to a bigger tree in Dan 4:12). The *hyperbole Jesus applies to the best image of growth from tiny to large that he had available does not change the point, however; the *kingdom might begin in obscurity, but it would culminate in glory.

4:33-34
Secret Teachings

Sometimes Jewish (and other ancient) teachers had some special esoteric teachings that they could confide only in their closest pupils, because they were not for public knowledge. People could not be ready to grasp the secret of the nature of Jesus' *kingdom until the secret about the nature of his *messiahship had been revealed (see the introduction to Mark in this commentary).

4:35-41
Lord of Creation

Rousing a sleeping prophet to secure his prayers may have reminded the *disciples or first hearers of Jonah 1:5-6, but Jesus appears quite different from Jonah here. Some ancient pagan stories told of powerful individuals able to subdue even the forces of nature, but these were nearly always gods or, rarely, heroes of the distant past. Many Jewish people believed that angels controlled the forces of nature, such as winds and sea; yet such angels did have one to whom they must answer. In Jewish tradition, the one who ruled the winds and sea was God himself (Ps 107:29; cf. Jon 1:15). The disciples' surprise at Jesus' power is thus easy to understand.

Storms often rose suddenly on the lake called the Sea of Galilee; these fishermen had usually stayed closer to Capernaum and are unprepared for a squall this far from shore. The only place one could sleep in a small fishing boat with water pouring in from a storm would be on the elevated stern, where one could use the wooden or leather-covered helmsman's seat, or a pillow kept under that seat, as a cushion for one's head. Jesus' sleep during the storm may indicate the tranquillity of faith (Ps 4:8; cf. 2 Kings 6:16-17, 32; Prov 19:23); in some Greek stories, the genuineness of philosophers' faith in their own teachings on tranquility was tested in storms.

5:1-20
Overpowering a Legion of Demons

Jesus could bind the strong man no one

else could bind (3:27; 5:3-4).

5:1. Matthew's "Gadara" (Mt 8:28), nearly eight miles from the lake, is more accurate than Mark's "Gerasa," a prominent city over thirty miles southeast from the lake by a straight line and a longer journey by road. But both towns were in the same general region, the area of the Decapolis, a predominantly non-Jewish area, and Mark appears to be writing for readers who were far from this area and who would be less concerned with details of Syro-Palestinian geography than Matthew's readers would be.

5:2. Jewish people considered tombs unclean for Jews and a popular haunt for demons. People in many ancient cultures brought offerings for the dead, which might also appeal to these spirits. The time is night (4:35), when evil spirits were thought to exercise the greatest power. Mark thus sets the stage for ancient readers to feel the suspense of the ensuing conflict.

5:3-5. Some pagan worship had involved cutting oneself with stones (1 Kings 18:28), and both self-mortification and supernatural strength occur in conjunction with spirit possession in many cultures today.

5:6-8. In ancient magic, higher spirits would be invoked to drive out lower spirits, and the demons here appeal to the only one higher than Jesus to keep Jesus from driving them out: "I adjure you by God" (not "Swear to God"—NIV). This language invokes a curse on Jesus if he does not comply. (Phrases like "I adjure you" and "I know you"—Mk 1:23—appear in ancient magical exorcism texts as self-protective invocations to bind the spiritual opponent.) The attempt at magical self-protection proves powerless against Jesus. Not only Jews but also *Gentiles sometimes called Israel's God "the Most High."

5:9. Identification of spirits' names or the names by which those spirits could be subdued was standard in ancient exorcism texts (see ancient magical texts and the *Testament of Solomon); but this case, where many demons are present, is the only recorded example of Jesus seeking a name, and here he does not seem to use it in the exorcism.

A legion included four thousand to six thousand troops. This man is therefore hosting a large number of demons; they probably outnumber the pigs (5:13).

5:10. Ancients were familiar with demons pleading for mercy or other concessions when they were about to be defeated (e.g., *1 Enoch 12—14; Testament of Solomon 2:6). Perhaps they wish to stay in the area only because of the tombs, but in ancient lore spirits were often associated with particular local areas.

5:11-12. Only *Gentiles (or very nonobservant Jews) raised pigs, and Jewish readers would think of pigs as among the most unclean animals and rightful hosts of evil spirits. Ancient exorcists found that demons often asked for concessions if the pressure for them to evacuate their host was becoming too great for them to stay.

5:13. Jewish tradition often taught that demons could die, so many ancient readers would assume that the demons had been destroyed (or at least disabled) with their hosts. (Some traditions also portrayed at least some demons as fearing water—Testament of Solomon 5:11-12; but in other traditions, certain demons lived in water. What is significant in the Gospel accounts is the much greater dependence of demons on their hosts than in most other sources from the period.)

5:14-17. The opposition to Jesus arises from both economic interests—the loss of a large herd of swine—and some Greek conceptions of dangerous wonderworking magicians, whom the people would fear.

5:18. In ancient stories, those recovering from madness might be unaware of their prior state (e.g., Leucippe in Achilles Tatius), but this was not always the case (Dan 4:34-37).

5:19-20. Because his *messiahship would be misunderstood, Jesus kept it a secret in predominantly Jewish areas. In the predominantly non-Jewish Decapolis, however, where people would perceive him as a magician, he urges his new *disciple to spread word about what *God* had done, thereby correcting the people's misunderstanding (cf. 2 Maccabees 3:36).

5:21-43
Healing a Girl and an Outcast Woman

This passage includes two cases of uncleanness: a woman with a continual flow of blood and a corpse (see Lev 15:19-33; Num 19:11-22). Even after the flow stopped, the first woman would be counted unclean for seven days (Lev 15:28); the dead girl was even more unclean (Num 19:11).

5:21-24. "Rulers of the *synagogue" were the chief officials in synagogues (distinct from the attendant, Lk 4:20) and were prominent members of their communities. Jairus's daughter had been a minor until that year and on account of both her age and her gender had virtually no social status. One would fall at the feet of someone of much greater status (like a king) or prostrate oneself before God; for this prominent man to humble himself in this way before Jesus was thus to recognize Jesus' power in a serious way.

5:25. This woman's sickness was reckoned as if she had a menstrual period all month long; it made her continually unclean under the *law (Lev 15:25-28)—a social and religious problem on top of the physical one. The ailment probably started after puberty; given an average ancient life expectancy of about forty years and the "twelve years" that she had been ill, she may have spent half or all her adult life with this trouble.

5:26. Many practices of both Jewish and *Gentile physicians in biblical times were no more than superstitious remedies, so it is not surprising that they had proved ineffective (cf. 2 Chron 16:12; Tobit 2:10; *Qumran *Genesis Apocryphon* 20:19-20). Although many physicians in the Greek world were slaves, Palestinian Jewish sources suggest that physicians in Palestine had ample incomes.

5:27-29. If this woman touched anyone or anyone's clothes, she rendered that person ceremonially unclean for the rest of the day (cf. Lev 15:26-27). Some uncleanness was unavoidable, but it was inconvenient to fulfill the required bath, and men avoided uncleanness when they could. Because she rendered unclean anyone she touched, she should not have even been in this heavy crowd. Later Jewish tradition made this danger even more serious than Leviticus had (e.g., *Mishnah *Toharot* 5:8), so many teachers avoided touching women altogether, lest they become accidentally contaminated. Thus she could not touch or be touched, was probably now divorced or had never married, and was marginal to Jewish society.

5:30-34. Jewish people believed that only teachers closest to God had supernatural knowledge. Jesus uses his supernatural knowledge to identify with the woman who had touched him—even though in the eyes of the public this would mean that he had contracted ritual uncleanness. Given the frequent failure of the male *disciples' faith (8:17-21; 9:19), Mark's record of this woman's faith (cf. 7:29; 12:44; 15:40-41) is all the more striking, especially for readers whose culture considered women less stable and emotionally weaker than men.

5:35-39. Several professional mourners were required even at the funeral of the poorest person; more mourners would assemble at the death of a member of a prominent family like this one. Because bodies decomposed rapidly in Palestine, mourners had to be assembled immediately upon someone's death, and they had gathered before word even reached Jairus that his daughter had died. Messengers were normally dispatched immediately to bring a parent or spouse the sad news.

5:40-43. In that culture, at the age of twelve the girl was a virgin probably soon to be married (women were not able to continue in education or public employment as they do today). Young girls usually looked forward eagerly to their wedding day as the most joyous event in their life, and to die unmarried—especially just short of it—was lamented as a particularly great tragedy. Jesus spoke to her in *Aramaic, perhaps her first language, although Greek was widely spoken in Palestine. (On the use of Aramaic in healings, see comment on 7:34-35.)

6:1-6
Jesus' Rejection in His Hometown

The *Old Testament often reiterates the principle of the prophet without honor: Jeremiah, Moses, Joseph and so forth; subsequent Jewish tradition emphasized this concept even more. That Jesus is "unable" to do works because of their unbelief presumes a limitation not of his power but of his mission: to heal without morally directed faith would be to act like the pagan magicians of antiquity.

In 6:3, Jesus is called a "carpenter." Early in Jesus' childhood, Sepphoris, then capital of Galilee, had been destroyed by the Romans, and rebuilding had begun immediately. Thus carpenters were no doubt in demand in Nazareth, a village four miles from the ruins of Sepphoris; and Joseph, Jesus' father, probably taught his son his own trade, as was common for fathers to do in those days. After Sepphoris had been rebuilt, they probably did most carpentry work from their home, as most Galilean carpenters did. The observation that Jesus is a carpenter is meant to identify him, not to suggest the unlikelihood of a carpenter being a teacher, for we also know of other carpenters who became famous teachers (e.g., *Shammai).

"Brothers" and "sisters" are the usual terms for siblings; a different term for more general "kinfolk" (e.g., Rom 16:11) is not used with regard to Jesus' siblings. This text undoubtedly refers to children born to Mary after Jesus.

6:7-13
Traveling Representatives of Jesus

6:7. It was customary to send heralds, or messengers, by twos, in both Greek and Jewish culture. In Judaism, such pairing also provided validation for their testimony (Deut 17:6; 19:15).

6:8-9. They are to travel light, like some other groups: (1) peasants, who often had only one cloak (though they did not travel much); (2) some traveling philosophers, called *Cynics; (3) some prophets, like Elijah and John the Baptist. They are to be totally committed to their mission, not tied down with worldly concerns. The "bag" would have been used for begging (like the Cynics' bags).

6:10. Hospitality was highly valued. Like some of the early *synagogues, early *churches found it most practical to meet in homes and to use them as a base of operation in reaching the rest of the community.

6:11. "Shaking the dust off" meant essentially treating these Jewish cities as if they were unclean, pagan cities, no dust of which the true followers of God would want remaining on them.

6:12-13. Oil was sometimes used medicinally, and in the *Old Testament it was often associated with divine commissioning. Thus it was a useful symbol in prayer for healing (Jas 5:14).

6:14-29
The Politician Murders the Prophet

6:14-16. Herod Antipas was technically tetrarch (with Matthew and Luke), not "king"; Mark may use the latter term loosely or ironically. Herod's appeal for the title "king" under Herodias's influence led to his banishment in A.D. 39; this could support Mark's use of the term ironically.

Some Greeks (and Jews influenced by them) believed in reincarnation; but John's return is said instead to be a "rising from the dead" (as a few persons had been raised by Old Testament prophets); Elijah had never died, and many Jewish people anticipated his return (Mal 4:5). Reincarnation is thus not in view here.

6:17-19. Herod's affair with his sister-in-law, whom he had by this time married, was widely known. Indeed, the affair had led him to divorce his first wife, whose father, a king, later went to war with Herod over the issue and defeated him. John's denunciation of the affair as unlawful (besides being adultery, it violated incest prohibitions; see Lev 18:16; 20:21) was an attack against Herod's adultery, but Herod could have perceived it as a political threat, given the political ramifications that later led to a major military defeat. (*Josephus claims that many viewed Herod's humiliation in the war as divine judgment for his executing John the Baptist.)

It has been suggested that Herod's half-brother Herod Philip may be called by the secondary name Philip here to avoid confusing him with the main Herod in the story, Herod Antipas.

6:20. Despite Antipas's grounds for animosity toward John (6:17-19), it is not incredible that he would enjoy hearing him (cf. Ezek 33:31-33). Many well-to-do Greeks, fancying themselves *patrons of intellectual pursuits, supported philosophers more for cultural and entertainment purposes than for ethical edification. Influenced by upper-class Greek ideals, Herod undoubtedly considered himself as open-minded culturally as he was brutal politically.

6:21. Celebrating birthdays was at this time a Greek and Roman but not a Jewish custom, although the Jewish aristocracy had imbibed plenty of Greek culture by this period. Herod held tight, centralized control over Galilee, and the officials he invites are probably local village and regional leaders loyal to his government; in all Galilee, only Tiberias and probably Sephoris were cities organized after the Greek model.

6:22. It is otherwise known that the Herodian court was given to excesses like those described here. Some scholars suggest that Herodias's daughter Salome is at this point no longer a young girl and is already married to the tetrarch Philip. Other historical data about her, however, suggest that she may be no older than twelve or fourteen (which was a common age for virgins to marry in Jewish Palestine); it is possible that she is even slightly younger. On any reading, Herod's vulgarity is perverse; after taking his brother's wife (cf. Lev 20:21), he lusts after his wife's daughter (cf. Lev 20:14).

6:23. This is the sort of oath one might make while drunk, but it is especially reminiscent of the Persian king stirred by Queen Esther's beauty (Esther 5:3, 6; 7:2), though this girl's request is far less noble than Esther's. But Herod's oath is not backed up with adequate authority; as a Roman vassal he has no authority to give away any of his kingdom.

6:24. The girl has to go "out" to ask her mother. Excavations at Herod's fortress Machaerus suggest two dining halls, one for women and one for men. Herodias has thus presumably not been present to watch Herod's reaction to the dance. *Josephus characterizes Herodias the same way Mark does: a jealous, ambitious schemer (she and Antipas ultimately did themselves in; see comment on 6:14-16).

6:25. Beheading by the sword was the method of executing Roman citizens and other individuals of status; lower-class individuals were usually executed by crucifixion or other means, unless the matter were urgent. Salome's asking for John's head on a platter means that she wants it served up as part of the dinner menu—a ghastly touch of ridicule.

6:26-28. Although an oath like Herod's was not legally binding, breaking an oath before dinner guests would have been embarrassing; it is known that even the emperor would not lightly do it. *Tacitus, who despised Nero, reports how this despicable man had heads of his victims brought to him; Mark's readers are meant to get the same revolting impression of Herod and Herodias that Tacitus wished to convey of Nero. Unlike Judean Jewish leaders who needed Pilate's approval to enact legal executions, Herod Antipas was acting ruler in his own domain.

6:29. If a man had sons, the eldest son was normally responsible for his father's burial; here John's *disciples must fulfill this role for him. Because he had been executed, the disciples perform a dangerous task unless they had Herod's permission to take the body (contrast the absence of Jesus' male disciples in 15:42-47!).

6:30-44
A Shepherd Feeds His Sheep

6:30-34. Jesus' care for the sheep (6:34) is modeled on God's care for his people in Ezekiel 34:5, 15; this care is likewise expressed by providing sound teaching (cf. Ezek 34:4; Jer 23; Num 27:17).

6:35-38. Fish and especially bread were central components of the Palestinian diet; meat was rarely available except at feasts. Food was always sold in village markets, and the Galilean countryside was full of villages (6:36); but Jesus had withdrawn his followers some distance from the nearest villages (6:32). Even the larger villages would have under three thousand inhabitants; despite Galilee's agricultural self-sufficiency, feeding the crowd in the villages would thus have been difficult. But it would have taken more than two hundred days of an average person's wages (around seven months of hard labor) to feed the great multitude that had assembled.

6:39. That the grass is green indicates that it is spring, around Passover.

6:40. Jesus' followers are organized in ranks like armies in the *Old Testament and in the *Dead Sea Scrolls. The purpose is to facilitate the distribution of food, but some people in the crowd may have thought that Jesus was organizing them as ranks for a *messianic army (cf. Jn 6:15). (Mark records this organizing, however, simply to emphasize the great numbers fed.)

6:41. It was customary to begin a meal by giving thanks for the bread and then dividing it.

6:42-44. The multiplication of food is reminiscent of the miracle of God supplying manna for Israel in the wilderness, and especially of Elisha multiplying food (2 Kings 4:42-44, where some was also left over). Ancient ethics frowned on wasting leftovers, although aristocrats often flaunted such waste. The term for "baskets" here was often used for wicker food baskets but could also mean the large baskets in which Roman soldiers carried their supplies.

6:45-52
Walking on Water

6:45-48. The language of "passing by" may refer to how God's glory "passed by" in the *Old Testament (Ex 33:19; Job 9:11), which also described God as "treading" upon the waves (Job 9:8).

6:49. Although not all Jewish teachers sanctioned a belief in ghosts, it existed on the popular level and contradicted the standard Jewish (and *New Testament) teaching that the righteous and wicked dead are separated at death in view of the coming *resurrection.

6:50-52. "It is I" (NIV, NASB, KJV, etc.) is literally "I am." Although the former is the primary meaning here, in this context it is possible that Jesus (or Mark) also intends to allude to a particular nuance of the latter meaning: "I am" may refer back to the God of the Old Testament (Ex 3:14; cf. comment on Mk 6:45-48).

6:53-56
Crowds Seek Healing

Carrying the sick on their mats or touching Jesus' cloak imitated earlier expressions of faith (see comment on 2:3-5; 5:27-29). Evidence from ancient pagan healing shrines suggests that once someone was healed in a particular way or at a particular place, others often tried to get healing by the same method. The marketplaces (6:56) constituted the largest open area of a town or village, where larger crowds could gather. In contrast to Greek cities, market areas in Galilean towns were not always located in the center of the town.

7:1-23
True and False Religion

Controversy over Jesus' treatment of uncleanness (1:40-45; 5:21-43) and other religious issues (e.g., 2:1—3:35) climaxes in a confrontation over the failure of Jesus' *disciples to wash their hands.

7:1. It is not clear why *Pharisees, most of whom were centered in Jerusalem, would have come to Galilee. Some commentators have suggested that they came to evaluate Jesus' teaching, to see if he were a false teacher leading people astray (see Deut 13:13-14). This suggestion is possible; but had their mission been so serious, Mark would probably have mentioned it. They may have simply wished to hear and evaluate this popular teacher in a general way; or perhaps these represent a small number of Pharisees who did live in Galilee. Plenty of *scribes already lived in Galilee.

7:2-3. The *Pharisees were scrupulous about washing their hands as part of ritual purity, though this rule was not found in the *Old Testament and may have originally derived from Greek influence. Mark gives his *Gentile readers only a cursory summary of a much more complex custom (which some scholars think was limited to particular days), although his readers may have been familiar with related Jewish purity practices in their own parts of the world (*Diaspora Jews were known for washing their hands).

7:4. Washing the hands removed partial ceremonial impurity picked up in the marketplace; hands were apparently immersed up to the wrist or purified by having water poured over them from a pure vessel. The Pharisees also had rules about immersing vessels to remove impurity.

7:5. The *Pharisees held their traditions in high regard; unwilling to innovate more than necessary, they grounded everything they could in the teachings of their predecessors. Thus they want to know where Jesus, as a popular teacher, stands on issues on which their tradition commented (such as washing hands), so they can evaluate his teaching accordingly.

7:6-8. Jesus quotes a prophecy of Isaiah decreed against the Israel of Isaiah's day (Is 29:13), which had been religious in form but not close to God in heart (Is 1:10-20). The very thing the Pharisees prized as spiritual—traditions derived from many pious and wise teachers who had tried to interpret and apply God's *law—Jesus claims is undercutting the plain message of God.

7:9-13. Many Jewish teachers regarded the commandment to honor father and mother as the most important in the *law. Jewish interpreters included in this commandment providing for one's parents when they were old. At the same time, tradition allowed that various items could be sacrificed or dedicated to the use of God's temple. ("Corban" appears on sacrificial vessels and means "consecrated to God"; in popular usage, it could also mean "forbidden to so-and-so.") One school of Jewish teachers in Jesus' day declared that a vow that something was consecrated and forbidden to others applied even to family members, even if those to whom it was forbidden included them only accidentally.

Some apparently religious people had been using this practice to withhold what should have otherwise gone to the support of their parents—against *Pharisaic belief that one should support one's parents. Jesus attacks here not the Pharisees' religious theory but their inconsistency with that theory in practice: their love for the *law had led them (like some modern Christians) to such attention to its legal details that it created loopholes for them to violate the spirit of the law.

7:14-15. Other teachers are occasionally reported to have uttered sayings similar to Jesus' statement here, but only rarely and in private. If Jesus' words are taken literally, they declare the whole clean/unclean distinction emphasized in the law as of only symbolic value. Because this distinction constituted one of the main barriers between Jews and *Gentiles (see Rom 14), Jesus' statement opens the way for racial and cultural reconciliation in table fellowship.

7:16-19. Jesus says that food does not affect what a person really is; writing in a day of conflict between the customs of Jewish and Gentile Christians, Mark applies this point to the kosher laws of Leviticus 11: pigs, dogs, bats, owls and so on are now "clean," or acceptable to eat. Mark's proposal would not have been popular among most Jewish people. Liberal Alexandrian Jews who no longer believed in literal observance of the food laws (Lev 11; Deut 14) were particularly despised by their more conservative colleagues in Egypt and certainly found few allies in Palestine.

7:20-23. Other Jewish teachers would have agreed that the vices listed by Jesus were evil and that they came from the heart. (Vice lists were also a common teaching technique of ancient moralists.) But they would not have agreed with Jesus that most of themselves were more concerned about legal details than ethics, even though as lawyers they necessarily spent more time dealing with legal issues than with transforming the heart.

7:24-30
A Gentile Woman's Faith

If "unclean" foods such as pigs and dogs were no longer unclean (7:16-19), neither were *Gentiles. Although Jesus wins all his controversies with the religious authorities in Mark, he allows himself to be persuaded by a Gentile woman's desperate retort. This story would encourage Mark's Gentile readers, who were being persecuted for a faith that many simply regarded as a Jewish heresy.

7:24-26. Jewish people did not expect much faith from pagans, especially from pagan women. Like Sidon, Tyre belonged to ancient Phoenicia, and the most prominent woman from Phoenicia in the *Old Testament was the wicked Jezebel. But another Phoenician woman who petitioned Elijah in the same generation received God's favor for her son (1 Kings 17:17-24). Greek culture had long influenced Syria, and many Greeks had settled there; the citizen class of the Phoenician republics Tyre and Sidon was thoroughly *Hellenized. Thus she is both Syrophoenician and Greek.

7:27-28. "Dog" was often a bitter insult. Worthless food would be cast to the dogs (cf. Ex 22:31). In Jewish Palestine, dogs were regarded as scavengers, but in well-to-do houses influenced by Greek custom (more familiar to the Syrophoenician woman), dogs were sometimes pets. Jesus is making an illustration: the children must be fed before the pets, and the Jewish people therefore had first claim (e.g., Ex 4:22). "Greeks" were the ruling class in Syrophoenicia, taking others' "children's bread"; now the woman must humble herself.

He is saying that he will not heal like pagan magicians; he wants her to demonstrate faith, specifically faith in the supremacy of the true God. (Her reply takes up his illustration: she concedes the priority of the Jewish people, the children, but protests that even the dogs get to eat crumbs. In so arguing, she indicates her faith that only the smallest fraction of his power is necessary to heal her daughter.)

7:29-30. In the *Old Testament, faith was often expressed in bold zeal, holy chutzpah, by women of faith (2 Kings 4:14-28), prophets (Ex 33:12—34:9; 1 Kings 18:36-37; 2 Kings 2:2, 4, 6, 9) and other heroes (Gen 32:26-30). These examples all combine humble respect for God or his prophet with boldly urgent entreaty, and God answers these prayers.

7:31-37
A Deaf-Mute Healed

7:31. The Decapolis, literally "ten cities" (see 5:1-20), was predominantly inhabited by non-Jews, though many Jews also lived there.

7:32-33. Deaf-mutes were protected under Jewish law but classed with other groups (women, slaves, imbeciles, minors) not educated enough to keep the law. Crowds normally gathered to see magicians do their tricks, and this crowd would have preferred to have seen Jesus heal a man in front of them, though he does not do so. On the spittle see 8:22-23; here Jesus may be acting out "healing," "speech" and (7:34) "from God," to let the man know what he is about to do (Jewish law recognized that deaf-mutes could communicate via signs). Mark's term for "mute" occurs in the *Septuagint only at Isaiah 35:6, referring to the blessings inaugurated in the *messianic era.

7:34-35. Some scholars point out that magicians often spoke unintelligible phrases during healings. Here, however, Jesus speaks *Aramaic, which would have been known to most people, Jewish or *Gentile, in Syria-Palestine (cf. also Mk 14:36).

8:1-13
Feeding the Four Thousand

See 6:30-44 for more background on this passage. Jesus was not limited to doing a miracle only once; he could repeat them whenever necessary (8:19-21; cf. 2 Kings 2:19-22; 4:1-7, 38-41, 42-44; 7:16).

8:1-4. Galilee was full of towns and villages, so Jesus purposely withdraws his *disciples some distance away, presumably to secure privacy for instructing his disciples.

8:5-7. Bread and fish were basic staples; it was customary to give thanks before a meal.

8:8-10. The term for basket here (different from the one in chap. 6) refers to a reed basket often used for carrying fish. This feeding miracle, like the earlier one, is reminiscent of Elisha.

8:11-13. Most ancient peoples, including most Jewish people by this time, believed that signs in the heavens could portend events about to take place; unusual signs could portend the death of a ruler, the fall of a city and so forth. The specific nature of the *Pharisees' request for a sign here is unclear. If they want him to call down fire from heaven or to perform a similar cosmic sign, they are requiring a sign that none of the would-be prophets of the day had offered. If they are asking Jesus to predict and interpret an event in the heavens, they are requesting astrological prognostication, which Deuteronomy 18:10 forbade (as divination). Because "heaven" was a Jewish title for God, it is also possible that they simply mean a sign "from God."

In view of Mark 8:1-10, the reader recognizes how foolish Jesus' opponents are. Ancient literature sometimes used the denseness of opponents to underline the protagonist's virtue.

8:14-21
Disciples Still Blind

Mark's Christian readers are confronted with a point less comfortable than the one in 8:11-13: not only Jesus' opponents but even his *disciples are dense.

8:14. The disciples' concern over not having brought bread is reasonable in human terms; they are apparently headed for the east side of the lake, which was less heavily populated (though they could find bread in Bethsaida—8:22). Their concern is heightened because bringing provisions had been their responsibility; teachers often delegated such matters to some of their disciples.

8:15. Yeast is used to represent various things in the Bible (unleavened bread in Ex 12:15-17 represents haste; in Mt 13:33, the *kingdom; in 1 Cor 5:6-7, someone's sin); the point here seems to be that it is something that spreads (as in Mt 13 and 1 Cor 5). Both *Pharisaic piety and Herod as an agent of political power are corrupting influences.

8:16-18. The *disciples are still spiritually half-blind, which is a moral fault in Mark 4:12 (and in the Old Testament: e.g., Is 29:9-10; 42:19-20; 44:18; Ezek 12:2).

8:19-21. The disciples should have

seen enough bread miracles not to worry about earthly bread and to catch Jesus' plain point. Instead, they appear more like the Israelites in the wilderness, who never learned faith despite all that God had done for them.

8:22-26
Blindness Half-Cured

8:22-23. Spittle was sometimes associated with healing; it was also often considered disgusting and may have tested the blind man's desire to be healed.

8:24-25. This is the only two-stage healing in the Gospels, and miracle stories in antiquity usually stress the suddenness of the miracle; healing by degrees was quite rare. This narrative is therefore significant and probably represents an acted *parable: unlike Jesus' opponents, the *disciples have begun to see but remain blind (8:16-18) until he touches them again at his *resurrection (9:9). The *Old Testament prophets sometimes acted out parables to get people's attention and communicate their point (e.g., Is 20:2-6; Jer 19:1-15; Ezek 4:1—5:17; 12:1-11).

8:26. Prophets usually presented healed persons to their families (1 Kings 17:23; 2 Kings 4:36), but Jesus' private action here emphasizes the *messianic secret (see the introduction to Mark in this commentary). Had the man returned to the town, everyone would have known of the miracle.

8:27-30
The Disciples Half-See

8:27. Caesarea Philippi was a pagan city known especially for its grotto dedicated to the worship of Pan, a Greek nature god. Thus we might think this region an unlikely place for the *disciples' first recognition of Jesus' *messiahship. "Villages of Caesarea Philippi" accurately depicts the area; throughout the *Hellenistic world, villages were dependent on the city in whose territory they were located.

8:28. Because many Palestinian Jews believed that prophets in the *Old Testament sense had ceased, ranking Jesus among the prophets would have been radical—but it was not radical enough to grasp his true identity.

8:29-30. The "*Messiah," or "Christ," is literally the "anointed one"—not just any anointed one but the anointed king, descended from David, who would restore sovereignty to Israel (Is 9:6-7; 11:1-10; Ps 2). There were many different views of the Messiah (or messiahs) in Jesus' time, but they all revolved around an earthly deliverance and earthly kingdom. Peter is right to call Jesus "Messiah," but what Peter means by the term and what Jesus means by it are entirely different at this point (see Mk 8:31-32). Although Jesus' future *kingdom would transform the world irresistibly, the present aspect of his messianic mission in the Gospels is to transform human hearts to live out the values of the kingdom in the face of the opposition of this age.

8:31—9:1
Jesus Explains His Messianic Mission

8:31. People throughout Greco-Roman antiquity commonly believed that someone about to die could make predictions about the future, and many believed that holy men could forecast their own death. This background may not be relevant here, however; some have proposed other interpretations of Jesus' foreknowledge here. Knowing the character of the temple authorities and their likely response to his actions in the temple (11:15-18) could have enabled Jesus to predict his death; his actions virtually provoked it. Some of Mark's hearers may have thought in either of these terms here; but another observation explains more of the evidence. Jesus' words here are shaped especially by his mission, which accords with Old Testament *prophecy (Is 52:13—53:12).

8:32. The *New Testament writers interpreted some Old Testament texts as referring to the *Messiah's suffering, but most Jewish people in the first century did not recognize these texts as referring to the Messiah, who was to reign as king. Most Jewish people believed in the *resurrection of all the righteous dead at the end of the age, and the inauguration of a *kingdom under God's appointed ruler afterward. Jesus' explanation of his mission in 8:31 thus seems to Peter to contradict his confession of Jesus' messiahship in 8:29.

8:33. "*Satan" originally meant "adversary" and could be used in the plural (though the plural is extremely rare); but in early Christian and most early Jewish writings it refers specifically to the devil. One could be said to act like someone else, however (e.g., John "in the spirit and power of Elijah"—Lk 1:17), and Jesus probably uses *hyperbole to make the point: Peter is just like Satan in preferring the worldly to the divine (cf. Mt 4:8-10). Calling Peter by the name of the ultimate tempter and accuser underlines the seriousness of his failure as a *disciple at this point.

The proper position of a disciple is "behind" his master, "following" him; "get behind me" may call Peter back to his rightful position of subservience. In Greek circles a person could be reproached for thinking in human rather than divine terms.

8:34-37. The cross was an instrument of violent and painful execution. To "take the cross" was to carry the horizontal beam of the cross out to the site of execution, generally past a jeering mob. In rhetorically strong terms, Jesus describes what all true disciples must be ready for: if they follow him, they must be ready to face literal scorn and death, for they must follow to the cross. Because life is worth more than the world itself, giving one's life in this world to gain it in the world to come is a wise transaction (cf. *2 Baruch 17:2-3; 51:15-16); there was nothing else one could give in exchange for it (Ps 49:7, 15).

8:38. "*Son of Man" here may refer back to Daniel 7:13-14. The *kingdom for which the *disciples are hoping would ultimately come; but it will be preceded by a period of great suffering and wickedness. Many others in Jesus' day believed that great suffering and sin would precede the kingdom; but Peter and his colleagues prefer the easier view that it would not, or at least that their side would triumph supernaturally at no cost to themselves.

9:1. This verse points to the future glory mentioned in the preceding verses by way of an anticipatory revelation of that glory they are to experience in 9:2-13. Because the future *Messiah had already come, the glory of his future *kingdom was also already present.

9:2-13
Glory on the Mountain

God had revealed his glory to Moses on Mount Sinai, so that Moses had come down from the mountain reflecting God's glory (Ex 32—34). In Mark 9:2-13, the glory of Jesus, who is greater than Moses and Elijah, is revealed on the mountain; he is thus the ultimate spokesperson for God (Deut 18:18-19).

9:2. Mount Sinai was where God revealed his glory. Jesus waits "six days" to ascend a mountain to make the same point (Ex 24:16). That Jesus takes three companions may allude to Exodus 24:1,

9, although this is less clear (70 elders were also present in that account). Transformation or transfiguration appears in both Greek myth and Jewish *apocalyptic literature, but the background of Jesus' transformation here must be Moses' glorification on Mount Sinai.

9:3. Jewish literature often described angels and other heavenly beings as being clothed in white. Laundering (cf. NIV "bleach") was normally a housewife's task, but this text refers to professional launderers, who could be men or women.

9:4. Elijah reportedly never died; Moses was buried by God himself, and some (unbiblical) Jewish traditions even claimed that Moses was still alive (cf. comment on Rev 11:6). These two figures were both expected to return in some sense before the time of the end.

9:5-6. Peter's suggestion of erecting shelters on the mountain may allude to Israel's tabernacles in the wilderness, recognizing God's presence among the Israelites in Moses' day.

9:7. The heavenly voice repeats the basic message of Mark 1:11 but may add another biblical allusion. "Hear him" may refer to Deuteronomy 18:15, where the Israelites are warned to heed the "prophet like Moses," the new Moses who would come.

9:8. One may compare Elijah and Moses' vanishing with a Jewish belief assumed especially by the later *rabbis that Elijah could come and go at will, like an angel.

9:9-10. Given their cultural presuppositions, it was difficult for the *disciples to understand what had happened; they assumed that all the righteous dead would be *resurrected simultaneously at the end of the age (cf. Dan 12:2).

9:11. The Jewish people expected Elijah to come at the time of the end (Mal 4:5), to prepare the Lord's way (Mal 3:1; Ecclus 48:1-10), though they held different views on his exact function.

9:12. Elijah would come "to restore all things," that is, to reconcile families (Mal 4:6; later *rabbis interpreted this restoration as straightening out Israel's genealogies, but the text was probably understood more broadly in this period).

9:13. Most Jewish people were expecting the real Elijah (whom the *disciples saw speaking with Jesus), but by applying the promise of Elijah to John, Jesus interprets it much more symbolically than most of his contemporaries would.

9:14-32
Insufficient Faith for Exorcism

9:14-15. Most *scribes did not claim the power to work miracles, in contrast to Jesus' *disciples (6:12-13). Teachers of the *law knew the Bible better than the disciples did, so if the disciples could not demonstrate God's power in other ways, they risked their credibility.

9:16-18. The possessed person's lack of control over his own motor responses is paralleled by examples of spirit possession in many cultures through history and is attested in anthropological studies of spirit possession today. Some writers have noted parallels between this form of demonized activity and epileptic behavior (though epilepsy and demonic possession are distinguished in Mt 4:24); the parallels could indicate that the spirit gained access to the same centers in the brain where seizures could also be induced by other means.

9:19. Mature *disciples were supposed to be able to carry on in their teacher's absence; sometimes a teacher would delegate lectures to his advanced pupils. The matter at hand requires a different sort of preparation than lectures did (9:29), but Jesus had already prepared them (6:7-13).

9:20-22. Demoniacs were often self-destructive (cf. 5:5), which again characterizes many cases of spirit possession in diverse cultures. See also comment on 9:16-18.

9:23-27. Exorcists usually tried to subdue demons by incantations invoking higher spirits, by using smelly roots or by pain-compliance techniques. Jesus here uses only his command, showing his great authority.

9:28-30. Jewish teachers often explained more mature subjects to their *disciples in private. Some *rabbis were seen as miracle workers, but not often did they expect their disciples to be able to do miracles—and certainly not in the rabbi's name (v. 39). Exorcists' methods normally focused on their own power or, more precisely, their ability to manipulate other powers; Jesus here emphasizes prayer instead (9:29).

9:31. The context of Daniel 7:13-14, which speaks of God entrusting his *kingdom to one like a *Son of Man, declares that suffering at the hands of the evil world ruler precedes exaltation (7:18-27).

9:32. Suffering was not part of the contemporary expectation for the *Messiah; to understand Jesus' message, the people need a paradigm shift in their categories and values (cf. Mk 8:29-33). *Disciples always strove to be respectful toward their *rabbis. They would regard their fellow disciples as their peer group and thus might not include the rabbi in a dispute among themselves.

9:33-37
The Greatest Is the Child

9:33-34. Those with capital could advance economically, but most people in ancient society lacked sufficient capital for advancement and were thus locked into roles determined by birth. Even those who improved economically could not break into the aristocracy. In other circles, rank was assigned by noble birth, by age or by advancement in the *law; thus, for example, the *Qumran sect annually reevaluated each member's rank, which determined their seating and speaking order. By whatever means it was determined, rank was a critical issue in ancient life (cf. comment on 1 Cor 14:27). Many Jewish people hoped for a new status in the world to come, based not on noble birth but on faithfulness to God's covenant.

9:35. In antiquity, as today, heroes or benevolent people with power were eminent. *Rabbis stressed humility but expected their *disciples to serve them.

9:36. Much more than today, in antiquity children were especially powerless in society and dependent on parents.

9:37. In Jewish custom, a person's agent, similar to a modern business representative, could act on behalf of the person who sent him. To the extent that he accurately represented the one who sent him, the agent was supported by the sender's full authority; the principle was applied in the *Old Testament to God's messengers, his prophets (1 Sam 8:7).

9:38-41
Turning Away a True Believer

Here the *disciples, who shortly before could not cast out a demon by using Jesus' name, criticize one of the "little ones" who did act in his name (cf. 9:37) by casting out demons (cf. Num 11:28). The format of this discussion resembles stories in which a famous teacher refutes the contentions of the less informed.

9:38. Sectarian attitudes were common in Judaism, as the *Dead Sea Scrolls testify. (Some Jewish groups would break away from others over such issues as the correct day for Passover.)

9:39. Merely recognizing Jesus' name is one thing, but having the faith to do a miracle in that name indicates that this man was not just a typical exorcist trying to use a more powerful name to accomplish miracles, as exorcists often did (Acts 19:13-16).

9:40. "He who is not against you is for you" may have been a proverb (cf. several sources, including Cicero, a first-century B.C. Roman author); Jesus adapts it to make his point.

9:41. Here Jesus refers to those who are so poor that they have only water to give when a *disciple comes to them (cf. 6:8-11). Such people are very poor even by ancient standards (1 Kings 17:12). This action reflects faith and hospitality one would normally show to teachers one respects (1 Kings 17:12-16; cf. Lk 11:5-6) but not to those one thought to be false (2 Jn 10). Jewish teachers often spoke of receiving one's "reward" when God judged the world.

9:42-50
The Penalty for Turning a Believer Away

9:42. "Stumble" was often used metaphorically to refer to sinning or falling away from the true faith. Millstones were extremely heavy; one would certainly drown with a millstone tied around one's neck. Further, this term refers to the heavier kind of millstone turned by a donkey, rather than the lighter kind a woman would use. Jewish people regarded this punishment as the awful sort that pagans might execute; thus the image is all the more dreadful. Death without burial (including death at sea) was regarded as the worst kind of death; pagans even believed that the spirit of the deceased hovered eternally over the waters where the person had died (see comment on Acts 27:20).

9:43-47. The imagery here is corporal punishment (cutting off appendages, e.g., Ex 21:24-25) versus capital punishment, the decree of eternal death pronounced by the heavenly court. Some Jewish thinkers believed that one would be *resurrected in exactly the form in which one had died (e.g., with limbs missing, as in the case of many martyrs) before being made whole.

9:48. Here the imagery is from Isaiah 66:24. Although one could read Isaiah as applying only to the eternal destruction of corpses (cf. Ecclus 10:11; 19:3), the imagery had nevertheless already begun to be applied to eternal torment (Judith 16:17).

9:49. Salt was used on sacrifices (Lev 2:13; Ezek 43:24; cf. *Jubilees 21:11), so the image may be related to the burning of Mark 9:48.

9:50. Here Jesus apparently changes salt to a positive metaphor, perhaps meaning "peace." That real salt (as opposed to the impure salt mixtures available from some inland sea deposits) by definition does not lose its saltiness only reinforces the strength of the image (cf. comment on Mt 5:13). Being "at peace with one another" contrasts with the divisiveness related in Mark 9:33-38.

10:1-12
Divorce Forbidden

Because 10:1-12 addresses the treatment of spouses, 10:13-16 deals with the treatment of children, and 10:17-31 relates to one's true household in the *kingdom, some scholars have compared 10:1-31 to the ancient literary form "household code," except that this passage is in *narrative form. If this comparison is apt, Mark's point runs precisely counter to the values of those codes in his culture, which stressed the absolute submission of wives, children and slaves (see comment on Eph 5:21-33).

10:1. Most teachers who taught in public did so in specific localities. Only figures popular with the masses drew such crowds as Jesus did wherever they went, and these popular teachers would naturally arouse the envy of many local professional scholars and the discomfort of the authorities.

10:2. Matthew's wording (Mt 19:3; see comment there) is closer to the exact wording *Pharisees would normally have used at that time; the issue was the *grounds* for divorce, not whether divorce was ever valid. Because Moses had assumed the practice of divorce (Deut 24:1), Jewish interpreters debated only the grounds for divorce; to ask whether Jesus thinks divorce is permissible at all is to ask whether he knows or agrees with Moses' law.

10:3-5. *Rabbis distinguished between what Scripture commanded and what it allowed as a concession; by asking what Moses "commanded" Jesus forces them to recognize that Moses explicitly only "permitted," not "commanded," divorce, on any grounds.

10:6-9. Jewish interpreters commonly appealed to one clear text of Scripture to show that another text could not mean what its interpreters claimed that it meant. Some interpreters, like the *scribes who wrote the *Dead Sea Scrolls, appealed to the creation *narrative to show God's original plan for marriage. These interpreters used Genesis 1—2 to argue against polygamy; Jesus uses it to argue against divorce. (Reflecting Greek custom against polygamy, the *Septuagint had substituted "two" for the original Hebrew "they" in Gen 2:24.)

10:10. *Disciples often sought more detailed explanations from their teachers privately.

10:11. Like many wisdom sayings of ancient Jewish teachers, this saying is a general rule; Matthew (Mt 5:32) and Paul (1 Cor 7:15) give exceptions (on behalf of the innocent party divorced against his or her will). The saying is *hyperbolic—that is, it has exaggerated, intensified force: because God does not accept divorce as valid, any man who divorces his wife is not really divorced, and if he marries someone else, he commits adultery. No one else in antiquity spoke of divorce in such strong terms. (Because most Jewish teachers allowed polygamy, they would not have seen marrying a second wife as adultery, even if they had agreed that the man was still married to the first wife. But Jesus eliminates the double standard; a man consorting with two women is as adulterous as a woman consorting with two men. Jesus' point is to advocate fidelity to one's first wife, not to break up existing polygamous unions.)

10:12. Unlike Roman law, Palestinian Jewish law did not permit a woman to divorce her husband (although under extreme circumstances she could request that the court force him to divorce her). The only Jewish women who flouted this law were aristocrats like Herodias (6:17), who paid more attention to Greek custom than to Jewish custom. Mark, who writes for readers living where wives could divorce their husbands, brings out the implications of Jesus' teaching for them too. (Like modern preachers, ancient writers had the liberty to paraphrase sayings to bring out their meanings.)

10:13-16
Images of the Kingdom

10:13. Children were loved but were socially powerless; the high infant mortality rate meant that they were physically powerless as well, many dying before attaining maturity. (In the poorest places, like Egypt, perhaps half of those born died by the age of twelve. Poorer *Gentile families often discarded babies if they thought they could not support them.) Eager to get on with the business of setting up the *kingdom, the *disciples have little time for people who do not wield political power.

10:14-15. Some thought that the *kingdom would be achieved by force of arms; others, by radical moral reform, and so on. But although Jewish people (unlike Greeks) respected humility, no one expected the kingdom to come by becoming powerless like children. The totally powerless can depend on no one but God.

10:16. In Genesis some of the patriarchs conferred blessings by the laying on of hands (Gen 48:14), and their prayers were answered. We may be sure that these children were truly blessed.

10:17-31
A Rich Man and the Kingdom

10:17. A pious man customarily sought out his own teacher; a man of wealth could normally find the best or most popular teacher for himself. For a man of wealth to bow before a teacher indicated tremendous respect. We know that at least some *disciples asked their teachers questions like the one this rich man asks Jesus. To "inherit *eternal life" meant to share in the life of the coming world, the life of the *kingdom of God.

10:18-19. Without denying that he himself is good, Jesus reminds the man of the standard Jewish conception of God's goodness (others could be good, but no one compared with God); he then lists select commandments from the *Old Testament (five from the Ten Commandments) dealing with human relations (rather than directly with God) that people could test (not, for instance, a prohibition against a sin of the heart, coveting).

10:20. If only God is good, the man will have to admit he has broken some commandment; but the commandments Jesus had listed were kept by most well-raised, educated Jewish people.

10:21-22. Judaism stressed charity heavily, but Jewish teachers did not normally require a prospective *disciple to divest himself entirely of funds. Several teachers, especially some radical Greek teachers, made such demands on rich students to see if they would value true teaching above their wealth; a few rich persons would give up their goods, but most disappointed such teachers.

10:23-24. Jesus turns the social order upside down. The well-to-do were often hailed for their generosity (they had more to give); being less educated in the law, the poor were sometimes seen as less pious (although poverty itself was certainly not seen as a sign of impiety, especially by the poor themselves).

10:25. This image reflects a Jewish figure of speech for doing something impossible (a large animal going through a needle's eye). The saying, a *hyperbole, refers to a literal needle. (Those who think Jesus refers here to a gate in Jerusalem called the "eye of a needle" are mistaken, because that gate was built in medieval times.) A wealthy person could relinquish wealth only by God's grace (10:26-27).

10:26-30. Most of Jesus' *disciples had not been poor (being fishermen and *tax gatherers) but had abandoned their economic position to follow him. Their reward would be found in believers sharing possessions as a family in this world (cf. 6:10; Mt 10:42; Acts

2:44-45) and receiving the life of the *kingdom in the world to come.

10:31. Most Jewish people understood that the day of judgment would turn things upside down; those who appear great in this world will be nothing in the next, and those who were nothing in this world will be great in the next. Jewish people applied this principle to the exaltation of Israel over the other nations, the oppressed righteous over their wicked oppressors, but Jesus applies it also to individual rank and status.

10:32-34 Third Passion Prediction

10:32. Despite their expectation of the coming *kingdom, the *disciples recognize the danger of going to Jerusalem and confronting the high priestly aristocracy there. Perhaps they are aware of Jewish traditions about a terrible war preceding the final establishing of the *Messiah's kingdom—a war in which the Jerusalem aristocracy would prove as evil as the Romans (cf. the *Dead Sea Scrolls). Or perhaps they trust the Jerusalem leaders but fear the Roman garrison in Jerusalem.

10:33-34. Jesus warns against both the Jewish aristocracy and the Romans, who will execute him in the manner customary for revolutionaries. On the suffering *Son of Man, see comment on 9:31.

10:35-45 The Greatest Is the Servant

10:35-37. James and John want the status of viceroys in an earthly kingdom; this desire again reflects a popular conception of the *Messiah and God's *kingdom that Jesus has repeatedly repudiated (see comment on 8:31-38).

10:38. Jesus elsewhere refers to the cross as his cup (14:23-24, 36), which may allude to the cup of judgment that appears often in the *Old Testament (Ps 60:3; 75:8; Is 51:17-23; Jer 25:15-29; 49:12; Lam 4:21; Zech 12:2). His baptism in some way also prefigures his death (see comment on Mk 1:11; cf. Lk 12:50; Ps 69:2, 14-15).

10:39-40. The positions on either side of a king's throne (especially the right side) were the most prestigious in a kingdom. But Jesus may be alluding instead to those crucified on his right and his left (15:27). James was later the first of the twelve martyred (Acts 12:2), but according to church tradition John lived into the nineties.

10:41-42. Jewish people knew well the *Gentile model of authority: ancient near Eastern kings had long claimed to be gods and ruled tyrannically; Greek rulers had adopted the same posture through much of the eastern Mediterranean. The Roman emperor and his provincial agents (who often showed little concern for Jewish sensitivities) would have been viewed in much the same light: brutal and tyrannical. Jesus' reminding the *disciples that seeking power was a Gentile (i.e., pagan) practice was tantamount to telling them they should not be doing it; Jewish teachers used Gentile practices as negative examples.

10:43-44. It was radical for Jesus to define greatness in terms of servanthood; despite Jewish rules requiring that slaves be well treated, Jewish free persons, like their Gentile counterparts, considered slaves socially inferior.

10:45. By calling himself a "servant" and defining his mission as "giving his life a ransom for the many," Jesus identifies himself with the suffering servant of Isaiah 53:10-12 (despite the contrary view of some interpreters today). Although the servant's mission had been given to Israel as a whole (Is

41:8; 43:10; 44:2, 21; 49:3), Israel through disobedience could not fulfill it (42:19), so that the one who would fulfill it had to restore Israel as well as bring light to the *Gentiles (49:5-7; 52:13—53:12). Because hardly anyone else had yet applied this passage to the *Messiah, Jesus is trying to redefine their expectation about his messianic mission. On the "many" see comment on Romans 5:15.

10:46-52
Stopping for a Blind Beggar

The *disciples want to get on with the business of setting up the *kingdom (10:37; 11:9-10), not understanding that stopping for a blind beggar is the sort of thing Jesus' kingdom is all about.

10:46. The blind, the lame and others who could not engage in the traditional occupations of the day could support themselves only by begging, normally on a busy roadside. Judaism considered it righteous to help them. Jericho was a prosperous town with a good climate, and Timaeus's son no doubt received adequate support there.

10:47-48. Except for what they had learned from listening to others recite, blind people in that time were illiterate in the *law (Braille had not been invented yet, so they could not read). They were thus not respected as religious persons, although they were protected under the law of Moses. They were also socially powerless, and Jesus' followers view this blind man's loud pleas as an intrusion, the way they had viewed the children (10:13). The *disciples may have viewed Jesus' final journey to Jerusalem as a royal procession, and it was foolhardy and impudent to interrupt a royal procession.

10:49-52. By "stopping" and standing still, Jesus allows the blind man to come to where Jesus' voice had last sounded. The "cloak" (10:50) is an outer garment, used as a coat in cold weather and as bedding at night, and might have been spread before him for use in his daytime begging if he had no pouch. On the *narrative level, the act of casting it aside may signify his forsaking dependence on anything else and trusting only in Jesus.

11:1-11
Jesus Enters Jerusalem

Although later Jewish teachers understood "the king coming on a donkey" (Zech 9:9) *messianically, it is not clear that the whole crowd understands Jesus' claim to messiahship here. Had members of the Roman garrison been present outside the gates and recognized the implications of Jesus' claim, they would have arrested him.

11:1-2. Heralds or messengers were typically sent two by two (6:7; cf. 14:13). That Jesus chooses a colt over a grown donkey reinforces Mark's portrayal of his humility.

11:3. Residents of the area around Jerusalem had to be particularly hospitable with their property around Passover season, when Jewish pilgrims from the whole ancient world came for the feast. The response to the potential question could have meant, "Lend these to Jesus, the teacher" (*Aramaic *rab* can be translated as "master" or "lord"), or "Lend these to the service of God."

11:4-6. In many cities, the doors of homes faced a courtyard shared by neighbors; in a small village, the doorway may have just faced a dirt road through the town. People would normally ride the adult, not the colt never before ridden, so the *disciples' purpose in untying the colt may not have been immediately obvious even had they owned it themselves.

11:7-8. The spreading of garments

represents royal homage (2 Kings 9:13). Branches were also waved in homage to rulers (cf. 1 Macc 13:51; 2 Macc 10:7). The larger palm branches used for the Feast of Tabernacles (in the fall) would not be available at Passover time (in the spring), unless brought from Jericho; the branches described here are small enough for the colt to walk on. (Carrying branches was also part of the worship at the feast depicted in Ps 118:27.)

Pilgrims to the feast were typically welcomed by crowds already there, so it is unlikely that the whole crowd recognized the significance of Jesus' entry. In view of the crowd's acclamation in 11:10, however, the image that may have come most readily to the minds of Mark's ancient readers is probably that of a royal entrance procession.

11:9. "Hosanna" means "O save!" and both this and the next line of verse 9 come from Psalm 118:25-26. Psalms 113—118, called the Hallel, were regularly sung at Passover season, so these words were fresh in everyone's minds; hopes for the restoration of the Davidic kingdom also ran high at this time of year.

11:10. The coming of the *kingdom when David or his descendants would again reign (e.g., Is 9; 11; Jer 23) is here associated with the hope of one coming in the Lord's name. (David is their "father" in the sense of "deliverer," not their ancestor: cf. Is 9:6; 2 Kings 13:14.) Passover commemorated God's deliverance of Israel from slavery in Egypt; consequently, Jewish hopes for a future deliverance from their current problems ran high during this season, and Rome had troops in Jerusalem ready in case riot control became necessary. By treating Jesus as the object of any of these hopes, the crowds are beginning to see in this teacher a possible *messianic figure who could lead them against the Romans.

11:11. The ancient workday began at sunrise; the "evening" offering in the temple was what we call afternoon (about 3 p.m.). "Late" may mean not "dark" but rather that the daily activity in the temple had begun to subside.

11:12-25
The Temple and the Tree: Judgment Coming

Jesus' prophetic act against the temple is enclosed by the story of his cursing the fig tree, also an acted *parable of judgment. Fig trees were one of the most common kinds of trees in Palestine.

11:12-14. At this time of year, edible figs were still about six weeks away, but the bland fruit had recently appeared on the tree in late March; they would become ripe by late May. These were the early figs that preceded the main crop of late figs, which were ripe for harvest from mid-August into October. If only leaves appeared, without the early figs, that tree would bear no figs that year—early or late. Because everyone would know that it was "not yet the season for [real] figs," Jesus is making a point about trees that only pretend to have good fruit (cf. Jer 24). In some Jewish stories, exceptionally holy men could curse others or objects and so destroy them; Jesus exerts genuine authority to curse only here, as an acted *parable to his *disciples.

11:15. Jewish people from other parts of the empire or even from different towns in Galilee would have local currencies that needed to be converted to some standard for use in the temple. Further, one was not to bring sacrifices from long distances but to follow the more convenient prescription of Moses' law: buy the sacrifices in Jerusalem. Moneychangers and sellers of doves were thus necessary and in some sense biblical. The issue is not whether there should have been money-changers; it is whether it was valid to turn much of the outer court into a place emphasizing commerce rather than worship. With hundreds of thousands of pilgrims at Passover, the merchants' strip in the temple must have been quite large; disturbing a significant portion of this business would have attracted everyone's attention.

11:16. Later *rabbinic law also warned against defiling the temple courts by carrying unnecessary items through them, but no one protested as strongly as Jesus does, and no one seems to have questioned the necessity of commercial activity in the outer court at a feast.

11:17. Jesus cites two texts as the basis for his attack. The first is Isaiah 56:7. God's house was intended to be for all peoples (1 Kings 8:41-43; Is 56:7), and in the *Old Testament the only separation in the temple was between priests and people. But in Jesus' day the temple was also segregated by race and gender for purity reasons, with Jewish women on a lower level outside the Court of Israel and non-Jews in the outermost court. Jesus shows his concern for the worship of the *Gentiles and protests racial segregation in a religious institution.

The second text he cites is from Jeremiah 7:11, where Jeremiah condemns the idea that the temple is a safe haven for Judah in its sin; although those who have exploited the poor think that the temple will protect them, God will destroy his temple (Jer 7:3-15). Robbers' "dens" were where robbers kept their loot; in A.D. 66 rebel brigands or "robbers" (for whom *Josephus uses the same term as Mark) took possession of the temple and slaughtered the priests, further inviting God's impending wrath (see comment on Mk 13:14).

11:18. Knowing the priestly aristocracy, one can easily recognize that they saw in Jesus' attack on the temple establishment a threat to their own economic and social interests. Their position in relation to both the Romans and their own people depended in large measure on their authority and keeping order in the temple.

11:19. Jerusalem was too crowded at Passover season to accommodate all the pilgrims during this period, though the pilgrims would seek to eat the Passover meal itself within the city's walls.

11:20-24. Some Jewish texts speak of "removing mountains" as an infinitely long or virtually impossible task, accomplished only by the most pious (the *rabbis applied it to mastering studies that appeared humanly impossible to master). Thus Jesus is saying that nothing will be too hard for the person of faith. The image of God's *Spirit bringing down a mountain before a faithful servant also appears in Zechariah 4:6-7 (where the faithful one is the anointed king). The promise of one's commands coming to pass probably presupposes *Spirit-inspired speech (cf., e.g., 2 Kings 2:21-22; 4:3-7, 41-44; Lam 3:37; Acts 3:6, 16).

11:25. Standing (often with uplifted hands) was the normal posture for prayer; kneeling was much rarer.

11:27-33
By Whose Authority?

11:27-28. As guardians of the temple and the status quo with the Romans, the chief priests would see Jesus' act as a direct challenge to their authority.

11:29-30. Here Jesus argues that his authority and John's derive from the same source, from "heaven" (one Jewish way of saying "God"). This argument follows the Jewish legal principle that a commissioned messenger acts on the full authority of the one who sent him. If John's authority were merely human (cf. Deut 18:20; Jer 23:16), they should have taken a firmer stand against him (Deut 13:1-11); if it was divine, God would hold them to account for not having listened (Deut 18:18-19).

11:31-32. The chief priests were politicians—less popular than the politically powerless *Pharisees—who had to balance the interests of both their people and the Roman authorities. Thus they had to keep popular opinion in mind when making decisions that might incur the displeasure of the people (11:32).

11:33. Counterquestion (11:29) was a legitimate means of debate; their withdrawal from the rules of debate *rhetorically frees Jesus from the responsibility to continue in dialogue with them.

12:1-12
The Greedy Tenant Farmers

Jesus still addresses those who fancy themselves rulers of Israel, reminding them that they are merely custodians appointed by God (like the shepherds of Jer 23 and Ezek 34) over his vineyard.

Much of the rural Roman Empire, including parts of Galilee, was controlled by wealthy landowners, whose land was worked by tenant farmers. Landowners had great status in society, whereas tenant farmers had little except, perhaps, among their own peers.

12:1. Here Jesus describes a normal way to prepare a vineyard, but he clearly alludes to Isaiah 5:1-2, where Israel is the vineyard. Some Jewish interpreters by the time of Jesus saw Isaiah 5 as a prediction of the temple's destruction in 586 B.C.; if such an allusion was in the mind of any of Jesus' hearers, it would communicate his warning all the more forcefully.

According to the most likely reconstructions, the "wall" was a rugged stone hedge, and the vat was a pit into which juice would run when workers trod down newly picked grapes. The top of the "watchtower" was a sentry post against intruders, but the building itself, probably a crude hut, undoubtedly also housed workers during harvest season.

12:2. Payments were rendered at harvest time, often one-quarter to as much as one-half the produce.

12:3-5. Landowners always had power, socially and legally, to enforce their will on the tenants; a few reportedly even had hired assassins to deal with troublesome tenants. Here the tenants act as if they are the ones with power, and they exploit it mercilessly (as opposed to the ideal of a *benevolent* landowner). Their behavior fits the Jewish tradition that Israel martyred many of the prophets God sent.

12:6. In the light of 1:11 and 9:7, the "beloved son" clearly represents Jesus and probably alludes to Genesis 22:2, where similar Hebrew words were used by Jewish readers to emphasize the pathos involved in Abraham's willingness to give up his precious son Isaac.

12:7-8. The tenants presume too much about the inheritance; although they could have seized it under certain legal conditions, the owner could also stipulate—and after their misdeeds certainly would—that someone else inherit the vineyard; or representatives of the emperor could have seized it. The story paints the tenants as more wicked and stupid than one would expect any *real* tenants to be; but it is transparent that the tenants represent the religious leaders who serve themselves rather than God (12:12).

12:9. The ancient hearers would wonder why the landowner had not come and thrown out the tenants earlier.

12:10-12. This text is from Psalm 118:22-23, part of the Hallel, like 118:25-26 cited in Mark 11:9-10. The building referred to is the temple (Ps 118:18-21, 25-27); as the cornerstone of a new temple, Jesus is a threat to the builders of the old one.

12:13-17
Caesar and God

*Rabbis dealt with questions concerning legal, moral and exegetical issues as well as mocking questions posed by opponents (e.g., *Sadducees, *Gentiles, apostates and schismatics). Parallels to these basic categories of questions appear in Mark 12:13-37, where Jesus' answers prove him a proficient rabbi.

12:13. *Pharisees tended to be nationalistic, whereas Herodians were clients of Herod, the Roman vassal; they worked together only in extraordinary situations. Pharisees would be concerned about Jewish legal requirements to have witnesses for a charge but would be ready to investigate charges concerning Jesus' disloyalty to the *law. That they would try to test his teaching here is not surprising. The Herodians, who hoped for a restoration of Herodian rule in Judea (which Pilate currently governed), were naturally disturbed by *messianic figures who challenged their idea of Herodian rule and might cause Rome to tighten its direct control over the land.

12:14-15. They pit the obligations of peace with Rome against the nationalistic, messianic fervor that they assume Jesus has generated; a disastrous tax revolt two decades earlier had shown where such fervor could lead. If he publicly takes the view characterized by those later called *Zealots (no king but God), he can be arrested; if he rejects that view (which he does), he may compromise his following.

12:16-17. Jewish Palestine circulated copper coins that omitted the image of the deified emperor, which was offensive to Jewish tastes. (Although King Agrippa later used both the image of the emperor and his own, Herod Antipas, current ruler in Galilee, avoided any images on his coins, and so did local Jewish coinage.) But Jesus' opponents have a silver denarius—which bore the emperor's image—available when he requests one. They are therefore hardly in a position to challenge his lack of nationalistic zeal.

12:18-27
Sadducees and the Resurrection

12:18. One of the basic points of contention between *Pharisees and *Sadducees was that the latter did not accept the future *resurrection of the bodies of the dead.

12:19. The Sadducees' question to Jesus concerns the custom called levirate marriage (Deut 25:5-6), which was meant to protect widows economically. It is practiced in many societies where women are not permitted to earn wages.

12:20-23. The Sadducees probably take this story line from the Jewish book of Tobit, where seven husbands of pious Sarah die one after the other.

12:24-27. Jesus' response resembles standard *Pharisaic responses. When Pharisees debated this issue with Sadducees, they argued for the *resurrection from the *law of Moses; they typically read a text for all they could get out of it. Standard Jewish interpretive technique would have read Exodus 3:6 as present tense, "I *am* the God of the patriarchs"—implying that the patriarchs still lived. Phrases like "in the passage about the bush" were standard, because the Bible had not yet been divided into chapters and verses.

12:28-34
The Love Commandments

12:28. *Rabbis would often discuss the question of which commandments were heavier (i.e., more important) and which were lighter.

12:29-34. Following Jewish interpretive technique, Jesus links the two commandments (Deut 6:5; Lev 19:18) by a common key word, "love." These passages were also linked in Jewish tradition (e.g., *Philo), and some other teachers felt that these were the greatest commandments that summarized the law. This was especially true of "Love the Lord your God," which followed directly on and applied the basic confession of Judaism, "Hear, O Israel, the Lord . . . is one" (Deut 6:4). That many of Jesus' hearers would recognize the truth of his reply makes it all the more difficult to dispute with him on the matter.

12:35-37
David's Lord

When Jewish teachers challenged their hearers to resolve apparent discrepancies in Scripture, they assumed that both texts were true (in this case, Jesus knows that he is both David's son and David's Lord) and were asking how to harmonize them. Jesus' opponents apparently have no answer, because Jewish interpreters did not apply Psalm 110:1 to the *Messiah.

12:35. By definition, the Christ, or anointed one, was the royal descendant of David (Is 9:7; 11:1; Ps 2; 89; 132). But this view of *messiahship lent itself to a revolutionary view of the *kingdom (see Mk 11:10) and was thus inadequate by itself.

12:36-37. The one who would reign in God's *kingdom was David's "lord," not merely his descendant; he would thus be greater than the *resurrected David. Writing in Greek, Mark may want his readers to connect this verse (Ps 110:1) with a verse he has cited in the preceding section, because Jewish interpreters often linked verses with a key word—there was only one Lord: God (Mk 12:29). If so, Mark makes a claim for Jesus' deity here (cf. 1:3).

12:38-44
The Pious Poor and Their Religious Oppressors

12:38. Like their Greek counterparts, some Jewish teachers wore a special identifying garb; this seems to have been a long, white linen robe, similar to those of priests and temple officials. Teachers were normally greeted with titles of honor; marketplaces, which were full of people, would provide many opportunities for these teachers to receive such recognition.

12:39. *Synagogues were not all of the same shape or size, but in many later synagogues, teachers could take a seat in full view of most of the rest of the assembly (like ministers in most churches today). What is significant is their status in a status-conscious society; synagogues were the most important assembly places for the community. At banquets, those seated nearest the host were in positions of honor; ancient literature is full of complaints from those snubbed by being given socially inferior seats.

12:40. Widows had little means of support, were socially powerless and honorless in a society emphasizing status and honor, and were to be protected under Jewish law.

Jesus could mean that these teachers exploit widows' resources by seeking extensive tithes (which they could set at 20-30 percent, on top of the heavy land taxes levied by the government); or he could mean that they follow the letter of the law in legal decisions rather than showing mercy to the poor. Whatever their specific crime, the charge of "devouring widows' houses" portrays them as worse than *tax gatherers.

They may have lingered long in their individual prayers in the *synagogues; it is not the longevity of prayers but the motive of this longevity that Jesus criticizes here. Like the *Old Testament prophets, Jesus sees social injustice and religious hypocrisy as inextricably linked (e.g., Amos 2:7; 8:5-6), and he stands on behalf of the economically powerless (Is 1:17).

12:41-44. A later tradition claims that thirteen receptacles for such gifts stood in the Court of Women, accessible to Israelite women as well as to men. The temple sported ostentatious wealth, and its officials would probably waste this widow's money; but this powerless woman, ignorant of that likelihood, acts in good faith and is the greatest giver in God's sight. The widow would not starve, given provisions for the poor in Jewish *synagogues (cf. comment on Acts 6:1-4). The widow's "mite," or *lepton*, represented the lightest and least valuable coin of the period.

13:1-4
Setting of Jesus' End-Time Discourse

Mark could have gotten in serious trouble with the Roman authorities for writing this chapter; Jewish underground tracts about the time of the end usually included Israel's exaltation, and Rome distrusted any threat to its power. But this chapter before Jesus' arrest climaxes Jesus' warnings to his *disciples in Mark: true followers must be ready to follow to the cross and share his sufferings.

13:1. Greek texts often portray Greek philosophical teachers conversing with their *disciples while strolling about; this may have been a common teaching technique.

The temple complex consisted of many buildings and was one of the largest, most magnificent structures in the ancient world; it was twice the size of Solomon's temple. Construction had begun under Herod the Great before Jesus' birth and was still continuing at this time. Jewish people all over the world contributed to the temple, and so much was received that officials kept adding on to a golden vine that was part of its ostentatious glory. It was sacred to Herod's enemies as well as to his allies.

13:2. In A.D. 70, the Romans destroyed the temple. The wording here is only slightly *hyperbolic: some stones remained in place, but most of the temple was obliterated. As exemplified in the *Dead Sea Scrolls, some other goups also expected God to judge the temple authorities; but no one before A.D. 66 was as accurate concerning the timing as Jesus was (13:30).

13:3-4. Although Greek teachers often instructed their pupils while walking, they also often instructed them while sitting in front of a temple. The *disciples question to Jesus about the sign of the temple's destruction sets the scene for Jesus' answer in the rest of the chapter, in which he describes both the imminent end of the Jerusalemites' world and the ultimate end of the age.

13:5-8
Not Yet the End

13:5-6. False *messiahs were common and often drew significant Jewish followings in Palestine as late as Bar Kochba, whom Rabbi Akiba hailed as the Messiah around A.D. 130.

13:7-8. Ancient Jewish prophecy teachers usually listed these events among the signs of the end; the end was often portrayed as preceded by great sufferings or a final war, and was sometimes compared with birth pangs. Jesus says that instead these events characterize normal life until the end; history until the final time is only the *beginning* of birth pangs.

13:9-13
Sufferings to Expect Before the End

13:9. Before A.D. 70, local courts, or councils deciding cases, were probably run by local elders or priests; in later times *rabbis would staff them. *Synagogues were the local places of public assembly and thus provided the natural place for hearings and public discipline. Sometimes discipline was administered in the form of flogging; under second-century rules, this meant thirteen harsh strokes on the breast and twenty-six on the back; the smiter was to strike as hard as possible. These words would have particularly pained Jewish Christians, because they signified rejection among their own people.

13:10. In context, this preaching will be carried out before officials of all nations ("kings"—v. 9—could refer just to Rome's vassal princes, but "all nations" suggests that Parthian and other rulers from the East are also in view), indicating virtually universal persecution.

13:11. Jewish people thought of the *Holy Spirit especially as the Spirit of *prophecy who had anointed the prophets to speak God's message.

13:12. See Micah 7:5-7 (more explicit in Mt 10:35-36).

13:14-23
The Prerequisite for the End

About a decade after Jesus uttered these words, his *disciples had good reason to remember them. When the Roman emperor Caligula declared himself divine and tried to set up his image in the Jerusalem temple (A.D. 39), Jesus' sayings about the impending abomination that would cause desolation must have been circulated with renewed vigor. These sayings were available to Paul a decade later (2 Thess 2:1-12) and to Mark when he wrote his Gospel (perhaps A.D. 64). The abomination that would bring about desolation was finally fulfilled in A.D. 66-70.

13:14. *Josephus, who lived through the war of 66-70, thought the "abomination of desolation" (the reference is to Dan 9:27; cf. 11:31; 12:11) happened in A.D. 66, when *Zealots shed the blood of priests in the temple. Others date the abomination of desolation three and one-half years later, in 70. The Jerusalemites had considered it a sacrilege for the Roman standards, which bore the image of the worshiped emperor, to enter Jerusalem. But in the year 70, when the temple was destroyed, the Romans erected these standards over the desolate site of the temple. Both views may be true: if the phrase means "abomination that *causes* desolation," then the abomination of A.D. 66 may have led to the desolation of A.D. 70.

The mountains were full of caves and represented the safest place to flee; both David and the second-century B.C. Jewish revolutionaries, the Maccabees, had earlier practiced guerrilla warfare from them, and Jewish refugees hid there in the war of A.D. 132-135. It is reported that the Jerusalem Christians, warned by prophecies before Jerusalem's fall, fled to a place called Pella, hewn from foothills far to the north.

13:15. Housetops were flat and used for prayer, drying vegetables and so forth. Because one approached them by an outdoor staircase, one who fled in haste would descend without entering the house to retrieve any possessions.

13:16. Workers would wear their outer coats in the cool of the early morning but leave them on the edge of the field as the day grew warmer. This exhortation again indicates haste.

13:17. The difficulties of bearing or nursing a child under these circumstances are obvious in any culture, especially to mothers. Mothers often nursed their babies for the first two years of life. The text may also indicate grief over the loss of the children (cf. *2 Baruch 10:13-15).

13:18. In addition to the colder nights and rains, in winter the dry Judean creek beds were filled without warning with rainwater from the hills, and they became difficult to cross. *Josephus wrote of a group of Jewish fugitives from Jerusalem who were delayed by the recently flooded Jordan in the spring of 68 and as a consequence were slaughtered by Roman soldiers.

13:19. Daniel 11 ends with Antiochus Epiphanes in the second century B.C., and the final distress to which no other tribulation could be compared (12:1) seems to occur at that time, to be followed by the *resurrection of the dead (12:2). But sometimes events in Israel's history (like the promise to Abraham or the conquest of Canaan) were deferred, and Daniel 9:24-27 better fits a date in the first century A.D. than in the time of Antiochus.

Jesus' addition of "never shall be" (Joel 2:2) to Daniel's "such as never occurred" suggests that other tribulations after 66-70 could follow in history.

13:20. "The days" refers presumably to Daniel's 1,260 days; given the severity of sufferings, the full period was too long to permit survivors.

13:21-23. False prophets and false *messiahs had gained Jewish followings all through this period and usually challenged the authority of Rome, leading to the death of their followers. Some such prophets continued claiming that God would deliver Jerusalem up to their slaughter by the Romans at the fall of Jerusalem. After the temple's demise, hopes for the *Messiah's coming were presumably even more intense.

13:24-27 The End of This World

13:24-25. Here Jesus uses the language of the end (Is 13:10; 34:4; cf. 24:23; Ezek 32:7-8). Sometimes this cataclysmic language was used for historical events (the *Sibylline Oracles use it for an earthquake; cf. Jer 4:20-28), but usually ancient literature reserves it for the end or transformation of the present world order and the establishing of God's eternal *kingdom.

As in Daniel, the end Jesus predicted seems to have been deferred; the temple was destroyed just as Jesus predicted, but he did not then return. Because *Old Testament *prophecies blended together events according to the kind of event rather than the time they would occur, Jesus likely means that the end would follow the temple's destruction and the ensuing tribulation; hence the end remains imminent.

13:26. Jesus describes the *Son of Man in terms that Jewish literature usually reserved for God (coming in glory, sending his angels). The text clearly alludes to Daniel 7:13-14, where "one like a son of man" (i.e., like a human being) receives the *kingdom from God. This Son of Man functions as a representative on behalf of Israel, who in the same context suffers and also receives the right to rule the world (7:25-27).

13:27. One of the most prominent features of Jewish future expectation was the regathering of the dispersed tribes of Israel. (Mark probably means the dispersion of believers in Jesus here; cf. 2 Thess 2:1).

13:28-31
The End Is Imminent

13:28-29. The signs Jesus lists show that the end is imminent, just as a fig tree's leaves show what season it is: because fig trees lack smaller branches they appear barren in winter, but they bloom in late March and are ideal for shade in the summer. This image could refer back to Jesus' acted-out *parable with a fig tree, implying the imminent destruction of the temple (see comment on 11:12-25).

13:30. The length of generations varied but was often represented in the *Old Testament by forty years (in the *Dead Sea Scrolls, forty years represents the suffering of the final generation). Jesus speaks these words near A.D. 30; the temple would be destroyed in A.D. 70.

13:31. Others also noted that it was easier for heaven and earth to pass than for God to forget his covenant or his words (e.g., Jer 31:35-37). Here Jesus speaks of his own words in the same manner.

13:32-37
The Time of the End Is Unknown

13:32-34. Other Jewish teachers also told *parables of kings or householders going away and returning to find spouse or servants faithful or unfaithful. First-century readers heard enough stories about such events (including in the Bible—Prov 7:19-20) to relate to the image well. Slaves held many different roles, but the doorkeeper's role was a prominent one, because he held the master's keys, kept out unwanted visitors and checked other slaves leaving the premises. But with the relative prestige of the doorkeeper's position (some were married to *freedwomen) came great responsibility as well.

13:35. The times of night which Jesus mentions represent the Roman division of the night into four watches, Jesus' only guarantee being that he will come at night while the servant is posted on guard duty. In most of the ancient Mediterranean a rooster's final crowing could function like a modern alarm clock, signalling the advent of dawn; but in this context it refers to the "watch" by that name, the quarter of the night after midnight (see comment on 14:30, 72).

Because the roads were infested with robbers, one would not expect the master to travel at night when it was unnecessary. Thus a slave could be caught off guard if the master returned at night.

13:36-37. Falling asleep at one's guard post would lead to punishment.

14:1-11
Anointed for Burial

14:1. Jewish literature reports that many high priests bullied those who opposed them. Thus they would certainly not tolerate someone who said that God had directed him to attack their temple cult or who threatened impending judgment on its unwatchful servants.

14:2. Jerusalem was crowded during the feast, with perhaps five times its usual population. Riots were known to occur; *Josephus reported that at one Passover several decades after the events of this verse, thirty thousand persons were crushed or trampled. Thus extra Roman troops were garrisoned in Jerusalem during the feast, and the Roman governor came from

Caesarea to be on hand in case of trouble. The danger of arresting Jesus at the feast (i.e., during the festal time, in public) reflects an important concern for the temple leadership.

14:3. Bethany was one of those villages near Jerusalem where Passover pilgrims could spend the night with hosts. One "sat" at normal meals; one "reclined" on couches at special meals like feasts or banquets. If Simon had been a "leper" (nicknames usually had some basis but were not always meant literally; e.g., a tall family was nicknamed the "Goliaths"), he was certainly not one by this point; no one would have joined him for dinner if he had been. Jesus may have healed him.

14:4-5. It was customary to anoint the heads of important guests, but this woman's action is extreme. Whatever her economic status, this perfume (an oil from a root probably imported from India or South Arabia) was worth a year of a common laborer's wages; her family had probably kept it as a status symbol. Its fragrance was preserved by sealing it in alabaster (the favored container for perfume), and once the flask was broken its contents had to be used immediately. Her anointing of Jesus represents a major sacrifice and indicates the depth of her love, but given the great numbers of landless or tenant-farming peasants, some people present think the worth of the perfume could have been put to better use.

14:6-7. Jesus' reply probably contains an allusion to Deuteronomy 15:11, which urges generosity to the poor, who will always be in the land. He does not play down giving to the poor; rather he plays up what follows.

14:8-9. In Jewish tradition kings (including, by definition, the *Messiah, or "anointed one"), priests and others had to be anointed for service. But Jesus here stresses a different kind of anointing, which the woman undoubtedly had not intended: anointing a body for burial. This woman's act of love was the only anointing Jesus would receive (16:1).

14:10-11. Judas could easily locate the chief priests, although they would not have been accessible to him had his mission been less in line with their plans. His mercenary motives would have appeared as vile to ancient readers as they do to us, and they contrast with the behavior of the unnamed woman of 14:1-9.

14:12-26
The New Passover and the Betrayer

14:12. By this period the Feast of Unleavened Bread, which immediately followed Passover, had been extended in popular parlance to include the Passover itself. Representatives from each family would have the priests slaughter a lamb for them in the temple, then return with it to feed the whole family that night.

14:13. Many commentators point out that water jars (as opposed to wineskins) were nearly always carried by women; a man carrying one would therefore be a noticeable sign. Households that could afford slaves always had them carry the water; in many cities, servants were sent to the public fountains to bring rainwater that had been stored in cisterns.

14:14-16. Anyone with a two-story house, the second story containing a "large" upper room, would be considered well-to-do. This family presumably resided in the area of Jerusalem known as the Upper City, near the temple, rather than the poorer Lower City, downwind of Jerusalem's sewage. Because the Passover had to be eaten within Jerusalem's walls, most homes would be crowded with guests; but the accommodations for Jesus' last meal with his disciples would be quite adequate.

14:17. The Passover was to be eaten at night. April's sundown in Jerusalem came by 6 p.m., so the meal could have started then. Table fellowship was intimate at the feast; one or two families normally shared the meal, but here Jesus and his closest *disciples make up a family.

14:18-20. That someone "dipping in the bowl" (dipping bowls were especially used at Passover as part of the ritual) with a person would betray that person would have horrified ancient readers, who saw hospitality and the sharing of table fellowship as an intimate bond (cf. Ps 41:9, cited in Jn 13:18). Some scholars have also suggested that someone dipping "with" Jesus could mean that the person was denying Jesus' superior rank, because many Jewish groups required the leader to act (hence to dip) first (see the *Dead Sea Scrolls; cf. Ecclus 31:18).

14:21. Most of Judaism acknowledged both God's sovereignty and human responsibility.

14:22. The head of the household customarily gave thanks for the bread and wine before any meal, but special blessings were said over bread and wine at the Passover meal (though probably not in quite the same form as became standard later). Jewish people broke rather than cut their bread. We should not understand "This is my body" literally (in *Aramaic the phrasing would be ambiguous: "is" or "represents" would not be distinguished), just as we do not take literally the standard Jewish interpretation spoken over the Passover bread: "This is the bread of affliction our ancestors ate when they came from Egypt." (Taken literally, that bread would have been centuries old, and it had already been eaten.)

14:23. Four cups of red wine came to be used in the Passover meal; if they were in use by the first century, this cup may be the fourth, which followed the blessing of the bread. (Other scholars have suggested that the third cup is in view. By the end of the first century the four cups seem to have been both Jewish and Greco-Roman practice at feasts.) Each person did not have an individual cup; they customarily passed around one cup.

14:24. Covenants were ratified by the blood of sacrifice; God had redeemed his people from Egypt by the blood of the Passover lamb; "on behalf of the many" probably alludes to Isaiah 53 (see comment on Mk 10:45). Passover ritual interpreted the cup but did not interpret it as blood, because Jewish law and custom were revolted by the idea of drinking any creature's blood—especially human blood.

14:25. Vows of abstinence were common in Palestinian Judaism: "I will not eat any such and such until this happens," or "I vow that I will not use this until that happens." Jesus apparently vows not to drink wine again until the *kingdom comes, and he perhaps abstains from the fourth cup. Jewish tradition commonly portrayed the time of the kingdom as a banquet, when the Bible had promised an unending supply of wine (Amos 9:13). Jewish blessings over the wine called it "the fruit of the vine."

14:26. After the meal, it was customary to sing psalms from the Hallel, which consisted of Psalms 113—118. The walk to the Mount of Olives took at least fifteen minutes.

14:27-31
Other Betrayers Predicted

14:27. Here Jesus cites Zechariah 13:7, which is not clearly *messianic;

Jesus may refer to the principle it reports: a flock is scattered without the shepherd to guide them. (The *Dead Sea Scrolls do, however, apply this text to the future time.)

14:28. Jewish people in this period were not expecting a *resurrection of a given person distinct from the resurrection of the whole nation. Further, they certainly would not have expected a migration to Galilee to follow it: God's people would gather in Jerusalem in the time of the end (cf. Joel 2:32). These expectations may be why the *disciples ignore this part of Jesus' statement.

14:29-31. Ancient sources typically regarded the rooster as a reliable reporter of the advent of dawn (e.g., the second-century A.D. Roman writer Apuleius in *Metamorphoses* 2.26; *3 Maccabees 5:23; Babylonian Talmud *Berakot* 60b), but commentators report that in Palestine nocturnal crowings are familiar to the night watchmen beginning at 12:30 a.m.; the second was about 1:30 a.m. In either case the point is that the denial is imminent.

14:32-42 Watchmen Asleep

14:32-34. Jesus and his *disciples may have arrived at Gethsemane by 10 or 11 p.m. (which was late in that culture). It was customary to stay awake late on Passover night and to speak of God's redemption. The disciples should have been able to stay awake to keep watch; they had probably stayed up late on nearly every other Passover of their lives.

14:35-36. "Abba" is the *Aramaic word for "Papa," a term of great intimacy and affectionate respect. It was normally the first word a child would utter, but adults could use it for their fathers as well, and students sometimes used it of their teachers. Perhaps because it implied such intimacy, Jewish people never used it of God (though they did call him a heavenly father) except in an occasional *parable by a charismatic teacher. On the cup of judgment see comment on Mark 10:39; Jesus cries to be spared this cup (cf. Ps 116:3-4, 15).

14:37. The *disciples were to "stand watch" like the porters, the slaves in charge of the door, in the *parable in 13:34-36.

14:38. "Temptation" here is "testing"; given the common Jewish religious uses of the word, Jesus is saying: "lest you fall prey to the testing you are about to face." The contrast between "spirit" and "body" is not meant in the later *Gnostic or Neo-Platonic sense (the soul is good and the body is evil); rather that though one may mean well on impulse (14:31; cf. the use of "spirit" in many cases in Proverbs), the body is susceptible to exhaustion.

14:39-42. Jesus' use of "sinners" (v. 41) to refer to the men dispatched by representatives of the *Sanhedrin is strong language, especially in view of the way most people would use the word (2:16).

14:43-52 The Betrayal

14:43. Because they had been sent by prominent men of Jerusalem, the band that comes to arrest Jesus is probably the temple guard. This guard is known to have possessed the weapons mentioned here (swords and clubs); clubs were said to have characterized the corrupt priestly aristocracy in charge of the temple, as well as being useful in controlling rioters. Clubs were not supposed to be carried on holy days, including the Passover festival.

These men come prepared for armed resistance from one they suppose is a *messianic revolutionary—

because they had interpreted Jesus' act in the temple in terms of the cultural categories of their day, rather than in terms of the rest of his teaching (14:48).

14:44-46. A kiss was a sign of special affection among family members and close friends, or of a *disciple's honor and affection for his teacher. Thus Judas's kiss is a special act of hypocrisy (cf. Prov 27:6).

This band believed they needed Judas to lead them in person to the appropriate spot; had they searched for Jesus only on the basis of general directions, their search would have become evident and given Jesus time to escape. The kiss is necessary because darkness made it harder to recognize Jesus; under normal conditions the guards could have recognized him (he had been teaching in the temple).

14:47. Being well-to-do, high priests had ample servants. Although the servant mentioned here is probably not a Levite and thus unable to minister in the temple anyway, it is worthy of note that those who were missing appendages such as ears were barred from serving in the sanctuary. (Jesus' disciple is probably *aiming* for the neck or something more substantial than an ear, however.) Although the object of the expedition was only to arrest Jesus, had the sword struck again many of the *disciples would likely have been killed in the ensuing conflict.

14:48-49. Subversives (e.g., the later assassins who slew Jewish aristocrats under cover of the crowds in the temple) did their acts secretly or so as to avoid capture; Jesus' supposed subversion had been public and unconcealed. An arrest in the temple would have been politically disadvantageous and possibly aroused a riot (cf. comment on 14:1-2).

14:50-52. Except for some Jews overwhelmed by Greek culture and considered apostates, Jewish people generally abhorred nakedness. At night, one might have expected the *disciple to have an outer garment as well as the linen cloth, and he is probably already chilly (cf. 14:54). (Although one could sleep naked inside one's home in Palestine in April, Jerusalem's higher elevation makes 14:54 a likely indication that it was a cool night; Passover pilgrims who camped outdoors had coverings.) The point is that the man is in a hurry to escape.

14:53-65
The Sanhedrin's Mock Trial

This trial breaks a number of Jewish legal rules, if later documents correctly indicate the state of Jewish law in this period. Mark probably knew most of these rules, though many of his readers probably did not.

14:53. "Leading priests," "elders" and "*scribes" were the three groups represented on the *Sanhedrin, the ruling religious court of Israel. The full Sanhedrin, with seventy-one members, normally met in the assembly hall in the temple called the Chamber of Hewn Stone, where they sat in a semicircle with the high priest in the center. In this case, many members of the Sanhedrin (twenty-three members were necessary for a quorum) hold a secret night meeting without advance notice in the high priest's home (14:54), although they are investigating what they will claim is a capital offense.

Such a meeting is illegal on all these counts, although they would no doubt have explained it as only a preliminary inquiry before a real investigation (cf. Lk 22:66). The lack of advance notice could have been excused because it is during a feast and all necessary officials are in town; but because Jewish law forbade trials on the sabbath, they were probably also forbidden on feast days. The officials who gather seem more concerned with convicting Jesus quickly than with legal technicalities.

14:54. Peter's trespassing on private property—that of the high priest himself—required serious commitment from a Galilean fisherman. The guards could be the priest's night watchmen, but presumably they would immediately recognize that Peter does not belong there; more likely, these are members of the temple guard, waiting to see the results of the trial inside. Regardless of whether they had been assigned night duties in the temple, they may have planned to stay up late for Passover anyway.

14:55-56. Despite the high priest's certainty of Jesus' subversiveness, at least some members of the council, perhaps *scribes, follow the virtuous Jewish tradition of diligent cross-examination of witnesses. But once these witnesses had contradicted one another, all understandings of Jewish law unanimously demanded that they be declared false and the case be rejected as contrived; under Jewish law, in a capital case, false witnesses were to be put to death (see Deut 19:16-21 and the *Dead Sea Scrolls). Even though Rome had not given the *Sanhedrin jurisdiction to execute false witnesses, the Sanhedrin should have at least disciplined them; that the case just goes on demonstrates severe bias among the council members gathered there.

14:57-59. Many Jewish people expected that God would establish a new, purified temple at the time he put down the Romans. Outsiders had naturally misinterpreted Jesus' teaching about a new temple and warning about the old temple's destruction as the threat of a mad, *messianic revolutionary. But the witnesses still fail the cross-examination.

14:60-61. At least according to later *rabbinic law, the high priest could not legally force Jesus to convict himself out of his own mouth, but the testimony of other witnesses is so far not working; had the later law been in effect in Jesus' day, the priestly aristocracy might choose not to observe it. The high priest finally asks whether Jesus thinks of himself as a *Messiah—hence, to the high priest's mind, as a revolutionary.

"The Blessed One" was a common paraphrase for "God." "*Son of God" was an unusual phrase for a high priest to use, but not an impossible one; or Mark may have put the high priest's question in his own words, a common technique in writing at that time. Most likely he had heard that Jesus had adopted the title for himself, possibly in a messianic sense (12:6).

14:62. Jesus' statement is a claim to be not only a mortal *messiah but the cosmic ruler of Daniel 7:13-14, the embodiment of Israel's call, who would come in glory and reign forever. (The seating may allude to Ps 110:1.)

14:63. Tearing clothes was a sign of mourning or *repentance, and was required if one heard the sacred name blasphemed. But the high priest must be desperate for a conviction; unless Jesus mentions the sacred Hebrew name of God or summons them to what would be presumed to be idolatry (e.g., by calling himself God, which he does not at this point), he is not technically guilty of blasphemy (certainly not as it came to be defined by second-century *rabbinic teaching but also not by the broader popular sense; cf. 2:5-7). A Jewish court would have been more likely to have pronounced him insane; how could this arrested upstart teacher from Galilee think that he would come in the clouds of heaven?

14:64. Under Jewish law, the high

priest is not permitted to judge the case alone; he has to solicit the council's vote (if later recorded rules were already in effect, this vote would begin with the youngest and conclude with the high priest). Although they cannot have genuinely believed that Jesus has committed blasphemy according to its technical Jewish definition, they have an important reason to deal with him quickly: he poses a clear threat to the temple establishment (11:15-18), and as a *messianic claimant he threatens the whole Roman power structure that they, the Jewish aristocracy, represent.

14:65. Unlike public flogging, the behavior represented here—spitting on, blindfolding, striking and taunting a prisoner—was, of course, against Jewish law. While they ridicule Jesus as a false prophet, Peter fulfills Jesus' *prophecy concerning him (14:66-72); Jesus thus passes an important test for true prophets (Deut 18:22).

14:66-72
Peter's Denials

14:66-69. Slaves in aristocratic households exercised more power and status than the average free person. Although the high priest undoubtedly had many servants, the slave girl would have recognized that Peter and the guards (14:54) were not from the high priest's household. As a servant in an aristocratic household near the temple, she had perhaps been at the temple and could have gotten a good look at Jesus' *disciples in the temple courts. Peter's withdrawal from the court to the vestibule perhaps anticipates the need to escape.

14:70. Galilean accents differed from Judean accents, certainly in *Aramaic and presumably (as undoubtedly here) in Greek. The high priest's servants and temple guard would have lived in Jerusalem and regarded themselves as Judeans.

14:71. The "curses" Peter utters are not vulgar words; rather, he vows that he does not know the man, invoking curses on himself if he is lying. The temple hierarchy is interested in eliminating the ringleader; unless Peter poses a further threat, his *life* is probably in no danger (although he would be punished for following Jesus onto the high priest's property). But Peter would not know that.

14:72. For most people in the ancient Mediterranean, rooster's crowing marked daybreak. Some scholars have suggested that this refererence is to an earlier Palestinian rooster crowing between 12:30 and 2:30 a.m.

15:1-15
Pilate and the King

15:1. The night trial having been illegal, the officials reconvene somewhere around the first light (about 4:30 a.m.) or dawn (about 5:30 a.m.) to quickly make their conclusion official. Roman officials like Pilate would meet with clients and members of the public from dawn till about noon, so they must have Jesus ready for Pilate very early. Pilate lived in Caesarea but during the Passover stayed in Herod the Great's old palace in Jerusalem; the Roman governor needed to be in Jerusalem to forestall troubles at Passover.

15:2-4. Claiming to be the Jewish king, the *Messiah, would lead to a charge of sedition and treason against the emperor. The only offense for which the Jewish leaders could automatically execute any transgressor was profanation of the temple; to them, Jesus' act in the temple had at least approached that, but the leaders know that his claim to messiahship would threaten Pilate more. Pilate had not been particularly cooperative with these leaders in the past, and they need to have a strong case for him now.

15:5. Jewish accounts of martyrs testify frequently to *Gentile judges' astonishment that the martyrs refuse to cooperate (e.g., 2 Maccabees, *4 Maccabees). Roman law did not, however, interpret silence as an admission of guilt.

15:6-10. Releasing a prisoner at the feast is one local custom on which the surviving historical records are silent, but it fits the culture of the time (e.g., a governor in Egypt in A.D. 85 handed someone over to "the multitudes"). Unlike Jesus, Barabbas is a violent revolutionary; but he does not claim to be a king or boast such a large following.

15:11. Ancient writers often criticized the fickleness of crowds.

15:12-15. A severe flogging normally preceded crucifixion, but it was customarily administered along the way or even after the condemned was fastened to the cross. Crucifixion was the most agonizing form of criminal execution known in antiquity.

When Pilate became governor, he immediately enraged Jerusalem by bringing the imperial standards into the city; more recently, he had built an aqueduct with funds from the temple treasury. His insensitivity had only provoked Jewish hostility, and he had apparently become less eager to clash with the local officials.

15:16-20
Hailing the King

15:16. The Praetorium was Herod the Great's enormous palace, which Roman governors used when they came to Jerusalem.

15:17. Purple was always expensive (see Acts 16:14), but more significantly here, purple robes and garlands of leaves marked the Greek vassal princes. The soldiers may have had to improvise from a scarlet Roman cloak.

Many scholars think that the crown of thorns, perhaps from the branches of the thorny acanthus shrub or from the date palm (which would look more like a crown), may have been meant to turn mainly outward rather than painfully inward; thus the crown would have mimicked the wreaths worn by *Hellenistic rulers. Because the wreath was twisted, however, some thorns or spikes must have scraped inward, drawing blood from Jesus' scalp. Only the highest king would wear an actual crown instead of a wreath, so they are portraying Jesus as a vassal prince.

15:18. The Roman emperor was greeted with "Hail . . ." Thus the Roman soldiers mock Jesus ("King of the Jews") here; they would have had little respect for a Jewish king even had they believed Jesus was one.

15:19-20. One paid homage to a king (including Caesar) by falling on one's knees.

15:21-32
The Crucified King

15:21. Cyrene was in what is now Libya in North Africa and included a large Jewish community. "Simon" was a typical Jewish name, and devout Jewish pilgrims from throughout the Mediterranean came to Jerusalem during Passover. Roman soldiers could impress anyone into service to carry things for them. Because it is a feast and work is forbidden, Simon is not coming from "the field" (literally) as a worker; perhaps he is late for the festival, only now arriving from Cyrene or from where he is residing temporarily in the countryside.

15:22. The site of the crucifixion might have been named "Place of the Skull" because so many deaths occurred there. (The suggestion that the place was shaped like a skull is possible, but the inference that it is thus the purported site of Calvary proposed by

Charles Gordon around 1884 is unlikely; the contours of the ground there were created subsequent to the time of Jesus.)

15:23. Pious women of Jerusalem normally prepared a solution like this one and offered it to those being executed to dull their pain (cf. Prov 31:6-7); Jesus chooses to endure the full force of the agony of crucifixion. Myrrh is said to have had narcotic effects.

15:24. Roman soldiers customarily divided the executed criminal's apparel.

15:25. The third hour began shortly after 8:30 a.m. and ran till shortly after 9:30 a.m. (The exact time of hours would vary according to the time of sunrise from which they were reckoned, hence according to the season of year.)

15:26. The charge was often posted above the head of the person being crucified. The claim to be a king would be sufficient to incur Roman wrath; ironically, however, Jesus is called not a royal pretender but "King of the Jews," perhaps reflecting an anti-Jewish sentiment of Pilate or his agents.

15:27. The term for "robbers" here (NIV, NASB; cf. "bandits"—NRSV, TEV) is the same one *Josephus used for revolutionaries. Thus these two men were probably colleagues of Barabbas and were originally meant to be executed with him that day.

15:29-32. Some people observing a crucifixion would normally curse those being crucified, but these people should have been Jesus' allies (15:26). Many ancient writers used irony, and Mark is no exception, reporting unintended truth in the words of Jesus' enemies (v. 31).

15:33-41
The Death of the King

15:33. The "sixth hour" began before noon, the "ninth hour" before 3 p.m. Jesus dies around the time of the evening offering in the temple. Stories were told of catastrophes occurring at the deaths of pious *rabbis, especially those whose intercession had been vital to the world; but the biggest point of these signs is that judgment is imminent. Darkness had signified judgment in the past (Ex 10:21-23) and would in the future (Is 13:10; Ezek 32:7; Joel 2:2, 10, 31; 3:15; Amos 5:18; 8:9; Zech 14:6).

15:34. Jesus' cry is an *Aramaic quotation of Psalm 22:1, which was sometimes recited at this time of day in prayer but receives special significance when Jesus prays it. The first line would evoke this whole psalm of the righteous sufferer—and its hope of divine vindication. (Jesus probably quoted the psalm in Hebrew, as in Matthew; Mark uses the Aramaic form because the saying was transmitted in an Aramaic milieu. "Eli" could be mistaken for "Elijah" much more easily than "Eloi"; cf. 15:35-36.)

15:35-36. Members of some circles of Jewish tradition believed that Elijah was sent like an angel to rescue famous teachers, in addition to his role in the time of the end.

15:37. Crucifixion generally killed by asphixiation: one became too weary to keep pulling one's frame up on the crossbeam, the diaphragm was increasingly strained, and eventually one became unable to breathe. But death usually took a few days—much longer than the few hours Jesus suffered.

15:38. The holy of holies, which the priest could enter only once a year, was the ultimate symbol of God's dwelling place. God's rending the veil meant that he was now available apart from the temple system and that the old temple order stood judged and abolished.

15:39. A non-Jew might use a phrase like "son of God" with reference to a pious philosopher or, more commonly, a hero whose father was a deity; but in Mark's Gospel, "*Son of God" means much more than that (14:61). Because Romans viewed the reigning emperor as a son of the deified Augustus, the centurion might be recognizing Jesus not only as "king of the Jews" (15:26) but also as a rival to the emperor. Whatever the specific nuance intended, Mark's irony (cf. 15:29-32) is plain: only a *Gentile is impressed by Jesus' death.

15:40. The women followers were much less likely to be indicted than male followers, but they were still courageous to show up at the crucifixion. The epithet of James, "the Less" (NASB, KJV), is better translated "the younger" (NIV, TEV, NRSV), as the usage of the word in the ancient papyri indicates.

15:41. By the standards of the religiously strict, it would have been scandalous for women (especially married women) to travel with an entourage of male *disciples; apart from members of the Hellenized aristocracy, Palestinian Jewish women were expected to limit their public activity, keep their heads covered and fulfill their domestic duties. The idea of women *patrons (sponsors) is elsewhere known, though again it is striking that these women traveled with Jesus. In this one verse Mark hints at an aspect of Jesus' ministry that potently challenges the social order, especially if these women "followed" as disciples, which they presumably did (cf. comment on Luke 10:39; common use of "follow" in the Gospels).

15:42-47
The Burial of the King

15:42. The sabbath would begin at sundown, within several hours of Jesus' death. It was not lawful to prepare the body for burial on the sabbath (cf. comment on Mt 27:57-58 for what was permitted).

15:43. That the *Sanhedrin included pious members like Joseph, and not just the sort who appeared in the trial *narrative (as pious as even they may have supposed themselves), fits the known diversity within even the Jewish aristocracy of the period. Because he awaited the future *kingdom, Joseph was probably not a *Sadducee, unlike many of his colleagues.

15:44. Crucifixion often took several days to kill a person unless hurried along (cf. Jn 19:31-32).

15:45. That excavated tombs include few crucifixion victims suggests that the bodies were not generally made available for burial—a horror to most Jewish sensitivities. One exception found in a wealthy family tomb suggests that then, as now, those with wealth and social power had extra influence, which they could use for good or ill.

15:46-47. Joseph must have bought the linen quickly, just before sundown (about 6 p.m.) when the sabbath began. Linen shrouds were customary for burial; tombs cut from virgin rock were the best. Large disk-shaped stones could be rolled in a groove over the mouth of a tomb, making entry difficult. After a body had been prepared for burial it would be left to decompose for one year; then the eldest son or other closest family member would return, gather the bones for burial in a box and deposit them in a slot on the tomb wall.

16:1-8
The Women at the Tomb

Having predicted the *resurrection appearances (14:28), the Gospel of Mark would be complete with or without 16:9-20; Mark does not need to narrate them. Many ancient documents were content simply to predict and foreshadow events certain to come after the *narrative itself had closed (e.g., the *Iliad,* perhaps the most popular book in Greek antiquity, foreshadows Achilles' death and Troy's fall without narrating them). Such suspension was a literary and *rhetorical technique in this period. Some books (e.g., the Jewish historiographic work known as *Pseudo-Philo) and speeches and essays (some of *Plutarch's) also end abruptly. Mark may have wished to end just short of the resurrection appearances themselves because his persecuted readers were still sharing in Jesus' cross but needed to be reminded of the foolishness of their present doubts of their ultimate triumph.

16:1. Bodies were normally anointed with oil (then rinsed with water) before burial, but because Jesus had died on Friday just before the sabbath began (at sundown, around 6 p.m.), this anointing had been postponed. Men were allowed to dress only men for burial, but women could dress men or women. Spices may not have been used for everyone but were often used for the bodies of special persons (e.g., Herod). They reduced the immediate stench of rapid decomposition in the hot Mediterranean days. After one day and two nights, the women could expect that the body would already stink. But Jerusalem is over two thousand feet above sea level and is cool enough in April that in a sealed tomb the body would have still been approachable.

16:2. The time is around 5:30 a.m.; it was customary to arise at dawn. At least some merchants are already selling wares, because the women buy spices (16:1) before coming to the tomb.

16:3-4. The disk-shaped stone rolled in a groove across the entrance to a tomb, and several strong men would be needed to roll it back. Tombs were normally opened only for the secondary burial of bones a year later and for subsequently deceased family members to be buried there.

16:5. In Jewish literature, angels are normally garbed in white. These women need not have automatically assumed that this figure is an angel; the priests in the temple and some others also wore white.

16:6-8. Throughout Mark, people spread news that they were supposed to keep quiet; here, when commanded finally to spread the word, people keep quiet. If the original Gospel of Mark ends here, as is likely, it ends as suddenly as it began, and its final note is one of irony. Many other ancient works (including many treatises and dramas) also had sudden endings.

16:9-20 The Commission (An Appendix)

The manuscript tradition and style suggest that these verses were probably an early addition to the Gospel of Mark, although a few scholars (such as William Farmer) have argued the case that they are Markan. In any case, most of the content of these verses is found elsewhere in the Gospels.

16:9-11. The witness of a woman was considered unreliable, as both *Josephus and the *rabbis attest. Given this view and the fact that Judaism was not expecting an individual *resurrection of the *Messiah, it is not surprising that the *disciples do not believe Mary Magdalene.

16:12-14. According to Jewish tradition, supernatural beings like angels and Elijah were capable of disguising themselves in different forms. The resurrected Jesus apparently shares this trait, which helps convince some male disciples.

16:15-18. Among the signs of the *messianic era, Isaiah predicted that the sick would be healed and that mute tongues would speak (Is 35:5-6), and that God's people would be witnesses for him (Is 43:10). The powers here attributed to believers are the sort that characterize many of the *Old Testament prophets (cf. this theme in Acts).

16:19-20. Both Jewish and Greek readers could relate to the idea of an ascension of a great hero to heaven (like Heracles or, in postbiblical Jewish tradition, Moses), but for Jesus to sit at God's right hand goes beyond this idea—it means that Jesus reigns as God's agent (Ps 110:1).

LUKE

Introduction

Authorship. Early tradition, verified by second-century witnesses and the early title of the book (see the discussion of authorship in the introduction to Mark), favors Luke, traveling companion of Paul, as the author of Luke-Acts. Although the case for Luke's use of medical language has been exaggerated, there is some evidence for it, and it is consonant with the tradition of Lukan authorship.

Date, Purpose. See the introduction to Acts; some of the specific emphases of Luke-Acts are clearer in Acts than in the Gospel. Luke and Acts together made up a single two-volume work.

Setting. Luke writes to readers in the Greek world or Greek-speaking upper-class Rome. His readers are well-to-do and literarily sophisticated, and possibly require confirmation in their faith or arguments they can use to defend it. See comment on 1:3-4 and the discussion of purpose in the introduction to Acts.

Genre. See the introduction to the Gospels. Whereas the other

Gospels are closer to the genre of Greco-Roman biography, Luke's Gospel is the first volume of a two-volume work, Luke-Acts, which is in many ways closer to a Greco-Roman history than to a biography. Because Mark is one of Luke's sources, I treat many of the passages where they overlap more thoroughly in Mark than in Luke.

Luke's Message. Various themes are especially prominent in Luke: Jesus' ministry to the outcasts, the religiously unfit, the poor and women; this emphasis paves the way for his treatment of the *Gentile mission in volume two, the book of Acts. The plot movement is from Galilee to Jerusalem in Luke (though the book is framed by scenes in the temple), and from Jerusalem to the ends of the earth in Acts.

Commentaries. Two of the most helpful commentaries are I. Howard Marshall, *The Gospel of Luke,* NIGCT (Grand Rapids, Mich.: Eerdmans, 1979), and F. W. Danker, *Jesus and the New Age: A Commentary on St. Luke's Gospel* (Minneapolis: Augsburg/Fortress, 1987); these works were particularly useful in preparing this commentary. Cf. also Joseph A. Fitzmyer, *The Gospel According to Luke,* 2 vols. (Garden City, N.Y.: Doubleday, 1981), and Craig A. Evans, *Luke,* NIBC (Peabody, Mass.: Hendrickson, 1990). Besides general works mentioned in the introduction to Matthew, Kenneth Bailey, *Poet and Peasant* (Grand Rapids, Mich.: Eerdmans, 1976), is helpful on the background of much of Luke (especially Lk 15).

1:1-4
The Literary Prologue

In Luke's day the more sophisticated writers would often introduce their books with a piece of stylish prose written in the classical style. (Those with literary pretensions generally imitated the Greek of a much earlier period than was commonly spoken.) Luke's introduction here is superb in this regard.

1:1. Luke's word here for "account" was used for a *narrative of many events, as distinct from a narrative of a single event, and was most characteristically (though certainly not only) applied to works of history.

Writers compiling a work usually started with one main source and wove in secondary material from another source or sources. (Most scholars agree that Luke begins with Mark as his main source and weaves in other material, including "Q"). Writers also normally explained why they were writing a work if other books on the same subject had appeared. Some writers invoked length (see 2 Maccabees) or stylistic considerations (see *Theon) to explain the need for a new work; other authors thought earlier writers had investigated matters inadequately (*Josephus, Artemidorus) or had embellished them *rhetorically (*Tacitus); still others simply wished to compile earlier works more thoroughly (*Quintilian).

1:2. "Handed down" was sometimes a technical term in the ancient world. *Disciples of *rabbis normally passed down first-generation traditions carefully. Oral storytellers were also adept at memorizing and passing on stories accurately. Because Luke writes while eyewitnesses are still alive, and because they were accorded a place of prominence in the early *church, we may be sure that his traditions are reliable. (Eyewitness sources were accepted as the best.)

1:3-4. Literary introductions often specified the purpose of the work (e.g., in *Josephus's *Against Apion:* "to teach all who wish to know the truth" about the Jewish people); here Luke wishes to provide "exact information" ("exact truth"—NASB; "certainty"—NIV).

It was proper for a good historian to check the data that had come to him. Books would often open with a dedication to the wealthy *patron who sponsored the writing project. (Luke-Acts is not just a private work; Luke's Gospel is within 3 percent of the length of Acts, both fitting the standard size of scroll for publication.)

Theophilus, the name of the sponsor, was a common Jewish name. "Most excellent" could literally mark him as a member of a high class in Roman society (the equestrian order), although Luke may use the title only as a courtesy. Theophilus's desire for verification was reasonable in view of the many competing claims to religious truth in the Roman Empire.

1:5-25
The Angel and the Priest

After the much more classical Greek prologue of 1:1-4, here Luke establishes himself as a master of various literary styles by adapting to *Septuagint style, reflecting its Hebraic rhythms, which dominate chapters 1—2.

1:5. Historians customarily introduced a *narrative by listing the names of reigning kings or governors, which provided the approximate time of the narrative. Herod the Great was officially king of Judea from 37 to 4 B.C. Twenty-four "orders" (NRSV, TEV) or "divisions" (NIV, NASB) of priests (1 Chron 24:7-18, especially v. 10) took turns serving in the temple, two nonconsecutive weeks a year. Priests could marry any pure Israelite, but they often preferred daughters of priests ("daughters of Aaron").

1:6. The terms Luke uses to describe Zechariah and Elizabeth are the same that the *Old Testament used for some other righteous people, such as Noah (Gen 6:9), Abraham (Gen 17:1) and Job (Job 1:1). One who reads those *narratives understands that although they may not have been morally perfect (Gen 9:21) or complete (Job 42:3-6), they did not violate any stated commandments in the *law. Thus Luke uses these terms to challenge the misconception that could arise from conventional wisdom concerning barrenness (Lk 1:7).

1:7. To be childless was economically and socially disastrous: economically, because parents had no one to support them in old age (cf. comment on 1 Tim 5:4, 8); socially, because in the law barrenness was sometimes a judgment for sin, and many people assumed the worst possible cause of a problem. Most people assumed that barrenness was a defect of the wife, and Jewish teachers generally insisted that a man divorce a childless wife so he could procreate. "Aged" may suggest that they were over sixty (*Mishnah *Abot* 5:21); age itself conferred some social status and was sometimes listed among qualifications or virtues.

Contrary to conventional wisdom, however, Zechariah and Elizabeth are clearly righteous (1:6; cf. Wisdom of Solomon 4:1), and the Jewish reader would immediately think of righteous Abraham and Sarah, who was also barren. The Lord also opened the wombs of other matriarchs, Rachel and Rebekah, and those of Hannah and Samson's mother; yet Elizabeth is especially like Sarah, who was not only infertile but also too old to bear.

1:8-9. There were many more priests and Levites than necessary (perhaps eighteen thousand) for any given function in the temple, so they were chosen for specific tasks by lot, during their appointed time of service (besides service on the three major festivals, they served about two weeks out of the year). Given the number of priests, a priest might get the opportunity in 1:9 only once in a lifetime; this would have been a special occasion for Zechariah.

Incense offerings (Ex 30:7-8) had been standard in ancient Near Eastern temples, perhaps to quench the stench of burning flesh from the sacrifices in the closed buildings. This offering in the temple preceded the morning sacrifice and followed the evening sacrifice. It is said that the officer who ministered regularly in the temple signaled the time to begin the offering and then withdrew; the priest cast incense on this altar, prostrated himself and then withdrew himself—normally immediately (cf. 1:21).

1:10. The hours of morning and evening sacrifices were also the major public hours of prayer in the temple (cf. Acts 3:1). Except during a feast, most of the people praying there would be Jerusalemites; unable to enter the priestly sanctuary, they were presumably men in the Court of Israel, and some women outside that in the Court of the Women.

1:11. The altar of incense was in the center of the priestly sanctuary, outside the holy of holies.

Zechariah 3:1 reports an Old Testament apparition in the temple. There *Satan appears to the high priest, standing at his right to accuse him; but the high priest stands before the angel of the Lord, who defends him and brings him a message of peace for his people.

1:12. People usually reacted with fear to angelic revelations in the Old Testament as well.

1:13. Angelic annunciations, often complete with names, also preceded some major births in the Old Testament (e.g., Gen 16:11; 17:19; Is 7:14). Childless people throughout the ancient world entreated deities for children.

1:14-15. The closest Old Testament parallel to Luke 1:15 is Judges 13:4-5, 7, where Samson, as a Nazirite from birth, is warned to abstain from strong drink (cf. Num 6:3-4). Cf. Luke 7:33. Ancient Judaism especially viewed the *Holy Spirit as the Spirit of *prophecy.

1:16-17. Elijah was to return before the day of the Lord, turning the father's hearts to the children (Mal 4:5-6; cf. Ecclus 48:10). Although later *rabbis interpreted this event as Elijah, master of intricate legal questions, straightening out Israelite genealogies, the point in Malachi is probably familial reconciliation; cf. Micah 7:5-6. On "prepared for the Lord," see Luke 3:4. On coming in Elijah's measure of the Spirit, cf. Elisha's request for a "double portion" (the inheritance right of a firstborn son) of this in 2 Kings 2:9; although John claimed no miracles, he was a great prophet—for he was Jesus' forerunner.

1:18. Like Zechariah here, Abraham (Gen 15:8; cf. 17:17), Gideon (Judg 6:17, 36-40; 7:10-11) and others in the Old Testament (2 Kings 20:8; cf. Is 7:10-14) asked for signs in the face of astounding promises, but they were not punished. That Zechariah's sign should be harsher to him (1:20) suggests only that this revelation is much greater than those which preceded it.

1:19. Although Judaism had developed quite a list of angelic names, the *New Testament mentions only the two who also appear in the Old Testament: Gabriel (Dan 8:16; 9:21) and Michael (Dan 10:13, 21; 12:1). These became the two most popular angels in contemporary Jewish lore, in which Gabriel was sent on many divine missions. Jewish literature typically portrayed the chief angels as before God's throne.

1:20-21. Casting incense on the heated altar of incense normally took little time, after which the priest emerged immediately. The delay here may have troubled the crowds; perhaps they thought Zechariah had been disrespectful and struck dead, or that something else had gone wrong. If Zechariah's offering had failed, their prayers were also in jeopardy.

1:22. The term here for "mute" can, but need not, include deafness.

1:23. Because his term of service was only two weeks a year, and he had no son to support him in his old age, Zechariah probably worked a small farm or did other work in the hill country of Judah. (Priests were supposed to be supported by others' tithes, not by working the land, but high taxes on the poor and unfair practices by the priestly aristocracy—especially in the decades just prior to A.D. 66—combined to make it harder on less wealthy priests.)

1:24-25. Praise such as Elizabeth utters here was common among the barren whom God visited (Gen 21:6-7; 1 Sam 2:1-11) but especially recalls Rachel's exultation, "God has removed my reproach!" (Gen 30:23).

1:26-38
The Angel and the Girl

Luke here contrasts the simple faith of a teenage girl, Mary, with the genuine but less profound faith of an aged priest, Zechariah (cf. the severer contrasts between Hannah and Eli in 1 Sam 1—2; though the story line is quite different, in both cases God uses a humble and obscure servant to bear an agent of revival to the coming generation). This section has parallels not only with *Old Testament birth annunciations but also with Old Testament call *narratives: Mary was called to fill the office of Jesus' mother.

1:26-27. Because Joseph was of David's line and Jesus would be his legal son, Jesus could qualify as belonging to David's royal house. In Judaism, "virgins" were young maidens, usually fourteen or younger. The term Luke uses here for "virgin" also indicates that she had not yet had sexual relations with a man (1:34-35). Nazareth in this period was an insignificant village of an estimated sixteen hundred to two thousand inhabitants. On Gabriel, see comment on 1:19.

1:28-29. God often encouraged his servants that he was "with" them (e.g., Jer 1:8). Greetings (like "hail") were normal, but rank and status within society determined whom one should greet and with what words. As both a woman and a young person (perhaps twelve or fourteen years old) not yet married, Mary had virtually no social status. Neither the title ("favored" or "graced one") nor the promise ("The Lord is with you") was traditional in greetings, even had she been a person of status.

1:30. "Do not fear" (cf. 1:13) was also common in Old Testament revelations (e.g., Josh 1:9; Judg 6:23; Jer 1:8; Dan 10:12; cf. Gen 15:1). Mary here joins the list of those in the Bible who found favor before God (Gen 6:8; 19:16, 19; Ex 33:13).

1:31. This verse follows the typical Old Testament structure for a divine birth announcement and especially resembles Isaiah 7:14, the Immanuel promise (on which see Mt 1:23).

1:32-33. This language ultimately derives from 2 Samuel 7:12-16 and also identifies Mary's future son with the "Mighty God" *Messiah of Isaiah 9:6-7 ("Mighty God" is clearly a divine title; cf. Is 10:21). On the eternal *kingdom, cf. also Daniel 2:44; 4:3; 6:26; 7:14.

1:34-35. Jewish tradition used the language of "overshadowing" for God's presence with his people.

1:36-37. The point of 1:36-37 is that God, who acted for Elizabeth as he did for Sarah, could still do anything. On 1:36, cf. Genesis 18:14 (on Sarah having a child); Mary has more faith than her ancestor (Gen 18:12-15).

1:38. Mary expresses her submission to the Lord's will in regular Old Testament terms for submission or acquiescence (e.g., 1 Sam 1:18; 25:41; 2 Sam 9:6, 11; 2 Kings 4:2; cf. Bel and Dragon 9; see especially 2 Sam 7:25).

1:39-56
Miracle Mothers Meet

1:39-40. The journey from Nazareth to the hill country of Judea may have taken three to five days, depending on the precise location of Elizabeth's home. In view of bandits on the roads, young Mary's journey was courageous, although she may have found a caravan with which to travel; otherwise her family may not have allowed her to go. Greetings were normally blessings meant to bestow peace, hence the response of verse 41.

1:41. Like dancing, leaping was an expression of joy (e.g., Wisdom of Solomon 19:9). Jewish people recognized that the fetus was able to sense and respond to stimuli; while occasionally suggesting that the fetus's gender could be changed by prayer up until birth, some *rabbinic tradition also believed that infants could sin, sing and so forth in the womb. Some pagan stories also told of babies dancing in their mother's wombs or speaking in infancy, but pagans generally regarded these events as evil omens; here John's activity is instead a result of his prenatal sensitivity to the prophetic Spirit. On the *Holy Spirit see 1:15.

1:42-44. For praising another indirectly through a secondary blessing, see comment on Matthew 13:16-17 (cf. also, e.g., the *pseudepigraphic 2 Baruch 54:10-11).

1:45. Abraham also believed the promise of a son (Gen 15:6).

1:46-47. Verses 46-55 emphasize the exaltation of the poor and humble and the casting down of the proud and wealthy. This emphasis of Mary's song strongly resembles the praise song of Samuel's mother, Hannah, in 1 Samuel 2:1-10; Hannah celebrated when the Lord opened her barren womb. (Luke omits the imagery of military triumph that Hannah had applied to her rivalry with Peninnah.) Hebrew poetry commonly uses synonymous parallelism (in which a second line reiterates the statement of the first); thus "soul" and "spirit" are used interchangeably here, as often in Scripture; joy and praise are also linked (cf. Ps 33:1; 47:1; 95:2; 149:1-5).

1:48. The Old Testament spoke of those who obeyed God, especially the prophets, as God's servants. It also emphasized God's exalting the humble and reveals the importance ancient culture placed on one's honor and name enduring after one's death.

1:49-50. In verse 50 Mary alludes to Psalm 103:17, which in context emphasizes God's faithfulness, in spite of human frailty, to those who fear him.

1:51. This is the language of vindication through judgment; often in the Old Testament, God's "arm" would save his people and "scatter" their (his) enemies. Mary weaves together the language of various psalms.

1:52-53. The principle that God exalts the humble and casts down the proud was common in the Old Testament (e.g., Prov 3:34; Is 2:11-12, 17; cf. Ecclus 10:14). "Filling the hungry" comes from Psalm 107:9, where God helps those in distress, because he is merciful.

1:54-55. God had promised to be faithful to his people Israel forever, because of the eternal covenant he had made by oath with their ancestor Abraham (e.g., Deut 7:7-8). Israel is God's "servant" in Isaiah 42—49 (cf. comment on Mt 12:15-18).

1:56. Although ancient texts sometimes speak of pregnancy as lasting ten months, it was known that it normally lasted nine; the three months mentioned here plus the six of verse 26 suggest that Mary was present long enough to see John's birth.

1:57-66
The Birth of John

This account lacks the *hagiographic details found in many Jewish birth stories of the period, especially those about Noah and Moses, where the baby illumined the room or (newborn Noah) spoke.

1:57-58. Neighbors customarily joined in celebrations (cf. 15:6), and the birth—especially an unusual one like this one—and circumcision of a son in the family home (typically performed by the father in this period) were such occasions; Jewish tradition suggests that guests assembled every night from a boy's birth to his circumcision. On the special cause for the celebration here, see comment on 1:7. Jewish people viewed sons as essential because they carried on the family line, although in practice they seem to have loved daughters no less.

1:59. The *law required that circumcisions be performed on the eighth day; this was a special event, and Jewish custom included a charge to raise the child according to biblical law. Jewish children had customarily been named at birth; the evidence for naming a child at circumcision is late, apart from this text. But Roman infants were named eight or nine days after birth (for girls and boys, respectively), and Luke may either accommodate Greco-Roman practice for his readers or, more likely, indicate the Greco-Roman influence on Palestinian Jewish custom. Zechariah's muteness may have delayed the normal naming, but cf. 2:21.

1:60-62. Children often were named for grandfathers and sometimes for fathers. The father rather than the mother had ultimate say in the matter; in Roman (as opposed to Jewish) society the father even had the legal right to decide whether the family would raise the child or throw the infant out on the trash heaps.

1:63. The writing tablet was a wooden board coated with wax; one would inscribe the message on the wax surface.

1:64-66. Prophetic speechlessness and the restoration of speech once the *prophecy had been fulfilled are found also in Ezekiel 33:22.

1:67-79
Zechariah's Prophecy

In the *Old Testament only a fine line existed between inspired praise and *prophecy (e.g., 1 Sam 10:5-6; 1 Chron 25:1-3), and often, as in Psalms, one could move from one to the other (46:1, 10; 91:1, 14).

1:67. The *Spirit of God was especially (though not exclusively) associated with prophecy in the Old Testament, and this perspective continued in various Jewish circles around the time of Jesus.

1:68. "Blessed be God" occurs in Old Testament praise (e.g., 1 Chron 16:36; 2 Chron 6:4; Ps 41:13; 72:18) and became a standard opening prayer for Jewish blessings. The prophets and later writers (cf. the *Dead Sea Scrolls) spoke of God visiting his people for redemption and judgment. The use of "redeem" here compares this new event to when God saved his people from Egypt; the prophets had promised future deliverance in a new exodus.

1:69. Because a horn could give an animal the victory in battle, it indicated strength. "Horn of salvation" parallels the meaning of "rock" and "strength" in Psalm 18:2. Thus the Davidic *Messiah would be their deliverer (cf. Ps 132:17).

1:70-75. God had promised salvation from their enemies in his covenant with Abraham and his descendants. The language here thoroughly reflects the Old Testament.

1:76. "Prepare his way" alludes to Isaiah 40:3 (predicting the herald of a new exodus) and perhaps Malachi 3:1 (probably connected with Elijah in 4:5); cf. Luke 3:4.

1:77. Future "salvation" in Isaiah includes deliverance from political oppressors; but, as here, it is predicated upon Israel's restoration to divine favor through forgiveness.

1:78. "Sunrise" (NASB) or "rising sun" (NIV) could allude to God as the Sun of righteousness in Malachi 4:2 (cf. Ps 84:11). Some commentators have suggested a Greek play on words referring to the *Messiah as both a "shoot" and a "star" in the Old Testament.

1:79. Although Zechariah weaves in various allusions here as elsewhere in the chapter, Isaiah 9:2 is especially in view the context of this passage is explicitly messianic (Is 9:6-7).

1:80. The summary statement is especially reminiscent of 1 Samuel 2:26 and 3:19 for the maturation of the prophet Samuel. The desert was the expected place for a new exodus and thus for the *Messiah; some groups, seeking greater purity, withdrew from common Judaism into the desert. Whether John may have studied among such groups for a time is debated, although it is probable if his aged parents died before he reached maturity (the *Essenes reportedly adopted children and trained them from age ten on).

2:1-7
Journey to Bethlehem

By A.D. 6 wide-scale censuses were taken every fourteen years; before that time, periodic censuses seem to have occurred at less regular intervals. A tax census instigated by the revered emperor Augustus initiates the contrast between Caesar's earthly pomp and Christ's heavenly glory in 2:1-14.

2:1. Censuses were important for evaluating taxation; they were generally conducted locally, so all local governments in all regions probably did not simultaneously implement Caesar's decree.

2:2. Some scholars dispute whether Quirinius was governor of Syria at this time. Quirinius was certainly governor of Syria during the much-remembered later census of A.D. 6, when Sepphoris and some Galilean patriots revolted against the tax census of that year. This passage seems to refer to an earlier census while Herod the Great was still king (before 4 B.C.); thus Luke's "*first* census under Quirinius."

Some commentators have suggested that Luke blended the two events or that Quirinius was governor of Syria at the earlier time Luke describes as well as in A.D. 6, for which there is some (though currently incomplete) evidence. Historians dated events by naming current officials, so Quirinius may have been in office at the time without being associated with this census. The governor of Syria is mentioned because the Roman province of Syria included Palestine under its jurisdiction at this time.

2:3. Although Egyptian census records show that people had to return to their homes for a tax census, the home to which they returned was where they owned property, not simply where they were born (censuses registered persons according to property). Joseph thus must have still held property in Bethlehem; if the tax census of A.D. 6 is any indication, he might not have had to register for any property in Galilee.

2:4. Pottery samples suggest a recent migration of people from the Bethlehem area to Nazareth around this time; Joseph's legal residence is apparently still Bethlehem, where he had been raised.

2:5. Betrothal provided most of the legal rights of marriage, but intercourse was forbidden; Joseph is courageous to take his pregnant betrothed with him, even if (as is quite possible) she is also a Bethlehemite who has to return to that town. Although tax laws in most of the empire required only the head of a household to appear, the province of Syria (then including Palestine) also taxed women. But Joseph may simply wish to avoid leaving her alone this late in her pregnancy, especially if the circumstances of her pregnancy had deprived her of other friends.

2:6-7. The "swaddling clothes" were long cloth strips used to keep babies' limbs straight so they could grow properly (cf. Wisdom of Solomon 7:4). Midwives normally assisted at birth; especially because this was Mary's first child, it is likely (though not clear from the text) that a midwife would assist her. Jewish law permitted midwives to travel a long distance even on the Sabbath to assist in delivery.

By the early second century A.D. even pagans were widely aware of the tradition that Jesus was born in a cave used as a livestock shelter behind someone's home, and they reported the site of this cave to the emperor Hadrian. The manger was a feeding trough for animals; sometimes these may have been built into the floor. The word traditionally translated "inn" probably means "home" or "guest room"; with all Joseph's scattered family members returning home at once, it is easier for Mary to bear (or care for the child after birth) in the vacant cave outside.

2:8-20
The Real King's Birth

2:8. Due to the proximity to Jerusalem, some scholars have suggested that the flocks here are the temple flocks raised for sacrifice. This narrative would have challenged the values of many religious people, who despised shepherds; shepherds' work kept them from participation in the religious activities of their communities. Pasturing of flocks at night indicates that this was a warmer season, not winter (when they would graze more in the day); Roman Christians later adopted December 25 as Christmas only to supersede a pagan Roman festival scheduled at that time.

2:9. Angelic appearances, the revelation of God's glory and consequent fear among the humans present were common in the Old Testament when God was acting in history in special ways.

2:10-12. For "Do not be afraid" see comment on 1:13, 30. "Good news" could refer to the proclamation of God's salvation (Is 52:7), but pagans applied it also to celebrations of the cult of the emperor among all people in the supposedly worldwide empire. Particularly in celebration of his birthday (pagans publicly celebrated deities' birthdays), the emperor was hailed "Savior" and "Lord." But Jesus' birth in a lowly manger distinguishes the true king from the Roman emperor, whose loyalists in Luke's day would have bristled at (and perhaps responded violently to) the implicit comparison. "Signs" are common in prophetic literature (e.g., Is 7:14; Ezek 12:11) and function as much to provoke and explain truth as to prove it.

2:13-14. This choir contrasts with the earthly choirs used in the worship of the emperor. The current emperor, Augustus, was praised for having inaugurated a worldwide peace. The inverted parallelism (God vs. people, and "in the highest" vs. "on earth") suggests that "in the highest" means "among heaven's angelic hosts."

2:15-18. The shepherds probably checked the animal stables till they found the one with the baby; Bethlehem was not a large town.

2:19-20. Mary kept these matters in her mind as Jacob had Joseph's revelations in Genesis 37:11 (for the idiom, cf., e.g., Ps 119:11; Prov 6:21; Wisdom of Solomon 8:17).

2:21-40
The Infant and His Witnesses

2:21. See comment on 1:57-59.

2:22-24. These verses refer to Exodus 13:2, 12 and Leviticus 12:8. Jesus' parents fulfill the *law of Moses properly and piously. The particular sacrifice they offer indicates that they are poor (Lev 12:8). Following the custom, Mary would lay hands on the pigeons, then a priest would take them to the southwest corner of the altar, wringing one bird's neck as a sin offering and burning the other as a whole burnt offering.

2:25-26. This encounter with Simeon no doubt occurs in the Court of Women. God's future intervention for Israel was described as "consolation" or "comfort" (cf., e.g., Is 49:13; 51:3; 52:9; 66:13). The "*Holy Spirit" was especially associated with *prophecy. On living to see God's *grace before dying, cf. Psalm 91:16, Tobit 10:13 and 11:9; sometimes in the Old Testament the righteous would be spared seeing disaster and the wicked would not experience good (e.g., 2 Kings 6:2; 22:20).

2:27-32. Simeon's praise reflects Old Testament piety such as Genesis 46:30, and prophecies like Isaiah 42:6 and 49:6.

2:33-35. *Prophecies in Jewish and Greco-Roman tradition were often obscure, easier understood in hindsight than at the moment they were given. Simeon's words probably allude to the stumbling stone of Isaiah 8:14-15 and the anticipated *resurrection. The "sword" reflects either Mary suffering over Jesus' pain or her heart being bared, probably the former (a mother's grief can symbolize a son's suffering, e.g., Judg 5:28).

2:36. Although the Old Testament did include prophetesses, they were much less prominent than male prophets in the Jewish tradition of this period. The name "Anna" (Tobit 1:9) is the Hebrew name "Hannah" (1 Sam 1:2).

2:37-38. Jewish and Greco-Roman culture often viewed widows who never remarried as pious and faithful. Judith, a famous widow in Jewish tradition, was said to have lived as a widow till her death at 105. If one adds the two numbers given in the text here, seven and eighty-four (taking eighty-four as the length of Anna's widowhood rather than her age), and she was married at the common age of fourteen, one could see her as 105 also.

2:39-40. See comment on 1:80.

2:41-52
The Boy in the Temple

Where possible, ancient biographers would tell significant anecdotes about their subjects' youth, sometimes about spectacular child prodigies (e.g., Cyrus, *Josephus). In 2:21-40, Jesus intrigued prophets; in 2:41-52, he intrigues teachers of the law.

2:41. The *law required an annual pilgrimage to Jerusalem at Passover (Deut 16:6), although most Jewish people living far away could not come annually. Although Jewish teachers did not always require women's attendance at the festivals, many women attended. This verse may be another allusion to Hannah in 1 Samuel 1:7 and 2:19.

2:42. "Twelve years old" would have been one year before Jesus officially became an adult Israelite and accepted responsibility for fulfilling the law. (Although the official Jewish *bar mitzvah* ceremony may not have existed in Jesus' day, its analogy to Roman coming-of-age rituals supports other evidence for an official entrance to adulthood around this age.)

2:43-45. Caravans, which afforded protection from robbers, were common on pilgrimages for the feasts in Jerusalem. Traveling with a caravan, in which neighbors from their town would watch the community children together, Mary and Joseph might assume that the near-adult Jesus was with companions, especially if by now they had younger children to attend to. If we assume a pace of twenty miles per day (though perhaps slower, depending on transportation and the children), Nazareth would be a little over three days' journey along the shortest route.

2:46-47. Some Jewish teachers in this

period reportedly conducted their classes in the temple courts; the famous *Hillel and *Shammai may have been two such teachers. Asking questions was used both in teaching and in learning, but it was important for learners to ask intelligent questions, as Jesus does. Teachers could answer questions with questions, and Jesus' answers are also intelligent.

2:48-51. The commandment to honor one's father and mother was regarded as one of the most important in the law, and children not yet considered adults were to express this honoring in part by obedience. On Mary's heart, see comment on 2:19.

2:52. See comment on 1:80; cf. Judith 16:23; for the wording, cf. also Proverbs 3:4.

3:1-6
Introduction of John

3:1-2. It was customary to begin historical narratives by dating them according to the years of rulers and officials, both in Greco-Roman and Old Testament historiography, and often in introducing prophetic oracles or books (e.g., Is 1:1; 6:1). Luke thus shows that John began preaching somewhere between September of A.D. 27 and October of A.D. 28 (or, less likely, the following year). Tiberius reigned from A.D. 14 to 37; Herod Antipas, son of Herod the Great (see comment on 1:5), was tetrarch (governor) of Galilee from 4 B.C. to A.D. 39; Pontius Pilate was in office from A.D. 26 to 36. On "Annas and Caiaphas" see comment on John 18:13, 19.

3:3. Non-Jews who wished to convert to Judaism were required to immerse themselves in water to remove their impurity as *Gentiles; John requires this act of conversion even of Jews. See comment on Mark 1:5.

3:4-6. On the quotation see Mark 1:3; Isaiah promised a new exodus in which God would again save his people Israel. Luke extends the quote to more of Isaiah 40, possibly to conclude with seeing God's salvation; cf. Luke 2:30.

3:7-20
John's Preaching

See comment on Matthew 3:7-12 for more details.

3:7. Vipers (e.g., the Nicander's viper) were commonly believed to eat their way out of their mother's womb; thus John's calling the crowd "viper's offspring" was even nastier than calling them "vipers." Serpents would flee a burning field.

3:8-9. The Jewish people believed that they were saved by virtue of their descent from Abraham, which constituted them the chosen people. The idea of raising people from stones appears in Greek mythology. Some scholars have suggested that John makes a wordplay between the Aramaic words for "children" and "stones."

3:10-11. The poorest people (such as most people in Egypt, who were peasants) had only one outer tunic; by such standards, anyone with two tunics had more than necessary. "What shall we do?" occurs throughout Luke-Acts as a question about how to be saved.

3:12-13. *Tax gatherers sometimes collected extra money and kept the profit; although this practice was not legal, it was difficult to prevent.

3:14. Some commentators think these "soldiers" are Jewish police who accompanied tax gatherers or Herodian mercenaries, but more likely these are the light auxiliary non-Jewish troops that Rome recruited from Syria. Although the large legions were stationed in Syria, not Palestine, some soldiers were stationed in Palestine (Caesarea and Jerusalem) and smaller bands no doubt marched through. The frequency of Roman soldiers' illegal concubinage with native women also indicates that all soldiers did not remain in their garrison at all times. Jews were exempt from required military service due especially to their dietary laws.

Soldiers occasionally protested their wages, creating trouble with the government (e.g., the frontier mutiny of A.D. 14); they were known for extorting money from local people they intimidated or for falsely accusing them (see, e.g., the *papyri; *Apuleius).

3:15-17. On John's *messianic preaching, see comment on Matthew 3:11-12. The *Old Testament prophets had declared that in the end time the righteous would be endowed with the *Holy Spirit and that the wicked would be burned with fire. The Jewish people generally viewed the Holy Spirit as the Spirit of *prophecy, and some circles viewed the Spirit as a force that purified God's people from unholiness.

3:18. On his "many other words" see comment on Acts 2:40.

3:19-20. John's preaching to Herod Antipas fits prophetic morality, but Herod and his advisers may view it as a political statement, especially given the political cost of Herod's illicit liaison with Herodias (see comment on Mk 6:17-20). Herod's nemesis, a Nabatean king, also found ethnic allies in Herod's subject territory of Perea, and Herod may have viewed John's preaching in that region (Jn 3:23) as especially damaging.

In ancient Israel prophets normally enjoyed an immunity from persecution that was virtually unparalleled in the ancient Near East (prophets of other nations rarely denounced living kings; at most they suggested more funds for their temples). But some Israelite rulers did imprison (1 Kings 22:26-27; Jer 37—38) and seek to kill or silence them (1 Kings 13:4; 18:13; 19:2; 2 Kings 1:9; 6:31; 2 Chron 24:21; Jer 18:18, 23; 26:11, 20-23). John's costly stand prefigures Jesus' death at the hands of the authorities.

3:21-22
Jesus' Sonship Declared

Jewish tradition stressed that God communicated in this era by voices from heaven; most people believed that he no longer spoke by prophets, at least not as he once had. The prophetic ministry of John and the voice from heaven thus provide a dual witness to Jesus' identity. See further comment on Mark 1:9-11.

3:23-38
Jesus' Ancestry

Greco-Roman biographers included lists of ancestors, especially illustrious ancestors, whenever possible. Like Greco-Roman genealogies, but unlike Matthew and *Old Testament genealogies, Luke starts with the most recent names and works backward. This procedure enables him to end with "*Son of God" (cf. 1:35; 3:22; 4:3).

For more details on genealogies, see comment on Matthew 1:2-16. Scholars have proposed various explanations for the differences between the genealogies of Matthew and Luke, of which the following are most prominent: (1) one (probably Matthew) records the genealogy of Joseph, the other of Mary; (2) one (probably Matthew) spiritualizes the genealogy rather than following it literally; (3) the lines of descent cross but are different because one list includes several adoptive lines through levirate marriages (Deut 25:5-10).

In Greek society, men often entered public service at the age of thirty; Levites' service in the temple also began at thirty. Like a good Greek historian,

Luke says "about thirty" (3:23) rather than stating an estimate as a definite number, as was more common in traditional Jewish historiography.

4:1-13 Tested in the Wilderness

See comment on Matthew 4:1-11 for more details. Jesus here settles issues as good *rabbis did, by appeal to Scripture. But this text also shows that Jesus does not just use Scripture to accommodate contemporary views of its authority; he uses it as his authority and the final word on ethics even when dealing with a supracultural adversary. (It should go without saying that the original writer and readers would have viewed the devil as a literal, personal being; some modern readers' figurative treatment of the devil as a generic symbol for evil reads into the text something entirely foreign to it.)

The three texts from Deuteronomy (6:13, 16; 8:3) cited here (4:4, 8, 12) were commands given to Israel when Israel was tested in the wilderness. Unlike Adam, another "son" of God, who sinned (3:38), Jesus overcomes the tests (cf. Gen 3).

4:1-2. Moses also fasted forty days and nights; Israel also was in the wilderness forty years.

4:3. The devil's first test of Jesus is the sort of feat ancient thought attributed to magicians, who claimed to be able to transform themselves into animals and to transform other substances, like stones into bread.

4:4. Other Jewish circles (evident, e.g., in the *Dead Sea Scrolls and later *rabbinic texts) also used the phrase "It has been written" to introduce Scripture.

4:6-7. The world did not technically belong to the devil (Dan 4:32), who owned human hearts and societies only as a usurper. The most he could do would be to make Jesus the political, military sort of *Messiah most Jewish people who expected a Messiah were anticipating.

4:8. Deuteronomy 6:13, which Jesus cites, prohibits idolatry (Deut 6:14), a commandment anyone who worshiped the devil would obviously violate.

4:9-11. The devil takes Jesus to a part of the temple overlooking a deep valley; a fall from there would have meant certain death. Later *rabbis acknowledged that the devil and demons could handle Scripture expertly; here the devil cites Psalm 91:11-12 out of context, because 91:10 makes clear that God's protection is for events that *befall* his servants, not an excuse to seek out such dangers.

4:12. Jesus cites Deuteronomy 6:16, which refers to how the Israelites had tested God at Massah by refusing to accept that God was among them until he wrought a sign for them (Ex 17:7).

4:13. To most ancient readers, the devil's departure would have implied at least his temporary defeat (cf. the *Testament of Job 27:6; Life of Adam 17:2-3, of uncertain date).

4:14-30 Preaching in His Hometown Synagogue

Luke, who follows the order of his sources quite meticulously (probably according to the pattern of biography he is using), departs from that order here (cf. Mk 6:1-6), because this section becomes his programmatic or thesis statement for the *gospel. (Cf. Peter's sermon in Acts 2, which functions analogously for Acts.)

That Jesus would quote Scripture against the devil (4:1-13) would hardly have disturbed his contemporaries; that he would use it to challenge traditions that his contemporaries believe are scriptural, however, enrages them.

Jewish teachers officially welcomed debate, examining all views from the Scriptures; but they generally interpreted Scripture in such a way as to support views sanctioned by tradition (a frequent practice in many churches today).

4:14-15. Visiting *rabbis were often given opportunities to teach; but Nazareth, a village of sixteen hundred to two thousand inhabitants, already knew Jesus and would be less open to thinking about him in new ways.

4:16. The people would have known that Jesus was devout and skilled in Hebrew from his previous readings in his hometown *synagogue. One customarily sat while expounding Scripture (Mt 5:1) but stood while reading it.

4:17. Synagogues later followed regular lectionary readings, but in this period readers had more freedom to choose the reading from the Prophets; even later, readers in the Prophets were allowed to "skip" passages. The synagogue attendant (*chazan*—v. 20) presumably chose which book to read (different books of the Old Testament were on different scrolls). "Opening" the book meant unrolling the Hebrew scroll to the right place.

4:18-19. Isaiah in this passage (61:1-2; cf. 58:6) seems to describe Israel's future in terms of the year of Jubilee, or year of release, from Leviticus 25; the *Dead Sea Scrolls read Isaiah 61 in this way. Some scholars have suggested that a recent Jubilee year may have made this text fresh in the minds of Jesus' hearers; some other scholars dispute whether this even remained a current practice in mainstream Judaism. That Luke ends the quote on a note of salvation is probably intentional, but his readers who know Scripture well would know how the passage continues.

4:20. Teachers normally sat to expound Scripture. The *synagogue attendant was the *chazan*, the official responsible for the upkeep of the building, the scrolls and so forth; this position was eventually a paid one (but lower in authority than "rulers" of a synagogue). Synagogues were probably less formal then than churches or synagogues generally are today, so the attentiveness of those present is significant.

4:21-22. Immediacy ("today"; cf. 2:11; 19:5, 9; 23:43) is the initial key to the coming offense; the text Jesus reads is supposed to be fulfilled in the messianic era, and the inhabitants of Nazareth saw neither *Messiah nor messianic era before them. Because they lived only four miles from Sepphoris, they were well aware of how the Romans had destroyed that Galilean capital after a messianic-style revolt in A.D. 6; that this region was thereafter cautious about messianic announcements is clear from the fact that the rebuilt Sepphoris did not join in the later revolt of A.D. 66.

Writers of the *Dead Sea Scrolls, who believed that they lived on the verge of the end time, often stressed the immediacy of biblical *prophecies, applying descriptions of Nahum, Habakkuk and others to their own day. Interpreting the Bible this way was thus not in itself offensive to first-century Palestinian Jews; the offense was implying that the end time had arrived in Jesus' own ministry.

4:23-24. The tradition that Israel rejected its own prophets was strong in Judaism; for instance, Jeremiah was persecuted by his own priestly town, Anathoth (Jer 1:1; 11:18-23). The proverb in 4:23 is attested in some form in Greek classical and medical literature, and some *rabbis cited a similar *Aramaic proverb.

4:25-27. Jesus mentions the socially

weak (widows) and marginalized (lepers) here, but the main point is that non-Jews were the ones to accept two of the major signs prophets of the *Old Testament. Sidon and Syria were among the particularly despised areas. Jesus' point: Nazareth will not receive him, but non-Jews will.

4:28-29. A mob could not legally execute capital punishment in Jewish Palestine; the crowd is thus unusually angry—especially to attempt this execution on the sabbath (v. 16). Although Nazareth does not appear to have been built on a hill per se, like many ancient cities it was set in the hill country, with plenty of jagged rocks and cliffs nearby. Stoning began with throwing the criminal over a cliff, then hurling rocks nearly the size of one's head on top of the victim. One aimed for the chest first, but at such a distance one's aim would not be particularly accurate.

4:30. Whether the Lord hides him (cf. Jer 36:26), his attitude silences them, or his townspeople suddenly realize what they are doing to one of their own, Jesus walks through the crowd unharmed—his hour had not yet come.

4:31-37
Preaching in Capernaum's Synagogue

A pericope about Jesus' inhospitable reception in a house of prayer and study (4:14-30) is followed by his confrontation with a demoniac in one. Yet the people's response in Capernaum, which by the second century A.D. had become a center for early Jewish Christianity, contrasts with that of Nazareth in 4:14-30. See comment on Mark 1:21-28.

4:31. Archaeologists have found the site of Capernaum's *synagogue.

4:32. Most teachers would try to expound the *law by explaining the proper way to translate it or by appealing to their legal or *narrative traditions; Jesus goes beyond such practices.

4:33-34. Demons were often associated with magic, and magicians tried to subdue other spiritual forces by invoking their names. If the demon is trying to subdue Jesus in this way ("I know who you are" was used to subdue spiritual powers in magical texts), as some scholars have suggested—his ploy does not work.

4:35-37. Exorcists had two main methods of expelling demons: (1) scaring the demon out or making it too sick to stay—for example, by putting a smelly root up the possessed person's nose in the hope that the demon would not be able to stand it—or (2) invoking the name of a higher spirit to get rid of the lower one. The people are amazed that Jesus can be effective by simply ordering the demons to leave.

4:38-44
Popularity Increases

See comment on Mark 1:29-39 for more details.

4:38. Simon's father-in-law had probably passed away, and Simon and his wife had taken her widowed mother into their home. Caring for one's extended family was more common then than it is today.

4:39. Waiting on guests was an important element of hospitality normally assigned to the adult women of the household (most free families could not afford slaves).

4:40-41. The sabbath (4:31) ended Saturday at sundown. "As the sun was setting" indicates that the sabbath is ending; thus people could carry the sick to Jesus for healing (carrying was considered work, thus forbidden on the sabbath). Greeks used laying on hands as a point of contact for healing more often than Jewish people did, but it had a rich symbolism in Jewish tradition as well (see comment on Acts 6:6). Jesus could also heal without it if the people could believe (see Lk 7:6-9).

4:42-44. It was nearly impossible to find a place to be alone in ancient towns, with their narrow streets and sometimes (often in poorer places like Egypt) twenty people living in the common one-room houses. Most blocks in Capernaum consisted of four homes facing a common courtyard. Villages were also often close together, though one could find a place alone if one arose early enough (most people arose at dawn).

5:1-11 Fishers of People

Like Moses' experience as a shepherd, David's as a commander and Joseph's as an administrator, the background of these *disciples as fishermen can provide them a perspective that will help them for their new task.

5:1-2. Nets would collect things other than edible fish, thus requiring cleaning. Edible fish in the inland "Sea" of Galilee (the Lake of Gennesaret) today include varieties of carp; *Josephus says that the lake of Galilee held several kinds of fish.

5:3. The shore of the lake functioned acoustically like an amphitheater; withdrawing a little from the crowd and addressing them from the boat thus would have made Jesus much easier to hear.

5:4-5. Peter's obedience is exemplary; a fisherman might trust a *rabbi's teaching on religious matters but need not do so in his own field of expertise, fishing. The fishermen had labored with a dragnet at night, which should have caught them many more fish than Jesus' instructions in 5:5. Sources suggest that fish were more easily caught at night than in the day in the lake of Galilee; they would be sold in the morning.

5:6. Jesus' multiplication of food and of creatures has *Old Testament precedent (e.g., food—Ex 16:13; 2 Kings 4:1-7, 42-44; creatures—Ex 8:6, 17, 24; 10:13).

5:7. Because the overhead cost of equipment was high, fishermen often worked together in cooperatives; families would sometimes work together to increase their profits. Other fishing cooperatives are known from ancient Palestine, so it is not unusual for Simon and Andrew to be in business with the family of Zebedee (5:10). Men working from more than one boat could let down larger nets than those working from only one; fish could then be emptied onto the boat or the nets hauled ashore.

5:8-9. Moses, Gideon and Jeremiah were all overwhelmed by their initial calls; but Peter's excuse is especially like Isaiah's (Is 6:5) and fits Luke's emphasis (Lk 5:20, 30-32).

5:10. "Fishers of people" could allude to two Old Testament texts (Jer 16:16; Hab 1:15), transforming an image of impending judgment into one of rescue from that judgment; but Jesus is probably just transforming their vocation as fishermen, as God made Moses and David "shepherds" of his people.

5:11. Fishermen made a better-than-average income (even if they had had a bad night—5:5), so leaving their job is an act of radical commitment that they would expect to adversely affect them economically.

5:12-16 Cleansing a Leper

See comment on Mark 1:40-45 for more details. Lepers were outcasts from society, and most nonlepers would not have wanted to touch them, even had Jewish law permitted it. The Bible had prescribed particular sacrifices if someone's leprosy were cured (Lev 14:1-32).

By complying with these regulations, Jesus does nothing to violate the *law or to offend the priests.

Teachers thought to perform miracles usually drew large followings, because many people were sick; the number of people who flocked to hot springs in Galilee that were thought to relieve ailments attests to the large numbers of people who suffered from various afflictions.

5:17-26
Healing a Paralytic

For more details, see comment on Mark 2:1-12.

5:17. *Pharisees seem to have been located especially in Jerusalem and Judea; thus the Galileans probably consisted mainly of the other group Luke mentions, the teachers of the law. All Galilean villages would have had *scribes schooled in Jewish law, who could execute legal documents and train children in the law of Moses.

5:18-19. The average Capernaum home may have allowed only about fifty persons standing (the span of the largest excavated homes there is eighteen feet). One gained access to the roof by an outside staircase, so these men could reach it unimpeded. The roof of a single-story Palestinian home was sturdy enough to walk on but was normally made of branches and rushes laid over the roof's beams and covered with dried mud; thus one could dig through it.

Luke changes this Palestinian roof structure to the flat roof of interlocking tiles more familiar to his own readers, as preachers today change details when retelling biblical stories to make them relevant to their hearers. For the same reason, Luke does not mention their digging through the roof. The paralytic's "bed" would have been the mat on which he always lay.

5:20-21. Judaism believed that only God could forgive sins, but most Jews allowed that some of God's representatives could speak on God's behalf. Technically, "blasphemy" involved pronouncing the divine name or perhaps inviting people to follow other gods; less technically, it had to involve at least dishonoring God. Strictly speaking, therefore, these legal scholars are mistaken in interpreting Jesus' words as blasphemy, even by their own rules.

5:22-26. Some Jewish teachers accepted miracles as verification that a teacher was truly God's representative; others did not regard miracles as sufficient proof if they disagreed with that teacher's interpretation of Scripture.

5:27-32
Partying with Sinners

See comment on Mark 2:13-17 for more details. In the Old Testament, God instructed "sinners" in his way, i.e., the humble who knew their need (Ps 25:8-9).

5:27-28. Customs officials were employees in Herod's civil service; they made good wages and were not likely to get their jobs back once they left them, especially on such short notice.

5:29. Jesus' invitation for Levi to follow him constituted a great honor, especially for one who would have normally been excluded from religious circles. That Levi should respond by throwing a party for him is not surprising; repaying honor was an important part of social life in antiquity. Table fellowship indicated intimate relations among those who shared it, and given the nature of ancient banquets, it was natural for a well-to-do person to invite his (former) colleagues and also subordinates to a feast.

5:30. The *Pharisees (and the teachers belonging to their party) were scrupulous about their special rules on eating and did not like to eat with less scrupulous people, especially people like *tax gatherers and sinners. Most people regarded tax gatherers as collaborators with the Romans, and nationalistic religious people despised them. Because the Pharisees here attack only Jesus' table fellowship, we may be certain that Jesus and his own disciples conduct themselves properly in word, eating and drinking and so forth (e.g., they would not get drunk), whether or not all of Levi's other guests are doing the same.

5:33-39
Partying or Fasting?

See comment on Mark 2:18-22. The *Old Testament also recognized that some practices or objects once appropriate in worship or commemoration were no longer appropriate (2 Kings 18:4; Jer 3:16).

5:33. Although the Old Testament commanded many more feasts than fasts, fasting had become a widespread Jewish practice; *Pharisees often fasted twice a week. Although *ascetic fasting was forbidden, many people probably did fast for ascetic reasons. Fasting was an important practice to join with prayer or penitence, so it would have been unusual for *disciples (prospective *rabbis) to have avoided it altogether. A teacher was regarded as responsible for the behavior of his disciples.

5:34-35. Wedding feasts required seven days of festivity; one was not permitted to fast or engage in other acts of mourning or difficult labor during a wedding feast. Jesus makes an analogy about the similar inappropriateness of fasting in his own time.

5:36-38. Jesus uses two familiar facts to make his point. Older clothes had already shrunk from washing. Wine could be kept in either jars or wineskins; wineskins, unlike jars, would stretch. Old wineskins had already been stretched to capacity by wine fermenting within them; if they were then filled with unfermented wine, it would likewise expand, and the old wineskins, already stretched to the limit, would break. Watered-down wine was drunk with meals.

5:39. Although distillation had not yet been developed and wine could achieve only a certain level of alcoholic content, aged wine was generally preferred over fresh wine that had not yet begun to ferment (a proverb, e.g., Ecclus 9:10; *rabbis). Jesus is probably indicating why the religious people are objecting to the joy of Jesus' *disciples: it is something new.

6:1-5
Lord of the Sabbath

See Mark 2:23-28 for more details. Some scholars have suggested that "rubbing with their hands" (v. 1) by extension constituted threshing, a forbidden category of work on the sabbath. Although the law of Moses was especially authoritative for Jewish legal experts, the *narratives of other parts of the *Old Testament sometimes illustrate principles of the *law's spirit taking precedence over its normal practice (e.g., 2 Chron 30:2-3).

If Jesus could demonstrate his case from Scripture, his opponents technically could not prosecute him successfully, due to the variety of Palestinian Jewish views on how the sabbath was to be observed.

6:6-11
Lawful to Do Good

See further comment on Mark 3:1-6.

6:6. The muscles and nerves of a "dried" or "withered" hand were inactive; thus the hand, smaller than usual, was incurably nonfunctional.

6:7-10. Again, Jesus does nothing to violate the *law; although many religious teachers opposed minor cures on the sabbath, "stretching out one's hand" was not considered work, and God could answer prayer on the sabbath.

6:11. Unintentional violations of the sabbath, or issues of disagreement about what constituted the sabbath (matters that were debated) were normally treated lightly; capital punishment (Ex 31:14; 35:2) was thought appropriate only for those who willfully rejected the sabbath. Jesus' opponents go far beyond their own teachings here.

6:12-16
Choosing the Twelve

See comment on Mark 3:13-19.

6:12. Jesus may here follow a pattern in Moses' ministry. Moses prayed on a mountainside, receiving instructions about helpers (Ex 19:24; 24:1-2; cf. 31:1-2) and successors (Num 27:15-23; cf. 20:23-29).

6:13-16. People often had a secondary name, sometimes a nickname, which may account for the slight differences among the Gospels' lists of the Twelve, as well as for the distinguishing of two Simons, two Judases and the second James in the list (these names were common in this period).

6:17-26
Blessings and Woes

See comment on Matthew 5:3-12. Blessings and woes were a common literary form, especially in the *Old Testament and Judaism; here they may parallel the blessings and curses of the covenant given from the mountains in Deuteronomy 27—28. For the particular blessings and curses listed here, cf. perhaps Isaiah 65:13-16.

6:17-19. On this introduction to Luke's Sermon on the Plain (or "level place"), see comment on Matthew 4:23-25.

6:20. Some of Jesus' *disciples who had not been economically poor became poor to follow him (see 18:28). Behind Luke's "poor" and Matthew's "poor in spirit" probably lies a particular *Aramaic term that means both. "The poor" had become a designation for the pious in some Jewish circles, because they were the oppressed who trusted solely in God. The piety of the poor was emphasized especially after the Roman general Pompey redistributed Jewish lands about a century before Jesus; like most other people in the ancient Mediterranean world, most Jewish people were poor. The Jewish people longed for the *kingdom.

6:21. Being "filled" (sustained) was a hoped-for blessing of the *messianic era. Hunger struck poor families in times of famine (the situation in rural Palestine was better than that of rural Egypt but worse than that of Corinth or Italy). Weeping was a sign of mourning or repentance.

6:22-23. The Old Testament tradition that most true prophets suffered rejection was amplified further in Judaism, so Jesus' hearers would have caught his point. The separation or ostracism here might allude to being officially put out of the *synagogue (cf. comment on Jn 9:22) but is probably meant more generally.

6:24-25. "Comfort" was a blessing of the messianic era (e.g., Is 40:1; cf. Lk 16:25). Most of Jesus' hearers were poor, but Luke's urban, Greco-Roman readership was probably better off (1:3-4); Luke pulls no punches for his own audience (cf. *1 Enoch 96:4-5). Laughter was often associated with scorn.

6:26. Greek philosophers, who often

scoffed at the opinions of the masses, sometimes complained if the multitudes spoke well of them. But Jesus' comparison with the prophets is even more appropriate; the burden of proof was always on prophets who told people what they wanted to hear (Jer 6:14; 28:8-9). Although the hearers often suspected some truth in the genuine prophets' claims (Jer 21:1-2; 37:3; 42:2; cf. 1 Kings 22:27), false prophets were usually more popular (1 Kings 22:12-13; Jer 5:31; 23:13-14).

6:27-38
Treat Others Mercifully

6:27. The *Old Testament specifically commanded love of neighbor (Lev 19:18), but no one commanded love of enemies.

6:28. Although Jesus (23:34) and his followers (Acts 7:60) practiced this rule of blessing and praying for enemies, prayers for vindication by vengeance were common in the Old Testament (2 Chron 24:22; Ps 137:7-9; Jer 15:15; cf. Rev 6:10) and in ancient execration (magical curse) texts.

6:29. The blow on the right cheek was the most grievous insult in the ancient Near East. The clothing in the verse refers to the outer and inner cloak, respectively; the poorest of people (like the average peasant in Egypt) might have only one of each; thus here Jesus refers, perhaps in *hyperbolic images, to absolute nonresistance on one's own behalf.

6:30. Here Jesus may allude to beggars, quite common in the ancient East, and poorer people seeking loans. In Jewish Palestine beggars were usually only those in genuine need, and most were unable to work; farmers generally sought loans to plant crops. Jewish society emphasized both charity and responsibility.

6:31. In its negative form ("Do not do to others what you do not want them to do to you"), this was a common ethical saying in the ancient world.

6:32-33. Ideas like loving enemies and lending without hoping to receive again were unheard of, although many *Pharisees advocated peace with the Roman state (at least, tolerating enemies in some sense).

6:34-35. In the Roman world, interest rates sometimes ran as high as 48 percent, but the *Old Testament forbade usury, or charging interest. Because many Jewish creditors feared that they would lose their investment if they lent too near the seventh year (when the *law required cancellation of all debts), they stopped lending then, hurting the small farmers who needed to borrow for planting. Jewish teachers thus found a way to circumvent this law so the poor could borrow so long as they repaid. Jesus argues that this practice should not be necessary; those with resources should help those without, whether or not they would lose money by doing so.

Biblical laws about lending to the poor before the year of release (Deut 15:9; every seventh year debts were forgiven; cf. Lev 25) support Jesus' principle here, but Jesus goes even farther in emphasizing unselfish giving. Although the law limited selfishness, Jesus looks to the heart of the law and advocates sacrifice for one's neighbor. A good man's "sons" were expected to exemplify their father's character; thus God's children should act like him.

6:36. That human mercy should reflect God's mercy became a common Jewish saying (e.g., the *Letter of Aristeas 208; *rabbis). "Merciful" may reflect the same *Aramaic word translated "perfect" in Matthew 5:48.

6:37. "Judge," "condemn" and "pardon" are all the language of the day of judgment, prefigured in God's current reckonings with his people (e.g., on the Day of Atonement).

6:38. The image here is of a measuring container into which as much grain as possible is packed; it is then shaken to allow the grain to settle, and more is poured in till the container overflows. Pouring it "into the lap" refers to the fold in the garment used as a pocket or pouch. Because Jewish people sometimes used "they" as a way of avoiding God's name, here "they will pour" (NASB) may mean that God will do it; or the idea may be that God will repay a person through others. The Old Testament often speaks of God judging people according to their ways (e.g., Is 65:7). Proverbs and other texts speak of his blessings toward the generous (e.g., Deut 15:10; Prov 19:17; 22:9; 28:8).

6:39-45
True and False Teachers

6:39. Others also used this proverbial image about the blind. The point here is that one must learn the right way (6:40) and receive correction before seeking to teach others (6:41).

6:40. In ancient Judaism, the purpose of a *disciple's training was to make him a competent teacher, or *rabbi, in his own right. By definition, a disciple did not have more knowledge about the law than his teacher.

6:41-42. Here Jesus uses *hyperbole, and the exaggeration would probably draw laughter—and thus attention—from Jesus' hearers.

6:43-45. See 3:9. Figs and grapes were often cultivated together and were two of the most common agricultural products in Palestine, often linked in Old Testament texts. Thorns and thistles were always troublesome to farmers (cf., e.g., Gen 3:18; also Is 5:2, 4 *LXX).

6:46-49
Right and Wrong Foundations

Jesus again uses the image of the day of judgment. The idea of ultimately being judged for hearing but not obeying was familiar (Ezek 33:32-33). But no Jewish teacher apart from Jesus claimed so much authority for his own words; such authority was reserved for the *law itself.

Some commentators have suggested that "digging deep" (v. 48) implies that he built a cellar; although cellars were not uncommon in Palestinian houses, they were used more often in Greek architecture; cf. comment on 5:19.

7:1-10
A Pagan's Amazing Faith

7:1-2. The nearest Roman legion was stationed in Syria, but many troops were also stationed at Caesarea on the Mediterranean coast; perhaps smaller groups were stationed or settled (after retirement?) at various points in Palestine. Centurions commanded a "century" (i.e., 100), which *in practice* consisted of sixty to eighty troops. Centurions were the backbone of the Roman army, in charge of discipline.

7:3-5. Non-Jews who feared God and donated substantial sums to the Jewish community were well respected. Centurions' salaries were much higher than those of their troops, but for this centurion to have built the local *synagogue represented a great financial sacrifice. The main point lies in the contrasting views of worthiness (7:4, 6).

7:6. The centurion was not a full convert to Judaism and thus retained some of his uncleanness as a *Gentile, especially in regard to the food in his home. To invite a Jewish teacher into such a home would have been offensive under normal circumstances, but in this case the community's elders want to make an exception (7:3).

7:7. During their twenty or so years of service in the Roman army, soldiers were not permitted to marry. Many had illegal local concubines, an arrangement that the army overlooked and the concubines found profitable. But centurions, who could be moved around more frequently, would be less likely than ordinary soldiers to have such relationships; they often married only after retirement. By ancient definitions, however, a household could include servants, and household servants and masters sometimes grew very close—especially if they made up the entire family unit.

7:8. The centurion demonstrates that he understands the principle of authority that Jesus exercises. Roman soldiers were very disciplined and except in rare times of mutiny followed orders carefully.

7:9. "*Gentiles" were generally synonymous with pagans, with no faith in Israel's God.

7:10. Some Jewish stories circulated about miracle workers, but reports of long-distance healings were rare and were viewed as more extraordinary than other miracles. Thus people would view this healing as especially miraculous.

7:11-17
Interrupting a Funeral

Interrupting a funeral was a blatant breach of Jewish law and custom; touching the bier exposed Jesus to a day's uncleanness (Num 19:21-22); touching the corpse exposed him to a week's uncleanness (cf. Num 5:2-3; 19:11-20). But in Jesus' case, the influence goes in the other direction.

7:11-12. People customarily dropped whatever they were doing and joined in a funeral procession when it passed by. For a widow's only son to die before she did was considered extremely tragic; it also left her dependent on public charity for support unless she had other relatives of means.

7:13. According to custom the bereaved mother would walk in front of the bier, so Jesus would meet her first. Philosophers often tried to console the bereaved by saying, "Do not grieve, for it will do no good." Jesus' approach is entirely different: he removes the cause of bereavement (1 Kings 17:17-24).

7:14. By touching even the bier, a stretcher on which the body was borne (Jewish custom did not use a closed coffin), Jesus would contract corpse-uncleanness, the severest form of ritual impurity in Judaism. Only those closest to the deceased were expected to expose themselves to this impurity. The young man had not been dead long, because it was necessary to wash, anoint, wrap, mourn over and then bury the body as quickly as possible to avoid the stench of decomposition.

7:15-17. God had used several earlier prophets (Elijah and Elisha) to resuscitate the dead, but it was a rare miracle. The few pagan stories of resuscitations, especially from the third century A.D. (from Philostratus and *Apuleius), are later and not validated by eyewitnesses as the Gospel accounts are; they also often exhibit features missing here, such as reports from the underworld.

7:18-23
Encouraging John

7:18-20. Perhaps John is troubled that Jesus exposes himself to potential ritual uncleanness (e.g., with *Gentiles and corpses) for the sake of healings. Then again, perhaps Jesus' words simply do not fit John's picture of the coming one he had proclaimed in 3:15-17, although John has no doubt that Jesus is at least a prophet who will tell him the truth.

7:21-23. Jesus' answer makes use of language from Isaiah 35:5; these healings are signs of the *messianic era. Some teachers compared the blind, lame and lepers to the dead because they had no hope of recovery.

7:24-35
Vindicating John

John's and Jesus' styles of ministry differ; but both are valid, and the religious community rejects both equally.

7:24. Reeds were fragile (Is 42:3), so a "reed shaken by the wind" would be notoriously weak (1 Kings 14:15) and undependable (2 Kings 18:21; Ezek 29:6).

7:25-26. Prophets were rarely well-to-do, and in times of national wickedness they were forced to operate outside societal boundaries. Now imprisoned by Herod Antipas, John is no court prophet who simply tells powerful people what they want to hear.

7:27. By fulfilling Isaiah 40:3, John is more than just any herald of God; he is the direct announcer of the Lord, who will act in a decisively new way by leading his people in a new exodus. (The new exodus, a return from captivity, is a theme in Isaiah.)

7:28. This comparison elevates Jesus' *disciples rather than demeans John. One may compare the early *rabbinic saying that Johanan ben Zakkai, one of the most respected scholars of the first century, was the "least" of *Hillel's eighty disciples; this saying was not meant to diminish Johanan's status but to increase that of his contemporaries and thus that of his teacher.

7:29-30. Because the once-for-all kind of *baptism was essentially reserved for pagans converting to Judaism, the religious people are unwilling to accept it for themselves. They questioned the religious commitment of less observant Jews, especially the *tax gatherers.

7:31-32. The marketplace was the most public part of town. Spoiled children having make-believe weddings and funerals (one later game was called "bury the grasshopper") represent Jesus' and John's dissatisfied opponents; unhappy with other children who would not play either game, they are upset no matter what.

7:33-34. John the Baptist fits the role of an *ascetic prophet, like Elijah (cf. 1:14-15 for John's abstention from wine); Jesus follows a model more like David, but both are proper in their place. Demon possession (v. 33) was associated with madness. "Glutton and drunkard" (v. 34) was a capital charge (Deut 21:20), hence a serious accusation.

7:35. Jewish tradition often personified Wisdom as divine, usually as a holy woman exhorting the righteous to follow her; here she is the mother of the righteous.

7:36-50
The Pharisee and the Loose Woman

Jesus violated social taboos to reach out to those marginalized not only racially (7:1-10), economically (7:11-17) and religiously (7:24-35) but also morally (7:36-50). Since the classical Greek period, banquets had become a setting for moral instruction.

7:36. It was considered virtuous to invite a teacher over for dinner, especially if the teacher were from out of town or had just taught at the *synagogue. That they are "reclining" rather than sitting indicates that they are using couches rather than chairs and that this is a banquet, perhaps in honor of the famous guest teacher.

7:37. That this woman is a "sinner"

may imply that she is a prostitute (surely a Jewish one—cf. Psalms of Solomon 2:11—though many prostitutes in Palestine were non-Jews), or at least a woman known to be morally loose and probably seeking something disreputable. If the *Pharisee is well-to-do, he may have a servant as a porter to check visitors at the door; but religious people often opened their homes for the poor, and the woman manages to get in. In banquets where uninvited people could enter, they were to remain quiet and away from the couches, observing the discussions of host and guests. Alabaster was considered the most appropriate container for perfume.

7:38. Jewish people did not consider perfume sinful, but because this woman is a "sinner" and uses the perfume as a tool of her trade, Jesus' acceptance of the gift of perfuming would offend religious sensitivities. That she stands "behind him" and anoints his feet instead of his head has to do with the posture of guests reclining on the couches; he would have had his left arm on the table and his feet away from the table toward the wall.

7:39. Adult women who were religious were expected to be married and thus would have their heads covered; any woman with her hair exposed to public view would be considered promiscuous. That this woman wipes Jesus' feet with her hair would thus indicate not only her humility but also her marginal religious status, even had Jesus not been a prophet and had she not been known in the community's gossip. That the host allowed that Jesus might be a prophet at all suggests great respect, because Jewish people generally believed that prophets ceased after the *Old Testament period.

7:40-42. Some scholars have argued that *Aramaic lacks a term for gratitude, hence "Which will love him more?" rather than, as we might expect, "Which will be more grateful?" Although debts were to be forgiven in the seventh year, experts in the law had found a way to get around that requirement. Those who could not pay could be imprisoned, temporarily enslaved or have certain goods confiscated; but this creditor goes beyond the letter of the law and extends mercy.

7:43-46. Common hospitality included providing water for the feet (though well-to-do householders left the washing to servants); the oft-invoked example of Abraham's hospitality (Gen 18:4) would render the host without excuse. Oil for the dry skin on one's head would also be a thoughtful act. A kiss was an affectionate or respectful form of greeting. Jesus faces her finally in verse 44; cf. comment on 7:38.

7:47-50. Although the priests could pronounce God's forgiveness after a sin offering, Jesus pronounces forgiveness without the clear restitution of a sacrifice to God in the temple. This pronouncement contradicted *Pharisaic ethics, and most of early Judaism would have seen it at best as marginal behavior. (One story in the *Dead Sea Scrolls is a rare exception to pronouncing forgiveness and accompanies an exorcism, but it does not seem to reflect general Jewish practice.)

8:1-3
The Women Disciples

For the form of support mentioned here, cf. 2 Kings 4:42. Women sometimes served as *patrons, or supporters, of religious teachers or associations in the ancient Mediterranean. (Men outnumbered them more than ten to one, however, because men had more of the economic resources.) But for these women to travel with the group would have been viewed as scandalous. Adult coeducation was unheard of, and that these women are learning Jesus' teaching as closely as his male *disciples would surely bother some outsiders as well. Upper-class families had more mobility, but commoners would still talk, as they did when other teachers (such as Greek philosophers) were accused of having women among their followers.

8:4-15
The Sower, the Seed and the Soils

See comment on Mark 4:3-20 for more details.

8:5-7. Seed was often sown before the ground was plowed; it thus commonly befell any of the fates reported here.

8:8. Thirtyfold, sixtyfold and a hundredfold are tremendously good harvests from Galilean soil.

8:9-10. Jewish teachers normally used *parables to illustrate and explain points, not to conceal them. But if one told stories without stating the point they were meant to illustrate, as Jesus does here, only those who listen most astutely and start with insiders' knowledge could figure out one's point. Greek teachers like *Plato would leave some points obscure to keep them from outsiders; Jewish teachers would sometimes do the same. Thus only those who were serious enough to persevere would understand.

8:11-15. Many of Jesus' hearers would be farmers who could relate well to these agricultural images; although Galilee (which was full of towns) was more urban than much of the empire, the tenant farmers who made up a large portion of the Roman Empire were also common in rural Galilee.

8:16-18
Accountability for the Word

8:16. Jesus is a master of the graphic illustrations in which Jewish teachers sought to excel: invisible light is pointless, and God wants people to receive the light of his Word. The lamps Jesus mentions were small clay lamps that had to be set on a stand to shed much light in a room; anything placed over the lamp would have extinguished it.

8:17-18. If the crowds do not obey what light they receive, they will never receive more. The language of "measuring" is the language of weighing food and other commodities at the market; it was sometimes used for God measuring out just judgments in the final day.

8:19-21
Jesus' True Family

Thinking of one's coreligionists as brothers and sisters was common; respecting older persons as mothers or fathers was also widespread. But allowing ties in the religious community to take precedence even over family ties was unheard-of in Judaism, except when a pagan converted to Judaism and regarded his new family as more important than his old one.

8:22-25
Master of Winds and Sea

Some ancient stories told of powerful individuals able to subdue even the forces of nature, but these were nearly always gods or, less commonly, heroes of the distant past. In Jewish tradition, the one who ruled the winds and sea was God himself (Ps 107:29), though a few pious men were reputed to be able to persuade him to send rain. The surprise of the *disciples at Jesus' power is thus easy to understand.

Storms often rose suddenly on the lake called the Sea of Galilee; these fishermen had usually stayed closer to Capernaum and are unprepared for a squall this far from shore. The only place one could sleep in a small fishing boat with water pouring in from a storm would be on the elevated stern, where one could use the wooden or leather-covered helmsman's seat, or a pillow sometimes kept under that seat, as a cushion to rest one's head.

8:26-39 Subduing the Demonic Legion

See further comment on Mark 5:1-20.

8:26. Matthew's "Gadara" (Mt 8:28), eight miles from the lake, and Gerasa, about thirty miles from the lake, were in the same general region, the area of the Decapolis, a predominantly non-Jewish area.

8:27. Jewish people considered tombs unclean and a popular haunt for unclean spirits. Many ancient cultures brought offerings for the dead, which might also appeal to these demons.

8:28. In ancient magic, one could try to gain control over a spirit by naming it. The attempt at magical self-protection is powerless against Jesus.

8:29. The strength that this demoniac displays is reported in many cases of demon possession in various cultures today as well.

8:30-31. A legion included four to six thousand troops. This man is therefore hosting a large number of demons. According to Jewish tradition, many demons were imprisoned in the atmosphere or, as here, under the earth (in the "abyss").

8:32. Only *Gentiles or nonobservant Jews considered "apostates" raised pigs, which Jewish readers would consider among the most unclean animals and thus rightful hosts for evil spirits. Ancient exorcists found that demons sometimes asked for concessions if the pressure for them to evacuate their host became too great.

8:33. Jewish tradition often taught that demons could die, so in the absence of evidence to the contrary, many ancient readers would assume that the demons had been destroyed (or at least disabled) with their hosts.

8:34-37. The opposition to Jesus arises from both economic causes—the loss of a large herd of swine—and certain Greek conceptions of dangerous wonderworking magicians, whom most people feared.

8:38-39. Because his *messiahship would be misunderstood, Jesus kept it a secret in predominantly Jewish areas. In the predominantly non-Jewish Decapolis, however, where people would wrongly perceive him as a magician, he urges his new disciple to spread the word about what *God* had done, thereby correcting the people's misunderstanding.

8:40-56 Death and the Flow of Blood

See further comment on Mark 5:21-43.

8:40-41. "Rulers of the *synagogue" were the chief officials in synagogues and were prominent members of their communities.

8:42. The official's daughter had been a minor until that year and on account of both her age and her gender had virtually no social status, quite in contrast to her prominent father (vv. 40-41).

8:43. This woman's sickness was reckoned as if she had a menstrual period all month long; it made her continually unclean under the *law (Lev 15:19-33)—a social problem on top of the physical one. Just as Jewish interpreters linked texts by a common word, Luke's source may use "twelve years" to emphasize the relatedness of these stories (vv. 42-43).

8:44-45. If she touched anyone or anyone's clothes, she rendered that person ceremonially unclean for the rest of the day (cf. Lev 15:26-27). She therefore should not have even been in this heavy crowd. Many teachers avoided touching women altogether, lest they become accidentally contaminated. Thus this woman could not touch or be touched, was probably now divorced or had never married, and was marginal to the rest of Jewish society.

8:46-48. Jewish people generally believed that only teachers closest to God had supernatural knowledge. Jesus uses his supernatural knowledge to identify with the woman who had touched him—even though in the eyes of the public this would mean that he had contracted ritual uncleanness. Lest anyone be permitted to think that the healing had been accomplished by typical pagan magic, operating without Jesus' knowledge, he declares that it happened in response to "faith" (v. 48).

8:49. Once an event had occurred, it was too late to pray for its reversal. For example, the *rabbis claimed that it was too late for one hearing a funeral procession to pray that it was not for a relative.

8:50-56. Several professional mourners were required at the funeral of even the poorest person; the funeral for a member of a prominent family like this one would have many mourners. Because bodies decomposed rapidly in Palestine, mourners had to be assembled as quickly as possible, and they had gathered before word even reached Jairus that his daughter had died.

9:1-6
Authorizing the Twelve

9:1-2. Under Jewish law, a sender could authorize messengers to act with his full legal authority to the extent of the commission given them.

9:3. Jesus instructs the *disciples to travel light, like some other groups: (1) peasants, who often had only one cloak; (2) traveling philosophers called *Cynics; (3) some prophets, like Elijah and John the Baptist. They are to be totally committed to their mission, not tied down with worldly concerns. The "bag" would have been used for begging (as the Cynics used it).

9:4. Jewish travelers depended on hospitality, which fellow Jews customarily extended to them.

9:5-6. "Shaking the dust off" essentially means treating these Jewish cities as if they are unclean, pagan cities, no defiling dust of which a pious Jew would want to bring into the Holy Land. A place like the temple was so holy that those entering would (at least in pious theory) not want the dust of the rest of Israel on their feet.

9:7-9
John Returned?

Although a few Jews influenced by *Plato and other sources accepted reincarnation, most Palestinian Jews believed in bodily *resurrection. The idea here is probably like the temporary resuscitations Elijah and Elisha performed in the *Old Testament (1 Kings 17:22; 2 Kings 4:34-35) rather than the permanent resurrection anticipated at the end of the age (Dan 12:2). Herod the tetrarch was a son of Herod the Great; the latter had been king when Jesus was born.

9:10-17
Mass Feeding

9:10-12. The Galilean countryside was full of villages, but Jesus had withdrawn his followers some distance from the nearest villages. Even the larger towns would have under three thousand inhabitants; feeding the crowd in the villages would have been difficult (9:12). (If they were beyond Bethsaida in *Gentile territory, hospitality would be even harder to find.)

9:13. It would have taken two hundred days of an average person's wages (around seven months of hard labor) to feed the great multitude that had assembled.

9:14. The people are organized in ranks like armies. The purpose is to facilitate the distribution of food, but some people in the crowd may have thought that Jesus was organizing them as ranks for a *messianic army (cf. Jn 6:15).

9:15. They may have "sat" instead of "reclined"; people generally reclined at banquets and sat for regular meals.

9:16. It was customary to begin a meal by giving thanks for the bread and then dividing it. People often prayed "looking toward heaven" (1 Kings 8:22, 54; Jn 17:1).

9:17. The multiplication of food is reminiscent of the miracle of God supplying manna for Israel in the wilderness, and especially of Elisha multiplying food (2 Kings 4:42-44, where some was also left over).

9:18-27
The Cost of Following the Real Messiah

9:18-19. Because many Palestinian Jews believed that prophets in the *Old Testament sense had ceased, ranking Jesus among the prophets would have been radical—but it was not radical enough to grasp his true identity.

9:20-21. There were many different views of the *Messiah (or messiahs) in Jesus' time, but they all revolved around a deliverance on earth and an earthly kingdom.

9:22. The *New Testament writers took some Old Testament texts as referring to the Messiah's suffering, but most Jewish people in the first century did not recognize these texts as referring to the Messiah, who was to reign as king. Most Jewish people believed in the *resurrection of all the righteous dead at the end of the age and the inauguration of a *kingdom under God's appointed ruler afterward.

9:23-25. The cross was an instrument of violent and painful execution. To "take the cross" was to carry the horizontal beam (the *patibulum)* of the cross out to the site of execution, usually past a jeering mob. In rhetorically strong terms, Jesus describes what all true *disciples must be ready for: if they follow him, they must be ready to face literal scorn on the road to eventual martyrdom, for they must follow to the cross. From the moment of faith believers must count their lives forfeit for the *kingdom.

9:26. "*Son of Man" here may refer to Daniel 7:13-14. The *kingdom for which the *disciples are hoping will ultimately come; but it will be preceded by a period of great suffering and wickedness. Many others in Jesus' day taught that great suffering and sin would precede the kingdom; but Peter and his colleagues preferred the easier view that the kingdom would come without suffering (perhaps, as some believed, by a supernatural, costless triumph).

9:27. The future glory of the preceding verses is anticipated by way of a revelation of the glory they would experience in 9:32-35. Because the future *Messiah had already come, the glory of his future *kingdom is also already present.

9:28-36
A Taste of Future Glory

God had revealed his glory to Moses on Mount Sinai, and Moses had come down from the mountain reflecting

God's glory (Ex 32—34).
9:28. God revealed his glory to Moses on a mountain (see above).
9:29. Jewish literature often described angels and other heavenly beings as being clothed in white. Luke omits Mark's "transfigured" because of the pagan connotations this term could have to his readers (Greek gods and magicians transformed themselves into other forms, though Mark, like Luke, was alluding to Moses, not to magicians).
9:30. Elijah apparently never died (2 Kings 2:11; Mal 4:5; Jewish tradition); Moses was buried by God himself (Deut 34:6), and some (unbiblical) Jewish traditions even claimed that Moses was still alive (cf. comment on Rev 11:6). Both these figures were expected to return in some sense before the time of the end.
9:31. Jesus' departure here is literally his "exodus." Although this term was a natural way to describe death (Wisdom of Solomon 7:6), it may represent an allusion to Israel's future salvation, which the prophets and later Jews often viewed as a new exodus.
9:32-33. Peter's suggestion of erecting shelters on the mountain may allude to Israel's tabernacles in the wilderness, by which the Israelites recognized God's presence among them in Moses' day.
9:34-36. "Hear him" may refer to Deuteronomy 18:15, where the Israelites were warned to heed the "prophet like Moses," the new Moses who would come.

9:37-43a
Delivering a Demoniac

9:37-38. An only son was extremely important to a father in this culture, for social, economic (support in old age) and hereditary reasons (including the passing on of one's ancestral line).
9:39. The possessed person's lack of control over his own motor responses parallels examples of spirit possession in many cultures through history and is attested in anthropological studies of spirit possession today. Greek medical texts mention "foam" in connection with epileptic seizures, the symptoms of which are in this case (but not always—Mt 4:24) caused by demonic possession.
9:40-41. Jesus' response presupposes that he expected his *disciples to have enough faith to work miracles as he did. Some ancient Jewish teachers were seen as miracle workers, but not often did they expect their disciples to be able to do miracles also.
9:42-43a. Exorcists normally tried to subdue demons by incantations invoking higher spirits, or by using smelly roots or pain-compliance techniques. Jesus here uses only his command, thereby showing his great authority.

9:43b-50
Qualifying Misconceptions of Glory

9:43b-45. The glory on the mountain and Jesus' power over demons would confirm the *disciples' *messianic suspicions (9:20), so Jesus needs to reemphasize his definition of the messianic mission in contrast to theirs (see 9:22).
9:46-48. Status was a preeminent concern in ancient society; children had none. But Jesus declares that in God's sight they are like messengers in Jewish custom, who bore the full authorization of the one they represented (see comment on 9:1-2), so they did not need worldly status. Representatives of someone who had great authority exercised more authority than others who acted on their own.
9:49-50. Ancient exorcists often invoked more powerful spirits to drive out lesser ones. If this exorcist is genuinely effective (contrast Acts 19:15-16), he is probably on their side.

9:51-56
Jerusalem via Samaria

9:51. This is a turning point in the plot movement, as in Acts 19:21. Like modern writers, skilled ancient writers gave signals of plot movement. "Setting one's face" normally implied resolute determination, such as a prophet would display (cf. Ezek 21:2).

9:52. Galilean pilgrims to the Passover feast in Jerusalem often took the short route through Samaria, although some took a longer route around it. But this verse suggests that Jesus sought accommodations there, which would have offended many pious *Pharisees and most Jewish nationalists.

9:53. Even before John Hyrcanus, a Jewish king, had destroyed the *Samaritan temple in the second century B.C., Samaritans and Jews had detested one another's holy sites. Samaritans later tried to defile the Jerusalem temple. They were also known to heckle pilgrims to Jerusalem, a practice that occasionally led to violence.

9:54. James and John want to call down fire from heaven as Elijah had done on the altar on Mount Carmel and when two companies of troops came against him (1 Kings 18:38; 2 Kings 1:10, 12). Elijah did this under much severer circumstances than Jesus faces here; all three cases were life-threatening, and his opponents at Carmel had been responsible for the martyrdom of most of his disciples.

9:55-56. Ancient Jewish readers would probably view Jesus' merciful restraint as pious (1 Sam 11:13; 2 Sam 19:22), no matter how much they hated the *Samaritans.

9:57-62
True Discipleship

9:57-58. *Disciples usually sought out their own teachers. Some radical philosophers who eschewed possessions sought to repulse prospective disciples with enormous demands, for the purpose of testing them and acquiring the most worthy. Many Palestinian Jews were poor, but few were homeless; Jesus had given up even home to travel and is completely dependent on the hospitality and support of others.

9:59-60. Family members would not be outside talking with *rabbis during the mourning period, the week immediately following the death. The initial burial took place shortly after a person's decease, and would have already occurred by the time this man would be speaking with Jesus. But a year after the first burial, after the flesh had rotted off the bones, the son would return to rebury the bones in a special box in a slot in the tomb wall. Thus the son here could be asking for as much as a year's delay.

One of an eldest son's most important responsibities was his father's burial. Jesus' demand that the son place Jesus above this responsibility would thus sound like heresy: in Jewish tradition, honoring father and mother was one of the greatest commandments, and to follow Jesus in such a radical way would seem to break this commandment.

9:61-62. One needed to keep one's eyes on the path of the plow to keep its furrow from becoming crooked. The hand-held plow was light and wooden and often had an iron point.

When Elijah found Elisha plowing, he called him to follow but allowed him first to bid farewell to his family (1 Kings 19:19-21). Jesus' call here is more radical than that of a radical prophet.

10:1-16
Authorizing the Seventy(-two)

10:1. If Jesus chose twelve *disciples to represent the twelve tribes of Israel, he may have chosen the number of this larger group to represent the seventy (sometimes seventy-two) nations of Jewish tradition, prefiguring the mission to the *Gentiles. (Some Greek manuscripts here read seventy, others read seventy-two.) Cf. also the seventy prophetically endowed elders of Numbers 11:24-25, plus Eldad and Medad (Num 11:26).

Heralds were generally sent "two by two." The term for "send" suggests that these are *apostles just as the Twelve are (see comment on 9:1-2; cf. 1 Cor 15:5-7).

10:2. A *rabbi of the late first to early second century made a similar statement to Jesus' here, referring to training people in the *law; the urgency of harvesting while the fields are ripe was a natural image to first-century farmers.

10:3. Jewish people sometimes viewed themselves (Israel) as sheep among wolves (the *Gentiles). The image of a lamb among wolves was proverbial for defenselessness.

10:4. These apostles are to travel light, like some other groups; cf. comment on 9:3. *Essenes reportedly received such hospitality from fellow Essenes in various cities that they did not need to take provisions when they traveled. Greeting no one on the way indicates the urgency of their prophetic mission representing God and not themselves (cf. 1 Kings 13:9-10; 2 Kings 4:29; 9:3); it was offensive to withhold greetings, and pious people tried to be the first to greet an approaching person. (Jewish teachers agreed, however, that one should not interrupt religious duties like prayer in order to greet someone.)

10:5-9. Hospitality to travelers was a crucial virtue of Mediterranean antiquity, especially in Judaism. To whom and under what circumstances greetings should be given were important issues of social protocol, because the greeting, "Peace," was a blessing meant to communicate peace. Jesus cuts through such protocol with new directives.

10:10-11. Pious Jewish people returning to holy ground would not want so much as the dust of pagan territory clinging to their sandals.

10:12. Both the biblical prophets and subsequent Jewish tradition set forth Sodom as the epitome of sinfulness (e.g., Deut 32:32; Is 1:9; 3:9; 13:19; Jer 23:14; 50:40; Lam 4:6; Ezek 16:46; Amos 4:11; Zeph 2:9). The particular sin that Jesus mentions here is probably rejection of God's messengers, albeit lesser ones than Jesus (cf. Gen 19).

10:13. Jewish people thought of Tyre and Sidon as purely pagan cities (cf. 1 Kings 16:31), but those who were exposed to the truth had been known to repent (1 Kings 17:9-24). "Sackcloth and ashes" were characteristic of mourning, which sometimes expressed *repentance.

10:14. According to some Jewish stories about the time of the end ("the day of judgment," as it was often called), the righteous among the nations would testify against the rest of their people, making it clear that no one had any excuse to reject the truth about God.

10:15. Jewish literature often described judgment in terms similar to those Jesus uses here (Is 5:14; *Jubilees 24:31), especially against a ruler who exalted himself as a deity (e.g., the reference to the Babylonian king's death in Is 14:14-15).

10:16. See comment on 9:48.

10:17-24
The Real Cause for Joy

10:17. Exorcists usually had to employ various incantations to persuade demons to leave; thus the *disciples are amazed at the immediate efficacy of Jesus' name.

10:18. Although the texts often cited today as describing *Satan's fall (Is 14; Ezek 28) refer contextually only to kings who thought they were gods, much of Jewish tradition believed that angels had fallen (based especially on Gen 6:1-3).

But the context and the imperfect tense of the Greek verb ("I was watching") may suggest that something altogether different is in view here: the self-proclaimed ruler of this age (Lk 4:6) retreating from his position before Jesus' representatives. (One might compare, e.g., the Jewish tradition that the guardian angel of Egypt fell into the sea when God smote the Egyptians for Israel; the image of falling from heaven is usually not literal, e.g., Lam 2:1.)

10:19. The protection Jesus promises is similar to that which God had sometimes promised in the *Old Testament (cf. Deut 8:15; Ps 91:13; for scorpions as a metaphor for human obstacles to one's call, see Ezek 2:6). Here serpents, sometimes associated with *Satan, demons or magic, probably represent Satan's hosts.

10:20. The book containing the name of the righteous in heaven was a common image in Jewish literature (e.g., *Jubilees; *1 Enoch), with ample Old Testament precedent (Ex 32:32; Is 4:3; Dan 12:1; Mal 3:16; perhaps Ps 56:8; 139:16; Jer 17:3).

10:21. Jesus' prayer here might offend *scribes, who had worked long and hard to study the *law.

10:22. Jewish texts did speak of unique mediators of revelation (e.g., Moses), but in this period the role here ascribed to the Son as the sole revealer of the Father and as the content of the Father's revelation is held in Jewish texts only by Wisdom, personified as a divine power second only to God.

10:23-24. Some Jewish texts describe how the righteous in the Old Testament longed to see the era of *messianic redemption and a fuller revelation of God. Making a statement about someone (here, Jesus) by blessing someone else (here, those who saw him) was an accepted *rhetorical technique of the day.

10:25-37
Loving One's Neighbor

10:25. The lawyer's question about inheriting *eternal life was a common Jewish theological question, and legal and other challenges to *rabbis were common in ancient rabbinic debate.

10:26. Teachers often responded to questions with counterquestions. "How do you read?" was a fairly standard rabbinic question.

10:27. The legal expert offers the answers sometimes given by Jewish teachers (and by Jesus; see Mk 12:29-31), citing Deuteronomy 6:5 and Leviticus 19:18.

10:28. Some texts in the *law promised life for those who kept the law. This "life" meant long life on the land the Lord had given them, but many later Jewish interpreters read it as a promise of *eternal life. Jesus applies the principle to eternal life as well (cf. v. 25). "You have answered rightly" serves aptly as a prelude to a *parable's application, driving the point home in the respondent's own case (4 Ezra 4:20; cf. 2 Sam 12:7; 1 Kings 20:40-42).

10:29. Jewish teachers usually used "neighbor" to mean "fellow Israelite." Leviticus 19:18 clearly means "fellow Israelite" in the immediate context, but the less immediate context applies the principle also to any non-Israelite in the land (19:34).

10:30. Like most *parables, this story has one main point that answers the interlocutor's question; the details are part of the story and are not meant to be allegorized. Jericho was lower in elevation than Jerusalem; hence one would "go down" there. Robbers were common along the road and would especially attack a person traveling alone. Many people did not have extra clothes, which were thus a valuable item to steal.

10:31. Priests were supposed to avoid especially impurity from a corpse; *Pharisees thought one would contract it if even one's shadow touched the corpse. Like the man who had been robbed, the priest was "going down" (v. 31), hence he was heading from Jerusalem and did not have to worry about being unable to perform duties in the temple. But rules were rules; although the rule of mercy would take precedence if the man were clearly alive, the man looked as if he might be dead (v. 30), and the priest did not wish to take the chance. The task was better left to a Levite or ordinary Israelite. Jesus' criticism of the priesthood here is milder than that of the *Essenes and often that of the prophets (Hos 6:9).

10:32. Rules for Levites were not as strict as for priests, but the Levite also wished to avoid defilement.

10:33. Jews and *Samaritans traditionally had no love for each other; although violence was the exception rather than the rule, the literature of each betrays an attitude of hostility toward the other. Jesus' illustration would offend Jewish listeners, striking at the heart of their patriotism, which was religiously justified.

10:34-35. Oil was used medicinally and for washing wounds; wine was also apparently used to disinfect wounds. Jewish people commonly avoided *Gentile, and probably Samaritan, oil. "I will repay" was a standard formula guaranteeing a debt.

10:36-37. Jesus' questioner would hate Samaritans, yet he is forced to follow the moral example of a Samaritan in Jesus' story. This parable forced him to answer his own question, "Who is my neighbor?" (10:29).

10:38-42
The Woman Disciple

This passage challenges the role designations for women in the first century; the role of *disciple and future minister of Jesus' message is more critical than that of homemaker and hostess, and is also open to women.

10:38. Being one of Jesus' hostesses would be a lot of work for Martha; he had brought many disciples to feed. Martha's act may fall short of Mary's in this narrative, but her labor represents the best display of devotion she knows how to offer.

10:39. People normally sat on chairs or, at banquets, reclined on couches; but disciples sat at the feet of their teachers. Serious disciples were preparing to be teachers—a role not permitted to women. (The one notable exception in the second century was a learned *rabbi's daughter who had married another learned rabbi; but most rabbis rejected her opinions.) Mary's posture and eagerness to absorb Jesus' teaching at the expense of a more traditional womanly role (10:40) would have shocked most Jewish men.

10:40-42. Despite the cultural importance of hospitality (the food preparation for guests was normally incumbent on the matron of the house), Mary's role as a *disciple of Jesus is more important than anything else she could do.

11:1-13
Jesus on Prayer

11:1. *Disciples commonly asked their teachers for instruction, and some were known to have asked the proper blessings or prayers for different occasions. Yet it was considered rude and impious to interrupt someone's praying; thus here the disciples wait till Jesus finishes his own prayers before they ask. Different teachers might teach special forms of prayers to their own groups of disciples, although all Palestinian Jews had some prayers in common, except for radical sectarians like the *Essenes.

11:2. Jewish people commonly addressed God as "Our heavenly Father" when they prayed, although such intimate titles as "Abba" (Papa) were rare (see comment on Mk 14:36). One standard Jewish prayer of the day proclaimed, "Exalted and hallowed be your . . . name . . . and may your kingdom come speedily and soon."

God's name would be "hallowed," or "sanctified," "shown holy," in the time of the end, when his *kingdom would come. This idea was biblical (Is 5:16; 29:23; Ezek 36:23; 38:23; 39:7, 27; cf. Zech 14:9). In the present God's people could hallow his name by living rightly; if they lived wrongly, Jewish teachers observed, they would "profane" his name, or bring it into disrepute among the nations.

11:3. This petition alludes to God's provision of "daily bread" (manna) for his people after he first redeemed them (Ex 16:4). Prayers for God to supply basic needs—of which bread and water were seen as the ultimate examples—were common (cf. Prov 30:8).

11:4. Jewish people regarded sins as "debts" before God; the same *Aramaic word could be used for both. Jewish law at least in theory required the periodic forgiveness of monetary debtors (in the seventh and fiftieth years), so the illustration of forgiving debts makes good sense. Parallels with ancient Jewish prayers suggest that "Lead us not into testing" means "Let us not sin when we are tested"—rather than "Let us not be tested" (cf. 22:46 in context).

11:5-6. Hospitality was a crucial obligation; the host must feed the traveler who has graced his or her home by coming to spend the night. Although many homes would have used up their day's bread by nightfall, in a small village people would know who still had bread left over. In modern villages of that region, bread might last for several days, but one must serve a guest a fresh, unbroken loaf as an act of hospitality.

11:7. The children would sleep on mats on the floor of the one-room dwelling; unbolting the heavy bar that was laid through rings attached to the door was a bother and would make noise that would awaken them.

11:8. The continual pounding would awaken the children anyway; unbolting the door would thus no longer pose much problem. The word translated "importunity" (KJV) or "persistence" (NASB, NRSV) means "shamelessness" (sometimes like the impudence characteristic of the *Cynics; cf. TEV). This term refers either to the boldness of the knocker, lest he be shamed by having nothing to give his guest, or perhaps the shame of the father inside, because the whole village would be humiliated by a bad report about their hospitality.

11:9-10. In the context of the *parable, these verses mean that the knocker receives because of boldness or because the honor of God is inseparably connected with the honor of his servant, the knocker.

11:11-13. This is a standard Jewish "how much more" *(qal vahomer)* argument. Most people believed that the *Holy Spirit (1) had departed, (2) was available only to several of the holiest people, or (3) belonged to the community (*Dead Sea Scrolls). Thus the promise of verse 13 would have sounded profound; given common beliefs about the Spirit in ancient Judaism (based on the Old Testament), this was essentially a promise that God would make them prophets, anointed spokespersons for God.

11:14-26
Who Is Satan's Real Vassal?

11:14-16. Most pagan exorcists sought to remove demons by magical incantations. *Rabbis in the second century still accused Jesus and Jewish Christians of using sorcery to achieve the miracles they were performing. "Beelzebul" is related to the name of the pagan god called "Baal-zebub" in 2 Kings 1:2; used as an equivalent to "Belial" (2 Cor 6:15), it was a common Jewish name for the devil in the *Testament of Solomon. (The *rabbis often called him Sammael; *Jubilees called him Beliar or Mastema; the *Dead Sea Scrolls, Belial; by whatever name, ancient Jews understood who the prince of demons was.)

11:17-18. Jesus does not deny the existence of other exorcists here, but he need not be validating most of them, either: a demon's retreat to draw attention to another of *Satan's servants would be only a strategic retreat. Their exorcisms contrast with the wholesale exorcising of the masses that Jesus undertakes, which clearly signifies a defeat of Satan (11:20).

11:19. "Your sons" means "members of your own group" (just as, e.g., "sons of the prophets" meant "prophets"); because some of their associates also cast out demons (by methods that would look more magical than Jesus'), they should consider their charge carefully.

11:20. God's "finger" represented his power. Although the phrase occurs elsewhere, Jesus alludes especially to Exodus 8:19, where Pharaoh's magicians, attempting to imitate Moses' miracles, are forced to admit that the true God is working through Moses but not through them.

11:21-23. Many early Jewish sources report that *Satan or demons were "bound," or imprisoned, after God subdued them. Less relevant to this context, ancient magical texts also speak of "binding" demons by magical procedures. The *parable here about tying up a protective and armed householder (perhaps viewed as a Roman soldier or veteran, or simply an especially zealous householder) means that Jesus had defeated Satan and could therefore plunder his possessions—free the demon-possessed.

11:24-26. Here Jesus returns the charge: they, not he, are servants of Satan; he casts demons out, but they invite them back in even greater numbers. Skillful lawyers and *rhetoricians delighted in subverting an opponent's charge by showing that the opponent himself was guilty and unqualified to bring the accusation.

11:27-36
The Genuinely Blessed

11:27-28. It was customary to praise the child by blessing the mother; this figure of speech occurs in Greco-Roman literature (e.g., the first-century Roman satirist Petronius), *rabbinic texts (e.g., sayings attributed to Johanan ben Zakkai) and elsewhere (e.g., *2 Baruch 54:10).

11:29-30. Jonah's preaching was a simple message of judgment, but that was all that Nineveh required in his generation.

11:31-32. Jewish discussions of the end times included converts from among the poor who would testify against those who said they were too poor to follow God; and similarly converts among the rich, converts among the *Gentiles and so on. Here Jesus appeals to pagans who converted. Jewish people probably thought of the "Queen of the South," the queen of Sheba, as the queen of Ethiopia, which was considered the southernmost part of the world (cf. Acts 8:27).

11:33. Most Palestinian homes did not have "cellars," but Luke is relating the image to his audience; many Greek homes did have them. Greek houses often placed the lamp in the vestibule, and many Palestinian homes had only one room; whichever architectural style is in view, "those who enter in" would immediately see the lamp.

11:34-36. Jesus speaks literally of a "single" eye versus a "bad" or "evil" one. A "single" eye normally meant a generous one. A "bad" eye in that culture could mean either a diseased one or a stingy one. Many people believed that light was emitted from the eye, enabling one to see, rather than that light was admitted through the eye; here it seems to be admitted through the eye.

11:37-54 Denouncing Religious Colleagues

As in 7:36-50, a dinner becomes the occasion for moral instruction (this practice was so common in antiquity that it became a frequent setting in a type of philosophical literature called a *symposium).* Even more than in 7:36-50, it also becomes the occasion for confrontation.

11:37. The *Pharisee's behavior would have appeared honorable; see comment on 7:36. Prominent teachers would be invited to lecture at such meals, discoursing on wise topics with others who also liked to show off their education.

11:38. Pharisees were particularly scrupulous about washing their hands, a tradition not practiced in the Old Testament.

11:39-40. Ritual purity was important to the *Pharisees, so they washed their vessels as well as themselves in ritual baths. The school of *Shammai—the Pharisaic majority in this period—said that the outside of a cup could be clean even if the inside were not; the minority view of *Hillel's followers was that the inside of the cup must be cleansed first. Jesus sides with the school of Hillel on this point, but does so to make a figurative statement about the inside of the heart.

11:41. The *Aramaic word for "cleanse" (Mt 23:26) is similar to that for "give in charity"; it is possible that Luke adopts one nuance of an *Aramaic wordplay by Jesus, while Matthew adopts another.

11:42. Tithes were used especially to support the priests and Levites. "Rue" and Mathew's "dill" (23:23) are similar words in *Aramaic, possibly reflecting an original Aramaic source here. The written law did not explicitly require tithing these dry, green, garden herbs; the question among the *Pharisees was whether they counted as foodstuffs.

11:43. Pharisees were considered quite meticulous in their observance of the *law, and those regarded as superior in their knowledge of the law were hailed especially respectfully in the marketplaces.

11:44. Nothing spread ritual impurity as severely as a corpse; *Pharisees believed that one contracted impurity if even one's shadow touched a corpse or grave. Inconspicuous tombs (or limestone ossuaries) would be whitewashed each spring to warn passersby to avoid them and so to avoid impurity, but the Pharisees lack this telltale warning sign. They are impure on the inside, but look religious on the outside.

11:45. Luke is more concerned to distinguish Pharisees from professional legal experts than Matthew is (cf. Mt 23:13-29). Although some Pharisees worked as legal experts and some legal experts were Pharisees, these groups were not identical.

11:46-47. Ancient Judaism emphasized more often than the *Old Testament had that Israel had martyred its prophets; the Jewish community in this period built tombs as monuments for the prophets and the righteous (including some Old Testament servants of God who were not martyred, like David or Huldah).

11:48. The point of Jesus' saying here is "like father, like son"; corporate sin and guilt continued among the descendants of the wicked unless they repented (Ex 20:5; Deut 23:2-6; 1 Sam 15:2-3; Is 1:4; etc.).

11:49-50. Jewish people commonly believed that fully anointed prophets had ceased at the end of the Old Testament period and would be restored only in the end time. Bloodguilt was a serious matter, affecting the whole community and not just the individuals directly responsible (Deut 21:1-9). God would avenge it (Deut 32:43; Ps 79:10). The *rabbis considered the place between the porch and altar the holiest place on earth after the holy of holies and the priestly sanctuary.

The Hebrew Bible is arranged in a different sequence from our modern English versions of the *Old Testament; in it Zechariah is the last martyr (2 Chron 24:20-22) and Abel is the first, as in our Bibles (Gen 4:8). Jewish tradition expanded the accounts of both martyrdoms, declaring that after Zechariah's death a fountain of blood appeared in the temple that even the slaughter of thousands of priests could not appease. Zechariah prayed for vengeance (2 Chron 24:22), and Abel's blood cried out from the ground (Gen 4:10); to say that their vengeance would be requited on Jesus' generation was thus to promise unimaginable horrors. This judgment is because his generation would climax the terrible sins of their spiritual ancestors.

11:52-54. Experts in the law supposedly increased knowledge of the law; for Jesus to charge that their detailed expositions of it instead rendered its plain meaning inaccessible was a serious accusation.

12:1-12 Sound Speech and the Day of Judgment

Jesus warns his hearers to evaluate all their values and priorities in view of the day of judgment: their words, their lives and (in 12:13-34) their possessions. Although the world's hostility appears somewhat less pronounced in Luke (who, like *Philo and *Josephus on the Jewish side, wants his faith to make sense to the broader culture) than in Mark (who, like many *apocalyptic writers, experienced only opposition from the world), Luke reports Jesus' warnings no less plainly than other writers: following Jesus is costly. The costs of not following, however, are eternal.

12:1. From natural acoustic settings (e.g., coves or hills) a powerful speaker could address a vast crowd. A crowd of "many thousands" was rare; had the Romans known of such large crowds in the wilderness, they might have detained Jesus. They did not trust large gatherings of people who met without their sanction and whose potentially revolutionary *rhetoric they could not monitor. (The theater in the Galilean city Sepphoris seated 4,000-5,000 people, but because it was not in the countryside, any anti-Roman rhetoric would have been immediately reported.) The odds of Roman interference at this point are not particularly great, however; they did not patrol the Galilean countryside, and their highest officers are as yet unaware of Jesus (23:2).

12:2-3. The flat housetops would have provided the most conspicuous forum for shouting news to neighbors; they were in the open, as opposed to the inner rooms. The darkness of night was considered the easiest time to pass along secrets. In this context, 12:2-3 may either warn that one's confession or denial of Christ will be reported by deceptive betrayers (12:1, 4-5) or that it will be reported at the judgment (12:4-10). The day of judgment would bring all deeds to light (cf., e.g., Is 29:15); the wicked would be ashamed and the righteous vindicated (e.g., Is 45:16-17).

12:4-5. All Jewish readers would understand "the one who has authority to cast into hell" as God, the judge, whose power the wise are respectfully to "fear."

12:6-7. Sparrows were one of the cheapest items sold for poor people's food in the marketplace and were the cheapest of all birds. According to Matthew 10:29, one could purchase two sparrows for an *assarion,* a small copper coin of little value; here it appears that they are even cheaper if purchased in larger quantities. This is a standard Jewish "how much more" argument: If God cares for something as cheap as sparrows, how much more does he care for humans? The hairs of one's head being numbered was an *Old Testament way of saying that nothing could happen to a person without God allowing it (cf. 1 Sam 14:45; 2 Sam 14:11; 1 Kings 1:52).

12:8-9. Jesus is presented as both intercessor (defense attorney) and prosecutor before the heavenly court, a familiar Jewish image. In many Jewish accounts, the heavenly court consisted of angels; the angels would certainly be gathered for the day of judgment. God would pass final judgment, but the text implies that Jesus never loses a case before him.

12:10. When Jesus says people "will be forgiven," he means God will forgive them (Jewish people sometimes used passive constructions to avoid use of God's name). See comment on Mark 3:23-30. In this context, blasphemy against the *Spirit may refer to a denial of Jesus of which the denier (unlike Peter) never repents.

12:11. *Synagogues functioned as meeting places for Jewish local courts; transgressors were sometimes beaten there. Punishments meted out by Roman authorities were normally even harsher than Jewish punishments.

12:12. The Jewish people viewed the *Holy Spirit especially as the Spirit of *prophecy; thus when brought before the authorities (12:11) believers would be empowered to speak God's message as plainly as did the *Old Testament prophets. (Inspiration does not, of course, imply lack of general preparation or discipline in the subject about which one speaks; disciples memorized the sayings of their teachers in both Jewish and Greek culture, and Jesus' disciples would know his teaching as well as being inspired by the Spirit.)

12:13-21 Materialism and Hell

12:13. People often called upon *rabbis to settle legal disputes. The eldest son would always receive double what any of the other sons would receive. The proportion of inheritance was thus fixed, and the plaintiff in this case has every legal right to receive his share of the inheritance.

12:14-15. Jesus' answer would strike first-century hearers forcefully: the issue is not whether the plaintiff is legally in the right; the issue is that life, not possessions, is what matters. Even most peasants owned some property (a dwelling), so Jesus' words strike at the very heart of human desire. Only a few Greek philosophers (e.g., Epictetus) uttered words about possessions that sounded as harsh as Jesus' here.

12:16-18. Archaeologists have found large grain silos on farms where wealthy absentee landowners lived, such as in Sepphoris, one of the largest and most *Hellenized Jewish cities in Galilee. The image in the *parable here is that of a wealthy landowner, part of the extremely small leisured class (generally estimated at less than 1 percent), who need not labor in his own fields. Although many peasants may have taken pride in their labor and few could ever change their social status, the lifestyles of the rich and famous provided natural models for popular envy.

12:19. The *Epicurean-like complacency of the man who would "eat, drink and be merry" probably refers to the analogous folly of well-to-do Jews in Isaiah 22:13-14. It was the best that mortal life itself could offer a person (Eccles 2:24; 3:12; 5:18-19), but one needed also to consider God's demands (11:7—12:14). Many other Jewish texts also criticize the self-sufficient person who thinks that he or she has it all and does not reckon with death (e.g., Ecclus 11:18-19; Syriac Menander's *Sentences* 368-76; Pseudo-Phocylides 109-10; *1 Enoch 97:8-10).

12:20. The idea of leaving the fruit of one's labors to others more worthy appears in the *Old Testament wisdom tradition (e.g., Eccles 2:18); the fear of leaving it to someone who would squander it is also common in ancient literature; the image of life being loaned to a person and required back at death would have likewise been familiar (Wisdom of Solomon 15:8).

12:21. Jesus states that the sin is not how he gained his income but simply that he hoarded it rather than giving generously; the same emphasis appears in Proverbs.

12:22-34
The Unimportance of Possessions

12:22-23. Jesus reasons back to basics: one's basic needs relate to survival. Some philosophers taught that people should seek only these basic needs, although most philosophers felt that people could acquire possessions as long as they did not go out of their way to seek them. The *Cynics, however, owned nothing; and among Palestinian Jews, the *Essenes shared all their possessions communally. Jesus nowhere prohibits possessions, but he teaches priorities that challenge his followers' lifestyles; whereas people and their needs matter, possessions beyond one's needs are worthless.

12:24-28. Jewish (and Greek) wisdom teachers often illustrated their points from nature. Solomon's splendor, during what was undoubtedly the wealthiest period materially in Israel's history, was impressive by all human standards (1 Kings 10:5).

12:29-30. A Jewish hearer would not wish to be worse than the "nations," the godless *Gentiles. The Jewish people believed that God was their (not the Gentiles') father.

12:31-32. Here Jesus probably uses a Jewish "how much more" argument (if God gives you the *kingdom, how much more will he also supply all other needs); but Jesus could mean that the blessing of the future kingdom includes God's faithful provision now.

12:33-34. One should invest in eternal life rather than in possessions; see comment on Matthew 6:19-21.

12:35-40
Ready for His Coming

In context (12:22-34), this passage suggests that only those who travel lightly will be prepared. Although most of Jesus' Jewish contemporaries longed and prayed for the time of future redemption, they also seem to have been more preoccupied with daily needs than with extraordinary preparation for the future judgment (exceptions were the *Essenes and followers of *messianic figures and revolutionaries).

12:35. Like military watchmen or others who stay prepared when others sleep, Jesus' followers must be dressed and ready for action (Ex 12:11). Keeping lamps lit would literally mean having a ready supply of oil and staying awake so they could draw on this supply; this is a figure for preparedness (cf. Mt 25:3-10).

12:36. Well-to-do householders often had a special slave or slaves in charge of keeping the door; these slave-porters would keep unwanted persons out but admit members of the household. If Jewish banquets resembled Greek and Roman banquets, the feasting itself could last well into the night. Whether or not he had remained for the full seven days of the feast, it would be unusual for a well-to-do householder to return from a distant banquet (as opposed to one in the same city) in the night. Robbers made night travel more dangerous, though the danger was reduced by a large entourage.

12:37. Although a few philosophers argued that slaves were the moral equals of their masters, and one well-to-do Roman is known to have eaten on the same level as his freed slaves, masters' serving slaves was unheard-of. Such an image would offend the well-to-do but would be a powerful symbol of how Jesus would treat those who remained faithful to the end.

12:38. Here Jesus follows a Jewish division of night into three watches; contrast the division for Roman guard duty in Mark 13:35.

12:39-40. The term translated "broken into" is literally "dug through"; walls were often built of dried mud and thus one could dig through them (although it would be quicker to break in the door). More well-to-do homes could use stone instead.

12:41-48
For Ministers Too

Leaders in the *church must recognize that they are appointed only to serve their fellow servants, the rest of the church.

12:41. *Disciples often sought clarification from their teachers by asking questions.

12:42. Many well-to-do householders had a slave called a "steward," a sort of business manager who managed the estate. Such a high-level slave could be in charge of rations to the other servants.

12:43-44. Upward mobility existed among household servants; indeed, many such servants outranked free peasants in terms of real power or status, and even earned more money (which they could later use to buy their freedom).

12:45. Such a slave could abuse his authority only if the master were not present. Absentee landowners and householders were not infrequent, especially if they owned other estates at a great distance. In other stories of the period, absentee kings, landowners or husbands posed temptations to those remaining behind. Drunkenness was despised, especially when slaves became drunk at the master's expense. A slave who abused the other slaves was viewed as mistreating his master's property (see comment on 12:47-48); in some cases, slaves were also objects of a master's personal concern.

12:46. The punishment of "cutting in pieces" is attested elsewhere in an earlier period in the pagan Greek East; Luke's readers, who would view themselves as more civilized, would no doubt find this detail horrifying. Taken literally, the subsequent banishment with unbelievers could mean that he was deprived of decent burial; but in the *parable it especially points to the Jewish doctrine of hell (*Gehinnom) for idolaters.

12:47-48. Some ancient laws viewed slaves as persons; other laws viewed them as property. Although masters were allowed to beat slaves (as they also generally beat their children), it was in their economic interests not to do so often or severely. A major flogging (12:47), execution and disfigurement of the corpse (12:46) reflect the severity of the crime; a master legally had the power of life and death over his slaves. The *parable indicates that greater knowledge brings greater responsibility (see Lev 26:18; Amos 3:1-2).

12:49-53
Bringer of Division

Jesus' ethics differ so radically from those of the world that division is inevitable.

12:49. The fire probably refers to the impending end-time judgment. Fire in the *Old Testament could symbolize the end-time judgment and purging; cf. comment on 3:16.

12:50. Jesus' impending "*baptism" probably refers to undergoing the baptism of fire (12:49; judgment—3:16) on others' behalf, as does his cup (cf. comment on Mk 10:38).

12:51-53. Given the great emphasis on family harmony in Judaism, Jesus' words here would strike the hearers strongly. Extended family lived in the same household more frequently than today, although not everyone would have had in-laws present.

12:54-59
Signs of the Times

12:54. A cloud from the west would be coming from the Mediterranean Sea and thus would be full of rain.

12:55. A wind from the south would bring hot air from the desert.

12:56-57. Such weather predictors (12:54-55) were obvious; Jesus says that the truth of his message is equally obvious.

12:58-59. Here Jesus refers to the ancient practice of debt imprisonment (mentioned also in the *Old Testament, e.g., Lev 25:39-41; Amos 2:6). In debt imprisonment, one would have to depend on friends to come up with the needed funds; one would not be released unless they did so. Luke substitutes a Greek officer for Matthew's Jewish one (Mt 5:25), making the story more intelligible for his own readers.

13:1-9
Repent or Perish

13:1-5. As in most cultures, in ancient Judaism, when something bad happened to someone, people wondered what the person had done wrong. Pilate's cruelty here fits the sort of conflicts he had with the Jewish community and the presence of Galilean pilgrims at the holy days celebrated in Jerusalem. (Pilate was present at the feasts to ensure that order was maintained.) The "tower in Siloam" may have been on Jerusalem's city wall above the pool of Siloam; it may have been associated with Pilate's construction of an improved water-supply system for the city.

13:6. Palestinian vineyards often contained fruit trees in addition to vines.

13:7. That some fig trees did not bear fruit in a given year did not mean that they would never do so (cf. comment on Mk 11:12-14); in this *parable the vineyard worker asks the master to wait till the fourth year to make sure it was a worthless tree (cf. Is 65:8). According to *rabbinic interpretation of Leviticus 19:23, fruit from newly planted trees was forbidden for three years (though the Jewish tradition may have applied more strictly to olives than to figs). In later Jewish teaching, God examined Israel's sins once a year to decide their future for the coming year; but it is not clear if Jesus alludes to such an idea here.

13:8. The vineyard worker answers to the owner, perhaps as his servant, yet intercedes on behalf of the fig tree. Digging around a tree and putting manure around it to fertilize it were common procedures, but fig trees usually did not need manure; the worker does all he can to try to save the tree. Jewish teachers debated whether Israel's *repentance could change the set time of the end, but they agreed that God could suspend his judgment if he saw repentance.

13:10-17 Healing on the Sabbath

13:10. Visiting teachers were commonly asked to speak in *synagogues on the sabbath.

13:11-12. Ancient medical writers used words like "loose" to describe the removal of curvature of the spine and related ailments. The term was also used of freeing people from a demon's grip.

13:13-14. The synagogue leader's argument sounds logical: work is forbidden on the sabbath, but that still leaves six days a week for healings. The problem is that biblical sabbath laws did not restrict *God's* activity, and the only physical work Jesus performs on this sick woman is to lay his hands on her (though some *Pharisees considered this work). Even Pharisaic rules officially forbade only healing by a physician; they debated the propriety of prayer for the sick on the sabbath. But Pharisees may not have been present on this occasion anyway; most of the estimated 6,000 seem to have lived in Judea.

13:15-16. Here again Jesus uses the common Jewish "how much more" *(qal vahomer)* argument: if one could release an animal from a bond for its own good on the sabbath (one of the few kinds of tying and loosing permitted then), how much more could one release a "daughter of Abraham" (i.e., an Israelite) from her satanic bonds?

13:17. Arguments by analogy were accepted in Jewish legal debate; Jesus has skillfully outmaneuvered his opponents. Both Greek and *rabbinic controversy narratives typically culminated in the wise protagonist's response that silenced his opponents, so Jesus' triumph would be obvious to Luke's readers.

13:18-30 The Nature of the Kingdom

13:18. "To what shall we compare?" was a common *rabbinic way to introduce a *parable to illustrate a point.

13:19. Everyone regarded the mustard seed as very small; indeed, something smaller would be hard to see. It nevertheless yielded a shrub the size of a tree (around the Sea of Galilee, it can reach a height of 8-10 feet), with room for birds to perch in it (borrowing the language of Daniel 4:12, the splendor of a mortal ruler's kingdom). According to second-century Palestinian teachers the mustard seed was not sown in gardens (cf. Mt 13:31); but outside Palestine (where Luke's readers lived) it could be.

13:20-21. Leaven, or yeast, would be mixed with flour throughout the dough. The point of both *parables (13:18-21) is that the mighty *kingdom everyone expects could issue from apparently obscure beginnings—like Jesus and the *disciples.

13:22-24. The image of "the two ways" was common in Jewish (and other ancient) literature; some texts also stressed that more people would follow the way to destruction. Other Jewish groups besides Christians, like the *Essenes, also believed that they were the only saved group. But the general Jewish belief was that nearly all Israel would be saved in the time to come (cf. Mishnah *Sanhedrin* 10:1).

13:25. It was an essential social rule to greet by name or title those persons one knew. To deny knowledge of where they were from would be to deny knowing them.

13:26-27. Table fellowship created a social bond; hospitality bound its recipient to friendship (cf. comment on 14:1). In this *parable the fugitives from destruction try to remind the owner of the house who they are, but he reiterates that he does not know them, and therefore they will not enter his house. The final line is Psalm 6:8 (cf. 119:115; 139:19), where the workers of iniquity are the psalmist's own persecutors, against whom the Lord takes vengeance to vindicate the psalmist.

13:28. Jewish people assumed that God had prepared the *kingdom for Israel; they expected to participate in it with the patriarchs (Abraham, Isaac and Jacob) and the prophets.

13:29-30. Here Jesus could refer to the gathering of the Jews dispersed outside Palestine, but in the context of Luke-Acts (and the parallel in Mt 8:11-12) the point is much more shocking: *Gentiles will participate in the *kingdom, reclining (the posture used for feasts) at the *messianic banquet, from which many of the people who expected to be there would be excluded. The four directions were used together to mean "everywhere."

13:31-35
Lament of the Rejected Lover

13:31. Herod Antipas had considerably more authority in Galilee than the priestly aristocracy did in Jerusalem; he had executed John and could do the same with Jesus. If, however, Jesus leaves Antipas's jurisdiction (as the well-meaning *Pharisees here warn him to do), he will be safe.

13:32. Calling someone a "fox" in antiquity would not necessarily imply that the person is sly; instead, it could portray the person as worthless, slanderous, treacherous or (often) cunning in an unprincipled manner. Thus Jesus here does not offer Herod a backhanded compliment (cf. Ezek 13:4). Perhaps more to the point, foxes also would prey on hens (v. 34) when they got the chance.

13:33. In the *Old Testament some prophets were martyred, and Jewish tradition applied this fate to many other prophets as well. Jesus plays on this tradition; in several days he will enter the city that had murdered the most prophets (i.e., he is going to die soon, with or without Herod's help). Although the martyrdom of prophets matched Jewish tradition, that Jerusalem is the most appropriate site for it would shock many Jewish listeners, because most Jews except the *Essenes considered Jerusalem the center of Jewish piety.

13:34. Jewish tradition claimed that Jewish people were under God's wings, and when a Jewish person converted a *Gentile, he or she "brought the Gentile under the wings of God's presence." The Old Testament also portrays God as an eagle hovering over its offspring (Deut 32:11; cf. Ex 19:4) and protecting Israel under his wings (Ps 17:8; 36:7; 57:1; 61:4; 63:7; 91:4), and similarly terrifying Israel's foes (Jer 49:22). This is but one image of God's love for his people. Jesus here applies this divine role and image to himself.

13:35. The desolation of the "house" probably refers to the destruction of the temple in A.D. 70 (cf. Lk 21). The quotation is from Psalm 118:26, which was sung during this season at the Passover and which the crowds will sing to Jesus at his entry into Jerusalem (19:38).

14:1-6
Healing on the Sabbath

14:1. Eating bread together was supposed to be an occasion for intimate fellowship; treachery or less than friendly motives among those sharing a meal would repulse ancient readers. This feeling would be magnified at a sabbath meal, to which Jewish people considered it particularly virtuous to invite a prominent teacher.

14:2. Dropsy causes the body to swell from excess fluids, as ancient medical texts commonly mention. Because the man with dropsy here is in front of Jesus and not on the room's periphery, he may be an invited guest.

14:3-6. Jewish legal experts debated proper sabbath laws among themselves; if one side was silenced and unable to reply, they would be presumed wrong or at best too ignorant of the *law to defend their position. *Essenes did not permit rescuing an animal on the sabbath, but *Pharisees did. Jesus argues by analogy with a principle on which his opponents agreed, and extrapolates by a "how much more" argument; cf. 13:15-16.

14:7-14
Instructions to Guests and Hosts

14:7. Well-known teachers customarily lectured or participated in dialogues at banquets. Ancient writers sometimes arranged literary discussions as monologues or dialogues in the setting of such banquets; these writings were called *symposia.*

Social status was important in antiquity and was made obvious by the seating of dinner guests at banquets. This status was especially a problem in well-to-do Greco-Roman circles (see comment on 1 Cor 11:21), but seating by rank is well attested in Palestinian Jewish society, including in the *Dead Sea Scrolls.

14:8-10. Jesus states a principle directly from Proverbs 25:6-7—to which the guests were not paying much attention—that is repeated in other ancient Jewish texts. Yet as in Roman circles, no one of socially inferior status would be arbitrarily invited forward; one would be advanced only if one had sat in too low a position.

14:11. Here Jesus repeats a standard *Old Testament promise, applied especially to the day of judgment (cf. Is 2:12; Ezek 17:24; 21:26; cf. also comment on Lk 1:52-53).

14:12. Not to invite people of one's own social status would offend them; but Jesus says that the other's need, not one's own social standing, must determine the giving of gifts. The Old Testament forbade charging interest on a loan and so profiting by one's neighbor; but Jesus' principle here excludes looking for any repayment at all; cf. 6:34-35.

14:13. Well-to-do persons in the Greco-Roman world usually invited people of somewhat lower social status in return for receiving honor, but these invitees would still be relatively respectable, not absolute dependents or beggars, as crippled, lame and blind people would be in that society, or peasants (although many Jewish teachers might regard inviting beggars and peasants as an act of piety). The crippled, lame and blind were not permitted on the premises of the probably *Essene community at *Qumran.

14:14. Judaism taught that the righteous would ultimately be rewarded at the *resurrection of the dead; here Jesus applies this truth to distribution of resources. That God repaid those who helped the poor was already taught in the *Old Testament (Prov 19:17).

14:15-24
The Ultimate Banquet

Those one would have expected to attend God's banquet had turned him down; thus he has every right to invite the outcasts of society whose presence would offend the powerful.

14:15. Texts reflecting Jewish expectation (as early as Is 25:6-9) often portrayed the *kingdom of God as a banquet.

14:16. The man in the *parable would have invited well-to-do persons, though many of them would have been less well-to-do than himself.

14:17. Invitations were often R.S.V.P.; thus these invited guests had already confirmed that they were coming.

14:18. One would think that this man would have examined the land beforehand, even if he had bought it through an agent. The buyer may have been legally obligated to go to complete the purchase; deals were also sometimes made contingent on a later inspection. But like the excuses that follow, this late notice would be heard as a weak excuse that would serve as a grievous insult to the dignity of the host, who had prepared the feast at much expense.

14:19. Having even a total of five yoke of oxen would mean that this man had much land to plow; he must be a wealthy landowner in his own right. It would be inconceivable that he had no one working for him.

14:20. This man's excuse is a valid one for not going to war during the first year of marriage (Deut 20:7; 24:5; cf. 1 Macc 3:56), but it is not valid for skipping a feast one had promised to attend, even though women (including his new wife) were often not invited to such dinners. Banquets generally lasted into the night. Wedding feasts (which this feast probably is; cf. Mt 22:2) were planned far in advance, and the man should have known not to schedule two events at the same time.

14:21-24. Bringing in beggars from off the street was unheard-of (see comment on 14:13).

14:25-35
The Cost of Following Jesus

The demand that all Jesus' *disciples value the needy above respectability (14:7-24) deprives them of the right to remain socially respectable; to count the cost of following Jesus, one dare not value family approval (14:26) or any possessions (14:33) above God's call heard through the world's need.

14:25-26. "Hate" could function as a *hyperbolic, Semitic way of saying "love less" (Mt 10:37), but this point hardly diminishes the offensiveness of this saying in a society where honor of parents was considered virtually the highest obligation and one's family was usually one's greatest joy. Teachers regularly demanded great respect and affection, but in Jewish tradition only God openly demanded such wholesale devotion as Jesus claims here (Deut 6:4-5).

14:27. A condemned criminal would "carry the cross" (i.e., the horizontal beam of the cross) out to the site of the upright stake where he would be crucified, usually amid a jeering mob. No one would choose this fate for oneself, but Jesus calls true *disciples to choose it and thus to hate their own lives by comparison with their devotion to him (14:26).

14:28-30. Several years earlier (A.D. 27) a poorly built amphitheater had collapsed, with an estimated fifty thousand casualties. The failings of inadequate or half-finished structures were well-known. The crucial point here, however, is the builder's shame in a society obsessed with honor.

14:31-32. Herod Antipas had recently lost a war with a neighboring Roman vassal, so the image of foolhardy war should be meaningful to Jesus' hearers. Jesus' point (as in 14:28-30) is that one must recognize the cost when one enlists as a *disciple of Jesus (cf. Prov 20:18; 24:6).

14:33. The *Essenes devoted all their property to the community; some radical Greek philosophers espoused the same kind of teaching. But the rest of early Judaism and, even more, Greco-Roman society at large rejected such fanaticism; Judaism stressed giving to charity but not divestiture of possessions. Jesus' *disciples did not become propertyless but shared all that they had (Acts 2:44-45; cf. comment on 12:12). Nevertheless, Jesus would sound like one of the radical teachers, because he claims that anyone who values possessions more than people—and so holds onto them rather than meeting known needs—is not being his disciple.

14:34-35. Salt was particularly used as a seasoning agent for taste, and sometimes (probably not in Palestine) mixed in with manure to keep it fresh for use as fertilizer (although the salt itself would be counterproductive in fertilizing soil). The point is that disciples who do not live like disciples are worth as much as unsalty salt: nothing.

15:1-2
Sinful Friends

15:1. *Tax gatherers and sinners were excluded from the religious community; cf. comment on 5:29-32. Proverbs (1:15; 13:20; 14:7) warns of the danger of spending time with sinners. But it is clear in this text that the moral influence is from Jesus to the sinners, not the reverse. Many religious Jews emphasized talking about the *law whenever possible; no one could legitimately complain about Jesus, who here communicates God's message to his listeners during table fellowship (on lectures at meals, cf. comment on 14:7).

15:2. *Pharisees and legal teachers did not consider it proper to eat with those excluded from the religious community; besides such dangers as eating untithed food, intimate table fellowship connoted acceptance. "Grumbling" could remind biblically knowledgeable ancient readers of Israel's unbelief and murmuring in the wilderness.

15:3-7
The Lost Sheep

Jesus addresses three *parables to his religious accusers (15:1-2), in effect turning the tables on them and demonstrating that they were not truly God's friends. *Pharisees considered shepherds members of an unclean profession and thus would not readily identify with the protagonist of the story (but cf. 2:8-20).

15:3-4. One hundred was probably an average-sized flock. Because shepherds often traveled together, this shepherd could probably leave his flock with his companions without endangering the flock. That they remain in the open pasture at night makes it likely that this is the warm season, not winter. Other Jewish teachers stressed God's forgiveness for the *repentant, but did not stress God's seeking sinners out.

15:5. The easiest way to carry a lamb was across one's shoulders, with the legs crossed over one's chest (cf. God carrying his sheep in Ps 28:9; Is 40:11).

15:6-7. The moral of the story is: As the shepherd's friends rejoice when he finds that which was lost, so do God's friends rejoice when he recovers what was lost to him; thus Jesus' accusers, who resent his fellowship with sinners he seeks to restore, may not really be God's friends (15:1-2).

15:8-10
The Lost Coin

The relative value of the lost item increases in each *parable: one out of one hundred, one out of ten and finally (15:11) one out of two. *Pharisees were generally unimpressed with the moral character of women and would not readily identify with the protagonist of this story (but cf. 24:1-11).

15:8. The ten silver coins are most likely the woman's *ketubah*, or dowry—the only money she brings into the marriage that is technically hers even if the marriage is dissolved. That she has only ten coins (worth about ten days of a worker's wages) suggests that her father's family is not well-to-do; she would presumably have married into a household equally poor.

The lamp here is a small, hand-held oil lamp, which emits little light but is more helpful than the small (if any) window that may be in her wall. The rough stone floors of poor homes had many crevices between the stones, into which coins and fragments of pottery fell so often that archaeologists can now use coins in those crevices to date when people lived in these homes. By sweeping with a broom she might hope to hear the coin rattle against the floor.

15:9-10. See comment on 15:6-7 for the moral. In Jewish tradition the angels in heaven generally took great interest in God's workings on earth; each person was specifically assigned at least one guardian angel.

15:11-32
The Lost Son

15:11-12. To ask one's father for one's share of the inheritance early was unheard of in antiquity; in effect, one would thereby say, "Father, I wish you were already dead." Such a statement would not go over well even today, and in a society stressing obedience to one's father it would be a serious act of rebellion (Deut 21:18-21) for which the father could have beaten him or worse. That the father grants the request means that most of the hearers will not identify with the father in this *parable; from the start, they would think of him as stupidly lax to pamper such an immoral son.

The eldest son always received a double portion (Deut 21:17); in this case, he would have received two-thirds of the inheritance and the younger brother one-third.

15:13. Jewish law did permit a father to determine which assets (especially land) would go to which sons before he died, but they could take possession only on the father's death: the father was manager and received the land's profits until then. Thus this son could know what would be his but could not legally sell his assets; he does it anyway.

Many Palestinian Jews migrated, seeking fortune in less economically pressed areas. The younger son is presumably no older than 18 (he was unmarried) and had an older brother; he would thus have had little experience in managing finances. Moralists considered squandering very evil.

15:14. Famine was a common devastating feature of the ancient economy. (People often viewed famines as divine judgments, but because Jesus' story does not address the famine area as a whole, it does not apply this perspective to the story line.)

15:15. At this point, Jesus' Jewish hearers are ready for the story to end (like a similar second-century Jewish story): the son gets what he deserves—he is reduced to the horrendous level of feeding the most unclean of animals. The son is cut off at this point from the Jewish community and any financial charity it would otherwise offer him.

15:16. Some commentators have suggested that the "pods" here are the kind of carob pods that Israel would eat only in famine, which some teachers said drove Israel to *repentance. Others argue that these are prickly, wild pods that only swine's snouts could reach. Neither pod was considered appetizing, and given pigs' proverbially unclean eating habits, the thought of eating pigs' food would disgust Jesus' hearers. That the young man is jealous of pigs' fare also suggests that he is not receiving fair wages (cf. 15:17).

15:17. "Hired men" could be either slaves rented for hire or free servants working for pay; either one suggests that his father is well-to-do.

15:18-19. Jewish people often used "heaven" as a respectful way of saying "God." The son here returns simply out of hunger and the belief that his father may feed him as a servant, not because he is genuinely sorry that he disgraced his father. Given the magnitude of his sin and the squandering of one-third of his father's life's earnings, Jewish hearers might regard his return as an act of incredible presumption rather than humility.

15:20. It was a breach of an elderly Jewish man's dignity to run, though familial love could take priority over dignity after a long absence (cf. Tobit 11:9—mother and son). Given the normal garb, the father would have to pull up his skirt to run. Kissing was appropriate for family members or intimate friends.

15:21-22. The best robe in the house would belong to the father himself. The ring would probably be a family signet ring—a symbol of reinstatement to sonship in a well-to-do house. Slaves did not normally wear sandals, though they carried and tied a master's sandals. The father is saying, "No, I won't receive you back as a servant. I'll receive you only as a son."

15:23. The calf would be enough to feed the whole village; this would be a big party! Aristocratic families often invited the whole town to a banquet when a son attained adulthood (about thirteen years old) or a child married.

15:24. Ancient writers sometimes bracketed off a section of their work by repeating a particular line; this bracketing off is called an *inclusio.* So far this *parable has followed the course of the two that preceded it (15:3-10), but 15:24-32 are bracketed off to address the climactic issue: the elder brother represents Jesus' religious accusers (15:2).

15:25-28. Dancing was used in both religious and nonreligious celebrations. Elder brothers were to reconcile differences between fathers and younger brothers, but here the elder brother, returning at the end of a long day's work, refuses even to enter the house. This is also a grievous insult to the father's dignity and could have warranted a beating (cf. 15:12).

15:29-30. Failing to greet one's father

with a title (e.g., "Father, "Sir"; contrast even 15:12) was a grievous insult to the father's dignity. The elder brother here is a transparent metaphor for the *Pharisees, and the younger brother for the sinners with whom Jesus was eating (15:1-2).

15:31-32. Religious Judaism in this period considered prostitution sinful; both Jewish and non-Jewish sources considered squandering property, especially someone else's (16:1), sinful.

Because the inheritance had been divided, the elder brother was already assured of his share, effective on the father's death (15:12); he had nothing to lose by his brother's return. The final response of the elder brother is never stated, providing the *Pharisees with the opportunity to *repent if they are willing.

16:1-13
The Unfaithful Steward

16:1. Many well-to-do landowners had managers to oversee their estates; these managers, or stewards, could be slaves or, as here (16:3-4), free persons. Squandering another's possessions was considered a particularly despicable crime (cf. 15:13).

16:2-4. Although the master has dismissed this manager, the master gives him some time to get the accounts together before he leaves. The manager uses this time to procure favor for himself with others to whose houses he may join himself afterward; ancients were very conscious of favors they owed. He uses the master's authority even though he can no longer legally exercise it.

Both digging and begging were considered undignified professions. Digging was usually performed by captive slaves or those who knew no other skills, and was viewed as the most difficult form of labor.

16:5. These tenants may owe the landowner fixed amounts of their crops. They were not required to pay the sum until harvest.

16:6-7. The measure of olive oil (100 baths, about 850 gallons) represented the yield of nearly 150 trees and was worth about 1,000 denarii, no small sum. The measure of wheat (100 cors, about 1,000 bushels) represented the yield of about 100 acres and was worth about 2,500 denarii. The percentages of debt forgiven differ, but roughly the same amount of money is forgiven in each of the sample transactions (about 500 denarii). These renters are all relatively well-to-do in their own right, and thus might make use of a manager themselves in the future.

In hard times, masters would sometimes forgive part of the debt, writing it off as a loss, in return for being considered benevolent.

16:8. All these changes of notes required only small marks on the papers, made by the *clients themselves; and if the projected income thereby appears less, it will be harder to recognize that the master's profits affected by the manager's embezzlements are really diminished.

More important, the manager has gained public favor for himself and for the master as a generous benefactor; if the master punishes the manager now, it would appear to the public that he were doing so because of the manager's benevolent act. The criminal manager could be jailed, but he wisely stakes everything on his master's honor as a generous man. Ancient stories often portray powerful persons as appreciating and rewarding cunning, even if it had been used against them ("wisely"—KJV—can mean "shrewdly"—NIV, NASB, etc.; cf. Ex 1:10). Some stories (undoubtedly popular among slaves) portray slaves outwitting their masters; although this steward appears to be free (thus "begging" in 16:3), the story line may resemble one with which Jesus' hearers would be familiar.

16:9-13. The moral of the story is: Use possessions to serve people, because you are only God's managers of anything you have. "Mammon" (KJV) is an *Aramaic word for possessions or money.

16:14-18 The Radical Demands of the Law

16:14. Many *Pharisees may have belonged to the leisured class, but that description applied far more to the *Sadducees. Most Pharisees worked and praised the piety of giving. In this context, however, "lovers of money" refers to all who value money too much to give whatever of it they must to satisfy the human needs around them.

16:15. Jesus here cites a standard *Old Testament principle (1 Sam 16:7; Job 10:4), applicable especially to the practice of religion (Is 1:10-17; 58:1-14; Jer 6:13-14, 20; Hos 4:4-9, 19; 6:6; Amos 5:21-27).

16:16. Jewish people sometimes summarized the Bible as "the Law and the Prophets"; many of them believed that after the era of the prophets the prophetic voice had been muted until the *messianic time. Thus John introduces the messianic era.

16:17. Later *rabbis told the story that when God changed Sarai's name to Sarah, the *yod* (the smallest letter of the Hebrew alphabet) that was removed complained to God for generations till he reinserted it in Joshua's name. Jewish teachers used such illustrations to make the point that the *law was sacred and one could not regard any part as too small to be worth keeping.

16:18. Jewish law permitted men the right of divorce for almost any reason, although many *rabbis disapproved of divorcing on slight grounds. Jesus' statement, however, declares that divorce is invalid in God's sight, so that a subsequent marriage is adulterous. Here Jesus articulates a stronger view of the marriage bond than anyone else we know of in antiquity, and his statement thus intensifies the law of Moses. Like most other statements of general principle in the ancient world (e.g., Prov 18:22 with Prov 11:22; 12:4; 21:9; or Prov 10:15; 13:8; 14:20 with 10:2, 11:4; or 14:24; 16:6 with 15:16; 16:8; 30:7-9; or 11:8; 12:13, 21 with principles such as 2 Tim 3:12), this one does not exclude exceptions (for the innocent party who had no say in the matter, cf. Mt 5:32; 19:9; 1 Cor 7:15); Jesus' purpose is to protect an innocent party from being divorced, not to punish the party who has been so betrayed. His statement addresses especially the wife because in Jewish Palestine (in contrast to Roman custom) only the husband had full rights to divorce.

16:19-31 The Rich Man and the Poor Man

This story resembles a *rabbinic story of uncertain date, except that there the rich man did a good deed and made it into the world to come; here he allows starvation while he lives in luxury, and thus inherits hell. Some details about the afterlife here are standard features of Jewish tradition; a few are simply necessary to make the story line work (acceptable practice in the telling of *parables).

16:19. Purple was an especially expensive form of apparel (cf. comment on Acts 16:14); the lifestyle Jesus describes here is one of ostentatious luxury. Although this man may have become rich by immoral means (as people often did), the only crime Jesus attributes to him is that he let Lazarus starve to death when he could have prevented it.

16:20. Some Jewish *parables (including the *rabbinic one mentioned at the beginning of this section) named a character or two.

16:21. The crumbs here may be regular crumbs or the pieces of bread used to sop up the table. Had Lazarus gotten to eat them, these leftovers would still have been insufficient to sustain him. The dogs here appear to be the usual kind Palestinian Jews knew: scavengers, viewed as if they were rats or other unhealthy creatures (also in the *Old Testament, e.g., 1 Kings 14:11; 16:4; 21:24; 22:38). They were unclean, and their tongues would have stung his sores.

16:22-23. Jewish lore often speaks of the righteous being carried away by angels; Jesus spares his hearers the traditional corresponding image of the wicked being carried away by demons. Every person, no matter how poor, was to receive a burial, and not to be buried was seen as terrible (e.g., 1 Kings 14:13). But Lazarus, having neither relatives nor charitable *patron, did not receive one, whereas the rich man would have received great eulogies. True Israelites and especially martyrs were expected to share with Abraham in the world to come. The most honored seat in a banquet would be nearest the host, reclining in such a way that one's head was near his bosom.

16:24-26. Jewish literature often portrayed hell as involving burning. The formerly rich man hopes for mercy because he is a descendant of Abraham (see comment on 3:8), but the judgment here is based on a future inversion of status. Jewish people expected an inversion of status, where the oppressed righteous (especially Israel) would be exalted above the oppressing wicked (especially the *Gentiles), and also believed that charitable persons would be greatly rewarded in the world to come. But this *parable specifies only economic inversion, and its starkness would have been as offensive to most first-century hearers of means as it would be to most middle-class Western Christians today if they heard it in its original force.

16:27-31. If those who claimed to believe the Bible failed to live accordingly, even a *resurrection (Jesus points ahead to his own) would not persuade them. Jewish literature also emphasized the moral responsibility of all people to obey whatever measure of light they already had.

17:1-4
Proper Relationships

17:1-2. Those who caused others to stumble ("to sin"—NIV) are as doomed as the rich man of the preceding *parable; in contrast, *disciples should look out for one another's good. "Stumble" was often used metaphorically to refer to sinning or falling away from the true faith. Millstones, used to grind wheat and olives, were extremely heavy, and the term here refers to the heavier kind of millstone turned by a donkey, rather than the lighter kind a woman would use. Because Jewish people regarded this punishment as the awful sort pagans might execute, the image is all the more dreadful.

17:3-4. Private reproof, *repentance with restitution, and forgiveness were standard doctrines of Jewish piety. Jewish teachers did question the genuineness of repentance if one planned to sin again, but like Jewish legal experts exploring legal principles, Jesus offers here a theoretical case: if a person does genuinely repent repeatedly, you must forgive that person.

17:5-10
The Faith of Servants

17:5-6. Ancient Jewish writers sometimes observed that the black mulberry's roots are spread out, which makes it a difficult tree to uproot. Mustard seeds were proverbially small.

17:7-10. Most slaveholders had few slaves; thus the slaves did both fieldwork and food preparation. Masters regarded this work as their slaves' duty, not an option. Nor was it considered honorable for masters to eat with their slaves, and it was virtually never done. The point of the illustration seems to be: Faith grows as one uses it as a servant; its end is service, and it is never an end in itself.

17:11-19
A Samaritan's Gratitude

17:11-12. Leprosy was an unattractive skin disease (not limited to what is called leprosy today) for which the Bible had prescribed quarantine from the rest of society (Lev 13:45-46), although the Bible did not go so far as many Jewish teachers in blaming the disease on the leper's sin. Lepers were thus outcasts from the rest of society, the kind of people most healthy people preferred to ignore.

17:13. The lepers approach Jesus with humility, which was the proper *Old Testament way to approach God or one of his representatives for prayer.

17:14. The Bible had prescribed particular sacrifices if someone's leprosy were cured (Lev 14:1-32). By complying with these regulations, Jesus does nothing to violate the *law or to offend the priests.

17:15-19. On their own terms *Samaritans were quite pious, but Jewish people considered them irreligious, and religious Jews avoided intimate dealings with them. This tension supplies most of the punch of the story. That a Samaritan would travel with Jewish lepers in the area between Samaria and Galilee (v. 11) also illustrates the extremity of lepers' outcast status: it erases other social distinctions.

17:20-37
The Nature of the Impending Kingdom

17:20-21. Although Jewish people acknowledged that God ruled in the present, most especially longed for God's unchallenged rule, or *kingdom, in the future. Jewish teachers disputed when the kingdom would come: either at a set time unknown to mortals, or whenever all Israel *repented. By teaching that the kingdom as God's reign is somehow present, Jesus implies that something of the kingdom—such as the *messianic king—is already among them.

17:22. Jewish literature sometimes spoke of a future period called "the days of the *Messiah." Some texts spoke of a period (sometimes forty years) when the Messiah would lead Israel in war against its enemies before the final end; others, that the Messiah would come to reign for a period after those enemies were subdued.

17:23-24. The ultimate coming of the *kingdom would not be ushered in by just an earthly war (as some thought) but by a cosmic revelation to all the earth. (Various Jewish texts adopted either scenario.) "In his [Jesus'] day," if original, may allude to the *Old Testament "day of the Lord," the final time when God would judge the earth and bring about eternal justice.

17:25. Cf. the context of Daniel 7:13-14 (the future *Son of Man) for suffering preceding glory (in Dan 7:21-22, referring to the saints).

17:26-27. Jewish literature often used Noah's generation as a typical image of evil. None of the activities Jesus mentions here is evil (though Jewish teachers regarded some as necessary responses to the evil impulse); the crime of these people is simply that they ignore the most important issue.
17:28-30. Many Jewish texts used Sodom (Gen 19) as a typical image of evil (cf. comment on Lk 10:12) and often linked it with Noah's generation (cf. comment on 17:26-27).
17:31. The flat rooftop was used for a variety of purposes. Because the stairs from the rooftop led down the outside wall of the house, not inside, one need not go inside when descending. This is an image of haste: of forgetting possessions, property and worldly concerns to get to the street and greet the returning king, or to flee impending doom.
17:32-33. When Lot's wife looked back to her destroyed home in Sodom, it cost her her life, which had been of greater value to God than her possessions (Gen 19:15-16, 26).
17:34. The Greek language used masculine pronouns if any members of the group were male; thus the "two" likely refers to husband and wife (NIV, against NASB "two men"). Here Jesus undoubtedly refers to one being taken to judgment (as in an analogous second-century story about Israelites and Egyptians in bed during the last plague).
17:35. Part of the Palestinian Jewish woman's work was grinding at a mill; she would often do this with another woman. These women could normally work together regardless of religious convictions. Provided that the unreligious woman was not violating *Pharisaic rules, even the wife of a Pharisee and the wife of a nontither (whom Pharisees despised) could grind together.
17:37. The *Son of Man's coming would bring judgment as on Noah's and Lot's generations (17:26-30), leaving his enemies as food for vultures (Ezek 32:4-6; 39:17-20), which Jewish people considered a horrible fate (Deut 28:26; 1 Sam 17:44; Ps 79:2). Some commentators have suggested that the "eagles" here refer instead to the Roman standards, which could be represented thus. In A.D. 70 the Romans offered sacrifice to these standards on the site of the temple after they had destroyed it.

18:1-8
God the Faithful Judge

18:1-5. Under *Old Testament law, judges were to fear God (i.e., consider that he will judge those who break his law and mistreat others) and therefore defend the oppressed. Many ancient societies had severe legal penalties for unjust judges.

In the *law, the widow was the ultimate example of the oppressed person, because she had no means of support (e.g., Ex 22:22-24; Ps 146:9; Is 1:17, 23; Jer 7:6-7). She certainly could not afford a bribe; in Jesus' parable here the widow's opponent is presumably threatening something like taking her land in payment for a debt (cf., e.g., 2 Kings 4:1).
18:6-7. This parable is a standard Jewish "how much more" *(qal vahomer)* argument: if an unjust judge who cared not for widows can dispense justice, how much more will the righteous judge of all the earth, who was known as the defender of widows and orphans? In the context, God would administer his justice especially when Jesus came to judge the earth (17:22-37). The principle is familiar from the Old Testament: God is faithful to act on behalf of and to vindicate his people, by

his acts in the present and especially his final day of judgment.

18:8. Many Jewish writers predicted great sufferings in the end time, on account of which many people would fall away from the truth; Jesus warns his own to persevere (21:8-19, 34-36; 22:31-32, 40, 46).

18:9-14 The Pharisee and the Tax Gatherer

18:9-10. *Pharisees were the most pious people in regular Palestinian Jewish society; *tax gatherers were the most despicable, often considered traitors to their people. Pharisees did not want tax gatherers admitted as witnesses or given honorary offices. To catch the impact of this *parable today one might think of these characters as the most active deacon or Sunday-school teacher versus a drug dealer, gay activist or crooked politician.

18:11. Jewish people considered it pious to thank God for one's righteousness, rather than taking credit for it oneself. The first hearers of this parable would not think of the Pharisee as boastful, but rather as grateful to God for his piety.

18:12. Many of the most pious fasted—without water, despite the health hazard—two full days a week (Mondays and Thursdays), at least during the dry season. *Pharisees were meticulous about tithing to the full extent one could infer from the *law (several different tithes, together constituting more than 20 percent of one's income).

18:13. Standing with eyes and hands lifted to heaven was a common posture of prayer. Beating one's breast was a sign of great mourning or grief, in this case, in *repentance for sin (which in Jewish custom was expressed by mourning). The *tax gatherer's prayer for mercy involves no deliberate act of restitution, and hence many of Jesus' contemporaries would judge it invalid.

18:14. Jesus' conclusion to the *parable would shock the original hearers (cf. comment on 18:11); it fails to shock Christians today only because they are so accustomed to the parable. On the future inversion of present roles, cf. 14:11 and 16:25.

18:15-17 The Kingdom Is for Children

Children were people of no social status, and the *disciples would not want the important time of their *rabbi taken up with blessing them. But Jesus says that the *kingdom belongs to the nobodies, those who do not approach it on the merits of their own status.

18:18-30 Sacrificing Wealth for the Kingdom

18:18. Some *disciples asked their teachers questions like the one this ruler asks Jesus about *eternal life. To "inherit eternal life" meant to share in the life of the coming world, the life of the *kingdom of God.

18:19-20. Without denying that he himself is good, Jesus reminds the man of the standard Jewish conception of God's goodness (others could be good, but no one compared with God); he then lists select commandments from the *Old Testament.

18:21. If only God is good, the man will have to admit he has broken some commandment; but the commandments Jesus lists were kept by most well-raised Jewish people.

18:22-23. Judaism stressed charity heavily, but other Jewish teachers did not normally require a prospective *disciple to divest himself entirely of funds. A few teachers, especially some radical Greek teachers (Antisthenes, Zeno and Diogenes), made such demands on rich students to see if they would value true teaching above their wealth. A rich person would occasionally give up his goods, but rich prospective disciples usually disappointed such radical teachers, failing the test of discipleship and returning to their wealth.

18:24. Jesus turns the social order upside down. Often the well-to-do were hailed for their generosity (they had more to give), and the poor, being less educated in the *law, were thought less pious (although poverty itself was not seen as a sign of impiety, especially by the poor themselves).

18:25-27. Jesus' saying here reflects a Jewish figure of speech for doing something impossible (a large animal going through a needle's eye). The saying, a *hyperbole, uses the image of a literal needle (not a gate, as some have incorrectly thought).

18:28-30. Most of Jesus' *disciples had not been poor (being fishermen and *tax gatherers) but had abandoned their economic security to follow him. Their reward would be found in believers' sharing of possessions in this world (cf. Acts 2:44-45) and the life of the *kingdom in the world to come.

18:31-34
Jesus' Impending Suffering

Standard Jewish messianic concepts did not accommodate a suffering *Messiah (most Jewish references to that idea are from the second century or later). Although Jesus saw this idea in the Scriptures (24:44-46), Jewish tradition's different way of reading the Bible (normally passages about suffering were not applied to the expected triumphant Messiah) makes it difficult for the *disciples to square their belief in Jesus as the Messiah with the plain words he speaks.

18:35-43
Healing a Blind Suppliant

18:35. The blind, the lame and others who could not engage in the traditional occupations of the day could secure their living only by begging, normally on a busy roadside. Jewish people considered helping them a righteous deed. Jericho was a prosperous town with a good climate, and this blind man (Timaeus's son—Mk 10:46) no doubt received ample support there, especially when pilgrims were passing by en route to the festival in Jerusalem.

18:36-38. That the blind man shouts "Son of David" means that he recognizes Jesus as the *Messiah. Jesus characterizes his insistent, obstinate (v. 39) plea for mercy as "faith" (v. 42).

18:39-42. Blind people were socially powerless, and Jesus' followers see his loud pleas as an intrusion, the way they had seen the children (18:15).

18:43. Other miracle stories in this period frequently ended with the response of the crowds, a response generally characterized—as one would expect after a miracle—by awe.

19:1-10
A Tax Gatherer's Repentance

19:1-2. Being a border city, Jericho had a customs station. Because it was also one of the wealthiest cities of Palestine, in the most fertile part of Judea and boasting a Herodian palace, other tax income would also be extensive. The "chief" *tax gatherer would be the one who contracted for sales and customs taxes and hired collectors under him. Given this role, Zacchaeus could have become rich without cheating; but it seems that he had cheated anyway (19:8).

19:3-4. For Zacchaeus to be "short" by ancient Mediterranean standards probably means he was less than five feet tall. With its pleasant climate year-round, Jericho was especially noted for its palm trees but supported many other trees as well, including the well-known sycamore tree. The kind of "sycamore" tree described here is related to the fig tree and was easy to climb; it is not the North American sycamore or European-Asian sycamore maple. *Old Testament Jericho had many tightly packed houses, but the prosperous city of the *New Testament period had spacious villas and parks, where one could more easily climb a tree than get on a rooftop.

19:5. No matter how high their status, people did not normally invite themselves to someone else's home. Pious Jews would also be loath to enter the home of a *tax gatherer or to eat of his food (which Jesus' language also implies); because someone unreligious enough to collect taxes would not be careful about tithing his foodstuffs, *Pharisees would not trust what he offered. Jewish people normally considered the ability to call the name of someone one had never met—as Jesus does here with Zacchaeus—to be the sort of thing that only a prophet could do.

19:6-8. That Zacchaeus makes restitution in response to *grace, rather than to receive grace, fits Jesus' ministry but differs from the common view of his day (and in practice, probably from that of our own day as well). His promise to make restitution recognizes that his white-collar crime is just as serious as other kinds of theft (Ex 22:1-4). His restitution goes beyond Pharisaic law, which required fourfold or fivefold restitution only for stolen oxen and sheep, only if he slaughtered or sold it, and only if a sufficient number of people witnessed the act. In ancient accounts of *discipleship, a radical response with possessions was a certain sign of newly acquired devotion to the teacher.

19:9-10. Most Jewish people believed that salvation belonged to all Israelites by virtue of their descent from Abraham, except for those who excluded themselves by heinous crimes. In Ezekiel 34:6 and 11, God took over the mission of seeking out the lost sheep because the Jewish leaders had failed (less directly relevant, cf. also Wisdom of Solomon 6:16).

19:11-27
Making Use of the Delay

19:11. *New Testament Jericho is about seventeen miles from Jerusalem and about a mile south of the site of *Old Testament Jericho.

If Jesus were the *Messiah, proclaiming the *kingdom and saying things like salvation was "today" (19:9), Jewish hearers would naturally expect the kingdom right away (Acts 1:6). The most common expectation of the kingdom would include the subjugation of Rome and other *Gentiles.

19:12. The image Jesus uses here would be familiar: Herod the Great (40 B.C.) and his son Archelaus (4 B.C.) had to go to Rome to receive the right to rule Judea.

19:13. Each of the slaves was given a mina, the equivalent of about one hundred days' wages, which they would probably entrust to the moneychangers. Because of exorbitant interest rates in the Greco-Roman world and because only a few people had significant capital, those doing business could quickly multiply their investments.

19:14. What this verse describes happened to Herod's son Archelaus, who was not at all popular with the people. An embassy of fifty representatives of the people went to Rome to oppose him. Similarly, his father Herod the Great had to fight till 37 B.C. before his kingdom (already officially granted him by the Romans) was securely under his control.

19:15-19. It was not unusual for investors to make returns such as those these servants report; nor was it unusual for rulers to reward profitable servants who proved their administrative skills. Rome allowed its client kings to appoint their own local officials.

19:20. Not only was this servant's failure to invest the money contrary to the king's orders and common sense (19:13); he even failed to protect the money, as giving it to moneychangers, storing it in a temple treasury or even keeping it in a strongbox might have done. Wrapping money in a perishable handkerchief was considered one of the most irresponsible ways to take care of money and suggests that the servant was stupid or treasonous (cf. v. 14), or (most likely) both.

19:21. Objecting that the master "takes out what he does not supply" means that he took money that he had not deposited, perhaps misappropriating funds.

19:22-26. Knowing that the master liked to make money that he had not deposited, the slave should have understood that the master would certainly want good interest from a deposit.

19:27. Eastern kings coming to power often disposed of enemies in this manner; Herod the Great had taken some ruthless measures to quell opposition and bring peace, and his son Archelaus likewise brutally retaliated against those who had opposed him.

19:28-40 The Royal Entrance

19:28-29. Messengers were normally sent two by two. When Jesus' group reaches the Mount of Olives, they are just outside Jerusalem.

19:30-34. Readers might interpret Jesus' (as king) borrowing the animal in terms of Romans or royal emissaries temporarily impressing (demanding the service of) an animal. The donkey's owners probably see it as part of the hospitality to visitors to the feast, or perhaps as the honor of helping a famous *rabbi on his way.

In antiquity the vast majority of people, including Christians, were poor; knowing that their Lord Jesus had to borrow his royal mount would have encouraged them.

19:35. Officials used donkeys for civil, not military, processions (1 Kings 1:38). Thus this text is not a triumphal entry in the sense of Roman triumphal processions; it is Jerusalem's reception of a meek and peaceful king.

19:36-37. Festal pilgrims were often welcomed with shouts of joy, but 19:37-40 suggests that a greater recognition was taking place here.

19:38. With the addition of "the king," the first part of the people's cry is taken from Psalm 118:26. The Hallel, composed of Psalms 113—118, was sung regularly during Passover season and would be fresh on everyone's mind; later generations applied these psalms to the future redemption for which they hoped. Jesus will cite the psalm *messianically in Luke 20:17.

19:39-40. "Stones" could mean any stones (3:8), but they may refer to the stones of the temple (see 19:44; 20:17).

19:41-44 Jerusalem's Doom

19:41-42. Like Jeremiah or another prophet weeping for his people (e.g., Jer 6:26; 8:18—9:3; Lam 1:1-4), Jesus cries out a lament over his people.

19:43. "The days will come" was a common phrase used by *Old Testament prophets (e.g., 1 Sam 2:31; 2 Kings 20:17; Jer 31:31). The Romans besieged and destroyed Jerusalem in the war of A.D. 66-70, roughly forty years after Jesus spoke these words.

19:44. Here Jesus uses standard prophetic *hyperbole; the city was destroyed in A.D. 70 but not completely leveled. Further leveling (including the filling of an entire valley) took place after the Bar Kochba revolt, which was finally suppressed in A.D. 135. The Old Testament spoke of God "visiting" (KJV, NASB, NRSV; cf. "coming to"—NIV, TEV) his people in acts of deliverance or judgment (e.g., Is 23:17); here the term refers to Jesus' mission.

19:45-48 Transforming the Temple

See the more extensive comment on Mark 11:15-19.

19:45. Sellers were needed in the temple so foreign Jews could buy sacrifices to offer there. Psalms, prophets and Jewish teachers in Jesus' day agreed that prayer and a pure heart counted for more than sacrifices but did not oppose sacrifices per se. Jesus presumably would oppose not sacrifices (cf. Acts 21:26) but an emphasis on ritual without the true relationship with God that he had demanded in his own teaching (cf. Lk 19:47). Even if he clears out the whole temple, however, the sellers will not stay out.

19:46. One text Jesus cites in part, Isaiah 56:7, refers to the future restored temple when pious *Gentiles would come to worship in the temple too; but instead the temple has become like the "robbers' den" of Jeremiah 7:11. Jeremiah called it that because Israel thought the temple was a refuge from divine judgment despite the people's sins; injustice was taking place in the land, but the people did not expect judgment because of their ritual piety (Jer 7:1-15).

19:47. Other teachers also taught in the temple courts. The Jewish aristocracy who controlled the temple had vested interests in keeping down would-be *Messiahs (usually revolutionaries) and anyone who challenged the temple. Defiling the sacred inner courts of the temple was the one offense for which the Romans permitted the Jewish authorities to execute an automatic death penalty. Although Jesus' action in the outer court would not actually qualify as defiling the sacred precincts, it must have enraged the authorities and served as a direct challenge to their power there.

19:48. These leaders had official authority, but they lacked the measure of popularity with the common people in Jewish Palestine that the *Pharisees and Jesus possessed.

20:1-8 On Whose Authority?

20:1-2. The powerful priestly aristocracy who ran the temple exercised their own authority over it; they would know that Jesus has not received the authority from themselves or from the Romans. They would not accept any other human authorization as legitimate, nor regard other humans as divinely authorized; they presumably believed that God had authorized them rather than someone else to be in charge of the religious aspects of the temple.

20:3-4. Jesus' question about John the Baptist concerns the principle of agency: in Jewish law, an authorized agent acted on behalf of the sender, backed by the sender's full authority. "Heaven" was a Jewish circumlocution for God.

20:5-7. The temple authorities, who had to please the Romans on the one hand and the populace on the other, were already accustomed to considering the political consequences of their statements.

20:9-18
Judgment on Evil Leaders

Jesus still addresses those who fancy themselves rulers of Israel, reminding them that they are merely custodians appointed by God over his vineyard (like the shepherds over God's flock of Jer 23 and Ezek 34).

Wealthy landowners controlled much of the rural Roman Empire, including the rural parts of Galilee; tenant farmers worked their land. Landowners had great status, whereas tenant farmers had little; tenants were therefore normally quite respectful to the owners.

20:9. Absentee landlords were common.

20:10. Payments were rendered at harvest time. Some contracts specified that the tenants would pay the landowner a percentage of the harvest; other contracts called for a fixed amount.

20:11-12. Landowners always had power, socially and legally, to enforce their will on the tenants; a few even reportedly had hit squads to deal with troublesome tenants. Here the tenants act as if they are the ones with power, and they exploit it mercilessly (as opposed to the ancient ideal of a *benevolent* *patron or landowner). This description fits the Jewish tradition that Israel martyred many of the prophets God sent to it.

20:13. In the light of 3:22, the "beloved son" clearly represents Jesus. Ancient hearers of the *parable would regard the landowner as abnormal; naively benevolent, he counted on a kindness in his tenants that their behavior had already disproved. Rich or poor, all hearers at this point would agree that the landowner was in the right, and that he was benevolent—indeed, strikingly, foolishly benevolent.

20:14-15. The tenants presume too much about the inheritance; although they could have seized it under certain legal conditions, the owner could also stipulate—and after their misdeeds certainly would—that someone else inherit the vineyard; or representatives of the emperor could have seized it. If a dead body were left in a vineyard, it would render the harvested food impure if the food got wet (Jewish interpretation of Lev 11:38).

20:16. The ancient hearers would wonder why the landowner had not come earlier and killed the tenants. The people's negative response is only because they know how Jesus is applying it—against their own leaders (v. 19).

20:17. Here Jesus cites Psalm 118:22-23, another text from the Hallel (the crowd referred to 118:25-26 in Lk 19:38). The building here is the temple (Ps 118:18-21, 25-27); as the cornerstone of a new temple, Jesus is a threat to the builders of the old one.

20:18. "Falling on" the cornerstone reflects Isaiah 8:14-15 (cf. 28:16); the stone falling on the offender reflects Daniel 2:34, 44, where God's *kingdom, portrayed as a rock, crushes its earthly challengers. Jesus here uses a standard Jewish practice of expounding one text (cf. Lk 20:17) by citing others sharing the same key word or concept, in this case, the divine stone.

20:19-26
Both Sides of the Coin

20:19-21. Here Jesus' opponents seek to force him to choose between revolution—which would get him in trouble with Rome—and accommodation to the Romans—which they suppose he opposes (because he opposed their leadership in the temple).

20:22. They pit the obligations of peace with Rome against the nationalistic, *messianic fervor that they assume Jesus has generated; a disastrous tax revolt two decades earlier had shown where such fervor could lead. If he publicly takes the view characterized by those later called *Zealots (no king but God), he can be arrested; if he rejects that view (which he does), he may compromise his following (cf. 23:18-19).

20:23-26. Jewish Palestine circulated its own copper coins, which bore the name but not the image of the deified emperor. Nonetheless, foreign coins, which bore the emperor's image and mention of his divine status, were in common circulation in Palestine, where neither gold nor silver coins were permitted to be struck. Revolutionaries in A.D. 6 had violently protested the use of such coins and incurred terrible Roman retaliation.

20:27-40
God of the Living

20:27. In ancient Judaism the *Sadducees were especially notorious for not believing in *resurrection, and *rabbis who considered themselves successors of the *Pharisees classified Sadducees as heretics for this view.

20:28. The Sadducees' question to Jesus concerns the law of levirate marriage, practiced in many cultures both in antiquity and today. It provides economic and social protection to widows in societies where women cannot earn wages. Students of Jewish law were still expounding this *Old Testament principle (Deut 25:5) in Jesus' day and afterward.

20:29-32. The Sadducees borrow the story line from the Jewish book of Tobit, where the jealous demon Asmodeus killed righteous Sarah's first seven husbands.

20:33. *Rabbinic literature is full of examples of the "mocking question" posed by pagans, apostates or heretics like the *Sadducees.

20:34-36. Jewish people widely agreed that angels did not procreate (they did not need to replenish their numbers, because they did not die, and also because, in some other traditions, God regularly created new angels), nor did they normally eat or drink.

20:37-38. Against their *Sadducean opponents the *Pharisees commonly tried to prove the *resurrection from the law of Moses; Jesus here does the same. He argues that God would not claim to be the God of those who no longer exist; indeed, his faithfulness to his covenant demands that if he is their God after death, death is not the final word for them. One of the most common Jewish prayers of the period recites God's faithfulness to Abraham, Isaac and Jacob as a living reality for their own time (cf. also *4 Maccabees 7:19; 16:25).

20:39-40. Contemporary literature commonly reports hearers being overawed by a wise speaker's (usually the protagonist's) wisdom.

20:41-44
David's Lord

By definition, the Christ, or anointed one, was the royal descendant of David (Is 9:7; 11:1; Ps 2; 89; 132). But this view of *messiahship often lent itself to a revolutionary view of the *kingdom (see comment on 17:20-24) and was inadequate. The one who would reign in God's kingdom was David's "Lord," not merely his descendant; he would thus be greater than the resurrected David.

When Jewish teachers challenged their hearers to resolve apparent discrepancies in Scripture, they assumed that both texts were true (in this case, Jesus knows that he is both David's son and David's Lord) and were asking how to harmonize them. Jesus' opponents apparently have no answer, because other Jewish interpreters did not apply Psalm 110:1 to the Messiah (reacting against the Christian interpretation, some later Jewish interpreters even applied this text to Abraham).

20:45—21:4
The Powerful and the Weak

Some Jewish teachers were so concerned to prevent the exploitation of the poor that they criticized collectors of charity who asked for contributions from the poor. But then, as now, some people used their religion to exploit others.

20:45-46. Like their Greek counterparts, some Jewish teachers wore a special identifying garb, in this case a long, white linen robe, similar to those of priests and temple officials. People normally greeted teachers with titles of honor; marketplaces, which were full of people, would provide many opportunities for teachers to receive such recognition. Seating at banquets marked one's rank in society.

20:47. Widows had little means of support, were socially powerless and were to be protected under Jewish law (see comment on 18:1-5). Jesus could mean that these teachers exploit widows' resources by seeking extensive tithes (which they could set at 20-30 percent, on top of the heavy land taxes levied by the government); or he could mean that they follow the letter of the law in legal decisions, rather than showing mercy to the poor as the *law required.

These teachers may have lingered long in their individual prayers in the *synagogues; here Jesus criticizes not the longevity of prayers but the motive of this longevity. Like the *Old Testament prophets, Jesus sees social injustice and religious hypocrisy as inextricably linked.

21:1-4. A later tradition claims that thirteen receptacles for gifts to the temple treasury were in the Court of Women, accessible to Israelite women as well as to men. The temple sported ostentatious wealth, and its officials would probably waste this widow's money; but this powerless woman, ignorant of that likelihood, acts in good faith and is the greatest giver in God's sight.

21:5-7
Introduction to the Discourse on the Future

Jesus draws much of the language of this discourse from the *Old Testament.

21:5. The Jerusalem temple was one of the most splendid structures of all antiquity and seemed strong and invincible (cf., e.g., *Letter of Aristeas 100-101); cf. comment on Mark 13:1.

21:6. Other groups also expected the temple to be judged, but most Jews, regardless of their other differences, found in the temple a symbol of their Jewish unity and would have been appalled to think that God would allow it to be destroyed (as in Jer 7:4-15). Some stones were left on others (e.g., one wall still stands), but this fact does not weaken the force of the *hyperbole: the temple was almost entirely demolished in A.D. 70—roughly forty years after Jesus predicted it (Lk 21:32).

21:7. Old Testament prophets often grouped events together by their topic rather than their chronological proximity, and Jesus in this discourse does the same. He addresses two separate questions: the time of the temple's destruction and the time of the end.

21:8-19
Imminent Sufferings

21:8. False *messiahs were common and drew significant Jewish followings in Palestine as late as Bar Kochba, whom Rabbi Akiba hailed as the Messiah after A.D. 130.

21:9-11. Ancient prophecy teachers usually listed these events among the signs of the end; the end was often portrayed as preceded by great sufferings or a final war. Jesus says that instead these events characterize normal life until the end.

21:12. *Synagogues were the local places of public assembly and thus provided the natural place for hearings and public discipline. Sometimes discipline was administered in the form of flogging; under second-century rules, this meant thirteen harsh strokes on the breast and twenty-six on the back. Prisons were usually holding places until a trial rather than places of punishment; punishments included execution, enslavement, banishment, confiscation of property and so forth.

21:13-15. In context, this preaching will be carried out before officials of all nations ("kings"—v. 12—could refer just to Rome's vassal princes, but "all nations" suggests that Parthian and other rulers from the East are also in view), indicating virtually universal persecution and proclamation.

21:16. See Micah 7:5-7. In a culture with a heavy emphasis on family fidelity, betrayal by a family member would sound especially harsh.

21:17-19. Here Jesus offers a promise of protection (cf. 1 Sam 14:45; 2 Sam 14:11). Because hundreds, probably thousands, of Christians had been publicly murdered under Nero in Rome in A.D. 64, probably less than two decades before Luke wrote, it is clear that this is hyperbolic, not an unqualified promise (9:23-24; 21:16). (With most scholars I assume that Luke did not write before A.D. 64, although the case for this date is not conclusive.) This promise suggests either spiritual survival (12:4-5) or that God will often deliver physically, as in many cases in the Old Testament (e.g., Dan 3:27).

21:20-24
The Fall of Jerusalem

21:20. Luke's language is less ambiguous than Mark's "abomination of desolation": the war with Rome began in A.D. 66, and soon Roman armies had marched through the rest of Palestine and surrounded Jerusalem, then laid siege to it until it fell in A.D. 70. Those who tried to flee shortly after Jerusalem was surrounded found that it was too late; some who escaped the *Zealots inside Jerusalem were cut open by Syrian recruits outside, who were looking for jewels they might have swallowed.

21:21. The mountains of Judea were the safest place to evade invading armies, as the people in Judea had often learned (e.g., David and the second-century B.C. Maccabean guerrillas). When people in the countryside saw approaching armies, they often fled to the safety of city walls; but those trapped within Jerusalem's walls would be doomed (v. 24).

21:22. The prophets often spoke of judgment against Jerusalem. Although they usually pointed especially to the Babylonian captivity (about six centuries before Jesus), their principle of judgment and their demand for *repentance before ultimate restoration was still applicable.

21:23. The difficulties of bearing or nursing a child under these circumstances are obvious in any culture. The text may also indicate grief over the loss of the children (cf. *2 Baruch 10:13-15). The language of "great distress" echoes *prophecies about tribulation that would precede Israel's final repentance (Dan 12:1). The *Old Testament repeatedly describes God's judgments in history as "wrath" (e.g., on Jerusalem—Lam 1:12), as well as his future wrath in the day of the Lord (e.g., Zeph 1:14-15).

21:24. All the inhabitants of Jerusalem died in the war (by famine, disease, burning, Jewish factional fighting or fighting with the Romans) or were enslaved in the year 70. Jerusalem was left in ruins; after the second destruction in A.D. 135, Jerusalem was rebuilt as a pagan city, with a pagan temple on the site where God's temple had been.

21:25-38
Be Prepared

The destruction of Jerusalem constitutes the final, universally visible earthly sign before Jesus' return; after this sign, Christ's followers should be ready for his imminent return.

21:25-26. *Josephus and writers dependent on him spoke of portents in the heavens preceding the fall of Jerusalem. These portents were meant to give the wicked cause to fear (Is 19:16; Jer 4:9). This is the language of the end (Is 13:10; 34:4; cf. 24:23; Ezek 32:7-8). Some ancient Jewish literature used this cataclysmic language for historical events (the *Sibylline Oracles use it for an earthquake; cf. Ps 18:6-19; Jer 4:20-28), but most reserved it for the end or transformation of the present world order and the establishing of God's eternal *kingdom.

21:27. Jesus sometimes describes the *Son of Man's coming in terms Jewish literature usually reserved for God (cf. Is 19:1). Here Jesus clearly alludes to Daniel 7:13-14, where "one like a son of man" (i.e., like a human being) receives the *kingdom from God.

21:28. Unlike others, believers need not fear these heavenly signs (Jer 10:2); they merely signal that "redemption" is near. During the revolts against Rome, Jewish patriots declared the arrival of their "redemption," or liberation from Rome; but Jesus teaches that this redemption will come solely from heaven's intervention.

21:29-31. The signs Jesus lists show that the end is imminent, just as a fig tree's leaves show what season it is. (In winter the fig tree appeared more bare than other trees.)

21:32-33. The length of a generation varied but was often represented in the *Old Testament by forty years (in the *Dead Sea Scrolls, 40 years represents the suffering of the final generation). Jesus speaks these words near A.D. 30; the temple was destroyed in A.D. 70.

21:34-36. "Strength to escape" (v. 36) could refer back to the escape of verse 21 or to enduring the persecutions of verses 12-19; "standing before the *Son of Man" may mean persevering or being presented triumphant before him.

21:37. As sundown approached, about 6 p.m. in April, fewer and fewer people would be in the temple courts. Because thousands of pilgrims came to the Passover feast, many had to stay in surrounding villages at night.

21:38. "Early in the morning" could mean as early as sunrise, which would be by 6 a.m. in Jerusalem in April.

22:1-13
Preparing the Passover

22:1. The Jewish Feast of Passover was technically followed immediately by the Feast of Unleavened Bread; but because pilgrims made one trip to Jerusalem to celebrate both of them, in popular parlance they had come to be described as a single entity.

22:2-6. Jewish literature reports that the high priests bullied those who opposed them; they would certainly not tolerate someone who claims that God has directed him to attack their temple cult. But they have to be cautious due to Jesus' popularity (22:2;

cf. comment on 20:5-7).

22:7. See comment on 22:1.

22:8-9. Representatives from each family would have the priests slaughter a lamb for them in the temple, then return with it to feed the whole family that night.

22:10. Water jars (as opposed to leather wineskins) were almost always carried by women; thus a man carrying one would be a noticeable sign.

22:11-13. Anyone with a two-story home, the second of which contained a "large" upper room, would be considered well-to-do. This family presumably resided in the Upper City of Jerusalem, near the temple, rather than the poorer Lower City, downwind of Jerusalem's sewage. Because the Passover had to be eaten within Jerusalem's walls, most homes would be crowded with guests; but the accommodations for Jesus' last meal with his *disciples would be quite adequate.

22:14-23 Eating the Passover

Both the preparation for Passover and its eating are mixed with promises and foreshadowings of the betrayal, because the Passover here itself prefigures Jesus' death. Following the *Old Testament prophets, Judaism looked for a new exodus when God would again deliver his people from bondage, although contemporary Judaism was looking for a new Moses—not a new lamb.

22:14. The Passover was to be eaten at night. April's sundown in Jerusalem came by 6 p.m., so the meal should have started then. Table fellowship was intimate at the feast; one or two families normally shared the meal, but here Jesus and his closest *disciples make up the family unit. One "sat" for most meals but "reclined" for feasts, like Passover.

22:15-16. Vows of abstinence were common in Palestinian Judaism: "I will not eat any such and such until this happens," or "I vow that I will not use this until that happens." Jewish tradition often portrayed the time of the *kingdom as a banquet. It was customary to give thanks over the cup of wine at regular meals and also at Passover.

22:17-19. The head of the household customarily gave thanks for the bread and wine before any meal but said special blessings over bread and wine in the Passover meal. We should not understand "This is my body" literally, just as we do not take literally the standard Jewish interpretation spoken over the Passover bread: "This is the bread of affliction our ancestors ate when they came from Egypt."

22:20. Covenants were ratified by the blood of sacrifice; God had redeemed his people from Egypt by the blood of the Passover lamb. "On behalf of the many" probably alludes to Isaiah 53 (see comment on Mk 10:45). Passover ritual interpreted most elements of the meal and included blessings over the cup. But the ritual certainly did not interpret the cup as blood, because Jewish law and custom were revolted by the idea of drinking any creature's blood, especially human blood.

22:21. Ancient Jewish readers would view betrayal by one sharing a meal as particularly scandalous, because they saw hospitality and the sharing of table fellowship as an intimate bond.

22:22-23. Most people in ancient Judaism stressed both God's sovereignty and human free will, which they saw as complementary. (Modern views that see them as contradictory are based more on Greek logic than on Jewish thought or the Bible.)

22:24-30 Exaltation of the Servants

22:24-25. Jewish people were well familiar with the *Gentile model of authority: ancient Near Eastern kings had long claimed to be gods and had ruled tyrannically; Greek rulers had adopted the same posture through much of the eastern Mediterranean. Jewish people would view the Roman emperor and his provincial agents (who often showed little concern for Jewish sensitivities) in much the same light. Rulers and others who doled out favors from the vantage point of power were called "benefactors"; the practice of benefaction was widely praised in Greek circles. Jesus' reminding the *disciples that seeking power is a Gentile (i.e., pagan) practice is tantamount to telling them they should not be doing it.

22:26. In antiquity age often determined rank; the youngest had the least respect. A slave was always powerless and without social status compared to the master (regardless of the position slaves had relative to peasants and others who were socially inferior to their masters).

22:27. Slaves waited on masters at table. "Reclining" was the standard Greek posture for eating, which Palestinian Jews adopted at feasts.

22:28-30. Jewish literature often portrayed the *kingdom as a future time when Israel would partake of a banquet prepared for them; a standard Jewish expectation for that time was that the lost tribes of Israel would be restored. Those who "judged" Israel in the Old Testament ruled it.

22:31-38
Preparing for the Betrayal

22:31-32. Wheat would be sifted to separate the genuine wheat from other items that had gotten mixed in with it; for the image, see Amos 9:9. For winnowing away the chaff, see comment on Matthew 3:12. The background for *Satan's demand is presumably Job 1:6-12 and 2:1-6, where Satan tries to prosecute Job before the heavenly court (the Hebrew has "the satan," literally "the adversary," i.e., the accuser).

22:33-34. Ancient sources typically regarded the rooster as a reliable reporter of the advent of dawn (attested by Apuleius *Metamorphoses* 2.26; *3 Maccabees 5:23; Babylonian Talmud *Berakot* 60b). But commentators report that in Palestine nocturnal crowings are familiar to night watchmen beginning at 12:30 a.m.; the second was about 1:30 a.m. In either case the point is that the denial is imminent.

22:35. See comment on 9:3.

22:36-38. By mentioning the "sword" here Jesus is not inviting revolution like the *Zealots did (cf. *Pseudo-Phocylides 32-34). Instead, Jesus calls for a temporary and symbolic act—two are sufficient (v. 38)—so he may be charged as a revolutionary and hence "reckoned among transgressors" in accordance with Isaiah 53:12. (On the *messianic import of Is 53, see comment on Mt 12:15-18.) To be without one's outer cloak at night would leave one cold; yet Jesus suggests that it is better than being unprepared for the conflict these *disciples are about to face.

22:39-46
The Prepared and the Unprepared

22:39. The walk from the upper room to the Mount of Olives took at least fifteen minutes.

22:40. They may have arrived at Gethsemane by 10 or 11 p.m. (which was normally considered late in the evening, because agriculture and business operated by daylight). Jewish people customarily stayed awake late on Passover night to speak of God's redemption. The *disciples should have been able to stay awake to keep watch; they had probably stayed up late on nearly every other Passover of their lives.

"Temptation" here means "testing"; given the common Jewish religious uses of the word, Jesus is saying: "lest you fall prey to the testing you are about to face."

22:41-42. On the "cup of judgment" see comment on Mark 10:39.

22:43-46. The *disciples are to "stand watch" like porters (slaves in charge of the door) or sentries. Some ancient texts report the rare phenomenon of sweating blood; Luke may mean this phenomenon or simply that Jesus' sweat is profuse and dripping the way blood would.

22:47-53
The Betrayal

22:47. Because they had been sent by prominent men of Jerusalem, the band that comes to arrest Jesus is probably the temple guard. This guard is known to have possessed the weapons mentioned here (swords and clubs); clubs were said to have characterized the corrupt priestly aristocracy, as well as being useful in controlling rioters.

22:48. A kiss was a sign of special affection among family members and close friends, or of a *disciple's honor and affection for his teacher. Thus Judas's betrayal kiss is a special act of hypocrisy (cf. Prov 27:6).

22:49-50. Being well-to-do, high priests had many servants. Although the servant mentioned here is probably not a Levite and is thus unable to minister in the temple anyway, it is worthy of note that those who were missing appendages such as ears were barred from serving in the sanctuary. This attack on this servant would confirm the armed (22:47) expedition's suspicions that Jesus' followers are violent revolutionaries (22:36-38).

22:51. Many people associated *Messiahs with popular revolt and the overthrow of the *Gentile kingdoms that oppressed Israel; a Messiah who would heal his attackers was not part of anyone's messianic picture.

22:52-53. Subversives (e.g., the later assassins who slew Jewish aristocrats under cover of the crowds in the temple) did their acts secretly or in a way that would avoid capture; Jesus' alleged subversion was public and unconcealed. Night was commonly associated with evil; in popular superstition (later found in *rabbinic teaching as well), night was the time when the demons ruled and witchcraft operated.

22:54-62
Peter's Denials

22:54. This trial breaks a number of Jewish legal rules, if later documents correctly indicate the state of Jewish law in this period. Taking Jesus to the high priest's home at night was against the rules.

22:55. Peter's trespassing on private property—that of the high priest himself—required serious commitment from a Galilean fisherman. The guards are probably members of the temple guard, waiting to see the results of the trial inside. They may have planned to stay up late for Passover anyway.

22:56-58. Slaves in aristocratic households exercised more power and status than the average free person. Although the high priest had many servants, the slave girl would recognize that Peter and the guards are not from the household; further, Peter was not dressed like one of the guards. As a servant in an aristocratic priestly household near the temple, she had no doubt been at the temple and could have gotten a good look at Jesus' *disciples in the temple courts.

22:59. Galilean accents differed from Judean accents, certainly in *Aramaic and presumably (as undoubtedly here) in Greek; Galileans were especially noted for mispronouncing guttural sounds. The high priest's servants and temple guard lived in Jerusalem and would see themselves as Judeans. Regional accents were difficult to hide (cf. Judg 12:6).

22:60-62. For most people in the ancient Mediterranean, a rooster's crowing marked daybreak. Some scholars have suggested that this crowing refers to an earlier Palestinian rooster crowing between 12:30 and 2:30 a.m.

22:63-71
The Decree of the Sanhedrin

22:63-65. Jewish law permitted public flogging of a condemned person; it did not permit the treatment described here—mocking and beating—certainly not before a person had been proved guilty in a trial. Jewish law meticulously guarded the rights of the accused and erred on the side of mercy in official decisions; thus the behavior described here would have revolted the *Pharisees and other pietists.

22:66. By at least waiting till morning for an official hearing (as opposed to any informal interrogations that may have taken place earlier), those representatives of the *Sanhedrin present maintained some semblance of legality in the proceedings; night trials were illegal.

"Leading priests," "elders" and "*scribes" were the three groups represented on the Sanhedrin, the ruling religious court of Israel. The full Sanhedrin, with seventy-one members, normally assembled in a meeting hall in the temple called the Chamber of Hewn Stone, where they sat in a semicircle with the high priest in the center. Although the body acted as a whole, not all its members concurred (23:51); writers would often make a general statement about a group without listing explicit exceptions (cf. Jer 26:16, 24).

22:67-68. If extant reports of ancient Jewish law are accurate, the high priest could not legally force Jesus to convict himself out of his own mouth. Nevertheless, he asks whether Jesus thinks of himself as a *Messiah—hence, to the high priest's mind, as a revolutionary.

22:69. Jesus' response is a claim to be not a merely mortal messiah but the cosmic ruler of Daniel 7:13-14. "Power" was sometimes used as a Jewish title for God; Luke simplifies the phrase for his Greek readers as "power of God."

22:70-71. The religious authorities serve as their own witnesses that Jesus claims to be a subversive, a revolutionary (23:2).

23:1-12
Accusations Before Pilate and Herod

23:1. The visit to Pilate would be early in the morning, because Roman officials met the public only from sunrise to noon.

23:2. "King *Messiah" became a standard title of the Messiah; "Messiah" meant simply "anointed one," but in popular parlance it was most often used for the king from David's line who would be associated with the restoration of the *kingdom to Israel.

Despite 20:22-25, the leaders interpret Jesus' messianic claim the only way they know how: according to the category of prophetic revolutionaries. Such revolutionaries had become common in their day and would climax in Bar Kochba, the purported messianic warrior who would lead his people to a bloody defeat in A.D. 132-135. Such political messiahs threatened the religious authorities' power and security and were especially troublesome to Rome.

23:3-4. Pilate apparently understands Jesus' claim in a religious rather than a political sense and therefore does not feel that it comes under Roman civil jurisdiction. Further, Pilate's relationship with the priestly aristocracy is known to have been strained. On Luke's theme of Roman authorities exonerating Christians, see the discussion of Luke's legal purpose in the introduction to Acts.

23:5. A Galilean had led the tax revolt of A.D. 6; Judeans also tended to view Galileans as inferior to themselves, although much of Galilee was urban and in touch with the larger Mediterranean culture, as Jerusalem was.

23:6-7. Herod Antipas would be in Jerusalem for the feast and was probably staying at the old Hasmonean (Maccabean) palace. Pilate had the authority to try Jesus if he had committed a crime in Pilate's area of jurisdiction; but sometimes the right of extradition was allowed, and Antipas might thus be free to try Jesus for a crime committed in Galilee. By refusing jurisdiction, Pilate could take the matter off his own hands.

23:8-10. This Herod was the one who had murdered John; cf. comment on Mark 6:14-29. Many people wanted to see signs; in some popular stories, their curiosity got them in trouble with sorcerers. Of the four Gospels, only Luke reports two hearings before the governor separated by one before a Herod; Acts reports two trials of Paul before procurators with a trial before another Herod, Agrippa II. Ancient Greco-Roman historians liked to point out parallels between related figures in history.

23:11. The "bright" or "elegant" (NIV, NRSV) robe may be a white one, characteristic of Jewish kings. This apparel would be an appropriate mockery from Antipas's bodyguard.

23:12. Herod and Pilate had had plenty of opportunities to become alienated; for instance, Antipas had intervened in a matter concerning votive shields (reported in *Philo); on another occasion Pilate had pilfered the temple treasury for funds for an aqueduct; even the event of Luke 13:1 could have been the provocation. Giving the ambitious Herod Antipas a sign of influence in Jerusalem would certainly create a "friendship," which in upper classes often meant a political alliance.

23:13-25
Pilate and the Crowds

23:13-17. On the Lukan motif of Roman authorities exonerating Christians, see the introduction to Acts.

23:18-25. As a clearly violent revolutionary, Barabbas appeared to Pilate to be a greater danger than Jesus. Romans were known for their emphasis on justice, but Romans were also politicians concerned with crowd control: the emperor himself pacified the masses with shows in the arena and free grain, and public outcry had previously forced Pilate to withdraw the Roman standards from Jerusalem. Efficiency in ruling provinces and keeping peace took precedence over individual justice; for instance, a Roman soldier who had burned a law scroll was executed to pacify Jewish antagonism, not because the Romans cared about burning a religious book.

23:26-32
Road to the Cross

23:26. Condemned criminals normally bore their own crosses (i.e., the horizontal beam of the cross), but in this case someone else is drafted, perhaps due to the severe precrucifixion beating often administered, which the other Gospels report Jesus had received.

Cyrene was in what is now Libya in North Africa and included a large Jewish community; "Simon" is a typical Jewish name. Devout Jewish pilgrims from throughout the Mediterranean came to Jerusalem during Passover. Roman soldiers could impress anyone into service to carry things for them. Because it is a feast and work is forbidden, Simon is not coming from "the field" (literally) as a worker; perhaps he is late for the festival, only now arriving from Cyrene, or perhaps he has rejoined the day's festivities from where he is residing temporarily in the countryside.

23:27. Crowds generally went to view an execution. The pious women of Jerusalem often went to mourn the executed, providing a narcotic drink to dull the victim's pain. (After condemned persons died, it was not legal to mourn them publicly; but nationalistic Jews would sympathize with fellow Jews executed by the Romans for being revolutionaries.) In antiquity women usually expressed mourning more dramatically than men.

23:28. "Daughters of Jerusalem" designates Jerusalemite women but could also recall some judgment oracles (Is 3:16). The admonition to "mourn for yourselves" was also a prophetic cry of judgment (Is 32:9-14).

23:29. Jesus' statement is the sort of lament mothers would offer when their children died (*2 Baruch 10:13-15). *Josephus reports that some mothers were reduced to eating their children during the famine in Rome's siege against Jerusalem, A.D. 66-70 (cf. Lev 26:29; Deut 28:53; 2 Kings 6:29).

23:30. The prophets had used the same image Jesus uses here as an image of awful judgment (cf. Hos 10:8; Is 2:10, 19-21).

23:31. Unlike a green one, a dry tree would easily catch fire. The point may be that Jesus is "green" wood, not really a revolutionary; how much greater would be the Roman judgment against the dry wood, the real revolutionaries? Or that if they murdered the innocent, how much more would they destroy themselves (the Jewish leaders fought one another as well as the Romans in 66-70)? Or the saying may simply mean that Jerusalem is becoming more ripe for judgment. Jesus may also allude back to the trees and Jerusalem's fall in 21:24, 29-30, though this option is less likely.

23:32. It was less work for the soldiers if they could execute several convicts at once.

23:33-43
On the Cross

23:33-34. Despite the precedent of *Old Testament prayers for vengeance (e.g., 2 Chron 24:22; Ps 137:7-9; Jer 15:15; 17:18; 18:23; 20:12), Jesus prays that God will forgive his persecutors. Those who were executed were supposed to say, "May my death atone for all my sins"; but Jesus confesses instead the sin of those who falsely convicted him, who under Old Testament law were liable for his penalty before God. Ancient biographers often paralleled different figures, and Luke parallels with Jesus the first martyr of his second volume, Stephen (Acts 7:60). Roman custom awarded the soldiers the victim's clothes.

23:35. Ridicule was one of the sufferings inflicted on the naked man hanging on a cross. Ancient writers liked irony; the double irony here is that Jesus does save others, and that the leaders utter lines like *Satan's (4:3, 6-7, 9).

23:36. One might view the soldiers' offer of "sour wine" or "wine vinegar" (NIV) as an act of mercy, because sour wine could act as a painkiller and was also often used as a remedy for thirst; but Luke declares that it is done only as part of their ridicule.

23:37. The soldiers' taunt may include a touch of Roman cynicism toward Judaism, which was widespread despite (or partly because of) Roman conversions to Judaism.

23:38. The condemned person often carried the charge (Latin *titulus)* to the site of execution.

23:39-42. Jesus' interaction with his fellow victim is Luke's ultimate example of Jesus receiving sinners and outcasts, although Luke (unlike Mark) has called them "evildoers" or "criminals" (NIV) without specifying that they were revolutionaries.

23:43. Jewish literature typically contrasted "paradise" with "*Gehenna," or hell. Although Jewish texts disputed the location of paradise (e.g., in the third heaven; or on the perimeters of the circle of the earth—like a Greek view of the Elysian Fields), they often mentioned it as the abode of the righteous after death or after the *resurrection. Thus both Jesus and this condemned man would proceed directly to the abode of the righteous after death.

23:44-49
Jesus' Death

23:44. "All the earth" (KJV) means simply "the whole land" (NIV, NRSV, TEV). The "sixth hour" would come shortly before noon, the "ninth hour" shortly before 3 p.m.; crucifixions rarely ended so quickly. The latter time, when Jesus dies, is close to the time of the evening offering in the temple. Darkness was one of the plagues in Egypt (Ex 10:22) and occurs in the prophets as a judgment for the end time (often due to clouds of rain, locusts, smoke, etc.; Is 13:10; Ezek 30:3, 18; 32:7-8; Joel 2:2, 10, 31; 3:15; Amos 5:18; Zech 14:6).

23:45. The "veil" (KJV, NASB) or "curtain" (NIV, TEV, NRSV) is probably the one between the holy of holies—inhabited only by God, and where no mortal could enter except the high priest once each year—and the sanctuary where the priests ministered (Ex 26:33). Although the point of the veil's rending may be that God provides access for all people into his presence, it is more likely that it indicates instead the departure of God from the temple, as in Ezekiel 10—11.

23:46. This line from Psalm 31:5 is said to have often been recited at the period of the evening offering—about the time of Jesus' death. (Roman readers might, but probably would not, have read this verse in the light of a Roman custom in which the nearest of kin receives the dying person's breath in his own mouth, ensuring the spirit's survival.)

23:47. Whereas Mark has "*Son of God," Luke emphasizes an implication of that claim: "innocent." Roman pronouncements of innocence were important to Luke's audience; see the introduction to Acts.

23:48. Beating breasts was a characteristic sign of mourning (cf. 18:13); Jewish women bystanders would offer this as the only public mourning these criminals could get, because none was permitted after the disposal of their bodies.

23:49. Family and friends would usually be present at an execution; only the male *disciples would be in danger as potential revolutionaries. No one stood too close to the cross, because that could obstruct the view; most crosses were lower to the ground than many modern pictures depict. To Palestinian Jews, the fact that these women accompanied Jesus' group of disciples could have been scandalous.

23:50-56
Jesus' Burial

23:50-51. Luke, whose readers are not clashing with Palestinian Jewish leaders (as are Matthew's), is more apt to distinguish different elements within that leadership than Matthew. In Jesus' day, Judaism was quite diverse, because no one group could lay claim to all the power; but after A.D. 70, when much of the competition had been eliminated by the destruction of the temple (the Sadducees' power base) and the scattering of other groups, some of the Palestinian leaders sought to consolidate their religious power.

23:52-53. Condemned criminals did not normally receive such honorable burials; but exceptions seem to have been made on the intercession of well-to-do family or friends, as the skeleton of a crucified man buried in another aristocratic Jewish tomb of this period testifies.

23:54-56. Because bodies decomposed rapidly, mourners were allowed to anoint, wash and wrap the body in its shrouds even on the sabbath. More elaborate arrangements that these loyal women *disciples wish to bestow on Jesus, however, might wait until the sabbath (sundown Friday evening to sundown Saturday evening) has passed.

24:1-12
The First Announcement

24:1. The sabbath ended at sundown Saturday evening; as soon as daylight breaks (by 6 a.m. at this time of year) these women head for the tomb. (In popular superstition, night was dangerous due to the predominance of demons at that time, but the women probably do not travel at night because it would be too hard to find the tomb.)

24:2-3. The stone was probably a large, disk-shaped stone rolled along a groove in front of the tomb. That it had been rolled back could have suggested tampering or a tomb robbery, although nothing valuable had been buried with the body.

24:4-5. Angels often appeared as human beings in the *Old Testament (Josh 5:13) and also often appeared in radiant garments or bodies (cf. 2 Kings 6:17; Dan 10:5-6). The latter was especially the case in contemporary Jewish texts (i.e., in the expectations of the people to whom this revelation is being given).

24:6-12. Part of the reason for the apostles' unbelief is that a *resurrection of this nature contradicted their *messianic expectations; another reason may have been that Jewish officials considered the witness of women nearly worthless, because they regarded women as unstable and undependable.

24:13-35
The Emmaus Appearance

24:13. Sixty stadia was about seven miles. More than one place in Palestine was called Emmaus (1 Macc 3:57; 4:3; *Josephus reports a different one). The exact site of Luke's Emmaus is no longer known.

24:14-17. Jewish travelers would not consider it unusual for a stranger, who is also a fellow Jew, to join their small company walking for some distance, especially if they assume him to be a Passover pilgrim on his way home. Jesus' feigning ignorance to ask a question does not mean that he does not know the answer (cf. Gen 3:9, 11; 4:9-10). On their lack of recognition, see comment on 24:31-35.

24:18. News spread quickly by word of mouth, and public executions at a feast would be widely discussed. No matter where a Greek-speaking pilgrim visiting Jerusalem for the feast was from, he or she would probably have heard something about these matters. (The description of Cleopas's surprise resembles astonished characters in ancient stories confronting people awakening from many years of sleep and unaware of recent events.) Cleopas does, however, suppose too much to presume that everyone would regard these events as the most obvious of the past several days.

24:19-21. Cleopas's words reflect the confusion all Jesus' followers must have felt: Jesus was a prophet, as in the *Old Testament, or maybe the *Messiah; but the religious leaders of the nation, who of all people should have embraced and followed him, had rejected him. In Galilee and outside Palestine, where the priestly aristocracy was not as directly known as in Judea, respect for the temple leadership no doubt ran higher.

24:22-24. See comment on 24:6-12.

24:25-27. Jesus surely includes references to Deuteronomy 18:15-18, Isaiah 9, 11 and 53; but the implication is that Jesus adduced principles applying to his *messiahship from throughout the Old Testament. *Rabbinic literature regularly praised interpreters with the deep insight into Scripture that Jesus demonstrates here.

24:28. It is polite for Jesus to make as if he would go on, unless they invite him to stay with them; such behavior could also test a person's hospitality (Gen 19:2).

24:29. Hospitality demanded no less than the lodging these *disciples offer Jesus, especially because it is approaching sundown; night travel, particularly as one got farther from Jerusalem, would be dangerous due to robbers. Jewish people throughout the ancient world welcomed fellow Jews who were traveling to spend the night, and insistence was part of hospitality (e.g., Judg 19:5-9; 1 Sam 28:23).

24:30. It was also part of hospitality to offer bread to a guest, no matter how late in the evening (see comment on 11:5-6). After the long walk, these *disciples would be hungry anyway. But by giving thanks and giving bread to them, Jesus takes the role usually held by the head of the household, which he had exercised among his disciples.

24:31-35. Angels were sometimes said to come in disguises and reveal themselves only at the end of their mission (e.g., Raphael to Tobit and Tobias in the book of Tobit). But this was not the case with humans, including dead persons restored to earthly life in the *Old Testament. Although one reason these disciples do not recognize Jesus may be that their eyes have been blinded (24:31; cf. 2 Kings 6:17), Jesus' subsequent disappearance also seems to indicate that he has a new kind of body, the sort of body promised the righteous in the future *resurrection.

24:36-43 The Nature of Jesus' Resurrection

24:36-38. Because the *resurrection of all the dead had not yet occurred, the *disciples think Jesus might be a "ghost" or some other spirit. On the popular level, some people held a belief in ghosts without considering that it contradicted the idea of afterlife in paradise or hell (*Gehenna) and the doctrine of the bodily resurrection. But Jesus assures them that he is not an example of a ghost but of the bodily resurrection.

24:39-40. Some victims were tied onto crosses; others were nailed on. The nails would have been driven through the wrists (which could be called part of the hand). A nail through the ankles may not have been common (the evidence of one excavated example

is in dispute), but there was nothing to have kept soldiers from doing it.
24:41-43. In most Jewish traditions, angels did not eat earthly food.

24:44-53
The Final Commission

24:44-46. See comment on 24:25-27. Other Jewish writings mention the threefold division of the *Old Testament. Jewish interpreters sometimes spoke of God "opening their eyes" to his truths, language with Old Testament precedent (Ps 119:18). Although the Gospels report Jesus' disagreement with his contemporaries on many issues, every stratum of Gospel tradition reports his appeal to the Old Testament to define his mission. Although he may have disagreed with many of his contemporaries on Old Testament interpretation, he agrees with them concerning its authority.
24:47-49. Isaiah spoke of Israel being witnesses to (or against) all the nations in the end time (43:10; 44:8), by means of the endowment of the *Spirit (42:1; 44:3). The Spirit was especially associated with the ability to prophesy, to speak as God inspired a person to speak.
24:50. Priests lifted their hands to give the priestly benediction over the people ("May the Lord bless you, and keep you . . ."—Num 6:24-27).
24:51. See comment on the ascension in Acts 1:9-11.
24:52-53. Many of the temple courts were used for prayer. Ancient writers often framed literary units by starting and ending on the same point; Luke frames his whole Gospel by starting and ending it in the temple.

JOHN

Introduction

Authorship. Early tradition is almost unanimous that "John" wrote the Fourth Gospel. The Gospel itself claims to come from an eyewitness (19:35), whom the internal evidence suggests is the "beloved disciple," whose role best fits John, son of Zebedee, in the other Gospels. The arguments that nineteenth-century scholar B. F. Westcott raised for John's authorship (based on internal claims for an eyewitness, and internal evidence that narrows the possible author to only one member of Jesus' inner circle) are still sound, although many scholars today are not persuaded by them. (One mediating solution has been the proposal that a Johannine "school" composed the Gospel using traditions John had passed on to them; most famous teachers had disciples to pass on their teachings in such settings.)

Archaeological discoveries since Westcott have further demonstrated the appropriateness of the Fourth Gospel's traditions to a Palestinian Jewish milieu—that is, the place where both Jesus and

John had lived. The two strongest objections to Johannine authorship of this Gospel are its date and its differences from the other extant Gospels. The argument based on date objects that the son of Zebedee would have been in his eighties or nineties when the Gospel was written. This challenge is not particularly cogent, however; although most people did not live that long, mortality was highest in early childhood. That one of the Twelve should have survived into his nineties and would then be pressed to record his experience of Jesus is not inherently unlikely. The other objection, based on differences from Matthew, Mark and Luke, is more persuasive but would lose most of its force if John represents an independent tradition or witness to Jesus, writing in his own style (see the discussion of genre).

Although *pseudonymous works existed in antiquity, they stated their purported author rather than implied him; unless we want to argue for John's *implicit* pseudonymity, the internal evidence supporting an eyewitness author should be allowed to stand. For this reason, I believe the Fourth Gospel's claim to authorship by John is stronger than the claims for the other Gospels, which are ultimately dependent only on Christian tradition external to the text itself.

Date. Tradition holds that the Gospel was written in the 90s of the first century; that it could have been written no later (against some nineteenth-century scholars' views) has been confirmed by a manuscript fragment of the Gospel dating to the early second century. A date in the 60s has also been proposed, but most scholars hold to the mid-90s, which best fits the setting described below and the probable setting of the book of Revelation, which stems from the same Christian circles as the Fourth Gospel.

Where John Was Written. Because John is preoccupied with the *Pharisees as opponents, it is reasonable to suppose that his Gospel is written in Galilee or Syria, where conflicts with the Judean Pharisees would be most easily felt in the 90s of the first century.

Tradition strongly holds, however, that John lived in Ephesus, although he had originally come from Palestine and probably maintained awareness of issues in Palestine through contacts there. Two of the seven churches in the book of Revelation grapple with precisely the issues that his Gospel tackles: Smyrna (Rev 2:9-10) and Philadelphia (3:7-9). The church in Smyrna, a center of Johannine tradition in the next generation, might be his main audience. It is possible that the Gospel circulated in different forms in both Galilee and these churches in Asia Minor (western Turkey).

Setting. After A.D. 70, the strength of many Jewish religious groups in Palestine was broken; the *Pharisees began to take more leadership in religious matters, and the influence of their successors eventually became felt throughout Mediterranean Jewry. They engaged in conflicts with their main competition, the Jewish Christians, and (according to the most likely reading of the evidence) even added a line to a standard prayer that cursed sectarians, among whom they included the Jewish Christians. John's antagonism toward the Pharisees in his Gospel suggests that their opposition is somehow related to the opponents his readers face in their own communities.

After the war of A.D. 70, many Jews in the Roman Empire wanted to distance themselves from sects emphasizing *Messiahs, the *kingdom and *prophecy. The Johannine Christians (John's readers) had been made unwelcome by local *synagogue authorities, treated as if their very Jewishness was held in question because they believed in Jesus as Messiah and kingdom-bringer. The Roman authorities were also suspicious of people who did not worship the emperor but were not Jewish (see the discussion of setting in the introduction to Revelation). John writes his Gospel to encourage these Jewish Christians that their faith in Jesus is genuinely Jewish and that it is their opponents who have misrepresented biblical Judaism.

Genre. For the *genre of Gospels in general, see the introduction to the Gospels. Although all four Gospels fall into the general ancient category of biography, that genre was broad enough to allow considerable differences of style. For instance, Luke writes like an ancient Greek historian; Matthew's heavy use of the *Old Testament shows his interest in interpreting such history. But

John seems to be the most interpretive of all, as has been recognized since the early church fathers.

Jesus' discourses in this Gospel also require special comment. The style of Jesus' speaking in John differs from his words in the first three Gospels; it may be helpful to observe that ancient writers were trained to practice paraphrasing speeches in their own words. Some scholars have also argued that John applies Jesus' words to his readers' situation under the *Spirit's guidance; Jewish teachers and (more thoroughly) storytellers often developed different kinds of Old Testament *narratives by describing them in terms most relevant to their audience. Most of Jesus' discourses in John 3—12 are conflicts with the Jewish authorities and thus bear some resemblances to the briefer *rabbinic accounts of arguments with opponents. All in all, however, John remains a Gospel—an ancient biography of Jesus (see the introduction to the Gospels in this commentary).

Message. One emphasis in the Fourth Gospel concerns God's law and word. The *Pharisees claimed that God's law supported their positions; but John emphasizes that Jesus himself is the Word (1:1-18) and the appointed messenger of the Father, and that to reject him is thus to reject the Father.

Another area of emphasis is the *Spirit. The Pharisees did not believe that the Spirit, which they associated especially with the ability to prophesy, was active in their own day; thus they did not claim to have the Spirit. In contrast, John encourages the believers to argue not only from the law but also from their possession of the Spirit. The Pharisees claimed to know the law through their interpretations and traditions; the Christians claimed to know God personally and therefore claimed to understand the law's point better than their opponents did.

One recurrent set of characters in the Gospel, identified with these opponents of Jesus, is "the Jews." Although Jesus and the *disciples are clearly Jewish, John usually uses the term "Jews" in a negative sense for the Judean authorities in Jerusalem, whom he identifies (to update for the language of his own day) with "the *Pharisees." Anti-Semites have sometimes abused the Gospel of

John to deny Jesus' Jewishness, ignoring the situation in which John writes. But John often uses irony (a common ancient literary technique), and by calling the Jewish authorities "Jews" he is probably ironically answering these authorities who say that the Jewish Christians were no longer faithful to Israel. He concedes the title to them, but everything else in his Gospel is meant to argue just the opposite: that the heirs of Israel's faith are the Jewish Christians, even though they have been expelled from their Jewish communities.

John uses many images common in his culture, especially contrasts between light and darkness (common in the *Dead Sea Scrolls), above and below (common in Jewish *apocalyptic literature), and so on.

Commentaries. The multivolume commentaries by Raymond Brown (*The Gospel According to John,* 2 vols., AB 29 and 29A [Garden City, N.Y.: Doubleday, 1966-1970]) and Rudolf Schnackenburg (*The Gospel According to St. John,* 3 vols. [New York: Herder & Herder/Seabury/Crossroad, 1968-1982]) and the single-volume commentary on the Greek text by C. K. Barrett (*The Gospel According to St. John,* 2d ed. [Philadelphia: Westminster, 1978]) are especially helpful for advanced studies; a more useful commentary for the lay reader is J. R. Michaels, *John,* NIBC 4 (Peabody, Mass.: Hendrickson, 1989).

1:1-18
The Word Becomes Flesh

The Greek term translated "word" was also used by many philosophers to mean "reason," the force which structured the universe; *Philo combined this image with Jewish conceptions of the "word." The *Old Testament had personified Wisdom (Prov 8), and ancient Judaism eventually identified personified Wisdom, the Word and the *Law (the Torah).

By calling Jesus "the Word," John calls him the embodiment of all God's revelation in the Scriptures and thus declares that only those who accept Jesus honor the law fully (1:17). Jewish people considered Wisdom/Word divine yet distinct from God the Father, so it was the closest available term John had to describe Jesus.

1:1-2. Beginning like Genesis 1:1, John alludes to the Old Testament and Jewish picture of God creating through his preexistent wisdom or word. According to standard Jewish doctrine in his day, this wisdom existed before the rest of creation but was itself created. By declaring that the Word "was" in the beginning and especially by calling the Word "God" (v. 1; also the most likely reading of 1:18), John goes beyond the common Jewish conception to imply that Jesus is not created (cf. Is 43:10-11).

1:3. Developing Old Testament ideas (e.g., Ps 33:6; Prov 8:30), Jewish teachers emphasized that God had created all things through his Wisdom/Word/ *Law and sustained them because the righteous practiced the law. (Some even pointed out that Gen 1 declared "And God said" ten times when he was creating, and this meant that God created all things with his Ten Commandments.) Ancient Jewish teachers would have agreed with verse 3.

1:4. Developing Old Testament promises of long life in the land if Israel obeyed God (e.g., Ex 20:12; Deut 5:16; 8:1; 11:9), Jewish teachers emphasized that the reward for obeying God's word was *eternal life. John declares that this life had always been available through God's word, which is the same word that he identifies with Jesus. Jewish teachers called many things "light" (e.g., the righteous, the patriarchs, Israel, God), but this term was most commonly applied to God's law (a figure also in the Old Testament, e.g., Ps 119:105).

1:5. That darkness did not "apprehend" the light may be a play on words (it could mean "understand" [NIV] or "overcome" [NRSV]). Similarly, in the *Dead Sea Scrolls, the forces of light and darkness were engaged in mortal combat, but light was predestined to triumph.

1:6-8. "Witness" was especially a legal concept in the Greco-Roman world and in Jewish circles. Isaiah used it in relation to the end time, when the people God delivered would testify to the nations about him before his tribunal (43:10; 44:8). This image recurs throughout this Gospel. On John the Baptist himself, see 1:15.

1:9-10. Jewish tradition declared that God had offered the law to all seventy nations at Mount Sinai but lamented that they had all chosen to reject his word; only Israel had accepted it. In the same way, the world of John's day has failed to recognize God's Word among them.

1:11. Here John breaks with the image in Jewish tradition, according to which Israel alone of all nations had received the law. Jewish people expected that the faithful of Israel would likewise accept the revelation when God gave forth the law again in the end time (Is 2:3; Jer 31:31-34). (In most Jewish tradition, the law would, if changed at all, be more stringent in the world to come.)

1:12-13. The emphasis is thus not on ethnic descent (v. 11) but on spiritual rebirth; see comment on 3:3, 5 for details on how ancient Judaism would hear the language of rebirth.

1:14. Neither Greek philosophers nor Jewish teachers could conceive of the Word becoming flesh. Since the time of *Plato, Greek philosophers had emphasized that the ideal was what was invisible and eternal; most Jews so heavily emphasized that a human being could not become a god that they never considered that God might become human.

When God revealed his glory to Moses in Exodus 33—34, his glory was "abounding in covenant love and covenant faithfulness" (Ex 34:6), which could also be translated "full of *grace and truth." Like Moses of old (see 2 Cor 3:6-18), the *disciples saw God's glory, now revealed in Jesus. As the Gospel unfolds, Jesus' glory is revealed in his signs (e.g., Jn 2:11) but especially in the cross, his ultimate act of love (12:23-33). The Jewish people were expecting God to reveal his glory in something like a cosmic spectacle of fireworks; but for the first coming, Jesus reveals the same side of God's character that was emphasized to Moses: his covenant love.

"Dwelt" (KJV, NASB) here is literally "tabernacled," which means that as God tabernacled with his people in the wilderness, so had the Word tabernacled among his people in Jesus.

1:15. Scholars have suggested that some people may have thought too highly of John the Baptist, a mere prophet, at the expense of Jesus the *Messiah (cf. Acts 19:3-5); such a situation would invite the writer to put John in his place. In the Fourth Gospel, John always defers to Jesus, as a proper prophet should.

1:16-17. *Grace and truth were clearly present in the law (Ex 34:6), but their ultimate expression would come in the Word/law enfleshed.

1:18. Even Moses could see only part of God's glory (Ex 33:20), but in the person of Jesus God's whole heart is fleshed out for the world to see. "In the Father's bosom" (KJV, NASB; cf. "side"—NIV) means that Jesus was in the position of greatest possible intimacy (cf. Jn 13:23). Ancient writers often framed a narrative by beginning and ending it with the same phrase or statement; this framing device is called *inclusio.* In John 1:1 and (according to the most likely reading of the text) 1:18, John calls Jesus "God."

1:19-28
John's Witness to the Jewish Leaders

1:19. Although a few priests were *Pharisees in Jesus' day, there was generally little cooperation between them (v. 24), and the Pharisees certainly had never had power to send priests on missions from Jerusalem. But by the time John writes, the Pharisees represent Palestinian Christians' main opposition. It was within the tradition of Jewish writing John follows to update the language, the way preachers often do today to bring home the point of the text. John thus focuses on the Pharisaic element of Jesus' opposition.

1:20-21. Elijah had been caught up to heaven alive, and Jewish people anticipated his return, which was predicted in Malachi 4:5. (The later *rabbis thought of him as a master of Jewish law who would sometimes show up to settle rabbinic disputes or be sent on angelic errands to deliver rabbis in trouble. They expected him to settle legal issues when he returned; others expected him to perform great miracles or to introduce the *Messiah.) "The Prophet" undoubtedly means the prophet like Moses (Deut 18:15-18).

1:22-23. Applying Isaiah 40:3 to himself means that he is the herald of a new exodus, announcing that God is about to redeem his people from captivity, as he had in the days of Moses. This theme appears in many of the *Old Testament prophets and was part of Jewish expectation in Jesus' day. Indeed, would-be prophetic leaders usually gained followings in the "wilderness."

1:24-25. Of the many kinds of ceremonial washings in Jesus' day, the most significant once-for-all kind of washing was *proselyte *baptism. *Gentiles were usually baptized when they converted to Judaism; this was widely known and even mentioned by the Greek philosopher *Epictetus. By reporting that John asks Jews to be baptized in an act of conversion, the Gospel writers declare that John treats Jews as if they are pagans, which was unheard-of (see comment on 3:3-5). The Fourth Gospel often contrasts water rituals and the *Spirit (3:5; see comment on 4:7-26).

1:26. John employs the common ancient technique of irony: that they do not "know" the coming one speaks ill of them spiritually (1:10, 33-34).

1:27. Slaves carried their master's sandals; John claims that he is not worthy to be even Christ's slave. Prophets were often called God's servants in the Old Testament (e.g., 2 Kings 18:12; 19:34; 20:6; 24:2; Jer 35:15; 44:4).

1:28. "Beyond the Jordan" means Perea, one of the territories controlled by Herod Antipas. Because *Josephus tells us that John was later imprisoned in the fortress Machaerus in the same region, it makes sense that this is where he ministers and is later arrested.

1:29-34
John's Witness to His Disciples

1:29. John's saying probably alludes to the Passover lamb (19:36), likely with the *Old Testament image of sacrificial lambs blended in. He may also allude to Isaiah 53:7, 11.

1:30-31. The whole purpose of John's *baptism is to "prepare the way" (cf. v. 23). To "come after" a person sometimes meant to be his *disciple, so some scholars propose that Jesus actually followed John for a time, as well as being baptized by him; others interpret "come after" in this passage only chronologically.

1:32-34. Most Jewish groups believed that the *Spirit was not as active in prophetic inspiration as in the Old Testament period. The emerging *rabbinic movement and many of their allies, who linked the Spirit almost exclusively with *prophecy, emphasized that the direct prophetic endowments of the Spirit had ceased when the last Old Testament prophets (Haggai, Zechariah and Malachi) died. For many of John's hearers, a claim that the Spirit is being restored would be a claim that the *messianic era is at hand.

1:35-39
John's Disciples Take the Bait

1:35-37. See 1:29. Teachers normally trained *disciples, who then went out to teach others; to recommend disciples to a greater teacher was rare, required great humility and denoted confidence in the other teacher's superiority.

1:38-39. Asking such indirect questions (they want to come home with him) was characteristic of ancient politeness and hospitality. The "tenth hour" by usual reckonings would be about 4 p.m., possibly too late in the afternoon to walk a long way home before dark and thus implying that a hospitable person would invite them to spend the night. (By another system of time reckoning, unlikely here, the "tenth hour" could mean 10 a.m.; this system fits 19:14 better but not 4:6.)

1:40-51
The Disciples Witness Too

Like John the Baptist, the *disciples learn that the best witness is simply to introduce people to Jesus and let him do the rest.

1:40-41. Of the four Gospels, only John uses the Hebrew or *Aramaic title, *Messiah, although he also translates it into Greek because that is the language of his Jewish readers. (Outside Palestine, most Jews in the Roman Empire spoke Greek.)

1:42. "Cephas" is Aramaic and "Peter" Greek for "rock." Nicknames were common, and *rabbis sometimes gave characterizing nicknames to their *disciples. In the Old Testament, God often changed names to describe some new characteristic of a person (Abraham, Sarah, Jacob, Joshua; as a negative declaration see Jer 20:3).

Greeks and Romans would attribute supernatural knowledge (like knowing the name of a person one had never met, as Jesus does here) to miracle workers (usually magicians); Jewish people would attribute it to prophets or prophetically endowed teachers; but see especially comment on 2:24-25 for John's point.

1:43. Some radical Greek teachers were said to have called disciples to follow them (e.g., Socrates called Xenophon), but normally ancient students or their parents chose their own teachers. As often in Matthew and John, "following" could mean "becoming a disciple," because disciples could show respect to masters of Torah (*law) by walking behind them. In the Fourth Gospel, however, this term also has greater significance (see 10:4).

1:44. Bethsaida was known for its fishing industry. Mark says that Simon and Andrew were from Capernaum (1:21, 29; 2:1), and excavations confirm that early Christians thought that Peter's home was there. It is not unlikely that as fishermen in a fishing cooperative with James and John (Mk 1:19) they took their boats back and forth between Capernaum and Bethsaida.

1:45. By the one predicted in "the Law and the Prophets" (a common Jewish designation for the Old Testament), Philip no doubt means the *Messiah (e.g., Deut 18:15-18; Is 9; 11; 53).

1:46. Nazareth seems to have been a very traditional, orthodox town; priests later considered it ritually clean enough to move there. But Nazareth was relatively small and obscure, with about sixteen hundred to two thousand inhabitants. It lay about four miles from the massive city of Sepphoris, which rivaled Tiberias (6:23) for its urban Greek character in Jewish Galilee.

1:47. Jesus here makes a wordplay on the Old Testament Jacob, or "Israel," who *was* a man of guile (Gen 27:35; 31:26).

1:48. Teachers often taught *disciples under trees, which were popular for this and other purposes because of their shade. But Jesus' knowing *which* tree Nathanael had sat under is a demonstration of genuine supernatural knowledge (cf. Susanna 54, 58). On this knowledge see comment on 1:42 and 2:24-25.

1:50-51. The opening of the heavens indicated a major revelation (e.g., Ezek 1:1). Jesus' words allude to Genesis 28:12: Jesus is the new way between heaven and earth (Jacob's ladder) on whom angels ascend and descend; like Jacob of old, this "genuine Israelite" Nathanael (Jn 1:47) would receive this new revelation.

2:1-11
Jesus' First Sign

2:1. "Third day" here does not refer

to the third day of the week, because virgins were married on the fourth day (Wednesday) and widows on the fifth; nor does it seem to fit the count of days in 1:29, 35, 43. But ancient writers often bracketed off segments of their work by starting and ending on the same note (a practice called *inclusio);* thus John may use this designation to point toward 2:19 and link this story (2:1-11) with the prediction of Jesus' death and resurrection (see on 2:4).

"Cana" may be Kefar Kanna (over three miles from Nazareth), but most scholars prefer Khirbet Kana (over eight miles from Nazareth). Either site would be close enough to Nazareth to explain how the host knows Jesus' family.

2:2. Weddings lasted seven days, and hosts invited as many people as possible, especially distinguished guests like prominent teachers.

2:3. To run out of wine at a wedding was a social faux pas that would become the subject of jests for years; the host was responsible to provide his guests with adequate wine for seven days.

The women's quarters were near the place where the wine was stored; thus Mary learns of the shortage of wine before word reaches Jesus and the other men. Her words probably suggest that he should do something; guests were to help defray the expense of the wedding with their gifts, and it seems that their friend needs some extra gifts now.

2:4. "Woman" was a respectful address (like "Ma'am") but hardly customary for one's mother. Jesus' statement here establishes polite distance (though "What have I to do with you" is usually a harsh, not a polite, expression in biblical language). Because Jesus' "hour" in John refers especially to the cross, here Jesus is saying, "Once I begin doing miracles, I begin the road to the cross."

2:5. Like many Old Testament seekers of God who would not take no for an answer (Gen 32:26-30; Ex 33:12—34:9; 1 Kings 18:36-37; 2 Kings 2:2, 4, 6, 9; 4:14-28), Mary acts in confidence that Jesus will hear her entreaty. Ancient Jewish readers, who told stories of miracle workers who insisted that God would send rain, would read Mary's action as demonstrating strong faith.

2:6. The description of the stone jars indicates that they contained enough water to fill a Jewish immersion pool used for ceremonial purification. Although *Pharisees forbade storing such water in jars, some Jews were less strict; thus these large jars were being reserved for ritual purposes. Stone jars were common because they were less likely to contract ritual uncleanness than those made of other substances.

2:7. Using the jars for another purpose would temporarily defile them; Jesus shows more concern for his friend's wedding than for contemporary ritual.

2:8. "Master of the banquet" was a position of honor (Ecclus 32:1-2); one of his primary duties was to regulate the distribution of wine to prevent excess that would (especially in a Jewish context) ruin the party. At least in Greek banquets, guests elected this person to preside over the entertainment and to control the level of dilution for the wine; thus some observers might have held him partly responsible for the host's running out of wine prematurely.

2:9-10. Soon after the grape vintage, all wine would contain some alcohol (neither refrigeration nor hermetic sealing existed). But the alcohol level of the wine was not increased artificially (distillation was not in use); rather, the wine was watered down, with two to three parts water to one part wine.

Sometimes at Greek parties drunkenness was induced through less dilution or the addition of herbal toxins, but Jewish teachers disapproved of such practices; that drunkenness is part of the celebration at Cana is unlikely. Yet one would normally serve the better wine first because, drunk or not, guests' senses would become more dulled as the seven days of banqueting proceeded.

2:11. God had often manifested his glory by doing signs (Ex 16:7; for glory, cf. comment on Jn 1:14). Moses' first sign was turning water into blood (Ex 7:20; cf. Rev 8:8); Jesus' first sign is turning water into wine.

2:12-25 The Raising of a New Temple

2:12-13. All Jews who could attend the Passover in Jerusalem customarily did so; unlike Jewish people in distant lands, Galileans could make the pilgrimage regularly.

2:14. The sheep and doves (and, to a lesser extent, the cattle; cf. Lev 1:3-9; 4:2-21; 8:2; 22:21) were necessary for the people's sacrifices; moneychangers were needed to standardize foreign and Galilean currencies into coinage useful to the sellers of the sacrificial animals.

2:15-16. Jesus insists on a different priority for activity in the temple; cf. Malachi 3:1-6.

2:17. The *disciples recall Psalm 69:9, a psalm of a righteous sufferer. Psalm 69:21 speaks of vinegar being given him to drink (cf. Jn 19:29). In the context of John, Jesus' zeal "consumes" him by bringing about his death for the world (cf. 6:51).

2:18-20. Many groups in Judaism expected a new or transformed temple. But the old temple was one of the most magnificent buildings in antiquity, the symbol to which the rest of Judaism looked. To most Jews, and especially to the aristocracy who controlled Jerusalem's temple, Jesus' words here would sound blasphemous. Herod the Great began work on the temple in 20-19 B.C., and work continued until A.D. 64; its forty-sixth year mentioned here places Jesus' words in A.D. 27.

2:21-22. A prophetic word was often understood only in retrospect (e.g., 2 Kings 9:36-37). Many Jewish interpreters (attested especially in the *Dead Sea Scrolls) interpreted Scripture in this way.

2:23-25. Miracle workers were often thought to know some hearts, but only God, who was called "Searcher of hearts," was thought to know the hearts of all people.

3:1-8 Conversion as Birth from Above

Jesus explains to Nicodemus that religious knowledge and ethnicity are not a sufficient basis for a relationship with God; one must be born into his family by the *Spirit. John often contrasts water rituals and the Spirit (3:5; see comment on 4:7-26).

3:1. A wealthy and prominent Nicodemus is known in Jerusalem in this period, though we cannot be sure that John means the same one. As a highly educated "ruler" or leader in the Jewish community, John's Nicodemus was surely well-to-do.

3:2. One might come by night to avoid being seen, or because Jewish teachers who worked during the day could study only at night (cf. Ps 119:148; the latter was undoubtedly not the case with Nicodemus, who would not need to work—v. 1). But John includes the detail because it serves the theme of light and darkness (11:10; 13:30) that brackets this narrative (3:19-21).

3:3-4. Jesus speaks literally of being

born "from above," which means "from God" ("above" was a Jewish circumlocution, or roundabout expression, for God). One could also construe the phrase as meaning "reborn," which Nicodemus takes literally. (Ancient writers, including those of the Old Testament—Jer 1:11-12; Mic 1:10-15—often used plays on words, and John includes quite a few other puns; they also sometimes used other characters as less intelligent foils for a *narrative's main spokesperson.) Because Jewish teachers spoke of *Gentile converts to Judaism as starting life anew like "newborn children" (just as adopted sons under Roman law relinquished all legal status in their former family when they became part of a new one), Nicodemus should have understood that Jesus meant conversion; but it never occurs to him that someone Jewish would need to convert to the true faith of Israel.

3:5. Converts to Judaism were said to become "as newborn children" when they were *baptized to remove *Gentile impurity. "Born of water" thus clarifies for Nicodemus that "born from above" means conversion, not a second physical birth.

The Greek wording of 3:5 can mean either "water and the *Spirit" or "water, that is, the Spirit." Ezekiel 36:24-27 used water symbolically for the cleansing of the Spirit (cf. especially the *Dead Sea Scrolls), so here Jesus could mean "converted by the Spirit" (cf. 7:37-39)—a *spiritual* *proselyte baptism. Whereas Jewish teachers generally spoke of converts to Judaism as "newborn" only in the sense that they were legally severed from old relationships, an actual rebirth by the Spirit would produce a new heart (Ezek 36:26).

3:6-7. The "spirit" that is born from God's Spirit may reflect the "new spirit" of Ezekiel 36:26.

3:8. One could also translate "sound of the wind" as "voice of the Spirit" (for plays on words, see comment on 3:3-4). The wind is unpredictable and uncontrollable (see Eccles 8:8; cf. Eccles 1:6, 8, 14, 17; 2:11, 17, 26; 4:4, 6, 16; 6:9). The Spirit was symbolized as wind in Ezekiel 37, which some Jewish interpreters linked with Genesis 2:7 (cf. Jn 20:22).

3:9-21
The Revealer from Above

Jesus as incarnate Wisdom (see comment on 1:1-18) is the only one fully qualified to reveal God and reconcile the world to him.

3:9-10. Nicodemus's denseness makes him a foil for Jesus the revealer. For this theme in some ancient literature, see the discussion of Mark's message in the introduction to Mark.

3:11-13. Only an eyewitness of heaven could fully testify about heaven. Jewish literature provides other parallels to John 3:11-13, but the closest are Jewish texts that speak of divine Wisdom coming down from God, seeking to reveal the ways of heaven (God) to people. Jesus may imply a contrast with the Jewish tradition that Moses ascended not only Mount Sinai but up into heaven to receive God's law; now Wisdom/Word/*Law has come down from heaven in the flesh (see comment on 1:14-18).

3:14-15. "Lifting up" is another play on words (3:3-4): Jesus returns to heaven by way of the cross, "lifted up" like the serpent Moses lifted up to bring healing (Num 21:4-9; for "lifting up" see comment on Jn 12:32-33).

3:16-18. The tenses of the Greek verbs indicate the sense: "This is how God loved the world: he gave his son." "Only begotten" is literally "special, beloved," and was often applied in Jewish literature to Isaac, to emphasize the greatness of Abraham's sacrifice in offering him up. *Eternal life is literally the "life of the world to come"; John's present tense ("have") indicates that those who trust Jesus begin to experience that life already in the present time.

Despite ancient Jewish literature's mention of God's love for humanity and its emphasis on God's special love for Israel, nothing compares with this sacrifice, especially not for "the world," which in John normally means those not yet following God's will. The *Old Testament also emphasizes God's immeasurable love (e.g., Ex 34:6-7; Deut 7:7-8; Judg 10:16; Is 63:9; Hos 11:1-4, 8-11; cf. Is 16:11; Jer 48:36).

3:19-21. Ancient texts (especially the *Dead Sea Scrolls) often contrast light and darkness as good and evil in the same way John does here. Everyone would have understood John's point. Bracketing off a *narratve by starting and ending on the same point (3:2) was an ancient literary device.

3:22-36
The Witness and the Son

3:22-24. On John's *baptism see comment on Mark 1:4-5. Away from the Jordan River, water was not plentiful, so in their itinerant ministry Jesus' *disciples (4:2) probably do not baptize everywhere, although ceremonial immersion pools were widespread in Palestine.

3:25-26. On Jewish ceremonial purification, cf. 2:6 and 11:55. This theme runs through the Gospel: ceremonial washing (2:6), *proselyte baptism (3:5), perhaps Jacob's well (chap. 4) and the healing waters of Bethesda (chap. 5), Siloam's water for the Feast of Tabernacles (7:37-38; 9:7) and perhaps 13:5-11 and 19:34.

3:27-28. In Jewish law, one person who represents another acts on his sender's authority but must adhere to the constraints of his mission; the real authority always stems from the sender.

3:29-30. The "friend of the bridegroom" refers to the Jewish custom of the *shoshbin,* who was much like the best man in weddings today. The most significant emphasis of Jewish weddings was joy.

3:31. One who originates from heaven, as opposed to others who were from earth, most naturally applies in Jewish texts to divine Wisdom (see comment on 1:1-18).

3:32-33. Prominent individuals had distinctive marks on their signet rings, which they would press into hot wax seals on the outside of documents to attest that they were witnesses to the execution of the document.

3:34. Because many thought that the *Spirit had been quenched in Israel till the future restoration of Israel, and many thought that only a few had merited the Spirit, to say that someone had unlimited access to give the Spirit indicates that he is greater than any person who had ever lived (the *most* anyone else could have would be unlimited access to *receive* the Spirit).

3:35-36. Again, the language of the Father authorizing the Son and judging the world by their response to him portrays the Son more highly than any mere human was viewed in Jewish literature; cf. 3:31.

4:1-6
Jesus Travels Through Samaria

In John 4:1-42, Jesus crosses strict cultural boundaries separating races (in the general sense of culturally distinct peoples), genders and moral status, pointing to the new and ultimate unity in the Spirit.

4:1-2. On Jesus' *baptism see comment on 3:22-23. Although ceremonial washings were common in Judaism, those who practiced initiatory baptisms (those which initiated people into a particular Jewish group) were viewed by other Jews as sectarian.

4:3-4. One could travel around Samaria, but many pilgrims to and from the feasts in Jerusalem took the shorter route straight through Samaria. *Samaritans and Jews worshiped the same God and both used the law of Moses (although the Samaritans made a few changes in it). But they despised one another's places of worship and had remained hostile toward one another for centuries.

4:5-6. The site of Jacob's well is still known; it is within view of Mount Gerizim, which was holy to the Samaritans. This site begins a *narrative that emphasizes holy geography (especially 4:20). Although this concept is foreign to most modern Western readers, ancient people were widely attracted to special "holy sites"—which Jesus here supersedes.

The "sixth hour" normally means noon; thus Jesus and the *disciples had been journeying for perhaps six hours. (According to another system of time reckoning, less likely here, "sixth hour" would mean 6 p.m.—cf. 19:14—in which case Jesus and his disciples would be ready to settle down for the night and lodge there—4:40.) The local women would not come to draw water in the midday heat, but this woman had to do so, because she had to come alone (for her reasons, see comment on 4:7).

4:7-26
A Gift for a Samaritan Sinner

In the Fourth Gospel, Jesus' gift of the *Spirit supersedes the ritual waters of John the Baptist (1:26, 33), ceremonial purification (2:6), *proselyte *baptism (3:5) and the Feast of Tabernacles (7:37-39; 9:7). It also apparently supersedes water having other religious symbolism associated with holy sites, such as healing sanctuaries (5:2-8) and Jacob's well (4:7-26). For John's readers, who have the Spirit but lack many of the rituals of their opponents, these contrasts would constitute an encouragement.

4:7. That this *Samaritan woman comes to the well alone rather than in the company of other women probably indicates that the rest of the women of Sychar did not like her, in this case because of her sexual activities (cf. comment on 4:18). Although Jewish teachers warned against talking much with women in general, they would have especially avoided Samaritan women, who, they declared, were unclean from birth. Other ancient accounts show that even asking water of a woman could be interpreted as flirting with her—especially if she had come alone due to a reputation for looseness. Jesus breaks all the rules of Jewish piety here. In addition, both Isaac (Gen 24:17) and Jacob (Gen 29:10) met their wives at wells; such precedent created the sort of potential ambiguity at this well that religious people wished to avoid altogether.

4:8. *Pharisees considered many of the foods of the *Samaritans unclean.

4:9. The woman first confronts this encounter in racial terms: under Jewish law, even her water vessel (same term as in 2:6) was considered unclean for Jewish drinking. Ironically, in John's Gospel only non-Jews recognize Jesus' Jewishness (here and 18:33-35).

4:10. "Living water" simply meant "fresh" or "flowing" as opposed to stagnant or well water, but given John's propensity for double meanings (see 3:5), here the term may also mean "water of life."

Some scholars have pointed out that the *rabbis spoke of Torah, the *law, as

God's gift and as living water. But John uses the symbolism differently to refer to the *Spirit (7:37-39). The background here is God as provider of the source of genuine life (Is 12:3; Jer 2:13).

4:11. Jesus has no jar to lower into the well; moreover, even with a jar he could not get "living" (i.e., fresh or flowing) water from a well (see comment on 4:10).

4:12. Her saying "our father Jacob" is an affront to the Jewish teaching that the Jewish people were children of Jacob, and the *Samaritans were at best half-breeds. The one who is greater than Jacob does not argue the point with her; it is peripheral to the issue he wishes to drive home.

4:13-15. The images of water and wells were often used symbolically in antiquity; like many other characters in John, however, she takes Jesus literally when he is speaking figuratively.

4:16-17. In view of the ambiguity of the situation (see comment on 4:7), her statement, "I have no husband," could mean "I am available." Jesus removes the ambiguity, which stems from his refusal to observe customs that reflected ethnic and gender prejudice, not from any actual flirtation on his part.

4:18. Jesus clarifies her ambiguous statement: she had been married five times and is not married to the man with whom she now lives. *Samaritans were no less pious and strict than Jews, and her behavior would have resulted in ostracism from the Samaritan religious community—which would have been nearly coextensive with the whole Samaritan community.

4:19. Prophets were considered capable of knowing others' thoughts (see comment on 1:42). Although this frequent designation for Jesus is inadequate (4:44; 6:14; 7:40; 9:17), it at least moves the conversation beyond 4:17. The Samaritans awaited not just any prophet, however, but the greatest prophet, one like Moses (Deut 18:15-18); see John 4:25.

4:20. Mount Gerizim, the *Samaritans' holy site equivalent to Judaism's Jerusalem, was in full view of Jacob's well. She uses the past tense for "worship" precisely because of her continuing consciousness of Jews' and Samaritans' racial separation: roughly two centuries before, the Jewish king had obliterated the Samaritan temple on that mountain, and it had remained in ruins ever since. Samaritans mocked the Jewish holy site and once, under cover of night, even sought to defile the Jerusalem temple. Jews similarly ridiculed Mount Gerizim and even built many of their *synagogues so worshipers could face Jerusalem.

4:21. "A time is coming" was common prophetic language (1 Sam 2:31; 2 Kings 20:17; Jer 31:31); because she accepts him as a prophet (4:19), she has to listen to his message.

4:22. Jesus is not neutral; he accepts the correctness of the Jewish position, although he does not allow that to remain as an ultimate barrier to racial reconciliation (4:23). In a Gospel addressing Jewish Christians rejected by their *synagogues (see the introduction), this point is significant.

4:23-24. When he speaks of "worship in Spirit and truth," Jesus may have in view the common identification of the *Spirit with *prophecy in ancient Judaism, as well as *Old Testament passages about charismatic, prophetic worship (especially 1 Sam 10:5; 1 Chron 25:1-6). Given the general belief that the prophetic Spirit was no longer active, Jesus' words would strike ancient ears forcefully. The future hour (4:21) is present as well as future; Jesus makes the character of the future world available to his *disciples in their present lives (see comment on 3:16).

For oppressed Jews and Samaritans longing for the future promise, this was also a striking statement.

4:25-26. Later *Samaritan documents explain the Samaritan concept of a *messiah: the *Taheb,* or restorer, was a prophet like Moses (Deut 18:15-18).

4:27-42 Reaping Among the Samaritans

4:27. Jewish piety warned men not to talk much with women (some *rabbis added, even with one's own wife!), both because of temptation and because of what others might think. That the *disciples are amazed yet trust their teacher enough not to ask about this situation is a sign of their respect for him, an attitude considered appropriate for faithful disciples. (A few later Jewish traditions report rabbis who disintegrated disrespectful disciples into heaps of ashes with their eyes, but such stories are meant only to illustrate the general principle that one ought not to challenge one's teacher!)

4:28-30. Judaism did not have much regard for the witness of a woman, and the witness of an adulteress would be worthless; the situation was probably the same among the *Samaritans. Nevertheless, she witnesses the way Philip had (1:46). That she is distracted from her original purpose for coming to the well (4:28) and leaves behind her water pot suggests that Jesus' water has replaced the water of Jacob's well for her.

4:31-33. Ancient teachers sometimes used food as a metaphor for spiritual food (see comment on 6:32). In the *Old Testament, this metaphor sometimes related to one's calling (Jer 15:16; cf. Ezek 2:1-3).

4:34. Jewish teachers regarded God's work in one sense as finished (his creative work—Gen 2:2) but in another sense continuing (his work of sustaining his creation; see comment on Jn 5:17). Jesus refers here to a work that climaxes all God's work: Jesus completes the Father's work on the cross (19:30; cf. 17:4).

4:35. "Lifting up one's eyes" (KJV, NASB) was a common Old Testament expression, although it became rarer in later Hebrew; it often simply meant looking. The main wheat harvest ran from mid-April through the end of May; the barley harvest, which made fields "white" (literally, as in KJV, NASB; cf. "ripe"—NIV, NRSV) was in March. Some scholars think that Jesus here cites a Jewish proverb that refers to four months between planting and harvesting.

4:36-38. In this context, Jesus and the *Samaritan woman sow, and the *disciples see the harvest (v. 39). Verse 37 seems to adapt a popular proverb based on ideas such as Ecclesiastes 2:18—changing an image of sorrow to one of joy.

4:39-42. The Samaritans believe because they meet Jesus (cf. 1:46-49), but the woman's relationship to her community also changes through her having become his first witness there.

For Jesus to lodge there, eating *Samaritan food and teaching Samaritans (v. 40) would be roughly equivalent to defying segregation in the United States during the 1950s or apartheid in South Africa in the 1980s—shocking, extremely difficult, somewhat dangerous. The Jesus of the Gospels is more concerned with people than with custom.

4:43-54 Faith and Healing in Galilee

4:43-45. See comment on Mark 6:4; but here the "home country" is apparently Judea (cf. Jn 1:11).

4:46. For Cana see 2:1. Capernaum was close to a full day's walk from there. "Royal official" (NASB, NIV) probably means that this man is one of Herod Antipas's court officials, although Herod's official title was tetrarch rather than king. Jesus was extremely unfavorable toward Antipas (Lk 13:32; 23:9; for reasons, cf. Mk 6:17-29); this man who comes to Jesus would be a wealthy aristocrat, probably much influenced by Greco-Roman culture and not very religious by general Palestinian Jewish standards.

4:47. "Come down" (KJV, NASB, NRSV) is more accurate than "come" (NIV) because Capernaum, on the Sea of Galilee, was lower in elevation than Cana.

4:48-49. On Jesus' rebuff and a suppliant's insistence, see comment on 2:4-5.

4:50-54. Long-distance miracles were rare by *Old Testament, other Jewish and Greco-Roman standards; people generally believed prophets and Greek magicians more easily if they were present in person. The rare stories of long-distance miracles suggested to ancient readers that these miracle workers had extraordinary power. For Jesus, the only prerequisite for such miracles is seekers' faith in his power.

5:1-9a
Healing at Bethesda

Healing shrines were common throughout the ancient world, especially for the worship of Asclepius and other popular deities renowned for healing powers. Most of these shrines required the supplicants to purify themselves at the adjoining fountain or other source of water. This passage portrays Jesus as greater than such healing sanctuaries of his day.

5:1. John does not specify which Jewish feast is the occasion for Jesus' trip to Jerusalem, although some manuscripts have "the feast," which would mean the Feast of Tabernacles, as in Jewish tradition (not Passover). But the real issue for this narrative is that the day on which Jesus heals is a sabbath (5:9b).

5:2. Although scholars do not agree on the site of Bethesda (or its exact spelling), the site most scholars currently favor is under St. Anne's Monastery in Jerusalem. This site had two twin pools, surrounded by four porches, or porticoes, and one porch down the middle separating the pools. Although John writes after Jerusalem was destroyed in 70, his recollection of the site is accurate.

5:3. This site was later used as a pagan healing shrine; given the ancient tendency to reuse older shrines, the Jewish community in Jesus' day probably viewed this pool as a place of healing. The temple authorities undoubtedly did not approve—after all, sacred pools at healing shrines characterized Greek cults like that of Asclepius—but popular religion often ignores religious contradictions that are clearer to the official religious leaders.

5:4. This verse may not be original (see notes in most translations) but was probably added early by a scribe familiar with the tradition of healing at Bethesda; it explains the otherwise enigmatic verse 7.

5:5. The man had been sick there longer than many people in antiquity lived—for about as many years as Israel had wandered in the wilderness. Ancient reports of healings often specified how long the person had been sick to emphasize the greatness of the healer's cure. Obviously nothing else, including this pool, had succeeded in restoring him.

5:6-9a. In 2:6 and 3:5, Jesus replaces the water of ceremonial purification; in 4:13-14, he replaces the "holy water" of a *Samaritan holy site. Here he, not the supposedly healing waters, restores the man.

5:9b-18
Betrayal on the Sabbath

*Narratives often made points by contrasting characters; John contrasts the man healed in 5:1-9 with the man healed in 9:1-7. Local authorities may have been pressuring John's readers to follow the example of the former; John urges them to emulate the latter instead (cf. 1 Jn 3:16; a few decades later, a Roman letter indicates that apostate Christians in the region of Asia Minor were betraying others).

5:9b-10. Biblical rules forbade work on the sabbath, even so much as gathering wood for a fire (Num 16:32). By Jesus' day, Jewish law explicitly forbade carrying things on the sabbath, viewing this as a form of work.

5:11-13. Many teachers also forbade minor cures—physicians' cures not necessary to save a life—on the sabbath. That Jesus acts in God's name with a miracle rather than a physician's cure should make that discussion irrelevant; but law is often argued by analogy, and these particular authorities reason that Jesus' cure is just like a physician's cure.

5:14. The man may have been in the temple for worship. In the Bible sufferings were sometimes (not always—cf. 9:2-3; e.g., 2 Sam 4:4; 1 Kings 14:4; 2 Kings 13:14) judgment for sin (e.g., 1 Kings 13:4; 2 Kings 1:4; 2 Chron 16:12). Jesus warns of greater judgment here—the *resurrection for judgment (cf. 5:29).

5:15-16. This man does just the opposite of the faithful healed man in 9:30-34, with whom John contrasts him. His behavior is like those who left the *churches of John's readers and sided with their opponents, betraying them to persecution (see introduction to 1 John in this commentary).

5:17. Everyone recognized that God had continued to work since creation, sustaining the world even on the sabbath. Jesus reasons by analogy that what is right for God in sustaining his creation is also right for himself.

5:18. Because Jesus appears to usurp prerogatives solely attributed to God (5:17—the right to work on the sabbath), his hearers think that he thereby claims a position equal to that of God, a claim that naturally sounds blasphemous to them. Second-century *rabbis accused many Jewish Christians of believing in two gods. One could "annul" a biblical law by disregarding it, so they feel that Jesus is (literally) "destroying" the sabbath.

5:19-29
Jesus' Relation to the Father

Jesus seeks to qualify their understanding of his relationship to the Father; far from usurping God's honor (5:18), Jesus acts only on the Father's authority and in conjunction with his will.

5:19-20. Jesus qualifies their understanding by applying another analogy: it was common wisdom that sons imitated their fathers. But the offense remains in that Jesus claims to be God's Son in a unique way that does not include them.

5:21-22. Although some *Old Testament texts spoke of a king who would reign under God's authority (Dan 7:13-14; cf. Jn 5:27), raising and judging the dead was a divine prerogative reserved for God alone, as rehearsed daily in Jewish prayers ("God who raises the dead").

But by claiming that the Father "gave" him this authority, Jesus claims to exercise delegated authority as the Father's agent (Judaism accepted the legal principle of agency). The idea of the Son as the Father's agent runs throughout this section and disarms their objection in verse 18. (In trinitarian terms, Jesus is equally deity with the Father but distinct in person and submits to the Father in role.)

5:23. God sometimes gave others honor as his representatives (Ps 2:11-12), but no one was ever to be honored to the same degree as God (Is 42:8; 48:11; cf. Ex 20:5). Jesus' hearers could easily construe Jesus' statement here as a claim to deity.

5:24-25. *Eternal life, the life of the world to come, was supposed to be available only when the dead would be raised; but Jesus provides new life already for those who trust in him.

5:26. Non-Palestinian Jewish texts held God to be the only one with life "of himself" ("uncreated," "self-begotten," etc.); as in some Greek writings, they described the supreme God as existing without any source outside himself. Although John can also use the phrase more generally in other contexts (6:53), this passage compares Jesus' prerogatives with those of the Father, suggesting that, as in *Diaspora Jewish sources, the term here refers to Jesus' uncreated eternality.

5:27. The *Son of Man in Daniel 7:13-14 was to rule for God in the future *kingdom; ruling included executing judgment.

5:28-29. The Old Testament (Dan 12:2) and much of ancient Judaism taught a *resurrection of both the righteous and the unrighteous, which would take place at the last day. (Some circles in ancient Judaism taught only a resurrection of the righteous; others taught that the wicked would be resurrected only temporarily for judgment and then destroyed; still others held that the wicked would be resurrected to eternal judgment.)

5:30-47
Jesus' Witnesses

5:30. Jesus is thus a faithful *shaliach,* or agent; Jewish law taught that a man's agent was as a man himself (backed by his full authority), to the extent that the agent faithfully represented him. Moses and the *Old Testament prophets were sometimes viewed as God's agents.

5:31. Here Jesus cites the Old Testament principle, central to later Jewish law (both that of the *rabbis and that of the *Dead Sea Scrolls), that two witnesses are necessary to prove a (capital) case (Deut 17:6; 19:15).

5:32. Jewish teachers sometimes spoke of God in roundabout terms (here, "another").

5:33-35. On John the Baptist as a witness, see comment on 1:6-8. The hand-held oil lamps of the Herodian period were too small to give forth much light (they normally produced as much as a candle), and thus one would symbolize only a small reflection of "the light."

5:36-38. The witness of the Father should be all that is necessary. Israel at Sinai supposedly saw his form and heard his voice, and accepted his word through his agent Moses; Jesus says that his own generation rejects the fuller revelation of God sent to them (cf. 1:11, 14-18).

5:39-40. Scripture said, "Do this and you will live," which Jewish teachers read as: "Do this and you will have life in the world to come." Thus they believed that one had *eternal life through the Scriptures; but Jesus says that the Scriptures witness to him, hence to reject him is to disobey the Scriptures.

5:41-44. The Father's agent comes in the Father's name, not in his own; to reject a person's agent was to reject the authority of that person himself.

5:45-47. Moses witnesses to Jesus in his writings (the first five books of the Old Testament were attributed to him). Ancient Judaism viewed Moses as an intercessor for Israel (e.g., *Josephus, *rabbis, the *Testament of Moses); but Jesus says that Moses will instead be their prosecutor. Jewish teachers regarded Moses as the central prophetic figure of their history, and even many pagans knew of Moses as Israel's lawgiver.

6:1-15
A New Passover Meal

After speaking of Moses (5:45-47), Jesus goes on to perform a sign that might be expected of a new prophet like Moses (Deut 18:15): providing manna.

6:1-2. Those thought to be wonder-workers drew large followings in the ancient world, but most wonder-workers in this period did not emphasize teaching over miracles, in contrast to Jesus (6:26-27).

6:3-4. If the events of chapter 5 took place at the Feast of Tabernacles (see comment on 5:1) and those of this text occur at Passover, and if this section of John is in chronological order, half a year has elapsed between these chapters.

6:5-6. Teachers quizzed their *disciples with questions, and they occasionally tested their resolve or understanding of a matter by posing a difficult situation.

6:7. The bread needed to feed the crowd would cost two hundred days' wages for a peasant or unskilled laborer; although fishermen could have earned the same amount faster, it still represents a substantial sacrifice to the disciples' communal treasury (12:6; 13:29).

6:8-9. The "barley" loaves are reminiscent of 2 Kings 4:42-44, where Elisha multiplies such loaves. Philip's and Andrew's skepticism also mirrors that of Elisha's prophet disciples (2 Kings 4:43). (Some scholars also point to the presence of Elisha's assistant in 2 Kings 4:38, 41; the *LXX there uses the same word for "lad" as Andrew does here.) Fish and bread were basic staples; few people could afford meat.

6:10. Grass would flourish especially around Passover season (cf. 6:4); it would also make the ground more comfortable for sitting. John numbers five thousand "men" (the Greek term here is gender-specific, and only men were usually numbered); the whole crowd, including women and children, may have been four times that number. Thus Jesus addresses a crowd nearly as large as the seating capacity of the theater for the citizen assembly of a major city like Ephesus, and at least four times the seating capacity of the theater in Sepphoris, a major Galilean city; to address such a crowd was no small feat.

6:11. The head of the Jewish household customarily gave thanks before (and normally after) the meal. Miracles of multiplying food appear in the *Old Testament (cf., e.g., 1 Kings 17:16; 19:8) and occasionally in Jewish tradition (cf. the oil in late traditions about the Maccabees) and Greco-Roman texts; the background here is 2 Kings 4 (see comment on Jn 6:8-9) and especially the manna of Exodus 16 (see comment on Jn 6:31-33).

6:12. Greco-Roman moralists and Jewish teachers abhorred waste; although the extra bread has been provided miraculously, its provision is not to be taken for granted and squandered.

6:13. The leftovers are considerably more than they started with. It was a Roman custom always to have some food left over after a meal to indicate more than adequate provision. Jesus reveals himself as the ultimate host.

6:14. "The Prophet" implies the prophet like Moses of Deuteronomy 18:15-18. In Moses' day, God had miraculously provided bread from heaven, manna. At Passover season (Jn 6:4) hopes for deliverance ran high, because the Jewish people rehearsed how God had delivered them from their oppressors by the hand of Moses.

6:15. Some other first-century leaders gathered large followings in the wilderness who believed that they could perform signs like Moses or Joshua and overthrow the Romans; see comment on 6:14. The crowds wanted a worker of earthly miracles and an earthly leader like Moses (some Jewish traditions—*Philo, the *rabbis, etc.—viewed Moses as a king; cf. Deut 33:4-5); but this was not Jesus' mission (6:63). Perhaps threatened by the earthly emperor's claims to authority (see the introduction to Revelation), John's readers may have taken warning from this passage.

6:16-21
Lord of the Sea

In the context of John's discussion of Jesus as the New Passover, new manna and one greater than Moses, Jesus' miracle on the sea may have reminded his first readers of Israel's crossing the sea in the days of Moses.

6:16-19. Squalls were frequent on the lake. Given where they are traveling, they had probably already gone over halfway when caught in the storm; turning back is no longer an option. Fishing boats were equipped with oars; the sail would be counterproductive in this storm.

6:20. "It is I" (v. 20) is literally "I am." "It is I" is a legitimate way to translate the phrase, and no doubt how Jesus intends the *disciples to understand it; but given the context of Jesus walking on water, the nuance of deity in "I am" (Ex 3:14; Is 41:4; 43:10, 13) is probably present. Several pagan miracleworkers claimed to be able to walk on water, but these were not part of Palestinian Jewish tradition. In the Old Testament, Moses, Joshua, Elijah and Elisha all parted bodies of water, but only God trod upon the water (Job 9:8; cf. Ps 77:20).

6:21. The boat being instantly at its destination has no exact Old Testament parallels, but the *Spirit had sometimes carried prophets from one place to another almost instantly (e.g., Ezek 8:3; 11:24—probably in a vision; cf. 1 Kings 18:12; 2 Kings 2:16).

6:22-29
Proper Motives

6:22-23. A large, culturally Greek-oriented city on the lake of Galilee, Tiberias was named for the emperor Tiberius and built by Herod Antipas on the site of a graveyard. This site effectively kept the most religious Jews out of the city and allowed Herod to dole out favors to allies without interference from other powerful Jews. It does not appear in the *New Testament record apart from this mention and, like Sepphoris, the other large city of Galilee (also very *Hellenized), does not seem to have been frequented by Jesus.

6:24-26. The crowd wants to follow a prophet who will provide free food and political deliverance—another Moses. But they miss the central thrust of Jesus' mission (cf. 6:15).

6:27-29. The dialogue between Jesus and the crowd plays on the term *work;* Judaism stressed righteous works, but Jesus singles out one work: faith in him (Jewish teachers praised Abraham's "work" of faith in God, but Jesus' demand is more specific). They then demand from Jesus a "work," which now means a sign (v. 30), as it sometimes does in Jewish literature. The "seal" (v. 27) means that God has attested Jesus; cf. comment on 3:33.

6:30-59
Jesus as the New Manna

This passage is a regular Jewish *midrash, or homily, on Exodus 16:15 and Psalm 78:24, which Jesus quotes in John 6:31. Jesus paraphrases, explains and expounds in a manner characteristic of ancient Jewish teachers, yet his hearers fail to understand him. Ancient teachers sometimes made their lectures hard to understand to sort out genuine followers from the masses.

6:30-31. The crowd still wants him to act as the new Moses they expect—on an earthly, political level. Many Jewish people expected manna to be restored in the world to come. Like other ancient writers, John was free to paraphrase his material in his own words; here the crowd cites Scripture as if they are *rabbis in a debate (Ex 16:4, 15; cf. Ps. 78:24; John seems to know and use both Hebrew and Greek versions of these texts).

6:32-33. One method of Jewish exposition was "Do not read this text as saying *x*, but rather *y*." Jesus says, "Not Moses, but God really gave this bread." His hearers would have to agree; that was technically how Moses had put it (Ex 16:4, 15; cf. Deut 8:3). Like many other interpreters of his day (see, e.g., the *Dead Sea Scrolls), Jesus is concerned to apply the biblical text to their present situation.

6:34. They hear him on a different level from the meaning he intends (cf. 4:15), so he explains further. The ignorance of opponents or minor characters was often used as a foil to further a main argument throughout ancient literature (*Plato, *rabbis, novels, etc.).

6:35-40. Jewish expositors had already often used manna as a symbol for spiritual food, God's *law, or Torah/Wisdom/Word. The dead would be raised to *eternal life "on the last day," the day of the Lord, when God would transform the world and inaugurate his eternal *kingdom.

6:41-43. They continue to hear him on the wrong level, even though he clearly refers to *eternal life and not literal bread. Their "grumbling" alludes to the grumbling of Israel in the wilderness against the first Moses.

6:44-46. Most Jewish people believed in both human choice and God's sovereignty. The argument here stresses that those in relationship with the Father will recognize Jesus; those who do not recognize him do not know the Father either.

6:47-51. Jesus contrasts the new and old manna in good *midrashic style, like a good Jewish expositor.

6:52. Again they interpret him too literally. Jewish people had many forbidden foods, but all the Greco-Roman world abhorred cannibalism (which some abominable cults and some barbarians reportedly practiced occasionally). Romans later misinterpreted Christian language about the Lord's Supper: "eating the body and blood of their Lord" sounded like cannibalism to outsiders and thus aroused more persecution against the *church.

6:53. Eating the flesh of the Passover lamb was required (Ex 12:8); but drinking the blood of the lamb (or of any creature) was always forbidden (Lev 17:10-11). A thoughtful interpreter, however, might have also recalled the expression "the blood of grapes," meaning wine (Gen 49:11), which was essential to the Passover meal.

6:54-59. On the literal level (cannibalism and drinking blood) obeying Jesus' statement should have merited judgment, not salvation; thus they are confused.

6:60-71
Perseverance and Apostasy

6:60-61. The *disciples' grumbling recalls how the Israelites treated Moses in the wilderness. "Stumbling" was a common figure of speech for sinning or falling away.

6:62. Here Jesus may use a standard Jewish "how much more" argument: If you cannot receive the message of the cross, how much more difficult will it be for you to accept my *resurrection and return to the Father?

6:63. Jesus provides here the interpretive key to what preceded: he is not speaking literally, as if they are to eat his literal flesh; he speaks of his gift of the *Spirit. Many Jewish interpreters were masters at figurative interpretation; but his followers still fail to understand him (6:66).

6:64-65. On Jesus' knowledge see 2:23-25.

6:66. John portrays the departure of these *disciples as apostasy, which Judaism regarded as one of the worst sins.

6:67-71. Even among his closest followers, one is a betrayer. That even Jesus faced such betrayal would encourage John's readers, who had experienced some apostates in their own churches (see the discussion of setting in the introduction to 1 John).

7:1-9
The Unbelief of Jesus' Brothers

7:1. In Jesus' day, Galilee and Judea were under separate jurisdictions (that of Antipas and the Roman prefect, respectively), so that someone in trouble in one part of the country would be safer to remain in the other part. In John's day, regional religious differences seem to have been increasing, with Christians being concentrated in Galilee and the *rabbinic movement gaining more allies in Judea.

7:2. The Feast of Tabernacles was one of the three most important festivals of the Jewish year and was celebrated for eight days in Jerusalem. Jewish pilgrims from throughout the Roman and Parthian world would gather. The men would live in booths constructed on rooftops or elsewhere, commemorating God's faithfulness to his people when they lived in booths in the wilderness (women and children were not required to live in the booths). This feast was known for its joyous celebration.

7:3-4. From the standpoint of general ancient political theory, the advice of Jesus' brothers is correct; they may not know the specific matter of the Jerusalem authorities' opposition. Most teachers taught in public places. Frank or open speech (v. 4) was considered virtuous, secret acts deceitful.

7:5. But Jesus' brothers lack the proper faith to understand his mission; their unbelief could encourage John's readers in their own struggles with unbelieving families.

7:6-9. Pious Jewish men who lived as near as Galilee were supposed to go to the feast. It would be normal for Jesus to travel with his extended family (*Josephus spoke of whole towns going). The issue is not that he will not go, but that he will only go "secretly" at first, so as not to hasten the appropriate time of his execution (cf. 7:6 with 2:4).

7:10-36
Divided Opinions

7:10. Greco-Roman biographers often liked to describe their subjects' appearances, flattering or not. That none of the Gospels does so suggests that Jesus' appearance may have been average enough to allow him to pass unnoticed in a crowd: probably curly black hair, brown skin, perhaps a little over five feet in height—unlike the Aryan pictures of him that circulate in some Western churches. (The *Shroud of Turin, which is purported to be Jesus' burial cloth, makes him taller, in the epic Hebrew tradition—1 Sam 9:2. But its authority is disputed.) Although *Diaspora Jewish men, like Greek and Roman men, were normally clean-shaven, coins portray Palestinian Jews in this period with full beards and hair down to their shoulders.

7:11-12. "One who leads astray the multitude" (cf. NASB) or "one who deceives the people" (cf. NIV, NRSV) was a serious charge, applied to those who led other Jews to idolatry or apostasy. Deuteronomy 13 prescribes death as the penalty, and some *rabbis even felt that such persons should be given no chance to *repent, lest they be able to secure forgiveness though their followers had perished. Some Jewish sources as early as the second century charged Jesus with this crime.

7:13. The "Jews" here are clearly the Jerusalem authorities, who correspond in John's day to the leaders repressing not only the Jewish Christians but also any other views within Judaism that they saw as competing with their own position.

7:14. Teaching was often done in public places, including in the temple courts. Some popular teachers drew large crowds there.

7:15. Most children in the Greco-Roman world could not afford even a primary education. But Palestinian Jewish children, except perhaps from the poorest homes (which a carpenter's family was not), would learn how to read and recite the Bible, whether or not they could write. The issue here is not that Jesus is illiterate (he is not), but that he has never formally studied Scripture with an advanced teacher, yet he expounds as well as any of the scholars without citing earlier scholars' opinions.

7:16-17. Learning by doing was a standard part of Jewish education, which included imitating one's teacher. (Sometimes this may have been taken too far. One *disciple was said to have hidden under his *rabbi's bed to learn the proper way to perform the marriage act. When the rabbi caught him, however, he did not commend this disciple for his thorough aspiration to learn.)

7:18-19. False prophets were technically to be executed; but the prophet like Moses was to be followed (Deut 18:9-22).

7:20. Demoniacs were often thought to act insanely; in this case the crowd thinks Jesus is paranoid. But even this charge could imply the suspicion that he is a false prophet (7:12): false prophets were also thought to channel spirits (indeed, many pagan magicians claimed such spirit-guides). The penalty for false prophets was death. *Josephus tells of one true prophetic figure in this period (he does not quite label him a "prophet") who was regarded as insane and demon possessed; the Gospels mention another (John the Baptist—Mt 11:18).

7:21-24. Jesus asks the crowd to reason consistently (sound and fair judgment was paramount in Jewish teaching): why is it wrong for him to heal supernaturally on the sabbath, when circumcision (which wounds) is permitted on the sabbath? A later first-century *rabbi argued similarly: If circumcising on the eighth day takes precedence over the sabbath (and it does), saving a whole life also does (as was commonly agreed). Some practices at the festivals (such as killing the Passover lamb and waving the lulab, i.e., palm branch, at the Feast of Tabernacles) likewise took precedence over the sabbath.

7:25-27. Some scholars have pointed to a tradition attested in later sources that the *Messiah would be hidden for a time before he appeared, and thus no one would know where he was from (cf. the irony in 9:29).

7:28-29. Jesus declares that where he is "from" is obvious: he is "sent from" the Father. This expression means that he is a commissioned agent, an authorized representative, of the Father.

7:30-31. In most Jewish traditions, the Messiah was not a miracle worker, except to the extent that the works of a new Moses figure would validate his prophetic claim to lead the people.

7:32. In Jesus' day the *Pharisees as a whole had no authority to arrest anyone, although the chief priests did; but John updates the language for readers of his own day. The main Palestinian opposition that Jewish Christians faced in the decades after A.D. 70 came from Pharisees. The officers are the Levitical temple guards.

7:33-36. John again employs the motif of misinterpretation: if the Jewish authorities misinterpret Jesus so badly, how can they claim to understand the Scriptures rightly? The "Dispersion" (NASB) refers to the Jewish people scattered throughout the Greek world; Jesus' hearers suspect that he will use the foreign Jews as a base of operation for reaching the *Gentiles to whom they seek to be witnesses. (The book of Acts indicates that this outreach actually occurred.)

7:37-39
Rivers of Water

7:37. The "last day" of the Feast of Tabernacles (7:2) probably refers to the eighth day. For at least the first seven days of the feast, priests marched in procession from the Pool of Siloam to the temple and poured out water at the base of the altar. Pilgrims to the feast watched this ritual, which Jews throughout the Roman world thus knew; it was even commemorated on souvenir jars they could take home with them.

7:38. The public reading of Scripture at this feast included the one passage in the Prophets that emphasized this feast, Zechariah 14, which was interpreted in conjunction with Ezekiel 47. Together these texts taught that rivers of living water would flow forth from the temple (in Jewish teaching, at the very center of the earth, from the foundation stone of the temple), bringing life to all the earth. The water-drawing ceremony (7:37) (originally meant to secure rain) pointed toward this hope.

Because the water of verse 38 flows to and not from the believer (v. 39), 7:37-38 may be punctuated to read: "If anyone thirsts, let this one come to me; and let whoever believes in me drink. As the Scripture says . . ." (The original manuscripts had no punctuation.) Verse 38 may thus declare that Jesus fulfills the Scriptures read at the feast, as the foundation stone of a new temple, the source of the water of life (cf. 19:34; Rev 22:1).

7:39. Most of Judaism did not believe that the *Spirit was prophetically active in their own time but expected the full outpouring of the Spirit in the *messianic age or the world to come. Water usually symbolized Torah (*law) or wisdom in Jewish texts, but John follows *Old Testament precedent in using it for the Spirit (Is 44:3; Ezek 36:24-27; Joel 2:28).

7:40-52
The Division Deepens

7:40. "The Prophet" is the "prophet like Moses" (see on 6:14-15), in whose time God also gave living water in the wilderness.

7:41-44. Contradicting what others had said in 7:27, some people cite the place where the *Messiah was to originate, based on Micah 5:2; that the Messiah was of Davidic descent was unanimously held. Although John included no birth *narratives, the conjunction of Matthew, Luke and widespread Christian traditions known by the early second century (to pagans interrogated by Hadrian) suggests that John's readers know that Christ was born in Bethlehem. They would thus regard Jesus' opponents here as ignorant.

7:45-46. Powerful and wise speech was highly regarded in antiquity; in that era, listening to public speakers was a form of entertainment as well as of learning (the former function has been largely replaced in affluent societies by television). The temple guards would have heard many teachers in the temple, yet they are particularly impressed by this one.

7:47. On the "misleader" see comment on 7:12.

7:48. The *Pharisees are clearly mistaken here (cf. 3:1-2). John uses irony, a common ancient literary technique, to underscore his point: Jesus' opponents are closed-minded and dense.

7:49. Trained *rabbis often looked down on the *'amme ha'aretz,* "the people of the land," common people who did not even try to follow rabbinic interpretations of the *law. Many texts indicate the animosity between Pharisaic rabbis and *'amme ha'aretz* (e.g., Akiba contended that before becoming a rabbi he was an *'am ha'aretz* and wanted to beat up rabbis). On a lesser scale, analogous attitudes may sometimes be observed among educated elites today; but the rabbis reasonably believed that one could not live the law without knowing it, and they did not think that *'amme ha'aretz* knew it.

7:50-51. Given their attitude to those who do not know the law (7:49), John's irony (cf. comment on 7:48) is eloquent here: Nicodemus calls them on a basic matter of legal procedure accepted by Moses and all Jewish interpreters.

7:52. This response reflects regional prejudice rather than knowledge of the Scriptures: 2 Kings 14:25 demonstrates that they were mistaken. Later *rabbis admitted that prophets arose from every tribe in Galilee.

7:53—8:11
The Woman Taken in Adultery

Omitted by all the earliest manuscripts, this passage is generally agreed to be a later addition to the Fourth Gospel. Although it may be a true story, as many scholars think, it should not be read as part of the context in John.

7:53—8:1. For Jesus spending nights on the Mount of Olives, cf. 18:1-2; Luke 22:39; cf. also Mark 11:1, 11.

8:2. Teachers often taught in the temple courts; cf. 7:14.

8:3. John, who deals only with "*Pharisees" and chief priests, nowhere mentions "*scribes," who are more frequent in the other Gospels; scribes functioned as teachers of the *law.

8:4-5. The law demanded the execution of this woman, but Rome had removed capital jurisdiction from Jewish courts, except for temple violations. Thus the Jewish leaders test whether Jesus will reject the law, compromising his patriotic Jewish following, or reject Roman rule, which will allow them to accuse him to the Romans.

8:6-8. God wrote the Ten Commandments with his finger (Ex 31:18; Deut 9:10); perhaps Jesus writes the first line of the tenth commandment in the *Septuagint of Exodus 20: "You shall not covet your neighbor's wife." This text would declare them all guilty of adultery (Mt 5:28). This proposal is at best speculation, but we have no better clues concerning what Jesus might have written with his finger; perhaps the most reasonable other option is that he is merely passing time until they leave.

The witnesses were normally the first to throw the stones, but false witnesses were to pay the same penalty they had hoped to inflict on their victim (Deut 17:7; 19:19).

8:9-11. It was a commonplace of Jewish teaching that even the most pious had committed sins. God had the power to judge or forgive sins.

8:12-29
Accepting the Witness of the Light

In the likelihood that 8:1-11 is not part of the context, 8:12—10:21 still takes place on the last day of the Feast of Tabernacles (7:2, 37).

8:12. Jewish literature was generous with the title "light of the world," applying it to Israel, Jerusalem, the patriarchs, the *Messiah, God, famous rabbis and the law (cf. 1:4-5); but always it refers to something of ultimate significance. One of the most spectacular celebrations of the Feast of Tabernacles involved torches that lit up the city; this feast, along with Hanukkah (10:22), was thus known for splendid lighting. That Jesus offers his light to the whole world, to all the nations, may suggest an allusion to Isaiah 42:6. Walking in darkness (cf. Jn 9:4; 11:9) is a natural metaphor for stumbling (Is 59:10; Jer 13:16), falling from the right way (Jer 18:15; Mal 2:8) or being destroyed (Ps 27:2; Jer 20:11).

8:13-18. The law of Moses required two witnesses to confirm any case (Deut 19:15; cf. 17:6), and subsequent Jewish interpretation made this requirement stricter; Jesus employs the standard Jewish argument "how much more": if the witness of two men is valid, how much more that of Father and Son?

Jews spoke of the *law as "God's law" or "our law"; *rabbis presented only their pagan and heretical challengers as calling it "your law" (8:17). In John (who argues that Jesus fulfills the law), however, this expression is surely ironic: see the introduction on "the Jews."

8:19-20. Their response is (v. 19): If he is a witness, he must appear in the court; and they complain that they have no access to the voice of God. Jesus' reply is: I know; that is the problem. The "treasury" (v. 20) was next to the Court of Women, where the lighting ceremony (8:12) and dancing took place throughout the nights of the festival. The treasury itself may have been used only for storage, but 8:20 can be read, "near the treasury."

8:21-22. Most Jewish pietists disapproved of suicide; they do not see Jesus as a particularly pious person here. Yet John's irony is again at work: Jesus does return to the Father through his death on the cross.

8:23. The contrast between the realm above (God's realm) and the realm below (where mortals lived) was common in Jewish *apocalyptic literature, and its meaning should be plain to the hearers if they are open to hear his point.

8:24-25. Dying in sin was a serious matter, for at death one's final opportunity for *repentance had passed (cf. Ezek 18:21-32). (For this reason, Jewish teachers exhorted those being executed to confess their sins and believe their death would atone for their sins.) Jesus agrees that one must repent but insists that genuine repentance must include faith in him.

8:26-27. According to Jewish law, an agent must accurately represent his sender, and to the extent that he did so was backed by his sender's full authorization.

8:28-29. "Lifting up" (cf. 3:14; 12:32)

is from the *Septuagint of Isaiah 52:13—which in context refers to the crucifixion (Is 52:14—53:12).

8:30-47
Debating Parentage

8:30-31. Although Jesus' listeners initially believe, they are ready to kill him by the end of the passage (8:59; cf. Ex 4:31; 5:21). John's readers would reflect on this report and be encouraged that their Lord had faced what they were facing; some members of their *churches had also defected and begun to betray Christians to persecution (see comment on 6:67-71; 1 John).

8:32. The Greek concept of truth emphasized reality; the *Old Testament word translated "truth" had more to do with integrity or faithfulness to one's word or character. Jewish thought characterized God as the Truth, so Jesus' hearers should realize that he refers specifically to God's truth in the Jewish sense.

8:33. Although Jesus' interlocutors were never themselves slaves, their reference to Abraham shows that they understand Jesus as referring to the Jewish people as a whole. Jewish teachers generally acknowledged that their people had been subjected under the yoke of at least four kingdoms: Babylon, Persia, Greece and Rome. But many teachers believed that these kingdoms were only servants of God, and that he would ultimately break the yokes of the other nations (an extreme form of this belief led to the revolt of A.D. 66-70). They taught that the other nations were ruled by guardian angels and the stars, but that Israel was ruled by God alone.

8:34. Philosophers often used "free" to mean free from false ideas or from concern; Judaism spoke of being free from sin. Jewish teachers believed that because Israel had the *law, the evil impulse that made the *Gentiles so sinful could not enslave them.

8:35. Old Testament law mandated that Jewish slaves be freed in certain years, and under Gentile laws slaves could be freed or sold to other households; a son, however, was always part of a household. Jesus may also make another allusion here: "house" (which can mean "household," "family" or "home") may include a wordplay with God's house, the temple (2:16); only the "sons" will have a permanent share there (Ezek 46:16-17; cf. also Is 56:5).

8:36-37. In popular Jewish belief, descent from Abraham virtually guaranteed salvation except for the most wicked; Israel was chosen and destined for salvation in him.

8:38-39. "Father" could mean "ancestor," and on that level Abraham was their father (v. 37—although most had some *Gentile converts in their ancestry). But metaphorically a father was someone whose ways one imitated, often a teacher, or whose nature one revealed, such as a spiritual progenitor.

8:40. Abraham was used as the ultimate model for Jewish piety and hospitality, and Jewish tradition celebrated his reception of God's disguised messengers in Genesis 18.

8:41. To suggest that someone had one father by law but another father by nature was to suggest that one's mother was guilty of adultery. Recognizing this implication, the interlocutors insist on the purity of their descent: "children of Abraham" was equivalent in Jewish literature to "children of God" (cf., e.g., Ex 4:22), because God had adopted Abraham's descendants. (Some scholars have also seen here an allusion to the later *rabbinic charge against Jesus that his mother bore him to a Roman soldier rather than as a virgin, though this is not clear in this debate.)

8:42-47. That the devil was the original murderer (cf. 8:37, 40) and denier of truth (cf. 8:32) is irrefutable; Jewish tradition stressed that his lie had led to Adam's death (cf. Gen 3). Because Jesus' interlocutors want to kill him and reject his truth, their behavior demonstrates who is their real father; the issue is not ethnic but spiritual.

8:48-59
Greater Than Abraham

8:48. Jesus' fraternizing with *Samaritans (4:40) would not play well to a Jerusalem audience, but his hearers are probably unaware of that. The basis for this charge is apparently similar theology: Samaritans insulted the temple and challenged the Jewish people's exclusive heritage in Abraham (cf. comment on 4:12). The charge of demon possession (also 10:20) challenges his prophetic credibility (see comment on 7:20). The discussion is thus becoming quite hostile at this point. It also reflects John's irony: only the Samaritans (4:9) and Pilate (18:35) recognize that Jesus is *Jewish.*

8:49-50. According to Jewish law, one who rejects a person's appointed agent also insults and rejects the one who sent that agent.

8:51-53. Most Jewish people except the *Sadducees would have agreed that Abraham and the prophets were spiritually alive with God; but Jesus' opponents here take his reference to death as literal, physical death. (Even in one Jewish tradition where Abraham did not want to die, God made special arrangements to get him to give in.)

8:54-55. "He is our God" was the basic confession of the covenant in the *Old Testament (e.g., Ex 6:7; Lev 26:12; 1 Chron 17:22; Jer 31:33; Ezek 36:28); those loyal to the covenant—those who truly keep God's law—were said in the Old Testament to "know" God (e.g., Jer 9:24; 31:31-34; Hos 2:20).

8:56. Jewish tradition emphasized that Abraham had been shown the future kingdoms that would oppress Israel and the *messianic era beyond them.

8:57-58. Fifty was the minimum age for involvement in some kinds of public service.

If Jesus merely wished to imply that he existed before Abraham, he should have said, "Before Abraham was, I *was.*" But "I am" was a title for God (Ex 3:14), which suggests that Jesus is claiming more than that he merely existed before Abraham. This title of God may have been fresh on the minds of Jesus' hearers at the feast: during the Feast of Tabernacles, the priests were said to utter God's words in Isaiah: "I am the Lord, I am he" (Is 43:10, 13). (It is not certain, however, whether this tradition is early enough to serve as background for the Fourth Gospel.)

8:59. Jesus' hearers do not miss his point in 8:58 and take his words as blasphemy (a mere claim to *messiahship was not considered blasphemous, although it could be offensive; they understood him to claim deity). But their reaction to Jesus puts him in good company (Ex 17:4; Num 14:10; 1 Sam 30:6). The temple was constructed from massive stone blocks, not the sort of stones that people could throw; but in Jesus' day construction was still going on, and a mob could have found objects to throw, as *Josephus says *Zealots later did in the temple and a crowd did in a *synagogue.

God had hidden some of his servants under similar circumstances before (Jer 36:26); here Jesus hides himself. Jesus' departure from the temple is portrayed as *Ichabod:* the glory had departed (Ezek 10—11); the departure of God's presence on account of Israel's sin was a common theme in later Jewish texts.

9:1-12
Healing the Blind

9:1. Blind people could make a living only by public charity, and they could make it best near the temple, where many people passed and people would tend to think charitably (cf. Acts 3:2). The *disciples see this blind man as they are leaving the temple area (8:59).
9:2. Jewish teachers believed that suffering, including blindness, was often due to sin; one could suffer for one's parents' sins or even for a sin committed by mother or fetus during the pregnancy.
9:3-5. Jesus uses commonplace images: no one (except night watchmen and shepherds) works in the dark (v. 4); on the light of the world, see comment on 8:12.
9:6. Spittle was sometimes used for healing in pagan circles, so it would naturally represent an agent of healing in popular thought. But spittle was still more widely considered vulgar and gross, and its application would make the man uncomfortable if he knows what it is.
9:7. It is not clear whether "Siloam" meant "sent," but Greek teachers as well as Jewish teachers from *Philo to the *rabbis commonly made arguments based on wordplays, which were often based on fanciful etymologies.

Although Siloam was used as a water supply and for *baptizing converts to Judaism, it has more direct significance here. This was probably still the last day of the Feast of Tabernacles (7:2, 37), and the water of Siloam was the sacred water used for this feast (see comment on 7:37-38). Here Jesus employs the ritual water (cf. 2:6; 3:5), but it works only because the man is "sent."
9:8-12. Those blind from birth (9:1) were not known to recover (9:32)—at least not without direct supernatural intervention. On healing through washing, cf. 2 Kings 5:10-14.

9:13-23
Interrogating the Witnesses

The key word in 9:12-31 is "know": everyone claims repeatedly what they know and do not know. The *Pharisees, who supposedly know the law, turn out to know nothing; whereas the healed man, who knows only Jesus, has had an experience with God that his more scholarly interrogators cannot refute.
9:13. Local elders (or in some places, like *Essene communities, priests filled this role) served as judges in local communities before A.D. 70; but *Pharisaic teachers gradually began to take on this role in Palestine after 70. Writing in the 90s, John uses the language of his day to communicate the point to his readers, many of whom have faced opposition or expulsion from their own *synagogues (cf. comment on 9:24-34).
9:14-16. This is a natural Pharisaic response on the sabbath (5:9-12; see comment on Mk 2:23—3:6). Kneading (dough, and by analogy clay) was one of thirty-nine classes of work forbidden on the sabbath. Pharisees were divided among themselves on many issues in Jesus' day, and they had still not settled those issues by the end of the first century, when John was writing.
9:17. "Prophet" is an inadequate but positive title (cf. 4:19, 44; 6:14; 7:40).
9:18-21. The blind man could have remained under his parents' roof at night and earned his keep by begging in the day, although this is not clear. But the reason the Jewish leaders ask his parents about his blindness is that they would know if he was born blind. Both Greek and Jewish courts of law could compel persons to witness against their will. After age thirteen a Jewish boy became responsible for his own keeping

of the commandments (this point is especially clear in later *rabbinic texts but was probably already implied in coming-of-age rituals in this period).

9:22-23. *Pharisaic law was scrupulous about cross-examining witnesses fairly and without prejudice; these interrogators thus violate Pharisaic ethical teaching. Excommunication was one of the severest forms of discipline administered by a *synagogue community and was apparently rare and thus very harsh in the time of Jesus.

9:24-34
Excommunicating a Disciple

John's readers had faced the danger or reality of expulsion from their *synagogues (Jn 16:2; cf. 12:42-43). The faithfulness of this man (in contrast to the betrayal of the man in 5:14-16) would encourage them to remain faithful too.

9:24. "Give glory to God" may be an oath or confession formula demanding truthful witness (cf. Josh 7:19).

9:25-27. Diligent cross-examination was important in Jewish law.

9:28. *Rabbis spoke of students of Scripture as *disciples of Moses; *Philo often spoke of being Moses' student. John's point, however, is that these interrogators are wrong (5:45).

9:29-30. The interrogators confess that they do not know where Jesus is from. The circumstances of birth of a person accused of leading people astray would sometimes be investigated to determine if the misleader was an illegitimate child; if this point is in view here at all, the interrogators have failed to investigate the matter.

9:31. This view reflects good Jewish piety: everyone taught that God heard the pious but rejected the prayers of the ungodly (cf. Ps 34:15; Prov 15:8, 29; 21:27; 28:9). This is the major premise in the healed man's argument.

9:32-33. The minor premise of the argument (9:31) is that an extraordinary miracle was done; the conclusion is that Jesus is a righteous man. Syllogism—the practice of demonstrating a conclusion from two accepted premises—was a common way of arguing a case in antiquity.

Blindness from birth was thought an especially difficult ailment to cure; in the rare instances when such extraordinary healings were claimed at a pagan healing shrine (e.g., empty eye sockets filled), they became a cause for much praise to the pagan god held responsible for them. (The man's "never since the world's beginning" is emphatic, and probably rhetorical overstatement; there were a few claimed exceptions in the *Gentile world of which he was probably unaware.)

9:34. Later *rabbis emphasized being humble and teachable; but despite the proper Jewish argument he gave in 9:31-33, the authorities expel this man on the premise that he was born in sin—which the reader knows to be false (9:2-3). How formal excommunications were in this period is unclear, but he is certainly expelled from participating in the local center of religious life (cf. comment on 9:22-23).

9:35-41
The Seeing and the Blind

9:35-38. The healed man responds like John's Jewish Christian readers: in faith, unlike their opponents.

9:39-41. The reversal of physical and spiritual blindness is a motif in the prophets (e.g., Is 42:16-19; Jer 5:21); the religious authorities, who are sure they are not spiritually blind, are the blindest of all.

10:1-18
Shepherd, Sheep and Robbers

The original text of the Bible had no

chapter breaks; this passage continues Jesus' words to the *Pharisees in 9:41. It is based on *Old Testament images of God as the shepherd of Israel (Gen 48:15; 49:24; Ps 23:1; 28:9; 77:20; 78:71; Is 40:11; Ezek 34:11-31), of Israel as his flock (Ps 74:1; 78:52; 79:13; 100:3) and of abusive or unfaithful religious leaders as destroyers of his flock (Jer 23:1-2; Ezek 34). Faithful human shepherds (Jer 3:15) included Moses, David (2 Sam 5:2; Ps 78:71-72) and the Davidic *Messiah (Mic 5:4).

10:1-2. During the cool winter months, sheep were kept inside a pen at night; the pen usually had a stone wall, which might have briers on top of it. (Winter was approaching at the time of this feast.) Jewish law distinguished thieves from robbers: the former broke in, whereas the latter often lived in the wilderness and assaulted passersby. Shepherds continually had to guard against losing sheep to either kind of enemy.

10:3-4. In the Old Testament, Israel "heard God's voice" when they obeyed the *law and his message through his prophets. Those who were truly his sheep—in covenant relationship with God—knew him (see comment on 10:14-15). (John's readers hear him through the *Spirit, a practice that most of Judaism did not believe was possible in their own day; cf. 16:13-15.) It is said that shepherds customarily knew each of their sheep by name. In the Old Testament, God called his special ones, his closest servants, "by name" (Ex 33:12, 17; cf. Is 43:1).

10:5. In this context the strangers are the thieves and robbers (v. 1)—the Pharisees—who have sought to mislead the sheep (9:40-41). The *synagogue leaders who expelled John's Jewish Christian readers claim to be true shepherds, but when John's audience hears this passage they will think of them quite differently.

10:6-9. Sheep were led "in" and "out" (Num 27:17; 2 Sam 5:2) of the sheepfold to and from pasture. Several scholars have cited a modern example of shepherds sleeping across the gateway to serve both as shepherd and door, but Jesus probably alternates between images simply because he fulfills more than one role; like God in the Old Testament, he is Israel's shepherd, but he is also the way to the Father.

10:10-11. The thief (in the context, unfaithful leaders; cf. v. 5) acts for his own good, not that of the flock (hungry thieves might steal sheep for food); a shepherd risks his life to protect his flock from animals and thieves. *Pharisees considered shepherds members of an unclean profession, and aristocrats despised them as vulgar lower-class workers; thus Jesus' opponents would not readily identify with the protagonist of the story. "Life" was short for "eternal life," the life of the world to come, in Jewish parlance; Jesus provides this relationship with himself in the present. See comment on 3:16.

10:12-13. A hired helper was not responsible for attacks from wild animals (Ex 22:13) and worked for pay, not because the sheep were his own. Religious leaders who let God's sheep be scattered are not his true agents or representatives, because they are not concerned with what concerns him (Jer 23:1; Ezek 34:6).

10:14-15. The Old Testament often described Israel's covenant relationship with God as "knowing" him, which meant having an intimate and obedient relationship with him (e.g., Jer 31:34; Hos 6:6). See John 10:3-4 and 16:13-15.

10:16-18. The image of gathering the folds together into one flock in Old Testament language meant gathering the dispersed sheep of Israel, scattered among the nations (cf. Ezek 37:21-24;

Mic 2:12). The regathering of Israel in the end was one of the basic hopes of ancient Judaism, reflected in writings and prayers. But Jesus may here refer to the *Gentiles.

10:19-21. The Jewish community again experiences schism over Jesus' identity (cf. also 7:43; 9:16), as it was also experiencing in John's day. On charges of demonization see comment on 7:20.

10:22-42
In the Temple at Hanukkah

10:22. Hanukkah, the Feast of Dedication, was not a required pilgrimage festival, but the eight-day celebration of lights in the temple was beautiful, and many pious Jews from nearby Galilee would come to Jerusalem. It was the next festival after those immediately connected to the Feast of Tabernacles (7:1—10:21).

10:23. The outer part of the temple had porches on all four sides; the Royal Porch, on the south, had four rows of pillars. Solomon's Porch was on the east side of the temple, with two rows of pillars (as on the west and north sides). The south portico was called Solomon's because people thought that it contained remains of Solomon's temple. Greek public buildings often included such porches, and they had long been a popular place for public lectures and discussions. It was cool in Jerusalem in winter, so people would be especially inclined to walk under the colonnades.

10:24. See 8:25; cf. also the discussion of the theme of the *messianic secret in the introduction to Mark. These Jews would have either misunderstood his claim or used it to charge him with sedition (cf. 18:29-35).

10:25-27. On hearing Jesus' voice, cf. 10:3-4.

10:28-29. A shepherd who would protect his sheep against any thief or predator would have to be ready to pay a great price (10:12, 15), but this is the price of faithfulness (Jer 23:4).

10:30. His hearers might think of the relation between Israel and God, but Jesus' wording about his unity with the Father is too explicit for that: instead he echoes the basic confession of Judaism that God is one (Deut 6:4). For Jesus to be one with the Father (albeit distinct from him) is tantamount to a claim to deity.

10:31-33. Cf. 5:18, 8:59; as in the other instances, Jesus' opponents understand his claim to deity, even if they do not catch all the ramifications.

10:34. On "your *law" cf. 8:17. Psalm 82:6 in context refers to powerful people, probably the kings of the earth viewed as God's divine council; those kings considered themselves divine, but they would perish like mortals. In Jewish tradition, however, this verse was sometimes applied out of context to Israel as recipients of the divine law, as Jesus apparently knows.

10:35-36. Jesus responds with a standard Jewish "how much more" *(qal vahomer)* argument: if (as you read it) Israel was loosely called "gods," how do you object to me saying that I am God's Son, without even understanding my point?

Many commentators have argued that Jesus' being "sanctified" or set apart to his mission (cf. also 17:17) may relate to the context of the Feast of Hanukkah, or "Dedication" (10:22). Hanukkah commemorated the consecration, rededication or setting apart (as again holy) of the Jerusalem temple in the time of the *Maccabees in the second century B.C.

10:37-38. Jewish tradition emphasized right motives but allowed that obeying a commandment from inadequate motives was better than not obeying at all.

10:39-42. "Beyond the Jordan" presumably means Perea, in Jesus' day ruled, like Galilee, by Herod Antipas—and well outside the jurisdiction of the Jerusalem leaders.

11:1-16
Announcement of Lazarus's Sickness

11:1. Bethany was close to Jerusalem (v. 18); emphasizing Jesus' Galilean ministry, Mark omits this miracle and is followed by Matthew and Luke.

11:2-5. Visiting and praying for the sick was a pious obligation in Judaism, but Jesus' reputation as a healer is undoubtedly the main reason for informing him of Lazarus's sickness. Informing him would serve as a polite request (cf. 2:3).

11:6. It is a long walk from where Jesus is to Bethany, but Lazarus is already dead, perhaps by the time the messengers reach Jesus (11:14, 17)—it was only a day's journey each way, just over twenty miles. For temporary rebuffs to test faith, cf. 2:4.

11:7-8. Although the Jerusalem priesthood was respected in Galilee, it wielded more power and influence in Judea; Antipas, the ruler of Galilee, did not tolerate direct interference in his territory. (In John's day, the *Pharisaic establishment was also settled in Judea, where it undoubtedly wielded more influence than in Galilee.)

11:9-10. On walking in darkness and stumbling, see comment on 8:12.

11:11-16. Again the *disciples interpret Jesus too literally (v. 12)—although "sleep" was a common metaphor for death in Jewish texts and throughout the ancient world (Greek myth even portrayed Sleep and Death as twin brothers). But even though they may not understand that Jesus' death is the cost of giving Lazarus (and others) life, they are prepared to die with him (v. 16). As much as disciples loved their teachers, this is a rare expression of commitment in practice; in general, Jewish people emphasized only being prepared to die for God and his *law.

11:17-37
Comforting the Mourners

11:17-19. Visiting and consoling the bereaved in the days immediately following a close relative's loss was an essential duty of Jewish piety. The neighbors would provide the first meal after the funeral. Lazarus would have been buried on the day of his death.

11:20. The first week of deep grief after a close relative's burial would be spent mourning in one's house, sitting on the floor and visited by friends. This custom, called *shivah* (for "seven" days), is still practiced in Judaism today and is very helpful for releasing grief. Mourners abstained from adornment for the next three weeks and from common pleasures for the next year.

11:21-24. Prayers for comfort were standard, and this may be the import of verse 22. Conversely, Martha may be asking in verse 22 for her brother's resuscitation, and verse 24 may test Jesus, pressing him further for the favor (2 Kings 4:16; cf. 4:28). Ancient Near Eastern peoples often sought favors from benefactors in such self-effacing ways, as opposed to the more direct modern Western approach ("Hey, can I have . . . ?").

11:25-27. The common belief of Judaism in this period was that the dead would be raised bodily at the end; indeed, *Pharisees considered those who denied this doctrine (specifically *Sadducees) to be damned for doing so.

11:28-37. The time and consolation of an important religious teacher who had come a long distance would be especially meaningful, though local students and teachers of the law joined in funeral processions when it was possible for them to do so. Greek and Roman philosophers emphasized sobriety and remaining calm and untroubled by bereavement; Jesus prefers the traditional Jewish form of expressing grief.

11:38-44 Raising Lazarus

11:38. People were often buried in caves; stones, usually disk-shaped, would be rolled along a groove into place in front of the tomb, protecting its contents from animals, the elements and occasionally robbers.

11:39. The body would be wrapped and left lying on the floor in the tomb's antechamber; only after a year, when the flesh had rotted off, would family members return to collect the bones into a box, which they would then slide into a slot on the wall. After four days (11:17), decomposition was well under way, especially because it was no longer winter (11:55). Whatever spices they may have used to delay the stench (cf. comment on Mk 16:1) would no longer be effective.

11:40-42. On the preliminary prayer, cf. 1 Kings 18:36.

11:43-44. The deceased would be wrapped in long cloth strips. This wrapping was thorough, binding the limbs to keep them straight and even the cheeks to keep the mouth shut; the facecloth may have been a yard square. This tight wrapping would have made it hard enough for a living person to walk, not to mention a formerly dead person coming forth from the entrance to the tomb; this difficulty further underlines the miraculous nature of this event. Men could not wrap women's corpses, but women could wrap both men and women, so Lazarus may have been wrapped by his sisters.

11:45-57 The Religious People Plot to Kill Jesus

11:45-46. On the *Pharisees here, see comment on 7:32.

11:47-48. The Pharisees and chief priests call together literally a "*sanhedrin," probably referring here to the supreme court of Israel or those of its representatives who are available.

Their concern is a legitimate one validated by history: those perceived as political *messiahs threatened their own power and Judea's stability, inviting Roman intervention; the Romans accepted only one king, Caesar. *Josephus testified to this concern of the priestly aristocracy, and one reason Joseph Caiaphas maintained his office longer than any other high priest of the first century (A.D. 18-36) was that he kept the peace for the Romans. But this is another touch of John's irony (a common ancient literary device): this was their view, not that of the Romans (18:38; 19:12); and although they killed Jesus, the Romans ultimately did take away their temple and nation, in A.D. 70, anyway.

11:49. The high priesthood, like some Greek priesthoods (e.g., at Eleusis), had originally been a lifelong office. It had never been reduced to an annual assignment, like most priesthoods in Syria or Asia Minor, but John's "priest that year" may poke fun at how the Roman governor had power to change the high priests, or at how the high priest's deposed relative could still meddle so much in these affairs (18:13); or he may simply mean "high priest in the particular year of which we speak," because officials' terms were used to date events.

The high priest presided over the *Sanhedrin. To have a high priest inform his colleagues, "You do not know anything," is the epitome of John's irony.

11:50-53. Here the high priest means one thing on the level of his own hearers, but his words have another meaning that would be more obvious to John's readers: others (both Greeks and Jews) also believed that those appointed as God's representatives could sometimes prophesy (speak God's truth) without meaning to do so. Some Jewish traditions seem to associate *prophecy with the priesthood.

Sacrificing the few for the many makes good politics but bad religion: *Josephus claimed that King Agrippa II urged his people to forego vengeance for injustice for the sake of peace; but Jewish teachers said not to betray a single Israelite to rape or death even if the result would be the rape or execution of all.

11:54-55. The temple courts had countless pools for ritual purification; on this point, cf. also 2:6 and 3:25.

11:56-57. They could not believe someone as pious a religious teacher as Jesus is popularly supposed to be would not show up for one of the great pilgrimage festivals required by the *law, especially when he had to come only from Galilee.

12:1-8
Mary's Gratitude, and Dying to Live

For more details, see comment on Mark 14:1-11.

12:1-2. One "sat" at normal meals; one "reclined" on couches at special meals like feasts or banquets. Unless the Gospel writers simply adopt Greek language for the meals consistently (Greeks normally reclined), Jesus was invited to many banquets—this one probably in his honor. Early traveling teachers were often invited to lecture at meals in return for free meals and lodging.

12:3. The "pound" (NASB) or "pint" (NIV) may have been about twelve ounces. A flask would normally contain not more than an ounce, so Mary is tremendously extravagant here.

It was customary to anoint the heads of important guests, but a host would provide only water for their feet. Further, religious Jews resented married women who uncovered their heads and exposed their hair to men's gazes; because Mary's brother and sister but not her husband are mentioned, she may have been unmarried (thus young, widowed or divorced); but acting thus toward a famous (albeit single) *rabbi might still raise some pious eyebrows.

12:4-5. Some *rabbis delegated their school's financial concerns to their *disciples; some other groups, like the *Essenes and some Greek philosophers, held property in common. Only those whose virtue was most trusted were permitted to keep group funds (cf. 13:29); thus Judas's treachery is all the more scandalous.

12:6-7. On anointing corpses see comment on Mark 16:1; they were first anointed to clean them and then washed with water. This was an important act on Mary's part; those executed as criminals may have sometimes been denied anointing before burial (though not Jesus; see 19:39).

12:8. Jesus' reply probably contains an allusion to Deuteronomy 15:11, which urges generosity to the poor, who will always be in the land. He thus does not play down giving to the poor but plays up his impending death; he must be his followers' first commitment.

12:9-11. John's irony: those who receive life by Jesus' death must die because of it; witnesses get martyred. That the religious leaders put out a contract on Lazarus is further irony. Irony was a common ancient literary device.

12:12-22
The World Follows

12:12-18. See comment on Mark 11:8-11.

12:12-13. Those already present in Jerusalem typically welcomed pilgrims to the feast and strewed branches in their path. Palm branches were used at the Feast of Tabernacles but had to be brought from Jericho. They had been one of the nationalistic symbols of Judea since the days of the *Maccabees, were consistently used to celebrate military victories and probably stirred some political *messianic hopes among the people. "Hosanna" means "O save!"; both this and the next line of verse 9 come from Psalm 118:25-26. Psalms 113—118, called the Hallel, were regularly sung at Passover season, so these words were fresh in everyone's mind.

12:14-16. One expected military heroes to ride horses or be drawn in chariots; Jesus came as a meek, nonmilitary official would, following Zechariah 9:9. (Later *rabbis also took Zech 9:9 as *messianic, due to the mention of the king.)

12:17-19. Again employing irony (a literary technique common in antiquity, as it is today), John lets the *Pharisees curse themselves: "You do nothing profitable!" Their complaint that the world has begun to follow Jesus leads into 12:20.

12:20. Although these could be Jews who live in the Greek East, they are probably ethnic Greeks, God-fearers not yet fully converted to Judaism who nevertheless would come to worship at Jerusalem (cf. Acts 8:27). Jews and Greeks were known for their mutual hostility in Palestine, nearby Syria and Egypt.

12:21-22. Philip is one of the only *disciples of Jesus with a Greek name; being from Bethsaida, he may also have had *Gentile trade contacts, because it was near predominantly Gentile cities, including the Decapolis. The announcement of verse 21 prompts Jesus' knowledge that his hour has arrived (v. 23); his mission has begun to touch the whole "world."

12:23-34
Jesus' Death Approaches

12:23-27. On "the hour" see 2:4; on "glory" see 1:14. "Glorified," like "lifted up" (v. 32), refers back to the *Septuagint of Isaiah 52:13, to the death of the suffering servant (Is 53), whom early Christians recognized to be Jesus.

12:28-30. Jewish tradition often discussed voices from heaven, which were frequently regarded as a substitute for *prophecy. (See comment on Mk 1:11 for more detail.) In ancient Jewish stories, God often answered prayers by sending angels, which may have seemed less dramatic to some of his hearers than a voice from heaven. (On the persistent misunderstanding of the crowds, see comment on 3:9-10.)

12:31. God is the ruler of the world in nearly all Jewish texts, but these texts also speak of fallen angels ruling much of the world under his decree and recognize that the prince of the evil angels (equivalent to *Satan) ruled most of the world except Israel. John would agree that God has always been ultimately sovereign over all; but here he speaks of Satan's dominion in human affairs and of the present defeat of demonic spiritual forces, which Judaism expected only in the time of the *kingdom.

12:32-33. The "lifting up" (also 3:14; 8:28) alludes to Isaiah 52:13 and refers to being lifted up on the cross.

12:34. The *Old Testament predicted that the *Messiah's rule would be eternal (Is 9:6-7; cf. 2 Sam 7:16); so also the *Son of Man's (Dan 7:14). (Especially in the time of John and later, some Jewish teachers moved away from identifying the Son of Man with the Messiah; no less a *rabbi than Akiba was reproved by his colleagues for supposing that the Son of Man, like God, would receive his own throne.)

12:35-50
Belief and Unbelief

12:35-36. The *Dead Sea Scrolls also contrast light (symbolizing good) and darkness (symbolizing evil), calling the righteous "children of light" and their opponents "children of darkness." Jesus' hearers would easily understand his language.

12:37-38. Isaiah 53:1 is from the same passage to which "glorified" and "lifted up" refer (Is 52:13). The point is: Israel's very unbelief in the servant-*Messiah fulfills Scripture.

12:39-41. On the text (Is 6:10), see comment on Mark 4:12. Isaiah 6:1-5 refers clearly to Isaiah seeing a vision of God, the Lord of hosts, in his glory when he received this message, but John explains that this manifestation of God was the Son, Jesus (v. 41).

12:42. Because John selects details most applicable to his own day, it appears that not even all the *synagogue leaders of his time are of one mind about believers in Jesus. Those who are not hostile to the Jewish Christians, however, seem to remain publicly silent on the issue. The admission that even some of their opponents recognize the truth would encourage John's readers.

12:43. The Greek word translated "glory" (NRSV) or "praise" (NIV, KJV) can also be translated "reputation" or "honor" but contrasts here with Jesus' glorification (12:23). Ancient moralists often condemned those who sought much glory; but honor was the goal of high society and considered critical in a status-conscious culture obsessed with shame and dignity.

12:44-45. Jewish literature portrayed personified, preexistent divine Wisdom as the image of God; others, like Moses, could reflect his glory, but Jesus is the glory Moses and others saw (12:41, 46; cf. 1:18).

12:46. On the "light" see comment on 8:12; on the contrast of light and darkness as a common image for God's kingdom versus that of his opponents, see comment on 12:35-36.

12:47. Judaism believed that God's *law was the standard by which he would judge his people at the end time; Jesus thus presents his words as equivalent to those of God.

12:48-49. One was to receive an agent or ambassador with the honor due his sender. An agent or ambassador was also expected to represent his sender accurately.

12:50. *Rabbis sometimes explained that keeping even the smallest of God's commandments warranted *eternal life (by which they meant life in the world to come), whereas disobeying even the smallest forfeited that life. Jesus describes his personal commission from the Father in the same terms.

13:1-11
Footwashing

John intertwines foreshadowings of the betrayal and cross with the footwashing. Jesus follows Mary's example of servanthood (12:3).

13:1-2. Meals were common settings for teaching sessions.

13:3-8. The couches would be arranged around tables containing the food, with the upper part of each person's body facing the food and their feet away from the table. Jesus would go to the outside of this circle to wash each person's feet.

After travelers had come a long distance, the host was to provide water for their feet as a sign of hospitality, as exemplified by Abraham (Gen 18:4). Yet loosing sandals and personally washing someone else's feet was considered servile, most commonly the work of a servant or of very submissive wives or children (cf. also 1 Sam 25:41). (Travelers' sandals would not be covered in dung, as some scholars have suggested. Side roads were very dusty; the main streets of Jerusalem, however, would have been kept as clean as the city could make them, especially the Upper City, where Jesus ate this Passover meal.) Jesus' removing his outer garments to serve them would also appear as a sign of great humility before them.

By so serving, Jesus prefigures his death as the suffering servant of Isaiah 53 on behalf of the many. Unlike Greco-Roman society, Judaism stressed humility; but like other societies, it also upheld societal roles. Jesus overturns even positions of social status. Rabbi Judah ha-Nasi (about A.D. 220) was said to be so humble that he would do anything for others—except relinquish his superior position; seating according to rank was crucial. Jesus goes beyond even this.

13:6-8. Jesus' act violates cultural status boundaries so thoroughly (see comment on vv. 3-5) that Peter finds it unthinkable.

13:9-11. The "bath" here presumably alludes to ceremonial washing that Jesus and the *disciples had undergone before the feast (11:55), but Jesus applies it in a spiritual sense. This figurative sense of cleansing was common enough that the disciples should have been able to understand his meaning.

13:12-20
The Meaning of Footwashing

13:12-14. *Disciples normally served their teachers, after the model of Elisha serving Elijah and Joshua serving Moses.

13:15. Disciples were to learn especially by imitating their teachers.

13:16-17. Some slaves were prominent when compared with free peasants, but any authority slaves exercised was derived from their masters, and slaves were always subordinate to their masters. An agent was always subordinate to his sender, his authority limited to the extent of his authorization.

13:18. Here Jesus cites Psalm 41:9, a psalm of a righteous sufferer; one scholar has pointed out that lifting up one's heel is an act of disdain in cultures similar to ancient Judaism. Table fellowship was considered an intimate bond, and betrayal following it was particularly perverse.

13:19. Cf. Isaiah 41:26, 44:7, 11 and 48:3-7: God predicts the future so when it comes about his people will finally acknowledge that he, unlike the gods of the nations, is true.

13:20. In ancient cultures, one responded to agents, ambassadors or other representatives according to one's feelings toward the person who authorized them.

13:21-30
The Betrayer's Mission

13:21-22. Greek philosophers stressed remaining always tranquil and untroubled in spirit, but not everyone in antiquity shared this value. Although the Fourth Gospel stresses Jesus' deity, it also stresses and frequently illustrates his humanity (1:14). In the *Old Testament God's passionate feelings also frequently surface (e.g., Judg 10:16; Is 63:9-10; Jer 2:30-32; 9:1-3; Hos 11:8).

Hos 11:8).

13:23. Men would recline on couches at feasts (women would not dine in the same room with a gathering of men outside their family). Each person would recline slightly behind the person to his right; thus John could lean his head back and be even with Jesus' chest. (They would lean on the left elbow with the right arm free and so could not cut up their food; it would come presliced at the banquet.) This beloved *disciple (presumably John) has one of the most honored positions at the feast, along with the person on the left—perhaps Judas, as some commentators have suggested, given verse 26.

13:24-27. For the host to dip a piece of bread in the common bowl (or on Passover, no doubt bitter herbs in a container of something sweeter) and hand it to someone was normally a sign of honor to the person who received it. Jesus is in complete control here (cf. Mk 14:20).

13:28-30. Some pietists would do a charitable work before Passover to secure God's favor. It would not have been customary to go outside on Passover night (Ex 12:22), but in John's *narrative (unlike Matthew, Mark and Luke) Passover apparently begins the following day (18:28; see comment there).

13:31-35
Glory and Love Defined

The context of these verses is betrayal and Jesus' death.

13:31-32. On glorification see comment on 1:14 and 12:23-27.

13:33. Teachers sometimes called their *disciples "children" (cf. 1 Jn 2:1), and disciples called teachers "my father." Jewish literature also included "testaments" of dying or departing famous heroes of the past giving important teachings to their children, to be read by future generations. Because Jesus is leaving, it is natural for him to provide final instructions to his disciples, whether or not John consciously follows the testamentary form here.

13:34-35. The *Old Testament had commanded love (Lev 19:18); what makes Jesus' commandment new is the new standard and example: "as I have loved you"—in the context, to the point of laying down one's life for others.

13:36—14:1
Following to the Cross?

13:36-37. Although Peter is sure that he will follow Jesus to the death, he does not understand that death is precisely where Jesus is going (14:5). For the misunderstanding motif, see, for example, 3:4; for background on it, see the introduction to Mark.

13:38. The first night cock crowing in Jerusalem occurred by about 12:30 a.m., according to some reports (others place it later), though only night watchmen were awake to hear it (most people went to sleep at sundown). That the rooster crowed to mark the advent of dawn is more widely reported because this was the cock crowing most people knew. In either case the point is that Peter's denial will follow almost immediately after his promise not to deny Jesus.

14:1. "Your" is plural, and thus Jesus addresses all the *disciples; in the *Old Testament God often told his servants not to fear. But to pair faith in Jesus with faith in God would sound blasphemous to most ancient Jewish readers (although they could have found a less offensive way to interpret the phrase; see 2 Chron 20:20).

14:2-7
Where Jesus Is Going, Enigmatic Version

As the chapter proceeds, one learns

that the coming again in verse 3 refers to Jesus' coming after the *resurrection to give the *Spirit (v. 18); but this point is not immediately clear at the beginning (v. 5).

14:2. The "Father's house" would be the temple (2:16), where God would forever dwell with his people (Ezek 43:7, 9; 48:35; cf. Jn 8:35). The "dwelling places" (NASB, NRSV) could allude to the booths constructed for the Feast of Tabernacles but probably refer to "rooms" (cf. NIV, TEV) in the new temple, where only undefiled ministers would have a place (Ezek 44:9-16; cf. 48:11). John presumably means this language figuratively for being in Christ, where God's presence dwells (2:21); the only other place in the *New Testament where this term for "dwelling places" or "rooms" occurs is in 14:23, where it refers to the believer as God's dwelling place (cf. also the verb "dwell"—15:4-7).

14:3-4. In this context, John probably means not the Second Coming but Christ's return after the *resurrection to bestow the *Spirit (14:16-18). In Jewish teaching, both the resurrection of the dead (which Jesus inaugurated) and bestowal of the Spirit indicate the arrival of the new age of the *kingdom. Jesus explains where he is going and how they will come to be there in 14:6-7.

14:5. *Disciples asked their *rabbis questions to clarify the teaching. That four questions were also asked in the extant household Passover celebration may be mere coincidence (13:36-37; 14:5, 8, 22).

14:6-7. The "way" in many Jewish texts refers to the righteous way to behave but here possibly echoes Isaiah's way back to the new Jerusalem through the wilderness (cf. Jn 1:23). In this case the background is less critical than the force of the image, however. Jesus answers Thomas's question thus: The Father is where I am going, and I am how you will get there.

"Truth" later came to be a Jewish title for God; it is uncertain if it was in use this early. The primary significance of the statement, however, is that Jesus is the embodiment of the truth, God's covenant faithfulness (1:17), which was embodied in God's "word" in the *Old Testament (17:17; Ps 119:142, 151). Just as Judaism affirmed that there was only one God and thus one right way (his *law, either in the short version supposedly given to the Gentiles or the full version given to Israel), Jesus here affirms that he is the only way to the only God.

14:8-17
Revealing the Father Clearly

14:8. John may wish his readers, most of whom were more immersed in the Bible than most modern readers, to think of Exodus 33:18, where Moses asked to see God's glory; cf. comment on John 1:18 and 14:21-22.

14:9-11. The *Old Testament sometimes spoke of God's *Spirit inspiring or anointing the prophets for his work. Jesus' words here go beyond that idea, but it is the closest parallel available.

14:12-14. Here "works" (KJV, NASB, NRSV) could refer to righteous deeds, as often in Judaism (e.g., 8:39), or to miraculous works such as Jesus wrought (5:17; 10:32), or to both. (The works are quantitatively greater because Christ's work is multiplied through *all* his followers.) In this context Jesus' words are an invitation to radical faith: Jewish tradition allowed that some very pious teachers could receive from God almost anything they asked because of their intimate relationship with him, but never applied this possibility to the majority even of the pious. This promise also goes beyond claims made for most charms in pagan magic. Magic had no emphasis on relationship with the power addressed and sought only to manipulate forces for the manipulator's ends (contrast 14:15).

Ancient Judaism used "name" in so many overlapping senses that the context tells us more here than the background. In the *Old Testament "name" often meant reputation or renown, and when God acted "on account of his name" it was to defend his honor. "In the name of God" could mean as his representative acting on his behalf (Ex 5:23; Deut 18:19-22; Jer 14:14-15), according to his command (Deut 18:5, 7), by his help (Ps 118:10-11; Prov 18:10) or using his name in a miraculous act (2 Kings 2:24). (When *rabbis passed on traditions "in the name of" other rabbis it simply means that they were citing their sources, their basis of authority for the tradition.) In prayer, calling on a deity's name simply meant addressing him (1 Kings 18:24-26, 32; 2 Kings 5:11; Ps 9:2; 18:49). In the Old Testament and later Judaism "Name" could also simply be a polite and roundabout way of saying "God" without uttering his name.

In this context "name" means something like: those who seek his glory and speak accurately for him, who are genuinely his authorized representatives. Nothing could be further from the pagan magical use of names that sought to manipulate spiritual forces for one's own ends.

14:15. Here Jesus cites another Old Testament idea (e.g., Ex 20:6; Deut 5:10, 29; 6:5; 11:1, 13, 22; 13:3-4; 19:9; 30:6, 14). In Ezekiel 36:27, the gift of the *Spirit enables one to keep the commandments (Jn 14:16).

14:16. The background for calling the *Spirit "Counselor" (NIV) or "Helper" (NASB) is debated, but it is probably a courtroom image: one sense of the term is "advocate," "defending attorney," "intercessor"; see comment on 16:8-11. In Jewish depictions of God's heavenly court, angels and divine attributes could serve as accusers or advocates, but *Satan is the primary prosecutor, and God (or his favored attribute of mercy, or Michael) defends Israel. Here the Spirit is "another" advocate like Jesus (cf. 9:35-41, where Jesus defends the man put out of the *synagogue and accuses his accusers); Judaism was also familiar with the idea of a "successor" who carries on a predecessor's work.

14:17. The Spirit of truth guides God's people in the way of truth—into fuller revelation of Jesus, who is the truth (14:6; 16:13). The *Dead Sea Scrolls contrast the spirit of truth with the spirit of error (cf. 1 Jn 4:6).

14:18-31
Jesus' Coming and Revealing

14:18-20. In the *Old Testament, "orphans" (NASB, NIV) were powerless and needed a legal defender. The context here refers to Jesus' coming to them and leaving his presence in them by the *Spirit (20:19-23).

14:21-22. Israel believed (rightly) that God had given them a special revelation in the *law that the nations did not have. The language of "manifesting" (KJV) or "revealing" (NRSV, TEV) himself to them recalls God's revealing himself to Moses on Mount Sinai (see comment on 1:14).

14:23-24. Jewish teachers spoke of God's presence residing in a special way among those who studied his law; Jesus speaks of God's presence residing in each believer continually as an individual temple for his presence. That God dwelt in his temple and among his people was standard Old Testament teaching; that his laws were written in the hearts of his faithful and that his *Spirit moved among his prophets were also taught in the Old Testament. But Jesus broadens and personalizes this perspective in a manner unparalleled in extant ancient literature. The *Dead Sea Scrolls speak of the Spirit being active among God's people, but this activity is not nearly as extensive as the prophetic and charismatic activity found in the *New Testament.

14:25-26. Some of the functions Jesus lists here for the *Spirit were attributed in Judaism to divine Wisdom, which was associated with God's Spirit as well as his law in some popular, pre-Christian Jewish writings (cf. also Neh 9:20; Ps 143:10). In a Jewish context, "teaching" could include elaborating and expounding; rote memorization was also an important part of ancient learning.

14:27. Jewish teachers highly extolled peace (especially in terms of relationships with others).

14:28-31. For verse 29, see comment on 13:19; for verse 30, see comment on 12:31; for "love" and "commandments" in verse 31, see comment on 14:15. Jesus' obedience to the Father includes his mission to the cross in 14:31, where he also summons his followers to participate in that call ("let *us* go"). Thus the world could know Jesus' true identity (12:32-33; 17:21).

15:1-8
Dwelling in the Vine

The word "abide" (KJV, NASB, NRSV), "remain" (NIV, TEV) or "dwell" (15:4-10) is the verb form of "dwelling place" (on which see comment on 14:2, 23). In the *Old Testament God had promised to dwell with his obedient covenant people always (Ex 25:8; 29:45; Lev 26:11-12; Ezek 37:27-28; 43:9).

15:1. The Old Testament and Jewish literature sometimes portrayed Israel as a vineyard (e.g., Is 5:7), or less frequently as a vine (e.g., Ps 80:8; Hos 10:1), and God as the vinegrower. A golden vine in the temple symbolized Israel's power, and Jesus may here portray the *disciples as the remnant of Israel (see comment on 15:16). The most basic point of the imagery is the obvious dependence of branches on the vine for their continued life.

15:2-3. Here is another of John's plays on words (cf. comment on 3:3): "prunes" also means "cleanses," which is a motif in John (cf., e.g., 2:6; 13:10). The Old Testament prophets often called on Israel to "bear fruit" for God (e.g., Is 27:6; Hos 14:4-8).

15:4-8. Dead, fruitless branches of vines are obviously of no use for carpentry; their only possible value is for fuel. Jewish teachers believed that God had awful punishments in store for apostates, because those who had known the truth and then rejected it had no excuse (cf. 15:22-24).

15:9-17
Abiding in Love

15:9-11. Keeping the commandments (here epitomized as love) was supposed to bring joy (Ps 19:8 and often in later Jewish teachings).

15:12-13. Dying for others was considered heroic in Greco-Roman stories, and friendship to the death was considered a high moral value (see comment on vv. 14-15). But Judaism did not share this general Greek perspective, although it emphasized dying for the law if need be. Rabbi Akiba (within a few decades of John) argued that one's own life took precedence over another's. Although it is unlikely that Jesus is directly influenced by the Greek view of friendship, John's *Diaspora readers would have been familiar with it and so grasped his point quickly.

15:14-15. There were different kinds and levels of friendship in antiquity, and Greco-Roman writers often commented on the topic. Friendship could involve political or military alliances and was often pursued in self-interest; kings or lesser *patrons who supported dependents called *clients were (especially in Roman circles) said to be engaging in "friendship"; *Pharisees also met in circles of "friends." The traditional Greek concept of friendship emphasized equality among companions, and some philosophical schools like the *Epicureans especially emphasized such friendship.

The main ideals of friendship in ancient literature included loyalty (sometimes to the death), equality and mutual sharing of all possessions, and an intimacy in which a friend could share everything in confidence. Jesus especially emphasizes the last point in verse 15, where he distinguishes a friend from a servant, who might also be loyal but would not share intimate secrets. Jewish writers like *Philo sometimes contrasted being friends of God with being servants of God.

The *Old Testament called two people friends of God: Abraham and Moses. Jewish tradition amplified on the friendship and intimacy of both of them with God. If an Old Testament allusion is in view here, it may be to Moses (cf. comment on 14:8). If this text emphasizes Jesus' sharing his heart with his followers, the context communicates the character of his heart: love.

15:16-17. Jewish teachers emphasized repeatedly that Israel was chosen and commissioned by God (in Abraham, the other possible allusion in v. 15); see comment on 15:1. On asking "in the name" see comment on 14:12-14.

15:18—16:4
The World's Hatred

15:18-21. Jewish people believed that the *Gentile nations hated them because they were chosen and sent by God and suffered on his account. They would resent Jesus' grouping most of them with "the world," but other persecuted minority sects in Judaism (like the *Essenes at *Qumran) also included the majority of Israel, whom they regarded as apostate, as among the world, their enemies.

15:22-24. Judaism taught that greater knowledge brought greater responsibility; the nations were accountable to keep only seven commandments, whereas Israel, who had received the *law, had 613 commandments. Jesus also teaches that revelation increases moral responsibility (elsewhere, e.g., Lk 12:41-46).

15:25. Here Jesus quotes from a lament of a righteous sufferer (Ps 69:4; cf. 35:19), which Jesus elsewhere applied to his sufferings (cf. Jn 2:17). On "their law" see 8:17 and 10:34.

15:26. On the forensic work of the *Spirit as advocate, see 14:16; here he is not only advocate but witness.

15:27. The believers are also witnesses for Jesus before the court of the world (cf. 16:2) and God's tribunal. The Jewish people viewed the *Holy Spirit especially as the Spirit of *prophecy (usually in the Old Testament and even more often in later Jewish literature); God would thus anoint the *disciples to speak as prophets. (This promise also fits the idea that God's people would be anointed by the Spirit to witness God's truth against the nations before God's final tribunal; cf. Is 42:1; 43:10-12; 44:3, 8.)

16:1. Advance warning was helpful; cf. comment on 13:19.

16:2-4. Christians in John's day were being expelled from many local *synagogues, perhaps under the influence of Palestinian *Pharisaic propaganda (see the introduction to John; cf. comment on 9:34 and 12:42). Hostile Jewish non-Christians in Asia Minor do not appear to have killed Christians directly; but their participation in Christians' deaths was no less significant. By betraying Jewish Christians to the Roman authorities and claiming that Christians were non-Jewish, they left Christians with no legal exemption from worshiping the emperor. Worried that Christians were a *messianic and *apocalyptic movement that could get them in trouble with Rome, many synagogue leaders may have thought their betrayal of Christians would protect the rest of their community (cf. 11:50). On persecution being viewed as worship to God, see Isaiah 66:5.

16:5-15
The Spirit's Witness

The *Spirit testifies of Jesus to the world (16:8-11, duplicating the earthly witness of Jesus) and to Jesus' followers (16:13-15). The opponents of John's readers did not claim to have the Spirit or to hear the Spirit speaking to their hearts as he had spoken to the prophets (many may have claimed to feel close to God but did not claim to hear him directly, in contrast to Christians and some *apocalyptic visionaries). John encourages his readers that their intimate, personal relationship with God in the Spirit distinguishes them from their opponents.

16:5-7. The Advocate comes to the believers, which implies that his ministry to the world (16:8-11) is through them (cf. Neh 9:30). This idea fits the common *Old Testament and later Jewish perspective on God's *Spirit as the Spirit of *prophecy.

16:8-11. The believers' Advocate becomes a "prosecutor" of the world, as sometimes in the Old Testament (Jer 50:34; 51:36; Lam 3:58-66; cf. Ps 43:1; 50:8). Many Jewish people believed that God would make Israel prevail over the nations before his tribunal in the day of judgment; for John, the judgment has already begun (Jn 3:18-19). Roman courts had no public prosecutors and depended on an interested party to bring charges, although trained *rhetoricians then debated on behalf of those who could afford them. The Spirit here brings charges against the world before God's heavenly court (see Mt 5:22).

Verses 9-11 probably mean that the world's unbelief constituted their sin; Christ being the heavenly Advocate (1 Jn 2:1) constituted the believers' righteousness; and the judging of the world's ruler (see comment on 12:31) spelled the judgment of the world. Thus for John it is not Jesus and his people (chaps. 18—19) but the world that is now on trial. One may compare a common motif in the Old Testament prophets: the covenant lawsuit where God summons his people to account for breach of the covenant.

16:12-13. The Psalms speak of God leading his people in truth, in his way of faithfulness (Ps 25:5; 43:3; cf. 5:8); in John, this language implies a fuller revelation of Jesus' character (14:6). The *Spirit will relate to the *disciples as Jesus has (15:15), so that believers' relationship with Jesus in John's day (and in subsequent generations) should be no less intimate than relationships with him were before the cross.

16:14-15. This intimacy (v. 13) is expressed in a sharing of possessions that characterized ideal friendship in antiquity (see comment on 15:15); the point of the language in this context, however, is that God shares his heart with all his people, as he once shared his word with his prophets (Gen 18:17; Amos 3:7).

16:16-33
Seeing Jesus Again

After his *resurrection, Jesus would

return to the *disciples to impart life (14:18-19), and through the gift of his *Spirit he would remain with them forever (20:19-23).

16:16-22. Women often died in childbirth. The prophets commonly used birth pangs as an image of suffering, often stemming from judgment (Is 13:8; 21:3; 26:17; 42:14; Jer 4:31; 6:24; 13:21; 22:23; 30:6; 49:22-24; 50:43; Mic 4:9-10; cf. Ps 48:6). In some *Old Testament texts, these pangs signified the birth pangs of a new, *messianic era (Is 66:7-10; Mic 5:1-4; cf. Is 9:6; 53:12—54:1; 62:5; Hos 13:13-14).

Early Judaism sometimes came to apply these birth pangs specifically to the final period of suffering before the end of the age, which would be followed by the *resurrection of the dead. Jesus' tomb is the womb of his resurrection, and his resurrection inaugurates a new age; Jesus' resurrection means that the life of the coming world is now available to the *disciples in the present (see comment on 3:16).

16:23-24. See comment on 14:12-14, especially on the use of the "name" in prayer.

16:25-28. Following the Old Testament wisdom tradition, Jewish teachers often used proverbs and riddles. Although the *disciples are not ready for the full understanding of the new relationship with God that Jesus describes (16:12), he is getting them ready.

16:29-30. In the context of the Fourth Gospel, that Jesus knows their question before they ask reveals his special insight; see comments on 1:42 and 2:24-25.

16:31-32. The scattering of sheep may refer to Zechariah 13:7 (cf. Mt 26:31). The *Old Testament often reports that God's flock was scattered for want of a devoted shepherd (cf., e.g., Is 53:6; Jer 23:1; 50:17; Ezek 34:6, 12, 21), as one would expect with flocks (e.g., Ps 119:176; 1 Macc 12:53).

16:33. This verse reveals the dramatic situation of early Christians who recognized that final victory would come, as Jewish prophets and teachers said, when the *Messiah comes in the future; but they also recognized that the Messiah had already come and therefore had inaugurated triumph in the midst of present tribulation.

17:1-5
Jesus Reviews His Mission

Jesus here reveals his unique relationship with the Father, sharing his glory as divine Wisdom (cf. 1:1-18). From 12:23-33 it is clear that he returns to this full glory only by way of the cross.

17:1. Lifting one's eyes to heaven was a common posture of prayer (cf. perhaps Ps 121:1; 123:1). "Glory" here has a double sense, another instance of wordplay; see comment on 1:14 and 12:23-27. Moses reflected God's glory in Exodus 33—34, but Jesus is to be "glorified" in the same sense as the Father, with his preexistent glory (17:5).

17:2. The *Old Testament also often used "flesh" (KJV) in the sense of humanity ("people"—NIV; "mankind"—NASB). Only at the end, in the final *kingdom, did God promise to delegate his authority to a particular ruler (Is 9:6-7; Dan 7:13-14); this background suggests that Jesus' death and *resurrection represent no mere temporal event but the climactic inbreaking of a new world.

17:3. On knowing God see 10:4-5. Other Jewish texts written in Greek also identified knowing God with *eternal life (e.g., Wisdom of Solomon 15:3); here one must have a personal relationship with Jesus Christ.

17:4-5. On finishing the work see 4:34 and 19:30. The Old Testament declared that God would not give his glory to another (Is 42:8; 48:11); Jesus' sharing the Father's glory in this sense is a claim that he is divine. Judaism did have a category in which to understand Jesus' divine claim here: God's Wisdom was related to and in some sense identified with his glory (Wisdom of Solomon 7:25-29). John's Jewish Christian readers may have understood Jesus' identity in analogous (albeit superior) terms (see comment on 1:1-18).

17:6-19
Jesus Prays for His Disciples

This passage addresses the inevitable conflict between Jesus' followers and the world. Jesus' followers here assume the role assigned to Israel in most extant Jewish portrayals of the end times and that assigned to the remnant (the children of light) in the *Dead Sea Scrolls; they constituted the whole number of the righteous and as such were a persecuted minority within society.

17:6. God had told Moses to reveal his name (Ex 3:13, 15); when God revealed his name, he revealed his character and attributes (Ex 33:19; 34:5, 14; for the future, see Is 52:6).

To "hallow" or "sanctify" God's name was to demonstrate its holiness, its sacredness. In contemporary Jewish teaching, righteous deeds hallowed God's name, and wicked ones dishonored it; most Jewish people prayed for the future time when God would sanctify his name throughout the earth (see comment on Mt 6:9).

17:7-11. Moses received God's words and passed them on to Israel, who alone of the nations received his *law; the ideas of Jesus' being glorified among the *disciples and the use of God's name (17:11) may also expound Jewish traditions related to Moses in the book of Exodus. On unity see comment on John 17:20-26.

17:12. Here Jesus might allude to Psalm 41:9, which he cited in John 13:18. Jewish teaching recognized that God dealt more severely with apostates than with those who were born pagans, because apostates had known the truth but turned away from it.

17:13-19. The *Old Testament and Jewish tradition emphasized Israel's separation from and often hatred by the world. God had "sanctified" or "set apart" Israel for himself as holy, especially by giving them his commandments (e.g., Lev. 11:44-45). (Today Jewish people still celebrate this sanctification by the commandments in the blessing over the lighting of sabbath candles.)

If God had sanctified his people, or set them apart among the nations by giving them the law, how much more are followers of Jesus set apart by his coming as the law made flesh (see comment on 1:1-18); Jesus treats his *disciples here as the true remnant of Israel, i.e., the saved covenant community within Israel. (Throughout most of the Old Testament, only part of Israel in any given generation followed God; in some times, like those of Joshua and David, the remnant was large; in other times, like Moses' generation or that of Elijah, it was small.) Other Jewish groups, like the *Essenes who likely authored the *Dead Sea Scrolls, also felt that the rest of their nation had gone astray and that they were the true remnant; the theme appears in the Old Testament prophets (cf. Is 10:20-22; Joel 2:32; Amos 9:8-12).

17:20-26
Jesus Prays for Future Disciples

The unity of Father and Son models the unity to be experienced by their people in whom they dwell. Israel acknowledged that their God was "one" and recognized the importance of this factor in their own solidarity among the nations, in a world hostile to them. This passage stresses the same idea but in a manner more related to the idea of God's personal indwelling introduced in chapter 14 (see especially comment on 14:23-24). For an example of the passing on of glory to a people in whom the Lord would be glorified, see Isaiah 46:13; God also sanctified his dwelling places with the glory of his presence (Ex 29:43).

The emphasis on unity would also speak to John's readers, who are troubled by opposition from the *synagogue and perhaps from secessionists from their own ranks (see introduction to 1 John); it is also likely that ethnic or cultural unity—perhaps among John's [emigrant?] Galilean and Asian constituencies (see the introduction to John)—is partly in view (10:16; 11:52; 12:20-23); John clearly emphasizes ethnic reconciliation in Christ in chapter 4 (the Samaritans). At any rate, followers of Jesus constitute a small minority in a hostile world and need each other to survive as much as other minorities normally do. On concern for coming generations compare, e.g., Psalm 78:3-7.

18:1-11 The Betrayer Arrives

18:1-2. "Kidron Valley" is literally the "winter-swollen Kidron": this brook flowed only in the rainy season—winter—so crossing it in April would not involve even getting wet. The site is still identifiable. Jesus and his *disciples had met there other times; cf. Luke 22:39.

18:3. Many scholars have noted that this military contingent is described in a manner much like Roman cohorts (so NASB). Nevertheless, the same language was equally used of Jewish units, and this unit is undoubtedly Jewish—the temple guard. (Roman troops would not be used for a routine police action like this one, and Romans would not have taken Jesus to the house of Annas—18:13—whom they had deposed.)

A full cohort in the Roman sense could have involved eight hundred soldiers, but a detachment from the cohort is all that John need mean here. Both the temple police and Romans carried torches (two kinds are mentioned here) at night, although only a few need have carried them, especially since the moon would be nearly full at Passover.

18:4-6. "I am" can mean "I am he (whom you seek)," but it can also allude to Exodus 3:14, translated literally. A Jewish tradition, purportedly pre-Christian (attributed to the early *Diaspora Jewish writer Artapanus), said that when Moses pronounced the name of his God, Pharaoh fell backward. (If Jesus' hearers had thought he was pronouncing the divine name, they might have also fallen back in fear, because magicians were said to try to cast spells in that name.)

18:7-9. That Jesus' word (17:12) should be fulfilled just as Scripture is suggests his divine rank and mission. Although some Jewish writers allowed that *prophecy continued in their own time, they never accorded such revelations the same status as Scripture.

18:10. As slave of the high priest, Malchus would be a powerful person with much authority. On the symbolic effect of his disfigurement, see comment on Mark 14:47.

18:11. On the possible background of the "cup," see comment on Mark 10:39.

18:12-27 At the House of Annas

18:12. The officer mentioned here is literally "one in charge of a thousand men" (a cohort, which in practice was probably fewer than eight hundred men); but see comment on 18:3.

18:13-14. Annas was high priest from A.D. 6 to 15, when the Romans deposed him. According to Jewish law, the high priest was entitled to rule for life; thus some Jews no doubt considered the Roman deposition of Annas invalid, and he continued to command great respect. He was wealthy and powerful, but later Jewish literature (written by successors of those he opposed) does not speak well of him. The high priesthood had been the most powerful office in Jewish Palestine until the Roman period.

Capital cases were to be heard by a plurality of judges (according to later tradition, a minimum of twenty-three). No individual could legally act as judge in a capital case, but this law did not stop Annas from exercising his political power and privately interrogating Jesus. Perhaps he would have excused himself by a law that those tried by the supreme *Sanhedrin for misleading the people first had to be tried by two lower courts. But that law may be *Pharisaic and may be later than the first century, and it is doubtful that Annas is attempting to follow any law. The predominantly *Sadducean priestly aristocracy would certainly not follow the Pharisees' rules: they had to please the Romans, not the Pharisees.

18:15-18. For more detail see comment on Mark 14:66-69. According to later *rabbinic teaching, Jewish people were permitted to deny their Jewishness, especially by evasion (cf. Mk 14:68), to save their lives. Direct denial that allowed God's name to be reproached, however, was considered shameful. Peter probably does not know these specific rules, but they may illustrate his cultural setting, which did not always regard denial as severely as Jesus regards it. Like most people, Peter is influenced by his culture and does not yet grasp the radical demands of Jesus in practice.

18:19. The changing of scene back and forth was a standard suspense-building technique in ancient novels; then, as today, it was good writing.

John does not claim that the "high priest" here is the official one Rome recognized (see 18:13, 24); like other *New Testament writers and *Josephus, John follows the common practice of labeling all prominent members of the priestly aristocracy "high priests."

18:20. Although *rabbis offered particular special teachings only to small groups of *disciples (e.g., teachings on creation and on God's throne-chariot), they had a tradition that one must teach the law openly, in contrast to false prophets, who taught "in secret."

18:21. According to what we know of Jewish law, interrogators were not supposed to force the accused to try to convict himself. But if this law is in effect in Jesus' day, the priestly aristocracy, upheld by Rome and acting on what they believe to be right for the people, does not concern itself with it.

18:22-24. Striking a captive was certainly against Jewish law. This act shows how abusive and uninterested in any form of Jewish legality Annas is; his interest in the case is political, not legal. This also fits the picture of the high priests supplied by other minorities in Judaism who did not like them (*Pharisees and *Essenes). See comment on Mark 14:1, 43. Jesus has not violated Exodus 22:28; cf. Acts 23:3-5.

18:25-27. On the cock crowing see comment on 13:38.

18:28-38a
Jesus Before Pilate

18:28. Roman officials began meeting the public (especially their *clients) at daybreak; "early" is no exaggeration.

The priestly aristocracy, who controlled Judea for the Romans, would be able to secure an audience with him on short notice. Clamoring before Pilate in large numbers was usually effective, because a riot was the last thing he wanted. The "Praetorium" (NASB) here was Herod the Great's old "palace" (NIV), used by the Roman prefect when he came to Jerusalem from Caesarea during the feasts. He came precisely to ensure that order was maintained during the feasts, when Jerusalem was overcrowded and riots were most apt to break out.

That observant Jews (including the priestly aristocracy) would not enter this palace, lest they be defiled and thus unable to eat the Passover, fits Jewish practice. But a possible conflict with the other Gospels at this point has led to considerable debate as to when the Passover described in the Gospel passion narratives occurred. According to Matthew, Mark and Luke, Jesus had already eaten the Passover with his *disciples this night; whereas according to John, the priests plan to eat it the following night.

Of the many explanations for the apparent discrepancy, the two most prominent are probably these: (1) Several Jewish groups had different calendars and did not celebrate Passover on the same day. A dispute about when the month had begun (based on the appearance of the new moon) would also affect when the feast would be eaten. Some scholars have suggested that Jesus' *disciples celebrated it a day early, thus without a lamb slaughtered in the temple. (2) Either John or the other Gospels—probably John—is making a symbolic point (John stresses that Jesus is the Passover lamb; cf. 19:14, 36). Later Jewish tradition also reports that Jesus was crucified on Passover, but this report could be based on the approximate time in earlier tradition. Another proposal is that John here uses "Passover" loosely for the Feast of Unleavened Bread, which immediately followed; but although this usage was common, "eat the Passover" is a very odd way to speak of eating the bread during the rest of the feast.

18:29. Precedent exists for a Roman official's having to go outside to respect Jewish sensitivities (on the sensitivities, see comment on 18:28). An official charge would be necessary before Pilate would be required to hear the case. Roman law had no public prosecutor in the modern sense and depended on private accusers to bring charges (although *rhetoricians could be hired to debate a case, they were not supplied by the state).

18:30-32. Pilate regards the matter as one of religious law, hence to be tried in a Jewish court if the person claims to be Jewish and so submits to a Jewish court's jurisdiction; this was Roman practice throughout the empire (also, e.g., Acts 18:14-15). Pilate is also known not to have been cooperative when dealing with Jewish religious matters; unless the situation got out of hand, he did not need to cooperate as long as his *patron Sejanus controlled the emperor Tiberius in Rome (see comment on 19:12).

Although scholars have debated the matter, Rome apparently did not permit Jewish courts to exercise the death penalty, except in the case of a *Gentile intruding into an inner court of the temple. They could flog and probably decree a person worthy of death; but executions not authorized by the Romans were illegal. The Romans had to try all other capital offenses; they used not stoning but crucifixion for executing noncitizens charged with treason (thus fulfilling Jesus' word about being "lifted up"—12:32-33). (Some later *rabbinic sources place the abolition of Jewish courts' right to execute the death penalty in A.D. 70 [other rabbis place it about A.D. 30], but this would have given Palestinian Jewish leaders a right not shared by most other local officials under Rome, a right we would therefore expect contemporary apologists for Judaism like *Josephus to attest. Normally only governors and client rulers exercised the "right of the sword." The Sanhedrin's possession of it is not attested early, and later rabbis often idealized the earlier legal situation, even reading their own authority back into the pre-70 period. The right to execute violators of the temple was also permitted in the case of violators of other sacred shrines, like the sanctuary at Eleusis; but the right was rarely extended beyond this violation.)

18:33-35. Pilate follows a Roman procedure called *cognitio,* an inquiry to determine what really happened. As prefect, he would make the final decision and answer to no one for it unless a complaint were sent to Rome; but he investigates the matter nonetheless.

The priests charge Jesus with claiming to be a king, which is a charge of treason against the emperor. (Herod Antipas was exiled for simply requesting the title, which an earlier emperor, Augustus, had granted Herod the Great.)

18:36-38a. The idea that Jesus' *kingdom is not based on military or political force is repeated throughout the Gospels, but Jesus' Jewish hearers never grasp that meaning in his words (after all, why call it a "kingdom" if it was nonpolitical?). Pilate hears the term "truth" and interprets Jesus in another sense: a philosopher or some other teacher. As an educated Roman, Pilate may have known that many philosophers portrayed themselves as ideal rulers (see comment on 1 Cor 4:8); although he probably had little attachment to philosophers himself, he would have viewed them as harmless. No one could be more nonrevolutionary in practice than a *Cynic or *Stoic philosopher, no matter how antisocial Cynic teachings might be. "Truth" in *Old Testament and Jewish tradition was God's covenant integrity; the concept was much more abstract to Greek ears and perhaps impractical to many Romans.

18:38b—19:3
Pilate Meets the Masses

18:38b. Roman law prohibited treason, not wandering, antisocial philosophers. From Pilate's Roman perspective, he had no reason to condemn Jesus.

18:39. Although unattested in extant Palestinian sources (as are many customs), the specific custom mentioned here is the sort of custom the Romans would have allowed. Roman law permitted two kinds of amnesty, the *indulgentia* (pardoning a condemned person) and—what Pilate probably has in mind here—*abolitio* (acquitting a person before judgment). Romans and Greeks seem to have granted mass amnesty at some other regular feasts, and Romans occasionally acquitted prisoners in response to the cries of crowds; Roman provincial officials were also permitted to follow previous officials' precedents or provincial customs.

18:40. The term translated "bandit" (NRSV, TEV) or "robber" (KJV, NASB) suggests that Barabbas is a revolutionary (cf. NIV)—the kind of person Rome *would* want to execute. The irony cuts deeply: the people preferred a real revolutionary to Jesus, who was denounced for treason as a would-be king but had no actual record of participation in insurrection.

19:1. Severe scourgings often preceded crucifixions. Beatings were a regular punishment themselves, but flogging and scourging, much more severe, were part of the death sentence. Because Pilate has not yet pronounced sentence, the beating Jesus receives is a lesser one. Pilate may hope that the blood it draws would satisfy Jesus' accusers (19:5)—but this is an unlikely supposition (18:31).

In the provinces, soldiers normally administered this punishment. Free Romans were beaten with rods, soldiers with sticks, but slaves and probably despised non-Romans with whips whose leather thongs enclosed sharp pieces of metal or bone. Jewish law allowed only thirty-nine lashes; Roman law allowed scourging till the soldier grew tired, and texts report that bones or entrails were sometimes bared.

19:2. Soldiers played games like throwing knucklebones, coins or dice; the chance to play games with this prisoner would come as a welcome respite from their customary boredom in a foreign land. Common, coarse street mimes seem to have often included mock kings arrayed in mock splendor; the Jewish ruler Agrippa I was ridiculed in this manner in Alexandria.

Greek vassal princes typically wore a purple chlamys—purple dye being the most expensive—and a wreath of gilded leaves. The "purple robe" that the soldiers put on Jesus may have been a faded scarlet lictor's robe or an old rug. The crown of thorns, perhaps from the branches of the thorny acanthus shrub or from the date palm (the latter would have looked more realistic), may have been meant to turn mainly outward (mimicking the wreaths of Hellenistic kings) rather than painfully inward; nevertheless, some thorns must have scraped inward, drawing blood from Jesus' scalp. Only the highest king would wear an actual crown instead of a wreath, so they are portraying him as a vassal prince.

19:3. "Hail" is sarcasm derived from the customary salutation of the Roman emperor, "Ave (Hail), Caesar!"

19:4-16
Politics over Justice

19:4. The governor's investigation has yielded a verdict: not guilty (18:35-38a). Under normal circumstances, this verdict would stand.

19:5. The garb of a mock king, as in the case of the Alexandrian dressed up to ridicule Agrippa I (see comment on 19:2), portrays Jesus to the mob not as a true king but as a harmless fool. His title "man" contrasts ironically with their charge: "God's Son" (19:7); it may be a mock royal acclamation, as in "Behold the king!" (contrast the opening acclamation of the Gospel—1:29).

19:6. Pilate's challenge is derisive: the Jewish authorities did not have the legal right to execute capital offenders, and if they had they would normally have stoned them rather than crucified them.

19:7-9. The *Old Testament called the *Messiah (and all David's line) the *Son of God (2 Sam 7:14; Ps 2:7; 89:27); in a more general sense, all Israel was called God's child (Ex 4:22; Deut 8:3 Hos 11:1). But even falsely claiming to be the Messiah was not a capital offense in standard Jewish teaching, as long as one were not a false prophet advocating other gods. On their own terms, Jesus' accusers are thus mistaken about the *law's teaching about him (10:34-36); but John may intend more irony: he believed the Old Testament predicted that God's Son would die (cf. Is 53).

Pilate hears the charge very differently. Although many wandering philosophers claimed to be sons of gods and were not taken seriously, some teachers were thought to actually possess divine wisdom or power, and Pilate may be cautious not to offend such a powerful being. Some Romans were cynical about the gods, but most believed in them, and Pilate may be especially cautious, given the reputation of Jewish magicians for being among the best in antiquity.

19:10. Pilate's decree was legally binding in all capital cases; he did not even have to accept the recommendations of his *consilium,* or council. He was authorized to judge in all cases regarding public order, even if no specific laws had been violated. Roman law did not take silence as an admission of guilt, but the issue with Pilate is no longer guilt or innocence but weighing the religious and political consequences of both decisions.

19:11. Judaism understood that rulers held authority only temporarily delegated them by God, who would judge in the end; "above" was sometimes a Jewish way of speaking of God (frequent in John). Here Jesus may imply that the authority of Caiaphas, unlike that of Pilate, is illegitimate; the high priesthood was to be for life, but high priests had been deposed and others installed at the whim and for the political expediency of the Romans.

19:12. Romans respected courage in the face of death (e.g., one praises an ancient Spartan boy who silently let a fox eat away his entrails rather than break the rules of military training). Jesus' answer may also confirm Pilate's fear that Jesus is a genuinely divine messenger, not simply a deluded street philosopher who thinks himself divine.

On October 18, A.D. 31, Sejanus, Pilate's political sponsor in Rome, fell from power, and Pilate had much to fear from any bad reports about him. But Jesus' trial may well have taken place before A.D. 31, and the accusation of 19:12 would be a fearful one even with Sejanus in power: the emperor Tiberius was suspicious of the least talk of treason, and a delegation to Rome providing the slightest evidence that Pilate had supported a self-proclaimed king could lead to Pilate's beheading. *Philo tells us that Pilate also backed down much earlier in his career when the Jewish leaders threatened to petition the emperor against him.

"Friends" of powerful *patrons were their political dependents, and to be the "friend of the emperor" (NRSV, TEV) or the "friend of Caesar" (KJV, NASB, NIV) was a special honor. "Friend of the king" had been an office in Greek and ancient Near Eastern palaces (including Israel, from David through Herod the Great); "friend of the emperor" was likewise an official title with political implications.

19:13. Some commentators have thought that the "Stone Pavement" is the pavement in the fortress Antonia on the temple mount, but that pavement seems to date from a later period. Instead the text undoubtedly refers to the raised, outdoor paved area near Herod's palace, where the governor resided. Both Pilate and a later governor are known to have addressed audiences from this platform. Evidence suggests that the governor had to pronounce death sentences from the judgment seat (see comment on Rom 14:10-12).

19:14. The "day of Preparation" was the day that the Passover lamb would be slaughtered to be eaten that night (cf. comment on 18:28). (Jewish people reckoned days from sunset to sunset, so what we would call Friday night they considered the beginning of the sabbath, or Saturday.) Later *rabbis estimated that offerings began earlier on

Passover eve, but the slaughter of Passover lambs probably had to continue all day and was finally completed about the time the evening offering was slaughtered, roughly when Jesus died (about 3 p.m.).

The "sixth hour" should mean noon but by a different reckoning could mean 6 a.m., close to dawn. Or John could use it for a symbolic connection with 4:6 or a symbolic connection with Passover (many scholars argue here that the slaughter of Passover lambs began about noon). (John's other large work, Revelation, also uses time symbolically.)

19:15-16. For Pilate to free someone accused of treason or of insulting the emperor's *maiestas* would invite the same accusation against himself, especially at this time under Tiberius, one of the most paranoid rulers of the first century. Although not accommodating when he did not need to be, Pilate is known to have acceded to mob demands on other occasions. As a provincial governor he officially had full discretion to decree the penalty. Crucifixion was the standard Roman method of execution for slaves, revolutionaries or other provincials who were not Roman citizens (such as most Palestinian Jews).

The authorities' cry is typical of the irony of John: Jewish people prayed daily for the royal *Messiah, and one Jewish prayer that came to be part of the Passover celebration at least in later times acknowledges no king but God (cf. also comment on 8:33).

19:17-22
The Crucifixion

19:17. Condemned criminals normally carried their own cross (the horizontal beam, the *patibulum*, not the upright stake) to the site of the execution; the victim was usually stripped naked for the procession and execution as well, although this full nakedness must have offended some Jewish sensibilities in Palestine.

The probable site of Golgotha was outside the city wall and not far from Herod's palace—perhaps a thousand feet north/northeast of it. Roman custom placed crucifixions, and Jewish custom located stonings, outside towns rather than at their center (in the *Old Testament, cf. Lev 24:14, 23; Num 15:35-36; Deut 17:5; 21:19-21; 22:24; in the New Testament, cf. Luke 4:29; Acts 7:58).

19:18. Several stakes, at most about ten feet high, stood in Golgotha ready to be reused whenever executions occurred. On the top of the stake or slightly below the top was a groove into which the horizontal beam of the cross would be inserted after the prisoner had been fastened to it with ropes or nails.

According to Jewish tradition dating from the second century or earlier, Passover lambs would be hung up on iron hooks and flayed. Jesus here is hanged.

19:19. The condemned man was often required to carry a *titulus* stating the reason for his crucifixion, although it is not clear that it was usually displayed above the cross in this period. The charge against Jesus: one who attempted to usurp the prerogatives of royalty, which were properly dispensed only at the decree of Caesar. Jesus is charged with high treason against the majesty of the emperor.

19:20. The site of execution was necessarily outside the city, although the soldiers preferred that it be nearby (see comment on 19:17). Jewish people in the Roman Empire dealt with three or four basic languages: Greek, Latin, *Aramaic and Hebrew (of these, Greek especially was spoken outside Palestine and shared its prominence with Aramaic inside Palestine). Jewish inscriptions to foreigners were written in Greek and Latin.

19:21-22. No longer faced with the possibility of mob unrest or a complaint to Tiberius, Pilate returns to his characteristic lack of cooperation. In about this same year, Pilate minted a cheap coin of Tiberius bearing the augur's wand—a pagan symbol quite offensive to Jewish sensibilities.

19:23-37
Jesus' Death

19:23. Roman law as later codified in their legal Digests granted the soldiers the right to the clothes the executed man was wearing; it was customary to execute the condemned man naked. The basic unit of the Roman army was the *contubernium,* composed of eight soldiers who shared a tent; half-units of four soldiers each were sometimes assigned to special tasks, such as execution quads.

19:24. John's mention that the soldiers do not want to "tear" it might allude to the high priest's garment in the *Old Testament (Lev 21:10), which *Josephus mentions was also seamless; but this interpretation probably reads too much into the text. John finds two distinct acts in Psalm 22:18 (a very Jewish method of interpretation), as Matthew does in Zechariah 9:9 (see comment on Mt 21:4-7).

19:25-26. The evidence is disputed as to whether relatives and close friends were allowed near crucifixions; they probably were. In either case, the soldiers supervising the execution would have looked the other way in practice if they had no reason to forbid it; the prerogatives of motherhood were highly respected in the ancient world. Because Jesus may not be elevated far above the ground, Jesus' mother and *disciple can hear him without being extremely close to the cross.

19:27. Jesus makes an oral testament in front of witnesses, which makes it binding, and formally places his mother under his disciple's protection, providing for her after his death. Dying fathers could exhort sons to take care of surviving mothers (which they normally would do); for a disciple to be accorded a role in his teacher's family was a great honor to the disciple (disciples sometimes called their teachers "father").

A primary responsibility which Jewish custom included in "honoring one's father and mother" was providing for them (cf. 1 Sam 22:3) in their old age. Jesus' mother is probably in her mid to late forties, is probably a widow and lives in a society where women rarely earned much income; she is therefore officially especially dependent on her eldest son, Jesus, for support, although after his death her younger sons would support her.

19:28. Some scholars have suggested that Jesus may have recited the rest of Psalm 22 after the verse cited by Mark (15:34); in the light of Mark 15:35, this suggestion is not likely, but John could nonetheless allude here to the same psalm (Ps 22:15).

19:29-30. "Hyssop" was not the most natural instrument to use for this purpose. If this plant is identified as the *Origanum maru l.,* its stalk is over three feet long; others claim that it is a very small plant that could not have reached far, and they suggest a play on words with the similar-sounding term for "javelin." In either case, John *mentions* hyssop because of its significance in the Passover (Ex 12:22), fitting the symbolism of John 19 as a whole. "Sour wine," consisting of wine vinegar mixed with water, was often used by soldiers to quench their thirst.

19:31-33. Those bound with ropes often survived on the cross several days. The dying man could rest himself on a wooden seat (Latin *sedile*) in the middle of the cross. This support allowed him to breathe—and prolonged the agony of his death. When the soldiers needed to hasten death by asphyxiation, they would break the legs of the victims with iron clubs so they could no longer push themselves up; the skeleton of a crucified Jewish man recovered in 1968 confirms this practice attested in ancient literature. Romans would have allowed the bodies to rot on the cross, but Deuteronomy 21:23 and Jewish sensitivities about the sabbath require that these executions be speeded up, and Romans accommodated Jewish wishes particularly during the crowded festivals. (*Josephus declares that Jewish people always buried crucifixion victims before sunset.)

19:34. According to (probably) first-century Jewish tradition, the priests were supposed to pierce Passover lambs with a wood pole from their mouth to their buttocks.

Jewish tradition required certification that a person was dead before the person could be treated as dead, but Jewish observers would not treat the body as disrespectfully as this Roman does.

A foot soldier was armed with a short sword and a *pilum*, or lance; the *pilum* was of light wood with an iron head, and was about three and a half feet long. Such a lance could easily penetrate the pericardial sac which surrounds and protects the heart and contains watery fluid. A Greek might read this description as referring to a demigod, because Greek gods had ichor (which looked like water) instead of blood. But the person who has read the Gospel from start to finish would see in it a symbol rooted in *Old Testament and Jewish hopes; see comment on 7:37-39.

19:35. Eyewitness accounts were considered more valuable than secondhand accounts, and narrators who were eyewitnesses (like *Josephus) make note of that fact.

19:36. Although John here could allude to Psalm 34:20, he probably refers instead to the Passover lamb (Ex 12:46; Num 9:12). Jewish law (second century or earlier) stipulates the maximum corporal punishment for breaking the Passover lamb's bones.

19:37. Although a late rabbinic passage interpreted Zechariah 12:10 *messianically, the passage itself seems to refer to *God*'s having been pierced by the people of Jerusalem (before the coming of Jesus one would have assumed a figurative sense, "pierced with sorrow"). (Pronouns with divine referents seem to change readily in Zechariah; cf. 2:8-11 and 4:8-9, unless an angel is in view—4:4-6.)

19:38-42
Jesus' Burial

19:38. Crucifixion victims were usually thrown into a common grave for criminals and were not to be mourned publicly after their death; had the Romans had their way, the corpses would not have been buried at all. But exceptions seem to have been made at times if family or powerful *patrons interceded for the body. Burying the dead was a crucial and pious duty in Judaism, and an important act of love; being unburied was too horrible to be permitted even for criminals. To accomplish his task before sundown and the advent of the sabbath, Joseph of Arimathea has to hurry.

19:39. If this measure of Nicodemus's mixture is one of weight, it is as much as seventy-five of our pounds (Roman pounds were lighter); if it is a measure of volume identified with the Old Testament *log*, it may be less than seventy fluid ounces. In either case it is a lavish expression of devotion, as in 12:3; but other accounts of lavish devotion for beloved teachers are occasionally reported (a *Gentile convert allegedly burned eighty pounds of spices at the funeral of Gamaliel I, Paul's teacher), so the numbers need not be doubted. Myrrh was used for embalming the dead, and aloes for perfume.

19:40. John mentions the Jewish custom; Jewish people did not burn dead heroes, as Greeks and Romans did, or mutilate them for embalming, as Egyptians did. Bodies were wrapped in shrouds, sometimes expensive ones, especially prepared for burials. Jewish sources are emphatic that none of these actions may be undertaken unless the person is clearly dead; thus those burying Jesus have no doubt that he is dead. Here strips of linen rather than a full shroud are used, perhaps because of the imminent approach of the sabbath at sundown.

White linen garments were worn by Jewish priests, by some other ancient priests (devotees of Isis) and by angels in Jewish tradition (e.g., 2 Macc 11:8); they were also wrappings for the righteous dead.

19:41. On the locale, cf. "near the city" in verse 20: according to Jewish custom, burials had to be outside the city walls (one may compare the outrage of pious Jews over Antipas's building Tiberias on a graveyard). To be buried in a tomb not yet used was no doubt a special honor and would make the tomb difficult to confuse with others in the vicinity.

19:42. The sabbath (or in this case, the coming of Passover—18:28) interrupted all other activities. Joseph and Nicodemus did not need to "lay" Jesus there very carefully; this would have been only a preliminary burial even had the sabbath not approached, to be completed a year later, after the flesh had rotted off the bones.

20:1-10 The Discovery

Some have doubted the empty tomb story simply because Paul does not mention it (although he presupposes it; cf. 1 Cor 15:3-4), but the *disciples could not have credibly proclaimed the *resurrection in Jerusalem if Jesus' body were still in the tomb. Although ancient laws of evidence differed from modern ones (they depended heavily on probability), ancients, like moderns, would not have staked their lives on a report without investigating the tomb! Given how readily holy sites were venerated, believers in the resurrection themselves would have at least checked the tomb. Those modern critical scholars who have suggested that the original *disciples meant only that they had a spiritual experience but did not claim that Jesus rose bodily read their own modern culture into the *New Testament: "resurrection" meant bodily resurrection and nothing else, and no one would have persecuted the disciples for claiming that they had had merely a spiritual experience. Mere belief in ghosts and apparitions was widespread and would not have gotten them in trouble with anyone.

20:1. The nearest of kin would remain home mourning for seven days; Mary Magdalene, who would have grieved as much as the family, might have remained inside had it not been necessary to complete the work left unfinished due to the sabbath (19:42). But Jewish mourners as well as pagans were often known to visit tombs within the three days after the burial.

The first day of the week began at sundown on what we would call Saturday night, so the sabbath had ended hours before she approaches the tomb; that Mary would approach the tomb before daylight demonstrates her eager devotion to Jesus. Disk-shaped stones were often rolled in front of the entrances of tombs and were so heavy that they frequently required several men to roll them away.

20:2-3. That the authorities would have moved even the body—perhaps to a criminal's grave—is troublesome news. Ancient Jewish men did not accept women as reliable witnesses for most legal purposes (their witness was limited, but less so, in Roman courts), and this cultural tendency may further move John and Peter to look for themselves.

20:4-5. Comparison of characters was important in ancient writing and a standard *rhetorical technique. That the beloved disciple (on the traditional view taken in this commentary, John, but perhaps also meant to represent *disciples in general through his anonymity) is faster than Peter fits some other comparisons in the Gospel (13:23-24; 21:7). Depictions of physical prowess were part of *narratives extolling characters (e.g., *Josephus outswims most others in *Life* 15.3), so comparison may be in view here, showing that a normal disciple is as important as the famous Peter.

20:6-7. Had robbers stolen the body (a rare practice) they would have taken it in its wrappings; had they left the wrappings, they would have left them in disarray. Whoever left them, left them there neatly. The face cloth separate from the linen is not merely "folded up" (NIV) but "rolled up" (NASB, NRSV, TEV), which could be an indication of neatness, or that it was still rolled the way it had been when it was wrapped around Jesus' head—that his body had risen straight out of the wrappings and cloth.

The skeptic's proposal that Jesus had only swooned and then recovered would not explain how he could have loosed the strips tied around him or escaped a sealed tomb, but it also ignores the nature of crucifixion: *Josephus had three of his friends taken down alive from a cross, but two of them died *despite medical attention* because their bodies had been so weakened from the crucifixion.

20:8-10. This *disciple's faith may have been due to parallels with John 11 or to the way the cloths were laid (20:6-7); John implies that they would have already believed it from Scripture had they understood.

20:11-18
The First Appearance: Mary Magdalene

The witness of women was worth little in Judaism; that Jesus first appears to a woman would not have been fabricated and shows us how Jesus' values differ from those of his culture. Even the later church did not always maintain Jesus' countercultural stance, and they would hardly have chosen such initial witnesses in an environment where this account would reinforce pagan prejudices against Christians (see comments on Eph 5:22-33).

20:11. Jewish people took the first seven days of mourning so seriously that mourners could not wash, work, have intercourse or even study the *law. Jewish culture was serious about expressing rather than repressing grief. That the body is missing and thus people are prevented from bestowing final acts of love would be regarded as intolerably tragic; even tomb robbers usually left the body behind.

20:12-13. On the "white" clothing see 19:40; black garments were used for mourning.

20:14. In Jewish tradition, angels could appear in different forms. Jewish traditions in *Pseudo-Philo also speak of God changing the appearance of some *Old Testament human characters so they would not be recognized, and this evidence might reflect more widespread Jewish tradition.

20:15. Gardeners were at the bottom of the social scale, and a gardener there would have tended to the gardening, not to the tomb itself. But Mary has no better guess concerning his identity. (That he could be a tomb robber does not occur to Mary; tomb robbers were unlikely to come during the mourning period, when visits to the tomb were still frequent, and he would have reacted with more fear or hostility at seeing her if he were one.)

20:16. "Rabboni" means "my teacher" and is more personal and less formal than the title "*Rabbi."

20:17-18. The verb translated "Touch me not" (KJV) is a present imperative and is probably better translated "Stop clinging to me" (NASB). The reason she must release him is that she must go testify for him in the short time remaining in view of his coming ascension—despite the cultural opposition to sending a woman to testify to such an important event and one so impossible for unbelievers to accept. "Brothers" suggests that 3:3 is now in effect.

20:19-23
Appearing to Other Disciples

20:19. The *disciples would remain inside to mourn; the Feast of Unleavened Bread is also still going on, so none of them would have left Jerusalem for Galilee yet anyway. Proper residences were equipped with bolts and locks. Bolted doors would prevent anyone from entering (a heavy bolt could be slid through rings attached to the door and its frame), unless one could walk through closed doors. Jesus' appearance in the locked room suggests a *resurrection body whose nature is superior to that normally envisioned in ancient Jewish literature. "Peace be with you" was the standard Jewish greeting, but it was meant to communicate peace (like a thoughtful "God bless you" today).

20:20. Wounds were sometimes shown as evidence in court; here their function is to identify that it is the same Jesus who died. In much of Jewish tradition, the dead would be resurrected in the same form in which they died before God healed them, so that everyone would recognize that the person who stood before them was the same one who had died. "Hands" includes one's wrists, which was where the spikes would have been driven; a nail through the palm would not have secured the person in place on the cross, since the victim's weight would have ripped the hand open.

20:21. In Jewish tradition prophets often appointed their successors. Judaism sometimes conceived of prophets as God's agents; the sender authorized agents with his authority to the extent that they accurately represented him.

20:22. Jesus' breathing on them recalls Genesis 2:7, when God breathed into Adam the breath of life (it might also be relevant that later Jewish tradition sometimes connected this passage with Ezek 37, when God's Spirit or wind revives the dead). Jewish literature especially connected the *Holy Spirit with the power to prophesy, or speak for God.

20:23. Acting as God's agents (20:21) the *disciples could pronounce the divine prerogative on his authority (i.e., pronouncing it when he would do so).

20:24-31
Appearing to Thomas

20:24-25. Only the evidence of his

senses could persuade Thomas that the other disciples had not seen merely a phantom or apparition; a ghost or spiritual vision as in pagan tradition, or an image produced by a magician, would not be corporeal. The *resurrection body, by contrast, was clearly corporeal, although the exact nature of such corporeality may have been debated among early Christians. Thomas does not doubt that his friends think they saw something; he doubts only the nature of their experience.

20:26. See comment on 20:19. Now that a week had passed, the feast would be over and the *disciples would thus soon be ready to return to Galilee unless they received orders to the contrary.

20:27-28. Thomas's response is a confession of Jesus' deity; cf. Revelation 4:11. Pliny, a governor writing near the probable location of John's readers two or three decades after John, reports that Christians sing hymns to Christ "as to a god."

20:29-31. Jesus' blessing (v. 29) applies to the readers of John who believe through the apostolic testimony (v. 31); verse 30 is the culmination of John's signs motif: signs sometimes lead to faith and sometimes lead to opposition.

21:1-14
Appearing in Galilee

Some modern scholars have thought that John 21 was not part of the original Gospel of John because it seems anticlimactic. But the conclusion (book 24) of the most popularly read work of Greco-Roman antiquity, the *Iliad,* is also anticlimactic; ancient readers and writers would not have viewed epilogues in these terms.

21:1-3. Fishing was often done at night (cf. Lk 5:5). Some people have reported that fish are more easily caught at night than in the day on the Sea of Galilee (here called Tiberias); they could then be sold in the morning.

21:5-6. Jewish tradition recognized God as sovereign over fish (e.g., Tobit 6:2-5), which no doubt encouraged many fishermen's prayers. Nets were probably made of rope woven from substances like flax or hemp; it is thought that nets had a narrow end pulled by the men in the boat and a wider end sunk by attached weights.

21:7. Peter should not need help recognizing Jesus, but cf. 20:4-5. "Naked" was used as a relative term (it could mean "without an outer garment"); religious Palestinian Jews avoided nakedness in public. Peter has an inner garment or at least a loincloth on; but even in the cool of dawn he may have worked up enough of a sweat to have kept his outer garment off. (The Sea of Galilee is lower in elevation than Jerusalem.) His outer garment is wrapped around his waist or tucked over his belt.

21:8. A hundred yards is too far out for Peter to have waded; he must have been swimming when he first jumped from the boat.

21:9-10. Although Jesus provides as he did in chapter 6, this time he gives them a chance to share as the lad had in 6:9. The very small class of leisured, wealthy landowners in the Roman Empire despised manual labor, but most manual laborers seem to have taken pride in their work (they mention their occupations on their tombstones); Jesus affirms their fishing, even though that, too, had been his provision (21:5-6).

21:11. Jerome claimed that ancient zoologists counted 153 kinds of fish, but extant copies of their writings do not support his hypothesis, which may have been his attempt to explain this verse. Various symbolic interpretations of "153" have been offered (from Hebrew words that total "153" when their numerical value is reckoned, to it being a triangular number that would have impressed ancient *Pythagorean philosophers). But ancient miracle stories would stress numbers to heighten the reality of the miracle (e.g., 2 Kings 19:35); 153 is no doubt used because the *disciples were impressed enough to have counted the fish. The risen Lord has provided them more fish than they could possibly eat by themselves.

21:12-14. The host or the head of the household would usually pass out the bread; cf. 6:11.

21:15-23
Two Commissions

21:15-17. The two Greek words for "love" here are used interchangeably elsewhere in John and generally in the literature of this period; the point is not (against some interpreters) in the different terms, but that love for Jesus must be demonstrated by obedience to his call and service to his people. As a "follower," Peter is one of the sheep himself (10:4; on "sheep" see comment on Jn 10:1-18; for the background on faithful shepherds to feed them, see Jer 23:4; cf. Ezek 34).

21:18-19. Predictions in antiquity were often enigmatic; this one indicates that Peter will not have control even over dressing himself for a journey—in this case, being prepared for execution. For "glorifying" God like Jesus in martyrdom, see 12:23-27; strong tradition declares that Peter was crucified in Rome under Nero about A.D. 64.

21:20-23. The tradition about the beloved disciple's call was that Jesus told Peter, "It's none of your business," but this tradition was misinterpreted to mean that the beloved disciple would live till Jesus' return. The point is that Jesus has the right to choose who will be martyred and who will survive. According to strong (though not unanimous) tradition, John was one of the few original *apostles to escape martyrdom.

21:24-25
Attestation of Witnesses

21:24. Greco-Roman and Jewish legal documents typically ended with attestation by witnesses. "We know that his witness is true" may be a postscript added by John's own *disciples, attesting to the veracity of his eyewitness, although it is not beyond John to write such words himself (19:35; cf. the plural witness in 1 John, e.g., 1:1-4).

21:25. When writers had more data before them than they could record, they often noted that they were being selective. Greek, Jewish and *Samaritan writers included *hyperboles like this one as well, sometimes speaking of how the world could not contain the knowledge a particular *rabbi had of the *law, and so forth.

ACTS

Introduction

Authorship. The tradition that Luke is the author of Luke-Acts has nothing against it and fits what little we know about Luke. The style and themes of Acts clearly reflect the same authorship as those of the Gospel of Luke do. Luke varies between Greek literary prose style and a Jewish style of Greek heavily influenced by the *Septuagint.

A number of terms in Luke-Acts are frequent in medical literature, although most of these terms also occur elsewhere, so this terminology alone would not prove Lukan authorship. Physicians could be lower class, even slaves, but were generally well educated; the presence of women in that field (especially midwifery) may have made some physicians more conscious of women's concerns (which Luke-Acts is).

Date. Because Acts breaks off before Paul's death, some scholars have suggested that Acts (and hence Luke or its hypothetical earlier draft, proto-Luke) was written before A.D. 64. Others, reading

Luke 21, suggest a date after A.D. 70, saying that Acts breaks off about A.D. 62 for literary reasons or because Luke only needed *positive* legal precedents. The evidence is not conclusive on either side, but because Luke clearly used Mark as a source, dating Luke-Acts to A.D. 62 would call into question the usual dating of Mark to A.D. 64. Most scholars therefore date Luke-Acts later, sometime after 70. Neither the dating of Mark nor that of Luke-Acts is secure, but this commentary tentatively accepts a date for the latter in the early seventies.

Purpose: Legal. One purpose of the work is to record consistent legal precedents in favor of the early Christians. In Acts every Roman court declares Christians not guilty, and this record has so impressed some scholars that they have suggested Luke wrote Acts as a court brief on Paul's behalf. More likely, Luke cites a wide range of legal precedents from different local courts (which would be helpful but not binding) for the same reason that *Josephus does on behalf of Judaism: to argue that Christianity should enjoy continued legal protection in the empire. Luke thus gives Christians legal ammunition (Lk 21:15) and paves the way for later Christian lawyers and philosophers like Tertullian and Justin, who would argue for the toleration of Christianity.

Purpose: Apologetic. All history was written with a purpose; it was influenced by the literary conventions of the theater and also used to illustrate moral principles. *Josephus uses it to justify God and Israel after the war of A.D. 70; *Plutarch and *Livy use it to teach morals; even *Tacitus writes as an aristocrat longing for the grandeur of old Rome. History with a theme or focal point (church history, social history, African-American history, etc.) is no less history for having an interest or editorial perspective. Luke's apologetic purpose is especially advanced in the book's speeches.

Acts works on several fronts: the gospel confronts Roman law courts, Greek philosophers, rural Asian farmers and others on their own terms, and nothing can stop it. A major theme is the relationship of Christianity to Judaism. Ancient religions were respected by virtue of their age, and Christians needed to demonstrate that the *Old Testament was their book and that they were the authentic voice of Judaism (despite the opposition of much of the Jewish community of Luke's day to this claim). Luke develops this theme by displaying the fulfillment of Old Testament motifs.

Genre: History. Historians were permitted a wide degree of latitude on details, although they were expected to get the bulk of a story right insofar as their sources were accurate. Luke is meticulously careful with his sources in the Gospel (Lk 1:1-4), and we may regard him as no less trustworthy in Acts, where we can often check him against letters of Paul (few if any of which would have been available to Luke). Some sections of Acts also include eyewitness accounts of someone who journeyed with Paul; contrary to the opinion of some scholars, "we" normally *did* literally mean "we" in ancient *narratives. Luke is a careful enough editor that had he not meant to include himself in the company of Paul, he would not have allowed an earlier source's "we" to stand. It appears in historical writing (like *Josephus) as well as novels, but only historical works had historical prologues (Lk 1:1-4; Acts 1:1-2). Many historical writers also sought an entertaining, lively style just as novelists did; thus the mention of "plot devices" in the following commentary means only that Luke was a good writer, not that he was an inaccurate historian.

The question of the speeches' historicity invites special comment. Ancient writers never recorded speeches verbatim (cf. even Acts 2:40); they took notes if they were present, got the gist and were guided by their knowledge (when available) of the speechmaker's style and proper speechmaking technique. Historians sometimes fabricated speeches (as *Josephus does for a speech at Masada with no surviving witnesses) but used the basic thrust of the speech when data about it was available. Luke's editing brings out some consistent themes in the *apostolic-proclamation speeches in Acts, but we may also be confident that they reflect the substance of messages given on those occasions, to which Luke should have had access. Acts' speeches are significant for the book's purpose; they make up roughly one-fourth of the book.

Luke-Acts may be closer to standard forms of Greco-Roman historical writing than are the other Gospels, which resemble ancient biography. Whereas Matthew, Mark and John wrote forms of ancient biography, Luke's second volume shows that he wrote history as well. Luke and Acts are each roughly the same length as Matthew, with Mark one-half and John two-thirds that length, indicating scrolls of standardized lengths (Matthew, Luke and Acts were each close to the maximum length for scrolls, between thirty-two and thirty-five feet). In the first volume, Luke writes about Jesus; in the second volume, Luke writes about the *Spirit's activity in the Jewish and *Gentile *churches, especially through the figures of Peter and Paul. Many ancient writers would make comparisons between figures as part of their historiographic technique. (*Plutarch is especially known for paralleling Greek and Roman figures in his biographies; perhaps more to the point, 1 Kings 17—2 Kings 13 seems to compare Elijah and his successor Elisha.)

Message. Aside from the themes already mentioned and typical Lukan emphases on prayer, signs and wonders, and the *Spirit, Luke's whole book is structured around world evangelization (1:8), with six or eight summary statements throughout the book displaying the spread of the gospel (see 6:7; 9:31; 12:24; 16:5; 19:20; 28:31). For Luke, the ultimate goal is crosscultural communication and world evangelization, and the requisite power to carry out the task is only the *Holy Spirit.

Commentaries. Particular commentaries most helpful in preparing this commentary were Kirsopp Lake and Henry J. Cadbury, *The Acts of the Apostles: English Translation and Commentary,* vol. 4 of *The Beginnings of Christianity,* ed. F. J. Foakes Jackson and Kirsopp Lake, 5 vols. (1933; reprint, Grand Rapids, Mich.: Baker Book House, 1979); and F. F. Bruce, *The Book of the Acts,* NICNT, rev. ed. (Grand Rapids, Mich.: Eerdmans, 1988). Other useful commentaries include David J. Williams, *Acts,* NIBC (Peabody, Mass.: Hendrickson, 1990); I. Howard Marshall, *The Acts of the Apostles,* TNTC (Grand Rapids, Mass.: Eerdmans, 1980).

1:1-5 Preparing to Go

In a two-volume work it was customary to recapitulate the theme or the end of the first volume in the beginning of the second. Thus Luke 24:36-53 is recapitulated in Acts 1:1-14, repeating many points in greater detail. Historians had freedom to arrange materials in their own words and to paraphrase, and readers would have regarded different wording in two volumes of the same work as variation for the sake of readability, not as an accidental oversight.

1:1. This is not an uncommon way to begin a second volume. "Began" may indicate that Acts continues a report of Jesus' works through the *church, but it is common Lukan style and may simply reflect a Semitic or Koine (the common Greek dialect) figure of speech. Theophilus seems to be the *patron, or sponsor, of the work, to whom Luke formally dedicates it (as was the custom; see comment on Lk 1:3-4).

1:2-3. Sample evidences were reported in Luke 24, and the forty days here allows for the Galilean ministry reported in the other Gospels. Greeks also wanted eyewitnesses to document the epiphanies (or appearances) of their gods or goddesses, but those appearances were not clearly physical or sustained over such a long period of personal contact.

1:4. "Gathering together" (NASB) is literally "took salt together," an idiom for table fellowship. This act was the ultimate sign of physicality (in many Jewish traditions, angels could not genuinely eat human food) and intimacy (see comment on Lk 5:29-32).

1:5. The *Holy Spirit was associated both with purification (thus "*baptism") and wisdom or *prophecy in segments of ancient Judaism. But the emphasis was usually on the ability to prophesy (speak for God under his inspiration), and Luke emphasizes this aspect of the Spirit almost to the exclusion of others.

1:6-11 Coming and Going

1:6. This question was the most natural one for the *disciples to ask Jesus. He had been talking about the *kingdom (1:3), and the references to the outpouring of the *Spirit in the *Old Testament were all in the context of Israel's restoration (Is 32:15; 44:3; Ezek 36:25-28; 37:14; 39:29; Joel 2:28—3:1).

1:7. See Matthew 24:36. Jewish *apocalyptic writers often saw history as divided into epochs determined by God, yet they sometimes used their calculations of the epochs to predict that they were near the end. Jesus says that the Father has determined the time but not revealed it.

1:8. Although the time of Israel's restoration might be unknown, the end-time mission given to Israel, to be Spirit-anointed witnesses (Is 42:1, 4, 6; 43:10-12; 44:3, 8), is being given now. The *disciples are thus to serve as the prophetic remnant within Israel. (When Israel had disobeyed God, he had always kept a remnant; see comment on Rom 11:1-5.)

Different ancient texts referred to different places by the phrase "ends of the earth." Writers commonly meant Ethiopia (8:27), but in Acts the short-term strategic goal is Rome (the *Psalms of Solomon 8:15 uses "ends of the earth" thus), to make an urgent impact on the empire. From a long-range perspective, however, all peoples are meant (Ps 67:1, 7; Is 45:22; 49:6; 52:10; so Acts 13:47).

1:9-11. In Greek stories, various heroes ascended to heaven, usually by dying and becoming gods (like Heracles on his funeral pyre). For Luke, however, the ascension is only a confirmation of Jesus' status at the *resurrection, a coronation of the king who was both human and divine all along. Jewish accounts of Elijah (from the Old Testament) and others (from later traditions) taken up to heaven show that Jewish readers would understand the ascension, but again, the difference is between the exaltation of a pious man and the exaltation of the Lord, to faith in whom they are to summon humanity. Angels ascended and descended, but Luke's contemporaries did not regard these angelic movements as special events. (Judaism also spoke figuratively of divine Wisdom ascending or descending but never in a *narrative context, because Wisdom was a personification, not a historical character.)

Moses had passed on his work to Joshua, Elijah to Elisha, and *rabbis and philosophers to their *disciples. This model of succession created occasional "succession narratives" that described the passing on of a teacher's call. Jesus' ascension immediately after the commission of 1:8 leaves believers as his successors, responsible for the job of world evangelization, until his return in the same glorified body (1:11).

1:12-14
The Prayer Meeting

Given the fifty days from Passover to Pentecost, and subtracting Jesus' time in the tomb and the forty days of 1:3, this meeting may have lasted close to a week. (In church tradition, possibly based on this passage, it is ten days before Pentecost.)

1:12. Mount Olivet was the place of the *Messiah's expected coming (Zech 14:4). It was about half a mile east of the temple and several hundred feet above it—close to "a sabbath day's journey," which was two thousand cubits. (This expression is used as a measure of length, not to indicate that it was the sabbath.)

1:13. The wealthy part of Jerusalem was the Upper City, where upper rooms were more common and more spacious. Although upper rooms in many Palestinian homes were nothing more than attics, ancient texts report gatherings of large numbers of sages in more spacious upper rooms.

The list of the names of the Twelve varies slightly in different *New Testament texts, indicating that the list had not been standardized. But business documents from the period show that it was common for people to have two identifying names, either or both of which could be used. The insertion of "brother" before Judas in the KJV is unlikely; ancient inscriptions use Greek phrases like "Judas of James" to mean "Judas *son* of James."

1:14. Given the culture's usual downplaying of women's public roles, the equal participation of women is noteworthy, especially their apparent mixing with the men. (However, women were not necessarily segregated from men in synagogue services, as some have maintained.) "Prayer" frequently meant "prayer house," or "*synagogue," outside Palestine, and some commentators have suggested that meaning here; but Luke usually uses the term "synagogue" for that meaning. The text need not imply uninterrupted prayer, but it must mean more prayer than usual (i.e., more than several hours a day) or Luke would have no reason to mention it.

1:15-26
Replacing an Apostate Apostle

When the probably *Essene community of the *Dead Sea Scrolls chose a group of leaders which included twelve special officials, it was meant to symbolize that this community was the true remnant of Israel, faithful to God even though the rest of the nation was apostate. Jesus had chosen twelve special *disciples to make the same point, so the number had to be restored to twelve official leaders at least until the point of having twelve had been effectively communicated. Judas had forfeited his place by apostasy.

1:15. According to a Jewish tradition of uncertain date, 120 elders first passed on the law in the time of Ezra. Then again, the *Dead Sea Scrolls required one priest for every ten men, so 120 may be the number of people a team of twelve leaders could best accommodate; other disciples may not have all been present at one time. But Luke's point may be simply that the upper room is full (see comment on 1:13).

1:16-17. Jewish people believed that Scripture "had to be fulfilled" and that God was sovereign over the events of history. Greco-Roman writers used fate as a plot-moving device, but Luke sees history moving in accordance with God's revealed purposes in Scripture.

1:18-19. *Digressions were common in ancient literature; Luke makes a brief one here. The account has features in common with and diverging from Matthew 27:1-10; these similarities and differences can be explained on the basis of two authors reporting different details and ancient historians' freedom on such details. (Some ancient spoofs on suicide attempts report ropes breaking while a person was attempting to hang himself or herself, but these accounts were normally fictitious and at best would have been uncommon in real life!)

1:20. Here Peter uses the Jewish interpretive principle *qal vahomer,* or "how much more," argument: if the psalmist (Ps 69:25; 109:8) could speak thus of prominent accusers of the righteous in general, how much more does this principle apply to the epitome of wickedness, the betrayer of the *Messiah? (*New Testament writers appropriately apply many of the points of Ps 69, a psalm of the righteous sufferer, to Jesus.)

1:21-22. Eyewitnesses (cf. 1:8) were very important in ancient times, as they are today; hence the need to select someone who had been with Jesus from his *baptism to his *resurrection.

1:23-26. The lot was often used to select people for special duties in the Old Testament (1 Chron 24:7; 25:8) and in the *Dead Sea Scrolls. It was also used to decide other matters (so the *rabbis, the Jewish historian *Josephus and others), and as a form of divination in Greek circles. Jewish people used the lot because they believed in God's sovereignty (God even made it work for pagans in Jon 1:7, to expose Jonah's disobedience), although they forbade all forms of divination.

Double (in the case of Joseph Barsabbas, triple) names were quite common, especially with common names (like Joseph) that required qualification. "Barsabbas" is *Aramaic for "son of the sabbath," perhaps because he was born on the sabbath.

2:1-4
The Proof of Pentecost

Jewish people associated the outpouring of the *Spirit especially with the end of the age (1:6), and several signs God gave on the day of Pentecost indicate that in some sense, although the *kingdom is not yet consummated (1:6-7), its powers had been initiated by the *Messiah's first coming (2:17).

2:1. Pentecost was celebrated as a feast of covenant renewal in the *Dead Sea Scrolls; some later texts celebrate the giving of the law on Mount Sinai. (Some commentators have suggested that Luke intends a parallel between Moses' giving the law and Jesus' giving the Spirit, but the law-Pentecost connection may be later than Luke, and little in Acts 2 suggests that Luke makes the connection, even if some Jewish Christians before him might have. More significant is the crowd drawn by the feast; see comment on 2:5.)

2:2. God elsewhere used wind to symbolize his *Spirit, who would revive the dead at the future restoration of Israel (Ezek 37). This symbol shows the eruption into history of what was anticipated for the future.

2:3. God cast his glory on each tabernacle in which he chose to dwell before the exile (Ex 40:34-35; 1 Kings 8:10-11). But fire was also used to describe God's impending judgment in the day of his fury and thus could serve as a sign of the future (Is 66:15; cf. comment on Lk 3:16). (Others have paralleled the fire on Sinai when God gave the law—Ex 19:18—or fire's use in purifying metals.)

2:4. Some scholars have adduced instances of incoherent speech in other cultures as parallels to this speaking in tongues, but the purported parallels from Greco-Roman antiquity are weak. Luke presents this speech not as incoherent but as worship in languages they do not know, and he points to an *Old Testament background in the gift of *prophecy (see comment on 2:16-18).

2:5-13 The Peoples of Pentecost

The most sensible setting for the encounter Luke describes here is the temple courts. If the *disciples are still meeting in the "upper room" of 1:13 (this point is debated), they would be near the temple; very large upper rooms were found only in Jerusalem's Upper City, near the temple.

2:5. Jewish people from throughout the Roman and Parthian worlds would gather for the three main feasts (Tabernacles, Passover and Pentecost). Because Pentecost was only fifty days after Passover, some who had spent much to make a rare pilgrimage to Jerusalem stayed between the two feasts. Pentecost was probably the least popular of the three pilgrimage festivals, but *Josephus attests that it was nevertheless crowded.

2:6-8. The Jews from Parthia would know *Aramaic; those from the Roman Empire, Greek. But many of them would also be familiar with local languages spoken in outlying areas of their cities. (Even most Palestinian Jews were functionally bilingual, as are people in many parts of the world today.)

2:9-11. Although these are Jews, they are culturally and linguistically members of many nations; thus, even from the *church's inception as an identifiable community, the *Spirit proleptically moved the church into multicultural diversity under Christ's lordship.

Some commentators have thought that this list of nations corresponds to ancient astrological lists, but the parallels are not very close. More likely is the proposal that Luke has simply updated the names of nations in the table of nations (Gen 10). Those nations were scattered at the tower of Babel, where God judged them by making them unintelligible to each other (Gen 11); here God reverses the judgment in a miracle that transcends the language barrier.

2:12-13. Writers (whether writing fact or fiction) often used questions to set up a response. Ancient writers sometimes described inspiration in terms of drunkenness; Greeks believed in frenzied inspiration by the gods, and *Philo, a Jewish writer thoroughly in touch with Greek ideas, wrote of divine intoxication more than any other extant writer. Thus experiences of the transcendent (whether God-inspired or moved by base spirit possession) sometimes appeared to outsiders as ecstasy similar to drunkenness. (Although drunkenness was common among Greeks, it would have been a grievous accusation in Jewish Palestine, where it was regarded as obnoxious and sinful.)

2:14-21
The Prophecy of Pentecost

2:14-15. In Greco-Roman society, public speakers would normally stand to speak. Peter answers the questions (2:12-13) in reverse order. People usually got drunk at night (cf. 1 Thess 5:7), at banquets, not at 9 a.m.; people might have a hangover in the morning, but they would hardly act drunk.

2:16-18. "This" (2:16) refers to the speaking in tongues (2:6, 12), which Peter says fulfills Joel's message about the *Spirit of *prophecy, perhaps by means of a Jewish *qal vahomer* ("lesser to greater") argument: If the Spirit can inspire them to speak languages they do not know, how much more could he inspire them to prophesy the word of the Lord in their own language? Visions and dreams were especially prophetic activity, and Peter underlines this point by adding "and they will prophesy" at the end of 2:18 (not in Joel).

Peter reads Joel's "afterward" (2:28) as "in the last days," a phrase that in the prophets normally meant after the day of the Lord (Is 2:2; Mic 4:1), which fits Joel's context (Joel 2:30—3:3). Because the future age was to be inaugurated with the *Messiah's coming, it has been inaugurated in at least some sense because the Messiah, Jesus, had come—a point the outpouring of the Spirit on his followers is meant to demonstrate.

2:19. Joel 2:30 has "wonders" but not "signs"; Peter may add "signs" because he wishes to show that at least some requisite signs took place on earth (Acts 2:22; cf. Deut 26:8). "Blood, fire and columns of smoke" is the language of war.

2:20-21. In Joel the sun would be blotted out and the moon discolored especially by the locust (and/or human) invasion (Joel 2:2, 10; 3:15). Peter suggests that in some anticipatory sense, this final time of God's salvation for Israel has begun. Tongues prove that the *Spirit of *prophecy has come, which proves that salvation has come, which proves that the messianic era has come, and thus that the *Messiah has come.

Peter breaks off his quote from Joel here, but resumes with the final line of Joel 2:32 ("as many as the Lord calls") at the end of his sermon (Acts 2:39). Thus his sermon is a standard Jewish (*midrashic) exposition of the last line he quoted, and answers the question: What is the name of the Lord on whom they are to call? In the Hebrew text, "Lord" here is the sacred name of God (Yahweh), which readers in the *synagogue would pronounce as the word for "Lord" (Adonai); in the Greek text that Peter probably cites to communicate with hearers from many nations, it is simply the Greek word for "Lord," but everyone would know that it means "God" here.

2:22-40
The Preaching of Pentecost

As Kenneth Bailey has pointed out, Peter's sermon here involves an extensive chiasm, a reverse-parallel literary structure: A. Jesus whom you crucified

(2:23, 36b); B. David said, "The Lord . . . is at my right hand" (2:25, 34b); C. David died/did not ascend (2:29, 34a); D. David prophesied/the *Spirit is evidenced (2:30a, 33c); E. God swore/ the promise of the Spirit (2:30b, 33b); F. Christ enthroned (2:30c, 33a); G. David foresaw/the eleven testify (2:31a, 32b); H. Jesus' *resurrection (2:31b, 32a); I. Jesus did not rot (2:31cd). Point G connects the disciples' witness with prophetic empowerment (see comment on 1:8).

2:22-28. Peter quotes Psalm 16 to establish his point (developed in Acts 2:29-32): God would raise the *Messiah from the dead. Some anti-Semites have used texts like 2:23 to attack Jewish people in general, but Peter's critique of their corporate responsibility (cf. 2 Sam 12:9) is no harsher than that of *Old Testament prophets (e.g., Amos, Isaiah, Jeremiah), and cannot rightly be used as if it were.

2:29-31. Peter argues that the psalm cannot refer to David, because David did see corruption (rot). (A tomb in David's honor had been dedicated outside Jerusalem, along with one of Huldah the prophetess.) Rather, the psalm refers to David's ultimate descendant, whom everyone agreed to be the *Messiah (the anointed king), by definition (Acts 2:30; Ps 132:11; cf. Ps 89:3-4).

2:32. The Scripture was clear; they were eyewitnesses that Jesus fulfilled it, and their witness is confirmed by the outpouring of the *Spirit, which has no other biblical explanation (2:16-21, 33).

2:33-35. Jewish interpreters often linked texts using the same word or phrase (the principle was called *gezerah shavah*). Peter thus introduces Psalm 110:1, a clearly *messianic passage that includes "right hand" and speaks of exaltation just as Psalm 16 does. (Those commentators who see a link with Moses here point out a Jewish tradition that Moses ascended to heaven to receive the law; but the text makes better sense as a simple exposition of the psalm in question.)

2:36. From Psalm 110:1 Peter shows that the *resurrected one is the one whom David called "the Lord." Thus he bears the name of "the Lord" that Joel mentioned (2:32; see comment on Acts 2:21).

2:37-38. Peter instructs the people how to call on the Lord's name (2:21): be *baptized in Jesus' name. Because baptism was a sign of conversion to Judaism normally reserved for pagans, Peter's demand would offend his Jewish hearers and cost them respectability. He calls for a public, radical testimony of conversion, not a private, noncommittal request for salvation with no conditions. "In the name of Jesus Christ" distinguishes this sort of baptism, requiring faith in Christ, from other ancient baptisms; this phrase simply means that the person being baptized confesses Christ. (Acts always uses this phrase with "be baptized"—the passive, never the active; it does not denote a formula said over the person being baptized, but rather indicates the confession of faith of the person receiving baptism; see 2:21 and 22:16.)

Although different segments of Judaism tended to emphasize different aspects of the *Spirit (e.g., purification and wisdom in the *Dead Sea Scrolls, or *prophecy by the *rabbis and many others), and Luke's writings specifically emphasize the Spirit of inspiration and prophecy, Luke concurs with other *New Testament writers that the Spirit's work is theologically all one package (cf. comment on 8:14-15).

2:39. Those who read the whole book of Acts will suspect that those who "are far off" are the *Gentiles (Is 57:19;

cf. Acts 2:17), but Peter undoubtedly is thinking of Jewish people scattered outside Palestine. This universal outpouring of the *Spirit was reserved in the Old Testament for the end time and was expected to continue throughout that time.

2:40. Ancient historians edited and arranged speeches; they did not cite them verbatim (nor could anyone have done so unless the speech was short—rhetoricians sometimes continued for hours—and the speaker provided the author his prepared manuscript). Luke thus summarizes Peter's point.

2:41-47
The Power of Pentecost

2:41. Considering *Josephus's estimate of six thousand *Pharisees in all Palestine, three thousand conversions to the new Jesus movement in Jerusalem is no small start! The temple mount had many immersion pools that worshipers used to purify themselves ritually; mass *baptisms could thus be conducted quickly.

2:42. Most special groups in antiquity ate together (*mystery cults, Pharisaic fellowships, burial associations, etc.). Many Greek associations met for communal meals only once a month, however (contrast 2:46). This earliest Christian practice of daily meals (later reduced to weekly) is thus noteworthy.

Table fellowship denoted intimacy, and discussions or even lectures at meals were common. Given the topic of discussion recommended by Jewish pietists and what this text says about teaching and prayer (possibly including participation in the temple prayers—3:1), early Christian fellowship undoubtedly centered more on intimate worship, sharing and learning the Scriptures than its modern Western counterpart tends to do.

2:43-45. The Greek language Luke uses here is language that *Pythagoreans and others used for the ideal, utopian community. Those who have argued that the early *church made a mistake in 2:44-45 are thus reading their own views into the Bible, not hearing Luke's message, because Luke portrays this radical lifestyle as the result of the outpouring of the *Spirit.

Some Jewish groups, like the group that lived at *Qumran, followed the Pythagorean model and turned all their possessions over to the leaders of the community so they could all withdraw from society. That is hardly the case here, although the economic sharing is no less radical. The early Christians acknowledge that Jesus owns both them and their property (cf. 4:32); they sell off property to meet needs as they arise (4:34-35) and open their homes as meeting places for fellow Christians (2:46). These actions do not reflect an *ascetic ideal, as in some Greek and Jewish sects, but instead the practice of radically valuing people over possessions. Such behavior reportedly continued among Christians well into the second century, and it was long ridiculed by pagans until pagan values finally overwhelmed the *church.

2:46-47. Temples were among the best public places to gather, and people often congregated there. There were hours of public prayer at the morning and evening offerings (3:1).

3:1-10
Healing in His Name

Luke here provides the most prominent example of the wonders he mentioned in 2:43.

3:1. There were hours of prayer at the morning and evening offerings (cf. 2:42); the time of prayer for the evening offering mentioned here is about 3 p.m. (The *Dead Sea Scrolls and later sources suggest also a third time of prayer, probably at sunset.)

3:2-3. The "Beautiful Gate" was probably a popular title for the Nicanor Gate (named for its Alexandrian donor), the main and largest gate, made of the most expensive bronze. It was in the Court of the Women on the east, facing the gate of the sanctuary, and must have been especially beautiful in the light of the rising sun. Situated above fifteen steps, beyond which neither women nor the maimed and unclean could pass, it may have hosted beggars on its steps who could appeal to those going to the Court of Israel.

Begging alms at public places was common in antiquity, although other peoples did not stress charity as the Jewish people did. In Judaism only those who could not work made their living this way, but charity was highly regarded, and the lame or blind would not have to go hungry, especially if they were near the temple. Congenital infirmities were thought harder to cure than other kinds (Jn 9:32).

3:4-10. Ancient miracle workers usually prayed or invoked spirits rather than commanded the sick person to be healed (the *New Testament also recommends prayer—Jas 5:14); but the *Old Testament has ample precedent for doing miracles by simply declaring the word of the Lord, as a prophet speaking God's will (e.g., 2 Kings 1:10; 2:14, 21-22, 24; 4:43; 5:10). "In the name of Jesus Christ" here probably means "acting as his representative, (I say to you)" or "Jesus cures you" (Acts 3:16; 4:10-12; cf. comment on Jn 14:12-14).

3:11-26
A Preaching Opportunity

Signs and wonders often provide opportunity for witness in Acts, but the emphasis is always on the proclamation of the good news itself.

3:11. From the steps of the Beautiful Gate Peter, John and the beggar pass through the temple courts to the eastern colonnade, which supposedly remained from Solomon's temple (see comment on Jn 10:23).

3:12. Jewish people often thought wonderworkers did miracles (e.g., causing rain) by their great piety, which required God to pay attention to them. Luke emphasizes that the *apostles were normal people, filled with God's *Spirit (Acts 14:15).

3:13. The "God of Abraham, Isaac and Jacob" was celebrated in the daily prayers; "servant" alludes to Isaiah (see comment on Mt 12:15-18).

3:14. "Holy One" applied especially to God in Jewish literature; "Righteous One" was also usually a title for God, although it applied to Enoch, Noah, some *rabbis and others as well; the *Dead Sea Scrolls spoke of their founder as "the teacher of righteousness." The context would indicate to whom the title applied.

Because the healing did not occur during a feast, most of Peter's audience is now Jerusalemite or Palestinian (contrast 2:23); but the corporate accusation against his hearers here is no stronger than denunciations of *Old Testament prophets (e.g., Amos 2:6—3:8). Calling a revolutionary (Barabbas) a "murderer" (cf. Lk 23:19) would have alienated those with revolutionary sympathies.

3:15. "Prince" (NASB) or "author" (NIV) was used for founders and protectors of Greek cities, for heads of clans or military judges (Old Testament), or for commanders who lead the way; it was sometimes applied to Greek divine heroes such as Heracles. Here it may mean the leader who pioneered the way of (*resurrection) life (contrast the murderer of 3:14), who forged on ahead of others to make the way for them to live as well. Luke's language employs irony (a frequent literary device): when the Jerusalemites accepted a murderer (3:14), they killed the author of life.

3:16-17. The *Old Testament and Judaism regarded willful sin (Num 15:30-31) as far more heinous than sins of ignorance (Num 15:22-29), but both were sinful, and they also regarded ignorance of God's truth as sinful (e.g., Is 1:3; 29:11-12; Hos 4:6).

3:18. Later Jewish teachers sometimes said *hyperbolically that the entire message of the prophets dealt with the messianic era or Jerusalem's restoration, or with other favorite topics. Later teachers often said that a *Messiah would suffer and spoke of two Messiahs, one who would suffer and one who would reign, but the Christians seem to have been the first to proclaim the concept of a suffering Messiah.

3:19. Jewish teachers differed on whether Israel's *repentance had to precede its ultimate restoration, or whether God would simply bring it about in a predetermined time. In the Old Testament prophets, Israel's repentance had to precede it; following the Old Testament, some later Jewish traditions (e.g., *Jubilees 1:15-18; 23:26-27) stressed Israel's repentance as the goal of history.

3:20-21. Christ would not return again until the time to restore Israel (1:6) and the world had come. Many Greek writers spoke of the universe's "cycles": it was periodically destroyed by fire and reborn. But Jewish people expected Israel's restoration; this was a central message of the Old Testament prophets (e.g., Is 40:9-11; Jer 32:42-44; Ezek 37:21-28; Hos 11:9-11; 14:4-7; Amos 9:11-15), and Peter seems to have it in view here.

3:22-23. Other *New Testament texts also apply Deuteronomy 18:15 and 18 to Jesus. Some other sources (e.g., *Samaritan documents and the *Dead Sea Scrolls; not usually the *rabbis) also applied this text to a future prophet like Moses; some leaders whose followers thought they were prophets tried to duplicate miracles of Moses or Joshua, probably indicating that they sought this role. *Josephus states that their miracles failed, however.

3:24-26. Peter's hearers are spiritually "heirs of the prophets"; on the *prophecies see 3:18. Because Abraham's blessing for the nations (Gen 12:3) was to come through them, the servant (3:13) had been sent to be the blessing to them first.

4:1-12
Arraigned by the Temple Authorities

4:1. The *Sadducees controlled the temple hierarchy and most of the resident priesthood. The *sagan,* or captain of the temple guard (a local police force permitted by the Romans and made up of Levites), is known from other sources and is probably the same official called "the king's captain" in Herod the Great's day.

4:2. Sadducees disagreed with the *Pharisaic doctrine of the *resurrection, but Pharisees posed less of a threat to them than the Christians, for the Pharisaic doctrine was only a theoretical hope for the future. From the Jewish perspective, the apostolic witness that one person had already been raised would proclaim that the resurrection had been inaugurated. By guaranteeing rather than simply teaching the future hope of the resurrection, the *disciples threatened the Sadducees' security as leaders of the people.

4:3. Peter and John had come up to the temple about 3 p.m. (cf. 3:1), hence sundown is near. No longer dealing with someone overturning tables in the temple, the aristocracy is content to follow the law and wait till the next day to try them (night trials were illegal).

4:4. Estimates of Jerusalem's population at this time vary from 25,000 to 85,000, and *Josephus said that there were only 6,000 Pharisees in Palestine. A total of 5,000 Jewish Christian "men" in Jerusalem, not including women and children (so the Greek here), is thus quite substantial. Because they were in the outer court, the converts surely included women as well.

4:5. The Jewish authorities mentioned here represent the *Sanhedrin, the Jewish ruling court of Jerusalem; presumably they gather in their meeting hall in the vicinity of the temple.

4:6. These officials were widely known. Like other writers of his day, Luke uses "high priest" loosely for any officials of the high priestly household; Caiaphas was officially high priest at this time (see comment on Jn 11:49; 18:13). The *rabbis and *Dead Sea Scrolls (as well as other sources like *2 Baruch) offer an unflattering picture of the final generations of the temple aristocracy, with whom they did not get along.

4:7. Trial scenes, as much as pirates and other hardships, were standard suspense-builders in ancient stories.

4:8. In the *Old Testament, the *Spirit often came upon God's servants for specific tasks (e.g., Ex 35:31; Judg 14:6) and is especially associated with *prophecy and prophetic speech (i.e., the ability to speak what God is saying).

4:9-12. Salvation "in the name" (v. 12) alludes to Peter's earlier exposition of Joel 2:32 (Acts 2:21); the term translated "saved" includes making whole (i.e., healing the man—so v. 9, literally). Peter learned this use of Psalm 118:22, cited here in verse 11, from Jesus; see Luke 20:17.

4:13-22 God's Authority Rather Than the Hierarchy's

4:13. "Unschooled" means not trained in Greek *rhetoric (public speaking), as the priestly aristocracy would be. (It could also mean that they were not trained under a recognized *rabbi, if the aristocrats were too arrogant to count Jesus as a recognized rabbi.) Popular Greek philosophers used to boast that they were not educated in rhetoric and lived simple lives, so what strikes the *Sanhedrin as a weakness of Peter and John would strike many of Luke's readers as a strength. But the reason for their "uneducated" boldness is obvious: they had been educated by Jesus, who was himself bold and "uneducated." (It was widely understood that disciples regularly reflected the lifestyle and character they had learned from their teachers.)

4:14-18. Both the disciples and the priestly aristocracy recognize that there is no valid basis for a legal charge. Still, as custodians of the temple, the priestly aristocracy has the police power to control teachings on what they consider their grounds. Some Jewish teachers argued that miracles would not validate another's teaching if it did not accord with their own reasoning from Scripture and tradition.

4:19-22. Philosophers often stressed obeying God rather than people, following truth rather than social convenience; Socrates, who refused to be silent even on pain of death, was a notable example. The *Old Testament prophets (such as Nathan, Elijah and Jeremiah, who confronted kings, or Uriah, who suffered martyrdom—Jer 26:20-23) are even clearer examples.

Whether the readers' background is Greek or Jewish, it would be clear to them who is on the side of right.

4:23-31 Praise in the Face of Persecution

4:23-24. Although choruses in Greek drama recited lines together, here "with one accord" (KJV, NASB) simply means "together, in unity" (the same word occurs in 1:14; 2:46; 5:12). This is not a unified liturgy as eventually became standard in *synagogues; scholars do not even all agree that prayers were recited in unison in most Palestinian synagogues in this period. Instead, the text probably means simply that someone inspired by the *Spirit led the prayer.

The prayer begins by confessing God's sovereignty (his power to answer prayer) with lines from Psalm 146:6 on God's faithfulness to vindicate the oppressed; he is greater than their opponents.

4:25-28. Psalm 2 refers plainly to a royal descendant of David, particularly the *Messiah against whom the rulers were gathered. (Later *rabbis applied this text to Gog and Magog, nations gathered against the Messiah and Israel). In verse 27 the believers recognize the fulfillment of that opposition in Jesus' opponents. This is a recognition that the opposition to Jesus (and to themselves) is according to God's will.

4:29-31. Prayers for vindication were common in the *Old Testament and Judaism (see 2 Chron 24:21-22; Ps 109:6-20; see also Rev 6:10), but this is a prayer for faithfulness and boldness (cf. Ps 138:3). Although Judaism boasted stories of rare miracle workers and paganism had local healing shrines and some magicians, a movement trusting God for such widespread miracles (cf. Acts 2:43; 5:12) is unparalleled.

4:32-37 Continuing Revival

As in 2:41-47, the outpouring of God's *Spirit here leads not only to miracles and inspired verbal witness but also to actively caring for one another and sharing possessions. For background see comment on 2:43-45.

4:32-33. In the *Old Testament, God's favor and the *Spirit could be "upon" individuals (cf. Num 11:24-29; Ezek 11:5).

4:34-35. In the *Dead Sea Scrolls, community officials distributed contributions to the community; in most of Palestinian Judaism, supervisors of charity distributed funds given them.

4:36. Many Jews lived in Cyprus. The *Aramaic "Barnabas" can mean "son of refreshment" or perhaps "son of the prophet." Nicknames were commonly given to describe personal attributes.

4:37. Donations like Joseph's happened often (4:34), but Luke wishes to state a positive example before the negative one (5:1-11) and to introduce an important character here (9:27). Contrasting positive and negative examples was a recommended technique of ancient writing. Although Levites did not own land under *Old Testament law, they commonly did own it in Jesus' day (cf. Barnabas's relatives in 12:12-13), and some, like the Sadducean priests, were even rich.

5:1-11 Addressing Sin in the Camp

The sin of one man who had kept spoils for himself had once brought judgment on all Israel and the death of many, and only the death of the transgressor allowed Israel to move forward again (Josh 7). God took the corporate purity of his people, and the importance of sincerity in claims to total commitment, far more seriously than most Christians do today.

5:1-4. Ancient groups that required members to turn over their possessions usually had a waiting period during which one could take one's property and leave (see the *Dead Sea Scrolls and the *Pythagoreans). The early Christians act not from a rule but from love, but this passage treats the offense of lying about turning everything over to the community more seriously than others did. The *Dead Sea Scrolls excluded such an offender from the communal meal for a year and reduced food rations by one-fourth; here God executes a death sentence. Both 2 Kings 5:20-27 and a Greek inscription from Epidauros show that most ancient people knew the danger of lying to God or one of his representatives.

5:5. Jewish tradition said that when an adulteress drank the bitter waters of the temple (Num 5) she immediately died; other stories are told of *rabbis who pronounced judgment or (in later stories) disintegrated foolish pupils with a harsh look. Judgment miracles also occur in Greek tradition and are frequent in the *Old Testament (e.g., Num 16:28-35; 2 Kings 2:24; 2 Chron 26:16-21).

5:6. It was customary to bury people on the day they died, although normally the wife would know of the burial (5:7). Perhaps Ananias and Sapphira owned no family tomb because they had handed over so much property to the *church.

5:7-11. The Old Testament (e.g., Deut 21:21) and later Judaism (*Dead Sea Scrolls, *rabbis, etc.) in many cases prescribed the death penalty so that others might "fear" (v. 11); it thus served as a deterrent.

5:12-16
Miracles Increase

Although a few ancient teachers were known as miracle workers, only the most prominent were reported to have done miracles like those attributed to the *apostles here, and these reports are not from contemporary sources. More contemporary sources credited such miracles to deities housed in temples (for the early Christian view of which, see 1 Cor 10:20).

5:12. On Solomon's "porch" (KJV) or "Colonnade" (NIV) see 3:11 and comment on John 10:23.

5:13. "No one else" seems to refer to nonbelievers rather than to other Christians (2:42, 47) (in contrast to some Greek sects like that of Pythagoras, which reportedly counted only selected people worthy of entering his presence). Many non-Jews attended *synagogue and believed in Israel's God without fully converting and keeping Jewish rules (see comment on 10:2); it is possible that a similar group of Jewish outsiders who respect the Jesus movement without converting to it is in view here.

5:14-16. Ancient people thought that one's shadow was attached to oneself; in Jewish law, if one's shadow touched a corpse one was as unclean as one who physically touched the corpse. The public's emphasis on needing to touch healers may be drawn from magical superstition (power as a substance was a pagan magical concept), but God still meets their need through his appointed representatives (cf. 19:11; Mk 5:28-30).

5:17-32
Arrested Again

5:17. The *Sadducees were powerful but never gained the popularity that the *Pharisees enjoyed. Although the political situation required them to maintain relations with the Pharisees, it is not surprising that they would be "jealous" (cf. Mk 15:10) and act with hostility toward the *apostles. *Josephus described the Sadducees as a "sect," the same term Luke uses here (so most translations; cf. "party"—NIV, TEV; see also Acts 15:5; 26:5); Josephus also wrote for a Greek audience, for whom the term could mean a philosophical school.

5:18. Jails were normally used for detention until trial, not for imprisonment as a punishment.

5:19. Stories of miraculous escapes from prison appear occasionally in Greek tradition (e.g., the Greek deity Dionysus, imprisoned by King Pentheus) and in one pre-Christian story about Moses in the *Diaspora Jewish writer Artapanus. Of course, even the exodus from Egypt was a miraculous deliverance from captivity (cf. also Lev 26:13; Ps 107:10-16).

5:20-21. The gates of the temple opened at midnight, but the people returned only at daybreak. The hearing for the *apostles had been scheduled for daylight, because trials were not to be held at night (4:3, 5).

5:22-26. These guards are fortunate that they are Levites policing for the Jewish temple aristocracy rather than recruits under the Romans or Herod Agrippa I, who might have executed them (see 12:18-19).

5:27. The high priest presided over the *Sanhedrin, or ruling judicial council.

5:28. The charge against the *apostles is that they are trying to incite unrest against the municipal aristocracy which the Romans approved, by accusing them of responsibility for Jesus' execution. (The Sanhedrin viewed Jesus' execution as eliminating a revolutionary who was creating unrest.)

5:29-30. See comment on 4:19-20. The apostles claim that the Sanhedrin *is* responsible for the execution.

5:31. See comment on 3:15. The *Sadducean leaders of the *Sanhedrin might view the *apostles' claim that Jesus is a king after all, reigning for God and vindicated by him after the Sanhedrin had executed him, as an error; but more significantly in this case they would view this claim as a direct challenge to their political power and wisdom.

5:32. On witnesses see 1:8; the *Holy Spirit is the Spirit of *prophecy inspiring them to witness, supposed to be available only in the end time or only to the extremely pious. The apostles' reply indicates that they do not regard the Sanhedrin as obedient to God.

5:33-42
A Pharisaic Moderate's Support

Whether *Sadducean aristocrats with political agendas or *Pharisaic teachers with pietistic agendas, all the *Sanhedrin members claimed to be followers of Israel's God and would not wish to oppose him.

5:33. Because it is not a festival and the procurator is thus out of town, the religious leaders probably could have accomplished their purpose, as illegal and against all protocol as it would have been (cf. chaps. 6—7). Pharisaic traditions reported that the leading priestly families in this period sometimes used force to guarantee their will.

5:34-35. That Gamaliel I, the most prominent pupil of the gentle *Hillel, was widely respected may be an understatement; he was probably the most influential Pharisaic leader of the time and held prestige as a Jerusalem aristocrat as well. Later *rabbis extolled his piety and learning, and accorded him the title "Rabban," which later belonged to the rulers of the Pharisaic courts. *Josephus mentioned Gamaliel's aristocratic son Simon, indicating the family's power in Jerusalem. (The later tradition that Gamaliel was Hillel's son is probably wrong.)

*Pharisees had little political power and did not believe in executing someone for political reasons. Even if the Christians were in serious error, as long as they kept the law of Moses the Pharisees would not believe in punishing them. Unlike many of the Pharisees in the Gospels, Gamaliel I is here portrayed as living according to the rules Pharisees believed (see also 22:3).

5:36. If *Josephus is accurate, Theudas arose about A.D. 44—ten years after Gamaliel's speech. The name Theudas is not a common enough name to make an earlier revolutionary named Theudas likely, although the name does occur (e.g., in a Jerusalem tomb inscription). Luke may simply fill in names of the most prominent revolutionary leaders known by his own period rather than a less-known name Gamaliel might have cited (historians sometimes adjusted characters' speeches in their own words); the alternative would be that either Luke or *Josephus is mistaken.

Theudas was a Jewish magician who gathered followers to the river Jordan, promising to part it. The Roman governor Fadus sent troops who killed and captured members of the crowd; Theudas was beheaded.

5:37. Judas the Galilean led the tax revolt of A.D. 6. The Romans retaliated by destroying Sepphoris; Judas's model led to the revolutionaries who later came to be called the *Zealots. Judas's sons also revolted in the war of 66-70; they were crucified. Judas was helped by a certain Saddok—a *Pharisee. Gamaliel would naturally view such revolutionaries more favorably than the *Sadducees would, since the Sadducees had more vested interests in Roman rule.

5:38-39. Continuance was often viewed as a proof of divine help; "fighting against God" may be a familiar Greek saying, perhaps originating with the Greek tragedian Euripides but quoted in anthologies for students learning Greek. Many of those in the *Sanhedrin might have used such anthologies and hence been familiar with this expression.

Waiting for the Romans to take care of this problem would appeal more to Pharisees, who in this period were more convinced than the Sadducees that a future *Messiah should intervene to establish God's cause and overthrow the current order. Like many of his successors, Gamaliel wants no trouble with Rome, but he is sure that the Romans could take care of revolutionaries themselves—unless God is with the revolutionaries. By comparing the Jesus movement to followers of Theudas and Judas, however, he shows that he still misunderstands it in merely political terms.

5:40. The Pharisaic element would especially listen to Gamaliel, having great respect for teaching of their elders; perhaps reconsidering the extremeness of an illegal lynching, the predominant Sadducean element also concurs. Scourging as a civil punishment unconnected with execution is well-known (Lk 23:16; see comment on Jn 19:1); because the Pharisees would oppose a Roman scourging, the discipline of as many as thirty-nine lashes administered by traditional Jewish courts may be in view here (see comment on Mt 10:17).

5:41-42. In Jewish tradition, the righteous could rejoice when they suffered, because of their reward in the world to come; nevertheless, disobeying a ruler's decree was considered courageous, and Judaism extolled martyrs who did so. (The *apostles' continuing to teach publicly in the temple courts is especially courageous.) Ancient readers would respect this description of the apostles. "Teaching" is primarily instruction; "preaching" is especially proclamation of the saving *gospel.

6:1-7 The Seven Distributors of Charity

Those with political power generally repressed complaining minorities; here the *apostles hand the whole system over to the offended minority. This may thus be the first recorded instance of what we might today call "affirmative action."

6:1. Some scholars think that the "Hellenists" (NRSV) here are simply Greek-speaking Palestinian Jews, but most Jews in Palestine were bilingual, and Greek was probably the first language for most Jerusalemites. The more likely proposal is that this text refers to *Diaspora Jews who have settled in Jerusalem, as opposed to natives of Jewish Palestine.

The Bible mandated caring for widows, who had no other means of support if they had no family nearby. Judaism took this responsibility seriously, in contrast to *Gentile cultures. But because it was considered virtuous to be buried in the land of Israel, many foreign Jews would come to spend their last days there, then die and leave widows. (Palestinian *rabbis eventually provided further theological incentive to immigrants; according to one common tradition, the dead would be *resurrected only in Israel, so the righteous dead of other lands would have to roll the whole way back to Israel underground, and this was thought to be a very unpleasant experience.)

Thus a disproportionate number of foreign Jewish widows lived in Jerusalem, which did not have enough foreign Jewish *synagogues (6:9) for their distributors of charity to supply all the widows adequately. This urban social problem of Jerusalem spilled over into the *church.

6:2-4. Distributors of charity filled an office in later Palestinian Judaism. Reputation was important for the sake of public credibility; see comment on 1 Timothy 3:7. There was *Old Testament precedent for having the people themselves choose these distributors and the leader ratify their choice (Deut 1:13), and the *Essenes reportedly elected their officials.

6:5. Tomb inscriptions show that many Jerusalemites had Greek names whether or not their parents or grandparents had lived outside Judea. But even in Rome, under 40 percent of Jews had any Greek in their name, and only one or two of the *apostles had a Greek name. That all seven of these men have Greek names suggests that they are known to be Hellenists (6:1), first-or second-generation Jewish immigrants to Palestine—hence members of the offended minority. One is even a *proselyte—a former *Gentile who had converted to Judaism; many of these lived in Antioch (cf. 11:19).

6:6. The laying on of hands communicated blessing in the Old Testament (still occasionally attested in the apostolic period), but the idea here seems to be that of ordination, as in Numbers 27:18, 23 (cf. 11:25), similar to the later practice for ordaining *rabbis, called *semikah* (cf. 1 Tim 4:14; 2 Tim 1:6). (Rabbis applied this rite of laying on hands only to sacrifices and to ordaining scholars.) If so, the *apostles considered their friends' office of social ministry quite important.

6:7. Although most upper-class priests were *Sadducees, the poorer priests, many of whom came to Jerusalem only several weeks of the year, were not;

some priests were even *Pharisees. Priests were accorded high status in the *Qumran community. Priests did not represent any given ideology or economic status, but their conversion here shows that the Christians are making inroads even into the temple establishment, or at least the lower eschelon of priests who served there.

6:8—7:1
Stephen Arraigned

Despite Jesus' orders to engage in the *Gentile mission (1:8), the *apostles had stayed in Jerusalem and remained there as late as 15:2. It is ultimately the bicultural minority within the Jerusalem *church that holds the promise for the future. Luke gives us examples of two leaders from that minority (6:5), Stephen (chap. 7) and Philip (chap. 8).

6:9-10. Stephen's fellow Hellenists felt local Jewish hostility more acutely than the *church's Hebrew faction (see comment on 6:1). Jerusalem had many *synagogues (though not the 480 of later tradition), including some of those mentioned here. Archaeologists have found the dedicatory inscription from a "synagogue of the *freedmen," those descended from former Roman slaves. (They constituted a particular class in Greco-Roman society in the first generation; Judaism ranked them just below *proselytes.) Later sources attest the synagogue of the Alexandrians and that of the Cilicians; the capital of Cilicia was Tarsus, Paul's hometown. Other ancient cities with large Jewish immigrant populations also sported diverse synagogues.

6:11. It seems to have been an ideal for people to be judged by one of their peers (a judge in a local court); a criticism by fellow Hellenists would receive more weight than one from those who would be less likely to know Stephen. "Blasphemy" here does not have the later technical sense of pronouncing the divine name of God but the more general sense of purported disrespect for God.

6:12. The *Sanhedrin was not likely to be favorably disposed toward Stephen; the Jewish law of rebuke required a warning, but the Sanhedrin had already warned the leaders of this movement (5:40), and from this point the Sanhedrin would have to take action.

6:13-15. Ancients viewed perjury as an affront to the god in whose name the false witnesses had sworn an oath. False witnesses in a capital case were to be executed if found out (Deut 19:18-19; also under Roman law), but in this case Stephen will seem to confirm half their charge in reply to the high priest's interrogation (7:1). He is for the *law (cf. the bulk of his quotations in chap. 7) but in some sense against the temple (chap. 7). Jewish tradition praised those who had suffered to preserve the ancestral traditions based on Scripture; its defenders would regard Stephen as apostate. The accusers spoke first in a case.

7:1. The high priest opens the questioning of the accused; his broad statement would give Stephen the opportunity to deny the charge.

7:2-7
The Abraham Narrative

Reciting Israel's history in ways to make points was common (historical retrospective, e.g., 1 Sam 12:7-12; 1 Macc 2:49-69; Ecclus 44—50), and one need not study Acts 7:2-53 long before the point becomes clear: Stephen answers the charges (6:11, 13-14) and denies that the temple or even the land of Israel is necessarily central to God's short-term working in history. Although *Old Testament prophets had made the same case (e.g., Jer 7;

Jonah), he is bound to draw at least as much opposition as they did. Where his points differ from the standard Hebrew text, they generally agree with the Samaritan text or the *Septuagint.

7:2-4. Palestinian Jewish tradition strongly emphasized the specialness of the land of Israel, and some teachers even claimed that God revealed himself directly only in the land of Israel. Here, although God calls Abraham to the Promised Land, he reveals himself to Abraham in Mesopotamia, far to the east.

7:5-7. Although Abraham was the ideal man of God, neither he nor his descendants for four centuries were able to possess the Holy Land.

7:8-16
The Joseph Narrative

*Samaritans viewed Joseph and Moses as the greatest leaders of the past. Jewish literature also spoke of them highly.

7:8-9. The patriarchs who opposed Joseph the man of God were the ancestors of most of the Jewish people. Thus Stephen begins the secondary emphasis of his sermon: you oppose the real leaders God gives you.

7:10. The place where God exalted and blessed Joseph was Egypt, not Palestine.

7:11-13. Joseph rescued his family, but at first they did not recognize him.

7:14. Citing the *Old Testament in Greek for a Jewish audience whose first language is Greek, Stephen follows the *Septuagint rather than the Hebrew text for the number of people in Joseph's family—seventy-five (the later standard Hebrew text has seventy; a *Dead Sea Scrolls Hebrew text agrees with the *Septuagint).

7:15-16. Jacob, Joseph and his brothers died in a foreign land, although their bones were later moved to the Holy Land (cf. comment on 6:1). Scripture does not record that they were all buried in Shechem. (Jacob was buried near Hebron—Gen 23; 49:29-32; 50:13; Joseph was buried at Shechem—Josh 24:32. *Josephus has the other sons buried at Hebron, but because they died after Jacob's burial, their burial at the same time and place as their brother Joseph seems slightly more likely.) But Stephen here agrees with *Samaritan tradition, which naturally accorded Shechem this honor because it had become the leading city of the Samaritans (see comment on 8:5).

7:17-34
The Moses Narrative

Stephen follows the *Old Testament closely, avoiding the extensive elaboration on Moses' life found in other writers of the period. Here he ties together both his preceding themes: God reveals himself outside the Holy Land, and Israel rejects its deliverers.

7:17-19. Israel's hard times in Egypt, during which a deliverer was needed, resemble the difficulties in first-century Palestine; many people were looking for another prophet like Moses to deliver them from oppression. In the *New Testament period, non-Jews often left their children out to die, but Jews abhorred this practice; here Luke uses the same term often used for child abandonment, increasing revulsion for Pharaoh.

7:20. Some writers (especially later *rabbis, perhaps adapting earlier stories about Noah) related fantastic stories about Moses' birth (that his beauty at birth was so great that it lit up the room, that he was born circumcised, etc.); Stephen reports exactly what the Old Testament says about Moses' birth.

7:21. *Josephus also interpreted Pharaoh's daughter's action in Exodus 2:10

as adoption (though using a less technical phrase for it than Stephen, who plays on the *Septuagint wording).

7:22. Like Josephus, other writers elaborated extensively on Moses' Egyptian education and legendary exploits as an Egyptian general. Stephen simply tells what needs to be told, but his emphasis on Moses' *Gentile education would not disturb his Greek-speaking hearers the way his geography had (e.g., 7:2-4, 10). His mention of Moses' Gentile education, though brief, contributes to Stephen's polemic that God planned to reach beyond Israel even from the beginning.

7:23-29. Although Moses sacrificed his standing in Egypt to identify with his people, as a bringer of deliverance (the word usually translated "salvation") for them, they rejected him. See comment on 7:35-37. (Like both the *rabbis and Greco-Jewish writers such as *Philo and Artapanus, Stephen presents Moses' murder of the Egyptian in a positive light; writing Jewish history for *Gentile readers, *Josephus omits the incident entirely.)

7:30-34. God not only revealed himself to Moses on Mount Sinai and sent him to Egypt, but he also called the mountain "this holy place" (v. 33), a term Stephen's accusers reserved for the temple (6:13).

7:35-41
A Rejected Savior like Moses

7:35. Like Jesus, Moses was rejected by his people as a deliverer.

7:36. Like Jesus, Moses did signs and wonders.

7:37. As many Jewish people and the *Samaritans recognized, God would send a deliverer like Moses (Deut 18:18). In the style of a good Jewish expositor of Scripture, Stephen asks, "In what way will the prophet be like Moses?" He answers: he will be rejected by his people (7:35, 39); his hearers' very opposition proves his point (cf. Is 53:1-3).

7:38. The Jewish people celebrated that Moses had received the *law and passed it on to Israel (Stephen uses terms that might translate those used for Jewish teachers receiving and passing on traditions, though not as strong as those in, e.g., 1 Cor 11:23).

7:39. Yet Moses' own generation rejected him; why is it so hard to believe that the one whom the Jewish leaders of Jesus' generation rejected might not also be a deliverer for them?

7:40-41. The episode of the golden calf was the incident in Israel's history of which the *rabbis were most ashamed; they felt it was the most sinful of Israel's acts. But they grew defensive when pagans queried them about it (*Josephus earlier even omitted the incident), and several centuries later they argued that the pagans who accompanied Israel, not Israel, made the calf (against Ex 32:1-6). Israel had worshiped idols right after deliverance under Moses; yet, Stephen is going to imply, his accusers also follow the "works of their [human] hands"—an expression often used for idols in the Bible and other Jewish sources but equally applicable to their humanly built temple (Acts 7:48).

7:42-50
God's View of the Temple

Now Stephen replies to the charge directly: Scripture does not support the importance his opponents attach to the temple. To the keepers of the temple—which was the symbol of the unity of Jewish people throughout the empire—Stephen's accusation sounds like the sort of accusation that *Samaritans would bring. Even the heretical *Essenes condemned only the impurity of the leadership in the temple, while longing for a restored temple.

7:42-43. In a *prophecy also favored in the *Dead Sea Scrolls (Amos 5:25-27), Stephen plays on the term translated "tabernacle" (KJV, NASB) or "shrine" (NIV): Israel carried the tabernacle of a pagan god in the wilderness.

7:44-47. Stephen quickly qualifies that God did tell Moses to build the tabernacle in a particular way (see comment on Heb 9), and the tabernacle had remained until David's time; the temple was not built till Solomon's time. Stephen does not deny that God blessed and approved the building of the Old Testament temple; but he denies that God meant it to be the idol that his hearers have made it.

7:48-50. Isaiah 66:1-2 attest that God does not need the temple made with human hands; his own hands made everything. It became customary to expound the Law with reference to a reading from the Prophets, but Stephen's relevant citations from the Prophets (Amos and Isaiah) strike as hard in this context as they did in Amos's and Isaiah's generation.

7:51-53
The Altar Call

The conclusion of a Greco-Roman deliberative speech was meant to produce change or decisive action. Stephen's speech also includes elements of forensic speech, however—more to convict his hearers than to defend himself.

7:51. "Stiff-necked" and "uncircumcised heart" are standard prophetic insults in the *Old Testament; Moses emphasized circumcision (7:8), but those who were spiritually uncircumcised were especially cut off from the covenant (e.g., Deut 10:16; 30:6). Stephen could hardly choose harsher words. His point is that his hearers, like their ancestors, reject God's messengers; the *Holy Spirit was especially seen as the Spirit who had inspired the prophets.

7:52. Jewish tradition had heightened Israel's responsibility for the death of the prophets beyond what was found in the Old Testament, so Stephen's hearers could not deny his charge. Like Socrates in Greek tradition, but more relevantly like Jesus, Stephen deliberately provokes his accusers to kill him, thereby proving his point: they are like their ancestors who killed the prophets.

7:53. Aside from the angel who appeared to Moses in the bush, the Old Testament does not say that God mediated the law through angels; Jewish tradition had added them to heighten reverence for the law (cf. also Gal 3:19; Heb 2:2). Stephen concludes that his accusers are wrong; they, not he, are guilty of breaking the law, and are thus uncircumcised in heart. Like Socrates who turned the charge of impiety against the gods upon his accusers, he knows what the result will be: martyrdom.

7:54—8:4
The First Martyr

Romans did not permit subject peoples to execute capital punishment, but Stephen's hearers are so enraged that they lynch him according to their own Jewish law. Stephen's death proves his point, laying the theological groundwork for the expansion of the Jesus movement outside Palestine; it also leads to further persecution and thus the direct spread of the faith (8:1); and it sows a seed in a certain Saul (7:58)—a seed whose fruit would later be reaped on the road to Damascus (9:3-4; cf. the similar themes shared by Stephen's and Paul's preaching in Acts).

7:54-55. Judges normally stood to render verdicts; Jesus, the true judge, is now vindicating his servant as his opponents prepare to condemn him. As elsewhere in the narrative, Luke leaves no doubt as to who is really on trial before God (see comment on 7:57-58, 60; cf. Is 54:17).

7:56. In Daniel 7:13-14, the coming of the *Son of Man would vindicate the righteous (Israel) against their oppressors (the nations); Stephen's hearers would know in which category he places himself and in which category he places them.

7:57-58. According to Jewish regulations, a condemned criminal would be taken out to the edge of a city and thrown over a drop at least twice the man's height. The witnesses would be the first to hurl large stones on top of him, aiming for the chest (though precision was impossible), till the victim died. Under Jewish law, they were to strip the *criminal* before killing him; here Stephen's accusers strip *themselves,* probably because they are hot, as Greeks stripped for athletic activities. But Luke records the detail to identify the guilty parties—those stoning Stephen figuratively admit their own guilt by stripping themselves. Under Mosaic law, false witnesses in a capital case were to be executed themselves.

Luke's first-time readers probably know the name Paul, but not his other name, Saul (13:9); like a good ancient (or modern) writer, Luke saves an important revelation for later. "Young man" or "youth" is not very precise; the usual sense of "youth" extends from fourteen (or twenty-one) to twenty-eight years old, but the word used here can extend up to forty. In Jewish tradition (based on Num 4:35) one did not qualify for some offices before age thirty, but this point is probably irrelevant to Saul's mission in 9:2, especially if he is single (a common Jewish tradition also encouraged men to marry by age twenty). That Saul is in his twenties (the most common age to which the term translated "youth" referred) is reasonable.

7:59. Stephen's prayer parallels Jesus' cry in Luke 23:46. Ancient writers often liked to draw parallels between different figures; Luke wants his readers to see that Stephen, an ideal representative of the *church, follows in the steps of his Lord in martyrdom.

7:60. His final cry parallels Luke 23:34; see comment on Acts 7:59. At a stoning, the executed person was to confess his sin and pray, "May my death atone for all my sins." Stephen confesses not his own sin but that of his false accusers (see 7:57-58).

8:1. It took persecution—mainly the scattering of the bicultural, foreign Jews—to get the *church to begin to do what Jesus had commanded them back in 1:8. As the second-century North African theologian Tertullian pointed out, "the blood of Christians is the seed" of the church's growth.

8:2. Dying unburied was the greatest dishonor possible in the ancient Mediterranean world; even risking one's life to bury the dead was considered honorable and heroic. Adult sons or those closest to the deceased would take charge of burial. Jewish law forbade public mourning for a condemned criminal, but for anyone else it was considered a pious duty. Stephen's pious friends ignore the illegal ruling of the highest Jewish court to honor their friend.

8:3. Prison was normally a holding place till trial; that Saul detains women as well as men indicates that he is more zealous than most of his contemporaries would have felt necessary (Gal 1:13-14; Phil 3:6). The only charge against the church members seems to be an assumption of their opposition to the temple, aroused by Stephen's speech.

8:4. Most ancient religions were spread

by traveling merchants or other travelers more than by prominent individuals.

8:5-13 The Conversion of Samaria

Having finished his first example of the Seven (Stephen), Luke now turns to his second example, one of those "scattered" in 8:4.

8:5. "The city of Samaria" could refer to the *Old Testament site of Samaria, now a pagan Greek city called Sebaste, dedicated to the worship of the emperor and full of occult influences (cf. comment on 8:10-11). But Sebaste's people were Greeks rather than *Samaritans, so the phrase probably refers to the main Samaritan city of the district of Samaria, Neapolis, on the site of ancient Shechem (cf. 7:15-16). This was the religious center of the Samaritans.

8:6-8. Signs were accorded high evidential value in antiquity. That the modern Western educated elite tends to denigrate them is more a commentary on our culture than on theirs; most cultures in the world today (virtually all cultures not influenced by deistic rationalism or atheistic Marxism) accept diverse forms of supernatural activity. Thus those who reject miracles merely on the basis of philosophical a prioris may do so as ethnocentric dogmatists rather than as genuinely open-minded intellectuals.

8:9. Magicians usually drew large followings in antiquity; given the prominence of Jewish magicians in Greco-Roman antiquity, a Samaritan magician should not surprise us. Like the Old Testament, official leaders in mainstream Judaism opposed magic, but even some later *rabbis indulged in sorcery, claiming simply to exploit insight into the secrets of God's laws of creation.

8:10-11. In nearby Sebaste many Greeks were synthesizing the various Greek gods into one universal male deity and the goddesses into another female one. This synthesis followed a trend that had been developing among some educated Greeks for centuries. A second-century Christian writer suggested that Simon claimed to be the avatar, or incarnation, of the male form of the deity, while his consort Helena was its female form.

8:12. Familiar with *Samaritan opposition to Judaism, Jewish people would have found this scenario remarkable. Already circumcised, Samaritans would have converted to Judaism by *baptism alone; but such conversion rarely if ever occurred, because it would have been tantamount to denying one's own people. For Philip, a Jew, to present the *gospel in such terms that a Samaritan could follow a *Messiah proclaimed by Jews would be viewed by many Jews as a betrayal of Judaism. Philip follows the same theological program of decentralized witness argued by Stephen in chapter 7 and outlined by Jesus in 1:8.

8:13. Judaism acknowledged that pagan sorcerers could do miracles, which most segments of Judaism would attribute to Belial (*Satan). The *Old Testament taught that pagan sorcerers could duplicate some of God's signs on a small scale (Ex 7:11, 22; 8:7), but that their power was definitely limited (Ex 8:18-19; 9:11). Some writers have argued that Simon was not genuinely converted, given his subsequent behavior (8:18-24), but this issue depends on the meaning of "conversion"; like Judaism in the same period, early Christianity lamented not only false converts but also apostates (e.g., 1 Sam 10:6; 16:14; 2 Pet 2:21; 1 Jn 2:19).

8:14-25 Apostolic Ratification of the Samaritan Conversions

Philip's crosscultural ministry has broken new ground, of the sort which might draw opposition from some conservative elements in the Jerusalem *church (8:12). It is thus important for Luke to describe the response of the Jerusalem *apostles and the blessing of God on the work.

8:14-15. From a theological standpoint, the work of the *Spirit is one package (2:38-39), but in the experience of the church not all aspects of his work are necessarily manifested simultaneously. Luke emphasizes the prophetic-empowerment dimension of the Spirit so much that he rarely mentions other aspects of the Spirit's work known in the *Old Testament and early Judaism; this prophetic-empowerment aspect is no doubt in view here, although Philip's hearers were already converted in 8:12.

8:16. "Into the name" (NIV) is a literal translation that may reflect the language of ancient business documents, meaning that the converts have transferred ownership of their lives to Christ (or it may simply reflect the increasing ambiguity of Greek prepositions in this period).

8:17. Ancient Judaism provides rare examples of laying on hands for prayer (one in the *Dead Sea Scrolls), but in the Old Testament hands were laid on to impart blessings in prayer (Gen 48:14-20).

8:18-24. The only category into which many Greeks could fit the miracles wrought by the *apostles would have been that of magical works, but this text clearly distinguishes an amoral, magical interpretation of the miracles from the apostolic miracles, which are much more like those of *Old Testament prophets. Sorcerers could buy magical formulas; no one could buy the *Spirit.

8:25. After the new mission was pioneered by the bicultural witnesses of Acts 6, the *apostles finally begin to catch on to their own mission (1:8). Far from the apostles fixing or correcting Philip's inadequate conversion of the Samaritans (as some commentators have suggested), the whole *narrative indicates that they recognize and ratify the propriety of his work.

8:26-40
Conversion of an African Official

Luke devotes nearly as much space to the conversion of this one foreigner, who can function as an indigenous witness in his own culture, as to the revival in Samaria. Because *Samaritans were considered half-breeds, this is the first fully *Gentile convert to Christianity (probably unknown to most of the Jerusalem *church—11:18).

8:26. Two roads led south from near Jerusalem, one through Hebron into Idumea (Edom) and the other joining the coast road before Gaza heading for Egypt, both with plenty of Roman milestones as road markers. Old Gaza was a deserted town whose ruins lay near the now culturally Greek cities of Askalon and New Gaza. Philip might have no one to preach to on a little-traveled road that would lead by a deserted city, and after the revival in Samaria this command must seem absurd to him; but God had often tested faith through such commands (e.g., Ex 14:16; 1 Kings 17:3-4, 9-14; 2 Kings 5:10).

8:27. Ethiopia figured in Mediterranean legends and mythical geography as the very end of the earth (sometimes extending from the far south to the far east), and the most commonly mentioned feature of Ethiopians in Jewish and Greco-Roman literature (also noted in the *Old Testament—Jer 13:23) is their black skin.

"Candace" *(kan-dak'a)* seems to have

been a dynastic title of the queen of Ethiopia and is mentioned elsewhere in Greco-Roman literature; tradition declares that the queen mother ruled in that land. She seems to have ruled a black Nubian kingdom south of Egypt partly in what is now the Sudan, a kingdom that had lasted since about 750 B.C. and whose main cities were Meroe and Napata (this should not be confused with Abyssinia, which came to be called Ethiopia in more recent times and converted to Christianity in the fourth century A.D.). This kingdom had *some* trade with Rome, but this official and his entourage must have been among the few Ethiopian visitors this far north. He is probably a *Gentile "God-fearer" (see comment on 10:2). As the queen's treasurer, this man is a high and powerful official.

When meant literally (which was not always the case—Gen 39:1 *LXX), "eunuch" referred to a castrated man. Although eunuchs were preferred court officials in the East, the Jewish people opposed the practice, and Jewish law excluded eunuchs from Israel (Deut 23:1); the rules were undoubtedly instituted to prevent Israel from neutering boys (Deut 23:1). But God could certainly accept eunuchs (Is 56:3-5, even foreign eunuchs; Wisdom of Solomon 3:14). An Ethiopian "eunuch" in the Old Testament turned out to be one of Jeremiah's few allies and saved his life (Jer 38:7-13).

8:28. Most people walked, the more well-to-do rode animals, but only the most well-to-do had chariots. People were occasionally known to read while sitting in expensive carriages; thus the chariot may be moving while the eunuch is reading.

8:29-30. Although taught along with reading aloud in modern times, the skill of reading silently was not developed in antiquity; those who could read nearly always read aloud. The situation here is obviously divinely arranged (cf., e.g., Gen 24:13-27).

8:31. Often only one attendant would accompany the official in a chariot; the wealthy eunuch may have more, but there is still room for Philip.

8:32-35. Earlier servant passages in Isaiah refer explicitly to Israel, but 49:5 distinguishes the servant from the rest of Israel, and in 53:1-3 he is rejected by Israel; in 53:4-12 he bears the sins of Israel, although he himself is not guilty (53:9) and suffers voluntarily (53:12). The official's confusion is understandable, but Philip's exposition is correct. (Luke does not report all of Is 53, but the context is implied; because chapter and verse references had not yet been assigned, one had to cite part of a passage to let the readers know where one was reading.)

8:36-38. There are some wadis near Gaza (wadis are dry creek beds that fill with water during the rainy season); because Jewish *baptism presupposed full immersion, this is no doubt what Luke intends here. As a God-fearer, the Ethiopian may understand the Jewish view that full conversion includes baptism, even if Philip does not require him to be circumcised. (If he is a literal eunuch, circumcision may be impossible for him anyway, although castration sometimes involved only the testicles. But Jews did not let any physical eunuchs become full proselytes.)

8:39. Christianity especially began to expand in Abyssinia through lay witness in the third century, and that empire was declared "Christian" about the same time as the Roman Empire was. Nubia converted later; no certain record of this Ethiopian's witness remains, but with Luke we may suppose that he testified of his faith in high places.

Some magicians claimed the ability

to fly, but the language of Philip's removal suggests supernatural movement more like that mentioned in the *Old Testament (1 Kings 18:12; 2 Kings 2:16; Ezek 3:12, 14).

8:40. The Judean Azotus, the ancient Ashdod, was twenty-five miles north of Gaza and about thirty-five miles west of Jerusalem. Caesarea Maritima (the coastal Caesarea, not Caesarea Philippi) was over fifty miles to the north of Azotus, just off the same coastal road; this city will become significant in 10:1 (cf. 21:8).

9:1-9
Jesus Arrests Saul

The three accounts of Paul's conversion in Acts display some differences (chaps. 9, 22, 26; all fit the accounts in his letters). Classical literature often reports messages given to messengers and then repeats them verbatim on their delivery. Fortunately, *rhetorical style by Luke's day preferred variation, which makes the repeated *narratives much less repetitious, hence more interesting to read.

9:1-2. Official letters of introduction authorizing or recommending their sender were common, and *Josephus confirms that Palestinian agents could take orders from the Jerusalem *Sanhedrin. Jewish communities outside Palestine respected the high priest, and letters from him authorize Saul to carry out his mission with the full cooperation of *synagogues there. Because the high priest had exercised extradition rights over fugitive Judeans when he ruled Palestine under the Romans, local synagogues in Syria likely still recognized this right, although the local ruler would probably not. These synagogue communities could cooperate with Saul in his mission to weed out the Jewish Christians.

The *Essene sect at *Qumran also described itself as "the way"; this was a natural designation for a group that believed that it alone followed the way of righteousness. Essenes had apparently also settled in Damascus, if their writings on this point are meant literally. Tens of thousands of Jews lived in Damascus (as many as eighteen thousand were massacred there in A.D. 66).

9:3. The light from heaven indicates the Shekinah, God's presence (related to the concept of *yeqarah,* "glory"), as God often revealed his glory in the *Old Testament.

9:4. In the Old Testament and Jewish literature, people often fell to the ground when confronted with divine or angelic revelations. In Jewish literature names are often repeated when God calls to someone, drawing special attention to what is about to be said. Given the nature of the revelation, "Lord" here means more than "Sir"; perhaps Saul wonders if God or an angel is addressing him, or perhaps he simply cannot believe he is opposing God.

9:5-6. Persecuting his followers is persecuting Jesus, because they are his representatives (Lk 10:16).

9:7. The reaction of Saul's companions is similar to that in Daniel 10:7.

9:8. God sometimes struck people with blindness to stop them from an evil purpose or as a temporary measure to get their attention (Gen 19:11; 2 Kings 6:18-20, contrast 6:17).

9:9. Three days was not uncommon for a fast; but without water one would become dehydrated, and to continue without water would eventually lead to death. *New Testament examples usually conjoin fasting with prayer, but fasting was commonly an expression of mourning or *repentance. According to this *narrative, Saul does not change religions; he learns the true way to follow his Jewish religion.

9:10-19a
Ananias's Mission

9:10. Another individual bears the name Ananias elsewhere in Acts (23:2), but this was a common name, the Greek form of the Hebrew Hananiah (e.g., Jer 28:1; Dan 1:6). His response is the proper one for an obedient servant of God ready to obey orders (1 Sam 3:10; Is 6:8). (Damascus, capital of modern Syria, was then the capital of the Nabatean Arabs.)

9:11-12. Each is informed about the other in a vision. Such twin visions occur rarely in ancient literature (e.g., *Apuleius *Metamorphoses* 11.13; cf. Tobit 3); when they occur they allow no misunderstanding that the event was divinely coordinated (cf. Gen 41:32). Ancient Jewish hospitality was great, and accommodations with a fellow Jew in Damascus would not be hard for Saul to secure, whether or not Judas has advance notice of Saul's coming. Straight Street is probably the long street that ran east-west through Damascus, where tradition still places Judas's ancient home.

Jews are attested in ancient Tarsus, the capital and most prominent city of Cilicia, which had prominent schools and boasted many philosophers. But cf. comment on 22:3.

9:13-14. Ananias is naturally less eager to obey his orders (9:10) after he finds out what they are. On commands that seem absurd, see 8:26.

9:15-16. The language here is that of *Old Testament call or commissioning *narratives; Saul is apparently converted already and is about to be called to ministry. "On behalf of my name" or "for my name" (NIV) means either for Jesus' honor or that these sufferings would be incurred while Saul is acting as his representative (cf. comment on Jn 14:12-14).

9:17. "Brother" was often used for coreligionists, fellow members of the same Greek association or fellow Jews.

9:18-19a. Saul's healing resembles the healing of Tobit's blindness in a popular Jewish story, which would underline the sense of the miraculous for Saul.

9:19b-31
Confrontations in Damascus and Jerusalem

9:19b-21. Although Saul had carried the letters authorizing his mission (9:2) on his own person and presumably not delivered them, word of his mission had gotten around in Damascus's Jewish community. "*Son of God" is characteristic of Paul's style, not Luke's; writers tried to imitate the style of those whose speeches they reported, and it is not likely that Luke would know Paul's style this early unless he knows him personally (which he undoubtedly did; see the introduction to Acts).

9:22. Saul's position presupposes that he is already expert in the Scriptures; now he turns this expertise against his former mission.

9:23-24. Saul's Jewish opponents plan to assassinate him, not to execute him legally; but his own account in 2 Corinthians 11:32-33 indicates that they had secured the cooperation of high officials in the Damascus government. Saul's preaching in other Greek cities under the control of Aretas IV of Nabatea (9 B.C.-A.D. 40) for as long as three years (Gal 1:17) had possibly aroused opposition.

9:25. Houses were sometimes built into city walls; Saul's escape method has biblical precedent (Josh 2:15; 1 Sam 19:12). That he has gained *disciples there indicates that he has worked like a Christian *rabbi, or teacher, and that he has the requisite training to present himself as such (cf. 22:3).

9:26-31. As provocative as his evangelistic predecessor Stephen, Saul appears headed for the same fate, until he is sent to Tarsus. Because he had been born there (22:3), he possibly had relatives there; but his training had been thoroughly Palestinian Jewish (Phil 3:5), so it is during this period in his life that Saul begins to relate especially to *Gentiles from Asia Minor (modern Turkey). The only representatives of the *apostles he gets to know well are Peter and James (Gal 1:18-19).

9:32-43
Continuing Miracles Through Peter

9:32. Lydda, capital of one of the Judean districts that included non-Jews, later hosted many prominent *rabbis and a rabbinic school.

9:33-35. Sharon is not a town but the coastal plain that extended from Lydda toward Mount Carmel in the north. The Christian presence was still notable in Lydda in the second century A.D.

9:36. Joppa, now part of Tel Aviv-Jaffa, was a profitable port city. It was under Jewish control for about forty years until it came under direct Roman authority in A.D. 6. Tabitha is a Semitic name and Dorcas a Greek one (both meaning the same thing, "gazelle").

Jewish women were active in charity projects. In Greco-Roman culture in general women were sometimes *patrons, and it has been suggested that Tabitha may have been a patron or benefactor of the widows mentioned in verse 41. But whether officially (as a benefactor) or unofficially, she was looking out for their interests.

9:37. Jewish dead were always washed before burial. Only women prepared women's bodies for burial.

9:38. It is important that Lydda is near Joppa, because corpses had to be buried right away. The distance of ten miles meant perhaps three or four hours' journey each way (for the messengers to Peter and Peter to Joppa); because it was customary to bury the corpse before sundown, even if Tabitha had died early in the day they could afford no delay.

9:39. Upper rooms were usually small (1:13 is an exception), generally attics built on the flat rooftops; this one is at least large enough to accommodate a few people. Making clothing was one of the domestic tasks assigned to women in that culture. Well-to-do Roman women had maids to do it but were still considered responsible for it getting done.

9:40. In accordance with Jewish scruples, Tabitha's body would be covered before Peter is brought into the room. On Peter's sending the others out, cf. 2 Kings 4:33.

9:41-42. The resuscitator normally presented the raised person to the suppliants who had requested the resuscitation (1 Kings 17:23; 2 Kings 4:36; Lk 7:15).

9:43. It was customary to name people by their occupation or parentage. Strict observers of *Pharisaic opinions avoided tanners whenever possible, because their stripping of animal hides continually involved them with unclean carcasses. Second-century teachers reported (not necessarily accurately) that tanners had been forbidden in Jerusalem (many *rabbis were more lenient if the tannery were near water, as Simon's house is—10:6). But Judaism stressed hospitality, and Peter, who probably never followed Pharisaic opinions anyway, is happy to receive it.

10:1-8
Cornelius's Vision

Compare comment on the twin visions of Paul and Ananias in 9:12.

10:1. Herod the Great had renamed

Strato's Tower "Caesarea" in honor of the emperor. The residence of the Roman governor of Judea (23:23-24), it held a regular Roman garrison. Centurions commanded units of roughly eighty men (rather than their official designation of 100). Unlike the aristocrats who could directly become tribunes or legates, centurions were generally soldiers who worked their way up through the ranks.

His century was part of a "regiment" (NIV, TEV) or cohort (NASB, NRSV), one-tenth of a legion, made up of six hundred men. Five cohorts were stationed in Caesarea and another in Jerusalem. This particular cohort is known to have been in Palestine in A.D. 69, though not specifically attested here in this period; from A.D. 41 to 44 Agrippa I had his own troops in Caesarea, so these events must be before A.D. 41.

Military service was the preferred occupation; only roughly half those who enlisted survived the twenty years of service (generally ages seventeen to thirty-seven; it became twenty-five years of service later in the first century), but the rewards for survivors were high. Noncitizens could not join legions but could become auxiliary troops who received citizenship upon their discharge.

10:2. Cornelius is clearly not yet a full convert to Judaism (10:28), but his almsgiving and the appreciation of Jews who know him (10:22) testify to his devotion. Although the term "God-fearer" had a broader usage, it generally functions technically in Acts and in some other Jewish sources for righteous *Gentiles who had not been circumcised. *Josephus, *Philo, inscriptions and even the pagan philosopher *Epictetus mention this class of incomplete converts. Inscriptions indicate a high level of religious interest among many of the soldiers.

If these events are before 41 (see comment on 10;1), Cornelius would probably be retired (centurions could retire at the age of sixty) by the war of 66-70. Nevertheless, most of Luke's Jewish readers after A.D. 70 would not be fond of Roman officers stationed in Syria-Palestine, and this account would challenge their prejudices. Recruits had all sworn oaths of allegiance to the divine emperor.

Cornelius's "household" (NASB, NRSV) or "family" (NIV, TEV) is of interest. Luke would certainly know that military personnel were not permitted to marry. Soldiers commonly had illegal concubines whom superiors ignored, but centurions were frequently moved around and thus could rarely hope to maintain long-term informal marriages with local concubines. Thus while Cornelius may have unofficially married a concubine, the weight of probability does not favor it. It was considered proper for a wife to share her husband's religion, so if he *was* married, her shared devotion here would be natural. But the term translated "household" could include servants or *freedpersons; although a cheap slave would cost about one-third of a regular soldier's annual pay, centurions received fifteen times the pay of rank-and-file soldiers. "Household" here may just mean "servants" (v. 7).

10:3. The "ninth hour" (KJV, NASB) is about 3 p.m.—he keeps the Jewish hours of prayer, which corresponded to the morning and evening offerings in the temple (3:1).

10:4-8. In the *Old Testament as well God looked out for many *Gentiles who were seeking him, whether or not they had yet become full converts (e.g., Josh 6:25; 2 Sam 12:9-10), and revealed himself to individuals other than Abraham's descendants (Gen 5:24; Num 22—25). "Memorial" (v. 4) may be the language of sacrifice (Lev 2:2), which would be fitting for prayers offered during the time of sacrifice in the temple.

10:9-16
Peter's Vision

Compare Cornelius's vision in 10:1-8; on such cases of "double vision," compare the comment on 9:12.

10:9. Caesarea was about thirty miles north of Joppa. If Cornelius's messengers left even immediately after 3 p.m. (10:3), they must have traveled part of the night on foot, or (less likely) Cornelius must have found horses for them to ride, because here they approach Joppa by noon ("the sixth hour"—KJV, NASB). Thus their task must be urgent.

The flat rooftops were used for drying vegetables and for prayers. If one reclined under a canopy, the rooftops were cooler even at midday than the poorly ventilated rooms of most Palestinian homes (although this home may be larger than most; cf. 10:17). Noon was not a regular hour of prayer (3:1), so Peter prays in addition to the traditional hours followed by many of his contemporaries.

10:10. Peter is not hungry from any special fast; noon was the normal time for a meal in Rome and may have been in Joppa as well. *Philo described the state here attributed to Peter as "divine intoxication," when the soul is so filled with God that one loses touch with one's surroundings; but in contrast to Philo and *apocalyptists who sought mystical experiences, Peter has done nothing intentionally to bring it about.

10:11-13. Even Palestinian Jews most lenient in other regards kept kosher. Thus this vision would present a horrifying situation for any first-century Palestinian Jew (and the vast majority of foreign Jews as well): God commands Peter to eat all these unclean, forbidden creatures. Hungry he may be (10:10), but he is not *that* hungry!

10:14-16. In another vision half a millennium before, God had similarly called Ezekiel, a priest, to eat something unclean, and he had offered the same protest; God's response was but a small improvement (Ezek 4:13-15). Jewish people had preferred death to eating unclean (nonkosher) food in the time of the *Maccabees; thus Jewish readers would be appalled that God would require anything so disgusting (from the perspective of cultural cuisine) and impious (from an *Old Testament perspective). The point of the vision, that God can declare anything clean, applies especially to the *Gentiles Peter is about to meet (10:28; 15:9). Repetition of a revelation is not unusual (1 Sam 3:4-10).

10:17-23a
Receiving the Gentiles

10:17. Joppa was a large town, but knowing Simon's profession and that his house was near the sea would make it easy to find him. (In many cities of the Roman world, people of the same trade would live in the same district.) That Simon has an outer gate indicates that he is a man of some means.

10:18. Being knowledgeable about Judaism themselves (10:2), Cornelius's messengers "call out" rather than simply going up to the house to enter (10:28), although as representatives of a Roman centurion they could surely have done so with impunity under Roman custom.

10:19-21. Peter "went down" to them by the outside staircase leading from the flat roof.

10:22. Although many stories tell of Jewish teachers talking with *Gentiles, strict Jews would not enter a Gentile's house or allow a Gentile in theirs.

Thus Peter faces a problem in being invited to Cornelius's house. Although more lax Jews would probably not object (v. 23a), Peter has to be concerned about stricter elements within the Jewish *church, which eventually included even *Pharisees (15:5).

10:23a. Pharisees and other pietists were concerned about impure table fellowship; lodging Gentiles overnight, no matter how exhausted the guests may have been, contradicted strict Jewish piety. Eating with them was forbidden on the principle that they were evil company (*Jubilees 22:16). Perhaps Simon, being a tanner, is less concerned with strict rules; although most of his customers were probably Jewish, Joppa was a mixed town and his was a profession despised by strict pietists anyway. (Even later *rabbis allowed some short-term business contacts with Gentiles and recognized that some shops employed both Gentile and Jewish workers.) But Peter's vision probably has something to do with the treatment the guests receive.

10:23b-33
Cornelius Receives Peter

10:23b. Peter's companions are no doubt brought partly to serve as witnesses that he behaves properly (10:45; cf. Deut 17:6; 19:15).

10:24. Had they left around sunrise, after the *Gentiles had lodged in his house overnight (NASB "he arose"—v. 23), and walked without stopping, they would have arrived at Cornelius's house that evening. "The following day" here means that they all stopped for overnight lodging along the way (v. 30), presumably in a mixed town (perhaps in Apollonia, just under halfway along the Mediterranean coast). That Cornelius is patiently "waiting" (NASB, TEV) for them means not only that he trusted his servants not to run off but also that he is eager to hear Peter's message.

The term translated "relatives" (NASB, NIV) can also mean "countrymen" and probably does here. If it means relatives, it could mean distant relatives who were soldiers stationed in the same city, although that coincidence is unlikely. It is not the usual way to describe one's immediate family (cf. also on 10:2), but it is even less likely to include servants. That he had "called them together" suggests that they are not infants (cf. also v. 46), and nothing in this passage supports the reference to infant *baptism that some writers have seen here (v. 48).

10:25-26. Greco-Roman paganism believed not only in gods but in semidivine men, often sons of the gods, who had supernatural powers (14:11; 28:6). One would offer obeisance to gods by falling at their feet and worshiping them, as Cornelius does to Peter here. Cornelius should know better (10:2) than to treat Peter with such reverence; perhaps he intends only a special form of homage, which a servant of Jesus finds inappropriate (cf. Lk 22:25-27).

10:27-29. Devout Jews would not enter into idolaters' homes lest they unwittingly participate in idolatry; they apparently extended this custom to not entering any Gentile's home. It was considered unclean to eat Gentiles' food or to drink their wine; although this purity regulation did not prohibit all social contact, it prevented dining together at banquets and made much of the Roman world feel that Jews were antisocial. Cornelius is undoubtedly accustomed to accepting reluctant (10:22) snubs, so Peter's statement in 10:28 would mean much to him.

10:30-33. See comment on 10:3-6.

10:34-43
Peter's Message

10:34-35. Judaism heavily emphasized

God's impartiality; cf. Romans 2:11.

10:36. Jewish people in general would call *God* "Lord of all." "Preaching peace" alludes to the concept of Israel's redemption, found in Isaiah 52:7 and similar passages, although even God-fearing *Gentiles might not catch this allusion (but perhaps cf. Is 57:19 in Acts 2:39).

10:37. "Judea" here apparently includes Galilee and is used in the broader sense of "the Jewish land" instead of its usual more narrow sense as the southern region of Palestine.

10:38. "Doing good" is literally "benefacting"—the sort of thing a ruler, deity, or some other powerful person would do when bestowing gifts or mercy on those of lower status. Depending on how much Cornelius knows about Judaism, he may recognize that anyone anointed with the *Holy Spirit in his own time would be considered extraordinary by his Jewish contemporaries.

10:40-41. Some Greeks seem to have believed that heroes or gods who had founded cities visited them but remained invisible. But Peter has no thought here of Jesus' remaining selectively invisible; rather, he comes only to those whom God had chosen.

10:42. In most Jewish literature, God himself is the judge.

10:43. Many prophets had messianic *prophecies, but only a few of them (e.g., Is 53) directly connected the *Messiah and the forgiveness of sins. Peter probably means this in a general sense: all the prophets testify of forgiveness through God's *grace, which will be provided in the time of the Messiah (c.f., e.g., Jer 23:5-6).

10:44-48
Saved Gentiles

10:44. Interruption was a common literary device; when enough has been said, the author allows the speaker to be interrupted. (Of course, it happened in real life as well as in literature; public speakers were often interrupted by individuals in the crowd.) "Fell upon" is equivalent to "filled" here (cf. 2 Chron 7:2-3).

10:45-47. Most Jewish teachers felt that the *Spirit inspired only the most pious with divine utterances, or that the Spirit would mark God's people in the future age. *Gentiles obviously could not receive the gift if God had not accepted them, so he clearly *had* accepted them—even without circumcision.

10:48. *Baptism was used as a public declaration of conversion; see comment on 2:37-38. Peter's lodging at a Gentile home for several more days would compound the offense to Jewish piety but drives home Peter's lesson (10:28).

11:1-18
Called to Account

11:1. On "brethren" (KJV, NASB) or "brothers" (NIV) see comment on 9:17.

11:2-3. Peter's colleagues do not object that the members of Cornelius's household are not God-fearing (10:2); the problem is that they are not fully Jewish—*Gentiles had to be circumcised to convert fully to Judaism. (This requirement is a natural inference from the *law and continues to be an issue as late as 15:1, 5.) Nor do they object that Peter preached Christ to Gentiles; the issue is that he ate with them even though as Gentiles they were ritually unclean (10:28; cf. Gal 2:12).

11:4-15. See comment on 10:9-46. On repeating a story in slightly different words, see the introduction to 9:1-9. Claiming (truly or falsely) divine authorization or sanction (v. 12) was a common means of defending one's actions in antiquity; Peter's ultimate evidence, then, is in 11:16-17.

11:16-17. Because Judaism used *baptism alongside circumcision to signify conversion, if God had baptized someone in his *Spirit, he had certainly accepted their conversion—with or without circumcision.

11:18. The believers in Jerusalem marvel that God has given "even the *Gentiles" (NIV, NRSV; not "also"—KJV, NASB, TEV) the gift. Jewish people believed that Gentiles could be saved by converting to Judaism; many also believed that Gentiles could be saved simply by being righteous and keeping the seven laws God gave to Noah (according to Jewish tradition). But until now no one had believed that Gentiles could be saved on the same terms as Jewish people, who had been chosen for salvation by God's sovereign *grace.

11:19-30
The Ministry at Antioch

The Jesus movement shifts from a predominantly rural movement in Galilee to an urban movement in Jerusalem to a cosmopolitan movement in Antioch. Such a rapid transition is virtually unparalleled in antiquity and indicates considerable social flexibility. That Judaism had already adapted to these various settings over the centuries provided a conduit for these rapid transitions within the Jewish Christian community.

11:19. The large Jewish communities in Phoenicia, Cyprus (4:36) and Antioch were natural places for Jewish Christians to settle after 8:1-4.

11:20-21. Antioch on the Orontes in Syria was the third largest urban center of antiquity (after Rome and Alexandria), with an estimated population of half a million, and was the headquarters of Rome's Syrian legion. With a famous cult center of Apollo within walking distance and Seleucia, its port city off the Mediterranean coast, only a brief river journey, it boasted numerous *mystery cults and was known for its pagan religious diversity.

Because of its cultural pluralism, it included an upwardly mobile and *generally* accepted Jewish element with many "God-fearers" (see 10:2) and was far less segregated than Alexandria. Some more liberal non-Palestinian Jewish people saw their witness to the God of Israel among the *Gentiles as making monotheism reasonable and contacting the best in pagan philosophy; circumcision was to them a lesser issue. Thus Antioch was a more natural place for Gentiles to hear the *gospel without circumcision than Judea was (15:1).

11:22-24. Barnabas trusts God's work in people (9:27; 15:37-39). Later sources often extolled an earlier Jewish sage named *Hillel for his gentleness and for being willing to accept Gentiles as they were and to lead them on from there, unlike many of his contemporaries.

11:25. Tarsus was about a hundred miles to the north; this trip would be a major undertaking.

11:26. "Christians" occurs in the *New Testament only here, as a nickname given by outsiders, and in 1 Peter 4:16, as something like a legal charge. The title is formed on the analogy of adherents to a political party: the "Caesarians," the "Herodians," the "Pompeianians" and so forth. Antiochans were known for making fun of people, but Christians in the second century decided to adopt the title with pride. No one would have guessed how long the name would last!

11:27. That the movement had a number of *prophets would impress those outside the movement; few if any movements had many prophets acting together, although Greek oracles still operated at cultic centers (less popular than in the past), and *Josephus said that many *Essenes could prophesy. Syria was known for its oracles, so Antiochans are probably also impressed by Christian prophets.

Some commentators have pointed out that these were traveling prophets and compared them to wandering *Cynic philosophers; but given the frequent mobility of many other people in Greco-Roman antiquity, their mobility need not be related to their office. Most prophets were probably relatively stationary (1 Cor 14:29).

11:28. A series of famines devastated Mediterranean agriculture in the time of Claudius: papyri show high grain prices around A.D. 46; a grain shortage in Rome nearly led to Claudius's being mobbed in the streets (about A.D. 51); Queen Helena of Adiabene bought Egyptian grain "for large sums" (due to famine there) to help Judea (about 45-46). Some commentators have connected this *prophecy with the image of an end-time famine common in *apocalyptic texts; although that suggestion is possible, this prophecy was fulfilled in the reign of Claudius.

11:29-30. Most Jewish relief efforts were local except in severe cases, for instance, when Queen Helena helped famine-stricken Palestinian Jews. But this local focus was due more to the nature of the Roman Empire—where multiprovincial organizations were suspect—than to the nature of Judaism; cf. comment on 2 Corinthians 8—9. What is significant here is that the believers act in advance of the famine through faith in the *prophecy (cf. Gen 41:33-36).

12:1-17
Peter's Deliverance

12:1. This Herod is Agrippa I, brother-in-law and son of a half-brother of Antipas, the Herod of the Gospels whose attempt to gain as much power as Agrippa cost him his own kingdom. (Antipas's fatal jealousy of Agrippa was instigated by his own consort Herodias—*Josephus *Antiquities* 18.7.1-2, 240-44, 250-54—although she had helped her brother Agrippa out after he had wasted all his money in Rome and returned to Palestine in debt—*Antiquities* 18.6.1-2, 143-49.) Herod Agrippa I had partied with Gaius Caligula in Rome; when Caligula became emperor, Agrippa I became the first official Jewish "king" since his grandfather Herod the Great. Because his grandmother Mariamne was a Hasmonean princess, he was Jewish as well as Idumean (in contrast to Herod the Great). He was thus very popular with the people, on behalf of whom he used his influence. He was pro-*Pharisee and frequented the temple.

12:2. Formerly performed with an ax, in this period beheading was performed with the sword and was the more merciful form of execution given to Roman citizens and others for whom crucifixion was considered too cruel. As king, Agrippa had the right of life and death that had been denied the *Sanhedrin before and after him. Like Judaism, early Christians believed that death did not come apart from the sovereign purpose of God.

12:3. Luke may mention the Feast of Unleavened Bread to recall to the reader the time of Jesus' execution (Lk 22:7) or because Peter could not avoid being seen in Jerusalem during the feast; if Luke had meant it only as a chronological detail, he would probably have also indicated the year in Agrippa's reign. Although Agrippa gave generously to *Gentiles outside Judea, his policies made him much more popular with his Jewish subjects (to whose majority whims he catered) than with his pagan subjects.

12:4. Agrippa I resided in Jerusalem. Luke does not mention the specific place of Peter's imprisonment, but the fortress Antonia on the temple mount is one possibility. As a trusted *client ruler of Rome, Agrippa also had his own army, so the soldiers mentioned here need not be Romans, although they are described in terms of Roman organization. The basic unit of the Roman army was the *contubernium*, composed of eight soldiers who shared a tent; half units were sometimes assigned to special tasks, as here (sixteen soldiers total). Agrippa perhaps feared armed resistance. Luke uses "Passover" in its general sense in this period to refer to the whole Feast of Unleavened Bread. The expression "bring before the people" (NASB) was used for public judicial assemblies in Greek cities.

12:5-6. Prisoners who were chained between guards (as often they were—21:33; cf. 28:16, 20) had no human hope of escaping.

12:8-11. On miraculous escapes see comment on 5:19-20. Agrippa wielded much more direct power than the *Sanhedrin had, and his guards were much more efficient. In a popular Greek story, Dionysus had made chains drop off and locked doors open; doors opening "by themselves" appear in ancient literature from Homer to *Josephus. Thus we can understand why Peter might think he is dreaming.

12:12-13. A home with an outer gate, a servant girl who could serve as a porter and a gathering much farther back in the house would suggest the home of a fairly wealthy resident of Jerusalem's Upper City. (For another indication of the family's wealth, cf. Col 4:10 with Acts 4:36-37. As Levites—4:36—they may have had ties with the priestly aristocracy; many well-to-do priests lived in the Upper City.) Thus the home is not far from the temple mount (hence not far from the fortress Antonia, where Peter may have been held). Believers met in homes rather than *church buildings for the first three centuries of the church (e.g., Rom 16:5), just as some poorer Jews did who could not afford *synagogues.

"Mark" is a Latin name, but as a *praenomen* it need not indicate Roman citizenship; still, the use of the name hardly indicates antipathy toward Rome or its interests in Jerusalem, and may again suggest the family's wealth.

12:14-16. Because these believers had probably prayed after James's capture, and he had been executed, their uncertain faith is perhaps understandable. But given the purpose for this prayer meeting (12:5), their surprise (and Peter's having to keep pounding on the gate—which could wake up some of the other neighbors, who are probably from aristocratic priestly families and hence dangerous) is ironic enough that ancient readers may have laughed. In some popular Jewish traditions the righteous would become like angels after death.

12:17. "James" (literally "Jacob," as with every use of "James" in the *New Testament) was a common name; this is not the James of 12:2, but the James of 15:13, 1 Corinthians 15:7 and Galatians 2:9. Jewish sources tell us that this James, Jesus' younger brother, was highly reputed for his devoutness in Judaism (cf. Acts 21:18-20), and when he was later martyred the people of Jerusalem protested his death. *He* would thus be safe from Agrippa, who catered to the Jewish masses (12:1-3).

12:18-19. Given the soldiers' precautions (chains, doors and different guards posted for each—12:6), it was humanly impossible for Peter to have escaped without all the guards having aided him. Agrippa examines them for information, perhaps under torture, but they have none. Under Roman law, a guard whose prisoner escaped would pay for it with the penalty due the prisoner—in this case, his own life (cf. 16:27; 27:42), a custom Agrippa, deprived of a favor for the masses, chooses to follow.

12:20. The Hellenistic (culturally Greek) cities of Tyre and Sidon were dependent on Agrippa's territories for vital food supplies; he had been withholding trade from them.

12:21. Agrippa I liked to flaunt his power; his self-display had unfortunately led to anti-Jewish riots in Alexandria earlier. His public meeting with these emissaries is in the theater of Caesarea, built by his grandfather Herod the Great; the foundations of this theater still remain today. According to *Josephus this speech occurred on a festival day in honor of the emperor (probably his birthday, but perhaps a rare festival held in March A.D. 44).

12:22-24. The first-century Jewish historian *Josephus reports that on this occasion Agrippa flaunted his power, and his flatterers praised him as a god—the sort of flattery toward royal patrons common for centuries in the Greek East. But in the Roman period Caesar expected even pagans who were not emperors (such as the general Germanicus in Egypt) to humbly deflect such praise. Because Agrippa does not repudiate their praise, he collapses immediately. Josephus reports that he was carried to the palace, where he died at the age of fifty-four, after five days of stomach pains. Deaths from bowel diseases and worms were thought among the most horrible.

12:25—13:3 Antioch Sends Out Missionaries

Despite the commission of 1:8, the Palestinian *apostles are still in Jerusalem (15:6). The leaders of the church in Antioch, however, discovered success in the *Gentile mission (11:19-26) and are moved to ratify the apostolic call of two of their number.

12:25. The journey from Jerusalem to Antioch was roughly four hundred miles. It was customary for ancient teachers to take *disciples with them, and it was safer to travel in groups.

13:1. All the overseers of this *church are probably understood to be both prophets and teachers. What sounds normal in early Christianity would sound phenomenal to its culture, for prophets were thought to be rare. Simeon and Manaen (Menahem) are Jewish names, suggesting strong Jewish representation still in the leadership of the church (no doubt because they had better background for teaching Scripture). But Simeon's surname "Niger" was a very respectable and common Roman name; he may be a Roman citizen, although this is not clear—the name was also used by Jews and is here a *nickname*. Nicknames were common and usually significant in antiquity; the meaning of Simeon's Latin nickname suggests a dark complexion and may indicate that he was descended from *proselytes from the Romanized coast of North Africa (perhaps also Lucius). Cyrene, on the North African coast, had a large Jewish population.

That Manaen was "brought up" with Herod may mean they had the same wet nurse. Slaves who grew up in the master's household with the son who would inherit them were often later freed by the son, who had been their companion at play; even as slaves they were powerful because of their relation to the owner. Other boys brought up with princes at the royal court also attained prominence. Especially in

Greek culture, friendships from youth determined political alliances and favors. Thus, until the fall of Herod Antipas ("the tetrarch") perhaps a decade before, Manaen had held a socially prominent position (and is probably Luke's main source for the Antipas material unique to his Gospel).

13:2-3. Jewish people fasted to mourn or *repent, and some fasted to seek revelations; special fasts for prayer related to mourning were called in the face of great crises such as droughts. Here they are probably simply seeking God in prayer. The *Holy Spirit was especially known as the Spirit of *prophecy, so "the Holy Spirit said" probably means that one of the prophets prophesied. For the laying on of hands see comment on 6:6.

13:4-12 The Pronconsul of Cyprus Believes

Messengers customarily traveled by twos. Students of the *law also preferred having companions to study with; Saul, Barnabas and Mark (v. 13) no doubt discussed Scripture during many of their long walks. Roman roads were good and generally safe during the day, and travel was easier than it ever had been or would be again until close to the modern period.

13:4. Seleucia was Antioch's port city on the Mediterranean, less than twenty miles to the west. The island of Cyprus is a natural destination if Barnabas knows the culture and has relatives there (4:36).

13:5. Salamis, the chief town of Cyprus, was a port city only about a hundred miles from Seleucia, a straight voyage by ship. As visiting teachers skilled in the law, Barnabas and Saul would be asked to speak in local *synagogues (with its large Jewish community, Salamis must have had several synagogues). In the early second century, the Cypriot Jewish community is said to have attacked Salamis in a revolt and to have itself been destroyed.

13:6. New Paphos, a Greek harbor town on the north and west of Cyprus, had long been the provincial capital and maintained some trade relations with Judea. Jewish magicians were reputed to be among the best in the Roman Empire (though forbidden in Scripture and mistrusted among pious Jews). It was not unusual for Roman aristocrats to attach philosophers to their court; while magicians would be less appealing, the proconsul probably sees Bar-Jesus ("son of Joshua") as a useful adviser from a "Jewish" perspective. (Romans generally distrusted magic, but *Josephus said that Felix, a Roman governor of Judea, counted among his friends a Cyprian Jew reputed to be a magician. His name is not Bar-Jesus, but Bar-Jesus and he attest to the same activity of Jewish magicians on Cyprus and their appeal to some Roman officials.)

13:7-8. Sergius Paulus was proconsul of Cyprus (the highest Roman official on the island) about A.D. 45-46. As always, Luke has the correct, specific local title of the Roman official, even though these titles varied from place to place and decade to decade, and the only way to check all the proper titles would be to go to those places. It is uncertain if this is the Sergius Paulus whose family is known from later inscriptions.

13:9. Roman citizens had three names. As a citizen, Saul had a Roman *cognomen* ("Paul," meaning "small"); his other Roman names remain unknown to us. As inscriptions show was common, his Roman name sounded similar to his Jewish name (Saul, from the name of the *Old Testament's most famous Benjamite). This is not a name change; now that Paul is moving in a predominantly Roman environment, he begins to go by his Roman name, and some of Luke's readers recognize for the first time that Luke is writing about someone of whom they had already heard.

13:10-11. Paul's rebuke of Elymas sounds like an Old Testament judgment oracle or the utterance of a signs prophet. In Jewish literature, temporary blindness was sometimes a judgment to prevent further damage from sin (the *Letter of Aristeas 316); see comment on 9:8.

13:12. The proconsul's employ of a Jewish "prophet" demonstrates his openness to Judaism (v. 6), but Paul and Barnabas show superior power and a better presentation of Judaism than Bar-Jesus had provided.

13:13-41
Sermon in Pisidian Antioch

The cities that Paul and his companions visit in 13:13—14:26 were along the same Roman military road, the Via Augusta, which was built roughly half a century before.

13:13. They probably landed at Attalia, the main harbor, then proceeded by road to Perga, twelve miles north and at least five miles from navigable water. It was part of the district Pamphylia-Lycia in this period (A.D. 43 to about 68).

13:14. Antioch near Pisidia was a Roman colony; if Sergius Paulus (13:12) had supplied them with letters of recommendation (cf. 9:2) to the local aristocracy, they would receive immediate hospitality. Regular Jewish public gatherings at the *synagogue in this period were normally only on the sabbath and feast days.

13:15. In a later period, the biblical readings (especially from the law) would be fixed, and the synagogue sermon would be a homily on the texts read, similar to the one in this chapter; homilies (expositions of texts) were probably already used in this period. "Rulers of the synagogue" were the highest officials of local synagogues and are attested in Jewish inscriptions throughout the empire.

13:16. Many scholars have drawn parallels between Paul's speech here and the synagogue teaching form that came to be known as the "proem homily"; others have questioned whether the proem homily can be documented this early so far from Palestine. Whichever is the case, Paul's Scripture-laced exposition in 13:16-43 contrasts plainly with 14:15-17 and 17:22-31, showing that Paul adapted to different audiences in his speeches, as he did in his letters. In Jewish Palestine, one sat to expound the *law; here Paul stands because he is exhorting rather than expounding, or because the custom may have differed outside Palestine.

13:17-19. Four hundred fifty years is a round number, apparently presupposing that Israel was in Egypt for four hundred years (see 7:6) and wandering in the desert for forty years.

13:20-21. The forty years of Saul's reign is taken from early Jewish tradition, also preserved in *Josephus.

13:22-25. David's reign is the climax of centuries of waiting through other models of leadership; Jesus is the descendant of David, the *Messiah of whom the prophets spoke. Thus they proclaim one greater than the ancient hero David.

13:26. "Children of Abraham" are his Jewish hearers; "God-fearers" here may refer to interested *Gentiles (cf. 10:2) or perhaps full *proselytes (cf. 13:43).

13:27-29. For the Jerusalemites' fulfilling the Scriptures in condemning Jesus, see especially Isaiah 53, which states that the servant would be rejected by his own people; early Christians also cited psalms of righteous sufferers (Ps 22 and 69). Luke does not cite all Paul's references, because he would not have room in his scroll to record the whole speech (see comment on 2:40).

13:30-32. Paul needed to bolster especially this section of his proclamation with Scripture (13:33-35), because Judaism did not expect the death and *resurrection of a *Messiah *within* history.

13:33. Psalm 2:7 was already applied to the messianic enthronement in Judaism (most clearly in the *Dead Sea Scrolls). Psalm 2 celebrated the promise made to David of an eternal dynasty, a promise that was repeated regularly in the temple worship, in the hope of the ultimate Davidic king who would fulfill it completely.

13:34. Paul cites Isaiah 55:3 (and perhaps originally 55:4, with its hope for the *Gentiles) to indicate that Israel's future hope was bound up with the promise to David.

13:35-37. *Rabbis used a technique called *gezerah shavah* to connect passages that used the same key word; thus here Paul may use "holy" in Isaiah 55:3 to lead into a citation of Psalm 16:10, which guarantees that the object of David's promise would never rot (cf. also Acts 2:25-28).

13:38-41. Paul concludes with Habakkuk 1:5; he says "in the Prophets" (NASB) because some of the smaller books of the prophets were grouped together and treated as a single book. Habakkuk refers to impending judgment under the Chaldeans (1:6), which only the righteous remnant will endure by faith (2:4); here the principle is applied to the judgment of the end. The *Dead Sea Scrolls apply the text to those who violated God's covenant by disbelieving the Teacher of Righteousness (the founder of the *Qumran community).

13:42-43. According to *Josephus, many *Gentiles attended *synagogues with great interest. Even as late as the fourth century, the Christian preacher John Chrysostom complains that Gentiles—in this case Christians—were still attending synagogue services. Those who were interested in Judaism but unattracted to circumcision might well find Paul's message appealing.

13:44. When famous speakers (e.g., Dio Chrysostom) would come to town, much of the town would go to hear him. Word spreads quickly about the new speaker at the synagogue in Antioch, and Paul, probably originally more comfortable giving expositions of Scripture than public speeches in the Greek style, is billed as a *rhetorician or philosopher.

13:45-46. Paul and Barnabas's response to their opponents here has some *Old Testament precedent (cf. Lk 4:24-27; Amos 9:7) but goes further. It had always been God's purpose to bless the Gentiles in Abraham (Gen 12:3), but the tenacity of ancestral religions as part of cultural tradition is well known; when ethnic religion loses its uniquely ethnic component it may attract outsiders but simultaneously weaken its own constituency.

13:47. Here they quote the mission of the servant of Isaiah 49:6. The servant is clearly Israel in 49:3-4; in 49:5-7 it is the one who fully carries out the servant's mission and suffers on behalf of Israel (as in 52:13—53:12), whom the early Christians recognized to be Jesus. As followers of Jesus, Paul and Barnabas take up the servant's mission, part of which was revealing the way of salvation to the Gentiles.

13:48-49. Because the Jewish people believed that they were predestined for salvation by virtue of descent from

Abraham, the idea that many *Gentiles had been "ordained to *eternal life" (KJV) could be offensive—but was exactly what Isaiah 49:6 implied (see Acts 13:47).

13:50. Ancient sources report that many prominent women were interested in Judaism (partly because their wealth gave them leisure to consider it, partly because they, unlike men, did not have to face circumcision if they became serious about it); these women in turn could influence their powerful husbands. Local aristocracies made up a fraction of the population but held great wealth and most of the political power; from them came *decurions* for the local councils, and their opposition could drive someone out of town. But their authority was only local, and by going to Iconium Paul and Barnabas move out of their jurisdiction.

13:51-52. Iconium was further along the same road, at the very east end of Phrygia-Galatia (assuming, as is probable though disputed, that this region was called "Galatia" in this period).

Many Jewish people on returning to the Holy Land would shake the dust of a pagan land from their feet; because the temple was considered holier than the rest of Israel, they would also shake the dust from their feet when they entered the temple. Paul and Barnabas probably imply that those who reject their message are pagan and stand under God's judgment. Jesus had commanded his *disciples to follow this practice even in Jewish Palestine (Lk 10:10-12).

14:1-7
Opposition in Iconium

14:1-4. Although Iconium was a wealthy and prosperous town, it was hardly the size of a city like Ephesus or Smyrna. Whereas urban culture in the empire tended to be uniformly Greco-Roman, rural society preserved local language and customs, and a town like Iconium would have its share of both. Traveling teachers would undoubtedly have drawn more attention in a town like Iconium than in larger cities. Because the native language of Iconium was Phrygian, Paul and Barnabas may address mainly the Greek-speaking upper social strata, or they may speak through interpreters (cf. 14:11, 14); but it is more likely that most of the crowd understands Greek, even if it is not their first language.

Among the deities that the *Gentiles of Iconium worshiped, the most prominent was Cybele, the Phrygian mother goddess; Phrygian *mystery cults were also common. But inscriptions testify that the Christian faith spread and Iconium later became a major center of Christianity in Asia Minor.

14:5. Under law, city magistrates could do whatever necessary to quell disturbances; in the case of Paul and Barnabas, the officials could quell the disturbance simply by legally banning them from the city. Thus the plot to kill them goes beyond the law.

14:6-7. Iconium was in Phrygia near the border of Lycaonia, which contained Lystra and Derbe. Some people considered flight undignified, but Jewish teachers preferred it to death, unless flight required denying the *law of God.

14:8-20a
Preaching at Lystra

14:8. For half a century Lystra had been a Roman *colony; its own citizens were accorded privileges as citizens of Rome. It emphasized its local culture and its Roman character alongside Pisidian Antioch and against the Greek cities of the region.

Although some philosophers lectured in halls or served wealthy *patrons, most preached their philosophical wares on street corners or in marketplaces; powerful speakers like Dio Chrysostom criticized philosophers like *Epictetus who reserved their lectures for the classroom. Like an ancient philosopher, Paul here preaches on the street rather than in a *synagogue (perhaps Lystra has none; see 14:19). Paul's approach should not surprise us; his own letters indicate that he shares some of this philosophical ideal (1 Cor 4:11-13), and he often uses the *Cynic-*Stoic preaching style in them. What is surprising is not that Paul would occasionally preach this way but that he draws such a vigorous response; perhaps the controversy his opponents create helps him. Secluded philosophers tended toward academic discourse, while those on the streets were ready to denounce the folly of their hearers to secure their attention.

14:9-11. Local Phrygian legend told of an ancient visitation by Zeus and Hermes to Phrygia. In the story only one couple, Baucis and Philemon, received them graciously; the rest of the population was destroyed in a flood. Knowing some form of the story in their own language, the Lycaonians are not about to make the same mistake ancient Phrygia had made; they want to honor Paul and Barnabas, whom they mistake for gods. People sometimes considered miracle workers as gods.

14:12. Hermes was the messenger of the Olympian gods who spoke for the more dignified Zeus (though in other stories Zeus was less dignified and out chasing women or occasionally boys for his sexual delights). Like most early Jewish and Christian writers (cf. also Is 46:5-7), Luke is not above making fun of paganism's stupidity.

14:13. Inscriptions show that Hermes and Zeus were worshiped together in the Phrygian region. Sacrificial animals were often decorated with garlands before being offered. Temples "outside the city gates" or "just outside the city" (NIV) were quite common in Asia Minor. The lame man had probably been healed at the gate, because lame people made their living by begging, and beggars normally found their best income at such places of transit (cf. 3:2).

14:14. Villages of the East usually kept their own ancient language after Greek had become the language of the cities. Landowning citizens of Lystra spoke Latin, but Paul and Barnabas are preaching to the masses, the abundant Anatolian noncitizens who lived there; only at verse 14 are they informed of what the crowds are saying. Jewish people were required to tear their robes when they heard blasphemy.

14:15-16. Although using biblical language, Barnabas and Paul preach to these Anatolian farmers in terms they would not need to know the Bible to understand, emphasizing the God who rules nature, who was already recognized by paganism. Jewish people often pointed to pagan philosophical teachings on the supreme god, which Jews felt contradicted the pagan worship of idols. Jews called idols "vain" (futile), in contrast to the "living" God. Jewish people believed that God allowed a lower moral standard for *Gentiles, who had only seven laws to keep; but idolatry, like sexual immorality, was not an issue on which God would permit compromise.

14:17. Phrygia was fertile, and Phrygians especially worshiped the mother goddess who was supposed to provide fertility to the earth. Various philosophers, especially *Stoics, believed that nature itself testified to the character of the supreme god. Jewish teachers agreed that nature testifies to God's character (this is biblical; cf. Ps 19:1; 89:37) and taught that he provides all peoples with health, food and so forth.

14:18-20a. The visitors from Antioch had no legal authority outside their own territory, but they are able to persuade the mob to accomplish what had failed in Iconium (14:5-6). A mob could change its views quickly (cf. Lk 23:18), especially in a case like this one: when Paul and Barnabas deny the gods, they would be considered impious and hence would appear to fit a different category of ancient paganism: they were not gods after all, but dangerous magicians. (Whereas gods were popularly regarded as generally beneficent, sorcerers were viewed as secretive and usually harmful.)

Antioch was nearly a hundred miles from Lystra by road, but it is known that the cities were in contact with each other, considering themselves sister cities. See 7:58 for details on Jewish stoning, but stoning was also the most common form of urban mob violence in the *Gentile world. Stones, tiles and cobbles were readily available in ancient streets. When Jewish crowds stoned a transgressor, they sought the transgressor's death; Paul's survival undoubtedly points to divine protection. Normally such executions were performed outside the city, and they may have dragged him out of the city for purity reasons; that he not only survived but could walk afterward must be understood as miraculous.

14:20b-28 Consolidating the Work

14:20b. Derbe was the frontier city on the imperial road and thus probably profited from customs duties charged there. Yet it was a rude and poorly educated city, reflecting Greek language and perhaps some Greek culture but little contact with Roman society.

14:21-22. Much traditional Jewish teaching spoke of a period of intense suffering before the time of the *kingdom; Paul may allude to this idea in verse 22, although "tribulation" (KJV, NASB) here may be more generic.

14:23. Elders had always governed and judged in towns and villages in the *Old Testament (and in much of the rest of the Mediterranean world as well), and the evidence is abundant that this form of rule continued in the *New Testament period. Most ancient *synagogues had several elders who filled a religious office (acting as councils rather than as individuals). The title generally called for respect; the Greek East accorded much influence to the *Gerousia,* clubs made up of elders.

14:24. It was known that Pamphylia was near Pisidia; both peoples were reputed to be especially adept in augury (predicting the future by the flights of birds)—forbidden by the Old Testament prohibition of divination (Deut 18:10).

14:25. Attalia was Pamphylia's main port on the mouth of the Catarractes.

14:26-28. When they return to Antioch, Paul and Barnabas report on their missionary work to the sending *church. Although Jewish people in the *Diaspora were concerned to propagate a favorable impression of their religion and to gain converts when possible, they do not seem to have engaged in a concerted effort at what we call "missions." Yet *synagogue communities throughout the Diaspora informally remained in contact through travelers who reported news, and reports of large numbers of converts to Judaism would have been considered news when it occurred. The Antiochan church's commitment probably goes beyond such interest, because the early Christians' interest in missions was far more central than that of other Jewish sects; Luke-Acts is clear that missions is at the heart of Jesus' purpose for his church.

15:1-5
The Controversy

15:1. Many Jewish people believed that *Gentiles were saved simply by keeping the seven laws given to Noah (prohibiting idolatry, sexual immorality, etc.); others believed that Gentiles had to convert to Judaism by being circumcised (if male) and (according to most of this group) *baptized (whether male or female). (*Josephus reported that some of his colleagues demanded the circumcision of Gentiles who had come to them for refuge, but Josephus himself forbade this requirement; this report would commend Josephus to his Gentile readers.) Of course, even those Jewish people who believed that righteous Gentiles could be saved without converting to Judaism did not accept them as part of God's people Israel unless they converted (cf. comment on Galatians, where inclusion in God's people, rather than salvation, may be in view).

15:2. These believers would "go up" because Jerusalem is higher in elevation than Antioch (the image of "ascending" to Jerusalem recurs often in the *Old Testament). The *churches of the *Diaspora, like the *synagogues, were ruled by local elders, not by a hierarchy in Jerusalem; but just as synagogues respected messengers from the temple authorities in the homeland, the non-Palestinian churches need to resolve the issues raised by those purporting to speak for Judean Christians (15:1). (*Josephus pointed out that Jerusalemites, priests and those who knew the *law well were given great respect by others. He reported that some who were qualified in this way were sent to subvert his own similar qualifications as an officer in Galilee.)

15:3-4. Their testimonies, like Peter's (11:12; 15:8), appeal to divine attestation, which was widely accepted in both Jewish and *Gentile circles. But many strict *Pharisees believed that signs were insufficient attestation if they contradicted traditional interpretations of the law (15:5).

15:5. Among the Pharisees, the stricter school of *Shammai may have prevailed at this time; the school of *Hillel, which predominated later, was much more generous toward Gentiles. Other Jews respected Pharisees for their piety, and the Jerusalem *church no doubt accorded them high status for their knowledge of the law.

15:6-11
Peter's Response

Having the backing of the leading minister to the traditional constituency (Gal 2:7) on one's side (Acts 10—11) is certainly strategic in granting credibility to the very different ministry of the Antioch *church.

15:6-7. The *apostles do not rule without the elders, and both engage in vigorous debate, as Jewish teachers did in their schools. In later rabbinic schools, *rabbis often had to agree to disagree; this assembly seeks to achieve consensus (v. 22).

15:8-9. *Gentiles were continually impure by virtue of their state as Gentiles; for this reason, they were expected to undergo *proselyte *baptism when they converted to Judaism. Here, however, Peter says that God enacts that "cleansing" (NASB, NRSV) or "purifying" (NIV, KJV; cf. 10:15) simply through their faith.

15:10-11. Here Peter may refer to the common Jewish tradition of the "yoke" of God's *law or his *kingdom as opposed to the yoke of worldly care. Most Jewish people saw the law not as a burden but as a gracious gift; they believed that its duties freed them from real burdens (cf. Mt 11:29-30). If he refers here to the law, Peter may think of its inadequacy only in the sense found in Jeremiah 31:32: the fathers broke it, but under the new covenant God would write the law in their hearts (Jer 31:33-34). Later *rabbis sometimes offered more lenient rulings for the sake of the majority of their people, who could not live by the stricter ones.

15:12-21 James's Response

15:12. See comment on 15:3-4. "The multitude" (KJV, NASB) means "the assembly" (NIV, NRSV), as in the *Dead Sea Scrolls.

15:13-14. In the *Old Testament "a people for his name" (KJV, NASB, NRSV, literally; or "a people for himself"—NIV) normally meant Israel; James derives this title for *Gentile Christians from Amos, whom he cites in verse 17.

15:15-16. James refers to "the Prophets" (plural) in this case because he is speaking of the scroll containing the twelve smaller books of the prophets, including Amos.

"Tabernacle of David" (Amos 9:11) probably means the "house [line] of David," fallen into such pitiable disrepair that it is called merely a tabernacle (KJV, NASB), or tent (NIV). Rebuilding David's house would mean raising up a *Messiah after the Davidic line's rule had been cut off. The *Dead Sea Scrolls also cited this text as messianic, along with 2 Samuel 7:10b-14. (Since the Old Testament rarely explicitly associates the tabernacle with the prophetic worship David instituted in 1 Chron 25, the interpretation that reads this passage as a restoration of Davidic worship is less likely. Amos and Acts refer to the restoration of the splendor of David's kingdom, and the charismatic worship of 1 Chron 25 presumably was already occurring around the time of Acts 15; cf. 1 Cor 14.)

15:17-18. Amos 9:12 says "the remnant of Edom," but by slightly changing the spelling (as Jewish interpreters often did to make points; James or Luke here follow the *LXX) James can say "the remnant of Adam," meaning "of humanity" (cf. "of men"—NIV). Amos 9:12 refers to "possessing" Edom, and nations being "called by my [God's] name" (NASB) could refer to conquest rather than willing submission. But the point is that the nations will come under the rule of God, and the context (Amos 9:7) suggests that God is concerned for the nations themselves.

15:19-20. The few requirements James suggests they impose are representative of the handful of laws Jewish tradition declared that God gave Noah. According to the more lenient Jewish position, any righteous *Gentiles who kept those basic laws would have a share in the world to come. Because even stricter *Pharisees had to get along with the majority of more lenient people, these teachers did not try to invalidate other teachers' rulings if they had majority consent.

15:21. James's statement here could mean that Moses already has enough observers of his *law; but more likely it means that believers are to abstain from the practices in verse 20 lest they offend the many people of verse 21.

15:22-35 The Church's Decree

15:22. When views were disputed in the later *rabbinic academies, the majority view always prevailed; here a partial compromise (in favor of the Antioch *church) seems to command consensus. Other Jewish groups also had "general sessions," such as at *Qumran, where the priests, elders and people would gather. "Silas" is the *Aramaic form of the Hebrew name "Saul"; its nearest Latin name is "Silvanus" (1 Thess 1:1).

15:23. That ethnic *Gentiles should be called "brothers and sisters" is significant. The greetings are standard for Greco-Roman letters; the address shows that it is a circular letter, to be copied and circulated by its messengers to these different regions. Both novels and historical works sometimes cited the contents of letters.

15:24-27. The messengers they send to deliver the decree will be widely respected as trustworthy and representative of the council (analogies occur elsewhere, e.g., the *Letter of Aristeas 40).

15:28. Because the *Holy Spirit was usually associated with prophetic inspiration or special enlightenment, readers would understand that the apostles and elders are claiming that God directly led the decision of their community. "It seemed good" (also v. 22) occurs in Greek decrees in the sense, "Be it resolved," often associated with votes in citizen assemblies.

15:29. See comment on verse 20. The Jewish high court was permitted to issue temporary decrees to alleviate specific problems not directly settled in Scripture, and the assembly in Jerusalem may act on analogy with this tradition. Greco-Roman letters normally ended with "Farewell," as here.

15:30-35. The frequency with which *prophets turn up in Acts would seem phenomenal to ancient readers. Although some people in ancient Judaism claimed to be prophets, this was a rare phenomenon and no group boasted prophetic activity to the extent that Christians did; most Jews felt that there were no genuine prophets in their own time.

15:36-41
Returning to the Mission Field

That Israelite literature reported the failings of its heroes even during the epic period may be noteworthy, but by this time it had long been standard for Greco-Roman biographers to admit their heroes' weaknesses. Luke surely intends us to see God's blessing on the new Paul-Silas team (15:40; cf. 16:37), but this does not signal his approval of the dispute between Paul and Barnabas, handled so unlike the council in 15:22.

16:1-5
Spreading the Word

On Derbe and Lystra see 14:8, 20. Palestinian Jews considered intermarriage between Jews and pagans a horrible sin (Tobit 4:12; 1 Esdras 8:68-96; 9:7-9), but views were no doubt more lenient in places like Lystra, where the Jewish community was smaller. Under Jewish law at least as early as the second century, a person was presumed Jewish if his or her mother were Jewish; but even if that ruling was in effect in Paul's day, Timothy would not have been accepted as fully Jewish, because he had not been circumcised. (Wives were expected to submit to their husband's religion, and Timothy's father had probably refused to let him be circumcised.)

Paul makes him a full Jew for the sake of his witness to the Jewish community (cf. the different situation addressed in Gal 2:3-4, where the issue is not witness but coercion). The *Gentile community already recognized Christians as proclaimers of a form of Judaism; thus, offended as many of them were by the idea of circumcision, they would not be more offended by a circumcised Jewish Christian than by an uncircumcised Christian.

16:6-10 The Spirit's Guidance

16:6. The Greek phrase here may view Phrygia and Galatia together as a unit (though cf. 18:23); many scholars believe that Paul's letter to the Galatians covers the Phrygian regions included in Acts 14. Most Jewish groups believed that the *Holy Spirit was no longer active in the *Old Testament sense, and none paralleled the magnitude of the Spirit's working regarded as normal among the early Christians.

16:7-8. Troas was directly to the east of Mysia; Bithynia was a senatorial province northeast of Mysia. Thus Paul and his companions go from eastern Mysia (near Bithynia and just north of Phrygia) westward toward Alexandria Troas, which was ten miles south of the more famous ancient Troy. Troas had a mixed population of Roman citizens and natives who never quite adjusted to one another's presence; it was also where two major routes from the East toward Rome converged, and those traveling from Asia to Macedonia or the reverse regularly passed through the port of Troas.

16:9. Macedonia had been a Roman province since 146 B.C. It was strategically more important to Rome than Achaea (most of Greece) was, because it was the link between Rome and the whole eastern part of the empire along the Via Egnatia (the Egnatian Way), a road originally constructed about 148 B.C. The narrow body of water between Troas and Thrace was the famous divider of Asia and Europe. Because deities in Greek religion used visions to send people on missions, even unconverted *Gentile readers would understand Luke's point here.

16:10. In contrast to the views of some scholars (who regard "we" as a fictitious literary device because it appears in novels as well as in historical works), "we" in ancient texts normally *meant* "we." Luke is writing a historical work (novels did not have historical prologues), so he is no doubt reporting that he was with Paul as an eyewitness on this and subsequent occasions when he uses the term. Personal eyewitness experience was considered the most dependable source for history.

16:11-15 A Response in Philippi

16:11. The mountainous and thus easily visible island of Samothrace is the first port travelers would reach; it was a major landmark. Neapolis was one of the two best ports of south Macedonia, directly serving Philippi (the other was Thessalonica). A two-day voyage indicates favorable winds (cf. 20:6), probably from the northeast. Except during the winter (mid-November to early March), sea travel was quicker and less expensive than land travel, allowing one to cover perhaps a hundred miles a day.

16:12. Neapolis was the port of Philippi, which lay about ten miles to the northwest across Mount Symbolum. This was the eastern end of the Via Egnatia, which led westward to Dyrrhachium, an Adriatic port from which one could sail to Italy. Philippi had been a Roman colony (see comment on Phil 3:20) since 42 B.C.; thus it included among its inhabitants full citizens of Philippi, who were thereby honorary citizens of Rome. It was more an agricultural than commercial center, unlike many urban areas Paul visited.

Thessalonica, not Philippi, was Macedonia's capital, but Philippi was considered in the "first part" or "first district" (TEV) of Macedonia, which was divided into four districts. Philippi was also a "first" or "leading" city of the province in the sense that it was one of the most eminent there (alongside Thessalonica).

16:13. "Place of prayer" was a customary non-Palestinian Jewish term for a *synagogue, but the gathering here seems to be without a building. According to Jewish pietists concerned about assimilation, a minimum of ten Jewish men was necessary to constitute a regular synagogue and thus indicate a city where Jewish people would be likely to form their own community; this number of Jewish men may not have lived in Philippi. But in places with no official synagogue, Jewish people preferred to meet in a ritually pure place near water; ritual washing of hands before prayer seems to have been standard in *Diaspora Judaism, and excavations show the importance of water to synagogues.

The nearest body of flowing water, the Gangites (a tributary of the Strymon), is about one and a quarter miles from Philippi. It was thus more than a "sabbath day's journey" by *Pharisaic standards, suggesting that they were more concerned with assembling near a pure place than with the technicalities of Palestinian legal ideals. The "gate" is probably the colonial archway of the city, through which the Via Egnatia (cf. 16:9) went out to the Gangites.

16:14. Conservative Roman writers often complained that women pursued religions from the eastern Mediterranean, and *Josephus attests that tremendous numbers of women (far more than men) were attracted to Judaism. The sphere of religion was the one sphere in Greek culture where women were given some public responsibility, and the Diana cult in Philippi may have made women more prominent than in other Greek centers (Macedonian women traditionally exercised more freedom than Greek women). But Greek religion consisted of ritual, not teaching; thus these women would have had little training in the *law and would welcome Paul's teaching—although his teaching a group of women might violate traditional Palestinian protocol.

The name "Lydia," though common, would be especially natural for a woman from Thyatira, which was in the region of ancient Lydia. Thyatira was known for its dyers' guilds and textiles, and inscriptions show that other Thyatiran business agents also sold purple dye in Macedonia, becoming prosperous (although Macedonians, like inhabitants of most of the Empire, were generally poor, Macedonia had historically been one of the more prosperous provinces). Her name and trade may indicate that she was a *freedwoman (former slave); many traders in purple dye were freedwomen who continued to work as agents of their former masters' businesses.

16:15. By this period, some women were engaged in business; even slave women could become managers, just like slave men. Lydia probably did not gain wealth by becoming a widow; Roman law allowed a widow to inherit only 10 percent, although widows could inherit more than that from a deceased father. More than likely Lydia is well-to-do as a seller of purple, a luxury good associated with wealth throughout Mediterranean culture for over a thousand years. (The dye had been especially procured from the murex shellfish near Tyre, but in Macedonia it could have been procured from the mollusks near Thessalonica.) Well-to-do women sometimes became *patrons, or sponsors, of pagan religious associations; those attracted to Judaism helped support Jewish causes.

Paul and his companions may have been staying at an inn till the sabbath, but Lydia immediately offers the proper Jewish hospitality and invites the *apostles into her home, thus serving as a *patron of their work (cf. 1 Kings 17:13-24; especially 2 Kings 4:8-11). She appears to be the head of a household consisting mainly of servants, but it is also possible that she is married to a husband who simply leaves her religious activities alone (contrast the usual custom in Acts 16:31-32; cf. 2 Kings 4:8-23).

16:16-22
Exorcisms and Economics

16:16. This slave girl (as in 12:13, the Greek implies that she is very young) has literally a "spirit of a pythoness"—the same sort of spirit that stood behind the most famous of all Greek oracles, the Delphic oracle of Apollo whose priestess was called a pythoness (she was named after the "Pythian Apollo," slayer of the great Python). Thus Paul and his companions confront a powerful demon here.

16:17. "Most High God" is a common designation for God in Jewish texts but also occurs in pagan sources for Zeus or for the Jewish God with whom pagans sometimes identified Zeus. Magical texts show that pagans respected this supreme God, typically identified with the Jewish God, as the most powerful.

16:18. Exorcists often tried to use names of higher spirits to evict lower spirits (see comment on 19:13); but for the use of "the name of Jesus Christ" here, see comment on 3:6 (cf. also comment on Jn 14:12-14).

16:19. The "authorities" here are the "magistrates" (v. 20), the most common Greek title for the Latin *duoviri,* the two Roman officials of Philippi, who probably called themselves by the more dignified title of "praetor." The marketplace, the rectangular agora at the center of a Greek town, was the center of all civic activity.

16:20. The Jewish-Roman contrast (16:20-21) is a taste of common ancient anti-Judaism, although the assumption that one could not be both Jewish and Roman will not hold up in this case (16:37). Proponents of traditional ways always demanded avoidance of new or alien gods, and one of the main complaints Romans brought against Jews was that they were always converting people to their religion. Although the Jewish population of Philippi was very small, there was a large native non-Roman population, and other immigrants from the East had settled there, increasing official xenophobia (fear of foreigners).

16:21. Philippi was extremely Romanized; despite its location, over 80 percent of its inscriptions are in Latin (twice the percentage in Pisidian Antioch, also a Roman *colony). As a Roman colony (16:12), the citizens enjoyed Roman rights, used Roman law, were exempt from tribute and modeled their constitution on that of Rome. Foreigners and noncitizen residents did not acquire Roman rights simply by settling in Philippi.

16:22. Unless the accused were Roman citizens, they were normally beaten before the trial as a means of securing evidence (this was called the *coercitio);* in practice, lower-class persons had few legal protections. Roman magistrates' attendants, called lictors, carried rods in bundles, and with these rods they beat the foreigners here. Sometimes, as here, the accused were stripped first. Public beatings served not only to secure evidence but also to humiliate those beaten and to discourage their followers.

16:23-34 Prison Ministry

16:23. The job of jailer may have been assigned to a retired soldier settled in this Roman *colony; veterans often settled in such colonies. The evidence for the jailer's being a veteran is ambiguous, however; veterans were also often given land, diminishing their need for other resources.

16:24. Stocks were often used for torture as well as detention, with extra holes so the legs could be forced into painful positions.

16:25. Jewish sources praised the ability to glorify God amidst suffering and shame, and Greco-Roman philosophers praised the wisdom of being content and thankful in one's situation. Most people were usually well into their sleep around midnight, which was not a customary time for Jewish prayers; the other prisoners listening to Paul and Silas must either be upset at the missionaries' timing or glad for some distraction from jail monotony.

16:26. Miraculous deliverances are common in Jewish and other traditions (cf. the exaggerated deliverance of Abram by an earthquake in *Pseudo-Philo 6:17). An earthquake severe enough to split the staples of prisoners' bonds from the wall could have brought down the roof as well but miraculously does not.

16:27. When confronted with execution (in this case, for letting prisoners escape), Romans considered suicide a noble alternative (contrast Mt 27:5).

16:28. The other prisoners may have remained for fear of the guards (the jailer "calls for" torches—v. 29—hence he has subordinates) or because of the missionaries' witness (v. 25).

16:29-30. Asking how to be saved is a motif in Luke-Acts (Lk 3:10; 10:25; 18:18; Acts 2:37); the jailer in this case may view Paul and Silas as representatives of the gods, who can "save/deliver/heal" (all potentially implied in the same Greek word); more likely, he is familiar with their teaching of the one true God known in Judaism.

16:31-32. Romans expected the whole household to follow the religion of its head; they also expected the head to lead his household to the worship of Roman gods. Here conversion is not automatic; the whole household must hear the word.

16:33-34. In view of 16:20-21, the jailer risks getting in serious trouble here. If he is a retired soldier (which is not clear—v. 23), he may have young children (soldiers were not permitted to marry officially until retirement); but this is far from certain and therefore cannot be used to prove infant *baptism (as some have attempted).

16:35-36. The magistrates could have regarded the earthquake as a sign, perhaps from the gods or dangerous magicians; then again, the intercession of wealthy Lydia may have helped; or perhaps the magistrates felt that public humiliation would have been sufficient to silence the troublemakers.

16:37. Roman citizenship in the provinces in this period was a mark of high status (especially because Paul's family was from Tarsus, not a Roman colony, and thus must have received it for special service or as *freedpersons of a well-to-do Roman). The Julian law forbade binding or beating Roman citizens without trial. Falsely claiming citizenship was a capital offense.

16:38. *Cicero and *Quintilian tell of a Roman citizen who cried out that he was a citizen during a scourging, thereby humiliating his oppressors, who had not properly recognized his high status. By waiting until after the beating (cf. 22:29) to inform the authorities that they were citizens, the missionaries had placed the magistrates themselves in an awkward legal position: now the magistrates, not the missionaries, are forced to negotiate. Reports of their deed could even disqualify them from office and (in theory, at least) deprive Philippi of its status as a Roman *colony. This strategy would help secure the future safety of the fledgling Christian community.

16:39-40. The magistrates had no legal authority to expel Roman citizens without trial, but a trial would bring up their own breach of law; thus they are reduced to pleading.

17:1-9
Turmoil in Thessalonica

17:1. Amphipolis on the Strymon, Apollonia (a day's travel beyond it), and Thessalonica (thirty-five miles west of Apollonia) were all on the Via Egnatia (16:9, 12); this road continued further westward into Illyricum (Rom 15:19), but Acts reports only Paul's turn to the south, off this road, to Berea (17:10). Roads were usually no more than twenty feet wide, but they were better and safer than most European roads before 1850, and especially inviting to those who traveled on foot or with donkeys or mules.

Thessalonica was an important city in this period, Macedonia's largest port, capital of its old second district and now residence of the provincial governor.

17:2-3. Thessalonica's non-Greek religious importations included not only Judaism but the Egyptian cult of Serapis and Isis. Paul had to be there long enough to receive support from Philippi (Phil 4:15-16), about a hundred miles away; until then, his occupation, which would allow him to set up shop in the agora, must have supported him (1 Thess 2:9).

17:4. Macedonian women had earlier gained a reputation for their influence, which they probably still exercised in this period. As *patrons within *church or *synagogue, upper-class women could also enjoy higher status than was available to them in society at large due to their gender. Social conditions thus made it easier for well-to-do women than for men to convert.

17:5. The idle unemployed of the marketplace could be stirred to mob action, as other ancient examples attest. Jewish inhabitants were a small minority in Thessalonica, so those Jews whom Paul did not persuade (v. 4) would need help to oppose Paul effectively. "The people" (KJV, NASB, TEV) means the citizen body (cf. "assembly"—NRSV); as a "free city," Thessalonica's gathered citizen body performed judicial functions.

17:6. Jason was a common Greek name but was also common among *Hellenized Jews, as inscriptions and business documents alike testify. He is probably a Jewish host with whom Paul and Silas stay while working there. *Delatores,* or accusers, were necessary to open a case under Roman law.

17:7. Romans could understand proclaiming another king (i.e., the *Messiah—v. 3) as treason against the majesty of the emperor; they could take mention of signs indicating this new ruler's coming (see 1-2 Thessalonians) as predictions of the current emperor's demise, and such predictions violated imperial edicts. That Jesus had been crucified on the charge of sedition only lent further credibility to the charge against Paul and his associates. Citizens who pledged loyalty to Caesar also pledged to report any possible treason. Like John, Luke likes to show the denseness of the *gospel's opponents; cf. 17:18.

17:8. Luke uses the precise designation for Thessalonica's city officials, "politarchs" (also v. 6), a term virtually restricted to Macedonia; there were five or six in Paul's day. Rome gave them a free hand to run the city, although they ultimately had to answer to Rome for inappropriate actions. Evidence indicates that local officials in the eastern Mediterranean were responsible for enforcing loyalty to Caesar.

17:9. As their host (v. 6), Jason is held responsible for their actions and required to post bond for them, as if they were members of his household. A fine was a lenient penalty as far as Roman courts went, and a bond to curtail troublemakers would not have been unusual. But given the charge (v. 7), had Paul himself been caught, he might not have been so fortunate. The politarchs' decision would stand till they left office (cf. 1 Thess 2:18).

17:10-15
Response at Berea

17:10. The Via Egnatia (17:1) continued westward, but the road south, to Greece, led through Berea, sixty miles west of Thessalonica and the Via Egnatia.

17:11. Judaism regarded nobly those who checked everything against the Scriptures and diligently listened to teachers; Greek philosophers likewise praised those who listened attentively.

17:12. For the special mention of women (especially before men), see comment on 17:4.

17:13. Thessalonians had no legal jurisdiction in Berea, but mobs are not prone to follow the law.

17:14-15. Messengers rarely traveled alone, and travelers over long distances were safer to travel in the company of those they knew. Cf. 1 Thessalonians 3:1.

17:16-21
Entering Athens

Athens' fame rested mainly on the glories of its past; even as a philosophical center, its primacy was challenged by other centers in the East like Alexandria and Tarsus. But Athens remained the *symbol* of the great philosophers in popular opinion, so much so that later *rabbis liked to tell stories of earlier rabbis besting Athenian philosophers in debate. Romans did not always trust philosophers, but Acts records other speeches to appeal to those with less philosophical tastes. This speech is Paul's defense of the *gospel before Greek intellectuals.

17:16. City streets were often lined with statues of men and gods, and Athens was especially decorated with the *Hermae,* pillars mounted with heads of Hermes; many visitors wrote of the evidences of Athenian piety. From an aesthetic standpoint, Athens was unrivaled for its exquisite architecture and statues. Paul's concern is not aesthetics, however, but the impact of idols on human lives.

17:17. Inscriptions attest the Jewish community in Athens, but it was not prominent.

17:18. *Epicureans were influential only in the educated upper classes, and their views about God were similar to deism (he was uninvolved in the universe and irrelevant); if there were gods, they were only those known through sense knowledge, like stars or planets. Life's goal was pleasure—the lack of physical pain and emotional disturbance. *Stoics were more popular, opposed pleasure, and criticized Epicureans (though not as much as they had in previous times). Here, as in 23:6, Paul practices the maxim "divide and conquer": 17:22-29 is calculated to gain a Stoic hearing, but Paul and the Epicureans have little common ground.

Although Stoics still professed belief in the gods, philosophers were often considered impious, because they questioned the old traditions, although allowing them for the masses. The charge against Paul, "proclaimer of strange deities" (NASB), would remind Greek readers of the charge of impiety against Socrates (cf. 17:19-20). Many centuries before, a priestess had been stoned to death for this charge, and it still violated the Athenian psyche in Paul's day.

"Babbler" (NIV, NASB) translates a Greek expression applied originally to birds pecking up grain but came to apply to worthless persons; an English equivalent to the reproach might be "birdbrain." But in the same verse Luke lets these critics demonstrate their own stupidity: they think Paul is preaching *gods* (plural), because he preaches Jesus and *resurrection—"Resurrection" (Anastasis) was also a woman's name.

17:19-20. Socrates had also been "led" or "brought" to the Areopagus many centuries before, as was well known. Socrates was the ideal philosopher, and Luke may portray Paul as a new Socrates for his Greek audience; given the outcome of Socrates' speech (which, like Stephen's, provoked his hearers to martyr him), this allusion builds suspense.

The Areopagus is here the council, not the site earlier used for this council (the literal hill of Ares). In this period the council may have met in the Stoa Basilicos, in the Agora where Paul had already been ministering (v. 17). Some scholars have suggested that the council was an accrediting board that tested lecturers; whether or not this is true, it is clear that they still serve some official function, and Paul's speech there is of pivotal importance.

17:21-31
Before the Areopagus Council

Paul's views are quite different from those of the *Stoics, but he emphasizes the points of contact, even when they are only verbal (e.g., Paul believed that God's presence was everywhere, but not in the Stoic sense, which could divinize creation itself)—until the climax of his sermon. Defenders of Judaism had worked for centuries to make their faith philosophically respectable, and here, as in his letters, Paul draws heavily on his Jewish predecessors' arguments.

17:21. Athens was proverbial for the curiosity of its inhabitants. By the first century, Athenian desire for entertainment also extended to gladiatorial shows, drawing the criticism of several famous moralists.

17:22. It was customary to begin a speech by complimenting the hearers in the opening *exordium,* designed to secure their favor. This practice seems to have been forbidden at the Areopagus, but this would not prevent Paul from starting on a respectful note. "Religious" meant that they were religiously observant, not that he agreed with their religion (KJV "superstitious" does not convey the right idea). His hearers may not have been extremely religious, though Stoics accepted the existence of the gods. Philosophers in Roman times dealt mainly with ethics, whereas pagan religion involved ritual rather than ethics.

17:23. During a plague long before Paul's time, no altars had successfully propitiated the gods; Athens had finally offered sacrifices to an unknown god, immediately staying the plague. These altars were still standing, and Paul uses them as the basis for his speech. Paul does avoid, however, the practice of some of his Jewish predecessors and some second-century Christian successors, of accusing pagan philosophers of plagiarizing their good ideas from Moses!

17:24. Some philosophical trends in this era combined deities, moving toward a single supreme god. Non-Palestinian Jews sometimes identified their God with the supreme God of the pagans, hoping to show pagans that their highest religious aspirations were best met in Judaism. *Stoics believed that God permeated all things and therefore was not localized in temples (cf. Is 66:1, cited in Acts 7:49).

17:25. Stoics and Greek-speaking Jews emphasized that God "needs nothing," using the same word Paul uses here.

17:26. Jews and many Greeks agreed that God was creator and divider of the earth's boundaries and of seasons' boundaries. *Stoics also believed that the universe periodically dissolved back into God, but on this belief they had no point of contact with Judaism.

17:27-29. Jewish people usually spoke of God as a father to his people (in the *Old Testament, cf. e.g. Deut 32:6; Is 63:16; 64:8; Jer 3:4). But Greeks, *Diaspora Jews and some second-century Christian writers spoke of God as the world's father in the sense of creator, as here. The quote from the Greek poet Epimenides (v. 28) appears in Jewish anthologies of proof texts useful for showing pagans the truth about God, and Paul may have learned it from such a text. (Greeks cited Homer and other poets as proof texts in a manner similar to how Jewish people cited Scripture.) Some philosophers criticized poets as too mythological, but others freely used their wording to prove their own case.

17:30. Here Paul breaks with his audience's views; although philosophers spoke of conversion to philosophy through a change of thinking, Paul here clearly communicates the Jewish doctrine of *repentance toward God.

17:31. The Greek view of time was that it would simply continue, not that history had a future climax in the day of judgment. Most offensive is Paul's doctrine of the *resurrection; see comment on verse 32.

17:32-34
Response of the Intellectuals

Although Paul's message to the university community of his day does not produce massive immediate results, his ministry to the Areopagus is clearly effective.

17:32. Among major schools of Greek thought, only *Epicureans denied the soul's immortality: they believed that the soul was material, like the body, and died with it. Most Greeks believed in a shadowy afterlife in the underworld (perhaps similar to the *Old Testament *rephaim*), sometimes coupled with reincarnation (as in *Plato); under Plato's influence some Greeks sought to free the immortal soul from worldly existence so it could escape back to the pure heavens from which it was created. *Stoics believed that the soul lived on after death (although, like everything else, it was eventually absorbed back into God), but like other Greeks they could not conceive of a *resurrection of the body.

17:33-34. The Areopagus included only those of highest status in this university community, so the conversion of Dionysius is significant. Modern readers who judge Paul's work in Athens a failure on the basis of 1 Corinthians 2:1 have missed Luke's point entirely (the emphasis of Acts is on his success, and the original readers of Acts could not simply turn to 1 Corinthians).

It is unlikely that women would be permitted in gatherings of the Areopagus; indeed, the most educated and publicly seen women in Athens were probably still prostitutes and foreigners. Whatever her background, Damaris may have been in the marketplace listening to Paul's speech to the Areopagus (see 17:19-20).

18:1-11 The Church in Corinth

18:1. Corinth was one of Athens's ancient rivals; the capital of Achaea, it had long since surpassed Athens. Roman Corinth was the political and economic center of Greece, still proverbial for its immorality.

18:2. Like Tiberius, an earlier emperor, Claudius expelled the Jewish community from Rome (possibly around A.D. 49). *Suetonius, a Roman historian, is often understood as indicating that the Jewish community was expelled because of disturbances about the *Messiah, perhaps caused by opposition to Jewish Christians. Given Luke's emphasis on legal precedents in favor of Christianity (18:14-16), it is easy to see why he would omit that detail.

18:3. In the ancient economy, people of the same trade did not compete with one another as they do today. They usually lived together in the same part of town and formed trade guilds. Their trade guilds normally adopted a *patron deity, and they ate sacrificial food at their regular banquets together. This cultic orientation of trade guilds would exclude practicing Jews from the fellowship, making Jews delighted to find other Jews of their own trade.

By this period, the term translated "tentmaker" was also applied to leatherworking in general. As a leatherworker, Paul would have been an artisan. Artisans were typically proud of their work, despite the long hours they had to invest to succeed, and were higher than peasants in status and income; but they were despised by higher classes, who thought labor with one's hands degrading (see the conflicts described in the introduction to 1 Corinthians). Their long hours in their shops afforded them much time to talk while doing their work, but Paul apparently is able to discontinue the labor (1 Cor 4:12) when his companions bring a gift from the Macedonian *church (v. 5; 2 Cor 11:7-8; 12:13; Phil 4:15). Corinth's *agora* (central marketplace) had the longest line of colonnaded shops in the empire.

18:4-5. Many foreign religions had settled in Corinth, including Egyptian religions (mushrooming in popularity by the second century). An inscription from a Corinthian *synagogue has also been recovered near the *agora* (central marketplace) where Paul had probably worked; its location suggests that some members of this synagogue had wealth and social status (see vv. 7-8).

18:6-7. The *church met in houses for the first three centuries (12:12; Rom 16:5). *Synagogues also sometimes gathered in homes until the Jewish community could afford a special building, and between persecution and the need for funds to free slaves, feed the poor and support missionaries, the churches had no money left for buildings anyway. *Patrons' homes in Corinth normally seated nine in the *triclinium* (the best room) and as many as forty others in the adjoining *atrium* (the largest furnished room).

The status and thoroughly Latin name of "Titius Justus" identify him as a Roman citizen and part of the Roman culture (Corinth was both Greek and Roman in this period); he may have been from one of the Roman families established there in the time of Julius Caesar. His first name may be Gaius (Rom 16:23; 1 Cor 1:14).

18:8. "Crispus" is a typical Roman name. It was not uncommon for Jewish people to have Latin names ("Crispus" and "Crispina" appear several times in Jewish inscriptions), but the proportion of Latin names among Paul's associates is so much higher than generally in inscriptions (even though inscriptions were normally made by the well-to-do) that it is likely that a number of Paul's Jewish and Greek associates were also Roman citizens. To be "*synagogue ruler" means that Crispus is a person of status and wealth, responsible for the synagogue services.

18:9-11. Assurance oracles such as "I will be with you" were standard in the *Old Testament (e.g., Gen 15:1; 26:24; 28:15; Jer 1:8; 15:20). In Greek literature gods or goddesses often appeared to people at night, frequently while they slept; but such revelations from God or his angels are no less common in the Old Testament (e.g., Gen 26:24; 28:12-15; 31:24).

18:12-17
Gallio's Refusal

18:12. A proconsul governed Achaea (most of Greece) from 27 B.C. to A.D. 15 and from A.D. 44 on. Gallio began his two-year term of office July 1 of A.D. 51; it was cut short by sickness, so we may reasonably date this appearance in A.D. 51-52, probably before the end of 51. Like his brother, the *Stoic philosopher Seneca, he was ultimately killed by Nero. Luke could not have had access to names of such officials at precise dates unless he learned them from Paul; there were no reference works listing them.

As proconsul, Gallio would decide important cases at his judgment seat in the morning. This "judgment seat" (KJV, NASB) is probably the ceremonial rostrum on the eastern end of the Corinthian forum, in full view of the public, although some scholars have suggested a tribunal (cf. NRSV) in an administrative building (cf. NIV). Juries decided cases about murder, adultery and several other offenses; a magistrate had to try other crimes.

18:13. If Paul's views put him outside Judaism, his followers would not have the protection Roman tradition gave to Judaism by virtue of its antiquity.

18:14. A Roman magistrate's first decision was whether to accept a charge and so decide a case.

18:15. Gallio dismisses the case. Roman courts decided violations of Roman law; but various individual edicts throughout the empire had given Jewish courts jurisdiction over internal Jewish affairs, and Gallio is not about to meddle in them. Gallio thus accepts Paul's religion as a variant form of Judaism, rather than a new and illegal religion *(religio illicita)*. Although precedent was not binding in Roman law, it was important and would likely be followed by other provincial governors; if involved in legal cases, Luke's Christian readers can cite this case on their own behalf.

18:16. That Gallio "drove them away" (NASB), perhaps with the force of his lictors' (attendants') rods, betrays more than a tinge of Roman impatience for Jewish religious disputes. Many upper-class Romans viewed Jews as uncultured troublemakers, classing them alongside other religions from Syria and Egypt (cf. 16:20-21).

18:17. Law courts (especially if held at the forum, or *agora*) were typically loud and crowded, and tempers flared. Luke may mean that the Jewish community disciplined a leader who was a Christian sympathizer (if this is the same Sosthenes as in 1 Cor 1:1—it was a common name), or that they beat their leader for getting them into political trouble. Or Luke may mean that, given Gallio's expression of his anti-Jewish sentiments, some local Greeks felt free to vent their own. Other Roman officials had encouraged or done worse. If the *synagogue officials had publicly charged Paul to dissociate themselves from a potential troublemaker, the plot backfired.

18:18-23
Paul Returns Home

18:18. Cenchrea was Corinth's main port on the isthmus; it also harbored temples of Isis, Artemis, Aphrodite, Asclepius and Poseidon. Travel was easier, faster and cheaper by ship than by land. But ships were generally meant as cargo transports, so seafarers had to bring their own bedding.

Some pagan priests (e.g., of Isis) shaved their heads; hence a pagan observer who did not know Paul could have taken him for such a priest. But Jewish people shaved their heads after completing a Nazirite vow, and Paul's faith in Jesus had not diminished his own Jewishness in the least (21:23-24). That Palestinian teachers demanded that Nazirites fulfill the vows in Jerusalem shows only that Paul had taken the less Jerusalem-centered approach of *Diaspora (non-Palestinian) Jews who had not the time or money to travel to Jerusalem very frequently.

18:19-21. Ephesus had a very large Jewish community. "If God wills" was a standard statement of pious Greeks and some Jews.

18:22. Summer winds were generally northerly but often east of north, which made Caesarea easier to reach than Antioch's port city of Seleucia.

18:23. Only by late spring or early summer was the land route from Antioch through Galatia and Phrygia open, another indication of the time of year.

18:24-28
Apollos's Enlightenment

18:24. Many Alexandrian Jews had names compounded with "Apollo," a prominent Greek god (Apollos may be a contraction for Apollonius). As in other ancient uses of the term, "eloquent" (NASB) or "learned" (NIV) most likely means "formally skilled in *rhetoric," the more practical form of advanced learning to which well-to-do pupils could attain (the other was philosophy).

Alexandria may have had the largest Jewish community in the empire outside Syria-Palestine, with numerous *synagogues. The Jewish aristocracy had worked hard to be culturally acceptable to the Greek privileged class, and they resented their own inferior status. (Most of the ethnocentric Greeks in Alexandria despised Jews and Egyptians, who made up the other two-thirds of their city; thus they spoke of "Alexandria near Egypt.") The clash of cultures and oppression of Jews ultimately led to a Jewish revolt—and the massacre of the entire Jewish community.

18:25. Ancient readers would most naturally take the phrase "fervent in spirit" (NASB) as referring to Apollos's own spirit.

18:26. Aquila and Priscilla apparently accompanied Paul on his voyage, then stayed to help in the *synagogue at Ephesus, which was open to teaching about Jesus.

18:27-28. Letters of recommendation were standard in Greco-Roman society. Apollos's learning might well appeal to the educated elite of the Corinthian *church (see the introduction to 1 Corinthians).

19:1-7
The Spirit Poured Out in Ephesus

19:1. Ephesus afforded an opportunity to influence all of Asia (not meaning the continent, but the Roman province "Asia" in what is now western Turkey). It was the most populous city of the most prosperous and populated province in the empire. Although Pergamum remained the official capital of Asia, Ephesus became the chief city with the real seat of provincial administration. Paul's approach by the "upper country" (NASB) probably means that he took a higher road from the north instead of the customary route by the Lycus and Meander valleys.

"*Disciples" means students, or learners, here apparently of John (19:3; but cf. 18:25). The Roman world was cosmopolitan, and other Palestinian Jews also settled in Ephesus, which had a large, ancient and influential Jewish community.

19:2. In most of ancient Judaism and in Luke-Acts, the *Holy Spirit is the Spirit who inspired the prophets. Paul can somehow tell these disciples lack this measure of inspiration, despite much sound knowledge (18:25).

19:3-5. For John's *baptism see comment on Mark 1:5; for baptism in Jesus' name see comment on Acts 2:38.

19:6-7. The tongues and *prophecy, as inspired speech, evidence their reception of the Spirit of prophecy; see comment on 19:2.

19:8-12
Word Spreads in Ephesus

19:8-9. Philosophers often lectured in rented halls; this could have been a guild hall as easily as a "lecture hall" (NIV). (If the former, Tyrannus is simply the owner; if the latter, he is the customary lecturer. Public life in Ephesus, including philosophical lectures, ended by noon; so if Tyrannus lectured in the mornings Paul used it in the afternoons; if no one else lectured there, Paul probably lectured there in the mornings, and did his manual labor afterward.) Either way, residents of Ephesus would view Paul as a philosopher or sophist (professional public speaker). Many early Greco-Roman observers thought that Christians were a religious association or club (like other such associations in antiquity), or a philosophical school that took the form of a such an association.

19:10. Ephesus was a cosmopolitan center from which word would spread quickly, especially if Paul were training *disciples (as philosophers and *rabbis typically did) and sending them out to spread the message.

19:11-12. Paul's "handkerchiefs and aprons" (NIV) are rags tied around his head to catch sweat and his work aprons tied around his waist; they could have been taken without his knowledge. Magicians often healed by such means; *Old Testament examples are rare but do occur (e.g., 2 Kings 13:21; contrast uncleanness, which was regularly communicated by touch in the Old Testament).

19:13-20
The Inadequacy of Magic

Although some Ephesians who knew no better may have regarded Paul as a magician, God seems to have healed them anyway to draw their attention to his message (19:11-12); but God would not tolerate unauthorized use of Jesus' name. Ephesus was widely reputed for its trade in magic and the need for exorcisms and protection against evil spirits.

19:13. Magical exorcists often invoked the names of higher spirits to cast out lower ones. According to magical theory, exorcists could coerce a deity or spirit to do their will by invoking its name. Ancient magical texts show that many exorcists were Jewish or drew on some knowledge of Judaism, and these texts include every possible permutation of vowels as guesses for pronouncing the unpronounced name of God (cf. comment on 2:20-21). Some later ancient magical texts invoked the name of Jesus alongside other formulas, recognizing, as do the exorcists in this narrative, its efficacy when employed by Christians to expel demons.

19:14. "Sceva" is a Latin name; as loosely as Jerusalem Jews used "high priest" for the highest members of the priestly aristocracy, it is likely that Sceva simply appropriated the title for himself. Inscriptions and texts testify to other irregularities in Jewish priestly claims outside Palestine. Because Jewish chief priests would be thought to have access to the sacred name (v. 13) and hidden names, especially of the supreme god, were thought to wield great power in magical circles, Sceva is probably highly reputed in those circles. "Sons" could mean they were part of Sceva's guild, although it is probably meant literally.

19:15. Ancient literature indicates that demons were typically unimpressed with orders from those who had no power over them, although they feared God and could be controlled by the manipulation of spirits more powerful than themselves (who apparently liked the influence this gave them with the magicians).

19:16-17. This incident indicates that Paul, the humble leatherworker, has more power than the magicians (cf. Gen 41:8, 39; Ex 7:11).

19:18. Despite the popularity of Jewish magicians, most prominent Jewish teachers officially condemned magic. When people recognize that Paul's Jesus cannot be manipulated like lower spirits, they understand that he is a servant of God and not a mere magician. "Confessing practices" (NASB, NRSV) can also be translated "divulging spells," an activity which was believed to deprive the spells of their power.

19:19-20. Magical papyri were rolled up in small cylinders or lockets used as amulets around the neck; Luke's term "books" or "scrolls" (NIV) probably refers to these magical papyri. These magical incantations were so common in Ephesus that rolls of these formulas are called *Ephesia grammata,* or Ephesian writings, in other Greco-Roman literature. Books were commonly burned in antiquity to repudiate their contents (in the *Old Testament, cf. analogously 1 Chron 14:12). The total price of what is burned comes out to about fifty thousand days' wages for an average worker.

19:21-22
Changing Course

Paul had already planned to leave Ephesus before he knew that trouble was coming (19:23-41); Luke here sets the pace for the rest of the book (cf. Lk 9:51), outlined as one more trip through Greece, then to Rome via Jerusalem. Philosophers and *rabbis expected *disciples to serve them, a model which also has *Old Testament precedent in Joshua serving Moses; Elisha, Elijah; and Gehazi, Elisha. Erastus may have been the *aedile,* or commissioner of public works, in Corinth for a time (see comment on Rom 16:23); if so, this text shows that status in the *kingdom and in the world are not determined on the same terms.

19:23-41
Artemis and Economics

As often, religious piety becomes a thin cloak for personal economic interests. The temple of Artemis served as a bank as well as a temple, and people from all over the world deposited funds there. About A.D. 44 (roughly a decade before Paul's arrival), inscriptions there show that the proconsul had to get involved in the temple treasury due to some serious financial irregularities: temple monies were being funneled to private individuals. In Ephesus, politics and religion were as heavily intertwined as religion and economics, and local civic pride was inseparable from the worship of the Ephesian Artemis.

19:23. The month of Artemis's reputed birth was called Artemisium and hosted a major festival in her honor, at which Asiarchs (see comment on 19:30-31) would be present (v. 31). Some scholars have suggested that this *narrative makes the most sense if it happened at that time; although this theory is possible, loyalty to Artemis ran strong all year long, and the Asiarchs who knew Paul best were those who resided in Ephesus anyway.

19:24-25. Members of the same trade united to form professional guilds, or *collegia,* which set standards for their own trade and united to defend their economic interests. Miniature shrines were made as souvenirs and amulets; most of the ones we know about were terra cotta, so Demetrius seems to be gathering other shrine makers, rather than other silverworkers. Small gold and silver images of Artemis weighing three to seven pounds were also made to be dedicated in her temple.

19:26. "Not gods at all" was the refrain of Isaiah (e.g., 44:920; 46:1-11) and Judaism. By the early second century the Roman governor of a nearby province complained that the temples of the gods were being forsaken due to conversions to Christianity. After the arrest of many Christians, the governor reported, more people did buy animals for sacrifices again.

19:27. "The world worships" reflects the fact that the Ephesian Artemis, distinct from other forms of Artemis, had cult centers dedicated to her in at least thirty-three places in the Mediterranean world. Her fame is widely attested in antiquity: she commanded followers in visions to spread her cult; her temple, around 350 feet long and over 150 feet wide, was listed as one of the seven wonders of the ancient world; forty-five residents of Sardis accused of assaulting a group of followers of the Ephesian Artemis received the death penalty; Jewish texts also mention her temple. It was a mile and a half northeast of Ephesus proper.

19:28. Crying out "Great is [such and such a deity]" seems to have been a standard way of expressing devotion.

19:29. News and trouble spread quickly in ancient cities, which were very crowded (perhaps two hundred people per acre, a population density found today in the West only in slums). The citizen assembly held its normal meetings in this open-air theater, which accommodated nearly twenty-five thousand people, was almost five hundred feet in diameter and contained many statues of deities.

19:30-31. Asiarchs were the most prominent men of the province, who were presiding or had presided in one-year terms over the cult of the emperor and the goddess Roma. Different cities in the Greek East competed for the honor of having the largest imperial cult, so Asiarchs were important to local civic pride. They had authority over the theater, but here they cannot quell this riot; they can only try to stop their Jewish Christian friend from entering. (In accordance with Roman customs, they may have viewed their "friendship" with Paul in terms of providing him support as patrons; in any case, Luke wants us to recognize that their concern for Paul indicates the high social circles Paul had begun to impact in some way.)

19:32. Greek comedy frequently parodied people's stupidity; Luke's readers would laugh at the crowd not knowing the purpose of their rioting, even though this ignorance characterizes mob psychology well. Luke no doubt uses the Greek term for "citizen assembly" here ironically: it is in fact a mob, not a legal gathering (v. 39).

19:33-34. Jewish people in Roman Asia were careful not to offend the local residents, and Alexander no doubt intends to explain that the Jewish community did not instigate the current confusion. But typical Greek anti-Judaism and the knowledge that the Jewish community accepted only one God leads to the assumption that the Jewish community instead wishes to explain their *responsibility* for the riot. (This event may help explain the Jewish community's dislike for Paul in 21:27.) Controversial public trials were also often punctuated with shouts.

19:35-36. The clerk here makes a deliberative speech, intended to change the mob's course of action (v. 36). The "city clerk" (NIV) was the top civic official, who made known the citizen assembly's rulings and represented the city to the Roman provincial officials also headquartered in Ephesus. The term for Ephesus being "guardian" of Artemis's temple is a technical one also found on inscriptions. Other statues worshiped in ancient Asia Minor also purportedly fell from heaven.

The bulbous appendages on pictures of the statue have been variously identified as breasts, castrated appendages, fruits, or bee or ostrich eggs; these interpretations suggest an Asian fertility goddess related to the local mother goddess and quite different from the Greek virgin Artemis. (Other scholars suggest that the objects represent planets, which fits the picture of Artemis as deliverer from Fate and its astrological agents.)

19:37. "Temple robbery" was considered one of the most impious of crimes, and the term eventually came to stand for sacrilege in a broader sense.

19:38. The financial scandal surrounding the temple of Artemis at this time was being addressed through the courts and by appealing to the proconsul; the economic dispute that had provoked this illegal gathering should be addressed in the same manner.

The proconsul met with the gatherings of citizens on various days in nine different cities of the province. Each province had only one proconsul, but Luke may use the plural because the proconsul of Ephesus died about A.D. 54, and several officials may have been carrying out his administrative functions till the new proconsul arrived.

19:39. A later source declares that this assembly met three times a month. The lawful gathering of the citizen assembly differed significantly from a mob (as here): the former met with Rome's favor, but the latter could lead to Roman disciplinary measures against the city.

19:40-41. Other examples show that leaders of cities warned their people that Rome would hear of their riots; other riots are recorded as having happened in Ephesus, although Rome never did crack down on them. But the special privileges Ephesus enjoyed as a "free city" (including its own senate) depended completely on Rome's favor, and other cities had had such privileges revoked. A famous late-first-century *rhetorician named Dio Chrysostom warned the citizens of another Asian city that those who abused the right of free speech had that right taken away.

20:1-6
To and from Greece

The *narratives of Acts 20 and 27 presuppose correct data on the length of travel between the places listed and take into account seasonal wind patterns and so forth. In short, they read like the report of an eyewitness.

20:1-2. Hinted in Acts only at 24:17 but clear in his letters, Paul's purpose is to collect the offering of the Macedonian (Philippi, Thessalonica) and Achaean (Corinth) *churches to help the poor Christians in Jerusalem, to demonstrate the unity of Jewish and *Gentile Christians (see comment on Rom 15:26; 1 Cor 16:1, 5; 2 Cor 8—9). He may have gone through Illyricum from Macedonia's Via Egnatia (Rom 15:19; cf. comment on Acts 16:9); if so, many months pass before he reaches Achaea.

20:3. Paul wrote Romans from this area (Rom 15:26-28). Although some sailors and shipowners were Jewish, most were *Gentiles. On a ship to Syria, however, many travelers may have been Jewish—especially if the ship planned to reach Syria-Palestine by Passover.

20:4. Just as prominent representatives from each of the Jewish communities would bring the annual temple tax to Jerusalem, so Paul has traveling companions from different Christian communities serving the poor in Jerusalem (20:1-2). This offering would show the Jerusalem *church that the Gentile Christians still recognize the Jewishness of their faith (see Rom 15:26-27).

20:6. The "we" picks up where it left off; Paul had left Luke in Philippi. They spend the week in Philippi for the Passover and Feast of Unleavened Bread. When one adds the remaining days (with parts of days reckoned as wholes, as generally in antiquity) presumed in the *narrative, from their arrival in Philippi to their arrival in Jerusalem requires over thirty days. Thus they would arrive in Jerusalem before Pentecost (fifty days after Passover) and would still make one of the three major pilgrimage festivals (20:16). "Five days" (i.e., parts of five—perhaps four) was a slow voyage to Troas (16:11) but may include the half-day land journey from Philippi to Neapolis.

20:7-12
Resurrection at Troas

20:7. Most religious associations in the Greco-Roman world met together once a month. Although some early Christians may have met daily (2:46), they seem to have gathered especially on the first day of the week (Sunday), probably because of the *resurrection (Lk 24:1) and to avoid conflicting with *synagogue gatherings on the sabbath (Saturday).

Christians may have met early, before sunrise, but would have to work Sunday mornings like everyone else in the empire; so this meeting may have have begun late Sunday afternoon or Saturday at sunset. (It depends on whether one reckons days from midnight to midnight, like the Romans and modern Westerners, or from sundown to sundown, like ancient Jews. In the former case, the first day means Sunday; in the latter, it started on what we consider Saturday evening.) Whatever view one takes, because most people went to bed not long after sunset, midnight was well into one's sleeping time, and Paul is certainly being long-winded.

20:8. The odor or heat of the oil lamps may have helped produce drowsiness.

20:9. Open windows were generally blocked off in the winter, but during summer one would sit in them to cool off. Either the heat from the lamps (midnight in April at Troas was not normally hot) or the crowdedness of the room had forced Eutychus to take a window seat. If he was old enough (cf. v. 12; but the term translated "boy" or "lad" there could also mean "slave"), he may have been tired from a hard day's work. Homes in much of the empire were a single story, but they were often two stories in more crowded urban areas. This is a fall from what Americans would call the second floor (which most languages call the "third floor"), which is not necessarily fatal; but Eutychus may have landed headfirst or hit his head on a hard object.

20:10. For Paul's action, cf. 1 Kings 17:21-22 and 2 Kings 4:34-35.

20:11-12. When people had not seen each other for a long time, it was customary to stay up late filling each other in on one another's lives.

20:13-17
Continuing the Journey

20:13. Assos was about twenty miles overland from Alexandria Troas, the main port, about a day's journey on foot. For short distances, especially if one had to wait at ports for ships that could take on passengers, a land journey might not take much longer, and traveling on foot was cheaper than buying passage on a boat.

20:14. Mitylene was the main town of the island of Lesbos.

20:15-16. They take the customary sea route, across from the island of Chios (probably near Cape Argennum), enabling them to avoid a longer voyage hugging the coast of the long promontory jutting forth into the Aegean Sea between Smyrna and Ephesus. From Chios it was much quicker to sail by the island of Samos and straight to Miletus, rather than cutting in toward the Asian coast to Ephesus. They put in at the Lion Harbor at Miletus, which sported a temple of Apollo; the city also had a sizable Jewish community (as did Samos, where the worship of Aphrodite and Isis was prominent).

20:17. Their ship had avoided the busy harbor of Ephesus, which was out of the way by the route across Chios and Samos; this ship had been the only one available going the right direction, but had not been going to their exact destination. The land route for messengers to reach Ephesus was over thirty miles, so they would have to travel quickly to arrive by Paul's third day; for those who could leave their work, to do so would be a big sacrifice. But Paul's mission to Jerusalem was urgent; he needed to present the offering at a festival, when Jerusalem would be full and this symbol of the *church's ethnic unity would make the loudest statement.

20:18-35
Paul's Farewell Speech

Farewell speeches developed a standard form in antiquity, related to the literary form called "testaments" (in which a dying or departing figure left important, wise instructions for his children or followers). The language of the speech is more like Paul's than Luke's. Although historians tended to rewrite speeches in their own words, regular *rhetorical training included practice in imitating others' styles (*prosopopoïa*). Because Luke presumably had little access to Paul's letters (they were not collected from various churches till long after Paul's death), he must have learned Paul's style from direct contact with him.

20:18-21. Many philosophers customarily appealed to their hearers in endearing terms, such as Paul uses here, and reminded them that any reproofs were given as signs of true friendship, as opposed to the flattery of false friends. That this language was common means only that it was culturally relevant to the hearers' needs, not that it was merely an empty *rhetorical form; Paul and most others who used such language also meant it sincerely.

20:22. True intellectual heroes in Greco-Roman tradition were those who believed their teaching so much that they were willing to die for it; philosophers who died for their beliefs were considered noble and brave. Paul stands in the *Old Testament prophetic tradition of speaking God's message no matter what the cost, but he also presents his message in a manner that resonates with the best in his hearers' culture.

20:23. "The *Holy Spirit's testimony" surely means *prophecies (21:4); early Judaism viewed the Spirit especially as the agent that had inspired the prophets.

20:24. "Finish the course" (e.g., NASB) or "finish the race" (NIV) are athletic images; philosophers often used such images to describe their own mission (cf. TEV).

20:25-27. The image of secondhand guilt for someone's blood is common in the *Old Testament (e.g., Deut 21:1-9), but here Paul refers especially to the watchman who does not warn the wicked to turn from his or her way (Ezek 3:18-20; 33:8-9).

20:28. "Overseer" was usually a Greek term for a ruling officer, although the *Dead Sea Scrolls include a Hebrew equivalent. Even though the image of shepherd as a leader is not exclusively Jewish, it is especially Old Testament language for the leaders of God's people. God would call shepherds to account for how they watched over his flock; see comment on John 10:1-18. "Take heed" was standard language for moral exhortations.

20:29-30. Jesus had warned of false prophets, and Jewish *apocalyptic texts foresaw great trials for the righteous before the end; Paul's prediction is hardly original. In the biblical sense, however, what made a person a prophet was the accuracy—not the novelty—of his or her prediction. (Deut 13:1-5; 18:20-22).

20:31. Exhortation often appealed to people to remember. "Night and day" was a standard way of saying "all the time"; parts of a night and of a day could be reckoned as the whole. Good public speakers were supposed to feel their speeches enough to express proper emotion and to move the crowds emotionally.

20:32. "An inheritance among all those who are sanctified" (NASB) (i.e., "set apart" or "separated" for God) refers to the Jewish hope that they as God's people would inherit the world to come, just as Israel had "inherited" the Promised Land.

20:33. Philosophers were often accused of seeking personal monetary gain, and many (especially those who acted from sincere motives) had to deny it, providing supporting evidence for their denial. "Clothes" (NASB) were part of one's substance in the ancient East, just as silver coins were.

20:34-35. Working with one's hands was not humiliating to an artisan, but the small upper class (who drew their income from landowning) and most of the philosophical elite despised manual labor. Many *rabbis had trades, but philosophers preferred charging fees, sponging off rich nobles or begging. The motives of those who gave freely (what ancients called benefaction) were harder to question, as philosophers who lived off charity and moralists who demanded no return often pointed out.

20:36—21:6
The Affection of Paul's Friends

20:36-38. Brief kisses might be used

in momentary greetings, but repeated kissing and embraces were signs of great affection, such as one would bestow on a family member, a dear teacher or a close friend; thus Paul had bonded deeply with these Christians (cf. 1 Sam 20:41). Many Romans and Greek philosophers believed that it was not proper for men to cry, but *narrative sources often report it in extreme circumstances, such as a sad parting.

21:1-2. They put into Cos overnight; a small island, it was on the usual route to Rhodes and had a large Jewish community. Rhodes was a regular stopping place for ships; it also had a sizable Jewish community. Alexandrian grain ships hugging close to the coast of southern Asia Minor frequently made tedious stops at each port, due to the uncertainty of land breezes; thus after they have put in at the Lycian port of Patara in southern Asia Minor, Paul and his companions find a ship sailing across open water directly for Phoenicia, cutting along the south of Cyprus, still under a slight time constraint (20:16).

21:3. The southern shore of Cyprus, by which they passed, was shallow and had no harbors, so the ship did not try to put in there. The Roman province of Syria included not only Antioch to the north but also Phoenicia and Judea to the south; they had saved considerable time by sailing across the open sea toward Tyre, which would provide safe harbor throughout the year.

21:4. Jewish people and Christians could expect hospitality from their own wherever they went; it was a required part of their culture, honored their host and was an incomparably superior alternative to spending the night in inns, which usually doubled as brothels.

In light of the standard Jewish view that God's *Spirit especially inspired *prophecy, prophecy is surely somehow involved in their exhortation. Yet this phrase is not Luke's usual description of prophecy and probably indicates that they were simply warning him not to go *on the basis of* their prophecies about what would happen (20:23; 21:11).

21:5-6. Tyre was known for its smooth sand beaches.

21:7-16
Agabus's Prophecy

21:7. Ptolemy II had made Ptolemais, a strong fortress and now a Roman colony (once named Acco), an important harbor.

21:8. Caesarea was about forty miles south of Ptolemais, and if the text indicates that they made the journey in one day, they must have gone by boat.

21:9. Paganism sometimes associated virginity with spiritual power (as with a special Roman order of celibate women called the Vestal Virgins), but the point of "virgins" here is probably that Philip's daughters are young, under the age of sixteen. The verb tense indicates that they prophesied regularly or habitually. The Jewish tradition about Job's prophetically endowed daughters (in the *Testament of Job) may be later, but it illustrates the high esteem in which such prophetesses would have been held in antiquity.

21:10. Agabus could have left for Caesarea from Jerusalem (he "came down" from the mountainous part of Judea, including Jerusalem) about the time that Paul arrived in Caesarea and could have easily gotten there in several days. (Caesarea was the Roman headquarters for Judea, but Luke here uses "Judea" in the sense of Jewish Palestine or ancient Judah, rather than the stricter Roman sense.)

21:11. *Old Testament prophets often acted out their *prophecies in ways similar to Agabus's action here (e.g., Jer 27:2). Some commentators point out that the details were not all fulfilled literally (it was the *Gentiles who bound him, although his accusers were Jewish), but one need not study the Old Testament prophets long before it is clear that they were allowed a large measure of poetic license, even though the essential message had to be accurate (e.g., 2 Kings 19:7, 28, 33, 35). The girdle was a long cloth wrapped around the waist several times and used as a pocket.

21:12-14. Greeks and Jewish people under the influence of Greek oracular thinking saw predictive oracles especially as preventive warnings; but the text gives no indication that Agabus himself wishes Paul to avoid what he is called to face. Accounts of martyrs frequently include exhortations to avoid the martyrdom (on account of age, youth, etc.). But Paul's friends, knowing what he will face, act out of love for him, although they turn out to be wrong (v. 14).

21:15. The journey from Caesarea to Jerusalem would take two days; they lodge overnight with Mnason (v. 16).

21:16. Cyprus had a large Jewish community, some of whom had migrated to Jerusalem and been among the first *disciples (4:36). The name "Mnason" was more common among Romans, "Jason" among Jews and Greeks, but Jews occasionally used "Mnason" too (e.g., a later *rabbi in Rome).

21:17-26
Paul's Jewish Identity Affirmed

21:17. This gracious reception would necessarily include hospitality for the whole delegation—including offering lodging in Jewish Christian homes to uncircumcised *Gentile Christians (although Paul himself might have stayed with his nephew's family—23:16). This line thus has more significance than would normally strike the modern reader (see comment on 10:28).

21:18-19. Paul delivers the collection from the Gentile Christians at this time (24:17; cf. comment on 20:1-4).

21:20-22. The Jerusalem Christians accept the *Gentile work but in so doing are confronted by a conflict with their culture. Jerusalem is not what it had been in Acts 2; tensions are rising, and in the temple *sicarii,* or assassins, are murdering aristocrats suspected of collaborating with the Gentiles. Jewish nationalism is on the rise, and nationalism's exclusivity makes it intolerant of supposedly faithful members of its people who have fellowship with members of other peoples. Thus it is incumbent on Paul to prove the integrity of his Jewishness; he cannot compromise the Gentile mission, but he will intentionally affirm his Jewish heritage at any cost short of unbiblical exclusivism.

The Jerusalem *church is providing an effective indigenous witness within its culture. Modern Gentile Christians who oppose Jewish Christians' keeping the *law while these Gentile Christians observe church and cultural traditions of their own are out of keeping with the spirit of the *New Testament, which calls people to forsake their sin, not positive or neutral elements of their culture. (The second-century Christian apologist Justin Martyr notes this controversy in his own day but clearly maintains the earlier Christian view that Jewish people could both practice the law and follow Jesus—*Dialogue with Trypho* 47.)

James says literally that "many tenthousands" believe (v. 20)—a minimum of fifty thousand, which, if taken at face value, would be one-tenth of Palestine's estimated Jewish population and over eight times the estimated number of *Pharisees. James himself was martyred by the pro-Roman aristocracy a few years after this time, but his witness to his culture had been so effective that the populace of Jerusalem demanded the removal of his killer from office.

21:23-26. These precautions are to protect Paul from false accusations, especially if he is going to move about publicly in the temple courts. Paul pays the fees for the devout Jerusalem Christians who are completing a Nazirite vow; the Greek language here suggests that he may also be paying for an earlier vow he completed while unable to come to Palestine (18:18). One shaved one's head on the seventh day of a vow and offered sacrifice in the temple on the eighth day (Num 6:1-21), but the minimum period of the vow according to ritual law seems to have been thirty days, so he did not join them in vows only at this point. Those (like Agrippa I) who used their own funds to pay the expenses of Nazirites were considered pious.

21:27-36
Riot in the Temple

Under Cumanus, the Roman governor immediately preceding Felix (23:24), a Roman soldier lewdly exposed himself in the temple area; *Josephus estimated that ten thousand people were trampled to death in the ensuing riot. When another soldier burned a Jewish law scroll, Cumanus acceded to the crowds' demands and executed him. Hostility against *Gentiles and collaborators with Gentiles had been mounting, and in less than a decade would lead to a war that would produce massacres (over twenty thousand Jews slaughtered in Caesarea in an hour) and culminate in the temple's destruction.

21:27. See 19:34. "Asia" means the Roman province of Asia, in what is now western Turkey.

21:28. The barrier between the outer court, open to the Gentiles, and the Court of the Women was about four feet high, with warning signs posted at intervals in Greek and Latin: "Any foreigner who passes this point will be responsible for his own death" (the inscriptions are reported in ancient literature and one has been found by archaeologists). This was the one offense for which Jewish authorities could execute capital punishment—even on Roman citizens—without consulting with Rome. (This special privilege was also accorded the Greek temple at Eleusis; but Rome delegated the right of execution only in rare cases like these, because local nationalists could otherwise use the penalty against Rome's own supporters.)

21:29. Ephesus was the chief city of the Roman province of Asia, and the Jewish community there knew Paul and his companions well (19:33-34; cf. 18:19-21, 26). Although the assumption of these Jews from Asia is false, it is occasioned by Paul's relationships with *Gentile Christians, which he would not compromise.

21:30. They drag Paul "out of the temple" into the outer Court of the Gentiles. The *sagan,* or chief of the temple guard, apparently ordered the doors at the Court of the Women shut to keep the violence certain to ensue from spilling into the temple proper. (*Josephus regarded the shedding of blood in the sanctuary as the "abomination of desolation," so keeping bloodshed from the sacred precincts was important.)

21:31. On the northern part of the Temple Mount was the fortress Antonia, which housed a permanent Roman garrison of six hundred men (a cohort); from its towers guards would readily notice disturbances. To rush into the outer court of the temple, they had only to rush down the stairs from the fortress. The "commander" is a *chiliarch,* or tribune, literally commander of one thousand but actually of six hundred troops. Tribunes were drawn from the small, well-to-do Roman "middle" class.

21:32. Because "centurions" (KJV, NASB, NRSV) is plural, we should think of at least 160 soldiers (a centurion commanded about eighty troops) and probably more. These troops would be enough to disperse a crowd, although they had not always been effective in the recent past.

21:33. Paul is apparently bound between two soldiers (12:6). He reasonably asks for coherent witnesses with specific charges; there are none.

21:34. The "barracks" by the temple is the old castle Antonia, called Baris by the Hasmoneans but renamed for Mark Antony by his friend Herod the Great.

21:35. The steps of the fortress Antonia led directly down to the outer court.

21:36. Some Greek writers of this period liked to draw parallels between analogous historical figures; Luke's record here parallels Jesus and Paul (Lk 23:18).

21:37—22:2
Paul and the Tribune

21:37. In the eastern part of the empire, Latin was confined to use in the military and in documents concerning Roman citizens. The public administration of Syria-Palestine used Greek, which was also the first language of the Jerusalem aristocracy, and most Jewish people in Palestine knew at least some Greek. The "tribune" (NRSV) or "commander" assumes that Paul is a particular troublemaker (v. 38); most rabble-rousers he would know would have spoken Aramaic by choice. But most Egyptian business documents of this period were in Greek, which seems to have been the main language there; he thus should not be surprised that one he supposes to be an Egyptian speaks Greek. The point is not that Paul speaks Greek; it is that he speaks it without an accent, like someone educated and fluent in the language, which the tribune assumes the Egyptian Jew who had caused problems would not be.

21:38. *Josephus wrote of a false prophet from Egypt who gained a following of roughly thirty thousand (a figure less realistic than those given in Acts). The Roman governor Felix (23:24) defeated him, but the Egyptian himself escaped. Most of the messianic-prophetic figures reported in this period gained followings in the "wilderness" ("desert"—NIV), perhaps expecting deliverance to come like a new exodus under a new Moses.

The word for "assassins" (NASB) here is *sicarii.* These were Jewish terrorists who carried curved daggers under their cloaks and brutally stabbed to death aristocrats in the midst of crowds in the temple, then slipped away unseen. A few years after this encounter they kidnapped people to secure the release of their own adherents held by the procurator. Josephus's final reports of them are at the fortress Masada, where they finally perished in A.D. 73.

21:39. Citizenship in a Greek city gave one higher status than the many who were merely "residents" of the city (who were in turn considered above transients and rural people). One became a citizen only by birth in a citizen family or as a grant from the city authorities. City pride and rivalry were fierce in antiquity, especially in Asia Minor, and Tarsus was a prominent city. Tarsus's citizens were not automatically *Roman* citizens (it was not a Roman *colony), but Paul saves his disclosure of Roman citizenship as a trump card in case he needs it later.

21:40. The tribune grants Paul permission to speak, probably hoping that he will clarify his identity to a crowd he thinks has wrongly supposed him a leader of temple assassins. "Hebrew" here is probably a loose expression for *Aramaic (so NIV), the vernacular of much of rural Syria-Palestine and all lands to the east. It is especially significant for Paul's purposes that Aramaic was the vernacular of the Jewish nationalists, and that Paul speaks it as well as they. The tribune would not understand any of what Paul is saying, however; Aramaic is similar to Hebrew, but bears little relation to Latin and Greek (see 22:24).

22:1. This typically Greek way to begin a speech reflects the extent to which Greek culture had permeated Palestine (Greek loanwords even occur throughout rabbinic Hebrew; Paul's hearers would not automatically associate his words with *Gentile culture). The parallel with Stephen (7:2), who provoked his audience to martyr him, also builds suspense for Luke's readers.

22:2. Those who thought that they had caught a *Diaspora collaborator with the *Gentiles must have reconsidered after they heard his fluent *Aramaic (see comment on 21:40).

22:3-21
Paul's Speech in the Temple

Of the three accounts of Paul's call, this is the one clearly designed for a nationalistic Jewish audience. Despite his clear Jewishness, however, his refusal to compromise God's call to the *Gentiles in the end incites the crowd's wrath. Paul was always sensitive to his audience but never willing to compromise the *gospel. Speeches usually included a *narrative component; this component takes up Paul's whole speech, perhaps because he is not permitted to complete it.

22:3. In ancient statements, "brought up" and "educated" (NASB) normally refer to different periods in a person's life; thus Paul was raised in Jerusalem (cf. 23:16; see comment on Phil 3:5) and studied to become a teacher of the *law under Gamaliel I—the famous pupil of *Hillel (see comment on Acts 5:34-35). Although he was born in another country, he can therefore explain that he is really a Jerusalemite by upbringing and an orthodox *Pharisaic teacher by training.

As a son in an educated and perhaps aristocratic home (his father being a citizen; cf. also 9:1), Paul probably began to learn the law around his fifth year and other Pharisaic traditions around his tenth year, and was sent to pursue training to be able to teach the law sometime after turning thirteen (cf. also Gal 1:14 and his letters' debate style). People normally sat on chairs (or reclined on couches for banquets); sitting at someone's feet was taking the posture of a *disciple. Paul's model for "zeal" may have been Phinehas, who killed for God (Num 25:13), and his successors in the *Maccabees. Within eight years of Paul's speech the revolutionaries were calling themselves "*Zealots," those zealous for God; this title may thus have appealed to Paul's more nationalistic hearers.

22:4-5. See comment on 9:2. Calling on the testimony of the high priest and the *Sanhedrin may indicate that he trusts their integrity; but unknown to Paul, a different high priest is now in office anyway (23:5).

22:6. People normally tried to avoid the noonday sun if possible, but it was unavoidable on urgent missions and on long journeys which required that much of the day be spent traveling.

22:7-16. The background is essentially the same as in 9:4-17, although this speech emphasizes different features, like Ananias's Jewish piety, which would commend themselves to Paul's nationalistic hearers.

22:17. The ancient Near East had a long tradition of receiving revelations (often dreams) in sanctuaries or holy places. God had revealed himself to his servants in such places in the *Old Testament (1 Sam 3:3-10; 1 Kings 3:4-5), and Paul's hearers would regard the temple as the most appropriate place to receive revelations (cf. comment on 7:2-7).

22:18. If Paul had been in danger in the past, he is in even more danger now, with hostilities rising against *Gentile collaborators; Paul would not be able to speak long after this point and could not realistically intend to get past the *narratio* of his speech (the *narrative part occurred early in a speech).

22:19-20. The *chazan,* or synagogue attendant, was normally responsible for beating wayward Jews as public discipline for their crimes, after judges (probably elders; *rabbis in a later period) pronounced judgment. If Paul had been given this responsibility, it was due to some respected authorization (similar to that mentioned in 22:5).

22:21. Like Jesus (Lk 4:22-30), Paul knows that this statement will offend his hearers, given the escalation of Jewish-*Gentile tensions in Palestine in these years. But he feels that multiethnic inclusiveness is a crucial part of the *gospel.

22:22-29
Examining Paul

22:22. The reaction is predictable; see comment on 21:20-22.

22:23. Throwing dust on one's head was a sign of mourning; removing it from one's feet meant removing what was unholy (13:51); here it is probably simply that they have nothing else to throw at him at the moment (cf., e.g., 2 Macc 4:41). They may throw off their cloaks for the same reason (perhaps they also tore them, as one would after hearing blasphemy), although Luke no doubt records it ironically as indicating their guilt: see comment on 7:58.

22:24-25. Even had Paul not been a Roman citizen, the tribune would have no authority to try a provincial belonging to another jurisdiction (21:39), after he had quelled the unrest. But it was legal to scourge slaves or aliens to extort confessions or to determine the truth concerning a situation. Paul had experienced Jewish *synagogue beatings and lictors' rods. But this scourge is with the *flagellum*—leather thongs into which pieces of metal or bone were woven. It could easily lead to the victim's death, and would certainly scar and probably maim him. Centurions were sometimes left to supervise executions and related duties.

But the Porcian and Julian laws exempted Roman citizens from such beatings without trial. Paul's citizenship excluded him from being tortured for information, and together with his being untried, it excluded him from punishment.

22:26-27. Paul waits until he has been chained for the same reason as in 16:37: he now has legal room to maneuver against *them.*

22:28. Scholars note that one could achieve Roman citizenship in several ways: one could be (1) born to a Roman father (so Paul); (2) a citizen of a Roman *colony; (3) a retired auxiliary soldier; (4) part of a municipal aristocracy or other group honored by Rome; or (5)—and this was most common after being born in Rome or in a colony—a slave freed by his or her owner.

This tribune or commander is either a former slave who acquired enough funds to buy his freedom (as often happened), or he bought his citizenship by a bribe, which was common under the preceding emperor, whose name he took (23:26). He had to be a citizen before he could be part of a legion; to have the status of a tribune, he must have had a powerful *patron or been one of the rare individuals who toiled his way up through the ranks to this position.

Being freeborn normally gave one higher status than being a *freedperson did, and a slaveborn citizen had limited rights. (This was true from the aristocratic standpoint of status, although it was not necessarily true economically. Still attached as *clients to their former owners, freed slaves had economic advantages that freeborn peasants lacked.) Paul thus has superior status in some sense. He may have replied in Latin: he was *ingenuus*, a citizen by birth (though cf. his family in 16:37).

22:29. See comment on 22:26-27. Not all officials would have cared about violating the law—some Roman procurators crucified Jerusalem aristocrats who were Roman citizens—but this tribune or commander has already shown his concern for Roman law (21:38-40).

22:30—23:10
Before the Sanhedrin

The *Sanhedrin was the highest religious court of Jewish Palestine. The *Pharisees and *Sadducees disagreed on many points. The Pharisees had less power and representation on the council, but some of them (like the aristocratic Simon son of Gamaliel I) would have had some power.

22:30. Because Paul's offense is clearly a religious one related to the temple, the perplexed official is going to try to ascertain the charge by consulting the Sanhedrin.

23:1. Paul's claim here (cf. also 24:16) may suggest that even when he was persecuting Christians, he was doing what he thought was right rather than knowingly opposing the truth (Phil 3:6). Whenever the accused could claim to have lived his life previously free of reproach, it counted in his favor *rhetorically.

23:2-3. Ananias was high priest A.D. 47-52 and about 53-59. Thus Paul here meets Ananias shortly before Agrippa II would remove him (see comment on 24:27). Ananias was a Roman vassal, known for his greed and for stealing the tithes belonging to the poorer priests. The *Zealot revolutionaries killed him in A.D. 66, about eight years after this hearing. Jewish law forbade condemnation before the accused was proved guilty. A "whitewashed wall" was one whose weakness or ugliness might be concealed—but not changed—by a veneer of whitewash: an appropriate condemnation of Israel's leaders (Ezek 13:10-11). Walls facing the street in the eastern Mediterranean were often whitewashed.

23:4-5. The high priest normally sat in a special place and wore distinctive robes; either he does not do so here because the gathering is informal, or Paul answers ironically, because of the official's corruption and improper claim to power. Socrates and others had endeavored to show themselves more pious in the matter concerning which they were accused than their judges were, which naturally led to condemnation by an angry court. Paul is content to show his piety by citing Scripture.

23:6. The *Sanhedrin sat in a semicircle, so most of the members of the court could see each other. Other sharp-witted Jewish strategists of this period, like *Josephus not many years later (*Life* 139, 28), also practiced this method of "Divide and conquer." The hope of the *resurrection was central to Judaism, and many martyrs had died staking their hope on it. Paul's views did not violate any central tenets of Pharisaism; he was now a "Pharisee plus," who taught that the resurrection had already been inaugurated in Jesus. Pharisees knew that no true Pharisee would have committed the crime with which Paul had been charged by the original crowd (21:28).

23:7. *Pharisees and *Sadducees were notorious for their disagreements, especially over the doctrine of the resurrection; Pharisees taught that Sadducees had no part in the world to come, because they did not believe in life after death (at least not in a form acceptable to most other Palestinian Jews).

23:8. Some scholars contend that the Sadducees believed only in the five books of Moses; but even if this were the case, they must have believed in the angels that appeared in Genesis. Luke's parenthetical comment here probably refers to the Sadducees' denial of the developed angelology and demonology of the Pharisees (12:15 is not Pharisaic). The Sadducees did not believe in life after death.

23:9. From the Pharisaic standpoint, if Paul were being condemned for being consistent with his doctrine of the *resurrection, then it is natural that the Sadducees want him convicted and likewise natural that the Pharisees and Sadducees should oppose each other on this matter. Later Pharisaic reports declare that the Sadducees would have no share in the world to come, because they did not believe in it.

23:10. Although Greek tragedy provides some parallels to the commander's fear for Paul (e.g., a story of two suitors who inadvertently killed their beloved by pulling on her), Greeks would most naturally read this account in the light of Greek *comedy*, laughing at the ludicrous character of the situation. Disputes in courtrooms chaired by high officials rarely came to blows.

23:11-22
The Plot Against Paul

23:11. See comment on 18:9-10.

23:12-13. Revolutionary-minded Jews considered some assassinations pious acts; Herod the Great had once executed ten *Pharisees who had formed an association by oath for the purpose of killing him. If Paul's enemies eventually broke their oaths to kill him, Jewish law would simply require them to bring atonement offerings to the temple; thus their oath here does not mean they would literally starve.

23:14-15. Ambushes by robbers and terrorists were common, especially at night. During these years shortly before the Jewish war with Rome, the *sicarii* (21:38) regularly assassinated Jews suspected of collaboration with the Romans, and all Palestine was uneasy; this report is thus quite believable. That aristocratic priests, who in the war of 66-70 turned out to have their own violent agendas, would cooperate in this plot is not surprising. (These priests would be some high *Sadducean members of the council, not *Pharisees.)

23:16-22. The *Diaspora Jewish writer Artapanus reported that Moses learned of a similar plot against himself and was thus able to thwart it. If Paul's sister was raised with him in Jerusalem, the whole family had presumably moved there from Tarsus after Paul's birth, rather than only having sent him there to study.

23:23-32
The Commander's Counter-measures

23:23. The commander's assignment of two hundred soldiers with the centurions (perhaps a paper strength; two centurions might command only 160 troops in practice) to guard Paul would weaken the garrison in Jerusalem's fortress Antonia by as much as one third; thus they must return quickly (23:32). The two hundred spearmen are non-Roman light auxiliary infantry. If the Antonia cohort included a regular cavalry unit, it had as many as one hundred horsemen—hence the commander sends most of them with Paul. Given the unrest in Palestine and night attacks by robbers, a smaller contingent would not be safe in the hills of Judea at night.

The Roman procurator or governor resided in Caesarea, visiting Jerusalem only for the feasts (to insure order). Caesarea was the military headquarters for Judea (the Roman overseer for all Syria-Palestine resided in Syria.)

Leaving at 9 p.m. (the night's "third hour"), only a protracted march would get them well on their way overnight; Caesarea was sixty miles away.

23:24. Shortly after Tiberius Antonius Felix (*Tacitus said Antonius, *Josephus said Claudius; an inscription may support Josephus's position but the matter is disputed) became procurator of Palestine, he convinced Drusilla to divorce her husband and marry him (24:24). He secured his position because his brother was Pallas, a powerful *freedman of Emperor Claudius. Tacitus reported that Felix was corrupt, having a king's authority but a slave's mind (from a Roman aristocrat, the latter was hardly a compliment). Josephus likewise condemned him as thoroughly corrupt, accusing him of bloody massacres and repression. He remained procurator from A.D. 52 to 59 or 60.

23:25. The empire (except perhaps for Egypt) had no postal service except for official government business; most people sent letters via slaves or friends. The commander sends this letter with the soldiers.

23:26. This was the standard greeting in letters, and the respectful title was standard for an equestrian official (equestrians were the so-called knight class). Although Felix was not equestrian, his power and status as procurator made that fact irrelevant. Indeed, despite his low birth, his three successive wives (Drusilla probably being the final one) were all from royal households.

23:27-30. Subordinate officials sometimes put their own slant on a story to make themselves sound good to their superiors; this commander, who has probably worked his way up through the ranks (22:28), knows how to play the game well. Local officials (and as Rome's chief representative in Jerusalem, this military tribune was an official) had to determine which cases should be referred to the procurator. This was obviously such a case.

23:31. Troops were able and trained to undertake all-night marches when necessary, as *Josephus testifies. Antipatris was some twenty-five miles south of Caesarea, about a day's march. But by the shortest route Antipatris was thirty-five to forty miles (fortunately downhill) from Jerusalem, hence the troops would have to march all night at a much faster pace than normal travelers.

23:32. The return journey need not have been undertaken so rapidly, nor with so much protection, because it would be in daylight and brigands more frequently and dangerously struck at night.

23:33—24:9 The Hearing Before Felix

The technical details of the trials here accord so well with other evidence on Roman legal procedure that noted Roman historians use them as major source material for understanding Roman provincial judicial proceedings.

23:33-34. It was good protocol to check the jurisdiction to which a person belonged before deciding a case. Officials had the authority to try the accused, wherever he might be from, for crimes committed in their region of jurisdiction; but the reverse was also true, and it would be easier for Felix to expel Paul from his own region than to take time to try him. Some ancient writers liked to draw parallels between related historical figures; here, cf. Luke 23:6-9.

Cilicia was an imperial province, the capital of which was Tarsus. But during Paul's period (not, however, Luke's period), Cilicia was governed as part of Syria. The Syrian legate had too much territory to concern himself with a relatively minor case, so Felix assumes jurisdiction he might otherwise have deferred.

23:35. Hearings for Roman citizens arraigned on capital charges required painstaking examination, if Felix were to follow the law. The procurator's residence in Caesarea was a palace built by Herod the Great; Paul was thus kept elsewhere in Felix's own residence.

24:1. Although Tertullus bears a fairly common Latin name, he could easily be a Jewish Roman citizen like Paul.

24:2-3. The prosecution would always begin first, both in Roman and in Jewish trials. Tertullus begins his speech with a standard *captatio benevolentiae*—flattery to secure Felix's favor. (*Rhetoric manuals emphasized winning the judge's favor, and speeches before public officials always opened by praising them.) Although flattery was sometimes true, this example is blatantly false: revolutionaries had escalated under Felix's corrupt and repressive administration, bringing neither peace nor reforms.

24:4. Speakers could apologize for wearying the official as if they had not really finished praising him (e.g., the *Letter of Aristeas 8); this was a *rhetorical technique for flattering someone even beyond the limits of one's own rhetorical skills or credibility.

24:5-6. Compare the analogously triple charge of Luke 23:2; some historians liked to parallel different historical figures. Paul's accusers make themselves out to be allies of the Romans, who especially in these years were concerned about Jewish unrest throughout the empire. Profaning the temple was a capital charge, and inciting people to riot against Rome was *maiestas,* high treason. Tertullus could accuse Paul only of *trying* to desecrate the temple, because no witnesses could prove that he had actually taken Trophimus inside (21:29).

If one's opponent in court were known to be a persuasive speaker, it was also common to warn about his crafty speaking ability; and character defamation was a major part of winning Roman lawsuits.

"Sect" is not a derogatory term in itself. "Nazarenes" (a term Jewish Christians in time generally applied to themselves) was perhaps originally an insult, calculated against the obscurity of Jesus' hometown (cf. Jn 1:46).

24:7-8. The text of verses 7-8a is questionable (see marginal notes in translations); if these verses are original, they refer to a conflict over whether the *Sanhedrin or the Roman commander has jurisdiction over the case; from all that we know about Felix, he would certainly side with the commander.

24:9. This verse means either that there is a cry of popular assent or that others present supporting arguments in turn; given usual proceedings in which first the accuser and then the defendant spoke, the former may be more likely.

24:10-21
Paul's Defense Before Felix

Paul's *rhetorical skills prove as effective as, or more effective than, those of his paid accuser Tertullus.

24:10. The defendant spoke after the accuser in Roman trials, as soon as he was given permission to do so. Paul also includes a *captatio benevolentiae* (see comment on 24:2-3), although a much more modest and believable one than that of Tertullus. Proclaiming one's confidence in the judge's fairness was an implicit statement of innocence, and other trained speakers appealed to this in court cases as well.

24:11. Here Paul begins a *narratio,* a stating of the case's facts. Paul shows himself skilled in the *rhetoric of his day.

24:12. This verse is a *propositio,* the proposition or thesis of Paul's speech; this was a standard part of ancient speeches.

24:13. Although ancient courts preferred arguments from probability over eyewitness accounts, proof was essential. For example, Herod's son Antipater, after much proof of his guilt, offered only oaths in favor of his innocence, so the Syrian legate Varus had him executed.

24:14. Roman lawyers also had defenses for those who confessed their guilt, admitting that the deed was wrong *(concessio);* they could claim they meant well *(purgatio)* or simply beseech pardon *(deprecatio).* But when Paul admits a deed, he does not admit that it is wrong or ask pardon for it. Instead, he creates a masterful defense: First, this is an issue of internal Jewish law, not a crime under Roman law, and therefore worthy neither of Roman trial nor of Roman execution at Jewish instigation. Further, the Christian faith springs from the *Old Testament and is thus an ancient religion, which should be protected as a form of Judaism under Roman toleration. Confessing what was not a crime was a typical masterful *rhetorical move; it would heighten one's credibility while doing nothing for the opponents' charge that the defendant had broken the law.

24:15. *Pharisaism and the rest of Judaism that believed in the *resurrection of the righteous were divided on the resurrection of the wicked. Some believed that the wicked would be raised for judgment (either temporary torture followed by annihilation, or eternal torture); others believed that they would not be raised. The early Christians who comment on the matter accept a resurrection of the wicked to judgment (Jn 5:29; Rev 20:5), the most natural way to read Daniel 12:2.

24:16. Here Paul means that one who truly believed the hope stated in verse 15 would be careful to do right before God and people. This is an implied argument from probability, a strongly favored line of argument in ancient law courts.

24:17. Almsgiving was highly regarded in Judaism but would not impress Felix, although he would regard it as harmless. More impressive is its value as clear proof of Paul's solidarity with his people and their ancestral customs. Again on a probability argument (v. 16), this point would make the charge of violating the temple absurd.

24:18-19. Paul had appeared publicly but had not spoken publicly before the riot, and the lack of eyewitnesses in such a public place refutes his opponents' argument, especially when the chief witnesses had conveniently returned to Asia after the feast. The uprising was their fault, not his.

24:20-21. Roman magistrates would view this as a matter of internal Jewish religious disputes, nothing on which to judge a case of Roman law.

24:22-27
Felix's Procrastination

24:22. Lysias, the commander, is the independent witness, who would not be expected to have bias for either side.

Neither Paul nor his accusers mention Jesus, and Paul's words are acceptable *Pharisaism; but Felix recognizes the religious issue involved. It would have been difficult for Felix not to have known of the massive Judean Jesus movement (21:20), but he and the Romans by this period were treating it as politically innocuous; the difference between Christians and the brigands who were assassinating people was finally clear.

24:23-24. Paul is probably still kept in the procurator's own palace (23:35), making it easy for Felix to visit him—and also for Paul's friends to provide him money, some of which might later be used to Felix's advantage (v. 26). Corrupt officials might keep someone imprisoned for their own ends; a later but partly analogous story is told of the Roman emperor Domitian acquitting a philosopher for his wisdom—then retaining him in detention so he could question him in private.

Drusilla was Herod Agrippa I's youngest daughter and Agrippa II's sister. She married the king of a small region in Syria, but at the age of sixteen divorced him at Felix's instigation to marry him instead. Although it violated normal Roman policy for a governor to marry a woman from his province, Felix had much power as long as his brother Pallas remained in favor in Rome (cf. comment on 23:24). Drusilla is about twenty years old here, and her Jewish faith may help influence her husband to listen to Paul.

24:25. Although wealthy households often kept philosophers around for their interesting insights, God's prophets were not quite as pleasant as most philosophers (Jer 38:14-23). Self-control was one of the favored topics of many moralists, but the future judgment was strictly Jewish teaching and probably not the side of Jewish teaching the procurator was accustomed to hearing. (Although there were Egyptian Jewish judgment oracles, most upper-class Jews under Greek influence would think like *Sadducees or like a handful of aristocratic *Pharisees such as *Josephus [who could accommodate *Platonic views of the afterlife] or like *Philo, whose views accommodated *Hellenism to the furthest possible extent.)

24:26. Felix was not known to be particularly just; *Josephus complained that he sent priests to Caesar on a trifling charge. Josephus also complained that the procurator Albinus, several years after Felix, released anyone—including revolutionaries—from jail whose relatives paid him something. Although Felix was not *that* corrupt, all ancient sources agree that he was corrupt, and this verse should not surprise us.

24:27. Cases often became backlogged, and it seems to have been unusual for procurators being removed to concern themselves with judging all cases still pending before their departure.

When Felix was being replaced by Porcius Festus (probably summer of A.D. 59), Jewish leaders from Caesarea finally went to Rome and accused him (Roman law had permitted provincials to accuse their governors since 149 B.C.). Fortunately for his sake, his powerful brother Pallas, although no longer in power in Nero's court, may have retained sufficient influence to protect him from Jewish retribution. "Wishing to do the Jews a favor" here (NASB) may mean that he needs all the Jewish mercy he can get.

25:1-12
Hearing Before Festus

*Josephus's portrait of Festus is much more positive than his portrait of Felix or Albinus; Festus corrected disturbances and caught many of the revolutionaries. It also appears from Josephus that Festus died in office, having served in Palestine only a year or two. Extensive parallels between Jesus' hearings in Luke 23 and Paul's in Acts 25—26 indicate that Luke wishes to parallel them, as some other historians paralleled figures; his point is that Christians must follow in Jesus' footsteps.

25:1. Festus's residence would be in Caesarea, but it was politically appropriate to visit the local authorities centered in Jerusalem.

25:2. Relations between Felix and the Jewish authorities had been strained; a new governor, however, meant a new chance to introduce agendas previously deferred.

25:3-5. They wanted Paul moved; given the frequent assaults by revolutionaries throughout the country, the priestly aristocracy would not necessarily appear to have sponsored the violence against Paul (as violent as some of their own agendas were reported to be, according to early Jewish sources).

25:6. Sitting on his tribunal (NASB), *pro tribunali,* means that this is an official hearing.

25:7-8. The accusations against Jewish law and temple (21:28) would be relevant to a Roman magistrate only if Paul had violated the sanctity of the temple, a charge that had not been demonstrated. An implication of treason *(seditio)* against Caesar, however, would be fatal.

25:9. History reports that Festus was a fairer and more cooperative governor than most who ruled Judea; he undoubtedly wishes to engender a good relationship with the provincials here.

25:10-11. Roman citizens had the right to appeal to Caesar's tribunal *(provocatio ad Caesarem),* although the emperor in this period normally delegated the hearing and judging of cases to others. Later, the governor Pliny in Bithynia executed many Christians but sent those who were citizens to Rome for trial. Noncitizen provincials had no automatic right to appeal a governor's decision (except to accuse the governor of extortion or on a capital charge).

25:12. A Roman judge normally had a *consilium,* or council, with whom to confer; because a governor might not be learned in the law *(iuris prudentes),* it was important for him to have some advisors who were, although he was ultimately free to disregard their counsel. A citizen could appeal a capital sentence *(appelatio),* but appealing before a case had been heard *(provocatio),* as Paul does here, was less common, because it was not necessarily advantageous. Festus has reason to comply with Paul's request. The political implications of dismissing an appeal to Caesar were unpleasant, whereas the benefits of sending Paul to Rome free Festus from having to disappoint the Jerusalem leaders if his own juridical conclusions differ from theirs.

25:13-22
Festus and Agrippa II

25:13-14. When Agrippa I died (12:23), his son, Agrippa II (here), was only seventeen; his daughters were Berenice (sixteen), Mariamne (ten) and

Drusilla (six). Agrippa II ruled a small part of Palestine and worked with the Roman administration. He was an advocate for his people but was also loyal to Rome and later struck a coin in A.D. 89 commemorating Rome's triumph over the Jewish rebels. *Josephus's record shows that Agrippa visited Roman officials frequently, especially when they first arrived. Festus later took Agrippa's side in a dispute with the priests.

Berenice (also spelled Bernice) was Agrippa's sister. Some ancient writers maligned her close relationship with her brother Agrippa, slandering it as incestuous, but their charge is unlikely. Berenice later became the mistress of the Roman general Titus, who besieged Jerusalem, but once he became emperor so much scandal arose about his consorting with a Jewish woman that he was forced to ignore her; she finally left Rome brokenhearted. She was fifteen years older than Titus.

25:15-16. Roman law required that the accused be permitted to confront his accusers and defend himself against charges in a public hearing.

25:17-21. The real issue here is one of Jewish law—one not tried by Roman courts. Luke again shows the Roman impression that Christianity was part of Judaism and thus should be accorded legal toleration.

25:22. Compare Luke 23:8. As a newcomer, Festus would naturally want the counsel of Agrippa, who knew Judaism but was more sympathetic to Roman interests than the priestly aristocracy was proving to be. Agrippa had a good Greek education, and Festus might have gravitated to him as one of the few local people with whom he could talk.

25:23—26:1
The Hearing Before Agrippa Begins

25:23. The pomp Luke mentions here was characteristic of royal families, including Jewish ones (e.g., 1 Macc 11:6). The "commanders" (NASB) or "officers" (NIV) are the five tribunes, Roman commanders of the five cohorts in Caesarea and each equal in rank to the one tribune in Jerusalem (21:31).

25:24-26. When Greeks called the emperor Nero "lord" (v. 26), they often meant it as a divine title; but no Roman would yet use it thus.

25:27. The charge against Paul is political, but all the evidence involves Jewish religion, which would be incomprehensible to Roman procurators. Agrippa II is the first official competent in both Roman and Jewish law to hear Paul's defense; he will thus supply the evaluation for Festus's letter to Nero.

26:1. On receiving permission from the judge (in this case, unofficially Agrippa), one could speak. Paul's hand is stretched forth in customary *rhetorical style; gestures were an important part of ancient training in public speaking.

26:2-11
Paul's Pious Background

Standard defense speeches varied somewhat in form but had general consistency, as exhibited here: the address to the judge (26:2-3), the *narratio* (narration of events—26:4-18) and finally the *argumentio* (proof of the case—26:19-23).

26:2-3. Here Paul offers the *exordium* of the speech, in which it was customary to praise the judge *(captatio benevolentiae).* Paul is able to do so honestly; Agrippa's interest in the *law was known, and his realm became a safe haven for Jewish practice after the Jewish-Roman war of 66-70.

26:4. On Paul's youth in Jerusalem see 22:3.

26:5. The appeal to many potential witnesses is not unusual; it occurs even

in *Plato's version of Socrates' defense.
26:6-7. Two of the most basic future hopes of most Jews were the *resurrection of the bodies of the righteous and the restoration of the twelve tribes at the same time.
26:8. Ancient courtrooms counted arguments from probability more heavily than they counted what we would consider hard evidence (such as reliable witnesses); Paul must thus counter the supposition that a resurrection is improbable by reminding his hearers of God's power and that resurrection is rooted in the most basic Jewish hope.
26:9-10. "Casting a vote" could also be used of unofficial decisions; Paul himself was probably too young to belong to the *Sanhedrin, but he could still have exerted influence on others' opinions. If Paul refers to more executions than Stephen's, members of the Sanhedrin or unofficial courts may have voted for their execution while the procurator was in Caesarea, but the executions themselves, like Stephen's, were illegal. Thus Paul's account here paints his accusers, for whose cause he once worked, in a rather anti-Roman light.
26:11. Pliny, governor of Bithynia in the second century, noted that former Christians could easily be moved to worship the gods, but complained that genuine Christians could not be forced to do so, even on the pain of death. Pagan rulers who had earlier tried to force Jews to abandon their ancestral customs had encountered the same resistance, which pagan officials generally considered obstinate.

26:12-23
The Risen Christ Calls Paul to the Gentiles

26:12-13. On "midday" or "noon" (NIV), see 22:6. In 26:13 Paul uses clearly Jewish language for a theophany, a revelation of God's glory.
26:14. Falling down was a common response to such revelations in the *Old Testament and Jewish tradition. The "heavenly voice" (which some segments of Judaism thought had replaced *prophecy) was often thought to speak in Hebrew or *Aramaic. "Kicking against the goads" was a Greek proverb about fighting a god, possibly originating with the classical Greek playwright Euripides. It is not cited in the other accounts of Paul's conversion, but it is appropriate in an address to Agrippa, who had an ample Greek education.
26:15-18. Jesus' words to Paul evoke Old Testament passages about prophets' calls (Jer 1:5-8) and Israel's call to the *Gentiles (Is 42:7, 16). "An inheritance among those who have been sanctified" (NASB) or "the set-apart ones" refers to the Jewish hope that they as God's set-apart people would inherit the world to come, just as Israel had "inherited" the Promised Land.
26:19-21. A Roman aristocrat like Festus may dislike Paul's mission to move Gentiles to *repent, but he would not understand the Jewish opposition. Agrippa II, who had pagan friends and knew well the mounting animosity of Judean Jewry against Gentiles, would understand Paul all too well, and it is to him that Paul directs these words.
26:22-23. Paul begins marshaling evidence at this point (26:8) that the faith he represents is in continuity with the *Old Testament religion tolerated by the Romans as an ancient and ethnic religion.

26:24-32
The Court's Evaluation

26:24. Undoubtedly referring to Paul's Jewish learning (26:4-5) but perhaps also to his mastery of Greco-Roman *rhetoric, Festus gives the usual answer that educated Romans gave to concepts so foreign and barbarian to them as *resurrection. In Greek circles, madness was sometimes associated with prophetic inspiration, but Festus, a Roman, undoubtedly means it less charitably.

26:25. A term in Paul's reply ("utter"—NASB; "saying"—NIV) may imply that he *is* speaking under inspiration (the same term is used in Acts only at 2:4, 14). But "sober" (or "reasonable"—NIV) speech was a virtue appreciated by Romans, related to the ideas of dignity and respectability.

26:26. The charge "speaking in a corner" had long been used to deride philosophers who avoided public life. By the second century Christians were often charged with being secretive (although sometimes they were meeting secretly to avoid being arrested), but Paul argues that Christian claims are public facts, dismissed or ignored by others only because of the others' bias.

26:27. Paul returns to his argument from Scripture, directed toward Agrippa although incomprehensible to Festus (26:22-24).

26:28-29. Although some commentators have read this as an ironic question (see, e.g., NIV), the whole apologetic structure of the *narrative suggests that Agrippa instead takes Paul's case seriously; this could thus be a statement or a rhetorical overstatement ("You are so convincing that you may soon convert me!").

26:30-31. Paul is not guilty before Roman law, and this is the only conclusion to which Roman hearers could come. Nor is he offensive to Agrippa's more liberal form of Judaism, which cared nothing for revolutionaries and did not accede to the demands of the Jerusalem aristocracy.

26:32. Because Paul had used his Roman right to appeal to Caesar's tribunal, Agrippa and Festus can only refer him there with a letter specifying their own opinion. This appeal had earlier saved Paul's life (25:3), and now it provides him free passage to Rome (19:21) and a public forum for the *gospel there.

27:1-8
The Voyage to Rome Begins

Some commentators have suggested that the "we" here characterizes fictitious sea voyages; but it was used just as often in genuine historical *narrative. Greek writing had long included passages describing other lands from the vantage point of ships voyaging by their coasts, and these included genuinely historical accounts. This narrative is clearly eyewitness history; the details of the voyage, including the number of days it took to reach particular harbors given the winds mentioned, fit exactly the report of one who had undertaken such a voyage. This point was shown already in the nineteenth century by an experienced Mediterranean mariner, James Smith, whom most subsequent commentaries follow on the nautical details.

27:1. "Augustan" (NASB, NRSV) was often an honorary term, and one cohort known in Syria-Palestine before and after this period bore that name. Centurions could be moved around; this one may have had his full company of eighty troops (27:31), although it might be hard to fit eighty more persons on the average Mediterranean cargo ship (cf. 27:37). The "other prisoners" may have been sent for trial as Roman citizens, but a higher number of those sent normally were convicted criminals to be killed in the games for the entertainment of the Roman public.

27:2. Shippers had low status but often made large profits. Ancient Mediterranean ships were quite small by modern standards; most of them weighed less than 250 tons, although Alexandrian grain ships (27:6) were much heavier (often estimated at eight hundred tons or more). Adramyttium was southeast of Troas. Imperial messengers normally traveled by land, unless a ship were convenient, as this one proved to be.

27:3. Sidon had a double harbor and was about seventy miles north of Caesarea, where they had started.

27:4. The ship is opposed by the usual summer winds from the west or northwest. Thus, remaining close to the Syrian coast east of Cyprus, and northward to the south of Asia Minor, their voyage is much slower than the reverse voyage across open sea (21:1-3), although aided by land breezes.

27:5. Myra was two miles from its harbor. The soldiers and their prisoners might have gone on by land (27:2), but the centurion is able to find another ship (27:6).

27:6. Rome's grain fleet dominated Mediterranean trade; ships from Alexandria, Egypt, would travel northward and then westward to bear their cargoes to Rome. This journey took from as little as fifty days to over two months, although the reverse voyage from Rome to Alexandria could take as little as nine to twelve days. The Egyptian grain ships were about 180 feet long, 45 feet wide and (at their deepest) over 40 feet deep; the fleet may have transported some 150,000 tons of Egyptian grain to Italy each year. This was the largest mercantile fleet known to Europe before the 1700s. The Alexandrian fleet was the quickest means of transportation from Syria to Rome.

27:7. Ships that sailed over against Cnidus were keeping north of Rhodes. Crete was the largest island of the Aegean Sea. It had few harbors in the north, and a north wind from the Aegean there could wreck a ship against the coast. A wind that would drive their ship toward Salmone (on the eastern end of Crete) would be a northwesterly wind, normal for late summer. But the south coast of Crete had more harbors, and the south winds there were more gentle.

27:8. Shortly beyond Fair Havens, Crete's southern coast veers sharply northward, exposing a ship to the full harshness of a northwesterly wind blowing across the land.

27:9-19
The Crisis at Sea

27:9. The "fast" here refers to Yom Kippur, the Day of Atonement, which occurs in September or October. Sea travel became more dangerous as winter approached (2 Tim 4:21; Tit 3:12). Shipping was completely closed down from around November 10 to as late as March 10, but September 15-November 10 and March 11-May 26 were risky periods as well.

27:10. Pagans undertaking sea voyages always sacrificed to the gods and sought their protection. Bad omens, astrological interpretations or dreams sometimes prevented a ship from sailing if they were taken seriously. Before going to war Romans would check the entrails of animals, the flight of birds and other forms of divination; religious advice was always important to those contemplating a potentially risky venture. Paul would sound to them like the kind of seer who could predict the future without divination. Unlike Greeks, Romans respected divination more than this kind of prophecy.

27:11. Being a practical Roman, the centurion respects the nautical knowledge of the captain more than a Jewish prisoner's religious insights. Yet such a decision was often made more on economic than nautical grounds. Grain ships sometimes traveled together; this one is making the voyage alone and is probably one of the latest vessels of the shipping season. But the captain at best hopes to make it to a better harbor before the seas close down for the winter; he cannot hope to reach Italy this late in the year (27:9). The captain is probably also the ship owner here, but because his vessel is part of the imperial grain fleet, the centurion functions as a Roman official with greater authority than the ship owner, just as he would on land in Egypt.

27:12. Phoenix was probably a common winter harbor; its site is either in southwestern Crete or, more likely, on the north of Crete.

27:13-14. A south wind is what they need and should have brought them to their destination within hours. But the south wind often changes suddenly to a dangerous northerly wind in this region; the conflicting air currents increase the danger.

27:15. With a favorable wind in their mainsail, these ships could cover about fifty nautical miles in daylight, or ninety miles in twenty-four hours; but they had little resistance to a powerful wind going in a direction they wished to avoid.

27:16. The only place to anchor at Cauda is also exposed to the east-northeast wind and thus could not help them. The "boat" or "lifeboat" (NIV) was used for landings, to maneuver the ship for tacking and so forth. Sometimes these boats were kept on deck; at other times, as here, they were towed behind. Here, filled with water or in danger of breaking loose from the ship, it has to be brought on deck to be rescued.

27:17. The "supporting cables" (NASB) or "ropes" (NIV) were used to undergird the hull against the raging sea in times of fierce storms; they must have been slipped around the stern or prow and worked backward to brace the whole hull.

If they continued on their present course too far to the south, they would eventually be destroyed in Syrtis Major (modern Gulf of Sidra), a shoal west of Cyrenaica along the African coast. Even in good weather, Alexandrian grain ships sailed northward to Asia and then westward to Italy, rather than directly northwest, because a sudden change in winds could wreck them on this shoal.

27:18. Jettisoning the bulk of the cargo is the natural step at this point; in crises like this one no distinction is made between valuable and cheap cargo (Jon 1:5; also *Josephus, *Achilles Tatius).

27:19. It would take most of the manpower on deck to lower the yard ("tackle"—NIV)—a spar that could be nearly the ship's own length—down to the deck. One would secure it if possible, but in the severity of this storm, they cannot afford the encumbrance created by retaining it.

27:20-44
The God of Safety on the Sea

27:20. Pagans felt that those who died at sea never entered the realm of the dead; instead their souls wandered aimlessly forever above the waters in which they perished.

27:21-22. Ancient people evaluated the sincerity of philosophers (e.g., Aristippus) according to how calm they stayed under pressure. A true philosopher consistent with his teachings would remain calm in a dangerous storm at sea (so Pyrrho the Skeptic), whereas as a false prophet like Peregrinus would not. The others' lack of eating may be due to seasickness.

27:23-25. It was not unusual for ancient writers in the middle of a story to report earlier events they had not yet mentioned.

A story is told that even some unreligious men began to supplicate the gods during a raging storm; the philosopher Bias, aboard the same ship, urged them to be quiet, lest the gods recognize they were aboard and sink the ship! Like Jonah's behavior in the *Old Testament (Jon 1:6-16), this attitude contrasts sharply with Paul's concern for all aboard. (A few other people, like Caesar, were said to have claimed that a ship could not sink with them on it, but Paul's claim is because of God's mission and message, not because he is personally indispensable.) Various deities claimed the role of protector at sea, like Isis or the Dioscuri (28:11); but God is the true protector.

27:26. Running aground was not normally good news; Paul's advance notice of that crisis would make faith easier when the time came.

27:27-28. The sea around Malta (28:1) is far south of what is called the "Adriatic Sea" today but was included in the "Sea of Adria" in antiquity. The rate of drift per day and the trajectory they would have followed from Cauda to avoid Syrtis has been calculated; it was exactly fourteen days to reach Malta (28:1). The soundings in verse 28 indicate that they were at this point near Koura, east of Malta. They can hear the water breaking against land here, because they are only perhaps half an hour from what is now called St. Paul's Bay.

27:29. Anchors were used as brakes and were normally cast from the bow. Here they are cast from the stern, as was occasionally done if the winds would otherwise blow the ship around.

27:30. Other cases are known of crew members' trying to escape a doomed ship in a small boat; these boats were not meant as lifeboats and fitted only a handful of people.

27:31. By this point, Paul (whose advice was originally disregarded, perhaps as the impractical concerns of an eccentric Jewish teacher) is now in virtual command of the ship, because he has the centurion's ear.

27:32. On the next day they could have used the small boat to ferry people to land (although it would have taken many trips); without it, they would have to run the whole ship aground.

27:33-34. "Not a hair of one's head" was a proverbial expression in the *Old Testament (1 Sam 14:45; 2 Sam 14:11; 1 Kings 1:52); but it would make sense even to hearers who were not familiar with it.

27:35-36. The meal here is done in the traditional Jewish manner: the head of the household thanked God and distributed the bread.

27:37. Large ships frequently carried several hundred people; *Josephus even claimed that he had traveled aboard a ship with six hundred people.

27:38. They need to lighten the ship further (27:18), in order to run aground as close to land as possible. They had so far retained some of the cargo as ballast (heavy material kept in the hold of a ship to steady it). An Alexandrian ship's cargo would be wheat.

27:39. The traditional site of St. Paul's Bay on northern Malta fits all the details of the *narrative.

27:40. These actions are normal for a disabled ship trying to come near land.

27:41. Between St. Paul's Bay and the island of Salmonetta on the northwest is a shallow channel about three hundred yards wide. The ship wedges on a sandbar there, while waves pound the immobilized rear of the vessel.

27:42-43. Guards were responsible for the prisoners' safe custody. They would be less liable for their charges if the prisoners "died at sea" than if they escaped.

27:44. In Greco-Roman literature, someone's escape from disaster at sea could serve as evidence of that person's religious purity even before a court.

28:1-10
Miracles on Malta

28:1. Malta (ancient Melita) was on the shipping route from Rome to Egypt, whereby empty ships would sail quickly to Alexandria to load up more cargoes. It was the stop immediately after Syracuse in Sicily. The alternative proposed site for this island near Dalmatia (Meleda, modern Mljet) is based on a misreading of "Adria" in 27:27 and has no merit; winds from the north could not have driven them there.

28:2. The Maltese were of Phoenician descent, and commoners there spoke and read only Punic (the late Phoenician dialect of the Carthaginians). But Roman citizens and retired soldiers also lived there, and the island was certainly not considered culturally primitive. Anyone who did not speak Greek was called a "barbarian," and Greeks did not expect kind treatment from them. But Luke's use of the term translated "barbarous" (KJV) in this context (cf. "natives"—NASB; "islanders"—NIV) is not derisive; he indicts Greek racial prejudice at the same time that he displays God's providential care through them.

28:3. In cold weather some snakes can look like twigs until the heat of a fire stirs them.

28:4. Ancients argued in courts that their survival of troubles at sea proved their piety and hence innocence; on the importance of arguing Paul's innocence, see the introduction to Acts. In some stories, the impious escaped one form of terrible death (e.g., at sea) only to face something worse (besides Greek stories, see Amos 5:19). "Justice" was a goddess who executed the will of Fortune or the Fates; although the Maltese observers refer to some Punic deity, Luke translates their idea into the idiom of Greek poets. Several groups of Jewish catacombs dating between the second and fifth centuries A.D. have been found on the island; but if Jewish people were on the island in the first century, this *narrative does not mention them.

28:5. Adam's rule over the beasts (Gen 1:26) was cut short by the Fall, but Jewish interpreters of Isaiah 11:6-9 believed that this rule would be restored in the *messianic time, and a few holy men were believed to have that power in the present age. Some Greek initiates to *mystery cults may have practiced snake handling. Paul simply deals in faith with a situation thrust upon him.

28:6. Whenever similar stories were told, those who survived bites from poisonous snakes or lizards were considered holy men (e.g., the pious Jewish holy man Hanina ben Dosa); Greco-Roman paganism often considered such holy men to be divine or semidivine. The change of mind on the part of Paul's viewers could strike the ancient reader as humorous, as in some similar accounts in antiquity where a human was mistaken for a particular divinity.

28:7. Hospitality was an important virtue, especially toward people who had been shipwrecked and were stranded without possessions. Publius is a Latin *praenomen,* and as the top official he had probably received a grant of Roman citizenship; the title assigned to him here has been found in Greek and Latin inscriptions as the proper title of the island's governor.

28:8-10. In subsequent times the Maltese were affected by a special sickness due to a microbe in the milk of the goats there; although such organisms would have mutated over the centuries, perhaps a similar illness is in view here. The attacks are intermittent, and the sickness described here is similar to malaria.

28:11-16
Journey to Rome

28:11. The seas opened as early as February 8 or as late as March 10, depending on the weather; in the year in view here they seem to open toward the earlier date. On Alexandrian ships see comment on 27:6; like most ships, this one would have harbored on the other side of the island. Ships were named for their patron deity (e.g., "the Isis") in whose protection they trusted and whose image was used as the ship's figurehead. The Dioscuri (Castor and Pollux, twin heroes, sons of Zeus who had been deified) were considered special protectors of ships, on whom one might call in a storm.

28:12. Syracuse was the chief city of Sicily, with a rich Greek and Roman heritage.

28:13. Rhegium was the Italian harbor closest to Sicily. In the first century, mercantile vessels, including the Alexandrian grain fleet, put in at Puteoli just west of Naples; to have reached it in two days meant that they had made optimum time (about ninety miles a day).

28:14. The Jewish community in Puteoli had been there a long time, as had Egyptian and Phoenician cults. As the regular port receiving visitors from the East, it naturally received foreign religions as well as goods. Thus it is not surprising to find Christians there; but readers of Luke's day might be more surprised that these Christians offer hospitality to Paul's captors, who accept it from them.

28:15. In older times, isolated inns had grown into larger settlements that retained the names of the inns. One of these was the Tres Tabernae, or Three Inns, thirty-three Roman miles from Rome on the ancient and famous Appian Way. The "Market of Appius," or Appii Forum, was about forty-three miles from Rome on the same paved road. Jewish communities had existed in Italy for a long time and may have formed the basis for the first Christian groups there (cf. 2:10).

28:16. Along the Appian Way, Paul and the others would enter Rome's Porta Capena. Paul was loosely chained by the wrist to a soldier (28:20), who would be a member of the Praetorian Guard, Caesar's elite personal guard in Rome, which consisted of nine or twelve cohorts.

The Praetorian Guard was commanded by the Praetorian prefect, one of the most powerful men in Rome, who was at this time Afranius Burrus. Burrus was officially responsible for all prisoners from the provinces to be tried by Caesar's court, although the task itself was probably delegated to a lower officer, the *princeps castrorum,* who administered the Praetorian Guard's *officium.* Burrus later died with Nero's philosopher-tutor *Seneca during Nero's purges (A.D. 62).

28:17-31
Paul, Jews and Gentiles in Rome

28:17. The "leaders of the Jews" (NIV) are leaders of different *synagogue communities; no single body ruled over the whole Jewish community in Rome. The Jewish congregations in Rome were all autonomous, and

Christians could spread their views among the various synagogues with relative freedom. The Jewish community there had also made many Roman converts and sympathizers (to the chagrin of many male Roman aristocrats). Many of these sympathizers would be happy to embrace a version of the Jewish faith that accepted them fully without circumcision.

28:18-20. Imprisonment and chains were not used as punishments but as a means of detention until trial. Paul continues to emphasize the continuity between the *Old Testament message and his own; this point would be important to Jewish leaders and also to Roman readers, who needed to understand that the Jesus movement was rooted in an ancient religion worthy of toleration (even if, after 70, Judaism was unpopular in some circles).

28:21-22. Unable to win their case in Judea, Paul's accusers would have even less chance in Rome. By A.D. 62, the Jewish community in Rome had an advocate with the emperor in his wife (former mistress) Poppaea Sabina—until Nero kicked her to death while she was pregnant. It is by no means clear that the Roman Jewish community was uniformly hostile to the Christian movement (28:24), but they naturally had questions, especially if their previous expulsion in 18:2 was due to Christian teachings.

28:23-27. Paul's citation of Isaiah 6 climaxes a theme throughout Acts: that most of God's own chosen people reject their *Messiah while *Gentiles accept him is not amazing but the fulfillment of Scripture.

28:30. At the end of two years, if no accusers had arrived and no charges had been sent against him (28:21), Paul would normally be automatically released. Paul was later arrested again and beheaded, but Luke wishes to end on a note of positive legal precedent, before the corruptions of Roman law introduced by Nero's tyranny. A number of ancient works had sudden endings; and following the pattern of other Jewish and Christian works (but in contrast to many Greek works), Luke wishes to end happily.

28:31. That Paul could preach under the very nose of the Praetorian Guard suggests that, before Nero instituted his persecution against Christians for political reasons, they were tolerated under Roman law. Luke's defense of Christianity on legal and philosophical grounds paved the way for second-century defenders of Christianity and points the way for Christian lawyers, statespersons and others to work in society today.

NEW TESTAMENT LETTERS

Rhetoric. Good letters were written according to the standard conventions of *rhetoric, which was the study and use of proper forms for public speaking. Greek higher education usually concentrated on rhetoric, although some students specialized in philosophy instead. Those who could afford it learned basic reading and writing under a *grammaticus,* beginning around age eleven or twelve, and the fewer who could afford the next stage proceeded to the *sophistēs,* or rhetorician, around the age of eighteen.

Rhetoric was the indispensable tool of politicians, lawyers and other public figures, an essential focus of upper-class education. Its training included speech imitation and composition, oratory, practice in extemporary exposition on diverse topics, gestures, grammar, proper citation technique and so forth. Those not specifically trained in rhetoric picked up its basic outlines from listening to public speeches; those who wished to learn technical details had a variety of handbooks from which to choose.

Types of Rhetoric. There were three main types of rhetoric: epideictic (or encomiastic), praising or blaming someone in the present; deliberative, convincing someone to act in a particular way (directed toward the future); and judicial (or forensic), the rhetoric of law courts (dealing with actions of the past). Attempts to strictly classify Paul's letters according to any one of these forms usually fails because in practice letters mixed the forms.

Letters. Letters imitated oral forms of rhetoric. Rhetoricians followed the typical Greek penchant for categorization and provided guidelines for the educated to write different types of letters: letters of rebuke (e.g., Galatians), letters of friendship or family, aesthetic letters (read among the elite for enjoyment), official letters and letter essays. Most of the *New Testament letters (except Philemon, 2-3 John and Jude) are long even by the standards of literary letters; some, like Romans, are extremely long (about seventy-one hundred words compared to an average of about three hundred in *Cicero and about one thousand in *Seneca).

Rhetoric in New Testament Letters. Because certain rhetorical conventions were simply part of formal speaking in their day, many writers like Paul may not have been conscious of their own rhetorical artistry. It is nevertheless helpful for the modern reader, accustomed to different forms of public speaking and argumentation, to understand the rhetorical techniques that New Testament writers often used. Paul was undoubtedly more conscious of and concerned for his technique in his most formal letters (e.g., Romans) or when challenged by upper-class readers (e.g., in 1 and 2 Corinthians), and my treatment of the rhetoric of these letters is accordingly more detailed than that of his other letters.

Purpose of Letters. Some were written with a long-term purpose, intended for publication and wide circulation even if addressed to an individual. The prophetic letters in the Old Testament (2 Chron 21:12-15; Jer 29; 36; cf. also Rev 2—3) show that in Jewish circles letters could be viewed as inspired if dictated by a prophet (1 Cor 7:40; 14:37).

Letter essays were general treatises that depended more on the author's context than on the situation of the readers. Most letters, however, were addressed to the audience's situation; ancient epistolary theorists stressed adapting letters to the situation of the readers. James is probably a letter essay; probably all of Paul's extant epistles (including Romans) are addressed to specific situations.

Stereotypical Forms in Letters. Different kinds of letters addressed different standard themes (now loosely called *topoi*). Rhetoricians provided standard forms for different topics so that speakers and writers could best adapt their message to the situation they needed to address. For instance, ancient letters of consolation repeated some basic themes, just as modern sympathy cards, epitaphs or eulogies do. But rhetoricians like Cicero emphasized that one should *feel* what one was preaching, rather than merely reproduce stereotypical forms emotionlessly. For information on introductions and conclusions of letters, see comment on Romans 1:1-7, 16:21-24 and 25-27.

Reception of Letters. According to some estimates, literacy in the Roman world was around ten percent; although reading was more common than writing, and urban areas had more education than rural areas, many persons in the congregation would be unable to read. Reading was nearly always done aloud even in private; *churches receiving Paul's letters would have them read publicly in the congregation's services, probably by those who normally read Scripture in the services.

How to Understand Letters. Letters had no chapter or verse breaks when they were first written (these were added later); thus one should read the whole letter to catch the flow of thought and never extract verses from their context. Ancient readers recognized that one should try to understand the author's purpose in writing, and they already knew their own cultural situation. When we read the letters, we must try to assume the original situation and then catch the writer's flow of thought by reading through the whole context.

Collections of Letters. Sometimes the letters of a famous person would be collected for publication. Paul's letters were collected some time after his death, but possibly as early as the end of the first century as local churches shared their own treasures.

Tensions Among Letters. Because most letters addressed specific situations, similar phrases could be used to address very different problems. Most writers were eclectic philosophically, drawing from a variety of different sources; even the *Dead Sea Scrolls testify that the same readers could accept different kinds of religious language (law, ritual, apocalyptic, hymns, *narrative). It is therefore difficult to determine differences of authorship, or to argue for the presence of apparent theological contradictions, based on differences among Paul's or other early Christian letters.

Works on Ancient Letter Writing. The most readable introductions to the genre are Stanley K. Stowers, *Letter Writing in Greco-Roman Antiquity,* LEC 5 (Philadelphia: Westminster, 1986); and David E. Aune, *The New Testament in Its Literary Environment,* LEC 8 (Philadelphia: Westminster, 1987), pp. 158-225.

ROMANS

Introduction

Authorship. All *New Testament scholars accept this as a genuine letter of Paul. *Churches naturally preserved letters of Paul; it would have been unnatural for anyone to have forged letters in his name during his lifetime or until long after his genuine letters had become widely known and circulated as authoritative. On the basis of letters clearly written by Paul to address specific situations of his day (e.g., 1 Corinthians) and other letters that share a common style with them, even the most critical New Testament scholars rarely dispute the Pauline authorship of particular letters (including Romans, Galatians, 1-2 Corinthians, Philippians, 1 Thessalonians and Philemon).

Rome's Jewish Community. Rome's Jewish community was predominantly poor, although some groups of Jewish people there were wealthier than others and better educated; different groups lived in different parts of the city and had their own leaders. It is thought that many of the predominantly Jewish house churches existed in the Jewish ghetto across the Tiber.

The primary language of the Jewish community in Rome was not Latin but Greek, the language in which Paul writes (76 percent of their burial inscriptions are in Greek, 23 percent in Latin and 1 percent in Hebrew or *Aramaic.) The Jewish community here was perhaps fifty thousand strong; many Roman conversions to Judaism created resentment among other aristocratic Romans and led to tension between the Jewish and *Gentile elements in the city.

Situation. Many of the founders of the Roman church were Jewish Christians (Acts 2:10). But sometime in the 40s A.D., the emperor Claudius, like the earlier emperor Tiberius, expelled the Jewish community from Rome (see Acts 18:2 and the Roman historians Suetonius and Dio Cassius). The Roman church was thus composed entirely of Gentiles until Claudius's death, when his edict was automatically repealed, and Jewish Christians returned to Rome (Rom 16:3). Jewish and Gentile Christians had different cultural ways of expressing their faith in Jesus; Paul thus must address a church experiencing tension between two valid cultural expressions of the Christian faith.

Theme. Given this situation, what the Roman Christians needed was what we would call racial reconciliation and crosscultural sensitivity. Paul reminds Jewish readers that they are as damned without Christ as Gentiles (chaps. 1—3); that spiritual, not ethnic, descent from Abraham is what matters (chaps. 4, 9); that Jews are also descended from the sinner Adam (5:12-21); and that the *law does not justify Israel (chaps. 7, 10). He reminds Gentiles that they were grafted into Judaism and therefore dare not be anti-Semitic (chap. 11) and that they must respect the practices of their Jewish siblings (chap. 14). Christ (15:1-13) and Paul (15:14-33) are agents of racial reconciliation, and unity (16:17-20) is the paramount issue.

Genre. Some scholars have argued that Paul's letter to the Romans is a letter-essay, explaining his *gospel without relating to the specific needs of the Roman church. In view of the previous discussion of situation and theme, however, it seems that Paul lays out the facts of the gospel in chapters 1—11 and then summons his readers to reconciliation and mutual service in chapters 12—15; thus the letter is "deliberative" rhetoric, an argument intended to persuade the readers to change their behavior.

Subsequent History. Protestants have traditionally stressed justification by faith, a doctrine emphasized in Romans and Galatians, because Luther found this doctrine helpful in addressing indulgences and other ecclesiastical corruptions in his day. But it is important to understand not only this doctrine but also why Paul needs to stress it. Most Jews already believed that the Jewish people as a whole were saved by God's grace, and Jewish *Christians* recognized that this grace was available only through Christ; the issue was on what terms *Gentiles* could become part of God's people. In arguing for the ethnic unity of the body of Christ, Paul argues that all people come to God on the same terms, no matter what their ethnic, religious, educational or economic background; Jesus alone is the answer to all humanity's sin. Paul stresses justification by faith, a truth most of his readers would know, especially so he can emphasize reconciliation with one another, a reality they still need to learn.

Commentaries. Two of the most useful shorter commentaries are A. M. Hunter, *The Epistle to the Romans,* Torch Bible Commentaries (London: SCM, 1955), and John A. T. Robinson, *Wrestling with Romans* (Philadelphia: Westminster, 1979). James D. G. Dunn, *Romans,* WBC 38A and B, 2 vols. (Dallas: Word, 1988), is a helpful detailed commentary. For views on the background, see especially Karl P. Donfried, ed., *The Romans Debate,* rev. ed. (Peabody, Mass.: Hendrickson, 1991); Krister Stendahl, *Paul Among Jews and Gentiles and Other Essays* (Philadelphia: Fortress, 1976). E. P. Sanders, *Paul and Palestinian Judaism* (Philadelphia: Fortress, 1977), provides a helpful corrective to earlier criticisms of Jewish views on the *law; for Paul's view on the law in Romans, see especially C. Thomas Rhyne, *Faith Establishes the Law,* SBLDS 55 (Atlanta: Scholars, 1981).

1:1-7
Introduction

Letters customarily opened with the name of the sender, the sender's titles (if any were necessary), the name of the addressees and a greeting. For example: "Paul . . . to the church at . . . greetings." Persuasive letters and speeches often began by establishing the speaker's credibility, what the Greeks called *ethos*. This beginning did not prove the speaker's point but disposed the audience to hear him respectfully.

1:1. A slave of someone in high position had more status, authority and freedom than a free commoner; the emperor's slaves were some of the highest-ranking people in the empire, as the Roman Christians would know. In the *Old Testament, prophets from Moses on were generally called "servants" or "slaves" of God.

Paul, who had once been an agent or commissioned messenger (*apostle) of the high priest (Acts 9:2), was now a representative for God. The ideas of being "called" and "set apart" go back to Old Testament language for Israel and, more important here, Israel's prophets.

1:2-3. Paul's words here would appeal to Jewish readers. "Through his prophets" concurs with the Jewish doctrine of the Old Testament's inspiration and final authority; "according to the flesh" (NASB) means simply that Jesus was physically descended from David.

1:4. "Spirit of holiness" was a common Jewish name for the *Holy Spirit, the Spirit of God. A regular *synagogue prayer regarded the future *resurrection of the dead as the ultimate demonstration of God's power. The phrase "*Son of God" meant many things to many different people in the ancient world, but it could strike Roman pagans as portraying Jesus as a rival to the emperor; in the *Old Testament it referred to the Davidic line, thus ultimately to the promised Jewish king (see 1:3; cf. 2 Sam 7:14; Ps 2:7; 89:27). Paul here regards Jesus' resurrection as the Spirit's coronation of him as the *Messiah and as humanity's first taste of the future resurrection and *kingdom.

1:5-6. The Old Testament promised that a representative remnant from among the nations would turn to God; Isaiah associated this remnant with the mission of the servant (42:6; 49:6; 52:15). Because the Roman *church clearly included Jewish Christians, "*Gentiles" (NIV, NASB, NRSV) is better translated here "nations" (KJV; cf. TEV); the term was used to mean both "nations," excluding Israel, and "peoples," including Israel. Representatives of all Mediterranean cultures resided in the great urban center, Rome.

1:7. "Saints" or "those who have been set apart" goes back to the *Old Testament image of God's people as set apart for himself. Like Paul (see comment on 1:1), they too are "called" (1:6-7); Paul embraces them as fellow heirs in the mission, not as inferiors.

The standard Greek greeting was "greetings" (*chairein*—Jas 1:1) a Greek term related to "grace" *(charis);* Jewish people greeted one another with "peace," and Jewish letters often began, "Greetings and peace." Paul adapts this standard greeting, a well-wishing, into a Christian prayer: "The grace and peace of God and Jesus be with you." (On "wish-prayers" see comment on 1 Thess 3:11.) Placing the Father and Jesus on equal footing as providers of grace and peace elevated Jesus above the role given to any mere human in most of Judaism. "Father" was also a title for God in Judaism (usually "our Father").

1:8-17
Paul's Thanksgiving

If one follows all the "fors" or other "cause" words (in some translations, e.g., NASB, NRSV), Paul's argument continues without pause through the chapter. Like prayers, thanksgivings were fairly standard in the openings of the bodies of ancient letters, and when Paul omits one (Galatians) it is conspicuous.

1:8. "All roads lead to Rome"; due to the connections of the whole empire with Rome, Christians everywhere knew about the faith of believers in the capital.

1:9. For "in my spirit" (NASB) the modern idiom would be "from the bottom of my heart," "with all my heart" (TEV; cf. NIV). It was common to call as witness the one who knew one's heart—God—although Paul avoids oath formulas like those mentioned in Matthew 5:33-37 (swearing by something). Recurrent prayer was sometimes described as "remembering," "reminding" or making mention to God.

1:10. Devout Jewish people might spend several hours a day in prayer; many did so at the times of morning and evening offerings in the temple. On "by God's will" or "if God wills" see comment on Acts 18:20; on Paul's plans to go to Rome see Acts 19:21 (the following chapters of Acts relate how he finally got there).

1:11-12. Longing to see a friend was a conventional matter to mention in ancient letters, which were used to convey a sense of one's presence when the writer and reader were (as often) far apart.

1:13. Addresses such as "beloved" or "brothers and sisters" were common in letters. On "*Gentiles" see comment on 1:5-6, although in 1:13-15 one should keep in mind Paul's special call to the Gentiles (11:13). Ancient cities were cosmopolitan, but the closing of sea travel for winter, needs of other *churches and the expense of travel could all have delayed Paul's coming.

1:14-15. Greeks considered everyone else in the world "barbarians" (cf. "non-Greeks"—NIV); they also usually considered themselves wise and others foolish. Some educated Jewish people classed themselves as Greeks, but Greeks considered them barbarians. Paul will introduce the Jewish division of humanity in verse 16, but here he uses the Greek one; in both cases, he affirms that God is for all peoples, regardless of race or nationality.

1:16. Verses 16-17 seem to be the *propositio,* or thesis statement, which begins Paul's argument. Paul stresses that the good news is for all peoples (see discussion of the situation in the introduction to Romans); if to both Jews and Greeks (Greeks were the most anti-Jewish), then to all peoples between Jews and Greeks.

1:17. In the *Old Testament (and in the *Dead Sea Scrolls), "God's righteousness" is that aspect of his character on account of which he vindicates his people and shows their faithfulness to him to be right. Thus it relates directly to "justification," or legal acquittal and vindication. (In Romans, many English versions translate the same Greek word as both "righteousness" and "justification.")

The Hebrew and Greek versions of Habakkuk 2:4 differ on a pronoun, which Paul thus omits (since the disputed detail is irrelevant to his argument anyway). In the context of Habakkuk 2:4, the righteous are those who will survive the judgment because they have faith (i.e., are faithful to God). (Biblical saving faith was not passive assent but actively staking one's life on the claims of God. It was a certainty sufficient to affect one's lifestyle; cf. Rom 1:5.) Paul applies this text to those who trust in Christ and so are saved from the final judgment. That his contemporary readers would understand his application is made clear by the similar application of Habakkuk 2:4 in the *Dead Sea Scrolls.

1:18-23
Willful Idolaters

Paul's argument is similar to one in the Wisdom of Solomon, a popular Jewish work widely circulated by this period. His arguments would thus have been timely and easy for his readers to follow.

1:18. "Heaven" was a Jewish circumlocution for God, and the phrase is a typically Jewish way of saying "God is angry." (Paul uses "revealed" to parallel v. 17.) The truth that the wicked suppress is the truth of God's character (1:19-20), which they distort by idolatry (1:23).

1:19-22. *Stoic philosophers argued that the nature of God was evident in creation; *Cicero at that time could even assert that no race of humanity was so uncivilized as to deny the existence of the gods, and along with others he argued that the human mind points to what God is like. Jewish people scattered throughout the Greco-Roman world used this argument to persuade pagans to turn to the true God. Even the *rabbis tell delightful stories about how Abraham reasoned back to the first cause and showed his fellow *Gentiles that there was really only one true God. According to Jewish tradition, God had given seven laws to Noah, for which all humanity was responsible (including the prohibition of idolatry). But unlike Israel, who had to keep all 613 commandments in the *law (according to rabbinic count), most Gentiles disobeyed even the seven laws of Noah.

1:23. In later Jewish tradition, idolatry was the final stage of sin to which the evil impulse (see comment on 7:10-11) would reduce a person; it was one of the worst sins. Yet the language Paul uses to describe *pagan* idolatry is drawn from *Old Testament passages about *Israel's* idolatry (Deut 4:16-20; Ps 106:20; Jer 2:11); this is a setup for his argument for Jewish readers in chapter 2.

1:24-32
Other Pagan Deeds

Pagan gods acted immorally in the popular myths; one who worshiped them (1:23) would end up acting the same way. Paul argues that distorting one's view about God's character perverts one's sexual treatment of other people; ancient Jewish people recognized that both idolatry and sexual immorality characterized *Gentiles.

1:24-25. The refrain "God gave them over" (1:24, 26, 28) tells how God's wrath (1:18) works: he lets people damn themselves as they warp their own humanity. As in the Old Testament, God can turn people over to their own hardness of heart (e.g., Is 6:9-11; 29:9-12; Jer 44:25-27; some writers have called this "penal blindness"); cf. Psalm 81:12 (about Israel).

1:26-27. Greek men were commonly bisexual; not only was homosexual behavior approved (some writers, like speakers in Plato's *Symposium,* preferred it to heterosexual behavior), but elements of the culture socialized boys in this direction. Men and women were segregated growing up, and male bonds became close. Apparently due to a deficiency in the number of women (which many attribute to female infanticide), marriages were often made between thirty-year-old men and fourteen-year-old women, whom the men saw as children. Men had access to only three forms of sexual release until such late marriages: slaves, prostitutes and other men. (Introducing boys to homoerotic pleasure was a favorite pastime of Greek men in this period.)

Although many upper-class Romans were affected by Greek ideals, many other Romans, especially Roman philosophers, regarded homosexual practice as disgusting. Greco-Roman moralists sometimes opposed gender reversal as "against nature," which would resemble the Jewish argument from God's original purposes in creation (Gen 2:18). Although Jewish texts speak of Jewish adulterers and thieves, they nearly always treat homosexual behavior as a *Gentile practice. (Socialization clearly affected one's sexual development.)

Paul did not choose this example of sin to be controversial with his readers; his Jewish and Roman Christian readers alike would have agreed with him that both idolatry and homosexual behavior are sinful. But this example is a setup for his critique of sins less often denounced (Rom 1:28-32).

1:28-32. Ancient writers (Greek, Roman, Jewish; cf. also Lev 18) sometimes employed "vice lists," as here. But unlike idolatry and homosexuality (Rom 1:18-27), sins like greed, jealousy, slander, arrogance and ignorance also occur in Jewish lists as sins some Jewish people committed. Like Amos (see Amos 1—2), Paul here sets up his readers for chapter 2: pagans are not the only ones who are damned.

2:1-11 No Partiality

Paul engages in a lively *diatribe style (a style ancient philosophers often adopted), challenging an imaginary opponent and thereby demolishing possible objections to his position in a vivid manner.

2:1-3. Speakers typically argued on the basis of syllogisms, which consisted of a major premise (here, 2:1), a minor premise (2:2) and a conclusion (2:3). Both philosophers and Jewish teachers accepted that people should live what they preach, hence few could dispute Paul's point. Philosophers saw sin as a moral folly, and Jewish teachers saw it as an affront to God but as something everyone did. Paul demands that people be consistent with their denunciations, which meant taking sin more seriously than most people did.

2:4. The *Old Testament and Judaism agreed that only God's *grace made *repentance possible (e.g., Deut 30:6). This principle never denied a person's responsibility to respond to that grace once it was offered (e.g., Deut 5:29; 10:16).

2:5. The Old Testament prophets often referred to "the day of wrath" (the "day of the Lord"), when God sat as judge in his court and judged the world by his justice (e.g., Is 2:11-12; 13:6, 9, 13; Ezek 30:2-3; Joel 1:15; 2:1-2, 31; 3:14; Amos 5:18-20; Obad 15; Zeph 1:7; 1:14—2:2; Mal 3:2; 4:5). Some Jewish traditions speak of treasuring up good works against the day of wrath, but the *rhetorical opponent Paul addresses here has stored up the opposite (cf. Deut 32:34-35; Hos 13:12).

2:6-11. On verse 6 cf. Psalm 62:12 and Proverbs 24:12. The structure of this passage is chiastic (i.e., inverted parallelism, an ancient literary form): God's impartiality (vv. 6, 11); to doers of good (vv. 7a, 10b), future rewards (vv. 7b, 10a); to the wicked (vv. 8a, 9b), punishment (vv. 8b, 9a).

Justice in judging was widely emphasized, and God's impartiality was one of the most commonly stressed doctrines of Judaism (although Israel's preferential treatment at the day of judgment was also explained as righteous). Judaism also acknowledged that the wise person worked for long-range rewards (2:7; cf. Prov 21:21; 22:4).

2:12-16
Stricter Judgment

Paul's point is that everyone should know better than to sin, but those with more access to the truth will be judged far more strictly than those without. Woe to those who thought themselves righteous by comparing themselves with others! Judaism was right that most pagans did evil; but Jewish people knew God's standard better than the pagans and still did evil. This point underlines Paul's argument of the common predicament of Jews and *Gentiles under sin.

2:12. Paul is stricter than most of Judaism here. Most Jews acknowledged that Gentiles could be saved simply by keeping the Noahide (also spelled Noachian) commandments (see comment on 1:19-20), because they did not have the whole *law. Paul argues that anyone who has sinned with or without the law will be strictly judged (unless atonement for the sin is accepted in Christ, as he argues in 3:24-26).

2:13. Jewish teachers agreed that hearing the law was not enough; one must also obey it. Few would challenge Paul's argument on this point.

2:14-16. Paul plays on the Greco-Roman philosophical view of the law of nature written in people's hearts, according to which all people had some measure of innate knowledge of right and wrong, although it was less explicit than the written law. (Greek moralists and especially *Stoic thinkers heavily emphasized the knowledge of the "conscience.") That they could know enough to do right some of the time renders them without excuse for ever doing wrong. Only when God's law is fully written on the heart in Christ (8:2; Jer 31:33) will it be internalized enough for people to live out God's righteousness.

2:17-24
Disobeying the Law

This *diatribe style often used by philosophers was meant to teach and exhort rather than to attack; the imaginary opponent represents an idealized wrong position, which the speaker or writer destroys *reductio ad absurdum* (by reducing it to its absurd logical conclusion). The opponent of 2:17-29 is the idealized hypocrite but points up the evils of any measure of hypocrisy. (Similar attacks were made on "pretentious philosophers" in Greco-Roman diatribes.)

2:17-18. Jewish sages often warned that sages should be humble and not boast in their knowledge. But Israel could boast in their sole possession of the *law, because they alone worshiped the one true God.

2:19-20. Some of Paul's language here comes from the *Old Testament (cf. Is 42:6-7, 18-20) and some from typical *Cynic-*Stoic philosophical terminology, which was probably adapted by Jewish teachers outside Palestine. Paul again shows his mastery in relating to his ancient readers.

2:21-23. *Diatribe often used brief, pointed rhetorical questions. Philosophers typically reviled the inconsistency of their hearers' lifestyles. Temple robbery was considered one of the most impious crimes, and even though Jewish teachers warned against disturbing pagan temples, pagans sometimes thought Jews inclined toward such crimes (Acts 19:37). But those who would rob temples would have to value their contents.

2:24. See Ezekiel 36:20-23. Jewish teachers complained that public sin profaned God's name among the *Gentiles; misbehaving Jews could bring reproach on the whole Jewish community. (A case in point was a charlatan in Rome earlier in the century whose behavior had led to the expulsion of Jews from Rome under Tiberius.)

2:25-29
True Judaism

Moses had complained that Israel was uncircumcised in heart (Lev 26:41), and the prophets had reinforced this conviction (Jer 4:4; 9:25-26; cf. Is 51:7). God's people were responsible to circumcise their hearts (Deut 10:16), and someday God would circumcise their hearts (Deut 30:6). The *rabbis commented little on this issue; Paul makes it central and defines religious Judaism in terms of possession of the *Spirit (Rom 2:29; an internalized law—8:2; cf. Ezek 36:27). Both Jewish and Greco-Roman writers emphasized caring what the deity thinks, not what other people think (Rom 2:29).

3:1-8
God's Justice: Why Then Israel?

Jewishness was special—but not for salvation. Some might object that Paul thinks God had been unfaithful to his covenant, in which case God would be unjust; but the issue here is that Israel had been unfaithful to the covenant, not that God had been.

3:1. These are the objections of the imaginary interlocutor, a common device for furthering one's argument in a *diatribe (see comment on 2:1-11). The objections are reasonable: was not Israel a special, chosen people? Determining "profit" (KJV) or "benefit" (NASB) was a common device among philosophers for evaluating the worth of a behavior or idea.

3:2. *Digression, even long digression, was a normal part of Greco-Roman writing; Paul develops and completes this "first of all" only in chapter 9. Judaism often emphasized that God entrusted his *law to Israel, and Paul here agrees.

3:3. "What then?" was a common *rhetorical question used to further the argument of a *diatribe. God's faithfulness to his covenant was good long-term news for Israel as a whole; as in the *Old Testament (e.g., in Moses' generation, contrary to some Jewish tradition), however, it did not save individual Israelites who broke covenant with him.

3:4. "May it never be!" (NASB) or "Not at all!" (NIV) was also a common rhetorical retort to the rhetorical questions of imaginary opponents (especially in some philosophers like *Epictetus). It was used to show the absurdity of the opposing objection. Paul declares that God's justice is ultimately unassailable, as wrongdoers must confess (Ps 51:4; cf. 116:11).

3:5-6. "In human terms" (NASB) or "a human argument" (NIV) is similar to a *rabbinic phrase meaning "a secular argument." God's "righteousness" here is his "justice" (NRSV), as defined in terms of his faithfulness to his covenant word to Israel (3:3).

3:7. "Sinner" was an awful insult in Jewish circles; for Paul to call *everyone* sinners (Rom 1—2) would be shocking. God could be glorified and his justice vindicated even by its contrast with human rebellion, but this point in no way vindicated the rebellion.

3:8. Philosophers also often had to clear up misrepresentations of their teaching.

3:9-18
Proof from Scripture

Stringing together texts ("pearl stringing") was common at the opening of *synagogue homilies and in the *Dead Sea Scrolls.

3:9. Another objection from the imaginary protester allows Paul to return to his argument that Jew and *Gentile are equally in need of salvation. To be "under" sin was idiomatic for being subject to its rule.

3:10-12. Here Paul quotes Psalm 14:1-3 (=53:1-3; cf. 1 Kings 8:46; Ps 130:3; 143:2; Prov 20:9; Eccles 7:20).

3:13-18. The principle for attaching these proof texts to one another is similar to the *rabbinic principle of *gezerah shavah* (which linked Old Testament texts by a key word). All these verses mention body parts: throat, tongue, lips and mouth (3:13-14; respectively, Ps 5:9; 140:3; 10:7); feet (Rom 3:15-17; Is 59:7-8); and eyes (Rom 3:18; Ps 36:1). Jewish teachers emphasized that the evil impulse (see comment on Rom 7:10-11) ruled all the parts of the body (by later enumeration, 248 parts). The preponderance of mouth-related sins here may be intentional, especially if Roman Christians are complaining about each other (see chap. 14).

3:19-31
The Law and Righteousness

3:19. The Jewish people were those "under" (see comment on v. 9) the *law; "the law" could loosely include the Psalms and the Prophets (the rest of the *Old Testament), as in 3:10-18. People were "silenced" in a law court when they could raise no objections in their own defense (cf. Ps 107:42; Job 40:4-5; 42:6).

3:20. Most of Judaism also agreed that all people sinned sometimes and that they needed God's *grace; although some Jews suggested exceptions, they considered them extremely rare. Paul here forces his readers to be consistent and to recognize that *Gentiles would thus be saved on the same terms as Jews. This verse echoes Psalm 143:2, a psalm that goes on to praise God's righteousness and faithfulness. The Greek text has literally "all flesh will not be justified" (for which most translations use some variant of the less awkward English "no flesh will be justified"—NASB); "all flesh" is a standard Hebrew expression for all humanity (or, in some contexts, for all creatures).

3:21. "The Law and the Prophets" was one way to speak of the whole Old Testament; in chapter 4 Paul will argue how these texts teach righteousness by faith (v. 22). But God's justice is not dependent on human performance of the law and thus not based on an advantage available only to Israel (3:2). Jewish teachers believed that Israel was special with regard to salvation and that their reception of the law at Sinai vindicated God's choice of them.

3:22. "No distinction" (NASB, NRSV) refers to Jew and *Gentile; both must approach God on the same terms, through Jesus Christ. This statement directly challenges the values behind the tensions in the Roman *church (see discussion of the situation in the introduction to Romans).

3:23. Judaism viewed "sin" as a moral offense against God (in contrast to the less dramatic usual Greek sense of the term). Jewish sources agreed that everyone sinned (with rare exceptions, like a young child); Greek moralists said that some faults were inevitable. "Falling short of God's glory" may allude to the Jewish idea that humanity lost God's glory when Adam sinned (cf. 5:12-21), hence each generation repeats Adam's sin; or it may simply mean that no one lives up to God's standard of justice.

3:24. "Redemption" (freeing a slave) was a standard *Old Testament concept; the Old Testament terms always involve the paying of a price, sometimes to get something back. God "redeemed" Israel, making them his people by *grace and by paying a price for their freedom (the Passover lamb and the firstborn of Egypt), before he gave them his commandments (cf. Ex 20:2). In Paul's day, the Jewish people were looking forward to the *messianic redemption, when they would be delivered from earthly rulers; but the malevolent ruler here is sin (3:9).

3:25. To "propitiate" (KJV, NASB) God was to turn away his wrath; although in Jewish tradition prayers, alms and other good deeds could turn away wrath (Ecclus 3:3, 20; 32:1-3; Wisdom of Solomon 18:20-21), the *law also required bloodshed: something had to die to appease the wrath properly due a person's sin. The term here may refer to the mercy seat (Ex 25:22). God mercifully "passed over" (Ex 12:13) sins before the cross, in anticipation of the sacrifice that would take place there. (One might compare the *rabbinic view that *repentance defers judgment until the Day of Atonement atones for sin, although nothing in the text suggests that Paul has this idea in mind here.)

3:26. To the Greek mind, justice meant "fair [but not necessarily equal] distribution" (the inequality of justice may be illustrated in that Roman law assigned higher penalties to lower social classes); it was nevertheless agreed that magistrates should rule according to "justice." Judaism emphasized God's justice and recognized that he, like a just judge, could not simply acquit the guilty. Jewish texts in time developed a rift in God's character: his attribute of mercy pleaded before him on Israel's behalf, triumphing over the accusations of his attribute of justice.

Paul allows no such rift; he says that God could be just and simultaneously vindicate as just those who depend on Jesus, only because the sentence of wrath was executed on Jesus in their place (3:25). The rest of Judaism believed in God's *grace; the differences between Paul and his Jewish contemporaries here are that Paul insists that this grace came at such a great price to God, and that *Gentiles can receive it on the same terms as Jewish people.

3:27-28. "Principle" (NIV) is a mistranslation; Paul poses two ways of approaching the "*law" (NASB): by human effort or by faith (cf. 7:6; 8:2; 9:31-32). Faith is the right way, which the law itself teaches (3:21, 31).

3:29-30. The basic confession of Judaism was God's oneness. Paul thus argues: if there is only one God, he must also be God of the *Gentiles (see Is 45:21-25).

3:31. Jewish teaching contrasted "annulling" and "establishing" the law. Because the law teaches righteousness by faith (as Paul goes on to argue in chap. 4), anyone who teaches this idea upholds the law.

4:1-22
Abraham Made Righteous by Faith

As Israel's ancestor, Abraham was regarded as the model for their faith; he was also regarded as the model *proselyte (convert to Judaism), because he was considered a *Gentile before his circumcision. Jewish readers believed that they had been chosen in Abraham and that virtually every Israelite would be saved by God's *grace if they maintained the covenant. Gentiles who wished to become part of the chosen community, however, had to be circumcised and join Israel in doing the righteous deeds of the *law, as Abraham did.

This chapter is a good Jewish *midrash, or commentary, on Genesis 15:6. Jewish and Greco-Roman debaters often proved their cases by examples, and this text was a favorite example used by ancient Jewish teachers.

4:1. *Diatribes typically used rhetorical questions such as "What shall we say then?" as transitions to the next point. Jewish tradition spoke repeatedly of "our father Abraham."

4:2. If anyone was righteous in Jewish tradition, it was surely Abraham. The model *Pharisee, he served God from love; the model *proselyte, he brought many other *Gentiles to faith in the one true God. He destroyed idols and stood for God's truth. These extrabiblical Jewish traditions often declared that Abraham's merit sustained or rescued Israel in subsequent generations.

4:3. *Rabbis appealed to biblical citations, sometimes prefacing them with, "What does Scripture say?" Jewish teachers often commented on Abraham's faith as reflected in Genesis 15:6, which they read as "faithfulness," one of his works. Paul reads it contextually as dependence on God's promise and stresses the word "reckon" (NASB) or "credit" (NIV), a bookkeeping term used in ancient business document for crediting payment to one's account.

4:4-5. Still expounding Genesis 15:6, Paul refers here to Abraham. This "reckoning righteousness" is comparable to the kind of justification one has in a law court—acquittal as one not guilty. But this idea goes beyond a mere declaration of forgiveness, and no ancient Jewish reader would have limited God's pronouncement of acquittal to merely legal terms: when God speaks, he creates a new reality (Gen 1:3); see Romans 6:1-11.

4:6-8. Using the Jewish interpretive principle *gezerah shavah*, which links different texts containing the same key word or phrase, Paul introduces Psalm 32:1-2, which explains what "reckons" means. Omitting the next line on moral righteousness (not yet relevant to his point), Paul recognizes that the "reckoning" of the psalm is based on God's grace rather than on the psalmist's perfection (Ps 32:5). Psalm 32 was ascribed to David.

4:9. The "blessedness" (NIV) or "blessing" (NASB) here is that of which 4:7-8 spoke; in standard Jewish fashion, Paul expounds the details of the text he has cited.

4:10. Here Paul appeals to another Jewish interpretive rule—context. Abraham was made righteous by faith over thirteen years before he was circumcised (Gen 15:6; 16:3-4, 16; 17:24-25; some Jewish interpreters made this even longer—twenty-nine years). This fact challenged the great significance Judaism gave to circumcision, although Jewish teachers were correct that the *Old Testament had used it as the mark of the covenant.

4:11-12. Circumcision was the "sign" of the covenant (Gen 17:11; *Jubilees 15:26); but Paul interprets it also as a sign of Abraham's *prior* righteousness according to Genesis 15:6. Jewish ears would recoil at Paul's argument, which makes *Gentile Christians full heirs of Abraham without circumcision. It is one thing to say that uncircumcised Gentiles could be saved if they kept the seven Noahide laws, as many Jews believed; it is quite another to put them on the same level as the Jewish people.

4:13. Abraham was told that he would inherit the "land"; but in Hebrew the word for "the land" also means "the earth," and Jewish interpreters had long been declaring that Abraham and his descendants would inherit the whole world to come.

4:14-16. Paul forces the reader to choose between completed righteousness by faith (based on God's *grace; Judaism acknowledged grace) and completed righteousness by a knowledge of the *law, which would have made Israel more righteous than the Gentiles, regardless of faith.

4:17. Judaism agreed that God could speak things into being (e.g., Gen 1:3). Paul says that God's promise to Abraham was thus enough to transform Gentiles into his children (especially because God decreed Abraham father of many nations just before telling him to be circumcised—Gen 17:5).

4:18-22. Faith as defined in Abraham's experience is not passive assent to what God says; it is an enduring dependence on God's promise, on which one stakes one's life and lives accordingly. On the level of meaning, Paul and James (Jas 2:14-26) would agree. It is possible, although far from certain, that Paul's analogy here alludes to the offering and survival of Isaac, Abraham's son (Gen 22).

4:23—5:11
The Believer Declared Righteous

No one could boast before God (2:17; 3:27; 4:2), but there is cause for a different kind of boast in hope of restored glory (5:2; cf. 3:23), in tribulation (5:3) and in God through Christ (5:11).

4:23-25. Paul begins to apply his exposition about Abraham to his readers (the application carries through 5:11). Ancient teachers (Jewish and Greco-Roman) often used examples to exhort their hearers or readers to think and act differently.

5:1. "Peace" meant a relationship of concord between two persons much more often than it meant individual tranquillity; thus here Paul means that the believer is always on God's side.

5:2. "Hope of God's glory" may imply the restoration of Adam's "glory" (3:23); it probably alludes to the *Old Testament *prophecies that God would be glorified among his people (e.g., Is 40:3; 60:19; 61:3; 62:2).

5:3-4. Progressions like this one (tribulations, endurance, character, hope) represent a special literary and *rhetorical form called concatenation, also found in other texts. Again Paul demonstrates his skill in making his point in culturally relevant ways. Philosophers emphasized that hardships proved the quality of the wise person, who knew better than to be moved by them; the truly wise person should be tranquil in hardships. The Old Testament and Jewish tradition show men and women of God tested and matured by trials (although the Old Testament also includes the internal struggles of its heroes, like David and Jeremiah, rather than their continual tranquillity).

5:5. Jewish people viewed the *Holy Spirit especially as the Spirit who had enabled the prophets to hear and speak for God. In this context, Paul means that the Spirit points to the cross (5:6-8) and so enables Christians to hear God's love for them. In many Jewish traditions, the Spirit was available only to those most worthy; here he is bestowed as a gift. On the Spirit being "poured out" see Joel 2:28.

5:6-9. Well-educated Greco-Roman readers were aware of the Greek tradition in which "the good man" was extremely rare. Greeks considered laying down one's life for someone else heroic, but such sacrifice was not common; among Jewish people it was not particularly praised.

5:10-11. Greeks spoke of people in opposition to each other being "reconciled," being made friends again, but did not speak of people being reconciled to *God*. The Jewish members of the Roman *church would be more familiar with this sort of language (from the Old Testament and some early Jewish texts like 2 Maccabees), hence it could strike the *Gentile members more forcefully (if they had not already heard it in *church).

5:12-21
A Common Heritage in Sin and Righteousness

Paul's Jewish readers might have argued for their unique descent from Abraham the righteous, but Paul points them instead to their common descent with the *Gentiles from the line of Adam the sinner. His argument would have greater force to his Jewish readers than Genesis alone might imply, because their traditions had made Adam much more prominent than he had been in the *Old Testament (he is hardly mentioned outside Genesis).

Jewish people in this period sometimes spoke of Adam's immense size (he filled the whole earth!), or more often of his glory, which he lost at the Fall. They believed that his sin introduced sin and thus death into the world, and that all his descendants shared in his guilt.

Jewish interpreters generally believed that Adam's glory would be restored to the righteous in the world to come. (The structure of Genesis, from Adam to Noah [5:29; 9:1-2, 7] to Abraham [12:1-3] and so on, suggests that God was working to restore humanity, and from Abraham's line the deliverer of Gen 3:15 would finally come.)

5:12-14. "All sinned" (v. 12), even those who, unlike Adam (v. 14), had no direct law to disobey (v. 13). Paul is not, however, denying personal responsibility for sin on the part of Adam's descendants. Jewish writers claimed that Adam brought sin and death into the world (4 Ezra 7:118; *2 Baruch 54:15), but they also believed that each of his descendants made his or her own choice to follow in Adam's footsteps (4 Ezra 7:118-26; 2 Baruch 54:15), becoming each "our own Adam" (2 Baruch 54:19).

5:15. "The many" here could refer, as in the *Dead Sea Scrolls, only to the elect; but if Paul meant this, he would also only be claiming that the elect were damned in Adam. More likely, "the many" is an allusion to Isaiah 53:11, where the suffering servant would justify "the many" by becoming a sacrifice on their account. All who were in Adam by birth became sinners; all who were in Christ by true *baptism (6:4) became righteous.

5:16-21. Much of the argument of 5:15-21 is a standard Jewish argument, *qal vahomer,* an argument from lesser to greater ("how much more"). Greco-Roman logic also used this interpretive technique; many Jewish ways of arguing from Scripture were part of the general interpretive methodology of antiquity.

Jewish people believed that Israel would reign in the life of the world to come (cf. 5:17), as Adam and Eve reigned before the fall (Gen 1:26-27).

6:1-11
Dead to Sin

6:1-5. For Jewish people, *baptism was the act by which non-Jews converted to Judaism, the final removal of *Gentile impurity; by it one turned one's back on life in paganism and sin, vowed to follow God's commandments, and became a new person with regard to Jewish law. A person who became a follower of Jesus likewise gave up his or her old life; through participation with Christ's death, Paul says, their death to the old life in sin, which was crucified in Christ, is an accomplished fact.

Ancient Near Eastern religions had long had traditions of dying-and-rising gods, general vegetation deities renewed annually in the spring. Some ancient sources, especially early Christian interpretations of these religions, suggest that initiates into various *mystery cults "died and rose with" the deity. Scholars early in the twentieth century naturally saw in this tradition the background for Paul's language here. Although the evidence is still disputed, it is not certain that the mysteries saw a once-for-all dying-and-rising in baptism, as in Paul, until after Christianity became a widespread religious force in the Roman Empire that some other religious groups imitated. More important, the early Christian view of *resurrection is certainly derived from the Jewish doctrine rather than from the seasonal revivification of Greek cults.

6:6-7. The "old man" ("old self" in many translations) is life in Adam versus life in Christ (5:12-21). When a Gentile slave escaped from a Jewish owner and converted to Judaism by baptism, in Jewish legal theory his or her new personhood made the slave free from the former owner.

6:8-11. Jewish teachers believed that the "evil impulse" (see comment on 7:14-25) would trouble even the most pious until the time of the *Messiah, when the evil impulse would be slain. For Paul, the Messiah has come, and sin's power has been killed. The finished work of Christ means that the believer has already died to sin and now needs to acknowledge this—to "reckon" it done in faith (6:11; this is the same term for God's reckoning righteousness in chap. 4). Such faith in God's complete work was not common in ancient religion, nor is it in most religions today.

6:12-23
Free from Sin, Servants of Righteousness

6:12-13. "Instruments" (NASB, NIV) could be more specifically translated "weapons," as in 13:12. If that image is in view here, the image of presenting oneself (more than in 12:1) could allude to soldiers presenting themselves for battle (although it is as slaves reporting for duty in v. 16).

6:14-21. Some scholars have seen here the idea of "sacral manumission": a slave could be freed from the service of one master by officially becoming the property of a god and the god's temple. What is much more clear is that many philosophers regularly used "slavery" and "freedom" in the sense of slavery to false ideas and pleasure, and freedom from such ideas and pleasure as well as from their consequences, like anxiety. Philosophers often emphasized being one's own master.

Judaism could speak of being free from sin. Jewish teachers believed that because Israel had the *law, the evil impulse that made the *Gentiles sinful could not enslave them. They also taught that Israel had become God's slaves when they were freed from slavery in Egypt.

6:22. In the *Old Testament, Israel was "sanctified" (NASB, NRSV) or set apart as special for God; in standard Jewish teaching, *eternal life was the life of the world to come, inaugurated at the *resurrection from the dead.

6:23. Slaves could and often did receive some "wages." Although the slave's owner legally owned the slave's possessions, the slave could use this property or money (called a *peculium*), sometimes even to purchase freedom. That such wages were normally a positive symbol makes Paul's words here all the more striking.

7:1-6
Dead to and Freed from the Law

The Jewish people believed that they

were saved by God's gracious choosing, not by meticulous observation of the commandments. Nevertheless, with few exceptions they kept the commandments as best they knew how, and this set them apart from *Gentiles, who did not behave as righteously as Israel did. Paul here addresses another major divider between Jew and Gentile in his effort to bring the two together (see the introduction to Romans), because even a Gentile who converted to Judaism would take years to know the *law as well as a Jewish person who had been raised in it did.

7:1. Some later Jewish teachers argued that one who converted to Judaism was a new person—to such an extent that one's former relatives no longer counted as relatives. Paul can use this line of reasoning differently: just as a person became dead to his or her old master (here, sin) at conversion (see comment on 6:1-5), that person became dead to the old law in which he or she was held.

7:2-4. According to biblical law, both death and divorce severed previous relationships; Paul emphasizes the one that fits his analogy in the context. (Because one never spoke of a woman's former husband as her "husband" after the divorce, no one would have understood Paul's words here as ruling out certain kinds of divorce; cf. 1 Cor 7:15.)

7:5. Philosophers often contrasted reason (which was good) with the passions (which were bad); Jewish teachers came to speak of these in terms of the good and evil impulse. See comment on 7:15-25.

7:6. Most of Judaism felt that the *Spirit had departed from Israel with the prophets and would only return with the *Messiah's coming; here Paul contrasts the new act of God in the coming of the Spirit with the old instructions only written on tablets (cf. Ezek 36:26-27). Greek interpreters had traditionally distinguished between interpreting laws according to principles and according to exact wording; Palestinian Jewish interpretation was very interested in the exact wording (sometimes even literally to "letters" and spellings of words).

7:7-13
Sin Unfairly Exploited the Law

Scholars dispute whether Paul here refers literally to his own past life or uses "I" generically for sinners under the *law. Because there is more precedent for teachers using themselves in illustrations (e.g., Phil 3:4-8) than for them using "I" (as opposed to a *rhetorical "you" or "one") generically (but cf. 1 Cor 13:1), Paul probably uses his own previous experience under law, viewed in retrospect, to illustrate life under law in general.

7:7-8. The opening rhetorical question is the natural one after the parallelism of 6:1-23 with 7:1-6. "You must not covet" is the tenth of the Ten Commandments, the only one that goes directly beyond one's actions to the state of one's heart. The point is that one might not regard coveting as transgressing God's law if one were not so informed by the law.

7:9. When a Jewish boy came of age around thirteen (as in the later *bar mitzvah,* similar to Roman coming-of-age rituals), he became officially responsible for keeping the commandments. Paul may refer to something even earlier in his life, because Jewish boys in upper-class Jewish homes began to be schooled in the law at age five.

7:10-11. Jewish teachers recognized the power of human sin (the evil impulse), but said that study of the law enabled one to overcome it, and that the law brings life. Paul says that the law became instead the vehicle of his death. (Some scholars think that "deceived" alludes to Gen 3:13, where Eve was deceived and death entered the world. If Adam were speaking in the verse, it would fit Rom 5:12-21 better. Although "sinned and died" alludes back to 5:12-21, it is less clear that Paul alludes to Adam here.)

7:12-13. Paul argues in Romans that Jew and *Gentile come to God on the same terms (see the introduction to Romans), and that the law is not a direct advantage for salvation (2:12-15), although it is valuable for knowing more *about* salvation (3:2). His whole purpose in this section is to explain that the problem is not the law; it is human sinfulness that leads people to disobey the law in their hearts.

7:14-25
The Struggle of Human Effort Under the Law

Many commentators have thought that 7:14-25 describes Paul's struggle with sin at the time he was writing the passage, because he uses present-tense verbs. But *diatribe style, which Paul uses in much of Romans, was graphic in its images, and Paul in the context has been describing his past life under *law (7:7-13). Thus it is more likely that Paul contrasts the spiritual worthlessness of religious introspection and self-centeredness (count the "I's" and "me's") in Romans 7 with the life of the *Spirit by *grace in Romans 6 and 8.

Jewish teachers said that *repentance and learning the law were the only present cures for the evil impulse; here Paul replies that knowing moral truth had not freed him from sin. But Judaism also believed that in the day of judgment the evil impulse would be eradicated. As some *rabbis later put it, "God will take the evil impulse out in the sight of the nations and slay it"; or as Paul put it, Christians are dead to sin and freed from its power (chap. 6). Paul's point in the context is that one must receive righteousness (including the power to live rightly) as a gift of God's grace, not as an achievement by human effort (cf. 1:17; 8:4). (This reading of the passage accords with most Greek, as against most Latin, church fathers.)

7:14. On "flesh" (NASB, NRSV) in the sense of human sinfulness, see comment on 8:1-11. The *Old Testament spoke of God's selling his people into bondage to their enemies, and of God's redeeming his people from slavery to their enemies. Selling into bondage is the opposite of redemption, of freedom from sin in 6:18, 20 and 22. That the law is "spiritual" means that it is inspired by the *Spirit (see comment on Spirit in 8:1-11).

7:15-22. Philosophers spoke of an internal conflict between the reason and the passions; Jewish teachers spoke of a conflict between the good and evil impulse. Either could identify with Paul's contrast between his mind or reason—knowing what was right—and his members in which passions or the evil impulse worked.

7:23. Other moral teachers also described the struggle between reason and passions (or against the evil impulse) in military terms; see comment on 13:12 (cf. also 7:8, 11: "opportunity" was sometimes used in terms of military strategy).

7:24. "Wretched man that I am!" was a standard cry of despair, mourning or self-reproach; some philosophers complained that this was their state, imprisoned in a mortal body. When they spoke of being freed from their mortal bodies, however, they meant that they would be freed simply by death; Paul's freedom came by death with Christ (6:1-11).

7:25. Paul summarizes 7:7-24 here:

the dual allegiance of the person trying to achieve righteousness only by human effort, without becoming a new creation in Christ.

8:1-11 People of the Spirit Versus People of the Flesh

In the *Old Testament "flesh" could designate any mortal creature but especially designated human beings. It connoted weakness and mortality, especially when contrasted with God and his *Spirit (Gen 6:3; Is 31:3; cf. Ps 78:39). By the *New Testament period, this connotation of weakness was extended to moral weakness, as in the *Dead Sea Scrolls, and could be translated "human susceptibility to sin," or "self-centeredness" as opposed to "God-centeredness." A life ruled by the flesh is a life dependent on finite human effort and resources, a selfish life as opposed to one directed by God's Spirit. Paul's use of "flesh" and "Spirit" refers to two spheres of existence—in Adam or in Christ—not to two natures in a person.

"Flesh" per se is not evil in the New Testament writings; Christ "became flesh" (Jn 1:14), though not "sinful flesh" (Rom 8:3). (The NIV translation "sinful nature" can be misleading, because some people today think of spirit and flesh as two natures within a person, whereas "Spirit" here is *God's* Spirit—it is not a special part of a person but the power of God's presence. Romans 7:15-25 describes a struggle of two aspects of human personality—reason and passions—trying to fulfill divine morality by human effort; but this struggle is not in view here, where people either live that struggle by the flesh or accept God's gift of righteousness by the Spirit. The radical bifurcation of a human being into a morally upright "spiritual" part versus an immoral "bodily" part is a Neo-Platonic idea foreign to Paul. It was first introduced into the interpretation of the New Testament by *Gnostics and would not have been the natural interpretation to Jewish readers or to *Gentile Christians who knew about the Spirit.)

But flesh, mere bodily existence and human strength, is mortal and inadequate to stand against sin (which abuses bodily members that could have been harnessed instead by the Spirit). Although the term is used flexibly in the Bible, in one sense we *are* flesh (especially in the Old Testament use of the term); the problem is not that people are flesh but that they live life their own way instead of by God's power and *grace. The New Testament does sometimes distinguish the human body from the soul, but this distinction is not the point of the contrast between walking according to the flesh and walking according to the Spirit (8:4).

The Spirit especially anointed God's people to prophesy in the Old Testament but also endowed them with power to do other things. Here, as in the *Dead Sea Scrolls and occasionally in the Old Testament, the Spirit enables a person to live rightly (see especially Ezek 36:27). In Judaism, the Spirit indicated God's presence; here the Spirit communicates the very presence, power and character of Christ.

8:1-4. Paul's point here is that whether the law brings life or death depends on whether it is written in one's heart by the Spirit (Ezek 36:27) or practiced as an external standard of righteousness, which is unattainable by human effort (cf. 3:27; 9:31-32; 10:6-8).

8:5-8. Philosophers often urged people to set their minds on eternal things rather than on the transitory affairs of this world. *Philo condemned those whose minds were taken up with the matters of the body and its pleasures. Philosophers divided humanity into the enlightened and the foolish; Judaism divided humanity into Israel and the *Gentiles. Paul here divides humanity into two classes: those who have the *Spirit (Christians) and those left to their own devices.

Some people believed that inspiration came only when the human mind was emptied, as in some Eastern mysticism. But Paul speaks of the "mind of the Spirit" as well as the "mind of the flesh." Instead of opposing reason and inspiration, he contrasts reasoning that is merely human (and thus susceptible to sin) with reasoning that is directed by God's inspiration.

8:9. Most Jewish people did not claim to have the Spirit; they believed that the Spirit would be made available only in the time of the end. After the *Messiah had come, all those who were truly God's people would have the Spirit working in them (cf. Is 44:3; 59:21; Ezek 39:29).

8:10. Jewish people in this period usually distinguished soul and body, just as the Greeks did, although for Jews the division usually functioned only at death. (Some Jewish writers were more influenced by Greek categories than others.) But Paul does not say here that the (human) "spirit is alive" (NIV, NASB); literally, he claims that the "Spirit is life" (KJV, NRSV, TEV). Thus he means that the body was still under death's sentence, but the Spirit who indwells believers would ultimately resurrect their bodies (8:11).

8:11. Jewish people believed that God would raise the dead at the end of the age. Paul modifies this teaching by only one step: God has already raised Jesus, and this event is a sure sign that the rest of the *resurrection will happen someday.

8:12-17
Led by the Spirit

The Jewish people looked back to their deliverance from Egypt as their first redemption and looked forward to the *Messiah's coming as a new exodus, God's ultimate act of salvation. In this hope they were prefigured by the prophets, who often portrayed the future deliverance in terms of the exodus from Egypt (e.g., Hos 11:1, 5, 11).

8:12-13. Those who lived according to the flesh (as bodily creatures in their own strength) would die, but those who lived by the *eschatological *Spirit (the Spirit who in most Jewish thought and often in the *Old Testament prophets characterizes the life of the age to come) would be *resurrected by him; see comment on 8:1-11 and 8:10-11.

8:14. The Old Testament often comments that God "led" Israel through the wilderness (Ex 15:13; Deut 3:2; Ps 77:20; 78:52; 106:9; 136:16; Jer 2:6, 17; Hos 11:4; Amos 2:10; for the new exodus, see Is 48:20-21; Jer 23:7-8) and called Israel his "sons" or "children" when he redeemed them from Egypt (Ex 4:22; Deut 14:1; 32:5, 18-20; Ps 29:1; Is 1;2, 4; 43:6; 45:11; 63:8; Jer 3:19, 22; Hos 1:10; 11:1, 10). In both devotional and historical language, God's leading was sometimes associated with his Spirit (Neh 9:20; Ps 143:10; Is 63:14).

8:15. Here Paul again plays on the idea of the exodus from Egypt; God's glory led his people forward, not back toward slavery (cf. Ex 13:21; Neh 9:12; Ps 78:14; for new exodus, Is 58:8; Zech 2:5). He adopted them as his children (cf. 9:4). On "Abba" see comment on Mark 14:36; although only a few Roman Jews spoke *Aramaic, Jesus' special address for his Father as "Papa" had become a name for God in early Christian prayers (Gal 4:6), perhaps by

Jesus' design (Mt 6:9). Roman adoption—which could take place at any age—canceled all previous debts and relationships, defining the new son wholly in terms of his new relationship to his father, whose heir he thus became.

8:16. Philosophers spoke of conscience testifying (cf. 2:15; 9:1); Jewish people believed that the *Spirit had testified to God's truth against Israel and the nations by the prophets. But here the Spirit's prophetic message is good news to the believer's heart. As a legal act, Roman adoption (cf. 8:15) had to be attested by witnesses; the Spirit is here the attesting witness that God adopts believers in Jesus as his own children.

8:17. God had promised Israel an "inheritance" in the Promised Land, and Jewish people spoke of "inheriting the world to come"; on inheritance and adoption, see comment on 8:15. Many Jewish people believed that a period of suffering would precede God's revelation of glory at the end.

8:18-27
Birth Pangs of a New World

8:18. Jewish readers would agree with Paul that the righteous would be greatly rewarded for any sufferings in this world. (Many Jewish teachers went beyond Paul and even said that one's suffering atoned for sin; but Paul accepted only Christ's atonement as sufficient for sin—3:25.)

8:19. Following *Old Testament tradition (Is 66:17-18), Jewish people generally believed that the whole world order would be transformed at the time of the end (although not all believed that it would be cosmic in scope or cataclysmic in scale).

8:20. Greek tradition declared that the world had been declining from its past Golden Age to the present. Jewish tradition debated whether it was good that humanity had been created, and suggested that Adam's sin had brought harm and the domination of evil powers to all creation. *Stoic philosophers believed that the elements would come unraveled and nothing but the primeval fire was really eternal. Cosmic pessimism was rampant in the first century; most people believed that decay and Fate reigned supreme. Paul's point that God had subjected creation to this worthless temporal state is bearable only in the light of the future hope he attaches to it (v. 21); like most Old Testament prophets, he includes the assurance of God's faithfulness.

8:21. The Greco-Roman world dreaded "corruption" (NASB) or "decay" (NIV); only the eternal, unchanging things in the heavens would last—the human body and everything else on earth would decompose. The language of "being set free from slavery" (NASB, TEV), "God's children" and probably "glory" alludes to the Old Testament exodus *narrative (see comment on 8:12-17).

8:22. In Exodus, God's people "sighed" or "groaned," and their groaning under hardship was an unintended prayer that hastened God's redemption of them (Ex 2:23). Paul also connects "groaning" (Rom 8:22, 23, 26) with birth pangs here. Some Jewish traditions portrayed the time just before the end as birth pangs (see comment on Mt 24:6-8), the great suffering that would bring forth the *Messiah and the messianic era. For Paul, the sufferings of the whole present time are birth pangs, meaningful sufferings that promise a new world to come.

8:23-25. "First fruits" was the actual beginning, the first installment, of the Palestinian harvest (Lev 23:10); the presence of the *Spirit in believers is thus the actual beginning of the future world. Believers had experienced redemption (Rom 3:24) and adoption (8:15), but still awaited the fullness of that experience at the *resurrection of their bodies by the Spirit (8:11).

The Israelites were redeemed from Egypt, but the consummation of their salvation was delayed a generation by their disobedience in the wilderness; it was nearly forty years before they entered the Promised Land. Paul can explain Christ's salvation in the same way, because it is a new exodus (see comment on 8:12-17): the beginning and completion of salvation are separated by the period of God's leading through the tests of the present age (8:14, 18).

8:26. Judaism usually viewed the *Spirit as an expression of God's power rather than as a personal being; like John (chaps. 14—16), Paul views the Spirit as a personal being (cf. 2 Cor 13:14). Jewish teachers portrayed God's personified mercy or angels like Michael as intercessors for God's people before his throne; Paul assigns this role to Christ in heaven (Rom 8:34) and to his Spirit in his people (8:26). The Spirit joins here in the birth pangs, as eager for the new creation as God's children are (see comment on 8:22-23).

8:27. All Jews agreed that God searches hearts (1 Kings 8:39; 1 Chron 28:9), an idea that occurs repeatedly in the *New Testament, and in some later *rabbinic texts even appears as a title for God ("Searcher of Hearts").

8:28-30
God's Eternal Purpose

8:28. *Stoic philosophers believed that everything would work out for the best—from the vantage point of God, although no other individual being (including lesser gods) would continue. Judaism believed that God was sovereign and that he was bringing history to a climax, when he would vindicate his people and turn their past sufferings to their advantage as he rewarded them (see comment on 8:18). For Paul, the ultimate good of these hardships is their work in conforming believers to Christ's image in the end (8:29).

8:29. Some Greek thinkers emphasized becoming like the deity, but the "image" ("likeness"—NIV) idea is most prominent in Jewish sources. In Jewish thinking, Wisdom was God's purest image (see comment on Col 1:15), but Jewish texts often speak of Adam or humanity in general as made in God's image (following Gen 1:26-27; for the sense in Genesis, cf. Gen 5:3). God's children will all be conformed to the image of the firstborn of the new creation, the new Adam (Rom 5:12-21).

8:30. On predestination, see chapter 9. The predication of predestination on foreknowledge (8:29) does not cancel free will; most of Judaism accepted both God's sovereignty and human responsibility. (The idea that one has to choose between them is a post-New Testament idea based on Greek logic.)

8:31-39
God's Triumphant Love

8:31. The *Old Testament often speaks of God being "with" or "for" his people (Ps 56:9; 118:6; Is 33:21; Ezek 34:30; 36:9); anyone who challenged them challenged him (see Is 50:8; cf. 54:17).

8:32. On the idea of inheriting all things in the world to come, see comment on 4:13; cf. comment on 5:17.

8:33-34. Here Paul applies the advocacy of God in 8:31 to God's heavenly court in the day of judgment. Jewish texts express confidence that God would ultimately vindicate Israel, as he did each year on the Day of Atonement; Paul bases his confidence of believers' vindication on the advocacy of

Christ (see comment on 8:26).

8:35-36. Lists of hardships were common in Greco-Roman literature (especially used to show that the wise man had passed all tests and lived what he believed). "Nakedness" was applied to insufficient dress, not only to complete exposure. "Sword" was the standard mode of citizen execution in this period, and the citation from Psalm 44:22 (applied by second-century *rabbis to martyrdom) reinforces the certainty that martyrdom is in view here (8:36).

8:37. Verses 35-39 form a chiasm (an ancient literary structure based on inverted parallelism): nothing can separate us from Christ's love (8:35a, 39b), no matter what it is (8:35b-36, 38-39a), which makes believers more than overcome their opposition (8:37). The center of a chiasm, this verse, would be especially significant to the ancient reader. Israel believed they would triumph in the day of judgment because God was for them; Paul assures believers that they triumph in their present tests because of what God has already done on their behalf (8:31-34).

8:38. Given the context of cosmic opposition here, we should take "principalities" and "powers" (KJV, NASB) with "angels" as referring to the spiritual forces ruling the nations and bringing opposition against God's people. Many ancient Jewish writers used these terms in this way.

8:39. "Height" and "depth" may simply personify the heavens above and Hades (the realm of death) below. Other scholars have suggested that they are astrological terms; the spiritual forces who ruled the nations were often believed to do so through the stars, and most first-century Greeks feared the inevitable power of Fate working through the stars. For Paul, it is not fate, the stars, angelic powers, or heaven or hell that determines the lives of believers; rather, the faithfulness of Jesus (8:31-34) does.

9:1-5
Israel's Rightful Place

9:1-3. Paul's love and willingness to sacrifice himself for his people would remind his biblically informed hearers of Moses (Ex 32:32), although God did not permit Moses to sacrifice himself, either (Ex 32:33-34).

9:4-5. "Covenants" may be plural to include an allusion to God's covenants with the patriarchs, or to his frequent renewing of his covenant with his people in the *Old Testament, also recognized in later Jewish texts.

The blessings Paul had assigned to believers in Jesus (8:2, 15, 18, 29) belonged to Israel, according to the Old Testament. By recognizing Christ as God (NIV and other translations of 9:5; cf. 1:25 for the same construction), Paul makes the point even more emphatically: God himself came to humanity through Israel.

9:6-13
Not Saved by Ethnic Descent

Most Jewish people believed that their people as a whole was saved, in contrast to the *Gentiles. Israel's salvation began with God choosing Abraham (chap. 4). Paul argues here that ethnicity is insufficient grounds for salvation, as the *Old Testament also taught (e.g., Num 14:22-23; Deut 1:34-35; Ps 78:21-22; 95:8-11; 106:26-27); God can save on whatever terms he wishes.

9:6-9. Abraham had two sons while Sarah was alive, but only one received the promise (Gen 17:18-21).

9:10-13. Isaac had two sons, but only one received the promise. This was determined before their birth (Gen 25:23; cf. Mal 1:2-3). Although God may have chosen Jacob because he foreknew Jacob's heart (8:29), the point here is that God has the right to choose among the chosen line. Not all Abraham's descendants received the promise; the rest of the Old Testament was clear that many Israelites broke the covenant (Ex 32:33-35; Num 11:1; 14:37; 16:32-35; 25:4-5; Deut 1:35). Why do most of Paul's contemporaries act as if things are different in their own time?

9:14-18
God's Choice in Moses' Time

9:14-15. In Exodus 33:19, God has the right to choose whom he wills. In the context, he has forgiven Israel as a whole because Moses has found favor in his sight (33:12-17), and God would show Moses his glory (33:18-23) because Moses is his friend (33:11). God's choice of individuals, however, was not arbitrary but was based on people's response to God (32:32-34), although God had initially called both Israel and Moses unconditionally.

9:16-18. God raised up this particular Pharaoh for the purpose of showing his power, that "the Egyptians may know that I am the Lord," as Exodus repeatedly says (e.g., 9:16). God clearly hardened Pharaoh's heart (Ex 9:12, 35; 10:27; 11:10), but not until Pharaoh had hardened his own several times (Ex 7:22; 8:15, 32). In other words, God elevated a particular person to fight against him; but that person also made his own choice, which God foreknew, before God punished him with a continuously hard heart (cf. Rom 1:24-25; 2 Thess 2:10-12). The *Old Testament affirms both God's sovereignty (e.g., Deut 29:4) and human responsibility (e.g., Deut 5:29), assuming that God is sovereign enough to ensure both (although human choice could not nullify God's word; cf., e.g., 1 Kings 22:26-30, 34-35).

9:19-29
God Chooses Gentiles

9:19-21. Paul here uses the language of Isaiah 29:16, 45:9 and 64:8, which the *Dead Sea Scrolls often used in prayers. The point is that God made people, and God can therefore do with them as he wills. In the context this means that he can choose either Jews or *Gentiles, not that his predestination is arbitrary.

Some nineteenth-century churchgoers reasoned that God would save them if he chose and hence made no effort to seek salvation. Their view misrepresented the point of this passage. Although Paul teaches "predestination," we must understand what he means by that term in the light of what it meant in his own day, not what it has meant in recent centuries' theology (or, as in the case just mentioned, in distortions of that theology).

Most Jewish people believed that their people as a whole had been chosen for salvation; they viewed predestination in corporate, *ethnic* terms. Paul here discusses predestination only in the context of the salvation of Israel (9:1-13) and the Gentiles (9:23-29); thus he means only what both context and culture suggest: God can sovereignly choose to elect whom he wills, and that need not be on the basis of descent from Abraham. God's sovereignty means that he is free to choose on another basis than his covenant with ethnic Israel (3:1-8); he can choose on the basis of (foreknown) faith in Christ (4:11-13; 8:29-30).

Some older New Testament scholars, like Rudolf Bultmann, thought that Romans 9—11 had nothing to do with the argument of the letter; but these scholars misunderstood Romans. In this letter Paul puts Jews and *Gentiles on the same spiritual footing (see the introduction), and Romans 9—11 is in fact the climax of his argument.

9:22-23. Here Paul means that God tolerated those who would remain in evil for the sake of those who would be saved, rather than ending the world immediately (cf. 2 Pet 3:9; cf. Prov 16:4).

9:24-26. In context Hosea 2:23, which Paul cites here, refers to God's restoring Israel, despite his temporary abandonment of them (1:9). If God could abandon but then restore Israel, he could also graft Gentiles into Israel if this were his will.

9:27-28. Here Paul quotes Isaiah 10:22-23: the prophet warned that only a remnant would survive and return to the land after judgment. If God saved only a remnant in the *Old Testament and promised that only a remnant would survive judgment, Paul asks what makes Jewish people of his own day feel secure that their Jewishness will save them.

9:29. Now Paul cites Isaiah 1:9, which makes the same point as Isaiah 10:22-23 (which he just quoted). In the context in Isaiah, Israel has acted like Sodom, the epitome of sin (1:10); they are fortunate to have any survivors (1:7-9), because God demands justice (1:16-17), not mere sacrifices (1:11-15).

9:30—10:4
Israel's Wrong Righteousness

Why had Israel so often failed God in the *Old Testament, with only a remnant surviving? Because they pursued the *law in terms of human effort (see comment on 9:29) instead of trusting in God, who transforms the heart. Although the term "faith" is rare in translations of the Old Testament (Paul already used most of the references in 1:17 and 4:3), Paul believes that the idea permeates the Old Testament, where God's people must respond to his *grace from their hearts.

9:30-32. Israel rightly sought the law but missed its point by stressing works rather than faith (see comment on 9:29)—faith was the law's point (3:21, 31). The two approaches to the law (one right and the other wrong) are essential to Paul's argument (3:27; 8:2; 10:5-8).

9:33. Here Paul follows a common Jewish interpretive practice of blending texts together (Is 8:14; 28:16). Because Isaiah 28:16 probably alludes back to Isaiah 8:14, Paul's blending of the two is especially reasonable, although perhaps only his Jewish readers caught what he was doing. The point is that the same stone that caused Israel to stumble (Is 8:14, which also speaks of the stone as a sanctuary) would save those who believed (Is 28:16).

10:1-2. Jewish literature from this period often praises zeal for the law, even to the point of violently resisting those who wished to repress Jewish practice of the law.

10:3-4. On God's righteousness see comment on 1:17. "End of the law" can mean the "goal" or "climax" to which the law points.

10:5-10
Two Approaches to Righteousness

10:5. One approach is based on a particular Jewish interpretation of Leviticus 18:5: those who keep the commandments merit *eternal life. (This view appears in Jewish texts alongside the view that God elects Israel as a whole to be saved.) This kind of righteousness was unavailable to *Gentiles without years of study of the *law. Paul also established in Romans 1—3 that this kind of righteousness does not work (see comment on 9:30-32).

10:6-7. Paul here does *midrash, expounding a text in good Jewish fashion. In context, "Who will ascend?" in Deuteronomy 30:12 means, "Who will ascend again on Mount Sinai, to bring the law down again?" "Who will descend?"

in Deuteronomy 30:13 means "Who will descend into the Red Sea to cross it again?" God had redeemed his people at the Red Sea, according to the *Old Testament and Jewish tradition; now, God has consummated his saving acts in Christ, and the same principle applies to him.

10:8. Deuteronomy 30:14 refers to the law; as long as it is written in the heart (cf. 30:6), God's people could live out its righteousness (cf. Jer 31:31-34). Paul says that this principle applies all the more to the message of faith that the law teaches (3:31); *grace, not human effort, leads to righteousness (8:2-4).

10:9-10. Paul emphasizes "mouth" and "heart" here because he is expounding Deuteronomy 30:14 (cited in the previous verse), which speaks of the message of faith in one's mouth and heart.

10:11-21
Salvation for All Peoples

10:11-12. Paul again cites Isaiah 28:16 (see Rom 9:33), which he is still explaining. His emphasis is on the "whoever" (NASB, TEV), by which he argues that the text must apply literally to *Gentiles as well as Jews.

10:13. Jewish teachers commonly expounded a text by citing other texts that shared the same key word; hence Paul ties in another verse (Joel 2:32) that has the word "whoever" to explain that in Isaiah 28:16 "not be disappointed" (NASB) or "not be put to shame" (NIV) means "be saved."

10:14. Paul expounds the implications of Joel 2:32: salvation is meant for whoever will seek it, Jew or *Gentile, but this availability of salvation presupposes that they must have the opportunity to hear the message.

10:15. Paul also has Scripture to verify that bearers of the good news must be "sent" (this term is the verb form of the noun translated "*apostle," hence "apostled"); people are not saved without the opportunity to hear. Isaiah 52:7 announced that there was good news, but heralds still had to bring it to the people.

10:16. Several verses after Isaiah 52:7, Isaiah reports the response to the good news the heralds bring (53:1), and Paul's readers probably know how this text continues: Israel rejected the good news (53:2-3).

10:17. Paul confirms his earlier interpretation of Deuteronomy 30:14 (in Rom 10:8): the saving message is none other than the proclaimed message of Christ.

10:18. Jewish teachers often grappled with the question of whether *Gentiles who had not heard the truth could be held responsible for it. They concluded that Gentiles could at least infer the oneness of God from creation and thus should avoid idolatry (see comment on Rom 1:19-20). The Gentiles may not have heard all of Christ's message (10:17), but creation itself made them hear enough of it to be responsible for doing right. (Psalm 19:4 refers in context to the testimony of creation.) The Jewish *Diaspora had more knowledge than the Gentiles had; having the *law, they had every reason to believe, and word about Christ had already begun to penetrate most Jewish centers of the ancient world.

10:19. God had promised in the law to provoke Israel to jealousy by another nation. Israel had rejected him for that which was not a god; God would reject them for that which would not be a people—to provoke them to jealousy (Deut 32:21; cf. Rom 11:11, 14).

10:20-21. Here Paul quotes Isaiah 65:1-2, which occurs in the context of God's judgment on Israel (64:8-12), of *Gentiles being accepted into God's household (56:3-8) and of God restoring the remnant of Israel to himself (65:8-9).

11:1-10 Always a Remnant

"Remnant" does not presuppose any particular percentage; it is simply the current state of "some" Jewish people following Jesus, rather than "all Israel" (11:26). A few other groups of Jewish people, as represented in the *Dead Sea Scrolls, also felt that they alone were serving God and the rest of Israel was in apostasy. Because the early Christians believed that Jesus was the *Messiah, they believed that rejecting him was like rejecting the law or the prophets, and like the prophets they accused their people of apostasy from Israel's true faith.

11:1. Ancient writers often adduced examples for their arguments, sometimes using themselves. But Paul turns quickly to an example from Scripture (11:2-4).

11:2-4. The Elijah *narrative in 1 Kings 19:10, 14 and 18 indicates that at the time of Israel's deepest apostasy, a remnant had still avoided idolatry. It may be relevant that some Jewish traditions presented Elijah as zealous for God but not patriotic enough for Israel.

11:5-7. Paul now expounds on 11:2-4: if there was a remnant even in Elijah's day, there will always be a remnant (i.e., "how much more" now, a common form of argument in ancient times). That God chooses the remnant follows directly from 9:19-29 and from the other texts Paul will marshal in 11:8-10.

11:8. Here Paul cites Isaiah 29:10, which makes clear that God hardened Israel; but this hardening again does not exclude Israel's responsibility. God silenced the prophets (Is 29:10) because Israel refused to hear them (30:10-11); thus God would make his message plain through the Assyrian invasion (28:9-13). Israel had become blind and deaf to God's word (29:9-10), having excuses (29:11-12) and a pretense of righteousness (29:13-14); but someday they would see and hear again (29:18, 24).

11:9-10. In Psalm 69:22-23, the righteous psalmist prays for the judgment of blindness on his persecutors, implying that God was sovereign over blindness—spiritual (Rom 11:8) as well as physical.

11:11-14 Provoking Israel to Jealousy

Paul here begins to expound Deuteronomy 32:21, which he cited in Romans 10:19. He does not say that the only purpose for the salvation of the *Gentiles is to turn Israel back to God (cf. the missionary purpose of *Israel* in Gen 12:2-3), but he recognizes that it is their primary purpose relating to Israel. Paul's argument in Romans places Jew and Gentile on the same level with regard to salvation (see the introduction); but now he reminds the Gentiles to remember whose faith they have adopted. Gentile racism against Jewish people is as contrary to the focus of Christianity as Jewish prejudice against Gentiles; racism of any sort opposes the message of the *gospel. Ancient *rhetoricians considered it acceptable to praise oneself only if the purpose were to stir others to emulation (as here) or to defend oneself.

11:15-24 The Jewishness of Christianity

*Gentile Christians must remember that they are grafted into a Jewish faith, and that when they are grafted into the *Old Testament people of God, they accept not only Israel's spiritual history as their own but also Jews as in some sense their siblings, even if those who do not follow Jesus are fallen siblings. Earlier in Romans Paul had opposed Jewish arrogance against Gentiles; here he opposes Gentile arrogance against Jewish people.

11:15. In the biblical prophets, the turning of the Jewish people back to God's ways coincided with Israel's restoration and the end time (which included the *resurrection of the dead).

11:16. The mention of "dough" alludes to the first fruits of the dough offering in Numbers 15:20-21, which sanctifies the whole offering; Israel's beginnings were holy (Jer 2:3), and God had not forgotten his plans for them. Paul's second illustration (root and branches), however, is the focus of 11:17-24. (Mixed metaphors were common in antiquity.)

11:17-24. *Gentiles could and did become part of the people of God in the *Old Testament (e.g., Ruth, Rahab, David's Cherethite guards, etc.); but they were clearly a small minority. Now that Gentile Christians in Rome have begun to outnumber Jewish Christians, it is easier for them to forget their heritage in Israel's history.

Israel was sometimes described as a tree, whose roots were the patriarchs (Abraham, Isaac and Jacob). Contrary to standard Jewish teaching, Paul had argued that uncircumcised Gentiles could become part of that people of God through faith in the Jewish *Messiah (chap. 4). Now he reminds Gentiles to respect the Jewish people, who had brought them their faith. It was easier for Jewish branches to be grafted back into the true form of their own faith than for pagans who had worshiped idols before their conversion to understand the faith they were now accepting. Like other Jewish teachers of his day, Paul does not regard any particular person's salvation as guaranteed from the human perspective till they have persevered to the end.

Grafting of trees (adding a shoot of one tree to another tree) is reported in both Jewish and Greco-Roman literature. Sometimes shoots from a wild olive tree would be grafted onto a domestic olive tree that was bearing little fruit in an attempt to strengthen or save the life of the tree. The unproductive original branches would be pruned off, and the new graft was considered "contrary to nature" (as in 11:24—NASB).

11:25-32
The Coming Salvation of Israel

God had promised that Israel as a whole (the surviving remnant after great afflictions) would someday turn to him (Deut 4:25-31; 30:1-6); at this time God would bring about the end (e.g., Hos 14:1-7; Joel 2:12—3:2). Paul's view of the end time here presupposes this return.

11:25. Some *Old Testament prophets had predicted God's witness spreading among the *Gentiles; because the final *repentance of Israel would usher in the end, God had delayed Israel's final repentance until the fullness of the Gentile remnant could be gathered in (cf. Mt 24:14; 28:19-20; 2 Pet 3:9).

11:26-27. The future salvation of Israel is repeated throughout the Old Testament prophets, although this is one of the few *New Testament passages that had occasion to address it. Jewish teachers commonly said that "all Israel will be saved," but then went on to list which Israelites would *not* be saved: the phrase thus means "Israel as a whole (but not necessarily including every individual) will be saved." In other words, the great majority of the surviving Jewish remnant will turn to faith in Christ. Paul proves this point from Isaiah 59:20-21: the remnant of Jacob who turn from sin will be saved by the coming of the new redeemer, when he puts his *Spirit on them (Paul paraphrases, as was common in ancient citations).

11:28-29. Unlike some interpreters today, Paul does not regard God's promises to ethnic Israel as cancelled—only deferred (cf. Deut 4:25-31); God still had a covenant with the fathers (Deut 7:8). Most readers today subscribe to one of two systems: Israel and the *church are separate and irreconcilable entities, and Israel will be restored; or Christians become the true Israel and ethnic Israel has no more purpose in God's plan. Paul would have rejected both extremes, believing that ethnic Israel as a whole would return to the covenant in the end time, joining the *Gentiles and Jewish remnant that already participate in it.

11:30-32. Paul's point here is that all peoples have sinned and all peoples must come to God through his mercy in Christ. This point addresses the cultural-ethnic conflict in the Roman *church (see the introduction to Romans).

11:33-36
Praising God's Wisdom

Like the writers of some *Hellenistic Jewish documents, Paul concludes this section of his letter with a doxology, or praise to God. Using the language of Isaiah 40:13 and Job 41:11 (which refer to God's sovereignty in and over creation), Paul praises God's wisdom in designing history as he has so that salvation would be available to all peoples (chaps. 9—11).

*Stoic philosophers believed that God controlled all things and that all things would ultimately be resolved back into him. In this context Paul's words in 11:36 mean instead what Jewish people normally meant by such words: God is the source and director of human history, and all things—even the evil choices of sinful humans—would in the end glorify him and the rightness of his wisdom.

12:1-8
Serve One Another

Having laid the theological groundwork for reconciliation in the Roman *church (chaps. 1—11), Paul now turns to practical counsel. (Some other ancient letters of exhortation followed this pattern.) He emphasizes that God's will is for believers to think rightly: to recognize the equal value of all members of the body and to use all of one's gifts to build up the body.

12:1. Ancient Judaism and some philosophical schools often used "sacrifice" figuratively for praise or for a lifestyle of worship; hence it would be hard for Paul's readers to miss his point here. When he speaks of "your rational [cf. KJV 'reasonable'; not 'spiritual'—NIV, NASB, NRSV] service," his word for "service" alludes to the work of priests in the temple, and "rational" to the proper way to think (as in 12:2-3). The *Old Testament called sacrifices that God accepted "pleasing" (NIV, TEV) or "acceptable"; people also spoke of sacrifices being "holy"; but "living" sacrifices strains the metaphor in order to present the sacrificial lifestyle as a continual experience.

12:2. Judaism generally believed that evil powers dominated this age but that all peoples would acknowledge God's rule in the age to come. Here Paul says literally, "Do not be conformed to this *age*." In contrast to some ecstatic Greek worship that played down rationality and the amoral ritual formalism of most Roman and many public Greek cults, Paul emphasizes the proper use of the mind: those who discern what is good, acceptable (v. 1) and perfect will know God's will.

Jewish wisdom writers and Greek philosophers could have agreed with Paul's emphasis on renewing the mind; they understood that one's attitudes and values affected one's lifestyle. But Paul's basis for renewal is different from theirs; he bases it on the new kind of life available in Christ, which most of Judaism expected only in the world to come.

12:3-5. That each class in society had a special function, like members of a body, had long been argued by philosophers defending the status quo of the state; *Stoic philosophers had also applied the image of head and body to God and the universe. But Paul may be the first writer to suggest that each member of the religious community has a special function within the one body, abolishing the priesthood-laity distinction of most ancient religions. By affirming that each member has "a measure of faith" (NASB; not "*the* measure of faith"—KJV, NIV, NRSV) apportioned for different functions (12:6-8), Paul affirms diversity within unity. He will apply this principle to the ethnic conflict in the *church (see the introduction) in chapter 14.

12:6. Most of ancient Judaism regarded *prophecy as supernatural in a way different from the other gifts Paul lists here. God could use the other gifts here, but most of ancient Judaism saw them as activities one did *for* God, whereas they thought of prophecy as a divine "possession" that was very rare in their own day. That Paul regards all these gifts as divine empowerments and prophecy as one among many suggests how thoroughly he expects the God who worked miracles in the *Old Testament to continue to work this way regularly in the life of the *church.

12:7-8. Although "serving" may have a broad meaning (cf. 15:25), its position between prophecy and teaching suggests that it refers to an office in the church (*diakonos;* see comment on 16:1). "Showing mercy" probably refers to charity—caring for the sick and the poor, and so forth; although all Christians did this work to some extent, some had a special gift for it.

12:9-21
General Parenesis

One of the styles ancient moralists used is called parenesis, which strings together various moral exhortations that have little connection among them. Paul uses parenesis here but has a general theme that applies to most of his exhortations: Get along with one another. This theme fits the situation of Romans (see the introduction).

12:9-10. Ancients emphasized honor highly. Soldiers swore never to "give preference to another" in honor above Caesar. Some philosophers recommended that "inferior" people prefer "superior" people above themselves. Paul's admonition sounds more like that of Jewish teachers, who emphasized that each of their *disciples should look out for the others' honor as much as for the disciple's own.

12:11-13. Jewish people believed in taking care of needs in their community, and the Christians of Paul's day no doubt agree (v. 13); the modern phenomenon of well-to-do and hungry Christians in the same city would have shocked the moral sensibilities of ancient Jews and Christians (though not pagans). In antiquity "hospitality" meant putting up travelers (without charge) in one's home while they were in town; they would normally carry letters from those trusted by their hosts, attesting that they were to be accepted as guests.

12:14. Like some other exhortations

in the context, this one may well echo Jesus' teaching (Lk 6:28); it was common to repeat the sayings of famous teachers, and Jewish teachers always cited their own teachers and the *law. In a *Cynic or *Stoic context, the exhortation would sound like a call to ignore suffering; but although Cynic philosophers disregarded reputation, they were adept at returning wisecracks. The counsel of Jesus and Paul has more to do with the Jewish conviction of a final judgment and that believers could let matters rest with God's justice (12:17-21).

12:15. Weeping with those who mourned was a proper expression of sympathy in most of ancient culture. Although philosophers and moralists often warned against weeping too much, because it "does no good," Jewish weddings and mourning ceremonies (including funeral processions, in which the public joined) presupposed the principle Paul states here.

12:16. Humility was a Jewish virtue, definitely not a Greek one (except, Greeks thought, for the socially lowly, who *ought* to be humble). Whereas many writers emphasized knowing one's proper place, Christian literature goes beyond other ancient literature in suggesting that believers go out of their way to associate with the lowly.

12:17-18. Not repaying evil for evil may come from Jesus' teaching (Mt 5:39), although some other Jewish teachers had also recommended nonretaliation (as early as Prov 20:22). Doing what is respectable in the opinions of other people was a virtue not only to aspiring Greco-Roman politicians but also to Jewish people in their dealings with *Gentiles. But while Jewish people adopted stricter guidelines than the surrounding culture for the sake of witness, they never compromised their own beliefs; the point of the admonition is to protect their witness and prevent unnecessary opposition.

12:19. *Stoic philosophers opposed seeking revenge; they believed that Fate was sovereign, and one's best resistance to Fate was to cooperate with it and refuse to let one's will be manipulated by circumstances. Jewish pietists likewise condemned vengeance; they trusted God to vindicate them. The practice was, however, more difficult than the principle. The later Gentile massacres of Jews in Palestine invited bloody reprisals; unfortunately, only the most devout usually live out what to others are pious theories. Paul cites Deuteronomy 32:35, but the concept appears elsewhere in the *Old Testament as well (2 Sam 22:48; Prov 20:22; Jer 51:56).

12:20. Here Paul quotes Proverbs 25:21-22; although Solomon might have meant "heap burning coals upon his head" as the enemy's emotional misery, in Paul's context of vengeance (Rom 12:19) this expression may mean that one's enemy will be punished all the more severely in the day of judgment. This is also the sense in which the *Dead Sea Scrolls viewed nonretaliation.

12:21. Some Greek and Jewish thinkers suggested that one should turn an enemy into a friend instead of retaliating. Sometimes, however, the one who does good to the evildoer will be vindicated only in the future day (12:20).

13:1-7 Submission to Civil Authorities

Loyalty to the state was a standard literary topic among ancient writers (e.g., the Stoic writer Hierocles, *How to Behave Toward One's Fatherland*); it appears in lists and discussions alongside proper treatment of parents, elders and friends. Philosophers and moralists commonly wrote on how government officials should act but also wrote on how citizens should behave toward the government. According to *Plato, Socrates even refused to escape execution lest he undermine the state with its good laws as well as its bad laws.

When Jewish people felt repressed for their ethnic and religious practices, submission to civil authorities was the ultimate example of nonresistance (12:17-21), an attitude that they did not always achieve. Paul is well aware that only roughly a decade before his letter the Jewish community had been expelled from Rome—possibly in debates over the identity of the *Messiah that Jewish Christians provoked (see comment on Acts 18:2).

Jewish people had to be concerned about public opinion, especially in Rome, where their maintenance of economic ties with Palestine was viewed with suspicion. Because many people viewed Christianity as a minority sect within Judaism, Christians had even more reason to be cautious. Jews and Christians publicly stressed their good citizenship, against the popular slander that they were subversive. This emphasis does not mean, however, that they would avoid denouncing injustice (cf. 2 Thess 2; Jas 5; Jewish *apocalyptic).

13:1-2. Nero was emperor at this time, but he had not yet begun persecuting Christians or repressing other groups; he was still under the benevolent influences of *Seneca and Burrus, rather than the reprobate Tigellinus. Nero was always popular in Greece, from which Paul was writing.

Although some Palestinian Jews already advocated the revolt against Rome that would take place in little more than a decade, other Palestinian Jews reportedly swore to nonresistance, believing that God had ordained all civil authorities (in the *Old Testament, cf. Is 45:1; Jer 25:9; Dan 4:32). Jews in Rome certainly upheld this position and would have been embarrassed by any other. Judaism generally believed in submission (which is a matter of nonresistance or nonviolence, not always of obedience), unless it involved a conflict with obeying God's *law. The Old Testament clearly taught God's sovereignty over earthly rulers (Prov 16:10; 21:1).

13:3-5. Here Paul offers standard ancient moral exhortation. The Roman state did many evil things; even its court system was based on social class. But the Romans generally advocated justice and toleration, and at this point the Christians have nothing to fear from them. Paul thus does not need to qualify the general principle he is articulating at this time. "The sword" refers to the standard method of execution in this period (beheading); in earlier times the ax had been used. Swords were carried in front of Roman officials to indicate their authority over life and death.

13:6-7. The empire as a whole levied a property tax (often about 1 percent) and a head tax; local provinces or kingdoms added further taxes; there were also customs duties. Taxes were used to finance roads and run the government but also to support Roman armies and temples devoted to the worship of the emperor. Officials expected and received honor by virtue of their position.

13:8-10
Fulfilling the Law

Paul reminds his Jewish readers concerned about *Gentiles' lax observance of the *law that the best way for them to fulfill the law is to get along with each other (see the discussion of situation in the introduction to Romans).

13:8. Moralists often emphasized not being in debt (cf. Prov 22:7); sometimes even whole essays were written on the subject (e.g., by *Plutarch). Judaism always stressed love of one's neighbor and sometimes recognized it as a commandment that summarized God's law.

13:9-10. No readers, whether Greek, Roman or Jewish, would disagree with the commandments Paul cites here, except for some Gentiles who might disagree about coveting. Treating one's neighbor as oneself is a recurrent admonition of ancient ethics, although ancient moralists found many different ways to summarize ethics; Paul follows the specific summary advocated by Jesus (Mk 12:31).

13:11-14
Waking for the Dawn

13:11. Philosophers sometimes spoke of a soul inattentive to spiritual matters as being asleep. Paul's image of sleeping in the light of Christ's impending return probably harks back to Jesus' own teaching (Mt 24:43; Mk 13:36). Most Greeks expected history to continue as normal or believed that the universe moved in cycles; but most Jews, like Paul, were anticipating its climax in the imminent future.

13:12. Many Palestinian Jews were expecting an end-time battle that would include the overthrow of the *Gentiles, but Paul here intends this image much more in the sense that Jews outside Palestine would have used it. Philosophers often described their battle with the passions in athletic and military images. This imagery also influenced non-Palestinian Jewish writers; for instance, one document portrays Moses' armor or weapons as prayer and incense (Wisdom of Solomon 18:21). Some of these documents also use the image of clothing oneself spiritually, and Judaism could speak of persons' being "clothed" with God's *Spirit (cf. also *Old Testament images listed in comment on Eph 4:20-24).

13:13-14. Jews often characterized Gentile behavior in terms of wild drinking parties and premarital sex, and in general they were not far off the mark. These activities were done at night (drunken parties often lasted well into the night), like sleeping (v. 11) and burglaries.

14:1-23
Don't Be Divided over Foods or Holy Days

Paul's exhortation to unity between the Jewish and *Gentile Christians in Rome now reveals some of the cultural divisions being experienced there. Jewish people did not expect most Gentiles to observe their food laws or holy days but did expect Gentile converts to Judaism to do so, perhaps including Gentile Christians. (Leviticus 11:44-45 deals with holiness as separation and may suggest that God gave special food laws to Israel particularly to keep it separate from other nations, because most cultures had their own special dietary practices. This approach would no longer be productive in the *New Testament period in the light of Paul's missions strategy. Its principle of moral separation could be retained without cultural separation.)

Gentiles, particularly in Rome, had long ridiculed Jewish people for their peculiarities on especially these two issues (plus circumcision, which seems not to have been an issue in the Roman *church). Paul emphasizes primarily eating practices. (Although he addresses a different kind of division over foods in 1 Cor 8, he applies similar principles.)

14:1-4. Most distinct cultures in the ancient world had their own food customs; some philosophical schools also had their own food rules. But few cultures were as insistent as the Jewish people that a deity had assigned their food laws; in the two centuries before Paul many Jews had died for refusing to eat pork, a meat Greeks thought delicious. Although we know that some Hellenistically educated Jews in Egypt took the food laws symbolically, most Jews continued to keep these laws regardless of where in the Roman Empire they went.

14:5-6. The precise time for festivals was such an important issue in Judaism that different Jewish groups broke fellowship with each other over the issue. (Not much later in history, different Christian groups followed suit.) Pagans had their own festivals, with different nations having their own ancestral customs and calendars. But *Gentile writers especially reviled the Jewish sabbath. Romans reasoned that Jews were just lazy and wanted a day off from work. (This was not the first time in history that someone viewed Jewish worship in such terms—Ex 5:17.) Paul also alludes to the Jewish custom of giving thanks over food.

14:7-9. Like their separate food laws, their sabbath regulations forced Jews to form their own moderately self-sufficient communities in the Greco-Roman world, and Gentiles often regarded Jews as separatistic and unsociable. This situation increased the social distance between most Jews and Gentiles.

14:10-12. "Judgment seats" were common in the Greco-Roman world; officials like Pilate or Gallio would make their judgments from such a *bema* or rostrum (Acts 18:12). God judging all people before his throne was a common image in Jewish portrayals of the end. It is natural for Paul to apply Isaiah 45:23 to the final judgment, because the chapters around it speak of God delivering Israel in the end and calling the nations to account before him so that they acknowledge that he is God.

14:13. Other ancient texts also used the "stumbling block" as a metaphor. Jews called one another "brothers," as did members of Greek religious clubs. Christians regarded one another as spiritual siblings, and Paul reinforces the conviction that Jewish and *Gentile Christians must regard one another in these terms.

14:14. Jews classified foods as "clean" or "unclean," based on the Bible (Lev 11). For Paul to say that this classification is no longer literally relevant would put him in agreement with some philosophically minded Jews in the Greco-Roman world (most of whom nevertheless kept the food laws), but it would shock the vast majority of ancient Jews.

14:15-16. Precisely because foods do not matter, one should be willing to forgo eating them for the sake of what does matter: preserving the unity of the body of Christ. Paul is not telling *Gentiles to keep kosher; but he is telling them not to try to talk Jewish Christians out of doing so.

14:17-19. Jewish people often spoke of the perfect future time of God's *kingdom (see 1 Cor 6:9), when the *Spirit would be made available and all people would be at peace with one another (Rom 14:17). For Paul, the coming of the *Messiah and the coming of the Spirit have also inaugurated the working of the kingdom, hence believers should be at peace with one another (14:19).

14:20-21. The issue here is not eating meat or drinking wine per se, but that *Gentile meat (suspected of having been offered to idols or not having the blood properly drained) and Gentile drink (some of it possibly used for libations to gods) were suspect to Jews.

But like a good *rhetorician, Paul calls his readers to concede his point even in the most extreme case, requiring abstinence from all meat or wine (and if it applies to the extreme, "how much more"—following a standard style of argument—to all lesser cases). (Although some Jewish groups abstained from wine for periods of time—Num 6:3; cf. Jer 35:5-6—diluted wine was a normal part of meals; thus the language here is probably *hyperbolic; see comment on Jn 2:9-10.)

14:22-23. Jewish teachers erected a "fence around the *law" to keep people from areas of "doubt," areas that were unclear and where they *might* be sinning. Paul's point is that total commitment to God means doing one's best to find out what is right and avoiding what one does not know to be right.

15:1-13
Christ as a Minister of Racial Reconciliation

Ancient writers commonly used examples to argue their points. Opponents were more hesitant to challenge the example of a virtuous teacher. Continuing his argument from chapter 14, Paul begins with the ultimate and indisputable example for Christians: Christ.

15:1-3. Psalm 69:9 makes good sense in this context—Psalm 69 is a psalm of the righteous sufferer; thus the *New Testament often applies it appropriately to Christ (the ultimate righteous sufferer).

15:4. Paul's can say that Scripture "was written for our instruction" (NASB) because he believes, like his Jewish contemporaries, that it is God's Word and remains relevant to new situations. This statement does not mean that he thought it was intended only for his own generation, as some commentators have suggested on an analogy with their views of scriptural commentary in the *Dead Sea Scrolls; indeed, "for our instruction" could easily refer directly to Moses' words in Exodus 24:12. The Jewish people found comfort in the teaching of the Scriptures (2 Macc 15:9).

15:5. Being of "one mind" means thinking in unity (1 Chron 12:38)—in this case a unity of love, not of complete agreement (chap. 14).

15:6. Praising God "with one voice" means in unanimity; cf. Exodus 24:3 (this chapter may be fresh in Paul's mind; cf. Rom 15:4) and 2 Chronicles 5:13.

15:7-12. That Christ accepted not only Jews but *Gentiles Paul demonstrates from Scripture (Ps 18:49=2 Sam 22:50; Deut 32:43 [cf. Rom 12:19]; Ps 117:1; Is 11:10). Paul provides citations from different parts of the *Old Testament and could have provided others to make his case that God seeks the praise of the Gentiles as well as that of the Jewish people (e.g., 1 Chron 16:31; Ps 22:27; 96:10; 102:22; Is 49:23; 60:3, 9-14). His last citation, Isaiah 11:10, was a clear *prophecy of Gentiles turning to the *Messiah and being saved in the end time; Isaiah also has other prophecies about Gentiles being incorporated into God's people (19:23-25; 56:3-8).

15:13. Letters often included a prayer or well-wishing for someone's health, especially in the opening; Paul's letters, which focus on spiritual issues, naturally include more prayers than most ancient letters (15:5-6, 33, etc.). Jewish people customarily used wish-prayers like this one in the same way that they used direct intercession, and Paul no doubt means for God as well as his Roman audience to hear this prayer.

15:14-33
Paul as a Minister of Racial Reconciliation

Often a speech's epilogue would repeat

points made in the proem (opening); Paul employs such repetition in this letter but in a more personal tone characteristic of especially affectionate letters or speeches. The end of a speech was often the place to stress what the Greeks called *pathos,* or emotional appeals.

15:14. Greek writers often expressed their confidence in their addressees; this expression helped the readers to listen more favorably to the rest of the letter and sometimes served as a polite way to make a request. Although it was customary in letters of advice, it was less appropriate in letters of reproof (cf. Galatians). "Admonition" (KJV, NASB) was the gentlest form of correction offered by public speakers and by skilled writers in "letters of blame," and Paul here notes that they can supply this instruction to one another.

15:15. "Reminding" was a common feature of ancient moral exhortation.

15:16. One popular Jewish expectation of the end time was that Israel would rule over the *Gentiles, who would finally acknowledge the one true God, and the Gentiles would send tribute to Jerusalem (e.g., Is 60:11-14). Jerusalem Christians may have viewed Paul's collection for the saints there (15:25-27) as a fulfillment of this vindication of Israel's faith.

15:17-18. Philosophers used their lifestyle as well as their teaching to demonstrate their principles and could call attention to it as an example. Paul limits his credentials to what has been demonstrated in his life and ministry.

15:19. Illyricum was north of Macedonia, across from Italy on the eastern Adriatic coast, on the west of the Yugoslav/Serbo-Croation region. The Roman province was called Illyricum; Greeks included this region and some more territory farther south (including Dyrrhachium on the Via Egnatia in Macedonia) in what they called Illyria.

15:20. Illyricum (15:19) may have been one of these previously unevangelized areas; Spain would be another (15:28).

15:21. Here Paul quotes Isaiah 52:15, which in its context clearly refers to *Gentiles ("kings"), who contrast with the *Messiah's own people, Israel, who would not recognize him (53:1-4).

15:22-23. Ancient letters often dealt with business, including planned visits.

15:24. "Assist" (NIV) or "help" (NASB) implies that they would cover his expenses for the trip. This would be a great expression of hospitality, but one which the Roman *church would probably consider an honor if they could afford it. There is little evidence of any major Jewish settlement in Roman Spain before the third century A.D.; Paul's missionary work there would probably be among those who knew nothing of the Bible. At the farthest western end of the Mediterranean, Spain was counted by geographers such as Strabo as at the end of the earth (with India on the opposite, eastern side of the world); cf. Acts 1:8.

15:25-26. "The poor" became a title for the pious of Judea in some circles (especially members of the *Qumran community)—perhaps mainly because most of them were poor. Jewish teachers considered the laws requiring care for the poor to be a major test of whether a *Gentile convert had genuinely accepted God's *law. Sending money to Jerusalem was a common Jewish practice in the Mediterranean, especially with regard to the annual temple tax. Jews throughout the world expressed their solidarity with Jerusalem and the homeland through the temple tax; here the Gentile Christian offering for Jerusalem expresses solidarity between Gentile and Jewish

Christianity. This is a practical example of humble racial reconciliation, important to Paul's case in Romans.

Paul's letters more frequently identify *churches by cities in which they are located than by provinces. The churches probably viewed themselves in these terms because inhabitants of large urban areas identified themselves more by the cities in which they lived than by the political boundaries of Roman provinces. Regional cultural ties existed, however, and this passage may indicate regional cooperation among churches.

15:27. Jewish readers steeped in the *Old Testament had a much better sense of corporate responsibility from members of one people to another than is common in individualistic Western society (Deut 23:3-4; 2 Sam 21:1-9). The Roman government collected tribute from the rest of the world, but in the second century the *church in Rome was known for sending funds to needy churches elsewhere in the empire, to free Christian slaves from the mines and so forth.

15:28. Ancient letters often anticipated personal visits. It was impossible for any traveler to find a direct route from Syria or the East to Spain; eastern vessels would go to Rome, from which a traveler would have to transship to Spain. A seafarer would voyage to Tarraco there; one could also travel overland by roads to southern Gaul and across the Pyrenees to Tarraco. It was a trip of more than a thousand miles; overland from Rome to Cordova was about seventeen hundred miles. "Put my seal on this fruit" (NASB) refers to the seal used in commercial documents, guaranteeing the correct contents of merchandise (hence "made sure"—NIV); Paul would inspect and oversee the offering's delivery.

15:29-33. That Paul's journey to Jerusalem could involve some danger is attested by the account in Acts 21—22; see comment on that passage.

16:1-2
Letter of Recommendation for a Minister

Jewish travelers normally carried letters of recommendation attesting that they should be received; they were generally bearers of such letters themselves. (The only mail service was by imperial couriers for the government; Paul thus had to send the letter by a traveler.) Paul no doubt emphasizes Phoebe's spiritual qualifications for two reasons: Jewish and Greco-Roman circles did not usually have high regard for women's religious wisdom; and she will need to minister to them, explaining to them by word of mouth anything in Paul's letter that the hearers would not understand.

16:1. "Servant" (KJV, NASB, NIV) is the Greek *diakonos,* which is sometimes translated "deacon" (e.g., NRSV), probably the owner of a home in which *churches met. The term for "deacon" probably corresponds to the *chazan* of the *synagogue, who was in charge of the building (see comment on 1 Tim 3:8 for the meaning of "deacon"). If deacons filled this office or the office of charity overseers, they held an office that was respected in Jewish synagogues (and not normally assigned to women). But the New Testament usually applies the term *diakonos* to "ministers" of God's word, like Paul and his colleagues; Paul may have this meaning in view here (although ancient Judaism did not allow women to teach the law publicly to men).

Cenchrea was the eastern port city of Corinth, close to the isthmus. It had naturally come to host a variety of foreign religions and thus had an atmosphere of religious toleration.

16:2. "Helper" (NASB) or "help" (NIV) translates a Greek term applied especially to *patrons. A patron of a religious association was normally a well-to-do person who allowed members of a religious group to meet in his or her home. The patron was generally a prominent and honored member of the group and generally exercised some authority over it. Although most patrons of religious associations were men, some women patrons are known.

16:3-16
Greetings to Friends in Rome

"All roads led to Rome," and many people in the ancient Mediterranean migrated there; this would be especially true of Jewish Christians who had returned after Claudius's death annulled his expulsion order, such as Aquila and Priscilla (16:3; cf. Acts 18:2). Many ancient letters closed with greetings to friends, often by name, but this letter makes it clear how many friends Paul had, even in a city he had not yet visited.

Many of the names are Greek or Jewish, but this is not unusual; perhaps as much as 80 percent of the inhabitants of imperial Rome were descendants of freed slaves from the East. One could bear a Latin name without being a Roman citizen, although the list probably includes several indigenous Romans.

It is noteworthy that although Paul greets roughly twenty-eight individuals and only about eleven are women, he specifically commends the work of six (over half) the women and six (about one-third) the men. This disproportion may be because, in that culture, the women needed more affirmation in their ministry (see comment on 16:1-2).

16:3. Husbands were normally mentioned first unless the wife was of higher status, which may suggest Priscilla's superior status in society (by birth) or in the *church. "Prisca" is the Latin diminutive form of "Priscilla."

16:4. "Laying down one's neck" (KJV) seems to have been a figure of speech for risking one's life on someone else's behalf, probably derived from the Roman method of execution by beheading.

16:5. Small *synagogues sometimes had to meet in homes before they could purchase buildings; many Greek religious associations did the same; *churches did so for the first three centuries, using their income to buy slaves' freedom, feed the poor and so forth, rather than to build edifices. In Rome, many well-to-do apartments existed above shops in multistory tenement buildings; Aquila and Priscilla probably lived above their artisan shop. The Roman house churches might especially be threatened with disunity among themselves, because Rome (unlike the cities of the East) did not allow Jews to assemble on any level larger than local synagogues, and Christians were regarded as Jews. "Epenetus" was a common name among slaves and *freedmen, though not limited to their ranks.

16:6. "Maria" could be a Latinized form of the Jewish "Miriam" (normally translated "Mary" in the *New Testament), or possibly a Latin *nomen,* probably indicating citizenship.

16:7. "Andronicus" is elsewhere attested as a *Hellenistic Jewish name. "Junia" is a Latin *nomen* that should indicate her Roman citizenship. Against attempts to make "Junia" a contraction of the masculine "Junianus," this form is not attested in Rome; ancient Christian readers recognized that Junia was a woman. Because she and Andronicus traveled together without scandal, and singleness was unusual, they were undoubtedly a husband-wife team; husband-wife teams were known in some professions, like doctors and lower-class merchants. The most natural way to read the Greek phrase is that both were *apostles; some modern interpreters have rejected this reading mainly because they presuppose that women could never fill this office. "Kinsmen" (KJV, NASB) can mean countrymen (cf. TEV; see also 9:3; 16:11).

16:8-9. "Ampliatus" and "Urbanus" were common slave names in Rome.

16:10. "The household of Aristobulus" may refer to freed slaves of Aristobulus, Herod the Great's grandson, who spent his life in Rome. But "Aristobulus" is a common Greek name, so the phrase could refer to a house *church or family headed by a different Aristobulus.

16:11. "Household of Narcissus" may mean the *freedpersons formerly belonging to Narcissus, himself a freedman who was one of the empire's most powerful people under Claudius.

16:12. "Tryphaena" and "Tryphosa" are Greek names sometimes used by Jewish as well as Greek women. One scholar, noting that both names come from a root meaning "delicate," thinks that Paul may be playing on their names ironically when he says they "labor hard"; this proposal is weakened by the same phrase in 16:6. "Persis" is attested as a slave name but was also used by free persons.

16:13. "Rufus" is a Roman name, sometimes born by Jews (some commentators think this is the Rufus of Mk 15:21); it was a common slave name. Greetings at the close of letters could include affectionate terms of intimacy such as "father" or "mother" (e.g., one ancient letter addresses two older men as "fathers"). Here "mother" could be a simple mark of endearment toward an older woman, or it may imply that she was a benefactor who helped support Paul's ministry.

16:14. Like Greeks, Jewish people in the ancient Mediterranean often used Greek names compounded from the names of pagan gods, like Hermes or Apollo. "Patrobus" is short for the rare name "Patrobius"; some scholars have linked this name with the household of one of Nero's wealthy freedmen. "Phlegon" was also a common slave name.

16:15. "Julia" is a Latin *nomen* (not just a *praenomen*) and may indicate that she was a Roman citizen. (By contrast, other commentators have noted that it was instead a common name for female slaves.)

16:16. Kisses were a common form of affectionate greeting for family members, intimate friends or those who were objects of respect (e.g., Gen 33:4; 45:15; 1 Sam 20:41). Due to abuses, in subsequent centuries the *church limited the practice of the liturgical kiss of fellowship to men kissing men and women kissing women, although this was not the initial practice.

16:17-20 Concluding Exhortation

16:17. In keeping with the point of the letter (see the discussion of the situation in the introduction), those who cause schisms and divisions are Paul's main object of warning.

16:18. Philosophers ridiculed those who were "slaves" to their passions; on Paul's phrase here see comment on Philippians 3:19. Philosophers and moralists also distanced themselves from populist public speakers who sought to flatter their audiences; but they emphasized that they themselves told people what they needed to hear rather than what they wanted to hear.

16:19. Paul probably alludes here to Adam and Eve seeking fruit from the

tree of the knowledge of good and evil (Gen 2:9; 3:6); see comment on Romans 16:20. He may also intend a contrast with Jeremiah 4:22: "wise to do evil, but ignorant of how to do good."
16:20. Genesis 3:15 promised that the serpent who deceived Adam and Eve to partake of the fruit (cf. Rom 5:12-21) would ultimately be crushed beneath the feet of Eve's seed. In many Jewish traditions the serpent represented *Satan or his instrument. Some texts seem to have understood Eve's "seed" as Israel, others (perhaps including the *LXX of Gen 3:15) as the *Messiah; but here Paul applies it more broadly to the Messiah's followers as well. His point is that they should persevere to the end, and their opposition will be defeated.

16:21-24
Greetings to the Church in Rome

It was not uncommon to attach supplemental greetings; these, however, are from Paul's colleagues in Corinth to the *church in Rome. Although this is a basic list of greetings, it may have also served the purpose of attestation of witnesses, which also came at the end of documents.
16:21. "Lucius" was a Greco-Roman name sometimes used by Jews; its shortened Greek form is "Lucas" (i.e., Luke). For the names "Jason" and "Sosipater" (possibly but not necessarily the same people), see Acts 17:6, 9 and 20:4 ("Sopater" was another form of "Sosipater").
16:22. "Tertius" was a Roman name (often used for a third child), sometimes used by Jews. Most of the ancient world was too illiterate to write letters, certainly letters as sophisticated as this one; they depended instead on scribes. Those who were highly literate were also wealthy enough that they could dictate letters to scribes as well, sometimes their own secretaries, who were usually literate slaves. Paul's host may have lent him his scribe, or Tertius may have been a professional scribe; in any case, Tertius seems to be a believer, because scribes did not normally add their own greetings. That Paul followed the common practice of signing dictated letters (1 Cor 16:21; Gal 6:11; Col 4:18; 2 Thess 3:17) indicates that he used scribes regularly.
16:23-24. The *church in Corinth met in Gaius's home; Paul is probably also lodging there. For his house to accommodate "the whole church," it must have been larger than most of the house churches.

"City treasurers" (NASB) were often public slaves or *freedmen, but they were generally wealthy. In other cases public jobs like this one were assigned to well-to-do persons as part of their civic responsibilities. If this is the same "Erastus" who is attested in a Corinthian inscription as an *aedile* in this period (and this is likely), he must have been a wealthy benefactor of the city, part of the municipal aristocracy.

16:25-27
Closing Benediction

The conclusions of Greco-Roman letters varied considerably but often ended with a wish for the recipient's health and then "Farewell." *Synagogues, however, closed prayers, readings and services with benedictions, and Paul anticipates that his letter would be publicly read in house churches' worship services.
16:25-26. Some ancient Jewish texts like Daniel and the *Dead Sea Scrolls spoke of God revealing what were once mysteries, special knowledge previously unavailable except by divine revelation. For Paul, this mystery of *Gentile ingathering was already

taught in the Scriptures (Paul cites many of them in his argument in Romans; cf. also, e.g., Is 19:18-25; 56:3-8; Zech 2:11) and is finally being understood.

16:27. Here Paul offers the sort of standard Jewish doxology used to close *Hellenistic Jewish religious works (except, of course, for "through Jesus Christ"). "Amen" was the standard closing at the end of prayers and a number of Jewish books.

1 CORINTHIANS

Introduction

Authorship. All scholars accept 1 Corinthians as Pauline.

Corinth. Corinth was one of the major urban centers of the ancient Mediterranean and one of the most culturally diverse cities in the empire. A Greek city by location, the capital of Achaea (which made up most of ancient Greece), Corinth had been a Roman *colony for about a century, resettled by Romans after its destruction, and Greek and Latin cultures coexisted and sometimes clashed here. Its location on the isthmus of Corinth, a short land route across Greece that spared seafarers the more treacherous voyage around the south of Greece, made it a prosperous mercantile community. Its mercantile character contributed to the presence of foreign religions and may have accelerated the level of sexual promiscuity, although promiscuity was characteristic of Greek male culture in general. Corinth was known for its prosperity, and the proverbial sexual looseness of ancient Greek Corinth seems to have continued in Roman Corinth as well.

Language. Although Latin was used for official business, most people spoke Greek, especially most of the people who made up the Corinthian *church.

Situation. Roles were determined by social status in antiquity, and those with wealth and power preferred religious, philosophical and political ideologies that supported their base of power. A simple reading of 1 Corinthians in terms of a conflict of status ideals cuts through much of the speculation of older commentaries; although theological errors were involved, the biggest issue was that people were not getting along. The Corinthian Christians were basically like most Christians today. They had their own social interests, which seemed natural from their own perspective, but Paul summoned them to think instead as servants.

Thus higher-status members of the community seem to have preferred a more *rhetorically skilled speaker like Apollos; and, sharing the values of their peers they hoped to reach with the *gospel, they rejected manual labor as a suitable occupation for a moral teacher. Manual laborers in the *church, however, appreciated a voluntarily lower-status, working teacher like Paul, even if his personal delivery in speeches left something to be desired (chaps. 1—4). Philosophical ideals held by some higher-status members may have justified sexual offenses (chaps. 5—7); conflicts also arose over higher- and lower-status views of meat and communal meals (chaps. 8—11), high- and low-status views of head coverings (11:2-16), and possibly higher-status susceptibility to philosophical mystical currents (chaps. 12—14) and views of the body and immortality (chap. 15). In other words, the conflicting values of diverse groups in the broader society had been carried over into the church as divisive issues.

Commentaries. The best commentary is Gordon D. Fee, *The First Epistle to the Corinthians*, NICNT (Grand Rapids, Mich.: Eerdmans, 1987); C. K. Barrett, *A Commentary on the First Epistle to the Corinthians*, HNTC (New York: Harper & Row, 1968), is also helpful. More focused works on specific texts or themes, such as Gerd Theissen, *The Social Setting of Pauline Christianity* (Philadelphia: Fortress, 1982), or Dale B. Martin, *Slavery as Salvation: The Metaphor of Slavery in Pauline Christianity* (New Haven, Conn.: Yale University Press, 1990), are useful for specific studies on social relations at Corinth. Also helpful are general works on social relations in antiquity, such as Ramsay MacMullen, *Roman Social Relations* (New Haven,

Conn.: Yale University Press, 1974); for such relations in the *New Testament, see Wayne E. Meeks, *The First Urban Christians: The Social World of the Apostle Paul* (New Haven, Conn. Yale University Press, 1983); Abraham J. Malherbe, *Social Aspects of Early Christianity,* 2nd ed. (Philadelphia: Fortress, 1983); and other works in the LEC series cited in the bibliography in the introduction to this volume. On 1 Corinthians 7, see chapters five and six in my earlier book . . . *And Marries Another: Divorce and Remarriage in the Teaching of the New Testament* (Peabody, Mass.: Hendrickson, 1991); for 1 Corinthians 11:2-16 and 14:34-36 see my *Paul, Women and Wives* (Peabody, Mass.: Hendrickson, 1992), pp. 19-100; for 1 Corinthians 8 and 10, see Wendell L. Willis, *Idol Meat in Corinth: The Pauline Argument in 1 Corinthians 8 and 10,* SBLDS 68 (Chico, Calif.: Scholars, 1985); for parts of 1 Corinthians 2-3 and 15, cf. Birger A. Pearson, *The "Pneumatikos-Psychikos" Terminology in 1 Corinthians: A Study in the Theology of the Corinthian Opponents of Paul and Its Relation to Gnosticism,* SBLDS 12 (Missoula, Mont.: Scholars, 1973).

1:1-9
Opening Greetings

These verses follow a standard ancient way to open letters; see the introduction to New Testament letters and comment on Romans 1:1, 7.

1:1. Letters in antiquity were not usually coauthored; thus Paul may have authored the letter and Sosthenes served as scribe, writing it down (cf. 16:21); or Sosthenes may have contributed to the letter's contents or (more likely) merely concurred with Paul's message.

1:2. "Saints" means "set-apart ones," and "sanctified" means "set apart," "holy or separated for God." This language was applied to Israel in the *Old Testament; it meant that God had set apart Israel to himself when he redeemed them, and they were therefore to live for God, not like the nations around them.

1:3. "*Grace" adapts a standard Greek greeting, and "peace" a Jewish one. By pairing Jesus with the Father as the source of grace and peace in a wish-prayer (wish-prayers for the hearers were common in letter openings), Paul declares Jesus' divinity.

1:4. Thanksgivings were common in letters. As in speeches, letters might open with a proem praising the reader, which was designed to secure the reader's favor for the rest of the letter. Moralists who gave rebuking speeches or wrote rebuking letters also mixed in praise to make their advice easier to accept.

1:5. Opening sections of letters commonly introduced some of the themes that would recur throughout the letter. "Speech" and "knowledge" were important to the Corinthians. In fact, the nearby Isthmian Games (see comment on 9:24-25) included speech contests, and knowledge was associated with philosophical wisdom or the ability to speak extemporaneously on any topic (a skill in which *rhetoricians, or public speakers, were trained). Here Paul means spiritual, not merely natural, gifts, but the Corinthians had come to excel in these particular gifts precisely because these mattered most to them in their culture.

1:6-8. "The day of our Lord Jesus Christ" here fulfills the role assigned to "the day of *God*" in standard Jewish tradition. Some elements of Judaism, especially in the *Diaspora, played down the future aspects of biblical hope; Paul wants to reverse this tendency among the Corinthian Christians.

1:9. Ancient philosophers often spoke of human "fellowship" or "communion" with other people. Although Paul could mean fellowship with others in Christ, he probably means something far more unusual in antiquity: intimacy with the Lord himself. Greco-Roman religion tended to stress ritual (or, in some cults, nonrelational ecstasy). Judaism viewed God as intimate with his people, but it did not claim to experience him as indwelling and speaking to the believer by the *Spirit, as Paul does elsewhere.

1:10-17
Christ Not Divided

Ancient *rhetoricians would have classified at least 1 Corinthians 1:10—4:21 (addressing unity), and perhaps the whole letter, as a letter of admonition. Paul is not defending himself against opponents (as in 2 Corinthians) but addressing the misbehavior of the Corinthians. The context shows that they are favoring specific teachers (Paul and Apollos) on the basis of their respective rhetorical or philosophical skills (1:18—4:21).

1:10. For the first three centuries of its existence, the *church met mainly in homes; those belonging to more well-to-do members of the congregation could naturally hold the most people (see comment on 11:17-34). Because the size of these homes limited the size of congregations and forced Christians to meet in different house churches, divisions could easily arise among them. As the letter proceeds, however, it becomes clear that the *main* basis for division derives from differences of social stratification within the congregations. One type of ancient speech (known as a *homonoia* speech) lamented divisions and called for unity; Paul's readers would immediately recognize the nature of his argument.

1:11. These informants may have been agents of Chloe, a wealthy businesswoman in Corinth or Ephesus (16:8), traveling between the two cities on business. As such, they may have been high-status slaves or *freedpersons belonging to her household. Members of a Corinthian *church, they brought Paul the news; news and letters were most often carried by people traveling on other business. (Had they been her children rather than servants, they would have been named by their *father's* household, even were he deceased.)

1:12. People often gravitated toward particular teachers. Philosophers encouraged emotional attachment to themselves as a necessary part of developing morally and intellectually. *Rabbis had their own schools, and *disciples normally propagated their teacher's views. Paul probably mentions "Cephas" and "Christ" only hypothetically (cf. 3:5-6); his point is that any division is wrong, even one based on the claim to be of Christ alone and so rejecting Paulinists and followers of Apollos.

1:13. Paul here uses a common technique in argument: *reductio ad absurdum,* reducing an opponent's position to its natural but absurd conclusion.

1:14-15. In some Greek *mystery cults an initiate would reportedly call the one who had introduced him to the cult "father." "Crispus" and "Gaius" are Latin names and may reflect persons of high status in the congregation.

1:16. Paul may have recalled Stephanas separately because he may have met and baptized him elsewhere (16:15). A "household" normally followed the religion of the head of the household; 16:15 implies that Stephanas was a believer and a person of some means.

1:17. Judaism used "*baptism" as the final act of conversion for *Gentiles; early Christians followed this pattern. But Paul refuses to emphasize the act itself; his emphasis is on the message to whose reception baptism merely bears witness. Moralists commonly denied that they used skilled *rhetoric to persuade their hearers, and they pointed out that they appealed only to the truth.

1:18-25
God's Wisdom in the Cross

Judaism stressed the importance of divine Wisdom, which God revealed in his word; Wisdom was sometimes personified (1:30). Given popular Greek respect for philosophy and *rhetoric, it is probable that some educated members of the *church are especially interested in "wise speech." Apollos may have fit their preferred speaking style better than Paul did (1:12; see comment on Acts 18:24).

1:18. Greeks believed that some gods had died and returned (usually they were vegetation deities who returned annually), but they relegated this belief to ancient myth and sometimes even allegorized the myths. Romans regarded crucifixion as a death appropriate for slaves; Jews also saw it as shameful (Deut 21:23). Those viewed as "saviors" were normally gods, kings, wealthy benefactors or miracle workers. Roman society was built around power and status; power was concentrated in the male head of the household, in wealthy and aristocratic families, and so forth. Associating power with a crucified man—the epitome of weakness—thus made no more sense to ancients than it does to modern people outside Christ.

1:19. Here Paul quotes Isaiah 29:14 to show that the wisdom of those living by human tradition (Is 29:13-14) instead of by God's revelation (Is 29:9-12) would perish; cf. similarly Jeremiah 8:9.

1:20. Commentators rightly find models for Paul's wording in texts like Isaiah 19:12, 33:18 and Job 12:17 (cf. further the principle in Prov 21:30; Is 29:14; 44:25; 47:10; Jer 8:8-9; 9:12, 23). The "debater [or reasoner] of this age" probably refers to a trained *rhetorician, whom philosophers despised as devoid of genuine content. But Paul challenges the philosophers ("wise men") as well.

1:21. In Greek comedy the hero pretended to be stupid, but he proved to be wise in the end; in contrast to this hero was the fool who claimed to be wise and wanted credit for the wise man's triumph, but was rebuffed. *Plato said that human wisdom was worthless, and people should seek God's wisdom instead.

1:22-23. Greeks were known for their love of learning. Greeks and Jews alike might desire attesting miracles, but Paul keeps Jews and Greeks distinct here for *rhetorical effect. On the foolishness of the cross to both, see comment on 1:18.

1:24-25. In antiquity, divine power was typically associated with wonderworkers. Paul uses "the foolishness of God" and "the weakness of God" ironically: the least of God's wisdom is superior to the best of human wisdom. Irony was a common rhetorical device.

1:26-31
Inversion of Status

1:26-29. Roman social class was based on birth ("nobility") rather than on wealth; but by either criterion, most of the Corinthian Christians derived from the lower ranks of society, which made up the vast majority of ancient society. Paul's guarded language here ("not many"—NIV) suggests that some, however, were of higher status, no doubt including the owners of the homes in which the *churches met. This passage reflects Jeremiah 9:23, paving the way for Paul's explicit quotation of Jeremiah 9:24 in 1 Corinthians 1:31.

1:30. Both Jewish and Greek literature sometimes personified wisdom. Christ as divine Wisdom (8:6; cf. Jn 1:1-18) functions as righteousness, sanctification and redemption, changing the person completely for God. The *law was considered both wisdom (Deut 4:6) and righteousness (Deut 6:25).

1:31. Here Paul paraphrases Jeremiah 9:24: one should boast in knowing and understanding God rather than in human wisdom.

2:1-5
Saved by the Cross, Not by Rhetoric

Paul here appeals to the Corinthians' own conversion. It was the powerful preaching of the weakness of the cross, not humanly powerful *rhetoric, that had saved them (1:18).

Even most defenders of rhetoric, or skilled speech, admitted that it was sometimes abused. But they argued that it was necessary, because having truth but being unable to persuade others of it was not helpful. Philosophers commonly criticized rhetoric, claiming that truth, not skillful speech, should be the emphasis; but these same philosophers used forms of argument developed by rhetoricians. Paul here disapproves of *mere* rhetoric, but his own writing, including 1 Corinthians, displays extensive knowledge and use of rhetorical forms. Although Paul may not have matched the rhetorical prowess of Apollos or the standards of Corinthian leaders, he was a skillful writer in his own right.

2:1-2. Even the most renowned speakers (e.g., Dio Chrysostom) regularly disavowed their own speaking abilities in order to lower audience expectations; then they spoke brilliantly. Rhetoricians recommended this technique. Because Paul in the context is boasting in his weakness, he does not praise his speaking or philosophical ability (cf. Ex 4:10). But this reserve need not mean—and the skillfulness of his argumentation shows that it cannot mean—that his argumentation style was weak, even if his delivery (voice quality and gestures) were inadequate (which is likely—2 Cor 10:10).

2:3. "Fear and trembling" occur together as an expression in the *Old Testament and Jewish literature; although the expression was formulaic, it was used in a variety of different ways. In this context, this expression suggests that Paul's weakness was in his delivery, not in his awareness of contemporary *rhetorical style.

2:4-5. In rhetoric, "demonstration" was a form of argument proved from certain and undisputed premises; Paul does not offer a mere syllogism (a form that was logical but might be based on inadequate premises) or dialectic (which *Plato treated as defining and classifying data) or rhetorical tricks.

Here "power" is God's power resident in the preaching of the weakness of the cross (1:18, 24). This power might imply miraculous attestation (2 Cor 12:12; 13:4; Rom 15:19).

2:6-16 Genuine Wisdom Through the Spirit

Paul hastens to explain that he does not oppose genuine wisdom; but this wisdom is beyond human understanding and can be accepted only by those who know God's heart through the *Spirit.

2:6. Philosophers used the term for "mature" or "perfect" (KJV) here for those who had progressed to an advanced stage in wisdom. (Its use for full initiates to the *mystery cults is less relevant here.) The contrast in 2:6-9 is between temporal wisdom of those great in this age and God's eternal wisdom.

2:7. Judaism believed that God's Wisdom existed before the world and that God had created the world through this Wisdom.

2:8. Many scholars suggest that "rulers of the age" here refers to angelic powers in the heavens (cf. 15:24; Rom 8:38; Eph 1:21). In the context, earthly rulers are more likely, however; these are the powerful people of this age (1 Cor 1:26-28).

2:9. Here Paul quotes Isaiah 64:4, which was part of a prayer for God to intervene in history again on behalf of the remnant who hoped in him; Paul adapts the wording of the quotation slightly, as was common in ancient citations. (He may also slightly conflate this text with the *LXX of Is 65:17, which speaks of the present being forgotten in the world to come.) The point is that the things of the eternal God are inaccessible to mortals except by the means Paul articulates in verse 10.

2:10-13. Only God's *Spirit knows what is in his heart, but because believers have God's Spirit, they can know his heart too. This was a radical statement for most of ancient Judaism, because most Jewish teachers did not believe that the Spirit was active in their day. "Spirit" had a broad variety of meanings, including "attitude," "disposition"; hence "spirit of the world" need not refer to any particular spiritual being (unlike God's Spirit).

2:14-15. The spiritual person can evaluate all things, but the "natural" (KJV, NASB) person cannot evaluate the things or people of the Spirit. Paul's use of "natural" (literally, "soulish") may be based on a particular interpretation of Genesis 2:7 current in *Hellenistic Jewish circles; see comment on 15:45-46. (This Hellenistic Jewish use may borrow the language of some Greek philosophers, who contrasted the "natural," or earthbound, part of the soul with the mind. Paul's distinction is between those ruled by their earthly soul and those ruled by the Spirit of God. *Gnostics in the second century wrongly used 1 Cor 2:14-15 as a proof text to distinguish the human soul and spirit and to argue that they were an elite group who followed the incorruptible, immortal spirit.)

2:16. Paul turns the rhetorical question of Isaiah 40:13 (cf. Rom 11:34) around in the light of the coming of the *Spirit; believers do know something of the mind of the Lord because they know what the Spirit has revealed.

3:1-9
Do Not Follow Servants

With their partisan celebrity cults the Corinthian Christians are acting like "natural," "fleshly" people rather than people of the *Spirit. Paul and Apollos are mere servants; God is the one the Corinthians ought to follow.

3:1-2. Ancient writers often compared the unskilled in knowledge to babes who had to start out with the basics, with milk (*Philo, *Epictetus, etc.). If Paul intends the image to evoke all that it can, he portrays himself as mother or wet nurse (cf. 4:15; 1 Thess 2:7). Teachers always expected students to start with basics but also expected them to progress past basics.

3:3. "Fleshly" (not "worldly"—NIV) is slightly different from "as fleshly" (again, not "worldly," NIV) of verse 1: it means that they were *acting* fleshly, not that they were fleshly by nature. On "flesh" and Spirit, see comment on Romans 8:1-11.

3:4. Greek culture sometimes divinized heroes into gods; some scholars have also claimed that initiates to some *mystery cults were said to become gods. Later traditions divinized philosophers, and philosophers often claimed that people could be divinized by virtue, because they considered the soul a divine part within each person. Although some Jewish writers in the Greek world adopted the language of deification, the principle of one God generally kept Jews and Christians from following this concept that far (Gen 3:5). Here Paul says: If you follow humans, then you are not only not divine; you are not even following the *Spirit of God.

3:5-9. Paul uses the familiar image of sowing; at the end of verse 9 he introduces the familiar image of building, which will dominate his exposition through 3:17. Other writers like *Philo also described God as planter or builder; in the *Old Testament, cf. Ruth 4:11; Psalms 28:5; 51:18; 69:35; 147:2; Jeremiah 1:10; 18:7; 24:6; 31:4, 28; 45:4.

3:10-20
The Real Test of God's Servants

The Corinthians should follow God, not his ministers (3:1-9), because only the day of judgment would show the genuine character of ministers (3:10-15). The building on which God's servants are working is God's temple, representing God's people (3:16-17).

3:10-11. A "master builder" directed the construction; thus Paul was a strategist of sorts.

3:12-15. A few other ancient stories highlighted the competition among substances like those Paul mentions here; further, everyone knew which substances would endure testing by fire (cf., e.g., Num 31:23). Ancient Jewish writers sometimes compared the wicked to straw that would be consumed at the judgment (in the *Old Testament cf., e.g., Is 33:11). Only the judgment would test the ultimate value of each servant's work.

3:16-17. The *Dead Sea Scrolls also portrayed God's people as a building, the temple. This image was probably widely enough known that Paul's readers would understand it immediately.

3:18-20. Paul cites Job 5:13 and Psalm 94:11. The former is a wise principle, even though Eliphaz, who first articulated it, used it in an evil way against Job (Job 4—5). Psalm 94:11 in context stresses that God alone teaches people rightly; human wisdom is at best folly. Paul thus continues his proof from Scripture of human folly (e.g., 1 Cor 1:19).

3:21-23
All Things Are the Corinthians' Anyway

This passage would make good sense to ancient readers. Even Paul and Apollos are given to them by God; why follow just Paul or Apollos, when they should follow the God who gives everything? God's people would take possession of the world to come (Zech 8:12; Rom 4:13); at present they are heirs of the world and children of the God who rules it.

*Stoic and *Cynic philosophers often praised "having nothing" (see comment on 2 Cor 6:10) while emphasizing that the whole world belonged to them, so they could take whatever they needed. They often cited the proverb "Friends share all property in common" and claimed that because they were friends of the gods, who owned everything, everything was theirs.

4:1-5
Do Not Evaluate Before the Real Test

A sinful lifestyle always indicated sinful motives, but a godly lifestyle could sometimes mask selfish motives. Only God knows hearts, and Christian celebrities could be accurately evaluated only in the light of the final judgment (3:5-15). Paul adapts the language of philosophers respected by the Corinthian Christians.

4:1. "Stewards" ("those entrusted"—NIV) were often servants, as here, or *freedmen. These servants and freedmen were trusted to manage the master's estate, especially his financial affairs, and had great authority and prestige. Some philosophers saw themselves as stewards or managers of divine truths.

4:2. Because stewards were trusted to handle their masters' finances, purchasing slaves and goods and making wise investments, it was most important that they be "trustworthy" or "faithful."

4:3-4. The *Old Testament speaks of the day of God's judgment tribunal as "the day of God." "Day" sometimes meant "court," as Paul uses it and many translations render it here. Paul uses several legal expressions in these verses. Most philosophers, especially *Cynics, expressed disdain for what anyone else thought about them.

4:5. Jesus and other Jewish teachers spoke of God bringing secret thoughts to light at his judgment (cf. Is 29:15). Ancient *rhetoric was concerned with "praise" for those to be honored; Paul says that the only honor that counts is what God will assign at the final judgment.

4:6-13
Apostles Last of All

In Jesus' *kingdom, where the greatest is the least and the King died for his people, no one is more important than anyone else. Indeed, true *apostles take the lowest role, not the greatest; they should not be objects of a celebrity cult.

4:6. Philosophers advocating harmony often warned people not to "go beyond what is written" but to comply with a prior agreement; Paul may thus summon them to unity, reminding them of a contract implied in their acceptance of Christ. Some commentators have suggested that "not beyond what is written" refers to the learning of schoolchildren, who learned how to write by imitating what was written. Others think Paul refers to Scripture, perhaps texts he has cited so far in 1 Corinthians on the worthlessness of human folly.

4:7. Everything they have, God has given to them; they have earned none of it. Philosophers often liked to make this point to keep people from boasting.

4:8. Irony was a standard *rhetorical and literary device. Philosophers often claimed to be the only true kings, asserting that only they had character noble enough to rule rightly. They also claimed to possess the only genuine wealth. Paul ironically concedes the claims of his most educated readers: "You are true philosophers; I, your teacher in Christ, am foolish."

4:9. *Stoic philosophers believed that they evoked the admiration of gods and mortals as they persevered through suffering; but Paul declares that the suffering *apostles became a "spectacle," objects of scorn in the theater of the world. The person in charge of games in amphitheaters would exhibit the gladiators who would battle wild beasts there; here God himself exhibits the sufferings of the apostles. "Last of all" means that they were the final show for the day—normally reserved for the most wretched criminal condemned to die in the arena. Corinth's theater seated eighteen thousand.

4:10. Philosophers claimed to be wise, powerful and truly honorable, as opposed to the foolish masses. They meant that their conduct was wise, they were morally strong, and they were honorable in virtue. But society at large thought the opposite, especially of the homeless *Cynics: they were foolish, weak beggars. Paul's detractors think his behavior unbecoming of true wisdom; Paul uses irony to suggest that the true wisdom is on his side.

4:11. Greek moralists often presented themselves as models for others to imitate; a few philosophers, especially the Cynics, wandered around homeless and dependent on charity. Paul presents his own sufferings and sacrifices for the *gospel as a model for the Corinthians to imitate (4:9-16). Everything Paul describes in 4:11 fits the typical ancient depiction of the wandering Cynic philosopher.

4:12. Here Paul distinguishes himself from most kinds of philosophers and from the more aristocratic ideals of the higher-status faction within the Corinthian *church. Philosophers might beg, charge tuition or be supported by a *patron; to them, manual labor was the least honorable option. Because wealthy landowners also considered manual labor undignified, well-to-do people in the church would be embarrassed to invite friends of their own social circle to hear the teachings of Paul, who worked as an artisan (skilled laborer). Paul here supports the majority, lower-class faction in the congregation and boasts in his low social status.

4:13. Philosophers sometimes thought of the masses as "garbage" (TEV) and "refuse" (NIV); more often, the masses may have thought of wandering *Cynic philosophers in these same terms. It was a universally disgusting image for something worthless and rejected (Lam 3:45). Following Jesus, Paul goes beyond Cynics in answering slander gently (cf. Prov 15:1; 29:8); many Cynics were happy to revile their audiences, even without provocation, to prove their independence. *Stoic and Cynic philosophers believed that their perseverance in suffering authenticated them as genuine philosophers, and Paul wants his philosophically educated readers to recognize that on their own terms he can compete with the best of them.

4:14-21
A Father's Threat

4:14. "Letters of blame" could be written either to shame those who had acted dishonorably or (less harshly) to admonish them. Except in the most extreme circumstances, philosophers preferred to admonish rather than to rebuke and thereby humiliate. Moralists generally emphasized that they admonished people only because they cared for them, sometimes describing their concern in parental terms. Paul has already portrayed himself as a parent in 3:1-2; calling his readers "beloved children" here may reflect the fact that fathers were responsible for their sons' education.

4:15. "Guardian" (NIV; better than "tutor"—NASB—or "instructor"—KJV) refers to a slave who would accompany a child on his way to school; although respected by the child and responsible to teach him manners, this guardian was not a teacher per se. Students could affectionately call and treat special teachers as "fathers"; that Paul here calls himself their "father through the gospel" somewhat demeans other teachers by comparison, because slave aides were nothing like fathers.

4:16. Philosophers, *rabbis and teachers in general were models to imitate as well as to listen to. This is one of the most common ideas in Greek literature.

4:17. A *disciple of a teacher could be called his "child" (4:15); Timothy as an imitator of Paul can become a model for Paul's "children" in Corinth. Paul's "ways" (NASB) or "way of life" (NIV) may allude to the Jewish use of "ways" to mean divine laws or proper behavior.

4:18-21. Paul continues in the role of "father" (4:14-17) in this passage. Fathers were often portrayed as gentler than mothers, but they also used the rod for discipline, and in Roman political *rhetoric, the proper patriarchal figure was stern and uncompromising.

5:1-5
Discipline for Sexual Immorality

Paul now turns from issues of church unity (chaps. 1—4) to sexual issues (chaps. 5—7). Although most incestuous relationships today have innocent victims (molestation is never the victim's fault; cf. Deut 22:26), in chapter 5 Paul addresses the sin of two consenting adults.

5:1. The marriage of full brothers and sisters was considered immoral throughout the Roman Empire except in Egypt; parent-child incest was universally abhorred throughout the Roman world. From the revulsion against the idea exhibited in the Greek Oedipus stories to slanders leveled against emperors, it was one of those few crimes that all cultures agreed were terrible. Its Roman legal punishment was banishment to an island. Relations with stepmothers were treated like relations with mothers—as incestuous. Here Paul uses the language of Leviticus 18:6-8.

5:2. These people may have been boasting in their spiritual freedom. Committing a crime was considered bad in antiquity, but boasting about it in addition to committing it was considered even worse.

*Synagogues, which functioned as social centers for their communities, disciplined their members, especially those whose immorality threatened to bring *Gentile reproach on the whole Jewish community. Discipline could include corporal punishment (beatings), but the ultimate punishment was exclusion from the Jewish community—spiritual banishment. This expulsion was meant to be the spiritual equivalent of a death sentence, executed only by God; but it was reversible if the banned person *repented.

5:3. Letter writers sometimes expressed their intimate concern for the readers by saying that, although they were "absent in body," they were with them "in spirit" or in mind. In some cases, the letter itself communicated the effect of the writer's presence. But this expression was always meant as a statement of intimacy, not of metaphysical presence.

5:4. Jewish people believed that the judges in their courts judged cases on the authority of the heavenly court (see comment on Mt 5:22). Judaism seems to have used excommunication, or official exclusion from the community (attested in the *Dead Sea Scrolls and in *rabbinic literature), to replace the *Old Testament death penalty; Christians adopted the practice from Judaism.

5:5. One may compare the longstanding pagan custom of magical execration by devoting a person to the gods of the underworld or other avenging deities; curse tablets used for this purpose were widespread. In the Old Testament, God's servants were to place idolatrous items under the ban, devoting them to destruction; here Paul instructs the Corinthians to deliver this man to *Satan, the agent of destruction. Paul hopes that the resultant suffering (11:30) will lead to *repentance and thus salvation. Jewish teachers often felt that suffering plus repentance would expiate sin, or that (as here) suffering could lead to repentance.

5:6-13
Removing Immorality in the Church

Immorality inside and apparently sanctioned by the *church was far more likely to lead Christians astray than the immorality of nonbelievers would.

5:6. The most obvious characteristic of leaven, or yeast, is that it permeates the dough, making the whole batch of dough rise when baked. Paul uses leaven here as a symbol for sin.

5:7-8. Paul argues that the Corinthians should remain unleavened, just as bread does during the Passover season. (The Jewish people left Egypt in such haste after the first Passover that they did not have time to leaven their bread, and subsequent generations were commanded to celebrate the feast with unleavened bread in commemoration of the event.) The Jewish people were expecting a new redemption, like their first exodus from Egypt, when the *Messiah came; Paul believes that the Messiah has come, and that this Messiah was himself the new paschal lamb.

5:9-10. Jewish people typically considered *Gentiles sexually "immoral" and were probably correct about most Gentile men.

5:11. Jewish excommunication (5:3-5) also excluded people from communal meals, as in the *Dead Sea Scrolls.

5:12. Rome allowed local Jewish communities to judge Jewish offenders of Jewish laws. This judgment and the discipline were carried out in the *synagogues, the community centers for local Jewish groups (cf. comment on 2 Cor 11:24). Paul expects the Christians of his day to follow the same model, correcting the behavior of erring fellow Christians.

5:13. The *Old Testament often commanded God's people to purge evildoers from among their ranks, normally by execution (Deut 13:5; 17:7; 19:19; 21:21; 22:21, 24; 24:7). Otherwise, the unrepentant offender could remove God's blessing from the whole community and bring about the death of others (Josh 7:5, 25). Here the evildoer is purged from the community by being banished; banishment was a common punishment in the Roman period. In Judaism, exclusion from the community was a spiritual equivalent of execution, applied in the *New Testament period to capital crimes of the Old Testament (see comment on 1 Cor 5:2; capital sentences of Jewish courts could not be legally carried out without Roman permission).

6:1-11
Christians in Secular Courts

Having advocated that the *church act as a court with regard to sexual offenses (chap. 5), Paul now argues for the necessity of church courts in his society (6:1-8) and then returns to sexual offenses (6:9, 12-20). It is possible that the litigants of 6:1-8 are the father and son of 5:1; if so, such litigation would clearly be displaying the church's dirty laundry before the world. "Defraud" (6:7-8) favors this suggestion (cf. 1 Thess 4:4-6); "why not be wronged?" (6:7) may be against it.

Jewish communities throughout the Mediterranean world had their own courts in their *synagogues. Bringing internal disputes of the Jewish or Christian communities before secular magistrates was a luxury these minority religions could ill afford; there was already too much slander against them in the broader society. See comment on Acts 18:12-17.

6:1. Like modern North American society, Roman society was extremely litigious. Cases began to be heard at dawn and sometimes could be argued as late as sunset. Judges were always chosen from among the well-to-do, and most legal disputes revolved around money.

6:2. Members of the upper class received better treatment in the law courts; indeed, this preference was written into penalties prescribed in the laws. Further, social inferiors could not sue members of the upper class. But for Paul, even the lowliest believers are equipped to judge cases.

6:3. In many Jewish traditions, the righteous would judge the nations; this judging could also imply judging the angels who were believed to rule the nations. "Matters of this life" (NASB) normally referred to property matters, particularly concerning people who were well-to-do; but adultery (considered wife stealing) might also fit this general category in ancient thought (see comment on 6:5).

6:4. This verse may be read as a command (KJV, NIV) rather than a question: "appoint the lowliest," in contrast to the world (see comment on 6:2); this reading reinforces the idea that the least of Christians should be more competent in justice than the wisest of pagans (cf. 2:14-15).

6:5. Family disputes such as inheritances could be settled by private arbitration, although the arbitrators were usually socially prominent landowners. Juries judged cases like adultery, murder and treason; magistrates tried other cases. This case had apparently gone before a secular jury court, and, given the context (5:1-13; 6:12-20), adultery or voluntary incest could be the offense in view here.

6:6. The Jewish communities outside Palestine were very conscious of their minority status and did not wish to reinforce negative pagan conceptions of their morality. Consequently, they usually dealt with Jewish problems within their own community. Christians were an even smaller minority at this time.

6:7-8. Many philosophers who believed that property did not matter could advocate ignoring offenses rather than going to court. Paul prefers the Jewish method of settling disputes within the community, which serves both justice and the community's witness to the outside world.

6:9-10. That the unrighteous would not "inherit God's *kingdom," i.e., would not have a share in it, was standard Jewish and Christian teaching. Both Jewish and pagan "vice lists" often defined the "unrighteous"; Paul follows this practice. "Do not be deceived" appears in ancient moral exhortation and is common in the *New Testament. Scholars have disputed the meaning of the term translated "homosexuals" (NASB), but it seems to mean those who engage in homosexual acts, which were a common feature of Greek male life in antiquity.

Like the *rabbis, Paul engages in *rhetorical damnation: even though in practice he has expelled from fellowship only the most extreme offender (5:1-5), those who continue in the lifestyles he mentions here (whether premarital sex or materialism) will not make it into the *kingdom.

6:11. Unlike most ancient moralists, Paul reasons from what the Corinthians are (by God's action) to how they should live, rather than the reverse.

6:12-20
The Body Is for God, Not for Immorality

Biblical law forbade sex between people who were not married; the penalty for having sex with one person and then marrying another was the same as the penalty for adultery while married—death. Although this penalty was no longer strictly enforced by Paul's day, it was intended to underline the seriousness of the offense; premarital sexual immorality was adultery against one's future spouse (Deut 22:13-29).

Many Greek thinkers, however, reasoned that sex without marriage ("fornication"—KJV, NRSV) was fine as long as it did not control a person; the more vulgar *Cynics even relieved their sexual passions publicly. For most Greek men under the age of thirty, heterosexual sex was most available with slaves or with prostitutes. Roman law permitted prostitution, and it forbade fornication only if both parties were of aristocratic birth. Paul's response shows his mastery of his readers' culture and his ability to communicate biblical truth relevantly.

6:12. Philosophers used various tests for whether one should do an act, such as whether it was "lawful" or "permissible" (NIV) and, more important, whether it was "profitable" (NASB) or "expedient" (KJV). Many philosophers excused relieving their sexual appetites with prostitutes or by publicly stimulating themselves, explaining that they were in complete control of their own emotions!

As is common in *diatribe (an ancient teaching form), Paul cites the opinion of an imaginary opponent similar to that of his readers, and then refutes or qualifies it: " 'I can get away with anything.' Maybe so, but 'anything' is not good for you."

6:13-14. "Food for the stomach and the stomach for food" was a typical Greek way of arguing by analogy that the body was for sex and sex for the body (cf. also the general use of the "stomach" metaphor in comment on Phil 3:19). That God would do away with both reflected the typical Greek disdain for the doctrine of the *resurrection (chap. 15), because Greeks believed that one was done with one's body at death. Paul responds to this Greek position with the *Old Testament/Jewish perspective that the body is for God and he will resurrect it.

6:15-16. Here Paul argues from Genesis 2:24. Jewish interpreters normally applied this text to marriage, but because in Jewish law intercourse sealed a marriage union or betrayed it, Paul's argument from Genesis 2:24 would make sense to Jewish readers or to Gentiles conversant with the Old Testament.

Prostitution was considered a business like any other, disreputable as the occupation was thought to be (for prostitutes, not for the men who had sex with them). It was readily available in inns and taverns, and the ranks of prostitutes were especially stocked with slave girls raised from the vast number of abandoned babies. Jews strongly opposed prostitution (although a few engaged in it), and *Philo said that it was a capital offense in God's sight; but this Jewish view was hardly the pagan position. Some pagans even considered prostitution a useful deterrent to adultery.

6:17. The *Old Testament speaks of people being "joined" to God (Jer 50:5; Zech 2:11; cf. Num 25:3; Hos 4:17). Paul works here especially with the Old Testament doctrine that God is married to his covenant people. Applying the analogy from Genesis 2:24, Paul cannot say that God is "one flesh" with them (the Old Testament and Judaism did not believe God had flesh), but he can say they are "one spirit," united in an intimate, covenant relationship like husband and wife. Thus Christians uniting themselves with prostitutes would defile the sanctity of their relationship with God, as in the religious prostitution so common in pre-Roman Corinth.

6:18. Moralists often exhorted people to flee from vices (also in 10:14); a *narrative example in this case would be Joseph (Gen 39:12). "Every sin [KJV, NRSV; not 'other' sins, against NASB, NIV] . . . is outside the body" may represent the opposing position (6:12-14), to which Paul responds, "The sexually immoral person sins against his own body."

6:19. Compare comment on 3:16-17; but here the application to the individual Christian (and hence his or her sexual sanctity) is Paul's own.

6:20. Glorifying God with the body ran against the Greek thinking of many of Paul's readers; see comment on 6:12-14. "Bought" refers to redemption from slavery (7:23); here it is possible that Paul makes a wordplay on the price of freeing a slave prostitute.

7:1-7
Fulfilling Conjugal Rights

Different views on celibacy existed in the ancient world. Most ancient writers condemned it; many Jewish teachers even considered it sinful, because reproduction was essential and marriage was the proper deterrent from sexual offenses and distractions. ("Replenishing the earth" was considered a biblical commandment for all Jews. Abortion and child abandonment were widely practiced in antiquity; under Roman law, a newborn was not legally a person till the father accepted him or her as a member of the family. But ancient Jews and Christians—as well as some pagan moralists—unanimously condemned both as the taking of human life.)

A number of groups of philosophers and minor religious sects, however, as well as many *Essenes among the Jews, advocated celibacy or the rejection of marriage. Some philosophers rejected marriage but thought that sexual release with prostitutes was acceptable since it would not tie a person down (cf. comment on 6:12-20).

One may divide some of the ancient opinions roughly as follows: (1) Marriage and procreation are vital for all who are physically capable of it (the majority view). (2) Marriage is a distraction and should never be undertaken by the wise man except in the rare instances where one might find a spouse equally devoted to the philosophic lifestyle (the *Cynic position). (3) Marriage is good for most people, but one must make exceptions for those too committed to other spiritual pursuits to take time for it (an early-second-century *rabbi). Paul combines elements of the second and third views.

7:1. Now Paul responds to the position in their letter to him: "It is good not to touch [not 'marry'—NIV, TEV] a woman." Some members of the *church may be following an idea common among many Greek thinkers: sex was fine as long as one did not get tied down with marriage (cf. 6:12-20). Others, whom Paul addresses here, are already married (7:2-5) and abstain from relations with their spouses. Paul says that it is too late to choose celibacy once one is married (cf. v. 5).

7:2. "Let each have" reflects a Greek idiom for "Let them have sexual relations." Jewish people saw married sexual intimacy as the best deterrent to sexual immorality, and Paul here agrees (see also Prov 5:19-20).

7:3. Jewish marriage contracts stipulated a number of duties for the husband and a number for the wife; one major duty required of the husband was intercourse. Paul views intercourse as a mutual obligation; the meaning of "marital duty" (NIV) here is clear (cf. "conjugal rights"—NRSV).

7:4. Greek writers sometimes portrayed submitting to sexual relations or passion as bringing oneself under someone else's control.

7:5. Jewish teachers who were trying to formulate laws in this period differed on how long a man could vow to abstain from intercourse with his wife; one school said two weeks, and the other school said one week. Although Paul would not make longer abstinence grounds for divorce, as they did (7:10-13), he clearly wishes to limit even abstinence by mutual consent, leaving the specifics to the couple. For "temptation" here see comment on 7:2, 9.

7:6. Jewish law permitted concessions for human weakness; here Paul permits but does not require periods of abstinence, implying that it is those who wish to abstain (rather than those who do not) who are weak. Abstinence within marriage is their idea, not his.

7:7. Paul recognizes that not all are called to singleness and equipped for it.

7:8-16
Getting Married Versus Staying Married

Verses 8-9 are a *digression Paul uses

to establish a contrast between single persons concerned to stay single (7:8-9) and married persons wishing to become single (7:10-16). Digressions were a standard feature of ancient writing.

7:8. Singleness has advantages; see comment on 7:32-34. But not everyone is equipped for this lifestyle; others should pursue marriage (7:9).

7:9. "Burn" (NIV, NRSV and TEV interpret correctly by adding "with passion") was used throughout ancient romances to describe the arousal of passion, often (metaphorically) through Cupid's fiery darts. Whereas Greco-Roman literature in general saw nothing wrong with passion, Paul believes that its proper place is only in marriage, and he advocates two alternatives: either self-control or marriage.

7:10-11. This divorce prohibition—virtually unique in antiquity—is "from the Lord," from a saying of Jesus (Mk 10:11-12). (The terms translated "leave" and "send away"—NASB—or "separate" and "divorce"—NIV and NRSV—were often synonyms for divorce and probably function as such in this context. In 7:10-11, however, where Paul refers to Jesus' teaching, it may be significant that a wife in Jewish Palestine could only "leave," not "divorce"; in Roman society, either partner could divorce the other.)

7:12-13. In 7:12-16, Paul must address how Jesus' teaching relates to a specific situation; general statements of principle were regularly qualified for specific situations. What about the party divorced against his or her will? (Under Palestinian Jewish law, women could be divorced by a unilateral act of the husband; under Roman law, either party could divorce the other.) Because most first-generation Christians were converted after marriage (which was generally arranged by parents), this text is no indication that Christians knowingly chose marriages with pagans.

7:14. Both Greco-Roman and Jewish law debated the status of children of socially mixed unions; Jewish law also debated the status of children of religiously mixed unions. Here Paul argues that children of religiously mixed unions are within the sphere of *gospel influence and cannot be used as an excuse for divorce. In Roman society, the children normally went to the father in the event of a divorce; a Christian wife involved in a divorce would lose her opportunity to influence her children for God.

7:15. Paul addresses the specific situation not addressed in Jesus' general principle that he has just cited (7:10-11): the innocent party is free to remarry (see comment on 7:12-13). "Not under bondage" or "not bound" alludes to the wording of Jewish divorce documents, which told the woman, "You are free to remarry any man," and further applied to divorce the precise language of freedom from slavery. Being "bound" would mean that she was still married in God's sight; not being "bound," or being "free," meant that she was free to remarry.

7:16. Although the *Old Testament stressed God's faithfulness to the families of his servants, it is also clear that godly parents could have ungodly children, and ungodly parents could have godly children (c.f., e.g., 2 Chron 23—36 passim). Paul here agrees that the conversion of the spouse is not guaranteed.

7:17-24
Be Content with Present Circumstances

Whether persons are married or single, they should accept their present lot, although this acceptance does not mean that one can never change one's lot (7:21). Paul's argument here is so similar to *Cynic-*Stoic teaching that his educated, philosophically inclined readers would probably concede his point respectfully.

7:17. Greek philosophers, especially Stoics, emphasized accepting one's situation. But whereas Stoics identified the God who directed their lives with Fate, Paul trusts God as a loving Father.

7:18-20. Greeks exercised in the nude, and both Greeks and Romans regarded circumcision as a mutilation. For several centuries some Jews, ashamed of their circumcision in the predominantly Greek culture, had opted for a minor surgical operation that could pull the remains of their foreskin forward and make them appear uncircumcised.

7:21. Many ancient philosophers believed that slaves and masters could be moral and spiritual equals, but the philosophers also had to address the situation in which slaves lived. Even when such philosophers came to power (such as Marcus Aurelius, an emperor in the second century), they did not force their *Stoic morality on society. Every attempted slave revolt had been brutally repressed, so Paul's advice is the most practical he can give.

7:22. A *freedperson owed some continuing duties to his or her former master but was legally free. The former master remained a *patron, who would help the freedperson out financially and politically; the freedperson remained a *client, who would also look out for the former master's interests and reputation. Freedpersons were still considered part of their former master's household.

7:23-24. Slaves were expensive. They could be bought to be turned over to a temple ("freed" for service to a god) or, more often, to a new human owner.

7:25-38 Advice Especially to Virgins

Although this section addresses mainly virgins, Paul digresses here as elsewhere (7:8-9; 11:2-16), in this case to relate the virgins to groups he has just discussed (7:27-28, alluding back to 7:12-16).

7:25. The term translated "virgin" here was usually used for women, who were also the only ones expected to avoid premarital sex in Greco-Roman culture (outside Judaism). Paul seems to apply the term to both men and women, as do a few later writers.

7:26. Many Jewish people expected a time of great suffering just before the end of the world; in that time, marriage and procreation would be of little value. In other periods of great suffering, when one was liable to be bereaved of spouse and children, the same principle applied (e.g., Jer 16:2; this was not the norm—cf. Jer 29:6).

7:27-28. In the language of ancient divorce contracts, "do not seek to be released" (NASB) means "do not seek a divorce" (NIV). "Released from a wife" (NASB; not simply "unmarried"—NIV) can mean "divorced" or "widowed," and in the immediate passage must at least include the former (its meaning in the preceding line). Paul discourages both remarriages (v. 27) and first marriages of virgins for reasons given in the context, but he permits both.

7:29-31. The dangerous time that was upon them would affect all normal human relations; see comment on 7:26.

7:32-35. As a matter of principle, *Cynic philosophers eschewed marriage (though not intercourse) to avoid "distraction"; one could make an exception, however, if one found a wife who shared these convictions and who would thus not distract one from the

Cynic lifestyle (the only recorded exception is Hipparchia, wife of Crates). The context indicates that Paul is making a general statement here, not a rule without exceptions; see comment on 9:5. Paul allows that some would be distracted more by being unmarried (7:2, 5, 9), but reiterates the value of singleness for those who can live by it.

7:36-38. Scholars debate whether this passage addresses the fathers of virgins (see NASB) or their fiancés (see NIV, NRSV, TEV); evidence within the text can be read either way. Parents arranged their children's marriages, usually with some input from the children; the father had the greatest measure of authority in the matter. "Full age" (7:36—NASB) could mean midteens (parental arrangement of marriages allowed couples to wed at a younger age than in our culture); but the term normally means "beyond youth" and hence probably refers to a virgin older than usual. There is no evidence in this period for unconsummated "spiritual engagements," which became common in later Christianity, perhaps through the "fiancé" reading of this passage.

7:39-40
Widows and Remarriage

7:39. On "bound" and "free," see 7:15, 27; in discussions of divorce and widowhood "free" always meant "free to remarry." (Different Greek words are used for "bound" in 7:15 and for "free" in 7:27, but these are synonyms; variation was a standard *rhetorical technique and appears throughout the New Testament.) Those who argue that the first line of this verse excludes remarriage of all divorced persons ignore not only 7:15, 27-28, but also the language of antiquity: no one considered her former spouse "her husband" after a legitimate divorce had taken place. That a widower is to marry only "in the Lord" means that Paul is against Christians' marrying non-Christians (cf. Deut 7:3; Judg 3:6; Ezra 9:2); widows and divorcées, unlike virgins (whose parents arranged their marriages), had a great deal of say about whom they would marry.

7:40. Although Paul states his "opinion" (NASB, TEV) much less strongly than he proclaims the words of Jesus (7:10-12), he does not for this reason think it any less authoritative. The *Spirit was normally associated with the prophets of the past, and Paul here claims that he believes he writes under inspiration as a prophet would (cf. 14:37).

8:1-13
Food Offered to Idols

Meat was offered to idols before being served in temples' dining halls (often as part of worship) or being used for communal meals; some of the meat served at the marketplace had been offered to idols. One who ate in a temple would know the source of the meat; one who ate at a pagan friend's home could never be certain. In pagan cities with large Jewish populations, Jews normally had their own markets.

Palestinian Jewish teachers debated what to do in many cases of uncertainty (such as untithed food), but would never have taken a chance on food that might have been offered to an idol. They believed that Jews outside Palestine unwittingly compromised with idolatry when invited to pagans' banquets for their sons, even if they brought their own food. Following such teachings strictly (as some did) would have greatly circumscribed their relationships with pagan colleagues. The matter was more troubling for Christians converted from pagan backgrounds: could they meet over lunch with business associates or fellow members of their trade guild, or attend a reception in a temple for a relative's wedding?

In chapters 8—10, Paul works on an elaborate compromise between two factions in the Corinthian *church. The more educated and socially elite group, who unlike the poor ate meat regularly and not just when it was doled out at pagan festivals, had well-to-do friends who would serve meat. They probably represent the liberal faction, who consider themselves "strong" and the socially lower group "weak."

8:1-3. Paul probably opens with the issue of knowledge bringing freedom because the Corinthians' letter to him had raised it (cf. 7:1); they claimed that superior "knowledge" about idols not being real enabled them to eat. Paul disagrees with their application.

8:4-5. Verses 4-6 constitute a good monotheistic statement that the "strong" are using to claim that idol food does not matter, hence they can eat it. Paul agrees with the content of these verses but not the application of the content that these Corinthians make (8:7-13).

8:6. *Stoics and others used formulas similar to this one (many gods, but one true or supreme God), which Jewish apologists (defenders) for monotheism naturally exploited. But Paul's position differs from both the Stoic and the Jewish position. The basic confession of Judaism was that there was one God, who was also the one Lord (Deut 6:4); Paul portrays both Father and Son as deity here. Some Jewish texts said that God created the world through personified Wisdom; here Paul assigns this same role to Christ (cf. 1 Cor 1:30).

8:7. Meat was unavailable to most Corinthians who were not well-to-do except at the pagan festivals, when it was doled out to the masses. Many of the socially powerless (the "weak") thus inevitably associated meat with idolatry.

8:8. Here Paul probably states the view of the "strong," the Corinthian elite, with which he concurs except for his response in 8:9.

8:9. Philosophers generally believed that "all things" were theirs and that they had liberty and authority to do as they pleased. Some, like the *Cynics, paid no attention to social customs. But ancient Jewish *rabbis who felt certain that they were right nevertheless circumscribed their own rights and submitted to the majority opinion of their colleagues, for the sake of peace. Jewish teachers considered causing someone to "stumble" from the way of God worse than killing that person, because it deprived the person of the life of the world to come.

8:10-13. The person who associates meat with idols might think that eating it was all right even if it meant participating in idolatry, misunderstanding the "strong" person's convictions. (Similarly, *Pharisees said that if one saw a Pharisee accepting food from an unreligious person, that did not mean one could assume that the food had been tithed; the Pharisee might have simply committed himself in his heart to tithe on it when he got home.)

9:1-14
Worthy of Support

Having called on the more well-to-do Corinthian Christians to give up their rights (chap. 8), Paul illustrates this principle by how he had given up his own rights (chap. 9), then continues the discussion of meat offered to idols (chap. 10). Ancient moral teachers commonly used their own lives as examples to make moral points, and their followers observed their lives as well as their teachings to learn how to live. Jewish teachers' lives were sometimes even used as legal precedent by later *rabbis.

9:1-2. By "free," philosophers normally meant free from false values or free from property concerns and thus self-sufficient. The idea of freedom was often bound up with "authority" or "rights"; Paul, who calls on his readers to circumscribe their "freedom" (8:9), also sacrifices his own rights (9:4-5).

9:3. Paul's primary purpose here is to provide an example that will support his exhortations in chapter 8; but for this purpose he adapts the form of an "apologetic [defense] letter." Some well-to-do members of the congregation have been complaining about Paul's simple artisan lifestyle, which distinguished him from most traveling teachers (see comment on 9:6). What is a peripheral issue here later becomes central when this group's dissatisfaction is exploited by other traveling teachers (see comment on 2 Cor 12:13-18).

9:4. Here Paul states a simple right to sustenance; see comment on 9:1-2, 6.

9:5. Jewish *disciples who went away to study under a distant teacher would not bring their wives along; this was also true of the disciples in the Gospels. But just as the rare *Cynic who found a wife willing to share his lifestyle would take her with him (see comment on 7:32-35), so the *apostles took their wives as colaborers. Paul presents himself and Barnabas as exceptions to the general rule that apostles were married.

Although ancient Egyptian and Hebrew (Song 4:9-12; 5:1) love songs called wives "sisters" as a term of endearment (also Tobit 8:4, 7), the term here simply means a sister in Christ (i.e., a fellow Christian; thus some translations have "a believing wife"; KJV has "a sister, a wife").

9:6. Philosophers supported themselves in one of several ways: by attaching themselves to a wealthy *patron, who used them for ostentatious dinner lectures; by charging fees for instruction; by begging (generally despised, but practiced by the *Cynics); or, least desirable of all, by working as manual laborers. Although artisans normally prided themselves on their own work, aristocrats and those who shared their values despised manual labor. The socially "strong" faction in the *church undoubtedly wish that their founder-teacher did not work.

9:7. If laborers in secular occupations are paid, why not *apostles?

9:8-10. Deuteronomy 25:4 was intended as a principle to teach that the laborer should be fed; here Paul may argue in the sense of the common Jewish *qal vahomer* argument: if for an ox, how much more for a person. Some Jewish teachers felt that God's teachings about animals were only to teach people principles.

9:11-12. Paul refuses to use the right to material support lest anyone be offended by the *gospel. Many traveling teachers depended on others for support, and if hearers thought that Paul was such a teacher, they might challenge his motives for preaching the gospel or view him as a *client of the church's higher-status faction. Philosophers debated among themselves whether they should be concerned about public opinion. Some *Stoics and most *Cynics lived as they pleased, arguing that it mattered not what anyone thought; other philosophers felt that they should give no unnecessary cause of offense, because they wanted to draw others to the wisdom of philosophy.

9:13. Priests and Levites were supported by the tithes of the people (cf., e.g., 2 Chron 31:4) but were also entitled to certain portions of the sacrificial food offered on the altar (like priests in many ancient pagan temples).

9:14. Here Paul alludes to a saying of Jesus (Mt 10:10; Lk 10:7; cf. 1 Tim 5:18).

9:15-27
Paul Sacrifices His Rights

Far from pleasing all his hearers (9:19; cf. 10:33) here, Paul's explicit tactic of siding with the working class (9:12-15) would offend aristocratic-minded landowners who had never done any manual labor. His use of populist political imagery in 9:19-23 would further alienate this part of his constituency, which is the financial backbone of the *church. Paul's priorities are reaching all people with the *gospel, not satisfying the tastes of a societal elite.

9:15. Self-reliance was a basic characteristic highly extolled among philosophers.

9:16. "Woe is me" was a common *Old Testament and Greek phrase uttered by one confronted with terrible news.

9:17-18. *Stoic philosophers said that Fate imposed its will whether one accepted it or not; hence one might as well accept it. The Old Testament taught that one must submit to God's call, even if (as in the case of Moses, Gideon, Isaiah and Jeremiah) one felt unprepared or inadequate for it.

9:19-23. Aristocratic thinkers despised demagogues who tried to please the masses; they considered such demagogues "slaves." Paul borrows the language of populist politics, undoubtedly offending defenders of the aristocratic element in Corinth. Some Jewish teachers, like *Hillel, were similarly accommodationists, to win as many as possible to the truth.

9:24-25. Philosophers (followed by *Diaspora Jewish sources like *Philo and *4 Maccabees) commonly used athletic illustrations to describe their striving for truth and wise living. Paul portrays the discipline and self-sacrifice necessary to live the Christian life through the analogy of races (9:24-26a) and boxing (9:26b-27). (The footrace preceded the other four athletic contests of the pentathlon in the Panhellenic Games.) The clause "but only one receives the prize" (a wreath for the head, which would eventually rot) emphasizes how hard one had to work to win the race. (A long period of intense discipline was mandatory for any who planned to participate in the events. For instance, participants for the Olympic games had to swear by Zeus to follow ten months of strict training beforehand.)

Corinth itself hosted major games for all Greece every two years on the isthmus; these were the best-attended Greek festivals next to the Olympic games, which were held every four years. The pine garland was awarded at these Isthmian games (wild olive at the Olympic, parsley at the Nemean, etc.).

9:26-27. Boxing was one of the major competitions at Greek games; boxers wore leather gloves covering most of the forearm except the fingers, and boxing was a violent sport. Shadowboxing or "beating the air" was insufficient preparation for a boxing competition; a boxer had to discipline his body better than that to win. In the same way, Paul had to discipline his life to sacrifice what he needed to sacrifice for the sake of the *gospel, lest he himself be disqualified from the race and fall short of the wreath of *eternal life (9:25).

10:1-13
Israel's History as a Warning

Having established that those who eat idol meat ought to lay down their rights, Paul now proceeds to an argument from Scripture: the Corinthian Christians' sexual immorality and associations with idolatry were no different from those of ancient Israel and invited the judgment of God. Paul's conclusions might surprise his readers, but his style of argument would not: ancient teachers relied heavily on past examples, especially from sacred books; Judaism naturally drew its examples from the Scriptures.

10:1-2. Some later Jewish teachers also drew parallels between the Red Sea and Jewish *proselyte *baptism, but Paul could use this illustration whether or not anyone else had already thought of it in his period. He parallels the experience of salvation in the first exodus and salvation in Jesus to show that salvation does not render one invulnerable to falling (10:6-12). (Jewish people were awaiting a new exodus, promised by the prophets for the time of the *Messiah.)

10:3-4. Again, the Israelites in the wilderness had sacred food and drink, as the Corinthians do (10:16), but that did not save them (10:6-12). In some Jewish traditions the well followed the Israelites in the wilderness (some added, on account of Miriam's merit). In Paul's *midrashic application, what the rock did for Israel corresponds to what Christ did for the Corinthians.

10:5. Jewish teachers generally regarded early deaths as signs of God's judgment (in their view scholars of the *law, for whom God had a higher standard, could be so judged even for failing to study the law diligently enough).

10:6. The events recorded in the law were meant as a sign or warning to others (Num 26:10). The Israelites' evil desires consisted in desiring "better" food than the manna, the spiritual food God had provided (Num 11:4-6); they wanted meat (Num 11:18; cf. comment on 1 Cor 8:7).

10:7. See Exodus 32:4, 6. Just as Israel had once eaten in God's presence (Ex 24:11), so in Exodus 32:6 they ate and drank before an idol whom they called God. Later *rabbis considered this the most embarrassing episode in Israel's history (eventually some even found ways to blame it on the *Gentiles traveling with the Israelites). Jewish interpreters rightly took "play" in this text to mean idolatry (cf. "pagan revelry"—NIV).

10:8. The Israelite men had unmarried sex with Midianite women, who were acting as cultic prostitutes (Num 24:1-8), and God sent a plague in judgment (Num 24:9). Jewish traditions unanimously report that twenty-four thousand died, as does the *Old Testament text; perhaps Paul intends an allusion to the numbered Levites (Num 26:62) or mixes this with an allusion to the three thousand killed in an earlier judgment (Ex 32:28). But ancient writers would not have lingered or expressed concern over this sort of detail, although it has exercised modern readers (who usually suggest either a major mistake or that the other thousand died the next day).

10:9-10. Jewish traditions unanimously lament Israel's behavior in the wilderness, including their complaining against God's provision. Philosophers also warned against grumbling, noting that one ought to accept whatever the gods and Fate would send.

10:12-13. Ancient teachers often pointed out that adversities come to everyone, and that one should not be proud but submit to what comes one's way. But whereas pagan writers emphasized human will, Paul emphasizes

God's faithfulness.

10:14-23
Idol Meat Supports Demons

Here Paul gives a religious argument against eating meat offered to idols.

10:14. "Fleeing" vices was a fairly frequent moral exhortation in antiquity (cf. 6:18).

10:15. Ancient speeches and letters of admonition often opened with a compliment designed to secure the favor of the audience. Paul's purpose is to persuade the Corinthians, not merely to rebuke them.

10:16-17. To honor pagan gods in Greek religious ceremonies, small libations of wine would be poured out of cups before people drank from them. But here "cup" and "bread" allude to the Passover meal, which was celebrated in the Lord's Supper (11:23-26). Not only at the Passover meal but at meals in general the head of the Jewish household would say a blessing (thanks) over a cup of wine. Commentators report that the last cup at the end of the meal was called the "cup of blessing."

10:18. The priests ate some parts of the offerings in the temple; other kinds of offerings (such as the Passover lamb, which Paul also considers a sacrifice—5:7) were eaten by the rest of the people. "Sharers in the altar" (NASB) means that Israel was bound together in their sacrifice to the one God.

10:19-20. Like Isaiah, Paul says that physical idols are nothing (cf. Is 44:12-20; 45:20-25; 46:1-11). But like most of the *Old Testament passages that mention demons (at least in their Greek rendering—Lev 17:7; Deut 32:17, 37-39; Ps 106:28, 37) and most subsequent Jewish and Christian literature apart from the *rabbis, Paul believes that false gods seeking human worship are demons.

10:21. Pagans spoke of the offering tables of their gods (e.g., the table of Serapis); most ancient Near Eastern temples had been equipped with such tables. The expression "table of the Lord" occurs in the Old Testament as meaning the altar (e.g., Mal 1:7; cf. 1 Cor 9:13). Table fellowship connoted intimate relations.

10:22. Paul again provides a rhetorical objection against his own position, but his readers who are familiar with the *Old Testament know that the Lord is a jealous God who allows the worship of no other gods (e.g., Deut 32:17, 21; see comment on 1 Cor 10:19-20).

10:23. Greek teachers used criteria like "usefulness" to determine whether to undertake actions. Paul raises a rhetorical objection ("Everything is allowed") and then answers it ("But not everything is helpful"), as was common in ancient moral teaching.

10:24—11:1
Instructions for the Sake of Others

10:24-25. Whatever meat was left over from sacrifices was taken to the meat market in the large agora in Corinth (not far from where Paul had once worked—Acts 18:3). Not all meat in this market had been offered to idols, but some of it had. In comparatively large cities, Jewish people were often allowed to have their own markets so they could avoid such food. In other cities, they would ask about the source of the meat. But Jewish teachers considered inadvertent sins "light"; thus Paul can trust that the scrupulous will be satisfied with "What you don't know won't hurt you." Because most people could not afford to buy meat, subsisting instead on fish and grain, Paul here addresses the well-to-do in the congregation.

10:26. Here Paul quotes Psalm 24:1, which extolled the majesty and greatness of God; he was the only true and living God, and everything belonged to him, not to idols or demons. Jewish teachers, possibly as early as Paul, used this text to prove the need to give thanks at meals.

10:27-29. Most temples had their own dining halls, and people were invited to meals "at the table of Serapis" and other pagan gods. The meat at these meals would obviously have been offered to idols. But people were also invited to banquets in wealthy homes, where they could not be certain of the meat's source. Jewish people who avoided impure foods (like pork) were virtually excluded from such banquets, but they did not look down on *Gentiles who ate pork as long as they abstained from idols. Jewish people had sometimes faced martyrdom to avoid eating impure foods, and they would expect Gentiles who claimed to believe in God at least to avoid food that had certainly been offered to idols.

10:30. Like Jewish people, Christians always offered thanks over their food before (and, at least in pious Palestinian Jewish homes, after) the meal.

10:31. Some Jewish teachers emphasized that everything should be done for the sake of God, as Paul does here; some philosophers argued that one should invest one's life only in that which is of eternal significance. In the *Old Testament, God clearly desired his people to live wholly for him (Deut 6:4-5; Ps 63:1). Paul regards such convictions as appropriate and applies them to the credibility of the *gospel (1 Cor 10:32-33).

10:32-33. See comment on 9:19-23.

11:1. Paul had already presented himself (chap. 9) as an example of this principle, which he articulates in 10:32-33; philosophers often used their own lifestyles as models for their pupils.

11:2-16 Women's Head Coverings

Paul returns to the topic of food in 11:17-34 (cf. chaps. 8-10), but here he digresses briefly to address another issue in the Corinthian *church that involves those who are free surrendering their rights (11:10). *Digressions were standard in ancient literature.

Women's hair was a common object of lust in antiquity, and in much of the eastern Mediterranean women were expected to cover their hair. To fail to cover their hair was thought to provoke male lust as a bathing suit is thought to provoke it in some cultures today. Head covering prevailed in Jewish Palestine (where it extended even to a face veil) and elsewhere, but upper-class women eager to show off their fashionable hairstyles did not practice it. Thus Paul must address a clash of culture in the church between upper-class fashion and lower-class concern that sexual propriety is being violated. (That Greeks bared their heads for worship and Romans covered them might also be significant, given the dual affiliation of Corinth as a Greek and Roman city. But because this custom was not divided along gender lines, it is probably irrelevant here.)

Thus Paul provides a series of brief arguments, each of which relates directly to the culture he addresses. His arguments do not work well in every culture (he is not completely satisfied with all of them himself—11:11-12), but it is the Corinthian women, not modern women, whom he wishes to persuade to cover their heads.

11:2. Letters were often written to "praise" or "blame" the recipients; sometimes these points characterized the entire letter in which they occurred. "Traditions" (NASB, NRSV) were accounts or regulations passed on orally; for instance, *Pharisees in Palestine transmitted their special traditions in this way.

11:3-4. Ancient writers often based arguments on wordplays, as Paul does here. He uses "head" literally (for that which is to be covered) and figuratively (for the authority figure in the ancient household). (Some commentators have argued, perhaps rightly, that "head" means not "authority" but "source"—see 11:12—but the matter is vigorously debated and cannot be decided here.) On head coverings for women, see the introduction to this section. Women did not lead prayers in most *synagogues, and Jewish tradition tended to play down *Old Testament prophetesses; Paul's *churches allow considerably more freedom for women's ministry.

11:5-6. Paul uses the ancient debate principle of *reductio ad absurdum:* If they are so concerned to bare their heads, why not also remove the natural covering, their hair? Paul thereby reduces their insistence to the absurd: the greatest physical shame for a woman was to be shaved or have her hair cut like a man's.

11:7. Paul here begins an argument from the order of creation. He cannot be denying that women are also the image of God (Gen 1:27 plainly states that both male and female were created in God's image). Perhaps he means that women's uncovered heads are drawing men's attention to humanity instead of to God; as one would say today, they were turning men's heads.

11:8-9. According to Genesis 2:18 God created woman distinct from man partly so that man would no longer be alone; the phrase there translated "helper suitable" praises woman's strength rather than subordinates her. ("Helper" is used more often of God than of anyone else in the *Old Testament; "suitable" means "corresponding" or "appropriate to," as an equal in contrast to the animals.) Woman was thus created because man needed her strength, not (as some have wrongly interpreted this verse) to be his servant.

11:10. Here Paul says literally, "she ought to have authority over her own head because of the angels"; Paul means that she should exercise wisely her right to decide whether to cover her head in a way that will honor her husband (11:8-9), given the situation with "the angels." The "angels" have been interpreted as (1) the angels who (according to ancient Jewish interpretations of Gen 6:1-3) lusted after women and so fell; (2) the angels present in divine worship, who would be offended by a breach of propriety or affront to the husbands (cf. the *Dead Sea Scrolls); and (3) the angels who rule the nations but who will ultimately be subordinate to all believers, including these women (6:3; i.e., as a future ruler a Christian woman or man should exercise wise choices in the present, even regarding apparel).

11:11-12. Paul qualifies his preceding argument from creation (11:7-10); he wants to prove his case about head coverings, but nothing more. Women and men are mutually interdependent (cf. also 7:2-5).

11:13-15. Ancient writers, especially *Stoic philosophers, liked to make arguments from nature. Nature taught them, they said, that only men could grow beards; women's hair naturally seemed to grow longer than men's. Like all urban dwellers, Paul is well aware of exceptions to the rule (barbarians, philosophers and heroes of the epic past, as well as biblical Nazirites); but the "nature" argument could appeal to the general order of creation as it was experienced by his readers.

11:16. Paul reserves one final argument for those unpersuaded by his former points. One philosophical group called the Skeptics rejected all arguments except an almost universally accepted one: the argument from custom—"that's just not the way it's done."

11:17-34
Factionalized Fellowship

The *churches in Corinth met in well-to-do *patrons' homes (see comment on Acts 18:6-7). In Greco-Roman society, patrons often seated members of their own high social class in the special *triclinium* (the best room), while others were served, in plain view of this room, in the *atrium* (the couches in which might seat as many as forty persons). The guests in the larger room, the *atrium,* were served inferior food and inferior wine, and often complained about the situation. This societal problem spilled over into the church.

The background for the meal itself is the Jewish Passover, a sacred meal and celebration; see comment on Matthew 26:17-30. But the Corinthians seem to have lost sight of this background; they treat the meal as a festal banquet such as they knew from Greek festivals or meetings of Greek religious associations.

11:17-19. Paul could praise the Corinthians on some points (see comment on 11:2) but not on this one; like division by racism or cultural bias (see introduction to Romans), division by social class is contrary to the *gospel.

11:20. On the "Lord's Supper" see the "Lord's table" in 10:21. Paul intends an ironic contrast between the *Lord's* Supper (11:20) and their own (11:21).

11:21-22. Some are treated more honorably than others at the meal, and this treatment reflects the status values of the world. See the introduction to this section.

11:23. "Received" and "delivered" (KJV, NASB) were used especially for passing on traditions (11:2; 15:3). Some later *rabbis spoke of traditions received "from Moses"; although they believed they received them by means of their own predecessors, they meant that the tradition ultimately went back to Moses. Paul probably means that earlier *disciples told him about the Last Supper. It took place at "night," as the Passover meal always did.

11:24-25. The unleavened Passover bread was normally interpreted figuratively as "the bread of affliction that our ancestors ate" in Moses' time; Jesus had applied it to himself (see comment on Mk 14:22-24). Pagans sometimes ate funerary meals "in remembrance of" a dead person, but the sense here is as in the *Old Testament, where the Passover commemorated God's redemptive acts in history (e.g., Ex 12:14). As in the Passover ritual (cf. the principle in Deut 26:5), the "you" applied to all future generations.

11:26. "Until he comes" is the temporal limitation on the Lord's Supper that goes back to Jesus as well (Mk 14:25). Passover celebrations looked forward to the future redemption of Israel as well as backward to how God had redeemed them in the exodus of Moses' day.

11:27-29. "Eating in an unworthy manner" here refers to the status-conscious eating that is dividing the *church (11:21-22). By rejecting other members of Christ's body, the church (10:17), they also reject the saving gift of his body represented by the bread (11:24).

11:30-34. Jewish teachers stressed that in this world God punished the righteous for their few sins, but in the world to come he would punish the wicked for their many sins; thus Jewish teachers believed that suffering could free one from later punishment. Paul agrees at least that suffering *can* be the Lord's discipline; the idea here may be that those who do not embrace other members of the *church no longer receive healing through the church (12:9).

12:1-3
Qualifying the Gifts

Because Christian gifts like *prophecy are given by God's *Spirit (in both the Old Testament and the New Testament), cultural background is less important here than in some parts of 1 Corinthians (e.g., on meat offered to idols). But it can help the modern reader appreciate how the first readers might have viewed the functioning of some of the gifts in their culture.

Paul indicates that prophesying is not necessarily a sign of godliness; pagans prophesied, too, and at Greek oracular shrines possessed persons prophesied ecstatically, inspired by gods other than the Christian God. Although some felt that interest in oracles had declined in this period, oracles and other forms of divination remained a strong influence on pagan culture. Paul can thus point to his readers' former behavior in paganism as a warning that ecstatic activity *by itself* cannot constitute proof that they are obeying God. (Verse 3 probably hypothetically contrasts two extreme examples of evil and true utterances.)

12:4-11
Diverse Gifts

Paul emphasizes that all the gifts are different but all are useful; hence a Christian with one gift is not more or less important than another Christian with a different gift. Like many ancient writers, Paul composes a random list. Given the use of "word," "wisdom" and "knowledge" (12:8) earlier in 1 Corinthians, here these terms surely refer to God's providing speaking ability and teaching (see comment on 1:5). (Some modern readers have taken these terms to refer to supernaturally revealed knowledge. Although in the context of 1 Corinthians these terms probably do not have that meaning, such supernaturally revealed knowledge is often illustrated by prophets in the *Old Testament and may be considered a form of the gift of *prophecy.)

Some magicians sought to perform healings and miracles (12:9-10), but outside Christianity there are no ancient parallels to these events as a regular occurrence within a local congregation. The gift of "discerning spirits" was particularly useful for judging prophecy (cf. 14:29; 1 Jn 4:1). Although ecstatic babbling occurs in some pagan cultures today, the ancient Mediterranean has little evidence of this phenomenon and no parallel to "tongues" (inspired speech in a language one does not know—14:2) or inspired "interpretation" of tongues (the term can mean either translation or communication of the general sense).

12:12-26
All Members of the Body Are Necessary

Paul adapts an image commonly used for the Roman state or for the universe and applies it to the *church (as in Rom 12:3-5). When the plebeians (the lower class in earlier Rome) had proposed revolt, the aristocrat Menenius Agrippa convinced them that although they were less noticeable members (like the stomach), they were necessary; the upper and lower classes had different roles but equal importance. This argument was mere aristocratic sophistry to keep the masses down; but after him other writers, especially *Stoic philosophers, borrowed the image. Stoics said that the universe was like a body, and God's *logos,* or reason, was the mind or head that directed it. Paul here refers to the unity of the body not to keep one group down but to tell all the Christians in Corinth to respect and appreciate one another. Just as a solitary eye or foot is useless, so is any member of the *church apart from other Christians.

12:27-31
Different Gifts Again

12:27-28. "First . . . second . . . third" was normally a designation of rank; most of the gifts after the first three seem to be listed randomly.

12:29-30. Ancient Jews or pagans would consider it extraordinary that any person in a given congregation has some of these gifts, such as *prophecy or miracles, which were considered rare. The term translated "*apostles" probably means "commissioned messengers," backed by the full authority of the sender so long as they represented his message properly; although some philosophers considered themselves messengers of the gods and Jewish people often viewed the *Old Testament prophets in this light, early Christians respected this position as a present office in the *church. (See comment on Eph 4:11.)

12:31. The greatest gifts (also 1 Cor 14:1) are defined by the need of the rest of the body (chap. 13). Most Jewish people believed that only a very small number of very pious men could do miracles; the idea that any believer could seek God for whatever gifts are most useful for his people was unheard-of. Early Christians democratized the supernatural—they believed God could work actively in each believer's daily life.

13:1-3
Nothing Without Love

This chapter resembles praises of various virtues elsewhere in Greco-Roman literature; but that Paul chooses this particular virtue above all others is not dependent on his culture—love appears regularly as the supreme virtue in early Christian literature. As a brief *digression between 12:31 and 14:1 (digressions were common in ancient literature), this chapter explains the way to evaluate which gifts are "greater."

13:1. In some Jewish traditions, angels preferred to speak Hebrew, but most Jewish people would have agreed that angels understood human languages, especially since angels were appointed over various nations. Paul may believe that there are angelic languages in addition to human ones, in which case he would be saying, "Though I be so fluent in tongues that I could speak every conceivable language . . ." (Job's daughters at the end of the *Testament of Job spoke ecstatically in angelic tongues as they were inspired to think heavenly things; but it is not clear whether this text is pre-Pauline or was added by a tongues-speaking Christian in the second century.) Although cymbals were used in some pagan worship (as well as in Jewish worship), the point of Paul's comparison is undoubtedly simply that, though loud, by themselves they communicate nothing (like some *rhetoricians in his day). Corinth was famous for its "bronze," and bronze vases (not "gongs," as in most translations) were often used for amplifiers in the outdoor theaters of this period.

13:2-3. "Moving mountains" seems to have been a figure of speech for doing the impossible (cf. Comment on Mk 11:23; cf. Zech 4:7). If Paul said burn, readers might think of lovers' suicides or self-burning by Indian philosophers, but "giving one's body to be burned" no doubt alludes instead to the standard Jewish tradition of martyrs, some of whom threw themselves into the fire to avoid being forcibly defiled.

13:4-13
What Love Is

13:4-7. The point of Paul's *rhetorically polished description of love is its contract to what he has earlier said about the attitudes of the Corinthians. See comment on 13:1-3.

13:8-13. As in verses 1-3, Paul demonstrates here that love is a greater virtue than the gifts; in this case it is because love is eternal, whereas the gifts are temporary. Some *Old Testament prophets predicted the outpouring of the *Spirit in the final time, accompanied by ability to speak under the Spirit's inspiration (Joel 2:28); but other *prophecies noted that all the citizens of the world to come would know God, hence there would be no reason for exhortation (Jer 31:33-34). Paul believes that the time of the Spirit's gifts, including mere human knowledge, is the current time, between Jesus' first and second comings (cf. 13:10, 12).

Mirrors (13:12) were often made of bronze, and given the worldwide renown of Corinthian bronze, would perhaps strike the Corinthians as a local product (also 2 Cor 3:18). But even the best mirrors reflected images imperfectly (some philosophers thus used mirrors as an analogy to describe mortals' searching for the deity); contrast the more open revelation of Exodus 33:11, Numbers 12:8 and Deuteronomy 34:10.

14:1-20
Intelligible Versus Unintelligible Speech

Because Christian gifts like *prophecy are given by God's *Spirit, cultural background is less important here than in some parts of 1 Corinthians (e.g., on women's head coverings in 11:2-16). But it can help the modern reader appreciate how the first readers might have viewed the functioning of some of the gifts in their culture.

Although Paul is clearly not against speaking in tongues (14:5, 18), he emphasizes that the value of gifts must be judged by their utility in any given setting; intelligible speech profits others in public worship, whereas unintelligible speech, no matter how inspired, is profitable only privately or if interpreted. Neither somber Roman ritual nor ecstatic Greek celebration is the rule of spirituality; concern for others is (chap. 13). The term for "tongues" normally means simply "languages," but it is clear here (14:2, 14) that the person inspired to pray in these other languages does not know the languages; as in Acts, this gift presupposes a supernatural enabling.

14:1-3. In the Old Testament, *prophecy also served the functions Paul lists here: "edification" or building up (and tearing down, e.g., Jer 1:10, where God's word overthrows and restores nations); "exhortation" (KJV, NASB; cf. "encouragement"—NIV, NRSV, TEV), which can include reproof; and nearly all Old Testament prophets, no matter how focused on judgment, included a message of "consolation" (NASB, NRSV) or "comfort" (NIV, KJV, TEV) and hope.

14:4-5. Paul's wish that all could prophesy (cf. Num 11:29) is probably realistic; God had promised to enable all his people to prophesy once the time of the end (inaugurated by Jesus, according to the *New Testament) had come (Joel 2:28). If tongues were interpreted, they could also serve as a form of inspired speech useful to the *church.

14:6-7. Intelligibility is the key to edifying others (14:6-12). Paul mentions here the two primary musical instruments of antiquity: the "pipe" (KJV; not "flute," as in most translations), a wind instrument that sounded like an oboe and often had two pipes from the mouthpiece, was common in religious and emotional music; the "harp," a stringed instrument, was considered more harmonious and often accompanied singing.

14:8-9. "Trumpets" or "bugles" were used to call armies to battle, to march and so forth; an uncertain trumpeting would confuse the soldiers (14:8).

14:10-12. Greeks traditionally looked down on non-Greeks as "barbarians" or "foreigners," calling them "barbarians" because they spoke "inferior" (i.e., non-Greek) languages, but even those who did not believe in the superiority of Greeks divided the world into "Greeks and barbarians" (e.g., Rom 1:14), often on the basis of race but sometimes on the basis of language. Paul simply observes that those who cannot communicate intelligibly may each view the other as an alien (14:11).

14:13-14. The Jewish philosopher *Philo described divine inspiration as God possessing his prophets and completely overwhelming their rational faculties during the period of inspiration. By contrast, Paul believes that prophetic inspiration utilizes the rational faculties (as does interpretation); even with regard to glossolalia or inspired tongues, which are the prayers of a different, nonrational component of human nature, Paul does not indicate that the mind is forced to be inactive. Paul believes that both kinds of worship and both components of human nature are important. (In modern terms, these components of human nature are perhaps similar to the affective and cognitive components, or the subconscious and conscious mind. At any rate, neither the pure rationality of some modern churches nor the pure emotionalism of some churches in other traditions would have suited Paul; his view of worship engaged the whole person.)

14:15. Charismatic worship—that is, worship inspired by the *Spirit—was also practiced by the schools of the prophets in the *Old Testament (1 Sam 10:5; cf. 2 Kings 3:15); transferred to worship in what became the temple (1 Chron 25:1-5), it generated many of the psalms in the book of Psalms. Although worship in tongues had not been practiced in the Old Testament, charismatic worship in a more general sense had been.

14:16-17. Roman officials followed standard prayers exactly; Jewish services allowed more freedom. Paul here expects spontaneity in prayer and does not even object to prayer in tongues ("by one's spirit"), provided that it is interpreted. "Amen" was the standard Jewish response to an agreeable benediction.

14:18-20. In *synagogues, those who prayed could not always do publicly as they did in private; Paul likewise distinguishes between private and public practice of tongues (ten thousand is the largest number in Greek). Even so, he clearly does not forbid it in public (14:39), as long as there is an interpreter (14:28).

14:21-25
Effects on Visitors of Intelligible and Unintelligible Speech

14:21. Here Paul quotes Isaiah 28:11, which in context refers to a sign of judgment; because his people could hear nothing else, God would speak to them through the Assyrians (cf. 33:19; Deut 28:49). (Many Jewish teachers used "law" loosely to refer to anything in the Old Testament; later it was even applied to earlier Jewish traditions.)

14:22. On one view, Paul here refers to tongues as a sign of judgment that causes nonbelievers to stumble (cf. 14:21); on another, Paul quotes the Corinthians in 14:22 and refutes them in 14:23-25 (cf. 6:12-14).

14:23-25. *Prophecy was a known phenomenon in the ancient world, whereas tongues was not (or at least, its parallels were extremely rare); ancients respected prophecy, but if they did not know beforehand to expect speaking in tongues, they would not know what was happening (cf. Acts 2:13). Perhaps Paul would not object to a whole group simultaneously worshiping charismatically under other circumstances (e.g., Acts 2:4-11), such as if they were by themselves (cf. 1 Sam 10:5; 19:20); but these are not the circumstances of the Corinthian house *churches.

14:26-33
Regulations to Keep Order

That Paul had spent over a year and a half with them (Acts 18:11, 18) and had apparently not told them these rules before suggests that these rules are directed toward the specific situation in Corinth. The *rules* necessary to keep worship edifying to everyone might vary from one culture and setting to another, but the *principle* of keeping it edifying to everyone is much more universal.

14:26. Although prayer in the *synagogues may have been more spontaneous in Paul's day than later, he advocates more individual participation here than would have been natural in other worship settings of his day. We should keep in mind, however, that the house *churches in Corinth probably comprised at the most only fifty members. Psalms were used regularly in Jewish worship (here Paul may mean either biblical psalms or newly composed ones), as was teaching; but the revelations, tongues and interpretations are distinctly Christian features of worship.

14:27. Order was very important in lecture settings and public assemblies in antiquity, as is clear from the frequent practice of seating according to rank. In *Essene assemblies, one had to have permission to speak, and one spoke in order according to rank. Paul is not so strict here, but he wishes to balance spontaneity with order; not everything that was inherently good was necessarily good for the gathered assembly. In the *Old Testament, charismatic worship was not incompatible with order (1 Chron 25:1-5; cf. also *Philo's description of an Egyptian Jewish sect of worshipers called the Therapeutae).

14:28. "Speak to himself and to God" probably means "so that only he and God can hear it." It is also possible, however, that this expression implies that tongues could be used not only as prayer but also as a vehicle of God's *Spirit speaking to an individual's spirit (cf. *prophecy coming thus in 2 Sam 23:2-3; Hos 1:2; cf. Ps 46:10; 91:14), although perhaps this speaking is mainly in the form of inspired prayer.

14:29. Most Old Testament prophets were apparently trained in groups of prophets, with more experienced prophets like Samuel presiding over them (1 Sam 19:20; also in the Elijah and Elisha *narratives). The young *churches of Paul's day had few prophets as experienced or trusted as Samuel, so the experience and testing has to be carried out in the public service by all those prophetically endowed. Testing, examining and interpreting prophecies was not necessarily viewed as incompatible with their general inspiration (cf. *Plato on inspired poets, and Jewish sages answering Scripture with Scripture).

14:30. Ancient teachers practiced various customs with regard to sitting and standing; at least in later times, *rabbis would sit and *disciples stand to teach; those who read Scripture would stand. Among the *Essenes, each would speak in turn; often the person speaking to an assembly would stand, while others would be seated.

14:31. On "all prophesying" see comment on 14:5; Paul here adds "teaching" to possible functions of *prophecy (i.e., hearers could learn from it).

14:32. In most contemporary Jewish teaching, prophecy involved complete possession by the *Spirit; one dare not seek to control one's utterance. For Paul, however, inspiration can be regulated, and regulating the timing and manner of one's utterance is not the same as quenching it altogether. On regulating one's spirit, cf. Proverbs 16:32 and 25:28.

14:33. For an appeal to the conduct of the *churches, see comment on 1 Corinthians 11:16.

14:34-35
Interruptions at Lectures

While addressing the topic of church order, Paul briefly *digresses from his contrast of *prophecy and tongues and regulations concerning them to address the interruptions of some women occurring during the teaching period of the church service. Unless Paul changes the subject from women's universal silence (v. 34) to asking questions (v. 35a) and back to universal silence again (v. 35b), his general statement about women's silence in church addresses only the specific issue of their challenges in verse 34a. The issue here is thus their weakness in Scripture, not their gender.

14:34. Biblical *law includes no specific text that enjoins silence or submission on women, although Paul could refer back to his creation argument in 11:8-9 or to the effects of the curse in Genesis 3:16. But he can also use "law" generally (1 Cor 14:21); thus here he could be referring only to the generally subordinate position of women in *Old Testament times. (On this reading, Paul counters an objection of Corinthian prophetesses, who do not think they should be in subjection; although Paul may not believe they should be subjected in all cultures, that they were in the Old Testament period suggests that it is not wrong for them to be submissive in some cultural settings. According to another view, Paul cites the Corinthians' view in 14:34-35 and refutes it in 14:36; cf. comment on 14:22. Others object that 14:36 is too weak to supply a refutation for 14:34-35.)

14:35. Informed listeners customarily asked questions during lectures, but it was considered rude for the ignorant to do so. Although by modern standards literacy was generally low in antiquity (less so in the cities), women were far less trained in the Scriptures and public reasoning than men were. Paul does not expect these uneducated women to refrain from learning (indeed, that most of their culture had kept them from learning was the *problem*). Instead he provides the most progressive model of his day: their husbands are to respect their intellectual capabilities and give them private instruction. He wants them to stop interrupting the teaching period of the church service, however, because until they know more, they are distracting everyone and disrupting church order.

14:36-40
Final Exhortations on Gifts

14:36-38. Some prophets in the *Old Testament stood out as stronger spokespersons for God than their peers—Elijah, Elisha, Samuel and so forth. Most prophets in the early *church were not comparable in authority to *New Testament prophets like Agabus and *apostles like Paul; if some prophets at Corinth appeal to their prophetic capabilities to advance their views, Paul can do so even more to *refute* their views—he claims to speak for God.

14:39-40. Here Paul summarizes the rest of the chapter; concluding summaries were not uncommon, even though they were not always used.

15:1-11
Jesus Was Raised

Some of the Corinthians dispute the future *resurrection of believers. They cannot, however, dispute the past resurrection of Jesus, because this is an established fact and the very foundation of their faith. Yet Paul points out that this fact cannot be separated from the future resurrection of believers (15:12-14).

15:1-2. Paul follows the standard argument technique of beginning with an agreed-on premise; the Corinthians must agree with the very *gospel by which they were converted (see also 2:1-5; Gal 3:2-5).

15:3. "Handed on to you . . . what I had received" (NRSV) is the language of what scholars call "traditioning": Jewish teachers would pass on their teachings to their students, who would in turn pass them on to their own students. The students could take notes, but they delighted especially in oral memorization and became quite skilled at it; memorization was a central feature of ancient education. In the first generation, the tradition would be very accurate; this tradition may even be a verbatim citation in 15:3-5 or 15:3-7. That Jesus died for our sins "according to the Scriptures" may refer especially to Isaiah 53:4-6, 8, 11-12.

15:4. The mention of the burial presupposes an empty tomb after the *resurrection, because by definition "resurrection" meant a new body that did not leave a corpse behind; Paul's Palestinian Jewish sources could have meant the term no other way. Unlike the Gospels, Paul does not mention the empty tomb, because the witnesses provide stronger proof of what happened to Jesus (15:5-8). "The Scriptures" probably refers to an assortment of texts, such as Psalm 16 and Isaiah 53:12. If the "third day" is also in view in "according to the Scriptures," perhaps it alludes to Hosea 6:2, Jonah 1:17 or other texts, although Paul may include the phrase simply to say, according to Jewish custom, that Jesus was raised before he could "see corruption" (Ps 16:10).

15:5. Although arguments from probability counted best in ancient law courts, eyewitness accounts were also highly valued. The ancient epiphanies (revelations) of gods or spirits were normally said to have been attested by eyewitnesses, but these were generally long since dead. ("Epiphanies" of gods in later times often refer simply to dreams or miraculous activities. The *mystery initiation at Eleusis may have climaxed with some sort of ecstatic encounter with the deity, but this event again differs significantly from the sort of historical, unsolicited, mass revelation Paul describes here.) Multiple revelations like this one, and mass revelations as in 15:6, especially defended by a persecuted sect, are virtually unparalleled. Because by definition *resurrection meant a new body, and

Christians would not have been persecuted for claiming that they saw a mere spirit (most ancient people believed in ghosts), they are making a claim no one else made. "Appeared" was used in antiquity both for visions and for actual appearances (often of God or angels); but by all Jewish definitions of resurrection, especially in a Palestinian tradition such as Paul cites here, Paul must mean a literal appearance.

"Cephas" is *Aramaic for "Peter"; for the "Twelve" see comment on Acts 1:13 and the introduction to Acts 1:15-26.

15:6. Paul's purpose in appealing to witnesses still alive is to invite his readers to check his facts if they doubt his words. We may safely rule out the suggestion that the resurrection appearances were mass hallucinations, because such a mass hallucination of a demonstrably physical person is unparalleled in history. (Were this evidence being cited for a war, about which we often take the word of a single ancient author, or any other event in history, no one today would think to deny it; that some regard this evidence as insufficient proof of the resurrection's historicity may indicate more about their own presuppositions concerning the existence or activity of God or his vindication of Jesus.)

15:7. "The *apostles" clearly includes a larger group than the "Twelve" (15:5); see comment on 12:29-30.

15:8. "One untimely born" (NASB, NRSV) or "one abnormally born" (NIV, TEV) usually meant a dead fetus, by either abortion or miscarriage. Paul may be calling himself a freak compared to the other apostles (15:9); he is probably deprecating himself in some manner. This expression could refer to his being born at the wrong time (here, *postmaturely* rather than prematurely), after Jesus' initial resurrection appearances were complete; other commentators have suggested that Paul was chosen from the womb, but his persecution of the church had been annulling that purpose, making him like an aborted person till his conversion.

15:9-11. Greeks did not mind boasting, provided that it was not too conspicuous; Jewish piety emphasized the need to thank God for one's goodness or status. Judaism and most ancient religion believed in retribution for sin; Paul believes that God exalted him despite his sin simply because of God's loving heart.

15:12-19
Resurrection of Christ and of Believers

15:12-17. With the exception of the *Sadducees and some Jews greatly influenced by Greek conceptions, most Palestinian Jews believed in the future *resurrection of the body (Dan 12:2). The resurrection of Jesus was only the initial act of fulfillment in that hope; hence if one rejected the future resurrection, one also had to reject Jesus' resurrection. Following a typical *rhetorical form, Paul's argument forces the Corinthians to accept the resurrection of all believers, because they already agree with him (and objectively could not help but do so—15:1-11) that Jesus had been raised. Jewish teachers also often used the particular to prove the general principle that it presupposed.

15:18-19. These verses suggest that Paul rejects the Greek idea of an immortality of the soul without a bodily resurrection; if there is no resurrection, the *Epicurean denial of an afterlife also follows (15:32). (Despite a view of judgment, the typical Greek view of most people's afterlife as shades below the earth was dreary and unhappy to begin with, providing little of the incentive Paul found in the resurrection.) Paul could believe in the resurrection and in an intermediate existence for the soul, as many *Pharisees did. But if God had not provided future hope for the whole person, Jewish people like Paul, who acknowledged the bodily nature of human existence, would have doubted that he had provided any future hope at all.

15:20-28
God's Plan for History

15:20. The first fruits were the beginning of the Palestinian harvest (familiar from the *Old Testament feast of first fruits, Pentecost—Lev 23:15-21), guaranteeing the imminent ingathering of the remainder of the harvest.

15:21-22. See especially comment on Romans 5:12-21. Paul may here play on a non-Palestinian Jewish tradition (attested in *Philo), possibly adopted by some of the Corinthian Christians, that the ideal, spiritual man formed in Genesis 1:26-27 differed from the natural man Adam formed in Genesis 2:7.

15:23-24. Although Paul's language here is not clear, some think that he, like many Jewish writers of his day, accepted an intermediate *messianic era between the present age and the age to come; see comment on Revelation 20. On "first fruits" see comment on 1 Corinthians 15:20.

15:25. Paul begins expounding Psalm 110:1, which he will link with Psalm 8:6 in 15:27.

15:26. Many philosophers refused to grieve or to view death as an enemy. Jewish writers generally portrayed death as an enemy, sometimes as an angel sent by God, but never pleasant. Paul sees death as the final enemy to be subdued; the *resurrection of believers would thus be the final event preceding Christ's *kingdom.

15:27-28. As in *Old Testament texts, Paul states here that the Son will reign over all else as God's viceroy but remain subordinate in role to the Father (Ps 110:1; Is 9:6-7; Dan 7:14). The use of Psalm 8:6 alludes to Genesis 1:26-28, paving the way for Paul's comparison of Adam and Christ (15:45). Were Paul a *Stoic, God's being "all in all" could mean that all things would be absorbed back into the primeval fire, being part of his being; but when Jewish writers like Paul used such language, they meant merely that God is creator and ruler of all (Ecclus 43:27).

15:29-34
Suffering in Hope of Resurrection

The early Christian witnesses of the *resurrection were so convinced of the truth of their own claims to have seen Jesus alive from the dead that they were not afraid to seal their witness with martyrdom.

15:29. Here "*baptized for the dead" may mean that a Christian friend was baptized for symbolic effect on behalf of a new convert who had died (perhaps by martyrdom, although we know of no major persecution in Corinth; or perhaps on his or her deathbed, thus allowing no time for baptism) before being able to be baptized. (Although there is no evidence of vicarious baptism in ancient Judaism, posthumous symbols could be employed. For instance, if someone was to be executed, Jewish teachers said that his death could atone for his sins; if he died before he could be executed, however, the people placed a stone on the coffin, symbolically enacting his stoning so that his execution would still count with God.) Or this expression may refer to washings of the dead before burial, a standard Jewish custom; religious groups in the ancient Mediterranean supervised the burials of their own members. It could also be a roundabout way of saying "baptized so as to be able to participate in *eternal life with Christians who have already died," hence baptized in the light of their own mortality as well. Many ancient pagans sought to honor the dead, for example, by putting meals at their tombs. To whatever practice Paul alludes, it is not clear whether he agrees with the Corinthian practice; even if he does not, however, he can use it to make his point.

15:30. For the language of continual opposition, cf. Psalm 44:22 and 119:109.

15:31. In this context, "die daily" (KJV, NASB) is figurative speech for Paul's proleptic experience of martyrdom in his repeated sufferings for the *gospel.

15:32. Romans were often entertained by watching criminals, prisoners of war or slaves mauled by wild beasts in the arena, much as many North Americans today enjoy the violence of television or movie theaters (although ancient Christians refused to attend such events except when they themselves were forced to be the victims). Roman gladiatorial shows were also held in the theater at Ephesus during many festivals (as well as in Corinth). It is unlikely, however, that Paul was *literally* cast to beasts in that arena. The victims were not supposed to survive the maulings, and as a Roman citizen Paul would have been exempt from this punishment. Philosophers employed the image of battling such beasts, and Paul here probably describes his opposition in similarly graphic terms (cf. similarly Ps 22:6, 12-13, 16, 20-21). "In human terms" in verse 32 means "figuratively" (contrary to most translations; cf. 9:8; Rom 6:19; Gal 3:15).

But if Paul had no future hope, instead of facing affliction, he may as well have simply indulged his passions, a sentiment often attributed (with some distortion) to *Epicurean philosophers but lived out by many Greek and Roman men at wild parties. Cf. especially Isaiah 22:13 and Luke 12:19. (The *Old Testament often uses the language of eating and drinking in a neutral way [Eccles 2:24; 5:18-19; cf. 3:12], but without God it is never enough for life—Is 22:12-14; Eccles 11:7—12:14; cf. 7:2, 14.)

15:33-34. Here Paul cites a popular proverb, first attributed to the comic playwright Menander but in common circulation by Paul's day. It was the common advice of Greco-Roman moralists and Jewish wisdom teachers to avoid morally inferior company (in the Old Testament, Ps 119:63; Prov 13:20; 14:7; 28:7). Paul perhaps refers here to those who do not believe in the future *resurrection and hence do not have the basis for morals that those who believe in a final judgment of God do; other Jewish teachers who believed in the resurrection associated disbelief in that doctrine with immorality.

15:35-49
The Nature of the Resurrection Body

Ancient Judaism taught the *resurrection of the body, not just the immortality of the soul; Paul agrees but defines the nature of the new body differently from many of his contemporaries.

15:35-38. Ancient writers often raised *rhetorical objections from imaginary opponents; Jewish teachers presented questions like the one Paul raises here as the standard objections nonbelievers raised against the doctrine of the resurrection. For instance, what happened if someone died at sea, or the body was completely destroyed by fire? The *rabbis decided that the body would be resurrected from a particular bone in the neck which they held to be indestructible. Paul more reasonably argues that, regardless of what physical material remains, at least the pattern of the old body will always remain as the seed for the new body. His argument from analogy, a standard argument, is effective, and later rabbis also used the "seed" analogy. "Fool!" (15:36) was a standard rhetorical insult, Jewish as well as Greek, for someone who raised an ignorant or immoral objection.

15:39-41. Even in the present, not all bodies were made of flesh; some were made of glory. Heavenly bodies, sometimes identified with angels, were thought to be made of fire. Paul describes the different kinds of glory that various earthly and heavenly bodies have to explain how the *resurrected body will come in glory, yet each person will remain distinct from other people. Thus there is continuity between the old and new bodies as well as discontinuity. Paul's argument here may not fit modern astronomy very well, but Paul was not commenting on astronomy per se; his argument is meant to persuade ancient readers, whose views of heavenly bodies differed from those of most people today.

15:42-43. Many Jewish teachers believed that the body would be raised in exactly the form in which it had died, even if maimed, and only then be healed; this belief was meant to prove the continuity between the old and new body. But Paul clearly sees the resurrection body in different terms.

15:44-45. A "natural" or "physical" body is literally a "soulish" body, in contrast to a "spiritual" body. Paul does not teach a future body made out of "spirit" (although the *Stoics taught that spirit was a material substance), any more than a present body made out of "soul." Rather, the present body is adapted for current natural existence, and the future body for the life even now ruled by God's *Spirit. In verse 45 Paul cites Genesis 2:7, where God made Adam a soul, a natural man; but many non-Palestinian Jews thought that Genesis 1:26-27 referred to a different, ideal man, the pure form and model for humanity, and Paul may play on this tradition here.

15:46-49. The *Diaspora Jewish philosopher *Philo contrasted the incorruptible "heavenly man" of Genesis 1 with the "earthly man" of Genesis 2; the former represented the ideal spiritual state of the mind seeking heavenly things, the latter the carnal person devoted to temporal things. Paul reapplies the language of this view, which the Corinthians had probably adopted, to the *resurrection body, switching the order (natural then spiritual).

Jewish teachers often explained that Adam's descendants were created like him; his sin brought sin and death into the world for everyone (see comment on Rom 5:12-21). But they also often taught that Adam had incomparable glory and power before his sin, and that this glory and power would be restored in the world to come.

15:50-58
The Resurrection Hope

15:50. "Flesh and blood" was a common figure of speech for mortals.

15:51. "Sleep" was a common euphemism for death.

15:52. *Old Testament prophets often employed the image of the trumpet, which was used to assemble people for convocation or war; here, as in a daily Jewish prayer of the period, it refers to the final gathering of God's people at the end (cf. similarly Is 27:13). Paul undoubtedly takes the image from Jesus (Mt 24:31).

15:53-54. Here Paul quotes Isaiah

25:8, which refers to God's triumph over death at the time of the end, at Israel's final restoration.

15:55. Using common rabbinic freedom, Paul reads "punishment" in the Greek version of Hosea 13:14 as the rhyming Greek word for "victory." Jewish interpreters often linked different texts together on the basis of a common key word; "death" and "victory" occur in Paul's paraphrase of Isaiah 25:8 and also in Hosea 13:14, which Paul may therefore apply to the *resurrection as well. Although the latter passage is in the context of judgment, it does seem to say the same thing as Isaiah 25:8 (unless read as a question).

15:56. Jewish teachers typically expounded points of a text once they had cited it. Paul explains the meaning of "sting" and "victory" ("power") in Hosea 13:14 here (cf. comment on 15:55).

15:57-58. As in 14:39-40, Paul concludes with a sort of summary; here it is a closing exhortation. Just as Judaism often linked failure to believe in the future world with immoral living, and faith in future judgment with perseverance, Paul encourages believers to hold to the truth of the resurrection and so to right living.

16:1-4
Paul's Collection

16:1-2. That one should give "as the Lord has blessed" indicates that Paul is applying the teaching on serving the poor in Deuteronomy 15:14 (cf. also 16:10, 17). On meetings on the "first day" of the week, see comment on Acts 20:7.

16:3-4. When Jewish people from around the world were ready to send the required annual temple tax to Jerusalem, they would choose respected and trustworthy members of their own communities as representatives to take the money to Jerusalem. Jewish travelers often bore letters indicating their authorization, which would allow them to receive hospitality wherever they went; Christians seem to have continued this practice.

16:5-9
Paul's Travel Plans

16:5. The easiest way to travel to Corinth from Ephesus was to cross over by boat from Troas in Asia Minor to Philippi in Macedonia, then to take the westward road and turn south into Greece (as in Paul's second missionary journey in Acts; see Acts 16:7-9).

16:6. The seas were closed for travel in the winter; if Paul were in Corinth once the seas closed, he would stay there until they opened in the spring. Paul is writing in the spring (16:8), hence he anticipates spending considerable time with them (from when he arrives to the following spring). Hospitality was important in antiquity, and the Corinthians would feel honored to be able to provide hospitality to a prominent teacher (especially the founder of their *church). "Send me on my way" (NASB, NRSV) means that the church will provide for Paul's travel.

16:7-8. Paul's mention of Pentecost presumably means that he plans to keep the Jewish feast. Perhaps he will stay in Ephesus for the feast in part to refute his adversaries' accusations (16:9).

16:9. An "open door" (or "wide door"—NASB, NRSV) was used figuratively for freedom of movement or choice; here Paul refers to his ministry.

16:10-18
Recommendations and Exhortations

16:10-12. Persons of high status often wrote letters of recommendation, using their status to advocate the needs of those for whom they wrote. See comment on 2 Corinthians 3:1.

16:13. "Act like men" (NASB) usually meant "be courageous" (NRSV); the expression did not necessarily connote masculinity, although it was used for courage because most people in antiquity associated courage with masculinity.

16:14. Although ancient writers often stressed virtues, the supreme place of love (chap. 13), emphasized repeatedly throughout early Christian literature, is unusual in antiquity and especially characterized Christianity.

16:15-18. Here Paul makes another recommendation (cf. 16:10-12). Because mail in antiquity had to be carried by travelers, and these people are returning to Corinth from Paul, we may safely assume that they brought the letter we know as 1 Corinthians back to Corinth.

16:19-24
Closing Greetings

16:19. The Corinthians knew Aquila and Priscilla and that they had moved to Ephesus (Acts 18:2-3, 18, 24-27). *Churches met in homes, as many pagan religious associations did; this was a matter of convenience, economy and eventually of safety.

16:20. Letters often closed with greetings, because mail came infrequently and greetings had to be included whenever a letter was being sent out. Family members and close friends used kisses as signs of affection (e.g., 1 Sam 20:41); see comment on Romans 16:16.

16:21. Most letters were written down by amanuenses, or scribes, and usually signed by the author. A signature authorized the letter, as it does today.

16:22. Ancient people, including Jewish people, used curse invocations as the opposite of blessings. "Marana tha" (TEV) is an *Aramaic prayer, "Come, our Lord." That the Corinthians would understand it means that it is part of common tradition carried over from the early Palestinian-Syrian church, which already recognized Jesus as "Lord" and as the one who would come (cf. Rev 22:20). (Thus Christians described his coming in the way that Jewish tradition expected God's coming for judgment.)

16:23-24. Greek letters often included the greeting *chairein,* "greetings"; Paul consistently transforms this to *charis,* "grace."

2 Corinthians

Introduction

Authorship and Unity. Although virtually all scholars agree that Paul wrote 2 Corinthians, scholars differ over whether it is one letter or a composite of several. Some of the proposed partitions in the book have more in their favor than others; the most obvious break in tone is between chapters 1—9 and chapters 10—13, the latter chapters shifting to an outright heated defense. But although ancient letter collections often removed openings and closings of letters, such collections generally retained the distinction between one letter and the next (e.g., *Cicero, *Seneca). Dividing 2 Corinthians into two letters is a possible way to read the evidence, but the burden of proof should remain on those who wish to divide it rather than on those who argue for its unity.

Situation. Scholars vigorously debate the precise setting of some books in the *New Testament, including 2 Corinthians. Reconstructing the exact problem depends somewhat on the issue of the book's unity. Virtually everyone agrees that Paul addresses tensions caused by opponents, at least in chapters 10—13, but views on the nature of the opponents vary. Gnostics (though developed *Gnosticism first appears in extant sources over half a century after Paul), Palestinian Jewish Christians, non-Palestinian Jewish Christians and others have been proposed as Paul's opponents here. Paul's reference to their descent from Abraham in 11:22 at least makes clear that they are Jewish, but this need not make the division a particularly Jewish issue. The dividing issue seems to be over views of ministry more than over theology as it is usually defined: Paul came as a servant and labored among them, whereas his accusers have a high view of themselves more appropriate to upper-class ideals of leadership in antiquity than Paul's was.

Purpose. Paul wishes to reestablish his converts' trust in him and their role of intimate friendship. He thus writes a letter of self-commendation, a particular form of letter of recommendation especially necessary if one were defending oneself against charges. Chapters 10—13 are an ironic self-defense to the Corinthian Christians. The letter includes elements of various ancient letter styles: reproof, comfort and especially friendship. Another concern is also at issue: for the sake of the poor in Jerusalem, Paul needs the Corinthians Christians' money (chaps. 8—9). Unlike the opposing missionaries who have sought to replace him, Paul has never asked the Corinthians for money for *himself*, and this has offended upper-class members of the congregation who believed that the community should pay their teachers, who should not be self-supporting artisans (the well-to-do despised artisans).

Commentaries. Among the most helpful are C. K. Barrett, *A Commentary on the Second Epistle to the Corinthians*, HNTC 8 (New York: Harper & Row, 1973); and F. F. Bruce, *1 and 2 Corinthians*, NCB (1971; reprint, Grand Rapids, Mich.: Eerdmans, 1980). More detailed works like Victor Paul Furnish, *II Corinthians*, AB 32 (Garden City, N.Y.: Doubleday, 1984); and Ralph P. Martin, *2 Corinthians*, WBC 40 (Waco, Tex.: Word, 1986), are useful to more advanced students. Of more technical and specialized works, John T. Fitzgerald, *Cracks in an Earthen Vessel*, SBLDS 99 (Atlanta: Scholars, 1988), is one of the most useful (some of his insights are incorporated in this commentary); H. D. Betz, *2 Corinthians 8—9*, Hermeneia (Philadelphia: Fortress, 1985), is also useful on many points in chapters 8—9; see also Peter Marshall, *Enmity in Corinth: Social Conventions in Paul's Relations with the Corinthians* (Tübingen, Germany: J. C. B. Mohr, 1987).

1:1-7
Opening Greetings

1:1-2. Paul opens following standard letter-writing conventions; see the introduction to New Testament letters and comment on Romans 1:1-7.

1:3. It was customary in the ancient world to include a prayer or offering of thanks to a deity in letters of substantial length (as most of Paul's extant letters are). One of the most common forms of Jewish prayer was a benediction or praise that began, "Blessed [praised] be God, who . . ."; this was a way of glorifying God for his works. A regular *synagogue prayer addressed God as the "merciful Father" (so TEV here), which is what "Father of mercies" (cf. "Father of compassion"—NIV) means.

1:4. God would bring his final comfort to his people with the *Messiah's coming (e.g., Is 40:1; 49:13), but he also comforted them in their hardships during the present (e.g., Ps 94:19). The principle that suffering teaches one how to treat others is rooted in the *Old Testament (Ex 23:9). Paul's specific comfort in this verse is that he found Titus well and with good news about the Corinthians (2 Cor 7:4, 6-7, 13; cf. 2:2-3).

1:5. Some Jewish people spoke of the "pangs of the Messiah" as a period of tribulation for God's people before the end, and commentators have naturally read "we have a share in Christ's many sufferings" (TEV) in these terms (Paul seems to have meant this also in Rom 8:22-23). But more is at work here than this image alone. Jewish people also believed that they corporately shared the experience of those who had gone before them. They were chosen in Abraham, redeemed with their ancestors in the exodus from Egypt and so on. Paul believed that Jesus' followers became sharers in his cross in an even more intimate way by his *Spirit who lived in them.

Greek philosophers often taught that one should ignore pain; Paul taught that pain should drive one to trust God for help.

1:6-7. In Greco-Roman tradition, the way a sage endured the sufferings sent by God helped others by setting an example of virtuous conduct. Paul involves the Corinthians in Christ's mission being carried on by himself and Christ's other witnesses; they share Paul's sufferings and victory through prayer (1:11). Such an expression of solidarity may have parallels, but they are rare—and in practice the Corinthians may not have been as supportive of his mission as Paul was wishing (chaps. 10—13). One standard type of letter in antiquity was the "letter of consolation"; Paul may hope to communicate comfort in this letter (2:7), after having written the sorrowful one (2:4; 7:7-13).

1:8-11
Paul's Sufferings

Speeches and letters often included a brief *narrative section (1:8—2:13), usually following the introduction, that explained the circumstances necessitating the speech or letter.

1:8. "Asia" is the Roman province by that name, in what is now western Turkey. Its capital was Ephesus, Paul's missionary headquarters during this period in his life (1 Cor 16:8). Some scholars have argued that Paul was imprisoned in Ephesus during this period, but it is more likely that he simply refers to chronic opposition climaxing in the riot of Acts 19:23-41.

1:9-10. "Carrying about a death sentence" or "we had the sentence of death within ourselves" (NASB) may be a figurative allusion to the way a condemned man carried the charge that mandated his execution on the way to the cross; at the least it means that Paul had already embraced the martyr's call Jesus demands of all who will follow him (Mk 8:34-38). Jewish daily prayers celebrated God's power by noting that he was "mighty to raise the dead." Paul has accepted a proleptic experience of the power of *resurrection as well as of martyrdom, witnessed in his escapes from death; proleptic thinking was natural for early Christian readers of the *Old Testament who saw God's previous redemptive acts as a history of salvation that climaxed in Jesus.

1:11. That the Corinthian Christians' prayers could affect Paul's work and that God's ultimate glory through the work was his goal presupposes a radical trust in God's activity in the world. Many ancient pagans tried to barter with the gods through sacrifices and offerings; there is none of that here. But even by Jewish standards, Paul's faith and commitment would have shown him to be very devout.

1:12-22
Paul Had a Reason for Not Coming

Hospitality was important in antiquity, and it was an honor to host a prominent guest. For Paul not to have come could have seemed like both a breach of his word—and thus of his honor and integrity—and an insult to their hospitality. *Rhetoricians (trained public speakers) recommended that one defending himself defuse the audience's negative attitudes before addressing the more serious charges (chaps. 10—13).

1:12-14. Many ancient letters focused on praise or blame; many moralists both chided and encouraged their pupils. It was also normal to open a speech or letter with compliments, which helped the hearers to be more open to the point of the speech or letter. Ancient writers sometimes praised themselves discreetly (thus essays like *Plutarch's "How to Praise Oneself Inoffensively"), but Paul's boast (1:12a—NIV) is in his *students.* By this period moralists customarily defended their motives whether they had been attacked or not, because so many charlatans existed; but if chapters 10—13 are part of 2 Corinthians (see the introduction), Paul is already defending himself against real opposition here.

1:15. This verse means that Paul had been to Corinth once and had meant to return to benefit them spiritually again. Well-to-do benefactors were greatly extolled for bestowing gifts on persons of less means; hence Paul's certainty that he could bestow spiritual benefits is realistic, not arrogant. But unlike worldly benefactors (or the opponents of chaps. 10—13), he asks for no status in return (1:24).

1:16. From Troas in Asia (1:8), one could sail to Macedonia, and come overland down to Corinth, as Paul had done before (Acts 16:11-12) and planned to do again (1 Cor 16:5), and finally did later (Acts 20:1-3).

1:17. Paul had been unable to fulfill his stated intention. As he says in 1:23, his decision not to stop at Corinth was to "spare" them; instead he sent Titus ahead with a harsh letter (1:23—2:11; 7:7-12). When Titus did not return to the appointed meeting place in Troas, Paul feared for him (given the dangers of traveling in antiquity) and went on into Macedonia (2:12-13). There Paul met up with Titus again, who gave him good news about them (7:5-16).

1:18-20. *Digressions were standard in ancient writing, and Paul here digresses (1:18-22) to assure them that he indeed had a good reason for not coming; he was a representative of the God who always kept his word, and he proclaimed a faithful *gospel. "Amen" functioned as a positive affirmation at the end of a prayer, and Christ became the amen and yes to all the biblical promises of a truly faithful God.

1:21. The term translated "stand firm" (NIV) or "establish" (NASB, NRSV) or "confirm" was often a business term confirming a sale; it is thus related to "down payment" ("deposit"—NIV) in verse 22. In the *Old Testament "anointing," pouring olive oil over someone's head, attested that God had set that person apart for ministry (royal, priestly, etc.); Paul adopts that image here. Both 1:21 and 1:22 signify that God attests to Paul's integrity.

1:22. Documents and jars of merchandise were sealed to show that no one had tampered with their contents. The stamp of the person witnessing a document would be pressed into the hot wax, which then dried over the string tied around the rolled-up document. Paul means that God attested the contents of the ministry of himself and his colleagues (cf. 3:2-3). Judaism generally associated the *Spirit with the end of the age (e.g., Ezek 39:28-29; Joel 2:28); Paul says that they had the Spirit in the present as a "down payment" ("pledge"—NASB; "deposit"—NIV; "first installment"—NRSV), the first taste of the life of the world to come.

1:23—2:13
Paul Delayed Coming in Order to Spare Them

Paul's reason for changing his mind about coming and for only sending Titus with a letter was to spare them his harshness (1 Cor 4:21).

1:23-24. Social superiors often acted arrogantly toward their inferiors and expected praise or even groveling. Unlike the world's authority models (and those of his opponents in chaps. 10—13), Paul counts his converts as coworkers.

2:1-4. Paul's letter suggested severe discipline of the offender (2:5-10). Scholars dispute whether this offender is the same as the one in 1 Corinthians 5:1-5; but whether or not it is, Paul had written a letter after 1 Corinthians to tell the Corinthians to discipline him (this one sent with Titus). This letter has probably been lost. (Some scholars think this harsh letter between 1 and 2 Corinthians is 2 Cor 10—13, which they believe was originally a separate letter. This passage mentions nothing about a particular offender, however, and it is therefore more likely that the intervening letter was simply lost. One might not blame the Corinthians for misplacing this one.)

2:5-7. "The majority" is undoubtedly a way of saying the community of believers (as in the *Dead Sea Scrolls). *Pharisaic Judaism also stressed receiving back *repentant offenders. Groups like the one reflected in the Dead Sea Scrolls, however, required a time of punishment to elapse before the repentant could be fully restored to the community, and Roman and Greek law assumed the carrying out of a sentence. The Corinthian Christians may thus wonder what to do with the man now that he has repented.

2:8. "Confirm" (KJV; "reaffirm"—NASB, NIV, NRSV) was often used in legal settings with reference to confirming the verdict; here the Corinthians are to confirm their love instead.

2:9-11. Playing into the hands of *Satan's "devices" (KJV; "schemes"—NASB, NIV) might mean to leave the disciplined person in Satan's hands after his *repentance (cf. 1 Cor 5:5). One of Judaism's most basic convictions about Satan was that he was a deceiver and could come in various disguises.

2:12. But Paul received good news about their compliance and the man's repentance from Titus (2:12-13; 7:5-16). Troas is Alexandria Troas, the port in Asia from which one sailed across to Macedonia, and thence walked or sailed to Corinth. The "opened door" means freedom to minister (see comment 1 Cor 16:9); Paul stayed in Troas long enough to leave some possessions there (2 Tim 4:13).

2:13. Paul and Titus would be able to check for each other at any of the *churches along the way, just as Jewish people knew how to find fellow Jews through the local Jewish communities when they traveled.

2:14-17
Witnesses to Christ's Triumph

*Digressions were common in ancient letter writing. Paul begins a digression here defending the sincerity of his ministry—a common topic of Greco-Roman moralists—that lasts through 7:4.

The view that 2:14—7:4 is not a digression but a separate letter accidentally inserted into the middle of another Pauline letter has little to commend it, because the first copies were on scrolls (codices were later), which preclude accidental insertions. This section makes more sense as a natural digression than as a separate letter.

2:14-16. Roman conquerors would lead their shamed captives in a "triumphal procession." Christ had triumphed and now led believers in him as his captives (the image is similar to that of being Christ's servants); cf. Psalm 68:18, used in Ephesians 4:8. The Roman senate normally decreed public thanksgivings before the triumphal processions, so they were great celebrations for the victors and great humiliations for the defeated. But Paul glories in the image of Christians as peoples taken captive by Christ (cf. 1 Cor 4:9, etc.), and this prisoner of war himself offers the thanksgiving!

When sacrifices were offered in the *Old Testament and elsewhere in the ancient world, incense was burned to offset the stench of burning flesh, and the same would have been true at Roman triumphal celebrations. (Ecclesiasticus 24:15 described Wisdom as having a pleasant "aroma"; Paul and his fellow witnesses for Jesus Christ fulfill here the role which that book ascribed to Wisdom, but it is unlikely that he intends an allusion to that book here; the image was a natural one.) The Old Testament has precedent for acknowledging one's own inadequacy (Ex 3:11) but God's adequacy (Ex 3:14; cf. 2 Cor 3:5).

2:17. Professional speakers had long been accused of changing truth into error for gain (like a merchant providing impure products to save money). Philosophers had come under the same charge in some circles, because most made their living by their teaching or, in the case of the *Cynics, by public begging. The public often perceived wandering teachers and holy men as charlatans, no doubt because many of them were. Thus many philosophers and moralists felt the need to repudiate the charge, as Paul does here.

3:1-6
Adequacy from God

3:1. Jewish travelers often carried letters of recommendation indicating that Jewish householders could trust them and give them lodging on their journey. In Greco-Roman society, higher-class *patrons would write letters recommending their subordinates; such recommendations naturally carried more weight than the person's own claims. Anyone who was trusted could write letters on someone else's behalf (Acts 15:25-27; 18:27; 1 Cor 16:3), and by such letters a sender could also authorize a messenger (Acts 9:2). Self-commendation was considered acceptable when necessary to defend oneself or to make a point (see comment on 5:12).

3:2-3. The first *law was written by God's fingers on tablets of stone (Ex 31:18; Deut 5:22), but the prophets had promised a new giving of the law (Is 2:3) to be written on the heart (Jer 31:31-34), as it had always been meant to be (Deut 30:6, 11-14). Ezekiel had prophesied that God would remove his people's hard heart, a heart of stone, and write his word on soft hearts of flesh, by the *Spirit (Ezek 11:19-20; 36:26-27). *Old Testament prophets appealed to their divine calls, and some Greek philosophers, eager to distinguish themselves from charlatans (2:17), also claimed divine rather than merely human ordination.

3:4-5. Jews outside Palestine sometimes spoke of God as "the Sufficient One" (see v. 5—KJV; cf. 2:16).

3:6. Greco-Roman legal scholars distinguished between the letter and the intent of the law. Perhaps more relevant here, Jewish teachers sometimes gave detailed attention even to the very letters in the law; the letter was thus the written law by itself, which "killed" simply by pronouncing its death sentence on the morally guilty. The *Spirit, however, wrote the law's morality in the hearts of God's people, by God's own gracious gift (Ezek 36:26-27).

3:7-18
The Glory of Two Covenants

Anyone in the Roman Empire who knew much about Judaism knew that Moses had been an important Jewish leader; many people saw him as a "divine man," one of those ancient heroes with special powers from God. But the glory revealed in Christ is much greater—though more subtle—than that revealed to Moses; thus *apostles like Paul are in some sense superior to Moses. Here Paul responds to Corinthian criticisms (perhaps fostered by the arrogant opponents in 11:13); Paul is even greater than Moses—but only because he preaches a message greater than that of Moses. If his opponents were appealing to Moses for their authority (cf. 11:22), Paul effectively short-circuits their claims here.

3:7. When Moses returned from beholding God's glory, his skin was shining so much that the people were afraid of him (Ex 34:29-30, 35). Jewish tradition had expanded on this *narrative extensively, so Paul's readers have probably heard other expositions of this passage before, although they could understand his exposition simply from the *Septuagint of Exodus.

3:8. The prophets had compared the new covenant favorably with the old (Jer 31:31-34) and spoken of the *Spirit and the internalized *law to come as the ideal (Ezek 36:26-27). Thus no one could deny that the Spirit of God in one's heart was better than a law scroll before one's eyes.

3:9-11. Paul reasons according to the Jewish principle *qal vahomer*, "how much more": if the giving of the law on stone tablets was revealed in great glory, how much more the greater giving of the law of the Spirit?

3:12. Paul continues explaining his confidence throughout this section of the letter (4:1, 16). Moralists and other speakers commonly used his word for "boldness" (NASB, NRSV) here to explain that they spoke forthrightly; they thus contended that they were not flatterers like the demagogues who sought popular support but did not care about the masses.

3:13. Moses' glory had to be covered—unlike Paul's forthright speech

(v. 12)—and would always fade away—unlike the glory of Paul's message, revealed through the *Spirit who came to reside in believers. Jewish men in Paul's day did not cover their heads unless they were ashamed or mourning.

3:14. The law of Moses was read aloud regularly in *synagogues. Only in the new covenant in Christ could the glory be revealed openly, when it would come internally by the Spirit. The future coming of the Spirit (in contrast to the present dearth of the Spirit in the world) was a common Jewish belief.

3:15-16. Paul says that the full glory present in the law still cannot be heard (human nature being unchanged since Moses' day), until one turns to Christ (3:14, 16) and has the law written on one's heart (Jer 31:31-34). In the same way, Moses, who had an intimate relationship with God, did not need a veil (Ex 34:34).

3:17. Following a standard Jewish method of interpretation, Paul shows the correspondence between figures in the first giving of the law and those under the new covenant: "The Lord" in the text about Moses corresponds to "the *Spirit" today.

3:18. Greeks told many stories of people who became "metamorphosed" or "transformed," but Greek philosophers spoke of being transformed toward divinity by contemplating divine things. The *Dead Sea Scrolls spoke of the righteous reflecting divine splendor. But although Paul could be relating to his readers in such culturally relevant images (minus the divinization), the basis of his image is simply how Moses reflected God's glory, as in the context. Those under the new covenant behold God's glory even more plainly than Moses could (Ex 33:20); thus, like Moses, they are transformed to reflect God's glory by the Spirit. On the "mirror" (NASB, NRSV) see comment on 1 Corinthians 13:12.

4:1-6
True Messengers of God's Glory

4:1-2. Merchants sometimes "adulterated" (cf. NASB here) substances by mixing in something cheaper to cheat their customers; philosophers often accused professional speakers of doing the same, because they were more concerned about speaking ability than about correct content. Like a good Greco-Roman teacher, Paul denies that the charge applies to himself or to his colleagues.

4:3-4. Paul continues his exposition from 3:1-18: the good news remains veiled (3:13) to some; Christ is the complete revelation of God's glory (cf. 3:18). Christ thus fills the place assigned to preexistent, divine Wisdom in Jewish tradition. Other Jewish teachers did not explicitly speak of *Satan as the "god of this age" (NIV), but most of them recognized that the nations (everyone but themselves) were ruled by spiritual powers under Satan's command.

4:5. To be the slave of a high official in the Greco-Roman world often meant to hold more honor and to control more wealth than the majority of free people. When Paul calls himself a "slave of Christ" (e.g., Rom 1:1), this is a title of honor, similar to the *Old Testament's calling the prophets "servants of God." But here Paul uses the image of the hired servant: Jesus has lent him to them to serve them on Jesus' behalf. Moral teachers like Paul would always have to be ready to refute the charge leveled against some philosophers that they proclaimed themselves, a charge that Paul seems to refute here.

4:6. God spoke light into being at the

first creation (Gen 1:3); he similarly could make the light of his glory shine in the hearts of those who saw greater glory than Moses had—the glory in Christ. In various Jewish traditions the light in Genesis 1:3 represented the light of God's law, of the righteous or of God himself; cf. comment on John 1:4.

4:7-18
Fading Flesh but Enduring Glory

The message of Jesus' witnesses is greater than Moses' message because Moses' glory could fade and the *law could be ignored, whereas the glory of God lives through Jesus' witnesses even in death.

4:7. Many Greek writers felt that philosophers' contentment in suffering displayed special power. But whereas philosophers were often hailed as strong and unswayed by testing, Paul reminds his readers that his power is from God alone.

"Earthen" or "clay" jars, as opposed to bronze ones, were readily discarded; because clay was always available, such containers were cheap and disposable if they were broken or incurred ceremonial impurity—an odd container for a rich treasure. Some Greek writers similarly described the body as the soul's container; for Paul, however, the contrast is not between body and soul but between humanity and God.

4:8-9. As an example to others, *Stoic philosophers often listed their various sufferings to show their commitment to a life of contentment and perseverance. Thus they remained content in illness, in hardship, in death and so on. Jewish people often appealed to prophets and martyrs of the past as examples of endurance.

4:10-12. On Paul's proleptic experience of Christ's death and *resurrection, see comment on 1:9-10; here the glory is Christ himself living in Paul and other believers through the *Spirit, as the context makes clear. Paul's term for "bearing around" (cf. "carry around"—NIV) the dying of Jesus was typically used for pallbearers, implying that Paul not only preaches but also carries around Jesus' dying in the persecutions he faces daily. The word he uses for Jesus' "dying" (KJV, NASB) includes the stench and rotting of a person who was dead or dying; hence Paul describes his participation in Christ's sufferings quite graphically.

4:13. Paul here offers one way to translate Psalm 116:10, the way followed by the most common recension of the *Septuagint (the Greek translation of the Old Testament) in Paul's day. Jewish teachers accepted arguments based even on short phrases, and Paul simply uses the quotation to establish a principle explaining why he boldly proclaims Christ despite the opposition he receives.

4:14. Judaism believed in a *resurrection at the end time, when everyone raised would be presented to God for the judgment (cf. 5:10). While acknowledging Christ's resurrection in the past, some of the Corinthian Christians had been more skeptical about future resurrection and judgment, especially of the body; the idea was foreign to Greek thought (see comment on 1 Cor 15).

4:15. The *Old Testament had prophesied that the *Gentiles would also give thanks to God in the end time, and Paul is zealous to see this *prophecy fulfilled in his day (1:11).

4:16. Following *Plato's lead, some Greek thinkers (and a few Greco-Jewish writers) distinguished between physical decomposition and the survival of the soul. *Stoic sages emphasized that inner choices, not outer circumstances, were what mattered. Adapting the Corinthians' own Greek language where it is relevant, Paul the master missionary seeks to convince them with their own language that the glory of proleptic resurrection is present even in proleptic dying (see comment on 4:7-12).

4:17-18. Plato and many philosophers after him rightly contrasted the temporal and the eternal. (By Paul's day many Platonists thought that bodily things were heavy and weighed down the soul, but that the soul was light; once freed by the body's death, it would soar up to the pure heavens from which it had originated. Paul here inverts the image but perhaps partly for a play on words that a few Jewish readers skilled in Hebrew exposition might catch: "glory" and "weight, heaviness," represent the same Hebrew word.)

Plato also believed that the world of ideas was the real, unchanging world, whereas the temporal, changing world of sense knowledge was only a world of shadows. Paul does not deny the reality of the visible world but does agree that it is subject to decay, whereas the unseen world is eternal. In making this statement, however, Paul is still contrasting his ministry with that of Moses: he does not teach an outward law written on stones, but the law written in his inner person by the *Spirit (chaps. 3—4).

5:1-10
The Present and Future Life

*Pharisees accepted both the immortality of the soul and the future *resurrection of the body, and many Jewish writers described the experience of heaven after death as a proleptic experience to be completed in paradise after the resurrection. Unlike some modern readers, Paul has no problem accepting both the soul's continuance after death and bodily resurrection. (Those who think Paul's view changed after 1 Cor 15 should compare Phil 1:21-23 with Phil 3:20-21, where Paul includes both views in what is almost certainly the same letter.)

Although Paul finds some common ground with his Greek readers on the righteous soul's endurance (4:16-18), he is quick to bring them back to the future hope that is the basis for it. Like the Greek sages, Paul is ready to face death; unlike them, he has a hope of future bodily life.

5:1. Greek writers described the body as a vessel, a house, a tent and often as a tomb; Paul says that a better body awaits.

5:2-4. "Groaning" may allude to Exodus 2:23 (the same word in the *LXX); or it may relate to birth pangs (Rom 8:22-23), in the light of some Jewish teachings that the *resurrection would be preceded by a period of suffering described as birth pangs. At any rate, groaning was behavior characteristically ascribed to those in agony.

Paul's longing here is not for death (as in Greek views of the body as a tomb, which made even suicide acceptable if life became too difficult) but for the resurrection, when he will receive a new body. Although Greeks regularly exercised in the nude, all Jews except those who had surrendered to Greek custom abhorred nakedness in public. For Paul, the image of "nakedness" is thus an unpleasant one.

5:5. The term translated "pledge" (NASB) or "deposit guaranteeing" (NIV) was used in business documents for "down payment," a first installment. Because the Old Testament (e.g., Is 44:3; Ezek 39:29) and much of early Judaism associated the outpouring of the *Spirit with the future age, the present experience of the Spirit is the Corinthians' initial experience of the *resurrection life to come, "guaranteeing" (cf. NRSV, TEV) its fulfillment (1:22).

5:6-9. Jewish accounts of the righteous dead in heaven portrayed them as experiencing a measure of the future glory now, while awaiting the resurrection. Although this state was inferior to the resurrection (5:4), it meant an end to the present toils—and Paul's continual experience of gradual martyrdom (4:8-10).

5:10. As the Corinthians know, Paul had appeared before their governor's "judgment seat" (Acts 18:12), but Paul's allusion here is directly to the standard *Old Testament and Jewish image of the day of judgment, in which God's throne became the ultimate judgment seat. Paul's emphasis on judgment for deeds in the body reiterates his opposition to any remaining elements of common Greek ideas disparaging the body, which Paul had refuted in 1 Corinthians 6:12-14.

5:11-19 Paul's Ministry of Reconciliation

5:11. The "fear of the Lord" was a common motivation for righteousness in Jewish texts, often associated with a recognition that God would judge (5:10).

5:12. In ancient culture, self-commendation was generally offensive (see also 3:1; cf. Prov 25:27; 27:2); one needed a good reason to employ it, like defending oneself or bringing pride to a group of people who should identify with the speaker. Paul here employs the inward-outward contrast of 4:16-18 against his boastful opponents.

5:13. Greek sages often indicated that others considered their usual way of life "insane" (TEV here; the standard meaning of "beside oneself"—KJV, NASB, NRSV), although they believed that they themselves were the only truly sane ones (cf. also Wisdom of Solomon 5:4); similarly, ecstatics often described their experiences in these terms. Paul's contrast between his behavior toward the Corinthians and his behavior toward God probably derives from Moses' behavior in Exodus 34:33-34 (see comment on 2 Cor 3:7-18); he would have revealed more of his ecstatic side to them had he thought it helpful (see comment on 12:1-7; cf. 1 Cor 14:18-19).

5:14-15. Here Paul means that all who are in Christ participate in his death and *resurrection and should thus experience this proleptically in ministry; see comment on 4:10-12.

5:16-17. The new person on the inside, participating in Christ's resurrection, means more than the decaying outer person observable to human eyes (see comment on 4:16-18). Judaism applied the language of "new creation" in various ways. (For example, in later *rabbinic texts one who made a *proselyte was considered as if he or she had created the proselyte; the New Year was also given some significance as a new beginning, because sins were shortly thereafter absolved on the Day of Atonement.) But in early texts like *Jubilees and the *Dead Sea Scrolls, "new creation" language applies especially to the world to come.

This was the most obvious application of new creation language, since it referred to the life of the world to come in the *Old Testament (Is 65:16-18). For Paul, that the *Messiah Jesus has come means that believers have already begun to participate in the *resurrection life of the coming world (see comment on 4:10-12).

5:18-19. By "us" as "ministers of reconciliation" Paul refers to himself and his associates—not to the Corinthians in their present state (5:20). Paul styles his words here in a relevant way to a

Greek audience: Greek speakers often spoke on the subject of "concord," thereby urging reconciliation and unity. The term translated "reconciliation" applied especially to relations between people; but here, as in the *Old Testament, reconciliation between people and God presupposes *repentance and atonement by blood sacrifice (here by Christ's death).

5:20—6:10
A Plea from Christ's Suffering Ambassadors

Having established that he and his colleagues are Christ's representatives, Paul entreats the Corinthian Christians to be reconciled to God again by being reconciled again to himself (7:2; cf. Mt 10:40); treatment of a herald reflected one's attitude toward the sender.

5:20. An "ambassador" was a representative of one state to another, usually applied in this period to the emperor's legates in the East. This image fits "*apostles" as appointed messengers (see comment on 1 Cor 12:29-30), just as the Old Testament prophets had been (Ex 7:1). (The prophets frequently delivered messages in the form of a covenant lawsuit or in words to kings used by messengers of suzerain [supreme] kings to vassal [client] rulers.) In the context of a plea for reconciliation, Paul as an ambassador urges the Corinthians to make peace with God the King; emperors normally took action against unrepentant client states that had offended them, and no one took such warnings lightly.

5:21. Here Paul means that Christ became sin's representative when he bore its judgment on the cross, and Paul and his associates become righteousness's representatives when they proclaim his message. This verse carries on the representative idea set forth in 5:20.

6:1-2. Paul quotes Isaiah 49:8, which is in the context of the *messianic redemption, a time that Paul says has arrived in Christ (5:17). His argument would also be quite relevant to his readers: Greek sages frequently discussed appropriate moments for speaking, especially for bold speech about reconciliation (concord, harmony; see comment on 5:18-19).

6:3. "Giving no offense" (KJV) was important for those in public office or for those whose behavior would influence public perceptions of their group; this topic was widely discussed by ancient political theorists, public speakers and minority religions. (The "ministry" is the ministry of reconciliation—5:18.)

6:4-5. Philosophers often listed their hardships, sometimes in triads, as Paul does here; these catalogs of hardships verified their commitment to contentment and thus the sincerity of their message. Some of Paul's words are essentially synonyms; as in ancient *rhetorical style, they are repeated for effect.

6:6-7. Philosophers also often described themselves by catalogs of virtues, which made their lives models for those of their readers. Because charlatans were abundant, true teachers had to stress their pure motives and that they acted on knowledge of what was real. Paul's defense here would impress a Greek audience who thought that Paul was out of touch with their culture's proper speaking conventions (see 1 Cor 2). By "weapons" Paul may refer to the shield, which was carried on the left, and the spear or sword, which was carried on the right.

6:8-9. Paul again relates to issues that other speakers on moral issues faced in Greco-Roman society. Paradox, contrasting apparently irreconcilable opposites, was a standard literary and *rhetorical technique. Some philosophers (particularly *Cynics) often used paradox and the similar technique of irony, especially for turning the comments of their accusers (insane, foolish, shameful) against them, proclaiming themselves truly wise and rich (see comment on 1 Cor 4:8). They proclaimed that the opinions of foolish men (nonphilosophers) did not bother them; *Stoics often reflected on their lack of worldly honor.

But many philosophers avoided unnecessary criticism when possible, lest their message be dishonored; moralists often even sought to learn some truth from false accusations leveled against them. Both Greek and Jewish traditions stressed being honorable and irreproachable, and most people cared about public opinion. "Well-known" here presumably means known to the one who counts—God. On "dying" and "living," see 4:10-12 and perhaps Psalm 118:17-18.

6:10. Although usually better off than peasants, artisans (Paul had earned his living as a leatherworker—Acts 18:3) toiled, remained poor and had little social status; this was especially true of those who moved around, as Paul did. *Cynic philosophers gave up all possessions to pursue their lifestyle but considered themselves spiritually rich. Cynic and *Stoic philosophers claimed that, although they owned little or nothing, all the world belonged to them, because they were friends of the gods who owned it; as a servant of the true God, Paul has all the more reason to apply the phrase "possessing all things" to himself.

6:11—7:4
Receive Christ's Ambassadors

By refusing to be reconciled to Paul, the Corinthians are in effect refusing to be reconciled fully to God, whose agent Paul is (cf. Mt 10:40). In 6:14—7:1, Paul calls the Corinthians to give up their intimate ties with the world; in the context of 6:11-13 and 7:2-4, his point is that they should instead resume their intimate ties with him and other true representatives of God. Thus Paul here offers a calculated insult to his spiritual opposition in Corinth.

6:11-13. A "mouth speaking freely" and a "heart bared wide open" fit Paul's emphasis on "open speech," an important motif in ancient speaking (see comment on 3:12). Paul's words here are deeply affectionate, again beseeching them to return his love. Recording deep feelings and reasoning on an emotional level were not out of place but were a normal part of ancient public speaking and writing. Public speakers purposely appealed to their hearers' emotions; often they even claimed not to know what to say because they were so moved by their subject (cf. Gal 4:20). Of course, these speakers were supposed to feel these emotions genuinely, not merely pretend to have them.

6:14. In 6:14—7:1 Paul makes a *digression, a common literary device; given the close parallels with the *Dead Sea Scrolls and differences from Paul's own style here, in this section Paul might be using some sermonic material or ideas he gleaned from an earlier source. He bases 6:14 ("unequal yoking"—cf. KJV) on Deuteronomy 22:10 (cf. Lev 19:19), which may have been meant to reinforce the *law's prohibition of interreligious marriage with pagans (cf. Deut 7:3; Ezra 9:12; Neh 13:25).

The lack of concord between the wise and the foolish was a Greek proverb; more prominently, the division between wise and foolish, righteous and wicked, and Israel and the *Gentiles was central to *Old Testament and Jewish thought. Very religious and less religious Jews could work together, but the more religious Jews imposed some limitations. Rhetorical questions were a common part of *rhetorical style, and Paul has several successive ones in verses 14-16.

6:15. "Belial" or "Beliar" (NRSV) was another Jewish name for *Satan.

6:16-17. Jewish *law forbade doing business with *Gentiles on pagan festival days or in any other way that would bring associations with idolatry. Jewish people did not try to interfere with pagan temples, but when an emperor planned to set up an idol in Jerusalem's temple less than two decades before Paul wrote 2 Corinthians, the Jewish people were ready to revolt rather than to allow it.

Portraying the Corinthian Christians as God's temple (1 Cor 3:16; 6:19) who have no fellowship with idols (1 Cor 10:20-21), Paul can cite relevant *Old Testament texts: verse 16 cites Leviticus 26:12 (in the context of God dwelling among his people—26:11); cf. similarly Ezekiel 37:27-28 and 43:7. Verse 17 cites Isaiah 52:11, addressing the time of the new exodus of the *messianic salvation (52:7-15); cf. Leviticus 11:31, 44-45 and 22:4-6.

6:18. God's people were his sons and daughters (e.g., Is 43:6; Jer 3:19), who would be restored to their special relationship with him in the time of the end. Paul blends the language of several texts (probably including 2 Sam 7:14), as Jewish writers sometimes did; here he may also add his own prophetic word (cf. 1 Cor 14:37-38).

7:1. Non-Palestinian Jews often spoke of pure and undefiled hearts; undefiled flesh normally referred to ceremonial purity (hand washing or ritual immersion). Here Paul refers to purity in body as well as in spirit (see comment on 5:10 and on 1 Cor 6:20)—abstention from sin.

7:2-3. Paul uses language of great affection; see 6:11-13. The greatest expression of devotion in Greco-Roman literature was willingness to die with someone (which also makes sense outside Greek culture; see 2 Sam 15:21; Jn 13:37; 15:13).

7:4. Greco-Roman speakers often emphasized their confidence in their hearers for the purpose of establishing intimacy and to secure willing compliance.

7:5-16 Reconciliation Between Paul and the Corinthians

7:5-7. *Old Testament texts often emphasized God's comfort for his people (e.g., Is 49:13; 51:3; 52:9); Paul here continues his opening theme (1:3-6). Paul crossed over from Troas to Macedonia to find Titus, whom he had sent to the Corinthians with a harsh letter (2:12-13). He was comforted not only by Titus's safety but by their response.

7:8-9. Ancient teachers of speaking and letter-writing skills warned that open rebuke should be reserved for the most extreme circumstances; people were more likely to listen if one mixed in praise with blame. In the technical language of such teachers, "rebukes" were meant to generate shame and *repentance.

7:10. Like the Old Testament (e.g., Amos 5:6-11) and Judaism, pagan philosophers sometimes recognized that divine judgments were not only acts of justice but also attempts to bring the guilty to repentance.

7:11-12. Piling up related terms was an acceptable expression of Greek *rhetoric and simply added emphasis to the point of the terms.

7:13. Titus received great hospitality; hospitality to travelers was emphasized in antiquity, especially in Jewish and Christian circles.

7:14. Whereas self-commendation had

to be done discreetly, boasting about one's friends was always considered acceptable in antiquity.

7:15-16. If the Corinthian Christians received Titus with such respect, it means that they saw him as Paul's own representative; one was always to receive a representative with the same honor one would grant the person being represented.

8:1-9
Models of Giving

Concerned with an active symbol of the unity of Jewish and *Gentile *churches (Rom 15:25-26) and relieving genuine poverty (Gal 2:10), Paul is forced to do here the very thing that he has so assiduously avoided in his own ministry (1 Cor 9)—asking for funds. Although he had previously told the Corinthians about the need (1 Cor 16:1-3), higher-class members of his congregation would be offended at what they would see as inconsistency. They had wanted Paul to accept pay as a regular philosophical teacher rather than maintain himself as a low-status artisan (12:13; cf. 1 Cor 9); by identifying himself with the poor in the congregation, Paul had risked alienating their well-to-do friends who despised artisans. Paul thus defends the collection in chapters 8—9.

8:1. Moral writers frequently offered positive role models. Public speakers used a standard *rhetorical technique called "comparison," which often served to stimulate moral competition. Many speakers, including Paul, were willing to appeal to ancient city and other geographical rivalries to spur their hearers on to greater zeal. Macedonia and Corinth were such rivals.

8:2. Some Greco-Roman aristocrats ridiculed those who lived simply, but other writers praised the simple lifestyle that enabled its followers to give generously. Macedonia was not altogether poor, but persecution and ostracism may have increased the financial hardship of the Christians there.

8:3. One was to give alms according to one's ability (Deut 15:14; cf. Ezra 2:69; Tobit 4:8, 16), but the Macedonians went beyond this rule.

8:4-5. The term translated "participation" (NASB), "sharing" (NIV, NRSV) or "fellowship" (KJV) was used technically in business documents of Paul's day for a "partnership." It could also signify an institution of Roman trade known as the *societas,* by which members contracted to supply whatever they had to fulfill their goal. Whether Paul conceives of this "partnership" officially or unofficially, it is clear that the Macedonians saw support, like hospitality, as a privilege. Judaism used the term here translated "service" (NIV) or "support" (NASB) technically for distributing alms for the poor.

8:6. Titus had raised this issue of support as well as the issue of the harsh letter when he was among them.

8:7. They have important spiritual gifts (1 Cor 1:5-7; 12:28) and other expressions of God's work among them. Paul uses praise as a basis for exhortation, as moralists often did.

8:8. Because contributors in antiquity were often forced to support public works (occasionally this forced support could bankrupt someone less well-to-do than the tax roll had indicated), speakers and writers calling for funds had to be particularly careful to stress the voluntary nature of the contributions. (Later Jewish teachers even charged charity collectors who pressured the poor for contributions with "oppressing the poor.") Paul alludes to the *rhetorical technique of comparison he has used (8:1).

8:9. Moralists often appealed to role models, and Paul here uses the supreme one, insisting that the Corinthian Christians follow Christ's example of using their prosperity to enrich the poor. Like both Jewish and non-Jewish writers of his day, Paul can use the language of wealth figuratively as well as literally, but he may mean Christ's enrichment of believers literally, as provision through one another (8:14).

8:10-15
Give According to What You Have

8:10-12. The Corinthians had already eagerly committed themselves to supporting the Jerusalem *church (1 Cor 16:1-3). (Commentators note that the phrase translated "last year" or "a year ago" could mean from nine to fifteen months earlier.) Because their church was more prosperous than others (8:1-2), however, they had contributed more, and some felt that they were contributing an inordinate percentage of the collection. Paul employs a common argument for why they should continue what they have begun: many ancient arguments were weighed by a principle here translated "advantage" (NASB) or "what is best" (NIV) (see, e.g., 1 Cor 6:12); Paul explains the advantage in 8:13-15. The *Old Testament normally described gifts and sacrifices as "acceptable" only if they reflected the best one had to give (e.g., Lev 1—4).

8:13. The Corinthian Christians may have resented having to provide a large portion of the offering, but Corinth was a prosperous city. One common definition of friendship was that "friends share all things in common" and are "equal," even though this principle came to be applied even to wealthy *patrons who sponsored poorer *clients. Ancient speakers and writers stressed "equality" as much as "concord" (see comment on 5:18-19), and the Corinthians could not miss Paul's point: their conversion made them "friends" to other Christians and required a more equitable distribution of provision within Christ's body.

8:14. Jewish wisdom writers exhorted their readers to remember famine when they were prospering (Ecclus 18:25); although Corinth was extremely prosperous and the Christians there probably could not conceive of their own poverty, Paul's principle may be analogous to some forms of health insurance today: if *they* are ever in need, someone else will supply their need. God always supplies enough to the whole body of Christ, but it is up to Christians to make sure that the "enough" is adequately distributed.

8:15. In case 8:14 sounded too good to be true, Paul introduces the principle of God's provision by way of the manna in the wilderness: God meant everyone to have just what they needed, no more and no less (Ex 16:18).

8:16-24
Envoys for the Collection

8:16-18. Here Paul provides a letter of recommendation (3:1) for Titus and his companion.

8:19. Just as *synagogues throughout the Mediterranean would send their annual tribute to the Jerusalem temple via local representatives of high reputation, this offering is also to be administered in an irreproachable manner: envoys would be "appointed by the churches." The term for "appoint" could indicate election by a show of hands or (more loosely) a casting of ballots, as was common in Greek administration.

8:20-21. In a culture obsessed with shame and honor, Greco-Roman writers were quick to emphasize that leaders and other beneficiaries of the public trust must be open and of irreproachable moral credentials. Judaism also stressed that charity collectors must act irreproachably to prevent even false accusations. Verse 21 echoes the *Septuagint of Proverbs 3:4 and the proverbial saying that grew out of it; Jewish teachers stressed doing what was good in the sight of both God and people.

8:22. Both Jewish and Greco-Roman moralists recommended that potential leaders be "tested" in lower positions before achieving public office. This brother (distinct from the one mentioned in 8:18) had already been proved in ministry.

8:23-24. As "delegates" (literally "*apostles") of the churches, they were commissioned representatives of those churches. As such, they were like the representatives of local Jewish communities who would band together and travel to Jerusalem to deliver the temple tax each year. Titus is Paul's representative in the group. Thus they are to be received hospitably, as hospitably as Paul and the other churches would have been received. Throughout the ancient Mediterranean envoys were to be respected and received with honor. On "boasting" see comment on 7:14.

9:1-5
Boasting in Advance

Citizens' first loyalties were to their cities, and bitter rivalries often arose between cities. Paul appeals to their civic pride to make sure that the well-to-do Corinthians do their part. Corinth was the capital of the province of Achaea, south of the province of Macedonia (which included Philippi and Thessalonica). Thus Paul employs here the *rhetorical techniques of endearment (by boasting about them) and comparison. By boasting about the Corinthians, however, Paul has laid his honor on the line. If chapters 10—13 are part of the same letter, Paul may have some reason to worry (cf. especially 12:16-18)!

9:6-15
Sowing and Reaping

9:6. Reaping what one had sown reflects an ancient proverb, related to many other agricultural images prevalent in antiquity (cf., e.g., Job 4:8; Prov 11:18; 22:8; Hos 8:7; 10:12; Ecclus 7:3; Cicero; Aristotle); the specific image of sowing and consequently reaping sparingly seems to have also been in general circulation.

9:7. Paul here cites standard Jewish wisdom; the first part of his exhortation may allude to Exodus 25:2, 35:5, 21-22 and Deuteronomy 15:10 (cf. 1 Chron 29:6-9; Ezra 2:68), suggesting that Paul had a fairly developed theology of giving based on the *Old Testament. "God loves a cheerful giver" is from an addition to Proverbs 22:8 in the *Septuagint ("God blesses a cheerful and giving person"). The term rendered "cheerful" often applied in Jewish texts to gifts for the poor.

9:8. "Sufficiency" (KJV, NASB) is especially a technical term of Greek philosophers, usually applied to the sage's contentment in all circumstances. Although some Greek traditions emphasized that one could be self-sufficient without anything to live on, most Greek thinkers would have agreed with Paul that basic needs had to be met before a person could be self-sufficient. For views on possessions and wealth in antiquity, see comment on 1 Timothy 6:3-10.

9:9. This quotation from Psalm 112:9 refers in the context of that psalm to the behavior of a righteous person; thus Paul may be saying in 9:8-9 that their reward for sowing seed (giving money) to the poor is that their righteousness will stand forever.

9:10. Because the Corinthians are to be righteous "sowers" ("scattering" seed—v. 9), Paul cites Isaiah 55:10: "He who provides seed for the sower and bread for food," which proves that God will continue to supply them so they can continue to give and hence have a greater reward of righteousness (v. 9). Paul uses the second text (Is 55:10) to apply the first text (Ps 112:9, cited in 9:9) to their situation; linking together texts with a similar key word or concept was a common practice in Jewish interpretation.

9:11-15. Jewish people believed that God heard the cries of the poor (Deut 15:9-10); Paul's readers would understand his point that their aid to the poor brought direct glory to God in praise (2 Cor 9:11-12; cf. 1:11) and would also benefit the Corinthians through the prayers of the poor in Jerusalem (9:14). (God's "gift"—v. 15—may thus be his strategic provision to the Corinthians by which they can benefit the poor of Jerusalem.)

10:1-18
Not Like Paul's Opponents

Paul's drastic change in tone here, from a cautious affection to addressing opponents, has led many scholars to believe that chapters 10—13 belong to a separate letter. Others believe that Paul received new information just before penning these words, or that he saved his real *diatribe for the concluding chapters of the letter.

10:1-2. Paul's harsh letter (2:4; 7:8; letters of hortatory blame were reserved for the severest circumstances) had provoked a hostile reaction among some members of the congregation: ancient *rhetoricians insisted that letters ought to reflect the same personality that the person exhibited when present. Christ's "meekness and gentleness" probably alludes to Jesus' saying later recorded in Matthew 11:29; this was a good reply to the Corinthians' complaint that Paul was too meek (1 Cor 2:3); Greek culture did not usually regard meekness as a virtue (cf. the modern colloquial expression "wimp").

10:3-5. Greek sages sometimes described their battle against false ideas as a war, in terms similar to those Paul uses here. Like those sages, Paul claims to be doing battle with false ideas. "Arguments" (NIV, NRSV, TEV) or "speculations" (NASB) is a technical term for *rhetorical or philosophical reasonings; the prisoners of war in this extended metaphor are human thoughts. Cf. Proverbs 21:22.

10:6. Rulers generally executed vengeance on those who had rebelled against them after the war was finished (e.g., 2 Sam 12:31). Paul may mean that the believers must work harder to make up for time lost through disobedience.

10:7. The Corinthians' preoccupation with outward appearances matched that of sophists concerned with proper and persuasive speech, but true philosophers constantly ridiculed this attitude (4:16-18). The more well-to-do members of the Corinthian *church were enamored with Greek philosophy; Paul thus rebukes them on their own terms here.

10:8. Paul's "authority" was an issue in 1 Corinthians 9:5 (where the same term is generally translated "right"); some wealthier Corinthians are assailing him for not conforming to their cultural standards (i.e., for working as an artisan although he is a moral teacher). *Old Testament prophets were called both to build up and to tear down (e.g., Jer 1:10), but Paul is called only to build up the Corinthians (2 Cor 12:19; 13:10).

10:9-10. A basic rule of ancient letter writing was that one's letters should be appropriate to one's personality when present, because letters in some sense communicated one's presence. Philosophers who failed to be consistent in this manner were typically attacked verbally.

"Weighty and powerful" (KJV) letters would be the sort written by a respectable authority figure (Romans valued a virtue called *gravitas,* which included sternness), whereas Paul's speech reflects insufficient *rhetorical training to impress the powerful people of society. His (literally) "bodily presence" (KJV, NRSV) was also unimpressive, perhaps meaning that he did not dress as a good philosopher would, or (more likely) that he was awkward in gestures, an important element of delivery in public speaking that rhetoricians stressed. In other words, Paul was a better writer than public speaker.

10:11. Philosophers and Jewish teachers often contrasted words and deeds; deeds weighed more heavily. Even if Paul was an inferior speaker, his life backed up everything he said.

10:12. "Comparison" was a standard *rhetorical and literary technique; here Paul mocks his opponents: they are so foolish that they do not realize that one cannot compare oneself with oneself. Higher-class *patrons would usually write letters of recommendation for socially inferior *clients, but sometimes people were forced to commend themselves; self-commendation was to be accepted only if done discreetly, but Paul paints his opponents as pretentious—a vice in Greek culture.

Paul satirically declines to compare himself with such teachers—satire was a common argumentative device. One of the rules of "comparison" was that one could not compare dissimilar items; yet the dissimilarity turns out to favor him in 10:13-18.

10:13-16. Teachers of rhetoric and philosophy in cities throughout the Mediterranean competed for students and their fees. One means of self-advertisement was to compare oneself favorably to rival teachers; Paul uses the ancient literary device of irony and turns his opponents' advertising on its head, refuting them while satirizing their very form of boasting. The language of a "sphere" (NASB) or "proper limits" (NIV) was sometimes applied to the extent of a public servant's service in a district or region; Paul could also mean it in terms of the language of Roman imperial conquest (cf. 10:3-6).

10:17. On Jeremiah 9:23-24 see comment on 1 Corinthians 1:26-31.

10:18. Applying Jeremiah 9:24, Paul notes that self-commendation is obviously out of place—unless, like Paul, one were forced to resort to it by unpleasant circumstances (e.g., to defend oneself). Public speakers used self-commendation but recognized that it was offensive unless done carefully and with appropriate reasons.

11:1-15 Countering False Apostles' Boasts

In contrast to Paul, who humbled himself by taking a socially demeaning role (11:7), his opponents have boasted. Paul therefore parodies their boasting with his own brag sheet, following the form of ancient self-praise. At the same time, however, he inverts his opponents' values in the light of the values of God's *kingdom, using another common literary technique called satire (11:16-33).

11:1. In Greek literature "madness" (here, "foolishness") was sometimes a divine punishment for insolent arrogance, hence some commentators have suggested that the Corinthian opponents had charged Paul with arrogance and madness. More likely, he is simply implying that, while he assumes the guise of a madman for *rhetorical purposes (being able to assume various styles was part of rhetorical training), it is his opponents who generally boast and hence are truly mad.

11:2. Being jealous over God's people with God's jealousy (cf. Ex 20:5) would have been viewed as pious (cf. Num 25:11). Fathers normally pledged their daughters in marriage, and Paul compares the Corinthian *church with a daughter (1 Cor 4:14-15) whom he has pledged in marriage to Christ (cf. Jewish depictions of God marrying his son Israel to the *law). (Other commentators see Paul as presenting the bride, as the best man would, rather than as a father betrothing her.)

11:3. In some Jewish traditions, *Satan, disguised as a good angel (cf. 11:14), deceived Eve sexually. Given the image of the betrothed virgin (11:2, perhaps betrothed to Christ, the new Adam), Paul could have this tradition partly in view here. More certain is the biblical allusion to Genesis 3, where the serpent deceived Eve. Paul presents his opponents as adulterers who corrupt betrothed virgins—a crime punishable by banishment under Roman law and death under *Old Testament law (Deut 22:23-27).

11:4. The Old Testament and later Jewish literature often portrayed false prophets as those who claim to have God's *Spirit but are really moved by a different one. Paul offers mock praise of their acceptance of this bad treatment (cf. also 11:19-20), using the common ancient device of satire.

11:5-6. *Rhetoric was important in Greco-Roman society, including in Corinth (see comment on 1 Cor 1:5). By rhetoric one showed that he was educated and truly worthy of being heard by the well-to-do. Philosophers, however, stressed their genuine knowledge over others' persuasive speech, and their ideas had also gained influence in Greek society; Paul appeals to the latter model against the former one to defend himself.

Paul's statement that he is "unskilled in speech" (NASB) need not mean that he is a terrible speaker; even the best speakers played down their oratorical skills to lower audience expectations. He seems to have been accused of inadequate rhetorical skill by others, however; his writings attest a higher level of rhetorical sophistication than possessed by most people of his day, but no matter how hard he worked at it, he did not have the early rhetorical training of an aristocrat, and some elements of delivery would not come to him as naturally as they might to others (see comment on 10:10).

11:7. Teachers were supposed to gain support by a *patron's sponsorship, by charging fees or even by begging, but never by engaging in a working-class job (1 Cor 9:6). Paul's opponents appeal to higher-status Corinthian Christians embarrassed by Paul's labor as an artisan; they, at least, are professional enough to take payment. Paul may have avoided accepting payment to keep from appearing as a common sophist who is teaching for monetary gain, or to avoid appearing dependent on them as a *client. "Humility" was a Jewish virtue, but Greeks saw it as "humiliation" and considered it appropriate only to those of very low status.

11:8. Paul *embraces* low status: he became the Corinthians' servant (contrast whom his opponents serve—11:15). Accepting wages from one employer while genuinely working only for another was naturally viewed as dishonest, hence Paul's use of "robbed"; robbery was naturally considered even lower-status than manual labor! (The term could also be used for "plundering" a defeated enemy's spoils after a military campaign. In conjunction with this sense, "wages" [KJV, NASB] later in the verse may mean "soldier's wages.")

11:9. *Patrons could view *clients, their social dependents, as "burdens." Sometimes teachers were clients of wealthy patrons, but Paul is not dependent on, hence not a client of, the Corinthian *church. Thus he need not answer to them.

11:10-12. Boasting was considered acceptable if it was for someone else's sake and not simply for one's own. For example, *Plutarch permitted self-praise if it were mixed with praise of one's audience.

11:13-15. In some Jewish traditions *Satan disguised himself as an angel or in other ways (e.g., as a beautiful woman to some *rabbis or as a beggar to Job's wife; for one tradition, see comment on 11:3); Judaism regarded Satan as a deceiver. Although Isaiah 14 and Ezekiel 28 do not in context refer specifically to Satan (against a common view today), a large body of Jewish tradition taught that Satan and other evil spirits were originally angels who had fallen in Genesis 6:1-3.

11:16-21
Paul's Apology for Boasting

11:16-18. *Rhetorical teachers like *Quintilian and moralists like *Plutarch warned their readers never to boast of themselves unless forced to do so by the necessities of a defense or some other very good reason (like making oneself a model for moral imitation). Although some wise men felt it appropriate to boast, popular opinion disliked it. Autobiographers had to come up with ways to decrease the potential offensiveness of their own claims. Paul's opponents had apparently laid themselves open to Paul's attack—indicating their own lack of *rhetorical skill.

11:19-20. Irony was a common rhetorical technique. A blow on the face, like spittle, was a grievous insult to one's honor (see comment on Mt 5:39). Taking "advantage" (NASB, NIV) sometimes connotes sexual exploitation, an awful offense. The ideology of the upper classes (shared by Paul's opponents) held that persons of truly noble character, those suited for freedom, could never tolerate being slaves.

11:21. Continuing the irony (11:19-20), Paul confesses his "shame" or "dishonor"—one of the most grievous offenses one could endure in status-conscious society. He uses again the *rhetorical technique of "comparison" to mock the boasting self-appointed *apostles who have come to Corinth and undermined his own standing.

11:22-33
Boasting in Sufferings

Aristocrats typically boasted in their heritage, their accomplishments and so forth; but they did not normally boast in their sufferings. Some philosophers listed the sufferings they endured as a model for emulation. (In other contexts, lists of sufferings could prove one's devotion to another cause; e.g., in a romance novel by Chariton, Leucippe's letter recounts what she suffered for her beloved Clitophon.) But those who list sufferings to prove endurance do so to boast in their strength, not in their weakness. For Paul, if one boasts, one should boast in the values of the *kingdom (10:17), humbling oneself for God's glory.

11:22. Even in Greco-Roman Corinth, the *church recognized its Jewish roots; and traveling Jewish Christians, especially those with Palestinian roots, could claim authority in a tradition earlier than Paul. (This "Are they . . . ? So am I" reasoning seems to have been persuasive in antiquity; cf., e.g., *Josephus *Life* 40, §199.) "Israelites" and "descendants of Abraham" refer in the parlance of ancient Judaism to anyone Jewish; "Hebrews" may mean the same thing, although it might apply especially to Palestinian Jews (see comment on Phil 3:5).

11:23. The term translated "servants" here may be a term of respect ("ministers"—KJV, NRSV); if it means "slaves of Christ" in this case, they are high-status slaves (see comment on Rom 1:1). On "insane" (NASB) see comment on 2 Corinthians 11:1. Paul begins by boasting in the very cause of the Corinthians' reproach: his low-status "labors" (see comment on 11:7). Some philosophers boasted in ignoring beatings; Jewish people praised those beaten and martyred for their faith.

11:24. Under Jewish law, some sins (like sabbath violation or being a false prophet) merited stoning (because the Jewish people could not legally enforce this penalty in this period due to Roman restrictions, they usually just excluded capital offenders from the community). Other, lesser sins required only a beating of thirty-nine lashes with a whip (Deut 25:2-3); a *synagogue court decided such cases, and the synagogue attendant administered the beating. As in the case of violations of festivals or ritual laws, this penalty was administered only after the person had been warned and yet persisted in the offending behavior.

11:25. Roman citizens were not supposed to be beaten with rods, but officials sometimes overlooked these rules (see comment on Acts 16:22). On Paul's stoning see Acts 14:19. Frequent travelers were also well aware of the danger of shipwrecks, and death at sea was the most frightful form of death in antiquity (partly due to the pagan belief that the spirits of those who died at sea roamed forever because they were not properly buried). Because there were no lifeboats per se (see comment on Acts 27:30) or life jackets, shipwrecked victims could spend a long time in the water and often did not survive.

11:26. Travel was one of the more dangerous activities in antiquity; a later Jewish tradition even speaks of priests' praying and fasting two days a week for travelers' safety. Rivers were often used to navigate inland from the coast to cities, and robbers occasionally attacked incoming boats, especially in Asia Minor; or Paul could refer here to the danger of crossing swollen rivers. Robbers were one of the most dreaded dangers of land travel and one reason many parties did not travel at night. Pirates had become much less common on the sea than in earlier times; although land robbers had also decreased in the period of the Empire, they remained a frequent danger. The climax of Paul's "dangers," however, is probably ironically pointed at his opponents: "perils among false brethren" (KJV).

11:27. Sleeplessness is probably due to potentially dangerous night travel (ministry itself would be limited at night because nearly everyone went to sleep early except watchmen and those who went to drunken parties, although people might stay up to tell stories and converse); insomnia is possible (cf. 11:28-29) but less likely at this point in the list (one would expect that with the anxieties of v. 28). One traveling to the interior of Asia Minor would face "cold"; coupled with "nakedness" (sometimes used, as here, to mean inadequate clothing), this was a serious hardship.

11:28. Paul's "anxiety" (NRSV; the same term translated "worry" in Mt 6:34) over the state of God's people is motivated by love (11:29-30), as the *Old Testament prophets' concern for Israel had been. Philosophers emphasized that one should never be anxious (also Phil 4:6), but Paul's anxiety is one of love, not a selfish kind (2 Cor 2:13; 7:5-6; 1 Cor 7:32—same word; 1 Thess 3:5).

11:29-31. Paul's identifying with the "weak" would again offend the socially powerful leaders in the Corinthian *church, who would view it as a sign of low status. To boast in his weakness inverts his opponents' entire position.

11:32. Aretas IV controlled Nabataea, the region around Syrian Damascus, and may have controlled Damascus itself about A.D. 34-39 (he died about 39-40). If he did not actually control Damascus, he certainly wielded political influence beyond his immediate sphere of legal jurisdiction. Because most of the caravan trade from the east passed through his kingdom, it was the strongest and wealthiest of the minor kingdoms of the Near East.

11:33. The "window" Paul mentions would have belonged to a house built along the city wall; many houses were built on such walls. Paul's strategy was borrowed from the *Old Testament (Josh 2:15; cf. 1 Sam 19:12). Acts 9:25 mentions this escape. This was hardly the sort of heroism in which high-status people would boast, because they did not value being in trouble with the authorities, even for the cause of Christ.

12:1-10
Revelations and Weakness

12:1. Although Paul spoke of his spiritual experiences only when forced to do so (e.g., 1 Cor 14:18), it is clear that he, like many *Old Testament prophets, regularly experienced visions and revelations. Some Jewish writers of Paul's day diligently cultivated visionary experiences with fasting and sleep deprivation, but there is no indication that Paul *sought* visions; rather, he was "caught up" (v. 2; see comment on Rev 4:2).

12:2-4. "Fourteen years ago" was perhaps a decade after Paul's conversion. Because later Jewish teachers sometimes used "that person" as "you" or "I," it is possible that Paul here relates his own experience in the third person to avoid boasting. Some Greek writers suggested that one should describe one's experience as another's if one were ashamed to speak of it openly; analogously, some Jewish *apocalyptists may have transferred their own visions to those heroes of the past in whose name they composed their writings. Willing to boast only in his weaknesses, Paul will not accept any praise for his personal revelations (cf. Prov 27:2).

Greek writers spoke of ascents of the soul, especially after death, as did Jewish mystics and apocalyptists. Jewish visionaries sometimes described their mystical experiences of heaven as being "caught up"; although they could mean that only their souls saw heaven, the experience was sometimes so vivid that the whole person seemed to be caught up (Ezek 2:2; 3:14, 24; 8:3; 11:1, 24), and some texts explicitly included the body in this experience (as in *1 Enoch). (The Jewish ascent stories sometimes emphasized the danger of the ascent, as in the case of the four *rabbis, only one of whom reportedly escaped unscathed. But except for *Philo, all the Jewish stories are either pseudonymous or later than Paul, so it is difficult to reconstruct the exact nature of Jewish mystical experience in Paul's day.)

Visions given by God are not the same as the practice of some Greek sorcerers and wonderworkers and spiritist experiences in many cultures today, where the soul could travel abroad in astral projections; even Philo, the Jewish philosopher most influenced by Greek thought, saw ecstasy as the soul's experience with *God*, not simply wandering around on the earth.

In Jewish texts, "paradise," the new Eden that was the opposite of hell (*Gehenna), would exist on earth in the world to come but was reserved in the heavens in the present time. Different texts varied in the number of heavens they envisioned (from three to 365); three and seven were the most common numbers, and paradise was often thought to be located in one of these heavens. Paul's "third heaven" probably means he thought in terms of three heavens, with paradise in the highest. (The lower atmosphere was usually regarded as the lowest "heaven.") Many Greek readers thought that the pure soul would ascend to the highest heaven at death, so the Corinthian Christians would have no problem understanding Paul's words here.

Revelations of deities in the Greek *mystery cults were also "forbidden to be uttered"; some Jewish writers like *Josephus and *Philo applied this description to God's highest wisdom or to the divine name.

12:5-6. One common *rhetorical device was to say, "I could say this, but I won't"; Paul uses this device here (also in Philem 19). If his opponents are boasting about their visions, Paul here outdoes them while maintaining the foolishness of their boasting.

12:7-8. "Flesh" here need not indicate a physical ailment (like the one in Gal 4:13), as is often supposed (so TEV); Paul may allude to the "thorn in Israel's side," the Canaanites God left in the land to keep Israel from exalting themselves (Num 33:55; Judg 2:3; cf. Josh 23:13; Ezek 28:24). Scholars debate exactly what Paul's "thorn" was, but in view of the context and Paul's "buffeting" (KJV, NASB) in this verse (cf. 1 Cor 4:11), it may be continuing persecutions; or this "messenger of *Satan" might be an ironic insult against his opponents themselves (11:14-15). As in the *Old Testament and most Jewish thought, God is here sovereign even over Satan and his angels.

12:8-10. Philosophers spoke of self-sufficiency, either to endure trials or sometimes because there were none. Paul's idea here is quite different: God's grace is sufficient, providing the power Paul needs. In paganism, divine power was especially displayed in magical wonders; for Paul, it is God's power enabling one weak in himself to endure. Miracle reports in pagan temples often followed the same form as Paul's request (v. 8) but concluded with the deity's appearing to heal the person. Although Paul had performed many miracles (12:12), he would not boast in his miracles, as his opponents perhaps boasted in theirs; instead he boasts in his weakness.

12:11-18
Paul's Closing Irony

12:11. Many ancient writers advised that one could praise oneself inoffensively only if one were compelled to praise oneself, especially to defend oneself. Philosophers usually considered public speakers "nobodies," and someone may have applied this term to Paul.

12:12. Appealing to readers' own eyewitness knowledge was one way of deflecting some of the offensiveness of self-boasting (so, e.g., the earlier Greek *rhetorician Isocrates).

12:13. The well-to-do in the Corinthian *church want an *apostle they can be proud of—one who conforms to their high-society expectations for a professional moral teacher. Thus they want Paul to stop working and to accept support from them, to become their *client or dependent (see 1 Cor 9). Paul avoids playing into the hands of the well-to-do faction of the church (see the situation in the introduction to 1 Corinthians) by accepting support from others instead; here he replies in irony: "Forgive me!"

12:14-15. The well-to-do Corinthians want Paul to be their *client and they his *patrons (12:13), but Paul reminds them that he is their father (1 Cor 4:15). Thus he reverses their own position: he refused their support not because he was socially ignorant, but because they were his dependents rather than his being their dependent. (Once a Roman father declared a child to be his, parents supported the child growing up and helped young couples establish themselves. Clients and children were both viewed as dependents in the Roman household.)

12:16-18. The same people who criticize Paul for not accepting their support—so their faith could appear more respectable to their social peers—also apparently accept his opponents' arguments against his offering for the poor in Jerusalem (chaps. 8—9). Occurring this close to the end of Paul's argument, his request for funds for the poor may have been at the center of his opponents' accusations against him: this Paul would not accept your support when it was socially appropriate, but now he wants money to help others you do not know!

12:19—13:4
Paul's Coming to Discipline

Paul, who had been "weak" among them before, would now be strong (13:3).

12:19. An "apology," or defense speech, was a standard type of writing, but Paul explains his ironic defense and display of *rhetoric as motivated only by love for the Corinthians, rather than a genuine defense of himself.

12:20. One standard theme of Greco-Roman moralists was "harmony"; they commonly attacked strife, envy and so forth. Ancient writers also attacked anger, among other attitudes. The Corinthians cannot possibly defend their behavior even on the basis of their own culture's ethics.

12:21. The powerful members of the Corinthian *church despised humility, as did most of their pagan colleagues; but if they worried that Paul had been too humble before (11:7), their wretched spiritual state (12:20) is about to humiliate him further. So much for his boasting of them (9:3)!

13:1-2. Moses' law (Deut 17:6; 19:15) and all subsequent Jewish (and Christian—Mt 18:16; 1 Tim 5:19) law required a minimum of two witnesses in the case of a charge against someone. Paul is treating his next visit to Corinth as a courtroom battle (cf. 1 Cor 6:3-4), and promising them that he is going to win his case.

13:3-4. Because Judaism talked of God speaking by the prophets, Paul's appeal to "Christ speaking in" him is probably an appeal to his prophetic gift. Paul often drives home God's power revealed in the weakness of the cross to the Corinthians (1 Cor 1:18—2:8), mainly because the Corinthian Christians, like their pagan culture, valued *rhetorical and miraculous power that drew attention to speakers and miracle workers, not to the supreme God.

13:5-10
True Power and Weakness

13:5-6. Philosophers often urged self-evaluation or testing. Paul, who preaches the true *gospel, has Christ in him (13:3-4), but the Corinthians must decide whether Christ is in them; if Christ is in them, then he is certainly in Paul, their spiritual father.

13:7-9. Philosophers generally reasoned that it did not matter what others thought of them; but many reasoned that they should guard what others thought of them, not for their own sake but for the sake of bringing others to philosophy. Paul is unconcerned with what others think of him but wants his friends to be built up.

13:10. On Paul's authority in this regard, see comment on 10:8.

13:11-14 Closing Words

13:11. This closing exhortation to unity fits Greco-Roman "harmony" speeches well enough that even pagans in Corinth would agree with its moral message.

13:12. Kisses were used as a sign of affection among family or friends.

13:13. Letters often included greetings from others present where the writer was.

13:14. Most Jewish people thought of the *Holy Spirit as a prophetic, divine force from God. Thus, for Paul to parallel Jesus, the Father and the Holy Spirit as he does here probably indicates his belief that Jesus is also divine and that the Spirit is also a personal being like the Father and Son.

GALATIANS

Introduction

Authorship. Virtually all scholars recognize Galatians to be Pauline.

Type of Letter. Although Galatians has apologetic elements (i.e., points where Paul seems to defend himself), Paul is not concentrating on the kind of *rhetoric used in law courts. Rather, Galatians is predominantly "deliberative rhetoric," the kind of argumentation ancient speakers and writers used to persuade people to change their behavior. The argument itself is very rational, and the emotional language of the letter was standard rhetoric characteristic of stern letters (Galatians includes elements of ancient "letters of rebuke").

Date. Some scholars have argued for a very early date (making this one of Paul's earliest letters), because Paul does not explicitly appeal to the Jerusalem Council of Acts 15; but that Paul can refer to taking Titus to Jerusalem with him (Gal 2:1) means that he had already completed his first missionary journey (Acts 13—14) and thus that the Council had probably taken place (Acts 15). Galatians may thus date to the late fifties.

Situation. Paul is clearly battling opponents who have settled in Galatia (for the location, see comment on 1:2; if one adopts the South Galatian theory for the location of Paul's readers, Acts 13—15 provides especially helpful background for the letter). These are Jewish Christians who would rather circumcise the Galatians—thus alienating them from their own *Gentile culture—than allow Judean Jews back home to think that Christian missionaries were lax (4:29; 5:11; 6:12-13). Unlike Paul, a more seasoned missionary, these missionaries want to impose their own culture on the Galatians.

The Issue. At an earlier time, some Judean Christians had insisted that Phrygian (maybe Galatian; see comment on 1:2) believers be circumcised to be saved (Acts 15:1). Although the Jerusalem Council had apparently settled this issue, side effects lingered: could *Gentiles be part of God's people without circumcision? Some of the strictest *Pharisees may have required circumcision for salvation, but many Pharisees believed that any Gentiles who kept the few laws given Noah would be saved. But even for this more lenient class of Pharisees (cf. Acts 15:5), one could not become part of the *people of God* without circumcision; very few Jews were so lenient as to accept Gentiles on such terms. Indeed, circumcision had even become a major cultural symbol of fidelity to Judaism: attempts to restrict the practice led to revolts both before and after Paul's time.

Some Judean Christians were now arguing that one must become culturally Jewish to become a full Christian, fully righteous; after all, the Bible itself made this requirement for one who wished to belong to God's people (Gen 17:10-14). Further, they may have reasoned, if Paul argued for *baptism (a post-Old Testament Jewish addition to circumcision), why could Judean Christians not require circumcision, even though it drove away potential converts? Paul argues forcefully against this view.

Commentaries. Among the useful commentaries on Galatians are those by Donald Guthrie, *Galatians,* NCB (1973; reprint, Grand Rapids, Mich.: Eerdmans,

1981); F. F. Bruce, *The Epistle to the Galatians,* NIGTC (Grand Rapids, Mich.: Eerdmans, 1982); and Richard N. Longenecker, *Galatians,* WBC 41 (Dallas: Word, 1990). Helpful specialized works include George Lyons, *Pauline Autobiography: Toward a New Understanding,* SBLDS 73 (Atlanta: Scholars, 1985). Hans Dieter Betz, *A Commentary on Paul's Letter to the Churches in Galatia,* Hermeneia (Philadelphia: Fortress, 1979), has helpful insights, although his model of judicial (courtroom) *rhetoric for the book was severely criticized by George Kennedy, *New Testament Interpretation Through Rhetorical Criticism* (Chapel Hill: University of North Carolina, 1984), and others (see comment on "Type of Letter" above).

1:1-5
Introduction

Like many polite ancient letters, Paul's letters characteristically include a thanksgiving at the outset, but Galatians lacks one. This lack suggests that Paul is angry, and following the proper *rhetorical style for a letter of blame, he does not mind expressing his anger explicitly.

1:1. Letters normally opened with the sender's name; less often, they included a description of the sender, where that was necessary. An "*apostle" was a commissioned messenger; although Paul had once been a humanly appointed agent (Acts 9:2), he is one no longer. Already he challenges his opponents, who claim authority from Jerusalem (cf. also Judea in general—Acts 15:1). (The status that Jerusalemites had in the eyes of many other Jewish people may be illustrated by the authority others ceded to *Josephus's opponents from Jerusalem in one of his accounts.)

1:2. Scholars dispute whether Paul here addresses those in Galatia proper (which scholars often call North Galatia, a region in Asia Minor settled by Celts, not mentioned in Acts and only slowly Christianized) or the so-called South Galatian region (which some scholars call Phrygia-Galatica). If Paul uses the term technically, he must mean North Galatia (which includes Ancyra, Tavium and Pessinus); if he uses it generally, as some other ancient writers did, it may instead cover the Phrygian region addressed in Acts 13—14 (including Antioch, Iconium, Lystra and Derbe).

1:3. Paul here adapts standard Jewish greetings; see comment on Romans 1:7.

1:4-5. Nearly all Jewish people in this period divided history into two main ages: the present age (under the dominion of evil nations) and the future age (when God would rule unchallenged). Because the future *Messiah has already come the first time, Paul can argue that Christians are already citizens of the future age of God's *kingdom. On the ransom, cf. Isaiah 53:10-12 and 43:3-4.

1:6-9
True and False Gospels

Paul minces no words in these verses; although speeches and letters often opened with praise of the hearers or a polite thanksgiving, Paul begins with a direct rebuke. This literary convention is found only among the harshest of ancient letters.

1:6. Letters of blame, especially in their harsher forms, typically used the expression "I am amazed" (NASB). Paul's readers will have no doubt that he is quite upset.

1:7. Messengers who distorted the contents of their message were subject to legal penalties. Those familiar with the *Old Testament would think of those who distorted the divine message in terms of false prophets (e.g., Jer 23:16), for whom the penalty was death (Deut 13:5; 18:20).

1:8-9. Some Jewish mystics of the period claimed revelations from angels (especially in *apocalyptic literature). Oaths and curses were familiar in ancient religion, magic and everyday life. Paul may allude here to the curses of the covenant leveled against those who failed to keep Moses' law (Deut 27—28); more significant is the use of this same word for "curse" in the *Septuagint of Deuteronomy 13: false prophets and those who listened to them were to be destroyed.

1:10-17
Not Revealed by People

Speeches and letters often included a long *narrative section, normally in chronological order. Narrative could sometimes be autobiographical, and Paul here uses standard themes of ancient autobiography to bolster his argument. Themes in ancient argument included divine attestation, examination of character and behavior, and comparisons between figures personifying different values or sides of the dispute. In deliberative speeches, the speaker first had to demonstrate the integrity of his character and conduct if it were in question.

1:10. Pleasing God rather than people echoes a common theme of philosophers. Demagogues who flattered the masses were unpopular in aristocratic circles and were commonly denounced publicly. Paul paints his opponents as pleasers of people (6:12-13).

1:11. "I make known to you" or "I would have you know" (NASB) was sometimes used to introduce the *narrative portion of a speech. Like philosophers and moralists who presented themselves as models of the virtuous life, Paul can present himself as a model of the *gospel. But anything that could be interpreted as boasting or self-exaltation was offensive to ancient ears, unless one had proper reasons for it; defending oneself or claiming to be boasting on behalf of another (here, God) was, however, considered sufficient reason.

1:12. In argumentation, firsthand knowledge counted highly. "Received" was sometimes used for the passing on of human traditions, as Jewish scholars did; here Paul refers to his experience in Acts 9.

1:13-14. "Advancing" (v. 14) is the technical language of philosophical schools for progress in one's studies, but it was also current in *Diaspora Judaism and could naturally be applied, as here, to a *rabbinic student. The Palestinian Jewish image of "zeal" was commonly rooted in the models of Phinehas (Num 25:11) and the *Maccabees, who were willing to kill for God. "Traditions" could refer to general community customs, but given Paul's *Pharisaism (Phil 3:5), it probably refers to Pharisaic traditions, on which Jews discussing Pharisaism generally commented. (Pharisees were known for their adherence to oral tradition.) Paul actually understands the Palestinian Jewish piety of his day far better than his opponents do. His position and activities are reported in greater detail in Acts 8:1-3 and 9:1-2.

1:15. That God set his servants apart even before birth is clear from Jeremiah 1:5 (see also Gen 25:23; Ps 71:6; Is 44:2; 49:1); Paul presents his own call in the light of those of the *Old Testament prophets.

1:16. "Flesh and blood" (KJV, NASB) was a common figure of speech for "mortals" (see "any man"—NIV—and "any human being"—NRSV).

1:17. "Arabia" refers to Nabataea, the area around Damascus in Syria. This area was prosperous; Greek cities like Petra (Aretas's capital), Gerasa and Philadelphia (modern Amman in Jordan) belonged to the Nabataean Arabs, and Bedouins traveled through the land. Damascus was next to Nabataea and at this time may have been controlled by Nabataea's king, Aretas IV (see comment on 2 Cor 11:32).

1:18-24
Return to Judea

In 1:11-24 Paul makes clear that he did not receive his *gospel as a tradition from the Jerusalem *apostles; he is not, therefore, their subordinate (as a *disciple passing on tradition from his teachers would be). If his opponents claim direct tradition from Jerusalem, Paul can counter their claims by pointing out that he is an equal of the Jerusalem apostles and has his own information firsthand.

1:18-19. On ancient reckoning, where part of the first year counts as the whole, "three" can mean either two or three. Hospitality was important in Jewish homes.

1:20. Oaths like this one ("before God") could be used in court to underline one's integrity; breaking the oath invited divine judgment, and most people had enough piety to believe that God (or the gods) would execute judgment on one who took such an oath (i.e., called the gods as witnesses) in vain.

1:21. Whether or not Paul means the whole province of "Syria-Cilicia" (as he could have in this period), Paul spent time both in Cilicia (Tarsus) and Syria proper (Antioch, its capital); cf. Acts 9:30, 11:25-26 and 13:1.

1:22. Paul means "*churches of Judea" generally, not Jerusalem; his fluency in the highest and most *Hellenized circles of Palestinian Jewish education (evident from 1:14 and Paul's *rhetoric) almost certainly places his education in Jerusalem, as Acts 22:3 also suggests.

1:23-24. The few Jewish stories that culminated in the conversion of a persecutor always emphasized the greatness and power of God. Paul's genuine *repentance would naturally produce the same response among Jewish Christians.

2:1-10
The Jerusalem Council

Although the matter is disputable, it seems likely that Paul here reports the relevant features of the Council that Luke records in Acts 15. Paul uses a variety of ancient literary devices to make his point in this passage (e.g., aposiopesis or ellipsis, antithesis). Given the probable claims of his opponents that Paul is relaxing biblical requirements to gain more converts, and that their views emanate from Jerusalem, the Jerusalem *apostles' support bolsters Paul's case.

2:1. The "fourteen years" here probably refers to his previous visit to Jerusalem, about three years after his conversion; if the Council met around A.D. 48, Paul's conversion may have occurred around A.D. 31, within perhaps a year of Jesus' *resurrection.

2:2. Paul sought first the support of the Jerusalem leaders for his revelation, before the assembly gathered to make a decree. On the importance of majority rulings in ancient Jewish groups emphasizing consensus, see comment on Acts 15:22.

2:3-5. Although many Jews believed that nonidolatrous *Gentiles would be saved, almost no one believed that they were adopted into the covenant on equal terms with Jewish people until they were circumcised. That some Jewish Christians wanted to force circumcision on Titus is thus not surprising (cf. Acts 15:5); that Paul's side won out in the Jerusalem *church means that the Jewish Christians had diverged significantly on this issue from the majority views of their culture. Paul graphically describes the other side as "spies" (TEV), infiltrators who seek to betray the Christian camp and finally enslave them as prisoners of war.

2:6-8. Those of "reputation" (2:2, 6—NASB) are the Jerusalem *apostles (2:9). But Paul regarded God's opinion more highly than any human opinion, no matter how highly reputed. Whenever a Greco-Roman speaker argued against tradition or custom, that speaker had to assume the burden of proof; divine revelations were, however, regarded as important evidence even among pagans. Among Jewish teachers, the majority opinion of the sages was normative, weighed more heavily by some than a direct voice from heaven; but Paul circumvents an appeal to such tradition by appealing instead to the standard Jewish doctrine that God is an impartial judge. In 2:7-9, even the "pillars" themselves recognized Paul's equal (but different) task.

2:9. Ancient writers sometimes used "pillar" as Paul does here (occasionally for prominent *rabbis); Paul may refer to these apostles' place in the new temple (cf. Eph 2:20). Receiving one another's right hands usually connoted greetings and welcome; but sometimes, as here, it indicates an agreement or treaty. "Cephas" is *Aramaic for Peter.

2:10. Palestinian Judaism sometimes called the pious "the poor"; but the literal poverty of the Jewish Christian masses in Jerusalem is more likely in view here. The *Old Testament and Judaism heavily emphasized alms for the poor, and Paul's collection (e.g., 2 Cor 8—9) was undertaken to alleviate this need.

2:11-14
Confrontation in Antioch

2:11. Paul extends the *rhetorical technique of comparison (used positively in 2:7-8), contrasting Peter's refusal to comply with the decree of the Jerusalem Council with Paul's defense of it. The Galatians should thus recognize that even if Paul's opponents had been authorized by the Jerusalem *apostles—which is not the case (2:1-10)—the Jerusalem apostles would have been wrong to have authorized them. Antioch was the largest city of Syria-Palestine, a few hundred miles north of Jerusalem, and the center of the Jewish Christian mission to the *Gentiles (Acts 11:20; 13:1-3; 14:26-27).

2:12. Pious Jews were not supposed to engage in table fellowship with Gentiles (Acts 10:28; 11:3). The Jerusalem Jewish leaders may have agreed with Paul on paper (in theory), but they also had to keep peace within their own Jerusalem constituency and maintain their witness to their culture, with its rising anti-Gentile sentiments. Peter probably saw his actions here the way Paul saw his own in 1 Corinthians 9:19-22—appealing to everyone—but the qualitative difference is enormous: withdrawing from table fellowship with culturally different Christians made them second-class citizens, violated the unity of the *church and hence insulted the cross of Christ. Although Peter and others undoubtedly claimed to oppose racism, they accommodated it on what they saw as minor points to keep peace, whereas Paul felt that any degree of racial separatism or segregation challenged the very heart of the *gospel.

2:13-14. Jewish piety demanded that reproof be given in private; for Paul to reprove Peter publicly suggests that he regarded the offense as quite serious and urgent. "Hypocrisy" or pretense was universally regarded negatively; philosophers and Jewish wisdom writers alike attacked it. (Some scholars have argued that before the New Testament period the term occurs only in its literal usage for actors in the theater; but earlier use in Jewish wisdom sources contradicts this view.)

2:15-21
Paul's Case in Antioch

Paul seems to summarize the substance of Galatians here, whether or not this paragraph is the thesis statement of the book (as Betz, who classifies Galatians as judicial *rhetoric, thinks). Paul's response to Peter may continue through verse 21 (as in NIV), although this is unclear.

2:15-16. Paul argues that Jewish

Christians are also made righteous by faith, which does not give them any advantage over *Gentiles who must come to God on the same terms. Jewish people regarded Gentiles as different by nature, because they believed that Gentiles' ancestors were not freed from the evil impulse at Sinai as Israel was.

2:17-18. Paul then argues—refuting opposing arguments in advance—that righteousness by faith does not lead to sinful living. He uses the objection of an imaginary interlocutor to make his point, as was standard in ancient *diatribe.

2:19-20. The *law itself taught Paul the way of Christ and Paul's death to sin in Christ. The closest parallels to the divine empowerment of Christ's indwelling are *Old Testament teachings about empowerment by God's *Spirit (although the *New Testament writers develop these teachings much further).

2:21. Paul continues his point that righteousness (both before God and in one's behavior) comes through Christ's life in the believer (through the Spirit—3:1-2; cf. 5:13-25). Christ would not have died if salvation could have been provided another way. Jewish people normally believed that all Jews were chosen for salvation in Abraham and were saved unless they were very disobedient; by contrast, *Gentiles might be saved without conversion to Judaism but could attain to Israel's full status as members of the covenant only if they converted. By insisting that righteousness is through Christ alone, Paul places Jew and Gentile on the same terms with regard to salvation.

3:1-5
Consistency with Their Conversion

Paul's style here is *diatribe—a vivid teaching style often characterized by imaginary interlocutors, rhetorical questions and intense reasoning—which lasts through 4:31.

3:1. Good public speakers were known for their dramatic gestures and vivid accounts, enacting before their audience the very events they narrated. All major ancient writers on public speaking emphasized this vividness of speech, in which the events narrated seemed to appear before the hearers' "very eyes" (NIV, TEV). Here Paul no doubt means that he acted out the crucifixion through his own lifestyle (2:20). The term translated "bewitched" refers to the evil impact of spells (see TEV) or the "evil eye," a jealous look with magical efficacy.

3:2. Many Jewish sources link the *Spirit with human merit: for example, it was said that no one in a given generation could receive the Spirit because the generation was unworthy, even if the potential recipient were worthy. But the Galatian Christians had a different experience; they had received the Spirit shortly after leaving paganism, in keeping with the Christian teaching that the future outpouring of the Spirit on God's people had been made available to all in Christ.

3:3. Although Paul's opponents do not seem to have denied that the Galatians received Christ and the Spirit before knowing the *law, they insisted that "perfect" (cf. KJV, NASB) or complete Christianity included obedience to the law. Judaism stressed that the Jewish people had been saved through *grace, but that Jews who rejected the law were lost; in their view, *Gentile converts to Judaism also had to prove the genuineness of their conversion by obeying all the details of the law. Many philosophers and pagan cults spoke of "perfection" or "maturity" as the ultimate stage of moral or (in the case of the cults) religious advancement.

3:4. Here Paul asks whether their conversion by grace and consequent persecution were meaningless. An appeal to the readers' own experience would constitute the ultimate eyewitness argument and was *rhetorically effective.

3:5. Not only their conversion but also the miracles continuing among them were by *grace. Although ancient peoples were more open to miracles than modern secularists are, the idea of a religious community (in contrast to a pagan healing shrine of Asclepius) where miracles occurred regularly would have been spectacular even in antiquity.

3:6-14
Abraham's Blessing and the Law's Curse

Paul here refers five times to the law of Moses and once to the Prophets, making a case from Scripture that those who claimed to respect the *law had to accept. He contrasts the message of faith (3:6-9, 14) with works directed toward the law (3:10-13), as in 3:5. (The two major interpretations of this passage are that *Gentile Christians believe as Abraham did—the traditional position, followed here—or that they are saved by Abraham's faith [as in Judaism] and hence Christ's faith, i.e., Abraham's and Christ's fidelity to the covenant.)

3:6. Paul cites Genesis 15:6, a popular Jewish proof text for showing how Abraham modeled the work of faith. Paul will expound it differently from the traditional Jewish interpretation.

3:7. Jewish people used "sons" (so NASB here) both literally (genetically) and spiritually (those who acted like their moral predecessors). They normally applied the title "Abraham's offspring" (or "children"—KJV, NIV—or "descendants"—NRSV, TEV) to the Jewish people but occasionally referred specifically to those who excelled in righteousness—although Jewish people would never have applied this designation to *Gentiles. Here Paul demonstrates that those who believe as Abraham did are his spiritual offspring (Gen 15:6, quoted in Gal 3:6).

3:8-9. Because Gentiles could believe as Abraham did (3:7), they could also be made righteous as he was. (Jewish teachers saw Abraham as the model convert to Judaism and consequently would be forced to respect Paul's argument more than they would like.) Like a good Jewish expositor, Paul proves his inference from this passage by appealing to another text dealing with the promise to Abraham (Gen 12:3 = 18:18; cf. 17:4-5; 22:18). God's purpose all along had been to reach the Gentiles, too, as had been stated at the very opening of the Abraham *narrative. In Jewish thinking, the righteous (Israel) were saved in Abraham; here, believing Gentiles are saved (blessed) in him.

3:10. Both Genesis 12:3 and the blessings of the law in Deuteronomy 28 contrast the curses of those who oppose Abraham or those who break the covenant with the blessings of Abraham's descendants or those who keep the covenant. Reasoning by opposites was a normal Jewish method of interpretation. Paul thus gives the verdict on righteousness sought by the "works of" (KJV, NASB) or by "obeying" (TEV) the law: imperfect obedience brings a curse (Deut 27:26, the summary of the curses). According to Jewish teaching, human obedience was always imperfect, and God could therefore not require perfect obedience as a condition for salvation; but like a good *rabbi, Paul interprets Deuteronomy 27:26 for all that he can get from it—after all, God was in a position to demand perfection.

3:11. Paul quotes Habakkuk 2:4 (on which see comment on Rom 1:17) as evidence that a righteousness based merely on human obedience is inadequate. Paul's knowledge of the *Old Testament is thorough: he has selected the only two texts in the entire Old Testament that speak of both righteousness and faith together (in v. 6 Gen 15:6; here Hab 2:4).

3:12. Because Habakkuk 2:4 connects righteousness and life, Paul cites the other Old Testament text that refers to both, again demonstrating his Jewish exegetical skill (Jewish interpreters regularly linked texts on the basis of key words they shared). Paul contrasts the faith method (3:11) with the works method of Leviticus 18:5 (cf. Ex 20:12, 20; Lev 25:18; Deut 4:1, 40; 5:33; 8:1; 30:16, 20; 32:47; Neh 9:29; Ezek 20:11, 13; 33:19). Although these Old Testament texts speak of long life in the Promised Land, Paul knows that many Jewish interpreters applied these texts to the life of the world to come; hence he responds: "This is the works method." His opponents may have been using this text to make their case that faith was not enough. Paul agrees that the righteousness of the law has to be fulfilled, but he believes that it is fulfilled by being in Christ and living by his *Spirit (5:16-25); his opponents believe that a Gentile has to achieve it by obeying the details of the law, especially the initial act of circumcision.

3:13. Again following the Jewish principle of linking *Old Testament texts on the basis of key words they shared, Paul cites Deuteronomy 21:23 to show that Christ took the "curse" that belongs to all who fail to perform the whole law (Gal 3:10).

3:14. In Jewish expectation "the blessing of Abraham" includes the whole world to come; here Paul says that believers have the down payment of that world (cf. Eph 1:3, 13-14) in the blessing of the *Spirit (cf. Is 44:3). (For the relationship of the promise of land to the promise of the Spirit, cf. also Hag 2:5 with Ex 12:25; 13:5.)

3:15-20
The Law Does Not Annul Abraham's Covenant

Greeks usually used the term Paul uses for "covenant" for a "testament" or "will" (a legal document opened at someone's death). Although Paul means "covenant" in the *Old Testament sense rather than as "testament," he can play on the legal nuances of the latter. Judaism stressed the covenant made at Sinai, but most Jewish writers saw that same covenant foreshadowed (or, less accurately from an Old Testament standpoint, actually practiced in advance) in Abraham (Gen 17:9-14).

3:15. Like other legal documents, testaments or "wills" (NRSV) were sealed so they could not be altered. In Greek law, wills were irrevocable; one could not impose new conditions or remove an heir, even if one added a supplementary testament. (This was no longer true in Roman law of this period, but it applied to some Jewish wills; compare a possible precedent in Deut 21:15-17.) Under Greek law, testaments were confirmed by their deposit with the municipal records office; if a new testament would interfere with an older one, it was rejected.

3:16. Paul means that Christ is the ultimate seed of the promise through whom the nations will be blessed; this thesis makes good sense of the promise motif in Israel's history. But he argues his case the way the *rabbis often did: by attention to a grammatical peculiarity that was not actually peculiar. (As in English, the Hebrew term for "seed" could convey either the singular or the plural [a collective], which Paul well knew—3:29. But *rabbis argued in this manner, too; "sons of Israel" meant either "sons and daughters" or only the men, depending on what the rabbis needed it to mean in a given text. Paul's opponents no doubt read Scripture this way, and Paul responds in kind; he takes "seed" as singular, a sense that the term can have in general but that does not seem to fit any of the Genesis texts to which he may refer [13:15-16; 17:8; 24:7], because he already knows, on other grounds, that Christ is the epitome of Abraham's line. When later rabbis applied "Abraham's seed" to one person, it was naturally to Abraham's son Isaac.) Judaism nearly always took "Abraham's seed" as Israel, which Paul would agree is usually what it means (Rom 9:7, 29; 11:1). But his argument in Galatians 3:6-9 permits him to apply this expression to *Gentile Christians who are in Christ, hence in Abraham.

Roman law allowed testaments to stipulate that property be left first to one heir and then to another after the first one's death. If Paul expected his readers to know this sort of custom, this may explain how his argument for them can move in principle from Christ as the heir to all who are in Christ.

3:17-18. On the legal principle of 3:15, God would not institute a law that retracted his earlier promise based on faith. Paul might be responding to an opposing argument that the new covenant could not alter the old; if so, Paul responds that the new covenant (Jer 31:31-34) returns to the *original* covenant. "Four hundred thirty years" comes from Exodus 12:40.

3:19. The *law's function of restraining transgressions would have also made sense to non-Jewish readers: Greco-Roman philosophers felt that law was necessary for the masses but that the wise were a law for themselves. In his image of the guardian in 3:23-25 Paul elaborates on this function of the law, meant to last till the promise could be fulfilled; such an addition could not change the earlier covenant (3:15). According to post-*Old Testament Jewish tradition, the law was given through angels, and (as in the Old Testament) the mediator was Moses himself.

3:20. Mediators intercede between two (or more) parties; if the law was given through a mediator (3:19), therefore, it was adapted to the needs of both parties. But the promise was not given through a mediator; it was a unilateral enactment of the one God (God's oneness was the most basic belief of Judaism). Paul again argues from analogy in a manner that would be persuasive in his readers' culture.

3:21-29
Before Faith Came

3:21. Jewish teachers said that life did come by the *law, both in this world and in the world to come (cf. 3:12). But Paul here concludes his argument (3:15-20) that the law was never meant to do the work of the promise.

3:22. In contrast to Romans 3:10-18, Paul has not argued humanity's universal sinfulness from Scripture in Galatians (Gal 3:10-12 at most implies it). Humanity's sinfulness could be safely assumed, however, because Jewish teachers in his day agreed that all people had sinned; Paul simply takes the consequences of that sin far more seriously than other teachers did, in that the death of God's Son was needed to cancel them.

3:23. Jewish traditions divided human history into various stages; Paul does the same, viewing the law as a temporary guardian till the original promise was fulfilled.

3:24. "Put in charge" (NIV) is better translated "tutor" (NASB) or, better still, "guardian." The slave assigned to this role would watch out for the student on his way to school and help him with his manners and schoolwork, but he was not the teacher himself. Children sometimes resented but often grew fond of their slave guardians and later freed them. Such guardians were also normally better educated than the free masses; the image is not intrinsically demeaning. But it was hardly the way most other Jewish teachers would have described the law. (They occasionally describe Moses as Israel's "guardian" till Israel grew up. Philosophers spoke of philosophy as a "moral teacher," and Judaism spoke of the law as a "teacher.")

3:25. The coming of faith is described in terms of coming of age, when a boy would achieve adulthood (about thirteen or fourteen years old in various Mediterranean cultures).

3:26. Israel was called God's "children" in the *Old Testament and often in Judaism. In contrast to standard Jewish teaching, Paul says here that one becomes a spiritual descendant of Abraham (3:29) and child of God through faith, not through ethnic participation in the covenant.

3:27. Ancient writers sometimes spoke of being spiritually "clothed"; Judaism occasionally spoke of being "clothed" by the *Spirit (see also comments on Rom 13:12; Eph 4:20-24). *Gentiles who wanted to convert to Judaism were *baptized. By putting on Christ in converting to Christianity, Gentiles took his status as Abraham's seed (3:16, 29) and God's child (3:26).

3:28. Some Greco-Roman cults claimed to ignore social divisions like those Paul mentions here, although they rarely erased them (most cults were expensive enough to exclude all but the well-to-do). But the early Christians were especially distinctive in surmounting such divisions. They formed the only bridge between Jews and Gentiles and had few allies in challenging class (slave versus free) and gender prejudices.

3:29. The Jewish people were called "Abraham's seed" (KJV, NIV) or "offspring" (NASB, NRSV; see comment on 3:16), heirs of the promise; Paul's argument in this chapter has transferred this position to *Gentile Christians.

4:1-11
Sons, Not Slaves

Under ancient law, sons were heirs, destined to inherit what belonged to their fathers; in contrast, slaves were part of the inherited property. The contrast between slaves and children appears elsewhere in ancient literature. But in household codes, which explained the proper relations of all members of a household with the head of the household, minor children were subordinated just as slaves were; only after leaving the home did a child achieve freedom in practice. Paul here continues the image of the slave guardian versus the child (3:24).

4:1. Under Roman law, the status of the minor still under a guardian was roughly that of a slave.

4:2. Minors were required to be under legal "guardians" even if their father was deceased; this guardian was normally chosen from the father's will, or, if this were unspecified, the role fell to the nearest male relative from the father's side of the family. The "managers" (NASB) or "trustees" (NIV,

NRSV) or "stewards" of estates were often slaves or *freedmen but wielded considerable power.

4:3. In their previous, pagan state, the Galatians had reverenced the elements of the universe as deities (Judaism had long since demythologized them as angels who ruled over nature, like those implied in Ps 148:2-4). Most ancients feared the personified, tyrannical power Fate, which was thought to exercise its will through the astral spirits, the gods who ruled the stars. Paul believes that even the Jewish people were enslaved by such evil spiritual powers apart from Christ; see comment on 4:9.

4:4. Jewish texts often speak of the fulfillment of appointed times in history as a way of recognizing God's perfect wisdom in and sovereignty over history. (Some commentators have compared "the fullness of the time"—NASB—to how ripe Greco-Roman culture was for the spread of Christianity; yet others could counter by citing the almost insurmountable obstacles that this culture presented to the early Christians.) Here Paul compares this fulfillment to the point at which a boy attains maturity and is considered an adult (about thirteen or fourteen years old). "Born under *law" means that Jesus was obligated to keep the law of Moses.

4:5. Greek law combined adoption with heirship; the same seems to have been true in the case of childless persons in ancient Near Eastern law (cf. Gen 15:2). Paul uses common *Old Testament imagery to make his point, however; God had made Israel his children (e.g., Ex 4:22), and the Old Testament repeatedly speaks of the land as Israel's "inheritance," bestowed on them by God (without any thought of God's dying, of course).

4:6. Roman adoptions required a witness of the transaction: the *Holy Spirit performs this function here. That the Spirit should testify is natural, because Judaism understood the Spirit especially as the one who inspired the prophets; the Spirit here inspires believers, speaking to them as he did to the prophets, to remind them of their calling as God's children. "Abba" is the *Aramaic word for "Papa," a term of special intimacy rarely if ever used in Judaism to address God directly (see comment on Mk 14:36; Rom 8:15).

4:7. The Galatians are now freed from the slave guardian of 3:24-25, for the time has come (4:4).

4:8. Jewish people often said that the pagans did "not know God," and that their gods, which were creations of the true God, were "not gods at all." (Philosophers often decided the moral value of an idea or action by how it corresponded to nature; Paul and other Jewish and Christian writers recognized that worshiping a created object as if it were the Creator failed this criterion. Some pagan thinkers, following an ancient Greek philosopher named Euhemerus, distinguished between real gods, which were evident "by nature" [sun, moon, planets and stars], and those invented by people [other deities].) Jewish people, because they were in covenant with God, said that they "knew" God truly.

4:9. As was fitting in *rhetorical rebuke, Paul uses harsh language: he is not sure that the Galatians "know" God even now. The "elemental things" (NASB) or "principles" (NIV) to which they are returning are presumably the "spirits" (cf. NRSV, TEV) of nature they used to worship as gods (4:8). Foremost among these would be the astral spirits (4:3), associated with special days and seasonal rituals (4:10).

4:10. Judaism had its own special calendar of holy days, new moons, sabbatical years and so forth. Paul is saying that by returning to a ceremonial, calendrical religion, the Galatians return to pagan bondage under these spirits in the heavens (4:3, 9). From a technical standpoint, this argument is standard *rhetorical exaggeration: Judaism and paganism felt that they had little in common. From the standpoint of experience, however, they would relinquish the *Spirit (3:2; 4:6) for tradition and custom. Some commentators think that Paul here links the deified elements of paganism (4:8-9), which correspond to Judaism's angels of nature, with the angels who gave the *law (3:19); although that linkage is uncertain, Paul's image here is negative, at best that of an adult going back under the guardianship of a slave.

4:11. The prophets sometimes complained of pleading with Israel to no avail; disappointed servants of God hoped that their devotion was not "in vain" (so KJV, NASB here), that is, not unrewarded (Ps 73:13; cf. Is 49:4; 65:23); even God's judgments were "in vain" when Israel did not return to him (Jer 2:30). The image was always that of great labor expended with no return, due to the recipients' obstinacy (Phil 2:16; cf. 1 Thess 3:5) or the ineffectiveness of a message (1 Cor 15:2, 14, 17, 58).

4:12-20
Paul's Plea

Although Galatians is clearly a "letter of blame," it is not the harshest sort of blame; Paul does not intend to break fellowship with his readers. In this section, Paul employs standard themes found in "letters of friendship," emphasizing that he still loves the Galatians deeply. Ancient *rhetoricians emphasized appropriate expressions of emotion as well as logic in persuasion, and recognized the need to lighten the tone after a section of heavy reproof. Paul's words here would thus sound entirely appropriate.

4:12. Especially in Greek culture, "friends" (so NRSV here) were viewed as "equals" (although the Roman idea of friendship between *patrons and their dependents was likewise widespread). "I became as you are" means that Paul relates to them as equals, not only as their father in the faith (4:19).

4:13. Paul's first visit (Acts 14:1-20 as opposed to 14:21-25, if we follow the South Galatian theory; see comment on 1:2) or preaching was occasioned by some "infirmity" (KJV); the term could be applied either to sickness or to injuries inflicted by persecution. *Stoic philosophers said that sickness should not affect one's attitude, and the Galatians may have been impressed with how Paul bore up under an infirmity. Some scholars have suggested (on the assumption that South Galatia is in view; see the introduction) that Galatia was a good area for someone sick to go to recuperate.

4:14. Physical infirmities were quite often regarded as the curse or punishment of the gods; this belief in sickness as divine retribution appears often even in Jewish texts. Receiving Paul as God's "angel" (cf. Acts 14:12) or "messenger" (the term can refer to human as well as supernatural messengers) meant receiving him with the hospitality due the one who sent him, Christ Jesus. Messengers were to be received as representatives of their senders. (The wording need not imply that Christ is present as an angel; cf. 1 Sam 29:9; 2 Sam 14:17, 20; 19:27; Zech 12:8. Many second- and third-century Jewish Christians did portray Christ as the chief angel, because of the limited categories available in Judaism to communicate him to their culture. The image was discontinued in the fourth century due to its exploitation by the Arians, who regarded Christ as deity but created, although the image fit earlier use by Ebionites who rejected Christ's divinity. Some Jewish writers, like *Philo, portrayed the Word as the supreme angel, but earliest Christianity lacks any direct evidence for this portrayal.)

4:15. Sacrificing one's eye for someone else was a figure of speech for a great sacrifice (*Petronius attributes it to some *rhetoricians). Thus Paul's statement that the Galatians "would have dug out your own eyes to give them to me" need not mean that his infirmity (4:13-14) was an oozing eye sore, as some commentators have suggested. In Greek culture, friendship was especially demonstrated by sacrifice; Paul here reaffirms the bond that exists between himself and the Galatians.

4:16-17. Demagogues who told people what they wanted to hear became popular through their flattery. Moralists thus always pointed out that the flatterers were not concerned for their hearers' good; those who told them the truth openly were those who really loved them (cf. similarly Prov 27:6).

4:18. In contrast to the Galatians' response to his opponents' flattery (4:17), the Galatians had sought Paul in genuine love (4:13-15)—as long as he was with them to defend himself (4:16). In ancient thought, letters were a surrogate for one's presence; Paul here hopes to reverse their questioning of his teaching.

4:19. Teachers were often viewed as "fathers." Galatians well understood the Roman custom of the ruling father, whose authority over his children was absolute. But Paul appeals to a different aspect of ancient parenthood: that of affection and intimacy. Although the image of affection was also applied to the father, Paul here takes the role of the mother as well. Labor pains were regarded as the severest pains humans experienced, and even with skilled midwives, mothers often died in childbirth. Paul's image of his love and sacrifice—and of their apostasy—could not be more graphic.

4:20. *Rhetoricians like Isocrates recommended honestly confessing, "I am at a loss as to what to say," when confronting an emotionally stirring and painful situation. Letters were considered a surrogate for one's presence (4:18) and were supposed to reflect the same character the person would display if present. But it was easier for Paul to write stern letters than to be stern in person (2 Cor 10:10-11); indeed, even when he was writing a letter of blame, it hurt him worse than it hurt them (2 Cor 2:4).

4:21—5:1
The Hagar-Sarah Analogy

If Genesis derives from the period of Moses and the exodus, the literary function of the Hagar *narrative includes a warning to the Israelites against going back to Egypt (Gen 16:1), although Hagar is ultimately more a positive than a negative character. Further, the entire section of Genesis (chaps. 16—21) emphasizes that the child who came according to God's promise (the promise Abraham believed in Gen 15:6; cf. Gal 3:6, 14) was the key to everything else God had promised Abraham; the child conceived "according to the flesh," by merely human means, was blessed by God but had nothing to do with the promise. Unlike the interpretations of *Philo and some other interpreters of his day (and not a few modern sermon illustrations), Paul's "allegory" is an analogy controlled by the biblical text, not merely by what he wants to say.

4:21. "Tell me" was one way of addressing an imaginary opponent in a *diatribe. In common Jewish parlance, "the *law" included Genesis, hence the Hagar-Sarah story.

4:22-23. When Abraham and Sarah tried to have a son by human means (apart from a divine intervention), they had Hagar bear a son to Abraham (Gen 16:1-4, 15). (Some scholars have suggested that they were following an ancient Near Eastern custom of using the barren wife's handmaid as a surrogate mother.) But God still planned to send a son miraculously, a son who would inherit the covenant God had made with Abraham (Gen 17:15-21). Paul is still playing on the slave-free image of 3:23—4:11.

4:24. Given his pedagogical views, *Philo naturally interpreted Hagar as imperfect training, but Sarah as perfect virtue. Paul instead draws an analogy between the slave, who produced according to the flesh, and those who seek to fulfill the law's righteousness according to the flesh. Hagar was from Egypt (Gen 16:1) and thus could have reminded the first Israelite readers of Genesis of their own slavery in Egypt; Mount Sinai was near Egypt.

4:25. "Arabia" included Mount Sinai, south of Judea, as well as the northward area mentioned in 1:17. The Nabataean Arabs were viewed as Ishmaelites, descendants of Hagar, in Paul's day, thus making the connection clearer to ancient readers familiar with eastern Mediterranean geography. Commentators have suggested that Paul answers his opponents' claims here, because an allegorical style of argumentation is rare for him. His opponents may have identified Sinai with the new Jerusalem, the place from which the law would go forth in the future (Is 2:2-4; cf. 65:17-19).

4:26. Many Jewish texts in Paul's day reinforced the *Old Testament hope of a new Jerusalem, often speaking of a heavenly Jerusalem that would come down to earth. These texts also sometimes spoke of Jerusalem (present or future) as "our mother." Because Judaism associated the *Messiah and the *Spirit with the end time, Paul would naturally identify followers of the Messiah Jesus with the future Jerusalem rather than with the present one.

4:27. It was natural for some Jewish teachers to connect Isaiah 54:1 (which Paul cites here) with Genesis 21:2: Sarah's giving birth typified her descendants' giving birth after the suffering of the captivity to a restored Israel and Jerusalem. That Isaiah himself intended such an allusion is at least possible (Is 51:2).

4:28. Paul's opponents argued that one must be circumcised to enter the covenant of Abraham and Isaac and become their spiritual descendants. Although they could make a strong case from Genesis 17:10-14, Paul goes beyond Jewish tradition (which generally expected the law to be strengthened, not radically changed, in the end time). He believes that the coming of the Messiah has inaugurated a new era in which the old rules no longer strictly apply (Gal 4:4, 26). Under this new covenant, these *Gentile Christians are children of Isaac, and their circumcising opponents are spiritual Ishmaelites.

4:29. That the inferior are envious of the superior was a frequent moral in antiquity; cf. 1 John 3:12 or *Philo's work entitled "That the Worse Attack the Better"; the Old Testament likewise often illustrated that the wicked persecute the righteous (e.g., Ps 37:32). Paul uses this idea to explain why his Jewish Christian opponents are succumbing to the pressure of non-Christian Jewish opinion (cf. 5:11; 6:12-13).

4:30-31. Paul's opponents felt that

uncircumcised *Gentiles were excluded from the covenant; Paul here argues the opposite. Completing his analogy, he cites Genesis 21:10: Hagar's line could not inherit with Sarah's, and Sarah demanded that Abraham expel Hagar and Ishmael. Paul calls on his readers to do the same—to expel his opponents, the spiritual Ishmaelites.

5:1. On the "yoke" see comment on Acts 15:10.

5:2-6
The Real Law

In 5:2—6:3 Paul emphasizes that the real law is of the *Spirit and of love, not of the flesh.

5:2-3. Most Jewish teachers allowed that righteous *Gentiles could be saved by keeping merely the seven laws believed to have been given to Noah; but any Gentile who converted to Judaism was responsible to keep all 613 commandments given to Israel at Mount Sinai (according to rabbinic count). *Rabbis said that the *law was a whole, and one had to keep all of it; rejecting any part of it was tantamount to rejecting the whole thing.

5:4. Although most Jewish people believed that they were born into the covenant by virtue of being Jewish, they recognized that one could be cut off from the covenant by refusing to obey it. But because salvation is only by Christ (2:21), Paul declares that seeking it any other way leads to being "cut off" (NRSV).

5:5-6. Most Jewish people believed that the *Spirit had been active in the *Old Testament and would become active again in the end time. For Paul, the Spirit activates the power of the future *kingdom in believers' lives in the present, thus enabling them to experience the "righteousness" or "justification" that will be fully revealed at Christ's return. See comment on 6:15.

5:7-12
Paul Castigates His Opponents

5:7-8. Ancient writers on moral topics often compared the moral life to running a race. Paul here speaks of someone "cutting in" (NIV, literally; "hindered"—NASB), which throws the runners off balance and perhaps out of the race. *Rhetoricians liked to play with words, and Paul here alludes to circumcision (which involved cutting), as in 5:12 ("cut off"—KJV).

5:9-10. One of yeast's most basic properties is that it spreads throughout the dough; Paul uses the same idea, possibly an ancient proverb, in 1 Corinthians 5:6 to warn of the negative effects of an unchecked spiritual malignancy.

5:11. If Paul were simply converting *Gentiles to Judaism in the ordinary manner (circumcision for the men, *baptism for both men and women), he would not be experiencing Jewish opposition—to which his opponents in Galatia, more sensitive to their own culture's expectations than to those of the Galatians' culture, have succumbed (6:12-13). (If his readers are in South Galatia, Acts 13—14 records some of the persecutions.)

5:12. "They were cut off" (KJV) or "cutting themselves off" could mean to cut themselves off from the community, but most commentators take the words as meaning "mutilate" (NASB), "emasculate" (NIV) or "castrate" (NRSV, TEV) themselves: while they are circumcising others, they ought to make a full sweep of themselves and remove the whole organ. Although Paul's language purposely avoids being explicit, there is no reason to think that such an insult is beneath him; witty insults were the mark of good public speakers in the heat of debate, and Paul is far more impassioned in his criticism of his opponents than in his blame of the Galatians themselves. Many pagans thought of circumcision as a form of mutilation, and the Roman emperor Hadrian later outlawed it under an anticastration law. But as Paul knew, Jewish people particularly abhorred eunuchs, castrated men (Deut 23:1).

5:13-18
Fulfilling the Law

5:13-14. Other Jewish teachers also summarized the humanward commandments of the *law in terms of this quotation from Leviticus 19:18; Paul prefers this summary to all others, however, because this was the summary Jesus offered (Mk 12:31).

5:15. The ancients (especially in the *Old Testament and Jewish sources, e.g., Prov 30:14) used the metaphor of being eaten by others as a grotesque description of a horrible fate or inconceivable wickedness (literal cannibalism horrified ancient sensitivities even more than it does modern ones).

5:16. The Old Testament and Judaism spoke of "walking" (so KJV and NASB here) in the way of the Lord, in righteousness, in the law, etc. (e.g., Lev 26:3); it meant "behaving" in these ways. Jewish teachers described their moral laws derived from the Old Testament law as *halakah,* which literally means "walking." Although this expression was not common in Greek, Paul's readers (especially those becoming more acquainted with the Old Testament and Judaism) would understand his point. He may allude here to Ezekiel 36:27: when God put his *Spirit in his people in the end time, they would walk in all his commandments, even though they had failed to keep the law's righteousness in their own strength.

5:17. "Flesh" is human weakness and mortality ("human nature"—TEV; not merely "sinful nature"—NIV), and means the best (or worst) anyone can do in himself or herself. Because flesh has nothing in common with God's power, one can be either a person of the Spirit (a Christian) or a person of the flesh (one who runs his or her own life without depending on God); one cannot have it both ways (5:16, 18). See comment on the introduction to Romans 8:1-11.

5:18. Philosophers often said that the wise man needed no laws, because he would simply choose to do what was right by the law written in his heart; the Old Testament also speaks of the law's being written in one's heart, a benefit that characterizes especially the new covenant (Jer 31:31-34). The Old Testament often described Israel's being "led" by God, especially in the wilderness after he redeemed them from slavery in Egypt.

5:19-26
Flesh Versus Spirit

When "flesh" referred to people in the *Old Testament, it meant humans viewed in terms of their finiteness, creatureliness and mortality. The *Dead Sea Scrolls thus often apply this idea especially to the moral weakness of humans in themselves, their susceptibility to sin.

The *Spirit of God, however, energized people in the Old Testament to speak and do God's works miraculously. In the Old Testament, flesh and Spirit had nothing in common (Gen 6:3). (The view that Paul contrasts the human body with the human spirit, rather than human weakness and God's Spirit, is based on a *Platonic misreading of Paul, the sort that led to *Gnosticism. Despite its strong condemnation of Gnosticism, the later *church was influenced by some of the same Greek philosophical ideas.) Paul thus declares that those who have

God's presence living inside them by the Spirit have new moral ability and are able to reflect God's own character; for Paul, this was the only way for believers to live out the new life.

5:19-21. Ancient writers commonly used lists of vices, as here, although Paul is much more forceful (v. 21) than pagan writers (who said one merely needed to avoid excess in most vices). Ancient moralists also could use lists of virtues (5:22-23; in the *Old Testament, cf. Ps 15). Laying them side by side to contrast them would also relate to Paul's ancient readers; the standard moral image of the "two ways" (the good and bad ways) or two dominions is frequent in both Jewish and non-Jewish texts. "Works" (KJV) recalls the "works of the *law" that Paul has disparaged throughout the letter (e.g., 3:2), but "of the flesh" (KJV, NASB, NRSV; not "sinful nature"—NIV) tells why: they are merely human, without God's empowerment.

5:22. The Old Testament also uses the metaphor of God's people bearing "fruit" (e.g., Is 27:6; Hos 10:1; 14:8). Here Paul contrasts "fruit" with "works" (5:19) because fruit is simply produced by the nature of the tree, and for Paul, believers' nature has been made new in Christ (5:24).

5:23. Self-control was one of the virtues most emphasized by philosophers and respected in Roman society. Philosophers often taught that the wise needed no law to regulate them, because their virtue itself was a law. Paul says that people of the *Spirit fulfill the moral intent of the law (5:14) by means of the Spirit guiding their lives.

5:24. Philosophers warned about the dangers of unchecked passions. Paul speaks here not of controlling passions, however, but of a completed death with Christ (2:20; 6:14). Paul nearly always uses verbs in the past tense for this death; one does not die to sin gradually (which the imperfect or present tense would suggest) by works, but one accepts one's completed (the aorist and perfect tenses he uses signify the action is completed) righteousness by faith and learns to live accordingly (5:19-23).

5:25. Believers "live" or "have life" (cf. TEV) by the *Spirit; they should then "behave" or "walk" (KJV, NASB) the Spirit's way, which will fulfill the moral principles of biblical law (5:16).

5:26. Paul returns (5:15) to a call to harmony, a common theme of ancient speakers. For Paul, true depth of relationship with God must be expressed in one's relationships with others.

6:1-5
Restoring Others Meekly

Paul continues his exposition on the true law of the *Spirit, the law of Christ (6:2). The gentleness that comes from the Spirit (5:23) is the proper way to correct faults; conversely, the legalist who is obsessed with addressing his or her own spirituality by fleshly means will have little patience with the spiritual needs of others.

6:1. A variety of ancient sources, including Greek and Jewish wisdom traditions and the *Dead Sea Scrolls, stressed wise reproof for the other person's good, and often stressed examining oneself before correcting others. Judaism (unlike Greek culture) considered humility one of the greatest virtues, even for the most noble.

6:2. The image of bearing another's "burden" or "weight" (the term was also applied metaphorically to griefs) might remind readers of slaves or of impressment (Roman soldiers could require local people to carry something for them). In either case, it is an image of subservience that demands more than convenience. "Bear burdens" in this context must include helping a fellow Christian deal with sins (6:1). Many take "law of Christ" as referring to a saying of Jesus, but in the context of Galatians it more likely refers to his example and the character of Jesus imparted by the Spirit (2:20; 5:14).

6:3-5. Greek literature includes some maxims similar to "each one shall bear his own load" (6:5, NASB), which usually stress self-sufficiency; but Paul gives the idea a different twist. In the context of stressing humility in dealing with others (6:1, 3-4), bearing one's own load (6:5) means answering to God himself for what one has done (6:7-8).

6:6-10
Providing for Others

This passage seems to have a financial emphasis, although it is probably not limited to the collection for the Jerusalem *church (1 Cor 16:1), as some commentators have suggested.

6:6. Many teachers charged fees for their instruction; many Greek teachers insisted that they and their students should share all things in common, and some groups of teachers and *disciples lived communally. In Asia Minor (including Galatia), a fee was exacted from those entering temples. Here Paul urges the Galatian Christians to support their teachers who could provide sound teaching (unlike that of his opponents).

6:7. Reaping what one sowed was a familiar image in antiquity (in the *Old Testament, e.g., Job 4:8; Prov 22:8; Hos 8:7; 10:12; cf. Prov 11:18; Is 3:10; Jer 12:13; widespread in other Jewish literature). Paul elsewhere used sowing as a monetary image (2 Cor 9:6); thus here he probably continues the thought of 6:6. "Do not be deceived" was a familiar phrase in ancient moral exhortation.

6:8-9. On the flesh's mortality, see the introduction to 5:19-26; Paul often associates the *Spirit with *resurrection of the body.

6:10. With the exception of the *Cynics, philosophers and moralists advocated working for the common good; no one would have complained about a group that lived accordingly. Paul's emphasis is especially on (though not limited to) ministering to the needs of one's fellow believers.

6:11-18
Crucifixion, not Circumcision

Greeks and Romans viewed circumcision as a mutilation of the flesh, but it in no way compared with the most shameful and painful form of death employed in the Roman world—crucifixion.

6:11. Most letters of this length were dictated to scribes, who wrote small to finish the task quickly. Paul, who may be unaccustomed to writing full letters (or whose hands may have been weakened by leatherworking in cold artisan shops in the winter), cannot write small and quickly. Some documents also seem to have called attention to especially important points at their beginning or end by using larger letters. Whatever the purpose of "large letters" here, the main point is that not a scribe but Paul himself writes this section, as the handwriting shows. Paul's special effort indicates that they must pay special attention.

6:12-13. The metaphor here is grotesque: Paul has been assailing those who live "by the flesh," by merely human, mortal power, ignoring God; physical circumcision was commonly said to be "in the flesh" (so also KJV, NASB, NRSV here). Here Paul speaks of these culture-bound missionaries as if they want to take the Galatians' foreskins back to their senders. See comment on 4:29 and 5:11.

6:14. Paul boasts in a wounding far more severe than circumcision: crucifixion. He is thus unafraid to face persecution from unsatisfied Jewish leaders; see the introduction to this section.

6:15. "New creation" means that the life of the future world has begun in believers now (see comment on 5:5-6; 2 Cor 5:17). Again Paul appeals to the product of God's power, as opposed to any merely human effort.

6:16. Paul blesses those who "walk by this rule" (NASB) as opposed to the "rule" of Jewish *halakah* (see comment on 5:16). The phrase "peace be with/on" someone was common in Judaism; it is one of the most common phrases on Jewish tombs. "Peace be on Israel" was also a regular *synagogue prayer, the final benediction of the Amidah (its basis is as early as Ps 125:5; 128:6); it is a fitting antithesis to the curse against the *law's distorters in 1:8-9. Scholars dispute whether "Israel" here means the faithful Jewish remnant or all believers as spiritual heirs of Abraham (chap. 3), although more seem to favor the latter sense.

6:17. Some slaves, criminals and prisoners of war were tattooed, as were devotees of some religious cults in Egypt and Syria. Greeks and Romans normally associated tattooing with barbarians, and branding was usually reserved for horses. Paul's term is the one normally used for tattooing rather than branding, but could more commonly apply simply to any mark or puncture wound. In this context, Paul simply means that he was crucified with Christ (6:14)—probably as evidenced by "scars" (TEV) from his past persecutions (5:11; 6:12-13).

6:18. The term translated "brothers" means "siblings" (i.e., "brothers and sisters"—NRSV; in Greek, a masculine plural form can include women). It was regularly applied to those of one's race or nationality, but members of religious associations also typically addressed one another in this manner; see comment on Acts 9:17.

EPHESIANS

Introduction

Authorship. Although scholars often dispute the authorship of Ephesians, most of the so-called non-Pauline words, phrases and stylistic features appear at least occasionally in letters that everyone agrees were written by Paul. Many differences between Ephesians and earlier Pauline letters are insignificant. For example, some note that "the genuine Paul" speaks of Christ as the head (1 Cor 11:3) and the *church as his body (Rom 12:4; 1 Cor 12:12) only separately. But ancient philosophers sometimes used the body metaphor with the head and sometimes without it, and requiring Paul always to express himself the same way in his few extant letters, although other writers did not, is hardly fair to Paul.

Unlike many of his earlier letters, Ephesians, Philippians and Colossians seem to have been written after Paul had experience in presenting Christianity in an ancient academic context, where he would have used philosophic language to communicate to his hearers (Acts 19:9). That Paul could adapt his language to his audience, including those to whom the sort of *Stoic language in Ephesians appealed, is evident elsewhere in his writings (e.g., Rom 1; 1 Cor 8); such language is more pervasive in Ephesians and Philippians, with somewhat more Middle *Platonic language in Colossians. Although the dispute over the authorship of Ephesians will continue in scholarly circles, this commentary works from the position that Paul wrote it.

Genre. Paul's exhortations in the letter cover several main themes, all of which the recipients' situation seems to have elicited (although he uses standard forms to describe them). This point would argue against the idea that Ephesians is merely a "letter essay" communicating general truths.

The abundant parallelism and repetition in the letter have been compared with Hebrew poetry, but they were also used in epideictic *rhetoric (i.e., in orations of praise concerning gods or humans). Worship language is more common in the first three chapters of the letter, which elaborate the sort of introductory prayer and thanksgiving that often appeared in ancient letters. As he usually does, Paul here blends the different ancient categories of rhetoric: the exhortation parts of his letter are "deliberative," intended to persuade the readers to a particular course of action; other parts of his letter are "epideictic," such as where he praises God and praises the church that is to reflect God's glory to creation.

It is possible that Paul, drafting other letters at the same time (e.g., Colossians), used a scribe for some letters to help him adapt his basic message for different situations in different churches.

Situation. Paul writes this letter from prison, probably in Rome. As readers in the Ephesian region of Asia Minor would know, he had been arrested on the charge of having brought a *Gentile into the temple (Acts 21:28-29; 28:16). Racial or cultural division between Jew and Gentile was a major issue in the Ephesian church (cf. Acts 19:17), and Paul was one of the best qualified writers of antiquity to address both sides intelligently.

From his detention under Roman authorities (probably in Rome), Paul is also aware of the possibility of imminent persecution and the need for the church to be a good witness in society (cf. especially comment on Eph 5:21—6:9). He is also aware of the church's struggle with its own background in the occult practices of Asia Minor—magic (Acts 19:19), astrology and attempts to escape the astrological power of Fate (cf. comment on Eph 1:8-11, 19-23; 3:9-11).

Commentaries. The most thorough and useful are Markus Barth, *Ephesians,* AB 34, 34A, 2 vols. (Garden City, N.Y.: Doubleday, 1974); and A. T. Lincoln, *Ephesians,* WBC 42 (Dallas: Word, 1990). Those unable to wade through the Greek, however, may prefer another commentary, such as G. B. Caird, *Paul's Letters from Prison,* New Clarendon Bible (Oxford, U.K.: Oxford University Press, 1976); George Johnston, *Ephesians, Philippians, Colossians and Philemon,* Century Bible (Greenwood, S.C.: Attic, 1967). For a fuller discussion of Ephesians 5:18—6:9, the reader may consult Craig S. Keener, *Paul, Women and Wives* (Peabody, Mass.: Hendrickson, 1992), pp. 133-224, 258-79.

1:1-2
Introduction

As notes in most translations point out, not all manuscripts include "in Ephesus" (v. 1). Many scholars have argued that Ephesians was originally sent to a number of *churches, of which Ephesus was only the most prominent. (Thus it would be a "circular letter," like imperial edicts.) But because all these churches would presumably be in the area around Ephesus, the history of the Ephesian church will help us understand the background to this letter (see Acts 19:1-41).

"*Grace" and "peace" were variations of standard greetings; what is significant here is that they are "from God the Father *and* the Lord Jesus Christ." See further the introduction to Paul's letters and comment on Romans 1:1-7.

1:3-14
Praise for Salvation

The opening, or *exordium,* of Paul's letter includes a benediction ("Praise be to God"—NIV, or "God be praised") and a prayer; ancient letters commonly included either prayers or thanksgivings, although Paul's elaboration of them here is unusual. Many Jewish prayers would begin with "Praise be to God who [helps his people in some way]." In Greek, 1:3-14 is one long praise to God; this one recounts, as Jewish prayers often did, God's redemptive plans and acts on behalf of his beloved people.

In these verses as many as eleven different terms used for Israel in the *Old Testament are applied to believers in Jesus. Because the *church in Ephesus comprised both Jews and *Gentiles (Acts 19:17), and Jews and Gentiles had different cultural practices, the church may have had cultural and ethnic tension. Paul reminds believers that whatever their ethnic or cultural background, they are all one people in Christ and must work together for God's purposes.

1:3. Today we distinguish between "the heavens" in a scientific sense (i.e., the outer atmosphere and the rest of the universe except the earth) and the spiritual place God lives. But in Paul's day he did not need to make this distinction to communicate to his readers; they divided "the heavenly realms" differently from the way we do. Almost everyone in the ancient world believed that the heavens had numerous levels (often three or seven), that different spiritual beings (various kinds of angels, demons, stars, etc.) lived in different levels and that God or the purest spiritual beings lived in the highest heaven. In much Jewish teaching, the spirits of the righteous would live with God there after death. "Heavenly realms" (NIV) can thus mean both "where God is" (as here) and "where the angelic powers live" (as often in Ephesians).

1:4-5. The Old Testament declares that God "predestined" or (literally) "chose" Israel in Abraham to be his covenant people and adopted them as his children, but that his people often fell short of the covenant. Paul explains that in a practical sense one becomes a member of God's covenant by Christ, not by one's background.

1:6. One reason God chose Israel was for them to bring him glory (Is 60:21; 61:3; Jer 13:11); so central was revealing his glory that even his acts of judgment were meant to turn people to him (Ex 7:5; Amos 4:6), the real source of life (Jer 2:13).

1:7-8. God had redeemed Israel (i.e., freed them from slavery) through the blood of the Passover lamb. The blood of animal sacrifices in the Old Testament indicated that the price paid for forgiveness was a life. Paul blends these images here.

1:9-12. It was a common Jewish belief that history was moving through many stages to its climax, when everything would be put under God's rule. Some philosophers argued that the whole universe was permeated by God and would be absorbed back into him. Like Jewish writers who adapted the language of such philosophers, Paul believes that history moves toward a climax of subordination to God, not absorption into him. The Old Testament and Judaism recognized that God had a sovereign plan in history to bring it to this climax. On "inheritance" (KJV, NASB, NRSV) see comment on 1:13-14. On God's ultimate purpose here, see comment on 3:8-11.

1:13-14. A wax seal would have a mark of ownership or identification stamped in it, identifying who was attesting what was inside the container that had been sealed. Because it was commonly understood that the *Spirit would be made especially available in the time of the end, Paul here speaks of the Spirit as a "deposit" (NIV)—a term used in ancient business documents to mean a "down payment." Those who had tasted the Spirit had begun to taste the life of the future world that God had promised his people.

After God "redeemed" (see comment on 1:7-8) Israel from slavery in Egypt, he led them to their "inheritance" or "possession" in the Promised Land. Later Jewish literature viewed the world to come as Israel's ultimate "inheritance," and early Christian writers used this language the same way (Mt 5:5; 25:34; Rom 8:17; 1 Cor 6:9; Jas 2:5). For Paul, Christians are God's people, redeemed but waiting for the completion of their redemption; as with Israel of old, God's presence among them is the assurance that he will take them into the land he has promised (cf. Hag 2:5).

1:15-23
Prayer for Revelation

1:15-16. Like pious Jews, pious Christians apparently had a time set aside for prayer each day. Many pious Jews prayed several hours a day, and if Paul continued such a custom we can understand how he could pray for all his *churches.

1:17-18. Jewish people commonly prayed for enlightened eyes to understand God's Word; the *Old Testament also spoke of opening one's eyes to God's Word (Ps 119:18) or to other spiritual realities (2 Kings 6:17). Some Jewish sources characterized the *Spirit of God as the "Spirit of wisdom" (the Old Testament especially emphasizes this: e.g., Ex 28:3; 31:3; 35:31; Is 11:2; cf. Deut 34:9).

*Rhetorically skilled writers often introduced major themes in their introduction, and Paul is no exception. He is about to explain the points that he has been praying for them to understand. On "inheritance" see comment on 1:13-14.

1:19-20. A daily Jewish prayer viewed God's ability to raise the dead in the future as the ultimate example of his power. Paul agrees, but for Paul the decisive event has already happened: the first installment of the future *resurrection has taken place. The position to a ruler's right was a position of great honor and authority; to be seated at God's right hand was to be enthroned as ruler of the cosmos, even if not all his enemies had been destroyed (Ps 110:1). On "heavenly places" see comment on 1:3.

1:21-23. Exorcists and magicians tried to manipulate powerful spirits by invoking their names (see comment on Acts 19:13); the supremacy of Jesus' name above all other names means that he is higher than all the spirit-powers being invoked and could not be exploited.

Paul uses standard terms of his day for the demonic and angelic powers at work behind the political structures of the world, powers that were thought to direct the earthly rulers and peoples (v. 21). Most people in Paul's day believed that the world was run by Fate, which was usually expressed by the stars (which were viewed as heavenly beings), and most of these people did not believe one had any hope of escape from Fate. Some of the *mystery cults, however, like the cult of Isis, gained popularity by claiming power to free initiates from Fate.

Jewish people commonly believed that the heavenly powers ruled all the nations except Israel; some later teachers explained that Israel had been lifted above those heavenly powers in Abraham their ancestor. Paul says that those united with Christ had also been raised above those powers. His words would be a great encouragement to Christians who had been converted from an occult background (cf. Acts 19:18-20).

Jewish people especially viewed these heavenly powers as "angels of the nations," spiritual beings who stood behind earthly rulers and guided their rule (cf. Dan 4:35; 10:13). (Although the details are developed more in later Jewish texts, the roots of the idea are as early as Daniel and the *LXX of Deuteronomy.)

Such beings were the ultimate expression of the spiritual division among different peoples, but Paul says that this distinction has been transcended in Christ—again making a point relevant to a congregation experiencing ethnic or cultural tensions. Thus Christ's body is "that which is filled by him who fills all"—"all" indicating especially representatives of all peoples in the *church (4:6-10; cf. 3:19; 5:18).

2:1-10
Exalted with Christ Above Sin

Paul continues to explain God's gracious exaltation of the Christian with Christ.

2:1-2. Most Jewish people believed that *Satan or the chief of the heavenly angels of the nations ran the whole world except for Israel. "Ruler with authority over the realm of the air" was a natural title for his dominion; it was commonly believed that evil spirits dominated the lowest realm of the heavens (i.e., the atmospheric realm), far below the realm of God's highest angels and his throne. "Air" was the usual term for the atmospheric heaven.

2:3. Many Jewish people sought to explain all sin as the direct result of demonic activity (cf. especially the "spirit of error" in the *Dead Sea Scrolls). Paul does not see sin as always directly inspired by demons but thinks that the world is pervaded with the devil's less direct influence (including in racial division—1:21-23); one is not delivered from this influence by one's Israelite ancestry but (vv. 4-6) through faith in Jesus.

2:4-7. This picture of God's delighting to bestow his love on his people forever develops *Old Testament pictures of his special love for his people (e.g., Deut 7:6-9).

Scholars have compared the image of the exaltation of the believers in 2:6 with the fairly common Jewish image of the righteous enthroned in the world to come; Christians have begun to experience the life of the coming age in advance (see comment on 1:14). The context would drive an additional point home especially forcefully to readers once enslaved by fear of Fate or the stars: to be "seated with Christ" means in 2:6 what it meant in 1:20-21—to be enthroned over the evil powers. Christians need not fear demons, Fate or anything else; their lives are ruled by God.

2:8-10. Good works flow from what God does in us, rather than God's work in us flowing from our works. God redeemed Israel before he gave them commandments (Ex 20:1); it was always his purpose for good works to flow from his *grace, even if Israel (like many people today) did not always grasp that point (Deut 5:29; 30:6, 11-14). Most Jewish people in Paul's day agreed that they were saved by God's grace in the covenant, but they did not extend this idea to non-Jews, who could not inherit the covenant by virtue of birthright.

2:11-22 United in the New Temple

2:11-13. In ancient Jewish beliefs, non-Jews could never participate in the fullness of the covenant without circumcision, although they could be saved by keeping some basic commandments. To be circumcised was to be grafted into the community of Israel, to become part of God's covenant people.

2:14-16. Paul writes this letter from prison because he has been falsely charged with taking a non-Jew inside the temple in Jerusalem (Acts 21:28). Taking a non-Jew beyond a particular dividing point in the temple was such an important breach of Jewish law that the Romans even permitted Jewish leaders to execute violators of this law. Paul's readers in Ephesus and Asia undoubtedly know why Paul is in prison (Acts 21:27, 29); thus for them, as well as for Paul, there can be no greater symbol of the barrier between Jew and non-Jew than "the dividing wall" of verse 14. But Paul says that this dividing wall is shattered in Christ. "He is our peace" might (but need not) reflect the Hebrew of Micah 5:5.

2:17-18. Isaiah 57:19 could be understood as referring to the scattered seed of Israel as those "who were far away," but not long before this passage God had promised that his house would be for foreigners too (Is 56:3-8). This text thus fittingly expresses Paul's point concerning the unity of Jew and *Gentile in the new temple (cf. also Acts 2:39).

2:19-22. In the *Old Testament, the only division in the temple was between priests and laity, but by Paul's day architects had added barriers for non-Jews and for women (contrast 1 Kings 8:41-43); Paul says these barriers are abolished in God's true, spiritual temple. Some other Jewish writers spoke of God's people as his temple, but only Paul and other early Christians recognized that this new temple included non-Jews. (Paul derived the image of Christ as the cornerstone from Ps 118:22, probably via Jesus' teaching; see comment on Mk 11:10.)

Around the time Paul was writing these words, arguing for racial unity in Christ, Jews and Syrians were massacring each other in the streets of Caesarea, a city where he had been not long before (Acts 23:23). Here Paul does not simply mimic a common stand against racism in his culture; he condemns racism and segregation of a religious institution even though he has to challenge his culture to do so.

3:1-13 The Mystery of a Unified People

The Bible had already taught that God would seek out non-Jews to join his people (Rom 16:26; e.g., Is 19:25); King David and others had welcomed non-

Jews into the fellowship of God (e.g., 2 Sam 6:10-11; 8:18; 15:18-22; 18:2; 20:23; 24:18-24; 1 Chron 11:41, 46; 18:17). But to be full members of the covenant, male non-Jews had to be circumcised; by this period, men and women were also usually required to immerse themselves in water to become ritually pure. But the coming of Christ had made it clear to his *apostles and prophets that by faith in Christ everyone could now approach God on the same terms.

Public speakers and writers frequently used a standard element of persuasion called *pathos,* an emotional appeal. By reminding his readers of what he their apostle had suffered for the ideal, multiethnic people that God was building, Paul appeals to them not to nullify his labors. The universal *church should be all that it is called to be, a united interracial people in all its glory.

3:1-2. "Stewards" were household managers, often slaves or freedmen, with great responsibility and prestige in a wealthy home.

3:3-5. The term translated "mystery" was used in *mystery cults and elsewhere, but the main background for Paul's use of the term is in Daniel 2 and in Jewish writings (especially the *Dead Sea Scrolls) that follow Daniel. There it means especially God's plan for history, encoded in the Scriptures but understandable only to the wise or to those with the *Spirit's insight. Because most of Judaism believed that full-fledged prophets had ceased after the Old Testament prophets died, Paul's claim that God has now actively unveiled his truth through "*apostles and prophets" would underline for his hearers the uniqueness of the Christian claim.

3:6. "Heirs" refers to the Old Testament idea that the Promised Land was Israel's inheritance; the "promise" was also a sole possession of Abraham's descendants (and those who joined that nation by circumcision). To make uncircumcised *Gentile Christians part of this same covenant would have sounded like heresy to many Jewish readers, jolting their ethnic sensitivities.

3:7. The *Old Testament often spoke of divine empowerment for God's servants (e.g., Ex 31:3; Judg 15:14); see comment on Ephesians 3:16.

3:8-11. Some pre-Christian Jewish texts also speak of God showing the angels his power and glory through his people, and thus receiving their praise. Because these heavenly "rulers" were viewed as angels of the different nations, the unity of the *church displayed the rule of God, whose authority transcended that of the angels and all earthly boundaries. On "stewardship" see comment on 3:1-2; on "mystery" see comment on 3:3-5. The point is that the church, a people destined to bring eternal glory to God, represents God's ultimate purpose in history (see 1:9-12), and all Christians should find their life's purpose in their role in that ultimate purpose (see 4:11-13).

3:12. "Boldness" often applied to the sort of frank speech appropriate among friends; here, conjoined with "confident access" (NASB), it probably relates to the certain place all members have in the household of God (2:18).

3:13. Many Jewish and Christian writers believed that a certain measure of suffering would have to be fulfilled before the end would come (cf. Rev 6:11). If Paul alludes to this idea here, he may be encouraging his readers that, as their missionary, he is experiencing some of the *church's requisite suffering that is to usher in the end. He may also mean that they share his glory because they have helped him in his ministry (cf. Mt 10:41) or that he suffers for the purpose of serving the body of Christ as a whole. Cities could view their local athletes as competing on their behalf in regional contests.

3:14-21 Prayer for Empowerment

3:14. Jewish prayers were usually offered standing, but kneeling or prostration was sometimes used (in the *Old Testament cf. 1 Kings 8:14, 22, 54; *Gentiles typically prostrated themselves also before rulers). Greeks rarely knelt to pray; like Jewish supplicants, they normally stretched out their arms with hands facing the gods being invoked (in the heavens, in the sea or toward statues).

3:15. Here Paul may mean that all peoples and families ("every fatherhood"; see notes in NIV, NRSV) reflect God's own fatherhood over the world; thus one would have to expect God's concern for all peoples (e.g., Gen 12:3). (Families "in heaven" may refer to the guardian angels of the nations.) Ancient writers often spoke of God as father and sometimes spoke of paternal authority in families as deriving from the example of God. The Roman father was also a supreme authority figure, with the right to rule all descendants as long as he lived.

3:16-17. Although Paul derives some language from the Greek world (see comment on 2 Cor 4:16 for "the inner person"), his ideas here are not particularly Greek. *Old Testament accounts associated the *Spirit especially with prophetic endowment but also with purity, strength and prowess or ability to fulfill whatever God calls one to do; the Old Testament sometimes also presents internalizing the Bible as a way to overcome sin (e.g., Ps 119:11). Israelite piety also recognized God as the source of strength (e.g., Ex 15:2; Ps 18:1-2; 27:1; 59:17; 119:28; Jer 16:19). When Paul speaks of the ability to live rightly because Christ himself lives in the believer through the Spirit, these points from the Old Testament are probably the closest parallels to his idea in ancient literature; rarely did anyone suggest that one's moral life would be empowered by the presence and activity of God. Paul advocates total reliance on *grace, even in the believer's ability to perform righteousness.

3:18-19. Many take "breadth and length and height and depth" to describe how all creation is filled with God's glory or as a description of the immeasurable vastness of his love. Some have suggested that Paul continues the temple image (2:18-22), describing the perfect cube proportions of the holy of holies in the Old Testament, although the idea is not explicit here. But the text almost certainly applies the language of divine Wisdom (e.g., Job 11:5-9; cf. Job 28:12-28; Ecclus 1:3) to God's love; cf. "manifold" (multifaceted) wisdom in 3:10.

3:20-21. Jewish people customarily ended their prayers with a blessing to God; sometimes the blessings closed with "forever and ever" (cf. 1 Chron 16:36; Ps 106:48). It was likewise customary to respond to prayers and benedictions with "Amen."

4:1-16 One Body, Many Members

Ancient persuasive speeches and letters often engaged in a detailed argument, but Paul to this point has mainly used "epideictic," or "praise" *rhetoric. He has praised the *church, calling it to be what God had planned for it to be. He now turns to a standard part of persuasive rhetoric, however, the *exhortatio,* or exhortations. This type of argument fills the rest of the book until the closing *peroratio,* or rousing conclusion, of 6:10-20.

4:1-2. Although gentleness was a recognized virtue, most Greek writers viewed "meekness" in the sense of "humility" negatively, unless it was the socially appropriate self-abasement of a social inferior to a superior. On Paul's captivity (probably in Rome), see comment on 6:20.

4:4-6. Some Jewish texts (especially in *Philo and *2 Baruch) suggested that Israel was united because God was one. These texts would never have united Jew and *Gentile in one people, however, even though all the nations were admittedly joined in common humanity. Paul's language sounds closer to *Stoic philosophical language about the unity of creation. But even the common Greek *rhetorical theme of concord (unity, peace) does not match Paul's emphasis on the unity that believers in Jesus share and must live out.

4:7-8. Paul adapts the text of Psalm 68:18, as ancient expounders of Scripture often did, to make his point (a later *targum of the Psalms rewords it the same way he does). This psalm refers to God's "going up" at Mount Sinai, as Jewish interpreters recognized, and Paul applies the principle of God's arising to Jesus. (In some Jewish traditions, Moses ascended all the way to heaven to receive the *law; if Paul or any of his readers knew such traditions, it would make the application of this psalm to Jesus all the more vivid. But it is questionable how widely known this tradition was in Paul's day.) Paul's point is in harmony with the image of the psalm, although he changed its language; once a conqueror had received tribute and plunder from the defeated (as in Ps 68:18), he distributed most of these spoils to his soldiers (as here).

4:9-10. Paul interprets and applies the text just cited, the way a good Jewish teacher would. "Lower parts of the earth" probably means the realm of the dead, hence that Jesus had died (Ezek 32:24), although it could mean his descent from heaven to become a servant at his incarnation (Phil 2:7; cf. Ps 139:15).

4:11. "*Apostles" were literally commissioned messengers carrying out their sender's mission; as such, they were backed by the sender's authority to the extent that they accurately represented that commission; in the *New Testament, the term applies to commissioned agents of Christ authorized in a special way (more authoritatively than others) to declare and propagate his will. "Prophets" were spokespersons for God, whose role was known from the *Old Testament and continued in the *church; apostles were to prophets perhaps as prophetic judges (e.g., Samuel and Deborah) or leaders (e.g., Elijah and Elisha) were to other Old Testament prophets—with special rank and authority.

"Evangelists," as proclaimers of good news (the message of Christ), were seen as "heralds," again a type of messenger. "Pastors" were literally "shepherds" (used for overseers in the Old Testament, e.g., Jer 23:2-4), elsewhere in the New Testament identified as overseers of local congregations (Acts 20:17, 28; 1 Pet 5:1-2); they were called to shepherd God's people by declaring his message accurately (Jer 23:18-22). "Teachers" were expounders of the Scriptures and of the Jesus tradition; if they functioned like Jewish teachers, they probably offered biblical instruction to the congregation and trained others to expound the Scriptures as well.

As in many ancient lists, some of these terms may overlap considerably (the Greek indicates an especially strong overlap between "pastors" and "teachers"). They share a common focus and basis of authority as bearers of Christ's message. The authority is resident in their message and spiritual gifting; as in the case of Jewish teachers of God's message (as opposed to the chief priests), none represents institutional authority in the sense of a supralocal *church hierarchy, which does not seem to appear until the early second century. Together these ministers of God's Word were to equip all God's people for their ministry (4:12-16).

4:12. The term for "training" or "equipping" was used in the Greek world to describe the work of philosophers and teachers.

4:13-16. The images of a person growing into maturity and a ship being tossed about by waves were common in Paul's day. The image of growing to maturity was rarely applied to a whole community of people as here, but the point would have been no less easy to grasp. Paul's image is a generic one, lacking standard Jewish images for the end time; he probably therefore refers to the church's need for maturity in general, rather than specifically predicting its completion in the end time.

4:17—5:2
Living the New Life

4:17-19. Greek writers often developed their moral exhortation by contrasting opposites, as Paul does here. Literature from this period demonstrates that most Jewish people would have described non-Jews in language similar to that which Paul uses (cf. also Lev 18:3, 24-30; 20:23-24; Deut 26:16-19). What is significant is that Paul refuses to call ethnically *Gentile Christians "Gentiles" any longer; they may be ethnically Gentile, but they are to be *ethically* Jewish. Premarital sex, homosexual intercourse and idolatry were typically Gentile sins from which nearly all Jews abstained. By contrast, pagans were raised this way; many Greek boys were ushered into "manhood" by an older man's molestation. "Walk" (KJV, NASB) means "behave"; see comment on Gal 5:16; "hardness of heart" is common in the Old Testament (e.g., Ex 4:21; Ps 95:8).

4:20-24. The "new self" (v. 24) is literally "the new person," who is (literally) "created according to God," which means according to his image or likeness. Paul probably alludes to the way God originally made Adam and Eve in his image, and says that the new person that a Christian has become is equipped with moral purity because he or she is made like God morally. Thus, he points out, one should live like it—as blamelessly as Adam and Eve did before they disobeyed. "Clothing" and "unclothing" provide a natural image, used in the Old Testament and Greek literature, for "putting on" and "putting off" or "removing" some kinds of behavior (Job 29:14; Ps 109:18; especially Is 61:3, 10; see comment on Rom 13:12), other attributes (2 Chron 6:41; Ps 93:1) and so forth.

Jewish wisdom writers and Greek philosophers could have agreed with Paul's emphasis on "renewing the mind"; they understood that one's attitudes and values affected one's lifestyle. But Paul's basis for renewal differs from theirs; he bases it on the new kind of life available in Christ, a kind of life that most Jewish people expected only in the world to come (after the *resurrection of the dead).

4:25. Except for 4:30 and 4:32—5:2, most of Paul's moral exhortations in 4:25—5:2 are the sort that most ancient moralists uttered. Exhortations to truthfulness, labor, opposition to slander and so forth were standard. These are not sins attributed only to

*Gentiles (cf. 4:17-19) but those with which Jewish people also struggled.

Paul's way of overcoming moral problems differs from that of other ancient moralists (4:22-24, 32), but he can find common ground with many moralists in his culture who oppose the same wrongs that he does. Despite many points in common with the ethics of his culture, however, Paul often cites the *Old Testament as his ethical authority; his exhortation to truthfulness here echoes a line from the commandments listed in Zechariah 8:16-17, where truthfulness may be opposed to false witness in a legal setting.

4:26. The exhortation to avoid sinning while angry is from Psalm 4:4; on the wickedness of those who hold anger overnight, cf. Hosea 7:6; the *Essenes and some Greek philosophers also required that disputes be settled the same day. Learning to speak in the most helpful way (4:29) was also stressed.

4:27. The image here is probably one of warfare, and that the one who sins surrenders ground to the devil's side (cf. 6:10-20).

4:28. Judaism valued laboring with one's hands and sharing with the poor. Although Greek artisans no doubt prided themselves in their work, the aristocracy throughout the Mediterranean world disdained work with one's hands as the duty of the lower classes.

4:29. Ancient wisdom literature often emphasized learning to speak rightly (cf. 4:25; 5:3-4); many sayings in Proverbs emphasize the idea, including the encouragement to speak gracious, uplifting words (e.g., 12:25; 15:23; 25:11; cf. Zech 1:13).

4:30. "Grieving" the *Spirit reflects a serious offense; in Isaiah 63:10 (one of only two *Old Testament texts to use the title "holy spirit"), it refers to Israel's rebellion in the wilderness, which led to their rejection by God. Similarly, Israel's rebellion against the Spirit led Moses to sin with his mouth according to Psalm 106:33 (cf. Num 20:10; Deut 3:26). On "sealing" as a sign attesting that no one had tampered with the sealed merchandise, see comment on Ephesians 1:13-14. The Ephesians must preserve their attestation for the day when their redemption would be complete (the Old Testament "day of the Lord," when he would judge the world and vindicate his people).

4:31. Vice lists were a common literary form in the writings of ancient moralists; sometimes all the vices listed pertained to a particular topic, as here (anger).

4:32—5:2. Other moralists, including Greek and Roman non-Christians and *Philo, appealed to the imitation of God for a standard of ethics. But non-Christian writers of Paul's day could not cite the example of a god who had lovingly sacrificed himself for his people (4:32—5:2). (Some scholars have appealed to the example of the Titan Prometheus, who suffered for his betrayal of divine secrets to people. But it is not clear that Prometheus expected the severe punishment he received, and the example would not have been prominent; given the punishment of the Titans and wounds inflicted on immortals in Greek mythology [e.g., the wounding of Ares in the *Iliad*], Prometheus cannot offer a pre-Christian parallel to the Christian idea of Jesus, who, though divine, voluntarily offered himself for humanity. Furthermore, the qualitative difference between Greek and Jewish conceptions of deity makes comparison between the stories of Prometheus and Jesus even less likely.)

On God's accepting someone as a

fragrant aroma, cf. Ezekiel 20:41 (his saved people); Ephesians 5:2 means that God accepted Jesus as a sacrifice (see Gen 8:21; Ex 29:18).

5:3-20
More Exhortations

5:3-6. Premarital and other immoral sex, insolent speech and sexual humor were as common in ancient pagan society as they are today. Paul did not water down God's standards to accommodate the culture; instead he warned that those who engaged in this lifestyle would not be among God's people in the world to come. On vice lists and "inheriting" the *kingdom of God, see comment on 1 Corinthians 6:9-10.

5:7. Here Paul does not advocate total separatism (like that of the wilderness community of the *Dead Sea Scrolls), or even the partial separatism that Judaism's food and sabbath laws imposed on *Diaspora Jews. But many in Greco-Roman society would have branded Christians as antisocial for refusing to take part in immoral conversation and, even more, in the pervasive civic religious cults which were regarded as a mark of local loyalty.

5:8-13. Jewish texts often used "light" and "darkness" to contrast good and evil, and Paul milks this image here. Some Greek religious groups known as "*mystery cults" emphasized night initiations, and some of them were also connected with sexual immorality; because some Roman critics of all foreign religions associated Christians with immoral cults, Paul has all the more reason to wish to dissociate Christianity from cults he already regards as pagan. People could enact deeds in darkness of which they would have been ashamed in public (cf. Is 29:15; 47:10).

5:14. Some commentators have suggested that here Paul cites an expository paraphrase of Scripture, like a *targum on a text such as Isaiah 60:1 or perhaps Daniel 12:2. Others think that Paul cites an early Christian *prophecy or song, composed by either Paul or another prophet (cf. 1 Cor 14:37). Either suggestion is possible, or a combination of the two (a prophecy or song based on biblical texts); in any case the quotation was no doubt familiar to both Paul and the letter's first hearers.

5:15-17. "Redeeming the time" (KJV, literally) probably means "making the most of the time"; cf. Ps 90:12. The *LXX of Daniel 2:8 uses the phrase for trying to gain a delay. (The other possible interpretation is bringing redemption to the present evil age.) That a "time of evils" would affect how the prudent behaved is also expressed in Amos 5:13. In Jewish tradition "wisdom" and "foolishness" had much more to do with morality than they did in pagan thought (e.g., Jer 29:23).

5:18. In Greek, the commands of verses 19-21 flow out of Paul's command to "be filled with the *Spirit" and express the nature of Spirit-filled living. Drunkenness was scandalous behavior in Judaism (cf. Prov 23:20-35).

Many people in the ancient world believed that drunkenness could produce a sort of inspiration or possession by Dionysus, god of wine. Dionysus's most active worshipers yielded control of themselves to him and performed sexual acts or acts full of sexual symbolism (often to the distaste of conservative Romans). Here Paul may contrast this behavior with inspiration by God's Spirit. People did not think of Dionysus every time someone became drunk, however; drunkenness was more commonly associated simply with loss of self-control. It was standard practice in both the late-night banquets of the rich and the taverns of the poor.

5:19. Both Greeks and Jews commonly believed that music could come by inspiration, an idea that appears in the *Old Testament as well. Paul emphasizes the kind of worship that Jewish people celebrated in the temple (e.g., psalms and hymns); we cannot be sure whether most other Jewish gatherings, such as those in *synagogues, included the singing of psalms and hymns in this period. "Spiritual songs" probably refers to Spirit-inspired songs (cf. 1 Chron 25:1-6), possibly spontaneous, which would clearly distinguish Christian worship from nearly all worship in antiquity (cf. 1 Cor 14:15).

5:20. The only ancient writers (Jewish writers and some Greco-Roman, especially *Stoic, writers) who stressed thanking God for everything were those who believed that God (whether the Stoic Fate or the personal God of Judaism) ruled the course of events.

5:21-33
Wives and Husbands

The section 5:21—6:9 addresses what we call "household codes." In Paul's day, many Romans were troubled by the spread of "religions from the East" (e.g., Isis worship, Judaism and Christianity), which they thought would undermine traditional Roman family values. Members of these minority religions often tried to show their support for those values by using a standard form of exhortations developed by philosophers from *Aristotle on. These exhortations about how the head of a household should deal with members of his family usually break down into discussions of husband-wife, father-child and master-slave relationships. Paul borrows this form of discussion straight from standard Greco-Roman moral writing. But unlike most ancient writers, Paul undermines the basic premise of these codes: the absolute authority of the male head of the house.

5:21. The final expression of being filled with the Spirit is "submitting to one another" because Christ is one's Lord. All the household codes Paul proposes are based on this idea. But although it was customary to call on wives, children and slaves to submit in various ways, to call *all* members of a group (including the *paterfamilias,* the male head of the household) to submit to one another was unheard-of.

5:22-24. Most ancient writers expected wives to obey their husbands, desiring in them a quiet and meek demeanor; some marriage contracts even stated a requirement for absolute obedience. This requirement made sense especially to Greek thinkers, who could not conceive of wives as equals. Age differences contributed to this disparity: husbands were normally older than their wives, often by over a decade in Greek culture (with men frequently marrying around age thirty and women in their teens, often early teens).

In this passage, however, the closest Paul comes to defining submission is "respect" (v. 33), and in the Greek text, wifely submission to a husband (v. 22) is only one example of general mutual submission of Christians (the verb of v. 22 is borrowed directly from v. 21 and thus cannot mean something different).

5:25. Although it was assumed that husbands should love their wives, ancient household codes never list love as a husband's duty; such codes told husbands only to make their wives submit. Although Paul upholds the ancient ideal of wifely submission for his culture, he qualifies it by placing it in the context of mutual submission: husbands are to love their wives as Christ loved the *church, by willingly laying down their lives for them. At the same time that he relates Christianity to the standards of his culture, he subverts his culture's values by going far beyond them. Both husbands and wives must submit and love (5:2, 21).

5:26. This "washing" probably alludes figuratively to the bride's prenuptial washing (of course, washing was natural before any occasion on which one wished to impress another positively). After this washing the bride was perfumed, anointed and arrayed in wedding clothes. The betrothal ceremony in Judaism also came to be called "the sanctification of the bride," setting her apart for her husband. The "word" naturally refers to the saving *gospel of Christ (1:13).

5:27. After the bride's preparation (5:26), the next stage in a Jewish wedding was the bride's removal from her father's house to the groom's house, followed by the bride's introduction into the groom's home. "In glory" (NASB) or "splendor" (NRSV) also fits the image of the passage, appropriate to the bridal array.

5:28-32. Although Greek and Roman moralists sometimes alluded to the unity of husband and wife, the image was especially prominent in Judaism, which shared Paul's and Jesus' dependence on Genesis 2:24, mentioned explicitly in Ephesians 5:31. The head-body analogy of 5:23 here becomes an image of unity rather than one of authority.

5:33. Writers sometimes closed a book or section with a concluding summary; Paul here summarizes the point of 5:21-32: the wife should respect her husband, and the husband should love his wife. Although ancient moralists expected wives to respect their husbands (and Jewish teachers also expected the reverse), moralists usually also emphasized the wife's "obedience"; Paul's exhortation to wives here would thus strike most ancient readers as quite weak.

6:1-4
Children and Fathers

Jewish and Greco-Roman writers unanimously agreed that children needed to honor their parents, and, at least till they grew up, needed to obey them as well. The command to honor one's parents was in the *Old Testament (Ex 20:12; Deut 5:16) and included living in such a way as to bring honor on them in a godly society (Deut 21:18-21). Many Jewish writers believed that honoring one's parents was the most important commandment.

At the same time, children were often taught through beating, which was standard in child rearing and education; fathers were considered responsible for their education. Paul is among the minority of ancient writers who seem to disapprove of excessive discipline (6:4). (Greek and Roman society was even harsher on newborn children; because an infant was accepted as a legal person only when the father officially recognized it, babies could be abandoned or, if deformed, killed. Early Christians and Jews unanimously opposed both abortion and abandonment. This text, however, addresses the discipline of minors in the household.)

6:5-9
Slaves and Masters

Masters often complained that slaves were lazy, especially when no one was looking. Paul encourages hard work but gives slaves a new hope and a new motive for their labor.

Paul says that slaves, like wives, should submit to the head of the household as if to Christ, but this duty is again *reciprocal*. Only a few writers in the ancient world suggested that slaves were in theory their masters' spiritual equals (cf. Job 31:13-15), and so far as we know only Paul goes so far as to suggest that in practice masters do the same for slaves as slaves should do for them (6:9).

When *Aristotle complained about a few philosophers who thought that slavery was wrong, the philosophers he cited did not state matters as plainly as Paul does here. Paul confronts the practical issue of how slaves can deal with their situation, not whether slavery should be abolished (an issue not relevant to his point in the context of household codes); even a violent revolution could not have ended slavery in the Roman Empire. But the way he deals with the issue leaves no doubt where he would have stood had we put the theoretical question of slavery's abolition to him: people are equals before God (6:9), and slavery is therefore against God's will. For more on slavery in general, see the introduction to Philemon.

6:10-20
Divine Armor

Although Paul does not follow a formal *rhetorical outline in Ephesians, 6:10-20 functions as a *peroratio,* a rousing conclusion. Philosophers sometimes described their conflict with wicked ideas as wrestling in an athletic contest or a war; they also used lists of virtues, the general idea of which Paul incorporates here. Aspects of Paul's conclusion resemble the exhortations that generals gave to their armies before battle.

The *Old Testament has many pictures of Israel as God's warriors, and God himself appears as a warrior in full armor, dealing out his justice (Is 59:17; cf. Wisdom of Solomon 5:17-20). But although Paul borrows his language from the Old Testament, the image Paul's words in this paragraph would have evoked for most of his readers is that of a Roman soldier ready to do battle. Most adults who heard his letter read would have seen Roman soldiers and could relate this image to their spiritual warfare against the demonic powers at work in the world; God who fought for them had supplied them his armor.

Paul omits some pieces of the Roman soldier's armor in his description; for instance, since he mentions only one offensive weapon, he uses the sword but omits the lance (the *pilum*). Paul probably has no particular purpose in correlating specific strengths of the Christian with specific armor body parts (cf. 1 Thess 5:8); rather, he wants his readers to know that they need all of them to be victorious.

6:10-11. In the day of battle, Roman soldiers were to stand their ground, not retreat. As long as they stood together on a flat, open field and did not break ranks, their legions were considered virtually invincible.

6:12. Some people in the *Old Testament learned that the nature of their battle was spiritual (cf. Gen 32:22-32; Dan 10:10-21), although in both Daniel and Paul the battle was fought by prayerfully submitting to God and doing his will, not by directly addressing the hostile powers (Dan 10:12-13, 21). Some pagan deities were called "world rulers," and terms for high ranks of good and evil angels were becoming popular in this period; "spiritual beings of wickedness" is idiomatic Greek for "evil spirits," a Jewish and *New Testament term.

6:13. The "evil day" could refer generically to any time of judgment or testing (e.g., Amos 6:3), but some scholars think it applies specifically to the period of intense tribulation Jewish people expected prior to the end of the age (cf. Dan 12:1), which Paul elsewhere may have regarded as present (cf. Rom 8:22-23). For "stand" see comment on 6:10-11.

6:14. The "belt" or "girdle" may refer to the leather apron beneath the armor or to the metal belt protecting the lower abdomen. The "breastplate" normally consisted of leather overlaid with metal, and it protected the chest in battle; like the helmet (6:17), it was used only in battle, not for normal wear. Roman soldiers were to face forward in battle, side by side, so the armor needed to protect only their front. In view of Isaiah 59:17 (cf. Wisdom of Solomon 5:18), this "breastplate of righteousness" is truly "God's armor" (6:13).

6:15. Soldiers needed to wear sandals or boots (technically the Roman *caliga,* a half boot) so they could advance toward the enemy undistracted about what they might step on; this gear was essential to their "preparation" for battle. Paul takes the image especially from the herald of Isaiah 52:7 who announces good news: sharing the message of Christ advances God's army against the enemy's position.

6:16. Roman soldiers were equipped with large rectangular wooden shields, four feet high, the fronts of which were made of leather. Before battles in which flaming arrows might be fired, the leather would be wetted to quench any fiery darts launched against them. After Roman legionaries closed ranks, the front row holding shields forward and those behind them holding shields above them, they were virtually invulnerable to any attack from flaming arrows.

Because the Greek and Roman god of passion (called Eros and Cupid, respectively) was said to strike with flaming arrows, some of Paul's readers may have thought specifically of the temptation of lust in this verse, although Paul probably intended the image to cover more than that danger (cf. Ps 11:2; 57:4; 58:3-7; 64:3; perhaps 120:1-4; Prov 25:18).

6:17. The bronze helmet, equipped with cheek pieces, was necessary to protect the head; though essential garb for battle, it was normally not worn outside battle. For the phrase "helmet of salvation" see Isaiah 59:17; cf. comment on Ephesians 6:14. The sword (*gladius,* 20-24 inches long) was a weapon used when close battle was joined with the enemy and the heavy pikes that frontline soldiers carried were no longer practical. Thus Paul implies that the battle is to be joined especially by engaging those who do not know God's word (the *gospel) with its message, after one is spiritually prepared in the other ways listed here. Paul's ministry was thus particularly strategic, because it included close-range battle advancing into enemy ranks (vv. 19-20).

6:18-19. If prayer for one another (v. 18) continues the figurative image of warfare in the preceding context, it might relate to how the soldiers had to stand together in their battle formation, covering one another by moving as a solid unit. A Roman soldier by himself was vulnerable, but as a unified army a Roman legion was virtually invincible. "Watching" or "being alert" may also be military language (suggested by Jesus; cf. Mk 14:38). Prayer in the *Spirit probably implies *inspired* prayer (cf. 1 Cor 14).

6:20. Ambassadors were to be received with all the respect due the ones who sent them; as heralds, they were to be immune from hostility even if they represented an enemy kingdom. Paul, an "ambassador" of the greatest king and the greatest *kingdom (6:20) is instead chained in Rome for his mission of peace (6:15). In Greek literature, a true philosopher was characterized by his "boldness," or frank speech.

Like 3:1-13, this section adds *pathos,* or feeling; although its most important function is to solicit prayer, it also sets an example for the *church.

6:21-24
Closing Greetings

6:21-22. Mail and other news were normally carried by travelers, because the Roman Empire had no official postal service except for imperial business.

6:23-24. The *Old Testament promised God's covenant love to all who loved God (Ex 20:6; Deut 5:10; Neh 1:5; Dan 9:4; cf. 1 Kings 8:23); here the promise applies specifically to those who love the Lord Jesus Christ.

PHILIPPIANS

Introduction

Authorship. The vast majority of New Testament scholars accept Philippians as an authentic letter (or letters) by Paul.
Unity. Some scholars have divided Philippians up into smaller units. Sending letters by messengers was no easy task, and Paul was more likely to send one large than several short letters, unless travelers were going to Philippi for other purposes. The division of Philippians is not, however, impossible: short letters were often sent in antiquity, and Paul maintained regular contact with the Philippians. Two factors ultimately support the letter's unity: (1) the burden of proof is on those who would divide it, because different letters are usually distinguishable in letter collections; (2) the arguments for division are based on modern letter-writing conventions that completely overlook ancient *rhetorical and epistolary conventions.
Structure. Chapter 1 addresses topics of Paul and the Philippians' common labor in the *gospel (using motifs from ancient

friendship letters). Chapter 2 provides models for imitation (in which he includes letters of recommendation). Chapter 3 includes a *digression (common in ancient letters). Chapter 4 turns to the main business of the letter (a thank-you note eager to avoid any suggestions of the common ancient *patron-*client ideology).

Situation. Paul states that the purpose of Philippians is to thank them (4:10-20); but writing from prison (probably in Rome), he also wishes to address some other issues, including the likely further persecution the *church will face and an exhortation to work together. As much as the Philippian church (probably made up of several house churches) loved Paul, its members were divided among themselves; thus the recurrent exhortations to unity (1:27; 2:2, 14) and mutual service (2:3-11). At least part of the division revolves around disagreement between two of Paul's fellow laborers, possibly leaders of separate house churches (4:2-3). If opposition to Paul exists, it probably involves Jewish Christians who advocate circumcision, if Paul believes they have already arrived in Philippi (3:2-21).

Commentaries. Most useful are Fred B. Craddock, *Philippians,* Interpretation (Atlanta: John Knox, 1985); and Gerald F. Hawthorne, *Philippians,* WBC 43 (Waco, Tex.: Word, 1983). Ralph P. Martin, *Epistle of Paul to the Philippians,* rev. ed. (Grand Rapids, Mich.: Eerdmans, 1988), and F. F. Bruce, *Philippians,* NIBC (Peabody, Mass.: Hendrickson, 1989), can also be helpful.

1:1-2
Introduction

1:1. The title "servants" is not demeaning in either a Jewish (the prophets had been called "servants of God") or Greco-Roman (slaves of the emperor and other high officials wielded far more power than independent free persons) setting. On "overseers" and "deacons," see comment on 1 Timothy 3:1, 8, where these terms also occur together.

1:2. Paul here Christianizes a customary ancient greeting form (see comment on Rom 1:7).

1:3-11
Thanks to God for the Philippians

Thanksgivings were common in ancient letters; Paul is particularly fond of them, omitting them in congregational letters only to the Galatians, and there for obvious reasons.

1:3-4. Jewish language sometimes connects prayers with "memorials" or "rememberings" before God (as in Rom 1:9); here Paul probably means he thanks God during his regular prayers for the Philippians (cf. Phil 4:6).

1:5. The term translated "participation" (NASB) or "partnership" (NIV) was often used in an economic sense for those who "share" (cf. NRSV) monetarily. Here it includes the financial help the Philippians have given (4:10-20).

1:6. "Day of Christ Jesus" adapts *Old Testament language for the "day of the Lord," and so assumes that Christ is divine. Paul's confidence in their perseverance is based on 1:5, 7.

1:7. Letters of friendship often mentioned the writer's longing for his friends. Given his imprisonment and legal situation, Paul also naturally uses language common in legal proceedings: the "defense" and "confirmation," or vindication, acquittal.

1:8. Ancients commonly called on a deity as a witness, assuming the deity's knowledge; to lie under such conditions was to invite the deity's wrath.

1:9-11. As Paul does here, philosophers also stressed the need to discern what was good from what was bad. On the source of "righteousness" (v. 11), see also comment on 3:9.

1:12-26
The Profit in Hardship

Greek philosophers typically declared that neither imprisonment nor death mattered; only one's attitude did. Paul partly agrees with this view but for very different reasons: God's sovereign use of hardship for his glory (1:12-14, a Jewish and *Old Testament belief), and the superiority of undistracted devotion to Jesus (1:21, 23). Letters, like speeches, usually included a *narrative component leading up to the circumstances of writing or filling in the readers on recent news.

1:12. *Stoic philosophers argued that imprisonment, like death, was not a bad thing. On "progress" (NASB, TEV) see comment on Galatians 1:14, although the idea in Philippians 1:12 (unlike 1:25) would more naturally evoke the image of an army's "advance" (NIV) than a scholar's advance.

1:13. Some commentators have suggested that "palace" or "praetorium" here may refer to a provincial governor's residence, such as the place of Paul's detention in Caesarea (Acts 23:35); Paul was often detained (2 Cor 11:23), and a detention in Asia or in Syria-Palestine would clarify the presence of so many helpers in Colossians 4:10-15. Others, taking "Caesar's household" (4:22) literally, think that "praetorium" here refers to a Roman imprisonment by the "praetorian guard" (NASB), as in Acts 28:16; the centrality of Rome in the Empire attracted many people, which could account for the presence of the ministers in Colossians 4:10-15. No army was allowed in Italy, but the Praetorian Guard consisted of about thirteen to fourteen thousand free Italian soldiers. They were the emperor's elite bodyguard under the praetorian prefect. Viewed as *clients of the emperor (thus part of his household), they were kept loyal with the highest pay in the Roman military; they were also kept loyal by the leadership of a prefect who could never legally become emperor (being a knight rather than a senator).

1:14-18. Jewish teachers allowed that serving God from impure motives was better than not serving him at all. They also unequivocally insisted, however, that those who used the *law only for their own gain would not share in the world to come.

1:19. "Salvation" (KJV) often meant physical "deliverance," sometimes from prison, and in this context it must have this meaning. Citizens of Philippi were Roman citizens (see comment on 3:20) and as such enjoyed certain legal protections. But Paul's fate in court as a Christian who was also a Roman citizen would set a legal precedent that could affect their own legal standing, so they would have more than one reason for concern about how his case turned out.

1:20-23. Philosophers often argued that death was neutral, not evil; it was either annihilation or the migration of the soul from one place to another. Paul sees it as an evil (1 Cor 15:26) but also as a way to pursue Christ undistracted. Most Palestinian Jews emphasized the future *resurrection of the bodies of the righteous but believed that the souls of the righteous dead were meanwhile in heaven with God; Paul agrees with them. Many Greco-Roman writers expressed a desire to die and so be free from sufferings; *Old Testament writers did not usually take this position (Ps 30:9), but some became depressed enough to do so (1 Kings 19:4), or even to wish that they had never lived (Job 3:1-19; Jer 15:10; 20:14-18).

1:24-26. Paul's remaining would help them by virtue of his continuance as a teacher, and perhaps also for legal precedent: see comment on 1:19. Nero was not particularly interested in legal questions, and in A.D. 62 he freed Jewish hostages that the procurator Felix had previously sent him. Paul was likely released at this time (see comment on Acts 28:30-31).

1:27-30 Endure in Hope

1:27. "Conduct yourselves" uses the Greek language of a citizen in a free state (cf. 3:20), language that Jewish writers used to describe their people obeying God's *law (as in Acts 23:1). On the athletic image (here undoubtedly implied in the Greek word that KJV and NASB translate "striving together"), see comment on Philippians 1:30.

1:28. The confidence that Paul suggests here alludes to the *Old Testament and Jewish hope that God would destroy his people's enemies in the end time but vindicate and save his people.

1:29. Although Jewish people sought to avoid persecution when possible, they extolled the martyrs who preferred death to disobeying God. (One could perhaps distinguish public attitudes, such as praise for past heroes, from personal attitudes, such as the price individuals paid in daily life for their convictions. In the case of Paul, however, he was daily confronted with the personal choice and in his own life modeled commitment to the point of martyrdom.) Paul regards suffering for Christ as a privilege (cf. similarly Acts 5:41). The idea of sufferings indicating the nearness of the end (as in Jewish thought) might also be present here.

1:30. Like many Greek moralists, Paul applies the language of ancient athletic competitions ("contest" or "conflict"—KJV, NASB) to the life of the moral person. Here the issue is persecution; on the Philippians' sharing in Paul's fate, see comment on 1:19.

2:1-11
Be Servants like Christ

Paul continues his exhortation of 1:27-30, advocating unity (1:27) and fearlessness in the face of martyrdom's reward (1:28; 2:9-11; cf. 3:20-21). Ancient moral writers often adduced examples to prove their points, and Paul here adduces Jesus (2:5-11), himself (2:17-18), Timothy (2:19-24) and Epaphroditus (2:25-30). Correspondences between 2:6-11 and 3:20-21 indicate the extent to which Paul uses Christ as a model for believers here. (The majority of scholars accept Phil 2:6-11 as a pre-Pauline hymn, based on the structure and language of the passage. Others point out that Paul could be responsible for the hymnic features himself. Greek authors peppered their writings with quotations from Greek poetry, and Paul's use of an earlier Christian hymn is possible, although it cannot be regarded as proven.)

2:1-4. Paul borrows language commonly used in Greek *homonoia* speeches, which advocated harmony and unity among the hearers.

2:5-6. Some scholars suggest that Christ's being in the "form of God" alludes to Adam being formed in God's image (Gen 1:26). Unlike Adam, who being human sought divinity (Gen 3:5), Jesus, being deity, relinquished his rightful position of honor. Even more to the point here is that Jewish texts described divine Wisdom as the perfect, archetypal image of God ("form" may mean "role" more than "image" here; cf. 2:7b, "form of a servant," although this phrase parallels "likeness" in 2:7c).

2:7. The "servant" of Isaiah 53 also was "poured out" or "emptied himself," though not in incarnation but in death (Is 53:12; cf. Phil 2:8). (Paul, however, uses a more explicit Greek word for "slave" [so NRSV] here than appears in the *LXX of Isaiah.)

2:8. Judaism prized obedience to the point of death in stories about its martyrs. Crucifixion was the most degrading form of execution, reserved for non-Roman criminals who were slaves or free persons of the lowest status.

2:9. Some commentators have seen in the language of this verse an allusion to the exaltation of Isaiah 52:13. If, as is likely, that verse refers to suffering rather than glory (52:14—53:11), Paul either does not refer to it here or *contrasts* the exaltation accomplished by God with the suffering Jesus experienced among people.

2:10-11. Isaiah 45:23 ("every knee will bow . . . every tongue will declare") refers to the final submission of all nations to God; that Paul applies the text to Jesus (especially with an *Old Testament divine title, "Lord," in v. 11) is telling. Those "in heaven" would include the angels, probably the rebellious angels who rule the pagan nations (see comment on Eph 1:19-23). Greeks worshiped gods in the heavens, earth, sea and underworld; traditional Greek mythology also placed the shadowy existence of departed souls in the underworld. Paul announces that whatever categories of beings there are, they must acknowledge Christ's rule, because he is exalted above them. One often bowed the knee in obeisance before a ruler or deity.

2:12-16
Live Right

Paul here continues his exhortation to

the believers to live in unity (2:1-11).

2:12-13. Letters were often used as proxies for one's presence; Paul thus entreats the Philippians through the letter to obey his teaching as if he were present. They secure their ultimate "salvation" by persevering together (see 1:27-28). The reward of this obedience is implied by the parallel with Jesus' obedience in 2:8-9. The teaching that they are enabled to obey by God's power is virtually unparalleled in pre-Christian literature except for *Old Testament teachings on the *Spirit; see comment on Galatians 2:19-20.

2:14. "Grumbling" and "disputing" (NASB) had characterized Israel in the wilderness and were condemned in the Old Testament; see comment on 1 Corinthians 10:9-10.

2:15. Jewish tradition often compared the righteous with "lights" in a dark world; cf. especially Daniel 12:3 (the term Paul uses here was especially applied to heavenly bodies, reflecting an image like the one Daniel uses).

2:16. The "day of Christ" is modeled after the Old Testament "day of the Lord" (see comment on 1:6).

2:17-24 The Examples of Paul and Timothy

Paul continues to model the servant lifestyle by examples.

2:17-18. Ancient religions regularly poured out libations to the gods, usually wine but sometimes water or another substance. Paul is being poured out (cf. 2:7) as such a "drink offering" to the true God, a willing offering on their behalf that joined their own sacrifice.

2:19-21. Both Greek philosophers and *Old Testament prophets complained about the scarcity of those fully devoted to the cause. Paul offers many "letters [or passages] of recommendation," a common ancient form of writing (see comment on Rom 16:1-2), but he places Timothy, his special emissary, in a category by himself, offering the highest commendation.

2:22. Messengers were often sent as personal representatives, to be received with the same honor accorded the sender (e.g., 2 Sam 19:37-38). Teachers and *disciples often developed an intimate relationship described in terms of "father" and "son."

2:23. News was difficult to send, because it had to be carried by messenger—a sometimes dangerous undertaking given travel conditions at various times of the year (cf. 2:30). Paul therefore wants to wait until he can give a full report of the outcome of his trial.

2:24. Letters were used as surrogates for one's presence but also often announced one's coming.

2:25-30 Epaphroditus's Sacrificial Service

Epaphroditus had been the Philippians' messenger, bringing their gift to Paul in prison (4:18); he no doubt carried Paul's letter back to them. Travel conditions were dangerous and harsh, especially at sea in late fall and early spring, and these conditions decreased one's resistance to antiquity's many diseases (vv. 26-27). Because "Epaphroditus" is a common name, no conclusions about his origin may be drawn from it, but the context suggests that he was from Philippi.

Pagans prayed to their gods for healing (especially certain deities associated with healing, most notably Asclepius); Jewish people prayed to and praised the true God as the healer of body as well as the forgiver of sin. Jewish prayers for healing were sometimes described as prayers for "mercy." "Risked" (in "risked his life"—v. 30) was often used as a gambling term, and some scholars have noted that gamblers invoked Venus, goddess of gambling, with the term *epaphroditus;* Paul could be making a wordplay on his friend's name. Although God usually healed those in the Bible who prayed to him, his activity could not be taken for granted; even some of his most faithful servants had died from sickness (2 Kings 13:14; cf. 1 Kings 1:1; 14:4).

3:1-16 Righteousness Not from Human Works

The section from 3:1 to 4:1 is a clear *digression. A number of scholars have suggested that it was a different Pauline letter accidentally inserted into the middle of Philippians, or one combined with several other Pauline letters to the Philippians. But digressions were common in ancient speaking and writing, and this section need be nothing more than such a digression. Literary connections with the rest of the letter strengthen the suggestion that it is part of a unified letter.

3:1. The expression translated "finally" here sometimes indicated the end of a letter (cf. "in conclusion"—TEV), but just as often functioned as a transition device within a letter.

3:2. The opponents here are not Jewish persecutors, who would be unlikely in Philippi, which had a very small Jewish community. Rather, they are like the traveling Jewish Christian teachers Paul had encountered in Galatia who want to circumcise *Gentiles. It is not clear whether they have already come to Philippi or are simply traveling about, and Paul is warning that they may come there.

*Cynic philosophers were regularly called "dogs," but given the specific error Paul refutes in this passage, he clearly does not use it as a reference to these philosophers; that use merely illustrates to what a great extent the term was one of disdain. More to the point, Jewish teaching considered dogs unclean and sometimes sexually immoral; the *Old Testament applies the title to male cult prostitutes (Deut 23:17). Such a title would certainly make the pietists who were demanding circumcision recoil. There were "beware of dog" signs even in ancient Rome, where they were pets and watchdogs (Petronius *Satyricon* 29), no doubt reinforcing the biting sarcasm of Paul's phrase. Here Paul uses another word for "circumcision" (NASB), which means "mutilation" (NIV, NRSV; cf. the *LXX of 1 Kings 18:28); see comment on Galatians 5:12 for the cultural significance of this idea.

3:3. Paul says that spiritual circumcision (Deut 10:16; 30:6; cf. Lev 26:41; Jer 4:4; 9:25-26) is what really matters to God. Because ancient Judaism usually associated the *Spirit with *prophecy, "worship in the Spirit" (NASB, NRSV) may refer to charismatic worship of the sort depicted in 1 Chronicles 25:1-6; because most Jewish people believed that the Spirit was no longer available in that fullness in their own time, Paul lays claim to an experience of the *church that confirms the *Messiah's arrival and that most of Judaism would not pretend to match.

3:4. Lists of virtues or vices were common in epideictic (praise and blame) speeches, and in *narrative form they characterized epideictic biographies. Self-commendation was considered appropriate if one were defending oneself or using oneself as a legitimate model for others. By claiming to have greater merit than his opponents even on their own terms, he turns this self-commendation into an occasion to undermine them; professional speakers and writers often used the standard *rhetorical technique of "comparison" to accomplish this end.

3:5. Lists of virtues typically included items such as noble birth or beauty as well as character traits like prudence or steadfastness. Those born Jewish males were circumcised the eighth day; by this virtue Paul eliminates any competition from *proselytes converted by his opponents later in life—proselytes had lower social status in Judaism than those born Jewish. "Hebrew of Hebrews" could indicate a Palestinian Jewish origin, although this is not clear; however, that Paul lived in Palestine before his conversion is clear from the fact that he was a *Pharisee (in Acts, cf. comment on 22:3). Although Pharisaic piety was known elsewhere, Pharisees themselves seem to have lived only in Palestine and been concentrated around Jerusalem. They were noted for being the most meticulous observers of the *law—something his opponents now claimed to be.

3:6. "Zeal" for the law did not always include violence, but the chief models for such zeal included Phinehas (Num 25:7-13) and especially the Maccabees, and Jewish patriots called themselves "*Zealots" in the war against Rome not long after Paul wrote these words. By defining his legalistic righteousness in terms of his persecution of Christians, Paul associates his opponents' position of "zeal" for the law with opposition to the Philippian Christians' faith.

3:7. Appealing to the Christian faith shared by himself, his readers and (according to themselves) even his opponents, Paul dispenses with his worldly credentials—and thus the only credentials to which his opponents could lay claim at all; see comment on 2 Corinthians 11:16-18. "Gain" (or "profit"—NIV, TEV) and "loss" are marketplace terms, like other terms later in the letter (4:10-20); Paul had to sacrifice all his former spiritual assets to follow Christ, who was what really mattered.

3:8. "Dung" (KJV) or "rubbish" (NIV, NASB, NRSV) usually meant either excrement or food to be thrown away, which dogs might enjoy (3:2). (Ancient speakers valued skill in producing insolent insults.)

3:9. As in 3:6, the problem is not the law but that the righteousness is Paul's own, hence inadequate. Both biblical psalmists and later Jewish ones whose hymns appear in the *Dead Sea Scrolls waited on God for their vindication or acquittal, and Paul likewise had to receive his justification, or righteousness, from God alone.

3:10. The greatest yearning of *Old Testament men and women of God was to "know" him (Ex 33:13), a relationship available to all the people of the new covenant (Jer 31:34). This language reflects both the covenant relationship (on the corporate level) and intimate fellowship with God (on the personal level experienced by the prophets). But Paul also connects knowing Christ with sharing his sufferings and glory.

3:11. The ultimate sharing of Christ's *resurrection occurs at the future resurrection of the righteous (in which most Jews believed). Many Jewish people believed that a period of sufferings would precede the resurrection, and this seems to be Paul's view as well (clear in Rom 8:18-22, possibly reflected in Phil 3:10-11).

3:12-13. In the language of athletic competition—often used metaphorically by ancient moralists—Paul describes his striving for the future hope of 3:11. Greco-Roman sages sometimes admitted that they were not yet "perfect" but spoke of themselves as the "mature," the wise, as opposed to those who were still novices. (Commentators note that the *mystery cults described the highest stage of initiation as "perfection" or "completion," but this is probably less relevant here than the language of sages.) "What is behind" (NIV) belongs to Paul's image of the race; to win, one must keep one's eyes on the finish line; Greek runners normally ran in a straight line and back.

3:14. At the end of each race, officials had their heralds proclaim the winner and call him up to receive his prize (in the Olympic games, a palm branch). In Paul's metaphor, the prize is the full revelation of Christ at the *resurrection (3:10-11).

3:15. Advanced philosophers, as opposed to novice students, were described as "mature" (NIV, NRSV; "perfect"—KJV, NASB).

3:16. Although not looking back to one's past (3:13) and not yet complete (3:11-12), they were to maintain what they had already achieved. "Live" here can mean "walk" (KJV); perhaps here Paul adapts his race metaphor from 3:12-14, although this is not certain.

3:17—4:1
Judgment and Salvation

Teachers like Paul would make it to the *resurrection of the righteous by staking their righteousness on nothing but Christ (3:9-11); his opponents, however, like dogs interested in dung (3:2, 8), were headed for destruction, as were those who followed them (3:18-19).

3:17. Ancient teachers often used themselves as examples. (Paul had given four examples, using himself for one, in chapter 2, and again used himself in 3:4-14.)

3:18. Displays of emotion were considered appropriate in public speaking, but Paul's earlier expressions of outrage (3:2) fit the ancient norm better than "weeping." "With tears" (NIV, NRSV, TEV) or "weeping" (KJV, NASB) indicates his love for his opponents.

3:19. Greco-Roman philosophers and non-Palestinian Jewish writers (especially *Philo) repeatedly railed against those ruled by their passions, often remarking that they were ruled by their "belly" (KJV, NRSV) or their (sexual or culinary) "appetite" (NASB), disdaining their neglect of eternal things. Gluttony especially became part of Roman culture, and its practice by the aristocracy was a frequent butt of satirists' humor. But being ruled by one's "belly" meant more than gluttony; it was used to mean any fleshly indulgence (cf. "bodily desires"—TEV). This would be a serious insult to those who thought they were zealous for the *law; but Paul had already "shamed" their "glory" by his own example in 3:4-8.

3:20. Citizens of Philippi, a Roman *colony, were automatically citizens of Rome, sharing all the rights and privileges of Roman citizens even though most of them had never been there. (Not everyone who lived in Philippi was a full citizen of Philippi, but the citizenship held by much of the *church, especially owners of homes in which it met, would raise the status of the whole movement there.) Paul's readers in Philippi therefore understand quite well what it means to be citizens of the supreme city while not yet living there. ("Citizenship" is not "conversation," as in the KJV.)

Many deities in Philippi were called "saviors," as was the emperor; although this title for Jesus derives from *Old Testament language for God, it provides a stark contrast with the paganism Christians outside Palestine had to confront daily.

3:21. Paul's view of the *resurrection is that it involves the body, but one distinct in nature from the current body (Greek culture considered the idea of a bodily resurrection vulgar superstition; see comment on 1 Cor 15). As in Judaism, the resurrection occurs at the time of the ultimate battle, when God subordinates all his enemies (cf. also 1 Cor 15:25-28).

4:1. That the Philippians are Paul's "crown" indicates that they are in some sense his prize (cf. 3:14; 1 Thess 2:19 and comment on 1 Cor 9:24-25). They must stand firm against Paul's opponents and persevere if Paul is to receive the reward he seeks for his labor for them—their salvation. There were different sorts of crowns. Heroes could be rewarded with public crowns, but the term applied especially to athletes' wreaths; Judaism also used the image for rewards at the end time.

4:2-9
Work Together

Moral writers often strung together short, unrelated statements of moral advice. Paul similarly lists several admonitions here, although a common theme runs among them.

4:2. "Euodia" and "Syntyche" are Greek names; because Philippi was a Roman *colony, their Greek names might indicate that they are foreign merchants like Lydia (Acts 16:14; see comment on Acts 16:21), although this is only a surmise (some commentators suggest that one of them *is* Lydia). Their prominence as Paul's coworkers may have been more acceptable at Philippi than it would have been in some other parts of the Empire; inscriptions indicate heavy involvement of women in the religious activities of this city.

4:3. Clement may be the author of 1 Clement, a late-first-century Christian letter from Rome to Corinth, as tradition suggests, although Clement is a common Roman name. The "book of life" is an *Old Testament image further developed in ancient Judaism (e.g., Ex 32:32-33; Dan 12:1; Mal 3:16; the *Essene Damascus Document 20:19; *Jubilees 36:10).

4:4-5. "The Lord is near" could refer to the Second Coming (3:20-21) but more likely means that the Lord is close to his people and hears their cries (Deut 4:7; Ps 145:18).

4:6-7. "Peace" (v. 7) could indicate tranquillity, although in the context of unity it may have its usual meaning of peace with one another (as in Greco-Roman *homonoia* speeches). If any connotations of the latter use are present, the image of such peace "standing guard" (if pressed in a military sense) over hearts and minds is striking. Jewish prayers (some based on Num 6:24) often asked God to keep his people from harm.

4:8. Like many writers, Paul resorts to a full list of virtues, including *aretē*, "excellence," which was central to the Greek concept of virtue. Throughout this list he borrows the language of Greek ethics, although nothing he says would have been objectionable to Jewish or Christian readers. (He omits some traditional Greek virtues, like "beauty" and "goodness" per se, but the last omission need not be viewed as significant, because such lists were never intended to be complete.) Greek and Roman philosophers repeatedly emphasized thinking such virtuous thoughts, and Jewish writers repeatedly borrowed their language the same way Paul does to communicate to Greek-speaking Jewish readers.

4:9. Teachers often exhorted students to live what they had been taught and to follow the example set by the teacher.

4:10-20
Paul's Thank-You Note

Paul avoids a direct "thank you" in this section while expressing his appreciation. (Gratitude may have been particularly important in Macedonia, of which Philippi was a part; in earlier times an ungrateful man was said to have been liable to prosecution there—*Seneca *On Benefits* 3.6.2.) In the ancient world, *patrons showed hospitality to and looked out for their *clients; if Paul had said "thank you" forthrightly, he might have cast himself in the role of a subordinate, dependent client.

4:10. Letters of friendship, when responding to a friend's letter, generally opened with a statement of joy about receiving that friend's letter.

4:11-13. Greek moralists, influenced by *Stoic thought, praised those who could be content with little as well as with much. (*Cynics went so far as to prove their contentment in little by making certain that was all they ever had.) It was said that the wise man needed no one but himself and was completely independent. But although Paul uses the language of contentment in all circumstances (being able to do "all things," as in 4:13) common among Stoic philosophers and others, the idea of persevering and enduring for God's sake was commonly lived out by the *Old Testament prophets, Jewish martyrs and other servants of God.

Paul's "abundance" (NASB) would have been meager and simple by modern standards; artisans were better off than the poor, but far below the standard of living enjoyed by the modern Western middle class or by the well-to-do of antiquity. ("Moderation"—seeking a mean between two extremes—was central to most Greek discussions of virtue, especially in *Aristotle; it also appears in *Diaspora Jewish ethics. But Paul nowhere seeks such a mean; like the best of Greek philosophers, he can live in any situation. His language is thus *Stoic-*Cynic rather than Peripatetic [Aristotelian]. Unlike such philosophers, who depended only on themselves, however, he is "self-sufficient" only by virtue of Christ, who works in him.)

4:14-16. The language of "sharing" (partnership—4:14-15) is the language of ancient business documents; it may even suggest a special account from which the Philippians sent Paul help when he was in need. "For my needs" (NASB, NRSV) also occurs in business documents specifying the purposes of a disbursement. The form he uses for the title "Philippians" is bad Greek but was what the Roman citizens of Philippi called themselves; it is thus a mark of sensitivity to their local traditions and culture.

4:17. "Profit" (NASB, NRSV, TEV), "what may be credited to your account" (NIV), is literally "fruit" (KJV), but because many business transactions involved crops this was a natural extension; Paul trusts that God will reward the Philippians with interest for their sacrifice on his behalf.

4:18. "I have received" was the most common standard phrase in receipts; Paul acknowledges their gift in regular business terms. But he also uses *Old Testament language for a sacrifice ("sweet-smelling"—TEV, "acceptable"); in being partners with this missionary, they are partners with the God who sent him.

4:19-20. Verse 19 may be a wish-prayer, as some commentators have suggested (see comment on 1 Thess 3:11); others take it as a statement. On either reading, the point is much the same: Paul cannot pay back the Philippians, but he trusts that God will. Although ancient writers often used wealth as a metaphor for spiritual riches like wisdom, in this context Paul no doubt means that he trusts that God will reward them for their faithfulness to his work (cf. Deut 15:10;

Prov 19:17). "Needs" in the case of most of the Philippian Christians were genuine, basic needs (see 2 Cor 8:1-2), not "wishes" (as some readers take it today). "In glory" (KJV, NASB, NRSV) can be translated "in a glorious way" or "glorious riches" (NIV).

4:21-23 Conclusion

4:21. Greetings were common in ancient letters. Because Paul knows most of the believers in Philippi, he keeps his greeting general. Letters also commonly included greetings from others, because mail had to be sent via travelers and thus could not be sent frequently.

4:22-23. The "household of Caesar" could refer to anyone in the Roman civil service directly dependent on Caesar, including all his slaves and *freedmen; it always indicated great prestige. It most likely refers here to the Praetorian Guard (see comment on 1:13); if Paul was in Rome at this point, anyone who guarded him (Acts 28:16, 30) would naturally be exposed to his teaching. Even Caesar's slaves wielded more power and prestige than most well-off free persons; the Praetorian Guard itself held the prestige of the Roman military's elite, often rewarded by Caesar himself. Paul's greeting would impress his readers: his imprisonment has indeed advanced the *gospel (1:12-13).

COLOSSIANS

Introduction

Authorship. Not all scholars agree that Paul wrote Colossians. Some think that a *disciple of Paul wrote the letter in Paul's name (probably with his approval, or posthumously in faithfulness to his teachings). Others think that Paul simply dictated this letter to a scribe, as he did most of his previous letters (e.g., Rom 16:22); in either case the probable date of the letter was in Paul's lifetime (see "Situation," below).

Although Paul may borrow language from some of the false teachers to make his case against them, most of the language that is used in Colossians has parallels in his undisputed writings (which also differ from one another). Given the brevity of the letter, the possible use of a scribe, similarities with undisputed Pauline letters, and the lapse of several years since his earlier letters, the differences between Colossians and the undisputed Pauline letters need not require different authors. Pseudonymous letters existed but were normally written long after the death of the person in whose name they were written.

Colossae. Colossae was in Phrygia, where religion was practiced with intensity and sometimes frenzy (e.g., the famous mother-goddess cult of Cybele). There is evidence for a Jewish presence in Phrygia as early as the sixth century B.C.; this Phrygian Judaism seems to have mirrored its culture to a significant extent. Christianity likewise exhibited unorthodox tendencies in this region in subsequent centuries. Colossae was a small and socially unimportant city by this period; it is probably only one of many cities in which Paul's students had founded *churches (Acts 19:10). The city was severely damaged or destroyed by an earthquake in A.D. 61, hence many scholars think that Paul wrote before that date.

Situation. Colossians 2 may indicate that Christians were attracted to mystical or *apocalyptic elements in a Judaism thoroughly influenced by Phrygian culture. (A great number of backgrounds have been proposed for the error at Colossae: *mystery cults, broader *Hellenistic mysticism, Hellenistic Judaism, *Qumran-type Judaism and so on. The merit of considering these sources is that they all reflect some broader cultural ideas that played into the problems Paul confronted in Colossae; even Qumran parallels, while limited to Palestine, provide evidence for some more widespread Jewish beliefs in this period. The one suggestion with little merit to sustain it is *Gnosticism, since full Gnostic systems cannot be dated this early. But that the Colossian error reflects one synthesis of different streams of thought that later developed toward Gnosticism is quite possible.)

That some Jewish Sibylline oracles may issue from that region and the activity of later Christian Montanists there both suggest the possibility of ecstatic elements in local Judaism (2:18). Acts testifies that Paul was preaching Christ to philosophically minded audiences in this period (see comment on Acts 19:9), and letters like Ephesians and Colossians give us an indication of Paul's grasp of Greek philosophy and also some of the popular philosophical ideas that permeated both *Gentile and Jewish thought in mid-first-century Asia Minor.

Commentaries. J. B. Lightfoot, *Saint Paul's Epistles to the Colossians and to Philemon*

(1879; reprint, Grand Rapids, Mich.: Zondervan, 1959), is still helpful; Ralph P. Martin, *Colossians and Philemon,* NCB (1974; reprint, Grand Rapids, Mich.: Eerdmans, 1981), is also helpful. Both Eduard Lohse, *Colossians and Philemon,* trans. W. R. Poehlman and R. J. Karris, Hermeneia (Philadelphia: Fortress, 1971), and Eduard Schweizer, *The Letter to the Colossians: A Commentary* (Minneapolis: Augsburg, 1982), are important and useful scholarly commentaries, providing more detail for advanced work.

1:1-2
Introduction

The opening follows the standard form of ancient epistolary prescripts (name of sender, name of recipients and greeting). As is customary in Paul, "greetings" (Greek *charein*) becomes "grace" (Greek *charis*); "peace" was a standard Jewish greeting, sometimes combined with "greetings" in Jewish letters.

1:3-13
Thanksgiving and Prayer for the Fruit Bearers

Thanksgivings to God or gods were customary in the openings of ancient letters. In Paul's letters, they often introduce major themes, which were on his mind from the beginning of the letter. Thus they often function the way that *exordia* did, introducing what follows and beginning the letter with a positive relationship with the readers.

1:3. Regular Jewish prayer times included many blessings, and Paul's prayer times clearly include many thanksgivings to God; hence this is not merely a conventional expression of thanks for the purposes of the letter.

1:4. The Colossians' spiritual condition was reported to Paul by Epaphras, apparently Paul's student working among them (1:7; cf. Acts 19:10), who was originally from their city (Col 4:12).

1:5. Jewish texts spoke of future rewards already reserved for the righteous, hence early Christian readers would be familiar with the idea.

1:6. The image of God's message bearing fruit may go back to Jesus' teaching (Lk 8:11); the *Old Testament often compares Israel with a vine or other plant and summons them to bear fruit for God (e.g., Hos 10:1; 14:7-8; cf. Gen 1:28).

1:7-8. "Epaphras" was a common name; this may well be the same Epaphras of Philemon 23. But Philippi and Colossae are too distant geographically for us to think that this is the same person as Epaphroditus in Philippians 2:25, although that name could legitimately be contracted as "Epaphras."

1:9. For unceasing prayer see Exodus 28:30 and 1 Samuel 12:23. Although philosophers sought "wisdom" and "knowledge," Paul here emphasizes the Old Testament moral sense of the terms (e.g., Prov 1:2-7).

1:10-11. On fruit bearing and growing, see Genesis 1:28 ("growing" appears especially in the *LXX); and see comment on Colossians 1:6. On "walk" (literally; KJV, NASB) or "live" (NIV, TEV), see comment on Galatians 5:16. Greek temples expected priests to act in a manner appropriate to their priesthood, "worthy of the god" in whose temple they served, although it is not clear that Paul alludes to that language here. In Jewish tradition, "worthy" could mean "appropriate to" (2 Macc 6:23-24, 27), "deserving of (reward)" (2 Macc 15:21); Wisdom sought those worthy of her (Wisdom of Solomon 6:16), and the righteous who persevered would be "worthy for God," like an acceptable offering (Wisdom of Solomon 3:5).

1:12-13. In the *Old Testament, the "saints" or "holy" or "set-apart ones" were Israel. Israel's "inheritance" was first of all the Promised Land but in Jewish tradition pointed toward the ultimate possession of the world to come. Christians become heirs of these promises in Christ. "Light" and "darkness" were regularly contrasted as good and bad respectively (e.g., Ps 27:1; Is 9:2; 42:6; 49:6; 58:8-10; 59:9; 60:1), and this was often applied to the conflict between good and evil realms (in the *Dead Sea Scrolls and often in ancient literature). (Since many peoples in the ancient Near East had been uprooted by powerful rulers and settled elsewhere, some scholars have suggested that this image lies behind the "transferral" from one kingdom to another here. But the image of a provincial achieving Roman citizenship or *Gentiles accepting the yoke of God's *kingdom in Judaism might have been more natural images to Paul's readers; see also comment on 1:14.)

1:14-23
The Supremacy of Christ

Some of those in error at Colossae want to emphasize the forms of rigorous human spirituality found in their culture (see comment on 2:16-23); Paul insists that Christ is enough (cf. 2:6-15) and describes him in the language Judaism normally reserved for personified Wisdom. This image was a natural one for early Christians to describe Christ; Judaism personified God's Wisdom as divine, and the roots of the image in Jewish tradition go back at least as far as Proverbs 8. (It is possible, as some have suggested, that Paul cites a two-stanza Christian hymn in 1:15-20; such citations occur without notice in other ancient literature. But despite the evidence and scholarly consensus that favor it, the theory falls short of proof either for or against it.)

1:14. "Redemption" meant freeing a slave by paying a price for that slave; in the Old Testament, God redeemed Israel from their slavery in Egypt by the blood of the firstborn and the lamb. This would fit the image of transferring a captive people from one realm to another (1:13). *Philo also believed that the Logos, God's Word, participated in redemption; but this background might be more relevant if it were mentioned as part of 1:15-17.

1:15. Here Paul describes Christ in terms Judaism reserved for divine Wisdom, which was portrayed as God's archetypal image by which he created the rest of the world. Philo describes God's Logos, his Word, as his image and firstborn son.

"Firstborn" could refer to the position of authority and preeminence given to the firstborn son in the Old Testament (Gen 49:3-4). (A related word for "firstborn" could translate the Hebrew word for "chief" in 1 Chron 5:12 *LXX. Jewish texts most commonly applied the term to Israel. Ancient Near Eastern texts applied equivalent terms to other deities, e.g., Amon-Re in Egypt, and kings were sometimes acclaimed as sons of gods at their enthronements.) This term could also refer to the redemptive role of the firstborn (cf. Col 1:14) or be another title for God's "Son" (1:18; see Ps 89:27, although David was the youngest of eight sons). Both Greek and Jewish religion describe God or supreme deities as "First."

1:16. The "invisible" creations of God refer especially to the angels in heaven who correspond to earthly rulers (see comment on Eph 1:19-23). Ancient Judaism accepted that God created both visible and invisible worlds. Many Jewish writers, including *Philo, gave angels or subordinate divine powers a role in creation; other Jewish and Christian writers (like Paul) are prepared to combat that view, as here.

Many Greco-Roman thinkers said that all things derived from, were held together in and would return to the Logos or nature or the primeval fire. In Jewish tradition, all things were created through and for God's Word or Wisdom. (In variants of that tradition, they were created for the righteous who upheld his word in practice.)

1:17. Many Greco-Roman philosophers said that all things were held together by Zeus or by the Logos, divine reason; by this they meant to emphasize the unity of the cosmos. Greek-speaking Jewish writers like Philo also emphasized that God's Logos held the creation together, further identifying Logos with divine Wisdom. In *Stoic thought, the Logos gave form to the primeval fire; in Judaism, Wisdom existed before all things and through it God created and then shaped the world.

1:18. "Head" could mean "authority" (2:10), "most respected or honored part" or "source" (2:19); on "body" see comment on Romans 12:3-5 or 1 Corinthians 12:12-26. God was sometimes called "the beginning" in Jewish tradition, and the term was even more often applied to Wisdom and the Logos; it was a natural term for the one from whom all things began. (In v. 18, it could be applied to the beginning of the new creation, however, as with "firstborn" here.) On "firstborn" see comment on 1:15. The *resurrection of the dead was expected at the end of the age; Jesus' resurrection ahead of that time was seen as the proleptic beginning or inaugurating of that future event (1 Cor 15:23).

1:19. The *Old Testament speaks of God's choosing a place for his name to dwell, and delighting to dwell among his people, to dwell in Zion and so forth. "Fullness" may refer to God's wisdom or glory filling the world (as in the Old Testament and Jewish tradition), or to the fullness of God's presence or attributes (as in *Philo and other Jewish sources).

1:20-22. The reconciling even of the invisible powers (1:16) refers to their subordination rather than their salvation (2:15), "peace" being an end to hostilities. Paul denies not their continuing activity in the world (2:8) but their real power to challenge Christ's *kingdom. (One may compare Enoch's mission to proclaim judgment against fallen angels in some early Jewish stories.)

1:23. Paul may intend the statement that the *gospel was announced throughout creation to counter the false teachers who claim secret, esoteric revelations (2:18). If "all creation" is meant literally, it might refer to the witness of creation (Ps 8:1; 19:1; 89:37; 97:6; cf. Rom 10:18). But here it is almost certainly a cosmic way (Is 51:16) of portraying that the gospel of Christ is for all peoples (Rom 1:8, 13; Mt 24:14). Jewish people generally believed that a person who rejected the covenant would be cut off from God; Paul similarly requires perseverance from those who profess Christ.

1:24—2:5
Paul's Labor for Them

Because Paul can describe his labor in terms of conflict suitable to an athletic contest (1:29), it is significant that Greek athletes traditionally strove in pan-Grecian competitions not only for their own honor but also for that of the cities they represented. Paul's sufferings are thus on the *church's behalf (1:24; 2:1).

1:24. Many Jewish people believed that some suffering had to be fulfilled before the end would come. Many scholars have thus read 1:24 as saying that Paul was taking an extra share of these afflictions, sometimes called "the *Messiah's birth pangs" because they presaged the messianic era. (He suffers "for their sake" [NASB, NRSV], apparently meaning as their representative, because they are part of the church; it is certainly not vicarious suffering, because Paul clearly believes that Christ's suffering was sufficient in that regard; cf. 1:14; 2:8-10, 14.)

1:25. "Stewards" (cf. NASB) were managers of large household estates;

they were often slaves or *freedmen of high status. The phrase "fulfill the word of God" (KJV, literally) was sometimes used for obeying God's word, sometimes for being an instrument in bringing it to pass; Paul here both obeys and fulfills God's word by making it available to the *Gentiles.

1:26. The *Dead Sea Scrolls and other texts speak of "mysteries" in the Scriptures that only the spiritually enlightened can understand; for Paul, Christians are now enlightened (1:9, 12). This statement would refute mystics who claimed special, elite revelations belonging only to themselves (2:18).

1:27. That this mystery would be made known among the *Gentiles had been prophesied (e.g., Is 66:19) and was now being fulfilled (1:25). *Old Testament writers often said that God dwelled "among" his people Israel (Num 35:34), and on a personal level, "within" some of them (Gen 41:38; Num 27:18; Dan 4:8, 18; 5:11, 14; 1 Pet 1:11; more often, "filled," "rested on"). But no one expected him to dwell among the *Gentiles*—indeed, on the personal level, within them (Col 2:12; 3:4, 16).

1:28. This teaching leads to their maturity or completion; cf. 1:22, 2 Corinthians 11:2 and comment on Philippians 3:12-13. Thus teaching Christ would lead to the hearers being prepared for the final day (1:22-23). "We" includes Epaphras (1:7) and other proclaimers as well as Paul; "every person" again stresses the free inclusion of Gentiles in God's plan (1:27).

1:29. Philosophers commonly used metaphors from athletic competition, such as "strive" (KJV, NASB) here (the image is much rarer in the *Old Testament, e.g., Jer 12:5). Divine empowerment "within" (NASB, NRSV) has few ancient parallels apart from Old Testament texts about the *Spirit's enabling God's servants; Paul's language here would have impressed ancient readers in a special way (see introduction to Rom 8:1-11).

2:1. He continues the athletic image of 1:29 ("struggle"). Although Paul had never met most of the Colossian Christians personally, he expresses his longing for them; this was a normal element of ancient "letters of friendship."

2:2-3. Ancient sages (especially those in the *Old Testament and Jewish wisdom writers) often spoke of wisdom as the true wealth (in the Old Testament, see Job 28:12-19; Ps 19:10; 119:14, 72, 127, 162; Prov 3:13-15; Is 33:6). Writers sometimes also spoke of "hidden" treasures, a dream especially valued by the impoverished multitudes.

2:4. Sages often criticized professional public speakers for their unethical use of persuasion at all costs, regardless of truth. Many educated people in antiquity were trained and skilled in persuasive speech.

2:5. Letters were meant as a surrogate for one's presence while one was absent, as ancient writers sometimes pointed out. Saying that one remained with someone "in spirit" was an expression of intimacy and affection. The point is intimacy, not metaphysical unity (see comment on 1 Cor 5:3).

2:6-15
Complete in Christ

2:6. "Walk" (KJV, NASB) or "live" (NIV) was a regular term for behaving according to God's laws (see comment on Gal 5:16), and "receive" was often used for Jewish teachers of the *law passing traditions on to their students. Paul thus exhorts the Colossians to continue in what (and whom) they were taught, not according to mere human traditions (2:8).

2:7. Paul combines agricultural and building images here, as in 1 Corinthians 3:9 (see comment there). The *Old Testament prophets used this language for Israel (if they obeyed God, they would take root, be planted, built up, etc.), and early Christians probably took this language from their preaching of the Old Testament.

2:8. Paul uses philosophical language in his letters (including this one), but his source of knowledge is God's revelation in Christ (2:2-3, 6), not the finite human reasonings of philosophers (2:4). Even though only the most educated went on to study *rhetoric or philosophy, the influence of these disciplines permeated the ancient world. Because philosophy in this period grappled especially with moral and ethical issues, new Christians in the culture now struggling with the same questions would naturally be interested in philosophers' ideas. *Diaspora Jewish writers praised "philosophy," and some, like *Philo, combined it readily with ecstatic experiences (cf. 2:18). (*Josephus, a Palestinian Jew writing for a non-Palestinian *Gentile audience, even calls Judaism a "philosophy"—*Apion* 2.4, 47—and describes the different Jewish movements as philosophical sects. The *Letter of Aristeas, Philo, and even *Justin's Trypho approved of and were skilled in Greek philosophy, and many Jewish apologists, including Philo and Josephus, accused the Greek philosophers of plagiarizing Moses.)

On "traditions," which characterized especially *Pharisaic teachers in Palestine, see comment on 2:6; Greek *disciples also "passed on traditions" of their teachers' sayings. "Elementary principles" (NASB) or "basic principles" (NIV) translates a term that can refer to the personified forces of nature, spirit beings or "spirits" (NRSV, TEV), as in Galatians 4:9 (cf. Colossians 2:10); but here it may refer, as usually, to elementary principles (the term is often used of the alphabet). If this is the case, Paul affirms that the simple message of Christ is much more profound than the greatest secular wisdom could be.

2:9. *Stoics spoke of the deity as being filled by all things, usually in a pantheistic sense; Greek-speaking Jewish writers modified this language to refer to God's rule encompassing all things. For *Philo, the "fullness" can be the sum total of the powers manifesting God's rule, denoting God's all-sufficiency in himself; much later Jewish mystics spoke of the heavens around God's throne as his fullness. Other Jewish writings spoke of God's *Spirit, wisdom or glory filling the world, as in the *Old Testament, which may be more to the point here.

Whatever precise sense Paul means by "fullness," he clearly means that access to all that God is and does is available only through Christ, a function ancient Judaism often attributed to divine Wisdom.

2:10. "Rule and authority" (NASB) probably refers to the angelic powers thought to rule the nations of the world (see 1:16; see comment on Eph 1:19-23), a doctrine that is somehow central to the erring persons wishing to influence the Colossian Christians (see comment on 1:16; 2:18). Of the various possible meanings for "head" (1:18), "authority" or "ruler" makes most sense here, although Jesus is also their "source" (1:16).

2:11-12. Physical circumcision was normally said to be "in the flesh" (Gen 17:11). The *Old Testament and some Jewish (mainly *Essene) texts speak of "spiritual" circumcision (Deut 10:16; 30:6), which in the *Dead Sea Scrolls can enable one to overcome the evil impulse (see comment on Rom 7:14-

25). Paul may here play on the Greek idea of the body as a "tomb" from which one must escape for mystical experiences and for ultimate deliverance in death; if this view has been a temptation for his readers, Paul is saying that they have already experienced all the deliverance from flesh's power that they need.

2:13-14. The term translated "written code" (v. 14—NIV) was used for "handwritten" (see KJV) notes, usually "certificates of debt" (NASB) with penalties attached. Paul intends his readers to think of an IOU before God; Jewish tradition also portrayed sins as "debts" before God. Jewish people used the term translated "decrees" (NASB) or "regulations" (NIV) for God's laws. The Jewish people believed that their sins were forgiven when they *repented; records of sins would be blotted out on the annual Day of Atonement. Paul says the atonement occurred when the debt was nailed to the cross in Christ and thus paid.

2:15. On "rulers and authorities" (NASB, NRSV) see comment on 1:16 and 2:10. In 2:8 Paul used a word that could mean "take as a prisoner of war"; here the cosmic powers themselves are shown off as captives in Christ's triumphal procession, an image familiar to Romans and presumably known to others throughout the Empire (see comment on 2 Cor 2:14). In Roman triumphs, the general dressed as the chief god Jupiter and led behind him humiliated captives, stripped of their possessions; prominent captives were the most impressive. Here Christ displays his triumph over the most prominent captives possible.

2:16-23
Avoid Human Religion

Christ is sufficient (2:6-15); ascetic additions to the *gospel would only detract from faith in it.

2:16. *Asceticism was growing in paganism, and many viewed it as a means of achieving spiritual power or revelatory experiences. But this text clearly refers to Jewish customs; although much of Palestinian Judaism opposed asceticism, Judaism and Christianity in other parts of the Empire often took on the characteristics of the surrounding culture, and pagans sometimes associated local Judaism with asceticism (even linking the sabbath with fasting, although the forms of Judaism we know about would not have fasted on the sabbath). *Gentiles mocked Jews as separatists especially on three issues: circumcision (2:11), special laws about food and drink, and special holy days. The "new moon" celebration was used to greet each new month; the sabbath was a weekly festival.

2:17. *Plato distinguished the "real" world of ideas from the shadow world of sense experience. *Philo developed Plato's concept to argue that the invisible God was known through "shadows," or copies, of his character, rather than through sensory vision. Writers by this period distinguished substance or body, the original reality, from shadows or mere copies; adapting their language, Paul believes that the *Old Testament prescriptions testified to genuine principles, but that those principles are fulfilled in Christ.

2:18. Jewish literature often conjoined "humility" ("self-abasement"—NASB, NRSV) in a positive way with fasting. But when taken to an extreme, "humility" referred to ascetic practices designed to open oneself to "visions" and ecstatic experiences. Such practices became popular in second-century Christian *asceticism. (Insufficient protein and sleep deprivation are known to induce hallucinations today as well.)

"What he has seen" (NIV) is the language of visions. It suggests that the erring people in Colossae may have been like the Jewish mystics who regularly sought to achieve the heavenly vision of God through ecstatic revelations of God's throne. Although these were attempts to simulate the experience of biblical visionaries like Ezekiel, the biblical visionaries sought only to walk close to God, not to achieve mystic experiences per se. On vain visions cf., e.g., Jeremiah 23:32 and perhaps Ecclesiastes 5:7.

Jewish mystics and *apocalyptists sometimes claimed communications from angels (cf. Gal 1:8; in a positive vein, Acts 27:23; Rev 1:1). In Colossae, angels were probably being venerated; although this veneration was against the teachings of *Pharisaism, some evidence indicates that many common *Diaspora Jews addressed prayers and petitions to angels, a practice that overlapped with magical spirit invocations. (Some Jewish literature, especially the *Dead Sea Scrolls but also other texts, spoke of the earthly community entering into the worship of the heavenly community, and some scholars think Paul attacks that idea here; but the book of Revelation seems to approve of that idea, and it is unclear that Paul would have reason to attack the practice.)

2:19. Ancient medical literature sometimes described the head as the source of life for the rest of the body.

2:20-21. Union with Christ in death was sufficient (cf. 2:11-12); adding ascetic rules (2:18) was useless (on "elementary principles" see comment on 2:8). The "decrees" (NASB) or "rules" (NIV, TEV) may be Jewish "regulations" (NRSV), as in 2:14. (Although the language with which Paul describes them in v. 21 has been compared to descriptions of *Pythagorean *asceticism, the language could fit *Old Testament purity rules just as well.) Most Jews outside Palestine still kept the food laws, and some Jews forbade even touching particular foods (Letter of Aristeas 129); other Old Testament laws explicitly decreed one impure for touching some things. (This application would be especially appropriate if Paul thought of people adding to those rules, as Jewish teachers noted that Eve or Adam her tutor apparently added "Do not touch" to God's "Do not eat"—Gen 2:17; 3:3.)

2:22. Those influenced by philosophical thought recognized that transitory, perishable things were much less valuable than what was eternal. "Human commands and teachings" (NIV, NRSV) is an allusion to Isaiah 29:13, which Paul's hearers might recognize from the Jesus tradition (Mk 7:7).

2:23. Pagan philosophers (especially *Stoics) often spoke of freeing oneself from bodily pleasures so one could concentrate on the contemplations of the soul. Some elements of paganism were tending toward *asceticism, which became still more prevalent in the second century. (Pagans converted to Christianity may have also thought Christianity tended toward asceticism, with its countercultural emphasis on avoiding premarital sex and drunkenness; Judaism was sometimes similarly misinterpreted as ascetic. This misinterpretation of Jewish and Christian morality may have disposed some of the converts toward genuine asceticism after their conversion.) But for Paul, "beating down the flesh" is worthless for dealing with fleshly passions.

3:1-11
Living Out the Dead Life

Paul's premise is that the Colossians have died with Christ (2:20); therefore trusting the finished work of Christ and living as what they are in him, rather than following human religious regulations (2:21-23), will produce holy living.

3:1-4. In *Plato's famous parable of the cave, centuries before Paul, shadows on the wall merely reflected the real world above. Many people by Paul's day believed that the heavenly realms were pure and eternal, in contrast to the temporal and perishable world below. Jewish *apocalyptic writers also distinguished between the heavenly and earthly realms, emphasizing the purity of God's realm in the upper heavens.

The Jewish mystics creating problems at Colossae were probably seeking these upper realms through mystical experiences (2:18), but Paul only mentions one thing specifically in heaven: Christ. In the context, he includes heavenly values centered around Christ, available because those who died and rose with Christ were also exalted with him (cf. Eph 2:6). The phrase "heavenly matters" was sometimes used this way.

3:5-7. Other Greco-Roman writers (including Jewish ones like the author of *4 Maccabees) also listed vices and warned against passions. Paul speaks of their "earthly" body because the erring people influencing church members had adopted a Greek view in which one's soul was heavenly and eternal but one's body earthly, perishable and thus unimportant. Paul uses their own language ironically, to emphasize that it does matter what one does with one's body.

Paul does not believe in "beating down the body" (2:23), but he is willing to speak of amputating appendages or "putting them to death" in a *figurative* sense. Perhaps borrowing an image from Jesus (Mk 9:43, 45, 47), Paul here describes passions as "members of the body." (*Philo speaks occasionally of the soul's needing to extinguish the body; but most thinkers recognized that morally therapeutic amputations were ineffectual, such as postadolescent castration, which did not remove sexual desires; they would mean such statements metaphorically. The so-called Orphic view of the body as a tomb—*sōma-sēma*—was widespread in this period.) But one puts to death the sinful lifestyle by depending on one's finished death in Christ (3:3-4), not by harsh treatment of the physical body (2:18, 20-23). The sins Paul lists here are typical sins Gentile converts to Judaism would have committed before their conversion.

3:8. Greco-Roman (the *Stoic Zeno) and Jewish teachers (see *4 Maccabees and the rabbinic commentary Sifra) sometimes had a second list of subordinate or less obvious vices following the first list, announcing that these, too, should be removed. In contrast to the more obvious vices of 3:5 practiced primarily by Gentiles, even Jewish people grappled with the sins listed here.

3:9-10. "Take off" and "put on" (NIV) may reflect the image of armor used by Greco-Roman moralists or Jewish tradition's occasional image of being "clothed" with the *Spirit. But Paul could have simply concocted his own image of spiritual clothing (which he uses frequently; see comment on Rom 13:12); there is nothing profound in the fact that ancient peoples had to put on and take off clothes. (Some scholars have argued that this is a *baptismal image. Because *Pharisaic baptisms in Jewish ritual baths were performed naked, disrobing and being clothed again afterward would make sense. We can hardly imagine, however, that John's public baptisms in the Jordan [Mk 1:5]—which probably included men and women—were done in the nude, and we have no clear evidence of how non-Palestinian *churches practiced baptisms in this period.)

"Old person" and "new person" probably allude respectively to Adam, in whom the old humanity lived (in the light of Jewish concepts of corporate personality and the use of *'adam* as a term for "man" in Hebrew), and to Christ. An allusion to Adam is the likely import of "image" and "created" in 3:10 (see Gen 1:26). The language of "renewing" fits Jewish teaching about a new creation arriving at the end of the age, which Paul believes has been inaugurated in Christ, the new Adam (see comment on 2 Cor 5:17); it has come, but believers living out the life of the new age in the old age must continually realize their participation in this newness to behave accordingly. The renewal may also reflect the language of the *Old Testament (Ps 51:10; cf. Ezek 18:31), especially language about God's work in his people at the end (cf. Ezek 11:19-20; 36:26-27).

3:11. Of all peoples in the Empire, Greeks, fiercely proud of their own heritage, were usually the most intolerant of Jewish people. Circumcision divided Jews from non-Jews. In the Greek language, which was widespread by Paul's time, "barbarians" technically still meant all non-Greeks, although some non-Greeks broke down these categories differently (i.e., some Alexandrian Jews claimed to be Greeks, even though this claim infuriated Alexandria's ethnic Greeks). Scythians were generally considered the most barbaric, cruel and anti-Greek people (although some ancient writers portrayed them as "noble barbarians"). "Slave and free" was one major way of dividing humanity socially, although some slaves were more advanced socially than many free persons. "Christ is all" may mean thus that he, rather than any human divisions, rules all of human life.

3:12-17
Rules for the Christian Community

The parallels with Ephesians here are so close that many scholars believe that Ephesians copied and expanded Colossians. When a letter purportedly from Paul diverges significantly from another Pauline letter, some scholars attribute the different letter to another author. But when the letter with differences also exhibits similarities to another Pauline letter, some scholars say one writer copied the other one. Actually neither line of argument is adequate without substantial evidence for non-Pauline authorship. Paul may have sent out similar instructions to different *churches in this period of his life, or even allowed an assistant to revise some basic instructions for different congregations (see comment on 4:16).

3:12-13. "Chosen," "holy" and "beloved" (NASB, NRSV) were all terms that the *Old Testament applied to Israel. For "put on" (KJV, NASB) see comment on 3:10. Paul includes a list of virtues, also a standard literary form in his day.

3:14-15. Love often appears as an important virtue in antiquity (sometimes as the chief virtue in Judaism), but it appears repeatedly in early Christian literature as the supreme virtue, in a manner not consistently paralleled in any other body of ancient literature. "Peace" (v. 15) probably means "among one another," in unity (v. 14); this virtue was highly valued in both Jewish and other Greco-Roman literature.

3:16. Whereas Ephesians 5:18-19 emphasizes the *Spirit in worship, Paul in Colossians is concerned with erring persons who have not recognized the full sufficiency of Christ; he thus emphasizes the "word of Christ" here. On the worship see comment on Ephesians 5:19.

3:17. Ancient culture was pervasively religious, but most pagan religious practices were ritual observances that did not cast moral influence over one's daily life and ethics. For Paul, in contrast, every aspect of life must be determined by Christ's lordship.

3:18—4:1
Rules for the Household

*Aristotle had developed "household codes" directing a man how to rule his wife, children and slaves properly. By Paul's day persecuted or minority religious groups suspected of being socially subversive used such codes to show that they upheld traditional Roman family values. Paul takes over but modifies the codes considerably. See the more detailed discussion on Ephesians 5:22—6:9.

3:18. All ancient moralists insisted that wives should "submit" to their husbands, but few would have stopped short of using the term "obey," as Paul does here (cf. 3:20, 22; see comment on Eph 5:33).

3:19. Although the ancient instructions to husbands normally stressed how he should rule his wife, Paul stresses instead that he should love her.

3:20. Throughout the ancient world (including under *Old Testament law, Deut 21:18-21), minor children were expected to obey their parents; although Roman law allowed the father to demand obedience even of adult children, adults no longer living with their parents were normally expected only to honor their parents.

3:21. Most ancient fathers and educators beat their children as a matter of course; like a minority of ancient moralists, Paul advocates a more gentle approach to child rearing.

3:22-25. Ancient law viewed slaves as being property as well as people, and their obedience was expected. Many, however, considered slaves generally lazy (an attitude easy to understand, since slaves rarely shared the profit of their own labors). The admonition that slaves devote their work to the Lord relativizes the master's authority (cf. 4:1); "not as menpleasers" (KJV) was also common advice in ancient Jewish ethics. For more on slavery in general, see the introduction to Philemon.

4:1. Some Greek and Roman philosophers warned that masters themselves could become slaves someday (unlikely as this was), so they should treat their slaves rightly. *Aristotle attacked philosophers in his own day who said that slavery was against nature and therefore wrong. By contrast, Paul clearly believes all people are by nature equal before God; although he does not address slavery as an institution here, what he does write thus suggests that he does not favor it. Although he has no control over the system, he can warn masters to keep in mind their status before God. For an example of a situation in which he does have more potential influence, see Philemon.

4:2-6
Rules Beyond the Community

4:2-4. For an "open door" as opportunity, see comment on 1 Corinthians 16:9.

4:5. The *New Testament often uses "outsiders" for "those outside the *church." It may be related to a term used by later Jewish teachers for those who did not understand the *law, but it is a natural image by itself, perhaps more analogous to the way Jews viewed *Gentiles in general. "Redeeming the time" (KJV, literally) probably means "making the most of the time" (NRSV). (Cf. Ps 90:12. The *LXX of Dan 2:8 uses the phrase for trying to gain a delay.)

4:6. "With *grace" (KJV, NASB) can mean with gracefulness, pleasantness and so forth (closer to the classical Greek usage of "grace" than the usual New Testament usage); see comment on Ephesians 4:29. Salt was a preserving and flavoring agent; thus Paul probably refers to speech designed to make sense to outsiders and be relevant to them. When a particular *rhetorician recommended salting one's words properly, he seems to have meant sarcastic wit; in this context, Paul seems to mean instead a gentle answer (cf. Prov 15:1).

4:7-18
Closing Greetings

Letters often closed with greetings from others, because letters went out irregularly and undependably (whenever someone was traveling to the recipients' area).

4:7-8. News was often carried by word of mouth via travelers. Hosts usually asked their guests about people they both knew elsewhere. Such news bearing was thus normally only incidental, but Paul sent Tychicus for the purpose of bearing news.

4:9. Because Paul is writing from imprisonment (4:18), this Onesimus could be the same one as in Philemon 10 (cf. perhaps 2 Tim 1:16), at a later period. An Onesimus became bishop of Ephesus by the early second century, although we cannot be certain if it is the same one Paul mentions here.

4:10. Both Aristarchus (Acts 20:4) and Mark (Acts 13:13; 15:37-39; 2 Tim 4:11; cf. 1 Pet 5:13) were junior colleagues of Paul in ministry.

4:11. "Jesus" (which can also be translated "Joshua"—TEV) was a common Jewish name. Many Jewish people used a second Greek or Latin name resembling their more traditional Jewish name, and this "Jesus" bears also the Latin name "Justus." That Paul sent greetings from Jewish and Gentile workers engaged in spiritual ministry together would have struck ancient readers as far more profound than most modern readers can guess.

4:12. "Striving" ("wrestling"—NIV, NRSV; "laboring"—NASB) is a term of conflict or athletic competition signifying great exertion; philosophers often used it metaphorically (see comment on 1:29; cf. Gen 32:24?). Paul thus depicts prayer as a form of spiritual conflict or discipline crucial to their mission (4:2-4).

4:13. The three largest cities of the Lycus Valley in Phrygia were Colossae, Laodicea and Hierapolis; in this period Colossae was the least significant of the three. Hierapolis hosted healing cults, a temple to the emperor and the reported entrance to the underworld; it also had a significant Jewish presence in this period. Laodicea was a wealthy commercial center, despite its somewhat remote location.

4:14. Physicians were well educated but were often slaves or *freedpersons, with relatively low social status. Although most physicians were men, women physicians besides midwives are known. It is possible that Luke studied medicine in Laodicea (where there is evidence of a prominent medical practice) or practiced for a healing cult in Hierapolis (before his conversion); the readers seem to have heard of him. Demas's ethnic background is uncertain; *papyri attest that some Jews did bear the Greek name "Demas" (cf. 2 Tim 4:10), but in this context he seems to be a Gentile.

4:15. Early manuscripts differ on the gender of "Nympha," but scribes would more likely change a woman's name into a man's name here than the reverse; hence the feminine form "Nympha" is probably original, making her leader of a house church.

4:16. Paul's letter to the Laodiceans is no longer extant, although some scholars have suggested that it is our current letter to the Ephesians (but see comment on Eph 1:1); like Ephesians, it may have been similar to Colossians. Virtually all reading was done aloud, and letters to groups would naturally have been read to the whole group by one person, because most people could not read well. In a *church service, Paul's letter may have been read alongside *Old Testament Scripture, although it is unlikely that either Paul or his earliest readers guessed that some of his letters would become Christian Scripture.

4:17. Archippus may have been Philemon's son or at least a colleague in his house church (Philem 2).

4:18. Writers usually dictated letters to scribes but closed with a signature in their own handwriting.

1 THESSALONIANS

Introduction

Authorship. The vast majority of scholars acknowledge 1 Thessalonians to be Pauline, most recognizing it as Paul's first extant letter.

Date. First and Second Thessalonians may be the earliest of Paul's extant letters, written shortly after the evangelization of the Thessalonians, hence by about A.D. 50, within two decades of Jesus' *resurrection.

Situation. While preaching Jesus as *Messiah (the Jewish king) in Thessalonica, Paul had been accused of preaching another king besides Caesar (Acts 17:7). The very young Thessalonian *church continued to experience persecution after Paul's departure, but he encourages them with the promise of a future hope, which applies even to those who have already died (1 Thess 4:13-18). Paul borrows much of the language used by Jesus and Jewish *apocalyptic motifs that had become part of the early Christian movement.

Form. Most of Paul's letters include a thanksgiving, but some commentators think that his thanksgiving in this letter extends from 1:2 to 3:13; thus they characterize this as a "letter of thanksgiving," a particular epistolary category in antiquity. Others characterize it as a "letter of comfort" or a "parenetic letter" (a letter telling them how to behave); it also contains substantial elements of a "letter of praise," commending the Thessalonians, and features from "letters of friendship." Like most ancient letters, 1 Thessalonians is a mixture of various types, borrowing themes as necessary from each type without concern for formal categories; its closest parallels, however, are to parenetic letters.

Unity. Nearly all scholars today acknowledge that 1 Thessalonians is a unity (the change of tone in chaps. 4—5 is characteristic of Paul's and other letters of this type), except for 2:14-16, which some scholars think (on content grounds) were added later to Paul's letter. Chapters 1—3 seem to exhibit a slightly modified chiastic (inverted parallel) structure, however, which suggests that even these verses belong: thanksgiving (1:2-5; 3:9-10), victory in suffering (1:6-10; 3:6-8), apostolic care (2:1-13, 17-20) and suffering (2:14-16; 3:1-5).

Commentaries. I. Howard Marshall, *1 and 2 Thessalonians*, NCB (Grand Rapids, Mich.: Eerdmans, 1983), is very helpful; F. F. Bruce, *1 and 2 Thessalonians*, WBC 45 (Waco, Tex.: Word, 1982); and Leon Morris, *The First and Second Epistles to the Thessalonians*, NICNT, rev. ed. (Grand Rapids, Mich.: Eerdmans, 1991), are also helpful. The article by Abraham J. Malherbe, " 'Gentle as a Nurse': The Cynic Background to I Thess ii," *Novum Testamentum* 12 (April 1970): 203-17, represents a crucial advance in the study of this letter; see further Abraham Malherbe, *Paul and the Thessalonians: The Philosophic Tradition of Pastoral Care* (Philadelphia: Fortress, 1987).

1:1-10
Introduction and Thanksgiving

It is uncertain where (or if) Paul's thanksgiving breaks off; because Paul did not write in paragraphs but according to flows of thought and *digressions, one cannot always outline his letters as we might outline discussions of topics today.

1:1. This was the standard way to open a letter. "Silvanus" is Silas's Latin name as a Roman citizen; a Jewish Roman citizen's parents often chose for their child Jewish (*Aramaic) and Latin names that sounded similar.

1:2. Thanksgivings were a common feature of ancient letters. Verses 2-10 are a proem, the customary opening designed to secure the readers' goodwill, although Paul also wishes at the same time to encourage them; he is lavish in his epideictic *rhetoric (i.e., language meant to praise them). On "mentioning" in prayers see comment on Philippians 1:3-4.

1:3-4. "Chosenness" (v. 4) was a term the Jewish people applied exclusively to themselves; Paul applies it here to a *church that includes many *Gentile converts.

1:5. Parenetic letters often reminded readers of what they already knew. Appealing to readers' own eyewitness knowledge was an irrefutable technique of argument.

1:6. Philosophers often called on students to imitate them, and this call was common in parenetic letters; but Paul claims that they have already begun to do so. The common Jewish association of the *Spirit with divine inspiration might suggest inspired or even ecstatic joy (perhaps in jubilant worship), although the Spirit was associated with other activities as well. Most of pagan culture reacted angrily to Jewish people's converting pagans from the religion of their ancestors; because a greater percentage of Christians were converts from *Gentile backgrounds, they would face still greater hostility.

1:7. Achaea, south of Macedonia, was well aware of events in that nearby province.

1:8. Travelers usually carried news with them, and the other *churches may have heard of the Thessalonians through the Philippian messengers, also from Macedonia, who brought Paul support (2 Cor 11:9; Phil 4:15-16), or through any other Jewish or Christian travelers. Cf. Psalm 19:4.

1:9. Jewish texts often described the radical change required of pagans converting to Judaism in terms like those Paul uses here; the Roman writer *Tacitus also criticizes Judaism for making *proselytes despise the gods and so reject their own countries and families. Foreign religions could become accepted in Thessalonica, however. Among major cults in Thessalonica were the Egyptian cults of Serapis and Isis, as well as those of the more traditional Greek gods like Dionysus; some of the upper class sponsored the cult of Cabirus from the Aegean island of Samothrace.

1:10. Jesus' *resurrection was the advance installment of the resurrection of all the righteous dead at the end of the age (which figured prominently in Jewish teaching from Dan 12:1-2 onward); Jesus will thus deliver the Thessalonians from wrath at the time of their resurrection. The *Old Testament often applied the term "wrath" to God's judgments within history, but this term was often extended, as nearly always in Paul and the *New Testament, to the outpouring of God's wrath in the final day of the Lord, the day of judgment when, according to the New Testament, Christ returns to punish the wicked (e.g., Is 13:9, 13;

26:20; 30:27; Zeph 1:18; Rom 2:5).

2:1-12 The Nature of the Apostles' Coming

Speeches and letters often contained a strong *narrative element near the beginning, recounting the events leading up to the circumstances of the speech or writing. As in much other parenetic (i.e., moral exhortation) writing, Paul contrasts proper and improper lifestyles by antithetical parallels ("not . . . but").

Paul need not be responding to actual opponents in this section, as some earlier commentators thought (although given the persecution the *church in Thessalonica faces, it is not unlikely that he suspects that standard charges have been raised against him in his absence). Wandering philosophers were often criticized and hence developed some traditional themes that they emphasized whether or not they were defending themselves, themes that Paul also uses here. As Malherbe points out, Dio Chrysostom, a public speaker who lived a generation after Paul, accused most *Cynics (wandering beggar philosophers) of error, impurity, deceit (2:3), flattery (2:5), and love of honor (2:6) and money (2:5). In contrast, Dio Chrysostom also observed that a true philosopher is gentle, like a nurse (2:7).

2:1-2. Dio Chrysostom criticized false philosophers, who feared insulting treatment from the masses, and he described their speech as vain. True philosophers, he said, spoke with boldness even in the face of opposition. Paul and his companions were "insulted" (NIV, TEV) or "mistreated" (NASB, NRSV) in Philippi shortly before arriving in Thessalonica; this term means that they were scandalously treated in a humiliating manner, being publicly stripped and beaten without a hearing (Acts 16:22-23).

2:3. Spurious philosophers were charged with speaking out of error, impurity and deception. ("Impurity" here probably alludes to the philosophical idea that one should use reason to purify one's mind from its slavery to human lusts. In 4:7 it refers to sexual impurity, but that does not seem to be the context here. Given the complaints about Judaism and eastern cults seducing women away from their husbands' religions, it is possible that charges of sexual impurity could have been raised against the sponsors of Egyptian, Jewish and Christian religious associations in Thessalonica; cf. Acts 17:4. But the usual philosophical use of the term is more probable here and requires less speculation.) Religious and philosophical charlatans were widespread in the ancient Mediterranean, and genuine philosophers were thus at pains to distinguish themselves from the phony variety by denying these characteristics.

2:4. This contrasting style ("not . . . but") was a common way of emphasizing the point, whether or not these exact charges had been leveled against Paul and his companions. Pleasing God rather than people was an important part of *Diaspora Jewish ethics. Divine authorization and inspiration were accepted as a sure sign that one was not a charlatan, although not everyone who claimed such inspiration was believed.

2:5. Despite the encouraging proem (opening) in this letter (1:2-10), Paul disclaims dishonest flattery. False philosophers were often guilty of flattery, which could earn them more money by begging; demagogic politicians likewise catered to the masses, becoming "all things to all people" (cf. comment on 1 Cor 9:19-23). But most philosophers and moralists complained that flattery was not for the hearers' good; although one should speak gently, a true teacher ought to correct faults boldly. Contempt for flatterers is thus one of the most common characteristics of ancient moral literature (cf. also Prov 28:23; 29:5).

2:6. Sages claimed the right to rule all things because of their wisdom. Seeking honor for oneself was seen in a negative light.

2:7. Although flattery was to be avoided (2:5), Dio Chrysostom and others despised vulgar *Cynics who simply cursed those from whom they were begging; one should mix praise with the blame, making one's message gentle enough for the hearers to be able to respond to it. (Paul's extant letters include no complete "letters of reproach," the harshest form of blame in ancient *rhetoric.)

Well-to-do Romans often had slave or free wet nurses to care for young children, as did some, though fewer, lower-class Romans. According to the ideal of the educated Romans who could afford them, wet nurses should be educated so they could teach the young children; their most important trait, however, was their gentleness. They often endeared themselves to young children, who when they grew older frequently freed those nurses who had been slaves. The harshest *Cynics criticized those who were gentle like wet nurses or the aged; others, like Dio Chrysostom, insisted that such gentleness should be cultivated.

Many moralists, e.g., *Plutarch, recommended that mothers nurse their own children rather than delegate the task to nursemaids, and this was no doubt the common practice for most people, who could not afford wet nurses anyway. The image could thus be one of a nursing mother, although all Paul's readers would have known of the custom of wet nurses as well. The particular image—wet nurse or nursing mother—does not affect Paul's point: gentleness. People in the eastern Mediterranean, where nursemaids were less frequent, often considered mothers more affectionate than fathers (see *4 Maccabees 15:4), although Roman culture frequently emphasized mothers' severity.

2:8. Dio Chrysostom claimed that a true philosopher (like himself, he noted) would give no thought for personal danger but speak truth out of concern for his hearers. Passionate lovers also said things like, "I love you . . . as if you were my own spirit" (Apuleius *Metamorphoses* 5.6). In contrast to most writers who made such claims, Paul had demonstrated the truth of his claim to endanger himself for the Thessalonians while he was among them.

2:9. The Thessalonian Christians were poor (cf. 2 Cor 8:1-2) and did not share some of the Corinthians' objections to manual labor (see comment on 1 Cor 9:6). The Christians in Philippi had sent him funds while he was in Thessalonica (Phil 4:15-16), but Paul still had to labor as an artisan. Because he could have set up shop in the marketplace, he could have done work and gained customers even if he was there only a brief time (Acts 17:2). Many Jewish teachers in this period had another trade besides teaching, often learned from their fathers.

"Night and day" was a common phrase, which could mean parts of the night and parts of the day. A manual laborer began work around sunrise and could talk with visitors while working; but from the early afternoon on Paul could use his time for more direct evangelism.

2:10-11. Although Romans valued

the dignity of the stern father, most ancient portrayals of fathers (including Roman ones) stress their love, indulgence and concern for their children. True philosophers compared their concern for their hearers to that of a father as well as to that of a nurse (2:7), and *disciples often saw teachers as paternal figures.

2:12. "Worthy" can mean appropriate to the dignity or standards of the person being honored (see comment on Col 1:10-11); Jewish wisdom texts sometimes spoke of the righteous being "worthy of God." To new Christians who could no longer participate in the civic cult that honored the emperor in Thessalonica (1:9), God's "*kingdom" may have had political overtones; recognizing their exclusive allegiance to God's kingdom would be costly (see comment on Acts 17:7).

2:13-16
Nature and Cost of the Thessalonians' Reception

Far from being non-Pauline, as some scholars have suggested, this paragraph reflects Paul's *apocalyptic expectations of judgment on Israel. Against the interpretation of some scholars, Paul does not here deny that the remnant will be saved or that Israel will turn in the end time (Rom 11). His words instead fit the apocalyptic Jesus tradition (the body of Jesus' sayings about the end time) that Paul uses later in the same letter (1 Thess 4:13—5:11). *Digressions were a standard feature of ancient letter writing.

2:13. Antiquity was replete with stories about people who rejected divine messengers, thinking them only charlatans; Paul is grateful that the Thessalonians embraced himself and his companions more appropriately.

2:14. Virtue was often taught by advocating imitation of a good example. The Thessalonian Christians were persecuted by others in Thessalonica, as Judean Christians were by Judean non-Christians (as Paul of all people could attest—Gal 1:13). That Paul's readers have had some problems with the local Jewish community is also likely (Acts 17:5-7); although they did not make up the majority of the *church's opposition (Acts 17:8), they would account for the elaboration on Jewish opposition in verses 15 and 16.

2:15. The Jewish people nurtured the tradition that their ancestors had killed the prophets, intensifying the Old Testament account. Opposition to missions-minded, Greek-speaking Jewish Christians had been increasing among Palestinian Jews as Jewish-*Gentile tensions increased there (see comment on Acts 21:20-22 describing a situation that existed within a decade of this letter). Jewish practices led Jewish people to band together in an often hostile environment, leading many Gentiles to accuse them of hatred toward humanity; but Paul's meaning here is quite different, referring only to their opposition to the Jewish Christian missionary outreach to the Gentiles.

2:16. "Filling up the measure of sins" (NASB) is an *Old Testament idea (e.g., Gen 15:16) also used by Jesus (Mt 23:32). In keeping with Paul's teaching elsewhere (Rom 11), "wrath has come on them to the end" (the literal translation) may mean "wrath has come on them until the time of the end" (cf. Lk 21:9, 23), rather than "forever" or simply the equally natural "fully" or "finally" (cf. "at last"—NIV, NRSV, TEV). The Old Testament prophets said that after many judgments the remnant of Israel would turn with their whole hearts toward God, and then he would restore his people and bring in the new age of his rule (e.g., Jer 29:11-14; Ezek 34:11-31; Hos 14:4-7; Amos 9:11-15).

2:17—3:10
Longing for His Friends

Emotion was appropriate even in persuasive speeches, and still more in letters of friendship; Paul's letters are full of emotion, and this passage is one of the clearest examples of it.

2:17. Letters of friendship commonly expressed a longing to see the other person and often noted that they were apart only in body, not in spirit. (Today we would say, "My heart is with you.") Paul goes beyond these conventions by protesting (literally), "We were orphaned without you" (see NRSV); though emphasizing gentleness, most philosophers would have considered such language *too* passionate.

2:18. Ancients sometimes spoke of Fate hindering them. Given the geographical proximity of Paul to Macedonia, "*Satan's hindering" (KJV) here must refer to some concrete obstacle preventing his return to Thessalonica—either the Jewish opposition he mentioned in 2:14-16 or opposition from city magistrates and its consequences for his friends there (Acts 17:8-9).

2:19-20. Crowns and garlands were used for rewards throughout Jewish and Greco-Roman literature of this period; not a royal crown but a victor's wreath is in view. Crowns (cf. Is 28:5; 62:3) and garlands (cf. Is 61:3) sometimes appeared as symbols of future reward in the *Old Testament and in ancient Judaism. Paul's reward, however, is simply the perseverance of the Thessalonians themselves (cf. similarly 3 John 4).

3:1-2. Letters of friendship often expressed longing to see another person; even when the expressions were formulaic, however, they were no less genuine (compare modern greeting cards for various occasions). Timothy and probably Silas accompanied Paul to Athens, and he dispatched them back to Macedonia while he labored alone in Athens. Luke omits some of these details in the account in Acts (Acts 17:14-16; 18:5), as one would expect; any author who has written a readable *narrative knows that one cannot report every detail and must smooth the narrative out. But the correspondences between the accounts are striking, and the divergences indicate that Luke could not have simply derived his account from this letter.

3:3-4. Jesus, the *Old Testament and some Jewish *apocalyptic writers had predicted a period of sufferings just before the impending end of the age. These sufferings would accompany the *gospel's proclamation (according to Jesus; cf. Mk 13:9-11) and help bring about the *repentance of Israel (according to the Old Testament, e.g., Jer 30:7; Dan 12:1; cf. Deut 4:30; Is 26:20-21). If this is in view here, Christians were destined to endure this suffering but were also destined to escape the wrath at the Second Coming (1:10; 5:9; cf. Acts 14:22).

3:5-8. Ancient letter writers often complained that their feelings were hurt when they did not receive letters back promptly; this complaint was meant as a sign of their affection. Because letters had to be carried by travelers, however, Paul would not expect to have heard from them, especially if they had not known where to find him; it would be easier for him to send someone to them than the reverse. Yet his complaint about not knowing their situation expresses affection, like that of a worried parent. On "living" in verse 8, see comment on 2:8.

3:9-10. Paul resumes, completes or adds a thanksgiving (see comment on 1:2); cf. Psalm 116:12. Most people slept during the night, and prayer during the night was a mark of special devotion in the *Old Testament and Jewish literature (in the Old Testament, e.g., Ps 22:2; 42:8; 63:6; 77:2, 6; 119:55, 148). "What is lacking" in their faith (3:10) may be adequate hope (3:6; cf. 1:3; 5:8), which Paul seeks to supply in 4:13—5:11.

3:11-13
Paul's Prayer

In most letters, the prayer immediately follows the thanksgiving; because the prayer in 1 Thessalonians begins in 3:11, some commentators suggest that Paul finishes the thanksgiving only in 3:9-10. But Paul might simply be following a format in this letter different from his later, more customary one.

3:11. "Wish-prayers" ("Now may God . . ." addressed to those for whom the prayer is offered) were considered genuine prayers in Judaism and were offered with the expectation that God would hear them. Paul continues the motif of longing in verse 11.

3:12. Thanksgivings and prayers could introduce topics to be taken up later in the letter, especially in Paul's letters; he returns to "love" in 4:9 and to "outsiders" in 4:12.

3:13. The *Old Testament, Judaism and Jesus' teaching also looked forward to a future hope that gave meaning to endurance in the present. The "saints" or "holy ones" here could refer to God's people (4:14) or to the holy angels (Zech 14:5); both were called "holy ones" regularly in Jewish literature. Paul usually uses the term for the former.

4:1-8
Sexual Purity

The issue throughout this passage is adultery (4:6). Paul may have heard of a specific instance in the congregation, or he may still be concerned because of the known sexual looseness of pagans, reinforced during his stay in proverbially immoral Corinth. Unmarried Greek men (i.e., Greek men below the age of thirty) commonly indulged in intercourse with prostitutes, slaves and other males; Greek religion and culture did not provide any disincentive for doing so.

4:1-2. This is the ancient Jewish and Christian language that scholars call traditioning: passing on an earlier teacher's words. Paul and his companions spent much of their time in Thessalonica teaching the new believers Jesus' sayings, to some of which he plainly appeals in 4:13—5:11.

4:3. Greek and Roman practice allowed for intercourse with prostitutes and slaves; premarital sex was prohibited for males under Roman law only if an aristocrat were doing it with an upper-class woman (this was called *stuprum*). Judaism was much stricter, reserving sex for marriage (although the literature indicates that some Jewish men did fall prey to premarital and extramarital temptations). Paul condemns all sexual immorality, although he moves to a specific example in 4:6. He shares the *Old Testament view that premarital sex with someone other than one's future spouse is adultery against one's future spouse and thus as sinful as other adultery (Deut 22:13-29). (This statement does not imply that premarital sex with one's future spouse was not prohibited in Judaism by the Old Testament view of marriage as covenant; it is only to affirm that premarital sex with anyone else was viewed as a capital offense against one's future spouse.)

4:4. "Vessel" (KJV, NASB) was commonly used as a metaphor for one's "body" (NIV, NRSV) in Greek and *Diaspora Jewish literature; it was occasionally applied to one's wife (in some Jewish texts and, on one interpretation, in 1 Pet 3:7). It probably means "body" here, although the matter is not beyond dispute.

4:5. Adopting more *ascetic Greco-Roman ideals, some Diaspora Jewish writers decided that sex was permissible only for procreation, and passion even toward one's wife was unacceptable. Because Paul elsewhere sees marriage as the only appropriate place to release passion (1 Cor 7:2-9), it is more likely that he opposes only adulterous passion (1 Thess 4:6), not sexual pleasure in marriage. Jewish people viewed nearly all *Gentiles as sexually immoral (later *rabbis argued that one could not assume the virginity of a Gentile woman over three years and one day old); most Gentile men *were* immoral. Although many of Paul's readers are ethnically Gentiles, he expects them to recognize that they are spiritually non-Gentiles by virtue of their conversion to the biblical faith (cf. Rom 2:29).

4:6. Adultery, or "wife stealing," as it was often considered, was punishable by banishment under Roman law; in some circumstances, a couple caught in the act could be killed on the spot. Adultery seems to have been common and usually unpunished, however; but a husband who learned that his wife was committing adultery was required by law to divorce her or himself be prosecuted on the charge of *lenocinium*—"pimping." Palestinian Judaism could no longer execute the Old Testament death penalty for adultery, but Jewish people believed that what they could not execute, God would (especially on the day of judgment).

4:7. From the standpoint of temples throughout ancient culture, intercourse generally made one ritually impure for a time. This impurity could be extended metaphorically, however, to spiritual impurity in the case of sexual sin. "Sanctification" (NASB) or "holiness" means being "set apart" to God; Israel in the Old Testament was "set apart" and exhorted therefore to *live* as if they were set apart (to be holy as God was holy; e.g., Lev 20:24-26).

4:8. The *Holy Spirit's main roles in Jewish texts included inspiring *prophecy and purifying the righteous; the latter was particularly prominent in *Essene literature and based especially on Ezekiel 36:25-27. Even someone unfamiliar with this role of the Spirit, however, would catch Paul's point from the title (*Holy* Spirit); although Old Testament writers call the Spirit of God "the Holy Spirit" only twice, this had become a common title by Paul's day and could be rendered literally "the Spirit of holiness." Paul has in mind the Spirit who purifies and sets apart God's people (1 Thess 4:7).

4:9-12
Behavior Toward One Another and Outsiders

4:9-10. Moralists often wrote on the topic "on love of family" and similar themes. For Paul, all Christians were one family and the ethics of familial love should apply. Thessalonica was a prominent city of Macedonia.

4:11. Quietism—minding one's own affairs—and clinging only to one's own philosophical community were central to *Epicureanism but came to characterize many people in the first century who remained aloof from public or political life. Complete quietism of this sort drew criticism from the rest of society, just as Jewish allegiance to its own customs and people did.

In the broad sense of avoiding public controversies, however, "leading a quiet life" was wise guidance for a persecuted minority in the first-century Roman Empire. Some writers like *Plutarch advocated the involvement of wise men in the affairs of the state, but even they advised certain people (e.g., those who had already enjoyed a full political career) to withdraw from active service. Paul asks his readers to be inconspicuous, not monastic.

4:12. Landowning aristocrats despised manual labor, but for most of the ancient world manual labor was the only means of livelihood. Although the Thessalonian *church may have included a few well-to-do *patrons (Acts 17:4, 9), Paul seems not to have encountered there the opposition to his views on manual labor that arose in Corinth. Treating outsiders appropriately ("behaving properly toward outsiders"—NASB, NRSV) presumably means one's witness in giving, or perhaps avoiding begging, if Paul thinks that some would beg favors from more well-to-do benefactors. Begging on the street normally characterized only the poorest, often propertyless persons; but some may have been attracted to the lifestyle of begging adopted by the Cynic philosophers (cf. comment on 2 Thess 3:11-12).

4:13-18
Comfort for the Grieving

One common form of ancient nonbusiness letter was the "letter of consolation." Paul loads this consolatory section of his letter with Jewish *apocalyptic motifs taken directly from Jesus' teaching. (Given the vast number of apocalyptic motifs Paul omits, and that most of those he includes coincide with the oral tradition of Jesus' teaching later recorded in the Gospels, there can be little doubt as to his source—see 4:15. Given the many prophets and hence prophecies in the early church, it is quite improbable that Paul and the Gospel writers simply drew on the same prophecy of someone other than Jesus; it is also unlikely that the Gospel writers would have known of 1 Thessalonians, or if they had, that they would have modeled their reports of Jesus' teaching after it.) Appealing to Jewish future hopes was a natural approach in consolation, as Jewish tomb inscriptions attest.

In the light of the local persecution that this letter addresses (1:6; 2:14-16; 3:3-6), some scholars have suggested that those in the congregation who died since Paul's departure died as martyrs. Martyrdom must have been the exception rather than the rule around A.D. 50; it would not have taken many exceptions, however, to provoke questions among the Thessalonian Christians.

4:13. Philosophers often "consoled" the recipients of their letters by saying, "Do not grieve," or "Do not grieve too much," since "it will not do any good." This is not, however, Paul's point; rather, it is that Christians do not grieve for their fellow Christians as pagans grieve, because Christians have hope. Most pagans believed in a shadowy afterlife in the underworld and did not share the philosophers' optimism or neutrality toward death. Most pagans grieved, and Jewish and other Near Eastern peoples engaged in very cathartic grief rituals. "Sleep" was a common euphemism for death.

4:14. Like many Jewish people, Paul believed that the soul lived in heaven till the *resurrection of the body, and that soul and body would be reunited at the resurrection (2 Cor 5:1-10). Many ancient writers distinguished the upper atmosphere ("aether") where pure souls would reside, from the lowest heaven, the realm of "air." Thus Paul can speak of the Lord descending from "heaven," meaning the highest heavens (4:16), and meeting his people in the "air," the lower atmosphere (4:17).

4:15. "Word of the Lord" in this case means a saying of Jesus (cf. Lk 22:61;

Acts 20:35; 1 Cor 7:10). Jesus spoke of his "coming" (e.g., Mt 24:27), a term that could apply to the visit of a king or royal dignitary, which was celebrated with great pomp and majesty.

4:16-17. In the *Old Testament, trumpets (shofars, rams' horns) were used especially to gather the assembly or give orders for battle; in this context, both connotations must be in view. Roman armies also used trumpets in war; Jewish views of the end time included Israel being gathered with a trumpet and trumpets used in the final war at the same time (daily Jewish prayers; the *Qumran War Scroll). Michael, the chief archangel of Jewish literature, was considered Israel's guardian angel and thus figures in Jewish texts about the final battle; here Jesus seems to assume Michael's role on behalf of believers, God's people.

The "clouds," "trumpet" and possibly "archangel" allude to a saying of Jesus about the end time (Mt 24:30-31); the meeting in the air may be inferred from the gathering to join him (Mt 24:31). Judaism traditionally associated the *resurrection of the dead with the end of this age and the inauguration of the *kingdom, and readers would assume this connection in the absence of a direct statement to the contrary. When paired with a royal "coming" (see comment on 1 Thess 4:15), the word for "meeting" in the air normally referred to emissaries from a city going out to meet the dignitary and escort him on his way to their city. The contrast that this image provides with the honor thought to be particularly due to the "Lord" Caesar and his emissaries could well have provoked hostility from local officials (cf. 2:12; 5:3; Acts 17:7).

The "shout" is undoubtedly the commander's shout of war (Amos 2:2), an image applied to God as warrior in the *Old Testament (Is 42:13; cf. the shout of triumph with a trumpet in Ps 47:5, 8-9), as is his descent (Is 31:4; cf. Zech 14:3-4). From the earliest *New Testament sources, Old Testament imagery about God's coming in the day of the Lord is applied directly to Jesus; Judaism envisioned this role as God's, not the *Messiah's. "Clouds" were used both as imagery for the coming day of God's judgment (e.g., Ezek 30:3; 32:7; Joel 2:2; often the clouds are the smoke of battle and pillaging) and the coming of the *Son of Man (Dan 7:13).

4:18. Writers of letters of consolation sometimes urged their readers to "comfort" (KJV, NASB; or "exhort," "encourage") themselves and others with their words. In the same way, Jewish people recognized that committed servants of God could exhort one another to stand firm in the face of suffering and martyrdom (2 Macc 7:5). Even the majority of the Old Testament prophets who wrote most fiercely of judgment included words of comfort and hope for the righteous remnant, and hope is central to Paul's message about the future for his readers, who make up such a remnant.

5:1-11 Watchfulness

Paul continues his discussion of the Lord's coming (4:13-18), ending on the same exhortation to comfort or encourage one another (4:18; 5:11).

5:1. Here Paul cites another saying of Jesus (later recorded in Acts 1:7; writers normally paraphrased sayings when quoting them). The general thought—that the time of the end was unknown—was common enough in other Jewish circles; teachers debated whether the righteous could hasten the time of the end or whether it would simply come in the time that God had ordained, but most agreed that people could not know the time of the end. Some, however, worked up elaborate schemes to predict that it was about to occur; Paul does not subscribe to such theories.

5:2. This verse is another saying of Jesus (Mt 24:43; also used in 2 Pet 3:10; Rev 3:3; 16:15). "The day of the Lord" in the *Old Testament was the day of God, the judgment at the end of the age (sometimes prefigured in nearer judgments, but ultimately cataclysmic in its final form). Jewish *apocalyptic commonly spoke of an unexpected end, yet one that was preceded by signs. Paul does not mean that no signs can precede the day of the Lord (2 Thess 2:2-4)—only that they will not pinpoint the time or provide sufficient warning to the wicked (1 Thess 5:3-4).

5:3. These "birth pangs" are not the age-long ones of Matthew 24:8, but the final pangs of destruction in the day of the Lord, as in Isaiah 13:8. Birth pangs were a common image of agony and destruction (Ps 48:6; Is 21:3; 26:17-18; 42:14; Jer 4:31; 6:24; 13:21; 22:23; 49:22-24; 50:43; Hos 13:13). Sudden destruction was also a common biblical idea (Is 47:11; Jer 6:26), and unexpected judgment on the wicked became a regular motif of Jewish apocalyptic; but Paul may here especially reflect Jesus' teaching (Mt 24:36-44).

The Jewish people knew well about false peace: false prophets prophesying peace had led to Judah's judgment in the Old Testament (e.g., Jer 6:14); the first-century B.C. Roman general Pompey had entered Jerusalem pretending peace; and roughly two decades after Paul wrote this letter, false prophets of victory led the Jerusalemites to slaughter at the hands of Titus's Roman army. Paul's readers in Thessalonica, however, would take his words as an attack on claims of earlier Roman emperors to have established peace and security *(pax et securitas)* throughout the empire. Teachings like this one sounded subversive and may have aroused persecution against Christians (Acts 17:7).

5:4-5. The background to these verses is quite natural: Paul extends the image of the day of the Lord coming as a thief in the night (see comment on v. 2). Thieves normally broke in at night, but believers in Jesus were people of the day of the Lord. Paul parallels day with light and night with darkness, using common images for good and evil in his day. "Sons of" (NIV, NASB) or "children of" (KJV, NRSV) was a way of saying "people characterized by."

5:6-7. Night was the time for both sleeping and drunken parties. Paul may draw on the sayings of Jesus in Matthew 24:42, 49 and 26:45, besides the obvious Matthew 24:43. Other moralists also used "sobriety" metaphorically.

5:8. Roman guards and other kinds of night watchmen (such as shepherds) were the only people who stayed awake at night, apart from those engaging in drunken revelry. Paul's armor imagery may also reflect the standard Jewish idea of a final war preceding the end and the military imagery used by moralists concerning their struggle with the passions (see comment on Rom 13:12; cf. also comment on Eph 6:10-20).

5:9. Although "salvation" could mean "deliverance," in the context of the final salvation it would also be associated with the bodily *resurrection of the righteous, as here. Judaism juxtaposed this resurrection with the wrath God would pour out on the *Gentiles and disobedient Jews at his coming to judge the earth, which they expected would occur at the same time.

5:10. On the image of "sleep" see

comment on 4:13 (it cannot allude to the image of 5:5-7, where it refers to the people of darkness).

5:11. See comment on 4:18.

5:12-22
How to Behave Among God's People

Verses 12-15 deal with how to treat one another; verses 16-22 address corporate (and partly private) worship (cf. similar exhortations to corporate worship in Eph 5:18-21, followed by household codes).

5:12-13. The term for those who "have charge" (NASB, NRSV) or "are over" (KJV, NIV) the Thessalonian Christians was especially applied in the Greco-Roman world to *patrons, sponsors of *clients and religious associations. If that sense is in view here, these would be the Christians who opened their homes for the *churches to meet in them and sponsored them, providing what financial and political help they could (the Thessalonian patrons probably included Jason—Acts 17:5-9).

That they would also "admonish" (not just "instruct"—NASB, TEV) is not unusual, since they would probably be the wealthier members of the congregation and hence better educated. (Most people in antiquity were functionally illiterate; exhorting was generally easier for those with the training and leisure to read the Scriptures, since the Scriptures were the source of exhortations in both synagogue and church.) If no one was particularly well-to-do, those who were relatively better off would have to perform the functions of patron as best they could, requiring either smaller or more crowded house churches; but the congregation probably included relatively well-to-do people (Acts 17:4).

5:14. The "unruly" (KJV, NASB) are the undisciplined—"idlers" (NIV, NRSV) who can work but refuse to do so (cf. 4:11; 2 Thess 3:7-8). The word for "faint-hearted" (NASB, NRSV) or "timid" (NIV, TEV) referred especially to those who were self-denigrating, who had a low opinion of themselves. Cf. Isaiah 35:3-4.

5:15. Compare Jesus' teaching (Mt 5:39); some other Jewish teachers also advised nonretaliation (see comment on Rom 12:17).

5:16. Greek ethics often listed succinct statements one after another as Paul does here. Many biblical psalms associate rejoicing with celebration and worship (e.g., Ps 9:14; 33:1; 47:1; 95:2; 149:1-5); here it is thus naturally linked with prayer and thanksgiving.

5:17. Even the strictest pietists of Judaism did not pray all day; but they prayed regularly, much and faithfully. "Pray without ceasing" could mean this type of prayer or to carry the attitude of prayer with oneself throughout the day, not just in corporate worship or personal quiet times.

5:18. Pagans who recognized that Fate or some god was sovereign over everything acknowledged that one should accept whatever comes or even give thanks for it. For Paul, those who trust God's sovereignty and love can give thanks in every situation.

5:19-20. Most of early Judaism associated the *Spirit especially with *prophecy; Paul does not want anyone quenching genuinely inspired speech. The term translated "quench" was often used with fire, which appropriately fits one *Old Testament image of prophets unable to repress God's inspiration (Jer 20:9).

5:21-22. In the context, "test everything" (NIV) may mean test prophetic utterances (5:19-20), retaining the good but rejecting the bad. *Perhaps* because some Greek religious cults practiced ecstatic inspiration, Paul warns the Thessalonians not to confuse their inspiration with that of paganism; but judging prophecy was already an issue in the Old Testament. In the Old Testament, many prophets were trained under senior prophets, guided in their sensitivity to the Spirit's inspiration (1 Sam 19:20); because such senior prophets were not available to most early Christian congregations, mutual testing by others moving in the prophetic gift was necessary (see comment on 1 Cor 14:29).

5:23-28 Concluding Words

5:23-25. On "wish-prayers" see comment on 3:11. Although Paul emphasizes the *whole* person here by listing component parts in good Jewish fashion (cf., e.g., Deut 6:5; Lk 10:27), he uses the language of his culture to describe the parts (which he can divide differently elsewhere, e.g., 1 Cor 7:34; 14:14-15). He is quite unlike the philosophers who constructed detailed analyses, dividing the soul into two (*Cicero), three (*Plato, *Philo) or eight (*Stoics) components. Like most Jewish writers and the *Old Testament, Paul saw people as a whole, with body and soul separated at death, and distinguished various components only to make his point. (Valentinian *Gnostics, mainly under Middle Platonic influence, later made much more of the differences between soul and spirit, and thus "soulish" and "spiritual" persons, than Paul intended here; their radical distinctions led them to deny the full incarnation, or enfleshment, of Jesus the Word. Posidonius, Marcus Aurelius and others advocated a form of trichotomy [three parts], and later *Samaritans also held to a trichotomous division of the person, although they did not tend to use Paul's wording here. Much later Jewish mystics called cabalists divided the soul into ten parts, including a trinity of triads. Ancient Egyptian thought also seems to have recognized component parts, distinguishing body from *ba,* and *ka* and *akh.*)

5:26. Kisses were a common affectionate greeting for those with whom one had an intimate or respectful relationship; see comment on Romans 16:16.

5:27-28. Many people could not read, so reading his letter aloud was the only way everyone in the congregation could be acquainted with it.

2 THESSALONIANS

Introduction

Authorship. Some scholars have denied that Paul wrote this letter, because it differs in some respects from 1 Thessalonians; conversely, they attribute the similarities it has with 1 Thessalonians to imitation. But 2 Thessalonians is Pauline in style and moves in the same *apocalyptic world of thought that much of 1 Thessalonians 4—5 does; the differences are no greater than one would expect in two separate letters dealing with such a broad topic. It seems unlikely that 2 Thessalonians 2:3-4 was written after the temple's destruction (A.D. 70); because *pseudepigraphic letters were rarely written during or immediately after the lifetime of their alleged author, 2 Thessalonians was most likely written by Paul (who died c. A.D. 64). Most commentators today accept it as Pauline.

Relationship to 1 Thessalonians. Although scholars have debated which letter was written first, most scholars think that 1 Thessalonians was written before 2 Thessalonians (the original letters were not titled, of course). The bearer of his first letter has probably returned with news about the situation in Thessalonica; some of the Christians have embraced Paul's message about future hope without the qualifications he had attached to it, and have decided that the day of the Lord has already come (2:2).

Commentaries. See those listed in the introduction to 1 Thessalonians. Most commentaries cover both letters.

1:1-12 Introduction, Thanksgiving and Prayer

Paul's letters usually open with the basic introduction ("Paul . . . to . . ."), a thanksgiving and either a prayer or a mention of his prayers for the recipients. Each of these features was typical of letters in his day, but Paul adapts them in a Christian way. Paul also stocks his *apocalyptic language here with phrases from the *Old Testament.

1:1. The basic format of letter openings was: sender's name, to recipient's name; greetings.

1:2. The typical Greek greeting was *charein,* which Paul adapts to *charis,* "grace." Jewish letters usually added the typical Jewish greeting of "peace," which functioned as a wish-prayer: "May God's peace be with you," "May all be well with you." (On wish-prayers see comment on 1 Thess 3:11.) Paul makes this prayer more explicit by adding the source of grace and peace: both God the Father and the Lord Jesus. Both "God" and "Lord" are divine titles in the Old Testament.

1:3. Thanksgivings for the recipients were common in Greek letters and helped establish a friendly tone at the beginning of the letter.

1:4-5. A major theme in Jewish thought by this period was God's reward for the righteous who suffer. Developing this theme from the *Old Testament, Jewish writers emphasized that God would punish their persecutors in the end and deliver the righteous, no matter what they suffered now. This deliverance was intimately bound up with the hope of the *resurrection of the righteous at the end of the age. Often the present or imminent tribulation was viewed as the final "messianic birth pangs" that would usher in the era of the *kingdom. Some philosophers also spoke of sufferings proving one worthy of God.

1:6-7. As in Jewish literature, so here the righteous receive rest from their tribulation only at the same time that God vindicates them by his final judgment on the wicked (cf. also Deut 32:34-36, 41). Fire burning one's adversaries was a common image in the Old Testament (e.g., Num 11:1; Ps 97:3; Is 26:11; 66:15-16, 24; cf. Jer 4:4; 15:14; 17:4; 21:12; Ezek 21:31; 22:20; Nahum 1:6; Zeph 1:18; 3:8). This image was natural because of the use of fire in war and because "wrath" was often described in Hebrew and cognate languages in terms of "burning."

This also became customary end-time imagery in Jewish literature; in some Jewish texts the whole earth would be destroyed, in others the *kingdom would be established without such cosmic transformation. But the wording here is particularly from Isaiah 66:15. The "mighty" angels are envisioned as the Lord's army.

1:8. On God's vengeance or repaying his people's enemies, see Deuteronomy 32:41, Isaiah 35:4 and 66:6; it was also an important theme in post-Old Testament Jewish literature.

1:9. This verse directly echoes the *Septuagint of Isaiah 2:10, 19 and 21. That Jewish literature often describes God turning his "face" (literally) or "presence" from the wicked may be theologically significant, but Paul directly takes over the Semitic idiom ("from the face of" means "from before," "from the presence of") as the Septuagint of Isaiah rendered it. "Eternal destruction" in the *Dead Sea Scrolls and elsewhere usually meant that the wicked were completely destroyed, but in the contexts of many of these passages they also suffered eternally (both could be mentioned in the same passage, e.g., *Jubilees 36:10; cf.

Is 66:24, cited in Mk 9:48).

1:10. Kings' "glory" was their splendor and royal bearing; the glorification of God's people was to be at the time of Israel's restoration (Is 46:13; 60:1-2; 62:2), when God (here Jesus) would come to vindicate them. (Paul normally associates the saints' "glorification" with their bodily *resurrection—e.g., Rom 8:17-23; 1 Cor 15:43; Phil 3:21.) "When he comes" echoes the language of the Septuagint of Psalm 96:13, applying language about God to Jesus. "On that day" is the "day of the Lord" (see 2 Thess 2:2; cf. Is 2:11-12, 17, 20; 11:10-11; Joel 3:18—"in that day").

1:11. Ancient letters, including Paul's, often contained prayers or mentions of prayers on behalf of the recipients. On "worthy" see comment on 1:5.

1:12. The Lord could be glorified in his obedient people in the present (Jer 13:11), but the ultimate glorifying of God in his people would be on the day when he would bring all things to light (see comment on 1:10).

2:1-12
The Final Rebellion

Some Thessalonian Christians thought that the imminent day of the Lord had already come. To correct their misunderstanding, Paul reminds them of Jesus' sayings he taught them while he was there (2:5, 15): a final period of rebellion constituted an essential prerequisite for *Christ's return.

2:1. The "coming" (described further in 2:8; cf. 1 Thess 4:15) and "gathering" here are grammatically linked, and the use of both terms derives from the sayings of Jesus. "Coming" was a common word, but when applied to a king it took on special connotations of a glorious visitation. Some Jewish texts applied it to God's past theophanies and future revelation in glory; Matthew 24:3, 27, 37 and 39 use it for Jesus' return to judge the world. Many texts, both in the *Old Testament (e.g., Is 27:12-13) and later Jewish literature, speak of Israel's gathering as God's people; Paul probably takes the image of the gathering of the righteous from Jesus' saying later recorded in Matthew 24:31 (which uses a related term).

2:2. Those who heard Paul's first letter read only once in the congregation may have misunderstood its point. The Greek outlook included an afterlife in the underworld or an escape of the soul to the highest heavens, but not a future event when the dead would be *resurrected. Thessalonian Christians may have read Paul in the light of their own cultural predispositions: they may have assumed that the future reality was already fulfilled, not just initiated, in *Christ. Paul replies that the future "day of the Lord" is imminent or unexpected in its timing (1 Thess 5:2) but still preceded by the final rebellion (2 Thess 2:3-12).

2:3-4. The first prerequisite is either the "rebellion" (NIV, NRSV, TEV) or the "apostasy" (NASB). If it is a "rebellion" against God, it is the world's final insult to him (2:4); if "apostasy," it refers back to Jesus' sayings later written in Matthew 24:10-13. Both sins are characteristic of Jewish lists of end-time sufferings, but because Paul omits most of the signs found in such lists and focuses only on those cited by Jesus, the term here might mean apostasy. In either case, Paul indicates that the term does not apply to his readers (2:10-15).

The figure of a general future antichrist (as he is commonly called) seems to occur mainly in later Jewish texts, but contemporary Jewish texts do describe some past or present rulers in similar terms (cf. also the evil rulers in Dan 9—11); the tradition of pagan kings who made themselves out to be gods is also quite ancient (Is 14:13-14; Ezek 28:2; Dan 6:7). The *Dead Sea Scrolls speak of a "man of lies" who opposed the founder of their community; the *Psalms of Solomon portray the Roman general Pompey in such terms; and Roman emperors lent themselves to such portrayals in general. Nearly a decade before this letter, Gaius Caligula had tried to set up his image in the Jerusalem temple, nearly sparking a revolt. (Caligula immediately preceded Claudius, the current emperor in A.D. 41-54.) Two decades after this letter, when Titus destroyed the temple, his soldiers desecrated the temple by paying divine honors to the insignia of Emperor Vespasian on the site of the temple.

The imagery used here derives especially from Jesus, however (cf. Mt 24:15), who took it from Daniel (Dan 7:25; 8:11; 9:26-27; 11:31, 36; cf. 2 Chron 33:7; Ezek 8:3). Some scholars who have examined the prophecies carefully have concluded that Daniel 11 describes the abomination caused by Antiochus Epiphanes; yet the "end" seems to come at that time (12:1), about two centuries before Jesus. Like the promise of the land to Abraham's descendants, deferred repeatedly during the period of the judges, between David and Josiah, and afterward due to Israel's disobedience, this text might be an example of deferred *eschatology. If one counts the period of Daniel 9:24-27, however, the anointed prince (whom some held to be the Messiah) was to be "cut off" around the year that Jesus died; the destruction of the city followed forty years later, again indicating a delay of at least forty years. Evangelical interpreters differ as to whether (1) a specific future tribulation remains (perhaps 2 Thess 2:8-9), (2) the Jewish war in A.D. 66-70 fulfilled it completely (cf. Mt 24:15-21), (3) the whole course of history constitutes this period (cf. comments on Revelation, especially chap. 12). or (4) the language is reused in different ways, all of which are true.

2:5. The Thessalonians apparently misinterpreted Paul's talk about the future *kingdom (Acts 17:7), much of which seems to derive from teachings of Jesus that Paul is transmitting to them (2 Thess 2:15).

2:6-7. The interpretations of this passage are more diverse than those of most passages in the *New Testament. Even the translation is not certain (is the restrainer "taken out of the way" or does the lawless one "come forth from the midst" at the end of v. 7?). Views of the "restrainer" are plentiful. Some have thought that the "restrainer" is one prerequisite for the end stated by Jesus, the preaching to all the nations (Mt 24:14); this view makes some sense, but the completion of this preaching was technically to precede the end itself, not the rebellion that preceded the end.

The "restrainer" could be simply God's sovereign restraint (e.g., Ezek 5:11); it could be the archangel Michael, angelic protector of Israel in Jewish tradition (also Dan 12:1); it could be the presence of Christians in Jerusalem (Mt 24:16-21); or it could be, as many scholars have argued, the ruler preceding the self-deifying emperor or succession of emperors. (Those who hold the last view point out that the name of the emperor when Paul was writing this letter was Claudius, which was related to a Latin word for "restrain"; he immediately preceded the persecutor Nero, on whom see introduction to 1 Peter.) Many of the early church fathers took the view that the "restrainer" was the Roman Empire.

One popular modern view that has no specific contextual support is that the "restrainer" is the *church, which had inadequate social power in Paul's day to perform that function. The church's removal from the earth by the *resurrection described in 1 Thessalonians 4:15-17 does not fit this context, because the Thessalonian Christians were to receive rest from affliction only at the day of judgment (2 Thess 1:6-9), and be gathered (2:1) only in the day of the Lord (2:2), which was to be preceded by the rebellion (2:3-4), which in turn was to be preceded by the restrainer (2:6-7). Although no ancient Christian authors attest the view that the restrainer is the church (the idea of a rapture before the tribulation first explicitly appears in history around 1830, as a corollary of dispensationalism), the many adherents of this view today cite various other New Testament texts for its support.

In any case, the Thessalonians would apparently understand what Paul means (2:5), and his point is not in question: this event has not yet happened, so the rebellion and hence the day of the Lord and the church's gathering are still future.

2:8. Paul describes the end of the lawless one in terms borrowed from Isaiah 11:4 (cf. Hos 6:5) and similar to those in other Jewish texts. Paul contrasts Jesus' own coming (cf. 2 Thess 2:1) with the lawless one's (2:9); on such contrasts see comment on Revelation 13.

2:9. Deceptive signs already occurred in Paul's day. Sorcerers and shrines of healing gods were common; although healing was not the primary focus of the imperial cult, some people in the eastern Mediterranean also invoked the spirit of the emperor, who was worshiped as a god, to deliver or heal them. Propaganda circulated that the emperor Vespasian (to whose insignia homage was paid on the site of the temple in A.D. 70) worked miracles, but emperors themselves were not usually known as miracle workers. Although miracle-working false prophets appear early in the Bible (Ex 7:11), Paul's source for their association with the end is probably again Jesus' teachings (cf. Mt 24:24).

2:10-12. In the *Old Testament, God often punished people by giving them the very blindness they had chosen for themselves (Is 19:14; 29:9-10); in Jewish tradition, all the nations chose to turn away from God's truth, and only Israel accepted his *law. *Satan's primary roles in Jewish thought were accuser and deceiver or tempter; for Antiochus Epiphanes' deceit, see Daniel 8:25; for that of idolatry in general, see Isaiah 44:20 and Jeremiah 10:3-5. Philosophers characterized themselves as lovers of truth, and this characterization was accepted as a morally high ideal among the leisured class of Paul's day and probably among others who stopped to listen to public lectures. But Paul, like most Jewish people, believed that God's perfect truth came by revelation, not by the finite reasonings of the philosophers.

2:13—3:5 Thanksgiving, Wish-Prayer and Prayer Request

As in 1 Thessalonians 3:9-13, here Paul offers a second thanksgiving and a wish-prayer before moving into the hortatory (exhortation) section of his letter.

2:13-14. In the *Old Testament, God "chose" Israel; *Gentile believers grafted into his people are often called "chosen" in the *New Testament (see comment on Rom 9:14-29; cf. Mt 24:31). On the *Spirit (often linked with spiritual purification in segments of Judaism) and sanctification, see comment on 1 Thessalonians 4:7-8. On "glory" see comment

on 2 Thessalonians 1:10 and 12.
2:15. *Pharisaic Judaism emphasized the careful passing on of traditions from earlier teachers. Paul passed on to the Thessalonian believers the teachings of Jesus, many of which he has alluded to in this chapter.
2:16-17. Here Paul offers a "wish-prayer," a prayer to God addressed as a wish for a person. Although not directly addressed to God, such statements were meant as prayers for God to answer.
3:1-4. The prayer request that God's word may "run" (literally) or "spread" swiftly probably borrows the image from Psalm 147:15. The Thessalonians would think of runners in an athletic competition.
3:5. Paul concludes with another wish-prayer (see comment on 2:16-17).

3:6-15 Dealing with Idlers

3:6. Paul acts "in the name of Jesus"—as his representative. By this period "unruly" (NASB) usually meant "idle" (NIV, NRSV), the clear meaning in this context. The origin of this group of idlers in the *church might be the Greco-Roman aristocratic disdain for manual labor, or a mistaken belief that the day of the Lord had come and canceled the need for such labor (2:2). More likely, they may have pursued a philosophic, specifically a *Cynic, lifestyle (see comment on 3:11-12). Idlers were known to pass their days in the marketplaces of Greek cities (including Thessalonica—Acts 17:5); some may have been genuinely converted but not given up their previous lifestyle.
3:7-9. Teachers commonly exhorted their students to imitate them. On the labor of Paul and his companions, see comment on 1 Thessalonians 2:9. As some commentators point out, to "eat bread" seems to have been a Jewish figure of speech for "making a living" (e.g., Gen 3:19).
3:10. Although Paul's saying here has no exact parallel, some Jewish and Greek sayings had similar meanings. Judaism had a strong work ethic and a heavy emphasis on charity; Proverbs emphasized both the need to help those who have nothing and for those who are able to work to do so. "Eat" refers either to food provided by other believers (cf. 3:12), as *synagogues cared for needy Jews, or food provided at the *churches' communal meals (cf. 3:14), a practice standard among religious associations in the Greco-Roman world.
3:11-12. For "eat their own bread" see comment on 3:7-9. "Busybodies" could refer to those engaged in superfluous activity, wasting their time on irrelevant details, or to troublesome "meddlers" (see TEV), or to both. Some Christians had apparently decided to take up the lifestyle of traveling philosophers, like Paul and his companions. But although Paul and his companions had distinguished themselves from the "bad" *Cynic philosophers (see comment on 1 Thess 2:1-12), some Thessalonians may have continued fully in the Cynic vein: unlike Paul, Cynics begged rather than worked; and with their denunciations of passersby they were certainly "meddlers."
3:13. "Doing good" (NASB, TEV) includes charity, as in Judaism; Paul does not want his readers to misinterpret his limitation of charity.
3:14-15. The *synagogue community enforced different levels of discipline, which the *churches largely adopted (except for corporal punishment). Even under later *rabbinic rules, which allowed less diversity of practice than was common in Paul's day, full excommunication involved treating the person as an infidel, bringing him under a curse (cf. 1 Tim 1:20; 1 Cor 5:5; Mt

18:15-20), but lesser bans that still treated a person as part of the religious community were practiced as well. The *Essenes also had different levels of discipline.

3:16-18
Conclusion

3:16. This verse and 3:18 are final "wish-prayers"; see comment on 2:16-17.

3:17-18. In law courts, lawyers often had to argue that documents were forgeries (so *Quintilian), and some commentators have compared 3:17 with 2:2 to propose that Paul here reinforces the suggestion that the Thessalonians check to ascertain which letters were genuine. But most letter writers used scribes and signed their names at the end, and Paul often follows this practice elsewhere in his letters (e.g., 1 Cor 16:21). That he fears the work of forgers is thus possible but not certain.

1 Timothy

Introduction

Authorship. Among all Paul's letters, it is the authorship of the *Pastoral Epistles (1 Timothy, 2 Timothy and Titus) that is the most disputed, although they were widely attested as Pauline in the early church. The style is noticeably different from the usual style of Paul's earlier letters: a heavier use of traditional materials (sayings from prior Christian tradition, e.g., the "trustworthy statements" marked by 1:15; 3:1; 4:9; 2 Tim 2:1; Tit 3:8), various literary forms he rarely employs in his earlier letters (e.g., lists of qualifications) and so on. Although these differences alone would not necessitate different authors, they have led many good scholars to suggest either that Paul is not their author or (more often favored by conservative scholars) that he allowed a scribe or amanuensis considerable freedom in drafting the letter. (It is common knowledge that Paul, like most people, depended on scribes for much of his letter writing—Rom 16:22.) Some have compared the style of the Pastoral Epistles with that of Luke-Acts and concluded either that Luke was the author or that he was the scribe of these letters (cf. 2 Tim 4:11). Especially in 2 Timothy, where the nature of Paul's detention may not have permitted him the materials to write his own letters, an amanuensis (scribe) spending time with Paul, remembering Paul's words and transcribing them in his own terms would make sense. Nearly all the details of vocabulary and style have parallels in Paul's earlier letters; it is their cumulative effect that is different. Different authors could legitimately explain this effect, but so could the passage of time and different circumstances in Paul's life (as more conservative scholars often suggest).

*Pseudepigraphic letters (letters falsely ascribed to a great teacher of the past) were a common literary device but were rarely written close to the author's lifetime. The many personal allusions in 2 Timothy provide a strong argument against the thesis that the Pastoral Epistles are later pseudepigraphic epistles or early forgeries. If 1 Timothy and Titus are "official letters" (cf. comment on 1 Tim 1:2) meant to bolster their respective recipients' authority among their congregations, then the fact that they are more formal than 2 Timothy is understandable. Apart from the special literary forms in 1 Timothy and Titus, these letters may exhibit fewer persuasive *rhetorical devices than Paul's earlier argumentation to *churches because he is writing to his friend Timothy.

Situation. Various features sometimes used to argue lateness, such as church offices and the heresy addressed (some scholars read it as second-century *Gnosticism), generally fit as well or better in the circumstances of Paul's time (see comments on specific passages; the heresy need not be Gnostic). False teachers advocating *asceticism (4:3) based on the *law (1:7) are undermining the work of Paul and his companions in Ephesus (1:3). (Although Ephesus was in Asia Minor, it was culturally more Greek than Anatolian by this period; its particularly Greek culture is presupposed in the following treatment of the background.) Central to Paul's solution to this problem is the appointment of church leaders especially qualified to address the heresies spreading in the church. Paul employs the sorts of stereotypical language normally used to address such situations in his day (e.g., by philosophers against sophists or pseudophilosophers).

Date. On the premise of Pauline authorship, the Pastorals were written toward the end of his life, about A.D. 62-64. This would mean that Paul was released from his detention described in Acts 28:30-31 and completed the journeys presupposed in the *Pastoral Epistles, as suggested also by early Christian tradition. Those who date these letters later than Paul must date them late enough to allow for the reuse of Paul's name pseudonymously, and many date them to the mid-second century (although the Muratorian Canon assumes them to be Pauline not long after that date).

Commentaries. Especially valuable is Gordon D. Fee, *1 and 2 Timothy, Titus,* NIBC (Peabody, Mass.: Hendrickson, 1988); see also J. N. D. Kelly, *A Commentary on the Pastoral Epistles,* HNTC (Grand Rapids, Mich: Baker Book House, 1981). On 1 Timothy 2, see also Craig S. Keener, *Paul, Women and Wives* (Peabody, Mass.: Hendrickson, 1992), pp. 101-32; 1 Timothy 3:1-7 and chapter 5 are addressed in chapter 7 of Craig S. Keener, . . . *And Marries Another: Divorce and Remarriage in the Teaching of the New Testament* (Peabody, Mass.: Hendrickson, 1991), pp. 83-103. On the social location of the Pastorals, see also David C. Verner, *The Household of God: The Social World of the Pastoral Epistles,* SBLDS 71 (Chico, Calif.: Scholars, 1983).

1:1-2 Introduction

1:1. Letters customarily began with the name of the author. Many gods were described as "saviors" in antiquity, but the *Old Testament and Jewish literature reserved this title for the God of Israel (cf. Phil 3:20).

1:2. The next elements of a letter were the name(s) of the addressee(s) and the greeting (cf., e.g., Rom 1:7). Educated persons in antiquity often addressed a letter to a specific person, but intended for that letter to be published or to be an open letter to a group. Paul publicly supports Timothy's authority through this letter; it functions as an open "letter of recommendation" for him. (*Patrons often sent letters of recommendation on behalf of their *clients, or political dependents. Such letters, if meant to be used only once, would be sealed; Timothy's letter, however, could be publicly read in the house-church gatherings, reinforcing Timothy's *apostolic authorization.) "True child" (NASB) might echo legal terminology for a legitimate heir.

1:3-11 Scripture Twisters

1:3. Timothy stayed in Ephesus while Paul traveled northward through Troas (2 Tim 4:13) and across into Macedonia. Paul here reminds the readers (1 Tim 1:2) that he authorized Timothy to act on his authority.

1:4. *Plato and most other philosophers rejected or reinterpreted the "myths" that they believed misrepresented the gods, although some believed that myths could be used to illustrate truths. *Philo, *Josephus and other Jews argued that their Scriptures contained no myths; but extrabiblical elaborations of biblical accounts were common, and Paul probably has them in view here (cf. Tit 1:14). "Genealogies" might refer to expansions of biblical genealogies, as in some Jewish works from this period, or perhaps false postbiblical attributions of ancestry. The phrase "myths and genealogies" had been used pejoratively from Plato on.

1:5. Greek literature also praises a "good conscience"; the *Old Testament extols a "pure heart" (Ps 24:4; 73:1, 13).

1:6. Both Judaism and the philosophers condemned empty, worthless talk, including arguments about words and the verbal skills of wordy *rhetoricians unconcerned with truth. Some groups of philosophers from Protagoras on emphasized verbal quibbling more than seeking truth, regarding the latter as inaccessible; but most philosophers criticized these agnostics. Many professional speakers also valued important speeches above subtle disputes over trivialities, although training in public speaking included extemporaneous speeches on randomly assigned topics.

1:7. Although segments of Palestinian Judaism had standards for accredited teachers of the *law, there was nothing legally to keep anyone from claiming to be a teacher of the Bible, any more than there is in many Christian circles today. A perusal of the Gospels indicates that Jesus had conflicts even with those who were publicly recognized as teachers of the law.

1:8-9. Philosophers believed that wise people did not need laws, because their wise behavior itself modeled the moral truth on which laws were based. For Paul, this ideal was true for Christians; laws were necessary only to restrain those who were inclined to sin. Like many ancient authors, he includes a "vice list" to catalog the sorts of sins he means (1:9-10). Most of these were obvious as sins to ancient readers: for instance, killers of fathers and mothers were considered the most evil of sinners and executed in horrible ways under Roman law (sewn into a bag with animals, including a snake, and drowned).

1:10. On "homosexuals" (NASB; "perverts"—NIV) see comment on 1 Corinthians 6:9-10. "Kidnappers" (NASB, TEV) were "slave traders" (NIV, NRSV; this was the purpose for which people were kidnapped—cf. Ex 21:16; Deut 24:7); Paul's remark directly assaults the vicious slave trade of his day. Many kidnappers sought children to make them male and female slave prostitutes. Perjury was a special form of lying that involved the violation of a divine oath. *Stoics and others described reasonable teaching as "sound" (healthy, wholesome).

1:11. Only the "faithful" (1:12) were to be entrusted with money, tasks as messengers and so forth.

1:12-17
A Blasphemer's Conversion

Having condemned the false teachers (1:4-11), Paul nevertheless does not want to portray them as beyond hope; although blasphemers were to be excluded from *church fellowship (1:20), Paul himself had been a blasphemer but was converted.

1:12. Paul's letters to churches usually open with a thanksgiving for his readers (so also 2 Tim 1:3); these were common in ancient letters. Paul similarly praises God here (concluding in 1:17). This is not, however, Paul's regular epistolary thanksgiving, which would have normally occurred after the introduction (1:1-2). Perhaps he sticks mainly to official business because this is an official letter meant to authorize Timothy.

1:13-15. Jewish texts condemn blasphemers to hell (*Gehenna). Although ignorance never absolved one of guilt in Judaism, it did decrease one's guilt; in Jewish texts, this was even true of the *Gentiles, who had some, but only very limited, knowledge about God.

1:16. Both Jewish and Greco-Roman teachers used examples to make their points. Sometimes they used themselves as examples, and occasionally (though rarely) described negative aspects of their past (e.g., Rabbi *Akiba on his conversion to love of the *law; many philosophers despised their past before their conversion to philosophy).

1:17. In praising a deity, Greeks and sometimes Jews would list his or her titles and attributes. Jewish texts unanimously affirm everything Paul says about God in this verse; that God was the "only" God was the view of Judaism and a small portion of Greco-Roman society. Most people believed in all gods equally, so the Jewish and Christian view could sound intolerant to outsiders. "Amen" concluded prayers and praises in the *synagogues, indicating the assent of the other hearers. In context (1:16), this description might refer to Jesus, but this is not clear.

1:18-20
Removing a Blasphemer

1:18. Philosophers and moralists used battle imagery to describe their labor on behalf of truth. Claims of *prophecies were a rare (and sometimes marginalized) phenomenon in Judaism but were apparently common in early Christianity; prophecies to Timothy at his ordination (4:14) would thus be very meaningful.

1:19. Philosophers also used the image of shipwrecks; Christians needed to be good spiritual sailors as well as good soldiers (1:18).

1:20. Official *synagogue excommunication seems to have included a curse or execration against the person being banned from the community; it was meant to be equivalent to capital punishment under the *Old Testament law. By handing these blasphemers over to *Satan, Paul is simply acknowledging the sphere they had already chosen to enter (5:15). Paul's purpose here is restorative, however, "so that they might be taught not to blaspheme" (NASB), as God had taught Paul (1:13). See comment on 1 Corinthians 5:5. On Hymenaeus's views (Hymenaeus is not a common name, so it is no doubt the same one), see comment on 2 Timothy 2:17-18.

2:1-7
Public Prayers for All

2:1-4. The Romans permitted subject peoples to worship their own gods, but they had to show their loyalty to Rome by also worshiping the goddess Roma and the spirit of the emperor. Because Jewish people worshiped one God to the exclusion of all others, Rome allowed them to pray and sacrifice *for* the emperor's health without praying and sacrificing *to* him. Prayers were offered for him regularly in the *synagogues, showing the loyalty of these Jewish institutions to the Roman state. When the *Zealots decided to throw off the Roman yoke "for God," however, they abolished the sacrifices in the temple. This act in A.D. 66 constituted a virtual declaration of war against Rome, several years after Paul wrote this letter. Christian public prayers for the emperor and provincial and local officials showed Christians as good citizens of the society in which they lived (Jer 29:7). Paul's motive is more than keeping peace (1 Tim 2:2); it is also to proclaim the *gospel (2:3-4).

2:5-7. Both *Christ's mission and Paul's mission testified to God's purpose, his wish to save all. In Judaism, wisdom, the *law or, in a lesser sense, Moses was thought to have mediated divine revelation, but it was ultimately effective only for Israel, not for the *Gentiles. Most Gentiles believed in many mediators of revelation, just as they believed in many gods.

2:8-15
Proper Demeanor for Public Worship

Paul addresses women (2:9-15) in considerably more detail than men here, apparently because women are erring more severely in this congregation. Their culturally inappropriate behavior can bring reproach against the *gospel (something Christians could ill afford—5:14).

2:8. Apparently men were bringing their dissensions (1:6) into public worship; although "anger and disputing" (NIV) were bad in general, Paul addresses the men here because they were the ones engaged in these sins. Hands were normally lifted or outstretched for both praise and supplication in the *Old Testament, Judaism, the ancient Near East and the Greco-Roman world. *Diaspora Jews usually washed their hands before prayer, so "pure [or holy] hands" became a natural image for genuine worship (cf. also Ps 24:4).

2:9. Whereas many men in the Christian community were quarreling (2:8), many women appear to have been violating a different matter of propriety in public prayer: seeking to turn others' heads. Most Jewish teachers allowed wives to adorn themselves for their husbands, but both Jewish and Greco-Roman moralists ridiculed women who decked themselves out to turn other men's eyes. Jewish writings warn especially of the sexual temptation involved in such adornments; Greco-Roman writers also condemn wealthy women who show off their costly array. Hair was sometimes braided with gold, which Paul might have in view here; men were especially attracted by women's decorated hair. Like most other writers who condemned such gaudiness, Paul should be understood as attacking excess, not as ruling against all adornment.

2:10. Greco-Roman moralists often stressed that it was inward adornment rather than outward adornment that would please a good husband; Paul concurs. See also 1 Peter 3:3-4.

2:11. The proper way for any novice to learn was submissively and "quietly" (a closely related Greek term appears in 2:2 for all believers). Women were less likely to be literate than men, were trained in philosophy far less often than men, were trained in *rhetoric almost never, and in Judaism were far less likely to be educated in the *law. Given the bias against instructing women in the law, it is Paul's advocacy of their learning the law, not his recognition that they started as novices and so had to learn quietly, that was radical and countercultural. (In the second century, Beruriah, wife of Rabbi Meir, was instructed in the law, but she was a rare exception. Women could hear expositions at the *synagogues and did sometimes attend rabbinic lectures, but the vast majority of *rabbis would never accept them as *disciples, and *Hellenistically oriented Jews like *Josephus and *Philo were even more biased against them than the rabbis were. There is evidence for a few women filling higher roles in *Diaspora synagogues, in local cultures where women had higher social positions, but the same evidence shows that even there prominent women in synagogues were the rare exception rather than the rule.)

2:12. Given women's lack of training in the Scriptures (see comment on 2:11), the heresy spreading in the Ephesian *churches through ignorant teachers (1:4-7), and the false teachers' exploitation of these women's lack of knowledge to spread their errors (5:13; 2 Tim 3:6), Paul's prohibition here makes good sense. His short-range solution is that these women should not teach; his long-range solution is "let them learn" (2:11). The situation might be different after the women had been instructed (2:11; cf. Rom 16:1-4, 7; Phil 4:2-3). See comment on 5:14.

2:13. Paul argues for women's subordination in pastoral roles on the basis of the order of creation, the same way he argued for women wearing head coverings (1 Cor 11:7-12). Some writers take his argument here as universal, for all circumstances, even though that is not the most natural reading of the Genesis text to which he alludes (Gen 2:18 in Hebrew suggests a complementary partner). Other writers take Paul's statement here only as an ad hoc comparison (see comment on 2:14), as most writers take his same argument for head coverings in 1 Corinthians 11.

2:14. Paul refers to the account of Eve's fall as it is told in Genesis 3, although some later Jewish stories increased Eve's guilt or deception considerably beyond that account. That he compares the unlearned women of the Ephesian *church with Eve is clear; his earlier letters also compare the whole church of Corinth, both men and women, with Eve (2 Cor 11:3), the Corinthian church with Israel (1 Cor 10:1-22) and his opponents in Galatia with Ishmael (Gal 4:24-25). That he would actually apply this illustration to all women in all times, as some have thought, is less likely (if he did, he would be implying that all women are more easily deceived than men, and his illustration in 2 Cor 11:3 would lose its force; moreover, the local false teachers themselves were men—

1 Tim 1:20; 2 Tim 2:17).

2:15. Some scholars have argued that "saved" is meant theologically: Christian women will have *eternal life if they live godly lives, which includes following cultural propriety for the sake of the *gospel's witness. Paul probably means "saved" or "delivered" in a different sense, however—the sense it was usually given when related to childbearing. Women normally prayed to particular gods to "save" them, which meant bringing them safely through childbirth. (The curse on Eve came to be associated with death in childbirth in some parts of Judaism, so Paul might be qualifying his comparison in 2:13-14. In this case, he would be noting that Christian women are not daughters of Eve in every sense, thus implying that his illustration in 2:13-14 should not be pressed beyond the service for which he employed it.)

3:1-7
Qualifications for Overseers

Lists of qualifications for offices appear in both Jewish and *Gentile sources; lists of virtues appropriate to such offices are even more common. These lists were applied both to political or military offices and religious ones (e.g., judges in Jewish sources). Exceptions were not stated in general lists of qualifications but might be made in extenuating circumstances. The term translated "overseer" (NIV, NASB) or "bishop" (KJV, NRSV) was elsewhere in use in the ancient world for leaders, and Paul uses it synonymously with "elders" (Tit 1:5, 7), a leadership title used in *synagogues.

3:1. Many moralists urged any worthy men to become statesmen. Certain officials in the Greek world, in both cities and associations, were naturally called "overseers." The *Dead Sea Scrolls also use the Hebrew equivalent of the term for an office of leadership at *Qumran; here it is probably equivalent to the synagogue leaders responsible for the synagogue service. This office is identified with that of elders in the *Pastoral Epistles (Tit 1:5, 7), a situation that had changed by the early second century (Ignatius *Letter to the Trallians* 3) but that still obtained in Paul's day (Phil 1:1; cf. Acts 20:17, 28).

3:2-3. The office of overseer was open to all, but some qualifications needed to be observed, especially in view of the heresy in Ephesus. The qualification of being "above reproach" frames the other qualifications (3:2, 7); this was an ancient way of emphasizing that the qualifications focused on this issue. Political leaders were also expected to be "above reproach," but a persecuted minority sect needed to protect itself against public slander even more than politicians did.

Polygamy was not practiced in the Roman world outside Palestine, though illegal bigamy and certainly adultery were. "Husband of one wife" no doubt means a faithful husband and presupposes marriage; such a man would be helpful in standing against the false teachers who opposed marriage (4:3). (The injunction that married leaders be used would not apply to all situations; cf. comment on 1 Cor 7:8.) "Husband of one wife" refers to one's current marital status and behavior; validly divorced people who remarried were considered married to one spouse, the second one, not to two spouses.

"Hospitality" referred literally to taking in trustworthy travelers as guests. Such hospitality was a universal virtue, but because inns in antiquity usually functioned also as brothels, Jewish people in the *Diaspora were especially willing to take in fellow Jewish travelers, as long as the travelers bore letters of recommendation certifying their trustworthiness.

3:4-5. Politicians were often evaluated by how well their children obeyed them; it had long been accepted that the family was a microcosm of society and that a leader first needed to demonstrate his leadership skills in the home. Men in Paul's day exercised a great deal of authority over their wives and children. That children's behavior reflected on their parents was a commonplace of ancient wisdom (for society's view, see also the public shame reflected in Lev 21:9; Prov 19:13; 27:11; but contrast Ezek 18:9-20 for God's view when normal means of discipline failed). This factor may have been especially important for leaders of *churches meeting in their own homes; but again, it is based on a premise of patriarchal ancient culture (where properly disciplined children usually obeyed) not directly, completely applicable to all societies.

3:6-7. Ancient leadership ideology required leaders to be tested in lower offices, to demonstrate their skills before being promoted; the church in Ephesus had existed for over a decade, hence the Ephesians could insist on more seasoned leaders than some other churches could (the requirement is missing in Titus). The ever-present danger of false accusation required leaders to do everything in their power to avoid scandal; a solid reputation was helpful for church leaders, as it was for public officials.

3:8-13
Qualifications for Deacons

Lists of qualifications were common in antiquity; see the introduction to 3:1-7.

3:8. *New Testament texts use the term translated "deacon" in several ways. It usually means a servant-minister, generally a minister of the word, like Paul. But sometimes it is an office distinguished from "overseers" (Phil 1:1) and is probably parallel to the office of the *chazan* in the *synagogue. This synagogue attendant was responsible for the synagogue building and would normally have been the owner of the home in which a house synagogue met. Unlike elders (3:2), this sort of "deacon" may have fulfilled an administrative function without much public teaching.

3:9. "Keeping hold of the deep truths of the faith" (NIV) is a critical qualification given the prevalence of heresy in the Ephesian *church (1:3-7).

3:10. A common feature of ancient political life was that leaders (or new members of groups) were often tested in lower offices before being promoted to higher ones; see comment on 3:6-7. On being "beyond reproach" (NASB) see comment on 3:2.

3:11. Scholars debate whether "women" here refers to deaconesses or to male deacons' wives, although even the Roman government was aware of Christian deaconesses (female deacons) by A.D. 112. Thus Paul either requires upright behavior on the part of *church officials' wives (in ancient society, men were often ridiculed for their wives' behavior) or explains some different requirements for women deacons. Gossip was especially associated with and probably more often practiced by women than by men in the ancient world (cf. 5:13).

3:12-13. On "husband of one wife" see comment on 3:2-3; on "managers of their children" (NASB) see comment on 3:4-5.

3:14-16
Purpose of Church Administration

3:14-15. The *church, which met in homes, was modeled on the household, just as pagan political theorists compared the household to society in general (3:4-5). Paul's prior admonitions to Timothy, especially in 3:1-13, thus serve a function analogous to the household codes of many ancient writers: providing a specific framework of wisdom for administrating the family unit and society. "Pillars" were used to uphold structures, and support for the truth was needed given its challenge by false teachers (1:3-7).

3:16. Here Paul gives the standard of faith his readers were to uphold in the form of a creed or hymn (which Timothy probably already knows). If "taken up in glory" refers to Jesus' return (cf. Dan 7:13-14) rather than to his ascension, then the lines are in chronological order; but not all scholars think this proposal likely. "Justified" or "vindicated" in the *Spirit refers to the *resurrection, God's acquittal after the human judicial condemnation of the cross.

4:1-5
Errors of the Heretics

4:1. Ancient Judaism associated the *Spirit especially with *prophecy (speaking under divine inspiration), and Paul here either prophesies or reports an earlier prophecy. ("The Spirit says" is equivalent to the *Old Testament formula "Thus says the Lord.") As a prophet himself, Paul refutes false or errant prophets (cf. 1 Cor 14:37).

Some Jewish groups (including the *Qumran community) predicted widespread apostasy in the end time, influenced by evil spirits. "Later times" probably refers to the "last days," which by the Old Testament definition were normally understood as inaugurated by Israel's *repentance and deliverance (e.g., Is 2:1; but cf. Dan 2:28; 10:14); in the *New Testament these days have begun because the *Messiah has already come.

4:2. The "branding iron" was especially used on livestock; the "searing" may thus mean that the consciences of these apostates have become the property of evil spirits.

4:3. *Asceticism was on the rise in Greco-Roman paganism, and although most teachers (both Jewish and *Gentile) advocated marriage, the doctrine of celibacy was becoming more popular (especially among Gentiles, but some *Essenes also seem to have practiced it). "Abstaining from foods" probably refers to Jewish food laws (see comment on Rom 14:1-4).

4:4-5. Jewish people always praised God before their meal; the normal blessing included praise for the God who "created" the fruit of the vine. Another blessing, possibly standardized in the early second century, was used after meals and included the statement "God is good and does good." This Jewish custom was an appropriate way to show gratitude to God for his provisions. The food was in a sense sanctified by the word of God (Gen 1:30-31) as well as by such prayer; there was thus no need to abstain from it.

4:6-16
The Importance of Sound Teaching

4:6-11. Paul alludes to the sort of physical training undertaken especially by athletes and others in the Greek *gymnasia*, where men stripped naked for exercises (v. 7). This image would have been familiar to his Greek readers, because the gymnasium was the center of civic life in *Hellenized towns. The image of physical training was extremely common in the illustrations of Greco-Roman moralists and philosophers. Like them, Paul speaks of moral, intellectual and spiritual discipline rather than physical exercise, although he is not opposed to the latter. "Nourished" (KJV, NASB, NRSV) or "brought up" (NIV) in verse 6 may anticipate this image in verses 7-8.

Philosophers commonly demeaned the tales of old women as fit only for children, and they mocked irrational views as those suited only to old women. This perspective also presupposes the illiteracy of most older women in antiquity (even those who had learned to read in youth would usually have had little subsequent practice at it). Paul takes up the current figure of speech (v. 7; but cf. 5:2).

Jewish teachers especially praised study of the *law, which was profitable "both in this world and in the world to come." Paul emphasizes the same point about spiritual discipline (v. 8).

4:12. "Elders" were highly respected in Greek *gymnasia* and exercised a ruling function in *synagogues and *churches, as they had in communities in the *Old Testament. Because Timothy joined Paul before A.D. 50 (Acts 16:1-3; men entered adulthood around puberty, so Timothy may have been in his midteens) and Paul is writing in the early sixties, Timothy is at least in his mid-twenties and could well be in his early or mid-thirties; this term for "youth" (KJV) could apply up to the age of forty, although it usually applied especially to someone under twenty-nine. But those who were not elders were often considered inappropriate for leadership positions (cf. 1 Sam 17:33), and many offices even in Judaism became available only at age forty. Most stories about the appointment of young men were made up later to extol prodigies (postbiblical stories about Daniel, Solomon or several *rabbis); Timothy's appointment was thus a rare privilege in his culture.

But even though Timothy is younger than the elders he is advising, he is to take the role of the mature leader and act as an example for the community. Teachers normally asked *disciples to imitate them, and in so doing took the role of father figures.

4:13. As in the *synagogue service (both in Palestine and in the *Diaspora), public reading of Scripture was central to the service; the reading from the Law was probably generally accompanied by one from the Prophets. The reading was then expounded (exhortation and teaching) by means of a homily on the text that had been read. (This Jewish practice [cf. Neh 8:8] would be intelligible in a Greco-Roman context; in Greco-Roman schools, children translated texts from classical Greek into vernacular Greek, then expounded them in response to questions and answers.) By the mid-second century *apostolic writings (later officially recognized as the New Testament) were being read alongside the *Old Testament in *church services. "Until I come" authorizes Timothy: his exposition of Scripture would function as the equivalent of Paul's apostolic presence.

4:14. Oracular utterances had long been used to attest the divine rights of kings and other officials, and Paul's mentioning of *prophecies about Timothy's gift (probably teaching—4:13) at his ordination could help quiet the opposition (see comment on 1:18). The approval of the "presbytery" (KJV, NASB) or "body of elders" (NIV) also could silence criticisms about his youth (4:12). Mature Jewish teachers ordained other Jewish teachers through laying hands on them; this practice served as official accreditation.

4:15-16. "Progress" (v. 15) was the standard philosophical way to describe a *disciple's advancement in moral philosophy and was naturally applied to advancement in Jewish (Gal 1:14) and

Christian (Phil 1:25) truth as well. It is clear that Timothy's attention to his teaching is critical: his teaching would affect the salvation of his hearers (v. 16; cf. 2 Tim 3:15).

5:1-2
Honoring Elders

Given the preceding context (4:14), "older man" here may refer specifically to an "elder" (the same Greek word); the use of kinship terms for officers in the church accords with the description of God's household in terms of a family (3:4-5, 15). In this case, 5:3-16 refers to female elders, a special office of older widows devoted to prayer, just as 5:17-25 applies to male elders. Interestingly, prominent individuals in *Diaspora *synagogues were often called "fathers" or "mothers" of synagogues. It is also possible that 5:1-2 is a more general statement, of which widows and elders as *church leaders represent specialized examples. In either case, Timothy must address those older than he is (4:12).

Respecting elders was a standard feature of ancient wisdom and social custom, just as respecting one's parents was; treating elders as if they were one's parents, and peers as one's brothers or sisters, was also considered praiseworthy behavior.

Developing the admonitions of Proverbs, Judaism heavily emphasized expressing concern for one's neighbor by offering and accepting correction (see both *rabbis and *Dead Sea Scrolls). But it also emphasized the necessity of private as opposed to public rebuke unless all attempts at private settlement failed.

5:3-16
Honoring True Widows

Here Paul may refer to widows in general, but he probably refers to an order of widows who served the *church, as in second-century Christianity. (Commentators disagree on this point.)

We should keep in mind that Paul addresses the values of ancient society for the sake of the church's witness (5:7, 14; 6:1), not implying that all societies should share those values (which would, for example, look down on older women who had never married—5:10).

5:3. Honoring elders was important; "honor" here includes financial support (5:4, 16-18). By "widows indeed" (KJV, NASB) or "real widows" Paul means not simply those bereaved of husband but those both committed to the church's ministry of prayer (5:5) and experiencing the stereotypical Old Testament plight of widows: destitution (5:4).

5:4. Adult children or other close relatives were expected to care for destitute widows, who had no opportunity to earn wages in ancient society. It was believed that one owed this care to one's parents for their support during youth; Paul agrees. Judaism even understood this support as part of the commandment to honor one's parents (see comment on Mk 7:9-13). (Under Roman law, a father could discard a newborn child; the child was not regarded as a person and member of the household until the father agreed to raise and support the child. This way of thinking no doubt contributed to children's recognition of responsibility to parents. Early Jews and Christians, however, unanimously opposed abortion, infanticide and throwing out babies, seeing personhood as a gift of God, not of parents.) Caring for aged parents was a matter not only of custom but of law, and was common even in Western society until recent times.

5:5. The Jewish ideal for older widows, who received support from family or distributors of charity but whose only contribution to society was prayer (no small contribution), was that they be women of prayer (cf. Lk 2:37). (This is probably unrelated to the Roman image of Vestal Virgins' prayers supporting Rome, although that image shows the ease with which the idea could have been grasped even in pagan culture.)

5:6. Here Paul probably refers to some sort of sexual immorality, perhaps becoming a mistress or indulging in lust (once remarried—5:11—a woman would not be considered a widow).

5:7. The Greco-Roman world as a whole was happy to find cause for scandals in minority and foreign religions, and libeled especially any sexual irregularities. Being "above reproach" (NASB, NRSV; also in 5:14; see comment on 3:2) is crucial for the spread of the *gospel (6:1). Although conflicting ideals about widows' remarriage existed in antiquity (see comment on 5:9, 14), all would view negatively a Christian's committing immorality or violating a *vow* of celibacy (cf. comment on 5:11-12).

5:8. Even pagans believed in supporting destitute widows who were relatives; it was believed that one owed support to one's aged parents (cf. comment on 5:4).

5:9. The expression "put on the list" was often used of official registrations (e.g., for troops). "Sixty" was a Jewish figure for the beginning of old age (see comment on Lk 1:7). Some scholars think that the "wife of one man" may allude to the ancient ideal of remaining faithful to one's former husband after death by not remarrying; but the more popular ideal in this period was remarrying quickly (cf. 1 Tim 5:14). Another use of a related term is more likely: many husbands praised wives who had been "one-man wives," meaning faithful and good wives. In view of 3:2, 12 (there was no ancient ideal that *husbands* not remarry), and 5:14, Paul must simply mean "faithful and good wives."

5:10. Ancient writers (especially Aristophanes; see comment on 4:7) sometimes ridiculed older women, though they sometimes respected them (see comment on 5:2). Paul's qualifications here are to ensure that those "on the roll" are above reproach; the popular ideal standards for women of any age included rearing or having reared children (see comment on 5:14). Providing water for washing of feet was a sign of hospitality in antiquity; the actual acts of washing someone's feet indicated the posture of a servant or a subordinate (cf. 1 Sam 25:41 and comment on Jn 13:3-8).

5:11-12. *Pharisees became upset with those who reneged on their Pharisaic vows, and the *Essenes were even more angered by those leaving their way of life; the importance that such sects attached to committed membership was reflected in the testing of candidates before their admission into full fellowship. Public departure from a commitment to the order of widows could bring about scandal; the "condemnation" (NASB, NRSV) is that of outsiders, as in 3:6-7.

5:13. Here Paul's language reflects a popular perception of uneducated women's behavior (cf. also 3:11); because of inadequate education (which Paul seeks to remedy in 2:11) and cultural expectations, idle gossip commonly characterized women's daily lives. Jewish and Greco-Roman texts alike condemn gossiping or babbling women, including widows. The *Essenes were so sensitive about their reputation that an Essene who slandered their community would be excluded from fellowship for a year.

5:14. Since the time of Augustus over half a century before, the rapid remarriage of widows became a Roman social ideal; it was also the ideal maintained by Jewish teachers.

The popular standards for a young woman, stressed in writings of philosophers and moralists, were chastity, modesty, quietness, submission and obedience to her husband, and devotion to domestic duties, including the rearing of young children. In contrast to the ideal wife of Proverbs 31, the ideal wife of Greek society was socially retiring and restricted herself mainly to the domestic sphere, the only place where she had authority. "Keep house" (NASB) is better translated "manage their homes" (NIV); although subordinate to her husband, the Greek wife otherwise "ruled" her home. Paul here upholds some societal values for the sake of the gospel's witness.

5:15. "Turning aside" (KJV, NASB) is used in the *Dead Sea Scrolls for apostasy; see comment on 1:20.

5:16. Some women were well-to-do enough to become *patrons; they had social dependents, which could include blood relatives, slaves, *freedpersons or others willing to be her *clients. By requiring well-endowed Christians to fulfill their responsibilities to family members, Paul hopes to stretch the *church budget to help those who really had no other means of support.

5:17-25
Treating Church Elders Respectfully

5:17. "Honor" sometimes included payment, and this is the case here (5:18). "Double pay" (so TEV here) was sometimes given to worthy soldiers and is probably in view here. Because elders who did not have large property holdings would otherwise be at least partly dependent on working children, Paul advocates supporting them well (this support does not imply making them wealthy, of course).

5:18. Paul argues his case both from the *Old Testament (Deut 25:4) and from the sayings of Jesus (cf. Lk 10:7). Citations from authoritative or classical texts were used to prove one's point not only in Jewish but also in other Greco-Roman literature.

5:19. Greek culture also recognized the value of witnesses for legal decisions, but the testimony of two or three was one of the most crucial requirements of Jewish law (based on Deut 17:6; 19:15). For Paul, it is the other side of being "above reproach" (3:2): accusations must be properly examined and not uncritically accepted.

5:20. Judaism strongly emphasized reproof and correction; public reproof was to be a final resort only if private attempts had failed (see comment on 5:1-2).

5:21. Calling witnesses to a charge as Paul does here made it far more authoritative; Paul chooses the ultimate witnesses for such a charge. The angels are "*elect" or "chosen" (NASB) as opposed to fallen angels. The ancient world—especially the Old Testament and Judaism (which did not automatically favor upper classes in disputes, as Roman law did)—stressed that judges must be fair.

5:22. Jewish teachers would "lay their hands" on their *disciples to "ordain" them (see comment on 4:14), and that is what Paul has in view here: ordaining an elder who had not first been tested (see comment on 3:10) made one responsible for his subsequent exposure if he turned out to be ungodly. Keeping oneself "pure" (literally) "from sin" was a *Stoic virtue as well as a Jewish one.

5:23. Most people drank wine with their meals (albeit about two parts water to one part wine, and not distilled to a higher than natural degree of fermentation). Timothy has been abstaining (apart from, we may assume, the Lord's Supper), perhaps to avoid the criticism of those influenced by the false teachers (4:3; some *ascetics abstained from wine); Paul tells him to go back to using it. Wine was often helpful in settling stomachs and preventing dysentery (it disinfected water).

5:24-25. The sins that were secret or in the heart made evaluation (5:22) difficult, as many ancient writers acknowledged.

6:1-2
Advice to Slaves

In keeping with exhortations dealing with households (3:15), Paul naturally includes advice to slaves. This advice was important because a religion that the Romans thought might incite slave discontent would immediately be labeled subversive and subjected to outright persecution; Paul wants the slaves who are Christian, as well as free Christians, to engage in a culturally relevant and intelligent witness. When Paul says that masters "benefit" from their slaves (v. 2), he employs a term especially used of wealthy benefactors who bestowed gifts on social inferiors. Thus Paul, like the philosopher *Seneca, possibly portrays the slaves as persons free in God's sight who can choose to bestow a gift on their masters by serving them freely.

6:3-10
The Heresy of Materialism

The heretics were using the *gospel to get rich; Paul says that food and clothing should be enough for a Christian (6:8), who should seek no more than his or her basic needs (cf. Mt 6:25). This greed was one reason that Paul had to prohibit materialistic persons from *church office explicitly (3:3, 8). Some pagan philosophers also used their philosophy for personal gain, and this behavior drew the hostility and criticism of outsiders.

6:3. "Sound" means "healthy"; Greek and Roman writers often used medical imagery to describe the spiritual state of people's souls or beliefs. Perhaps Paul refers here to Jesus' teachings (cf. Mt 6:19-34).

6:4. Pseudointellectuals liked to quibble about detailed nuances of words rather than deal with crucial issues; see comment on 1:6.

6:5. Jewish people often recognized wealth as a sign of God's blessing, and many teachers taught that those who served God would become more prosperous. This teaching was, however, meant as a general principle, as in Proverbs: one who works harder earns more. But these teachers also said that wealth could be used for good or evil, and many warned of the dangers of wealth, or even linked piety to poverty. A similar ambiguity is found among Greco-Roman philosophers: many said that wealth was acceptable if put to good use, but others (most obviously the *Cynics) thought that it should be rejected altogether as burdensome. The philosophers did not, however, normally see wealth as a reward for doing good. It is not clear whether Paul's opponents *preach* that godliness is a means of gain or simply *use* religion as a means of gain.

6:6. Moralists sometimes used "gain" figuratively in a contrast to material wealth. Judaism often viewed present wealth as paltry compared with the true wealth of the world to come, which really mattered. One of the most common doctrines of philosophers and those influenced by them was contentment; people should be self-sufficient, recognizing that they need nothing other than what Nature has given them.

6:7. Here Paul cites a moral commonplace, phrased similarly by *Cicero; it is also attested in the Old Testament (Job 1:21), *Diaspora Jewish literature and other Greco-Roman writers.

6:8. Ancient literature usually recognized "food and clothing" as the basic needs, which even *Cynics and the poorest of peasants required (Cynics and most peasants had only one cloak each). On "contentment" see comment on 6:6 and Philippians 4:11.

6:9. Middle-class North Americans understand "rich" much differently from the way Paul's first readers would have; in the widespread poverty of the ancient Mediterranean, most people would have viewed the lifestyle of middle-class North Americans as "rich." Like many writers of his day, Paul addresses those seeking to accumulate wealth (cf. Prov 28:20) rather than those who had already become wealthy through inheritance or industry (6:17).

6:10. Paul cites here a widely used ancient proverb about loving money being the source of various evils. The idea was even more common than the saying, but the saying itself circulated among philosophers and those who respected them.

6:11-16
Fleeing the Evil Lifestyle

In contrast to the greedy preachers (6:3-10), Timothy is to seek righteousness.

6:11. Moralists often exhorted readers to "flee" from vices. Ancient Hittites used the expression "man of God" to describe religious figures, and the *Old Testament used it for men commissioned by God to function as his spokespersons. Its rare occurrences in subsequent Jewish literature are probably dependent on the Old Testament usage, as is Paul's use here.

6:12. Greco-Roman moralists often described moral struggles in terms of warfare, as did Jewish texts influenced by them (e.g., *4 Maccabees, where it refers to martyrdom). The image in the Greek here is not that of a war, however, but of another image the moralists equally exploited in a figurative manner: the wrestling match or athletic contest.

6:13. A charge with gods as witnesses was considered especially binding.

6:14. "Without stain or reproach" (NASB) may allude to the requirements for pure sacrifices to God as unblemished (e.g., Lev 1:3, 10; 3:1, 6; 4:3, 23, 32) or to "undamaged" merchandise and so forth; it was a natural image for virtual perfection. On "without reproach" see comment on 3:2. "Appearing" was sometimes used in Greek religion for manifestations of gods, but it would be a natural Jewish description in Greek for the revelation of God at the end time.

6:15. Jewish literature repeatedly described God as king. Rulers who claimed to be supreme kings, such as the Babylonian or the Parthian king, called themselves "king of kings and lord of lords." Greek writers like Dio Chrysostom occasionally applied the title to Zeus; Judaism quite often applied it to God, and Christians applied it to Jesus (cf. Rev 19:16).

6:16. "The Immortal" was a common title for God in *Hellenistic Judaism (borrowed from the Greek term for their own gods, which Jews and Christians recognized as an inappropriate epithet for them; thus Paul adds "who alone"). Jewish texts often mentioned the glory of light around God's throne; kings' great authority made them unapproachable for common people. The

*Old Testament declared that no one could see God's full glory and live (Ex 33:20), and later Judaism amplified this recognition (although some Jewish mystics, expanding the visions of the throne in Ezek 1 and Is 6, claimed to have penetrated the splendor around the throne and seen something of God).

6:17-19 Instructions for Those Who Are Rich

In 6:3-10 Paul condemned those who were seeking wealth, but in 6:17-19 he addresses those who are already wealthy. For Paul, wealth and property are not sinful in themselves, provided that one is not seeking them. Wealth can be used for good or for evil, for selfish or for beneficent causes; Paul says that Christians must use it for good.

6:17-18. The very wealthy usually derived their income from landowning; they rented out the land to tenant farmers or residents, or derived profits from crops grown on the land. A socially inferior but nonetheless wealthy class of merchants also arose, especially of ship owners. Wealth could be gotten by a variety of means, not all of them immoral.

The issue was not whether one had wealth but whether one used it for oneself or for others. This was the usual view in Judaism, which stressed charity, and a view held by many philosophers. Paul does not reject the world, as the *Cynics or (in the most extreme sense) later *Gnostics did; with Judaism, he affirms that creation itself is good (4:4-5). But he also recognizes that material wealth is transitory. Still more important, people matter more than possessions, and in a world of unending human need, possessions were ultimately worthless compared with more important things one could do with one's resources.

6:19. Jewish texts sometimes spoke of storing up treasures in heaven; see comment on Matthew 6:20-21.

6:20-21 Final Exhortation

"Entrusted" is the language of keeping a deposit; those with whom money was deposited were under sacred obligation to keep it secure or increase it, and this principle applied also to teaching (to which the image was extended by other ancient writers as well). Some scholars have seen the "false knowledge" here as a reference to *Gnosticism (which could indicate a date for the *Pastoral Epistles later than Paul), but this interpretation is unnecessary; many philosophers made claims to "knowledge," which other philosophers considered false.

2 TIMOTHY

Introduction

Authorship, Commentaries. See the introduction to 1 Timothy. Of the three *Pastoral Epistles (whose authorship is often disputed), 2 Timothy is the most difficult to dispute, because of the abundance of personal notes. *Pseudepigraphic letters could also contain personal notes (e.g., Diogenes' letter to Rhesus), but they rarely had many, whereas 2 Timothy is full of them. Pseudepigraphers had little reason to include these details.
Situation. For the general situation of persecution in Rome, see the introduction to 1 Peter. Assuming Pauline authorship, Paul writes 2 Timothy while imprisoned in Rome, awaiting probable execution; he wants Timothy to join him before it is too late (4:21). Paul was probably released after his imprisonment in Acts 28 (see comment on Acts 28:30) and undertook the missions presupposed in 2 Timothy; then he was rearrested, this time during Nero's massive repression of Christians. He was most likely beheaded under Nero in A.D. 64.

Paul's opponents have spread in the province of Asia, and the situation has become much worse since Paul wrote 1 Timothy (2 Tim 1:15). Paul could be discouraged; like Jeremiah in the *Old Testament, his life is to end while God's people are turned away from him, and he will not live to see the fruit of his ministry. His consolation, however, is that he has been faithful to God (4:7-8), and he exhorts Timothy to follow in his paths no matter what the cost. (That the letter was preserved almost certainly indicates that Timothy did persevere.) The letter is dominated by the themes of persecution from outside the *church and false teaching within, and Paul's final exhortation to a young minister is to focus on the Scriptures and the sound teaching to be found in them.

Genre. In many ways, Paul's final letter resembles the letters of moral exhortation written by philosophers to their *disciples. But as a letter sent before his death, it also resembles Jewish tracts called "testaments," in which a dying leader imparted his final wisdom to his sons or followers, wisdom also of value to subsequent readers. Although most testaments were pseudepigraphic and Paul may have written this letter only for Timothy, the similar situation envisioned gives 2 Timothy the force of a testament: Paul's ultimate wisdom for young ministers.

1:1-7
Introduction and Thanksgiving

1:1-2. Paul modifies the normal opening of letters (author, to addressees, greetings—a word related to "*grace") in his characteristically Christian way. Both *rabbis and philosophers could call their *disciples "sons."

1:3. Ancient letters frequently included thanksgivings to God or gods on behalf of the addressee, who was often praised in the thanksgiving. "Unceasingly" or "constantly" probably means in Paul's regular times of prayer. Many Palestinian Jews prayed during the morning and afternoon offerings in the temple; they also said special blessings on rising in the morning and going to bed at night. Palestinian Jews reckoned days from sundown to sundown, so "night and day" is not an unnatural sequence. (One should not read too much into Paul's sequence, of course; the same sequence occurs not only in Jewish texts like Judith and *4 Ezra but also in strictly Latin texts like Horace, *Quintilian and *Cicero. In contrast, *Josephus and usually the *Septuagint, as well as the Roman writer Martial, could say "day and night," and the *New Testament references are not consistent. "Night and day" seems to have been the more common idiom.)

1:4. Expressions of longing were common in ancient letters of friendship, signifying the deepest intimacy. (This is not, as one commentator thought, a poor imitation of Rom 1:11 or other passages!) In the East, tears were an appropriate expression of sadness for troubled or long partings.

1:5. Even though fathers were responsible for their sons' education, Judaism and Greco-Roman aristocrats wanted mothers to be knowledgeable so they could impart knowledge to their young children. (This is true even though Judaism did not provide women advanced education in the *law, and even though Greco-Roman society generally reserved *rhetorical and philosophical training for men.) Until the age of seven a Roman boy's mother was his main formative influence; many thought that children should not be taught reading until age seven, but others wished to begin it much earlier, even at the age of three. Jewish Scripture education began by the age of five or six, although this education always emphasized memorization and recitation more than reading skills.

The "faith" of Timothy's mother and grandmother was Jewish (Jewish Christian by the time Paul met them—Acts 16:1). Jewish fathers were primarily responsible for their son's instruction in the law, but Timothy's father was a *Gentile (Acts 16:1, 3). Those without a living religious father also learned from grandmothers if they were still living (cf. Tobit 1:8).

Most education included corporal discipline, but some ancient education experts stressed instead encouraging the child, making him or her feel successful, provoking competition and making learning enjoyable (*Quintilian). Ancient writers differed on whether public instructors or home schooling was better, provided the former held classes small enough to permit private instruction.

1:6. Laying on of hands was used for ordination (see comment on 1 Tim 4:14). The image of "rekindling" (NRSV) a fire is possible in this verse (cf. Jer 20:9), although the word for "kindle" (NASB) had been extended metaphorically so often by this period that it is not clear that its fire nuance would always be in hearers' minds.

1:7. Although *Essene texts sometimes linked evil behaviors with pervasive evil spirits, in Greek "spirit of" often meant simply "attitude of." The exhortation not to be afraid was one of the most prominent biblical assurances from God (e.g., Gen 26:24; Jer 1:8) and was a customary expression of assurance from others as well (Gen 43:23). Although Timothy may have been "timid," one should not therefore assume that this was his unique problem, as some interpreters have (Acts 18:9; 1 Cor 2:3).

1:8-14
Carry on Paul's Mission

Timothy is to maintain his ground (1:3-7), joining Paul in suffering for the *gospel entrusted to them.

1:8. *Disciples were called to follow in their teachers' steps. Paul's suffering here entails especially his imprisonment and impending execution.

1:9-11. The language of "calling" is especially *Old Testament and Jewish, that of "appearing" and "immortality" especially Greek (though long before already adopted by *Diaspora Jews), and "*Savior" was both. That Paul is equally conversant in both worlds is not surprising; most *Diaspora and many Palestinian Jews generally saw no contradiction between fidelity to the Old Testament and speaking the language of their culture.

1:12-14. The "entrusted deposit" (1:12, 14) was originally a monetary image, although other writers had also applied it to teaching; one was responsible to safeguard or multiply any money given one for safekeeping. Jewish teachers felt that they were passing on a sacred deposit to their disciples, who were expected to pass it on to others in turn (cf. 2:2).

1:15-18
Allies and Opponents in Asia

Paul briefly addresses the opposition that Timothy and he face in Asia, where Timothy ministers.

1:15. "Asia" refers to the Roman province of western Asia Minor, of which Ephesus was the most prominent city (cf. 1 Tim 1:3). "All" excludes the household of 1:16-18; in accordance with the flexibility of common language in antiquity, it means "most." Although many Jewish teachers predicted widespread apostasy for the end time or even felt that it characterized their own generation, they lamented it. This is hardly the sort of detail a later *pseudepigrapher writing in Paul's name would have made up about the end of his ministry. (Later *hagiographers sometimes described the rejection of their heroes, but the *narrative was normally accompanied by a description of the awful judgment that befell the apostates who rejected them.)

1:16. "Onesimus" (Philem 10) could be a contraction for Onesiphorus, but the person Paul describes here is hardly a recently freed slave. Because Paul speaks of a whole "household" of believers, the Onesiphorus to whom he refers probably had slaves and other dependents. "Refresh" is the language of hospitality, which included housing travelers; Onesiphorus must have had a large home and housed Paul whenever he came to Ephesus. He is a good example to Timothy of one not "ashamed" (1:8, 12; 2:15).

1:17. Very many people in the first century traveled to Rome; Onesiphorus, as a well-to-do *patron in the prominent Asian city of Ephesus, would naturally be able to do so. "Finding" Paul would mainly be a matter of finding local Christians who could tell him where to find Paul, whether during his earlier detention (Act 28:30) or the more severe current one. If the latter is in view, Paul might have gotten his news about Asia (1:15) from Onesiphorus.

1:18. Because Paul greets Onesiphorus's "household" in 4:19, some writers have argued that Onesiphorus is dead and that Paul here prays for his posthumous salvation (although the context makes it clear that Onesiphorus was already a Christian). Judaism often spoke of departed heroes as "of blessed memory," and some later tomb inscriptions eulogized the righteous dead with "May he [or she] be remembered for good." Posthumous acts of *atonement were sometimes offered for the dead, but prayers for the "salvation" of the dead in the strict sense seem to be either minimal or altogether lacking in first-century Judaism. Further, it is not clear that Onesiphorus is dead; Paul looks ahead to the day of judgment for himself as well (1:12; 4:8). Paul could speak of someone's "household," including the individual, while the person was still alive (e.g., 1 Cor 16:15, 17).

2:1-13
Persevere

2:1-2. *Pharisaism strongly emphasized the passing on of sacred traditions; second-century *rabbis stressed the passing on of traditions from one generation to the next, noting that the process had begun long before them. This passing on of tradition was also the practice of Greek philosophical schools, although they usually emphasized the views of the founder more than those of immediate predecessors.

2:3-4. Philosophers emphasized the total commitment involved in being a true philosopher. They also compared their task to that of soldiers and athletes fighting a war or running a race. Soldiers were not even allowed to marry during their term of service (although some had unofficial concubines while they were stationed somewhere) and were to be strictly devoted to their service for over twenty years; only about half survived to retire.

2:5. Philosophers often compared their task to that of athletes, whose intense discipline and preparation were proverbial. Athletes were pledged by oath to ten months of such preparation preceding their participation in the Olympic games. The winner's prize was a garland; see comment on 1 Corinthians 9:24-25.

2:6. As in 2:4 (pleasing the enlister) and 2:5 (receiving the prize), the emphasis here is on both hard work and future reward; one who labored for God would be rewarded in the day of God's judgment. (Some commentators have suggested that in 2:4-6 Paul wants ministers to be supported only by their congregations, as some philosophers were supported by *patrons, and never to work on the side; but this view would be surprising given Paul's explicitly contrary position in 1 Cor 9, where he allows both forms of support.)

2:7. Authors occasionally exhorted readers to "consider" (KJV, NASB) and hence understand (cf. Mt 24:15; Rev 13:18).

2:8. Appealing to examples was one of the main hortatory methods of ancient parenesis (moral exhortation); Paul here appeals to the example of Jesus, who endured much but received eternal glory (cf. 2:10-12).

2:9-10. Paul uses himself as an example, also a common form of moral exhortation among ancient philosophers and moral writers (cf. 2:8).

2:11-13. Although God's character is immutable, his dealings with people depend on their response to him (2 Chron 15:2; Ps 18:25-27). The faithfulness of God to his covenant is not suspended by the breach of that covenant by the unfaithful; but those individuals who break his covenant are not saved (see comment on Rom 3:3).

2:14-26
Persevering Versus Heretical Vessels

The Ephesian Christians must observe "these things," which are what Paul mentions in 2:3-13 as summarized in 2:11-13. They must persevere, avoiding the false teachings rampant in Ephesus (2:14-23), and when possible correcting those involved in serious error (2:24-26).

2:14. Many professional speakers gave nitpicky attention to irrelevant twists and turns of phrase; some philosophers believed that one could do no better than examine the logic of words; many Jewish teachers, seeking to be faithful to the letter of the *law, did the same (emphasizing even the slightest variations in spelling or possible revocalizations). But others criticized this method (see comment on 1 Tim 1:6).

2:15. To the images of soldier, athlete and farmer (2:4-6), Paul now adds the general one of the worker, perhaps thinking of his own background as a skilled artisan. Jewish readers would have understood an exhortation to be diligent in representing "the word of truth" rightly as an exhortation to study God's law, where his word was found (cf. Ps 119:43). Although Paul presupposes such investigation of Scripture (3:14-17), his emphasis here is on accurate representation of the *gospel in contrast to the empty words of 2:14 and 16.

2:16. See comment on 2:14.

2:17. The image of spiritual or moral gangrene also occurred to some other authors; gangrene's basic characteristic is that it spreads and poisons the whole body, ultimately killing it if it is not removed. Hymenaeus and probably Philetus had been officially cut off (1 Tim 1:20) but still retained a pervasive influence and probably a significant following. Then, as today, it was easy for almost any speaker to get a hearing, because only a few were skilled enough in the Scriptures to discern truth from error for themselves, rather than being dependent on others' teachings.

2:18. A future *resurrection of the body did not appeal to Greek thought, although the proleptic spiritual resurrection that believers experienced in Christ was far more amenable to Greek tastes. Some false teachers like Hymenaeus and Philetus had apparently "demythologized" the *gospel to make it more palatable to their culture (cf. 1 Cor 15:12; 2 Thess 2:2).

2:19. Although some stones might be removed, a foundation or cornerstone would remain secure. Seals were often used to attest the witnesses of a document or that merchandise had not been tampered with; here the seal is the inscription on a cornerstone, inscribed by the owner or builder.

2:20-21. Paul shifts to another image. When used figuratively in ancient literature, "vessels" (KJV, NASB) usually meant people (or their bodies as containers of their souls, which would be irrelevant here). Expensive vessels were reserved for special purposes like banquets; the cheapest vessels were expendable and in Jewish circles would be shattered if rendered impure.

One could interpret "purifies himself from these things" (NASB) in two ways. On the one hand, Paul may distinguish here the righteous from the wicked (as in Rom 9:22-23); but the righteous, like vessels reserved for honor, had to be separated from the vessels for dishonor in the same house (see comment on 2:17-18). On the other hand, one normally purified important vessels from dirt or, in the religious sense, from defilement (such as the heretics' talk—2:16). (Paul may intend both senses; under some conditions of Jewish law, a pure vessel brought into contact with something impure, including an impure vessel, had to be purified again.)

2:22. Moralists often exhorted readers to "flee" from vices. Certain passions were associated especially with "youth" (a category that could still include Timothy; see comment on 1 Tim 4:12).

2:23. On debates over trifling points see comment on 2:14.

2:24. Jewish teachers and philosophers like the *Stoics also advised patience in instructing others; in contrast, some moralists, like the *Cynics, verbally abused passersby with their "wisdom." Philosophers typically derided the unlearned (cf. 2:23; "ignorant"—NASB, TEV; "stupid"—NIV) in wisdom who were unwilling to seek knowledge.

2:25-26. Judaism emphasized correcting another person humbly and privately before giving public reproof, in the hope of restoring that person to the right way.

3:1-13
The Wickedness of the Last Days

Judaism generally characterized the end time as one of turmoil, apostasy, and increased sin and oppression. This view was widespread despite the common expectation that all Israel would return to greater standards of holiness, ushering in the end and the restoration of Israel; others (see the *Dead Sea Scrolls) believed that only the righteous Israelites would remain after these judgments. Like most Jewish writers, Paul does not anticipate a complete renewal of righteousness in the world until the day of God.

3:1. In "last days" Paul includes the time in which he is living (cf. 1 Tim 4:1); he no doubt alludes here to the Jewish idea that came to be called the *messianic woes, a period of great suffering preceding the end of the age. (The length of this period varied as widely as those Jewish texts that speculated on it; it was not fixed in Jewish tradition.)

3:2. Other ancient moralists also used "vice lists" (cf. Rom 1:28-32). "Lovers of self" (i.e., self-seeking people) were condemned by philosophers such as Musonius Rufus (a Stoic), *Epictetus and *Philo; the moralist *Plutarch warned readers to avoid even the appearance of self-love. Love and obedience toward parents was one of the most central virtues of antiquity (see comment on Eph 6:1-3).

3:3-4. Philo and other philosophers, especially *Stoics, repeatedly condemned "love of pleasure"; among philosophers, only the *Epicureans sought pleasure (which they defined as the absence of pain or disturbance), and they were not very influential. Philo even subsumed a long list of vices under the title "lovers of pleasure" and opposed pleasure to virtue.

3:5. Both Jewish religion and Greek philosophy condemned those who pretended devotion but whose hearts or lives did not match their professed devotion. For Paul, religion without God's power transforming the heart was useless.

3:6. Because women were usually uneducated, they were more susceptible than men to false teaching (see comment on 1 Tim 2:11-12). Women's penchant for switching religions was ridiculed by satirists like *Juvenal and offended conservative Romans. Women reportedly converted to Christianity, Judaism, and the cults of Isis, Serapis and other deities far more readily than men; and in the second century A.D. women were attracted to many heretical movements. Because they were less educated in traditional religion and had less social standing to lose, they more quickly changed religiously, sometimes for good and sometimes for bad.

The false teachers had to get into the homes because they had less access to the women in public (due to married women's partial segregation in Greek society). After they had gained access to a household, their male or female convert within the household could supply financial and other help to them. Greek and Roman men often thought of women as easily swayed by passion and emotion; many may have been, because of their lack of education and cultural reinforcement. But Paul here addresses particular, not all, women.

3:7. Philosophers stressed that change came through knowing the truth, and that this knowledge came through learning from them. These women were learning, but they were learning falsehood designed to play on their passions; Paul says that *repentance, not mere learning, frees those thus taken captive (2:25-26).

3:8. Paul here employs Jewish tradition not found in the *Old Testament. In a widespread Jewish tradition (various elements appear in *Pseudo-Philo, the *Dead Sea Scrolls, *rabbis, etc.), Jannes and his brother Jambres were Pharaoh's magicians who opposed Moses in Exodus 7:11. Even pagan accounts (Pliny the Elder and *Apuleius) record them as magicians of Moses' time. Because Paul's opponents appeal to Jewish myths (1 Tim 1:4; 2 Tim 4:4; Tit 1:14), Paul cites such stories to fill in the names for these characters.

3:9. "Progress" (NASB, NRSV) could be a technical term for advancement in learning a particular school of teaching, but here it probably refers simply to advancement of the opponents' movement. Jannes and Jambres ultimately could not match all Moses' signs (in Exodus and in most later Jewish accounts); God would also confound this heretical movement in time (1 Tim 5:24).

3:10. *Disciples of philosophers were to follow and emulate their teachers' words and lives. Some other ancient moralists also naturally used "but you" for moral contrasts (cf. also 3:14; 4:5; 1 Tim 6:11). Timothy's knowledge of Paul's sufferings in Antioch, Iconium and Lystra (Acts 13:50—14:19) apparently dates to his family's initial exposure to the Christian message, before he began traveling with Paul (16:1-3).

3:11. See comment on Acts 13—14. Timothy was from this area of Asia Minor (Acts 16:1).

3:12. Many Jewish people expected repression from the pagans, especially in the end time, but Paul virtually *promises* persecution to every Christian truly living in a holy way (cf. Jn 15:20, etc.).

3:13. Paul clearly shares the view of much of early Judaism that the end time would be characterized by evil, with sinners proceeding from sin to sin unchecked (cf. Jer 9:3). They would ultimately be stopped only by God's final wrath (cf. Gen 6:11-13). The Greek term here rendered "impostors" or "seducers" (KJV) was often used as a pejorative title for harmful or fake magicians (cf. 3:8).

3:14-17
Equipped by the Scriptures

3:14-15. "Sacred writings" (NASB, NRSV) was also used for pagan religious writings (e.g., in the cult of Isis) but is attested in Greek-speaking Jewish sources as a name for the Bible that then existed, what we call the *Old Testament. Although there were different ways of counting the books, it is clear from the listing in *Josephus (*Apion* 1.8, 39-40) and subsequent listings that these Scriptures correspond to our Old Testament *canon. The most common recensions of the *Septuagint also appear to have included what we usually call the *Apocrypha, although neither the *rabbis nor Josephus seems to have accepted this material as part of the Bible per se.

At least in pious Palestinian Jewish homes, boys were normally taught the "sacred writings" from around the age of five; teaching Scriptures to the children was commanded in the Old Testament (Deut 6:7; cf., e.g., Ps 71:17; 78:5-7). Other peoples were often amazed at how well instructed Jewish children were in their ancestral traditions.

3:16-17. The belief in the inspiration of *prophecy and (usually in a somewhat different sense) poetry and music was widespread in Mediterranean antiquity. This belief was naturally applied to books of prophecy, and most of the Old Testament was attributed to prophets. Paul's claim for Scripture's inspiration matches Old Testament designations for the law and divine prophecies as "God's word." Like Paul, Judaism virtually universally accepted the Old Testament as God's word.

Listing examples of "every good work" (3:17), Paul employs standard terms from ancient education (3:16); "training" especially characterized Greek education (the *LXX often used the term for discipline). Reproof was especially important in Judaism, where it had to be done privately and gently first. The proper authority, source and content for any of these works was Scripture. On "man of God" (in Timothy's case; more generally, "person of God"), see comment on 1 Timothy 6:11.

4:1-8
Preach the Word

After reminding Timothy of the source of his authority, the Scriptures (in his day, the *Old Testament; see 3:14-17; cf. 1 Tim 4:13), Paul tells him to engage in the ministry for which the Scriptures are profitable (3:16—4:2).

4:1. An oath sworn by a deity or deities was considered especially binding and dangerous to break; in the same way, a charge witnessed by a deity or deities was sacred and inviolable. A broken oath would be avenged by the god whose name was violated; for Jewish people and Christians, the ultimate judgment was in the coming day of the Lord.

4:2. As virtually always in Paul, "the word" here stands for the message of Jesus, which was the divine message, like the Law and the Prophets were (3:16). Greco-Roman moralists often discussed the "appropriate" time for speech, especially frank speech; Paul says that Timothy should announce his message whether or not people are willing to listen (4:3). Although Paul adapts Greco-Roman philosophical language, the idea is also a pervasive Old Testament one; prophets had to continue speaking regardless of opposition (Ex 6:9-13; Jer 6:11; 20:8-9).

4:3. Demagogues who told people what they wanted to hear were common among politicians, public speakers and philosophers in Greco-Roman society, and false prophets in the *Old Testament (prophets who told people what they wanted to hear were usually false; cf. Jer 6:14; 8:11; Ezek 13:10, 16; Mic 3:5; see also comment on Lk 6:26). "Desiring to have one's ears tickled" means desiring to hear only what one enjoys; Lucian describes in these terms people who like to listen to slander.

4:4-5. The term translated "myths" was usually used derogatorily for false stories; see comment on 1 Timothy 1:4.

4:6. On one's life being poured out as a libation, or drink-offering, see comment on Philippians 2:17. (Some Jewish texts, especially *4 Maccabees, assign atoning—hence in some sense sacrificial—value to the deaths of martyrs; in much contemporary Jewish teaching, suffering could expiate guilt, and martyrs could turn away some of God's wrath against the people as a whole. But it is not clear that this idea is present here.)

4:7. Paul's first image is the athletic contest, probably wrestling in the arena; moralists commonly borrowed this image to describe struggles on behalf of virtue (see comment on 1 Tim 6:12). "Completed the course" refers to a race, again popular athletic imagery. "Keeping faith" was a Greek expression for loyalty, similar to a Hebrew expression meaning remaining faithful to the covenant, or in some cases, guarding the true faith (thus "*the* faith" here).

4:8. The image of the "crown" refers to the wreath given to victors in Greek races (4:7).

4:9-18
Old Acquaintances

Some friends had proved faithless, others Paul had needed to send away; but God had proved faithful all along (4:17-18).

4:9. See comment on 4:21. It was important for close friends to come by and visit a dying person a final time, and this principle applied above all else to a son, even an adopted or surrogate son (1:2). (Sons normally also buried their fathers, but the officials might be reticent to hand Paul's body over to Timothy.) It was especially important to Paul that Timothy be with him before he died; compare, for example, those friends who spent Socrates' final moments with him.

4:10. Most of Judaism contrasted this present evil age (Gal 1:4) with the age to come, often insisting that those who valued this age too much would have no part in the next one. The persecutions Paul had faced earlier in Thessalonica had probably diminished, and Demas (probably an abbreviation for Demetrius, but the name Paul always uses for him) expected to find less suffering there than he would have faced had he remained with Paul.

The motives of Crescens (a Latin name) and Titus are not criticized. "Galatia" probably means the Galatia in Asia Minor to which Paul addressed his letter "to the Galatians." (It is also possible, though less likely, that it refers to the land of the Gauls to the north, in what is now France, which was the original "Galatia." If so, this would be the only explicit reference to non-Mediterranean Europe in the *New Testament.) Titus had gone to Dalmatia, which was near Nicopolis, where he had met or tried to meet Paul earlier (Tit 3:12). If Timothy came overland to see Paul (2 Tim 4:13), he would probably pass through at least Thessalonia and Dalmatia (the latter on the Adriatic coast), and Paul gives him advance notice that he would find some of his former companions in this area.

4:11. Although "Mark" was a common name, among the limited number of close associates of Paul it almost certainly refers to John Mark of Acts, as in Colossians 4:10. Others besides Luke were with him in Rome (2 Tim 4:21), but Luke was the only traveling companion he and Timothy had shared; he was probably also the only one in Rome specifically to be with Paul.

4:12. Tychicus is bearer of the letter (cf. 1 Tim 1:3), a mutual traveling companion of Paul and Timothy (Acts 20:4; Col 4:7). Because the only Roman mail service was by imperial envoys for government use, personal mail had to be carried by travelers.

4:13. The sort of cloak mentioned was like a blanket with a hole for one's head; the ease with which it could be donned probably made it popular with travelers. It was useful only in cold or rainy weather; Paul had apparently left it at Troas when it was becoming warm and had not been able to return for it. Now, imprisoned, Paul is cold and anticipates the approach of winter soon after Timothy's arrival (cf. 4:21). (Some commentators have suggested that the term refers here not to a coat but to a wrapping for books; although this meaning is possible, most of the purported evidence for it derives from comments on this verse!)

Some commentators have suggested that the "parchments" refer to certificates (e.g., to prove Paul's citizenship), but such documents are not widely attested in this period. The term was, however, already in use for codices (collections of papyrus sheets with a cover, as opposed to scrolls), a form of book already in existence but popularized by Christians. They were originally used for notebooks, account ledgers and other nonliterary purposes; Christians quickly began using them for the Scriptures. Paul may have notebooks for Scripture study in view; the other "books" would then be papyrus scrolls, the most common form of writing in this period.

Paul apparently expects Timothy to journey northward to Troas, from which he would cross over to Macedonia and take the main Roman road through Thessalonica and to Dalmatia, sailing thence to Italy (though cf. 4:21).

4:14. Many coppersmiths lived in the eastern Mediterranean, but working with copper produced so much noise that Alexander, unlike Paul the leatherworker, could not have engaged in much discussion at work. He thus could not have gained much of a following until his workday was ended (unless he was a former coppersmith now living off his false teaching).

Alexander may be the false teacher of 1 Timothy 1:19-20, although this name was common. The term Paul uses for "did me harm" was sometimes used of *delatores,* "accusers"; it is not clear whether Paul also refers to Alexander as the one who betrayed him to the Roman authorities. Paul was probably not arrested in Ephesus, because he had spent the preceding winter in Nicopolis; he may have been on his way to Rome and simply arrived in time for Nero's persecution (Tit 3:12; cf. 2 Tim 4:10).

The psalmist often prayed for God to vindicate him and repay his enemies (e.g., Ps 17:13-14; 35:1-8, 26; 55:15; 69:22-28). Paul here makes a prediction (future tense) rather than a prayer for vengeance (cf. Ps 52:5; 55:23; 63:9-10; 73:17-20; etc.); nevertheless, his point is that God will put things right on behalf of his servants in the end.

4:16. Here Paul probably refers not to the detention of Acts 28:30-31, which presumably ended favorably, but to a more recent hearing after his rearrest. This would have been a preliminary hearing, a *prima actio,* before a Roman magistrate (in practice, probably not the emperor himself).

4:17-18. Paul may allude to David's or Daniel's exploits of faith in the Old Testament (1 Sam 17:37; Dan 6:27; cf. 1 Macc 2:60); Daniel was sent to the lions by the decree of a king, albeit a reluctant one. The image of a lion in ancient literature is one of supreme strength, appropriately applied here to Nero's court. Under Nero's persecution in which Paul died, some Christians were literally fed to beasts in the arena, but Paul uses "lion" metaphorically, as often in the Old Testament (e.g., Ps 22:13, 21). The term translated "delivered" meant earthly rescue and safety (v. 17) but was also applied to ultimate salvation (v. 18). Prayers seemed natural in ancient letters, because ancient life was permeated by religious belief and practice.

4:19-22 Conclusion

4:19. Letters often closed with greetings. Aquila and Priscilla, who had left Ephesus (Acts 18:24-26) for Rome (Rom 16:3), had returned to the work in Ephesus—probably recently, because Paul did not comment on their help in 1:16-18 (contrast also 1 Tim 2:11-12 with Priscilla's ministry in Acts 18:26); only Paul's traveling companions, probably mainly single men, are mentioned in 4:10-12 and 20. On the household of Onesiphorus see comment on 1:16-18.

4:20. Letters customarily mentioned news about friends, who included these former traveling companions of Timothy (Acts 19:22; 20:4). For how Trophimus's illness might have been viewed, see comment on Philippians 2:25-30.

4:21. The seas were closed down to traffic in winter; shipping was completely closed down from around November 10 to as late as March 10, but the periods from about September 15 to November 10 and March 11 to May 26 were risky periods as well. Timothy thus could not sail from Ephesus in winter, but even if he took the overland route north of Greece, as Paul seems to expect (4:13), he would still need to sail across the Adriatic, which was also closed. If Timothy delayed, he would not be able to come until spring—and Paul might not still be alive then. Paul may have sent this letter by Tychicus in summer, leaving Timothy little time to set matters in order and come to him.

"Pudens," "Linus" and "Claudia" are Latin names. Jewish people could have Latin names ("Claudia" would fit a slave woman freed during Claudius's reign), but most Roman Jews had Greek names. Thus three out of four names' being Latin might suggest that Christianity was making inroads into new sectors of Roman society. If they are *church leaders (although only these are named, Paul appends "all the brethren" as a distinct group), the woman's name is significant. Second-century tradition declares that Linus succeeded Peter as the second bishop of Rome.

4:22. The final "you" is plural in Greek; Paul's final greeting includes Timothy's fellow servants in Ephesus (4:19).

TITUS

Introduction

Authorship, Purpose, Commentaries. See introduction to 1 Timothy. Like 1 Timothy, Paul's letter to Titus seems to function more as a letter authorizing Titus than as a personal letter only.

Situation. Paul left Titus behind in Crete to establish *church leadership in each city there (1:5). The description of the opposition (1:10-11, 14) sounds much like what Paul addressed at Ephesus in 1 Timothy, suggesting that the error addressed there is spreading rapidly among Christian congregations. Paul's old opponents, those of the circumcision group he encountered in Galatia, apparently continue to follow on his heels to "correct" his converts (1:10, 14). Although they won over many of his converts, their views eventually lost ground; but Paul did not live to see his views prevail (2 Tim 1:15).

1:1-4
Introduction

As in 1 Timothy, here Paul omits many features customary to his letters (such as thanksgiving and, less often, mention of prayer) and goes right to the point with his instructions.

1:1. Letters customarily opened with the name of the sender. It could be prestigious to be the slave in a high-status household, and the *Old Testament prophets were often called "servants of God." Judaism believed that Jewish people were chosen for salvation by virtue of their corporate participation in Israel; perhaps especially to counter false teachers in Crete (1:10), Paul applies the term to all believers in Jesus (though he usually does so anyway).

1:2-3. "*Eternal life" was literally the "life of the world to come," which (according to Jewish teaching) was to be inaugurated by the future *resurrection of the dead. That God could not lie, that he had spoken through the prophets from the beginning and that the future resurrection could be proved from the earliest parts of the Bible fit common Jewish teaching and could not be disputed by his opponents (1:10). (The *Stoics taught the immutability of divine decrees, but the Stoic form of the doctrine allowed God less freedom to interact with human will than Judaism did. By contrast, in Greek myths, deities readily deceived mortals, but such a view of divinity was rejected by the philosophers and ridiculed by Judaism.)

1:4. After naming the sender, letters named the recipient(s) and conveyed an expression of greeting. Philosophers and *rabbis spoke of their *disciples as their children; cf. 1 Timothy 1:2 and 2 Timothy 1:2.

1:5-9
Appointing Sound Elders

1:5. In the *Old Testament, cities were ruled and judged by their "elders," those with the greatest wisdom and experience in the community. By the *New Testament period, prominent older men in the *synagogues were called "elders." Paul followed the convenient, conventional forms of synagogue leadership in his culture rather than instituting entirely foreign leadership structures. "In every city" meant that the different house *churches in each city would each have their own leaders. Like much of old Greece, Crete had long been known for intercity rivalry.

1:6. The requirement for being "above reproach" (NASB) was vital for leaders in antiquity (see comment on 1 Tim 3:2). "Husband of one wife" probably meant "a faithful husband"; like the requirement about the children, this one suggests that he be a family man and a leader in his household. These were necessary aspects of being respectable in antiquity and were qualities often examined with regard to suitability for public office. (The *Old Testament also emphasized filial obedience under normal conditions; cf. Deut 21:20.) Because they are "elders," and "dissipation" (NASB; the term means wasting money, often on selfish pleasures like drunkenness) was a vice stereotypically attributed to young men, not children, these elders are apparently held responsible for the behavior of their adult children. In the Roman world, sons were to respect their fathers, who had legal authority to rule their sons as long as they lived.

1:7. "Stewards" were household managers, often slaves or *freedmen, accountable to the master for how they handled his property; this term fits particularly well the image of leaders of household churches. The drunken worship of Dionysus was known on Crete, and the Christian leaders' behavior must not be confused with it in any way (some people ignorantly confused Judaism with the cult of Dionysus, and Christians were generally viewed as part of Judaism). Those "given to wine" (KJV, NASB) were also often recognized as abusive and given to fighting as well.

1:8. "Hospitality" meant housing, feeding and treating graciously travelers needing a place to stay. (Christian travelers, like Jewish ones, normally carried letters of recommendation attesting that they could be trusted.)

1:9. Elders had to be trained to refute current false teachings before they were appointed; for the false teachings in view here, see comment on 1:10-16. The "word" in Judaism would be the *law, but Paul means the apostolic message (see comment on 2 Tim 4:2).

1:10-16
Evil Legalists

Although the opponents here are probably related to opponents Paul had faced elsewhere, they may have derived some of their appeal from local knowledge of Judaism and possibly a strong Jewish element within the *church. Crete was racially mixed, and a large Jewish colony was there.

1:10. "Empty talk" (NASB) characterized many pseudointellectuals in antiquity; see comment on 1 Timothy 1:6 and 2 Timothy 2:14.

1:11. "Upsetting whole families" (NASB) could mean that, by gaining entrance to families, these false teachers were disrupting whole households (cf. 2 Tim 3:6-7), but more likely Paul means that they are "subverting" (KJV) households. Perhaps they are undermining the authority structures current in the culture (Tit 2:4-5, 9-10); less likely, they may oppose marriage or sex within marriage on *ascetic grounds (see comment on 1 Tim 4:1-3; 1 Cor 7:1-7). Neither error was characteristic of Palestinian or *Diaspora Judaism, although many *Essenes advocated celibacy.

On those who taught for "gain," see comment on 1 Timothy 6:3-10; this accusation was commonly leveled against traveling teachers of morality, probably including Paul (1 Thess 2:5). A writer long before Paul charged that the Cretans were known to be more fond of gain, dishonest as well as honest, than any other people.

1:12. The saying Paul quotes here has been attributed to several sources, the earliest being the sixth-century B.C. teacher Epimenides of Knossos in Crete. (The real source may more likely be Hesiod by way of the third-century B.C. Callimachus's *Hymn to Zeus;* Crete claimed to possess both the birthplace and grave of Zeus. But that the words were often attributed to a Cretan in Paul's day is sufficient for him to make the point for Titus. Paul is clearly not citing his own view, because he would not consider a liar to be a true prophet. Greek logicians played with the claim by a Cretan that all Cretans were liars: if he had told the truth, he was lying; but if he was lying, then they reasoned that all Cretans told the truth—reasonable, except that this Cretan had not!)

By Paul's time Epimenides was reputed to have been a traveling wonderworker, teacher and prophet; as usual in Greek thought, the line between poetic and prophetic inspiration could be thin. Although the saying seems to have become proverbial (one commentator declares that "to cretize" became slang for "to lie"), it is possible that Paul knew either the works of Epimenides or, perhaps more likely, an anthology containing sayings attributed to him (see comment on Acts 17:27-29).

Crete also had a bad reputation for arrogance, treachery and greed. "Gluttony" was associated with love of pleasure as opposed to love of knowledge; see comment on Philippians 3:19.

1:13. Ancient ethnographers attributed certain characteristics (both good and bad) to various peoples whose cultures emphasized those traits. (That Paul could cite these negative characteristics of Cretans in a letter that Cretan believers would hear suggests that he must have been on very good terms with them and that Cretans recognized these characteristics of their own culture; he is not offering here a model for crosscultural sensitivity in normal situations.)

1:14. Jewish "myths" would especially be *haggadot,* stories amplifying or explaining biblical *narratives. *Pharisees and others who tried to expound and apply biblical law for their own times were forced to surround it with case law, detailing how the *Old Testament rules addressed specific situations; Paul apparently dismisses such legal traditions here.

1:15. The Old Testament *law considered some foods pure and other foods impure (cf. 1:14), but Paul applies the common figurative extension of purity language to moral and spiritual purity (see 1 Tim 4:3-5; cf. Rom 14:14).

1:16. In the Old Testament, "knowing God" was being in covenant relationship with him; on a personal level, this meant an intimate relationship of faithfulness to him. But the claim was worthless if not accompanied by just treatment of others and obedience to the Scriptures (Hos 8:2-3; Jer 22:16).

2:1-14
Sound Doctrine: Right Relationships

Because the Romans suspected minority religions, especially religions from the East with ecstatic elements to their worship, of subverting traditional family values, minority religions often followed the philosophers in exhorting adherents to follow "household codes." These codes instructed patriarchs of households how to treat each member of the household, especially wives, children and slaves. Under the broad topic of "household management," such codes also extended to treatment of parents, duties to the state (3:1) and duties to the gods. Because the *church met in homes and was viewed as a sort of extended family around the household of the *patron in whose home the believers met, the instructions naturally extended to categories of relationships in the church.

Early Christian adaptation of Roman social relations was important for the church's witness to society and for diminishing preventable opposition to the *gospel (2:5, 8, 10). Modern readers often recognize only the traditional values of their own culture (e.g., traditional family values of the nineteenth- to mid-twentieth-century U.S. middle class), but one should recognize that Paul addresses instead the traditional Roman values of his day (including the household slavery of his day, which differed from many other societies' models of slavery).

2:1. Because the false teachers were subverting the structure of households, the "sound" teaching (cf. 2:15) Paul supplies in this case applies especially to household relationships (2:2-14). Households were defined in terms of hierarchy and dependence (e.g., slaves to masters or *clients to *patrons) rather than strictly in terms of blood relationship.

2:2. This description matches the expectation for venerable older men in Roman culture: dignified, serious, sober.

2:3. Older women were often objects of ridicule in comedies and were especially mocked for gossip and foolish talk (see comment on 1 Tim 4:7).

2:4. It had long been customary for older women, especially mothers, to instruct their daughters in the ways of life (even in ancient Israel, e.g., Jer 9:20); some philosophers wanting to advise women even wrote *pseudepigraphic letters purportedly from women, telling women how to behave. The Roman mother's chief duty to her daughter seems to have been to help her acquire the appropriate education (especially to be a good mother) and a good husband. "Young women" were almost always wives, because Jewish and Greco-Roman society generally frowned upon women's singleness and men seem to have outnumbered women. Both Judaism and ancient moralists stressed that wives should love their husbands and nurture their children; many tomb inscriptions report these characteristics as a woman's crowning virtue.

2:5. The term translated "sensible" (NASB) means "self-controlled" (NIV, NRSV, TEV) or disciplined, one of the central Greek virtues; when applied to women, it meant "modesty" and hence indicated virtuously avoiding any connotations of sexual infidelity. In the Greek ideal, women were also to be secluded in the privacy of their home, because they were supposed to be the visual property of their husbands alone. They ruled the domestic sphere to which they were limited but had to obey their husbands in everything. Paul only says they are to be "submissive" (NRSV, TEV) rather than "obedient" (contrast KJV); women were also expected to be quiet, docile and socially retiring. To violate such social customs was to lend credence to the charge that Christianity was socially subversive, a charge that would provoke more persecution for the small but growing faith than most of them, both women and men, would have felt it worth.

2:6-8. The men also are to be self-disciplined, and Timothy was to provide a model for them, as a good teacher should. Paul uses the expression "good deeds" in a variety of ways (see 1:16; 2:14; 3:1, 8, 14; 1 Tim 2:10; 5:10; 6:18; 2 Tim 2:21; 3:17).

2:9-10. Although masters legally held absolute authority over household slaves, in most cases household slaves held freedoms that field or mine slaves did not, and they had more adequate provision than most peasants. In the popular stereotype entertained by their owners, slaves were lazy, apt to argue with their masters and liable to steal when they could. The stereotype was sometimes true, especially where the work incentive was least, but Paul urges Christian slaves not to reinforce the stereotype. Minority religions were already viewed as subversive, and to counter this prejudice Christians had to work especially hard to avoid the normal causes of slander. For more on slavery in general, see the introduction to Philemon.

2:11. The believers were to live in a respectable way to counter false accusations (2:8-10) so that all would have access to the *gospel according to which they lived. On prejudice against minority religions, see the introduction to 2:1-14. That God's grace had provided (though not automatically effected—cf., e.g., 1:10) salvation for all people ran counter to Jewish exclusivism and prevailing sentiments of cultural distinctions held by many people in antiquity (though Judaism allowed that some righteous Gentiles would be saved, and philosophers and some mystery religions challenged conventional cultural boundaries).

2:12. The ethical terms Paul employs here were cardinal virtues of ancient Greek philosophers and moralists. An almost identical list occurs in *Philo, a Jewish philosopher who wished to present Judaism favorably to the Greek society of Alexandria, to which he also felt he belonged.

Judaism contrasted the present age, dominated by evil and suffering, with the age to come, when God would rule unchallenged and reward his people. Although some oppressors through history have used such a doctrine to keep the oppressed subdued, it more appropriately found its first hearing among the oppressed themselves. Palestinian Jews felt discouraged by Roman repression and the lack of independence to practice their *law as they believed it; *Diaspora Jews and Christians found themselves a moral minority in a morass of paganism, subject to slanders and sporadic violence. Their hope for the future was rooted in their faith in God's justice.

2:13. In Judaism, the ultimate revelation or "appearing" of God would signal the end of the present age and the beginning of the new one (cf. 2:12). *Diaspora Judaism commonly called God "the great God" and saw him as a "*savior" (in Greek religion, the latter term often meant deliverer or benefactor). According to the most likely reading of the grammar here, Paul applies this divine title to Jesus.

2:14. In the *Old Testament God "redeemed" the people of Israel (i.e., freed them from slavery in Egypt) to make them "a special people" (Ex 19:5; Deut 4:20; 7:6; 14:2; cf. 1 Sam 12:22; 2 Sam 7:24; Ps 135:4); here Paul applies this language to the *church.

Judaism strongly praised "zeal" for God. Although zeal was associated particularly with the *Zealots in this period, it is doubtful that Paul would intend an allusion to that group, which was very probably unknown to the Cretans. He probably uses it in its more general sense of uncompromising zeal for the law or for God. (Although unlikely, it is possible that the Jewish colony in Crete was affected by the same tensions building in Cyrene, which was on the North African coast far to the south but under the same Roman administration. These tensions erupted into violence in Cyrene a little over a decade after Paul wrote this letter, and into a full revolt around four decades later. These revolutionary sentiments had been stirred by surviving Zealots from Palestine.)

2:15—3:8
The Purpose of a Lifestyle Witness

Paul here provides his reasoning for their lifestyle witness (2:5, 8, 10): God wants everyone to be saved, and he paid a great price to accomplish this salvation. Now the only way to counter the world's negative conception of Christianity is to live irreproachably.

2:15. Paul encourages Titus to pass on the sound doctrine of 2:1-14.

3:1. Allegiance to the state and submission to its authorities were often part of the same sorts of exhortations as the household duties (see the introduction to 2:1-14). They were as important as, or possibly more important than, household duties in undermining slander about subversiveness, because the Romans hated nothing worse than cults they deemed seditious.

3:2. The epitome of right relationships was being kind toward everyone, including one's enemies; this injunction is a fitting climax to Paul's rules on relationships.

3:3-4. Philosophers sometimes exhorted people to imitate God's character; Paul here uses God's kindness toward sinners in saving them to argue why Christians should be kind to all people, even their enemies. Philosophers described the majority of people as "enslaved by passions and pleasure," until they were freed from this bondage by the truth of philosophy; Paul agrees with their evaluation of the human plight but sees a different solution for it (3:5).

Paul's term for God's "love for humanity" here was used by pagan moralists especially for the sort of sympathy humans as humans necessarily have for one another; for Paul, God in *Christ has sympathy for humanity. (Sometimes the term was also applied to the supreme God, but more often it was applied to the benevolence of the emperor.) Paul shows how the most valued genuine virtues of his culture reflected God's own character.

3:5. The *Essenes and some other Jewish people associated the *Spirit with purification, especially based on Ezekiel 36:25-27, where God cleanses his people from their idolatry. Because *baptism was the decisive act of conversion in Palestinian Judaism, it figures as the natural image for conversion here (see comment on Jn 3:5).

3:6. For the Spirit being "poured out," see Joel 2:28 (cited in Acts 2:17).

3:7-8. "Justified" meant "judged righteous" or "acquitted" before God's court; according to the *Old Testament and Jewish teaching, one must condemn the guilty and acquit only the innocent. But in the Old Testament, God by his covenant love had also promised to vindicate his people and declare them in the right for their faithfulness to him; see comment on Romans 1:17. "Heirs" reflects the Old Testament image of inheriting the Promised Land, a picture naturally developed in early Judaism for entering the future *kingdom.

On "*eternal life" see comment on 1:2-3; on "hope" see also comment on 2:13. For Paul, as for Judaism, eternal life would be fulfilled at the *resurrection of the dead at the end of this age and beginning of the next. But for Paul the hope was already inaugurated by *Christ's resurrection.

3:9-11
Avoid Divisiveness and Divisive People

Part of maintaining a gentle, nonresistant life among members of the Christian community (3:1-2; cf. Gen 26:18-22) involved dissociating oneself from those who would violate one's witness by their disobedience.

3:9. Genealogies and details about the *law (including arguments of Jewish legal scholars over spellings or vocalizations of Hebrew words) were minutiae that missed the genuinely critical issues in the spirit of the *Old Testament (see comment on 1:10; 1 Tim 1:6; 2 Tim 2:14).

3:10-11. The term translated "factious" (NASB) or "divisive" (NIV) had not always been used negatively; the related noun came to designate different sects of philosophers, and *Josephus used it to designate different schools of thought within Judaism. But Paul uses it negatively here (also Gal 5:20; cf. 1 Cor 11:19) for sectarian or divisive tendencies. He presumably refers either to the false teachers or to their *disciples in the congregation (cf. Tit 3:9 with 1:10).

Jewish law required several private rebukes before bringing a person before the religious assembly for discipline; this procedure gave the offender ample opportunity to repent. One severe form of punishment against an unrepentant offender was exclusion from the religious community for a set time or until *repentance ensued. Because Paul uses this penalty only in the most extreme circumstances, the divisiveness in view here must be serious; the person has already excluded himself from the life of the community.

3:12-15 Concluding Business

3:12. Nicopolis was on the Greek side of the Adriatic coast, about two hundred miles east of Italy. Located near the coast and only about a century old, it was not a major city that would be likely to occur to a *pseudepigrapher. It was in this city that the *Stoic philosopher *Epictetus, banished from Rome, settled three decades later, so it might have also invited philosophical debates (and hence opportunities for Christian witness) in Paul's day. Apparently wishing to go on to Rome, Paul is going to leave Asia, cross Macedonia and wait in Nicopolis for Titus, who is to come up from Crete after receiving Paul's message. Sea travel was not possible during winter, so Paul would wait there (see comment on 2 Tim 4:21). Titus later walked northward to minister in Dalmatia (2 Tim 4:10), where some work had probably been initiated before (Rom 15:19, referring to the same region). Because Paul later sent Tychicus from Rome to Timothy (2 Tim 4:12), it was probably Artemas he sent to Titus. (Although the name "Artemas" was compounded on the name of the Greek goddess Artemis, one cannot draw any conclusions about whether he was Jewish or *Gentile. By this period Jewish names in Egypt and possibly elsewhere were compounded with "Artem-" roots; cf. the analogously Jewish Christian "Apollos," taken from the name of the Greek god Apollo.)

3:13. "Lawyer" could refer to a Jewish legal expert, but in the *Diaspora it more likely refers to a jurist of Roman law. Such jurists were trained *rhetoricians (like Apollos; see comment on Acts 18:24) and were prominent men. (In contrast to some other ancient professionals like physicians, who were sometimes slaves, lawyers were generally of higher social status.) Like most names, "Zenas" is attested as a name in Jewish funerary inscriptions, so his occupation need not rule out his Jewishness; perhaps both he and Apollos were from the educated Jewish elite in Alexandria.

This verse constitutes a miniature "letter of recommendation" to provide hospitality to Zenas and Apollos (see comment on 1:8), who must be the bearers of this letter to Titus. "Help" means to supply their needs, providing for them to continue their voyage to their destination, perhaps to the south in Cyrene or Alexandria.

3:14. Here Paul enjoins charity (see comment on 2 Cor 9:6-8; Gal 6:6-10).

3:15. Such greetings were customary at the end of a letter, at times including expressions like "those who love us" (to designate to whom general greetings most suitably applied).

PHILEMON

Introduction

Authorship. Almost all scholars accept this letter as Pauline; the style and substance are characteristic of Paul.

Slavery and the Setting of Philemon. Like all other slave law, Roman law had to address the dual status of slaves: by nature they were persons, but from an economic standpoint they were disposed of as property. The head of a household could legally execute his slaves, and they would all be executed if the head of the household was murdered. Slaves composed a large part of the agricultural work force in parts of the Empire (e.g., Italy); they competed with free peasants for the same work. The mine slaves had the worst life, dying quickly under the harsh conditions of the mines.

But slaves were found in all professions and generally had more opportunity for social advancement than free peasants; unlike the vast majority of slaves in the United States and the Caribbean, they were able to work for and achieve freedom, and some freed slaves became independently wealthy. This social mobility applied especially to the household slaves—the only kind of slave addressed in Paul's writings. Economically, socially, and with regard to freedom to determine their future, these slaves were better off than most free persons in the Roman Empire; most free persons were rural peasants working as tenant farmers on the vast estates of wealthy landowners.

A few philosophers said that slaves were equals as people, but they never suggested that masters should free their slaves. Nearly everyone took the institution of slavery for granted, except a few people who purportedly said that it was "against nature"; their views were so unpopular that they survived only in the critique of their enemies. Paul's message to Philemon goes beyond other documents of his time in not only pleading for clemency for an escaped slave but asking that he be released because he is now a Christian. So powerful was this precedent that many early U.S. slaveholders did not want their slaves to be exposed to Christianity, for fear that they would be compelled to free them; only in time was a distorted enough form of the Christian message available for use in sustaining slavery (see Albert J. Raboteau, *Slave Religion* [New York: Oxford University Press, 1978]).

Slaves, especially skilled or educated males, were often sent on errands and trusted as agents with their masters' property. Such slaves could sometimes earn enough money on the side to buy their freedom (although their earnings legally belonged to their master, they were normally permitted to control the money themselves); still, some took the opportunity of an errand to escape. Because a safe escape required them to get far away from where their master lived (in the case Paul addresses here, from Phrygia to Rome), they might take some of their master's money with them. (Such theft is probably the point of v. 18, but Paul might there account for the possibility that Philemon wants repayment for Onesimus himself. From the standpoint of ancient slave owners, the lost time of an escaped slave was lost money and was legally viewed as stolen property, to which one harboring him was liable. But more important, slaves themselves were not cheap, and

Philemon might have already bought another slave to replace him.) Recapture normally meant severe punishment.

Old Testament *law required harboring escaped slaves (Deut 23:15-16), but Roman law required Paul to return Onesimus to his master, with serious penalties if he failed to do so. Paul uses his relationship with Philemon to seek Onesimus's release: in a standard "letter of recommendation," one would plead with someone of equal (or sometimes lower) status on behalf of someone of lower status. Paul was not Philemon's equal socially or economically, but as his spiritual father he had grounds to claim the equality that characterized ancient friendship.

Structure and Form. This letter is a "letter of recommendation," the sort that a *patron wrote to social peers or inferiors on behalf of a dependent *client to ask a favor for him. It is also "deliberative *rhetoric," the type of speech or writing educated persons in antiquity used to persuade others to change their behavior or attitudes. Paul's *exordium,* or opening appeal (vv. 4-7), is followed by the main argument, consisting of proofs (vv. 8-16), which is followed by the *peroratio,* or summary of his case (vv. 17-22). Paul uses methods of argumentation common in his day to persuade well-to-do and well-educated Philemon, who would find such arguments persuasive. The preservation of the letter suggests that Paul succeeded in persuading Philemon, who would not have kept it and later allowed it to be circulated had he not freed Onesimus. The shortest of Paul's extant letters, this letter to Philemon would have occupied only a single sheet of papyrus.

Commentaries. See under Colossians. For Paul's views on slavery, see S. Scott Bartchy, *First-Century Slavery and the Interpretation of 1 Corinthians 7:21,* SBLDS 11 (Missoula, Mont.: Society of Biblical Literature, 1973); compare also Craig S. Keener, *Paul, Women and Wives* (Peabody, Mass.: Hendrickson, 1992), pp. 184-224, for some general considerations of Paul's words to household slaves.

1-3. On house *churches see comment on Acts 12:12 and Romans 16:5. Well-to-do owners of homes in which ancient religious groups met were normally granted positions of honor in those groups, as their *patrons. Ancient writers defined households not by blood relations but by hierarchical relationships: the free man and his wife, children and slaves (though only those with sizable incomes could afford slaves). The addressees are located in Phrygia (cf. Col 4:17). (This location is based on more helpful evidence than the character of the names. Although a much more common Phrygian name than "Philemon," "Apphia" is also attested elsewhere, including Palestine.)
4. Paul kept times of regular prayer, a normal pious Jewish practice (probably at least two hours a day); see comment on Romans 1:10. Thanksgivings were common in letters, and Paul here (vv. 4-7) follows his usual custom of using his thanksgiving as a complimentary *exordium*. Such *exordia* were commonly used in speeches to praise the hearers, thus securing their favor.
5-6. The term translated "fellowship" (NASB, TEV) or "sharing" (NIV, NRSV) was often used for business partnerships or for sharing possessions (see v. 7). Philemon acts as a *patron for the *church (v. 2).
7. Hospitality was considered a paramount virtue in Greco-Roman antiquity, especially in Judaism. Well-to-do hosts often gathered those one rung below them on the economic ladder, sometimes members of their own religious group, to their home and provided a meal; Philemon and other well-to-do Christians sponsored the meals in their house churches. Mention of a shared friendship between the writer and recipient was a common feature of ancient letters; it was especially important in letters of friendship or when the writer was about to request a favor from the letter's recipient.
8. Although Philemon has high social status—something particularly valued in his culture—he recognizes Paul's higher spiritual rank in the faith. Philosophers were often sponsored by such well-to-do persons as lecturers at banquets or teachers, but Paul claims a higher role than a mere philosopher would fill. Philosophers could be *clients of wealthy *patrons, but Paul implies that he is Philemon's spiritual patron here. Philosophers used the expression "what is proper" (NASB; "what you ought to do"—NIV) as a criterion for ethical judgments.
9. *Rhetoricians (those who specialized in public speaking) liked to argue this way: "I could remind you of this, but I won't"—thus reminding while pretending not to do so. Respect for age was important in his culture, so Paul appeals to his age. (According to one ancient definition, the term Paul uses here ["aged"—KJV, NASB; "old man"—NIV, NRSV] applied to ages forty-nine to fifty-six; but *New Testament writers usually use it loosely for anyone no longer "young." On the basis of other New Testament evidence, Paul is probably around fifty-seven, give or take five years.) Shared friendship was also used as the basis for a request; friends were socially obligated to grant and return favors.
10. Teachers often called *disciples "sons." The point of Paul's plea is that one could not enslave the son of one's own spiritual *patron. Appeals to emotion were a necessary part of ancient argumentation.
11. Here Paul makes a wordplay on Onesimus's name, which means "useful." It was a common slave name, for obvious reasons. The well-to-do had a stereotype that slaves—explicitly including Phrygian slaves—were lazy

and ill-disciplined.

12-14. Slaves were sometimes freed by their masters to become slaves of the temple of some god; here Paul asks that Philemon free Onesimus for the service of the *gospel. He appeals not to his own authority but to Philemon's honor as a friend. Runaway slaves were known to be fearful of being captured and taken back to their masters, and Paul's concern for Onesimus is here evident.

15-16. Roman law saw slaves as both people and property; but a full brother would naturally not be viewed as property. The phrase "receive him back" or "have him back" resembles that found in business receipts, but here it is not a property transaction in which Philemon receives Onesimus back as a slave, but like welcoming back a family member. "Parted from you" (NASB) implies the sovereignty of God, a doctrine accepted by Judaism and no doubt assumed by Philemon.

17. "Partner" was often a formal business term (see comment on v. 6). In status-conscious Roman society, Paul is telling a social superior who respects his ministry: we are equals, and if you accept Onesimus as my agent (authorized representative), you must accept him as an equal (see, e.g., comment on Mt 10:40). Ancient letters of recommendation commonly appealed to friends to consider the bearer of the letter "as if he were me."

18-19. Here Paul employs language normally used for formally assuming debts; letters acknowledging debt normally included the promise "I will repay" and were signed by the debtor in his own handwriting. Because it is in writing, this offer would be legally binding in the unlikely event that Philemon would take Paul up on it. But Philemon also owes a debt to Paul; again Paul uses the *rhetorical technique of "not to mention" something he then mentions (vv. 8-9). By ancient social custom, friends were bound by the reciprocal obligation of repaying favors; Philemon owes Paul the greatest favor—his "self," his new life in conversion.

20. Compare the "refreshing" of verse 7; Paul asks for the same hospitable character that Philemon shows the *church.

21. "Do even more than what I say" (NASB) means that Philemon will free Onesimus (cf. vv. 12-14). Professional speakers often sought favors in such terms: "Knowing your goodness, you will gladly hear me" or "grant me such-and-such a request."

22-25. Well-to-do *patrons offered hospitality, which Paul can expect as Philemon's spiritual peer. Indeed, providing lodging for prominent guests was regarded as an honor.

HEBREWS

Introduction

Style. Along with Luke-Acts, this document displays the best Greek style in the *New Testament; its author must have had sophisticated *rhetorical training and literary skills.

Date. Because Timothy was recently freed (Heb 13:23) and the work was apparently written from Italy (13:24), we may assume that Timothy was arrested in Rome during the Neronian persecution (probably shortly after he came to see Paul—2 Tim 4:21) and freed when Nero (and his policy) died in A.D. 68. The mention of Timothy but not Paul, who died about A.D. 64, also would make sense about A.D. 68. At this time, when the outcome of the Roman war in Judea would have been assured from Rome's vantage point, it would be quite appropriate to speak of the old temple system as "passing away" (8:13)—a process completed in A.D. 70 with the destruction of the temple. That the writer cannot declare that temple sacrifices are no longer offered (which he surely would have declared if he could have) suggests a date before A.D. 70.

Authorship. From a stylistic perspective, it is impossible to attribute the letter to Paul; of other New Testament writers, it is closest to Luke's literary abilities, but the style is not particularly Lukan. The writer seems to be an influential person traveling in the same circles as Timothy (13:23) and well heeded by this audience, who are probably in the eastern Mediterranean. Silas would thus be a natural candidate (in Rome about 64—1 Pet 5:12); that he is Jewish yet a Roman citizen (Acts 16:37) and probably a scribe (1 Pet 5:12) would suggest the educational level necessary for such a letter. It is more commonly suggested that the writer is Apollos, whose Alexandrian rhetorical and possibly philosophical training would have suited him especially well to write such a letter; he was certainly respected as Paul's peer in the Pauline *churches. (He seems to have been moving from Rome toward the east or south a few years before Hebrews was written—Tit 3:13—but he could have returned.) Other suggestions, like Barnabas or Priscilla, are possible but have nothing specifically to commend them.

Audience. The readers are obviously predominantly Jewish and are under pressure to give up their Christian distinctives (either from the *synagogue or from *Gentile persecution of Christians). The actual seizure of their property in earlier days (10:34) does not fit Corinth or Ephesus (against one commentator, who perhaps fancifully but nevertheless quite skillfully constructs a case for this letter being written to Corinth and 1 Corinthians responding to some features in it). But 13:23 suggests an audience in the Pauline circle (i.e., not in Alexandria, though Apollos was known there too). The early persecution fits Thessalonica and possibly Philippi in Macedonia, although a community in Asia Minor or Syria with more ethnic Jewish representation might fit better. (Some have suggested a Roman audience on the basis of 10:32-34 and 13:24; the quality of Greek may fit an audience more to the east, but this argument would hardly be decisive. If we read 13:24 as suggesting a Roman place of origin, however, a Roman audience is unlikely.) Wherever the readers are located, they resonate with the intensely Greek rhetoric and interpretation of Judaism that come naturally to this author; the closest parallels are with *Philo of Alexandria. (That the letter also has parallels with the *Dead Sea Scrolls in Palestine and *apocalyptic motifs should not be surprising; we must construct a composite picture of ancient Judaism based on as many diverse sources as possible. But the clear Philonic parallels point to *Hellenistic rhetorical training.)

***Genre.** Some scholars have suggested that this document is a homiletic *midrash on Psalm 110 (see Heb 13:22); one cannot deny that the interpretation of this psalm dominates the work. (The suggestion that it was specifically a midrash on the readings for the Feast of Pentecost is not impossible, but evidence for the triennial readings later adopted in Mediterranean synagogues is lacking in this period.) It is more like a treatise than a normal letter, apart from concluding greetings. But one ancient letter-writing form was the "letter-essay," which in early Judaism and Christianity would naturally have resembled a written homily or sermon; Hebrews is very likely such a "letter-essay."

Structure. *Christ is greater than the angels (1:1-14) who delivered the *law (2:1-18); this contrast contributes to the writer's argument that Christ is greater than the law itself. He is greater than Moses and the Promised Land (3:1—4:13). As a priest after the order of Melchizedek, he is greater than the *Old Testament priesthood (4:14—7:28) because he is attached to a new covenant (chap. 8) and a heavenly temple service (9:1—10:18). Therefore, his followers ought to persevere in faith and not go back, regardless of the cost (10:19—12:13). The writer follows his theoretical discussion, as many letters did, with specific moral exhortations tied into the same theme (13:1-17). Interspersed throughout the letter is the repeated warning against apostasy, noting that the penalty for rejecting the new covenant is greater than that for rejecting the old had been.

Argumentation. The writer argues from Scripture the way a good Jewish interpreter of his day would; his methods have parallels in the *Dead Sea Scrolls, the *rabbis and especially *Philo. His arguments sometimes confuse or fail to persuade modern readers, but he is making a case first of all for his original readers, who would be accustomed to the kinds of arguments he makes. Given the forms of argumentation he must use to persuade readers in his own cultural context, he argues his case brilliantly, although some of the arguments would have to be restructured to carry the same conviction in our culture. Because the writer's arguments are often complex, this volume's comments on Hebrews are necessarily more detailed than the comments on many other New Testament books.

Commentaries. The best commentary is William Lane, *Hebrews,* WBC 47 (Waco, Tex.: Word, 1991). Besides conservative commentaries by F. F. Bruce, *The Epistle to the Hebrews,* rev. ed., NICNT (Grand Rapids, Mich.: Eerdmans, 1990), and D. A. Hagner, *Hebrews,* GNC (San Francisco: Harper & Row, 1983), the old commentary by James Moffatt, *A Critical and Exegetical Commentary on the Epistle to the Hebrews,* ICC (Edinburgh: T. & T. Clark, 1924), is good; Hugh Montefiore, *A Commentary on the Epistle to the Hebrews,* HNTC (New York: Harper & Row, 1964), is helpful and culturally informed despite his eccentric construction of the situation.

1:1-14
Christ Greater Than the Angels

*Christ's superiority to the angels made him greater than the *law, which was said to have been mediated by angels (2:2-3). The writer may also offer this comparison to argue against toning down Christ's divinity to mere angelic status, a position the readers may have been allowing to appease non-Christian Jewish opponents.

1:1-2. These two verses represent some of the most articulate, Atticizing Greek prose in antiquity and include literary devices like alliteration (five Greek words beginning with *p* in v. 1). The author also appears to model some of his language on the opening of the prologue to Ecclesiasticus, a Jewish wisdom book in wide circulation by this period and almost certainly familiar to his readers (available to modern readers in what is usually called the Apocrypha).

Christ is presented here as the ultimate Word of God; ancient Judaism identified God's Word with his Wisdom. That God had created all things through Wisdom or his Word was noted in the *Old Testament (e.g., Prov 8:30; Ps 33:6, alluding to Gen 1) and developed further in Judaism. As the fullness of the Word, Christ was superior to the authentic but partial revelation of God in the law.

"Last days" was Old Testament language for the time of the end (Is 2:2; Ezek 38:16; Hos 3:5; Mic 4:1; cf. Deut 4:30, 32; 8:16), now inaugurated in *Christ. An "heir" held title to the property of the one who appointed him heir; cf. comment on "inherit" in verse 4.

1:3. Jewish authors writing in Greek often said that divine Wisdom was the exact "image" (so KJV here) of God, the prototypical stamp by which he "imprinted" (cf. NRSV here) the seal of his image on the rest of creation (the way an image was stamped on coins). Sitting down at the right hand of the supreme king was an image of the ultimate honor and alludes to Psalm 110:1, cited explicitly in 1:13. "Purification" of sins was the work of priests; mention of it here anticipates a theme that appears later in the book.

1:4. Some *Diaspora Jewish writers attributed to the angels a role in creation, but early Christian writers routinely denied them such a role (Col 1:16), as did many Jewish teachers. Here Jesus' exaltation grants him a title that entitles him to much more status than the angels: Son (1:5). (Although some Jewish teachers said that God honored Israel more than the angels by giving Israel the law, something greater than comparison with Israel is in view here, because Jesus himself is identified with the divine Word in 1:1-3, and is "son" in a sense in which the angels are not; the title is applied to angels generally, e.g., Job 1:6, but Jesus is distinguished as *the* Son. Those original readers who wished to compromise their divine view of Jesus but to retain him as superhuman may also have wished to identify him as an angel, as some second-century Jewish Christians did, but if this is the case, the writer rejects this compromise as inadequate—2:5-18.)

1:5. The author cites Psalm 2:7 and 2 Samuel 7:14, texts which had already been linked in speculations about the coming *Messiah (in the *Dead Sea Scrolls). Jewish interpreters often linked texts on the basis of a common key word; the word here is "Son." Like several other *messianic texts, Psalm 2 originally celebrated the promise to the Davidic line in 2 Samuel 7; the "begetting" referred to the royal coronation—in Jesus' case, his exaltation (cf. similarly Acts 13:33). The repetition of this verse's rhetorical question in verse 13 suggests an *inclusio,* or framing device, that brackets off verses 5-14 as a united thought (though *Diaspora Jews often introduced quotations from Scripture with rhetorical questions).

1:6. "Firstborn" specified further the inheritance rights of the oldest son, who received double the portion of any subsequent son (Deut 21:17); it is a title of the Davidic king of Psalm 89:26-27. To Jesus' coronation as king and consequent superiority to the angels the author applies a text from the *Septuagint of Deuteronomy 32, a favorite mine for texts among early Christian writers and a text *Diaspora Jews used for worship alongside the Psalms. (Although these words are not in the Hebrew manuscripts preserved in the later Masoretic text, their presence in a *Qumran Hebrew copy of Deuteronomy shows that the line was in some Hebrew manuscripts, from which the Greek translation may have derived it.)

The author probably reads the text according to Jewish interpretive practice: attending to grammatical details, he distinguishes "God" from "him." (Some of his readers might have also recalled a Jewish tradition in which God ordered his angels to honor Adam at his creation, because he was God's image.)

1:7. Although Psalm 104:4 could mean that God uses winds and fire as his messengers, Jewish writers in the first century commonly took the text the other way and often thus suggested that angels were made of fire. (This notion also fit some Greek speculations about the elements. For many, the soul was made of fire—like the stars—or breath; for *Stoics, the whole world would be resolved back into the primordial fire from which it had come.) The writer's point is simply that angels are subordinate to God in character, in contrast to the Son (1:8).

1:8-9. Psalm 45 may have been composed for a royal wedding celebration, but part of it speaks of God's blessing on the king and probably (certainly in the Greek version cited here) addresses God directly. Jewish interpreters read as much literal significance into a passage as they could, hence the writer of Hebrews forces his fellow Jewish-Christian readers to recognize the plain language of this psalm. Because God is addressed in Psalm 45:6 (cited in Heb 1:8), it is natural to assume that he continues to be addressed in Psalm 45:7 (cited in Heb 1:9). (Later *rabbis applied this text to Abraham, and a later *targum applied an earlier verse to the *Messiah; but probably neither tradition was known to the writer of Hebrews, and the former one may have represented anti-Christian polemic.) But Psalm 45:7 distinguishes this God from a God he worships, so that one may distinguish God the Father from God the Son. The writer of Hebrews explicitly affirms *Christ's deity in this passage.

1:10-12. Both Jewish and Greek writers sometimes separated quotations with "And he said" or "and." Interpreters often linked texts by means of a common key word or concept, and the writer cites Psalm 102:25-27 on the basis of God's throne being "forever" in Hebrews 1:8 (in context this *Old Testament passage also promised God's faithfulness to his covenant people, even though individuals were mortal).

1:13. It is natural for the author to cite Psalm 110:1 because God's "right hand" is envisioned in terms of a place beside his throne (1:8; cf. possibly Wisdom of Solomon 9:4; 18:15). The full citation also includes God addressing the priest-king (see comment on Heb 5:6) as Lord, similar to the citation in

1:8-9. The writer shows himself a master of Jewish exegetical technique.

1:14. He already proved to his readers that angels were "ministering spirits" in 1:7. That they minister not only on behalf of the one who inherited a greater name (1:4) but also for those who inherit salvation (v. 14) would resonate with Jewish readers, who would be familiar with the concept of guardian angels assigned to the righteous by God.

2:1-4
Rejecting Christ's Word

According to common Jewish thought, any Israelite who willfully rejected the *law was excluded from the world to come; according to some teachers, this sin was even unpardonable. In Judaism, deliberate acts always carried more liability than inadvertent ones.

In a widely recognized Jewish tradition, God had given his law through angels (Acts 7:53; Gal 3:19; *Josephus; and *Jubilees). (The *rabbis preferred to emphasize only the great number of angels present for the Israelites.) The tradition máy have some basis in the interchange between God and his angel in Exodus (cf. Ex 3:2), the association of Psalm 68:17 with the Sinai tradition, and especially Deuteronomy 33:2 (more so in the *LXX, which declares that his angels were with him on his right).

Because *Christ is greater than the angels (Heb 1:1-14), rejecting his word is a more serious offense than rejecting the word said to have been mediated through the angels (2:2). This is a Jewish *qal vahomer,* or "how much more" argument: if the lesser point applies, then how much more does the greater point apply. Some scholars have suggested a nautical image (a drifting ship) in verse 1, as well as significant juridical language in verses 2-4.

2:5-18
Christ Human, Not an Angel

Recognizing Jesus as suprahuman but not wishing to offend their Jewish colleagues who protested that God's oneness disallowed Jesus' divinity, some second-century Jewish Christians portrayed Jesus as a chief angel. The temptation to such a path was probably already present among the audience of this letter, so the writer warns forcefully against such a view. *Christ was divine and became human as well; but he was never an angel.

2:5. The *Old Testament and Jewish teaching declared that God's people would reign with him in the world to come, just as Adam and Eve had been designed to reign for him in the beginning. The writer proceeds to prove this point by appealing to a specific Old Testament text, Psalm 8:4-6, in Jewish *midrashic style.

2:6-7. "One has testified somewhere" (NASB) does not mean that the writer has forgotten what part of Scripture he is quoting; this was a way of expressing confidence that the important issue was that God had inspired the words. *Philo used similar phrases in this manner. The writer can introduce Psalm 8:4-6 naturally on the basis of the Jewish interpretive rule, *gezerah shavah,* the principle by which one was permitted to link key words or phrases. This text speaks of everything subdued under someone's feet, as had the text he had cited most recently (1:13).

Psalm 8:4-6 declares that although humanity is nothing in itself, God appointed humans as rulers over all his creation, second only to himself (alluding to Gen 1:26-27). The *Septuagint interprets this passage as "a little lower than the angels" instead of "a little lower than God" (the Hebrew word used there, *elohim,* sometimes did mean angels instead of God). That angels were more powerful than people in this age was true, but the writer of Hebrews is going to make a different point. In the verses that follow, he expounds the version of this passage with which his readers are familiar in traditional Jewish interpretive style. ("Son of man" was simply a Semitic way of saying "human being," and the writer here does not seem to try to get more out of it than this, although he could have had he wished to do so, because he applies the whole text to Jesus. Some scholars have also connected this passage with the binding of Isaac, the tradition known as the *Aqedah,* but the evidence cited may be too sparse and late for the points of contact here.)

2:8. Jewish interpreters often established that a text could not mean what it seemed to mean on face value (or could not mean only that) before proceeding to argue what they believed that it did mean. Here, because the creation is not currently subject to humanity, the author can argue that God's original intention in Adam will be fulfilled again for all the righteous only in the age to come (2:5)—a doctrine shared with the rest of Judaism. But he can also argue that one representative man has already gone ahead for all humanity, as a sort of new Adam (2:9).

2:9. In Jewish thought, angels ruled the nations in this age. Jesus had obviously been made lower than God and the angels, but after death he was crowned with glory (1:13); therefore this text was not only true of the past Adam and God's people in the future but also had been fulfilled in Jesus. (The author may read "a little lower" as "for a little while lower," which was an acceptable way to read the *LXX of Ps 8; he also distinguishes "a little lower" from "crowned with honor," though the lines are parallel in Hebrew. Ancient Jewish interpreters generally read passages whatever way fit best with their views.)

2:10. That *Christ had been made lower but then exalted shows him as the forerunner of the righteous who would inherit the coming world (1:14; 2:5). The term *archēgos,* translated "author" (NASB, NIV) or "captain" (KJV), means "pioneer" (NRSV), "leader" (cf. TEV) or "champion." The term was used for both human and divine heroes, founders of schools or those who cut a path forward for their followers and whose exploits for humanity were rewarded by exaltation. "For whom . . . and through whom are all things" was a phrase *Stoics used to describe the supreme God, but the idea fit Jewish thought about God and divine Wisdom and was widely used by *Diaspora Jewish writers, including Paul (1 Cor 8:6). The *Septuagint uses the author's term for "perfect" for the consecration of a priest; some contemporary Jewish texts also speak of a righteous person's life crowned with martyrdom as being "perfected" thereby.

2:11. Again the idea is that the text has been fulfilled in Jesus, who has gone on ahead, but will yet be fulfilled in the rest of the righteous; he is the "firstborn" (1:6) among many brothers.

2:12. To prove the thesis of verse 11, the writer cites Psalm 22:22, which can be applied to Jesus the one who suffered because it is a psalm of the righteous sufferer (the Gospels apply many of its verses to Jesus' crucifixion).

2:13. Here the author cites Isaiah 8:17-18. Isaiah 8:17 refers to the Lord who was a sanctuary to the righteous and a stumbling block to the rest of Israel (8:14-15), a text that, when linked with other "stone" texts by the Jewish interpretive principle *gezerah shavah* (linking of texts with the same key word, e.g., Is 28:16; Ps 118:22), could apply to the *Messiah. In Isaiah 8:18 the prophet explains that his own children have symbolic names to signify things to Israel. The writer can cite it because it immediately follows 8:17 and perhaps because its wording matches his point (see comment on Heb 2:12). He may also make the link, however, because one of Isaiah's children pointed toward Immanuel, God with us (Is 7:14-16; 8:1-4), and this text declared the other children brothers.

2:14-15. Jesus had to become part of humanity, as in Psalm 8:4-6, to become a forerunner, a new Adam for humanity. Ancient literature often spoke of the terrors of death, although many philosophers claimed to transcend it. Jewish literature had already connected the devil and death, especially in the Wisdom of Solomon (which this author and his audience probably knew well); some later texts even identify *Satan with the angel of death. Like Heracles in the Greek tradition and perhaps God the divine warrior of Jewish tradition (cf. Is 26:19-21; 44:24-26), Jesus is the "champion" (see comment on 2:10) who has delivered his people.

2:16. Still expounding Psalm 8:4-6, the writer reminds his readers that *Christ acted as forerunner for God's people ("Abraham's seed"; cf. perhaps Is 41:8-9) for the world to come, not for the angels. (The *Old Testament called Abraham's chosen descendants "children of God"—e.g., Deut 32:19; Hos 11:1; the writer is addressing Jewish Christians, members of a people who have long believed that a great destiny awaits them in the future.) Christ is already exalted above the angels (2:7, 9), as his people will be in the age to come (2:5).

2:17-18. The writer here gives a reason for Christ's becoming human to redeem humanity: identification of the sort that had to characterize a high priest (see comment on 5:1-3). Such an image might have intrigued many people of antiquity, whose agendas were generally low on the aristocracy's list of priorities; the aristocracies merely kept them pacified with gifts of free food, public games and so forth. On "faithful" see comment on 3:2 and 5.

3:1-6
Christ Greater Than Moses

3:1. The mention of a "heavenly" calling would have appealed to philosophically minded Jewish thinkers like *Philo, who regarded earthly reality as only a shadow of heavenly reality. The writer of Hebrews probably presents Jesus as superior to Moses, who was *not* a high priest. (*Samaritan writers saw Moses as an "*apostle," and some Jewish writers saw the high priest as such, although rarely. The author of Hebrews sees Jesus as an "apostle," a commissioned messenger of the Father, in a way greater than Moses or an earthly high priest. Philo regarded Moses as a high priest of sorts, but the *Old Testament and most of Judaism recognized that Aaron filled that role, and the writer of Hebrews probably assumes only the Old Testament perspective on the part of his readers.)

3:2. In verses 2-6 the writer constructs an implicit *midrash on Numbers 12:7-8, expounding the familiar text without citing it (cf. also 1 Chron 17:14 *LXX). In this passage, God honors Moses above Aaron and Miriam, claiming him to be greater than a normal prophet and noting that "he is faithful in all my household." Jesus is thus this special kind of prophet "like Moses," of whom there were no others (Deut 18:15-18).

3:3-4. In many Jewish traditions Moses was the greatest person in history, and in others he was certainly one of the greatest (i.e., next to Abraham). Jewish and Christian writers used the argument that the builder was greater than what was made (v. 3) to note that the Creator was greater than his creation (as in v. 4). This writer identifies Jesus as the Creator. Ancient writers often developed arguments based on wordplays; this writer plays on two senses of "house": God's "household" (3:2) and a building (3:3-4).

3:5. Past symbols could testify to future realities in Jewish *apocalyptic literature, the way that earthly "shadows" testified to heavenly realities in writings by *Philo and Jews influenced by Platonism. Jewish readers may have recalled the tradition that Moses foresaw and testified of the *messianic era (on his special visionary abilities see Num 12:8). A first-century reader could understand Numbers 12:7 the way later *rabbis also did: God was owner of the house, but Moses was the manager of the estate, and like many managers, was a servant.

3:6. A firstborn son was naturally heir and lord over the house, acting on his father's authority while the father lived and becoming master when his father died. In the *Old Testament, God's household was Israel; here it is the faithful remnant, those who have submitted to God's truth in *Christ.

3:7-19
Rejecting Christ like Rejecting Moses

Here begins an explicit *midrash (commentary) on Psalm 95:7-11, which continues until 4:14, where the midrash on Psalm 110:4 begins. Like other Jewish writers, this author gives attention to the details of the text. Israel was to have "rest" in the Promised Land, but the writer points out that this means not only in this age—when the promise was never completely fulfilled (4:8)—but in its completion in the age to come.

3:7. Ancient Judaism most often associated the "*Holy Spirit" with *prophecy, and the *rabbis and some others particularly associated this prophetic Spirit with the inspiration of Scripture.

3:8-11. The author cites Psalm 95:7-11, a text that later became familiar through its regular use in the synagogue liturgy, but that would have been already known to most first-century Jews who recited the Psalms. This psalm refers to Israel's rebellion in the wilderness and calls on its hearers not to be like their ancestors. Jewish teachers debated whether the wilderness generation might have inherited the life of the world to come, even though they did not enter the Promised Land; the *rabbis believed that God's people could *atone for their sins in this age by suffering. But the psalmist and the writer of Hebrews seem to have agreed that they also did not enter the world to come.

3:12-13. Like many ancient Jewish interpreters (especially those who wrote the *Dead Sea Scrolls), the writer points out that the psalmist's exhortation for "today" was still valid in his own generation.

3:14-15. The psalm states that God's people could be cut off from the covenant if they refused to heed it; thus the writer warns his readers that they become sharers in *Christ's *kingdom (2:5-16) only if they persevere to the end.

3:16-19. Following Greek argumentative practice, the writer produces a series of rhetorical questions and their obvious answers, reinforcing his point.

4:1-13
Only the Obedient Enter His Promise

4:1-2. The Israelites rebelled in the

wilderness because they did not believe the word Moses gave them; those who rebelled against the word of *Christ were acting like Moses' generation had.

4:3-5. The writer now attends to grammatical details as Jewish interpreters in his day normally did. What could the psalmist mean by "my rest," since God had already rested from his works on the seventh day of creation? (Linking texts by a shared key word was a common Jewish exegetical technique; Jewish liturgy later linked these two texts similarly.) Perhaps he uses this text to point to the future, too; some Jewish writers believed that the world to come would be the ultimate sabbath rest, the final stage of creation.

4:6-7. All of Moses' generation failed to achieve "rest" (3:16-19), settlement in the land. Indeed, all subsequent generations from Joshua on, with the notable near exceptions of David and Josiah, failed to subdue all the land promised to Abraham. Thus the psalmist (Ps 95:7-8) could warn his own and subsequent generations to obey God's word or the same thing would happen to them. (By the *New Testament period, with Palestine under Rome's authority and no end of the Roman Empire in sight, almost all Jewish people agreed that the restoration of their kingdom and consequently rest in the land would come only in the end time, which most hoped was soon.)

4:8-9. "Joshua" and "Jesus" are the same name (these are anglicized forms of the Hebrew and Greek, respectively); perhaps the writer thus intends the first Joshua to point to his later namesake. But his main point is that Joshua was not able to subdue the whole land (4:6-7; Josh 13:1-2); the promise is thus yet to be fulfilled.

4:10-11. Because the *Messiah, the *Spirit and other events that had arrived in Jesus were normally relegated in Judaism to the age to come, early Christian writers could say that believers in Jesus experienced a foretaste of the future world in their present relationship with God (see comment on 6:5).

4:12-13. God's word, received by Israel through Moses and by the readers of Hebrews in *Christ (4:2), left those who heard it no excuses. Judaism recognized the ability of God to search out every detail of one's heart and thoughts (e.g., Ps 139:23), and it was natural to apply this property to his word or wisdom.

The Alexandrian Jewish philosopher *Philo spoke of the power of the universal, divine "Word" (the Logos, divine reason that permeated the universe) to subdivide the soul into smaller and smaller units, especially into its rational and irrational components; but he sometimes identified spirit and soul, as the New Testament writers usually do. The point here is not an analysis of human nature, but that the Word searches the heart in such detail that it is like a sharp sword that divides even what is virtually (but not absolutely) indivisible, whether soul and spirit or joints and marrow.

4:14—5:10
Christ the High Priest

Although *Philo portrays the Logos, the divine Word or reason, as God's high priest, this is probably not in the mind of the author of Hebrews. (Indeed, the emphasis on Christ's participation in people's humanity contrasts with Philo's attempt to circumvent the high priest's full humanity when he interceded for Israel.) Instead, a more obvious source lies at hand: his interpretation of Psalm 110:4, which becomes explicit in 5:6. His citation of the first verse of this psalm in 1:13, applied by Jesus to himself (Mk 12:35-37), may have already called Psalm 110:4 to his biblically informed readers' minds.

4:14. See Psalm 110:4, cited in Hebrews 5:6. *Apocalyptic traditions portray heaven as a place of worship; the imagery of a heavenly temple is especially prominent in the book of Revelation. In later *Samaritan tradition, Moses (who in some Jewish tradition had ascended to heaven to receive the law) served as heavenly high priest; but the Christian portrait of Jesus fulfilling this role is probably earlier than the Samaritan tradition about Moses.

4:15. The writer continues the theme that *Christ had experienced humanness without compromising his obedience (2:14-18). In the unlikely event that his readers were familiar with the abuses of the high priesthood in Jerusalem, they might have recognized here a contrast with the high priestly aristocracy.

4:16. The ark of the covenant symbolized God's throne in the *Old Testament (e.g., 2 Sam 6:2; Ps 80:1; 99:1; Is 37:16; cf. Ps 22:3) and in the ancient Near East (where kings or deities were often portrayed as enthroned on winged figures). But the ark was unapproachable, secluded in the most holy part of the temple, which even the high priest could approach only once a year. Christ has opened full access to God to all his followers (10:19-20).

5:1-3. While continuing the theme of 4:15-16, the author also shows *Christ's superiority over other high priests, who sin (Lev 9:7; 16:6).

5:4. The writer follows the *Old Testament law on the high priestly succession; in Palestine in his own day, the office of high priest was a political favor granted by the Romans. Outside Palestine, however, this was not an issue; the writer speaks of the system God had appointed in the Bible.

5:5. Citing again Psalm 2:7 (see comment on Heb 1:5), the writer proves from it that *Christ's royal coronation was God's initiative. In the next verse he links this kingship with the high priesthood.

5:6. Although the Romans had a powerful high priest, too (the *pontifex maximus*), the writer's model for this high priesthood and all its nuances derive unquestionably from the Old Testament and Jewish tradition. Melchizedek was a Canaanite priest-king (Gen 14:18); to speak of a "priest like Melchizedek" was thus to speak first of all of a priest who was also king. Israel had known a dynasty of priest-kings only in Hasmonean times, after they threw off the Syrian yoke and before they were subdued by Rome; some Jews opposed this combination. The *Dead Sea Scrolls came to separate the anointed high priest from the anointed King *Messiah, which was a necessary distinction so long as one was from Levi and the other from Judah (cf. 7:14). But Melchizedek was not Levitical; one like him would be a priest-king without being descended from the Jewish priesthood.

The *rabbis later contended that Psalm 110:4 meant that God transferred Melchizedek's priesthood from Melchizedek to Abraham; they may have argued this point to counteract Christian claims that it referred to Jesus. Melchizedek appears in some other Jewish traditions (Dead Sea Scrolls) as a heavenly figure, perhaps Michael, and is sometimes associated in Jewish literature with the end time. The writer does not appeal to this extrabiblical tradition, however, which could play into the hands of those wishing to reduce *Christ to angelic status (2:5-18); the plain statement of Psalm 110:4 is sufficient for his case.

5:7. Judaism stressed that God heard the pious; God answered Jesus' prayers by the *resurrection, however, not by escape from death. Although the writer's source here could be Psalm 22:5 and 24, it is more likely that he and his readers are acquainted with the tradition of Jesus' struggle and commitment in Gethsemane.

5:8-10. Discipline, including beatings, was an essential part of most Greek education. Classical Greek writers stressed learning through suffering, and the *Old Testament and later Jewish wisdom traditions portray divine chastisement as a sign of God's love. The Greek paronomasia here, *emathen aph' hōn epathen,* "learned from the things he suffered," was already a common play on words in ancient literature. But the writer here challenges the Greek idea that the supreme God (with whom the writer in some sense identifies the Son—1:9; 3:3-4) was incapable of feeling, pain or true sympathy. Jesus' participation in human suffering qualified him to be the ultimate high priest; the *Septuagint applies the word used here for "made perfect" to the consecration of priests (v. 9).

5:11—6:12
Press Deeper or Fall Away

The writer complains that his readers' knowledge of the Bible is inadequate to follow the rest of his argument. But he insists that they must become more biblically informed if they wish to persevere—and he proceeds to give them the rest of his argument anyway (6:13—7:28).

5:11-12. Many Greek writers used "much to say" to indicate how important their topic was. Even philosophers agreed that one must begin with simple matters before leading students to the more difficult; but they were not above complaining about their pupils' slowness to learn. Greek moralists also used "milk" and "solid food" figuratively, contrasting basic and advanced instruction. The "elementary principles" (NASB) or "elementary truths" (NIV) are the rudiments or basics (summarized in 6:1-2); Greek writers often applied the term to the alphabet. Some writers frequently reproved their readers in similar ways ("You should be teachers by now!") to stir them to learn what they should already know.

5:13. Some philosophers, like *Pythagoras, distinguished between elementary and advanced students, calling them "babes" (cf. v. 13—NASB, KJV) and "mature" (cf. v. 14; "perfect"—KJV) respectively.

5:14. Whereas Platonists disparaged mere sensory knowledge and Skeptics (another philosophical school) valued it even less, *Stoics believed that one's senses (of which there were five, as in *Aristotle) were useful, and *Epicureans particularly trusted them. Those who thought the senses at all reliable, like *Seneca and *Philo, wanted them trained for moral sensibility. The ability to differentiate critically between good and bad, i.e. between truth and falsehood, was important to Greco-Roman writers in general, although the specific application to moral sensibilities is more often Jewish (2 Sam 14:17; 1 Kings 3:9; Ezek 44:23). The writer borrows the language of Greek ethics, which would impress his *Diaspora Jewish readers, and uses it to call them to study the Bible more thoroughly.

6:1. They had to get past the basics to biblical maturity (5:11-14), or they would fall away (6:4-8). The writer probably chooses these items as the "basics" because they were the basic sort of instructions about Jewish belief given to converts to Judaism, which all the author's readers would have understood before becoming followers of Jesus. These items represented Jewish teachings still useful for followers of *Christ. Judaism stressed *repentance as a regular antidote for sin, and a once-for-all kind of repentance for the turning of pagans to Judaism; Judaism naturally stressed faith as well. Although "dead" works could echo the common Jewish denunciation of idols as dead, that specific an allusion is unlikely in this context; cf. 9:14.

6:2-3. "*Baptisms" probably refers to the various kinds of ceremonial washings in Judaism, of which the most relevant to Christianity was *proselyte baptism as an act of conversion washing away the former impurity of a pagan life. Jewish worshipers laid hands on certain sacrifices, and Jewish teachers laid hands on *disciples to ordain them; the latter was more relevant to Christian practice. The *resurrection of the dead and eternal judgment were standard Jewish doctrines, though embarrassing to some *Hellenized elements in Judaism.

6:4. Early Judaism severely limited possession of the *Spirit. The *Dead Sea Scrolls limit the activity of the holy spirit to the congregation of the children of light, that is, those who agree with them; but besides these and Christian texts, others viewed the Spirit as even rarer. The *rabbis do so the most; they generally report that the Spirit was so rare that even when someone was worthy to receive it, the unworthiness of his generation prevented him from doing so.

"Illumined" or "enlightened" clearly means converted, as in 10:32; the Dead Sea Scrolls similarly speak of their teachers as the "illuminators" and their adherents as "children of light." "Tasted" also normally meant "experienced" (2:9), and both the use of "heavenly" in the letter (cf. 3:1; 8:1-5) and the limitation of the Holy Spirit to Christians in early Christian literature also indicate that this person was genuinely converted.

6:5. Most of Judaism regarded the present age as under sin, but believed that God would rule the coming age unchallenged, after he raised the dead and judged them. Christians recognized that they had begun to experience the life of the future world; they were the vanguard of the future *kingdom (see comment on 4:10-11). On the "word" see comment on 4:2 and 12.

6:6. God had a higher standard for those who should have known better (Num 14:22-23). Judaism generally believed that some people could rebel against God so brazenly, aware that they were doing so, that they would become unable to *repent; the offense had to be extremely serious, however. (The *rabbis were not unanimous; Rabbi Meir is said to have insisted that the notorious apostate Elisha ben Abuya could repent, for example. But the majority opinion seems to have been that some could go too far, including King Manasseh. The *Dead Sea Scrolls also attest that one who had been part of the community for ten years—and thus knew full well what he was doing—and then turned away was never allowed to return. But as some writers have pointed out, this verse refers to intentional apostasy, not a single sin or drifting away that can be addressed by repentance; drifting away may be covered under Jas 5:19-20.) The point here is not that God does not accept the repentant, but that some hearts become too hard to consider repenting, because they refuse to acknowledge Christ, the only means of repentance. By willfully choosing the kind of belief that nailed Jesus to the cross, they accept responsibility again for killing him.

6:7-8. Others had also used ground choked with thorns and thistles as an image for the wicked and their spiritual destination in barrenness and death (e.g., Is 5:6). Judaism treated apostates as spiritually dead, as did *Pythagoreans and some other groups.

6:9. Greco-Roman moralists often presented their exhortations as reminders, thereby toning down the possible harshness of their words and making them more palatable: "We know, of course, that *you* would never do something like that." When they did think that their readers were likely to pursue such a course, however, they would state matters more harshly, rebuking them.

6:10. "Ministry to the saints" (KJV, NASB) probably refers to financial help. It might refer to a continuing effort to help the poor Jerusalem Christians that Paul had initiated (Rom 15:25), although by A.D. 68, with Jerusalem surrounded and the Christians having escaped safely to the wilderness, the monies would have to be sent elsewhere in Judea. On charity see, for example, comment on Matthew 6:2-4.

6:11-12. Ancient moral exhortation often emphasized imitating positive role models (some of whom this writer will list in chap. 11). As Israel "inherited" the land, so Judaism said that the righteous would "inherit" the world to come.

6:13-20
The Unbreakable Oath to Jesus

The writer compares the promise (continuing the theme of 6:12) God made to Abraham with the promise he had made to one who would be high priest after the order of Melchizedek. Although he does not quote Psalm 110:4, which states this promise, he expects his readers to understand this point presupposed by his exposition.

6:13-17. God swore this "by himself" (Gen 22:16; Ex 32:13), just like the promise to the one who would be high priest after the order of Melchizedek (Ps 110:4).

This oath is one of several by God in the *Old Testament. God had sworn an oath to David (Ps 89:35, 49; 132:11), which Jewish people expected to be fulfilled in the *Messiah; he swore to judge Israel for their sins, and he did so (Ps 106:26). But the greatest human oaths were oaths sworn "by God," and when God swore "by himself" his words were guaranteed, especially in the few instances where the oath included a promise not to change his mind (Ps 110:4; Is 45:23). As in Psalm 110:4, God swore by himself and would not change his mind that everyone would have to acknowledge him in the day of judgment (Is 45:23); he likewise swore by himself judgment on the royal house of Judah (Jer 22:5), on the Jewish refugees in Egypt (Jer 44:26), on Israel (Amos 4:2; 6:8), on Edom (Jer 49:13) and on Babylon (Jer 51:14). (*Philo claimed that God alone was worthy to bear witness to his own veracity, although he also decided that any of God's words had the force of an oath, hence he had not literally sworn by himself.) The accumulation of standard legal terms in this context is not surprising, given the legal force and common courtroom use of oaths.

6:18. Although God swore more than these two promises, the writer emphasizes here the two he has just mentioned: the one to Abraham and the one to the priest like Melchizedek. Greek philosophers believed that the gods were immutable, unchangeable; most Jewish people believed that their God was absolute and unchangeable in his character, yet he dealt with human beings as they were (Ps 18:25-26). The oath is thus important, although both

Jews and Greek philosophers believed that the one who was truly God (as opposed to the mythical antics of Greek gods) did not lie.

6:19. The "anchor" was a frequent metaphor in Greco-Roman literature, especially for the secure hold on hope which moral qualities produced. "Inside the veil" means that believers have a secure hope in the "holy of holies" (cf. Lev 16:2), which only the high priest could enter once a year. (Later *rabbinic texts also portray God as "behind the veil," from which he utters his decrees. Although this parallel illustrates that the readers of Hebrews would have caught the author's Jewish expression for God's presence in heaven, the *Old Testament is his direct source.) The writer means not the earthly but the spiritual holy of holies, in the heavenly temple (see comment on 8:1-5).

6:20. Jesus appears as forerunner often in the book (compare the idea in 2:10; 5:9); the term could be applied to a military vanguard, to first fruits, to the first-place runner and so forth. It always signifies that the rest of the company is coming afterward.

7:1-10
The Nature of Melchizedek's Priesthood

Because Scripture declares David's lord to be a priest like Melchizedek (Ps 110:4, in Heb 5:6), a Jewish interpreter would naturally ask, In what ways is he like Melchizedek? The writer's point is to show that Jesus' priesthood is greater than and so supersedes the Levitical priesthood of contemporary Judaism. Psalm 110 invites the reader to look for traits of the ultimate king in Genesis 14.

7:1. Here the author summarizes Genesis 14:17-24, in which the Canaanite priest-king of the city that later became Jerusalem blessed Abram. (The identification of Salem with Jerusalem is corroborated by Ps 76:2 and Egyptian execration texts, and assumed in *Josephus, the *Dead Sea Scrolls, and the *rabbis.)

7:2. *Philo and others commonly interpreted *Old Testament names allegorically. Jews like Philo and Josephus also interpreted Melchizedek's name as the writer of Hebrews does (as *melek*, "king," plus *tzedeq*, "righteousness").

7:3. One Jewish interpretive principle was that what was not mentioned did not happen. (Philo especially, though not exclusively—cf. the rabbis—exploited this technique. Thus, for instance, Philo argued that the wise man's family consisted of his virtues, because at one point Moses listed virtues instead of listing all ancestors. Similarly, because Cain's death is not mentioned, Cain did not die [for Philo, Cain represents deathless folly]. This technique of arguing from silence was applied selectively, of course, because *most* possible details were not mentioned in a text.) The writer of Hebrews can thus argue that Melchizedek, for the purpose of the comparison, was without parents, because Genesis 14 does not mention them, and Genesis supplies parentage and genealogy for other important representatives of God. To Greek readers, to be without beginning or end was to be divine (e.g., an argument by the philosopher Thales).

7:4. Tithing was already an ancient Near Eastern custom before it was mandated in the *Old Testament, and a form of it is also attested in Greco-Roman literature. Here the author refers to Genesis 14:20, its first occurrence in the Bible.

7:5-6. Under Old Testament law, the tithes went to the descendants of Levi, who was a descendant of Abraham (e.g., Num 18:26; 2 Chron 31:4-6; Neh

10:37-38; 13:5, 12); but Abraham tithed to someone else.

7:7-10. The writer's point is that Melchizedek (and thus the one who has inherited his priesthood—5:6) is greater than Abraham and thus greater than Levi, for Abraham is greater than Levi. Seeking to get around this argument, later *rabbis said that God withdrew the priesthood from Melchizedek (for blessing Abram before blessing God) and gave it to Abraham in Psalm 110:4; but Psalm 110 clearly refers to the ultimate priest-king who would rule over the nations, not to Abraham. Like *Philo, the writer of Hebrews believes that the perfect priest is eternal; but this writer can prove his case from Genesis 14 (or even better, from Ps 110 on Jewish premises about the future *Messiah and the *resurrection of the dead).

7:11-28
The New Priesthood Supersedes the Old

The writer of Hebrews had a difficult task. Although history was ultimately on his side—as the destruction of the temple several years later proved—he wanted all the Bible on his side, too, and the Bible said that the Levitical priesthood was "perpetual" (e.g., Ex 40:15). Although some *narratives in Scripture could undermine a literal construal of that phrase (e.g., Ex 32:10), and one could interpret the old priesthood allegorically (as some Jewish people in the writer's day did) or recognize eternal principles merely expressed in transitory, culturally relevant forms (as do many interpreters today), the writer of Hebrews had a more useful approach for his own readers. For him, the new and superior priesthood clearly promised in Scripture makes the old priesthood obsolete.

7:11-19. The *Dead Sea Scrolls eventually recognized two "anointed" figures: a warrior *messiah descended from David, hence of Judah, and an anointed priest from the tribe of Levi. But Psalm 110 allows this writer to view both roles as fulfilled by one future figure; a priest "like Melchizedek" need not be descended from Levi, and was, in fact, greater than Levi (7:4-10).

*Philo spoke of the "perfection" of Levi as a model of the perfect priesthood; the author of Hebrews disagrees. Like *Plato and his successors, this writer notes that what changes is imperfect, for the perfect by nature does not need to change. Yet God had promised another priesthood, an eternal and hence changeless one (7:17; cf. 7:3), which renders the first, imperfect one obsolete. (The term for "setting aside" in v. 18 was even used in business documents for a legal annulment.)

7:20-21. This priesthood is also greater than the Levitical priesthood because, unlike the latter, it is guaranteed with a divine oath (see comment on 6:13-18). This point constitutes a partial answer for any possible appeal to the *Old Testament claim that the Levitical prescriptions were perpetual ordinances; God changed some points in the *law when such changes were necessary to accomplish his original, eternal purpose in the law (e.g., Jer 3:16), but in this case he had sworn and promised not to change his mind.

7:22-25. On the eternal priest's superiority to temporal ones, see also 7:11-19. In the unlikely event that his readers are familiar with the politics of the Jerusalem aristocracy, they would think of the Romans' appointing and deposing of priests. More likely, however, the only issue here is the priests' mortality. The term for "guarantee" (NASB, TEV) or "surety" (KJV) in verse 22 was used in business documents for a deposit, a security guaranteeing that one would carry through on one's word or obligation, or someone who made such a guarantee.

7:26. Levitical priests were to avoid defilement, and special precautions were taken to avoid the high priest's defilement before the Day of *Atonement. This was the one day a year on which the high priest would enter the holy of holies (although he may have entered several times on that day; cf. Lev 16:13-16). Even though later *rabbis' views may be stricter than the actual practice of the Jerusalem high priests, their elaborate care to avoid the high priest's defilement is instructive (he was secluded for the week preceding that day; precautions were taken to avoid a nocturnal emission the night before; etc.). But such earthly high priests could never compare with the heavenly high priest, just as the earthly tabernacle was only a shadow of the perfect one in heaven (see comment on 3:1; 8:1-5).

7:27. High priests did not directly offer up the daily offerings, but they were responsible for the priestly service that did offer them. Fire was to burn on the altar continually; Israel's sacrifices were offered day after day; priests offered daily morning and evening sacrifices on behalf of the whole nation in the temple. The writer may be conflating the duties of the whole priesthood with the duties of the high priest on the Day of Atonement, thus stressing the necessity of repetition in the Levitical cultus. Or he might mean "daily" *hyperbolically for "continually," year after year. Only on the Day of Atonement did the high priest make an offering for his sins and then for those of the nation (Lev 16:6, 11, 15-16).

7:28. By Jesus' *resurrection he naturally qualifies for the "eternal" priesthood like Melchizedek in Psalm 110:4 (Heb 7:17). Many ancient thinkers accepted only what was eternal as "perfect." (The writer cites the promise given after the law, hence a statement that the law could not supersede. Addressing a different line of reasoning in Gal 3, Paul speaks of a promise that came *before* the law and that the law cannot annul. Thus Paul and the author of Hebrews assert promise over law from different directions.)

8:1-5
The Heavenly Tabernacle

Parallels between the heavenly and earthly were common in Judaism (e.g., the heavenly and earthly court or Sanhedrin), as elsewhere in ancient thought (e.g., the Babylonian temple of Marduk, called Esagila, and the Canaanite temple of Baal). (Some ancient Near Eastern temples and later *mithraea* were also designed to reflect the structure of the whole cosmos, signifying the deity's universal rule. *Philo naturally applied the principle of heavenly prototype and earthly copy even more broadly, following Platonic models. When specifically comparing the heavenly and earthly temples, Philo allegorized in great detail, regarding the ideal heavenly temple as virtue, its altar as ideas, its linen as earth, etc.) Correspondences between heavenly and earthly temples were presumably intended in Exodus 25:8-9, part of which is cited in Hebrews 8:5.

Much of Judaism, from *Hellenized wisdom traditions (Wisdom of Solomon 9:8) to *apocalyptic visionaries and writers and later *rabbis, spoke of the earthly temple as an imitation of the heavenly one. The eternality and value of the old temple are relativized by comparing it with the true temple in heaven.

8:1. Jesus' seat at the right hand of God was proved by Psalm 110:1 (Heb 1:13), which clearly addressed the same person as the priest like Melchizedek (Ps 110:4, cited in Heb 5:6; 7:17).

8:2-5. See on the introduction to 8:1-5. Like followers of *Plato (including, on this point, *Philo), the writer of Hebrews sees the earthly as a "copy and shadow" of the heavenly reality (8:5). (The word for "copy" means "sketch" [NRSV] or "plan, outline," as in the *LXX of Ezek 42:15, which deals with the temple of the world to come; many of its details the author of Hebrews might interpret symbolically, an approach not necessarily out of harmony with the symbolic language of Ezekiel elsewhere, e.g., 31:2-9.) Unlike Plato, the writer of Hebrews does not see the heavenly reality only as an ideal world to be apprehended by the mind: Jesus really went there. Jewish *apocalyptic writers sometimes also spoke of the future earthly kingdom (which generally included a magnificent temple) as a present reality in heaven.

8:6-13
The New Covenant

The writer produces here an extended citation from Jeremiah 31:31-34 to demonstrate his case that the Bible itself predicted a change in the *law. This text was also stressed by the *Qumran sectarians who wrote the *Dead Sea Scrolls; they saw themselves as the people of this "new covenant." But they interpreted Moses' law more strictly, whereas this writer would have been considered a more liberal Jew on this point than *Philo was (13:9), valuing the principles as eternal but the forms as cultural and temporary.

8:6-7. The author picks up a hint he dropped in 7:12: the old priesthood was tied with the old law and its covenant, and both were shown to be imperfect if they were superseded.

8:8-9. The phrase generally rendered "new" covenant in Jeremiah 31:31 could also be translated "renewed" covenant. The first covenant was meant to be written on people's hearts (Deut 30:11-14), and the righteous actually had it there (Ps 37:31; 40:8; 119:11; Is 51:7); but according to Jeremiah, most of Israel did *not* have it in their hearts (cf., e.g., Deut 5:29). The difference between the former and the new covenant would be precisely that whereas the Israelites broke the first covenant (Jer 31:32), the new law would be written within them, and they would know God (Jer 31:33-34).

8:10-12. Jeremiah echoes the language of the first covenant: "I will be their God, and they will be my people" (e.g., Lev 26:12). "Knowing" God was also covenant language, but on a personal level it referred to the sort of intimate relationship with God that the prophets had.

8:13. The writer undoubtedly says "about to disappear" because the temple service had not been directly discontinued by Jesus' exaltation, but it was at that time on the verge of disappearing. If, as is likely, this letter was written in the late 60s A.D. (see introduction), many in the *Diaspora recognized that the Romans might soon crush Jerusalem and the temple. Apart from a few groups not very dependent on the Jerusalem temple (such as the *Essenes), most Palestinian Jews were forced to make major readjustments in cultic practice after the temple was destroyed in A.D. 70.

9:1-10
The Old Tabernacle

On the principle of correspondence between the heavenly and earthly tabernacles, see comment on 8:1-5. The writer follows the *Old Testament carefully in his description in 9:1-10, not conforming it at all to the modifications of his day. (Verses 4-5 were no longer true in his own day, elements having been removed. In many Jewish traditions, they would be restored in the end times.) These verses also refer grammatically to the holy of holies; even though some traditions favor the view that the incense altar was inside the holy of holies, the author must mean instead that it belonged to the holy of holies but was not inside, as the ark was. The *Old Testament text plainly places the altar of incense in the sanctuary outside the holiest place. The Old Testament itself elsewhere—the Hebrew of 1 Kings 6:22—can put the matter ambiguously, however, but the author of Hebrews says that these items "belong to" it, not "are in" it.

Most of the details of the original tabernacle were meant to communicate something within its ancient Near Eastern culture. Some features simply informed the Israelites that this was a "temple." The three-part structure of the tabernacle, with the holy of holies in the back approached in a direct line from the front entrance of the tabernacle, was the standard design of Egyptian temples in Moses' day. The placement of the most expensive materials (such as pure gold) and dyes nearest the ark was an ancient way of glorifying the holiness of the deity and signifying that one must approach this deity with awe and reverence. Some other features of the tabernacle signify merely that God was being practical: whereas the later temple was built of cedar wood (like normal Canaanite temples), the tabernacle was built from acacia wood—the only wood available in the Sinai desert. Tent shrines were also known among nomadic peoples.

But the greatest teachings of the tabernacle lay in its contrasts with the shrines of surrounding cultures. Like most ancient Near Eastern temples, God's temple had an altar of sacrifice, an altar of incense (to overpower the stench of flesh burning from the sacrifices), a table and so on. But pagan temples often had a bed and similar apparatus for the image of the god, which was dressed, "fed" and entertained each day. Yet God's house had none of this—he was not an idol. Similarly, larger Egyptian temples often had shrines on either side for tutelary deities, but this feature is missing in God's temple—he was the only true God. The holiest place in ancient Near Eastern temples was what corresponded to the ark, on which would be mounted (sometimes enthroned on winged creatures like the cherubim) the image of the deity. But the climax of God's temple is that, where one would expect an image, there was none, because nothing could adequately represent his glory.

In suggesting that the details of the present, earthly tabernacle are significant (he believes they point to a heavenly tabernacle), the writer of Hebrews is not distorting the text. His modest suggestions are quite in contrast with the allegorizing of *Philo, who explains each detail as a symbol of something none of Moses' original readers would have guessed (linen as earth, dark red as air, the seven-branched candelabrum as the seven planets, etc.). Unlike the writer of Hebrews, however, some readers of the *Old Testament today follow Philo's more fanciful method of interpretation.

9:11-22
The Final Blood Offering

Under *Old Testament *law, sin could technically be expiated—God's anger appeased by substitution—only by bloodshed.

9:11. In typical first-century thought,

the heavens were pure, perfect and changeless; the heavenly tabernacle, then, would be the perfect prototype for the earthly and the only one that was ultimately needed. On the temple "not made with hands," see comment on Acts 7:40-41 and 48-50.

9:12. The high priest on the annual Day of *Atonement brought the blood of a bull for himself and that of a goat for the people (Lev 16:6, 11, 14, 15-16). According to the *Qumran War Scroll, "eternal redemption" arrives only at the time of the end, after the final battle; here it is inaugurated through the permanently satisfactory offering of the eternal high priest (cf. Dan 9:24).

9:13-14. Had the author wished to cite a particular proof text for a priest offering himself up, he might have compared the one who sprinkles (as the *Old Testament priests did) the nations in Isaiah 52:15 with the following context of this person carrying the sins of Israel (Is 53:4-6, 8-12); but he is content to argue instead on the basis of his comparison with the Levitical offerings. He reasons by means of a "how much more" argument (a standard argument especially used by Jewish interpreters): if the blood of sacrifices on the Day of Atonement can remove sin (hypothetically; cf. 10:4), how much more effective is the blood of *Christ.

9:15. Here the author brings together the "new covenant" (see comment on 8:6-13), redemption and an "eternal" inheritance (as opposed to the temporal inheritance their ancestors had sought in the land—chaps. 3—4; the Old Testament image of "inheriting" the Promised Land was applied in ancient Judaism to inheriting the world to come).

9:16-17. "Covenant" (NASB) can also be translated "testament" (KJV) or "will" (NIV, NRSV, TEV), and ancient writers often argued their points by plays on words. "Testaments" were sealed documents, opened only on the testator's death; "covenants" were agreements between parties or imposed by a greater party on a lesser one. (Some scholars have drawn a connection between the two in terms of the suzerain-vassal treaty form reflected in God's covenant with Israel. Because these covenants would be maintained in force dynastically—the suzerain's son would execute it after his father's death—the covenant could perhaps be understood in some sense as a testament. But this connection involves a different cultural world from the one in which the author of Hebrews usually moves, and it is not likely that he would have this connection in mind.) Regardless of the play on words (puns were used in antiquity for argumentation as well as wit), his point makes good sense: ancient covenants were normally inaugurated with blood (e.g., Gen 31:54).

9:18-20. See Exodus 24:6-8. One of the writer's minor changes in wording is attested elsewhere (*Philo), but that may be only coincidence; ancient interpreters normally felt free to modify the text in minor ways to make more intelligible its relation to the writer's point. A more significant change is the addition of water, bright red wool, and hyssop: the writer apparently midrashically connects Exodus 24 with Leviticus 14:6 or Numbers 19:6, to arouse the association of purification—in the latter case, from sin (Num 18:9).

9:21-22. See, for example, Exodus 29:37, Leviticus 8:15 and 16:16-20. To the *Old Testament *Josephus added that even the priests' garments, the sacred utensils and so on were cleansed with blood; while the writer of Hebrews may not go this far, the whole cultus was in some sense dedicated through sacrifice. Blood was officially necessary for *atonement under the law (Lev 17:11); ritual exceptions were permitted for the poorest Israelites (Lev 5:11-13), but the general rule established the principle. (Jewish tradition also interpreted the sprinkled blood of Ex 24:8 as blood for *atonement.)

9:23-28 A Sacrifice Sufficient for the Heavenly Sanctuary

9:23. The writer returns to the parallel between earthly and heavenly tabernacles (see comment on 8:1-5; 9:1-10): if the earthly sanctuary could be dedicated only by blood (9:11-22), so also the heavenly sanctuary. But a perfect sacrifice was necessary for the perfect sanctuary.

9:24-26. The "eternal" priesthood of one like Melchizedek (7:17; Ps 110:4) was not based on annual sacrifices; had "eternal" involved perpetual sacrifices, they would have had no beginning as well as no ending. But his priesthood is based on a once-for-all, finished sacrifice on the cross. Jewish people frequently divided history up into many ages (they proposed a number of different schemes), but the most basic was the division between the present age and the age to come. The "consummation of the ages" (NASB) thus refers to the goal of history, climaxing in the coming of God's reign; in the decisive act of *Christ, the writer recognizes that the future age has in some sense invaded history (cf. 6:5).

9:27-28. The author's point here is that just as people die only once (a commonplace even of Greek classical literature, though *Plato taught reincarnation), Christ had to offer himself for sin only once. When he appears (cf. v. 24) again, it will be to consummate the future salvation (just as the emergence of the priest into the outer court traditionally assured the people that the sacrifice had been accepted and their sins forgiven; cf. 1:14). "Bear the sins of many" is from Isaiah 53:12.

Although *Josephus and probably some other Jewish thinkers dabbled with the language of reincarnation in *Plato's writings, the vast majority of first-century Jews expected instead one death, then *resurrection and judgment (the sequence of the latter two varied in different Jewish accounts). Like the *Old Testament (Ezek 18:21-32), Jewish people often felt that death was the cutoff point for judgment. (Thus a late-first-century *rabbi warned *disciples to repent one day before death; those being executed should say, "May my death *atone for all my sins" [but cf. Ps 49:7-9, 15]; the dying often expected to be judged immediately—e.g., the story of Johanan ben Zakkai's pious fear when he was on his deathbed; one tradition said that the righteous were escorted by good angels and the wicked by evil ones; etc. But although other traditions did not allow for reincarnation, they did allow for temporary punishments that expiated one's remaining sins: the view that the corpse's decomposition helped atone for sin, the placing of a rock on a coffin to symbolize the execution of one who died before being executed, and the view that no Israelite could spend more than a year in *Gehenna. These views of posthumous expiation have no clear parallel in the Old or *New Testament.) This writer follows the frequent Jewish and unanimous New Testament consensus that death ended one's opportunity for reconciliation with God.

10:1-18 The True Sacrifice of the New Covenant

Only *Christ could be a sufficient sacrifice for the heavenly sanctuary (9:23-28).

10:1. *Plato spoke of the earthly world, perceived by sensory knowledge (by the earthly senses), as consisting merely of shadows of the real world, apprehended by reason alone. By the first century, even many Jewish writers (in the *Diaspora) spoke of the heavens above as pure and perfect, and the earthly as bound by corruption. Such writers often spoke of the need of the soul to escape back to the upper regions from which it originally came. Without adopting a thoroughgoing Platonic worldview, the writer of Hebrews agrees that the earthly tabernacle, at least, is a shadow of the heavenly one (he has scriptural proof for this thesis—8:5), but he also echoes the view of Jewish *apocalyptic writers: heaven reveals what the world to come will be like. For this writer, however, the first stage (9:24, 28) of that future time had already invaded history (6:5).

10:2-3. The author again plays on the idea that what is perfect need not be changed or supplemented. Rhetorical questions were commonly used in ancient reasoning. "Reminder" may mean that the annual Day of *Atonement sacrifices remind people of their sins the way Passover reminded them of God's redemptive acts (Ex 12:14; cf. Lev 16:21)—in contrast to the policy of the new covenant (8:12).

10:4. Palestinian Judaism argued that the Day of Atonement, conjoined with *repentance, was necessary for the forgiveness of most violations of the *law.

Many philosophers had revolted against the idea of blood sacrifice, which they felt was unreasonable in a perfect temple focused on the mind. That is not the premise of this writer, however, who like people in most cultures in human history recognized the need for blood sacrifice (10:19); he merely felt that animal sacrifices were inadequate for human redemption in the heavenly sanctuary (9:23), and thus unnecessary now that *Christ had come. He has plenty of *Old Testament precedent for relativizing the actual value of animal sacrifices (e.g., 1 Sam 15:22; Ps 51:16; Prov 21:3; Is 1:11; Jer 11:15; Hos 6:6; Amos 5:21-27), as he points out in his sample citation (Heb 10:5-7).

Before A.D. 70, many *Diaspora Jews and some Palestinian Jews emphasized the spiritual, figurative use of sacrificial imagery, but only a few denied the necessity of sacrifices altogether. Everyone in the ancient world, whether they had visited Jerusalem's temple or not, was familiar with animal sacrifices, which were a standard part of religion; some philosophers opposed it, but most ancient temples included it. This writer saw their past value as symbolic, pointing to the perfect sacrifice of Christ (9:23).

10:5-7. Here the author cites Psalm 40:6-8.

10:8-9. He proceeds to expound the text he has just cited. Not only has God not desired sacrifices, but the offering of sacrifices can be distinguished from God's actual will; the latter is what the psalmist came to do.

10:10. Although the *Old Testament was written in Hebrew and some *Aramaic, most first-century Jews scattered throughout the Roman world read the Old Testament in its Greek translation. Where the extant Hebrew text says "you have opened my ears," most Greek versions read "you have prepared me a body" (to do God's will). Jewish interpreters generally chose whichever reading they needed to make their point (some interpreters even changed readings slightly to make their point); both the writer of Hebrews and his readers are using the Greek version here. Consequently he expounds: "Not sacrifices, but rather a body to do God's will"—the ultimate sacrifice of *Christ's body. Such argumentation fit ancient Jewish exegetical standards and is carried out quite skillfully.

10:11-14. The author returns to his basic text, Psalm 110:1, presupposing also 110:4. An eternal priest like Melchizedek (Ps 110:4) who was to remain seated until his enemies were put down (and the enemies were yet to be put down—Heb 2:8), must have already offered his once-for-all sacrifice; priests could not offer sacrifices in a seated position.

10:15-17. Like Christianity, Judaism attributed the inspiration of Scripture to the "*Holy Spirit," who was viewed in most circles of ancient Judaism as the Spirit of *prophecy. The author returns here to one of his earlier texts, Jeremiah 31:31-34 (Heb 8:8-12), a practice commonly used to expound more recently cited texts.

10:18. If the new covenant (8:6-13) involves forgiveness of sins and sins being remembered no more (8:12; 10:17), then there is no longer a need to *atone for sins. The writer does not address the image of sin offerings or guilt offerings in Ezekiel's future temple (Ezek 40:39; 42:13; 43:18-27; 44:29); he would presumably have interpreted it symbolically, in view of the sufficiency of *Christ's death (Is 53, etc.).

10:19-25
The New Worship

10:19-20. The sanctuary was reserved for the service of the priests, but the most holy place (the Semitic expression is "holy of holies")—which is probably in view here—could be entered by the high priest alone, and even he could enter only one day a year. But Jesus the forerunner (6:20; cf. 2:10; 5:9) had dedicated the heavenly sanctuary (9:23-28), so that his followers could join him in the full presence of God (cf. comment on Rev 21:16). The veil (see comment on 6:20; cf. Mk 15:38) had separated even the priests from the full holiness of God symbolized by the most holy place, but now believers in Jesus had complete and perfect access to God's presence (Heb 4:16). God dwelling among his people in the tabernacle had pointed to a personal relationship available to those who sought him even then (Ex 33:11), despite some limitations (Ex 33:23; 34:30-35).

10:21. This verse alludes to Jesus' superiority over Moses (Num 12:7); see comment on Hebrews 3:6.

10:22. "Drawing near" could be sacrificial or moral language in the *Old Testament; here it means entering the presence of God (10:19-20) and into relationship with God (7:19, 25) through Jesus the great high priest. "Hearts sprinkled" (9:13; see, e.g., Lev 14:7; cf. Ex 24:8 quoted in Heb 9:19-20) and "bodies washed" (e.g., Lev 14:9) are imagery from the Levitical order, but the writer has a spiritual cleansing in view (Ezek 36:25-29).

Like many other *Diaspora Jewish writers, the writer of Hebrews may accept the need for both inner and outer cleansing; but the bodily cleansing here is initiatory (the Greek perfect tense) and thus refers to *baptism. *Gentile converts to Judaism were baptized to free them from Gentile impurity; the *Qumran sect required everyone to be baptized (as the first of many washings) to forsake former worldly impurities; Christians baptized new believers as a mark of initiation into a wholly new life. The symbolic value of Christian baptism would not have been lost on Jewish observers.

The conjunction of faith, hope and love as the primary virtues (10:22-24) appears to have been a specifically Christian formulation (e.g., 1 Cor 13:13; Col 1:4-5; 1 Thess 1:3).

10:23. This exhortation to "hold fast" is important given the opposition the readers face. Their opponents insist that they return to the ritual observances practiced by other Jews in their city and compromise the absolute sufficiency of *Christ. (Paul was not opposed to Christians engaging in sacrifices as a means of cultural identification, worshiping by thank-offerings, etc.—see, e.g., Acts 21:26; but like this author he would no doubt deny that sacrifices were necessary for *atonement—Rom 3:24-26. Because these readers were *Diaspora Jews who probably could go to the Jerusalem temple only rarely, and no one in their community had gone to the temple since the war had started in A.D. 66, it is more the principle than the practice that is at issue here anyway. The issue is whether they will regard Jesus as an appendage to their Judaism or as its fulfillment who supersedes previous mandatory forms of practicing the law.) As the Israelites of old should have trusted God to bring them into the Promised Land, so should this author's readers. The "faithful" one in this case may be not God the Father (11:11) but Jesus (3:2, 5).

10:24. Some ancient groups like the *Epicureans engaged in mutual exhortation; it was a standard practice of early Christianity (Rom 15:14; 1 Thess 5:14).

10:25. Greek moralists often lectured on "concord" or "harmony," warning against individualism. Jewish teachers also warned against a spirit of separatism, and even Jewish separatists (such as the *Essenes) stuck together among themselves. *Diaspora *synagogues functioned as community centers, and Jews rarely in attendance would thereby exclude themselves from the active life of their community; given the hostile reception most Jews in many places received from the *Gentile community, community cohesion was an important coping response.

Religious associations in the Greco-Roman world met together at various intervals, normally about once a month. Jewish people in the Diaspora could use their synagogues at any time, but especially gathered on weekly sabbaths (e.g., Acts 13:14, 42; 16:13). Christians seem to have gathered at least weekly (Acts 20:7; cf. also Pliny *Epistles* 10.96, an early-second-century description of Asian Christians from a pagan governor). But persecution (cf. Heb 10:32-39; 12:4) may have dissuaded some people from attending even relatively private house *churches; the Romans were suspicious of private meetings, although they would not be investigated in the East unless brought to the authorities' attention by a *delator* (accuser).

10:26-31
The Danger of Apostasy

Those who do not engage in the true worship, who do not continue to persevere (10:19-25), would ultimately fall away and be lost.

10:26. Judaism had long distinguished intentional and unintentional sin (Num 15:29-31; cf., e.g., Lev 4:2, 22); one who knew better would be punished more strictly than one who was ignorant. Sacrifices atoned for sins of ignorance, but Judaism taught that no sacrifice availed for the person who knowingly rejected the authority of God's law. (For such persons, many Jewish teachers insisted that *repentance, the Day of *Atonement and death were all necessary. Jewish teachers also observed that those who sinned presuming that they would be automatically forgiven were not genuinely repentant and hence were not forgiven.) In the *Dead Sea Scrolls, slight transgressions required temporary penance, but deliberate rebellion against God's *law demanded expulsion from the community. The sin in this context is unrepentant, thorough apostasy (10:29).

10:27. Here the author borrows the language of Isaiah 26:11, referring to the day of the Lord (for which believers hoped to be prepared—10:25).

10:28. The law of witnesses is Deuteronomy 17:6-7 and 19:15; apostasy from obedience to the true God is addressed in Deuteronomy 13:6-11 and 17:2-7. Jewish teachers recognized that everyone sinned in some ways; but a sin by which a person declared "I reject parts of God's Word" was considered tantamount to rejecting the whole law and was reckoned as apostasy.

10:29. Compare 2:2-3; here the author uses a "how much more" argument. Garbage could be "trampled down," but what was sacred was to be approached only with reverence, and trampling it underfoot was the ultimate disrespect (e.g., Is 63:18; Mt 7:6). It was a great sin to treat the holy as merely profane or as unclean; Christians had been sanctified by *Christ's blood (see comment on 9:19-22), but other Jews would simply regard Jesus' dead body as an unclean corpse (Deut 21:23). Insulting the *Spirit invited judgment (Is 63:10).

10:30. The author cites Deuteronomy 32:35-36, reading the first line of verse 36 with verse 35 instead of with what follows, to reinforce the contextual point that God had promised this vengeance against his own people. Unlike most of his citations, this one is closer to the original Hebrew form than to that of the extant Greek versions.

10:31. David had preferred falling "into God's hands," depending on his mercy, but the mercy was preceded by severe and rapid judgment (2 Sam 24:14-16; this was the prescribed judgment of the law in Ex 30:12). "Falling into [someone's] hands" and "living God" were both regular Jewish expressions.

10:32-39
Confidence in Their Perseverance

Although apostasy was a genuine possibility (10:26-31), the writer is confident that his readers, who have already endured much, will not apostatize (cf. comment on 6:9).

10:32-33. The athletic language of "contest" (v. 32—NIV) or "conflict" (NASB; see comment on 12:1-3) conjoined with "being made a public spectacle" (v. 33—NASB) or "publicly exposed" (NIV) could mean that the readers were subjected to the gladiatorial games. Although the writer probably does not mean this reference literally (since they were still alive—12:4), the image suggests the intensity of their struggle. It is not possible to identify the specific persecution involved without identifying the location of the letters' recipients (a difficult task; see introduction).

10:34. The confiscation of Christians' goods might match a situation presupposed in Macedonia (2 Cor 8:2), where both the Thessalonian and Philippian Christians were persecuted; but we do not know where the particular persecution described here occurred. That it could happen in the Roman Empire is beyond dispute: Jews were expelled from Rome under Tiberius and Claudius, although (apart from those drafted by Tiberius) they could have taken moveable property with them. Disputes over the equality of Alexandrian

Jews as citizens led to a Jewish revolt in the early second century, a massacre of the Jewish population there and confiscation of their property; in the first century, many Jews there had been driven out or killed and their homes looted during urban violence. Still considered a small Jewish sect, Christians were even more susceptible to public hostility.

The readers had remained faithful despite this persecution (cf. Tobit 1:20; 2:7-8). On the "prisoners" (no doubt fellow Christians detained in jails), see 13:3; cf. 11:36. For the "better possession," see comment on 11:10).

10:35-36. Both Judaism and Christianity (11:26) spoke of the reward for perseverance for God. On the promise cf., e.g., 6:13-20; 11:9, 13 and 39-40.

10:37. This is a citation of Habakkuk 2:3, the wording slightly adapted to apply more specifically to the writer's point about the return of *Christ (possibly reworded by combination with part of Is 26:20, from the context of which the author took words in Heb 10:27).

10:38. Here the author quotes Habakkuk 2:4, on which see comment on Romans 1:17. He follows the *Septuagint (which speaks of drawing back) almost exactly, except that he reverses the order of clauses, mentioning the righteous first. (Also, like Paul, he omits the "my" in front of "faith," joining it instead to "righteous one." Although the most common Greek version had "my" faith, i.e., God's faithfulness, the Hebrew had "his" faith, presumably that of the righteous, as Paul and this writer take it.)

10:39. The writer expounds Habakkuk 2:4 (quoted in the previous verse) in inverse order, to end (as was normal in ancient *rhetoric) on the desired note: perseverance by faith rather than apostasy. In the following chapter he defines genuine persevering faith.

11:1-31
Heroes of the Faith

After defining faith in 11:1 and introducing his thesis in 11:2, the writer surveys biblical history for samples of faith. Faith as defined by this chapter is the assurance in God's future promises, an assurance that enables one to persevere (10:32-39).

In form, the chapter is a literary masterpiece. It follows the frequent literary practice called historical retrospective, a summary of Jewish history to make a particular point, as in texts like Acts 7, 1 Maccabees 2:49-69 and Ecclesiasticus 44—50. The retrospective consists of encomiastic biographies (favorable accounts of virtuous lives). (Ancient moralists normally used examples of people who embodied the virtue they advocated, and sometimes wrote biographies for this purpose.) The writer builds the chapter around a literary device called anaphora, beginning each new account with the same Greek word, "by faith."

11:1. The author defines faith in terms of future reward, as in 10:32-39 (the Greek word often translated "now" in this verse is literally "but" or "and"). Jewish people defined ultimate "hope" in terms of the future day of the Lord. This hope is, however, an unshakable conviction in the present: "assurance" (NASB, NRSV; "being sure"—NIV) appears in Greek business documents with the meaning "title deed." To the Greek reader, what was "not seen" was what was eternal, in the heavens; here it also means what was yet to happen, as in Jewish *apocalyptic expectation (11:7; cf. 11:27).

11:2. "Gained approval" (NASB) is literally "gained testimony," as in 11:4, 5 and 39: the evidence of their lives and God's advocacy guaranteed that they would be declared righteous on the day of judgment.

11:3. The *Old Testament often taught this principle (e.g., Prov 3:19-20), but because the writer starts at the beginning of biblical history, here he refers to the creation in Genesis 1. In Greek cosmology (e.g., Hesiod, Empedocles), as opposed to many of the Jewish sources (e.g., 2 Macc 7:28), the universe was formed out of preexisting matter in a state of chaos; *Plato and *Philo believed the visible universe was formed from visible matter. Yet Philo and many Jewish teachers believed that the material universe was formed according to God's invisible, ideal pattern, embodied in his "word" or his "wisdom." Although this view may betray some Greek (especially *Stoic) philosophical influence, it was also rooted in and defended by means of the Old Testament (e.g., Prov 8:22-31).

11:4. Jewish literature praises its martyrs and offers Abel as the first example of martyrdom. (See, e.g., 4 Maccabees 18:10-19; Mt 23:35. In the Testament of Abraham, a *pseudepigraphic work of uncertain date, Abel even replaces the Greek Minos as the human judge of the dead [the role belongs to Enoch in Jubilees]. The Ascension of Isaiah and the Apocalypse of Moses, also Jewish works of uncertain date, extolled Abel among the righteous. In Philo Cain's love of self leads him to eternal corruption; other early Jewish traditions, e.g., Jubilees and 1 Enoch, provide him with other punishments.) That he still speaks is evident from the writer's implicit use of Genesis 4:10 in Hebrews 12:24.

11:5. Jewish tradition came to be divided on Enoch. The most *Hellenized Jews identified him as Atlas or other figures. More prominently, *Essene and other traditions glorified Enoch as the most righteous saint and one who had never died (e.g., Ecclesiasticus, 1 Enoch, *Qumran's Genesis Apocryphon, Jubilees). Reacting against this consensus, many *rabbis eventually interpreted "God took him" as "God killed him" so he could die in a righteous state, since (they claimed) he alternated betweeen righteous and unrighteous behavior.

The writer of Hebrews follows the most common Jewish interpretation, which was also the most natural interpretation of Genesis 5:21-24: God took Enoch alive to heaven, because he "walked with him"—i.e., was pleasing to him. Like some writers (such as *Pseudo-Philo), the writer of Hebrews follows the biblical account exactly, omitting later elaborations.

11:6. Moralists characteristically drew morals from the examples they cited; here, if Enoch was pleasing to God, it is clear that he had faith. The moral that the author of Hebrews draws from the Enoch story (v. 5) is well adapted to the context in his own letter: besides faith, cf. "draws near" (10:22), "reward" (10:35; 11:26) and possibly "seeks" (13:14; cf. 12:17).

11:7. Noah was likewise a renowned hero of early Judaism, although later *rabbis emphasized him less than early storytellers did, transferring the stories about his miraculous birth to Moses.

11:8. Judaism always extolled Abraham's faith (see the introduction to Rom 4:1-22). Historically, Abraham may have been part of a larger migration (cf. Gen 11:31-32), but his own obedience to God's call, leaving his home and relatives behind, was an act of faith (Gen 12:1, 4). Abraham's obedience was applied as a model of faith as early as the writing of Genesis, when Moses called his people to turn their backs on Egypt; the writer of Hebrews calls his readers to be ready to forsake the favor of their own families.

11:9-10. *Diaspora Judaism often described God as "architect" and "builder" (cf. 3:4) of the world. Like philosophers who could compare the cosmos with a city, *Philo saw heaven (or virtue or the Logos, the divine Word) as the "mother city," designed and constructed by God; one could not look for the heavenly Jerusalem on earth. Other Jewish people saw the new Jerusalem as the city of God for the future age (*Dead Sea Scrolls, etc.; see comment on Gal 4:26); on its foundations, see comment on Revelation 21:14. Compare also Hebrews 13:14. *Old Testament texts like Psalm 137:5-6 and New Testament texts like this one suggest that Christians' future hope is inseparably connected with Israel's history, and Christians do biblical tradition a great disservice to cut it loose from its historical moorings in ancient Israel.

11:11. Sarah was a woman of faith in the Old Testament just as Abraham was a man of faith; subsequent Jewish texts also came to extol her greatness as a matriarch.

11:12. Here the author quotes Genesis 22:17, often echoed subsequently in the Old Testament.

11:13-16. The Jewish people in the *Diaspora saw themselves only as "sojourners" among the nations; the language here has Old Testament precedent (especially Gen 23:4; cf. Lev 25:23). Like *Philo, this writer believes that earth is not the home of the righteous; heaven is. But he envisions this idea in more traditionally Jewish terms than Philo, looking for a *future* city (see also comment on 11:9-10).

11:17-19. The offering of Isaac, after years of waiting for the promise of this son, was Abraham's ultimate test of faith (Gen 22), and is often stressed in Jewish sources. This act was regarded as a model of faith to be emulated when necessary (see *4 Maccabees 14:20; 15:28; 16:20). Although Jewish tradition also noted Isaac's willingness to be sacrificed (as early as *Pseudo-Philo), the writer of Hebrews does not add to the biblical *narrative, except to expound the nature of Abraham's confidence (that God would raise him from the dead if need be; God's power to raise the dead was celebrated daily in Jewish prayers). "Only" son (cf. Gen 22:2, Hebrew text and Jewish traditions) was sometimes used, especially with regard to Isaac, to mean "specially loved" (*LXX, other Jewish traditions), even though Isaac was never Abraham's only son.

11:20. Jewish readers recognized that Isaac's blessings were inspired and that they included predictions of the future (Gen 27:28-29, 39-40).

11:21. Genesis 49 was also regarded as prophetic, and Jewish writers later expanded the predictions (also writing testaments for each of the twelve patriarchs to the patriarchs' children).

11:22. See Genesis 50:24-25. Joseph's faith provided a hope in a promise that transcended his own mortality.

11:23. The writer of Hebrews follows the biblical account here (in its *LXX form—the Hebrew only mentions the mother's decision to rescue him—Ex 2:2-3), but many Jewish writers expanded the story of Moses' birth, especially his beauty, into reports that his glory illumined the room at birth and so forth. These stories became very popular as time went on.

11:24-25. Although the author here draws a moralist application, he does not go beyond the biblical account. Many Jewish stories of this period, especially *Diaspora Jewish stories, portrayed Moses as an Egyptian military hero and stressed his great learning and knowledge (see comment on Acts

7:22). Yet the writer of Hebrews may allow the view affirmed by Philo—that Moses as son of Pharaoh's daughter was his heir. If this is the case (following a Roman understanding of adoption), Moses' rejection of this status to maintain his identification with his oppressed people (11:26) is all the more significant. Greek philosophers and moralists commonly stressed the superiority of enduring hardship over succumbing to the rule of pleasure, as Jewish tradition stressed honoring God above all else.

11:26. Forsaking riches for something greater, like piety or wisdom, was a common moral in Jewish and Greco-Roman stories, and the biblical story of Moses' life certainly illustrated that motif.

11:27. Exodus 2:14-15 indicates that Moses was afraid of the king; if this text refers to Moses' first flight from Egypt after slaying the Egyptian, perhaps the writer means a particular kind of fear (i.e., Moses was not afraid enough to deny his people), or perhaps he relativizes that fear by emphasizing Moses' faith in the unseen God (other writers, like Philo and Josephus, minimize or eliminate fear as the cause of Moses' escape). But he may refer to Moses' second departure from Egypt, with Israel following him; verse 28 also speaks of him (singular) keeping the Passover, although it is clear that all Israel kept it. Diaspora Judaism often called God "the Invisible."

11:28. Compare Exodus 12, with which all Jewish people were familiar, especially from the annual Passover celebration. Because the nature of his account is biographical, the author yields only reluctantly to describing the general experience of Israel, as opposed to Moses (v. 29).

11:29. Compare Exodus 14:29 and Nehemiah 9:11. Exodus reports the completion of Israel's faith after the miracle (Ex 14:31), but Moses and his people had to act in some faith to enter the basin (cf. Ex 14:10-22). Jewish teachers debated the immediate cause of the exodus, some affirming Israel's faith but many attributing the miracle to the faith or merit of their ancestors.

11:30. Compare Joshua 6. Some scholars have complained that the site of Jericho was uninhabited in Joshua's period, because little remains of the city from that time. But the excavator attributed the loss of this level of the city's ruins to erosion, and she was undoubtedly correct: mounds are normally formed, and ruins preserved, only when city walls exist. If Jericho's walls fell down, one would expect most of that stratum of ruins to have eroded away.

11:31. Later Jewish literature often praises Rahab's beauty and sometimes sees her as a prophetess and as a model convert to Judaism; but although *Josephus speaks favorably of her, *Philo and most earlier Jewish literature comment little on her. Hebrews, like James 2:25, follows the biblical account.

11:32-40
A Summary of Other Exploits of Faith

11:32. The writer's theme is still "by faith," but like *Philo, *Seneca and other *rhetorically trained writers, he remarks that he could go on but will not do so, settling instead for a quick summary. This remark gives the impression (in this case quite accurate) that he could provide much more evidence or many more examples; but he determines not to strain the readers' patience by continuing long after he has made his point (as some ancient rhetoricians were known to do even in law courts, displaying their eloquence for several hours without a break). By mentioning what he protests he cannot describe, however, he outlines what he would have covered. This, too, was a standard rhetorical device, allowing him to hurry while mentioning what he claims he cannot mention.

He names several of the judges (commanded to shepherd Israel—1 Chron 17:6): David, the ideal king; Samuel, founder of the schools of the prophets and overseer of the transition from judges to monarchy; and he mentions other prophets. That Barak replaces Deborah in the list fits later *rabbinic tradition and its tendency to play down biblical prophetesses, although the *Old Testament mentions neither Deborah nor Barak outside Judges 4—5. From the perspective of first-century readers, Barak would be the official victor even though Deborah was the main leader of faith.

11:33. The first three statements in the verse are general, but the third applies specifically to Daniel (Dan 6:16-24; cf. 1 Macc 2:60); although this story was amplified in early tradition (Bel and the Dragon 31-32), the writer of Hebrews follows the biblical account. Other Jewish writers also presented the endurance of Daniel and his friends before the lions and the flame as models to be emulated (for martyrs see *4 Maccabees 13:9; 16:3, 21-22).

11:34. Quenching the power of fire refers especially to Daniel's three friends (Dan 3:23-27; 1 Macc 2:59; 3 Maccabees 6:6; cf. Is 43:2), although Jewish tradition also transferred elements of that story to Abraham (*Pseudo-Philo and later *rabbis). "Were strengthened from their state of weakness" may refer particularly to Samson's regaining his strength (Judg 16:28-31), or it may be a general statement like several that follow. Much of the language of this verse comes from 1 Maccabees, which contains much historical material about pious Jewish defenders of the *law after the *Old Testament period and before the *New Testament period. It was widely known among Jewish people throughout the ancient world.

11:35-36. Women received their dead back to life under Elijah and Elisha (1 Kings 17:21-24; 2 Kings 4:35-37). "And others" marks a transition: faith does not always bring deliverance (cf. Dan 3:18), as the author's readers already knew (Heb 10:32-39) and might learn further (12:4). Nearly all Jews knew the stories of Maccabean martyrs, who were tortured in various ways: scalded to death, having skin flayed off, stretched on the wheel and so on. Regular torture practices of the Greeks included fire, thumbscrews and (what is probably meant by "tortured" here) stretching on a wheel to break the person's joints, then beating the victim to death (sometimes pounding the stomach as if it were a drum) in that helpless position. The *Maccabean martyrs were scourged, a punishment that the Romans had continued to use as well. All Jewish sources that addressed the issue agreed that martyrs would receive preferential treatment at the *resurrection, and 2 Maccabees declares that this was the hope that enabled the martyrs to endure.

11:37. "Sawn in two" fits a Jewish tradition that was popular in the second century A.D. and later but probably already known in the writer's time. When Isaiah hid in a tree the wicked king Manasseh had it—and Isaiah—sawed in half. Those stoned to death include a prophet named Zechariah (2 Chron 24:20-22; Mt 23:35); some Jewish traditions added Jeremiah. Prophets who lived outside society sometimes wore coarse animal skins (see the *LXX for Elijah's "mantle"); Elijah and similar prophets also wandered in the wilderness, and the Maccabees were later forced to live in such circumstances.

11:38. The Maccabean guerrillas hid out in caves in the Judean mountains, as David's band had in the time of Saul long before. Elijah and other prophets were sometimes forced to live in the wilderness. The idea of righteous persons of whom the world was unworthy has many partial parallels, although this formulation is the author's own.

11:39. This verse is the concluding summary of 11:3-38, rehearsing the author's thesis in 11:2. Concluding summaries of one's thesis were standard *rhetorical practice.

11:40. "Made perfect" here refers to the consummation of salvation (1:14), the *resurrection of the dead (11:35). All the righteous would be raised together at the very end of the age (Dan 12:2, 13).

12:1-3
The Ultimate Hero of Faith

The image in 12:1-3 and possibly in 12:12-13 is that of runners disciplining themselves for the race. Athletic contests were a common image in Greco-Roman literature, often used for the moral battle waged by the wise person in this world; the *Hellenistic Jewish work 4 Maccabees sometimes applied the image to martyrs. This passage (Heb 12:1-3) is the climax of the narration of past heroes of the faith (chap. 11).

12:1. "Witnesses" can function as those watching a race ("cloud" was often applied figuratively to a crowd), but the particular witnesses here are those who testified for God or received his testimony that they were righteous (11:2, 4, 5, 39). (The image could be that of a heavenly court made up of faith heroes of the past, who would judge those now vying for the same honors; the image of the heavenly court appears elsewhere in ancient Jewish sources. The idea does not correspond to the picture sometimes found in writers like the second-century Stoic philosopher Marcus Aurelius [cf. *Philo], where souls of the departed floated around for awhile after death before being resolved into the fire.) "Laying aside weights" (KJV) may refer to removing artificial weights used in training but not in races, but more likely it refers to the Greek custom of stripping off clothes to run unencumbered. The image would represent anything that would hinder his readers from winning their race (ancient writers sometimes used "weights" figuratively for vices); this encouragement is significant, for like Israel of old in the wilderness, they may be tempted to turn back.

12:2. On "author" see comment on 2:10; for "perfecter" see 9:9, 11 and 10:14. Like most ancient moralists, the writer uses human models to illustrate his chosen virtue, but his climactic illustration of the virtue of faith is the initiator and fulfiller of faith, who suffered in the hope of future reward, as these readers are to do (10:32-39). *Maccabean martyrs were said to have "looked to" (same word as here—NRSV) God, thus enduring tortures to the point of death (*4 Maccabees 17:10). The cross was an instrument of "shame" in both Roman (the standard proclamation of execution) and Jewish (cf. Deut 21:23; Josh 10:26-27) thought.

12:3. The verbs translated "grow weary" and "lose heart" were sometimes used for the exhaustion a runner could face. (The call to endurance in 12:1 reflects the language of long-distance races.)

12:4-13
Accepting Suffering as God's Instruction

Rather than questioning their faith

when they are persecuted, the readers are to embrace the suffering as a gracious opportunity to learn God's heart better.

12:4. Although some Jewish teachers said that one could violate most biblical laws if necessary to save one's life, provided that one did not profane the name of God, the earlier martyrs felt that compromising the commandments to save one's life constituted public profanation of God's name. Jesus, the ultimate hero of their faith, had shed his blood (12:2-3; cf. 9:12); his followers have to be prepared to do the same. The ultimate test of Greek athletic contests (12:1-3) was boxing, which often drew blood; but the language here indicates the ultimate test that Jesus portrayed as an expected part of Christian discipleship (Mk 8:34-38): martyrdom.

12:5-7. This quotation is from Proverbs 3:11-12 but has many biblical (e.g., Deut 8:5; Ps 94:12) and postbiblical (e.g., *Psalms of Solomon 3:4; 7:3; 8:26; 10:1-3; 13:9-10; 14:1-2; 18:4) Jewish parallels; *Philo and some *rabbis used Proverbs 3 similarly. In the context of Jewish wisdom literature, discipline was a sign of a father's love for his children, his concern that they would go in the right way; Jewish teachers felt that God purged the sins of his children by sufferings designed to *atone and to produce *repentance. Although this writer would deny that any person's sufferings could have atoning value, except for those of God in the flesh (7:25-28; cf. Ps 49:7-9), he undoubtedly agrees that they can help lead one to repentance or to a deeper relationship with God (Ps 119:67, 71, 75).

In the Greek world, the term translated "discipline" (NIV, NASB) was the most basic term for "education" (although this usually included corporal discipline), so the term naturally conveyed the concept of moral instruction. Some philosophers like *Seneca also used the image of God disciplining his children for their good, just as Jewish writers did.

12:8. In antiquity, calling someone an "illegitimate child" ("bastard"—KJV, TEV) was a grievous insult; illegitimacy negatively affected one's social status as well as one's inheritance rights. Fathers were more concerned for their heirs and usually invested little time in illegitimate sons.

12:9. God was often called "Lord of spirits" (i.e., Lord over the angels); here he is called "Father of spirits" in contrast to "earthly fathers." Jewish people developed the Old Testament image of God as Israel's father (e.g., Ex 4:22), often speaking of him in these terms. This argument is a standard Jewish "how much more" argument: if we respect earthly fathers, how much more should we respect the superhuman one?

12:10-11. Jewish teachers recognized that God's discipline, even the suffering experienced in martyrdom, was temporary, and that he would afterward reward the righteous greatly (e.g., in the *Apocrypha: Wisdom of Solomon 3:5; cf. 2 Macc 6:13-17; 7:18, 32-33). They also believed that whereas he disciplined his people, he punished the wicked more severely (Wisdom of Solomon 12:22) or would do so in the time to come (most *rabbis, *apocalyptic visionaries and writers, etc.).

12:12. "Weak hands and feeble knees" was a common description of weakening and slackness (cf. Is 13:7; 35:3; Jer 47:3; 50:43; Ezek 7:17; 21:7; Zeph 3:16), applied to moral or religious concerns in the *Dead Sea Scrolls, in Ecclesiasticus 25:23 and elsewhere. It may apply to the imagery of the race

in Hebrews 12:1-3.
12:13. "Make straight paths for your feet" suggests the quickest course in a race; the words are taken from the *Septuagint of Proverbs 4:26 with few changes.

12:14-29
Rejecting the Greatest Revelation

Turning away from Jesus was worse than Esau's shortsighted apostasy (12:16-17) and more serious than rejecting the revelation of God at Sinai (12:18-21), for Jesus is greater than Moses and greater than Abel (12:24)—he is the true and rightful leader of Israel (12:23). The vast majority of ancient Jews sought to keep the *law and were embarrassed by their ancestors in the wilderness; the writer warns that if his readers turn their backs on *Christ, they are even worse than their ancestors.
12:14-15. The image of a bitter root that can spread to infect many is from Deuteronomy 29:18, although many texts use similar images (1 Macc 1:10; a *Qumran hymn; the *rabbis). The text in Deuteronomy is quite appropriate, for it refers to apostasy, as the writer of Hebrews does.
12:16. Here the author refers to Genesis 25:31-34. *Philo regarded Esau as enslaved by sensual and temporal desires because of actions such as this one. Esau did not act as if he viewed life from a long-range perspective, much less an eternal one (the rabbis inferred from this text that he denied the future *resurrection of the dead). "Immoral" here is literally "sexually immoral" (NIV; cf. "fornicator"—KJV), the view of Esau that prevailed in Jewish tradition, undoubtedly based on his initial preference for pagan wives (Gen 26:34-35; 28:8-9).
12:17. Despite the "tears," which reflect Genesis 27:38, Esau was unable to persuade his father Isaac to change his mind, probably because the first blessing could not be annulled. (One commentator points out that the expression "place for repentance" was used in Roman legal documents as "an occasion to reverse a previous decision." Although neither the author nor his readers would be thinking in terms of legal terminology, it might reflect a more general idiom, which could apply to Isaac's choice [although the commentator applies it to Esau].) Esau's disinheritance from the promise (cf. Heb 6:12-18) was settled. (According to one nonbiblical Jewish tradition, Jacob later killed Esau in a war, but the writer of Hebrews does not go beyond the biblical account.)
12:18. Here the author describes Mount Sinai at the giving of the law (Ex 19:16; Deut 4:11-12).
12:19. In Exodus 20:18-21, when God had given the Ten Commandments, the people were afraid of God's awesome holiness. They wanted Moses to mediate for them, fearing that if God spoke to them directly, they would die (Ex 20:19; Deut 5:25-27), for he came as a consuming fire (Deut 4:24; 5:24-25). But God's purpose was to scare enough sense into them to get them to stop sinning (Ex 20:20).
12:20. Here the author uses Exodus 19:12-13. God was so unapproachably holy that violation of his command not to approach the mountain from which he gave the law was punishable by death, even for animals that happened to wander that way unwittingly (cf. Num 17:13).
12:21. When God became angry at Israel for violating his prohibition of idolatry, even Moses was afraid of God's anger (Deut 9:19).
12:22. Mount Zion (Jerusalem or the Temple Mount in Jerusalem), as op-

posed to Mount Sinai, was to be the place of the giving of the new law in the end time (Is 2:1-4). On the heavenly Jerusalem see comment on 11:9-10; everyone in antiquity would regard a heavenly place of revelation as superior to an earthly place, no matter how glorious (12:18-21) the latter was.

Jewish tradition stressed the vast number of angels present at the giving of the law (eventually claiming thousands per Israelite); the writer of Hebrews probably takes the angels from Psalm 68:17, a text which probably refers to the giving of the law, as later Jewish tradition also understood it.

12:23. Long before the first century, the *Septuagint applied the term translated "*church" to the "assembly" (NRSV) or "congregation" of Israel in the Hebrew *Old Testament; thus the writer of Hebrews here contrasts the congregation led by Jesus with the one led by Moses (12:19). (On the "firstborn" see comment on 1:6; because the reference is in the plural, it may refer to God's people as a whole here—e.g., Ex 4:22). "Enrolled" (NASB, NRSV) means that their names were "written" (KJV, NIV, TEV) on the list in heaven; the Jewish image of heavenly tablets and the book of life was common (see comment on Phil 4:3; Rev 20:12). In *apocalyptic texts like *1 Enoch, "spirits" or "souls" referred to the righteous dead in heaven (various texts apply it even more commonly to angels, but it would not make sense in regard to "spirits of righteous men," which was a usual designation for the righteous dead, not for guardian angels). Many *Diaspora Jews believed that the righteous finally attained perfection in death (or in *resurrection; cf. Heb 11:40; it has been suggested that the righteous of 12:23 include the heroes of chap. 11).

12:24. Moses was considered mediator of the first covenant. As mediator of a new covenant (9:15; see comment on 8:6-13), Jesus had to inaugurate it through the sprinkling of blood (see comment on 9:15-22). Abel's blood spoke, bringing condemnation against his murderer (Gen 4:10; cf. Prov 21:28; see comment on Heb 11:4). (In *rabbinic tradition, the blood of all the descendants who would have been born from Abel cried out to God against Cain, and Cain thus had no share in the world to come. Blood crying out is also found in the *Sibylline Oracles, 2 Macc 8:3 and elsewhere; cf. Deut 21:1-9. See comment on Mt 23:35 for the traditions about Zechariah's blood testifying; other rabbinic stories also suggested that they believed the blood of a murdered person kept seething till it had been avenged.) Jesus' blood, dedicating a new covenant of forgiveness, thus speaks "better things" than Abel's blood.

12:25. The comparison between Mount Sinai and a heavenly Mount Zion returns to the writer's standard *qal vahomer* or "how much more" argument (a fortiori arguments, "from lesser to greater"—here worked in converse—were common, especially in Jewish argumentation, but also appear in Greco-Roman and other argumentation; cf. Prov 15:11). If the law was glorious, and profaning it was something to fear, "how much more" to be feared is profaning the more awesome glory of the new covenant given from heaven (12:25-29).

12:26. The land quaked when God came to give the law on Mount Sinai (Ex 19:18; cf. *2 Baruch 59:3); later Jewish tradition amplified this point to say that God shook the whole world. The idea of a great end-time earthquake has *Old Testament (Is 13:13) and later Jewish parallels (e.g., 2 Baruch 32:1), but the writer quotes Haggai

2:6 (cf. 2:21) directly.

12:27. The author expounds the text he has just cited. Because Haggai 2:5 mentioned a promise God made when he brought Israel out of Egypt, and "once more" in 2:6 refers to a particular previous shaking, it was natural to read the first shaking of 2:6 as what happened at Sinai. The second shaking was clearly the future one when God would subdue the nations and fill his temple with glory (2:7). The writer of Hebrews adds to this text an interpretive perspective he shares with his readers, a perspective stressed in Greek philosophy but not incongruent with the Old Testament: what cannot be changed is truly eternal.

12:28. Like many Jewish writers, the author of Hebrews uses the language of sacrificial offerings figuratively for the appropriate attitude of worship (cf. 13:15; see comment on Rom 12:1). For the unshakable *kingdom, cf. perhaps Psalm 96:10 (especially in the *LXX, numbered 95:10).

12:29. The author takes over Deuteronomy 4:24 directly; cf. also Deuteronomy 9:3 and Exodus 24:17. Deuteronomy 4:24 goes on to call God "a jealous God"; Hebrews 12:29 is clearly a warning against taking his ultimate revelation for granted.

13:1-17
Closing Exhortations

Parenesis, an ancient *rhetorical and literary style especially consisting of moral exhortations loosely fitted together, could be conjoined with other literary elements. Moral exhortations often followed argumentation, as in many of Paul's letters (e.g., Rom 12—14; Gal 5—6; Eph 4—6).

13:1. See comment on 10:25; cf. 12:14. The bonds of Christian community would also hinder apostasy from that community.

13:2. Hospitality normally involved housing and caring for travelers; the greatest example of this virtue cited in Jewish texts was Abraham, who welcomed the three visitors (Gen 18). Because at least two of them turned out to be angels, this text is the most natural referent of the exhortation. (Other stories, like the early Jewish story of Tobit or Greek stories about gods visiting people in disguise, are of more peripheral value, but illustrate how readily ancient readers might have received the exhortation.)

13:3. By the second century, Christians were known for their care for the imprisoned. Some philosophers regarded visiting those who were in prison as a virtue, although Palestinian Judaism was largely silent on the issue, compared to its emphasis on visiting the sick or helping the economically oppressed (except in the sense of Jews captured or enslaved by pagans). "The prisoners" probably refers to some Christians imprisoned for their faith or for practices related to it (as in 13:23). Roman law used prison as detention until punishment rather than as punishment itself; sometimes prisoners had to depend on outside allies for food.

13:4. Many ancient writers spoke of honoring the "(marriage) bed" (the "bed" was an idiom for intercourse); one story goes so far as to emphasize a virgin's purity by noting that no one had ever even sat on her bed. Male sexual immorality was rife in Greco-Roman society, which also accepted prostitution; pedophilia, homosexual intercourse and sex with female slaves were common Greek practices until a man was old enough for marriage. A few Greek philosophers even thought marriage burdensome but sexual release necessary. The writer accepts not typical Greek values, but God's values represented in Scripture and also upheld by Jewish circles in his day.

13:5. The author draws this quotation especially from Deuteronomy 31:6, 8 and Joshua 1:5, although the idea was common in the *Old Testament (cf. 2 Chron 15:2; Ps 37:28). Moses spoke it to all Israel in the third person, but the writer, who regards all Scripture as God's inspired Word, uses Joshua 1:5 (an assurance oracle, one form of Old Testament *prophecy, to Joshua) to adapt it to the first person. The reference to love of money is characteristic of general parenesis (moral exhortation) of the day but may be particularly related to the economic consequences of following Jesus in a hostile culture (Heb 10:34; 11:26).

13:6. Here the author cites Psalm 118:6; cf. Psalm 56:11. The author may add this quotation to Deuteronomy 31:6 and 8 as an implicit *gezerah shavah* (linking of texts with a common key word or phrase), because Deuteronomy 31:6 and 8 say that the hearers should not be afraid (although the writer of Hebrews does not quote that line).

13:7. Public speakers and moralists generally cited examples for imitation, especially those most closely known to both writer and readers. The past tense of the verbs here may indicate that some of them have died (though not by martyrdom—12:4). "Led" probably refers to local leaders rather than someone like Paul, who was likely martyred a few years before this letter was sent.

13:8. *Philo and probably many *Diaspora Jews particularly emphasized the *Old Testament picture of God's changelessness (Ps 102:27; Mal 3:6; cf. Is 46:4), because they had to communicate the truth about God to Greeks, who felt that only what was changeless was truly eternal.

13:9. Leviticus 11 and Deuteronomy 14:3-20 listed "unclean" foods that Jewish people were to avoid, thus differentiating them from the nations around them. Philo allegorized these food laws but argued that one should still keep them literally; at the same time, he also testifies that some extremely *Hellenized Jewish people in his day viewed them as only symbolic and did not practice them. The writer of Hebrews does not reject them by interpreting them nonliterally; he simply believes that a new time has come, and the foods previously forbidden did not directly benefit those who abstained, making the prohibitions no longer necessary.

13:10. Now the author addresses a special kind of food in the Old Testament: the priests' portion in the tabernacle/temple (see comment on 1 Cor 9:13). Believers, he says, serve as priests (13:15) at a different kind of altar (cf. 7:13).

13:11. Burning sacrifices outside the camp was part of several different rituals (cf. Lev 9:11; Num 19:3), but the reference here is to the Day of *Atonement, when the priest went into the holy of holies with the blood of the sacrifice (Lev 16:27). This is the sacrifice Jesus fulfilled for the heavenly altar mentioned previously in Hebrews.

13:12-13. Blood was sprinkled to "sanctify" (set apart as holy) or "cleanse" things under the law (9:22). (That Jesus could cleanse by his own blood may indicate his superiority to the *Old Testament high priest, who had to wash himself before returning to the camp after the sacrifice—Lev 16:28.) That Jesus was crucified and buried outside Jerusalem's walls fits both the Gospel accounts and the Jewish requirement that the dead be buried outside the city (so as to avoid contracting ritual uncleanness caused by contact with graves; cf., e.g., Lev 24:14; Num 15:35-36; Deut 17:5; 22:24). Roman law also required that crucifixions occur "outside the gate." (Some commentators have also noted that the sin offerings of the Day of Atonement were burned outside the camp—Lev 16:27—but it should be observed that they were also sacrificed in the temple or tabernacle—Lev 16:5-19.) Leaving the camp for these Jewish-Christian readers may imply being willing to be expelled from the Jewish community whose respect they value, to follow the God of Judaism wholeheartedly (cf. Heb 11:13-16).

13:14. See comment on 11:10 for the hope of the eternal Jerusalem in ancient Judaism.

13:15-16. The *Dead Sea Scrolls often use sacrificial language for praises, as do other ancient writers (see comment on Rom 12:1); Hebrews is probably especially dependent, however, on Hosea 14:2 here. For spiritual sacrifices, cf. also Psalm 4:5, 27:6, 40:6, 50:7-15, 51:17, 54:6, 69:30-31, 119:108 and Proverbs 21:3. *Pharisees also stressed God's acceptance of piety as a spiritual offering, a factor that may have helped Pharisaism survive the destruction of the temple in A.D. 70; only a few Palestinian Jewish movements, such as Pharisaism's successors and the Jewish Christians, survived without the temple.

13:17. The writer urges his readers to submit to present leaders (probably as they did to former ones—13:7), whom he presents as "watchmen" (see Ezek 3:17; 35:7; cf. Is 21:8; Hab 2:1). A theme of Greco-Roman moralists had long been advice to peoples on how to submit to rulers; this author gives a brief exhortation that functions as a "letter of recommendation," placing his own authority behind that of their *church's leaders. This author is not as leader-centered as some other groups like the *Qumran community were, however; the *Dead Sea Scrolls report that the leaders of the community would determine members' progress or lack of it, affecting members' standing in the community, hence before God.

13:18-25 Conclusion

13:18-19. This may be the prayer request of one unjustly imprisoned; cf. 13:23.

13:20-21. On Jesus as the "shepherd," see comment on the introduction to John 10:1-18. The *Septuagint of Isaiah 63:11 says that God "brought up the shepherd of the sheep" (Moses) from the sea. The prophets had also prophesied a new exodus (which could include coming up from the sea), which was fulfilled in *Christ (on comparing the sea and the *resurrection, see comment on Rom 10:7).

The first covenant was inaugurated by "the blood of the covenant" (Ex 24:8), sometimes called the "eternal covenant" (*Psalms of Solomon 10:4; *Dead Sea Scrolls). But the new covenant would also be called "eternal" (Is 55:3; Jer 32:40; Ezek 37:26), and it was the blood of this covenant to which the author of Hebrews refers (9:11-22).

13:22. Philosophers and moralists provided "messages of exhortation." Such spoken messages could also be given in writing, especially in letter-essays like Hebrews. Professional public speakers (*rhetoricians) often remarked that they had spoken briefly or poorly when such was clearly not the case, to claim for themselves less than was obvious.

13:23. If, as is likely, Timothy was arrested under Nero in Rome, he may well have been released on Nero's death, because the Praetorian Guard and the Roman aristocracy had long before lost faith in Nero's policies. This background would set the letter in the late 60s (see introduction).

13:24-25. "Those from Italy" could mean people from Italy now living elsewhere, possibly sending greetings back to Italy; most commentators who take this view think it refers to Aquila and Priscilla (Acts 18:2). More likely—especially given the probable place of Timothy's imprisonment (13:23)—is the view that he sends greetings from saints in Italy, and that the letter is written from Rome.

JAMES

Introduction

Authorship. That "James" need not further specify which James he is in 1:1 suggests that he is the most prominent and well-known James of the early *church, James the Lord's brother (Acts 12:17; 15:13-21; 21:17-26; 1 Cor 15:7; Gal 2:9, 12), as in church tradition. (James was a common name, and when one spoke of a less commonly recognized individual with a common name, one usually added a qualifying title, e.g., "Plato the comic poet," "James the lesser" in the apostolic list and many people in ancient business documents.)

The main objection to this proposal is the polished style of the Greek language of the letter, but this objection does not take account of several factors: (1) the widespread use of *rhetoric and more than sufficient time for James, the main spokesperson for the Jerusalem church, to have acquired facility in it; (2) that as the son of a carpenter he had probably had a better education than Galilean peasants; (3) the spread of Greek language and culture in

Palestine (e.g., *Josephus, Justin); (4) excavations showing that most of Galilee was not as backward as was once thought; (5) the widespread use of amanuenses (scribes) who might, like Josephus's editorial scribes, help a writer's Greek.

The situation depicted in the letter best fits a period before A.D. 66 (the Jewish war with Rome), and James was killed about A.D. 62. The letter probably should be viewed as genuinely from James; *pseudepigraphic letters usually circulated long after the death of the person the author claimed to be, and a date between A.D. 62 and 66 would allow insufficient time for this letter to be a pseudepigraphic composition.

James the Just. *Josephus and some later Jewish-Christian writers reported the great esteem that fellow Jerusalemites, especially the poor, had for James. Non-Christian as well as Christian Jerusalemites admired his piety, but his denunciations of the aristocracy (as in 5:1-6) undoubtedly played a large role in the aristocratic priesthood's opposition to him. About the year A.D. 62, when the procurator Festus died, the high priest Ananus II executed James and some other people. The public outcry was so great, however, that when the new procurator Albinus arrived, Ananus was deposed from the high priesthood over the matter.

***Genre.** Greek writers, including Jewish writers enamored with Greek thought, often listed loosely related exhortations in a style called parenesis. Some modern writers have argued that James is this sort of work (some even view the letter as a New Testament collection of proverbs), but they fail to observe the close literary connections running throughout the book. It may be that James or one of his followers has adapted his sermonic material into a letter, but the connectedness of the material demonstrates that the letter in its present form is a polished, unified work.

James reads more like an essay than a letter, but one kind of ancient letter in which moralists and skilled *rhetoricians engaged was a "letter-essay," a general letter intended more to make an argument than to communicate greetings. Writers like *Seneca and Pliny used literary epistles of this sort, which were published and meant to be appreciated by a large body of readers (1:1). The messenger who delivered it would presumably provide appropriate words of explanation; like letters from Jerusalem high priests to *Diaspora *synagogues, a letter from a respected leader in the Jerusalem *church would carry much weight. James draws on Greco-Roman rhetorical conventions, Jewish wisdom and Jesus' teachings (especially as now found in Mt 5—7).

Situation. Over a century before this time, the Roman general Pompey had cut Judean territory and made many Jewish peasants landless; the exorbitant taxes of Herod the Great must have driven more small farmers out of business. In the first century, many peasants worked as tenants on larger, feudal estates (as elsewhere in the empire); others became landless day laborers in the marketplaces, finding work only sporadically (more was available in harvest season). Resentment against aristocratic landlords ran high in many parts of the empire, but nonpayment of promised goods to them was hardly an option; a few landowners even had their own hit squads of hired assassins to deal with uncooperative tenants. The situation was less extreme in the cities, but even there the divisions were obvious (e.g., the aristocracy in Jerusalem's Upper City versus the poor living downwind of that city's sewers). When the aristocratic priests began to withhold tithe income from the poorer priests, their only means of support, economic tensions began to climax.

In Rome, grain shortages often led to rioting. Social and economic tensions in Palestine were contained longer but eventually yielded to violence. Pursuing peace with Rome through practical politics, the Jerusalem aristocracy became an object of hatred to *Zealots and other elements of resistance, who felt that God alone should rule the land. (*Josephus, who wished to minimize the anti-Roman sentiment that prevailed in Judea just before the war, tried to marginalize the Zealots as a fringe group; but other evidence in his *narrative shows clearly that revolutionary sympathies were widespread.) Various outbreaks of violence eventually culminated in a revolt in A.D. 66, followed by a massacre of priests and the Roman garrison on the Temple Mount. Aristocratic and proletarian patriots clashed inside the city as Roman armies surrounded it, and in A.D. 70 Jerusalem fell and its temple was destroyed. The final resistance stronghold at Masada fell in A.D. 73.

Audience. James addresses especially Jewish Christians (and probably any other Jews who would listen) caught up in the sort of social tensions that eventually produced the war of A.D. 66-70 (see comment on Acts 21:20-22). Although the situation most explicitly fits James's own in Palestine, it also addresses the kinds of social tensions that were spreading throughout the Roman world (1:1). During the Judean war of 66-70, Rome violently discarded three emperors in a single year (A.D. 69), and immediately after the Judean war resistance fighters continued to spread their views to Jews in North Africa and Cyprus. But as in the case of most general epistles, this letter reflects especially the situation of the writer more than that of any potential readership elsewhere.

Argument. James addresses the pride of the rich (1:9-11; 2:1-9; 4:13-17), persecution by the rich (2:6-7; 5:6) and pay withheld by the rich (5:4-6). He also addresses those tempted to retaliate with violent acts (2:11; 4:2) or words (1:19-20, 26; 3:1-12; 4:11-12; 5:9). He responds with a call to wisdom (1:5; 3:14-18), faith (1:6-8; 2:14-26) and patient endurance (1:9-11; 5:7-11). Once understood in the context of the situation, his supposedly "disjointed" exhortations all fit together as essential to his argument.

Commentaries. Peter Davids, *The Epistle of James,* NIGTC (Grand Rapids, Mich.: Eerdmans, 1982); and Ralph P. Martin, *James,* WBC 48 (Waco, Tex.: Word, 1988), are the best; the essay by Ralph P. Martin, "The Life-Setting of the Epistle of James in the Light of Jewish History," in *Biblical and Near Eastern Studies: Essays in Honor of William Sanford LaSor,* ed. Gary A. Tuttle (Grand Rapids, Mich.: Eerdmans, 1978), pp. 97-103, is also helpful on background. For those who do not work well with Greek, much of the same material in Davids's earlier work is found in his NIBC commentary on James (Peabody, Mass.: Hendrickson, 1989). James is more favored with helpful commentaries than most other books, from Joseph B. Mayor, *The Epistle of St. James,* 3rd ed. (1913; reprint, Minneapolis: Klock & Klock, 1977), to James Hardy Ropes, *A Critical and Exegetical Commentary on the Epistle of St. James,* ICC (Edinburgh: T. & T. Clark, 1916), and Sophie Laws, *A Commentary on the Epistle of James,* HNTC (San Francisco: Harper & Row, 1980), and, somewhat less helpful, H. Greeven's reissue of Martin Dibelius, *A Commentary on the Epistle of James,* Hermeneia, trans. M. A. Williams (Philadelphia: Fortress, 1976), all of which give detailed parallels to specific verses.

1:1-11
How to Face Trials

In this opening section James introduces the major themes of his letter, by which he responds to the trials of poverty and oppression faced by Jewish Palestinian peasants in his day.

1:1. The three basic elements of a letter's introduction were (1) the author's name; (2) the name of the recipient(s); (3) a greeting (usually the same greeting as here). Because this is a "general letter" (cf. comment on "letter-essays" in the introduction to James under "genre"), it proceeds immediately to the argument, without other epistolary features.

Because "James" is an English substitution for the original "Jacob" (as always in the *New Testament), some writers have surmised here a symbolic "Jacob" addressing the twelve tribes of Israel, as Jacob addressed his descendants in the testament in Genesis 49. This suggestion would work better on the assumption of *pseudonymity, but it is also possible that James would play on his own name. Plays on names were common (e.g., Mt 16:18). On the author and audience, see the introduction.

Most Jewish people believed that ten of the twelve tribes had been lost for centuries, and they would be restored only at the end of the age. They were thought to exist somewhere, however, so James's address may just mean, "To all my Jewish brothers and sisters scattered throughout the world." The "dispersion" or *Diaspora included Jews in the Parthian as well as the Roman Empire, and James would meet Jews from many nations at the pilgrimage festivals to Jerusalem. Some commentators believe that he means the term symbolically for all Christians as spiritual Israelites, on the analogy of 1 Peter 1:1, but given the letter's contents, James probably particularly addresses Jewish Christians.

1:2. The specific trials he addresses in this letter are the poverty and oppression experienced by the poor (1:9-11; 5:1-6; cf. 2:5-6).

1:3-4. Jewish tradition repeatedly stressed the virtue of enduring testings and occasionally stressed joy in them due to faith in God's sovereignty. (*Stoic philosophers also stressed contentment in them, because they affirmed that one could control one's response to them, but one could not control Fate.) Addresses like "friends," "beloved" and "brothers" were common in ancient moral exhortation; "brothers" was used both for "fellow countrymen" and for "fellow religionists." One point leading to another, yielding a list of several items (as here; 1:14-15; Rom 5:3-5; 2 Pet 1:5-7), was a *rhetorical form known as concatenation. Lists of vices and virtues were also a conventional literary form.

1:5. Jewish wisdom traditions often stressed endurance and gave practical advice concerning how to deal with trials. The prime *Old Testament example of asking God (cf. 4:2-3) for wisdom is 1 Kings 3:5 and 9 (cf. also in the *Apocrypha, Wisdom of Solomon 8:21; 9:5; Ecclus 51:13-14), and God was always recognized as its source (e.g., Prov 2:6). In Jewish wisdom, upbraiding or reproaching was considered harsh and rude under normal circumstances, although reproof was honorable.

1:6. The image of being driven on the sea was common in Greek literature and occurs in Jewish wisdom texts; cf. especially Isaiah 57:20 and the saying about the insincere in Ecclesiasticus 33:2. In the context of James, asking for wisdom in faith means committing oneself to obey what God reveals (Jas 2:14-26).

1:7-8. Jewish wisdom texts condemn the double-minded or double-tongued person (cf. also 1 Chron 12:33; Ps 12:2); like philosophers, Jewish sages abhorred the hypocrisy of saying one thing and living another, and speaking or living inconsistently. (See comment on Jas 4:8 for the function of this warning in James.)

1:9-11. Wealthy landowners exploited the poor throughout the Empire, and Palestine was no exception; such economic tensions eventually provoked a war against Rome, in the course of which less well-to-do Jewish patriots slaughtered Jewish aristocrats.

The Old Testament and Jewish wisdom literature stress that riches fade, that God vindicates the oppressed and the poor in the end, and that he judges those who keep their wealth and do not share with the poor. James's final statement here resembles Isaiah 40:6-7 and Psalm 102:4, 11 and 16, although the idea was by this time common. The "scorching wind" (NASB) might refer to the sirocco, an especially devastating hot wind blowing into Palestine from the southern desert. But the summer sun by itself was also quite effective in wilting Palestinian flowers, which were then useless except as fuel.

1:12-18
The Source of Testings

1:12. James uses the beatitude form common in ancient literature, especially Jewish literature: "How happy is the person who . . ." Distresses were viewed as temptations, providing opportunities to sin. The term translated "trials" (NASB, TEV; cf. NIV) or "testing" did not necessarily mean "temptation" (KJV, NRSV) in the modern sense, however; the tester could be interested in the distressed person's perseverance, rather than his or her defeat. Famines, poverty and oppression were among events viewed as testings.

1:13-16. God clearly "tested" people in the Bible and later Jewish literature (Gen 22:1; Deut 8:2; 13:3; Judg 2:22), but he never tested them in the sense that is implied here: seeking for them to fail instead of persevere. Jewish texts distinguished between God's motives in testing people (in love, seeking their good) and *Satan's motives in testing them (to make them fall). In most Jewish texts, Satan (also called Belial and Mastema) fills the role of tempter. Although James does not deny Satan's indirect role (4:7), he emphasizes here the human element in succumbing to temptation. He personifies "desire" (NIV, NRSV, TEV) or "lust" (KJV, NASB) as enticing a person, then illegitimately conceiving the child "sin," which in turn brings forth "death"; Jewish teachers occasionally applied the *rhetorical technique of personification to the "evil impulse" all people had.

That people "tested" God in the *Old Testament is also clear (Num 14:22; Ps 78:18, 41, 56; 95:9; Mal 3:15), but again these examples mean that they tried to put him to the test, not that they led him to *succumb* to temptation. James could adapt the term in the light of the Greek philosophical idea that God could not be affected or changed by human actions, nor could he cause evils in the world. But more likely James is simply working with a different nuance of the term for "test"; in the Old Testament God is clearly the direct cause of judgment (e.g., Amos 4:6-11), and he listened to human pleas (Gen 18:23-32; Ex 32:10-13). The meaning is thus as in Ecclesiasticus 15:11-12 and 20: people choose to sin, and they dare not say that God is responsible for their response to testing (by contrast, Greek literature was full of people protesting that their temptation was too great to resist).

1:17. Rather than sending testing to break people (1:12-16), God sends good gifts, including creation or rebirth (v. 18). That God is author of everything good was a commonplace of Jewish and Greek wisdom. That what is in the heavens is perfect was a common belief in antiquity, and Jewish writers sometimes used "from above" to mean "from God."

"Father of lights" could mean "Creator of the stars"; the pagans viewed the stars as gods, but Jewish people viewed the stars as angels. (Canaanites at Ugarit had long before called El the "Father of lights," and the *Dead Sea Scrolls call God's supreme angel "Ruler of lights." Various ancient Jewish texts call stars "the lights"—cf. Gen 1:14-19; Jer 31:35.) Ancient astronomers used words like "moving shadows" to describe the irregularities of heavenly bodies; but philosophers viewed what was perfect, what was in the heavens, as changeless and without direct contact with earth. Most of the ancient world believed in astrology and feared the powers of the stars. James is not supporting astrology; rather, like other Jewish writers, he is declaring God lord over the stars while denying God's inconsistency. To ancient readers his words would thus proclaim: testings are not the result of arbitrary fate, but the faithful workings of a loving Father.

1:18. Whether he refers to believers' rebirth through the *gospel (cf. 1:21; 1 Pet 1:23; see comment on Jn 3:3, 5) or to humanity's initial creation by God's word (Gen 1:26) is disputed; "first fruits" may favor the former meaning (the beginning of the new creation). The point is clear either way: God's giving birth is contrasted with desire's giving birth (1:15), and it illustrates God's grace toward people (1:17).

1:19-27
True Religion

James now turns to appropriate ways to *deal* with testing (1:2-18). The *Zealot-like model, which was gaining popularity in Jewish Palestine and would ultimately lead to Jerusalem's destruction, was not the appropriate response. James condemns not only violent acts but also the violent *rhetoric that incites them.

1:19. These are by far some of the most common admonitions in Jewish wisdom, from Proverbs on (e.g., 14:29; 15:18; 16:32; 19:11); Greek parallels are no less easy to adduce. James contrasts this biblical and traditional wisdom with the spirit of revolution sweeping his land.

1:20. The militant Jewish resistance emphasized striking out at the Romans and their aristocratic vassals, supposing that they would be acting as agents of God's righteous indignation. But James associates righteousness with peace (3:18) and nonresistance (5:7).

1:21. "Wickedness" (NASB) in this context must refer to unrighteous anger (1:20); "meekness" (KJV) is the virtue of the nonresistant.

1:22. Receiving the word (1:21) meant more than hearing it; they had to live accordingly (1:19-20). (The proposal that "the ingrafted word" refers to the *Stoic concept of "innate reason," using similar language, fails on this point: "innate" reason need not be "received.") Although most Jewish teachers (some disagreed) valued learning the *law above practicing it—because they held that practice depended on knowledge—they all agreed that both were necessary to fulfill the law. That one must not only know but must also obey truth was common moral wisdom, which the readers would not dispute. Hearing without obeying indicated self-delusion (cf.

Ezek 33:30-32).

1:23-24. The best mirrors were of Corinthian bronze, but no mirrors of that period produced the accurate images available today (cf. 1 Cor 13:12). Those with enough resources to own mirrors used them when fixing their hair; if James alludes to such people, he portrays the forgetful hearer as stupid. More likely, he refers to many people who had no mirrors and saw themselves rarely, who might more naturally forget their own appearance. In this case the reference is to the ease with which one loses the memory of the word, if one does not work hard to put it into practice. (Some moralists recommended use of a mirror to emphasize moral reflection. Perhaps one who heard in the word how a new creation should live—1:18-20—but failed to practice it was forgetting what he or she had become. But the mirror analogy probably means only the quick forgetting of the word, as above.)

1:25. The mirror is an analogy for the law (as at least once in *Philo), which was thought to bring liberty. Philosophers believed that true wisdom or knowledge freed them from worldly care; the liberty here, however, as in many Jewish sources, seems to be from sin (1:19-20). (On conceptions of freedom, see comment on Jn 8:33.)

1:26. James again condemns uncontrolled speech, such as the impassioned denunciations of Roman rule likely to lead to violence.

1:27. In contrast to the violent and unruly religion of the Jewish revolutionaries, true religion involves defending the socially powerless (Ex 22:20-24; Ps 146:9; Is 1:17) and avoiding worldliness (i.e., the values and behavior of the world; see comment on 4:4). Orphans and widows had neither direct means of support nor automatic legal defenders in that society. In Judaism, charity distributors made sure that widows and orphans were cared for if they had no relatives to help them; such charity is also part of the visiting envisioned here. Greek society did look out for freeborn orphans, but not other ones. Jewish people visited the bereaved especially during the first week of their bereavement but also afterward, and they likewise visited the sick. Many Greco-Roman writers also valued visiting the sick and bereaved.

2:1-13
No Favoritism Toward the Wealthy

In Palestine, as in most of the empire, the rich were oppressing the poor (2:6-7). But the temptation to make rich converts or inquirers feel welcome at the expense of the poor was immoral (2:4). The language of impartiality was normally applied especially to legal settings, but because *synagogues served both as houses of prayer and as community courts, this predominantly legal image naturally applies to any gatherings there.

2:1. Jewish wisdom stressed that those who respected God should not show "favoritism" toward (literally "accept the face of") people. The title "Lord of glory" (KJV, NASB; it means "glorious Lord"—NIV, NRSV, TEV) was normally applied to God (e.g., in *1 Enoch; cf. Ps 24:7-8).

2:2. Moralists and satirists mocked the special respect given to the wealthy, which usually amounted to a self-demeaning way to seek funds. Illustrations like this one could be hypothetical, which fit the writer's *diatribe style of argument. In Rome the senatorial class wore gold rings; some members of this class sought popular support for favors shown to various groups. But rings were hardly limited to them; in the eastern Mediterranean gold rings also marked great wealth and status. Clothing likewise distinguished the wealthy, who could be ostentatious, from others; peasants commonly had only one cloak, which would thus often be dirty.

"Assembly" (KJV, NASB, NRSV) or "meeting" (NIV, TEV) is literally "*synagogue," either because James wants the whole Jewish community to embrace his example, or because the Jewish-Christian congregations (cf. 5:14) also considered themselves *messianic synagogues.

2:3. Jewish legal texts condemn judges who make one litigant stand while another is permitted to sit; these hearings normally took place in synagogues (2:2). To avoid partiality on the basis of clothing, some second-century *rabbis required both litigants to dress in the same kind of clothes.

2:4. Roman laws explicitly favored the rich. Persons of lower class, who were thought to act from economic self-interest, could not bring accusations against persons of higher class, and the laws prescribed harsher penalties for lower-class persons convicted of offenses than for offenders from the higher class. Biblical law, most Jewish law and traditional Greek philosophers had always rejected such distinctions as immoral. In normal times, the public respected the rich as public benefactors, although the *Zealots recognized in the Jerusalem aristocracy pro-Roman enemies. The *Old Testament forbade partiality on the basis of economic status (Lev 19:15) and called judges among God's people to judge impartially, as God did.

2:5. For God hearing the cries of the poor, who were also the most easily judicially oppressed, cf. texts like Deuteronomy 15:9. One line of Jewish tradition stresses the special piety of the poor, who had to depend on God alone.

2:6. Roman courts always favored the rich, who could initiate lawsuits against social inferiors, although social inferiors could not initiate lawsuits against them. In theory, Jewish courts sought to avoid this discrimination, but as in most cultures people of means naturally had legal advantages: they were able to argue their cases more articulately or to hire others to do so for them.

2:7. Judaism often spoke of "the sacred name" or used other expressions rather than using the name of God; James may apply this divine title to Jesus here (cf. 2:1). In the Old Testament, being "called by someone's name" meant that one belonged to that person in some sense; it was especially applied to belonging to God. Some of the Galilean aristocracy (such as those settled in Tiberias) were considered impious by general Jewish standards. But this accusation may apply specifically to anti-Christian opposition: the opposition Christians faced in Jerusalem came especially from the Sadducean aristocracy (Acts 4:1; 23:6-10).

2:8. A "royal" law, i.e., an imperial edict, was higher than the justice of the aristocracy, and because Judaism universally acknowledged God to be the supreme King, his *law could be described in these terms. Christians could naturally apply it especially to Jesus' teaching; like some other Jewish teachers, Jesus used this passage in Leviticus 19:18 to epitomize the law (cf. Mk 12:29-34).

2:9-10. Jewish teachers distinguished "heavier" from "lighter" sins, but felt that God required obedience to even the "smallest" commandments, rewarding the obedient with *eternal life and punishing transgressors with damnation. That willful violation of even a minor transgression was tantamount to rejecting the whole law was one of their most commonly repeated views. (Ancient writers often stated principles in sharp, graphic ways but in practice showed more mercy to actual transgressors in the community.)

*Stoics (against the *Epicureans) went even farther in declaring that all sins were equal. The point here is that rejecting the law of economic impartiality in Leviticus 19:15, or the general principle of love behind it (Lev 19:18), was rejecting the whole authority of God (Jas 2:8). Jewish teachers often used "stumbling" as a metaphor for sin.

2:11. Jewish tradition sometimes compared oppression of the poor with murder (cf. also 5:6). But James might here allude to those *Zealot-like protesters, too religious to commit adultery, who would nevertheless not scruple at shedding the blood of Jewish aristocrats. At the time this letter was written, these "assassins" were regularly stabbing aristocrats to death in the temple (see comment on Acts 21:20-22).

2:12. Ancients could summarize a person's behavior in terms of words and deeds; see comment on 1 John 3:18. Some scholars have pointed out that many philosophers believed themselves alone wise, free and kings, and they connect "law of liberty" here with "royal law" in 2:8. Jewish teachers believed that the law of the heavenly king freed one from the yoke of this world's affairs. "Law of freedom," as in 1:25, probably implies deliverance from sin.

2:13. James's point here is that if his readers are not impartial judges, they will answer to the God who is an impartial judge; his impartiality in judgment is rehearsed throughout the *Old Testament and Jewish tradition. Jewish teachers defined God's character especially by two attributes, mercy and justice, and suggested that mercy normally won out over justice. They would have agreed with James that the merciless forfeited a right to mercy, and they had their own sayings similar to this one.

2:14-26
Faith Must Be Lived Out

James could be reacting against a misinterpretation of Paul's teaching, as some commentators have suggested, but more likely he is reacting against a strain of Jewish piety that was fueling the revolutionary fervor that was leading toward war (cf. 1:26-27; 2:19). James uses words like "faith" differently from the way Paul does, but neither writer would be opposed to the other's meaning: genuine faith is a reality on which one stakes one's life, not merely passive assent to a doctrine. For James, expressions of faith like nondiscrimination (2:8-9) and nonviolence (2:10-12) must be lived, not merely acknowledged.

2:14-16. God commanded his people to supply the needs of the poor (Deut 15:7-8); to fail to do so was disobedience to his *law. "Go in peace" was a Jewish farewell blessing, but Jewish people were expected to show hospitality to other Jewish people in need. "Be warmed" (NASB) alludes to how cold the homeless could become, especially in a place of high elevation like Jerusalem in winter. Moralists often used such straw examples ("if someone should claim") as part of their argument; the reader is forced to admit the logical absurdity of the conclusion of a particular line of reasoning and to agree with the author's argument. Jewish people held Abraham to be the ultimate example of such hospitality (cf. 2:21-23 and comment on Heb 13:2).

2:17. Writers like *Epictetus could use "dead" the same way as here; this is a graphic way of saying "useless" (see comment on 2:26).

2:18. "Someone will say" was a common way to introduce the speech of an imaginary opponent, the answer to whose objection merely furthered the writer's argument. The force of the objection is "One may have faith, and another works"; the answer is "Faith can be demonstrated only by works." "Show me" was a natural demand for evidence and appears in other moralists, especially *Epictetus.

2:19-20. The oneness of God was the basic confession of Judaism, recited daily in the Shema (Deut 6:4 and associated texts). Thus by "faith" James means monotheism, as much of Judaism used the term *('emunah).* He thus says, "You hold to correct basic doctrine—so what? That is meaningless by itself." That demons recognized the truth about God and trembled before his name was widely acknowledged, even in the magical papyri (which specialized in what from a biblical perspective was illicit demonology; cf. also *1 Enoch). Jewish teachers would have agreed with James that the oneness of God must be declared with a genuine heart; his oneness implied that he was to be the supreme object of human affection (Deut 6:4-5).

2:21-24. James connects Genesis 15:6 with the offering of Isaac (Gen 22), as in Jewish tradition. This event was the climax of his faith in God, not only in Jewish tradition but in the Genesis *narrative itself. (God entered into covenant with Abraham's descendants because he loved him and made a promise to him—Deut 7:7-9—which Abraham embraced in faith and thus obeyed; God accepted this obedient faith—Gen 26:4-5. This view was not quite the same as the second-century *rabbinic view that God parted the Red Sea on account of the merits of the patriarchs, but neither is it the same as a common modern conception that faith is a once-for-all prayer involving no commitment of life or purpose and is efficacious even if quickly forgotten.)

Abraham was "declared righteous" at the *Aqedah,* the offering of Isaac, in the sense that God again acknowledged (Gen 22:12) Abraham's prior faith, which had been tested ultimately at this point. The *Old Testament called Abraham God's friend (2 Chron 20:7; Is 41:8), and later Jewish writers delighted in this title for him.

2:25. Like the example of Abraham, the example of Rahab would not be controversial among James's Jewish readers. Like Abraham (see comment on 2:14-16), Rahab was known for hospitality; but her act of saving the spies saved her as well (Josh 2:1-21; 6:22-25).

2:26. Most ancient people, including most Jewish people, accepted the necessary cooperation of body and spirit or soul; all who believed in the spirit or soul agreed that when it departed, the person died.

3:1-12
The Violent Tongue

James now returns to his warnings against inflammatory speech (1:19, 26): one ought not to curse people made in God's image (3:9-12).

3:1. Jewish sages also warned against teaching error and recognized that teachers would be judged strictly for leading others astray. Some who wanted to be teachers of wisdom were teaching the sort of "wisdom" espoused by the Jewish revolutionaries, which led to violence (3:13-18).

3:2. That everyone sinned was standard Jewish doctrine; that one of the most common instruments of sin and harm was the human mouth was also a Jewish commonplace (as early as Proverbs, e.g., 11:9; 12:18; 18:21).

3:3-4. Controlling horses with bits and ships with rudders were common illustrations in the ancient Mediterranean, because everyone except the most illiterate peasants (who would also miss many of the other allusions if they heard James read) understood them. Jewish texts often cast wisdom, reason and God in the role of ideal pilots, but James's point here is not what *should* control or have power. His point is simply the power of a small instrument (v. 5).

3:5-6. Others also compared the spread of rumors to the igniting of what would rapidly become a forest fire. Here the image is that of a tongue that incites the whole body to violence. The boastful tongue plotting harm (Ps 52:1-4) and the tongue as a hurtful fire (Ps 39:1-3; 120:2-4; Prov 16:27; 26:21; Ecclus 28:21-23) are old images. That the fire is sparked by "hell" suggests where it leads; Jewish pictures of *Gehenna, like Jesus' images for the fate of the damned, typically included flame.

3:7-8. Made in God's image (v. 9), people were appointed over all creatures (Gen 1:26). But although other creatures could be subdued as God commanded (Gen 1:28; 9:2), the tongue was like the deadliest snake, full of toxic venom (Ps 140:3; cf. 58:1-6, the *Dead Sea Scrolls and other Jewish texts). *Stoic philosophers also occasionally reflected on humanity's rule over animals.

3:9-10. Some other Jewish teachers also noted the incongruity of blessing God while cursing other people, who were made in his image; even more often, they recognized that whatever one did to other humans, it was as if one did it to God himself, because they were made in his image. James's readers could not easily miss his point. This text makes clear the sort of perverse speech that 3:1-12 addresses: antagonistic speech, which fits the situation the letter as a whole addresses. Whether by incendiary *rhetoric or a battle cry, cursing mortal enemies was incompatible with worshiping God, no matter how embedded it had become in Jewish patriotic tradition (since the *Maccabean era).

3:11-12. James produces two other common examples of impossible incongruity. Figs, olives and grapes were the three most common agricultural products of the Judean hills, and alongside wheat they would have constituted the most common crops of the Mediterranean region as a whole. That everything brought forth after its kind was a matter of common observation and became proverbial in Greco-Roman circles (cf. also Gen 1:11-12, 21, 24-25).

3:13-18 Peaceable Versus Demonic Wisdom

The *Zealot paradigm of violent retaliation claimed to be religious and wise; James urges the poor to respond by waiting on God instead (5:7-11). That James was wiser than advocates of revolution was proved in the aftermath of the Judean revolt of A.D. 66-70, when Judea was devastated, Jerusalem destroyed and Jerusalem's survivors enslaved.

3:13. Those who wished to teach others as wise sages (3:1) needed to show their wisdom by gentleness: this is the antithesis of the advocates of revolution, who were gaining popularity in the tensions stirred by poverty and oppression in the land.

3:14. The term translated "jealousy" (NASB) or "envy" (NIV, NRSV) here is the term for "zeal" used by the Zealots, who fancied themselves successors of Phinehas (Num 25:11; Ps 106:30-31) and the *Maccabees and sought to liberate Jewish Palestine from Rome by force of arms. "Strife" (KJV; "selfish ambition"—NASB, NIV, NRSV) also was related to disharmony and had been known to provoke wars.

3:15-16. "Above" was sometimes synonymous with "God" in Jewish tradition; as opposed to heavenly wisdom, the wisdom of violence (3:14) was thoroughly earthly, human and demonic (cf. similarly Mt 16:22-23). The *Dead Sea Scrolls spoke of sins as inspired by the spirit of error, and folk Judaism believed that people were continually surrounded by hordes of demons. James's words suggest a more indirect working of demons through stirring up their own ungodly values in the world system.

3:17. Wisdom "from above," i.e., from God (1:17; 3:15), is "pure," not mixed with anything else (in this case, not mixed with demonic wisdom—3:14-16); it is thus also "unhypocritical." Many Jewish wisdom texts spoke of divine wisdom coming from above. God's genuine wisdom is nonviolent rather than given to lashing out: "peaceable," "gentle," "open to reason," "full of mercy" (cf. 2:13); it was also "unwavering" (NASB), better rendered "impartial" (NIV), or "without prejudice or favoritism" (cf. 2:1-9). This wisdom is neither that of the *Zealots nor of those wishing to accommodate the aristocracy.

3:18. The image of virtues as seeds and fruits has many parallels (e.g., Prov 11:18; Is 32:17), but James's point in the context is this: true wisdom is the wisdom of peace, not of violence. Although many *Pharisaic teachers extolled peace, many populists were advocating violence, and James's message was in many regards countercultural.

4:1-12
Choose Between God and the World's Values

God's wisdom was not the populist wisdom of the revolutionaries (3:13-18); thus those whose faith was genuine (2:14-26) could not waver between the two options. James addresses here many of the poor, the oppressed, who are tempted to try to overthrow their oppressors and seize their goods.

4:1. Most Greco-Roman philosophers and many *Diaspora Jews repeatedly condemned people who were ruled by their passions, and described these desires for pleasure as "waging war." Many writers like *Plato, *Plutarch and *Philo attributed all literal wars to bodily desires. In a somewhat similar vein, Jewish people spoke of an evil impulse, which according to later *rabbis dominated all 248 members of the body.

4:2. *Diatribe often included *hyperbole, or graphic, *rhetorical exaggeration for effect. Most of James's readers have presumably not literally killed anyone, but they are exposed to violent teachers (3:13-18) who regard murder as a satisfactory means of attaining justice and redistribution of wealth. James counsels prayer instead. (Later he has much harsher words for the oppressors, however; cf. 5:1-6.)

4:3. Jewish prayers typically asked God to supply genuine needs; see comment on Matthew 6:11. James believes that such prayers will be answered (cf. Prov 10:24), even though the oppressed will always be worse off than they should be (cf. Prov 13:23). But requests based on envy of others' wealth or status were meant to satisfy only their passions (see comment on 4:1).

4:4. In the *Old Testament, Israel was often called an adulteress for claiming to serve God while pursuing idols (e.g., Hos 1—3). Those who claimed to be God's friends (Jas 2:23) but were really moral *clients of the world (friendship often applied to *patron-client relationships)—that is, they shared the world's values (3:13-18)—were really unfaithful to God.

4:5. Here James may refer to the evil impulse that, according to Jewish tradition, God made to dwell in people; on this reading, he is saying, "This human spirit jealously longs," as in 4:1-3. Less likely, he could mean that one's spirit or soul longs and ought to long—but for God (Ps 42:1-2; 63:1; 84:2).

A third possibility is that he may be citing a proverbial maxim based on such texts as Exodus 20:5, Deuteronomy 32:21 and Joel 2:18, summarizing the sense of Scripture thus: "God is jealous over the spirit he gave us" and will tolerate no competition for its affection (4:4). (Like Jewish writers, *New Testament authors sometimes *midrashically meshed various texts together.) This view seems to fit the context somewhat better than other views, given that Scripture did not speak this "in vain" (4:5); but the "greater grace" of 4:6 could support the first view above.

4:6. James cites Proverbs 3:34 almost exactly as it appeared in the common form of the *Septuagint. This idea became common in Jewish wisdom texts. Humility included appropriate submission, in this case to God's sovereign plan for a person's life (4:7, 10).

4:7. Ancient magical texts spoke of demons' fleeing before incantations, but the idea here is moral, not magical. One must choose between the values of God and those of the world (4:4), between God's wisdom and that which is demonic (3:15, 17). The point is that a person who lives by God's values (in this case, his way of peace) is no part of *Satan's kingdom (in contrast to the religious-sounding revolutionaries).

4:8. *Old Testament texts exhorted priests and people in general to "draw near to God." Purification was also necessary for priests (Ex 30:19), but the image here is not specifically priestly; those responsible for bloodshed, even if only as representatives of a corporately guilty group, were to wash their hands (Deut 21:6; cf. Jas 4:2). "Purification" often came to be used in an inward, moral sense (e.g., Jer 4:14).

Using ideas like "sinners," James employs not only the harsh diatribe *rhetoric that Greco-Roman writers used against imaginary opponents when demolishing their positions; he also uses the rhetoric of Old Testament prophets. "Double-minded" again alludes to the general ancient contempt for hypocrisy: one must act from either God's peaceful wisdom or the devil's hateful wisdom (3:13-18; 4:4).

4:9-10. Old Testament texts often connected mourning and self-humiliation with *repentance (Lev 23:29; 26:41), especially when confronted by divine judgment (2 Kings 22:11; Joel 1:13-14; 2:12-13). The exaltation of the humble was also a teaching of the prophets; see comment on Matthew 23:12.

4:11. James returns to the specific worldly behavior his readers are following: violent speech (3:1-12). (He either addresses social stratification within the Christian community or, more likely, uses "brothers" in its more common Jewish sense of "fellow Jews." Jewish revolutionaries had already begun killing aristocrats, and inflammatory *rhetoric was certainly even more common.) His general principle was standard Old Testament and Jewish wisdom opposing slander, which many of his readers may not have been considering in this context. The *law declared God's love for Israel and commanded his people to love one another (2:8); to slander a fellow Jew was thus to disrespect the law.

4:12. That God alone was the true judge was a common Jewish and *New

Testament teaching. In Jewish teaching, earthly courts proceeded only on his authority, and those who ruled in them had to judge by the law. Investigations had to be conducted thoroughly, with a minimum of two witnesses; acting as a false witness, slandering someone to a court without genuine firsthand information, was punishable according to the judgment the falsely accused person would have received if convicted.

4:13-17
The Pride of the Rich

Having counseled the oppressed, James quickly turns to the oppressors, denouncing their self-satisfied forgetfulness of God. Most of the wealth in the Roman Empire was accumulated by one of two means: the landed gentry, of high social class, made their wealth from land-based revenues such as tenant farmers and crops; the merchant class gathered great wealth without the corresponding social status. James addresses both merchants (4:13-17) and the landed aristocracy (5:1-6).

4:13. Many philosophers (especially *Stoics) and Jewish sages liked to warn their hearers that they had no control over the future. "Go now" (5:1) was a fairly common way of proceeding with an argument (e.g., Athenaeus), addressing an imaginary opponent (e.g., *Cicero, *Epictetus) or prefacing harsh words in satire (Horace, *Juvenal).

The primary markets for manufactured goods were towns and cities; projecting commitments and profits was also a normal business practice. Traders were not always wealthy, but here they are at least *seeking* wealth. The sin here is arrogant presumption—feeling secure enough to leave God out of one's calculations (4:16; cf., e.g., Jer 12:1; Amos 6:1).

4:14. Here James offers common Jewish and Stoic wisdom to which few readers would theoretically object, although many were undoubtedly not heeding it.

4:15-17. "If God wills" was a conventional Greek expression but fit Jewish piety well; it appears elsewhere in the *New Testament (e.g., Acts 18:21; 1 Cor 16:7).

5:1-6
Judgment on Wealthy Oppressors

Throughout most of the rural areas of the Roman Empire, including much of rural Galilee, rich landowners profited from the toil of the serfs (often alongside slaves) who worked their massive estates. That feudalism arose only in medieval times is a misconception; it is simply less prominent in literature of Roman times because Roman literature concentrated on the cities, although only about 10 percent of the Empire is estimated to have been urban.

Most of James's denunciation takes the form of an *Old Testament prophetic judgment oracle, paralleled also in some Jewish wisdom and *apocalyptic texts. The difference between his denunciation of the rich and the violent speech he himself condemns (1:19, 26; 3:1-12; 4:11) is that he appeals to God's judgment rather than to human retribution (4:12; cf. Deut 32:35; Prov 20:22). His *prophecy was timely; several years later the Jewish aristocracy was virtually obliterated in the revolt against Rome.

5:1. Exhortations to weep and howl were a graphic prophetic way of saying: You will have reason to weep and howl (Joel 1:8; Mic 1:8; cf. Jas 4:9). On "come" see comment on 4:13.

5:2. Clothing was one of the primary signs of wealth in antiquity; many peasants had only one garment.

5:3. Some other ancient writers ridiculed the rust of unused, hoarded wealth. For "rust" and "moth" (v. 2) together, compare Matthew 6:19. As Jewish sources often noted, wealth would be worthless in the impending day of God's judgment.

5:4. The law of Moses forbade withholding wages, even overnight; if the injured worker cried out to God, God would avenge him (Deut 24:14-15; cf., e.g., Lev 19:13; Prov 11:24; Jer 22:13; Mal 3:5). That the wrong done the oppressed would itself cry out to God against the oppressor was also an *Old Testament image (Gen 4:10). In first-century Palestine, many day laborers depended on their daily wages to purchase food for themselves and their families; withholding money could mean that they would go hungry.

The income absentee landlords received from agriculture was such that the wages they paid workers could not even begin to reflect the profits they accumulated. Although the rich supported public building projects (in return for attached inscriptions honoring them), they were far less inclined to pay sufficient wages to their workers. At least as early as the second century, Jewish teachers suggested that even failing to leave gleanings for the poor was robbing them (based on Lev 19:9-10; 23:22; Deut 24:19).

Most crops were harvested in or near summer, and extra laborers were often hired for the harvest. Some *Diaspora Jewish texts (literary texts, amulets, etc.) called God "Lord of Sabaoth," transliterating the Hebrew word for "hosts": the God with vast armies (an epithet especially prominent in the *LXX of Isaiah). If it was a bad idea to offend a powerful official, it was thus a much worse idea to secure the enmity of God.

5:5. The rich consumed much meat in a day of slaughter, i.e., at a feast (often at sheep-shearing or harvest; cf. 1 Sam 25:4, 36); once an animal was slaughtered, as much as possible was eaten at once, because the rest could be preserved only by drying and salting. Meat was generally unavailable to the poor except during public festivals.

The picture here is of the rich being fattened like cattle for the day of their own slaughter (cf., e.g., Jer 12:3; Amos 4:1-3); similar imagery appears in parts of the early *apocalyptic work 1 Enoch (94:7-11; 96:8; 99:6). As often in the *Old Testament (e.g., Amos 6:4-7), the sin in verse 5 is not exploitation per se (as in v. 4) but a lavish lifestyle while others go hungry or in need.

5:6. Jewish tradition recognized that the wicked plotted against the righteous (e.g., Wisdom of Solomon 2:19-20), as the sufferings of many Old Testament heroes (like David and Jeremiah) showed. Judicial oppression of the poor, repeatedly condemned in the Old Testament, was viewed as murder in later Jewish texts; to take a person's garment or to withhold a person's wages was to risk that person's life. James "the Just" himself was later martyred by the high priest for his denunciations of the behavior of the rich.

5:7-12
Endure Until God Vindicates

The oppressors would be punished (5:1-6), but the oppressed have to wait on God (cf. 1:4) rather than take matters violently into their own hands. This exhortation did not mean that they could not speak out against injustice (5:1-6); it only forbade violence and personally hostile speech (5:9) as an appropriate solution to injustice.

5:7-8. Harvest here (cf. v. 4) becomes an image of the day of judgment, as elsewhere in Jewish literature (especially *4 Ezra; Mt 13). Palestine's autumn rains came in October and November, and winter rains (roughly three-quarters of the year's rainfall) in December and January. But residents of Syria-Palestine eagerly anticipated the late rains of March and April, which were necessary to ready their late spring and early summer crops. The main wheat harvest there ran from mid-April through the end of May; the barley harvest was in March. The main grain harvest came in June in Greece, July in Italy. Farmers' families were entirely dependent on good harvests; thus James speaks of the "precious" (or "valuable"—NIV) fruit of the earth.

5:9. On this kind of speech, see comment on 4:11-12.

5:10. Most *Old Testament prophets faced great opposition for their preaching; some faced death. Jewish tradition had amplified accounts of their martyrdom even further, hence no one would dispute James's claim. Virtuous examples were an important part of ancient argumentation (*Stoic philosophers often used like-minded sages as models of endurance).

5:11. The whole structure of the book of Job was probably meant to encourage Israel after the exile; although God's justice seemed far away and they were mocked by the nations, God would ultimately vindicate them and end their captivity. *Hellenistic Jewish tradition further celebrated Job's endurance (e.g., the *Testament of Job, and Aristeas the Exegete). (Various later *rabbis evaluated him differently, some positively, some negatively. The Testament of Job includes Stoic language for the virtue of endurance and transfers some earlier depictions of Abraham to Job; this transferral may have been the source of one later rabbi's rare conclusion that Job was greater than Abraham.)

5:12. Oaths were verbal confirmations guaranteed by appeal to a divine witness; violation of an oath in God's name broke the third commandment (Ex 20:7; Deut 5:11). Like some groups of Greek philosophers, some kinds of *Essenes would not swear any further oaths after they had completed their initiatory oaths (according to *Josephus, in contrast to the Essenes who wrote the *Dead Sea Scrolls); the *Pharisees, however, allowed oaths. On swearing by various items as lesser surrogates for God, see comment on Matthew 5:33-37. Oaths generally called on the gods to witness the veracity of one's intention and had to be kept, or invited a curse on the one who had spoken the untruth. Vows were a more specific category of oaths to undertake some duty or abstain from something for a particular period of time.

The difficulty is ascertaining what sort of swearing is in view in the context. Some scholars have suggested a warning against taking a *Zealot-type oath (cf. Acts 23:12); while this would fit the context of James very well, his readers may not have recognized something so specific as the obvious application of his words. The idea is probably that one should not impatiently (5:7-11) swear; rather one should pray (5:13). One should pray rather than swear because the fullest form of an oath included a self-curse, which was like saying "May God kill me if I fail to do this" or (in English preadolescent idiom) "Cross my heart and hope to die."

5:13-20
Depending on God

5:13. Nonresistance did not mean pretending that things did not matter (as the *Stoics did; see comment on Eph 5:20) or simply waiting unconsoled until the end time (as some Jewish *apocalyptic writers may have done); it meant prayer.

5:14. Wounds were anointed with oil to cleanse them (cf. Lk 10:34), and those with headaches and those wishing to avoid some diseases were anointed with olive oil for "medicinal" purposes (from the ancient perspective). Oil was also used to anoint priests or rulers, pouring oil over the head as a consecration to God. Christians may have combined a symbolic medicinal use with a symbol of handing one over to the power of God's *Spirit (Mk 6:13).

A general prayer for healing was one of the blessings regularly recited in *synagogues; on "elders" see comment on Acts 14:23; on "*church" in a Jewish context see the glossary. Visiting the sick was an act of piety in early Judaism that Christians probably continued (cf. Mt 25:36, 43, for ailing missionaries).

5:15-16. The *Old Testament prophets often used healing from sickness as an image for healing from sin, and Jewish literature often associated sin and sickness; for instance, the eighth blessing of a Jewish daily prayer, for healing (although the emphasis is not physical healing), followed petitions for forgiveness and redemption. James does not imply a direct causal relationship between all sickness and sin, any more than Paul or the Old Testament does (see comment on Phil 2:25-30).

Jewish wisdom also recognized that God would hear the sick (Ecclus 38:9) and connected this hearing with renouncing sin (38:10). But although only a very few pious Jewish teachers were normally thought able to produce such assured results in practice (cf. Jas 5:17-18), James applies this standard of faith to all believers.

5:17-18. Although all Palestinian Jews prayed for rain, few miracle workers were thought able to secure such answers to prayer (especially Josephus's Onias, called Honi the Circle-Drawer in the many *rabbinic traditions about him; Hanina ben Dosa, in rabbinic texts; in later traditions about earlier pietists, occasional pious men like Honi's grandson Abba Hilkiah or Hanan ha-Nehba, Johanan ben Zakkai, Nakdimon ben Gorion, Rabbi Jonah and occasionally an anonymous person). The miracle of securing rain eventually came to be viewed as equivalent to raising the dead. The piety of these miraculous rainmakers always set them apart from others in Jewish tradition, but here James affirms that Elijah, the greatest model for such miracle workers, was a person like his readers and is a model for all believers (1 Kings 17:1; 18:41-46; cf. 1 Sam 12:17-18; for Elijah's weakness cf. 1 Kings 19:4).

The "three and a half years," not mentioned in 1 Kings 17 may reflect tradition (cf. 1 Kings 18:1; Lk 4:25 and a rabbinic tradition of three years), perhaps through associations with ideas about famines in the end time, which were sometimes held to last for this period of time.

5:19-20. In Jewish belief, the former righteousness of one who turned away was no longer counted in his or her favor (Ezek 18:24-25), but (in most Jewish formulations) the *repentance of the wicked canceled out his or her former wickedness (Ezek 18:21-23), if conjoined with proper *atonement. Some Jews (*Dead Sea Scrolls, some rabbis) regarded some forms of apostasy as unforgivable, but James welcomes the sinner back. In this context, he is especially inviting revolutionaries to return to the fold.

"Covering a multitude of sins" comes from Proverbs 10:12. In that text, it probably refers to not spreading a bad report (cf. 11:13; 20:19), but Judaism often used similar phrases for securing forgiveness. One may compare the Jewish idea that one who converted another to the practice of Judaism was as if he or she had created that person.

1 Peter

Introduction

Authorship. Although some commentators question Petrine authorship, others have argued forcefully for it; the situation presupposed in the letter fits Peter's lifetime. The tradition of Peter's martyrdom in Rome is virtually unanimous. By the late first century 1 Clement accepted the letter's authenticity, and excavations indicate a second-century memorial in Rome to Peter's martyrdom. Other early Christian traditions also support this tradition as well as the view that Peter was the author of the letter, which is cited by authors from the beginning of the second century.

Given this tradition of his martyrdom in Rome, the likelihood that letters he wrote would be preserved, and the fact that most letters were either authentic or written long after the purported author's death, the burden of proof is on those who wish to deny that Peter wrote the letter. One commentator (Selwyn) thought he could detect parallels to Silas's (5:12) style in 1 and 2 Thessalonians. This argument alone is not conclusive, but arguments against Petrine authorship are even weaker (for those based on Greek style, see introduction to James).

Date. Three basic periods of persecution have been suggested as the background: the time of Trajan (early second century), the time of Domitian (see introduction to Revelation) and the time of Nero, which would be the time of Peter's martyrdom. First Peter implies an atmosphere of severe repression, but not the official court prosecutions of Trajan's time. *Church leadership in the epistle (5:1-2) also fits the first-century model better than a later date. A pseudonymous letter attributed to Peter as early as the Flavian period (after Nero but still first century) is unlikely.

Unity. The first section of 1 Peter (1:1—4:6) does not explicitly indicate that fatal persecution has begun; the second part (4:7—5:14) is more explicit. Some writers have therefore divided the letter into two parts, usually arguing that the former was a *baptismal homily (due to abundant parallels with other parts of the *New Testament). But the difference of situation presupposed between the two sections is not significant enough to warrant such a division, and there appear no other compelling reasons to divide them.

Provenance and Audience. It is widely agreed that "Babylon" (5:13) is a cryptic name for Rome, as in some Jewish works and undoubtedly in the book of Revelation. The situation of persecution described here fits Rome, and it would be appropriate for Peter to send advance warning of that situation to believers in Asia Minor, the stronghold of emperor worship. An audience in Asia Minor might consist mainly of Jewish Christians, but Peter's audience probably includes *Gentile Christians (cf. 1:18; 4:3-4).

Situation. A fire devastated Rome in A.D. 64 but suspiciously left unscathed the estates of Nero and his friend Tigellinus. Like any good politician, Nero needed a scapegoat for his ills, and what appeared to be a new religion, understood as a fanatical form of Judaism begun by a crucified teacher three and a half decades before, filled the need perfectly.

Romans viewed Christians, like Jews, as antisocial. Certain charges became so common that they were stereotypical by the second century: Romans viewed Christians as "atheists" (like some philosophers, for rejecting the gods), "cannibals" (for claiming to eat Jesus' "body" and drink his "blood"), and incestuous (for statements like "I love you, brother," or "I love you, sister"). Judaism was a poor target for outright persecution, because its adherents were numerous and it was popular in some circles; further, Nero's mistress, Poppaea Sabina, was a *patron of Jewish causes. By contrast, Christianity was viewed as a form of Judaism whose support was tenuous even in Jewish circles, and therefore it was an appropriate political scapegoat.

According to the early-second-century historian *Tacitus, who disliked Christians himself, Nero burned Christians alive as torches to light his gardens at night. He killed other Christians in equally severe ways (e.g., feeding them to wild animals for public entertainment). In all, he must have murdered thousands of Rome's Christians, although most Christians there escaped his grasp. Thus, even though the Greek part of the Empire loved Nero and the Jewish community generally favored him, Christians saw him as a prototype of the antichrist. Nero died in disgrace several years later, pursued by fellow Romans who hated him.

***Genre.** First Peter is a general letter, influenced more by the situation in Rome than by the current situation in Asia Minor (what is now western Turkey); thus Peter can address it as a circular letter to many regions of Asia Minor (1:1). Peter does, however, seem to expect that the sufferings of Rome will eventually materialize in other parts of the empire. On events in Asia Minor three decades later, see the discussion of background in the introduction to Revelation. Leaders of the Jerusalem priesthood sent out encyclicals, letters to *Diaspora Jewish communities, by means of messengers; Peter's letter is similar to these but on a smaller scale of readership.

Commentaries. The most helpful for those who do not work with the Greek text is J. N. D. Kelly, *A Commentary on the Epistles of Peter and Jude* (reprint, Grand Rapids, Mich.: Baker Book House, 1981). J. R. Michaels, *1 Peter*, WBC 49 (Waco, Tex.: Word, 1988), Peter H. Davids, *The First Epistle of Peter*, NICNT (Grand Rapids, Mich.: Eerdmans, 1990), and E. G. Selwyn, *The First Epistle of St. Peter*, 2nd ed. (New York: Macmillan, 1947), are also helpful. Two of the best specialized works are

David L. Balch, *Let Wives Be Submissive: The Domestic Code in 1 Peter*, SBLMS 26 (Chico, Calif.: Scholars, 1981), and William J. Dalton, *Christ's Proclamation to the Spirits: A Study of 1 Peter 3:18—4:6*, Analecta Biblica 23 (Rome: Pontifical Biblical Institute, 1965).

1:1-12
Present Testing, Future Hope

Verses 3-12 are one long sentence in Greek; such long sentences could be viewed as skillful in antiquity, when hearers of speeches were accustomed to following the train of thought for a longer time than North American and some other television-trained readers are today.

1:1. Jewish people spoke of Jews who lived outside Palestine as the "*Diaspora," or those who were "scattered"; Peter transfers this term to his readers (cf. 1:17; 2:11). On "resident aliens" see comment on 1:17; cf. 2:11. The five Roman provinces he mentions were geographically connected; he omits the southern coastal regions of Asia Minor, which could be grouped with Syria in this period instead of as part of Asia Minor. The sequence in which Peter lists the provinces of his intended readers reflects the route a messenger delivering the letter could take if he started from Amastris in Pontus. (Although messengers from Rome were more likely to start at the province of Asia, Peter may start in his mind with the province farthest from him and work his way around.) On encyclical or circular letters, see the discussion of *genre in the introduction.

1:2. In the *Old Testament and Judaism, God's people were corporately "chosen," or "predestined," because God "foreknew" them; Peter applies the same language to believers in Jesus. Obedience and the sprinkling of blood also established the first covenant (Ex 24:7-8).

1:3. Peter adopts the form of a *berakah,* the Jewish form of blessing that regularly began "Blessed be God who . . ." The rebirth may allude to language Jewish people normally used for the conversion of *Gentiles to Judaism (see comment on Jn 3:3, 5), with the meaning: you received a new nature when you converted. Believers were reborn to a living hope by Jesus' *resurrection, an inheritance (v. 4) and future salvation (v. 5), three ideas connected in Jewish views of the end of the age.

1:4. *New Testament writers followed Jewish teachers in speaking of "inheriting" the future world; the original source of the idiom is probably Israel's "inheritance" of the Promised Land subsequent to their redemption from Egypt. Some Jewish texts (like *4 Ezra, late first century) also spoke of a treasure stored up in heaven for the righteous, but whereas the emphasis for receiving that treasure is normally on one's obedience, the emphasis here is on God's work.

1:5. The *Dead Sea Scrolls and other Jewish texts speak of everything being "revealed" in the "last time"; the deeds of the wicked would be made known, but the righteous would be "saved," delivered, from all that opposed them.

1:6-7. God was sovereign over testings, but his purpose both in the *Old Testament and in Judaism was to strengthen the commitment of those who were tested (it was only *Satan whose object in the testing was to bring apostasy—5:8). See comment on James 1:12-16. (The Old Testament and Judaism also taught that sufferings could be discipline to bring persons to *repentance or punishments to fulfill justice and invite repentance; contemporary Judaism developed this concept into the idea of *atonement by sufferings. Although this view does not reflect Peter's emphasis, he does allow that the persecution believers face is also God's discipline to wake his people up—4:17.)

Many Jewish traditions also presented the end as preceded by times of great testing. The image of the righteous being tested like precious metals purified in the furnace comes from the Old Testament (Job 23:10; Ps 12:6; Prov 17:3; cf. Is 43:2; Jer 11:4) and continued in subsequent Jewish literature (e.g., Ecclus 2:5). Ores of precious metals (the most precious of which was gold) would be melted in a furnace to separate out the impurities and produce purer metal.

1:8-9. Testing could be joyous rather than grievous because these readers knew in advance the goal of the testing: when they had persevered to the end, the final deliverance would come, as in traditional Jewish teaching. Unlike the testing in James, the primary test in 1 Peter is persecution (see introduction).

1:10-12. Many Jewish interpreters (especially attested in the *Dead Sea Scrolls) believed that the Old Testament prophets had told especially about the interpreters' own time, and that their meaning for this time had thus remained cryptic until sages of their own generation were given special insight by the *Spirit. Peter here seems to assert that the prophets recognized that their *prophecies applied to the *Messiah who would suffer and be exalted, and that they knew that many details would make sense to the readers only once they had happened. It sounds as if Peter would, however, have agreed with the interpreters in the Dead Sea Scrolls that the Old Testament prophets did not know the "time or kind of time."

That Old Testament servants of God could have the Spirit of God in them is clear (Gen 41:38; Num 27:18), although the Old Testament usually preferred the Hebrew idiom for the Spirit resting "upon" God's servants, empowering them (as in 1 Pet 4:14). According to some Jewish traditions, some secrets were so important that God kept them even from angels until the end time; in other traditions, angels respected *rabbis' esoteric teachings and came to their lectures to listen; in still other traditions, angels envied Israel, who received God's *law.

1:13—2:3
Live the New Life

1:13. Men wore long robes and would tuck them into their belt, "gird up their loins," so they could move more freely and quickly. Although the image also occurs elsewhere in the *Old Testament, here Peter may specifically allude to the Passover (Ex 12:11): once God's people had been redeemed by the blood of the lamb (1 Pet 1:19), they were to be ready to follow God forth until he had brought them safely into their inheritance (cf. 1:4), the Promised Land. Thus they were to be dressed and ready to flee. "Sobriety" in ancient usage meant not only literal abstinence from drink but also behaving as a nonintoxicated person should, hence with dignified self-control.

1:14. "Obedient children" picks up the image of 1:3: born anew, they were no longer what they had been before, and they should obey God (cf. 1:2, 22) as children obeyed their fathers. The obedience of minors to their parents was highly valued, and Roman and Jewish law required it.

1:15-16. Israel was called to be holy as God was holy and thus to live in a manner distinct from the ways of the nations (Lev 11:44; 19:2; 20:7, 26). The daily *synagogue prayers also stressed holiness to God, hence the idea would have been one of the most familiar to Jewish readers and to *Gentiles who had learned Scripture from them. If Peter continues the image of father and children between 1:14 and 1:17, he may allude here to another feature of a child's relationship with a father that was stressed in antiquity: imitation.

1:17. The image of God as an impartial judge was standard in Judaism, which also addressed him as "heavenly Father" in most of its prayers. "Resident aliens" ("strangers"—NIV; "the time of your stay"—NASB) were distinguished from local citizens, but as legal residents of an area they were viewed more highly than newcomers. Jewish communities throughout the empire generally enjoyed a resident alien status, and although some Jews could achieve citizen status, in other places like Alexandria the Greeks met their attempt to do so with hostility.

1:18. Jewish people often spoke of idolatry as "futile" or "empty." To them idolatry was the most basic characteristic of pagans' lifestyle, thus the former way of life of Peter's readers ("passing down" of the ancestors' way of life by itself could refer either to paganism or to Judaism). Jewish sages contrasted the imperishability of true wealth (cf. 1:4, 7, 23) with the eternal wealth of righteousness or wisdom; here it refers to the price of the readers' redemption, for which money was insufficient (1:19). (That gold was devalued in this period due to inflation under Nero may have occurred to some of Peter's original readers but is probably peripheral to Peter's point about perishable gold; cf. 1:7.)

1:19-21. Redemption by the blood of a lamb recalls the annual Passover celebration, by which Jewish people commemorated their redemption (freedom from slavery) in Egypt, through the blood of the Passover lamb (cf. 1:13).

1:22. In *Old Testament purity laws, people purified themselves from defilement by ceremonial bathing; although Judaism continued to practice literal ceremonial washings, it often used the image of washing figuratively for spiritual or moral purification (as occasionally in Old Testament prophets, e.g., Is 1:16; Jer 2:22; 4:14).

1:23. The new life of obedient love (1:22) is natural for the person with a new nature; it was axiomatic in antiquity that children inherited the nature of their parents. (Many writers even remarked that adulterers gave themselves away because children bore their image.) The father's seed was especially important; followers of Jesus had been reborn through the living word, the *gospel (1:3; 2:2), and it was imperishable (1:24-25). (A variety of parallels could be adduced, including *Philo's perspective on the divine word as not only imperishable but as "seminal," or a seed; but most of these examples are individual and distinct cases rather than based on general tradition. The parallels may thus all be remote, drawn from the same sort of natural imagery as Peter's [except that Philo, unlike Peter, might draw on *Stoicism's seminal Logos]. Compare Lk 8:11; 1 Jn 3:9. That the Word of God was imperishable, however, was agreed throughout all of Judaism; cf. Is 40:6-8.)

1:24-25. Here Peter quotes Isaiah 40:6-8 (following the *LXX, which is more concise than the Hebrew text here), where the word is the future message of salvation in the time when God would redeem his people (e.g., 52:7-8).

2:1. Ancient writers sometimes employed "vice lists," indicating what people should avoid; Peter employs a miniature vice list. "Putting aside" (NASB) the old ways also follows rebirth in James, Ephesians and Colossians; together with other parallels to those letters, this similarity has suggested to some scholars a common *baptismal tradition in the early *church. It might also follow some teaching by Jesus no longer available to us; on possible background to "putting aside," see comment on Romans 13:12 and Ephesians 4:20-24.

2:2. This verse continues the image of rebirth (1:23). Babies were dependent on their mothers or nurses for nourishment by their milk; use of cows' milk was rare. It was believed that children were very impressionable at this nursing stage, and those who allowed them to be tended by nursemaids were advised to select the nurses with care. "Pure" milk meant that it had not been mixed with anything else; the term is used in business documents for sales of unadulterated foods. Pure "spiritual" (NIV, NRSV, TEV) milk is a possible translation, but the adjective here more often means "rational" and could well be rendered "milk of the word" (*logikon;* cf. NASB, KJV), i.e., the "word" of 1:25.

2:3. Here Peter alludes to Psalm 34:8. The term translated "kindness" (NASB) or "good" (NIV, NRSV) was sometimes used to mean "delicious" when applied to foods (as here, milk—v. 2).

2:4-12
Being Built Up as God's People

The *Qumran community (the Jewish monastic sect who wrote the *Dead Sea Scrolls) also portrayed themselves as a new temple. Whereas many of Peter's exhortations to this point are the sort of moral instructions philosophers could give for individual behavior, this section concerns the *church's corporate identity and hence corporate witness.

2:4. Peter derives this image from Isaiah 28:16 ("choice," "precious"), which he cites in 2:6.

2:5. The *Dead Sea Scrolls portray the Qumran community as a living temple, and one text speaks of the temple's components (pillar, foundations, etc.) as animate beings. "House" could refer to a building, like the temple, or to a household (4:17), even to a large family like the "house of Israel"; both senses are played on here, as sometimes in the *Old Testament (2 Sam 7:5-7, 12-16). The image of God's people as a "holy priesthood" is from Exodus 19:5-6 (cf. Is 61:6) and appears more explicitly in Hebrews 2:9 (Israel as a priesthood also appears in some contemporary Jewish texts based on Ex 19:6, including an insertion into the *LXX of Ex 23:22). As priests (as well as stones) in this new temple, they would offer sacrifices; others in Judaism also used the image of a spiritual sacrifice (see comment on Rom 12:1; Heb 13:15).

2:6. The *Qumran community applied Isaiah 28:16 to their own leadership; early Christians applied it to Jesus (Rom 9:33).

2:7-8. The Jewish interpretive principle *gezerah shavah,* which linked texts that had a common key word, makes it natural for Peter to cite Psalm 118:22 and Isaiah 8:14. Although this interpretive technique suggests that he is not dependent on Paul, both Peter and Paul may have depended on Jesus for the cornerstone image (Mk 12:10-11). Psalm 118 was sung during the Passover season (cf. 1 Pet 1:19), normally, at least among some Jews in this period, after thanking God for delivering Israel from slavery in Egypt into freedom, "from darkness to great light" (cf. 2:9).

2:9. Roughly half this verse is a direct quotation of Exodus 19:6, implying that all Christians, including *Gentile Christians, share in God's covenant with Israel. Jewish people on the Passover described their deliverance from Egypt as a call "from darkness into great light." *Old Testament prophets taught that God had redeemed his people for his praise (e.g., Is 60:21; 61:3; Jer 13:11).

2:10. Peter cites Hosea 1:10 and 2:23, which reverse God's earlier verdict against Israel (Hos 1:6, 8-9), promising the restoration of God's people in the end time. Like Paul, Peter believes that Gentiles converted to Israel's true faith, the message of Jesus, are part of this end-time people of God (Rom 9:24-26). Had he wished, he could have cited Old Testament passages to support his conclusion (e.g., Is 19:24-25; 56:3-8).

2:11. On "resident aliens" (the normal sense of the terms usually translated "aliens and strangers"), see comment on 1:17. *Philo spoke of souls as being "strangers" (using a term technically more foreign than "resident aliens") in their bodies, belonging instead to heaven. The image here is of God's people (2:4-10) dispersed among the nations; God's people in the Old Testament were sometimes portrayed in such terms (Lev 25:23), because of their mortality (1 Chron 29:15; Ps 39:12), because of zeal for God (Ps 69:8; cf. 119:19) or because of their wanderings (Gen 23:4; 47:9). Greek philosophers often viewed fleshly passions as "waging war" against the soul. Peter uses the same image, although not for the same reason that philosophers did (freeing the soul from earthly distractions); he demands proper living (2:12).

2:12. Jewish people living in the *Diaspora (1:1) always had to be concerned about *Gentiles' anti-Jewish slanders, for their safety and for their witness to the one true God. Just as Gentiles were more than happy to slander Jews living among them, they were happy to slander Gentile converts to what they viewed as a Jewish sect, Christianity (2:4-10). The behavior advocated in the following household codes (2:13—3:12) would undermine some of the most traditional slanders against such faiths, slanders that they subverted the public order and traditional family values. "Day of visitation" (KJV, NASB) was good *Old Testament language for God's coming day of judgment (e.g., Is 10:3); many texts reported that the Gentiles would recognize God's glory in the end time (e.g., Is 60:3).

2:13-17
Responsibilities Toward the State

Many ancient household codes were set in the context of discussions of city management and included instructions on how to behave toward the state (as well as toward parents, elders, friends, members of one's household, etc.). According to contemporary aristocratic ideals, the household mirrored the government of a city-state, so public obligations and obligations within the household (2:18—3:7) were commonly treated together.

*Stoic and other philosophers commonly used these ethical codes to delineate proper relationships with others. Jewish people and members of other slandered religious groups sometimes adopted these codes to demonstrate that their groups actually supported the values of Roman society; this demonstration was important in combating persecution. See comment on Romans 13:1-7.

2:13. Vassal kings in the East ruled their people with Rome's permission but were required to act in Rome's interests. Because most of Peter's readers (1:1) would instead be directly under governors (2:14), by "king" Peter may refer specifically to the Roman emperor. Although the emperor's title was technically *princeps,* i.e., "the leading citizen" or the first among equals (to preserve the myth of the republic in the early years of the Empire), everyone knew that he was the supreme earthly king in the Mediterranean world.

2:14. The term translated "governors" covers both legates (who governed imperial provinces as representatives of the emperor—2:13) and proconsuls (who governed senatorial provinces). Such representatives of Rome ruled most of the empire. Governors of imperial provinces were "sent by" the emperor and were expected to administer justice. "Praise" may refer to legal acquittal or may apply to inscriptions of praise dedicated to benefactors who provided wealth or services for municipalities.

2:15. "Ignorance" includes the false understanding of Christianity spread among outsiders (more than in 1:14); Roman aristocrats were much quicker to malign minority religions, whose worship did not assimilate to Roman values, than to seek to understand them. The *Old Testament taught God's sovereignty over rulers (Prov 16:10; 21:1).

2:16. Here Peter modifies a common exhortation of ancient philosophers: for them, freedom from the world's values meant not only authority to do as one pleased but also freedom to pursue virtue, freedom from desire and freedom to do without. Most philosophers (such as contemporary *Stoics) regarded the wise man as the ideal ruler but still advocated obedience to the state. For Christians, freedom meant freedom to be God's slaves rather than slaves of sin; it meant freedom from the tyranny of the state but also freedom to uphold the laws of the state as God's servants (v. 15).

2:17. Such brief lists of these kinds of duties appear in other ancient moralists (e.g., Isocrates, Marcus Aurelius, Syriac Menander). The Old Testament also associated honoring God with honoring those in authority (Ex 22:28; 1 Kings 21:10; Prov 24:21).

2:18-25
Duties of Servants

This passage addresses household slaves, who often had more economic and social mobility than free peasants did, although most of them still did not have much. Field slaves on massive estates were more oppressed; given the regions addressed (1:1) and the nature of household codes (see comment on 2:13-17), they are probably not addressed here and at *most* are peripherally envisioned. The most oppressed slaves, who worked in the mines, were segregated from the rest of society and would not have access to Peter's letter; they are not addressed here at all.

It should also be kept in mind that Peter does not address the institution of slavery per se, although his sympathy is clearly with the slave (2:21): no ancient slave war was successful, and abolition was virtually impossible in his day except through a probably doomed bloody revolution. In this situation, it was far more practical for a pastor to encourage those in the situation to deal with it constructively until they could gain freedom. On slaves and household codes, questions of subsequent application and so forth, see comment on Ephesians 6:4-9 and the introduction to Philemon.

2:18-20. Except those slaves who were able to save enough money on the side to buy their freedom (which many household slaves could do), slaves were not in a position to achieve freedom. Although slaves and masters cooperated in many households as members of a common family, laws viewed slaves as property as well as people, and some owners abused them as property; nearly all owners treated them as socially inferior. Philosophers (especially the popular *Stoics) generally counseled that slaves do their best in the situation in which they found themselves; this was also the view of *Epictetus, who had been a slave earlier in life.

2:21. Moralists commonly cited models for imitation. Philosophers also often prided themselves in their ability not to be bothered by insults or deprivation (e.g., one said that Socrates, when advised that he suffered unjustly, protested, "What—would you rather I suffer justly?"). Although ancient society was very status-conscious and associated power with greatness, Peter identifies *Christ with unjustly treated slaves.

2:22. Here Peter quotes Isaiah 53:9, the first of several allusions to Isaiah 53 in this passage. The passage describes "the suffering servant," a role fulfilled by Jesus.

2:23. This verse may reflect the idea of Isaiah 53:7: though oppressed, he did not open his mouth. In a society based on respect and honor, this was a painful experience; subordinates like slaves were accustomed to it, but it could not have failed to hurt many of them. Many philosophers also advocated enduring reviling without responding in kind.

2:24. Here Peter reflects the language of Isaiah 53:4-5. In this context (1 Pet 2:24, 25), Peter takes the "wounds" as the wounds of sin, as it often was intended in the prophets (e.g., Is 6:10; Jer 6:14; 8:11) and sometimes in later Jewish literature (as probably in the eighth benediction of the Amidah, a regularly recited Jewish prayer).

2:25. This verse echoes Isaiah 53:6. The image of Israel as sheep was common in the *Old Testament (e.g., Is 40:11), and the image of Israel as scattered sheep wandering from the shepherd also appears elsewhere (Jer 50:6; Ezek 34:6; cf. Ps 119:176). An "overseer" (NIV; "guardian"—NASB, NRSV) was one who watched over, protected and had authority; *Diaspora Judaism sometimes applied the term to God. In the Old Testament, God is the chief shepherd of his people (see comment on Jn 10:1-18).

3:1-7
Wives and Husbands

Although Peter upholds societal norms for the purpose of the *church's witness in society (see the introduction to the household codes in 2:13-17), his sympathy here is clearly with the woman, as it was with the slaves in 2:18-25. He continues to advocate submission to authority for the sake of witness and silencing charges that Christianity is subversive; husbands were always in the position of authority in that culture.

3:1. "In the same way" refers back to the passage on slaves (2:18-25). Like Judaism and other non-Roman religions, Christianity spread faster among wives than husbands; husbands had more to lose socially from conversion to an unpopular minority religion. But wives were expected to obey their husbands in Greco-Roman antiquity, and this obedience included allegiance to their husbands' religions. Cults that forbade their participation in Roman religious rites, including prohibiting worship of a family's household gods, were viewed with disdain, and Jewish or Christian women who refused to worship these gods could be charged with atheism. Thus by his advice Peter seeks to reduce marital tensions and causes of hostility toward Christianity and Christians. Silence was considered a great virtue for women in antiquity.

3:2. "Chaste and respectful" (NASB) is the behavior that was most approved for women throughout antiquity.

3:3. Hair was braided in elaborate manners, and well-to-do women strove to keep up with the latest expensive fashions. The gaudy adornments of women of wealth, meant to draw attention to themselves, were repeatedly condemned in ancient literature and speeches, and Peter's readers would assume that his point was meant in the same way. See comment on 1 Timothy 2:9-10.

3:4. Ancients considered a meek and quiet spirit a prime virtue for women, and many moralists advised this attitude instead of dressing in the latest fashions to attract men's attention, a vice commonly attributed to aristocratic women but imitated by those who could afford to do so.

3:5. Moralists normally added examples of such quietness to their exhortations; they especially liked to appeal to matrons of the distant past, who were universally respected for their chaste behavior in contrast to many of the current models in Roman high society. Jewish readers would think especially of the great matriarchs, extolled for their piety in Jewish tradition: Sarah, Rebekah, Rachel and Leah, Sarah being most prominent. The readers may think in terms of head coverings that were prominent in much of the East, meant to render the married woman inconspicuous (see comment on 1 Cor 11:2-16).

3:6. Although Peter explicitly advocates only "submission" (v. 1), he cites Sarah as an example even of "obedience," which was what Roman male society demanded of their wives. That Abraham also "obeyed" Sarah is clear in Genesis (the term usually translated "listen to" in 16:2 and 21:12 also means "obey," and in both passages Abraham submits to Sarah), but this point is not relevant to Peter's example for wives with husbands disobedient to the word (3:1; see the introduction to this section). (One should not read too much into Sarah's calling her husband "lord" here. The direct address "lord" may have been used in Hebrew to address husbands respectfully as "sir," e.g., Gen 18:12; Hos 2:16, though it is especially in later Jewish traditions such as the Testament of Abraham that Sarah addresses Abraham in this manner. Even in the Testament of Abraham, Isaac also addresses his mother with a similarly respectful title and Abraham so addresses a visitor, unaware that he is an angel. In another Jewish tale, Asenath calls her father "lord" yet answers him boastfully and angrily, although Peter certainly does not suggest such behavior here. In the patriarchal period, it was a polite way to address someone of higher authority or one to whose status one wished to defer, e.g., Jacob to Esau in Gen 33:13-14.) Jewish people were considered "children" of Abraham and Sarah; on Christians' fulfilling such a role, cf. 2:9-10.

Peter's advice is practical, not harsh as it might sound in our culture. Although philosophers' household codes often stressed that the wife should "fear" her husband as well as submit to him, Peter disagrees (v. 6; cf. 3:13-14). Husbands could legally "throw out" babies, resort to prostitutes and make life miserable for their wives, although sleeping with other women of the aristocratic class or beating their wives was prohibited. (In a mid-second-century account, a Christian divorced her husband for his repeated infidelity, so he betrayed her to the authorities as a Christian.) Christian wives were limited in their options, but Peter wants them to pursue peace without being intimidated.

3:7. Although his point is to address the many converted wives with unconverted husbands (3:1-6), he includes a brief word for converted husbands as well. Many philosophers, moralists and Jewish teachers complained about the moral and intellectual weakness of women; some referred to the weakness of their bodies. Women's delicacy was considered an object of desire, but also of distrust; even the traditional Roman legal system simply assumed their weakness and inability to make sound decisions on their own. Much of this was due to the influence of *Aristotle, who argued that women were by nature inferior to men in every way except sexually.

Yet this weakness (Peter may apply it only to social position) was often cited as a reason to show them more consideration, and Peter attaches no significance to this common term *except* that requirement; the rest of the verse declares women to be equal before God, which ruined any arguments of their inferiority "by nature." A husband who failed to recognize his wife's spiritual equality jeopardized his own prayers, for the reason Peter gives in 3:12.

3:8-12
Be Kind to One Another

Peter concludes his argument of 2:13—3:7 in the verses following 3:8, although this conclusion flows directly into his next argument. It reinforces the sense of mutual consideration Peter wishes to engender in household relationships, within limitations imposed by the culture he addresses.

3:8. Moralists often listed virtues. They also often lectured on the topic of "harmony" between husband and wife. Advocating peace in all relationships in the home would not have offended any Roman moralists (3:13). "Sympathy" recalls the exhortation to husbands in 3:7, which probably means to "understand" their wives.

3:9. Parallels with Jesus indicate that his teaching may be the source of part of this verse; see comment on Romans 12:17.

3:10-12. Having cited Psalm 34:8 in 2:3, Peter now cites Psalm 34:12-16, which instructs the righteous to pursue peace with others and to speak no evil, thus supporting what he has argued in 2:13—3:7. (Jewish teachers also emphasized that one should pursue peace actively, not just passively.) It also indicates that although God hears the righteous, he opposes the wicked and hence does not hear the prayers of those who mistreat others (3:7).

3:13-22
Be Prepared to Suffer for Doing Good

This section flows naturally from 3:8-12.

3:13-14. Peter alludes to the language of Isaiah 8:12, where God assures the prophet that he need not fear what the rest of his people feared, but should trust in God alone (8:13).

3:15. The *Septuagint (standard Greek version) of Isaiah 8:13 begins "Sanctify the Lord [i.e., God] himself"; here *Christ is the Lord. The "defense" (NASB, NRSV; the common translation "answer" is too weak) implies especially (though probably not only) the image of a legal defense before a court, given "judgment" and execution in the context (4:5-6).

3:16. Judaism also tried this tactic to undermine false accusations.

3:17. Ancient writers sometimes communicated points through special literary forms; one of these is called chiasmus, an inverted parallel structure, which seems to occur here:

A Your slanderers will be ashamed (3:16)
 B Suffer though innocent, in God's will (3:17)
  C For Christ suffered for the unjust (3:18)

D He triumphed over hostile spirits (3:19)
E Noah was saved through water (3:20)
E′ You are saved through water (3:21)
D′ Christ triumphed over hostile spirits (3:22)
C′ For Christ suffered (4:1a)
B′ Suffer in God's will (4:1b-2)
A′ Your slanderers will be ashamed (4:3-5)

3:18-19. On "flesh" and "*Spirit," see comment on Romans 8:1-11; the idea here is that Jesus was resurrected by the Spirit of God, by whom also he went (presumably after the *resurrection) to proclaim triumph over the fallen spirits. Of the many views on this text, the three main ones are (1) that between his death and resurrection, Jesus preached to the dead in Hades, the realm of the dead (the view of many church fathers); (2) that Christ preached through Noah to people in Noah's day (the view of many Reformers); (3) that before or (more likely) after his resurrection, Jesus proclaimed triumph over the fallen angels (the view of most scholars today). (In early Christian literature, "spirits" nearly always refers to angelic spirits rather than human spirits, except when explicit statements are made to the contrary. The grammar here most naturally reads as if, in the Spirit who raised him, he preached to them after his resurrection; further, v. 22 mentions these fallen angels explicitly. The view that these were instead spirits of the dead often rests on 4:6, but the point of 4:6, which caps the section, is that martyrs put to death in the flesh will be raised by the Spirit as Christ was in 3:18.)

Except for most later *rabbis, nearly all ancient Jews read Genesis 6:1-3 as a reference to the fall of angels in Noah's day (1 Pet 3:20); after the flood, they were said to be imprisoned (so also 2 Pet 2:4; Jude 6), either below the earth or in the atmosphere (cf. 1 Pet 3:22). Then, according to a commonly known Jewish tradition, Enoch was sent to proclaim God's judgment to them; here Christ is the proclaimer of triumph over them.

3:20. Ancient Judaism sometimes used the flood as a prototype of future judgment, as in 2 Peter 3:6-7. The emphasis on the salvation of "few" would encourage Christian readers, who were a persecuted minority. God's "patience" reflects Genesis 6:3 and is mentioned in connection with the final judgment in 2 Peter 3:9.

3:21. The act of faith indicated in *baptism, rather than the physical cleansing, was what was significant; baptism was an act of conversion in ancient Judaism, but Judaism insisted on the sincerity of *repentance for it to be efficacious.

3:22. "Authorities and powers" were angelic rulers over the nations, of which Jewish texts often speak (see comment on Eph 1:21-23). Thus even the evil powers behind the rulers who persecuted Christians had been subdued, and the final outcome was not in question.

4:1-11
Persevere in the New Life

4:1-2. "Arm yourselves" borrows the imagery of soldiers arming, training or otherwise preparing themselves for battle and possible death. The sense seems to be that those who died with *Christ through faith (cf. 2:24) are genuinely prepared to suffer with him in any other way, including martyrdom.

4:3. Unlike certain maligned religions, social clubs demanded orderly behavior at parties. Nevertheless, dinners at the homes of *patrons and probably those of social clubs lasted far into the night, with heavy drinking and men often pursuing slave women or boys; religious festivals were similar occasions for immorality. Social clubs, household cults and virtually all aspects of Greco-Roman life were permeated with the veneration of false gods and spirits. Although this behavior was not immoral from the general Greco-Roman perspective, Jews and Christians condemned it as immoral. Jewish people rightly regarded this behavior as typical of *Gentile men in their day—especially, though not exclusively, on pagan festivals.

4:4. Although Jewish people did not participate in the lifestyle characterized in 4:3, their pagan neighbors often portrayed them as lawless and subversive because of their alleged antisocial behavior. The earliest pagan reports of Christians testify that the same prejudices were applied to them, although the authorities never found evidence substantiating these rumors from those they interrogated under torture. Nero's accusation against the Christians he butchered was that they were "haters of humanity," i.e., antisocial. But rumors of Nero's own base immorality offended even the Roman aristocracy.

4:5. These pagans, not the Christians (3:15), would have to give "account" at the final trial. Since the *Old Testament period, the final day of judgment had often been portrayed in courtroom terms.

4:6. Although some commentators regard "those who are dead" as souls of the dead, they seem to be Christians "judged" by earthly courts and executed, who would nevertheless be raised by the *Spirit, as in 3:18. Compare Wisdom of Solomon 3:1-6.

4:7. In many Jewish traditions (including Dan 12:1-2), the end of the age would be preceded by a period of great suffering; the impending end, therefore, calls for exhortations to perseverance in seriousness and prayer.

4:8. Proverbs 10:12 seems to prohibit gossiping about one another's sins or slandering one another (cf. Jas 5:20). The implication here may be that love overlooks one another's faults, although some scholars have suggested that it means that those who love will themselves find grace in the day of judgment (1 Pet 4:5-6).

4:9. Hospitality was receiving others, especially taking in travelers of the same faith who needed a place to stay. As generally in the ethical ideals of antiquity, lodging and provisions were to be provided generously, not grudgingly.

4:10-11. Like Paul (Rom 12:4-8), Peter emphasized the diversity of gifts in the *church and the need for all of them until the end. Speaking as if one uttered divine "oracles" would no doubt refer to the gift of *prophecy, or at least prophetic inspiration in some form of speaking for God. On prophecy and serving, see comment on Romans 12:6-8 and 16:1.

4:12-19
Christians Judged First

In the *Old Testament (Dan 12:1-2) and much Jewish tradition, God's people would suffer greatly just before the time of the end; then the wicked would be judged. Jewish tradition often emphasized that the righteous experienced their sufferings in this age but that the wicked would experience theirs throughout the age to come. Such persecutions as are mentioned here continued for two more centuries in the Roman Empire and have continued periodically in various times and places throughout history; believers in each generation have had the occasion to feel close to the end of the age.

4:12. It is possible that Peter alludes to the fate that befell many Christians captured in Rome in A.D. 64: they were burned alive as torches to light Nero's gardens at night. But he more likely alludes again to the image of gold being tried by fire (1:7), and perhaps to the fire of judgment day being experienced in advance; the language of fiery trials was often used figuratively.

4:13. Some Jewish people described the time of tribulation before the end as the "*Messiah's travail"; Peter may therefore be saying that those who share the Messiah's sufferings also hasten the coming of the end (although the regular *New Testament idea of sharing *Christ's sufferings may be adequate to explain the passage).

4:14. The Old Testament and Jewish tradition often speak of the *Spirit resting "on" God's servants, empowering them for their task. In the light of "glory" in verse 13, Peter presumably means, "the Spirit who will raise you [4:6] is already on you."

4:15. As second-century apologists, or defenders of Christianity, pointed out, the only charge on which true Christians were ever convicted was the charge of being a Christian. The Greek term for "meddler" (NIV, NASB) could refer to sorcerers but probably refers to "busybodies" (KJV), those giving unwanted and ill-timed advice. Meddling tactlessly in others' affairs was a vice often attributed to unpopular *Cynic philosophers (to whom some Christian preachers had already been compared).

4:16. The nickname "Christian" was originally used only by those hostile to Christianity; see comment on Acts 11:26. Here it is parallel to legal charges like "murderer" and "thief." Early Roman descriptions of Nero's persecution use this title for Jesus' followers. Many wise men in Greek tradition pointed out that it was truly noble to suffer scorn for doing good; in Greco-Roman society, obsessed as it was with shame and honor, this was a countercultural insight.

4:17. The image of judgment beginning at God's household is an *Old Testament one (Ezek 9:6; cf. Jer 25:18-29; Amos 3:2), as is the ominous expression, "the time has come" (Ezek 7:7, 12). Believers experience the judgment of earthly courts (1 Pet 4:6), but Peter probably sees that suffering also as God's discipline, as Jewish teachers did. Throughout history, persecution has refined and strengthened the *church.

4:18. Peter proves his case in 4:17 by citing the *Septuagint of Proverbs 11:31, which may reflect what had become the prevailing Jewish conception by Peter's day, that the righteous suffered in this life, but the wicked suffered in the world to come.

4:19. Peter again echoes the familiar language of Jewish prayer: the final benediction of one regularly uttered Jewish prayer included the lines "Our lives are committed to your hand, and our souls are in your care," and some others also uttered similar prayers in the face of possible death (cf. 2 Macc 13:14); the prototype for all of them was probably Psalm 31:5 (cited in Lk 23:46).

5:1-5
Faithful Caretakers of the Flock

The behavior of *church leaders in the time of crisis could encourage or discourage the flock. The leaders, once known, would be the first targets of search, capture, torture and execution.

5:1. Elders, older and wiser men skilled in judging cases, ruled in most Israelite towns in the *Old Testament. In the *New Testament period, "elders" held a respected place in the *synagogues, from which the churches took over this form of leadership. Peter ranks himself among them as a fellow elder.

5:2. The image of a "shepherd" is that

of a concerned guide, not of a severe ruler (although the image of shepherds had been applied to rulers in parts of the ancient Near East). Charges of illegitimate gain were often made against moral teachers in the ancient world, and it was necessary for Christians to avoid even the appearance of impropriety. (Like certain officials in the Jewish community, these Christian leaders distributed the funds for the poor.)

5:3. Heads of Greek philosophical schools and Jewish schools of law presented their lives as models to their students, but some also exercised strict control. A closer parallel to this text would be elders in *Diaspora synagogues, who were responsible for the services and led the Jewish community but normally had no official power outside settling internal legal disputes.

5:4. In ancient texts a "chief shepherd" appears to have been an overseer of a group of other shepherds, although they were usually not well-to-do themselves. "Crowns" were garlands given to victors of athletic contests, benefactors or other heroes, and they were perishable; those faithful to Christ would receive an imperishable crown. The image was also used in Judaism.

5:5. Respect for parents, elders and, in Judaism, those more knowledgeable in the *law was socially obligatory in antiquity; some Jewish traditions regarded it as an expression of one's respect for God. Such respect included deferring to the wisdom of older men and allowing them to speak first. Peter advocates submission to the ruling elders (5:1), but he also urges—against Greco-Roman society's ideals—mutual humility, based on the teaching of the *Old Testament (Prov 3:34).

5:6-11
Persevere by Grace

Although 1 Peter 5:5-9 has sufficient similarities with James 4:6-10 to suggest a common source for the imagery, the application is different. In James, the test is poverty and oppression tempting people to retaliate. In 1 Peter, it is persecution tempting believers to fall away.

5:6. Following on Proverbs 3:34, cited in 1 Peter 5:5, Peter urges believers to "humble" themselves before God. In the *Old Testament, this idea often meant *repenting, sometimes when facing impending judgment (4:17), or learning one's complete dependence on God. Here the sense includes embracing and accepting the suffering until God provides the way out (cf. Jer 27:11). On present humbling and future exalting, see comment on Luke 1:52-53 and 14:11; the cries of God's people during unjust sufferings had always moved him to act on their behalf (Ex 2:23-25; 3:7-9; Judg 2:18; 10:16).

5:7. Although the promise of complete relief from persecution is future (5:6), Peter encourages believers to pray and trust God's love for them in the present. Judaism learned to see God's love in Israel's sufferings (as disciplines of love), but most pagans, who bartered sacrifices and vows to get benefactions from the gods, had difficulty with this concept.

5:8-11. In the Old Testament, "*Satan" (in the Hebrew of Job, a title, "the satan") was the accuser, the prosecuting attorney before God—the "adversary," as Peter says. In Jewish tradition, Satan accused God's people before God's throne day and night (except, in later accounts, on the Day of *Atonement). The "devil" is literally the "slanderer," carrying the same connotation as the adversarial accuser. Jewish teachers recognized that, as in the book of Job (where he "went about" over the face of the earth—2:12), Satan sought in this present age to turn people to apostasy from the truth, although his power was limited because he ultimately had to answer to God. The *Dead Sea Scrolls called the present evil age the "dominion of Satan."

Lions were viewed as the most ferocious and mighty beasts, and from Psalm 22:13 (probably the background here) they came to be used as figures for enemies of God's people. In the time of Nero, Christians were fed to some literal lions as well. The small, isolated Christian communities could take heart that their other spiritual siblings—starting with the *churches Peter knew in Rome—were experiencing the same trials (1 Pet 5:9), until the end (v. 10).

5:12-14
Conclusion

5:12. Silvanus (the full Roman name for which the similar name Silas served as a short equivalent) appears to have been the amanuensis, or scribe. Most letters were written through the agency of scribes. As a Roman citizen (Acts 16:37), Silas presumably came from a fairly well-to-do Jewish family that provided him a good literary and *rhetorical education; Peter may have given him some degree of freedom in wording the letter. On assertions of brevity, see comment on Hebrews 13:22; it was a polite closing formula in many ancient speeches and letters.

5:13. Some elements of contemporary Judaism had readily transferred *prophecies of Babylon's demise in the *Old Testament to the new empire of Rome. "Babylon" had thus become a fairly common cryptogram for Rome (although "Edom" was more popular with later *rabbis).

5:14. Kisses were a common affectionate greeting for close friends and relatives.

2 PETER

Introduction

Authorship and Date. Regarding authorship, 2 Peter is one of the most disputed letters in the *New Testament. The style differs so much from 1 Peter that the same person could not have written both unless he were purposely trying to alter his style. But Peter could have given literary freedoms to his amanuenses, using a different scribe (1 Pet 5:13) for each, with the second being more accustomed to bombastic Asiatic *rhetorical style. (Although many second-rate rhetoricians preferred flowery Asianism, Atticist style became predominant and ultimately flourished by the early second century. This style might provide a clue to the destination or, more likely, the date [before the second century], although it might reveal only the rhetorical training of the author or scribe. *Quintilian noted that a third style, the Rhodian, less redundant than the Asiatic school but less concise than the Atticist, was sometimes also used.)

The most important argument against Petrine authorship is the letter's clear dependence on Jude, yet this point is not absolutely decisive; Peter could have incorporated much of Jude's letter, instructed a scribe to do so or (much less likely) even used Jude as his scribe. (That Jude used 2 Peter is improbable, based on simplifications of imagery, expansions of allusions, etc.)

The attestation for 2 Peter is weaker than that for most other New Testament books but stronger than that of early Christian books that did not become part of the New Testament, especially those claiming to be Petrine. The early *church did debate its genuineness, although its *existence* is attested early. But *pseudepigraphic documents were generally written in the name of a hero of the distant past; although a second-century date for the letter is possible, no internal evidence necessarily precludes a first-century date. Second-century *Gnosticism is probably not in view, and the end's delay was an issue perhaps as early as the first New Testament document (1 Thessalonians).

Opponents. One suggestion of the heresy combated in this letter is second-century Gnosticism or a first-century proto-Gnosticism; "knowledge" (a favorite emphasis of the Gnostics, though hardly limited to them) is mentioned seven times in the letter. Gnostics denied the future coming of *Christ, and many of them believed that bodily sins did not matter. Gnosticism did not, however, create these ideas out of nothing; they developed earlier Greek (plus Jewish and Christian) ideas that were already evident in the first century.

Given the reports of charlatans so prominent in antiquity and parallels to all the ideas in existing Greek and Jewish conceptions in the first century, it is likely that the opponents are simply *Diaspora Jews almost completely overtaken by Greek thought (perhaps even more than *Philo was).

***Genre.** Second Peter is clearly one of those ancient letters intended for a wide circulation (1:1), although the style indicates that it was not directed toward the highest literary circles who normally read such letters. Besides being a "general letter," some scholars have found in it elements of the "testamentary" genre:

testaments were final instructions left by a dying father or leader (cf. 1:14).

Commentaries. The best is Richard J. Bauckham, *Jude, 2 Peter,* WBC 50 (Waco, Tex.: Word, 1983). J. N. D. Kelly, *A Commentary on the Epistles of Peter and Jude* (reprint, Grand Rapids, Mich.: Baker Book House, 1981), is also very helpful.

1:1-2
Introduction

The Greek text here reads "Simeon" (NRSV) rather than "Simon" Peter; this form of the name is less common but closer to the original Semitic form of the name than "Simon" is (also in Acts 15:14). Although "*Savior" was a divine title in Judaism and antiquity as a whole, it could be applied more generally; but applying the title "God and Savior" (the most natural translation) to Jesus was a clear statement of his divinity and would have offended most Jewish readers who were not Christians. Writers often established the intimate relationship between themselves and their readers at the beginning of a letter (thus, "faith like ours"). "Grace and peace" adopts a standard ancient greeting form but with *Christ at the center; see comment on Romans 1:7.

1:3-11
How to Persevere to Salvation

This section is sometimes said to adapt the literary form of a civic decree known from inscriptions honoring benefactors, but the evidence for this thesis is hardly compelling. Although the parallels demonstrate ideas in common between this passage and some decrees, such ideas were relatively widespread and can be identified in other literary forms as well.

1:3-4. "Divine power" and "divine nature" had been important phrases in Greek thought for centuries; they had also become standard in many *Diaspora Jewish writers. Many Greeks in this period wanted to escape the material world of decay around them, believing that their soul was divine and immortal and belonged in the pure and perfect heavens above; some Greek thinkers and cults provided this idea as a hope for the masses.

Many Greek writers, some Jewish writers like *Philo and generally later *Gnostics argued that one could become "divinized," a god, either in life or at death; in some systems this divinization involved absorption into the divine. But most of ancient Judaism rejected the idea of divinization; there was only one God (cf. Gen 3:5; and even Philo meant divinization in a very qualified sense). Many Diaspora Jewish texts used language like Peter's but nearly always only to indicate reception of immortality, not divinization. (Peter applies this language to the Christian view that a believer in Jesus receives a new nature; see comment on 1 Pet 1:23.) In the context of monotheistic early Christianity, embattled by polytheistic culture, Peter's subdued language could serve to refute claims of those who expected full divinization.

That Peter's immediate cultural context is Diaspora Judaism rather than Greek paganism may be indicated by how he defines physical "corruption" or "decay": its source is lust (v. 4; cf. 2:14; 3:3). Immortality was available, as the Greeks wished, but it was made available only through purification from sin (1:9); and the Greek concept of immortality is qualified by the biblical hope in the *kingdom and hence future *resurrection (cf. 1:11).

1:5-7. Lists of vices and virtues appear elsewhere in ancient literature. Adding one virtue, vice or some other next step to a former one, as here, was also a standard literary form that appears in Jewish, Greek and Roman texts (such progressions were called sorites). "Moral excellence" (NASB) or "goodness" (NIV, NRSV, TEV) was the catchall Greek "virtue" (KJV) representing nobility of character.

1:8. Greek philosophers saw philosophical knowledge as the key to changing people's behavior; Peter may, however, intend "knowledge" to include the sense of a personal relationship, as often in the *Old Testament.

1:9. Jewish texts also speak of moral corruption and defilement from which one must be "purified" (cf. 2:20).

1:10-11. Judaism often spoke of Israel's "calling" and "chosenness." Peter applies these terms to all who would persevere to *eternal life. The future transformation of the world and an eternal *kingdom established in the future were Jewish and Christian ideas foreign to pagan Greek thought.

1:12-21
Peter's Eyewitness Traditions

1:12. "Reminding" was a common part of ancient moral exhortation, especially when softened by the qualification "though you already know this."

1:13. A number of ancient texts compared the body to a tent, as here; Peter chooses an image that his readers would readily grasp.

1:14. Jewish writers generally believed that the righteous often were warned of their impending death in advance. In ancient Jewish stories, heroes often gave final exhortations to their heirs in "testaments" as their death approached. By announcing his imminent death (undoubtedly his execution in Rome), Peter informs his readers: These are my final instructions to you, so pay close attention. Cf. John 21:18-19.

1:15. Reminders were common in testaments (1:14), although they were also common in moral exhortations in general (1:12). "Departure" here is literally "exodus," a term occasionally used in Jewish and Christian texts for death (e.g., Lk 9:31).

1:16. The term translated "myths" (NRSV) was usually used negatively for untrue stories, such as slanderously false accounts about the gods; "myths" were contrasted with reliable accounts. Eyewitness testimony was important in establishing a case historically or legally, although Greek and Roman rhetoricians did not always give it as much weight as it bears today. (Some scholars have drawn attention to the point that the same term Peter uses for "eyewitnesses" here was used for initiates in the final stage of initiation in some pagan *mystery cults, such as the Eleusinian and Samothracian mysteries; but a related term was also applied to the higher philosophy by *Plato and *Aristotle, and it was a standard term for eyewitnesses, applied even to God himself in *Diaspora Judaism. Because Peter describes not his initiation into the faith but an eyewitness experience distinct from that initiation, the eyewitness element is the central point. Like Peter here, the Gospels are at pains to point out that the glory which Jesus' companions would see before death was the transfiguration, not the Second Coming; but the transfiguration prefigured the Second Coming; cf. 1:19.)

1:17. Some "testaments" (1:14) cited special revelations (often heavenly journeys) of the hero; Peter provides a more down-to-earth revelation: what he experienced at the transfiguration (Mk 9:2-13). Early Judaism often referred to God speaking from heaven (see comment on Mk 1:11 for the texts excerpted here). "The Glory" was sometimes a Jewish circumlocution for God; Peter probably intends an allusion to Sinai, where God revealed his glory to Moses.

1:18. Israel also experienced a revelation of God at a "holy" mountain, and Peter probably parallels his own witness of Jesus' glory with Moses' witness of God's glory on Mount Sinai. (The *Old Testament usually applies this title to Zion, but Zion was to be the site of the new Sinai, or law giving, in the end time; cf. Is 2:2-4.) Both revelations led to divine Scriptures (cf. 2 Pet 1:20 with 3:16), although Jewish teachers generally agreed that the *law had more authority than any mere voice from heaven.

1:19. The apostolic revelation in *Christ confirmed the revelations of the Old Testament prophets. Some *Dead Sea Scrolls texts present the "star" of Numbers 24:17 as *messianic, and an Old Testament text describes the coming day of the Lord in terms of a sunrise (Mal 4:2) because God would come like the sun (cf. Ps 84:11). The point here seems to be that the morning star (Venus) heralds the advent of dawn; a new age was about to dawn (cf. 2 Pet 1:11), but the Old Testament plus what was revealed by Jesus' first coming was the greatest revelation the world would experience until his return in the day of the Lord. "You do well" was a common way of suggesting that a person do something (i.e., "You *ought* to do this").

1:20-21. Ancient Judaism and Greek thinkers generally viewed prophetic inspiration as a divine possession or frenzy, in which the prophet's rational mind was replaced by the divine word. (The remark on the Jewish perspective is especially true of *Diaspora Jewish ecstatics, like *Philo and authors of the *Sibylline Oracles.) The various literary styles of different Old Testament prophets indicates that this was not quite the case; inspiration still used human faculties and vocabulary (cf. 1 Pet 1:10-12; 1 Cor 7:40; 14:1-2, 14-19), although there may have been different levels and kinds of ecstasy (cf. 1 Cor 14:2; 2 Cor 5:13; 12:4). On either model, however, inspiration could protect the inspired agents from error; contrast 2 Peter 2:1.

2:1-22
Damnation of Immoral Teachers

2:1. In contrast to the inspired prophets of 1:20-21, false prophets were those who spoke visions from their own mind instead of from God's heart; in many *Old Testament texts that define them as such, they falsely promise peace for sinners destined instead for judgment (e.g., Jer 23:16-32; Ezek 13:3-10).

2:2. Sincere philosophers complained that philosophy was ridiculed on account of pseudophilosophers; Jewish people and representatives of other minority religions also suffered from the negative publicity following wayward, profiteering members of their groups (cf. Rom 2:23-24). The same was true of early Christianity.

2:3. Traveling diviners, false prophets and moral teachers typically charged fees or begged funds and were thus frequently accused of having monetary motives unworthy of their professed callings (see comment on 1 Thess 2:5). False teachers in the *church were likewise exploiting Christians.

2:4. One of the most prominent themes of ancient Jewish tradition, though usually suppressed by the later *rabbis, was the idea that the "sons of God" in Genesis 6:1-3 were angels who lusted after women and so fell. The term for "cast into hell" here is from the Greek name Tartarus, a place not only of holding for the wicked dead (and especially the Titans, the pre-Olympian supernatural beings), but of the severest conceivable tortures; it occurs elsewhere in Jewish literature as the place where the fallen angels were imprisoned. Jewish writers also generally affirmed a current hell as a holding place for the wicked until the final judgment.

2:5. Noah stories, like fallen angel stories, were also popular in nonrabbinic Judaism. Judgment on the fallen angels was usually linked with judgment on Noah's generation because Genesis 6 recounted both. Jewish traditions also portrayed Noah as a preacher of *repentance (e.g., *Sibylline Oracles and Jubilees). Jewish teachers liked to use the flood generation as an example of impending judgment to warn their own generation to repent, and they believed that the flood generation was particularly wicked and would not have a share in the world to come.

2:6. Jewish teachers often coupled Sodom with the flood generation as epitomes of wickedness ("an example"—3 Maccabees 2:5; the *rabbis frequently; etc.); the Old Testament prophets also used Sodom repeatedly as an image of ultimate sin, often imitated by their own generations (cf. Deut 32:32; Is 1:9-10; 3:9; 13:19; Jer 23:14; 50:40; Lam 4:6; Ezek 16:46; Zeph 2:9).

2:7-8. Jewish tradition was quite divided on whether Lot was righteous (most of the rabbis and some others said that he was not). Genesis portrays him as personally righteous (Gen 18:25; 19:1-16); though not as wise as Abraham (13:10-11; 19:29, 32-35), he was too righteous for Sodom (19:9, 15).

2:9. In most Jewish traditions, the wicked were tortured in *Gehenna until the day of judgment (or until their annihilation, depending on which tradition one follows). In the Wisdom of Solomon 10:6, Wisdom "rescued the righteous one," Lot, when the ungodly perished in the fire of Sodom; 2 Peter probably alludes to this tradition.

2:10-11. A wide variety of Jewish texts mention those who reviled the stars of heaven or cursed *Satan or demons. Peter's opponents have presumably adopted this practice, perhaps as a form of "spiritual warfare." (By contrast, the Sodomites [2:6] tried to molest angels but were unaware that they were angels.) Although Christians had to be concerned for their public witness—charges of subversion in the Roman Empire led to severe persecution and repression—these false teachers reviled earthly authorities and the angelic authorities behind them (see comment on Eph 1:19-23).

2:12. Ancient writers regarded some animals as existing only to be killed for food; here the animals are objects of the hunt. Philosophers (e.g., *Epictetus and the second-century Stoic emperor Marcus Aurelius) characterized animals as creatures ruled by instinct as opposed to humans, who were ruled by reason, and considered unreasoning humans "wild beasts."

2:13. Reveling was part of all-night parties; accusing these people of partying in the daytime was portraying them as worse than the pagans. (The common suggestion that Peter's wording here depends on the early Jewish work called the Assumption of Moses is possible, but it is also possible that the Assumption of Moses depends on 2 Peter; the direction of dependence depends on the respective dates assigned to the two documents. It is also possible that both depend on some other source, or that the verbal parallel is coincidental.)

2:14. Some Jewish writers also spoke of adultery of the eyes; see comment on Matthew 5:27-28. Whereas philosophers spoke of moral "training" and avoidance of greed, these false teachers were "trained in greed" (NASB, NRSV). "Accursed children" (NASB, NRSV) could either represent the Semitic figure of speech for accursed ones or refer to disinherited children who received curse instead of blessing from parents.

2:15. According to Jewish tradition and the most likely interpretation of the *Old Testament, Balaam was a dishonorable character. For the sake of money, Balaam had led the Israelites into cultic prostitution with the Midianites, bringing God's judgment on them and leading to his own death (Num 31:8; Josh 13:22). Jewish literature considered him the ultimate prophet (and sometimes philosopher) of the pagans but did not reduce his role in Israel's sexual offense. His attempt to make Israel sin was considered worse than any other nation's military attack on them because it brought *God's* judgment against them. The contrast between "the way of Balaam" and the "right way" reflects the common ancient image of two paths, one leading the righteous or wise to life, the other leading the foolish to destruction.

2:16. Ecstatic prophets were often called "mad" or "possessed" (in the ancient Near East and ancient Israel as well as in Greco-Roman antiquity; cf. 2 Kings 9:11; Jer 29:26). But Balaam's insanity is even more evident: despite a miraculous warning through an animal that proved to be smarter than he was (cf. the implications in 2 Pet 2:12), he proceeded with his folly (Num 22:20-35). *Philo used Balaam as an allegory for foolish people; the *rabbis said that people who followed in Balaam's paths would inherit hell. Jewish tradition added to the donkey's speech, in which it reproved Balaam's folly in greater detail.

2:17. Barren wells were worse than useless; they promised water in the arid East yet did not deliver on their promise. Hell was sometimes described as outer darkness.

2:18-19. Greek philosophers often warned against being enslaved by one's passions; the image could extend to those who exploited those passions (such as prostitutes). Those defeated in battle and taken captive were enslaved. Most philosophers spoke of freedom from passion rather than freedom to indulge it; the *gospel spoke of freedom from sin, not freedom to engage in it.

2:20-21. Jewish texts often spoke of the "way of righteousness"; see comment on 2:15.

2:22. One of the proverbs Peter cites here is from the Bible (Prov 26:11, referring to a fool returning to his folly); the other proverb was extrabiblical (from the ancient story of Ahiqar) but would have been a familiar image. Both dogs and pigs were considered unclean (cf. Mt 7:6) and would have been regarded contemptuously by Jewish readers; they were also associated in other analogies like this one.

3:1-7
The Certainty of Coming Judgment

Like many *Hellenized Jews and like later *Gnostics, the false teachers here played down future judgment, thus leading people to sin like the false prophets of old (chap. 2; see comment on 2:1). Now Peter turns to address the root of their immoral error directly; like many Jewish teachers, he recognizes that lack of expectation of future judgment usually led to immoral behavior or even moral relativism (see also comment on Jude 3-4). Some commentators regard chapter 3 as a letter distinct from the one in chapters 1—2, but this is unnecessary: the transition is natural, especially in view of Peter dropping his dependence on Jude at this point.

3:1-2. Some philosophers spoke of a "pure mind" as one untainted by the physical senses; Peter means one untainted by the false teachers' views (2:20). On "reminder" see comment on 1:12. For Jesus' commandment here, cf. Matthew 24:42-44 (especially for 2 Pet 3:9).

3:3. In much Jewish literature, those who deny the age to come have no basis for morality (cf., e.g., *Pharisaic accusations against the *Sadducees). Ridiculing the righteous was also understood to be characteristically wicked behavior; *1 Enoch speaks of sinners who mock God, denying his revelation; the *Dead Sea Scrolls complain about those who mocked their community's righteous teacher.

3:4. Ancient writers vested "the ancestors" (NRSV) or "the ancients" with great prestige.

*Aristotle and his adherents (the Peripatetics) believed that the universe was eternal. His view caught on even outside Peripatetic circles, and *Philo had to address the idea. (Like *Plato, Philo believed that God created the world from preexistent matter, but unlike Plato, he believed that God had created that preexistent matter too.) *Epicureans denied that God acted in the world; they also believed that matter was indestructible (on the atomic level) and that the universe was infinite. The *Stoics believed that fire was eternal, that the universe would periodically be resolved into the primeval fire (see comment on 3:7) and that eternity was a cycle of ages. Whether matter was created out of preexisting substance in chaos (as in most ancient thought) or from nothing (as is most likely in Gen 1) was debated in *Diaspora Judaism.

3:5. In Genesis 1, God created the world through his word (also Ps 33:6-9). (Some later Jewish traditions counted ten commands in Gen 1 and suggested that they represented the Ten Commandments, the word of the *law on which God founded the world.)

3:6-7. God had promised after Noah's flood (Gen 6—9) never to destroy the earth by water again (Gen 9:15; Is 54:9), but the prophets did speak of a future fiery destruction and renewal of the present world (cf. Is 65:17; 66:15, 22); they were followed on this point by later Jewish writers (e.g., *Dead Sea Scrolls, *Sibylline Oracles). Jewish tradition thus declared that the present world would be destroyed not by water but by fire (e.g., *Josephus; Rabbi Meir, second century; Life of Adam). Jewish literature sometimes used the flood as a symbol for the future judgment by fire. Unlike the *Stoics, who believed that the universe (including even the gods) would be periodically resolved into fire and formed again, Jewish people hoped for a future day of judgment and then a new creation that would stand forever (2 Pet 3:10, 12-13). Though their source was the Old Testament, on this point their view was closer to that of *Plato, who thought that the world would end once by flood and once by conflagration.

3:8-13 The Timing of the Final Judgment

Delay should never be taken to indicate that Jesus is not coming back after all (3:4; cf. Ezek 12:27-28; Hab 2:3). Although many modern scholars think that 2 Peter addresses a second-century disillusionment with the earliest Christian *apocalyptic hope, questions over the delay of *Christ's coming arguably surfaced as early as Pentecost, and the book of Revelation, at the end of the first century, still cherished apocalyptic fervor. The *Dead Sea Scrolls also attest unexpected, continued deferment of hope for the day of God among the *Essenes, producing similar exhortations to endurance.

3:8. Peter appeals to Psalm 90:4 to make his point, as did many other Jewish writers of his day (who often took "the day as a thousand years" literally and applied it to the days of creation). Some apocalyptic writers lamented that God did not reckon time as mortals do and consequently urged perseverance.

3:9. The *Old Testament emphasized that God delayed judgment to allow opportunity for the wicked to *repent (cf. 2 Kings 14:25-27; Ezek 18:23, 32; 33:11). His patience with regard to the world's end was further emphasized in later Jewish texts like *4 Ezra; in Jewish texts, one could no longer repent once the day of judgment had come. Some Greco-Roman writers also praised the mercy of God or that of the gods in delaying divine vengeance.

3:10. The day of the Lord is a familiar Old Testament image for the ultimate day of God's judgment, his final day in court when he settles the injustices of the world (e.g., Is 2:12; Joel 1:15; Amos 5:18-20). That day's "coming as a thief" refers to a saying of Jesus (extant in Mt 24:43). Different ancient thinkers had different lists of elements (the *Stoics, who believed the world would be resolved into fire, had four, like most writers: earth, water, air and fire), but Peter's point is that everything will be destroyed. The destruction or purifying renewal of heaven and earth was also common in *apocalyptic tradition.

3:11. As usually in the *New Testament, Peter's discussion of the future is practical and suggests how to live in the present. This focus corresponds with the motives of some *apocalyptic writers but contrasts with what appear to be those of many others: impatient curiosity about the future. Those who suffered in the present order especially embraced apocalyptic hope, which gave them strength to persevere in the midst of seemingly insurmountable tests in this age.

3:12. *Rabbis disagreed among themselves as to whether the end of the age was at a time fixed by God or whether it could be hastened by Israel's *repentance and obedience. In this context, Christians hasten the coming of the end by missions and evangelism (cf. Mt 24:14), thereby enabling the conversion of those for whose sake God has delayed the end (2 Pet 3:9, 15).

3:13. This hope is from Isaiah 65:17 and 66:22, and was frequently reiterated in later Jewish literature. The Old Testament and Judaism agreed that righteousness would characterize the world to come (e.g., Is 9:7; 32:16-17; 62:1-2; Jer 32:40).

3:14-18
Preparing for the Final Judgment

3:14. Here Peter urges his readers not to be like the false teachers (2:13). See comment on 3:11.

3:15-16. God's patience allows salvation for those on whose behalf he delays; cf. 1 Peter 3:20 on Genesis 6:3, returning to the judgment image of the flood (2 Pet 3:5-7). Calling a writer's work "hard to understand" in antiquity was not an insult (as it often is today); it could mean that it was complex and brilliant. Jewish teachers said that the message of the Scriptures could be "distorted" by misinterpreting them. Second-century *Gnostics and many first-century Jewish and probably Christian groups were already distorting the Scriptures, some even to play down a future judgment (perhaps by allegorizing it).

By the late first century, another early Christian writer (1 Clement) asserted the inspiration of Paul's letters; although Paul's early writings had undoubtedly not been collected before Peter's death, Peter may have known of some of them from his travels among the churches. Even though *Josephus and other writers asserted that Judaism had a closed *canon, some Jewish groups (such as the *Qumran community and *Diaspora communities that used various recensions of the *LXX) seem to have had a fluid idea as to where Scripture ended and other edifying literature began. Although some scholars have reasonably used this statement identifying Paul as Scripture to argue for a post-Petrine date for 2 Peter, it would not have been impossible for the real Peter to view Paul's writings as Scripture if he accepted Paul's apostolic status and hence the possibility that some of his writings were *prophetically inspired. Much that was prophetically inspired, however, never became Scripture (see "canon" in the glossary). If Peter wrote these words, they reflect a remarkable insight for his day.

3:17-18. Peter's readers are to resist the false teachers by growing in *Christ.

1 JOHN

Introduction

Authorship. The style of 1 John is so close to that of the author of the Gospel of John that no one questioned that they were written by the same person until the twentieth century. Some writers have pointed to minor stylistic differences and have proposed that 1 John was written by a different member of the "Johannine school." Sometimes disciples of famous teachers would seek to imitate their teachers' works (often even their style), so this proposal cannot be ruled out on a priori literary grounds.

One can account for the minor stylistic differences, however, simply by recognizing the difference between an epistle and a gospel; the latter *genre is literarily related to ancient biography, which went through several stages in the writing process before it was complete. Conversely, this epistle does not represent a major literary production (although literary epistles did exist).

One can explain the purported differences in theology and outlook by the different situation each addressed; by the standards used to suggest that the same person did not write both, different sermons of the average preacher today would often have to be attributed to different authors as well! Most important, the author claims to be an eyewitness (1:1) but does not claim to write in another's name (he provides no *pseudepigraphic preface).

Genre. The form is more like a homily than a letter (except 2:12-14). That the epistolary prescript (opening) and conclusion are missing need not surprise us; they were sometimes removed when letters were incorporated into collections (although 2 and 3 John retain standard elements of letters). But the whole document flows more like a sermon, albeit one not structured by the *rhetorical conventions of the day. It thus resembles the form of letter known as a "letter-essay," although it nevertheless addresses the specific situation of the readers.

Situation. If the setting of 1 John is the same as that of the Fourth Gospel, it is meant to encourage Christians expelled from the *synagogues, some of whose colleagues have returned to the synagogue by denying Jesus' *messiahship (2:19, 22; 4:2-3). The letter can be read in this way and makes sense on these terms.

But John was concerned about situations in cities other than those addressed in his Gospel. While Christians were expelled from synagogues and betrayed by the Jewish community in Smyrna (Rev 2:9-10) and Philadelphia (Rev 3:7-9), they were tempted with the heresy of compromise elsewhere, including compromise with idolatry advocated by false prophets (Rev 2:14-15, 20-23; cf. 1 Jn 4:1; 5:21). The form of idolatry may have especially been the imperial cult, to which people in the East needed to show their loyalty or pay serious consequences (cf. Rev 13:14-15), possibly including death (1 Jn 3:16). First John could address a community like Ephesus, where the *church had expelled the false teachers but needed love for one another (Rev 2:2-4).

On the one hand, the issue in view might be simply some false prophets (1 Jn 4:1-6) advocating compromises with the imperial cult to save one's life. On the other hand, the issue might be one of the heresies that was developing toward full-blown *Gnosticism. Docetists believed that Christ was divine but only seemed to become human (cf. 4:2); Cerinthians (followers of Cerinthus) believed that the *Christ-*Spirit merely came on Jesus, but denied that he was actually the one and only Christ (cf. 2:22). Gnostics also tended to define sin in various ways, hence some Gnostics believed that they were incapable of committing real sins, although their bodies could engage in behavior non-Gnostic Christians considered sinful. Any of the above backgrounds fits the letter itself; thus the commentary mentions all of them at relevant points below. But one point is beyond dispute: the primary troublemakers are clearly "secessionists," people who had been part of the Christian community John addresses but who had withdrawn from that community. John advocates testing the spirits by two main tests: a moral-ethical test (keeping the commandments, especially love of the Christian community) and a faith test (the right view of Jesus).

Commentaries. Among the best are I. Howard Marshall, *The Epistles of John*, NICNT (Grand Rapids, Mich.: Eerdmans, 1978); Stephen S. Smalley, *1, 2, 3 John*, WBC 51 (Waco, Tex.: Word, 1984); D. Moody Smith, *First, Second and Third John*, Interpretation (Louisville, Ky.: John Knox, 1991); and Kenneth Grayston, *The Johannine Epistles*, NCB (Grand Rapids, Mich.: Eerdmans, 1984). The most detailed commentary is Raymond E. Brown, *The Epistles of John*, AB 30 (Garden City, N.Y.: Doubleday, 1982).

1:1-4
The Basis for True Fellowship

The basis for fellowship as Christians (1:3) is precisely what divided John's readers from those who had withdrawn from the community. If (as many scholars think) 1:1 alludes back to the opening of the Fourth Gospel, John speaks of God's Word that had always been (see comment on Jn 1:1-18). Although philosophers and Jewish teachers alike spoke of the divine Word, none of them spoke of the Word's becoming human. By saying that Jesus' witnesses had touched and felt him, John indicates that Jesus had been fully human; he was not simply a divine apparition like the current "manifestations" of the gods in which the Greeks believed (though merely "testifying" what one saw "with one's eyes" could be used more broadly, e.g., 2 Maccabees 3:36).

1:5-10
The Reality of Sin

It is possible that the secessionists believe, like some later *Gnostics, that they have achieved a state of sinlessness. Given the emphasis on God's holiness in this passage and later statements about the secessionists, however (3:6, 9), it is perhaps more likely that they believe, like some later Gnostics, that they are sinless in a different sense—they do not regard the sins they commit as sinful. (On the sins they are especially committing, see comment on 3:6, 9.)

1:5. Other Jewish texts (especially the *Dead Sea Scrolls) also used the light-darkness image to contrast the followers of righteousness with those of sin, regarding God as wholly righteous. The *Old Testament also affirmed that God was wholly righteous (e.g., Ps 92:15).

1:6. The Old Testament often described "obeying" God's commands as "walking" in them—so often that Jewish teachers called their view of the way Jewish people should behave *halakah,* "walking." The image of walking about in darkness connoted the danger of stumbling (2:10-11). The Old Testament condemned mixing up light and darkness, right and wrong (Is 5:20; cf. 2:5).

1:7. Although water, not blood, cleansed in a physical sense, blood also purified in an Old Testament ritual sense (see comment on Heb 9:21-22). Sacrificial blood set apart what was sacred for God, purifying from sin by making *atonement (Lev 16:30).

1:8-10. The Old Testament prophets had often condemned false protestations of innocence as self-deception (e.g., Jer 2:35; Hos 8:2; cf. Prov 30:12); God required instead both admission of the sin and *repentance (cf. Lev 5:5; 16:21; Ps 32:1-5; Prov 28:13; Jer 3:13). (Some *synagogue prayers for forgiveness were also preceded by confessions of sin, indicating that Jewish people in the first few centuries A.D. generally recognized the idea; cf. also *Psalms of Solomon 9:6, etc.) On cleansing see 1 John 1:7. On the sins of the secessionists, see comment on 3:6 and 9.

2:1-11
The Moral Test

Christians were new people, and while they might not be living absolutely sinless lives yet (1:8-10), the newness of their life in *Christ would affect their lifestyles; because sin was real (1:5-10), moral behavior was a valid way of testing real commitment to Christ. This moral examination especially emphasizes the test of love (2:5, 9-11). Judaism also stressed that true participants in God's covenant obeyed his commandments.

2:1. Philosophers and Jewish teachers

sometimes addressed their *disciples as "children." "Advocate" meant "intercessor" or "defending attorney." In the *Old Testament, God could plead his people's case before the nations (Jer 50:34; 51:36); in ancient Judaism, such advocates as God's mercy or Israel's merit pleaded Israel's case before God. Jesus is naturally the advocate, as elsewhere in the *New Testament, because of his position, his righteousness and his work (v. 2).

2:2. A "propitiation" (KJV, NASB) was an *atonement, a way to appease or satisfy the wrath of a God whose standard had been violated; it alludes to the sacrifices offered for atonement in the Old Testament. In Judaism, the sacrifice on the Day of Atonement was for Israel alone; but Jesus' sacrifice was offered not only for Christians but even for those who chose to remain God's enemies, leaving them without excuse.

2:3-4. In the *Old Testament, Israel "knew" God—were in covenant relationship with him—when they obeyed his commandments (e.g., Jer 22:16; 31:33-34).

2:5. One was to demonstrate love for God by obeying his commandments (Deut 6:5-6); this idea was understood throughout ancient Judaism.

2:6. Moralists commonly appealed to imitation of God or of a famous teacher in ancient moral exhortation. John here alludes to Jesus' example of sacrificial love to the point of death (Jn 13:34-35).

2:7-8. In antiquity, paradox was one graphic way of forcing an audience to think through the meaning of one's words; John uses it here ("old, not new," "but new"). The love commandment was old, always part of God's word (Deut 6:5 and Lev 19:18, cited by Jesus—Mk 12:30-31), but also new, based on a new and ultimate example (Jn 13:34). Many Jewish traditions that used the light-darkness imagery for good and evil portrayed the present age as ruled mainly by darkness but the age to come in terms of the triumph of light.

2:9-11. The secessionists who have withdrawn from the Christian community John addresses have broken fellowship with true Christians, thus showing that they "hate" rather than "love" them. The *Old Testament and Judaism forbade "hatred of brothers and sisters" (Lev 19:17); in a Jewish context, this term referred to fellow Jews (though cf. also 19:34); in a Christian context, it refers to fellow Christians.

2:12-14 Exhortations to Different Groups

"I am writing" is probably not intended to convey a sense different from "I wrote"; it was common to vary style to make one's writing more interesting. One could write "I have written" in a letter one was presently writing; grammarians call this convention an "epistolary aorist."

On the one hand, "fathers," "young men" and "children" (John does not exclude women from consideration here but employs the language categories of his day, which used masculine forms for mixed groups) could refer to different stages of progress in the Christian faith; see comment on 2:1. On the other hand, some writers addressed different kinds of moral instruction to different age groups to which particular points were most relevant (e.g., the fourth-century Greek *rhetorician Isocrates; a letter of the Greek philosopher Epicurus; cf. Prov 20:29; 2 Tim 2:22).

Fathers held positions of honor and authority; children were in positions of learning and lacked status and authority. Young men were generally associated with strength and vigor; here they had overcome the evil one by participating in *Christ's victory (4:4; 5:4) over sin (3:10-12). Although some ancient writers often considered young men more vulnerable to particular temptations (especially sexual immorality), John expresses his confidence in them.

2:15-17 Do Not Love the World

2:15. "The world" could refer to everything but God; here it means the system in competition with God. Just as Israel in the *Old Testament repeatedly had to decide between allegiance to God and allegiance to the pagan nations around them, the Christians scattered among the nations had to choose *Christ above whatever in their cultures conflicted with his demands. In the case of John's readers, refusal to compromise might be a costly proposition (3:16).

2:16. The Old Testament often related the eyes to desire, especially sexual desire, and pride. Both Judaism and philosophers (e.g., *Aristotle, *Epictetus) condemned arrogant boastfulness. By listing the three vices together, John might allude, as some commentators have suggested, to Genesis 3:6, although the language here is more general.

2:17. Judaism spoke of the world passing away but of God's word remaining forever (cf. also Is 40:6-8). John's words here could encourage those who preferred death for the sake of *Christ over the survival that the world offered (cf. 1 Jn 3:16).

2:18-27 Discerning the Spirits: The Theological Test

John needs to assure his readers that they, not the secessionists, are true followers of God. To the ethical test (2:1-11) John now adds a theological test: they must hold the proper view of *Christ. John carries on the thought of the end time (v. 18) from 2:17.

2:18. It was a common Jewish belief that evil would multiply in the end time; the duration of this period immediately preceding the end of the age was often left indeterminate (as here), although some Jewish writers assigned a specific duration to it (e.g., forty years, four hundred years). Some Jewish people also appear to have envisioned a particularly evil figure as a high priest or ruler oppressing God's people, an idea that became much more prevalent in Christian circles (e.g., 2 Thess 2:3-4). John argues that by definition there are many "antichrists" already. (John is the only *New Testament writer to use this term. "Anti-" could mean "instead of," but he would probably call a substitute Christ a "false Christ," like "false prophets" in 4:1, if that were what he meant; the meaning "against" is more likely: hence, opposer of Christ. Cf. Paul's argument that the "mystery of lawlessness is already at work"—2 Thess 2:7.)

2:19. The *Old Testament was clear that the righteous could become wicked (e.g., Ezek 18:24-26) but also that one's deeds could reveal the sincerity or falsehood of one's heart (e.g., 2 Chron 12:14). Both Greek and Jewish teachers condemned *disciples who proved unfaithful or unable to endure the tests of discipleship, generally assuming that their initial commitment had been inadequate. Judaism recognized that many converts were false, although they regarded even more severely Jewish apostates who had once embraced but now rejected the law.

Some New Testament texts (e.g., Jn 6:70-71; 1 Jn 2:19) may view the issue from the standpoint of God's foreknowledge, and other texts from the standpoint of the believer's experience (e.g., Gal 5:4; 1 Tim 4:1-2). But unlike most modern interpreters, ancient Jewish interpreters would not see a contradiction between these two perspectives.

2:20-21. In the Old Testament people were anointed with literal oil to perform a specific task, especially for the priesthood or kingship; the term translated "anointed" is used figuratively for those ordained by God to particular tasks. Christians had been appointed to discernment (see 2:27).

2:22-23. Of themselves, these verses would counter equally well a non-Christian Jewish opposition and a Cerinthian opposition to Christian faith. Compromising the absolute uniqueness of Jesus as the *Christ and the only way to the Father would probably permit Jewish believers to remain in the *synagogues—thus delivering them from the direct challenge of the imperial cult and threat of persecution. That false prophets would advocate such compromise (cf. 4:1-6) is by no means difficult to conceive (see the introduction to Revelation). Cerinthus, who taught around A.D. 100, believed that the Christ-*Spirit came on Jesus but was not identical to him; the late-second-century Christian writer Irenaeus also attributed this view to many later *Gnostics.

2:24-27. Many commentators hold that the "anointing" (v. 27) is the Spirit (cf. Jn 14:17, 26; Acts 10:38); others suggest that it refers in context to the word, the message of the *gospel; in either case it alludes to the *Old Testament practice of God setting particular people apart for his calling, which here applies to all believers. The Old Testament used anointing oil symbolically to consecrate or separate people (such as kings) or objects (such as the tabernacle) for sacred use. The ultimate consecration for such use arose when the Spirit came on people (Is 61:1; cf. 1 Sam 10:1, 9; 16:13).

2:28—3:3
Readiness for His Coming

As the readers have been abiding in Jesus (v. 27), so they are to continue to do (v. 28); on abiding (dwelling, remaining), see comment on John 15:1-8.

2:28. In Jewish tradition, the coming of God to judge the world would be a fearful day for those who were disobedient to his will (cf. Amos 5:18-20).

2:29. It was an ancient commonplace that children inherited the natures of their fathers. So thoroughly was this belief held that many writers even warned that adulterers would give themselves away, because their image would be stamped on the children of the union.

3:1. No one who agreed with John that Christians were God's children would have disputed his point here. A roughly contemporary Jewish teacher, Rabbi Akiba, celebrated, "Beloved is humanity, since they were created in God's image; greater still is the love, that God made it known to humanity that they were created in the image." Rabbi Meir, later in the second century, proclaimed, "Beloved is Israel, for . . . they are God's children."

3:2-3. In some Greek thought, one's nature was transformed toward that of the divine by contemplating the divine; philosophers like *Plato believed that they accomplished this transformation through the vision of the mind rather than through knowledge derived through the senses. *Philo agreed that one attained the vision of God mystically, because he affirmed that God was transcendent; he believed that God endowed Israel and especially the prophets with this vision, that this vision was preceded by virtue and purity of soul, and that the vision would be made complete when one was perfected. The idea also occurs in some Palestinian Jewish texts, especially in Jewish mysticism. Perhaps more to the point, this vision of God was often associated with the end time, and some Jewish *apocalyptic thought seems to have envisioned transformation through beholding God's glory.

John may derive most of the image of transformation by beholding glory from the Old Testament (Ex 34:29-35; see comment on Jn 1:14-18). For him, one who knows God's character purifies himself or herself accordingly, and the final and ultimate purifying will take place when one knows God perfectly at the end.

3:4-24
Which Side Are You On?

In traditional Jewish fashion, John contrasts sin and righteousness, along with those aligned with either side (3:4-9). He then explains why the unrighteous oppose the righteous, appealing to a stock Jewish illustration for this principle: the righteous love one another, but the wicked, like Cain, hate the righteous (3:10-18). This was the test that would make clear who would ultimately triumph in the day of judgment (3:19-24).

3:4. Greeks saw sin as imperfection; the *Old Testament and Judaism saw it as transgression of God's *law. John wants everyone to understand that he means sin in the biblical sense.

3:5. Here John probably uses sacrificial language; cf. John 1:29. The point is that those who are in Jesus have their sins taken away, so they no longer live in them.

3:6-7. This verse again alludes to the transformative power of beholding God (cf. 3:2-3). Some commentators think that the claim to sinlessness here is ideal, "to the extent that" one abides in Christ. (In this way *Plato argued that to the extent one was a craftsman, one's craftsmanship would be perfect; but where one's craftsmanship failed, it was because one was not acting as a true craftsman at that point.) Others think it is potential: one is capable of living sinlessly (cf. Jn 8:31-36). But verse 9 is worded too strongly for either of these options.

More likely, John is turning the claims of the false teachers and their followers (1:8-10) against them: unlike those errorists who merely claim to be sinless, true believers do not live in sin. (Many commentators suggest that the present continuous tense of "sin" suggests "living in" sin, sinning as a natural way of life. This is different from living righteously but sometimes succumbing to temptation or deception and genuinely repenting.) The particular sins that dominate John's portrayal of these secessionists are violations of the two basic precepts John stresses in this letter: the right attitude toward members of the Christian community and the right view about Jesus (3:24). Thus John may mean that they commit the sin that leads to death, i.e., leading out of *eternal life (cf. 5:16-17).

3:8. In the *Dead Sea Scrolls, all sins were influenced by the spirit of error. Given the traditional Jewish view that the devil had introduced sin into the world, all sins were ultimately the devil's works and reflected his character.

3:9-10. On the claim to sinlessness, see comment on 3:6-7. Some scholars have suggested that John borrows the image of "seed" here from his opponents, since the idea is later attested among the *Gnostics; but the image was already widespread in Christian tradition (Jas 1:18, 21; 1 Pet 1:23; see comment on 1 Pet 1:23). A child was believed to inherit his or her father's nature through the seed, hence John is able to use this image to make his point: those who are born from God through conversion reflect his character now in them, and those who are not reveal this by their nature as well. In the *Old Testament one could overcome sin by the word written or dwelling in one's heart (e.g., Ps 119:11; Jer 31:32-33).

3:11-13. Cain's murder of Abel is often rehearsed with little adornment in Jewish tradition; at other times, Jewish tradition expounds on Cain's wickedness in great detail. He became a stereotypical prototype for wickedness (e.g., *Jubilees and *1 Enoch; *Pharisees sometimes associated Cain with the *Sadducees and their denial of the life to come); one pre-Christian Jewish text calls him "the unrighteous one" (Wisdom of Solomon 10:3). *Philo used Cain repeatedly as a symbol of self-love and made him an illustration that "the worse attacks the better," as here (cf. Gal 4:29). Some later antinomian Gnostics took Cain as a hero.

Murder of a brother was considered one of the most hideous crimes possible in antiquity (so, e.g., *Cicero, Horace); John applies "brother" or "sibling" to any member of the Christian community. A murderer was a child of the devil (3:10), for one of the devil's first works had been to bring death to Adam (see comment on John 8:44); some later *rabbinic texts claim that Cain's father was a bad angel, even the devil himself. Sibling rivalry (Gen 37:8; 1 Sam 17:28) was normally outgrown, but Cain's act did not allow that to happen.

3:14-15. Murder was a capital offense under *Old Testament law and thus merited *Gehenna in post-Old Testament Jewish thought. Jesus included as murder the attitude that generated the literal act (cf. Mt 5:21-22).

3:16-17. John's readers anticipated persecution and the possibility of death, although few had actually been martyred so far (Rev 2:13). Refusal to participate in the worship of the emperor would brand them as subversives, and their enemies would be more than happy to betray them to the government as such. Since noncitizen prisoners were routinely tortured for information, especially if they were slaves, Christians might have to pay a tremendous price to avoid betraying their fellow Christians to death.

But John also demands of them a practical commitment to love in the present. Their opponents, who had withdrawn from the community, perhaps to avoid persecution, are responsible for others' deaths as Cain was; but the true Christians are to live sacrificially on behalf of others daily. As in some Jewish thought, withholding goods from someone in need was equivalent to starving him or her (cf. Jas 2:15).

3:18. Ancient literature often coupled "word" and "deed" (e.g., in Isocrates, Demosthenes, *Quintilian, *Seneca, *Lucian, Wisdom of Solomon); one who did both was praised, but one who only spoke and did not act accordingly was viewed as a hypocrite.

3:19. The *Dead Sea Scrolls sometimes called the righteous "children of truth" or "the lot of God's truth."

3:20-21. Judaism repeatedly stressed that God knew the hearts of all people (cf. Jer 29:23); some texts even call him "Searcher of Hearts." As one Jewish wisdom writer expressed it, "Happy is the one whose soul does not accuse him" (Ecclus 14:2).

3:22-24. These commandments are precisely those which the secessionists are violating: by leaving the Christian community they have demonstrated their lack of love for their supposed brothers and sisters, and by not believing Jesus as the only true *Christ (2:22) they have failed the faith test as well. On the promise of answered prayer, see John 14:12-14.

4:1-6
Testing the Spirits

4:1. Judaism especially associated the *Spirit of God with *prophecy but acknowledged the existence of false prophets, who John says are moved by other spirits. His readers would understand his point; Jewish people were familiar with the idea of other spirits besides the Spirit of God (see especially comment on 4:6). There were many pagan ecstatics in Asia Minor, as well as Jewish mystics claiming special revelations; the need for discernment would be acute.

4:2-3. The issue may be the secessionists' denial that Jesus has come as the *Christ (if the opposition is Jewish); more likely it is a Docetic denial that Jesus was actually human and actually died (see introduction), a heresy an eyewitness would be well positioned to refute. It may simply be a relativizing of Jesus' role to the position of a prophet like John the Baptist, which allows enough compromise to avoid persecution. Whatever the error, the secessionists are claiming the authority of inspiration for it, as do some similar cults today. John does not deny the reality of the inspiration; he merely denies that the spirit working in them is God's Spirit.

4:4-6. The *Dead Sea Scrolls similarly distinguish between God's children and the rest of the world, though they go far beyond John in asserting that every act is determined by either the spirit of truth or the spirit of error. (The language of "two spirits" probably extended beyond the Dead Sea Scrolls, although the best attestation outside the Scrolls is in the *Testaments of the Twelve Patriarchs. These testaments contain a number of references to spirits of falsehood, but the closest to 1 John 4:6 is Testament of Judah 20, which, with the Testament of Levi, is one of the testaments most often suspected of harboring Christian interpolations. Thus the issue is not settled, although the Testament of Judah reference is *probably* pre-Christian, reflecting an idea similar to the general Jewish doctrine of the two impulses, which the *rabbis especially developed and expounded; on this doctrine see comment on Rom 7:15-22.) The promise that the one with them was greater than the one with the world (1 Jn 4:4) recalls an Old Testament principle (2 Kings 6:16; 2 Chron 32:7-8).

4:7-21
The Test of Love

4:7-10. Again (3:9-10) John argues that one's nature shows one's spiritual lineage; those who are like God are his children, and God's supreme characteristic is his love, revealed in the cross of *Christ. The secessionists proved their lack of love by withdrawing from Christian fellowship. On propitiation see comment on 2:2.

4:11-12. Even true Christians' love had to be perfected, but unlike the secessionists, they had remained within the Christian community, thus maintaining a commitment to love one another. The false teachers may have been claiming to have had mystical visions of God (see comment on 3:2-3; 4:1), but John includes a corrective: God was unseen (Ex 33:20), and the sense in which believers could envision him is in his character of love fleshed out in the cross (4:9) and in Christians' sacrificial love (4:12).

4:13-16. Although the *Qumran community as a group claimed to possess the *Spirit, most of ancient Judaism relegated the Spirit's most dramatic works to the distant past and future, or to very rare individuals. For John, all true believers in Jesus have the Spirit, who moves them to love (see comment on 4:11-12) and prophetically endows them to testify the truth about Christ (see comment on 4:1).

4:17. In the *Old Testament (e.g., Amos 5:18-20) and Judaism, "the day of judgment" was something to be feared by the disobedient (2:28). But those who continued in love could be confident of acquittal before God's tribunal in that day, for they are agents of his unselfish love.

4:18. It was understood that sin often leads to fear (e.g., Gen 3:8; *Epistle of Aristeas 243). Although *Stoic philosophers emphasized not fearing anything, because circumstances cannot ultimately destroy one's reason, John's assurance that true believers need not fear here is not explicitly directed toward all circumstances. His assurance applies specifically to punishment in the day of judgment (4:17).

4:19. The Old Testament also recognized that God's people learned how to treat others from God's gracious treatment of them (Ex 13:8; 22:21; Lev 19:34; Deut 10:19), although the ultimate expression of the principle is the example of *Christ (1 Jn 4:10; cf. Jn 13:34).

4:20-21. Principles like arguing on the basis of what was near at hand rather than from something related to the gods (e.g., *Plutarch) and that a new friend would treat you as he had treated others (e.g., the fourth-century B.C. rhetorician Isocrates) were also recognized by others in antiquity. In the *Old Testament, God accounted behavior toward those who could not repay it as if it were done to him (Prov 19:17; cf. Deut 15:9).

5:1-13
Triumph and Life Through Faith in Jesus

5:1. Families were often viewed as a unit, hence one could not love one member of a family while despising other members. This verse may also reflect the idea that children bear their parents' nature.

5:2. On love being demonstrated actively, compare 3:18.

5:3. God's commandments had never been too heavy for those in whose hearts they had been written (Deut 30:11-14). Many Jewish teachers regarded some parts of the *law as "heavier" or "weightier" than others (as in Mt 23:23), but they meant that some were more crucial for daily life, not that any of them were too hard to keep.

5:4-5. The image of achieving "victory" was used in military, athletic, debate and courtroom situations but always involved a conflict or test. John calls his readers to "overcome" or "triumph" in the face of opposition, persecution and possible martyrdom (probably including suffering for refusal to compromise with the imperial cult).

5:6-13. Many scholars have suggested that the secessionists, like Cerinthus and some later *Gnostics, said that the *Christ-*Spirit came on Jesus at his *baptism but departed before his death; or that, like the Docetists and some later Gnostics, the secessionists believed that Jesus was actually baptized but could not actually die, being eternal. It is also possible that some Docetists saw in the "water and blood" of John 19:34 the picture of a demigod: Olympian deities in Greek mythology had ichor, a watery substance, instead of blood. Thus they may have stressed his divinity at the expense of his humanity.

Ancient sale documents sometimes included the signatures of several witnesses attesting a sale, and the *Old Testament and later Jewish courts always required a minimum of two dependable witnesses (Deut 17:6; 19:15). John cites three witnesses whose reliability could not be in dispute. (The trinitarian formula found in the KJV of 1 Jn 5:7 is orthodox but not part of the text. It appears in only three manuscripts—of the twelfth, fifteenth and sixteenth centuries—out of the thousands available, placed there by scribes who knew it from the Latin Vulgate, which took it from an early marginal note based on a popular early interpretation of the text. The KJV includes it only because that translation was based on a recension dependent on the third edition of Erasmus's Greek text; Erasmus included the verse to fulfill a wager, protested it in a note and withdrew it in subsequent editions of the text.)

5:14-21
Avoiding Sin

5:14-15. For background applying to the general principle in these verses, see comment on John 14:12-14. But the specific issue emphasized here is prayer for an erring brother or sister, one attracted to the false prophets' ideas (4:1-6); see 5:16-17 (cf. Mt 18:15-20).

5:16-17. Given the use of "life" for *eternal life and "death" for its opposite in this epistle, a "sin unto death" (KJV) would seem to be a sin leading one away from eternal life (cf. Gen 2:17; 3:24). The two sins John would likely have in mind would be hating the brothers and sisters (the secessionists' rejection of the Christian community) and failing to believe in Jesus rightly (their false doctrine about his identity as the divine Lord and *Christ in the flesh); see comment on 3:23.

The *Old Testament and Judaism distinguished between willful rebellion against God, which could not be forgiven by normal means, and a lighter transgression. More relevant here, some ancient Jewish texts (e.g., the *Dead Sea Scrolls, *Jubilees) also spoke of a capital offense as "a matter of death," which was normally enforced by excommunication from the community rather than literal execution. Those who were sinned against could secure forgiveness for their opponents by prayer (Gen 20:7, 17; Job 42:8), but a sin of willful apostasy from God's truth nullified the efficacy of secondhand prayers for forgiveness (1 Sam 2:25; Jer 7:16; 11:14; 14:11). John is presumably saying: God will forgive erring believers at your request, but those who have gone completely after the heresy are outside the sphere of your prayers or (on another interpretation) simply must directly *repent to receive forgiveness.

5:18. *Satan could not touch Job without God's permission (Job 1:11-12; 2:3-6). Judaism recognized that Satan needed God's permission to test God's people, and that God rejected Satan's accusations against God's own people.

5:19-20. Judaism acknowledged that all the nations except themselves were under the dominion of Satan and his angels. The source of this idea is not hard to fathom; nearly all *Gentiles worshiped idols, and most also practiced sexual immorality and other sins.

5:21. "Idols" could refer to anything that led astray from proper worship of the true Lord (thus "idols of one's heart" meant falsehoods or sins in the *Dead Sea Scrolls), but a literal meaning (physical images of false gods) makes good sense to a congregation in Asia Minor. It may refer to worshiping the image of the emperor, to which Christians were eventually required to offer incense to show their loyalty to the state. It could also refer to compromise with idolatry in a broader sense—Asia Minor afforded plenty of temptation for former pagans. Ancient Jewish texts often condemned idolatry as the worst sin—surely a capital offense or a "sin unto death" (5:16-17); if the false prophets of compromise in 4:1-6 are like other false prophets affecting Asian *churches in this period (Rev 2:20), the idolatry may well be literal; see comment on Revelation 2:14, 9:20, 13:12 and 15.

2 JOHN

Introduction

Authorship, Date. See the introduction to 1 John and to the Gospel of John; there is little stylistic difference between 1 and 2 John. Although John himself might send a shorter personal letter resembling a longer one he had previously written, it is unlikely that a forger would try to produce such a short document that added so little to the case found in 1 John. Further, a later forgery of 2 John (or 3 John) would have drained it of its authority for the readers, since the contents of 2 and 3 John indicate that they knew the writer personally.

Nature of the Letter. Second John may function as an official letter, the sort that high priests could send to Jewish leaders outside Palestine. The length is the same as that of 3 John; both were probably limited to this length by the single sheet of papyrus on which they were written; in contrast to most *New Testament letters, most other ancient letters were of this length.

Situation. Second John addresses the problem of the same secessionists that 1 John addressed. The secessionists' inadequate view of *Christ was either a compromise with *synagogue pressure (see the introduction to Gospel of John) or a relativization of Jesus to allow more compromise with paganism (see the introduction to Revelation)—probably the latter. For the secessionists, Jesus was a great prophet like John the Baptist and their own leaders, but he was not the supreme Lord in the flesh (cf. 1 Jn 4:1-6; Rev 2:14, 20). They may have been affiliated with or forerunners of Cerinthus (who distinguished the divine Christ and the human Jesus, like some modern theologians) or the Docetists (who claimed that Jesus only seemed to be human). All these compromises helped the heretics better adapt to their culture's values what remained of Christianity after their adjustments, but led them away from the truth proclaimed by the eyewitnesses who had known Jesus firsthand.

Commentaries. See the introduction to 1 John.

1-3. "Elders" were given authority in local Jewish communities by virtue of their age, prominence and respectability; age was respected. John assumes this simple title (cf. 1 Pet 5:1) rather than emphasizing his apostleship here. The "chosen lady" (NASB, NIV) or spiritual mother could refer to a prophetess/elder (cf. 3 Jn 4; contrast Rev 2:23). But it more likely refers to a local congregation here (see v. 13); both Israel and the *church were portrayed as women.

4-6. The commandment John mentions here was an old one because it was in the law (Lev 19:18), although Jesus' example gave it new import (Jn 13:34-35). In the context of 1—2 John, "loving one another" means cleaving to the Christian community (rather than leaving it, as the secessionists were doing).

7-9. See the introduction.

10. Travelers were to be accorded hospitality and put up in hosts' homes (cf. 3 Jn 5-6; it is possible, though not certain, that the houses in question here may also be house *churches); early Christian missionaries had depended on this hospitality from the beginning (Mt 10:9-14). Traveling philosophers called sophists charged fees for their teaching, as some of Paul's opponents in Corinth probably did.

But just as Jewish people would not receive *Samaritans or those they considered impious, so Christians were to exercise selectivity concerning whom they would admit. Early Christian writings (particularly a text of mainly authoritative traditions known as the Didache) show that some prophets and *apostles traveled around, and that not all of them were true prophets and apostles. Greetings were an essential part of social protocol at that time, and the greeting ("Peace be with you") was intended as a blessing or prayer to impart peace.

11. In the *Dead Sea Scrolls, one who provided for an apostate from the community was regarded as an apostate sympathizer and was expelled from the community, as the apostate was. Housing or blessing a false teacher was thus seen as collaborating with him.

12-13. "Paper" is papyrus, made from reeds and rolled up like a scroll. The pen was a reed pointed at the end, and the ink was a compound of charcoal, vegetable gum and water. Written letters were considered an inferior substitute for personal presence or for a speech, and writers sometimes concluded their letters with the promise to discuss matters further face-to-face.

3 JOHN

Introduction

This is a "letter of recommendation" for Demetrius, a traveling missionary (vv. 7-8) who needs to be put up by a local *church while he is evangelizing in their area (cf. comment on Mt 10:11-13, 40-42). For authorship and date, see the introduction to 2 John. For the first three centuries of the church's existence, congregations met in homes; for further details on this practice, see Romans 16:5. In this letter to Gaius, a house-church leader, John is apparently attempting to counter the opposing influences of Diotrephes, a different house-church leader who is asserting his own authority and rejecting emissaries backed by John's apostolic authority.

Commentaries: See the introduction to 1 John.

1-2. This is a standard greeting in many ancient letters, which quite often began with a prayer for the reader's health, frequently including the prayer that all would go well with the person (not just material prosperity, as some translations could be read as implying). This greeting might be similar to saying "I hope you are well" today, but it represents an actual prayer that all is well with Gaius (see comment on 1 Thess 3:11).

3-4. *Rabbis and philosophers sometimes spoke of their *disciples as their "children"; here John probably intends those he led to *Christ (cf. Gal 4:19 and the later Jewish tradition that when someone made a convert to Judaism, it was as if the converter had *created* the convert).

5-6. Hospitality was a critical issue in the Greco-Roman world, and Jewish people were especially concerned to take care of their own. Most inns also served as brothels, making a stay there unappealing, but Jewish people could expect to find hospitality from their fellow Jews; to prevent abuse of this system, they normally carried letters of recommendation from someone the hosts might know to substantiate their claim to be good Jews. Christians had adopted the same practice.

7-8. Philosophers and sophists (traveling professional speakers, which is how many observers in the Greco-Roman world interpreted traveling Christian preachers) often made their livings from the crowds to whom they spoke, although others took fees or were supported by wealthy *patrons. Like Jewish people, Christians showed hospitality to travelers of their own faith, and these traveling preachers were dependent on this charity. Judaism spoke of the sacred "Name" of God; John is apparently applying this title to Jesus.

9-11. Diotrephes is apparently leader of another house *church; he refuses to show hospitality to the missionaries who have letters of recommendation from the elder. Scholars have speculated whether the issue was doctrinal disagreement, disagreement over church leadership structure or that Diotrephes was simply outright disagreeable; at any rate, he refuses to accept the authority of John that stands behind the missionaries he backs. To reject a person's representatives or those recommended by a person was to disrespect the person who had written on their behalf.

12. This is the recommendation for Demetrius, who has not only John's attestation but that of the rest of his home church(es). No one in Diotrephes' house church will receive him, so Gaius's house church must help him.

13-14. Sometimes ancient letters closed as John does here. Most letter writers employed scribes, and if John is writing by hand, he may well wish to close quickly. See comment on 2 John 12. If "friends" is here a title for a group, it probably refers to fellow Christians in the place from which the elder is writing; these Christians may have borrowed the idea from the *Epicureans, whose philosophical communities consisted especially of "friends."

JUDE

Introduction

Authorship. Although a *pseudepigrapher would want to clarify which Jude he was (i.e., Jesus' brother) or to write in the name of someone more prominent, this author does not specify which Jude he is, making it probable that the letter was genuinely written by Jude. At the same time, his lack of clarification as to which Jude he is and the fact that he seems to be already known to his readers (vv. 3, 5) suggest that he is the most prominent Jude, brother of the most prominent James—the younger brother of Jesus (Mk 6:3). Early *church tradition varied on which Jude wrote the letter, but this is the only Jude known to us whose brother was called James. His Greek is sophisticated, but the thought world he shares with his readers is that of popular Judaism; for a Palestinian Jew's knowledge of Greek, see the introduction to James.

Situation. The letter clearly opposes false teachers whose sexual lifestyles are immoral and who are teaching arrogantly. The thought world of Jude and his readers is popular Judaism; his opponents may be rooted in the same Jewish-Christian tradition that Jude is, but they have also sought to assimilate many values of immoral pagan culture. Given Jude's heavy use of *1 Enoch, that book may represent a tradition cited by his opponents, who apparently appeal to their own mystical visions as divine revelations like Enoch's (v. 8).

***Genre.** This is a letter-essay, a letter used as a sermon. Letters were meant as substitute speeches or surrogates for the presence of the writer.

Commentaries. The best are R. J. Bauckham, *Jude, 2 Peter,* WBC 50 (Waco, Tex.: Word, 1983), and (easier for those without Greek) J. N. D. Kelly, *A Commentary on the Epistles of Peter and Jude* (reprint, Grand Rapids, Mich.: Baker Book House, 1981).

1-2
Introduction

1-2. Jude's lack of elaboration on his office suggests that he is the well-known Jude, brother not only of James but of Jesus as well. Although a son of Joseph and Mary, he now describes his half-brother Jesus as "Lord" rather than as brother.

3-6
Falling from Grace

3-4. The heresy Jude addresses resembles that proclaimed by false prophets in the *Old Testament: judgment would not come on God's people because of his special favor for them—a doctrine that led to sin (Jer 6:14; 8:11; 23:17; Ezek 13:10, 16; Mic 3:5). Biblical *grace means forgiveness and power to overcome sin, not permission to act immorally. Ancient writers often applied the language of battle or athletic contests ("contend") to spiritual or moral battles.

5. All Jewish readers and even most recent *Gentile converts to Christianity knew the exodus story. That people had experienced God's redemption did not guarantee that they could not fall away and be destroyed.

6. In Jewish tradition (except most of the *rabbis), the "sons of God" in Genesis 6:1-4 were fallen angels who left their assigned place to have intercourse with women. In the earliest of these traditions, *1 Enoch, the fallen angels were imprisoned and bound; Azazel was thrown into "darkness" (which was applied to the realm of the dead in much ancient tradition). First Enoch uses "great day" for the day of judgment.

7-16
Sin and Judgment

7. Already in the *Old Testament and even more so in later Jewish tradition, Sodom came to be viewed as the epitome of wickedness. "Strange flesh" (KJV, NASB) here could mean angelic bodies, but because Jewish tradition would not call angels "flesh" and the Sodomites did not realize that they were angels (Gen 19:5), Jude may have their attempted homosexual acts in view. ("Strange" flesh is literally "other" flesh, but this may mean "other than what is natural," rather than "other than their own kind." Then again, "in the same way" as those of v. 6 might imply angels and people having intercourse with each other. Apart from *Philo, few ancient Jewish writers stressed the Sodomites' homosexual behavior; most instead stressed their lack of hospitality, arrogant sin or sexual immorality in general, which in the Jewish perspective included but was not limited to homosexual acts.)

8. "Dreaming" probably refers to the dreams of false prophets, who produce falsehood while claiming to speak truth (Jer 23:25); angelic "majesties" (literally "glories"; cf. NRSV, TEV) refers to the various ranks of angelic hosts, to which God has assigned authority over nations, nature and so on in Jewish tradition. Disrespect for earthly authorities and the spiritual powers behind them appointed by God would cause Christians to be labeled as subversive and produce widespread persecution of them in the Roman Empire. (Some scholars have also suggested that they reviled these angels as the angels through whom God gave the *law, because of their antilaw stance, but it is not clear that they argued for their immorality primarily on the basis of their rejection of the law.)

9. Michael (Dan 10:13, 21; 12:1) and Gabriel (Dan 8:16; 9:21) are the only two angels named in the *Old Testament, and they naturally became the two most popular angels in contemporary Jewish lore, with Michael as Israel's guardian and generally the most prominent archangel.

Jewish traditions about Moses' death (or lack of it, despite Deut 34) varied widely, and this report seems to have been one of these versions. In the Old Testament and Jewish literature, the devil acted as an accuser; here the great archangel Michael did not challenge his accusations; he deferred the issue to God the supreme judge. God's angelic messenger also cries, "The Lord rebuke you" in defending the high priest in Zechariah 3:2.

10. The false teachers, however, were ridiculing angelic powers, probably including *Satan. The *Dead Sea Scrolls show that some people cursed Satan, but Jude does not approve of that. Instead, he seems to agree with the moral embodied in a later *rabbinic story: a man named Pelimo went around making fun of the devil until one day the devil showed up and chased him into a bathhouse, whereupon he learned his lesson; cf. also Ecclesiasticus 21:27. Christians also should not speak authoritatively on secret or esoteric matters God has not chosen to reveal (cf. Deut 29:29).

11. More than in the Old Testament, in Jewish tradition Cain (see comment on 1 Jn 3:12) and Balaam (see comment on 2 Pet 2:15) had become symbolic for leaders of wickedness; Balaam was regarded as one of the most powerful prophets, as prophet of the *Gentiles, but he used his powers for evil. Korah revolted against the leadership of Moses (Num 16) and became a standard figure for rebelling against the law in Jewish tradition.

12. The Last Supper was a full Passover meal, and the early *church had continued the tradition of celebrating a meal ("the Lord's Supper") of which bread and wine were only a part. Communion as a full meal was also called a "love feast."

"Concealed rocks" (or "hidden reefs"—NASB) were deceptive and killed sailors who failed to navigate their vessels away from them; empty clouds promised rain to needy farmers but delivered nothing (Prov 25:14). The image of trees may be because harvesting would be complete by late autumn, when many trees shed their leaves before the advent of winter; or it may mean that they did not bear summer fruit and showed no signs of fruitfulness by early autumn; either way, these trees were plainly dead (on the future second death, see comment on Rev 2:11).

13. In Greek tradition, Aphrodite, goddess of desire, was produced from sea foam at the castration of the Titan Uranos (alluding to the teachers' immorality); waves appear in the *Dead Sea Scrolls as an image of casting up the filth of sin. "Wandering stars" referred to the erratic orbits of planets, sometimes attributed to disobedient angels, who were to be imprisoned under God's judgment and are called "stars" in *1 Enoch. Judgment as eternal darkness appears in 1 Enoch and elsewhere. The wicked as raging waves appear in Isaiah 57:20 and in subsequent Jewish tradition (Dead Sea Scrolls).

14-15. Jude quotes from 1 Enoch 1:9, citing a popular story that is still extant to make his point. This passage in 1 Enoch represents some themes that run throughout that section of 1 Enoch.

16. "Grumblers" may allude to Israel's murmuring in the wilderness, but especially to the wrong speech ("harsh words"—NIV) of verse 15, expounding the citation from 1 Enoch. Ancient moralists repeatedly condemned flattery and advocated forthright speech; politicians commonly used flattery to win people over with speeches, and flattery was a necessity for subordinates of many emperors to survive. Jude had already addressed both their lusts (vv. 6-8b) and arrogant speech (vv. 8c-10).

17-25
Call to Persevere

17-19. Later *Gnostics claimed to be spiritual, thinking that others were at best "worldly" (NASB, NRSV) or "natural" (NIV); under the influence of certain kinds of Greek philosophy, some false teachers were probably already moving in this direction. Because the false teachers claimed to be prophetically inspired (v. 8), they no doubt laid claim to the *Spirit (cf. comment on v. 20), but Jude says that they are altogether lacking in the Spirit.

20-21. Because the *Holy Spirit was usually viewed as the Spirit of *prophecy, "praying in [or by] the Holy Spirit" probably means inspired prayer (1 Chron 25:3; Psalms), very likely including tongues (cf. comment on Acts 2:4; 1 Cor 14).

22-23. Some of the language here is from Zechariah 3:2 and 4, but the reference is to those being led astray and others who are already astray or false teachers themselves, who are dangerous.

24-25. Jude closes with praise, as would be common in a *synagogue service; the emphasis is that, for all the danger of falling away (vv. 3-23), God is able to keep believers secure and persevering.

REVELATION

Introduction

Authorship. Many scholars today argue that different authors wrote the Fourth Gospel and Revelation; some do not even entertain the *possibility* that both were written by the same person. The style of Revelation is undeniably quite different from that of the Fourth Gospel, so some scholars as early as several centuries after their writing denied that they could have been written by the same author.

But a close examination of the works indicates that much of the vocabulary is the same, though used in different ways; one can account for most of the stylistic variations on the basis of the different *genres of the two works: gospel and *apocalypse (Revelation's style borrows heavily from Ezekiel, Daniel, Zechariah, etc.). That a single community could produce and embrace both a gospel (even one emphasizing the present experience of future glory) and an apocalypse is not difficult to believe; the *Dead Sea Scrolls contain similarly diverse documents. That a single writer could embrace multiple genres is no less possible (compare, e.g., *Plutarch's *Lives* and his *Moralia,* though their differences in genre and style are less pronounced than those of the Fourth Gospel and Revelation).

That one writer would use the same vocabulary but write two entirely different kinds of works from different perspectives seems more probable (at least to this modern author who does the same) than that two allied writers would differ in perspectives but share vocabulary. Theological communities and schools (see the introduction to 1 John) usually share perspectives more than vocabulary, whereas authors may adapt their style to the genre in which they write and emphasize perspectives according to the situation they address, while reusing much of the same vocabulary.

While the arguments against unity of authorship are not decisive, arguments in favor of Johannine authorship of both deserve more attention than they usually receive in modern scholarship. Most of early *church tradition attributes both documents to John the *apostle; the argument that Revelation was written by him is certainly strong (see comment on 1:1; for the Fourth Gospel's authorship, see the introduction to John).

Date. Some scholars have dated Revelation in the late 60s, shortly after Nero's death, as several emperors in a row quickly met violent deaths (cf. 17:10). In the book of Revelation, however, the emperor's power seems to be stable, and this situation does not fit the 60s. Similarly, the imperial cult in Asia (western Turkey) appears to be gaining in power and directly threatens the readers of the book; this situation fits the period of the 90s better. The church also seems to be entrenched in the major cities of Asia; thus a date in Domitian's reign in the 90s of the first century, reported in early church tradition and still preferred by most scholars, is most likely.

Genre. Revelation mixes elements of *Old Testament *prophecy with a heavy dose of the *apocalyptic *genre, a style of writing that grew out of elements of Old Testament prophecy. Although nearly all its images have parallels in the biblical prophets, the images most relevant to late-first-century readers, which were prominent in popular Jewish revelations about the end time, are stressed most heavily. Chapters 2—3 are "oracular letters," a kind of letter occurring especially in the Old Testament (e.g., Jer 29:1-23, 29-32) but also attested on some Greek pottery fragments.

Although the literary structure of such documents may have been added later, scholars are increasingly recognizing that many Jewish mystics and other ancient mantics believed that they were having visionary or trance experiences. Like the Old Testament prophets he most resembles, John may have experienced real visions and need not use them only as a literary device. (The apocalypses are usually pseudonymous, thus it is difficult to be certain to what extent they reflect religious experience. But other accounts of Jewish mystics seeking to invade heaven in visionary ascents—see comment on 2 Cor 12:1-4—and anthropologists' reports on the commonness of ecstatic trance states in a variety of cultures around the world today suggest that many such experiences were genuine. Early Christians generally accepted the reality of pagan inspiration as a phenomenon but attributed it to the demonic realm, while viewing their own inspiration as continuous with that of the Old Testament prophets. They held that there are many spirits in the world, but not all of them are good—1 Jn 4:1-6.)

Structure. After the introduction (chaps. 1—3), the book is dominated by three series of judgments (seals, trumpets, bowls), probably concurrent (they all culminate in the end of the age), and snapshots of worship in heaven (chaps. 4—16), then oracles against Rome (chaps. 17—18) and prophecies of the end (chaps. 19—22). The judgments may cover the (probably symbolic, but possibly deferred) period of 1,260 days to which the book repeatedly alludes (see especially comment on 12:6—if symbolic, this period may span history between Christ's first and second comings). The book is in logical rather than chronological sequence; John undoubtedly reports the visions in the sequence in which he has them, but every time he notes "And I saw/heard," he is receiving a new image. The new image, while connected with what preceded, does not always report an event that follows it chronologically.

Interpretations. There are several major categories of interpretation of this book: (1) Revelation predicts in detail the course of human history till the Second Coming, (2) Revelation reflects the general principles of history, (3) Revelation addresses only what was happening in John's day, (4) Revelation addresses only the end time, and (5) combinations of the above approaches (e.g., John addresses the principles of history in view of the ever-impending end time until it arrives, and originally articulated these principles to speak to the situation of his late-first-century readers).

Many interpreters of John's day (especially interpreters in the *Dead Sea Scrolls) reread *Old Testament *prophecies as symbols describing the interpreters' own generation, and the book of Revelation has similarly been reinterpreted by modern prophecy teachers in every decade of the past century. (For a sober rehearsal of the continual modification of prophecy teachers' predictions with each new series of events in the past century, see Dwight Wilson, *Armageddon Now!* [Grand Rapids, Mich.: Baker Book House, 1977]; for a longer historical perspective in less detail, see Stanley J. Grenz, *The Millennial Maze* [Downers Grove, Ill.: InterVarsity Press, 1992], pp. 37-63.)

Some prophecy teachers have interpreted and reinterpreted Revelation according to the whims of changing news headlines. But John's images would have meant something in particular to their first readers, and this commentary therefore investigates that sense, following the same procedure for interpretation that it follows elsewhere in the *New Testament. Thus it directly addresses the third category of interpretation mentioned above, although this data can be combined with the second category (as it often is for preaching) and, in a sense that becomes clear in the course of the commentary, the fourth category.

Method of Interpretation. John wrote in Greek and used *Old Testament, Jewish and sometimes Greco-Roman figures of speech and images; he explicitly claims that he writes to first-century *churches in Asia Minor (1:4, 11), as explicitly as Paul writes to first-century churches. Whatever else his words may indicate, therefore, they must have been intelligible to his first-century readers (see comment on 1:3; 22:10). Ancient readers had no access to modern newspapers, the basis for some popular methods of interpretation; but subsequent generations have been able to examine the Old Testament and first-century history while studying the book. Historical perspective therefore makes the book available to *all* generations.

This perspective does not deny Revelation's relevance for readers today; to the contrary, it affirms that its message is relevant to every generation, although it uses the symbolism familiar to the generation of its first readers. (Thus, for example, future opponents of the church might be described through the image of a new Nero, a figure more relevant to the original readers than to modern ones. But Christians oppressed in all times can take both warning—that such figures exist—and encouragement—that his end is prophesied—from this image, once they understand it.) By shedding light on the original point of the symbols, this commentary provides modern readers better access to the message of the book when they seek to apply it today.

Symbolism. As in the *Old Testament prophets, much of John's symbolic language is meant as evocative imagery, to elicit particular responses, rather than as a detailed literal picture of events. Readers steeped in the Old Testament and Jewish *apocalyptic literature would have understood this method of interpretation; sometimes older symbols could be reapplied to new situations but were meant to evoke the same sort of response. Sometimes John simply explains what the symbols mean (e.g., 1:20); in other cases the first readers would have understood from other clues in his book or because of cultural information or knowledge of how these symbols were used in antiquity, which he and his readers both understood. John plainly expected his readers to understand his points (1:3; 22:10).

Situation: The Imperial Cult. The line between human and divine had always been thin in Greek religion, and consequently peoples of the Greek East had built temples to Roman emperors from the first emperor on; the first shrines were in Ephesus and Smyrna. In Rome itself the imperial cult was viewed as a symbol of loyalty to the Roman state, and emperors were deified only after they died. But several emperors—all cursed instead of deified after death—claimed to be gods while still alive (Gaius Caligula, Nero and Domitian). The emperor at the time Revelation was written was the widely hated Domitian, who demanded worship while he was alive. In the eastern part of the Empire, worshiping the image of the emperor in his temple could be a test of loyalty to the state. Anyone refusing to participate in the worship of the state was considered subversive, and Rome was always brutally paranoid about subversive religions.

Domitian repressed the aristocracy, expelled astrologers from Rome (lest they predict his demise) and persecuted philosophers and religions that he perceived as hostile to himself. The sources also show that he repressed Judaism and Christianity, although they were not singled out. Evidence on the imperial cult in Asia and outright persecution of Christians in Asia on the provincial level in the early second century (pre-Trajanic repression continuing in Trajan's time) suggest that Domitian's own claims and behavior stimulated the environment in which provincial persecution of Christians in Asia Minor occurred.

Situation: Inevitable Conflict. Jewish people were unofficially exempted from emperor worship, but well-off Asian Jews, repressed by Domitian and embarrassed by the relatively recent revolt of Palestinian Jewry (A.D. 66-70), were paranoid about associations with potentially subversive groups. Many Asian *synagogues thus expelled Jewish Christians (2:9; 3:7-9), who would face Roman persecution if their Jewishness were in question.

The Romans repressed any groups whose prophets denounced Rome, but John stands well in the *Old Testament tradition of uttering oracles against oppressive nations and empires, especially those that oppressed God's people. Some other Jewish writers did pronounce judgment against Rome (often with cryptic names like Babylon, Edom or the Kittim), and many still wanted to revolt (this revolutionary fervor materialized in Egypt and Cyrene shortly thereafter); but Revelation is among the most explicit oracles of judgment against Rome's rebellion against God.

Message. Revelation provides an eternal perspective, by emphasizing such themes as the antagonism of the world in rebellion against God toward a *church obedient to God's will; the unity of the church's worship with heaven's worship; that victory depends on *Christ's finished work, not on human circumstances; that Christians must be ready to face death for Christ's honor; that representatives of every people will ultimately stand before his throne; that the imminent hope of his return is worth more than all this world's goods; and so forth. From the beginning, the Old Testament covenant and promise had implied a hope for the future of God's people. When Israel was confronted with the question of individuals' future, the Old Testament doctrines of justice and hope led them to views like the resurrection (Is 26:19; Dan 12:2). The future hope is further developed and embroidered with the imagery of Revelation.

Commentaries. See especially G. B. Caird, *A Commentary on the Revelation of Saint John the Divine,* HNTC (San Francisco: Harper & Row, 1966); G. R. Beasley-Murray, *The Book of Revelation,* NCB, 2nd ed. (1978; reprint, Grand Rapids, Mich.: Eerdmans, 1981); Gerhard Krodel, *Revelation* (Minneapolis: Augsburg, 1989). The reader may also find W. G. Morrice, "John the Seer: Narrative Exegesis of the Book of Revelation," *Expository Times* 97 (November 1985): 43-46, helpful in teaching the book. Many other works are useful for different points, including André Feuillet, *The Apocalypse,* trans. Thomas E. Crane (Staten Island, N.Y.: Alba House, 1965); Robert H. Mounce, *The Book of Revelation,* NICNT (Grand Rapids, Mich.: Eerdmans, 1977); Elisabeth Schüssler Fiorenza, *The Book of Revelation: Justice and Judgment* (Philadelphia: Fortress, 1985); Robert W. Wall, *Revelation,* NIBC (Peabody, Mass.: Hendrickson, 1991); and James Moffatt, "The Revelation of St. John the Divine," in *The Expositor's Greek Testament,* 5 vols. (reprint, Grand Rapids, Mich.: Eerdmans, 1979), 5:281-494. Apart from its eccentric view of Revelation's authorship, J. Massyngberde Ford, *Revelation,* AB 38 (Garden City, N.Y.: Doubleday, 1975), is quite useful and has been unduly criticized on account of that one point.

1:1-3 Title and Apocalyptic Introduction

Titles of documents often consisted of a statement like "the book of the words of so-and-so" (Tobit 1:1); John's title resembles that of some *Old Testament prophetic books (e.g., Is 1:1; Jer 1:1; Hos 1:1). Titles were normally affixed to the outside of a scroll, although by the mid-second century some people were using the codex, or modern form of book, and titles were put on the inside.

1:1. Most apocalypses were attributed to meritorious Old Testament characters of the distant past; like Old Testament prophetic books, Revelation is written by a contemporary *apostle who does not need such a pen name; he writes to real congregations that know him (1:4, 11). (Other apocalypses did not name specific recipients or use the epistolary form.)

Some revelations in the Old Testament (Dan 7:16; 10:5-21; cf. Ex 3:2; Judg 6:11-23) and many revelations in *apocalyptic literature (e.g., *1 Enoch and *4 Ezra) were mediated through angels. Old Testament prophets were called God's "servants," a title John aptly claims for himself at the opening of his book.

1:2. "Witness" was especially a legal term, although its sense had been widely extended beyond that. Christians were being betrayed to Roman law courts, but in the context of Revelation, "witness" is the Christian proclamation of knowledge about Jesus, providing evidence in the light of the court of God's final judgment (cf. Is 43:8-12; 44:8-9).

1:3. Most people in antiquity could not read, and there would not at any rate be enough copies of the book (which would have to be copied by hand) for everyone to have his or her own. Thus the blessing is for the one who reads aloud to the congregation (just as there was one reader in a *synagogue) and those who hear (just as the rest of the congregation listened to Scripture readings). The "blessing" form was common in the *Old Testament and Jewish literature (see comment on Mt 5:1-12), and here implies that the hearers were expected to understand and obey what they heard. (Revelation contains seven such "blessings" and seven curses or "woes," probably all oracular, i.e., prophetic.) *Apocalypses commonly predicted the imminent end of the age, or imminent events heralding that end (especially in the roughly contemporary work 4 Ezra).

1:4-8 Epistolary Introduction

Works that were not strictly epistles but were being sent to readers could include epistolary introductions, for example, the historical work 2 Maccabees (1:1—2:32, especially 1:1).

1:4. "Grace and peace" adapts a standard ancient greeting; see comment on Romans 1:7. On the encyclical nature of the letter (which could not be quickly recopied by hand many times over, and thus was read by the messenger to each *church in sequence), see comment on Revelation 1:11.

The "one who is, was and is to come" is related to an occasional Greek title for an eternal deity, but especially reflects a Greek exposition of the *Old Testament name "I AM" (Ex 3:14; the *LXX has "he who is"), in the same form in which it was also expanded by the *Targum. The "seven spirits" here might refer to the sevenfold *messianic *Spirit of Isaiah 11:2, but more likely refers to the seven holy archangels recognized by Judaism around the throne (Rev 8:2; see comment on 5:6). (Some

*Dead Sea Scrolls texts and some second-century Jewish Christians viewed the *Holy Spirit as an angel, although most usually recognized the Holy Spirit as the Spirit of God; we need not suppose such a confusion here, however. That the sevenfold Spirit imagery of Is 11:2 was current is suggested by *1 Enoch 61:11 [though this section of 1 Enoch, the Similitudes, is of uncertain date]; cf. *Psalms of Solomon 17:37, but see comment on Rev 5:6.)

1:5. A "faithful" witness (2:13; 3:14) was a reliable one (Prov 14:5, 25; Is 8:2; Jer 42:5). "Firstborn" and "ruler over the earth's kings" allude to Psalm 89:27. Under Old Testament ritual law, the blood of the sacrifice of the Day of *Atonement freed Israel from their sins; the Jewish people had also been freed from Egypt by the blood of the Passover lamb.

1:6. After God redeemed Israel from Egypt he called them "a kingdom of priests" (Ex 19:6), thus indicating that all of them were holy to him. The *Targum of this verse renders it "a kingdom and priests," as here (cf. *Jubilees 16:18).

1:7. Like Matthew 24:30, this verse blends Daniel 7:13 (coming with clouds on the day of the Lord; cf. also, e.g., Ezek 30:3) with Zechariah 12:10 (those who pierced him, i.e., God, will mourn for him). "Tribes of earth" extends the image beyond the tribes of Israel (cf. Zech 12:12) to all peoples; citizens of cities in the Greek East were divided into tribes.

1:8. Some Greco-Roman writers called the supreme deity the "first," but the *Old Testament (Is 41:4) and Judaism (e.g., *Josephus, *Philo, adapting *Stoic language) had already called Israel's God the "first and the last." This is the point of calling him by the first and last letters of the Greek alphabet, Alpha and Omega. (Some Jewish teachers similarly came to call him the *'Aleph* and the *Tav*, the first and last letters of the Hebrew alphabet. They further called God "truth," Hebrew *'emet*, spelled *'aleph-mem-tav*, which they said were the first, middle and last letters of the alphabet, showing that God was eternal and ruled over all time.) Greek-speaking Jews often called God "the omnipotent," or "all-powerful," as here.

1:9-20
The Opening Revelation

1:9. Governors of various provinces could exercise their own discretion as to whether those charged and found guilty should be banished to an island, executed or enslaved. Those of higher social status automatically received lighter sentences than others, but John was banished as opposed to executed (cf. 2:13) either on account of his age (as sometimes happened) or the clemency of the local governor. Banishments were of two kinds: *deportatio* (including confiscation of property and removal of civil rights) and *relegatio* (without such penalties); only the emperor could declare the former, but a provincial governor could declare the latter, as here.

The most common places of Roman banishment were some rocky Aegean islands called the Cyclades (around Delos) and the Sporades, off the coast of Asia, which included Patmos (forty to fifty miles southwest of Ephesus). Patmos was not deserted; it included a gymnasium and temple of Artemis (the island's patron deity). Because Babylon was the major place of exile in *Old Testament tradition (Ezek 1:1), John's own banishment puts him in a position to denounce Rome as the new Babylon (chaps. 17—18; see comment on 14:8).

1:10. Because the Old Testament and ancient Judaism especially associated the *Spirit of God with *prophecy, "in the Spirit" here may mean that John was in charismatic worship (1 Chron 25:1-6) or a visionary state (Ezek 2:2; 3:12, 14, 24; 8:3; 11:1, 24). Nevertheless, the revelation here, as in the Old Testament but in contrast to much Jewish *apocalyptic literature, is otherwise unsolicited (see comment on Rev 4:2). The "sound like a trumpet" may allude to God's revelation in Exodus 19:16, when the Lord was preparing to give forth his word.

One day a month was dedicated to the honor of the emperor in Asia Minor, but the Christians dedicated one day—probably each week—to Christ's honor, perhaps in view of the coming "day of the Lord." (According to some Jewish schemes for reckoning history, the seventh and final age of history would be an age of sabbath rest [cf. Rev 20]; some early Christian interpreters transferred the image to an eighth age, speaking of the Lord's day as the eighth day of the week. But it may be debated how early and how relevant these ideas are to John in Revelation.) Most scholars think that "the Lord's day" refers to Sunday, as the weekday of Jesus' *resurrection; the early Jewish Christians may have preferred that day to avoid conflicting with sabbath observance.

1:11. A messenger delivering John's book would arrive first in Ephesus; the other cities are arranged in the sequence a messenger would follow on foot to reach them. The distance between them generally varies from about thirty to forty-five miles. (Those who suggest that John meant the *churches symbolically for different stages of church history have to assume that churches before the final stage could not hope for Christ's imminent return; but John's letters to the churches display too much local color to represent merely church ages, and their precise geographical arrangement suggests that he means them literally.)

1:12. On the lampstands see comment on 1:20.

1:13-15. This passage draws on the picture of God in Daniel 7:9 (the white hair symbolizing the dignity accruing to age), features of the mighty angel in Daniel 10:5-6 and the title "one like a son of man" from Daniel 7:13 (where he would come to rule the nations). (The sound of the angel's voice "like a tumult" in Dan 10:6 is adapted by means of the divine imagery of Ezek 1:24; 43:2; later Jewish traditions also spoke of waters in the heavens.) The "robe" and "girdle" may allude to his role as high priest (Ex 28:4). Others could also wear robes and girdles, however; if the image is meant more generally, it may be significant that workmen wore their girdles around their waist while working, so a position around the breast would signify that his work is complete. But given the other biblical allusions here, it is probable that an allusion to the *Old Testament high priest is also in view. "Feet of bronze" could allude to the bearers of God's throne (Ezek 1:7) as well as to the angel of Daniel 10:6.

The cumulative impact of these images is to present the risen Jesus as the greatest conceivable figure, using biblical imagery. *Apocalypses employed some of this imagery (angels that looked like lightning, etc.), although John at this point avoids postbiblical elaborations that became common in such works (angels thousands of miles tall, etc.).

1:16. The mouth of God's spokesperson could be presented as a weapon (Is 49:2) and the *Messiah's just decrees of judgment would be the weapon of his mouth (Is 11:4). Some Jewish texts described angels shining as the sun (cf. also the angel's face like lightning in

Dan 10:6).

1:17. Terror was common during visions (Gen 15:12); those who received revelations of God (Ezek 1:28; 11:13) or of angels (Dan 8:18; 10:9, 15) in the *Old Testament often fell on their faces, unless the revealer touched and strengthened them (Dan 8:18; 10:10). (The image was continued in many later Jewish texts—e.g., Tobit, *1 Enoch and *4 Ezra—as well.) God often had to assure his servants not to be afraid (e.g., Deut 3:2; Josh 8:1; Jer 1:8), sometimes when he spoke to them (e.g., Gen 26:24).

1:18. In the Old Testament (Ps 9:13; 107:18) and Jewish literature, "the gates of Hades" referred to the realm of the dead and thus to the power of death; one who held the keys to these realms thus ruled over them. (Whoever held the keys in a royal house held a position of great authority in that house, as in Is 22:21-22; keys symbolized authority to control whatever they opened, and Jewish texts spoke of God dispensing keys to rain, etc.) Jewish literature said that God had authority over death and the gates of Hades (Wisdom of Solomon 16:13). *Christ's power over death, as the one who had risen, would encourage his followers now facing possible death.

1:19. *Prophecy in the *Old Testament involved speaking God's message and was not strictly limited to prediction of the future. But the Greek writer *Plutarch defined prophecy as predicting the future that is caused by the present and past; the Jewish Sibyl was said to prophesy the things that were before, were present and would come about (*Sibylline Oracles 1:3-4). Jewish *apocalyptic writers often divided history into ages as a prelude to their prophecies about the future (though often writing under a pseudonym, ostensibly before the history occurred).

1:20. Jewish texts often portrayed angels as stars (see comment on 12:4). Cosmic imagery was frequent; e.g., *Josephus and *Philo identified the "seven planets" with certain symbols in the temple, and Palestinian *synagogues later sported zodiacs around Helios, the sun god, on their floors (despite Old Testament prohibitions). Pagans believed that Fate controlled the nations through the stars, which were generally deified—an Eastern view introduced into Greco-Roman paganism under the guise of the science of the day. Many Jewish people concurred that the nations were ruled by the stars, which they took as angels under God's dominion. But if John uses this symbolism—and this is unclear—he is showing only that *Christ is Lord over the universe, including Lord over the angels who guide the churches as well as the nations.

A (usually) seven-branched lampstand, or menorah, was one of the most common symbols for Judaism and *synagogues in antiquity; by identifying the churches as lampstands, John claims that the Jesus movement is the true form of Judaism, no matter what many synagogue officials were claiming (2:9; 3:9). Because Revelation portrays heaven as a sanctuary (cf., e.g., comment on 4:6-8; 5:8-10; 7:9-12; 8:3), the lampstands may also allude to the spiritual representation of the churches in heaven (Ex 25:31-40).

There are four major views on the "angels" of the churches. One is that they are "messengers" bearing the scroll to the churches; although this meaning is possible (1 Macc 1:44), it is unlikely that John would have seven separate copies of the book or would send seven different messengers (see comment on Rev 1:11). A second view is that they are public readers in each congregation, like a corresponding kind of "messenger" in the synagogues. According to second-century teaching, if such a reader slipped in his reading of the biblical text, the whole congregation was held accountable before God because he acted as their agent. Third, they may be the guardian angels of each congregation, analogous to the Jewish view (rooted in Daniel) that not only each person but each nation was assigned a guardian angel, and the angels of the evil nations would be judged together with the nations they led astray. Finally (related to the third view), they may represent heavenly counterparts to earthly realities (the churches), symbolizing the heavenly significance of the churches as the lampstands did; this view would also fit *apocalyptic imagery.

2:1-7
Oracle to the Ephesian Church

Each of these oracle letters follows the same form, somewhat akin to imperial letter edicts posted as inscriptions in the cities of Asia Minor. Some scholars have compared the elements of the form to *Old Testament and ancient Near Eastern covenant formulas; if they are correct, the *prophecies here may act like the covenant lawsuits common in the Old Testament prophets (e.g., in Amos 2—4). They may also function analogously to series of oracles against the nations common in the Old Testament prophets (e.g., Is 13—23; Jer 46—51; Ezek 25—32; especially the 8 brief oracles of Amos 1—2). Some other ancient Near Eastern prophets also included judgment prophecies against other nations, but these were military oracles in the service of nationalism; unlike the Old Testament prophets, they did not condemn their own peoples. The exceptions are Egyptian moralist oracles after the fact, and Mari prophets' rebukes of kings for not supporting the temple better. There is no parallel outside Israel to an intergenerational succession of prophets calling their own people to *repentance for moral sins. Compare especially the *Sibylline Oracles, passim, for later examples of oracles against nations, including oracles against some of the cities Revelation lists, like Smyrna, Pergamum, Sardis, Laodicea and Ephesus.

William Ramsay long ago pointed to some local color in each of these oracles. Although some of his connections may be strained, others are quite appropriate. Ancient cities were fiercely proud of their own history and culture and would be more sensitive to local allusions than most readers today would be.

Ephesus had been one of the first Asian centers of the imperial cult, and Domitian had allowed Ephesus the title of guardian of his temple; on its notoriety in magic and the worship of Artemis, see comment on Acts 19. Inscriptions attest that Ephesus also had a sizable Jewish population, of which Christians had originally been a comfortable part (Acts 18:19-20, 26; 19:8-9). In practice, Ephesus was the leading center of Asia Minor in this period.

2:1. "Says this" (NASB) echoes the *Old Testament formula that prophets of God borrowed from royal edicts and typical messenger formulas: "Thus says the lord/king."

2:2-3. *Rhetorical experts (teachers of professional public speaking) recommended that speakers mix praise and blame for their hearers, to avoid closing them to the message while also avoiding populist flattery. Rhetoricians normally began with praise, as do most of the letters in Revelation 2—3. Edicts sometimes included "I know," although the allusion here is to the omniscience of the one who inspires *prophecy, a

standard ancient idea.
2:4. Sound doctrine and perseverance are inadequate without love. Whether love for other Christians (as in 1 Jn; cf. "works"—Rev 2:5, 19; "hate"—2:6) or for God (Jer 2:2) is in view is not clear.
2:5. Royal emissaries could threaten judgment on cities, but this threat is closest to God's warnings to the unrepentant in the *Old Testament. These oracles address the *churches rather than the cities they represented before God, but Ramsay's notes on the future of each city are nonetheless interesting. Eventually only a village remained of what was once mighty Ephesus, several miles from the original site of the city; due to silt deposits, it was already beginning to lose its geographical position as a coastal city in John's day.
2:6. This teaching may be related to that of "Balaam" (2:14-15); this sect may have advocated compromise with the imperial cult to avoid persecution. Later church fathers identified them as an immoral *Gnostic sect. As in the *Dead Sea Scrolls, the "hatred" here is hatred of sin, not private revenge (the Scrolls taught that vengeance should be left to God).
2:7. "The *Spirit" in Judaism was especially associated with prophetic enablement; thus the Spirit inspires John's vision and prophecy (1:10; 14:13). On having an "ear" see comment on Mark 4:9. Some moralists also exhorted hearers to "hear" sages of old they were citing, but the formula here resembles the common Old Testament formula "Hear the word of the Lord" (e.g., Amos 3:1; 4:1; 5:1). "Overcoming" (especially a military or athletic image of conquest or victory) here involves persevering in the face of conflict and hardship; this is all that the Lord requires to secure ultimate victory. Although the "tree of life" was used to symbolize the *law in later Jewish teaching, this vision alludes to Genesis 2:9 and a restoration of paradise (on which cf. 2 Cor 12:2-4). Each of the promises in these oracles to the churches is fulfilled in Revelation 21—22.

2:8-11 Oracle to the Church at Smyrna

Only Smyrna and Philadelphia are fully praised; Ramsay notes that of the seven these two cities held out longest before the Turkish conquest. Ephesus and prosperous Smyrna were the two oldest centers of the imperial cult in Asia. One of the oldest and most prominent cities in Asia, Smyrna sought but failed to achieve honor equal to that of Ephesus in this period. It was also known for its beauty. On the situation in Smyrna and Philadelphia, which apparently includes expulsion from the *synagogues, see the introduction to John.
2:8. On the description of Jesus here, see comment on 1:17-18. (Some commentators have argued that Smyrna was likewise dead and living, because it enjoyed only a shadow of its former reputation. This interpretation is unlikely in view of its prosperity, even if it had been overshadowed by Ephesus. According to Strabo, Smyrna had been razed by the Lydians and rebuilt with great beauty many centuries before, but this revival of a city was not commonly understood as death and *resurrection, and the occasion was now so remote in the past that the Smyrneans themselves would probably not have caught such a purported allusion. Furthermore, Sardis was once burned as well, but 3:1 says the opposite about it.)
2:9. The strength of the Jewish community in Smyrna is well attested. In

denying that his opponents are spiritually Jewish, he seems to return the charge they had made against the Christians; in calling them a "*synagogue of *Satan," his *rhetoric resembles that of the *Dead Sea Scrolls, where a persecuted Jewish sect that considered the rest of Judaism apostate called its opponents "the lot of Belial" (Satan).

People were betrayed to provincial officials by *delatores*, "informers," and by the early second century it is attested that Christians in Asia Minor were generally charged only if accused by such informers. By the early second century, Jews in Smyrna were reportedly fulfilling this function against Christians (such as Polycarp). But simply claiming publicly that Christians were no longer welcome as part of the *synagogue community was a form of betrayal; Christians who were not seen as Jewish had no protection against civil requirements for participation in the emperor cult.

2:10. Prison was merely a place of detention until trial and could therefore be a prelude to execution. "Testing" for "ten days" is a symbolic allusion to the minor test of Daniel 1:12, which preceded the major trials faced by Daniel and his three companions. "Behold" is common in prophetic literature and occurs repeatedly in Ezekiel (e.g., 1:4, 15).

Many Christians were martyred in Smyrna over the next several centuries. Jewish martyr stories praised those who were faithful to death and thus would be *resurrected at the end; "crowns" were victors' (2:11) rewards for athletes or military heroes. (A number of ancient writers also mentioned the "crown of Smyrna," possibly referring to the city's beauty.)

2:11. Other Jewish literature also refers to the "second death," although often meaning annihilation (Revelation uses it of eternal torment—20:10, 14). The text of *4 Maccabees portrays Jewish martyrs as fighting and triumphing by death and thus crowned as victorious athletes by godliness.

2:12-17 Oracle to the Church in Pergamum

There is some evidence for a Jewish community at Pergamum, but it was a strongly pagan city (see comment on 2:13). It was also a famous and prosperous city, and its rulers had been the first to invite the Romans into the affairs of Asia Minor. It was the center of the imperial cult for its province.

2:12. The "sword" in the *Old Testament and *apocalyptic literature often symbolized judgment or war; cf. 1:16, 2:16 and 19:13. Romans thought of the "sword" as the power to execute capital punishment (as in Rom 13:4).

2:13. Pergamum was traditionally known for its worship of Asclepius (whose symbol on Pergamum's coins was the serpent; cf. chap. 12), Demeter, Athena and Dionysus, along with Orphic elements. Its famous giant altar of Zeus (120 by 112 feet) overlooked the city on its citadel, and some have suggested that this is the background for "*Satan's throne" in this verse. A more likely allusion for "*Satan's throne" is the local worship of the emperor, celebrated on Pergamum's coinage in this period. Local rulers had been worshiped before the Roman period, and Pergamum was one of the first cities of Asia to build a temple to a Roman emperor (also on the citadel), making it a center of the cult. A further imperial temple was dedicated there within a decade or two after John wrote Revelation, so it is clear that the cult was popular there.

All citizens were expected to participate in civil religion or they would be suspected of disloyalty against the state; but Christians could not participate in imperial festivals or eat the meat doled out there, and as a group would thus naturally be suspected. Once one Christian was martyred, the legal precedent was set for the execution of Christians in other provinces.

2:14-15. The false teachers may be advocating compromise with the imperial cult, for humanly appealing reasons (2:13). "Balaam" was the most famous pagan prophet of the *Old Testament and Jewish tradition (see comment on Jude 11) and is thus provided as the pseudonym for the heretical leader of the compromisers, like "Jezebel" in Thyatira (2:20). Both claimed inspired authority for their views and may, like the Jewish Sibyls, have used their prophecies especially to commend themselves to some elements of pagan universalism.

Balaam, a prominent ancient figure also attested outside the Bible, was believed to have led Israel to eat meat offered to idols and to have sexual intercourse with pagans to whom they were not married (Num 25:1-3). Other nations could not destroy Israel, but Balaam knew that if he could subvert their morals, God would withdraw his blessing and judge them (see *Josephus and *Pseudo-Philo; cf. Num 25:8). God judged Israel, but Balaam, who acted from mercenary motives, also lost his life (Num 31:8; Josh 13:22). "Sexual immorality" may be meant literally here (it was common in paganism) or may refer, as often in the Old Testament prophets, to spiritual infidelity against God (perhaps to emperor worship; cf. 17:5).

2:16. Although there would be one ultimate end of the world, the Old Testament prophets and Jewish literature occasionally described judgments in history in the language of the final day of the Lord.

2:17. The original ark of the covenant was permanently lost in 586 B.C. (cf. Jer 3:16), and the manna inside it had vanished before then. But a wide spectrum of Jewish tradition declared that Jeremiah (e.g., 2 Maccabees, 4 Baruch) or an angel (2 Baruch) had hidden them and that they would be restored at the end time (a similar view took root among the *Samaritans, who dated the departure earlier). On the symbol of spiritual manna, see comment on John 6:35-40. Pebbles of various colors were used for admission to public celebrations; a black stone was the sacred symbol of the infamous Asian goddess Cybele; white stones used for medical purposes were associated with Judea; and perhaps most significant, jurors used black stones to vote for a person's guilt but white ones to vote for innocence. The *Old Testament associated change of name with a promise (e.g., Gen 17:5, 15).

2:18-29
Oracle to the Church in Thyatira

Thyatira's economy seems to have emphasized trades and crafts. The trade guilds each had common meals (normally about once a month) dedicated to their patron deities. Although Thyatira had a Jewish community, it does not appear to have been influential; Christians who refused to participate in the life of the guilds would thus find themselves isolated socially and economically (cf. 13:17). Thyatira was only beginning to achieve prosperity in this period, hence its citizens probably valued wealth highly.

2:18. Thyatira hosted a major cult of Apollo, son of Zeus and the deity associated with prophecy and the sun. The emperor was linked with Apollo and may have been worshiped in Thyatira as his earthly manifestation. Although bronze-working was not unique to Thyatira, some scholars have also pointed to the bronze-workers' guild in that city.

2:19-20. The biblical "Jezebel" was not a prophetess, but the name is used here for its related connotations (for false prophetesses cf. Neh 6:14; Ezek 13:17-19). Jezebel had nine hundred prophets (1 Kings 18:19) and led God's people into idolatry (see comment on Rev 2:14). She was accused of harlotry, a damaging charge against a king's wife (the term was probably meant spiritually, as one who led Israel from their commitment to God), and of witchcraft, no doubt for her occult involvement in pagan cults (2 Kings 9:22). As a harlot she becomes the prototype of the evil empire of chapters 17—18.

Some scholars have suggested that Thyatira was one of the Asian cities with an oracle of the Sibyl; this cult purported to involve female prophetesses in the Greek style, and its literary forms had come to be used by *Diaspora Judaism. Jewish *Sibylline oracles may at any rate have influenced the style and thinking of "Jezebel"; later Christian sources mention the Sibyl's prophecies frequently.

The compromises with sin here (as in 2:14) might be related to the imperial cult, although such compromises were less prominent in Thyatira than in some of the previously mentioned cities. It is known that the imperial cult employed some priestesses in first-century Asia Minor; but even if Jezebel was advocating compromise with the cult, it is unlikely that she could have had any credibility with Christians while being a priestess in it.

2:21-23. Jewish texts speak of judgment against children produced by illicit unions, but the children are meant figuratively here (cf. Is 57:3-4, 7-8): *disciples were sometimes called "children." Jewish texts regularly portray God's omniscience and sometimes call him "Searcher of Hearts and Minds" (based on *Old Testament descriptions of him); here this characteristic of God applies to Jesus. God gave false prophets opportunity to turn from their falsehood and hear the true word of the Lord (Jer 23:22-23).

2:24. *Mystery cults stressed deep secrets shared only among the initiates. For "no other burden" (NASB) cf. perhaps Acts 15:28-29.

2:25-27. Revelation cites here an enthronement psalm that celebrated the promise to David and pointed to his seed who would reign over the nations that sought to rebel against him (Ps 2:8-9). The *Messiah, to whom the psalm applied par excellence (and to whom it was generally understood to apply, as in, e.g., *Psalms of Solomon), here makes his people partakers of his rule over the nations. Someone who did not know the Old Testament would have applied this description to the Roman emperor; Revelation declares that Jesus is greater than the most powerful emperor the world had ever known.

2:28-29. The morning star, Venus, heralded the dawn, and great people could be compared to it as well as to the sun shining in glory (Ecclus 50:6); cf. Revelation 22:16. Because most of the Greco-Roman world believed that life was ruled by the stars, to be given authority over one of the most powerful of stars (a symbol of sovereignty among the Romans) was to share *Christ's rule over creation (2:26-27).

3:1-6
Oracle Against the Church of Sardis

Ramsay pointed out that the two *churches condemned most harshly belong to the only two cities of the seven that are completely uninhabited in modern times, Sardis and Laodicea. Sardis had a large, powerful and wealthy Jewish community that had long been a respected part of civic life.

Sardis hosted many pagan cults; Artemis, Cybele, Demeter and Kore (Persephone) were all worshiped there. The Greek goddess Demeter, absorbing the character of the old Asiatic goddess Cybele, had also been locally identified with the deified mother of an emperor. But mixing of deities was common in antiquity, and paganism permeated all the non-Jewish cities of the Roman Empire. Despite the city's paganism, the Christian community there seems to have experienced no persecution—and hence no spiritual life.

3:1-2. On the "spirits" and "stars" cf. 1:4, 16, 20; the "alive . . . dead" here reverses the imagery of 1:18 and 2:8. The past glories of Sardis as chief city of Lydia under Croesus were proverbial; its present prosperity could never regain for it the position it had once held.

3:3. This verse refers to Jesus' saying preserved in Matthew 24:43 (as do 1 Thess 5:2; 2 Pet 3:10). Sardis's acropolis had never been taken by battle, but twice in its history invaders had captured it by stealth unexpectedly in the night.

3:4. Inscriptions in Asia Minor indicate that many temples barred worshipers with soiled garments, whose entry would insult the deity. White robes were worn by priests (and purportedly other worshipers) in the Jerusalem temple, worshipers of most deities (e.g., Isis, Apollo, Artemis), celebrants in cult festivals for the emperor and so on.

3:5-6. All Greek and Roman cities had official rolls of citizens, to which new citizens could be added and from which expelled citizens would be removed. The "book of life" appears in the *Old Testament and figures prominently in Jewish *apocalyptic; see comment on Philippians 4:3. On confessing the believer's name before God's judgment tribunal, cf. Matthew 10:32 and Luke 12:8.

3:7-13
Oracle to the Church in Philadelphia

Philadelphia housed temples of Artemis, Helios, Zeus, Dionysus and Aphrodite. A third-century inscription from the Jewish *synagogue there has been recovered. The church in Philadelphia, like the church in Smyrna, had apparently been expelled from the Jewish community; the background resembles that for the Fourth Gospel (see introduction to John).

3:7-8. These verses clearly allude to Isaiah 22:22, which speaks of one who had David's key to open and shut, indicating full authorization to rule the house. To Jewish Christians excluded from the synagogue, this was Jesus' encouragement that he who rightly ruled the house of David now acknowledged them as his own people.

3:9. See comment on 2:9-10. Exclusion from the *synagogue could lead to more direct persecution by the Roman authorities, as in Smyrna. Jesus' claim that their opponents would know that he had loved them might echo Malachi 1:2, where God tells Israel that he loved them—but despised Esau/Edom; cf. Proverbs 14:19. Jewish people expected the kings of the nations to bow before them in the end time (Is 49:23; 60:11, 14; *1 Enoch; *Dead Sea Scrolls; cf. Ps 72:10-11).

3:10. *Apocalypses sometimes prophesied special deliverance (i.e., protection) for the righteous in the coming times of hardship; the *Old Testament also promised God's faithfulness to his people in such times (see comment on 7:3). Some texts spoke of the righteous being tested by the future time of suffering (e.g., the *Dead Sea Scrolls), although the motif of the righteous being tested in sufferings in general was a common one (see comment on 1 Pet 1:7). ("Keep from" could mean "protect from" [cf. Rev 7:3; cf. Jn 17:15, the only other *New Testament use of the construction] or "preserve from." The "hour of testing" is too universal for a local testing [2:10] and must refer either to the great tribulation or, as Allen Kerkeslager has argued, with attention to ancient parallels and the usage of "hour" throughout Revelation, to the final hour, the day of judgment.) Revelation contrasts the wicked "earth dwellers" with the righteous "heaven dwellers"; apocalypses (like *4 Ezra, the Similitudes of Enoch and *2 Baruch) also announce judgments on the "inhabitants of the earth."

3:11. "Crown" here alludes to the victor's crown, received at the end of a race or for military exploits.

3:12-13. God's remnant people appear as a new temple in the *Dead Sea Scrolls and in various other *New Testament texts. Pillars could be used to symbolize the people of God (Ex 24:4; see also comment on Gal 2:9) but were a natural feature of temples and often bore dedicatory inscriptions (also on the pillars of the Capernaum *synagogue, just as military standards and other items bore inscriptions). The primary allusion is probably to Isaiah 56:5, where those whom the Jewish community rejected (cf. Rev 3:8-9) received a place within God's house and a new name. On the new Jerusalem see 21:2; "coming down" was natural in the vertical dualism common in *apocalyptic literature and the Fourth Gospel, which typically contrasts heaven (where God rules unchallenged) and earth (where many disobey him until the day of judgment). Revelation portrays God's throne room in heaven as a temple (see, e.g., comment on 4:6-8).

3:14-22
Oracle to the Church in Laodicea

Laodicea became important only in Roman times. It was capital of the Cibryatic convention, which included at least twenty-five towns. It was also the wealthiest Phrygian city, and especially prosperous in this period. It was ten miles west of Colosse and six miles south of Hierapolis. Zeus was the city's patron deity, but Laodiceans also had temples for Apollo, Asclepius (the healing deity), Hades, Hera, Athena, Serapis, Dionysus and other deities. Many Jewish people lived in Phrygia.

3:14. "Beginning" is a divine title; see comment on 1:8 and 22:13. (It may also be relevant that the Roman emperor's primary title was *princeps*, "the first," i.e., among Roman citizens.) Jesus is also the "Amen," the affirmation of God's truth; cf. 2 Corinthians 1:20.

3:15-16. Cold water (and sometimes spiced hot water) was preferred for drinking, and hot water for bathing, but Laodicea lacked a natural water supply. Water piped in from hot springs six miles to the south, like any cold water that could have been procured from the mountains, would be lukewarm by the time it reached Laodicea. Although water could be heated, the natural lukewarmness of local water (in contrast with the hot water available at nearby Hierapolis) was undoubtedly a standard complaint of local residents, most of whom had an otherwise comfortable lifestyle. (Their imported water was also full of sediment, though better, said the geographer Strabo, than the water of Hierapolis.) Jesus says: "Were you hot [i.e., for bathing] or cold [i.e., for drinking], you would be useful; but as it is, I feel toward you the way you feel toward your water supply—you make me sick."

3:17-18. Laodicea was a prosperous banking center; proud of its wealth, it refused Roman disaster relief after the earthquake of A.D. 60, rebuilding from its own resources. It was also known for its textiles (especially wool) and for its medical school and production of ear medicine and undoubtedly the highly reputed Phrygian eye salve. Everything in which Laodicea could have confidence outwardly, its *church, which reflected its culture, lacked spiritually.

Although Greeks did not share Palestinian Jews' moral abhorrence of nudity, everyone except *Cynic sages agreed that the lack of clothing described here, that of poverty (here spiritual), was undesirable. Phrygian "eye salve" (KJV, NASB) was apparently not an ointment per se but was probably powdered and smeared on to the eyelids (contrast Tobit 6:8). On white garments cf. Revelation 3:4; here it may be a stark contrast with Laodicea's famous "black wool."

3:19. Compare the many prophetic rebukes of Israel in the *Old Testament.

3:20. Compare John 10:1-4, Matthew 24:33 and 42. Table fellowship was a sign of intimacy and committed the guest and host to friendly relations. Jesus here invites the Laodicean Christians to dine (cf. Rev 2:7; contrast 2:14, 20) in the present at the *messianic banquet (see comment on 19:9); it is an invitation to a genuinely lavish banquet, implying again their spiritual poverty (cf. 3:17-18). But the door to fellowship is presently closed—from their side (contrast 3:7-8).

3:21-22. The image here is one of sharing God's rule; Jesus shares as coregent or viceroy, whereas his people share because they are exalted to rule over the earth (as in *Old Testament and Jewish expectations for Israel's exaltation). God's preexistent and glorious throne was the subject of much discussion among Jewish *apocalyptic writers and mystics; see comment on 4:2.

4:1-11
John's Throne Vision

Jewish mystics (many of whom penned *apocalypses, like *1 Enoch) strove for visions of the invisible God, and modeled their views of what they would find on visions of God's enthroned glory in Isaiah 6 and Ezekiel 1 (cf. Ex 24:9-11; 1 Kings 22:19; Dan 7:9-10). In time these visions were embroidered with every fantastic magnification of the divine glory the mystics could imagine. In contrast to such elaborate reports of the preexistent throne of God, John's description is simple, like the *Old Testament accounts: just enough description to convey the point of God's majesty. The picture of the throne room, including the activity of those surrounding the throne, may also be a parody on the imperial court and the worship in the imperial temples—a daring revelation for a banished Jewish prophet like John.

4:1. "After these things" functions as a transition device to the next vision he would see (7:9; 15:5; 18:1; cf. 7:1; 19:1; 20:3; Jn 5:1; 6:1; 7:1); it was commonly used as such a transition. "I looked, and behold," is typical visionary language (e.g., Ezek 10:1; 44:4; Dan 10:5; also 1 Enoch, *4 Ezra and other writings based on this *genre). On the trumpet, cf. Revelation 1:10. Although elsewhere in Revelation John is told, "Come here" (17:1; 21:9; cf. Jn 1:39), in this instance "Come up here" may also allude to God's call to Moses to come up the mountain (in later Jewish tradition, to heaven) to receive revelation (Ex 19:24; 24:12; 34:2); the same language appears frequently in *apocalypses. The opened heavens are a figure for revelation as well (Rev 11:19; 19:11; Jn 1:51), again following an important Old Testament pattern for such visions (Ezek 1:1), developed in other Jewish apocalypses (including the door, e.g., 1 Enoch).

4:2. "In the *Spirit" means that John is prophetically inspired in his vision (see comment on 1:10); Ezekiel had similarly been carried elsewhere in visions (Ezek 11:1, 24). Jewish mystics stressed the mortal dangers of the ascent to see God's throne; they had to know special passwords, and many did not know enough to survive their purported ascent through the spirit realms (see especially *3 Enoch and the *rabbis). But some apocalypses allow that angels could immediately lift one into the heavens (*2 Baruch, *Similitudes of Enoch, 2 Enoch, Testament of Abraham). Like Ezekiel, John is simply caught up immediately by God's Spirit.

4:3. For this description of the throne, see Ezekiel 1:26, 28 and 10:1. (Thrones indicated the ruler's dignity and were generally approached by several steps; their bases could portray peoples subdued by the ruler.) This simple description contrasts with the Roman emperor's pomp. It also contrasts with other elaborations of heavenly palaces (1 Enoch 14), the magnitude of majesty (e.g., the later *rabbis' crowning angel is a five hundred years' journey tall), or a tour of earth, heaven and hell (especially in later works); John does not even elaborate by weaving together other available *Old Testament throne imagery (cf., e.g., Dan 7 in 1 Enoch 14).

4:4. "Elders" were those with authority in Old Testament cities and later Jewish communities who could function as representatives for their communities (e.g., Deut 21:6); see Isaiah 24:23. In the art of Asia Minor, a few priests could be used to represent thousands of worshipers. The number "twenty-four" has been related to the twenty-four books Jewish writers assigned to the Hebrew canon, to the twelve tribes plus the twelve *apostles and so forth, but it almost certainly alludes to the twenty-four orders of priests. These orders were fixed in the *Old Testament (1 Chron 24—25), continued in the *New Testament period and were still commented on by later rabbis and in later inscriptions. The faithful dead are thus portrayed as priests offering worship to God (Rev 1:6). (Jewish *apocalyptic literature often overlapped images of the future age with the present heaven for the righteous dead.)

Greek accounts sometimes portrayed deities as appearing in white (e.g., Demeter and Kore); at least some ancient thinkers, like *Pythagoras and some *rabbis, associated white with good and black with evil. This contrast no doubt arose in ancient thought through the contrast between day and night, the latter being more associated with witchcraft and (in Jewish thought) demons.

Romans and often Jews buried the dead in white. In Jewish tradition, angels were nearly always garbed in gleaming white. More significant here is the widespread tradition of worshipers dressing in white (3:4). Jewish teachers portrayed Israel as crowned at the revelation at Sinai; the righteous were sometimes viewed as crowned in heaven. (The Ascension of Isaiah has the righteous crowned, robed and enthroned in heaven, but it may well be a Christian work; the Odes of Solomon, which has a catching up to heaven by the Spirit—cf. 4:2—is a Christian work. But it is not always easy to distinguish early Christian works from Jewish works revised with Christian interpolations.) But the crowns here are probably victors' crowns for those who persevered to death (see comment on 2:10; 3:11). (Many Jewish traditions speak of a heavenly assembly—in the *rabbis, a legislative or judicial body—composed of angels or deceased scholars; the antecedents of the image go back to the angelic court of God in the Old Testament and the Canaanite images of El's pantheon of seventy gods, replaced by the angels of the seventy nations in Jewish tradition.)

The arrangement is undoubtedly significant. Greek choruses would often sing or dance in circles; amphitheaters surrounded stages; and the Jewish *Sanhedrin sat in a semicircle with the high priest in the middle.

4:5. The special effects rehearse the glory of God's self-revelation at Sinai (Ex 19:16; cf. Ezek 1:4, 13). Some *apocalyptic texts report the sources of lightnings and thunderings in particular levels of heaven.

4:6-7. The "sea of glass" (15:2) alludes to the sea in Solomon's temple (1 Kings 7:23; 2 Chron 4:2, 6). It had always been natural to speak figuratively of God's heavenly temple (e.g., Ps 11:4), given the ancient Near Eastern tradition of the earthly temple reflecting the heavenly one. John's emphasis on worship leads to a portrayal of God's throne room in exclusively temple terms: an altar of incense (5:8), an altar of sacrifice (6:9), the ark (11:19; cf. 15:5-8), which functioned as God's throne in the Old Testament, and so forth. The crystal firmament derives from Ezekiel 1:22. The cherubim were covered with eyes in Ezekiel 10:12; the four creatures had four faces in Ezekiel 1:10 (where, however, each creature had all the features). Ezekiel's imagery may be intentionally figurative (cf. 1 Chron 12:8) but may draw on Babylonian throne and temple imagery and indicate a God greater than any pagans could have conceived; cf. also 1 Kings 7:29.

4:8. Ezekiel also spoke of the six wings (Ezek 1:11). The trisagion ("Holy, holy, holy") is from Isaiah 6:3, where seraphim—fiery, holy angels modeled after the cherubim of the tabernacle—surround God's throne in the Jerusalem temple, symbolizing his universal glory (Is 6:3) and demonstrating the impurity of sinful mortals like the prophet (Is 6:5). Later Jewish texts also employ the biblical imagery of these creatures and this song, which came into use in *synagogue and later *church liturgy as well. One may contrast the permanently appointed imperial cult choir at Pergamum, where thirty-six members were to sing hymns in honor of the deified Augustus.

4:9-10. Prostration on one's face was a form of homage offered to gods and rulers in antiquity.

4:11. The emperor Domitian demanded worship as "our Lord and God" but never claimed the role of Creator. Jesus receives the same words of honor in John 20:28.

5:1-7
The Passover Lamb and the Scroll

5:1. Legal documents were sealed, often with seven seals imprinted with the attestations of seven witnesses. (The wax seals would have to be broken to loose the strings beneath them, which wrapped the scroll and guaranteed that it had not been opened and thus altered.) This form was used for contract deeds and wills; it became increasingly common in Roman documents of the period, and some Palestinian Jewish documents of this sort have been recovered. Scrolls were normally written on only one side of a papyrus sheet, reserving the outside for the title or address; but this scroll is particularly full and written on both sides (cf. Ezek 2:9-10). The writing side was called the *recto*, where the fibers were horizontal and easier for writing; the *verso* was used only when the *recto* had inadequate space. Documents written on both sides are rare enough to have a technical name, an opisthograph.

5:2-3. See Isaiah 6:8 for a similar call.

5:4. Loud wailing was normally reserved for intense mourning, such as for a person's death.

5:5. Lions were used on Torah shrines (containers which housed law scrolls) in early Jewish art and were regarded as figures of strength and authority, but a more direct background lies at hand. The "lion of Judah" alludes to Genesis 49:9-10, which predicted the Davidic dynasty and was understood messianically in later Jewish literature (*4 Ezra, the *rabbis). "Root of David" alludes to Isaiah 11:1 and 10 (Jesse was David's father), which suggests that the *Messiah would come after the Davidic line had seemed cut off. The image is also used messianically in later texts (e.g., Ecclesiasticus), and both these images are combined in the *Dead Sea Scrolls. *Apocalypses and other texts often included dialogue with heavenly particpants in the scenes revealed (e.g., Dan 7:16; Zech 4:11; 5:2).

5:6. Whereas a lion was the ultimate symbol of power in ancient views of the animal kingdom (cf. also, e.g., Is 35:9; 65:25), a lamb was considered powerless (cf. Is 40:11); a slaughtered lamb was a dramatic contrast with a reigning lion (cf. Is 53:7). Lambs were associated with a variety of sacrifices, but in Revelation this figure especially represents the Passover lamb, who delivers God's people from the plagues of the following chapters (cf. Ex 12:12-13).

Many texts mention lamb's horns, but the imagery of horns as symbols for authority is rooted in Daniel 8. The seven eyes ranging throughout the earth are from Zechariah 3:9 and 4:10. Because these may refer to angels (the image in Zechariah is modeled after Persian royal emissaries) in Zechariah 1:10 and 6:5-7, Revelation may apply the image to the seven traditional archangels of Judaism (8:2), subservient to *Christ, rather than representing the *Spirit of God. At any rate, the eyes in Zechariah are God's eyes; here they belong to the Lord Jesus.

5:7. Although Revelation is full of "sevens," it may be significant that Roman wills were normally sealed with seven seals; seals on legal documents guaranteed that no one had opened or tampered with them. A will could not be opened until the death of the person whose will it was could be attested; if a will is in view here, it is significant that it is the lamb who has been *slain* who is worthy to open it. (The book may well be the lamb's book of life; cf. 3:5; 20:12.) At any rate, under Roman law a document was valid only when the addressee had received it; it is thus ready to take effect.

5:8-14
Worshiping the Lamb

5:8. Prostration was particularly a sign of worship before gods and kings in antiquity; Jewish texts usually reserved it for God himself. The image of prayers as incense was not uncommon (e.g., Ps 141:2), but here it alludes to the altar of incense and its censer in the heavenly temple (Rev 8:3). In this context, the harps probably indicate worship as in the charismatic, Levitical temple choir of old (1 Chron 25:1, 3, 6; 2 Chron 5:12; 29:25; Neh 12:27; cf. 1 Sam 10:5).

5:9-10. Received in a context of worship (1:10) and offered to congregations presumably gathered in worship (chaps. 2—3), visions of heavenly worship would encourage the *church on earth that they stood in continuity with a much greater chorus than their persecutors in the imperial cult could muster. The *Dead Sea Scrolls show that earthly worshipers could envision themselves participating in heavenly worship with the angels. Inspired, spontaneous psalms composed by the temple worship leaders had been called "new songs" in the *Old Testament (Ps 33:3; 40:3; 96:1; 98:1; 144:9; 149:1).

The particular praise reflects the redemption of Israel from Egypt by the blood of the Passover lamb (see also comment on Rev 1:6), except that the people of God now explicitly include representatives from every people, celebrating redemption in their multiethnic, diverse styles of worship. Further, they would finally reign over the rest of the earth; Jewish traditions portrayed Israel as receiving the *kingdom and reigning over the nations in the end time.

5:11. Some Jewish texts were given to citing fantastically large numbers of people (e.g., they listed more slain in one battle than all the people who have lived in history); more reasonably, such texts estimated even larger numbers of angels. "Ten thousand" was the largest single number used in Greek, so "ten thousands of ten thousands" (myriads of myriads) is the author's way of calling them innumerable.

5:12. An early-second-century Roman governor confirms that Christians worshiped *Christ as a god. It is interesting that what became the official text of the Passover celebration, praising God for redemption from Egypt, also lists seven praises (as does a *Qumran text); John's predilection for sevens is broader than and independent of the Passover image, however, so it may be only coincidental.

5:13-14. Although the *Old Testament and Judaism believed that the world would submit to God's rule wholly in the end time, they recognized that all the elements of the universe answered to his authority in the present.

6:1-8
The Four Horsemen

The imagery is adapted from the angelic horsemen sent by God to patrol the earth in Zechariah 1:8-11 and 6:1-8, though used in a different way. (Some scholars suggest that the horsemen portray angels of judgment, others symbols for Christ coming in judgments, and still others simply symbols for judgments in general.) Although divine judgments in history are a major *Old Testament theme, pagans also recognized and would have understood John's point; most cultures in history have recognized the existence of divine judgments. Jewish *apocalyptic traditions associated some of these judgments, such as war and famine, with the time just preceding the end of the age; cf. Matthew 24:6-8.

6:1. A document could not be opened until all the seals were broken (i.e., in Revelation, after 8:1); the seals (in this case judgments) witness the validity of the document's contents. (Perhaps, as in the Old Testament covenant, heaven and earth are called to witness; cf. Deut 30:19; Ps 50:4.)

6:2. The very image of an archer on a white horse would strike terror into the heart of a pro-Roman reader. The only mounted archers of antiquity were the Parthians, whose tactics and skills had made them Rome's most feared enemies; old Persian armies, whose heirs the Parthians were, always included sacred white horses. Although the Old Testament uses the "bow" as a symbol of judgment by battle more generally, Roman readers would think of this eastern nation that had defeated them in some recent wars; Parthians' skill as archers was common knowledge. Other contemporary *apocalyptic writers (*Similitudes of Enoch) also suggested a dreaded Parthian invasion, hence ancient readers would have readily understood that this horseman meant conquest and war.

6:3-4. The "sword" was often a symbol of judgment by war in the *Old Testament and later literature, and red was the color most associated with war and bloodshed (hence the "red planet" is named Mars for the Roman god of war). The bloody unrest of A.D. 68-69, when three emperors were successively killed, would have been one illustration of the principle here.

6:5-6. The "scales" indicate rationing, or at least the caution of merchants to get every cent the food is worth. Barley and wheat were basic staples. Because a quart of wheat was a day's sustenance, and a denarius was a day's wage, a man with a family would have to buy the cheaper barley instead. Even then, three quarts of barley was hardly enough daily food for a whole family to subsist on; in the many peasant families with large numbers of children, several children would die. The famine also created a high inflation rate: this wheat costs more than ten times the average price of wheat.

Oil and wine were widely used, but not essential like wheat or barley. Oil was especially used for anointing the head, washing the body and lighting lamps; wine was mixed with water (one part wine for two to three parts water) for meals. The selective continuance of such items of relatively secondary importance while staples were barely obtainable would reinforce the reality of divine judgment. Because inflation was high at the end of the first century and some readers were no doubt aware of Domitian's unpopular restriction of land for vineyards in the provinces, readers would have readily resonated with the terror such prophecies implied. Asia Minor was hit especially hard by economic troubles during Domitian's reign.

6:7-8. This final specter may resemble the angel of death of Jewish tradition. Lists of judgments such as this horseman brought are common in the *Old Testament prophets (e.g., Jer 14:12; 24:10; 27:8; Ezek 6:11; 7:15; 12:16) and, less related in form, some judgment lists in the *Sibylline Oracles; this list is closest to Ezekiel 14:21.

6:9-11
The Fifth Seal

Comfortable people may not like the language of this passage, but oppressed and suffering people who trust God can resonate with the promise of vindication, as in the *Old Testament and often throughout history.

6:9. The blood of sacrifices was poured out at the base of the altar (Lev 4:7, 18, 25, 34; 5:9; 8:15; 9:9); the martyrs are thus viewed as sacrifices, like the Passover lamb of Revelation 5:6. (Paschal lambs had come to be viewed as sacrificial in some sense. Martyrs were also viewed as sacrifices in, e.g., *4 Maccabees and Phil 2:7.) Souls were "visible" to recipients of *apocalypses, due to the seers' visionary state.

6:10. The very fact of their shed

blood (6:9) cries out for the vindication of retribution (Gen 4:10; see comment on Mt 23:35); as in the Old Testament, a prayer for vengeance for corporate sin was ultimately a prayer for the vindication of the righteous and of God's name. Justice could ultimately be done, and the oppressed delivered, only when God arose to judge the earth. "How long?" was common in Old Testament prayers of entreaty (e.g., Ps 6:3; 13:1; 80:4), including prayers for vindication (e.g., Ps 79:5, 10; Zech 1:12); it also could address the duration of a judgment (Is 6:11; Jer 47:6).

6:11. Other Jewish texts also include prayers for vengeance and protests over delays (6:10); the souls of the righteous in *4 Ezra (probably from the same decade as Revelation) ask how long until the end and are told that they must wait until the full number of righteous dead is completed. Jesus and Paul had also earlier stressed that the good news must be preached to all nations—with the attendant suffering for witnesses involved in such proclamation—before the end. On white robes see comment on 4:4.

6:12-17
The Sixth Seal

Although cosmic, cataclysmic language is sometimes used for God's judgments in history (e.g., an already-fulfilled judgment in *Sibylline Oracles; cosmic exaggerations of Sinai phenomena in *Pseudo-Philo; cf. Ps 18; Jer 4:20-28), the language of this passage lends itself most naturally to the view that it, like the sixth and seventh trumpets and vials, represents the end of the age (as cosmic destruction generally does in the *Old Testament prophets and Jewish literature).

6:12-13. An Old Testament prophecy associated the end of the age with a powerful earthquake (Zech 14:4-5; cf. Ezek 38:20; Amos 8:8); because severe earthquakes had wrought devastation in first-century Asia Minor, this announcement would have special impact on the readers. Darkness was also an Old Testament judgment (Ex 10:21-23; Is 50:3), especially the judgment of the end (Is 13:9-10; 24:23; Ezek 32:7-8; Amos 5:18; 8:9; cf. *4 Ezra). The stars may symbolize angelic hosts (12:4; Is 24:21; Dan 8:10; 10:13), but in this context they probably depict simply the cosmic scope of the judgment (Is 34:4). The graphic language is not meant as literal astronomy: disappearing or shaken stars were used as poetic language for great devastations such as wars (Sibylline Oracles, *Petronius; cf. Is 13:10, 17).

6:14. A reader would unroll a scroll with the right hand to read, rolling up again the part just read with the left; the language here reflects Isaiah 34:4, which is also echoed in other Jewish judgment oracles (Sibylline Oracles). This sort of language was normally reserved for the end of the age.

6:15-16. The *Old Testament and *apocalypses also speak of judgment across social classes; the readers could be encouraged that God would ultimately vindicate them against the emperor and his governors who now judged them. Hiding in the rocks and crying for the mountains to conceal them from God's wrath reflects Hosea 10:8; cf. Isaiah 2:10 and 19-20.

6:17. This verse reflects especially Joel 2:11; cf. Malachi 3:2, referring to the day of judgment.

7:1-8
The Sealing of 144,000 Servants

One can take the 144,000 either consistently literally (literally twelve thousand male Jewish virgins from each tribe—14:4) or consistently symbolically (the spiritual people of God, not literally 144,000). (Those who take the number but not the ethnicity, gender and sexual history literally are inconsistent.) Against taking it literally is Revelation's usage elsewhere of "servants" (1:1; 6:11), suggesting that they constitute the whole of the saved community (7:3-4). But whether they represent the innumerable multitude of 7:9 or the restored remnant of ethnic Israel remains debated.

"After this I saw" (7:1) means that this vision follows the preceding one, not necessarily that the events it describes do (see comment on 4:1); if 6:12-17 represents the end of the age, 7:1-8 must precede that event chronologically (7:3), perhaps concurrent with the whole of 6:1-11.

7:1. *Gentiles often personified the elements of nature themselves or recognized gods attached to them; Jewish people believed that God had delegated his authority over various features of nature (including winds) to angels under his command (e.g., in *Jubilees; cf. Ps 148:1-12). "Four corners" of the earth was meant figuratively, even in ancient times. A few people thought that the world was sperical, but most people viewed it as circular; "four corners" was nevertheless conventional speech, as was the idea of four winds from the four directions of heaven (probably viewed as angels even in Zech 6:5). The winds had both positive and negative effects in ancient sources. According to some views, the wind carried along the sun and moon chariots (*1 Enoch 72:5; 73:2), or God founded the heavens on the winds (1 Enoch, Joseph and Asenath), and the stoppage of winds could signal the advent of a new age (Sibylline Oracles, on the postdiluvian era). Like writers today, the biblical writers used the language conventional to the *genre in which they were writing; this could include, as here, symbolic imagery.

7:2. In the most popular ancient conception, Helios drove his sun-chariot in a regular course above the earth, rising from the gates of the east and descending into the west to return by its path under the earth; the earth-circle was surrounded on all sides by the river Oceanus. Jewish people naturally modified the sun god into an angel; but any angel that would rise in the orbit of the sun would have been recognized as superior to the greatest of the kings of the earth.

"Seal" refers to the impress of a signet ring; an official who wished to delegate his authority for a task to a representative would allow that subordinate to use his signet ring.

7:3. Like documents or merchandise sealed and stamped to guarantee their contents and prevent tampering, God's servants were to be marked off as his (cf. Is 44:5). God had previously protected his people in Goshen during the plagues (Ex 8:28; 9:4; 11:7; see comment on Rev 5:6); the idea of a protecting sign is also an *Old Testament image (Gen 4:15; Is 66:19). Here it is taken directly from Ezekiel 9:4-6, where judgment could not begin until the foreheads of the righteous (those who mourned over the sin of their land) were marked. The forehead and the hand (Ex 13:9, 16; 28:38; Deut 6:8; 11:18) were the most natural and obvious parts of the body for this marking because they were most directly exposed to view.

With the possible exception of Genesis 4:15, all these Old Testament passages probably meant the sign symbolically (despite more literal postexilic Jewish practice of *tefillin,* phylacteries); Ezekiel 9:6 certainly did not mean a humanly visible mark, and Revelation presumably means it in the same sense as Ezekiel. In Hebrew, Ezekiel's mark was the Hebrew letter *tav;* in ancient script it looked like, and rabbis compared it with, the Greek letter *chi*—similar to English *x*—which some Christian commentators have compared (perhaps wishfully) with the cross sign. Comparisons have also been made with branding animals; with the occasional but well-documented tattooing of slaves and, later, soldiers; with religious tattooing (e.g., in Mithraism); with spiritual circumcision (circumcision was called a seal; and with the divine imprint on humans (*Philo), here applied specifically to those who live according to that image. See comment on Revelation 13:16-18 and on Galatians 6:17; cf. *4 Ezra 6:5; 10:23; *Psalms of Solomon 15:6-9; and *Testament of Job 5:2.

7:4. Because this is the full number of God's servants (7:3), the righteous (1:1; 2:20; 22:6), the number and ethnic designation may be meant figuratively for true followers of Israel's God (followers of Jesus; cf. 2:9; 3:9; 21:2, 14). Whether this number is meant figuratively or literally, however, the allusion is clearly to the *Old Testament and universal Jewish conception of Israel's restoration, which is pictured, as generally, in terms of the restoration of the remnant (survivors) of the twelve tribes.

7:5-8. The normal Jewish understanding was that the twelve tribes would inherit the land together (Ezek 48). Yet by counting Joseph and Manasseh (the tribe of Joseph was usually broken down into two tribes, represented by his sons Manasseh and Ephraim) without omitting Levi, Revelation has to omit one of the tribes, and omits Dan, the first in Ezekiel's list (48:1), in order to maintain the number twelve. (Jewish commentators as early as the second century associated Dan with idolatry, but no emphasis on that special association can be documented this early. Dan's sins [Judg 18:30; 1 Kings 12:29; Amos 8:14; cf. *Jubilees 44:28-29] are not the only ones mentioned in the Old Testament, and the association with the serpent [Gen 49:16-17] is too remote here.) This omission may underline the symbolic nature of John's point in the whole passage; one tribe may be omitted to indicate the danger of apostasy even among the people of God (cf. Jn 6:70; 1 Jn). The sequence of tribes itself is probably not significant—it varied considerably in the Old Testament.

The twelve tribes no longer existed as separate entities in the first century; with few exceptions, only Judah, Benjamin and Levi were recognized as ancestors, and today even most of those distinctions are no longer certain. The exact number, twelve thousand from each tribe, is another indication of the symbolic nature of the passage—twelve was the number of the people of God in Jewish texts (e.g., *Dead Sea Scrolls), and 144,000 is 12 × 12 × 10 × 10 × 10. Symbolic numbers were standard fare in Jewish views of the future. (Some numerical improbabilities worked their way into novels, too, e.g., the seven virgins who waited on Asenath, all born the same night she was; but symbolic numbers were standard in *apocalyptic texts; see especially comment on the times of Revelation 12.)

7:9-17
The Multitude of Overcomers Before the Throne

This section may represent a different group than the one pictured in 7:1-8, or another picture of the same group now in heaven (double versions of visions sometimes occur in the *Old Testament, too; cf. Gen 41:25-27; interpretations of visions also appear, e.g., in Daniel, *4 Ezra and *2 Baruch).

7:9-12. White robes were appropriate for worship in the temple and were also used for the worship of gods in Asia Minor. Palm branches were especially used in the celebration of the Feast of Tabernacles. In the future, the remnant of all nations would go up to Jerusalem to worship at the Feast of Tabernacles (Zech 14:16); as in *apocalyptic texts, the earthly future realm is in some sense presently fulfilled in heaven. Palm branches celebrated the victory of Israel's exodus from Egypt, and the feast commemorated God's faithfulness to them during their wanderings in the wilderness, when they were totally dependent on him.

Some scholars have suggested that these multitudes are the martyrs or martyr *church of 6:11, viewed from another perspective. "Innumerable" meant that the crowd was huge, too many to count—not infinite (*3 Maccabees 4:17; it could also represent a number so great that it could be pictured as the sands of the sea in number, as in Judith 2:20).

7:13-14. Jewish teachers sometimes asked questions they knew their *disciples could not answer; the disciples then responded by asking for the answer. The same teaching technique is employed here. Jewish *apocalypses and their occasional Roman analogues often included angelic guides (e.g., *1 Enoch and 3 Baruch) who asked the mortal observer rhetorical questions to guide him to a truer understanding (e.g., *4 Ezra and Testament of Abraham; cf. Dan 8:13-14; 12:6-7); in other texts confused visionaries simply had to ask to begin with (Dan 7:16; 12:8; 4 Ezra) or wait for an interpretation (Dan 8:16).

"The great tribulation" refers to Daniel 12:1, the period of great suffering that God's people were to experience before the end of the age. Making robes white with blood is clearly a ritual rather than visual image: sacrificial blood purified utensils for worship in the *Old Testament (see comment on Heb 9:21-22), and white was the color of robes required for worship in the *New Testament period.

7:15-16. God's tabernacle as a refuge over them directly echoes Isaiah 4:5-6, which in turn alludes to a new exodus of salvation in the future time. When God redeemed his people from Egypt and they wandered in the wilderness (the time commemorated in the Feast of Tabernacles; see comment on Rev 7:9-12), he made such a cloud over them as Isaiah describes. Revelation also borrows the language of Isaiah 49:10 (again the salvation of the future age); cf. Psalm 121:5-6. On God's throne room in heaven being portrayed as a temple, see comment on Revelation 4:6-7.

7:17. This verse alludes to Isaiah 25:8 (in the context of the *messianic banquet at the *resurrection at the end of the age) and 49:10 (in the age to come). For the imagery of the shepherd (here graphically juxtaposed with the lamb), see the introduction to John 10:1-18.

8:1-5
Preparing for the Trumpet Plagues

8:1. There are a number of possible ways to interpret "silence" here. In this context of worship (7:9-12) and intercession (6:9-11; 8:4) in heaven, "silence" could mean a brief delay in God's reception of his people's prayers for vindication (Ps 50:3, 21; 83:1), or silencing heaven's praises to receive his people's prayers (Rev 8:4), as in some later Jewish texts.

Perhaps more likely, it could be a form of awed worship (Ps 65:1) or perhaps of fear, grief or shame, as with the muzzled mouths of the guilty with nothing to say in their defense at the judgment (Hab 2:20; Zeph 1:7; Zech 2:13; cf. Ps 31:17-18; 76:8-10; Is 23:2; 41:1; 47:5). Silence could also characterize the end of the present world to form a new world (*4 Ezra and *2 Baruch; cf. Pseudo-Philo) or (often in ancient literature) the end of a speech, conversation or *announcement; it was also the appropriate state of a court before the accuser began to speak.

8:2. Trumpets were used for celebrations, to call sacred or military assemblies, and as alerts, often warning of impending invasions. It is in this last sense that the prophets usually employed the image, and this is probably also why Revelation uses it. Although John undoubtedly would have used "seven" anyway (given his three sets of seven judgments each), commentators note that series of seven trumpeters appear in the *Old Testament (Josh 6:6, 13), probably regularly in the temple cult (1 Chron 15:24; Neh 12:41). Between the Old Testament and the *New Testament Judaism had settled on seven archangels (adding five to the two important angels named in Daniel), and they are probably in view here.

8:3. The angel fulfills a task assigned to a priest in the earthly temple. For the heavenly temple in Revelation, see comment on 4:6-7; as in some other Jewish texts (including in the Old Testament, in Ps 141:2), prayers are presented as incense (some texts portrayed them also as sacrifices). For the heavenly temple in Jewish texts in general, see comment on Hebrews 8:1-5.

8:4-5. In this context, the continual prayers of the saints for vengeance (6:9-11) are the direct cause of their eventual vindication through judgments on the earth (8:6—9:21). On the image of atmospheric phenomena caused by angelic activity, see comment on 4:5; cf. 11:19 and 16:18.

8:6-12
The First Four Trumpet Plagues

The sorts of judgments characterizing the judgments of the trumpets and bowls are mainly taken directly from the ten plagues of the exodus (except that they are numerically adjusted to seven; see comment on Jn 2:11, the first of probably seven signs in John). As in other Jewish texts (e.g., *Pseudo-Philo, Artapanus), the sequence and even number of the plagues is not important for the point of the image. Some of the plagues are echoed in other judgment texts (especially *Sibylline Oracles) but never as systematically as here.

8:6. See comment on 8:2.

8:7. This plague echoes the seventh plague in Exodus 9:24-25.

8:8-9. Waters running with blood would normally indicate war (e.g., Is 15:9), but these verses also echo the first plague in Exodus 7:20-21. The mountain hurled into the sea characterizes the sort of imagery standard in this type of literature (e.g., the burning star hurled into the sea in a roughly contemporary oracle in Sibylline Oracles). (The suggested parallel to Babylon as a burning mountain in Jer 51:25, 42 is not as obvious, although it would have been more available than the Sibylline Oracles; it is doubtful if either Revelation or the Sibylline Oracles depends on the other, but the writers of both had access to Jeremiah.)

This plague addresses contamination of the water supply, effecting not only many swift deaths by dehydration but also long-term devastation by destruction of Egypt's irrigation and fishing

(Ex 7:18) resources.

8:10-11. Like the preceding plague, this judgment alludes to the poisoned water of Exodus 7:20-21, but through a sort of poisoning or embittering agent called "wormwood" (Jer 9:15; 23:15; cf. Jer 8:14), often used figuratively (for idolatry—Deut 29:18; fruits of adultery—Prov 5:4; suffering—Lam 3:19). This plague strikes local freshwater supplies and would naturally worry John's readers in Asia, especially in Laodicea (see comment on Rev 3:15-16).

8:12. This plague echoes the ninth plague in Exodus 10:22-23; many ancient texts speak of darkness as a dreaded judgment, and the *Old Testament (see comment on Rev 6:12-13) and some other Jewish texts also associate it with the end time.

8:13—9:11
The Fifth Trumpet Plague

8:13. The announcement of three impending woes indicates that as negative as the first four trumpet plagues were, the worst is yet to come. "Woe" often begins a new oracle in *1 Enoch and probably serves a similar function here.

The eagle was a symbol of imperial Rome carried by the legions and used on Herod's temple, but that symbolism is probably irrelevant here. Perhaps more to the point, eagles were used as messengers in some texts (4 Baruch); they could symbolize God's protection (Rev 12:14), or—most likely—the term here means (as it often does, including in the *LXX) "vulture," indicating a bird of prey (see 19:17), and thus imminent doom. "Midheaven" (NASB, NRSV) is the level of heaven between God's throne and the lowest atmosphere (in the minimal three-heaven scheme of some ancients—on which see comment on 2 Cor 12:2-4—but also in some other schemes, e.g., in 2 Enoch).

9:1-2. Many Jewish traditions spoke of evil angels imprisoned in dungeons or rivers, awaiting their time to come out and wreak havoc. Some ancient writers assumed that the "abyss" (NIV, TEV; "bottomless pit"—NASB, KJV, NRSV) was a real geographical place that could be found on earth (*1 Enoch); angels were assigned over such sites and given keys. The *Dead Sea Scrolls also spoke of the wicked as "men of" or "sons of the pit" (probably meaning those destined for death in the grave). Most pagans held stars to be divinities, and many Jews held them to be angels; stars could naturally symbolize angels in Jewish texts, as in this case. John exploits the standard imagery to make his point.

9:3. This plague recalls the eighth plague in Exodus 10:12, the locusts; but maintaining the imagery characteristic of much *apocalyptic and prophetic revelation, John's vision transmutes these locusts into something far more terrifying. Joel describes an imminent locust plague in terms of the armies of the final war (1:4—2:27) and also describes the final war (3:9-17). John borrows Joel's imagery here to amplify the imagery of a locust plague into a terrible invasion.

9:4. See comment on 7:3. Ordinary locusts would have feasted on the vegetation and left the people alone.

9:5. Scorpions' stings were among the most intense pains (1 Kings 12:11; 2 Chron 10:14); but a pain lasting five months (9:10, unless this is simply the duration of the plague; one commentator says that five months fits the approximate lifespan of a normal kind of locust) was unheard-of. Jewish texts often included scorpions as one of God's means of judgment.

9:6. Only the severest sufferings

prompted a preference for death over life (Jer 8:3); but even death will be withheld during this plague.

9:7. An invasion of locusts could be described as warhorses (Joel 2:4), and horses could be described as being as numerous as locusts (Jer 51:27; cf. 51:14). The crowns might reflect prior military exploits. The image of human-faced scorpions derived from nightmarish traditions from the East, and Mediterranean zodiacs eventually applied it to Sagittarius, who was often portrayed with long hair (see comment on 9:8). Although the image is not meant literally, it draws on the most terrible, repressed images of that culture's unconscious fears to evoke horror at the impending judgments.

9:8. Joel 1:6 described locusts with "teeth like lions" to emphasize their destructiveness to the crops and everything else. In Joel, the image would terrify an agrarian society; in Revelation, it would remind readers of the lion's proverbial ferocity. The "hair like women" would be a more obvious allusion to most of John's readers: everyone in the Roman Empire knew that "barbarians" outside the Empire, unlike most people in Greco-Roman society, had long hair. In the context of a military invasion, the readers would immediately think of the Parthians (or, in *apocalyptic terms, perhaps the evil spiritual realities behind them). By way of illustration, the reigning emperor Domitian's father was reported—perhaps fictitiously—to have joked about the Parthians' long hair in view of a long-tailed comet portending his death.

9:9. The "noise of chariots" is borrowed from the military imagery for locusts in Joel 2:5; the swarms would be so intense that they would sound like an invading army, a sound great enough to make a land quake (Jer 8:16). The scales of a kind of locust's thorax are compared with scaled armor in a later Jewish text; here John uses a more updated armor image.

9:10. Their tails may be mentioned simply because that was the weapon of scorpions (9:5), but the reverse could also be true; scorpions could be mentioned because of the tails. It may be of interest that the Parthians (9:8) had become famous for their rearward archery: they had retreated up hills mounted on horseback, and when unwary Roman legions had followed them, the Parthians had released a backward hail of arrows, wiping out several legions before the Romans learned not to follow them up hills.

9:11. "Abaddon" is a Hebrew name for the lowest depths of the earth, the realm of the dead (cf. Job 31:12; Ps 88:11; Prov 27:20); the *Dead Sea Scrolls also linked the "spirit of Abaddon" with the "angel of the pit." "Apollyon" means "destruction" in Greek. (Some scholars have secondarily connected the name to Apollo, a Greek deity one of whose totems was the locust, and whose incarnation the emperor claimed to be; cf. Rev 2:18. Because Apollyon as a name is otherwise unattested, it is not impossible that readers in Asia could have suspected this allusion; in this case, the emperor's supposed patron deity is in reality an evil angel who, in the sovereignty of God, will be used against him; cf. Ex 12:12; Num 33:4. But the allusion is not altogether clear.) The final, terrifying touch to this description of an army with elements from Joel's locusts, from Parthians and from scorpions is that these are the armies of hell, sent by death itself to fill its bowels.

9:12-21
The Sixth Trumpet Plague

Parthians were Rome's most feared

enemies in this period. They were portrayed as untrustworthy, and the authority of their monarchs was absolute. Older Greek prophecies about an eastern invasion of the Roman Empire still made some Romans nervous, and the Jewish *Sibylline Oracles prophesied that Nero would return, leading Parthian hordes in vengeance on Rome. (Many Jewish people lived in Parthian territory, and many Jews in the Roman Empire felt no more allegiance to Rome than they would have to Parthia; in the Jewish-Roman war of 66-70 many Jews expected Parthia to intervene on their behalf, but their hopes were disappointed.)

9:12. See comment on 8:13.

9:13. On the temple imagery, see comment on 4:6-7.

9:14. Ancient literature indicates that it was common knowledge that the river Euphrates (16:12) was, above all else, the traditional boundary between the Roman and Parthian empires. Some other Jewish texts speak of fallen angels being bound in the depths of various seas, able to be released only at the command of God or one of his angels.

9:15. For all their recognition of demonic forces in this age, *apocalyptic writers recognized also the standard Jewish doctrine that God ultimately rules all of history. Casualty statistics like this one are also familiar in Jewish judgment oracles (see the *Sibylline Oracles).

9:16. Parthians were noted horsemen; in contrast to Rome, whose only cavalry contingents were drawn from its auxiliary (non-Roman) units, the Parthians were renowned for their cavalry. "Two hundred million" would be a huge standing army even today (nearly the entire population of the United States, almost four times that of Great Britain, over twice that of Nigeria, and eight times that of Canada); in the first century it may have represented more than the population of the entire world.

9:17-18. The "dark blue" (NIV; "hyacinth"—NASB; or "sapphire"—NRSV) might allude to the color of the smoke of sulfur's flame. Cf. 9:7-8 for the source of the image of horses and lions; lions were considered the most ferocious and regal of beasts, which no one cared to meet. In a widely read Jewish wisdom book, a writer had declared that God could have punished idolatry by sending lions or newly created, fire-breathing and smoke-belching monsters (Wisdom of Solomon 11:17-20). But again this imagery may be mixed with the threat of a Parthian invasion: Parthian archers often used flaming arrows.

9:19. The power "in their tails" may allude to scorpions or to the Parthian cavalry's rearward archery (see comment on 9:10).

9:20-21. Jewish people commonly regarded the unrepentance of the world in the face of obvious judgments (e.g., Ex 7:22-23) as a sign of stupidity. (Even some pagan philosophers pointed out that divine judgments were acts of mercy, to bring the wicked to *repentance, as well as acts of justice; in this view they agreed with the *Old Testament—e.g., Ex 8:10; 9:14, 29; 10:2; 14:4; Amos 4:6-11.) Old Testament prophets and later Jewish writers frequently ridiculed the worship of idols (cf. Rev 2:14, 20) that were less powerful than those who made them (e.g., Ps 135:15-18; Is 46:6-7). That pagans worshiped demons was also widely accepted in Jewish circles (e.g., *1 Enoch; 1 Cor 10:20). Idolatry and immorality were standard parts of Greco-Roman culture; thieves and sorcerers were, however, considered dangerous by common consent.

10:1-7
The Mysteries of the End

10:1. Jewish literature pictures a number of angels as being as high as the highest heavens, often shining like the sun (2 Enoch; *3 Enoch; *rabbis; cf. Dan 10:6; cf. the Greek figure Atlas). Both evil angels (*1 Enoch) and good angels could be very tall. Sometimes they were crowned (e.g., 2 Enoch; 3 Enoch), in this case with a rainbow; in 3 Enoch, even the crown is more than a five-hundred-year journey high. (Sometimes such language was also used figuratively, e.g., for a particular high priest.) John borrows the imagery of his day for a powerful angel over creation (see comment on Rev 7:1).

10:2. The seals having been opened (6:1—8:1), the contents of the book may now be examined ("open"). The angel's enormity and his feet on both land and sea indicates how great his dominion is.

10:3-4. Something remains sealed (cf. 22:10), indicating that some mysteries must remain mysteries until the end (Deut 29:29). The thunders could be viewed as less ambiguous if they are identical with the contents of the book—10:2, 8-11—or, much less likely, if they are like seven commandments corresponding to the Ten Commandments, as Revelation's groups of seven plagues correspond to Exodus's ten plagues. On unspeakable revelations see comment on 2 Corinthians 12:2-4. The text implies that John is taking notes (as *rabbinic or Greek students sometimes did) or writing down what he hears and sees; one could write down visions or utterances as others were having them (e.g., * Testament of Job 51, a section admittedly of uncertain date).

10:5-6. Raising one's hand toward a god was used in solemn oath formulas in Greek culture as well as in the *Old Testament and later Jewish literature. Here John alludes to Daniel 12:7, where an angel lifted his hands toward heaven and swore by the one who lives forever that there would be only three and a half more years until the end; here this angel swears that the time has come, and there is no further delay. (Some *apocalyptic texts spoke of countable time itself ending, but the point here seems to be "time before the end," given Dan 12:7; cf. Rev 2:21; 6:11; 20:3; Hab 2:3.)

10:7. All the Old Testament promises, both of judgment and of restoration, came to a head in the day of the Lord.

10:8-11
A Bitter Message for the Nations

This account is based on Ezekiel 2:8-3:3, where a hand is extended to Ezekiel containing a scroll, written on both sides (cf. Rev 5:1) with a message of three kinds of judgment. Ezekiel ate the scroll, which tasted sweet to his mouth but was a message of judgment for Israel.

10:8-9. These verses are based on Ezekiel 2:8—3:3; another contemporary *apocalyptic writer (*4 Ezra) drew more loosely on the same imagery. Sin tasted sweet like honey but was poison because it led to judgment (Prov 5:3-4; cf. Num 5:23-31); but the sweetness here is the word of the Lord (cf. Prov 24:13-14; *rabbis), and the bitterness is the bitterness of judgment that John must proclaim. On an angel talking with the visionary, see comment on Revelation 7:13-14.

10:11. The Jewish Sibyl in the Sibylline Oracles conceived her task as prophesying concerning all nations (cf. Rev 11:2), but this was standard with many *Old Testament prophets, who uttered oracles against the nations, to which John's are much closer (Is 13—23; Jer 46—51; Ezek 25—32; Amos 1—2).

11:1-13
The Two Witnesses

John clearly uses *Old Testament language for prophets (Elijah, Moses) and a high priest and king (from Zechariah) to describe these witnesses. On a literal futuristic reading, they could refer to the new Moses and Elijah expected in Judaism; conversely, they could be read as joint aspects of the *church, as rulers and priests (Rev 1:6; 5:10), especially since this is the meaning of lampstands elsewhere in the book (1:20).

11:1. Measuring the courts of God's house (21:15) was one way of praising the magnificence of the building whose construction was meant as praise to God (Ps 48:12-13; Ezek 40:3—42:20; Zech 2:1-5; cf. the *Similitudes of Enoch, where paradise is measured). A "reed" (NIV, KJV) could be used as a surveyor's rule (hence "measuring rod"—NASB, NRSV, TEV).

11:2. The sanctuary had been trodden down before (Is 63:18; 1 Macc 3:45; 4:60), and its desolation was portrayed as the typical goal of pagans (Judith 9:8), but here only the outer court is trodden down. Yet the whole temple was destroyed in A.D. 70, and (with most scholars) Revelation was probably written in the 90s. Even the literal treading down of the outer sanctuary had taken place more than forty-two months before John's time, implying that the number was symbolic for the whole period from its devastation in some sense until its restoration (see comment on Rev 12:6).

If the heavenly temple is meant (11:19; see comment on 4:6), the outer court is meant symbolically. Perhaps as at *Qumran, the temple stands for God's chosen remnant (cf. 21:3). The outer court was the only court *Gentiles were allowed to enter. Although the literal outer court was in ruins like the rest of the temple, the reference here seems to be to some danger such as pagan spiritual domination over the *church as Israel's spiritual remnant (cf. 2:9; 3:9) or over the holy land or Jewish people, or to the lack of a temple; even while the temple stood, many felt that it was spiritually impure (e.g., *Dead Sea Scrolls).

11:3. On the 1,260 days see comment on 12:6; based on a 360-day year, this was the same as forty-two months or three and a half years (Daniel used all three figures). Sackcloth was proper *Old Testament apparel for mourning or *repentance; the two witnesses are apparently wailing over the sins of God's people (e.g., Joel 1:13; Jon 3:6; Joseph and Asenath; clothing for prophets in Ascension of Isaiah, etc.). Two witnesses was the minimum number acceptable under Old Testament law (Deut 17:6; 19:15).

11:4. The source of the image is clear: Zechariah 4:2-3 presented two seven-branched lampstands and two olive trees, which represented the two anointed ones (Zech 4:14): the king and the priest (Zech 6:13). In Zechariah's day they represented Zerubbabel and Joshua. (Thus *Qumran in some periods in its history stressed two future anointed figures, a *messianic king and an anointed priest.) John might connect the image with a kingdom and priests (Rev 1:6; 5:10).

That they "stand" (currently) could indicate, as some (e.g., the second-century North African Christian Tertullian) have suggested, an allusion to *Old Testament figures who did not die (cf. also *4 Ezra)—Elijah, Enoch (according to the most common reading of the Old Testament) and Moses (according to some Jewish storytellers, against the plain sense of Deut 34). They could also simply represent the *church, whose heavenly representatives are already before God (Rev 4:4; cf. Mt 18:10). The two anointed ones in Zechariah 4:14 "stand" by the Lord of all the earth.

11:5. Elijah seemed to have a spiritual gift for calling down fire from heaven (1 Kings 18:38; 2 Kings 1:10, 12; cf. Lev 9:24-10:2). But what appears to be an allusion to Elijah is slightly modified: the fire comes from their mouths (perhaps symbolic for efficacious proclamations of judgment—Jer 5:10, 14). (Later Jewish texts expand this gift to Joseph, Abraham and others; later *rabbis told stories of earlier pious rabbis, especially Simeon ben Yohai in the second century A.D. and Johanan in the third, who disintegrated disrespectful men by gazing at them spitefully.)

11:6. Elijah had "shut" the sky, bringing drought in obedience to God's word (1 Kings 17:1; 18:41); according to a probable Jewish tradition, this was for three and a half years (cf. also Jas 5:17; Lk 4:25). Authorization to turn water to blood clearly recalls Moses (Ex 7:14-25). Jewish people were expecting both a new prophet like Moses (Deut 18:15-18) and the return of Elijah (Mal 4:5); in the language of their power, Revelation describes the mission of the two witnesses, possibly the *church (see introduction to 11:1-13).

11:7. Developing *Old Testament pictures of the end (Zech 14:1-3), Jewish texts commonly expected this age to end with a long, climactic battle, which often included suffering for God's people but culminated in their ultimate triumph (cf. both sufferings of the final generation and spiritual battle plans in the War Scroll in the *Dead Sea Scrolls).

11:8. Refusing to bury the dead was the greatest cruelty one could offer throughout the ancient world (e.g., Is 5:25) and was usually a mark of grave impiety as well. As Paul contrasts the earthly and heavenly Jerusalem (Gal 4:25-26), so Revelation may do here (the place of Jesus' crucifixion); the Old Testament prophets often compared Jerusalem or Israel with Sodom (e.g., Is 1:9-10; Jer 23:14). As Egypt had oppressed Israel, so Jerusalem's authorities had oppressed the true followers of God. The association of Jewish authorities with the persecution of the church held true at least in Asia Minor (Rev 2:9; 3:9); compare this city with Babylon in chapters 17—18. (In contrast, some scholars have pointed to the use of the "city" for Rome elsewhere in Revelation, arguing that the city here is Rome, who martyred *Christ in Jerusalem, or the world system as a whole. When used figuratively, "the harlot" [Rev 17] in the Old Testament was almost always used for Israel or Judah betraying their covenant with God. It is possible that, besides Old Testament allusions, John also alludes to earlier Jewish-Christian *prophecies against Jerusalem, redirecting them toward Rome in Revelation. Because we do not have those prophecies, however, it is impossible to say; John may simply draw a link between the Jewish authorities and the Roman authorities who, as far as the early Christians experienced their activity, were conspiring together for their persecution.)

11:9. "Three and a half days" may be mentioned to signify that the dead bodies of the two witnesses were decomposing; or it may simply correspond to the three and a half years of their prophesying.

11:10. For "earth-dwellers" see comment on 3:10. The giving of gifts characterized some pagan celebrations and (probably not in view here) the Jewish

Feast of Purim, which celebrated Israel's deliverance from Persian enemies (Esther 9:19, 22).

11:11. The breath of life entering the two corpses alludes to Genesis 2:7 and perhaps Ezekiel 37 (cf. Jn 20:22; Testament of Abraham, recension A).

11:12. Elijah ascended to heaven in a chariot of fire (2 Kings 2:11), and as time went on, Jewish tradition multiplied the number of holy servants of God taken directly to heaven without death. Greek traditions pictured a very small number of heroes taken to heaven in death. But ascension after *resurrection refers in other Christian texts to Jesus (Acts 1:9-11) and the *church (1 Thess 4:15-16).

11:13. If "seven thousand" is understood as one tenth of the population, the description fits Jerusalem better than Rome (the latter is estimated to have had a population as high as one million, though some think this inflated). (Some commentators see it as a specific reference to the remnant of Israel—1 Kings 19:18.) On a final earthquake see Revelation 6:12.

11:14-19
The Final Trumpet and the World's End

11:14. See comment on 8:13; cf. 9:12.

11:15. The world system (in John's day, Rome) constituted a kingdom, but it would be handed over to God's people (Dan 7:17-18). On the eternal reign of Israel's final king, cf. Isaiah 9:7, Daniel 7:13-14 and 1 Maccabees 2:57. Trumpets were always blown on the accession of an Israelite king (1 Kings 1:34).

11:16. See comment on 4:4 and 10.

11:17. Although Judaism acknowledged God's present rule over the earth, it also awaited and celebrated his future rule unchallenged over all humanity, and it usually acknowledged Israel's rule over the nations on his behalf. In Jewish sources, this rule would be inaugurated at the very end of the age.

11:18. The raging of the nations, God's wrath and the rule of *Christ over the nations echoes Psalm 2. Judaism held that the righteous were rewarded at the end of the age (or at death). Destroyers and misusers of humanity's stewardship of the earth reversed the mandate God had originally given humanity (Gen 1:26). Many Jewish writers also believed that humanity's sin had corrupted the whole creation (e.g., *4 Ezra). More relevantly here, Babylon devastated the earth (Jer 51:25), meaning that they devastated the land (2 Kings 18:25).

11:19. The ark of the covenant (see comment on 3:17) was the piece of furniture in the tabernacle and temple that corresponded to a throne in ancient Near Eastern symbolism; the inclusion of the ark thus fits the dual image of heaven as a throne room and as God's temple. Jewish hearers of the book would also be aware that the covenant had been deposited in the ark and that the covenant was associated with stipulations and curses (plagues) against the disobedient. The *Dead Sea Scrolls and many *apocalyptic writers felt that the old temple had been defiled, but that God would supply a renewed, pure temple at the end of the age; on the heavenly temple here, see 4:6. The ark was kept behind a curtain in the holy of holies in the *Old Testament, seen only by the high priest one day a year; here it is exposed to open view. (One scholar has suggested that this verse evokes the image of the ark going forth to war, portrayed in terms Roman readers would readily catch, the numen of the state going forth from the temple of Janus for war, thus the opening of heaven here.) On the lightnings and related phenomena, see comment on 4:5; this exodus language (Ex 19:16; cf. Ezek 1:4) suggests that John's revelation is understood as a revelation on the same level as Moses'.

12:1-6 The Dragon, the Woman and the Child

This vision reapplies imagery that was widely known in ancient mythology. A pervasive Greek story, spread in several forms, presented Leto begetting the god Apollo while opposed by the dragon Python; Apollo then pursued the dragon Python and slew him. In an Egyptian story, the goddess Isis gave birth to the sun god Horus as the red dragon Typhon was pursuing her; Horus eventually killed Typhon. Such popular stories seem also to have been applied to the Roman emperor, whose rule is here linked with the evil dragon (in contrast with Roman tradition, which portrayed him in terms of the hero Apollo). Although these stories omit many details John includes from other sources (his whole account could be reproduced from the *Old Testament and Jewish sources), they indicate that all his readers could identify with a story line modern readers often find impenetrable. But ancient readers familiar with the Bible would especially recognize here the story of Israel giving birth to Jesus and *Satan's opposition to God's people.

12:1. Symbolic women occasionally appeared in *apocalyptic visions (e.g., *4 Ezra; Hermas probably reflects Roman influence here—*Plutarch has a woman in a man's visions of the afterlife). Ancient writers sometimes meant "signs" in heaven astrologically, but these signs were also fairly common as props in apocalyptic visions. The sun, moon and twelve stars help identify the woman as the twelve tribes of Israel (Gen 37:9). Judaism in this period (e.g., *Josephus, *Philo; later evident in *synagogue mosaics and the *rabbis) often associated the twelve signs of the zodiac with the twelve tribes, despite biblical prohibitions against astrological speculation; indeed, the romance novel Joseph and Asenath borrows twelve rays from typical Greek imagery for the sun god. But the Genesis reference itself is clear enough to show that the allusion is to Israel (cf. also Abraham and Sarah as sun and moon to Isaac in the Testament of Abraham).

The Old Testament portrayed faithful Israel (or Judah or Jerusalem) as a virgin or God's bride but their unfaithful equivalent as a prostitute; thus the tale of two cities that contrasts the heavenly Jerusalem (Rev 21:2) and Babylon the prostitute (17:5). (*2 Baruch and 4 Ezra also follow Old Testament models and contrast righteous Zion with its oppressor wicked Babylon, by which they meant earthly Zion.)

12:2. Righteous Israel was portrayed as the mother of the restored future remnant of Israel (Is 54:1; 66:7-10; Mic 5:3; cf. Is 7:14; 9:6; 26:18-19), an image freely mixed with the image of Israel as a bride (Is 62:5). The *Dead Sea Scrolls also spoke of the righteous remnant of Israel travailing to give birth (either to a saved Israel—cf. Rev 12:17—or to the *Messiah; the precise referent is disputed). Cf. John 16:21.

12:3. Ancient Mesopotamian myths portrayed seven-headed monsters; later Jewish tradition linked the worship of dragons to Babylon (Bel and the Dragon 23-27). The image of a seven-headed serpent or dragon was also part of Canaanite mythology that the Israelites symbolically turned to better purposes: God's parting the Red Sea was now symbolized as a defeat of the primeval serpent Leviathan or Lotan

(Ps 74:13-15; cf. also Ps 89:9-10; Is 27:1; 30:7; 51:9; Job 9:13; 26:12-13; Ezek 29:3; for the principle see Ex 12:12. Rahab in some of these texts had become a cipher for Egypt—Ps 87:4). The Greek hero Heracles also confronted a seven-headed dragon, the Lernean hydra, in Greek mythology, although the number of heads changed quickly! Serpents were also associated with Asclepius; their association with Athena is less relevant in Asia Minor. Serpent veneration is common in many cultures and prevailed in a *Gnostic sect called the Ophites in the second century.

Jewish people had many stories about the great evil reptile Leviathan, that he would even be killed and served up as part of the course at the *messianic banquet (cf. *2 Baruch and later *rabbis). Here the dragon is identified with the serpent of Genesis 3 and the devil (Rev 12:9).

12:4. The image of stars battling in heaven was used in the *Old Testament (Judg 5:20, figurative language for the heavens pouring out rain), the *Sibylline Oracles (catching the world on fire) and some Greek sources. Old Testament texts and later Jewish texts portrayed both Israel or the godly (Dan 12:3; cf. 8:10) and angels (*1 Enoch; probably also Is 24:21 and *2 Baruch) as stars. Jewish traditions usually assigned the fall of angels to the period of Adam (refusal to worship God's image in Adam) or, more often, to Noah's time (sexual sins), but Revelation links their fall especially with rebellion against *Christ.

12:5. Virgil and other Roman writers also extolled the birth of a divine boy who would bring deliverance to the world; the first emperor Augustus quickly filled the role of the divine *savior in imperial ideology. In Revelation, however, the emperor is a puppet of the dragon, whereas Jesus is the divine leader of a group persecuted for rejecting the imperial cult.

In the various forms of the Greco-Roman and Near Eastern myth, the divine child was sheltered until he returned to slay the dragon. Here he is kept at God's throne until he comes to destroy the dragon. In the light of Psalm 2:6-9, Isaiah 9:6-7 and Micah 5:3, the "birth" probably indicates Jesus' death, *resurrection and *messianic enthronement, not his literal birth (cf. Jn 16:21).

12:6. When God led his people from captivity, they wandered in the "wilderness" until their redemption was complete (i.e., until they possessed their inheritance in the Promised Land). As elsewhere in the *New Testament, the interim between Jesus' first coming and second coming is compared with Israel between Egypt and the Promised Land. The Jewish people were also expecting a new exodus of final deliverance in the wilderness.

More than 1,260 days had obviously already passed since Jesus' exaltation (see also comment on 11:2), but symbolic numbers were standard fare for *apocalyptic texts. Although "1,260 days" refers to the great tribulation of Daniel, Revelation apparently reapplies it as a general symbol for final tribulation to the whole course of the present age. Daniel's own numbers were a reapplication of Jeremiah (Dan 9:2, 24), and some other apocalyptic writers also described other periods of tribulation symbolically as "1,260 days" to characterize the kind, rather than the length, of time they described.

(The language of older *prophecies was commonly reused in Old Testament, later Jewish and Greek prophecy; sometimes prophecies and other texts sought to evoke the same meaning as the earlier texts, and at other times they simply borrowed earlier language as standard prophetic imagery, without implying that they referred to the same meaning. As to what happened to the literal 1,260 days, *Josephus and possibly the Gospels applied them to A.D. 66-70, the *Maccabean literature applied them especially to the time of Antiochus Epiphanes, and many early Christians probably expected a literal period of that length to precede *Christ's return, as became explicit in writings of some of the *church fathers of subsequent centuries.)

12:7-17 This Means War

That the 1,260 days of 12:6 symbolically covers the whole period between the first and second comings is clear from the structure of the context: it begins with Jesus' exaltation (12:1-6) and the coming of salvation (12:10), spans the period of persecution of Christians (12:11-17), and, given the story line Revelation uses (familiar to the first readers), undoubtedly ends with *Christ's return to slay the dragon (see comment on 12:1-6).

12:7-8. One of two angels mentioned by name in the *Old Testament, Michael was one of the chief heavenly princes, the guardian angel of Israel (Dan 10:13, 21; 12:1; each nation had its own angelic prince). In early Jewish literature and invocations, Michael was the chief prince of the heavenly host, God's main messenger (cf. Jude 9); in the *Dead Sea Scrolls, everyone was either in the camp of the Prince of Light or that of the Angel of Darkness. Mythical language from Jewish stories about a primeval, heavenly battle leading to the fall of the evil prince and his angels is here transformed: the ultimate battle was fought and won at Jesus' death and exaltation (Jn 12:31; 16:11). Because Michael was sometimes presented as Israel's advocate before God, and *Satan was generally presented as Israel's accuser, the image of war here may be one of judicial as well as of violent conflict.

12:9. The dragon is identified with the serpent of Genesis 3, who would be crushed by "the woman's seed" (Gen 3:15).

12:10. From his portrayal in the book of Job on, Satan is presented as an accuser of the righteous, a prosecuting attorney before God's court. In later texts, his role of tempter (gaining incriminating evidence) became more prominent, but he always retained his role as accuser; later *rabbinic texts declared that he accused Israel day and night before God, except on the Day of *Atonement. This verse declares that *Christ's finished work has ended Satan's power to accuse the righteous.

12:11. The believers' legal "testimony" counts more before the throne than *Satan's accusations, and the object of their testimony is the finished work of Christ on their behalf (1:2, 5, 9; 2:13). "Loving not one's life to the death" was the language of valor in battle (Judg 5:18), as was "overcoming"; they fought and won by faith to the point of martyrdom.

12:12. In many Jewish views of the end time, Satan/Belial would be unleashed against God's people in the final years (*Dead Sea Scrolls). His authority was always delegated by God, permitted for only a particular length of time, to give him and his followers full opportunity to prove themselves wrong.

12:13-14. When God led his people forth from Egypt and into the wilderness, he "bore them upon eagles' wings" (Ex 19:4; Deut 32:11), and other *Old Testament texts speak of God sheltering his people beneath his wings

(Ps 17:8; 36:7; 57:1; 61:4; 63:7; 91:4; cf. Jer 49:22); later Jewish texts speak of God's protecting his people, including converts to Judaism, under "the wings of his presence." "Time, times, and half a time" refer to three and a half years, as in Daniel (7:25; 12:7; cf. 4:32). The miraculous provision in the wilderness also recalls God's provision of manna for Israel of old there. The Old Testament prophets and Judaism looked forward to a new exodus like the first one in which God would ultimately deliver his people from all their oppressors; the early Christians applied this notion to their salvation by *Christ's first coming and entrance into the future era of the *kingdom by his second (see comment on Rom 8:12-17).

12:15. In the most common form of the Greek story about Leto and Apollo (see introduction to 12:1-6), the sea god hid Leto beneath the sea till she could bear the child; in another version of the story, the dragon stirred the waters against her but the earth helped her by raising up the island of Delos. "Floods" are a typical image of judgment (e.g., Jer 47:2—war) and tribulation (Ps 32:6; 69:15) in the Old Testament, but God had promised safety for the people of the new exodus, just as he had brought Israel through the Red Sea (Is 43:2).

12:16. In Jewish tradition, creation, loyal to God, sometimes helped the righteous against their wicked human oppressors; thus, for example, a tree hid Isaiah from his pursuers, and the earth swallowed and so hid the vessels of the temple; in the Old Testament, cf. Genesis 4:10 and Numbers 16:31-32.

12:17. The woman's "seed" alludes to Genesis 3:15; the woman's seed would ultimately crush the serpent's head, but only after the serpent had bruised the seed's heel.

13:1-10
The Worshiped Beast

Although Nero died, reportedly by his own hand, on June 9, A.D. 68, rumor circulated that he was still alive and ready to take vengeance on the Roman aristocracy for rejecting him. According to writers of the day, the majority of people in the eastern part of the Empire expected his return. Several impostors arose claiming to be Nero, hoping to gather followings in the eastern Empire, where he was most popular; one of them arose in Asia Minor during the reign of Titus (Domitian's older brother). During Domitian's reign, a Nero figure even persuaded the Parthians to follow him to invade the Roman Empire, but Domitian forced them to back down and execute the impostor instead.

Jewish oracles predicted the return of Nero, and Christians feared it. Although John clearly does not believe in a literal return of Nero, he may use the image of this popular myth, as many scholars think, to say: "You thought Nero was bad; wait till you see this!" (the way we today would use the image of Hitler, Stalin or Pol Pot). This image so shaped the views of early Christians—thousands of whose numbers had been eradicated under Nero in Rome—that "Nero" even became a term for "antichrist" in the Armenian language. Many later Christian writers, including Tertullian, Augustine and Jerome, connected Nero with the antichrist. The view that John here uses this Nero redivivus myth has continued through history and is widely held by modern scholars, such as F. F. Bruce, William Barclay and most commentators on Revelation. Politically dangerous oracles were known forms of Greek and Jewish protest, and Rome would have taken serious offense at the implications of this exiled prophet

John had the authorities read and grasped the symbolism of his book.

13:1. Rome came "from the sea" from the vantage point of the eastern Empire, although the image itself is borrowed from Daniel 7:3. (*4 Ezra 11:1 likewise has a symbol for Rome—an eagle with twelve wings and three heads—come from the sea, although in 13:1 a *messianic figure does the same.)

Emperors bore titles such as "divine" ("god," on Asian coins) and "son of a god" (i.e., of the preceding ruler), and Domitian demanded the address "Lord and God," thus "blasphemous names" here (see comment on Rev 13:5-6 for *Old Testament background). On seven-headed beasts see comment on 12:3; on the heads see comment on 17:9-10.

13:2. Daniel described four beasts, representing four successive empires (7:3-7); the fourth, the Greek empire of Alexander, was in John's day often interpreted to represent Rome instead. John uses components from several of Daniel's beasts (which were a winged lion, a bear, a winged leopard and a beast with iron teeth) to create a composite of oppressive evil, evoking the worst feelings his hearers would have toward Rome and all oppressive political powers.

13:3. Much of the passage can be explained by the beast's imitating God as a false god, hence the pseudoresurrection here. But many commentators have also seen reference here to the myth that Nero, who apparently died in A.D. 68, was alive and would return (according to some forms of the story, Nero was dead but would return from the dead; see introduction to 13:1-10).

13:4. The praise here offered to the beast mimics a praise often offered to God (Ex 15:11; cf. Judith 6:2-3; Ecclus 33:5, 10).

13:5-6. The proud mouth is the sort of imagery that later fed into the antichrist traditions (originally built around Antiochus Epiphanes and those after him who would be like him—Dan 7:8, 20, 25; 11:36; 1 Macc 1:24). On the forty-two months see comment on Revelation 11:2-3. The identifying of the tabernacle with the righteous heaven-dwellers matches the *Essene and early Christian picture of the righteous community as God's holy temple.

13:7. The antichristlike figure of Daniel 7:21-22 (applied first to Antiochus IV Epiphanes but necessarily reapplied to his successors in the role, with which history is replete) waged war against the saints ("holy ones," God's people—7:18, 25; 8:24) and "overcame" them—until the day of judgment and the *kingdom arrived. Nero burned Christians alive to light his imperial gardens at night, crucified others and fed still others to wild beasts; they were his political scapegoat for a fire in Rome for which he and his boyfriend Tigellinus were being blamed. Domitian does not seem to have instituted an empirewide policy of repressing Christians; but John's *prophecy came true soon enough, for some later emperors did so.

13:8. Antiochus Epiphanes, one of the earliest candidates for an antichrist figure (second century B.C.), had brought all the nations (in his part of the world) under his authority as one people (1 Macc 1:41-43) and demanded the worship normally considered due rulers in the East. The Romans had likewise unified much of the ancient world, and the ruler-worshiping East now worshiped the emperor. "All the earth" was used in other texts of John's time to mean all the "civilized" earth, all that was under a mighty empire (e.g., Judith 2:7; 6:4; 11:1; although everyone was aware, from legend, mythology and trade connections, of peoples outside the sphere of Rome, Parthia and the northern barbarians). This verse indicates the Jewish doctrine of predestination, which Jewish people held alongside the doctrine of free will (the early writers never saw enough tension between the two to explain the difference, although the idea of God's foreknowledge may have helped; see comment on Rom 9:19-21). On the "book of life" (cf. Dan 12:1), see comment on Philippians 4:3.

13:9. See comment on 2:7.

13:10. The language is from Jeremiah 15:2 and 43:11, where God promises to exterminate most of the Israelites by various means and to enslave the others in captivity; but the judgment here is against all nations who have rebelled against God. This judgment would encourage the martyred saints concerning their vindication (Rev 14:11-12).

13:11-18
Enforcing Imperial Worship

Although most of the details of 13:1-10 could apply to the emperor of John's day, and via him to totalitarian regimes throughout history, some of the details of 13:11-18 suggest that John consciously anticipates its ultimate fulfillment in an emperor yet to come (17:11).

13:11-12. The beast "from the earth," as opposed to "from the sea" (13:1), is often thought to be the local provincial council who supervised the imperial cult in Asia, as opposed to the Roman administration. It was called the *commune Asiae,* headed by the Asiarchs from local towns (see comment on Acts 19:31). John may not imply any great difference between earth and sea (cf. Dan 7:3, 17). The "horned lamb" probably parodies Christ (Rev 5:6); the two horns might reflect the power of ancient Persia in Daniel 8:6. Fire from heaven parodies and so apparently relativizes the miraculous power of God's witnesses (Rev 11:5), as Pharaoh's magicians tried to do with Moses' miracles as long as they could (Ex 7:11, 22; 8:7, 18; cf. 2 Kings 18:33-35).

13:13. Although the ancient Mediterranean world was full of self-proclaimed wonderworkers (some of whom were friends of emperors), and a few wonders had been attributed to Domitian's father (the emperor Vespasian), such wonders were not regularly associated with the imperial cult. Although some people did pray to Caesar for help (e.g., Lucius in *Apuleius's story of the ass and his transformation), most of the miracle reports are associated with temples like those of the healing deity Asclepius. John apparently envisions a future blending of anti-Christian state religion and occult power, both of which existed mainly separately in his own day. His source for this view is undoubtedly Jesus (Mt 24:24; 2 Thess 2:9), and he has *Old Testament precedent for the occult powers in the service of an anti-God ruler repressing God's people (Ex 7:11, 22).

(As crosscultural studies of shamanism and spirit possession become more available, the once popular tendency of commentators to rationalize away ancient reports of miracles, whether Christian or otherwise, will probably continue to diminish, although not all the reports, ancient or modern, are of equal value. Christianity has traditionally recognized the reality of other superhuman forces in the universe besides God [e.g., 1 Cor 10:20], although it would not agree with the increasingly accepted relativist position that all superhuman forces are of the same power or benevolent moral character, a position to which the data themselves would be hard pressed to point.)

13:14-15. Some magicians simulated the moving and speaking of idols (the skeptical *rhetorician *Lucian describes in detail the purported methods of a false prophet named Alexander). Hearing the extent to which the world can be deceived by false religion and state propaganda would evoke familiar discomfort in John's first Christian readers (cf. Deut 13:1-2). The demand to worship the image, which to the authorities symbolized appropriate loyalty to the state but to the Christians would symbolize apostasy, resembled the situation the *Maccabean martyrs had faced (cf. 1 Macc 1:50-51) and especially the conflicts faced by Daniel and his three friends (Dan 3, 6).

13:16-17. A Greco-Egyptian king had similarly required Jews to be branded with the ivy leaf, the emblem of Dionysus (*3 Maccabees 2:28-29); this is likewise a mark of ownership, a brand or tattoo indicating to which god or empire one belongs. The term for "mark" is, among other things, the regular term for the imperial stamp on documents and of the image of his head on coins.

Like the other markings in Revelation, it seems to be symbolic (see comment on 3:12; 7:3; cf. 14:1; 17:5; 19:12; 22:4); some Jewish texts speak of a symbolic mark of destruction on the forehead of the wicked (*Psalms of Solomon 15:9) in contrast to the mark of the righteous (15:6). Some interpreters have nevertheless seen a tangible expression of allegiance to the world system; in at least the last two major imperial persecutions of Christians, both in the third century, certificates were issued to those who had fulfilled the mandated rite of emperor worship. But the text may simply imply a figurative slave brand identifying to whom a person belongs—God or the world. Participation in idolatry appeared to be almost an economic necessity in many cities in Asia Minor (see comment on 2:18-29), and John warns that commercial discrimination would grow more severe, alongside t' e graver danger of martyrdom.

13:18. This verse is a typically cryptic *apocalyptic riddle (cf. Mt 24:15). Six hundred sixty-six is a triangular number, but most ancient readers would not know that. It has been thought a parody on the divine number, seven; this is possible, but scholars more often turn to another explanation. "Counting a name" or word was an easy practice in Greek and Hebrew, which used letters as specific numbers (later Jewish teachers often played with the numerical values of words; this form of calculation was known as *gematria.*) Many ingenious proposals have been made for the meaning of "666"; Irenaeus, a second-century Christian scholar, listed among the possibilities "Lateinos" (Rome as the final kingdom).

But the most popular proposal among scholars today is "Nero Caesar." Although his name comes out to 1,005 in Greek (which would have been obvious, because a familiar wordplay on that number of his name had circulated throughout the Empire's graffiti), his name comes out to "666" if transliterated into Hebrew. If John intends an allusion to Nero here (see comment on 13:1-10), either he expects his readers to know to switch to Hebrew letters (probably with the help of more skilled members of the congregation), or he and they had already used "666" in this manner. (This calculation requires using the Greek pronunciation Neron-Kaisar in Hebrew letters, with appropriate Hebrew numerical values: N = 50, r = 200, n = 6, K = 100, s = 60, r = 200. Hebrew used only consonants. But the *Sibylline Oracles, a Jewish document composed in Greek, does its *gematria* in Greek, not Hebrew; most of its readers would have been able to read only the former, being unable even to transliterate a name into proper Hebrew letters. Jewish scholars who used Hebrew incorporated many Greek loanwords, but John's readers would need either some help or prior knowledge to discern his point.)

14:1-5 Followers of the Lamb

14:1. "And I looked, and behold" indicates another vision (Ezek 10:1; 44:4; Dan 10:5). Mount Zion was the Temple Mount (sometimes loosely encompassing all Jerusalem), thus applied to the heavenly temple in the present (Rev 11:19) but pointing to the new Jerusalem of the future (21:2), a hope shared by nearly all ancient Jews, who longed for the restoration of their city and its sanctuary. Mount Zion thus figures prominently in *apocalyptic expectations (it appears by that title in *4 Ezra and *2 Baruch). The name on their foreheads contrasts with Revelation 13:16 (cf. 3:12; 7:3; 22:4); on the identity of the 144,000, see comment on 7:4-8.

14:2. Ezekiel heard the sound of many waters in heaven (Ezek 1:24; 43:2; cf. Rev 1:15), and thunder was heard at Sinai (Ex 19:16; cf. Ezek 1:4, 13; Rev 4:5; 19:6). Ancient meteorology, as reflected in *1 Enoch, placed waters (for rain) and thunders in the heavens. Harps had been used by priests and Levites in the worship of the earthly temple; it was natural to expect them in heaven's temple (Rev 5:8; 15:2).

14:3. Only these people could offer the song because it involved only them (5:9-10); on secret revelations in the heavens, see comment on 2 Corinthians 12:2-4.

14:4. The Greek term translated "virgin" here is hardly ever applied to men in Greek literature—probably partly because men in ancient Greek culture rarely were—but it means never having had sex with someone of the opposite gender, and hence includes not being married. In a literal sense, this virginity was practiced most often among a Jewish group known as the *Essenes. But the image here may here allude symbolically to the purity of priests for the temple service (Lev 15:16-18) or, less likely, to the purity required by the rules of a spiritual holy war (Deut 23:9-11). "Following" the lamb is John's idiom for the role of sheep (Rev 7:17; cf. Jn 10:4). "First fruits" were the beginning of harvest, offered up to God; the term declares their holiness (Jer 2:3) and perhaps that others like them would come after them.

14:5. "No lie" includes theological lies, i.e., false doctrine (3:9; 1 Jn 2:22). Truthtelling was important in ancient ethics, although it could be suspended even in the Bible to save life (e.g., Ex 1:19-20; Jer 38:25-27).

14:6-13 Vindication of the Righteous

14:6-7. On "midheaven" see comment on 8:13. The angel's "good news" is the vindication of God's people by judgment on the wicked (14:7; cf. Nahum 1:15). Because the activity of angels in heaven often corresponds to what happens on earth, however (12:7), this picture may refer, as some commentators have suggested, to the final proclamation of the good news of the *kingdom (including both salvation and vindication/judgment) preceding the end (cf. Mt 24:14).

14:8. In a taunting mockery of a dirge, Isaiah 21:9 announces, "Fallen, fallen is Babylon" (cf. Jer 51:8), referring to the historical Babylon that would later drag Judah off into captivity. But Jewish writers of John's day saw commonalities among all the empires that subjugated Israel, generally believing that Rome was the final such power (cf. Dan 2:35, 44). "Babylon" and its synonym, "the Chaldeans," were used as ciphers for Rome in Jewish texts such as the *Dead Sea Scrolls, *4 Ezra and the *rabbis (although the rabbis use "Edom" more frequently). The *Old Testament normally reserved the symbolic use of "harlot" for the sins of God's people (with only two exceptions), but the allusion here is to Babylon in Jeremiah 51:7, who made all the nations drunk with its wine (i.e., Babylon was God's judgment on them).

14:9-10. In the Old Testament, God passed around a cup of intoxicating wrath to all the nations (cf. Ps 75:8; Is 51:17, 21-22; 63:6; Jer 25:15; 49:12; Ezek 23:31; Hab 2:16; Zech 12:2; also the Dead Sea Scrolls; for infidelity, cf. Num 5:24). Fire and brimstone were appropriate for a spiritual Sodom (Rev 11:8; Gen 19:24), although the image may be broader than that (e.g., Ezek 38:22). (This text does not imply that they cannot *repent if they do so before death or the world's end—Rev 2:21; 11:10-13.) As often in *apocalyptic literature, the wicked get to see what they missed (cf. also Ps 112:10); but Revelation omits a common apocalyptic feature, in which the righteous also get to see and gloat over the fate of the damned (e.g., *1 Enoch 108:14-15).

14:11. The eternal smoking of Edom (night and day; contrast 4:8; 12:10) is described in similar terms in Isaiah 34:10, but there the meaning is desolation, whereas here it is eternal burning and torment.

14:12. Many comfortable people today (influenced in part by historical misapplications of biblical ideals of mercy) dislike the idea of judgment. But salvation/deliverance in the *Old Testament picture was not complete without vindication—removing the shame of the oppressed by punishing their unrepentant oppressors. The martyrs are here assured that they will be vindicated to the utmost (cf. 13:10).

14:13. Jewish texts spoke longingly of the day when the sufferings of the righteous would end. Greco-Roman letters of consolation stressed either that the dead were happy or that they were at least not sad, but Judaism especially stressed the peace of the righteous dead. The writer of *1 Enoch noted that the wicked would have no rest (99:13-14; cf. Rev 14:11), but the righteous dead would have great rewards (1 Enoch 103:3), and the idea of rest for the righteous dead occurs throughout Jewish texts (Syriac Menander, Wisdom of Solomon). Jewish funerary inscriptions regularly mentioned peace for the dead; over half the Jewish epitaphs recovered in Rome included the words "in peace" (hence "rest in peace" is not only a modern concept). The image of reward for works is from the Old Testament and is common in Judaism and in the *New Testament (see comment on Rev 22:12).

14:14-20
Reaping the Earth

14:14-16. Although the "one like a son of man" could refer to Jesus (1:13; Dan 7:13), it technically need only mean that this figure appeared human, in contrast to some of the other angelic figures in the book (Rev 4:7; Christ would not need to take orders—14:15-16). The harvest is also an image of judgment against Babylon in the *Old Testament (Jer 51:33); it is specifically appropriate for the final battle when blood would flow, as Joel 3:13 noted:

"Put in the sickle, for the harvest is ripe. Come, tread, for the wine press is full" (NASB).

14:17-19. Because crushed grapes could look like human blood (Gen 49:11), this image, playing on Joel 3:13 (cf. also Jer 25:30), was powerful for ancients, who were more familiar with viticulture than most modern peoples are (contrast *Christ and his people as a vine in Jn 15:1). This harvest image is particularly from Isaiah 63:1-6: God goes on to tread the wine press of his fury and tramples the nations, splattering his garments with their lifeblood. For angels over various elements of nature (including fire), see comment on Revelation 7:1.

14:20. Ancient reports of urban battles sometimes refer to streets flowing with blood due to the massive slaughter that occurred in a short span of time. For example, exaggerating the massacre at Bethar, the *rabbis declared that rivers of blood flowed from the city to the distant sea, rolling boulders from their place and submerging horses. Likewise, *1 Enoch reported God judging people by letting them slay one another till blood flowed in streams (100:1-2), so that horses walked up to their chests in it and chariots were submerged (100:3); cf. similarly other oracles of the end time (*Sibylline Oracles, several times).

The literal number here, "1,600 stadia" (NIV), which is about two hundred miles (NASB, NRSV, TEV), is a square number (40 × 40), probably used roundly for a large quantity (although it may be of interest that some ancients estimated the length of Palestine to about sixteen hundred stadia). The wine of God's wrath (14:10, 19) turns out to be human blood here, which is drunk in 16:6; other texts also speak of being drunk with blood (e.g., Judith 6:4).

15:1-4
Response of the Saints to Their Vindication

15:1. Ancient texts sometimes began and ended on the same point, thus bracketing it off (this design is called an *inclusio*). The heavenly perspective on the judgments on earth is bracketed by 15:1 and 8.

15:2. The saints celebrate their vindication in 15:2-4. Jewish texts often spoke of rivers of fire proceeding from God's throne, based on Daniel 7:9-10; this image is mingled here with the imagery of the heavenly temple (on the "sea" see comment on Rev 4:6). Their triumph over their oppressor may also suggest another connotation of the "sea": like Israel delivered from the Egyptians, who were slain in the Red Sea, they offer God praise (15:3-4).

15:3-4. The "great and wonderful" (TEV) works refer to the plagues (15:1; cf. Ex 15:11). The "song of Moses" could refer to Deuteronomy 32 (especially to the part where God avenges the blood of his servants—32:34-43), which was used alongside psalms in Jewish worship. But in this context Moses' song almost surely refers to his song of triumph and praise after his people came safely across the sea, where their enemies were drowned (Ex 15:1-18). "Song of the lamb" recalls redemption from the final plague (Rev 5:6).

The language here recalls Psalm 86:9-10; the *Old Testament often proclaimed the hope of the remnant of the nations turning to God. "King of the ages" (NIV) or "of the world" was a common Jewish title for God. Greco-Roman *rhetoricians praised gods who were universally recognized, but as Judaism also emphasized, God would be universally and solely worshiped in the final day of judgment (cf. Zech 14:9).

15:5—16:1
Preparing the Final Plagues

15:5. On the heavenly tabernacle/temple, see comment on 4:6 and Hebrews 8:1-5.

15:6. Ancient Jewish literature often viewed angels as wearing white linen, but such texts also described priests in this manner, and John portrays these angels as servants of the heavenly temple.

15:7. The image of the golden bowls is probably derived from the use of such incense bowls in the temple before its destruction several decades before; cf. 5:8 and 8:3. On the cup of wrath see comment on 14:9-10.

15:8. The temple filling with glory recalls the dedications of the earthly temple in earlier times (Ex 40:34-35; 1 Kings 8:10-11; cf. Ezek 10:3-4 for its withdrawal).

16:1. The *Old Testament commonly used the phrase "pour out wrath" (especially throughout Jeremiah and Ezekiel); the image of the cup may be related to this idea.

16:2-11
The First Four Bowls of Wrath

Like the trumpet plagues, the imagery for these judgments is especially borrowed from the judgments on Egypt in the *Old Testament book of Exodus, reminding John's hearers that they, like Israel of old, were protected from these judgments that would eventuate in the capitulation of their oppressors and their own deliverance.

16:2. Sores were the sixth plague in Exodus 9:10.

16:3. This plague was the first in Exodus 7:20 (the second plague in the listing in Rev 8:8).

16:4. This judgment also extends the first plague (Ex 7:20; cf. comment on the third plague in Rev 8:10).

16:5. The oppressed often cried to God to vindicate them; and when vindicated, they praised God for his justice (often in psalms; the language was also used for his mercy, e.g., Tobit 3:2). In the *Old Testament God often let people destroy themselves (the wicked fell into their own trap), and Judaism developed this theme, emphasizing the appropriateness of particular punishments against the wicked. Jewish people believed that angels had charge over different elements of nature, including over the seas (see comment on Rev 7:1).

16:6-7. Early Jewish tradition declared that God turned the water of Egypt to blood to requite them for shedding the blood of Israel's children (Wisdom of Solomon 11:5-7). (On the wicked being "worthy" of punishment, compare Wisdom of Solomon 16:1, 9; 17:4; 19:4; cf. *Josephus *War* 6.3.5, 216.) The image of drinking blood was sometimes used metaphorically for shedding it, so the justice of the judgment would be apparent even to the few hearers unfamiliar with the exodus story (some recent *Gentile converts). The altar speaks up as a witness to the lives of the righteous sacrificed on it by martyrdom (see comment on 6:9).

16:8-9. The Old Testament mentions being stricken by heat as a common suffering of field laborers and wanderers in the desert (e.g., Ps 121:6; cf. Ex 13:21), although it is not one of the plagues on Egypt. On unrepentance, see comment on 9:21; the purpose of judgments, up until final destruction, was to secure *repentance (Amos 4:6-11).

16:10-11. Darkness was the ninth plague (Ex 10:22; the fourth plague in Rev 8:12); the darkness in Egypt could be "felt" (Ex 10:21).

16:12-21
The Final Bowls of Wrath

16:12. Every informed reader in the

Roman Empire, especially in places like Asia Minor and Syria-Palestine near the Parthian border, would understand the "kings of the East" as the Parthians; the river Euphrates was the boundary between the Roman and Parthian empires (although some border states like Armenia kept changing hands); cf. 9:14. Swollen, large rivers could delay the crossing of armies until bridges or rafts had been constructed, but God sees to it that this army will encounter no delays. (The same image of difficulty in crossing major rivers is implied in the new exodus of the Euphrates' parting in *4 Ezra 13:43-47, but Revelation uses the image for an army [a natural usage], not for captivity and restoration.)

16:13-14. The writer of *2 Baruch mentions the release of demons to wreak havoc in the final period before the end. Frogs were negative symbols (*Apuleius, Artemidorus); one ancient writer even suggested tongue in cheek that Nero would be reincarnated as a frog. In this text the frogs may allude to one plague on Egypt which John had not had room to include up to this point (second plague—Ex 8:5-7); here the dragon is compelled to act as God's agent in bringing judgment. In Jewish texts like the *Qumran War Scroll, the army of Belial (the devil), consisting of the nations and apostate Israel, would gather to be destroyed by God and his faithful remnant (cf. 4 Ezra). Gathering the nations for judgment is the judgment language of the *Old Testament prophets (Joel 3:2, 11; Zeph 3:8; cf. Is 43:9), as is the "day of the Lord" (e.g., Amos 5:18-20).

16:15. Guards were to stay awake at their posts at night. It was common for people to sleep naked at night in the warm season, but most Jewish people would be horrified to be seen naked in public; perhaps the image is of a naked householder chasing a thief. The ultimate roots of the nakedness image are from the Old Testament, perhaps for the shameful stripping of a captive (Is 47:3; Ezek 16:37) or a drunken woman (Hab 2:16; cf. Rev 3:18); on the thief image, see comment on Revelation 3:3.

16:16. The Lord had promised to gather the nations (Joel 3:2, 11; Zeph 3:8; Zech 12:3; 14:2; cf. Is 13:4; Jer 50:29, against Babylon); Jewish tradition about the end time continued this image (*1 Enoch, *Dead Sea Scrolls). The nations and the dragon who led them might intend their gathering for other purposes, but God was gathering them to their own final destruction.

The Old Testament site of the end was the valley of Jehoshaphat (Joel 3:2, 12, 14), probably the strategic plain of Megiddo in the valley of Jezreel and Esdraelon. It was the corridor between the easily traveled coastal plain and the road to Damascus in Aram, and thus an essential crossing point for armies avoiding the difficult mountains (Judg 5:19; 6:33; 2 Chron 35:22; Zech 12:11; Pharaoh Thutmose III in 1483 B.C., etc.). Megiddo was a plain, not a mountain ("Har-Magedon," which the KJV read as "Armageddon," is literally "mountain of Megiddo"), but so transforming the site would not be incongruent with John's *apocalyptic geography (13:1; 17:1, 3, 9). John's exact referent is debated, but a site related to the valley of Megiddo remains the most common view and would allow the armies of the East to engage Rome in Palestine.

16:17-18. This language suggests preparation for a theophany, a manifestation of God's glory, as at Sinai (cf. Ex 19:16; Rev 4:5); the powerful earthquake may suggest the end of the age (6:12; 11:13).

16:19. The oppressed would cry out to God to remember their oppressors' deeds against them (Ps 137:7). On the cup see comment on Revelation 14:9-10.

16:20. This sort of language normally concerns the "end of the world" (6:14)—vast, cosmic devastation.

16:21. This hail is much more severe than that in Exodus 9:24; it would crush everything in its path, leaving no survivors; this language, too, must be relegated to the end of the age. People's unrepentance indicated how much they deserved the judgment to begin with (Ex 7:22); see comment on Revelation 16:9.

17:1-5 A Vision of the Harlot

Although the *Old Testament usually reserved the designation "harlot" for God's faithless people (e.g., Lev 17:7; Is 1:21; Jer 3:1-14; Ezek 16, 23; Hos 4:15), it was also appropriately applied to mighty mercantile or military centers. Thus Isaiah 26:16-18 portrayed Tyre as a harlot who served all the kingdoms of the world; Nineveh as capital of a world empire also was called a harlot and sorceress, who sold nations (into slavery) by both devices (Nah 3:4). (Sorcery and harlotry are also linked in Is 57:3; cf. 2 Kings 9:22.) The false prophetess portrayed earlier in the book appears to be an agent of the system (Rev 2:20). See comment on 18:23.

17:1. Angelic guides were common in *apocalypses, especially when the writer was given a tour of heaven or earth. Ancient art pictured cities as their patron goddess, often enthroned on the shore of a river; Rome, whose empire spread throughout the Mediterranean coasts, is naturally portrayed here as sitting on many waters (cf. Ps 65:7; Is 17:12-13).

17:2. Rulers of client states in Asia and Syria subservient to Rome were called "kings," even though they had to please Rome and cooperate with its agents; they also raised no objections to the imperial cult. Undoubtedly they did not think they were prostituting themselves, but any rare pockets of nationalistic resistance (such as in Judea, which was monotheistic besides) would have differed with their evaluation. For the nations' becoming drunk on Babylon's wine, see Jeremiah 51:7.

17:3. For being carried away in visions by the *Spirit, see Ezekiel 8:3, 11:1 and 24 (a "strong spirit" in *2 Baruch; angels in *1 Enoch). The wilderness was the place of the new exodus (Rev 12:14), although it was also associated with the demonic in some Jewish tradition; the point here may be that the woman who fancied herself seated on many waters would actually be "desolate" (using a Greek word related to the word for "desert," i.e., barren like the wilderness—17:16). The beast (13:1) might be related to the she-wolf of Roman legend associated with the goddess Roma (seated on seven hills) on some contemporary Roman coins (although John had ample Jewish precedent in representing kingdoms as beasts, e.g., Dan 8). The scarlet color of the beast is probably related to the blood of martyrs with which it was stained (Rev 17:6), or to the ostentation of the wealthy or of prostitutes (cf. Jer 4:30). (The allusion to the red heifer of Num 19 suggested by some commentators would work better if the heifer could be conflated with the scapegoat sent into the wilderness on the Day of *Atonement, bearing Israel's sins—Lev 16; but there is no evidence that such a conflation is in view.) On the blasphemous names see comment on 13:1 and 5-6.

17:4. True purple and scarlet required expensive dyes and were thus worn only by the wealthy, such as queens (18:7) like Jezebel, or by well-to-do prostitutes, who used purple attire to attract attention. Many ancient moralists reviled the ostentation of wealthy women, but John also intends a contrast between the earthly splendor of Rome, renowned throughout its provinces, and the true splendor of the heavenly woman (12:1) and heaven's court (4:3-11; comparison of characters was a major feature of ancient speech and writing).

17:5. As "mother" (cf. 2:23) of "harlots" and "abominations" (perhaps idolatries), "Babylon" is pictured as the most terrible of them all. (In the East, where married women generally covered their hair, a "harlot's forehead" [Jer 3:3; cf. Hos 2:2] might seem an obvious image in this period; of course everyone in Revelation is identified by his or her forehead or hand anyway [Rev 7:3; 13:16]. Older Greek literature reports the slander that Babylonian women were all required to play the harlot once in life, but it is doubtful that this association was popular in the *New Testament period; the imagery comes instead from the *Old Testament.)

17:6-18 The Meaning of the Harlot

17:6. Although the verse refers to Christians martyred under Rome in general, Rome's thirst for blood may have brought a special image to many minds. Rome's officials kept the multitudes happy with free grain and public amusements, the latter including especially bloodshed in the arena. Criminals and slaves were special candidates for satiating the public appetite for violent entertainment; once Christians were considered criminals, their large numbers would supply an inordinate proportion of victims. See comment on 16:6.

17:7-8. Again using the ancient *rhetorical technique of comparison, Revelation pictures the beast who "was and is not and is to come"—a parody on the eternality of God (1:4). *Apocalyptic texts often specialized in explaining cryptic revelations, frequently with the aid of an angel.

17:9. It was common knowledge that the original city of Rome sat on seven hills; this datum appears throughout Roman literature and on Roman coins and was celebrated in the name of the annual Roman festival called Septimontium. Here the hills have become mountains in characteristic apocalyptic *hyperbole. (The seven mountains of paradise in *1 Enoch 24:2 and 32:1 are probably unrelated, unless by way of radical contrast. But the *Sibylline Oracles also prophesied judgment against "seven-hilled Rome"—2:18; 11:109-16.) Like many Jewish interpreters who construed Old Testament language in a variety of ways, John here allows his symbolism to stand for more than one referent (Rev 17:10-11).

17:10-11. Some commentators count the kings starting from the first emperor (Augustus) but use up the seven before reaching the current emperor, Domitian, although the text itself claims that one of the seven was then reigning (v. 10). An allusion to the legendary kings who preceded the Roman Republic fails because obviously none of them is still living, either.

The real clue is that one king was then reigning, and one of the seven would return. Whether an author writing in the reign of the Flavian king Domitian would count the three brief rulers between Nero and Vespasian as "kings" is doubtful; hence Nero, probably viewed as less than seven kings before Domitian, would appear as one of the seven. Interestingly, Nero was also expected to return (see comment on 13:1-10). (Many commentators have missed this connection with what is widely accepted as background for Rev 13.)

17:12. Ten horns represented ten kings in Daniel 7:24, possibly successors of Alexander the Great's Greco-Macedonian kingdom (although most Jewish people in the Roman era read Daniel's fourth kingdom as Rome). It has been suggested that John reapplies the language for the fourteen Parthian satraps, but it would apply more naturally to Rome's client states in the East (cf. Rev 17:2).

17:13. The kings' unified conspiracy against God would come to nothing; this conviction had long been part of Jewish hope (cf. Ps 2:2; 83:5).

17:14. "King of kings" had long been applied to supreme rulers of the East (Ezek 26:7; Dan 2:37; cf. 2:47) and was now used as the title of the Parthian king. More significantly, Jewish people regularly applied these titles to God (from Deut 10:17).

17:15-16. The Roman Empire and its allies would eventually turn on Rome itself—a threat concerning the self-destructiveness and lack of faithfulness of those who pursue evil. The image is from the *Old Testament (Jer 4:30; Lam 1:2; Ezek 23:9). The burning derives from Daniel 7:11. Although fire was the standard method for destroying captured cities in antiquity (Amos 1:4), some knowledgeable readers might have remembered the rumor that Nero burned down Rome in A.D. 64 and blamed it on the Christians: Rome thus ought to be wiser than to embrace a new Nero. (The suggestion that Rome was burned like a priest's daughter guilty of harlotry in the Old Testament [Lev. 21:9] is also worthy of mention, although less likely than the interpretations just given.)

17:17. Jewish people recognized that the present world was dominated by evil powers but viewed them only as angels with limited authority; they recognized that God rules the ages. They also realized that, as in the Old Testament, he raises up one nation to judge another, but his purposes are far different from the purposes of the finite nations themselves (e.g., Jer 51:11, 29; 52:3; Joel 2:11).

17:18. In John's day, no one in the Roman Empire could have doubted that the city that "reigns over kings" meant Rome, any more than anyone would have doubted that the seven hills (17:9) alluded to Rome.

18:1-24
A Dirge over Babylon

Most of this chapter consists of funeral dirges over Babylon, following *Old Testament models; prophets sometimes ironically mourned a city's destruction, thereby prophesying its ruin. It is difficult for us to catch the impact today: an aged prophet, confined to an island for defying the whims of the mightiest empire the world had ever known, prophesied that empire's destruction. Yet the faith he proclaimed has spread throughout the world, and Rome has now been fallen for fifteen centuries. Although "Babylon" stood for Rome in John's day, other embodiments of the oppressive world system have risen and fallen since then.

Ancient *rhetoricians and writers often showed off their epideictic (praise) rhetorical skills by praising important cities, as in Aelius Aristides' lavish flattery of Rome. In contrast to such praises, John describes the city's power and wealth to condemn it, as the Old Testament prophets did with arrogant empires, and to produce a funeral eulogy that curses instead of blesses. Oracles of woe against the nations were common in the Old Testament and continued in some Jewish literature of John's day (particularly *Sibylline Oracles).

18:1. Powerful angels were frequently described as shining like lightning or the sun (Dan 10:6 and often in later Jewish texts).

18:2. *Old Testament prophets often pronounced an event as done even though it had yet to be fulfilled in practice. John takes this taunt lamentation directly from the Old Testament (Is 21:9; cf. Jer 51:8), as well as the description of a barren land possessed only by desert creatures (Is 34:9-15; cf. Jer 50:13; 51:29, 37; other cities—Jer 9:11; 49:33; cf. Baruch 4:33-35).

18:3. Later Jewish resistance oracles (some Sibylline Oracles) likewise portrayed Rome as lying with many suitors but headed for judgment.

18:4. In pronouncing judgment on Babylon, Jeremiah warned his people—who were supposed to be at home there in the short term (29:4-10)—to flee from the city's midst, because God would destroy it (51:6, 45; cf. Zech 2:7); even the presence of some of the righteous would not stay the judgment (cf. Gen 19:17). (In the *Dead Sea Scrolls, the righteous were to "separate" themselves from the "children of the pit"; in one *Essene commentary on Nahum, when the iniquity of those who were leading people astray was exposed, the righteous of Ephraim would flee from among them, joining the forces of the true Israel.) Getting out of an imminently doomed city was common sense for anyone who believed the *prophecy (cf. Tobit 14:8; Ex 9:20-21).

18:5. Jewish people recognized in the *Old Testament (e.g., Gen 15:16; 2 Kings 22:20) that if God's full judgment was delayed, it meant only that he was storing up retribution for the sins of many generations to pour them out on an even more wicked generation (also Mt 23:34-36).

18:6. Paying retribution to the wicked according to their mistreatment of others was a fairly common theme in the Old Testament (Neh 4:4; Esther 9:25; Ps 7:15-16; 35:8; 57:6; Prov 26:27; 28:10; Dan 6:24; Jer 50:15, 29—Babylon; Obad 15); paying someone back "double" indicated that the retribution would be more than complete (Is 40:2). For the cup with the wine of judgment, cf. Psalm 75:8, Isaiah 51:22 and other references in comment on Revelation 14:9-10.

18:7. Here John cites Isaiah 47:8-9 (also used by the *Sibylline Oracles), condemning Babylon's arrogance and smug security that it would never fall (cf. also, e.g., Is 32:9; Jer 48:11; 49:31; Ezek 16:49; Amos 6:1; Obad 3). Rome's luxury (including grain subsidies to keep the masses happy) came at the expense of other nations, such as the heavily taxed peasants of Egypt. The thoughtless extravagance of the Roman elite invited God's wrath; cf. Amos 4:1-2.

18:8. Beset by problems ignored by its king Nabonidus, ancient Babylon had fallen without battle to its conquerors in a single night, as Jewish people well knew (Dan 5:30). But this new "Babylon," the new site of the oppression of God's people, would be judged with fire (see comment on Rev 17:16).

18:9-10. Although the imagery is not totally consistent here (cf. 17:16; but *apocalyptic imagery did not have to be consistent), genuine mourning might be natural: client kings were normally appointed only with the favor of Rome, and Rome's fall would grant freedom and prestige to political competitors.

18:11. The imperial grain fleet, by

which the fertile soil around the Nile fed the masses of Italy, represented the largest form of transport in the Mediterranean world, but Revelation especially addresses the luxury trade (18:12-16), focusing on nonessential items secured for those who could afford them. The image of merchants mourning over a great trade center is from descriptions of Tyre in Isaiah 23:1-8 and especially Ezekiel 27, a passage that describes in more detail the city's greatness.

18:12-13. As commentators have pointed out, gold, ivory and this special kind of scented wood ("citron wood"—NIV, NASB) were imported especially from North Africa, precious stones and pearls particularly from India, purple dye mainly from Phoenicia, silk and cinnamon from China, the other spices from Arabia and slaves ultimately from subjugated peoples but in more recent times mainly from breeding slaves. "Human lives" (NASB, NRSV, TEV), distinguished from "slaves," probably refers to people reserved for gladiatorial shows and other forms of death to entertain the public; criminals, prisoners of war, the lowest of slaves and Christians were commonly used in such shows.

A second-century writer estimated Rome's imports just from China, India and Arabia at roughly thirty million denarii (a denarius was a day's wage in Palestine). Rome was a center of international trade, and no merchant marine existed like Rome's for a thousand years after its demise.

18:14-15. For "fear" at its fall, cf. the reaction predicted for Tyre's fall in Ezekiel 26:17-18; the merchants' investments are lost.

18:16. On the adornments cf. 17:4; these represent Rome's extravagance and wealth. Those who had never been to Rome often had an exaggerated opinion of its greatness (some later Mesopotamian *rabbis spoke of 365 sections of Rome, each with 365 palaces, each with 365 stories!). But it was the most powerful city that the ancient Mediterranean had ever known and that most of the world would know for many centuries after it. No one in the provinces could describe the judgment on Rome and not think of the destruction of great wealth (e.g., also the *Sibylline Oracles).

18:17-19. The merchants themselves had good reason to mourn—they were now out of business, perhaps with outstanding debts on their expensive cargoes that would lead to the loss of everything they had.

18:20. Judgment of the wicked is vindication of the righteous; cf. 6:9-11. The Greek phrase (literally "God has judged your judgment from her") may mean that God convicted Rome by applying to that city the judgment of its own law courts against the Christians. When Rome was later sacked by the barbarians of northern Europe after its acceptance of Christendom, the North African theologian Augustine explained that the judgment was due to Rome's past sins (cf. 18:5) and a *church too weak to avert judgment in its own time (cf. 18:4).

18:21. In Jeremiah 51:63-64, the prophet is commanded to hurl a stone into the Euphrates and declare that Babylon would likewise sink, never to rise again. Here the stone is the kind of millstone turned by a donkey, so heavy that it could never be retrieved from the sea (Mk 9:42).

18:22. The ghastly silence of Babylon here means complete devastation, as it meant in Isaiah 13:20-22: the city is without inhabitants.

18:23. The "voice of the bridegroom and bride" was the ultimate sound of joy; the prophets used the image of its stifling for terrible destruction (Jer 16:9; 25:10; Joel 1:8). Babylon, who would be left a widow (Rev 18:7, following Is 47:8), was a sorceress (Is 47:9) like Nineveh of old, a harlot who enslaved nations (Nah 3:4); the "sorceries" (KJV) here may refer to love potions or to the occult rites of their pagan priests.

18:24. God dealt vengeance against those stained with the blood of the innocent (Jer 2:34). Although it is not technically true that all the righteous were killed in Rome (cf. Mt 23:35), Rome assumed responsibility for their slaughter as the present embodiment of the oppressive empire, a trait of corporate human sin that recurs throughout history.

19:1-10
Praise over Babylon's Fall

The scene shifts immediately from mourning on earth to rejoicing in heaven; the martyrs have been vindicated at last. Although the reference is particularly to Rome, it looks beyond Rome to the oppressive elements of the world system that carry on Rome's role until the return of *Christ. (According to some commentators, chap. 19 applies only to Rome's fall, whereas chap. 20 presents the rest of human history until Christ's return. This view is also defensible; one's conclusion will depend on how figuratively one reads the language of chap. 19.)

19:1. "Hallelujah" is frequent in the Psalms (cf. Ps 146—50), a strong command to praise the Lord (a *piel*—it is the strongest possible command, probably originally uttered by the inspired Levite musicians summoning their hearers to worship); it was appropriate in all worship, especially in praising God for his magnificent acts (e.g., after deliverance—*3 Maccabees 7:13, or in end-time Jerusalem—Tobit 13:18). It functioned as a call to worship in the temple, and so functions in the heavenly courts of worship (Rev 19:1, 3, 6; cf. v. 5).

19:2. Vindication for the righteous included just punishments against their killers; see Deuteronomy 32:43; cf. Psalm 79:10 and Jeremiah 51:48-49 (on Babylon).

19:3. This quotation is from the description of the fall of Edom's leading city in Isaiah 34:10 but naturally applied to all cities that practiced the same wickedness, including the world system (cf. 66:24). (The application from city to society or world would have been as natural in the first century as application from one city to another; philosophers often viewed the whole state as a macrocity.) This language of smoking ruins was natural war imagery, and as an eternal devastation it is also repeated in the *Sibylline Oracles.

19:4. The *Old Testament pictures God enthroned both in heaven and above the cherubim on the ark in his temple; given the derivation of the four living creatures from Isaiah 6 and Ezekiel 1, the image may again be one of a heavenly temple as well as of a throne room.

19:5-6. For the "sound of waters" see comment on 1:15. Music and celebration were crucial at a wedding. God was often called "Almighty," and the Old Testament frequently celebrates his reign, especially with regard to his rule over creation (Ps 97:1), great deliverances (Ex 15:18) and the end time (Is 24:23; 52:7; Mic 4:7).

19:7. In Isaiah 25:6-7 God announces a great banquet for all peoples (cf. Rev 19:7), and in Isaiah 25:8 the promise of deliverance from death. In Isaiah 25:9 God's people celebrate their salvation, declaring, "Let us rejoice and be glad" in the salvation God had enacted on their behalf (slightly different in the *LXX). The Old Testament and later Jewish literature often compared Israel to a bride wedded to God; cf. Revelation 21:2. The *messianic age or world to come was also often portrayed as a banquet.

19:8. Pure linen was mandatory apparel for the high priest entering the holy of holies (Lev 16:4), extended in time to all ministers in the sanctuary; angels were often supposed to be dressed in linen too (probably based on Dan 12:6-7). Its symbolic use for purity and (here) righteous deeds would thus be natural.

19:9. The banquet here is from Isaiah 25:6, and the image of end-time reward was often developed in Jewish tradition (see comment on Rev 19:7).

19:10. Revelation seems to encourage the view that Christians on earth worship with the angels, in communion with the worship of heaven (a common Jewish view); but the book simultaneously rejects the views of those who prayed to and praised angels (amulets and incantations attest that some Jews invoked angels). Most of early Judaism associated the *Spirit of God with the spirit of *prophecy; for John, all witnesses of Jesus dependent on the Spirit (thus, ideally, all Christians) were prophets in the broadest sense of the term. It was, in fact, the proper witness to Jesus that distinguished true prophets from false ones (1 Jn 4:1-6), an important issue among some of the book's hearers (Rev 2:20).

19:11-16
The Final Invasion

This section is the ultimate climax of the book, for which readers have waited since 1:7. All the previous armies and other judgments were mere preludes to the coming of the final King of kings on a white horse.

19:11. Roman princes customarily rode white horses in military triumphs; the emperor Domitian had himself ridden one behind his father and brother in their Judean triumph after the Jewish war of 66-70. But the image of Jesus returning on a white horse, conjoined with the title "King of kings" (19:16), may mean that Jesus is portrayed like the *Parthian* king (cf. 6:2), his whole army coming on white horses (19:14). The pretentious claims of the emperor and all who were like him would be nothing before the true divine king from heaven.

The image may allude to God going forth as a warrior on behalf of his people (e.g., Is 31:4; 42:13; 59:16-18; Hab 3:11-13; Zech 14:3; cf. Ex 15:3). This is the ultimate "holy war," anticipated in the *Old Testament, in the *Dead Sea Scrolls, by the *Zealots and by other Jewish people, although not all these sources expected the deliverance and armies to come directly from heaven.

19:12. On "eyes like a fiery flame" see comment on 1:14 (Dan 10:6); diadems (in contrast to many *New Testament references to "crowns," most of which refer to victors' garlands) were for rulers. That his name is unknown may simply be a way of saying that no one has power over him (ancient magicians claimed that they could coerce spirits once they knew their names); compare Revelation 2:17.

19:13. The garments of God were stained with the blood of the winepress in Isaiah 63:2-3, when God was avenging his servants by judgment (cf. Rev 14:17-20); a later Jewish tradition naturally connects this text with the idea of Genesis 49:10-11, reading the latter as proclaiming that the warrior *Messiah will be stained with blood. Compare Wisdom of Solomon 18:15-16, where God's slaying the first-born of Egypt is figuratively described as his

Word leaping out of heaven like a mighty warrior; his commandment goes forth as a sharp sword (cf. Rev 19:15).

19:14. The armies of heaven were sometimes revealed in the *Old Testament (2 Kings 2:11; 6:17; Is 66:15; Hab 3:8; cf. Ps 68:17; Jer 4:13), although God's "hosts" were usually pictured on chariots there, whereas here they ride horses—the customary means of attack for the Parthians. In each case the portrayal matches the most devastating sort of aggressors known in the writer's time. White horses were often considered superior and associated with royalty, and were connected with the Parthians more than with other peoples. Most Palestinian Jews believed that Israel would participate in the final battle (*Dead Sea Scrolls; cf. Ps 149:6-9), but the image in this case seems to be the angelic host (also viewed as warriors on horseback, e.g., 2 Maccabees, *4 Maccabees).

19:15. The words of God's mouth could be described as a sword (Hos 6:5; cf. the *Similitudes of Enoch) and the *Messiah's decrees as a rod (Is 11:4); the mouth of Isaiah's servant also resembles a sharp sword (Is 49:2). (The writer of *4 Ezra 13 also describes a fire going forth from the Messiah to devour the wicked; the fire is said to represent the *law of God. In *Psalms of Solomon 17:24 and 35-36, the Messiah smites the nations of the earth with the word of his mouth. This is envisioned more literally than simply the image of a commander's orders going forth, as in Judith 2:2-3, although the latter may be what the image means.) God's sword is also described as his instrument of judgment (Is 34:5; Jer 12:12; 47:6), especially in the end (Is 66:15-16). The sword was a Roman symbol of an authority's right over life and death (capital punishment) but appears throughout the *Old Testament prophets as an image for judgment by war.

19:16. In Roman antiquity, horses and statues were sometimes branded on the thigh, but people were not (cf. Ex 28:36-38). This is a symbolic depiction; everyone in Revelation is identified by a name on his or her person (e.g., 7:3; 13:16). "King of kings" was the title of the king of Parthia but had been applied in Jewish tradition long before that Parthian usage to God himself, the suzerain King who rules over all the kings of the earth (see comment on 17:14; cf. Deut 10:17; Dan 2:47; Zech 14:9).

19:17-21
The Defeat of the Wicked

19:17-18. The saints have one feast (19:7-9), the birds of the air another (19:17-18). Revelation takes the image here from Ezekiel 39:17 (cf. Is 49:26; Zeph 1:7), which occurs after the final battle with Gog (cf. Rev 20:8). The description of such ultimate destruction of their mighty oppressors (cf. also *Sibylline Oracles) would have been a powerful encouragement to the persecuted Christians hearing the book.

19:19. In this depiction of the end, it is the armies, rather than the entire populations of the nations themselves, who are destroyed at this point (cf. 20:8); different Jewish views on the exact character of the final war tried to reconcile different Old Testament images of the end.

19:20-21. Some of these details (judgment by fire, the defeat of *Satan and his forces, with special attention to the evil leaders) are standard in accounts of the end time; others are unique to John's story line (the evil emperor and his sorcerer/propaganda minister being thrown into the furnace alive). Cf. Isaiah 30:33 and Daniel 7:11.

20:1-6
The Thousand-Year Kingdom

Many Jewish texts pictured an intermediate kingdom between the present and future eternal reign. (Whether this suggests that the period is literal or figurative in Revelation—and if figurative, figurative for what—has been debated since the first few centuries of *church history. "Amillennialists" like Augustine, Calvin and Luther usually have taken it as symbolic for the present age, whereas "premillennialists" like Irenaeus, Justin Martyr and Isaac Newton have read the period as future and after *Christ's return; "postmillennialists" like George Whitefield, Jonathan Edwards and Charles Finney have predicted a future millennial period preceding Jesus' return [this last view is generally rare today]. Those who take Revelation's millennium as in some sense future generally regard it as qualifying the absolute imminence of the final end, which might otherwise be supposed from 1:3. The structure of the *narrative here [19:20; 20:4, 10] is most naturally read as referring to a future period, but some have contended that this reading does not fit other biblical passages and have appealed to the cyclical structure of the rest of Revelation. The commentary follows the narrative as it appears to stand rather than taking sides on whether it should be read literally or figuratively, what the figure means or whether it is merely an *apocalyptic literary device. All three positions could use the presence of intermediate kingdoms in many ancient apocalypses to argue for their own position.)

Revelation 20 and what follows especially expound the later chapters of Ezekiel: Israel's *resurrection (chap. 37), the war with Gog and Magog (chaps. 38—39) and the new Jerusalem's temple (chaps. 40—48).

20:1-3. On the dragon/serpent see comment on Revelation 12:3 and 9. Many early Jewish texts spoke of wicked angels being "bound," meaning chained and imprisoned, until a particular time, usually the day of judgment (especially *1 Enoch; cf. Tobit, *Jubilees and *Testament of Solomon).

Many Jewish texts include an intermediate period between the present and future ages; in some, it is an age of *messianic peace, but in others it is the final tribulation, which came to be called the "messianic travail." The length of the final intermediate period varies in those ancient Jewish texts that include it, producing such diverse figures as forty years, three generations, four hundred years and nearly as many other calculations as there are opinions recorded, sometimes counted by "weeks" or jubilees of years. A few early Jewish traditions divided history into seven one-thousand-year periods, of which the final period would be an age of peace. (*Plato's figure of one thousand years between death and reincarnation as the intermediate state of the Greek afterlife might have influenced this Jewish figure [cf. also the phoenix of Greek mythology, discussed by *rabbis], but this is unlikely; the *apocalyptic penchant for dividing history into ages, plus the natural appeal of a round number like one thousand [cf. one hundred in Is 65:20], and especially the Jewish application of Ps 90:4 to the seven days of Gen 1, are sufficient to explain the length of the period on purely Jewish terms.)

20:4. The *resurrection of the righteous was a standard part of Jewish hopes; the subsequent reign of God's people with him is less frequent but also appears in Jewish literature (in the Old Testament, cf., e.g., Is 60:5; Dan 7:14, 18). Roman citizens were normally executed by beheading (with axes in previous times, but with swords by the first century); they were first beaten and blindfolded and then forced to kneel.

20:5-6. The punishment of the rest of the dead after an interim period may be suggested by Isaiah 24:21-22, even though Daniel 12:2 (like a number of New Testament texts) does not distinguish the time between the resurrection of the righteous (after the tribulation Daniel mentions—Dan 12:13) and that of the damned. Jewish texts sometimes spoke of the "second death" of the wicked at the judgment. On the reigning priests see comment on Revelation 1:6.

20:7-10 The Folly of Gog and Magog

20:7-8. Gog, prince in the land of Magog, appears as the final enemy of Israel in Ezekiel 38—39, after Israel's regathering and perhaps the time of the resurrection (chap. 37). Although scholars dispute whom Ezekiel has in mind, they agree that the enemies are from the north (like most of Israel's enemies in that period); *Josephus identified them with the Scythians. Gog and Magog thus recur often in Jewish texts as the final major enemies of Israel (*rabbis, *apocalyptic texts, *Dead Sea Scrolls).

Many Jewish teachers expected a mass conversion of pagans to Judaism in the *messianic time, to be followed by mass apostasy in the time of Gog and Magog. The army of the nations is called Belial's (*Satan's) army in the *Dead Sea Scrolls (although this text corresponds more to the battle of Rev 19).

20:9. Some Jewish texts portrayed a wall of fire around Jerusalem (based on Zech 2:5; cf. Ex 13:21), and some depicted fire falling from heaven to consume the enemies (the *Sibylline Oracles; based on such judgments as Gen 19:24; Lev 10:2; 2 Kings 1:10); here see especially Ezekiel 39:6. In the *Similitudes of Enoch, angels stir up Parthians to invade the Holy Land, but the ground opens to swallow them up. The Dead Sea Scrolls call the remnant community the "camp of the saints," a picture that also resembles Israel in the wilderness awaiting their final entrance into the Holy Land. For the gathering of the nations against God's people, see, for example, Zechariah 12:3 and 14:2; see comment on Revelation 16:13-16.

20:10. Judaism also anticipated the ultimate defeat and judgment of *Satan, a position in harmony with the *Old Testament view that God would reign unchallenged forever after the final day of judgment.

20:11-15 The Final Judgment

20:11. Although many writers also stressed a judgment of souls at death (some thoroughly *Hellenized writers like *Philo had little interest in a future *resurrection and judgment), Judaism had much to say about the day of judgment before God's throne at the end of the age. The image of a new heaven and earth (cf. Rev 21:2) is from Isaiah 65:17.

20:12. Many early Jewish texts refer to heavenly tablets (*Jubilees, *1 Enoch, 2 Enoch, 3 Enoch, Testament of Abraham), containing records of human history or God's laws; angels were continually writing down people's sins. The "opening" of the books meant that everything was about to be made known (see, e.g., also *4 Ezra). The final judgment would be a public judgment—there would be no way of hiding one's naked shame.

The image of the "book of life" appears in the *Old Testament (Ex 32:32-

33; Dan 12:1; Mal 3:16) and was developed in later Jewish literature (e.g., *Dead Sea Scrolls, *Jubilees). All would be judged according to their works (Ps 62:12; Prov 24:12; Jer 17:10; 32:19; Ezek 18:30), but former sinful works canceled by true repentance would not count against the righteous (Ezek 18:21-22).

20:13-14. Jewish texts often spoke of the final day on which the wicked would be cast into the abyss of fire (e.g., 1 Enoch). "Hades" (rendered "hell" in the KJV) was the abode of the dead (named for the Greek deity of the underworld, but not associated with him in Jewish texts), the equivalent of the *Old Testament realm of the dead, Sheol. In many Jewish texts, as here, the wicked were held there under judgment until their final destruction or place of torture.

20:15. Most Jewish people believed that all normal Jews (i.e., those who followed Judaism) would be saved, along with the small percentage of the righteous among the nations (*Gentiles); the rest would be damned. Israel's faith had always been exclusivistic (worshiping one supreme God; John would add here the further exclusivism that God was truly worshiped only through *Christ—cf. 1 Jn 2:23), and the Old Testament prophets had proclaimed a day of judgment that would call the nations as well as Israel to account. It would be too late to *repent in that time.

21:1-8
Promise of the World to Come

Some pagan oracles predicted a future age of bliss, but the hope for a future age of peace, ruled by God alone, is a distinctively *Old Testament, Jewish and Christian hope.

21:1. Isaiah had already predicted the new heavens and new earth (Is 65:17; 66:22); the focus of attention in this new creation would be the new Jerusalem (Is 65:18). Many Jewish depictions of the age to come (e.g., in *1 Enoch, *Jubilees and *Pseudo-Philo) emphasized the new heavens and earth. Some Jewish texts spoke of the renewal of the first creation; others spoke of its replacement by a new creation; Revelation holds to the latter position. Many texts described the end time in terms of the beginning, as a renewal of paradise (see comment on 22:1-5); so here the new creation recalls the goodness of the first creation before sin marred it (Gen 1:1).

Predictions of the sea's evaporation (perhaps in *Sibylline Oracles 5:157-59, although in 5:447-49 the drying of the seas for ships does not do away with water) were far less common for *apocalypses. Some commentators point to much earlier Canaanite myths, but these would not have been sufficiently contemporary to be obvious to John's readers. The sea's disappearance here may accommodate a literal (and typically ancient Jewish) reading of Isaiah 65:17, which mentions heaven and earth but does not mention the sea; another explanation may be the sea's symbolic link with evil powers earlier in Revelation (the borders of the Roman Empire in 13:1).

21:2. Like any city, "Jerusalem" meant both the place and the people who lived there; the new Jerusalem is thus a bride because its residents are a bride (19:7). Greco-Roman *encomia* (praises) of cities often turned to describing them as people, and Jewish people were familiar with *Old Testament personifications of Jerusalem and the Old Testament depiction of God's people as his bride. Contemporary Jewish writers (e.g., Tobit, 2 Maccabees, Ecclesiasticus, *Philo and *Josephus) and Jewish coins also called Jerusalem the "holy city" (in the Old Testament, cf. Neh 11:1, 18; Is 48:2; 52:1; 62:12); Jewish people (e.g., the *Qumran Temple Scroll) viewed it as the holiest of cities.

Pious Jews prayed daily for God to restore Jerusalem. The new Jerusalem, an Old Testament image (Is 65:18), had become a standard Jewish hope for the future, whether as a renewed and purified Jerusalem (Tobit, *Psalms of Solomon) or (as here) a new city from above (probably *4 Ezra); a city "from above" would be perfect, having been built by God himself (a hope found in some texts). In some *apocalypses (*2 Baruch), the righteous would dwell on high; in early Jewish literature like *Jubilees, God would descend and dwell with his people.

21:3. The tabernacle had always symbolized God's dwelling among his people (Ex 25:8-9; 29:45; 1 Kings 6:12-13); God had also promised to "dwell" among his people as part of his covenant (Lev 26:11-12), especially in the sinless world to come (Ezek 37:24-28; 43:7-10; Zech 2:11).

21:4. These depictions allude especially to Isaiah 25:8, 35:10, 51:11 and 65:16-19.

21:5. On the promise of a future new creation, see comment on 21:1; for divine Wisdom spiritually "making all things new" in the present, cf. Wisdom of Solomon 7:27.

21:6. On Alpha and Omega, see comment on 1:8. The future age was portrayed as having abundant water (e.g., Is 35:1-2; Ezek 47:1-12; see comment on 22:1); for the free offer of water to the obedient, cf. Isaiah 55:1.

21:7. God had called Israel his children in the *Old Testament (the language also continues in subsequent Jewish literature); those who had become his children were part of the covenant community and shared its promises for the future. God promised that his people who endured would inherit the world to come (Zech 8:12). The standard Old Testament covenant motif (also in *Jubilees) is "I will be their God and they will be my people."

21:8. Part of the promise in the Old Testament (e.g., Is 66:24) and Jewish literature was that the righteous who persevered would not have to share the world to come with their oppressors. Lists of vices were common in ancient texts. "Lying" may refer to idolatry (Is 44:20; Jer 10:3) or to false teaching (1 Jn 2:22) such as characterized the imperial cult and the false prophets Revelation opposes; most other sins in the list are sins committed by the *church's persecutors or by apostates.

21:9-27 The Glory of the New Jerusalem

*Rhetoricians often showed off their epideictic (praise) skills by describing and praising magnificent cities like Rome (Aelius Aristides) or Athens (Isocrates); John here describes the greatest of cities. His *encomium* is on a renewed city whose prototype was also loved and praised in the *Old Testament (e.g., Ps 48) and whose future glory was the hope of the prophets (e.g., Ezek 40—48). (Even the present Jerusalem's glory could be exaggerated and elaborated to conform to ancient Greek utopian schemes, as in Epistle of *Aristeas 116.)

Jewish literature after Ezekiel also delighted to describe the glory of the new Jerusalem (e.g., Tobit 13:9-18; 5Q 15, a written blueprint in the *Dead Sea Scrolls modeled on Ezek 40—48; *rabbis), often as part of their praise to God for his coming deliverance.

Some Jewish pictures of the end emphasized a return to Israel's pastoral/agricultural beginnings, without ruling out urban existence (*Sibylline Oracles 3:744-51), but the *New Testament and most contemporary Jewish literature are more urban than most Old Testament depictions of the end (Amos 9:13-15). The symbolic imagery for paradise was adapted to speak most relevantly to the cultures addressed.

21:9. Given the commitment involved in ancient Jewish betrothal, a betrothed woman and thus a bride could be referred to as a wife (as in 19:7).

21:10. The description of the revelation in 21:9-10 parallels exactly that in 17:1-3. Ancient *rhetoric commonly taught by means of contrasting characters, and the contrast between Babylon the harlot and new Jerusalem the bride is explicit and intentional. Those who instructed public speakers emphasized clarity and vividness in descriptions, and this description exemplifies those characteristics.

*Apocalyptic texts sometimes used a mountain reaching to heaven to provide visibility (*1 Enoch 17:2; cf. 18:6-8; 24:1-3; 77:4; Mt 4:8); Jerusalem was also regarded as atop a mountain (Epistle of Aristeas 83-84, 105-6; often in the *Old Testament, e.g., Joel 2:1); the image here is rooted in Ezekiel 40:2.

21:11. The emphasis on the wealth of the new Jerusalem would remind older Jewish readers of the glory of the temple, whose gates had been adorned with gold and silver; John declares that the whole city will share the glory of the temple. God would set his glory among his people in the end time (e.g., Is 60:1-3; Ecclus 36:14). Jewish writers spoke of supernatural precious stones that were luminous, or light-giving, by themselves.

21:12-13. The text of 1 Enoch links the twelve gates of heaven to the twelve signs of the zodiac, but Revelation links the gates to the twelve tribes, each tribe having its own position, as they did in the Old Testament during the wilderness wanderings and the settlement in the Promised Land. In the Temple Scroll (one of the *Dead Sea Scrolls), some Jewish pietists noted that the tribes would be commemorated on the twelve gates surrounding the new temple (three on each of the four sides). The image is from Ezekiel 48:31-35.

21:14. Jesus had made clear the continuity between the twelve tribes in the Old Testament and the first *apostles in the *New Testament by his initial numbering of those apostles (see the introduction to Acts 1:15-26); Asian Christians would easily recognize the symbolism (Eph 2:20).

21:15. The "measuring rod" comes from Ezekiel 40:3; the measurements of the city were to produce awe of God's great promises and thus *repentance (Ezek 40:4; 43:10-11). The *Dead Sea Scrolls also emphasize measurements of the future temple to call readers to endure for the future age.

21:16. That the dimensions are equal on all sides indicates that the city is shaped like a cube—like the holy of holies in the *Old Testament temple (1 Kings 6:20), indicating that the presence of God would always be with them in its fullest intensity. Ezekiel's city was also square, although not clearly cubed (48:32-34; cf. 45:2; 48:16, 20); but the cubing illustrates the point of Ezekiel 48:35—God's presence—all the more graphically. In some Jewish traditions, the future Jerusalem would expand in all directions (based on Is 54:2-3) and would become so tall that it would ascend to God's throne (based on Ezek 41:7). None of these descriptions is literal; if it is difficult to breathe atop the world's highest mountain (about five miles high), a city fifteen hundred miles high would not be very practical (at least under current laws of physics!). John elsewhere uses "twelve thousand" symbolically (7:4-8).

21:17. This wall is quite disproportionate with a city fifteen hundred miles high, but this point reinforces its symbolic use; important ancient cities always had walls, hence John includes one. Although John could have excluded walls (Is 60:18; Zech 2:4-5) as he does the temple (Rev 21:22), emphasizing that they were unnecessary given the lack of aggressors, he would then not have been able to include his symbolic use of gates (see comment on 21:12-14). *Apocalyptic texts (2 Enoch) sometimes called angels "men," and angels often appeared in human form in the Old Testament and Jewish literature.

21:18. Jewish descriptions of the costly stones used to build the new Jerusalem included miraculous elaborations, hence absolutely pure gold that looked like clear glass would have fit the *genre. Metal was used in mirrors, so it could mean that the gold gives a perfect reflection.

21:19-20. Twelve stones were normally used in the *Old Testament (Ex 28:17-20; Josh 4:2-3) and Judaism (e.g., *Pseudo-Philo) to signify the twelve tribes. The image is from Isaiah 54:11-12, where every part of the city (walls, foundations, gates, etc.) would be constructed with precious stones. Texts in the *Dead Sea Scrolls interpret this passage in Isaiah figuratively and apply it to the righteous, who displayed God's glory (including the twelve leaders of the community). Tobit applies it literally to the future Jerusalem but includes streets that cry out praises to God.

That the *Septuagint of Ezekiel 28:13 lists a variety of precious stones may inform Revelation 17:4, but the use of twelve different precious stones, each signifying a tribe of Israel, is from Exodus 28:17-20; John's list is roughly equivalent to the Hebrew one in Exodus. (Both *Josephus and *Philo also link the twelve stones on Aaron's breastplate with the twelve signs of the zodiac, but John characteristically avoids the astrological associations that some writers linked with the symbols he employs.)

21:21. In Tobit 13, the new Jerusalem's streets are paved with precious stones, and its walls and towers are of pure gold. Some *rabbis expounded that the new Jerusalem's gates would be made of giant pearls and precious stones; in one later story, a man who ridicules a rabbi's exposition about the pearls sinks to the bottom of the sea and sees the angels working on the gates of the new temple; he then pays the price for his mockery when the rabbi disintegrates him with his eyes. But the main source for the image of precious stones in the future city is Isaiah 54:11-12. "Street" (11:8) may be functionally plural but probably refers to the main street (cf. "great street"—NIV) running through well-planned towns on the Greek model.

21:22. One of the most basic hopes of ancient Judaism, recited daily in prayer, was the restoration and renewal of the temple (a hope from Ezek 40—48 onward). But for John, the whole city is God's temple or dwelling place (see comment on Rev 21:11, 16; Zech 14:21), and God is its temple as well.

21:23. The city's light being the Lord's glory rather than the sun or moon is taken directly from Isaiah 60:19-20 (cf. the image of 24:23; 30:26). Many Jewish teachers stressed that God's light would fill the world to come.

21:24. The nations will gather to Jerusalem to worship and bring tribute in the end time (e.g., Is 60:3-22; Jer 3:17; Zech 14:16-19; cf. Tobit 13:11-12;

see comment on Rev 3:9), bringing their glory into it (Is 66:12) and depending on its light (Is 60:1-3).

21:25-26. Like the gates of ancient cities, the temple's gates in the old Jerusalem were closed at night (cf. also the closing of gates in Ezek 46:1); but in the world to come, Jerusalem's gates will never need to be closed, because tribute rather than aggressors will come to them (Is 60:11). Revelation adds that the gates will also remain open because there will be no night, since the Lord will be the light (21:23; cf. Is 60:19-20). Night was also associated with sorcery, demons and robbers, and was considered a good time to stay inside. Contrast the city of wealth in Revelation 18:11-19.

21:27. Outcast groups (e.g., prostitutes) sometimes lived outside city gates, but an Old Testament allusion is in view here. There will be no more abominations in the house of God (Zech 14:21) or unbelievers in Jerusalem (Joel 3:17). The unclean had always been excluded from God's house so long as they remained in that state; this text refers to spiritual or moral uncleanness. The whole city is God's temple, or dwelling place (21:3, 16, 22).

22:1-5
The New Paradise

The *Old Testament sometimes figuratively described Jerusalem's restoration in paradise language (Is 51:3), but it was later Jewish texts that especially developed the picture of the end time as the restoration or amplification of the original paradise. Such texts present paradise as the home of the righteous, *Gehenna that of the wicked.

22:1. The rivers of paradise in Genesis 2:10 and the waters of Jerusalem (Ps 46:4) may supply some of the background for the image here; the immediate allusion, however, is to the rivers of water flowing from the new Jerusalem's temple in Ezekiel 47:1-11 (cf. Joel 3:18; Zech 14:8). (*Josephus *Antiquities* 1.1.3, 38, employed the Greek geographical concept of Oceanus and claimed that the garden in Eden was watered by one earth-encircling river that divided into four parts: Ganges, Euphrates, Tigris and Nile. *Philo naturally identified the river with virtue, flowing forth from Eden, which was wisdom—*Allegorical Interpretation* 1.19, 65. John might allude to the *Spirit; cf. Jn 7:37-39.)

22:2. The description of the "tree of life" is from Ezekiel 47:12, which speaks of many trees bearing fruit each month (as opposed to one season a year) and leaves for healing. John modifies Ezekiel's "trees" to incorporate an allusion to paradise: although treated elsewhere in Jewish literature (e.g., *4 Ezra), the "tree of life" is from Genesis 2:9. Later Jewish traditions further expounded the figure. (Some Jewish texts spoke of twelve trees, one for each month, in a four-river paradise, weaving together features of Ezekiel and Genesis in a manner similar to Revelation. Jewish texts frequently connected the twelve months with the twelve tribes and constellations, but John avoids astrological associations here, as elsewhere.)

22:3. The removal of the curse is from Zechariah 14:11, and in this context it refers to the reversal of the curse in Eden (Gen 3:16-19).

22:4. God's once-hidden face (Ex 33:20) will now be fully disclosed to his people (cf. comment on Jn 1:14-18). For writing on the forehead, see comment on Revelation 7:3; the point is that it will be clear that God's people belong to him alone.

22:5. Jewish visions of the future sometimes included the righteous shining like the sun or stars (*1 Enoch;

Ecclesiasticus; *4 Ezra; *rabbis; cf. Ex 34:29; Dan 12:3); for God shining on his people, see comment on 21:23. The righteous shining and also ruling in the future are combined in Wisdom of Solomon 3:7-8.

22:6-21
Final Announcements

Divine revelation and exhortation could go hand in hand. For instance, in Tobit's praise to God (Tobit 13:1-18) includes both a description of the final Jerusalem (13:9-18) and a call to *repentance for Israel (13:6).

22:6-7. "Faithful and true" may represent a testimony oath formula (cf. 3:14; 22:18; Jer 42:5), verifying the veracity of the revelation. "God of the spirits of all flesh" is an *Old Testament title for God (Num 16:22) attested in subsequent Jewish (e.g., *Jubilees; inscriptions) and *Samaritan texts; "Lord of Spirits" is also a divine title (*Similitudes of Enoch; cf. similar expressions in the *Dead Sea Scrolls). Here John especially identifies God with the prophets.

22:8-9. Ephesians and Colossians suggest that some Jewish Christians in Asia Minor had been assigning too prominent a role to angels; if that error is at all in view here, this passage refutes it (cf. also Rev 19:10).

22:10. Daniel had been instructed to seal up his words until the end time (Dan 12:4, 9); some of his visions had applied only to the future (8:26; 10:14; cf. Jer 23:20; 30:24; *1 Enoch 100:6). By contrast, John's revelation is meant to be understood in his own generation as well as subsequently (which should affect how subsequent generations understand his book). On opening sealed documents see comment on 5:1.

22:11. The righteous would stand, but the wicked would continue in their wickedness (Dan 12:10). John's exhortation here resembles an ironic invitation: let those who reject God's words do so, but they will pay the consequences (Ezek 3:27; cf. Jer 44:25; Amos 4:4-5; Eccles 11:9; *Sibylline Oracles 3:57-59).

22:12. The *Old Testament and Judaism stressed that God was righteous and would reward his people (e.g., Gen 15:1; Ps 18:20; 19:11; Is 49:4; *4 Ezra). That God would give each person according to his or her works was also Old Testament teaching (e.g., Ps 62:12; see comment on Rev 20:12).

22:13. A literary device called *inclusio* was used to frame a section of text by starting and ending on the same note; most of Revelation is framed by the announcement that the Lord of history is both Alpha and Omega, the beginning and the end (1:8; see comment on that verse).

22:14. On washed robes, compare 3:4-5 and 7:14, and see comment on 3:4; on the tree of life see comment on 22:2.

22:15. "Dogs" probably refers to the sexually immoral, specifically unrepentant prostitutes (Deut 23:17-18). Elsewhere in Revelation the imperial cult, combined with sorcery, martyrs Christians; immorality (both literal and spiritual) characterized the lifestyle of *Gentile men. See also comment on 21:8 and 27; cf. also Genesis 3:24.

22:16. "Root of David" comes from the "stem of Jesse" (David's father) in Isaiah 11:1—the shoot that would spring up from the stump of David's lineage, after his descendants had lost the throne. Some commentators suggest that "root" reverses the image, making him David's source. The morning star is Venus, herald of the dawn (cf. Rev 2:28), which in this case probably alludes to Numbers 24:17, the star descended from Jacob (Israel) and destined to reign and crush the enemies of

God's people. (The *Dead Sea Scrolls also applied Num 24:17 to a conquering *messiah.)

22:17. Ancient Judaism especially associated the *Spirit with *prophecy. Everyone who hears the invitation is to join in it, and the thirsty may come and drink freely (Is 55:1) of the water of 22:1.

22:18-19. The words of a divinely instituted covenant or book were not to be altered (Deut 4:2; 12:32; cf. Prov 30:5-6). Covenants often included curses against those who broke them; those who followed idols thus invited all the curses of Deuteronomy (29:20, 27). Such claims of completeness or inspiration of books were often made in later times (e.g., *1 Enoch; *Josephus and Epistle of *Aristeas made this claim for the *LXX) to uphold their authority or to secure them against later editors interpolating their own ideas—a practice common in books that were not treated as sacred Scripture or other inspired writings.

22:20. "Come, Lord" translates the *Marana tha* prayer common in early Christianity (see comment on 1 Cor 16:22), acknowledging believers' early recognition of Jesus' deity. For the testimony of witnesses at the end of a document, see comment on John 21:24.

22:21. This was an appropriate concluding greeting, often attached to Christian letters (see comment on Rom 1:7).

GLOSSARY

The most important terms and names are highlighted with an asterisk (*).

Achilles Tatius. A second-century A.D. *rhetorician who wrote *Cleitophon and Leucippe,* a Greek romance novel.

Akiba. A late-first- to early-second-century *rabbi whose opinions became very influential in rabbinic Judaism. After wrongly supposing Bar Kochba to be the *Messiah, he was flayed to death by the Romans and died reciting Judaism's basic creed: "The LORD is one."

***Apocalypses, apocalyptic literature.** The broadest use of the term today (usually followed in this commentary) refers to the thought world of literature dealing with the end time, often replete with symbols. The most precise sense of the term refers to a category of ancient Jewish literature growing out of *Old Testament *prophecy (especially Daniel and parts of Isaiah, Ezekiel, Zechariah, etc.) in which visions or travels through the heavens reveal divine secrets, usually including many about the future. Nonfuturistic Jewish mysticism was probably a truncated apocalyptic with future expectations played down.

Apocrypha. A group of books accepted as part of the Catholic *canon between the Old and New Testaments, but not part of the Protestant and Jewish canons. Most of these books circulated in the most common form of the *Septuagint, but ancient Jewish writers (e.g., *Philo, *Josephus and the *rabbis) did not treat them as Scripture. The *New Testament never expressly cites these books with Scripture formulas but alludes to them fairly often. The books are 1-2 Esdras, Tobit, Judith, Additions to Esther, Wisdom of Solomon, Ecclesiasticus (also known as Sirach or Ben Sira), Baruch, Letter of Jeremiah, Prayer of Azariah and Song of the Three Young Men, Susanna, Bel and the Dragon, Prayer of Manasseh, and 1-2 Maccabees.

***Apostle.** The term applies literally to a sent or commissioned messenger; in Judaism such messengers acted on the full authority of their sender, to the extent that they accurately represented the sender's message. The closest *Old Testament equivalent to God's "apostles" in this sense was the prophets, although the apostles seem to have added an overseeing and evangelistic function that prophets (both Old Testament and *New Testament) did not always incorporate. Those prophets commissioned with special authority to oversee prophetic awakening (e.g., perhaps Elijah, Elisha, Jeremiah) or to judge Israel (e.g., Deborah, Samuel) may provide the best Old Testament models.

Apuleius. A second-century A.D. *rhetorician who probably dabbled in magic and was initiated into the cult of Isis. He is most famous for his book *Metamorphoses,* now often called *The Golden Ass.*

***Aramaic.** A language related to Hebrew that was the standard international language of the ancient Near

East before Alexander the Great's conquests made Greek the standard; it was still widely spoken in different forms in Syria-Palestine and farther east in Jesus' day. Most Jewish people in first-century Palestine probably spoke both Greek and Aramaic.

Aristeas, Epistle of. The *pseudepigraphic story of seventy wise translators of the *Septuagint (*LXX) and how they impressed the ruler of Egypt. An Alexandrian document probably from the second century B.C., it seeks to portray Judaism in a positive light to Greeks.

Aristotle. A fourth-century B.C. student of *Plato who wrote treatises on logic, *rhetoric, nature and ethics. Many of his views became influential; his teachings were preserved especially by the school of philosophy known as the Peripatetics.

Ascetic. Austere and self-denying; some ancient religious and philosophical groups required this discipline as a matter of policy (often to show one's lack of attachment to mortal, bodily pleasures and pains). Asceticism grew in popularity in late antiquity, influencing the shape of later Christian monasticism.

Atone, atonement. The satisfaction of God's anger by venting it on a substitute instead of on the guilty person. Laying down one's life for another was highly regarded in Greek culture; some elements in Judaism came to emphasize that martyrs paid the price for others. But the concept especially derives from one kind of *Old Testament sacrifice, in which the death of a sacrifice appeases God's anger so the sinner can be forgiven.

***Baptism.** The *Old Testament and the ancient world emphasized ceremonial washings to remove various kinds of impurity; Judaism had developed these washings more fully by the time of Jesus, and some sects (particularly the community that authored the *Dead Sea Scrolls) were especially scrupulous. One once-for-all ritual designed to purify *Gentiles of pagan impurity when they converted to Judaism (attested in the *rabbis, in *Epictetus, and elsewhere) provided the most significant model for Christian baptism: it indicated an act of conversion, of turning from the old life to the new.

2 Baruch. A Jewish apocalypse from the late first or early second century A.D.

***Canon.** The minimum of books agreed to constitute the absolutely authoritative, divinely inspired body of literature, by which other claims to revelation may be evaluated. Most of ancient Judaism accepted the present *Old Testament as canonical; early Christians came to accept the books of the present *New Testament in addition to the Jewish canon.

***Christ.** The Greek equivalent of the Hebrew term for "*Messiah." Some *Gentile readers, unfamiliar with the Jewish sense of the term, may have taken it merely as Jesus' surname, a usage that became more common over time.

***Church.** The Greek term used in the *New Testament reflects the terms often used in the *Septuagint to translate the Hebrew word for the "congregation" *(qahal)* of Israel: "church" (assembly) and "synagogue" (gathering). Although some scholars have suggested that Jesus could not have spoken about the church during his earthly ministry, the *Dead Sea Scrolls used the Hebrew term for God's community; hence Jesus could use this word in talking about his future community (Mt 16:18; 18:17). The term was in common use in Greek culture for "assemblies," especially citizen assemblies in cities. (The popular modern surmise that the Greek word for "church," *ekklēsia*, means "called-out ones" is thus mistaken; that sense is actually more appropriate for "saints," i.e., "those separated [for God].")

Cicero. A famous Roman orator and statesman who wrote on a variety of subjects and flourished in the first century B.C.

***Client.** A person socially dependent on a *patron in Roman society.

Colony. A city either literally founded by the Romans or given honorary privileges as if it had been; its citizens were thus treated as citizens of Rome itself.

Cynic. One type of antiworldly philosopher who expressed independence from social needs by begging. Cynics owned only the barest necessities (e.g., cloak, staff, begging purse) and often greeted passersby with harsh, antisocial words.

***Dead Sea Scrolls.** Writings from a strict Jewish sect (usually agreed to be *Essenes) that lived in the Judean desert, near modern Khirbet *Qumran. The writings include the War Scroll, the Community Rule, the Damascus Document, the Thanksgiving Hymns, the Genesis Apocryphon, the Temple Scroll and commentaries on and expansions of various biblical books.

***Diaspora.** The Jewish dispersion outside Palestine. The technical term "Diaspora Judaism" is thus used interchangeably with "non-Palestinian Judaism" in this commentary.

Diatribe. A style of teaching used in ancient philosophical schools, generally characterized by rhetorical questions and imaginary interlocutors.

Digression. A change of subject (usually brief) before returning to the previous point; this was a standard technique in ancient speeches and literature.

***Disciples.** Students of *rabbis or philosophers, normally committed to memorizing and living according to their master's teachings.

Elect. Predestined, chosen. One of the most important tenets of Judaism was that the Jewish people were chosen in Abraham; the *New Testament applies the term to Christians, who are a chosen people in *Christ.

1 Enoch. An *apocalypse whose five sections may drive from different authors, 1 Enoch is mainly (excepting the *Similitudes) from the second century B.C. Probably written in *Aramaic, it circulated especially in *Essene circles and survives in part in the *Dead Sea Scrolls and in full in later Ethiopic manuscripts.

3 Enoch. An *apocalypse from the perspective of *rabbinic mysticism that is no later than the fifth century A.D. (probably the third century).

Epictetus. A first-century *Stoic philosopher, originally a slave.

Epicureans. A philosophical school that valued pleasure (the absence of pain and disturbance) and disbelieved in the gods of ancient myths; see comment on Acts 17:18.

Eschatological. Dealing with the end time.

***Essenes.** A strict group of pietists, some of whom withdrew into the wilderness as monastics. The *Dead Sea Scrolls are probably from one group of Essenes.

***Eternal life.** In Jewish texts, the term literally means "the life of the world to come," bestowed after the *resurrection from the dead; taken from Daniel 12:2, it became a standard concept in most of early Judaism and was sometimes abbreviated "life." Some *New Testament passages speak of it as a present as well as future gift, because Jesus' resurrection has inaugurated salvation for the present.

4 Ezra. The bulk of this work (chaps.

3—14) is a Jewish *apocalypse from the late first century A.D.

Freedperson. A former slave who had been manumitted, legally freed.

Gehenna. A Greek transliteration of the Hebrew *Gehinnom,* which in Judaism had come to describe the abode of the wicked dead in torment. Various Jewish sources differ on the duration of punishment in Gehenna and whether the wicked would eventually be annihilated, continue to be detained or be released; the Gospels, Acts and Revelation are much more united in their picture of a *resurrection to eternal judgment.

Genre. The kind of writing a work is: for example, letter, historical *narrative, biography, poem or bomb threat.

***Gentile.** Anyone who is not Jewish. In ancient Jewish parlance, this was often the equivalent of "pagan."

***Gnosticism.** A fusion of Greek, Jewish and Christian ideas that began by the early second century and presented a major challenge to early Christianity. Some scholars have seen tendencies toward developed Gnosticism in the opponents of Paul (especially in Colossians and the *Pastoral Epistles) and John. The same Greek ideas that later produced Gnosticism and Neo-Platonism were probably already at work in the first century, but we can reconstruct these from other sources without recourse to Gnosticism per se.

Gospel. The term so translated means literally "good news"; it was the sort of good news heralds would bring, and in Isaiah it refers to the specific message of God's restoration and salvation for his people. ("Gospel" as a literary *genre, a type of book in the *New Testament, is different; on this sense of the term see the introduction to the Gospels.)

Grace. In the *New Testament, the term generally represents the *Old Testament concept of God's covenant love, which was expressed in passages like Deuteronomy 4:37, 7:7-9 and 10:15.

Hagiography. A highly elaborated account of a holy person, meant to praise him or her.

***Hellenistic.** Although the commentary usually uses the term "Greek," "Hellenistic" is the more accurate technical term for the cultural fusion of classical Greek culture with Near Eastern cultures carried out in the eastern Mediterranean by Alexander the Great and his successors. "Hellenistic" Judaism is thus Judaism heavily influenced by Greek culture, i.e., "Hellenized."

Hillel. A famous Jewish teacher contemporary with *Shammai and with Jesus' early childhood; usually more lenient than Shammai, his school's opinions generally prevailed after A.D. 70.

***Holy Spirit.** Although used only twice in the *Old Testament (Ps 51, Is 63), this term became a standard title for the Spirit of God in *New Testament times. Many people believed that the Spirit had been quenched since the completion of the Old Testament and that *prophecy continued only in muted form; but the Old Testament had promised an outpouring of the Spirit in the end, when the *Messiah would come. Jewish people especially associated the Spirit with prophecy and divine illumination or insight, and many also (especially the *Essenes) associated it with God purifying his people in the end time. The New Testament includes both uses, although it also speaks of the Spirit as a person like the Father and Son (especially in John), which Judaism did not do.

Hyperbole. A *rhetorical exaggeration, a figure of speech often used by Jewish wisdom teachers to underline their point. The point of Jesus' hyperbolic illustrations is generally to grab the hearer's attention and force that hearer to take his point seriously.

Joseph and Asenath. An Alexandrian, *Hellenistic Jewish romance novel, describing the winning of Joseph's bride; probably non-Christian, it may derive from the first century A.D.

***Josephus.** A first-century Jewish historian who lived through the war of A.D. 66-70; his works *(The Jewish War, Antiquities of the Jews* and *Against Apion,* and his autobiography, the *Life)* are useful sources of information concerning first-century Palestine. Intended for a Diaspora audience, his writings are quite Hellenized.

Jubilees. A theologically shaped midrashic reworking of Genesis and part of Exodus. It circulated in (and probably derived from) *Essene circles in the second century B.C.

Justin Martyr. A philosopher both before and after his conversion to Christianity. Writer of two *Apologies* and the *Dialogue with Trypho,* he was a prominent Christian apologist (defender of the faith) in the second century A.D., until his martyrdom.

Juvenal. A Roman satirist of the late first through early second century A.D. He is especially known for his invective against women, foreigners and *freedmen who were encroaching on rights and privileges once reserved for aristocratic Roman males.

***Kingdom.** This term means "rule," "reign" or "authority" (not a king's people or land, as connotations of the English term could imply). Jewish people recognized that God rules the universe now, but they prayed for the day when he would rule the world unchallenged by idolatry and disobedience. The coming of this future aspect of God's reign was generally associated with the *Messiah and the *resurrection of the dead. Because Jesus came and will come again, Christians believe that the kingdom has been inaugurated but awaits consummation or completion. "Kingdom of heaven" is another way (Matthew's usual way) of saying "kingdom of God." "Heaven" was a standard Jewish way of saying "God" (as in Lk 15:21).

***Law.** "Torah" (the Hebrew word behind the Greek word translated "law") means literally "instruction" and "teaching," not just regulations. It was also used as a title for the first five books of the *Old Testament (the Pentateuch, the books of Moses) and sometimes for the whole Old Testament. This commentary uses the translation "law" because it is familiar to readers of most translations, even though the English term's semantic range is much narrower than the Jewish concept.

Livy. A first-century B.C. Roman historian.

Lucian. A second-century A.D. Greek satirist and *rhetorician.

LXX. The common abbreviation for the *Septuagint.

Maccabees. A priestly family who led the Jewish revolt against the *Hellenistic-Syrian empire in the second century B.C., they became the Hasmonean dynasty, an aristocracy that ruled Palestine until the time of Herod the Great.

3 Maccabees. A historical novel of Alexandrian Judaism; it may have been written in the first century B.C.

4 Maccabees. A Jewish treatise full of Greek (especially *Stoic) philosophy; probably written by an Alexandrian Jew in the early first century A.D.

***Messiah.** The rendering of a Hebrew term meaning "anointed one," equivalent to the original sense of the Greek term translated "*Christ." In the *Old Testament, different kinds of people were anointed, and some of the *Dead Sea Scrolls mention two main anointed ones in the end time, a king and a priest. But the common expectation reflected in the biblical Psalms and Prophets was that one of David's royal descendants would take the throne again when God reestablished his *kingdom for Israel. Most people believed that God would somehow have to intervene to put down Roman rule so the Messiah's kingdom could be secure; many seem to have thought this intervention would be accomplished through force of arms. Various messianic figures arose in first-century Palestine, expecting a miraculous intervention from God; all were crushed by the Romans. (Jesus was the only one claimed to have been resurrected; he was also one of the only messiahs claiming Davidic descent, proof of which became difficult for any claimants arising after A.D. 70.)

Midrash. Jewish commentary or exposition on Scripture. The forms varied considerably but often included reading a text in the light of other texts, with careful attention to all nuances of details supposedly filled with divine significance. Because such methods of reading Scripture were common, early Christians could employ them in relating their message to other ancient Jewish Bible readers.

***Mystery cults.** A diverse group of Greek cults entered only by special initiation. The details of the initiation were to be kept entirely secret, although one could join a number of these societies. Apart from secrets and initiations, they varied widely in popularity, antiquity and appeal to different social classes.

Narrative. Story form (applied to both true and fictitious stories), as opposed to other literary forms, like explanatory discourse.

***New Testament.** The common modern term for the early Christian literature finally declared *canonical by the *church and accepted by nearly all Christians today.

***Old Testament.** The common modern term for the Hebrew Bible (including *Aramaic portions) as defined by the Jewish and Protestant Christian *canons; Jewish readers generally call this the Tenach.

Papyri. Documents contemporary to the New Testament, especially business documents and correspondence, written on papyrus scrolls (writing material from the papyrus reed) and preserved especially in the dry climate of Egypt.

***Parable.** Jewish teachers regularly illustrated their teachings with brief stories, similar to the use of sermon illustrations today (though often with less verisimilitude). Jesus' parables, like those of other teachers, were meant to illustrate his points graphically, hence many details in these parables appear there only to advance the story line. Modern interpreters who read too much into such secondary details run the risk of overlooking the parable's real point or points. The Greek word for "parable" normally means a comparison; the Jewish practice behind Jesus' usage included a wide range of meanings (riddles, proverbs, fables, etc.).

Pastoral Epistles. Three Pauline letters—1 and 2 Timothy and Titus—that give Paul's advice to young ministers carrying on his work.

***Patron.** The social superior in the Roman patron-*client relationship, who granted favors to and acted as political sponsor for his clients, or social dependents. The obligations in the relationship were viewed as reciprocal; clients were to grant the patrons honor as their benefactors.

Petronius. A first-century A.D. satirist who indulged in pleasure. After incurring the jealousy of Nero's guide and reputed sexual partner Tigellinus, Petronius killed himself when it became obvious what his fate would be.

***Pharisees.** A movement of several thousand pious Jewish men who sought to interpret the *law carefully and according to the traditions of previous generations of the pious. They had no political power in Jesus' day but were highly respected and thus influential among the larger population. They emphasized their own version of purity rules and looked forward to the *resurrection of the dead.

***Philo.** A first-century Jewish philosopher committed to both Judaism and Greek thought; he lived in Alexandria, Egypt, and held a position of great influence and prestige in the Jewish community there.

Plato. A student of Socrates whose idealism and dualistic worldview became influential in subsequent Greek thought. He flourished in the fourth century B.C.

Plutarch. A Greek biographer and moralist whose writings illustrate many of the views prevalent in the first and second centuries A.D.

Prophecy. Speaking forth God's message by his inspiration. It can, but need not, involve prediction. Although "prophet" technically refers to anyone who prophesies, Judaism generally reserved this title for God's spokespeople of the distant past.

***Proselyte.** A convert (as used in this commentary, a convert to Judaism).

Psalms of Solomon. Jewish psalms from the mid-first century B.C., somewhat like the Qumran hymns. Probably all from one author, they *may* reflect early Pharisaic piety.

Pseudepigrapha. A broadly defined, modern collection of very diverse ancient Jewish texts outside the Jewish and Christian *canons and other collections such as the *Apocrypha, *Dead Sea Scrolls and *rabbinic literature. So named because most of them are *pseudepigraphic. These works include 2 Baruch; 1, 2 and 3 Enoch; Epistle of Aristeas; 4 Ezra; Jubilees; Life of Adam; 3 and 4 Maccabees; Martyrdom of Isaiah; Psalms of Solomon; Sibylline Oracles; Testament of Job; Testament of Solomon; and Testaments of the Twelve Patriarchs.

***Pseudepigraphic.** Purporting to be written by someone other than the real author, something like writing under a pen name today.

Pseudo-Philo. Pseudo-Philo's *Biblical Antiquities* retraces biblical history from Adam to the death of Saul. Possibly from Palestine, the work probably derives from the late first or early second century A.D., but betrays no specific Christian influence.

Pseudo-Phocylides. A probably Jewish work of moral wisdom, influenced by *Stoic ethics. It may date to the late first century B.C. or early first century A.D.

Publican. A mistranslation of a Greek term simply meaning *"tax gatherer." The Romans did not use literal *publicanoi,* a special kind of tax farmers, in the Palestine of Jesus' day.

Pythagoreanism. A mystical philosophy developed by Pythagoras, a Greek thinker of the sixth century B.C. Like other Greek philosophical schools, it had its own unique traits; one of its most basic tenets was the mystical significance of numbers.

Quintilian. An influential first-century Roman *rhetorician.

Qumran. The place where the *Dead Sea Scrolls were found (Khirbet Qumran); hence "Qumran community" is used to describe the people who lived there and wrote the Scrolls.

***Rabbi.** Jewish teacher. Sometime after A.D. 70 the term became a technical one for those ordained in the rabbinic movement, which probably consisted primarily of *Pharisaic scribes. (To accommodate customary usage this commentary sometimes applies the term to Jewish teachers of the *law in general, although such common usage may have technically been later; it also applies the term to the teachings of Jewish legal experts collected in *rabbinic literature.)

Rabbinic literature. The massive body of literature containing opinions attributed to various Jewish teachers considered part of the rabbinic movement; the bulk of the material used in this commentary is from the first few centuries A.D. Although all the written sources and most of the *rabbis they cite are later than the New Testament, this literature is useful to illustrate one stream of Jewish tradition. Rabbinic works include the Mishnah, Tosefta, Babylonian and Palestinian Talmuds, Mekilta on Exodus, Sifra on Leviticus, and Sifre on Numbers and Deuteronomy.

Repentance. In the *New Testament, this term does not merely mean "change of mind" (as some have gathered from the Greek term); it reflects the *Old Testament and Jewish concept of "turning around" or "turning away" from sin. Jewish people were to repent whenever they sinned; the New Testament uses the term especially for the once-for-all turning a *Gentile would undergo when converting to Judaism or any sinner would undergo when becoming a follower of Jesus.

***Resurrection.** Although some scholars earlier in the twentieth century derived the idea of Jesus' resurrection from Greek *mystery cults, it is now widely understood that early Christian belief shared little in common with the Mysteries' myths, which simply reenacted a seasonal revivification of fertility. Rather, Jesus' resurrection was rooted in a Jewish hope, which in turn was rooted in notions of God's covenant, promise and justice from early in Israel's history. Most Palestinian Jews believed that God would resurrect the bodies of the dead (at least the righteous, and many believed also the wicked), at the end of the age (Dan 12:2). There was, however, never any thought that one person would rise ahead of everyone else; thus Jesus' resurrection, as an inauguration of the future *kingdom within history, caught even the *disciples by surprise.

***Rhetoric.** The art or study of proper forms and methods of public speaking, highly emphasized in antiquity. Although only the well-to-do had much training in it, the rhetorical forms and ideas they used filtered down to the rest of urban society through public speeches, in a manner similar to that in which television permeates modern Western society.

***Sadducees.** Most belonged to the priestly aristocracy that had prospered due to its good relationship with the Romans; they pacified the people for the Romans and the Romans for the people. They controlled the prosperous temple cult, were skeptical of *Pharisaic traditions and supernaturalistic emphasis on angels and other spirits, and most of all were disturbed by talk of the *resurrection of the dead and other end-time beliefs. *Messianic beliefs about the end time could—and ultimately did—challenge the stability of their own position in Palestine.

Samaritans. A people of mixed Jewish and *Gentile ancestry who claimed descent from Jacob and worshiped the God of Israel, but felt that Mount Gerizim rather than Jerusalem was the holy site for worship. They engaged the Jews in bitter rivalry, often leading to political hostilities in Jesus' day, sometimes requiring Roman intervention.

Satan. Originally "the satan," "the adversary" (as in the Hebrew text of Job), but used as the devil's name by the end of Israel's exile (2 Chronicles, Zechariah) and standard by the *New Testament period, although many Jewish people also called him by other names. In contrast to some modern theologians, the first readers of the New Testament would have viewed him as a literal, personal evil spiritual being.

Savior. A title often used for gods and divine rulers in Greek culture but also used in the *Septuagint for Israel's God as the deliverer of his people.

***Scribes.** Throughout the Roman Empire, local executors of legal documents. In Jewish Palestine these would be the people who also taught children how to read the Scriptures; many of them were experts in the legal issues contained in the *law of Moses (i.e., they were predecessors of the *rabbis); some of them were *Pharisees.

Seneca. A Roman *Stoic philosopher, an adviser to Nero in that emperor's early days.

***Septuagint.** The Greek version of the *Old Testament widely circulated in the *New Testament period. (It is commonly abbreviated LXX because of the tradition that seventy scholars were responsible for it.) Although various recensions, or versions, of the Septuagint existed, this commentary refers to the most widely accepted standardized form (for the sake of avoiding technical questions beyond its scope).

Shammai. A famous Jewish teacher contemporary with *Hillel and with Jesus' early childhood; usually stricter than Hillel's, his school's opinions generally prevailed in the time of Jesus.

Shroud of Turin. The purported burial cloth of Jesus. Against its authenticity are the results of its radiocarbon dating; in its favor are its many Palestinian features (including traces of Palestinian plant fibers) and indications of first-century Jewish burial customs. The origin and character of the image have still not been resolved by investigators.

Sibylline Oracles. *Pseudepigraphic Jewish oracles modeled after pagan oracles of the same name, attributed to the ancient prophetess Sibyl and probably collected from Jewish circles in Alexandria, Egypt, and Asia Minor. Their composition spans a wide range of time, but they are mainly pre-Christian.

Similitudes of Enoch. The parables of 1 Enoch (1 Enoch 37-71), they may be from the first century B.C. or as late as the first century A.D. Because this section of Enoch alone is not represented in fragments from *Qumran, it remains disputed whether it is pre-Christian.

***Son of God.** The term was applied generically to all Israel (Ex 4:22) but specifically to the Davidic king (2 Sam 7:14), especially (following 2 Samuel) the ultimate restorer (Ps 2:7; 89:27). Although most Jewish texts from the time of Jesus do not use it to designate the *Messiah, some do (*Essene interpreters of 2 Sam 7:14).

***Son of Man.** Hebrew and *Aramaic used the expression to mean "a human being," but Jesus used it as a designation for himself, based on the particular use in Daniel 7:13-14. There "one like a son of man," a representative for the saints who suffer before receiving the *kingdom (7:25-27), receives the right to rule eternally. This passage was not usually applied to the *Messiah in Jesus' day, and not until he clearly cited Daniel 7 at his trial did his opponents fully understand the claim he was making.

Spirit. When capitalized in this commentary, it refers to the Spirit of God, the *Holy Spirit.

Stoicism. The most popular form of Greek philosophy in Paul's day. Although most people were not Stoics, many Stoic ideas were widely disseminated. For more detail, see comment on Acts 17:18.

Suetonius. A Roman historian whose early-second-century A.D. biographies of first-century A.D. emperors contain much useful information.

***Synagogues.** Assembly places used by Jewish people for public prayer, Scripture readings and community meetings.

Synoptic Gospels. Matthew, Mark and Luke; so called because they overlap so much, sharing common sources (probably especially Mark and "Q").

Tacitus. A Roman historian whose early-second-century history of first-century Rome is among our most dependable sources for that era (albeit often tainted with Tacitus's cynicism).

Targum. A paraphrase of the Hebrew Bible into the *Aramaic vernacular. Although it is impossible to date the extant written targums, the activity of translation is as old as Nehemiah 8:8 and could have developed into expanded paraphrases at an early date.

***Tax gatherers.** A despised group of Jewish people who collected taxes for the government at a profit. Rome allowed wealthy men to contract with their own cities or districts to see to it that taxes were paid; because they had to cover any shortfall themselves, they were not inclined to have mercy on their clients. Herod the Great had used local taxes to finance not only the Jerusalem temple and his palaces but also pagan temples in *Gentile enclaves in Palestine, an action that had undoubtedly further alienated the masses. Tax collectors thus appeared as collaborators with the occupying pagan power.

Testament of Job. A *Hellenistic Jewish account of Job's suffering and triumph, maybe from Egypt and probably from the first century B.C. or the first century A.D.

Testament of Moses. Some think this document derives from the *Maccabean era; it could also be dated after A.D. 70 (cf. 6:9), but probably it dates to around the mid-first century A.D. (it describes only *part* of the temple being burned).

Testament of Solomon. Probably a non-Christian Jewish work from about the third century A.D., possibly from Asia Minor; its exorcist rites reflect thorough familiarity with magical texts.

Testaments of the Twelve Patriarchs. Probably a mainly pre-Christian Jewish work with some Christian interpolations. Its date is uncertain. *Pseudepigraphic "testaments," or final instructions, are left by each of Jacob's twelve sons for their children.

Theon. A Greek *rhetorician whose manual of rhetoric is helpful in reconstructing ancient speaking and writing styles (along with handbooks by *Quintilian and others).

***Zealots.** Jewish revolutionaries who became prominent by this name especially shortly before the first Jewish war (A.D. 66-70). Seeking to exonerate his people before the Romans, *Josephus marginalized them as robbers and troublemakers, but Zealot sympathizers were almost certainly widespread, apparently even among many *Pharisees. Although *Zealots* technically refers to only one of the resistance groups, modern writers have often used the term as a convenient title for the whole resistance movement.

Maps & Charts

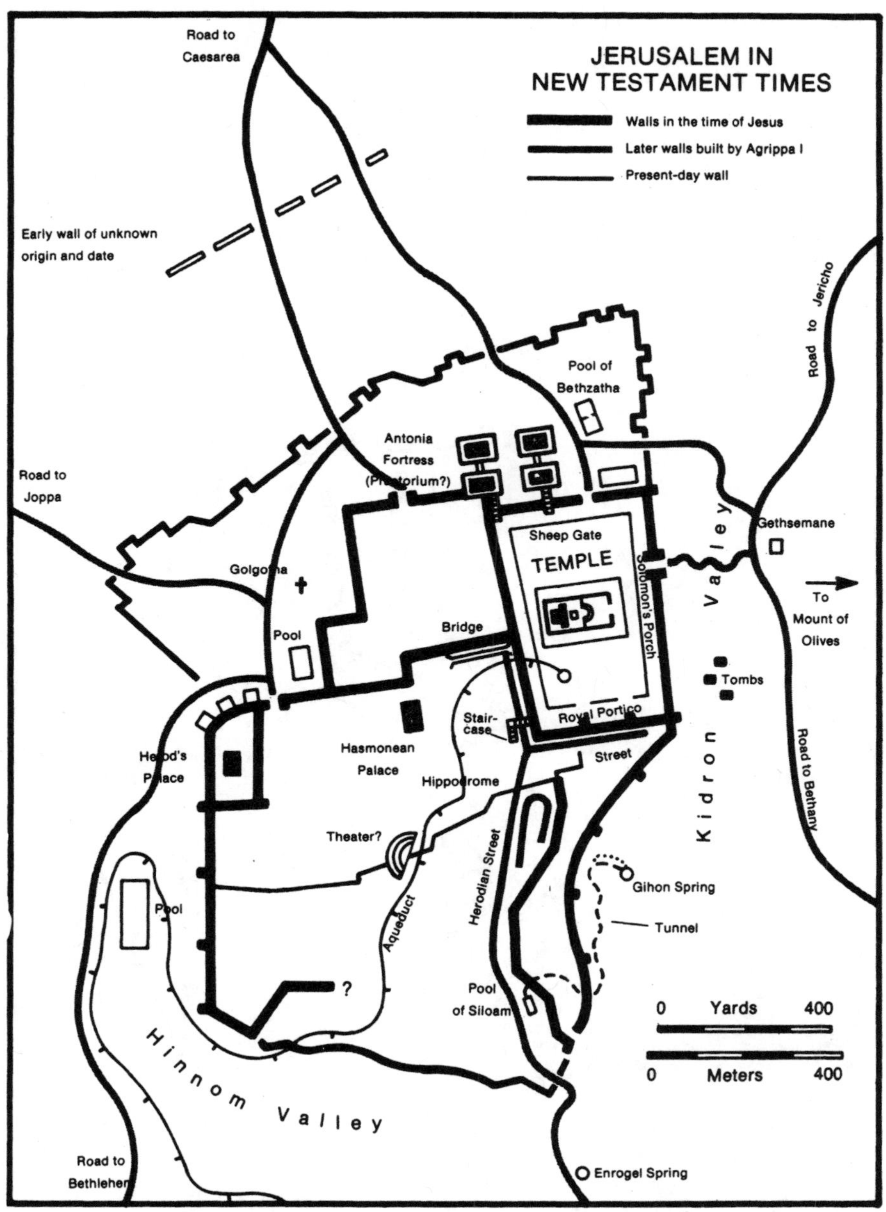

JERUSALEM IN
NEW TESTAMENT TIMES
Walls in the time of Jesus
Later walls built by Agrippa I
Present-day wall
Road to
Caesarea
Early wall of unknown
origin and date
Road to
Joppa
Road to Jericho
Pool of
Bethzatha
Antonia
Fortress
Sheep Gate
TEMPLE
Solomon's Porch
Gethsemane
To
Mount of
Olives
Pool
Bridge
Tombs
Road to Bethany
Kidron Valley
Stair-
case
Royal Portico
Street
Hasmonean
Palace
Theater?
Aqueduct
Herodian Street
Gihon Spring
Tunnel
?
Pool
of Siloam
0 Yards 400
0 Meters 400
Hinnom Valley
Road to
Enrogel Spring
Road to the
Dead Sea

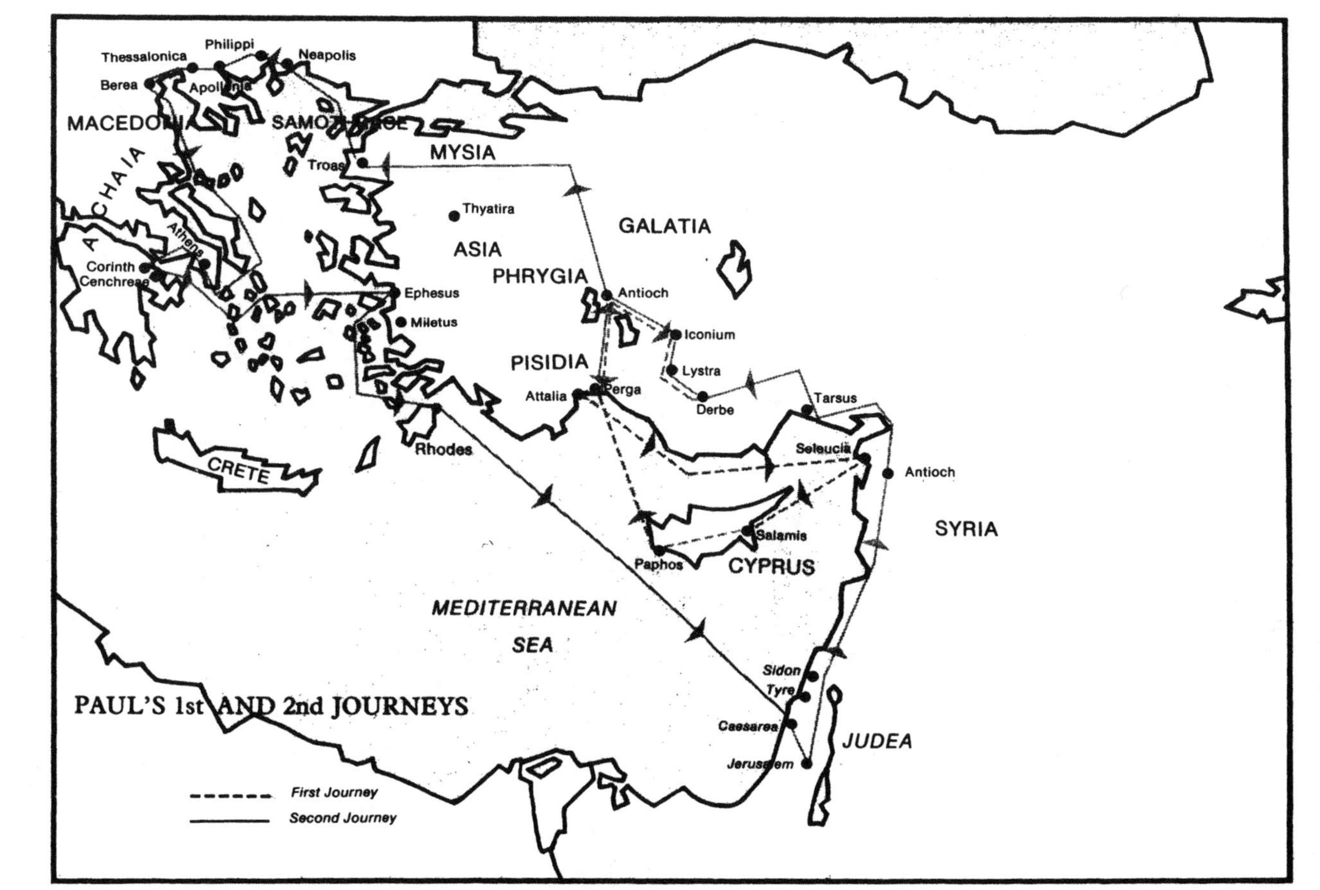
PAUL'S 1st AND 2nd JOURNEYS
First Journey
Second Journey
Thessalonica
Philippi
Neapolis
Berea
Troas
MYSIA
ACHAIA
Athens
Corinth
Thyatira
ASIA
GALATIA
PHRYGIA
Antioch
Ephesus
Miletus
Iconium
Lystra
PISIDIA
Attalia
Perga
Derbe
Tarsus
Rhodes
CRETE
Seleucia
Antioch
SYRIA
Salamis
Paphos
CYPRUS
MEDITERRANEAN
SEA
Sidon
Tyre
Caesarea
JUDEA

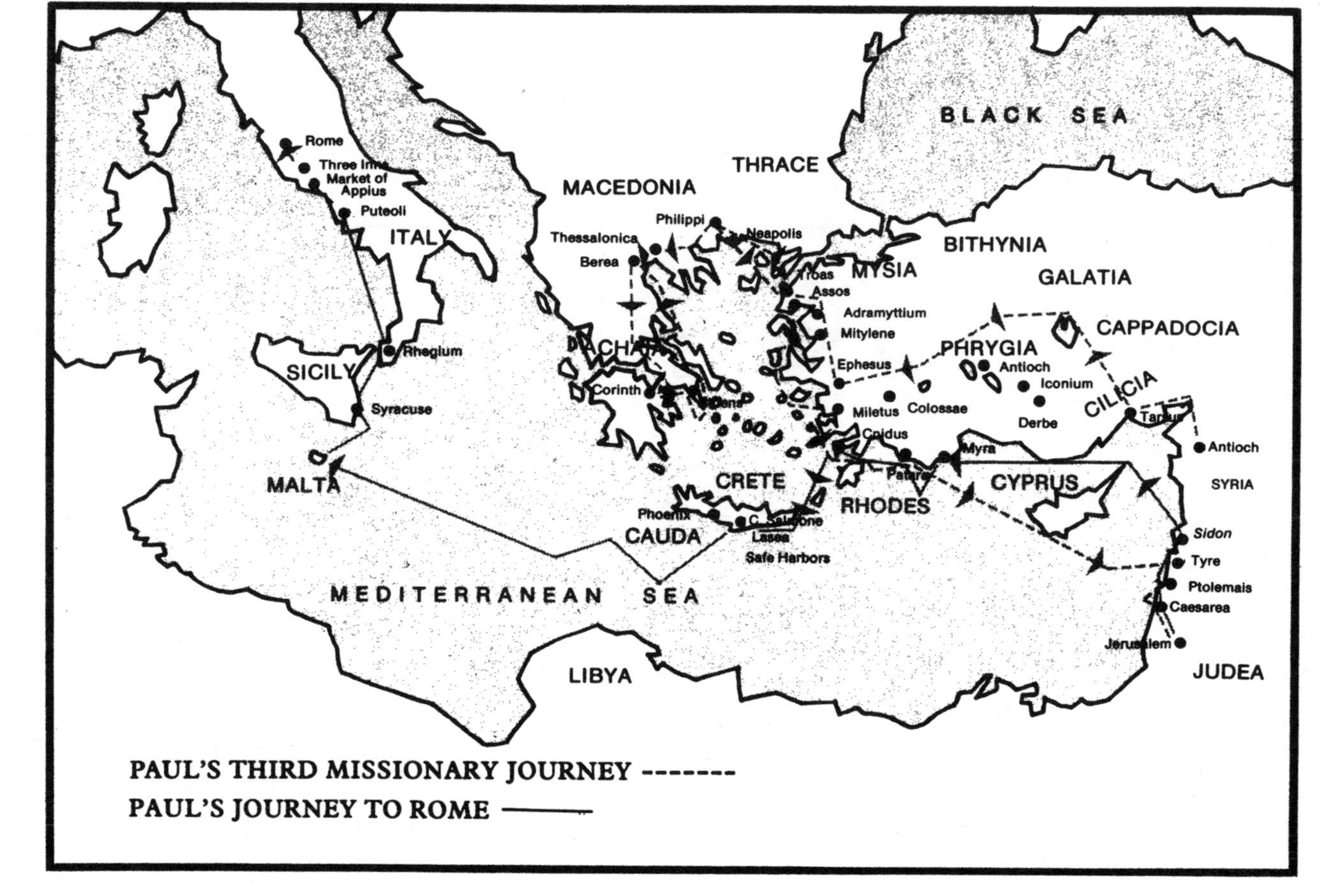
BLACK SEA
THRACE
MACEDONIA
Rome
Market of Appius
Puteoli
ITALY
Rhegium
SICILY
Syracuse
MALTA
Philippi
Neapolis
Thessalonica
Berea
Troas
Assos
MYSIA
BITHYNIA
GALATIA
CAPPADOCIA
Adramyttium
Mitylene
Ephesus
PHRYGIA
Antioch
Iconium
Corinth
Miletus
Colossae
Derbe
CILICIA
Antioch
SYRIA
Myra
CYPRUS
CRETE
RHODES
Phoenix
CAUDA
Lasea
Safe Harbors
Sidon
Tyre
Ptolemais
Caesarea
Jerusalem
JUDEA
MEDITERRANEAN SEA
LIBYA
PAUL'S THIRD MISSIONARY JOURNEY -------
PAUL'S JOURNEY TO ROME ———

The New Testament World: A Chronology

ROME (rulers)	PALESTINE (government)	JUDAISM	CHRISTIAN BEGINNINGS
		■ Dead Sea Scrolls (2nd century B.C. through mid-first century A.D.) Jewish teachers:	
■ Augustus (27 B.C.-A.D. 14) ◇ hailed as "Savior" ◇ Pax Romana	■ Herod the Great (c. 37-4 B.C.)	■ Shemaya, Abtalion ■ Hillel and Shammai	■ Birth of Jesus (c. 7 B.C.?)
	■ Archelaus, ethnarch (4 B.C.-A.D. 6)	■ Annas, high priest (A.D. 6-15)	■ Return from Egypt to Galilee ■ Work for carpenters in Nazareth (4 miles from Sepphoris)
	■ Judas's revolt and Sepphoris burned (A.D. 6)	■ Caiaphas, high priest (A.D. 18-36)	
■ Tiberius (A.D. 14-37) ◇ *patron of Sejanus ◇ expels Jews from Rome	■ Roman procurators over Judea (A.D. 6-37) ■ Herod Antipas, tetrarch of Galilee (4 B.C.-A.D. 39) ■ Pontius Pilate (A.D. 26 or 27 to 36 or 37); *client of Sejanus	■ School of Shammai predominates ■ Gamaliel I a prominent Pharisaic teacher (School of Hillel)	■ John the Baptist, Jesus begin public ministry (c. A.D. 27) (Lk 3:1; Jn 2:20) ■ Jesus crucified (c. A.D. 30) ■ Church begins in Jerusalem ■ Hellenist movement (Acts 6) ■ Stephen's stoning ■ Paul converted (c. 32) ■ Church in Antioch, Gentile expansion
■ Gaius Caligula (37-41) ◇ tries to set up his image in the temple	■ Herod Agrippa I, popular king (37-44) ◇ dies in Acts 12:23; Josephus (44)	■ Theudas's revolt (c. 45)	■ Apocalyptic ideas flourish probably due to Gaius (cf. 2 Thess 2:3-4)
■ Claudius ("Restrainer"?) (41-54) ◇ expels Jews from Rome over "Chrestus"	■ Procurators (44-66) and Herod Agrippa II (c. 50-92, over various territories)	■ Simeon b. Gamaliel ■ Rich (Sadducean) priests and Galilean landlords oppressing the poor	■ Paul's first missionary journey (45-48) ■ Jerusalem Council (Acts 15; c. 49) ■ Second journey (50-53): Philippi, Thessalonica, Corinth; 1-2 Thessalonians ■ Mid-fifties: 1 Corinthians, Romans
■ Nero (54-68) ◇ murders, orgies, bestiality, matricide ◇ *patron of Pallas	■ Felix: corrupt *client of Pallas (52-60)	■ Socioeconomic tensions building; *Zealots arise	■ Paul caught in temple, taken to Caesarea (c. 58-60) ■ James written?

ROME (rulers)	**PALESTINE (government)**	**JUDAISM**	**CHRISTIAN BEGINNINGS**
	■ Festus: fair procurator (60-62)		■ Paul sent to Rome (c. 60) ■ Prison Epistles (Ephesians, Philippians, Colossians, Philemon; c. 60-62) ■ Paul must address philosophy, Hellenistic and Jewish mysticism, and household codes
	■ Festus dies (62); replaced by corrupt governors		■ Paul probably released after 2 years (62) ■ James brother of Jesus martyred (62) ■ 1 Timothy, Titus
■ Fire of Rome (64) ■ Nero burns Christians alive (64)			■ Paul's reimprisonment ■ 1-2 Peter; 2 Timothy; Mark? (c. 64)
	■ Massacres in Caesarea, Decapolis		■ Peter and Paul executed (c. 64)
		■ War with Rome (66-70)	■ Jerusalem church flees
■ Nero dies; replaced by Galba, Otho, Vitellius (68-69)			■ Hebrews written (c. 68)?
■ Vespasian (69-79)		■ Jerusalem falls; temple destroyed (70)	■ False prophets say the End has come (c. 70)
		■ Sadducees, other groups disbanded ■ Johanan ben Zakkai reorganizes Pharisaism	■ Luke-Acts? (Greco-Roman)
■ Titus (79-81)			■ Matthew? (Syrian-Jewish)
		■ Gamaliel II, Samuel ha-Katon; troubles with "schismatics" (many possibly Jewish Christians; c. 85)	
■ Domitian (81-96) ◇ later in his reign, demands worship ◇ Christians and others persecuted			■ John (90s) ■ 1, 2, 3 John ■ Revelation
■ Nerva (96-98) ■ Trajan (98-117)		■ Akiba, Ishmael	■ Gentile Christianity overshadowing Jewish Christianity in many areas, understanding its roots less
■ Hadrian (117-138)	■ Jerusalem paganized (Aelia Capitolina, 135)	■ Bar Kochba revolt (132-135)	■ Justin Martyr
		■ R. Judah ha-Nasi I (c. 200) codifies the Mishnah (later Amoraic rabbis' opinions and rulings codified in the Gemara)	■ Irenaeus, Athenagoras, Clement of Alexandria, Origen, Tertullian

Major Figures in the Herodian Family

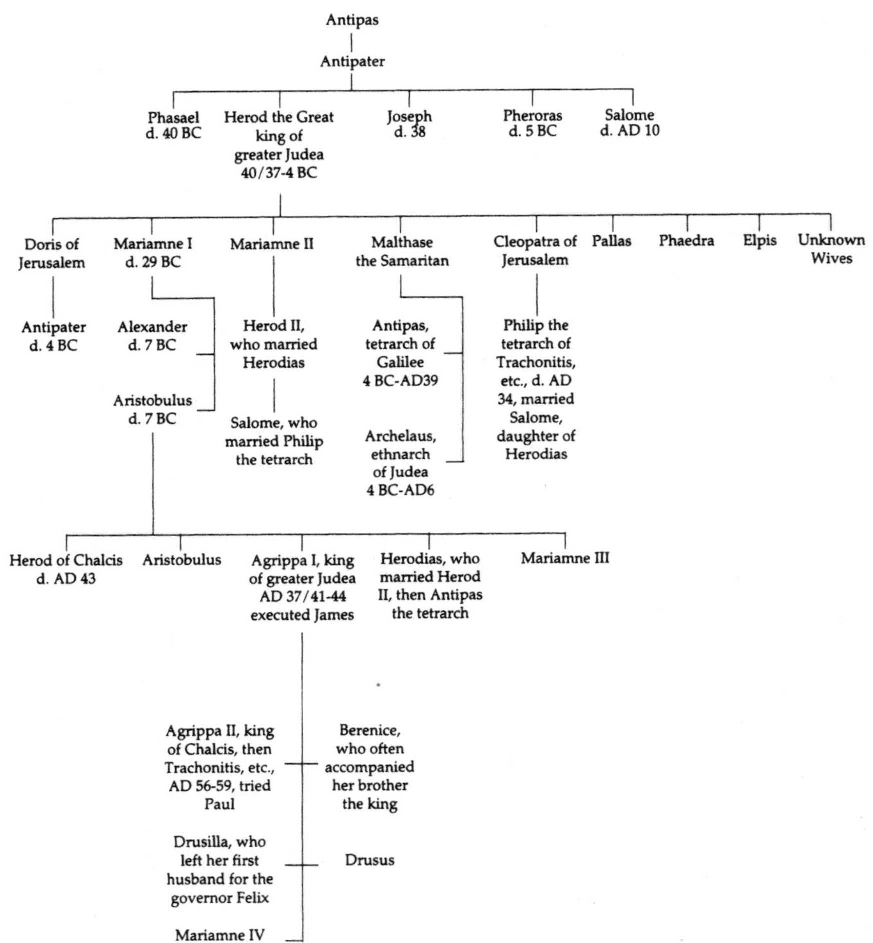

Jewish Eschatology

this age

age to come

Christian Eschatology

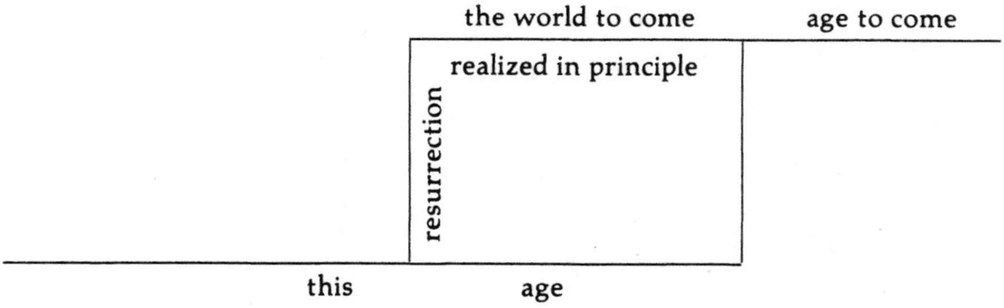

the world to come

age to come

realized in principle

resurrection

this

age

George Eldon Ladd, *A Theology of the New Testament* (Grand Rapids, Mich.: Eerdmans, 1974), p. 68. Used with permission.

A Chiasmus (Acts 2:22-36)

A This one [Jesus] . . . you crucified and killed
B But God raised Him up, having loosed the pangs of death
C David says . . .
MEN, BROTHERS, IT IS NECESSARY TO SPEAK TO YOU BOLDLY
D That the patriarch David died and was buried
(and his tomb is with us to this day)
E Being therefore a prophet, and knowing
F That God had sworn with an oath to him
G That He would set one of his descendants on his throne
H He foresaw and spoke
I Of the resurrection of Christ
J That He was not abandoned to Hades
J′ Nor did His flesh see corruption
I′ This Jesus God raised up
H′ Of that we are all witnesses
G′ Being therefore exalted at the right hand of God
F′ Having received from the Father the promise of the Holy Spirit
E′ He has poured out this which you see and hear
D′ For David did not ascend into the heavens
C′ David says . . .
ASSUREDLY, THEREFORE, LET ALL THE HOUSE OF ISRAEL KNOW
B′ That God has made Him Lord and Christ
A′ This Jesus whom you crucified

From Kenneth E. Bailey, *Poet & Peasant: A Literary Cultural Approach to the Parables in Luke* (Grand Rapids, Mich.: Eerdmans, 1976), pp. 65-66. Used with permission.